Management

A Focus on Leaders

Second Edition

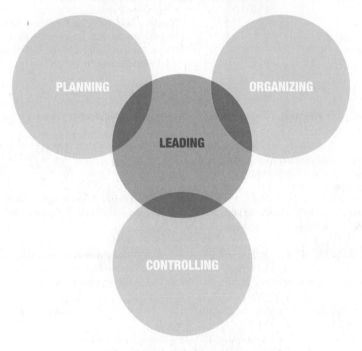

PLANNING

ORGANIZING

LEADING

CONTROLLING

Annie McKee

**The University of Pennsylvania
and Teleos Leadership Institute**

PEARSON

Boston   Columbus   Indianapolis   New York   San Francisco   Upper Saddle River
Amsterdam   Cape Town   Dubai   London   Madrid   Milan   Munich   Paris   Montreal   Toronto
Delhi   Mexico City   São Paulo   Sydney   Hong Kong   Seoul   Singapore   Taipei   Tokyo

Editor-in-Chief: Stephanie Wall
Senior Acquisitions Editor: April Cole
Director of Editorial Services: Ashley Santora
Editorial Project Manager: Claudia Fernandes
Development Editor: Laura Town
Editorial Assistant: Bernard Ollila
Director of Marketing: Maggie Moylan
Senior Marketing Manager: Nikki Ayana Jones
Marketing Assistant: Gianna Sandri
Senior Managing Editor: Judy Leale
Production Project Manager: Kelly Warsak
Operations Specialist: Cathleen Petersen
Creative Director: Blair Brown

Senior Art Director: Kenny Beck
Interior Designer: LCI Design
Cover Designer: Jodi Notowitz
Cover Image: Fariz Alikishibayov/Shutterstock.com
Permission Specialist: Brooks Hill-Whilton
Media Project Manager, Production: Lisa Rinaldi
Media Project Manager, Editorial: Denise Vaughn
Full-Service Project Management: Lori Bradshaw/S4Carlisle
  Publishing Services
Composition: S4Carlisle Publishing Services
Printer/Binder: R.R. Donnelley/Willard
Cover Printer: Lehigh-Phoenix Color/Hagerstown
Text Font: Minion Pro 10.5/12

Credits and acknowledgments borrowed from other sources and reproduced, with permission, in this textbook appear on appropriate page within text.

10 9 8 7 6 5 4 3 2 1

ISBN 10:   0-13-338201-X
ISBN 13: 978-0-13-338201-3

To salute wisdom and new beginnings, this book is
dedicated to
Murray Wigsten
and
Benjamin Renio

Brief Table of Contents

Contents

New to This Edition

Management: A Focus on Leaders has received high marks for writing style, up-to-date content, and existing and engaging treatment of current events. The author has also set a new bar and higher standards for sharing both original and new, innovative research, and high standards around sharing theories, and models. In this edition, enhanced these distinctive strengths by focusing even more deliberately on new knowledge and management practices. We have sought out the most current thinking and thinkers in the academy, business, government and not-for-profits and incorporated their research, views, and opinions throughout.

Students will find this book easy to read, easy to study, and enjoyable. Most importantly, they will find that the information, research, and engaging stories make it easy to *learn* from reading this book, engaging the discussion questions posed throughout, and doing the end-of-chapter exercises. The writing style invites them to explore all of the key concepts related to management while developing their own leadership skills and learning how to apply concepts to real-world situations.

Faculty will find seminal research—ideas, models, and concepts that all students of management should be exposed to—as well as the world's foremost business and thought leaders' best new ideas and research. Faculty will also find it easy to help students become educated consumers of knowledge: treatment of research, models, and management practices encourages critical thinking. Faculty will also be able to use the text to foster deep thinking about today's biggest opportunities and challenges, especially those related to ethics, globalization, diversity and inclusion and of course, what it means to be an outstanding leader today.

Both students and faculty will find that the way the book is written and the choice of content brings the study of management into the twenty-first century. This edition is packed with revisions that support ease-of-reading and new research, current events, and management practices. Students' learning and development is also enhanced through a variety of new tools, including provocative questions in the exhibits, reflection and discussion questions at the end of each section in each chapter, and creative, thought-provoking and fun individual and group exercises at the end of every chapter.

Features and content that have been strengthened and added to the second edition include:

- Key current events and thought provoking discussions about their impact on businesses, managers, and leaders;
- Brand new Leadership Perspectives that incorporate powerful guidance and wisdom on what it means to lead today's top organizations and institutions. All of the Perspectives are based on personal interviews conducted by the author;
- New interviews were conducted by the author with leaders who contributed to the Leadership Perspectives in the first edition. The updated Perspectives reflect these leaders' new thinking as the world has changed quite dramatically in the last year or two;
- New and updated examples of real leaders facing real opportunities and challenges in organizations today. These examples have been created as a result of the author's work with leaders around the world;

- Streamlined and updated section in each chapter on how human resources can impact chapter topic areas, as well as how the function can support leadership development and smoothly running businesses and institutions;
- Streamlined and updated section in each chapter on how all of us can become outstanding and ethical leaders;
- Clear, compelling learning objectives are tied directly to each major heading in each chapter;
- Pictures in the text are now accompanied by provocative and interesting questions to spark critical thinking;
- Discussion questions at the end of each major heading have been strengthened, streamlined, and updated;
- Major topics of our day, including globalization, the impact of technology, ethics, diversity and inclusion, ethics, and the need for emotional and social intelligence in leadership today are woven throughout the text in a powerful and even more thought provoking manner;
- A brand new section at the end of each chapter includes creative, fun learning experiences that students can do on their own and/or faculty can use as assignments. These exercises are designed to be fun as well as impactful learning experiences!

VISUAL Walk-Through

Leadership Perspective Each chapter contains at least one powerful and personal interview with a business leader, conducted by Annie McKee. These leaders offer their unique perspective and insights on today's challenging business environment.

Business Case Each chapter contains at least one case study about business challenges and leadership.

Leadership Perspective

Dan Nowlin is senior vice president, North America Store Operations and president, Sunglass Hut Global Culture. Throughout his career, Dan has focused on *people*: who they are, what they need, and how he can help them achieve personal and professional goals. When Dan walks into a store (which he does all the time), employees flock to him. He knows their names, when they started with the company, and personal details like their birthdays, their kids' names and whether the employee has decided to pursue a degree (and if not, he encourages them). As he puts it, "Little things don't mean a lot, they mean *everything*." Here's what else he has to say about leading people:

As a leader, you have choices to make: how you spend your time, what you say to people, how you communicate your ideas and your vision. How do you know what to do, when everything is complex and changing all the time? You need to be smart—but smart might not mean what you think it does.

There are at least three kinds of intelligence that matter today. You need intellect, of course. We measure intellect with things like SAT tests, final exams, and IQ. These might not be their place, but they don't measure the kind of intelligence that is really needed in today's organizations. That's because in most jobs, you don't need to be a genius. You need enough brain power to understand that the world is changing and you have to change with it. You need to think strategically and you need to make sense of what is going on now, so you can have a vision of tomorrow. All of these require keen intellect. But this is only a starting point.

The second kind of intelligence is common sense. This includes the basics: treat people the way you want to be treated; if you're mean, you'll get mean back, and if you're nice, you'll get nice back; if you choose to live a life of giving rather than getting, you will get more than you can possibly imagine. You also need to get out in front—if you want people to do something or act a certain way, do it yourself. You need to value each and every person equally. Diversity and inclusion is a hugely important strategy today. So, you need to learn about other people's views, cultures, and beliefs. You need to value them for who they are, not who you want them to be. These lessons look simple, but they aren't. And they certainly aren't "common" enough in our organizations.

The third kind of intelligence you need is emotional. People work for peo-

ple—that means that the people who work for you are going to be watching you. They want to know whether you are authentic and real. They will be checking to see if you care about the company, about your work, and especially about them. When they see you care, they care too.

Emotions matter. Your mood affects everyone. I used to work in a big department store, and by the time I got to my office on the third floor, every single person knew what kind of mood I was in. If I was happy, they were more likely to be happy. And if I was in a bad mood, they got there too. When people see their bosses in a bad mood, they can become scared or angry, and they don't focus on their jobs. They try to figure out how to deal with *you*—a waste of time and energy. But if they see that you are excited to be there, happy and ready to go, they pick up that state of mind and take it into everything they do.

Another thing about emotions: When people live in fear or anger they hold back. This goes for you, too. Your emotions impact what you and others contribute and where you can go in your life and as a leader. There are some things to learn here.

First, love what you do. Find meaning in your company's mission and what it does for the world. We love what we do at Sunglass Hut. We sell sunglasses which are practical and helpful. And sunglasses help people feel good about themselves. We also help the world through OneSight, a nonprofit organization which delivers vision care for people who could never afford it on their own. This program makes all of us feel good about our company.

Finally, no matter how much you love your job, never put it above your family, friends, or your health. When all is said and done, work is a part of life, not the other way around.

● **Dan Nowlin**
Senior Vice President, North American Store Operations and President, Sunglass Hut Global Culture
"Little things don't mean a lot, they mean everything."

Source: Personal interview with Dan Nowlin conducted by Annie McKee, 2012.

BUSINESS CASE **Unilever**

Transformation for Sustainability

Unilever's web site proudly states that "160 million times a day, someone somewhere uses a Unilever product."[4] You may be wondering what those products are, as Unilever is not yet a household name. For many years, it was a corporate name behind over 400 extremely well-known brands including household favorites like Axe, Dove, Lipton, Hellman's, Bertolli, Vaseline, Surf, and many more. Over the years, many of these brands have changed, and many haven't—both of which are equally important ingredients for success.

Some companies never change, and some change too much or in the wrong direction. Over the years, Unilever has gotten the equation right. The company's leaders read the local and global markets and respond fast and appropriately. What's as—if not more—impressive is that Unilever listens to more than just what customers and stakeholders want. They have mastered the local-global debate by providing products that local customers want while maximizing efficiency in their research, production, and supply chain processes.

Moreover, the company's leaders and all employees don't just blindly create new products based on fads: They seek to find out *why* customers and other interested parties want something new or different. Then, they go about trying to balance the multiple demands of many stakeholders and do the right thing.

Doing the right thing in business isn't always easy. This is because different constituencies often have different needs and place different demands on a business. For example, investors want growth and profits. Consumers want new, exciting products. And community groups want a business to behave in a responsible manner when it comes to jobs and the environment. These conflicting demands were exactly what Unilever and many other companies have faced in the past two decades. Unlike many other companies, however, Unilever has found a path to success. A path to success in today's complex

business environment starts with transformational *thinking*. And transformational thinking starts with refusing to see traditional conflicts in traditional ways. Transformational thinking means looking for solutions in new places and not falling prey to a win-lose mind-set.

In recent years, former chairmen Niall FitzGerald and Antony Burgmans engaged the entire company in transformational thinking as they streamlined their brands in the early 2000s. They also launched a tidal wave of passion and engagement in the company for examining how Unilever was impacting the environment—and making changes. This effort was expanded by the next generation of leaders, as was a complete overhaul of the supply chain. These actions are revolutionary in a business, and they are the outcomes of transformational leadership.

As CEO Paul Polman says, "The great challenge of the twenty-first century is to provide good standards of living for 7 billion people without depleting the earth's resources or running up massive levels of public debt. To achieve this, government and business alike will need to find new models of growth which are in both environmental and economic balance." He goes on to say, "In Unilever we believe that business must be part of the solution. But to be so, business will have to change. It will have to get off the treadmill of quarterly reporting and operate for the long term. It will have to see itself as part of society, not separate from it. And it will have to recognise that the needs of citizens and communities carry the same weight as the demands of shareholders."

This may not seem revolutionary to you, but it is. Many businesses have put the needs of one or two constituencies above all others. Unilever is not doing that. The challenges are not simple, of course. The company, like all responsible companies, is still struggling with answers to the complex questions around sustainability and success; at least they are boldly taking a stand. Unilever is paving a way to the creation of a new way of doing business that, the company's leaders and employees believe, will lead to happy, loyal customers, satisfied investors, safer workplaces, healthier communities, and sustainable environmental practices.

Clear, compelling Learning Objectives are tied to all main headings.

Objective 3.1
Define motivation.

1. What Is Motivation?

We spend almost a third of our *lives* working. We work as students, employees, carpenters, dancers, musicians, electricians, small business owners, artists, professional athletes, farmers, consultants, accountants, caregivers—you name it. We all work, and we work a lot. Including school, most of us will spend an astounding 60 years or more working during our lives. That's a good reason to understand what motivates us to do our best and find meaning and satisfaction in work. And if you happen to be a teacher, a parent, a manager, or a leader, it is essential to understand what motivates other people to contribute their very best to their families, teams, or organizations.

What, exactly, is motivation? Motivation is the result of a complex set of psychological and external factors or conditions that cause a person to behave a certain way while maintaining effort and persistence.[1] For example, consider yourself right now—you are reading this chapter and preparing for class. You may be slightly motivated because you have been told you must read. Perhaps you are cramming for a test, and you are motivated by a desire to achieve a good grade. Or, maybe you enjoy the class and are curious about management and leadership. These examples illustrate that you feel motivated to study—or not—based on what you believe others expect of you, your self-image, a desire for certain outcomes and/or because of how you feel about what you are doing.

Motivation
The result of a complex set of psychological influences and external forces or conditions that cause a person to behave in a certain way while maintaining a certain level of effort and persistence.

Key Terms are in the margin when the term is first mentioned and listed at the end of the chapter.

Visual Models We have created special visual models that we use throughout the book to support our most important concepts. For example, we have created an icon that reminds students of the importance of social and emotional intelligence, a key component of great leadership in our complex and global business world.

Visual Summary Each chapter ends with an engaging visual journey that highlights key points.

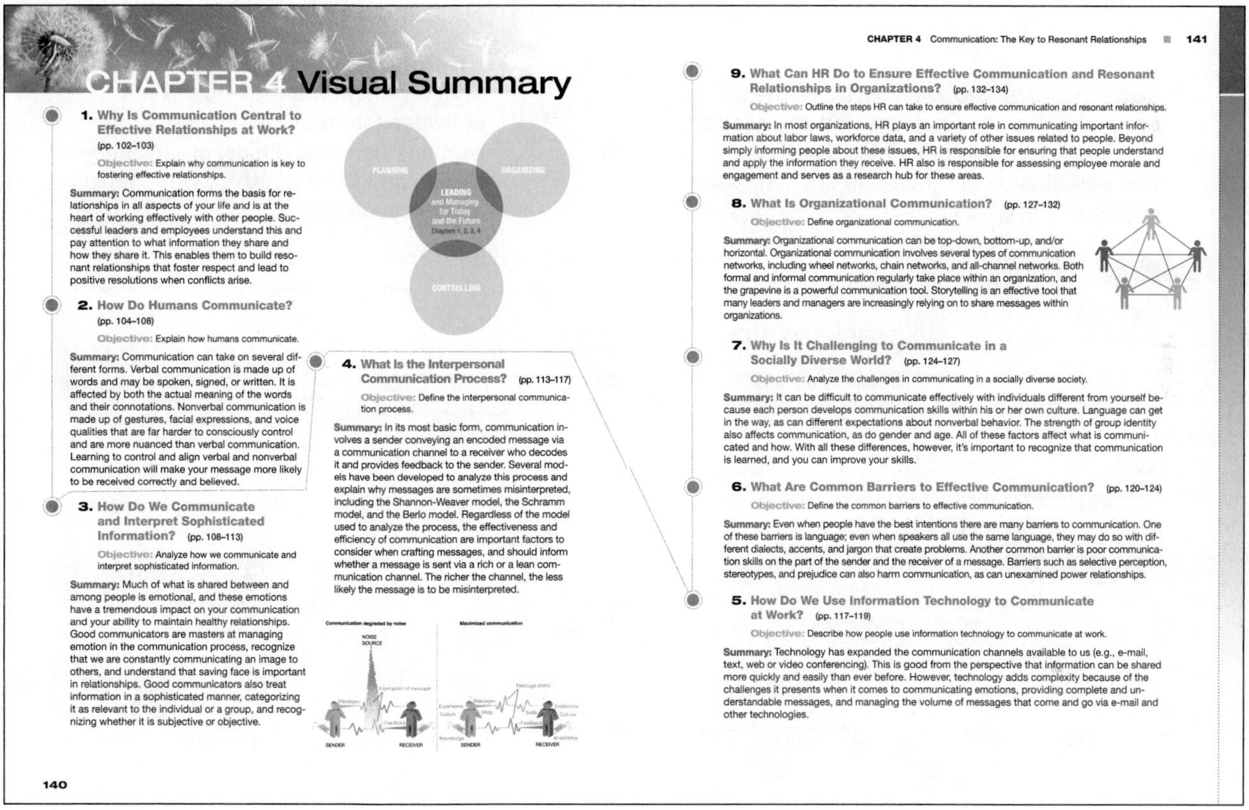

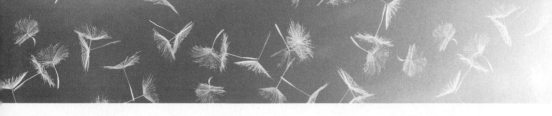

CHAPTER 4 Communication: The Key to Resonant Relationships ■ 141

CHAPTER 4 Visual Summary

1. Why Is Communication Central to Effective Relationships at Work? (pp. 102–103)

Objective: Explain why communication is key to fostering effective relationships.

Summary: Communication forms the basis for relationships in all aspects of your life and is at the heart of working effectively with other people. Successful leaders and employees understand this and pay attention to what information they share and how they share it. This enables them to build resonant relationships that foster respect and lead to positive resolutions when conflicts arise.

2. How Do Humans Communicate? (pp. 104–108)

Objective: Explain how humans communicate.

Summary: Communication can take on several different forms. Verbal communication is made up of words and may be spoken, signed, or written. It is affected by both the actual meaning of the words and their connotations. Nonverbal communication is made up of gestures, facial expressions, and voice qualities that are far harder to consciously control and are more nuanced than verbal communication. Learning to control and align verbal and nonverbal communication will make your message more likely to be received correctly and believed.

3. How Do We Communicate and Interpret Sophisticated Information? (pp. 108–113)

Objective: Analyze how we communicate and interpret sophisticated information.

Summary: Much of what is shared between and among people is emotional, and these emotions have a tremendous impact on your communication and your ability to maintain healthy relationships. Good communicators are masters at managing emotion in the communication process, recognize that we are constantly communicating an image to others, and understand that saving face is important in relationships. Good communicators also treat information in a sophisticated manner, categorizing it as relevant to the individual or a group, and recognizing whether it is subjective or objective.

4. What Is the Interpersonal Communication Process? (pp. 113–117)

Objective: Define the interpersonal communication process.

Summary: In its most basic form, communication involves a sender conveying an encoded message via a communication channel to a receiver who decodes it and provides feedback to the sender. Several models have been developed to analyze this process and explain why messages are sometimes misinterpreted, including the Shannon-Weaver model, the Schramm model, and the Berlo model. Regardless of the model used to analyze the process, the effectiveness and efficiency of communication are important factors to consider when crafting messages, and should inform whether a message is sent via a rich or a lean communication channel. The richer the channel, the less likely the message is to be misinterpreted.

140

9. What Can HR Do to Ensure Effective Communication and Resonant Relationships in Organizations? (pp. 132–134)

Objective: Outline the steps HR can take to ensure effective communication and resonant relationships.

Summary: In most organizations, HR plays an important role in communicating important information about labor laws, workforce data, and a variety of other issues related to people. Beyond simply informing people about these issues, HR is responsible for ensuring that people understand and apply the information they receive. HR also is responsible for assessing employee morale and engagement and serves as a research hub for these areas.

8. What Is Organizational Communication? (pp. 127–132)

Objective: Define organizational communication.

Summary: Organizational communication can be top-down, bottom-up, and/or horizontal. Organizational communication involves several types of communication networks, including wheel networks, chain networks, and all-channel networks. Both formal and informal communication regularly take place within an organization, and the grapevine is a powerful communication tool. Storytelling is an effective tool that many leaders and managers are increasingly relying on to share messages within organizations.

7. Why Is It Challenging to Communicate in a Socially Diverse World? (pp. 124–127)

Objective: Analyze the challenges in communicating in a socially diverse society.

Summary: It can be difficult to communicate effectively with individuals different from yourself because each person develops communication skills within his or her own culture. Language can get in the way, as can different expectations about nonverbal behavior. The strength of group identity also affects communication, as do gender and age. All of these factors affect what is communicated and how. With all these differences, however, it's important to recognize that communication is learned, and you can improve your skills.

6. What Are Common Barriers to Effective Communication? (pp. 120–124)

Objective: Define the common barriers to effective communication.

Summary: Even when people have the best intentions there are many barriers to communication. One of these barriers is language; even when speakers all use the same language, they may do so with different dialects, accents, and jargon that create problems. Another common barrier is poor communication skills on the part of the sender and the receiver of a message. Barriers such as selective perception, stereotypes, and prejudice can also harm communication, as can unexamined power relationships.

5. How Do We Use Information Technology to Communicate at Work? (pp. 117–119)

Objective: Describe how people use information technology to communicate at work.

Summary: Technology has expanded the communication channels available to us (e.g., e-mail, text, web or video conferencing). This is good from the perspective that information can be shared more quickly and easily than ever before. However, technology adds complexity because of the challenges it presents when it comes to communicating emotions, providing complete and understandable messages, and managing the volume of messages that come and go via e-mail and other technologies.

NEW! **End-of-Chapter Exercises** Students, like all adults, learn by reflecting, engaging in dialogue, creatively applying concepts, and DOING. The all-new individual and group exercises at the end of each chapter are powerful ways to engage students in developing their own leadership skills while deepening their understanding of the most relevant management concepts, ideas, and theories. These exercises can be done in class or assigned.

NEW! **Leading in a Global World** At the end of every chapter are exercises and activities on how the leadership principles discussed in that particular chapter can be applied to the challenges of globalization.

NEW! **Ethical Leadership** At the end of every chapter are exercises and activities that require the student to examine personal ethics, organizational ethics, and societal ethics when facing an ethical dilemma.

EXPERIENCING Leadership

LEADING IN A GLOBAL WORLD
Modular Planning on a Global Scale

These days, few companies don't have some kind of global presence. Planning and setting global strategy in uncertain times takes insight, coordination, and flexibility. In a highly competitive global marketplace, an organization must be able to change its strategy, or components of its strategy, quickly and effectively.

Today, there is much political, economic, and environmental instability that directly affects an organization's profitability and survival. For example, consider the problems Japanese businesses encountered following the 2011 earthquake and tsunami. How quickly these businesses recovered and resumed operations was partially determined by their disaster plans and the degree to which plans were modularized.

Select one of the global companies below and discuss how they can benefit from employing a modular planning approach to assist in quick strategic adjustments or changes. Be sure to include scenario planning as a key strategic element in identifying what a company can do to be prepared for natural disasters or political upheaval.

- Toyota
- GE
- Facebook
- Philips
- Siemens
- LG Corp

LEADING WITH EMOTIONAL INTELLIGENCE
SWOT You

A SWOT analysis is a useful tool for assessing what is going on both inside and outside an organization. Internally, a company can evaluate its strengths, such as excellent customer service, and its weaknesses, such as backlogged inventory. Externally, there may be opportunities, such as untapped markets, as well as threats, such as strong competition. If done thoroughly, a SWOT analysis can provide useful data for guiding a company's mission and vision toward success.

You, too, can be viewed as an organization: YOU, Inc. Your success as a student depends on both internal and external forces. For instance, if your strengths include self-awareness and self-management skills, the pressures of a rigorous course load may have little

effect on you. If your weaknesses include relationship management, for example, you may find it difficult working with others on collaborative projects. External forces, such as a teaching assistantship or scholarship opportunities can benefit you nicely. Threats, such as a tuition hike or a student loan rejection, might slow down your advance toward early graduation.

Do a SWOT analysis on YOU, Inc. When complete, answer the following questions:

1. What was the most difficult part of the SWOT analysis?
2. What was the easiest part of it?
3. How can your emotions work as both a strength and a weakness for YOU?

LEADING WITH CRITICAL THINKING SKILLS
Stereotypes and Sustainability

As sustainability movements gain momentum worldwide, more companies are revising their mission and vision statements to address environmental and social issues. Some companies are "going green" because it is fashionable *and* profitable to care about the environment and social injustice.

When it comes to sustainability and strategic planning, some industries face a bigger challenge than others. Chemical companies, for instance, tend to be associated with pollution, poison, and profits. Modern chemical companies may engage in safe, responsible practices, but the industry's checkered past has led to this negative stereotyping. So how do companies like DuPont or Dow Chemical strategically position themselves in a world that demands increasing accountability from businesses?

In a group or individually, choose two of the four major chemical companies (Dow, DuPont, BASF, and Union Carbide) and research their current market strategy. As you conduct your research, be sure to do the following:

1. Identify the mission, vision, stakeholders, and long-term and short-term strategic goals of the companies.
2. Determine how the companies address environmental sustainability in their mission and vision.
3. Describe any social components of the companies' strategies.
4. Outline any particular areas that these companies should focus on when doing environmental scanning as part of the strategic planning process.

176

ETHICAL LEADERSHIP
Planning for Disaster

What does a company do when it is involved in a major environmental and public relations catastrophe? When the Deepwater Horizon oil platform exploded in 2010 killing 11 men and injuring 17 others, BP found itself in this situation.

Over the course of three months, five million barrels of crude oil gushed from the ruptured pipe in the Gulf of Mexico. A government commission determined that BP and its partners were to blame for cost-cutting decisions that impacted well safety. After the spill, BP did major damage control of its image and revised its strategic plan.

Review the six steps in the strategic planning process and think about different ways that BP could rebuild its strategy in order to regain trust and credibility in the global community.

Consider these questions:

1. What does BP need to do in relation to its mission, vision, goals, and strategies to reestablish its reputation?
2. What information does BP need to analyze in regards to its internal business processes and its ongoing partnerships?
3. What strategies could BP craft to move the company forward and away from its legal and ethical problems?

KEY TERMS

Planning, p. 146	Retrenchment strategy, p. 162	SWOT analysis, p. 169
Goal-oriented planning, p. 1457	Divestiture strategy, p. 162	Strength, p. 169
Directional planning, p. 147	Differentiation, p. 162	Weakness, p. 169
Action orientation, p. 147	Core competency, p. 162	Opportunity, p. 169
Scenario planning, p. 152	Cost leadership, p. 162	Threat, p. 169
Mission statement, p. 153	Niche strategy, p. 162	Diversified company, p. 170
Competitive advantage, p. 154	Vertical integration, p. 163	BCG matrix, p. 170
Vision, p. 154	Supply chain, p. 163	Market share, p. 170
Vision statement, p. 154	Functional strategies, p. 163	Market growth rate, p. 170
Strategy, p. 157	Strategic planning, p. 163	Layoff, p. 172
Growth strategy, p. 159	Environmental scanning, p. 163	For-cause termination, p. 173
Acquisition strategy, p. 160	Industry, p. 165	Succession plan, p. 173
Joint ventures, p. 160	Stakeholder, p. 167	Recruiting, p. 173
Stability strategy, p. 161	Stakeholder analysis, p. 167	Selection, p. 174

MyManagementLab

Go to **mymanagementlab.com** for Auto-graded writing questions as well as the following Assisted-graded writing questions:

5-1. Choose a company that you respect. Perhaps it is one you buy from repeatedly or one whose products you have always dreamed of buying. What do you see as that company's competitive advantage?

5-2. How often do you think an organization should develop a strategic plan? What might cause an organization to change strategies?

5-3. Mymanagementlab Only — comprehensive writing assignment for this chapter.

NEW! **Leading with Emotional Intelligence** At the end of every chapter are exercises and activities on how one can use emotional intelligence to navigate today's leadership challenges.

NEW! **Leading with Critical Thinking Skills** At the end of every chapter are exercises and activities that require the student to think critically about how to handle opportunities and challenges within the workplace.

NEW! Writing Space in MyManagementLab

Auto-graded writing assignments use Pearson's Intelligent Essay Assessor to automatically score the quality of your students' written assignments. Students write and submit their work directly in the MyLab and get immediate contextual feedback.

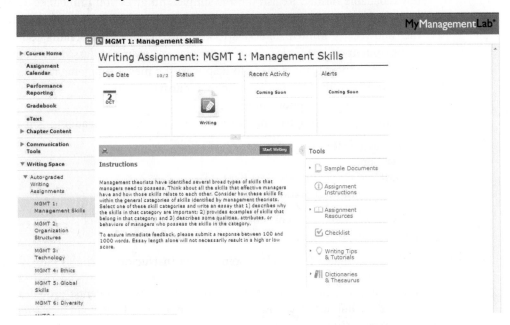

NEW! Assisted-Graded Questions

At the end of every chapter, you have the power to easily manage and assess your course using built-in content-specific rubrics to grade written assignment submissions in the gradebook.

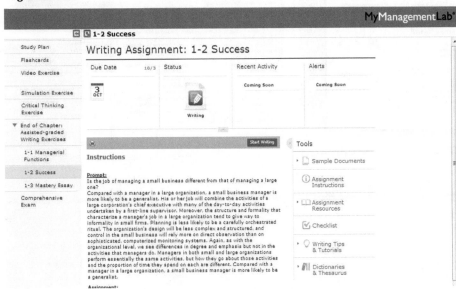

Updated Supplement Package

At the Instructor Resource Center, www.pearsonhighered.com/irc, instructors can access a variety of print, digital, and presentation resources available with this text in downloadable format. Registration is simple and gives you immediate access to new titles and new editions. As a registered faculty member, you can download resource files and receive immediate access to and instructions for installing course management content on your campus server. In case you ever need assistance, our dedicated technical support team is ready to help with the media supplements that accompany this text. Visit http://247.pearsoned.com for answers to frequently asked questions and toll-free user support phone numbers.

The following supplements are available for download to adopting instructors:

- Instructor's Resource Manual
- Test Bank
- TestGen® Computerized Test Bank
- PowerPoint Presentation

Video Library—Videos illustrating the most important subject topics are available in two formats:

- DVD—available for in classroom use by instructors, includes videos mapped to Pearson textbooks
- MyManagementLab—available for instructors and students, provides round the clock instant access to videos and corresponding assessment and simulations for Pearson textbooks

Contact your local Pearson representative to request access to either format.

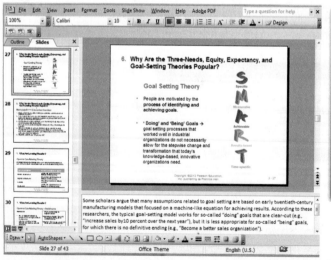

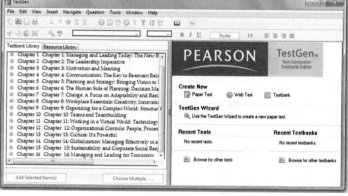

Acknowledgments

I would like to express my deepest gratitude to the many wonderful people who have helped create this book. Your contributions helped shape our vision at every step of the way, and your ideas, insights, expertise, enthusiasm, and support have been tremendously valuable—thank you. Most of all, thank you for your passion for learning and education, for your dedication to creating and sharing knowledge that will truly support the leaders of the future, and for your commitment to making a difference in the world.

To my **editorial team**, Laura Town, Chris Allen Thomas, Jim LoPresti, and Christina Yerkes: Your creativity and tireless commitment to excellence are inspiring. I am deeply grateful to all of you for your incredible writing, editing, research, ideas, passion, and good humor, and for helping shape our vision and this book at every step of the way. Thank you so very much.

 Laura Town, Founder, Williams Town Communications, and Development Editor, *Williams Town Communications*

 Chris Allen Thomas, Manager, Research and Knowledge, *Teleos Leadership Institute*

 Jim LoPresti, Adjunct Professor, Management *University of Colorado at Boulder* and President of CohereUs Consulting

 Christina Yerkes, Manager of Client Services, *Teleos Leadership Institute*

Special thanks also to Spenser Wigsten. I would also like to thank the team at **Williams Town Communications** for your professionalism and outstanding work on this book. To Rachael Mann, Amanda Boyle, and Sam Clapp, thank you!

To our **editorial review board**: You have each contributed to the vision of this book in so many ways, and your writing, research, editing, guidance, feedback, and advice have been outstanding. I appreciate all that you have done, and I feel honored to know you and to have worked with you on this book. Thank you. In addition to our core editorial review board, special thanks also to my editorial support team. Your talents, knowledge, and enthusiasm are much appreciated: Stephen Adams, *Salisbury University*; Gabriela Albescu, *Academy of Economic Studies in Foreign Languages, Bucharest, Romania*; Bella L. Galperin, *University of Tampa*; Ondrej Gandel, *University of Economics, Prague, Czech Republic; Alumni of AIESEC International*; Martha A. Hunt, *New Hampshire Technical Institute*; Mary Jo Jackson, *University of South Florida, St. Petersburg*; William T. Jackson, *University of South Florida, St. Petersburg*; Frances Johnston, *Teleos Leadership Institute*; Mary Beth Kerly, *Hillsborough Community College*; Jim LoPresti, *University of Colorado at Boulder*; Delores Mason, *2YourWell-Being*; Eddy Mwelwa, *Teleos Leadership Institute*; Bobbie Nash, *Teleos Leadership Institute*; Clint Relyea, *Arkansas State University, Jonesboro*; Mike Shaner, *Saint Louis University*; Steven Austin Stovall, *Wilmington College*; Charlotte D. Sutton, *Auburn University*.

Thank you as well to our **editorial reviewer team**. Your feedback on each and every edition is extremely helpful. As a writer, I truly recognize the value of outside review.

The time, attention, and professionalism you gave to this process was outstanding. I am deeply grateful for your review and feedback—and I acted on it! Thank you very much to Jeffrey Aizenberg, *Creighton University;* Michael Alleruzzo, *Saint Joseph's University;* Susan L. Alvarez, *Indiana University, Indianapolis;* Ron Anderson, *University of Oklahoma;* Kenneth Anderson, *Mott Community College;* Dr. Steven Austin Stovall, *Wilmington College;* Gene Blackmun III, *Rio Hondo College;* Stephen Braccio, *Vaughn College;* Michael G. Brizek, *South Carolina State University;* Michael J. Campo, *Regis University;* Wendy J. Casper, *University of Texas at Arlington;* Frank T. Clements, Jr., *State College of Florida, Manatee-Sarasota;* Dr. Aleta L. Crawford, *The University of Mississippi, Tupelo Campus;* Kathleen Davis, *Temple University;* Janice Ferguson, *Bryant and Stratton College;* Chuck Foley, *Columbus State Community College;* Pat Galitz, *Southeast Community College;* Dan Hallock, *University of Northern Alabama;* David Hearst, *Florida Atlantic University;* Mary Jo Jackson, *University of Tampa;* Syed Kazmi, *Brown Mackie College—Fort Wayne;* Martha Spears, *Winthrop University;* Jim LoPresti, *University of Colorado at Boulder;* Kimberly Lukaszewski, *State University of New York at New Paltz;* Dr. James Marcin, *Methodist University;* Antonio Papuzza, *University of Colorado at Boulder;* Douglas Scott, *State College of Florida;* Dr. Joanna Shaw, *Tarleton State University;* Miles Smayling, Minnesota State; Dr. Ronda M. Smith-Nelson, *Fort Hays State University;* Mary Tucker, *Ohio University;* Pamela A. Weldon, *Lehigh Carbon Community College;* Deborah Windes, *University of Illinois.*

The team at **Pearson Education** has worked tirelessly to bring this vision to life. Thank you all so very much. I have great respect for all that you have contributed—your great ideas, knowledge, and expertise. Special thanks to Stephanie Wall, April Kalal Cole, Claudia Fernandes, Bernard Ollila, Kelly Warsak, Judy Leale, Kenny Beck, Brooks Hill-Wilton, and Steve Deitmer. A special thank you as well to Sally Yagan.

Thank you, too, to the entire team at **S4Carlisle Publishing Services,** especially Lori Bradshaw, Cathy Seckman, Michael Rossa, and Julie Lewis.

This book is meant to bring "real life" into the classroom. To all of the **resonant leaders** who contributed time, wisdom, guidance, and real-life experience through your stories, heartfelt thanks: Bonaventure Agata, CSL Behring; Dolores Bernardo, Google; Vittorio Colao, Vodafone Group; Niall FitzGerald, British Museum and Hakluyt; John Fry, president, Drexel University; Michael Gaines, CSL Behring; Jill Guindon-Nasir, Ritz-Carlton Hotel Company; Mark McCord-Amasis, GlaxoSmithKline; Mary McNevin, Rafidah Mohamad Noor, Malaysia; Luis Ottley, Gavin Patterson, British Telecom Group; Charles H. Ramsey, Philadelphia Police Department; Sheila Robinson, Diversity Woman; Chade-Meng Tan, Google; Ivor D'Souza, National Institutes of Health; Connie Wayne, Eaton; Dan Nowlin, Sunglass Hut; Sandy Cutler, Eaton; Litha Giza, Eastern Cape Provincial Government, South Africa; Gavin Kerr, Joan Snyder Kuhl, Forest Laboratories; Frances Hesselbein, Leader to Leader Institute; John Reid-Dodick, AOL; Cathy Casserly, Creative Commons; Fred Hassan, Bausch + Lomb; Jane Luciano, Bristol-Myers Squibb; Mukul Pandia, The Wharton School; Ninan Chacko, PR Newswire; Henry Moniz, Viacom; Annette Rincke, Eaton; Mary Ellen Joyce, The Brookings Institution; Angela Scalpello, PR Newswire; Stefano Bertuzzi, American Society for Cell Biology; David Sutphen, Brunswick Group; Litha Giza, Eastern Cape Provincial Government, South Africa; and Gavin Kerr, Inglis House.

To my **Teleos Leadership Institute colleagues**: Thank all of you for all that you do to help others be the very best they can be. Your commitment to great leadership and resonant teams, organizations, and communities is inspirational! Thank you to the core team and our wonderful associates: Eddy Mwelwa, Frances Johnston, Bobbie Nash, Marco Bertola, Alberto Castigliano, Lee Chalmers, Fiona Coffey, Kaye Craft, Delores Mason, Cordula Gibson, Shirley Gregoire McAlpine, Judy Issokson, Janet Jones, Jeff Kaplan, Hilary Lines, Jochen Lochmeier, Gianluca Lotti, Robert McDowell,

Michael McElhenie, Nosisa Mdutshane, Bill Palmer, Laura Peck, Linda Pittari, Gretchen Schmelzer, Felice Tilin, Kristin von Donop, Lothar Wüst, Chantelle Wyley, Christina Yerkes, Greg Yerkes, Amy Yoggev, Lindsey Bingaman, Makenzie Newman, Laurie Carrick, Paul Thallner, Jim LoPresti, and Margret Klinkhammer.

To the many **friends and colleagues** who have helped shape the ideas and research in this book, I trust I have honored your contributions. Special thanks to my friends Richard Boyatzis, Peter Cappelli, Daniel Goleman, Peter Kuriloff, Greg Shea, and Kenwyn Smith. Thank you, too, to all the colleagues near and far who have influenced my thinking about leadership: Darlyne Bailey, Ann Baker, Laura Mari Barrajón, Diana Bilimoria, Susan Case, Cary Cherniss, Judy Cocquio, Luigi Cocquio, Harlow Cohen, David Cooperrider, Charlie Davidson, Arne Dietrich, Christine Dreyfus, Charles E. Dwyer, Ella L. J. Edmondson, Rob Emmerling, Jim Fairfield-Sonn, Ingrid FitzGerald, Mary Francone, Ronald Fry, Jonno Hanafin, Hank Jonas, Lennox Joseph, Jeff Kehoe, Toni Denton King, David Kolb, Lezlie Lovett, Carolyn Lukensmeyer, Doug Lynch, Tom Malnight, Jacqueline McLemore, Cecilia McMillen, Mary Grace Neville, Ed Nevis, Roberto Nicastro, Eric Nielson, John Nkum, Dennis O'Connor, Asbjorn Osland, Joyce Osland, Arjan Overwater, William Pasmore, Mary Ann Rainey, Peter Reason, Leslie Reed, Ken Rhee, Craig Seal, Joe Selzer, Dorothy Siminovitch, David Smith, Melvin Smith, Gretchen Spreitzer, Sue Taft, Scott Taylor, Ram Tenkasi, Tojo Joseph Thachankary, Felice Tilin, Lechesa Tsenoli, Bill van Buskirk, Kees van der Graaf, Susan Wheelan, Jane Wheeler, Judith White, Stanton Wortham, Andy Porter, Carolyn Merritt, Mahlubandile Qwase, Ariel Fishman, Shanil Haricharan, Eileen Meyer, Jalajakshi Krishnappa, Michael Johanek, Arianna Huffington, Jenn Moyer, Dr. Alecia Monroe, Alessa English, Erica Mahady, and Alan Otsuki.

Finally, to **my family**, you inspire me! Heartfelt thanks to Eddy Mwelwa, Rebecca Renio, Sean Renio, Sarah Renio, Benjamin Renio, Andrew Murphy, Toby Nash, Murray R. Wigsten Sr., Carol Wigsten, Murray R. Wigsten Jr., Karen Wigsten, Matthew Wigsten, Camille Wigsten, Mark Wigsten, Joyce Wigsten, Lori Wigsten, Jeff Wigsten, Juliane Wigsten, Spenser Wigsten, Samantha Hagstrom, Erik Hagstrom, Bobbie Nash, Mildred Muyembe, Ginny Lindseth, Jon Lindseth, Rita MacDonald, Warren Wigsten, Betty Wigsten, Ellie Browning, and Buzz Browning.

About the Author

Annie McKee has coauthored three groundbreaking books on leadership: *Primal Leadership* (with Daniel Goleman and Richard Boyatzis), *Resonant Leadership* (also with Boyatzis), and *Becoming a Resonant Leader* (with Richard Boyatzis and Frances Johnston). She is a Senior Fellow at the University of Pennsylvania. She is a guest lecturer at the Wharton School's Aresty Institute of Executive Education and speaks on leadership at businesses and institutions around the globe. McKee is the founder of the Teleos Leadership Institute, a consultancy serving managers and leaders of businesses and not-for-profits all over the world. She received her doctorate in organizational behavior from Case Western Reserve University and her baccalaureate degree, summa cum laude, from Chaminade University in Honolulu. Her life's work has been to support individuals in reaching their full potential as people, employees, and leaders, as they contribute to their families, organizations, and communities. As she puts it, "Today, every one of us needs to be an outstanding and resonant leader. Whatever we do, and wherever we are, we are called upon to bring the best of ourselves to support one another, our organizations, and our communities. My hope is that this book will help you to realize your dreams, to become a resonant leader, and to contribute to our world in a positive and powerful way."

Managing and Leading Today:
The New Rules

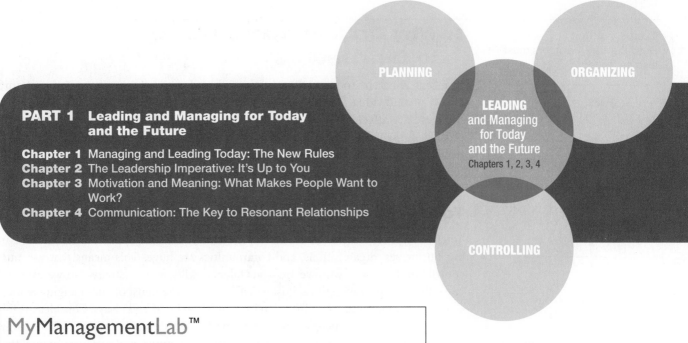

PLANNING

ORGANIZING

LEADING and Managing for Today and the Future
Chapters 1, 2, 3, 4

CONTROLLING

MyManagementLab™

⭐ **Improve Your Grade!**

Over 10 million students improved their results using the Pearson MyLabs. Visit **mymanagementlab.com** for simulations, tutorials, and end-of-chapter problems.

Chapter Outline

1. Why Do Managers Have to Be Leaders? (pp. 4–7)
2. What Is the Difference between a Manager and a Leader? (pp. 7–11)
3. What Is the Other Side of the Leadership Coin? (pp. 11–13)
4. What Is HR's Role in Managing and Leading Today? (pp. 13–14)
5. What Can We All Do to Become Excellent Managers, Leaders, and Followers? (pp. 14–15)
6. A Final Word: Changing World, Changing Expectations of Managers and Leaders (pp. 15–16)

Chapter Objectives

1.1 Describe why managers must also be leaders.
1.2 Differentiate between managers and leaders.
1.3 Explain what is meant by the "other side" of the leadership coin.
1.4 Summarize HR's role in managing and leading.
1.5 Describe what we can do to become excellent managers, leaders, and followers.

Objective 1.1
Describe why managers must also be leaders.

1. Why Do Managers Have to Be Leaders?

In recent years environmental, technological, and social changes have had profound effects on individuals, families, communities, and governments everywhere. These changes have affected the ways in which businesses and organizations are designed, organized, managed, and led, as well as the ways in which people do their jobs and relate with one another at work. Along with these changes come new responsibilities for leaders, managers, and employees alike.

Today, Everyone Needs to Be a Leader

Today, *everyone needs to be a leader*. The challenges and opportunities we face in our businesses, organizations, and communities are huge. This means that we must contribute the best of who we are—our talents, skills, and creativity—so we can successfully make positive, ethical business decisions in the midst of our changing world.[1]

Change is good, but it requires us to work and lead in different ways. Consider the following: More and more people around the world have access to information, technology, and a better way of life. Changes in global politics, economics, and societies demand that businesses be linked to social factors in ways never seen before. For example:

- The balance of world economic and political power is shifting from West to East, resulting in turmoil and uncertainty, as well as great hope.[2]
- Partly because of better access to food, clean water, and health care, the human population is growing at an unprecedented rate, as is the demand for resources such as land, water, education, and jobs (■ **EXHIBIT 1.1**).
- Open Educational Resources (OER) are rapidly expanding access to education and information around the world.[3]
- Rapidly expanding access to telecommunications means that people around the world are far more interconnected than in the past, but increased industrialization and globalization mean that environmental resources are at risk.
- Ongoing changes in the world's climate are cause for concern.
- Some groups and individuals continue to be left out of the advances and benefits that positive economic changes, computers, and advanced telecommunications can provide.
- Partly as a result of the Great Recession that began in 2007, capitalism itself is being challenged.[4]

The rapidly changing world we live in means that the days when some people led, some managed, and others just blindly followed orders are gone. In your career, you will be called on to do all three: lead, manage, and follow.

What Being a Leader Means for You

What do these changes mean for you at work? You will be called on to respond ethically, positively, and powerfully to the many transformations that are occurring in our world. This requires you to know your own values as well as your organization's ethical code and to make good decisions—often very quickly and without complete information. To do so, you

■ **EXHIBIT 1.1**
What benefits and risks accompany global population growth?

Source: Bildagentur/Glow Images

must engage in analytical thinking and rely on your intuition. You will also need to build strong, trusting relationships with others and communicate well with people at all levels of the organization. Developing your self-awareness, your capacity for empathy, and your ability to manage yourself well in stressful situations are key components for building these relationships. Understanding and managing your own and others' emotions are also invaluable in this endeavor. This is called emotional intelligence.[5] Self-awareness, self-management, and empathy, among other skills, enable you to inspire people; build powerful and effective teams; deal with conflict; and guide, coach, and mentor others.[6] People all over the world are working hard to understand what it means to be a great leader today.

You have choices about what you do, how you live your values, and how you influence others. You have opportunities all the time to *lead* other people, no matter what role you hold in an organization. Now, think about your own experience: Have you worked in a job where your manager directed *everything* you did every day? Were you also influenced by colleagues and your boss's boss? Did you manage *yourself* some of the time? It is highly unlikely that all your instruction and guidance came from your manager, and it's even less likely that you were influenced only by people above you, or that you yourself had no influence. Rather, you were guided by all the people around you, as they were by you.

Many dynamic young leaders understand that everyone needs to be a leader today. They lead—and live—in a way that inspires people. They help others succeed. Dolores Bernardo, leadership development manager at Google, is one such leader. Her wise and noteworthy advice is in the *Leadership Perspective* feature.

Just think about the implications of what Dolores Bernardo says. What if every one of us thought of ourselves as a leader? What if you decided to see yourself as a leader *now*, rather than waiting until you are more advanced in your career? What if

Leadership Perspective

Companies like Google truly understand that success depends on creating an environment where everyone can bring their best selves to work: their talents, their passions, and their leadership. Dolores Bernardo's mission is to bring this strategy to life and to ensure that Google's unique, diverse, and innovative culture enables every single person in the company to lead. Let's look at what she says about what it takes to be a great leader at work and in life today.

I think of leadership as a verb—it's about taking action. It's about inspiring others to come along with you. It's about taking the time to reflect. And it's about taking the time to build connections and relationships with people so they believe in what you are trying to do—and so they believe in you.

Anyone can be a leader at Google. That's the only way any of our companies will succeed today. If every single Googler feels empowered to innovate, to create new products and improve on existing ones, we'll not only keep up
with the changes that are happening around us, we'll be the change. Each one of us needs to think this way: we can't just respond to change, we have to lead change. Our success hinges on our ability to understand the needs of all Google's hundreds of millions of users. The unique perspective that each person brings to leadership is what makes Google's products serve our diverse user community.

Source: Personal interviews with Dolores Bernardo conducted by Annie McKee, 2009 and 2012.

● **Dolores Bernardo**
Leadership Development Manager at Google: "I think of leadership as a verb..."

we all took seriously our responsibility to inspire others, reflect on our actions, and build positive, powerful relationships? If we all acted this way, we'd have a much better chance of harnessing the brain power we need to face the challenges and opportunities in our organizations, our communities, and the world.

Still, many people don't see themselves as leaders. Part of the reason for this is that from the time we were small, we have been taught that leadership and authority go hand in hand with certain roles: parent, school principal, business owner. It's true: All of these roles require leadership. What's different today is that we can't simply rely on others to lead. We all need to be leaders, no matter what position we hold.

Discussion Questions

1. Think about the groups you are part of, including groups associated with your family, friends, school, and work. Who looks to you for leadership in these groups? What do they expect from you? How do you inspire them to follow you?

2. Complete the "Whom Do You Lead" exercise to discover the ways that you are a leader (◼ **EXHIBIT 1.2**).

◼ **EXHIBIT 1.2**

Whom Do You Lead?

1. On the chart on the following pages, brainstorm and write a list of several of the groups you belong to. Break these groups down as much as you can (e.g., instead of writing "family," note the various branches and groups within your family; instead of writing "work," describe your immediate team, the organization around it, and groups that you touch or have some responsibility for). Be sure to also list groups in which your authority is informal, and your "title" isn't the only source of your power. Finally, consider other arenas where you guide, advise, and help people.

2. Next to each group, label or name your role (e.g., "sister" or "brother"; "oldest cousin"; "team leader"; etc).

3. For each position, formal and informal, describe your role (e.g., "I am the person everyone comes to when there is a conflict in the family"; "I am the one who knows the professor"; "I am the designated team leader").

4. For each of your roles, write who looks to you for guidance, help, and vision and describe what they look for from you. Be as specific as you can (e.g., "My family looks to me to resolve problems"; "My team looks to me to understand their needs, provide help, remove obstacles, and share information"; "My boss looks to me to deliver on my promises").

My groups	My role	Description of my role	People and groups who turn to me for help, guidance, or direction	What people look for from me

Continued on next page >>

My groups	My role	Description of my role	People and groups who turn to me for help, guidance, or direction	What people look for from me

Source: Adapted from Annie McKee, Richard Boyatzis, and Frances Johnston. 2008. *Becoming a resonant leader*. Boston: Harvard Business School Press.

■ **EXHIBIT 1.2**
Continued

2. What Is the Difference between a Manager and a Leader?

Objective 1.2
Differentiate between managers and leaders.

What's the difference between a manager and a leader? Let's first consider what each of the words means. The verb *manage* comes from the Italian *maneggiare* (to handle). Back in the 1500s, the word referred to the handling of horses. The root of *maneggiare* comes from the Latin word *manus* (hand). Notice that *handle*—meaning *to control*—has a similar origin, in this sense: A person's hand is a tool for physically controlling the environment. The meanings of these words were eventually extended and are now used to refer to controlling and handling resources in organizations.

The word *leader* can be traced back to Old English *lædan* (to guide; to cause to go with one). It is also a form of *lian* (to travel). So, the word leader can be interpreted as someone who guides others on a journey. This way of looking at leadership is about *influencing* rather than forcing people to go in a particular direction.

So, a **manager** is an individual who makes plans; organizes and controls people, production, and services; and who regulates or deploys resources. A **leader** is a person who influences and inspires people to follow. There is no reason whatsoever that a manager can't be a leader, or that a leader can't manage. In fact, the political, social, and technological changes of recent years require all of us to do both (■ **EXHIBIT 1.3**).

Some leaders really *get* this—and they work to hone the skills that will enable them to both lead and manage effectively as the world changes rapidly. This is important in all industries, but particularly so in those that are technology dependent and tied to changes in societies, such as media. Viacom, which includes brands such as MTV, BET, Nickelodeon, and Paramount, to name just a few, is one such company. Henry Moniz, Chief Compliance Officer, Chief Audit Officer, and Global Head of Strategic Business Practices, shows us exactly how important it is to manage and lead for today's world, not yesterday's, in the *Leadership Perspective* feature.

As Henry Moniz points out, there are a number of skills that cross the boundaries between management and leadership: authenticity, vision, openness, and embracing change, to name just a few. These skills can't be reserved for leaders anymore.

■ **EXHIBIT 1.3**
What responsibilities does the Dalai Lama, the spiritual leader of Tibet, share with Nancy Pelosi, the first female speaker of the U.S. House of Representatives?

Source: Oliver Douliery/Abaca Press/MCT/ Newscom

My groups	My role	Description of my role	People and groups who turn to me for help, guidance, or direction	What people look for from me

Source: Adapted from Annie McKee, Richard Boyatzis, and Frances Johnston. 2008. *Becoming a resonant leader.* Boston: Harvard Business School Press.

■ **EXHIBIT 1.2**
Continued

2. What Is the Difference between a Manager and a Leader?

Objective 1.2
Differentiate between managers and leaders.

What's the difference between a manager and a leader? Let's first consider what each of the words means. The verb *manage* comes from the Italian *maneggiare* (to handle). Back in the 1500s, the word referred to the handling of horses. The root of *maneggiare* comes from the Latin word *manus* (hand). Notice that *handle*—meaning *to control*—has a similar origin, in this sense: A person's hand is a tool for physically controlling the environment. The meanings of these words were eventually extended and are now used to refer to controlling and handling resources in organizations.

The word *leader* can be traced back to Old English *lædan* (to guide; to cause to go with one). It is also a form of *lian* (to travel). So, the word leader can be interpreted as someone who guides others on a journey. This way of looking at leadership is about *influencing* rather than forcing people to go in a particular direction.

So, a **manager** is an individual who makes plans; organizes and controls people, production, and services; and who regulates or deploys resources. A **leader** is a person who influences and inspires people to follow. There is no reason whatsoever that a manager can't be a leader, or that a leader can't manage. In fact, the political, social, and technological changes of recent years require all of us to do both (■ **EXHIBIT 1.3**).

Some leaders really *get* this—and they work to hone the skills that will enable them to both lead and manage effectively as the world changes rapidly. This is important in all industries, but particularly so in those that are technology dependent and tied to changes in societies, such as media. Viacom, which includes brands such as MTV, BET, Nickelodeon, and Paramount, to name just a few, is one such company. Henry Moniz, Chief Compliance Officer, Chief Audit Officer, and Global Head of Strategic Business Practices, shows us exactly how important it is to manage and lead for today's world, not yesterday's, in the *Leadership Perspective* feature.

As Henry Moniz points out, there are a number of skills that cross the boundaries between management and leadership: authenticity, vision, openness, and embracing change, to name just a few. These skills can't be reserved for leaders anymore.

■ **EXHIBIT 1.3**
What responsibilities does the Dalai Lama, the spiritual leader of Tibet, share with Nancy Pelosi, the first female speaker of the U.S. House of Representatives?

Source: Oliver Douliery/Abaca Press/MCT/Newscom

Leadership Perspective

Henry Moniz is a remarkable man and an outstanding leader. His story is anything but ordinary, and he is dedicated to bringing what he learns from his life to his career. Here's what he has to say about being a great leader and manager:

"Great leadership starts with being authentic. If you aren't, and you don't really believe in what you are trying to accomplish, then no one will follow you. Position alone no longer confers authority. And staying authentic can be a challenge as you and your function and/or company evolve. If you lose sight of what you are and what really matters to you, and how that all relates to your pursuit of the broader goals, you can become perilously untethered.

At the same time that you are continually refining how to embody and inhabit those grander goals, you must also be able to communicate your vision in a clear way—even if it is not entirely clear as yet how you will realize it. In fact, it's impossible to predict all of the components you will need to achieve your big picture goals, but if you aren't authentic and your teams do not believe in you and understand and believe in your vision, they can't help you and you won't go anywhere good.

A key skill for executing against your vision is deciphering the context in which you are operating; that is, understanding the situation—in all its complexity—around you, your team, goals, company, industry, the market, relevant economies, etc. Understanding the context is critical to giving proper weight to the loads of information pouring over your desk and isolating the "relevant" pieces. This enables you to eliminate spurious variables and avoid being overwhelmed. It also takes a great deal of mental agility to be able to see things from many perspectives without getting lost. Can you stay open to new approaches, information and ideas without being side tracked by extraneous ones, and then go back and alter your assumptions even as you continually assimilate new data points? This is particularly relevant if you operate in diverse geographies, with people who are very different from you. In today's global markets, different people approach

work, rules, problem-solving, etc., very differently. For example, in some cultures one must have lunch, tea, and/or dinner many times before you even think of doing business, developing the relationship is key. In U.S. business culture, we tend to jump right in, and can become impatient in situations like those, much to our detriment ultimately.

While this all seems logical, it is of course, useless without the ability to drive people to work together on common goals. People often take positions which at first blush may seem to be at odds. When those positions are not aligned with the larger interests of the organization, the leader must step in to correct the distortions. Do you have the strong, core sense of self, confidence and patience required to confront others who are being excessively and perhaps, needlessly, oppositional, rigid and closed minded?

Finally, to be a great leader, manager and follower, you need to learn to embrace change, which is inevitable in this increasingly dynamic world. It has become a cliché, but too few people actually do it. It starts, of course, with a mindset of change representing opportunities, getting comfortable with taking calculated risks and accepting that you won't always succeed (at least not on the first try any way). But without risk, there is no real growth, or true success, in life or at work.

● **Henry Moniz**
Chief Compliance Officer, Chief Audit Officer, and Global Head of Strategic Business Practices at Viacom: ". . . if you aren't authentic and you don't have a vision, you won't go anywhere."

Source: Personal interview with Henry Moniz conducted by Annie McKee, 2012.

Manager
An individual who makes plans; organizes and controls people, production, and services; and who regulates or deploys resources.

Leader
A person who is out in front, influencing and inspiring people to follow.

We all need to manage *and* lead. However, historical views and much of the research have separated management and leadership and assumed that people are either one or the other. This type of differentiation between management and leadership is not useful in our complex organizations.

Let's look at the early research and perspectives on which this differentiation between management and leadership was based. Once we understand these assumptions, we can begin to adjust them to fit today's world.

Traditional Views of Managers and Leaders

Managers have been encouraged to focus their energies on problem solving and controlling resources, while leaders have been encouraged to focus on vision, inspiration,

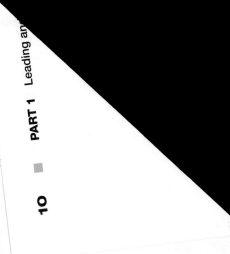

and the wider environment. Managers have been taught to see the *independence* their tasks and responsibilities in relation to their division or functional unit, where leaders have been encouraged to view and oversee the *interdependence* of all task people, and functions in the organization, rather than picturing them as isolated, self contained "silos."

Managers are expected to be tactical, implementing the strategic vision of their leaders like good soldiers. Managers are tasked with establishing and administering order and control to reduce complexity. In contrast, a leader is expected to thrive on chaos and possess a unique vision for the organization. Research has sought to articulate these perceived differences, as shown in ■ **EXHIBIT 1.4**.

In summary, one could say that managers have traditionally been expected to occupy themselves with the status quo. Leaders, on the other hand, have been called on to ask important questions about the organization's future: "Where are we going?" "How are we going to get there?" "What if?" Also, whereas a manager has historically been seen as someone who does things "right," a leader is more often pictured as someone who can be called on to "do the right thing."

■ **EXHIBIT 1.4**

A Traditional View of What Managers and Leaders Do	
Managers Tend to . . .	**Leaders Tend to . . .**
• Control resources.	• Create and provide resources through motivation.
• Be problem solvers.	• Be comfortable with uncertainty.
• Seek efficiency.	• Function well in chaotic environments.
• Be comfortable with order.	• Be concerned with what events and decisions mean to people.
• Be concerned with how things get done.	• Seek solutions that do not require compromise.
• Play for time and delay major decisions.	• Take highly personal attitudes toward goals.
• Seek compromises.	• Identify goals that arise out of desire.
• Identify goals that arise out of necessity.	• Inspire strong emotions.
• Adopt impersonal attitudes toward goals.	• Be comfortable with solitude.
• Coordinate and balance opposing views.	• Work from or seek out high-risk activities.
• Avoid solitary activities.	• Have meaningful, highly personal mentorship relationships.
• Work from low-risk positions.	• Be empathic and actively read others' emotional signals.
• Avoid displaying empathy.	

Source: Adapted from Zaleznik, Abraham, 1992. Managers and leaders: Are they different? *Harvard Business Review* (March–April): 126–35.

What Managers *Actually* Do

So what exactly does a manager do? Noted scholar Henry Mintzberg decided to answer that question by following managers on the job and recording their daily activities. Despite the fact that this research was conducted many years ago, Mintzberg's findings are important and continue to be relevant today. This is because we still have a mistaken image that managers spend their time on an orderly set of planning and organizing activities. In fact, as Mintzberg discovered, a manager's work is fraught with meetings, pressure to deliver performance results, and a great deal of "fire fighting," or constantly addressing unexpected issues. Managers, according to Mintzberg, put in long work hours and work at an intense pace.

Based on this research, Mintzberg came up with a solid outline for a manager's "job description" as described in ■ **EXHIBIT 1.5**. Each of the three broad categories—informational, interpersonal, and decisional—is a category into which multiple roles fall. The *informational* category includes the roles of monitor, disseminator, and spokesperson. The *interpersonal* category includes the roles of figurehead, leader, and liaison, and the *decisional* category includes the roles of entrepreneur, disturbance handler, resource allocator, and negotiator.[8]

Today, many of these roles and activities are expected of more people—people who may not formally be called "managers." That's because during the past two decades, many businesses and organizations have streamlined operations and decision making. Whereas it used to be that only managers—and many times, senior managers—did things like disseminate information, foster innovation, or negotiate contracts, nowadays nonmanagerial staff is often empowered to do these things.

Today's managers also *lead*. As you will see in Chapter 2, *The Leadership Imperative*, a vast amount of research has been done on leadership behavior. The early studies about leadership looked at personal characteristics and physical, intellectual, and psychological traits. Later research focused on leadership behaviors and styles and the importance of being able to adapt one's approach to a particular situation.

■ **EXHIBIT 1.5**

Henry Mintzberg's Managerial Roles

Category	Role	Organizational Function	Example Activities
Informational	Monitor	Responsible for information relevant to understanding the organization's internal and external environment	Handle correspondence and information such as industry, societal, and economic news and competitive information
	Disseminator	Responsible for the synthesis, integration, and forwarding of information to other members of the organization	Forward informational e-mails; share information in meetings, conference calls, webcasts, etc.
	Spokesperson	Transmit information to outsiders about organizational policy, plans, outcomes, etc.	Attend management meetings; maintain networks between the organization and stakeholders
Interpersonal	Figurehead	Symbolic leadership duties involving social and legal matters	Attend ceremonies; greet visitors; organize and attend events with clients, customers, bankers, etc.
	Leader	Motivate, inspire, and guide employees' actions; provide opportunities for training; support appropriate staffing	Build trusting relationships with employees; build effective teams; manage conflict
	Liaison	Build and maintain relationships between the organization and outside entities	Work on external boards; create and maintain social networks (real and virtual) with key stakeholders
Decisional	Entrepreneur	Scan the organizational environment for opportunities; foster creativity and innovation	Participate in strategy and review meetings for new projects or continuous improvement
	Disturbance handler	Manage organizational problems and crises	Participate in strategy and review meetings that involve problems and crises; get involved directly with key issues and people
	Resource allocator	Take responsibility for allocation of all types of organizational resources	Create work schedules; make authorization requests; participate in budgeting activities
	Negotiator	Represent the organization during any significant negotiations	Negotiate with vendors and clients; settle disputes about resource allocation

Source: Mintzberg, Henry, The Nature of Managerial Work, 1st Ed., © 1973. Reprinted by permission of Pearson Education, Inc., Upper Saddle River, New Jersey.

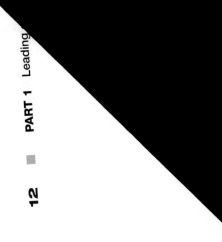

More recently, research has focused on bringing various fields of study together to help us understand what it means to lead effectively. For example, research in the areas of management, psychology, and neuroscience is helping us understand that social and emotional intelligence competencies, ethics, and the responsible use of power are key to great leadership. Emerging from this research is the growing understanding that one of the foundations of good leadership is self-awareness: the capacity to reflect on, articulate, and understand one's emotions, thought processes, and physical responses to certain situations (like stress). Throughout this book, we will encourage you to develop self-awareness as the first step in becoming an outstanding leader.

In this section, we have looked at the traditional views of what managers and leaders do, and we've made a case that at work, everyone needs to be both a manager and a leader. We all need to learn skills that will enable us to plan, organize people and resources, and control processes. We also need to learn to show people who we are and what we stand for and to demonstrate skills and competencies that will enable us to inspire others to follow our lead. Finally, we need to learn how to follow others. Leadership is not a one-way street. We all lead, and we all follow.

Discussion Questions

1. Think about the last time you worked on a project with a group at work or in school. What did you and others do that could be described as "managerial" behavior? What did you and others do that could be described as "leadership" behavior?

2. Consider Mintzberg's managerial roles in Exhibit 1.5. Which of these roles are easy for you to play or come to you naturally? Which roles do you think you need to learn more about or learn how to do better?

3. What Is the Other Side of the Leadership Coin?

Objective 1.3
Explain what is meant by the "other side" of the leadership coin.

Without followers, there are no leaders. So although we must strive to develop self-awareness, focus on our values and ethics, and learn to lead responsibly, we also need to learn how to follow.[9] Think about your own experience: More than likely you have been in the position of trying to lead a group in which some members simply didn't want to follow you. They wanted to do their own thing, they resisted being influenced, or they caused disruption. Often, this kind of behavior doesn't arise because people fundamentally disagree with what is being asked of them—they just don't want anyone else telling them what to do. In today's highly interconnected complex organizations, this attitude just doesn't work.

What does it mean to be a good follower? Bookstores and workshops are full of information on how to be a good leader, but there is less about what it takes to be an effective follower. That's partly because we simply don't know as much about followership. From Plato to Machiavelli to the researchers and philosophers of today, leaders and leadership have captured our imaginations, not followers or followership. For some, even the idea of following leaves a bad taste in the mouth. Why is that? It might be partly because in many cultures followership is seen in a very negative light.[10] How many times have you heard followers described as "mindless sheep"? This attitude is a significant problem in today's flatter, more networked organizations where the line between who is leading and who is following is often blurred.[11] When you think about it, *everyone* in an organization is a follower—even the CEO (chief executive officer). Despite being at the very top of the organization, he or she follows the wishes of customers, or the mandates of governing bodies like the board of directors. We all follow others, every single day of our lives.

So, what does it really mean to be a good follower? Does it mean we give up our power, our opinions, or our strength? Hardly. In fact, it's exactly the opposite. Being a good follower means being able to understand what we need to do to support leaders—and everyone else—in achieving our shared goals. Being a good follower means finding ways to teach and guide others, even when we don't have direct authority or the right to tell people what to do. Being a good follower means being *involved*.

Good followers, according to Harvard professor Barbara Kellerman, are actively engaged and supportive of their leaders and the organization's goals. She proposes a model that can help us understand how to be an effective follower that also includes what to be on guard against.[12] As you can see in ■ **EXHIBIT 1.6**, Kellerman's model includes five types of followers: isolates, bystanders, participants, activists, and diehards.[13]

Good followers know how to use their skills and enthusiasm in support of the work that needs to get done. They also help to create an environment that is full of excitement and shared commitment. They support their leaders, but they don't follow blindly: They respond appropriately to bad leaders, too. When, for example, a good follower is asked to engage in unethical behavior, or even questionable behavior, he or she finds a way to have the right conversations with the right people so no transgressions occur. Influencing our leaders like this is often called managing up—a useful skill you will want to learn and practice.[14]

Managing up
A followership tool that enables followers to influence leaders.

A final word, for now, on followership: One of the most respected leadership scholars in the world, Warren Bennis, notes that acceptable characteristics of both leaders and followers are often different from culture to culture.[15] For example, the concept of empowerment is highly culture dependent and means something different to employees around the globe.[16] As organizations become more globally integrated, these cultural differences are likely to become increasingly important.

Large organizations are complex systems, and their fate in a globally competitive environment may very well depend on how well leaders understand and respond to followers, as well as how we all learn to follow when things change and the rules of engagement are different.[17]

So, although we started this chapter with the statement "Today, everyone needs to be a leader," we now add ". . . and everyone needs to be an effective follower."

■ **EXHIBIT 1.6**

Types of Followers

- **Isolates:** Isolates are nonresponsive or indifferent to their leaders. They are typically found in large organizations. They do their jobs and make no effort to stand out.

- **Bystanders:** Bystanders are exactly what the name implies. They are not engaged in the life of the organization. They are observers and spectators rather than active participants, passively doing their jobs and offering little active support.

- **Participants:** Participants are actively engaged and make an effort to support and impact the organization. If they agree with a leader, they will support him or her. If they disagree, they will oppose the leader.

- **Activists:** Activists feel even more strongly about their organizations and leaders than participants and act accordingly. When supportive, they are eager, energetic, and engaged. When they disagree strongly with what a leader does, they are vocal and will take action.

- **Diehards:** Diehards are passionate about an idea, a person, or both and will give all for them. When diehards consider something worthy, they become dedicated.

Source: Kellerman, Barbara. 2007. What every leader needs to know about followers. *Harvard Business Review* 85(12): 84–91.

In the next two sections we will introduce ways that "people issues" can be dealt with and enhanced at work. In the first section, "What Is HR's Role in Managing and Leading Today?" we will focus on things that can be done by HR (human resources) to support people and skill development. In each chapter we will address HR issues relevant to the particular topics covered in the chapter. In the second section, "What Can We All Do to Become Excellent Managers, Leaders, and Followers?" we will explore ways that all of us can become better leaders.

Discussion Questions

1. When have you been a good follower? What inspired you or encouraged you to take up this role in a positive way?

2. What do you do when you are expected to follow someone, yet you know what he or she is doing is wrong or could be done better? How effective are you at influencing that person from the follower position?

4. What Is HR's Role in Managing and Leading Today?

Objective 1.4
Summarize HR's role in managing and leading.

Human resource (HR) management includes the strategic approach to managing and developing an organization's workforce. Unfortunately, the complexity of this endeavor is often underestimated because many people are unaware of the broad range of leadership roles HR plays within the organization. HR differs from other forms of management in that it focuses on the wider organization through implementation of recruitment, training, compensation, and labor relations strategies. It is important for you to understand these roles because no matter what your position in an organization, you will be touched by HR in some way. Additionally, reflecting on HR's unique leadership perspective may help you as you consider the type of leader you want to be.

Strategic human resource management has often been described as a cycle, at least since the early 1980s. The best known cycle was introduced in a seminal book in 1984, which defined the field of human resource management. In it, authors Fombrun, Tichy, and Devenna introduced a cycle that linked selection, performance, appraisal, rewards, and developments.[18] The model provided a framework for understanding the leadership roles that human resource managers play in their organizations. As the field has grown, so has our understanding of the complex interrelations of employees and their organizations.

With this new understanding, it is clear that the HR Cycle must take into account HR's role with regard to the company and organized labor, introducing new areas to the cycle like workforce management, labor relations, organizational design, and strategic support.[19] These additions have provided a more holistic and comprehensive view of the strategic role that HR plays.

As you can see in the HR Cycle in ■ **EXHIBIT 1.7**, HR is responsible for a number of key activities. These are often considered HR's areas of technical expertise. Let's take a closer look at each of these areas.

■ **EXHIBIT 1.7**
The HR Cycle.

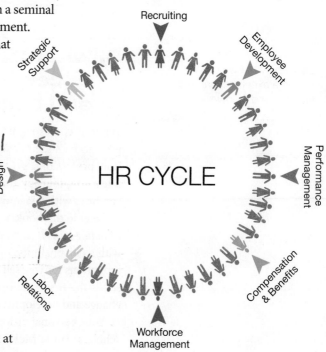

Recruiting: Handling employee selection, hiring, succession planning, and staffing.

Employee development: Providing leadership development and job or career-related training for employees through a variety of means, such as training programs, tuition reimbursement, seminars, cross-training, online learning, and self-directed learning.

Performance management: Providing processes and programs to identify, measure, and plan for the development of employees' skills.

Compensation and benefits: Providing schemas and technical processes to support employee compensation and benefits such as health care, flexible vacation time, flexible work schedules, travel, the company car, the executive washroom, the corner window, status, sense of purpose, etc.

Workforce management: Managing the size and shape of the workforce through activities such as organizational development and programs to support strategic issues.

Labor relations: Managing relations between internal and external groups (e.g., trade unions) that set standards for how employees are to be treated.

Organizational design: Studying organizational design issues and creating or re-creating job descriptions, work design, organizational structures, and interorganizational relationships.

Strategic support: Conducting research and providing support on people-related issues.

HR's role in supporting great leadership cannot be underestimated. As we move through this book, we will explore how HR uses these areas of expertise to foster leadership at all levels of the organization.

Discussion Questions

1. Look at the eight roles within the HR Cycle. In your opinion, are some of these roles more important than others? If so, which ones, and why?

2. Leaders of many organizations have said the now famous phrase: "People are our greatest asset." What do you think this means? Can you come up with an example from your own work experience or that of someone close to you where you found this not to be true? Explain.

Objective 1.5
Describe what we can do to become excellent managers, leaders, and followers.

5. What Can We All Do to Become Excellent Managers, Leaders, and Followers?

When it comes right down to it, great leadership doesn't happen by accident. If you want to be a great leader, manager, and follower, you will need to work at it. In addition, professional growth is not possible without personal growth. The best way to start a learning journey that will help you to become the best person and best leader you can be is with a vision.

Later in this book, you will develop a learning plan. Also, as you will learn in Chapter 5, *Planning and Strategy*, good plans start with a mission and a vision. A learning plan starts with a personal mission (what you believe to be your purpose in life) and a vision (your aspirations for yourself as a person). We call this your "ideal self." Articulating your ideal self is the first step in intentional change, which is a process that results in sustainable change and development.[20]

Your personal vision starts with your hopes and dreams for yourself as a person. As scholars Annie McKee, Richard Boyatzis, and Frances Johnston wrote in *Becoming a Resonant Leader*, "Our dreams help to determine what we become, because a compelling and meaningful vision provides us with the optimism, strength, energy, and efficacy we need to move confidently toward the future."[21] Our dreams feed our personal vision and our image of our ideal self. Hope—a belief in a more positive, feasible future, and a sense that we can make it happen—also feeds our vision. In addition, our core identity—our values, beliefs, and philosophy—is also a key element. As a way to begin to articulate a personal vision, reflect on the following questions and statements:

1. What is your highest purpose in life? What do you think you are meant to do and be?
   If I could accomplish only one thing in life, it would be to . . .
   Something I would like to do before I die is . . .
   If I could change anything in the world, it would be . . .
2. If I had as much money as I could ever need, I would . . .
3. In 10 years, my ideal life will include (reflect on loved ones, friends, work, lifestyle—anything that is important to you) . . .

Now, simply take the time to jot down a few themes you see in your responses to these questions. By doing this, you will begin to get a sense of what is most important to you. You will also practice pattern recognition, another key tool in planning.

Considering the themes you see in your writing, and thinking about your life holistically, write a few paragraphs that describe your ideal life in five years. Include key relationships, roles, work, where you live, your lifestyle, and anything else that is important to you.

Discussion Questions

1. Why is it important for you to create a personal vision now, while you are in college? How might this help you choose a career or find an organization where you will fit in well?
2. Who in your life today can help you think about your future? What advice do you think they might give you about your personal vision?

---

6. A Final Word: Changing World, Changing Expectations of Managers and Leaders

In this chapter we have made a case for learning to be a good leader, manager, and follower. Our world today requires this from all of us. People everywhere are facing great challenges and great opportunities, and business has a huge role to play in helping all of us create a better future.

We end this chapter with a few words from Niall FitzGerald, a distinguished and world-renowned leader. During the autumn of 2011, there were widespread protests calling attention to the difficulties people were—and are—facing as a result of the Great Recession. As *The Economist*, a well-respected magazine, reported, "Whether [the protesters] are inspired by the Occupy Wall Street movement . . . they burn with dissatisfaction about the state of the economy, about the unfair way that the poor are paying for the sins of rich bankers, and in some cases about capitalism itself."[22] This is not to say that capitalism has failed, or that business is solely at fault for the economic woes faced by many today. However, the situation is clear: Leaders everywhere need to take actions to build a more sustainable model—one that will bring the promises of capitalism, meritocracy, and democracy to many more people.[23]

Some leaders have been doing this for years, including Niall FitzGerald. Niall has had a long and distinguished career: former chairman and CEO of Unilever, chairman

Niall FitzGerald, Chairman of the Boards of the British Museum and Hakluyt & Co.: Acceptance Speech for the Business Alumnus of the Year Award.[24]

of Reuters, and deputy co-chairman of Thomson Reuters, to name just a few. Today, he is chairman of the Board of the British Museum and also chairman of Hackluyt & Company. In all of his roles, throughout his life, he has sought to learn and to have the courage to do the right thing, even when it wasn't popular.

In a speech given recently at his alma mater, University College, Dublin, Ireland, Niall shares wisdom you can take to heart and use at work and in life today. He calls on business and all of us to consider what it will take to rebuild our companies and, more importantly, trust. Here's part of what he says:

The financial crisis has left many disillusioned with bankers, business people, and politicians. There are questions about the equity of capitalism and free enterprise. People are angry—some would say enraged—there is little trust in leaders.

Young people face more expensive education, higher taxes, less generous benefits, and longer working lives than their parents. Homes are either expensive beyond reach or indebted beyond their value. Jobs are elusive or nonexistent. In Europe and the U.S. over 20% of those under 25 have no work—in Spain it is a horrific 50%.[25]

And it is not just the young. The middle aged face falling real wages and diminished pension rights. The elderly are seeing the value of their saving eroded while the cost of care escalates.[26] In the meantime bankers are back to huge bonuses, business leaders seem immune from austerity, and politicians are increasingly irrelevant. The gap between rich and poor widening—resentment between generations deepening—and no one holds themselves accountable.

So, why so bleak . . . ? I am an optimist.

It seems to me that the very problems we confront may present us with our biggest opportunity. A chance to look again at how we best combine wealth creation with the spreading of prosperity. A reminder to those of us in business that we have a wider responsibility than just the bottom line. You cannot over time have a successful business in a broken society. The renewed understanding that leadership is a privilege not an entitlement. A leader has a chance to leave a mark on society which is beyond their personal bank balance. A rediscovery that true and lasting satisfaction comes from giving rather than taking.

My generation was given freedom to pursue our dreams and the means to achieve them. We must now invest in the next generation so that we will be remembered with respect for what we helped others to achieve. It can no longer be about ME and ME but about leaving something behind which is truly sustainable. And in the era of the adoration of celebrity we should remember that:

There is no limit to what a man can achieve as long as he does not care who gets the credit.

EXPERIENCING Leadership

LEADING IN A GLOBAL WORLD
Your Global Team

Organizations worldwide are recognizing that their workforces are becoming increasingly more diverse every day as they hire people of every race, nationality, religion, and age group. So, how do you lead such culturally, religiously, and ethnically diverse groups?

Imagine you are a team leader for a major global organization. Eight team members report to you: two are American, two are from India, two are from the Middle East, and two are from Brazil.

Do some brief online research of these cultures. Be sure to note religious, political, and social differences that may have an impact on your management style. After you have some knowledge of cultural differences, answer the following questions in teams or individually:

1. What are the fundamental differences among my team members?
2. What are the fundamental similarities among my team members?
3. What things can I do as a leader to make my team comfortable, culturally speaking?
4. What can my team do to make me a more effective leader?

LEADING WITH EMOTIONAL INTELLIGENCE
What Kind of Follower Are You?

Mature leaders and managers are actively engaged in developing themselves and their relationships with their followers.

Think of a situation in which you were a follower. It could have been on a sports team, project team at school, or a work team at your job. Now think about the various characteristics you brought to your role as a follower. Answer the following questions:

1. What was right or wrong, good or bad with the leadership/management that led to you exhibiting these characteristics?

2. What could leadership/management have done to change the type of follower characteristics you exhibited?
3. Do you naturally gravitate to those follower characteristics? Why or why not?

LEADING WITH CRITICAL THINKING SKILLS
Leadership and Management—What's Different, What's the Same?

The daily operations of any organization require planning, organizing, controlling, and leading—all of which must be managed effectively. In other words, today's organizations require managers and leaders to share responsibilities. Still, leaders are often viewed as more strategic, while managers are viewed as more tactical.

Imagine you have been selected to identify key management and leadership duties for a new company that is manufacturing an electric car called the Mongoose. The company has already identified financial backers and acquired an automobile manufacturing facility from another car manufacturer. Your company wants to offer the Mongoose to the public in 10 months.

In teams or individually:

1. Make a list of responsibilities the **leadership team** must address immediately, the day the car is offered to the public, and in the months following the car's release.
2. Make a list of responsibilities the **management** team must address immediately, the day the car is offered to the public, and in the months following the car's release.
3. Look for overlaps in your two lists of duties and responsibilities. It may help you to create a matrix in order to identify shared responsibilities.

ETHICAL LEADERSHIP
Recognizing the Good and the Not So Good

The world has changed dramatically over the last decade, and in organizations today, everyone needs to be a leader. Now, more than ever, ethical leadership needs to become the rule, not the exception.

In teams or individually, choose two or three leaders from the list below. Perform a brief Internet search by typing the leader's name and "leadership" or "ethical" into your favorite search engine. Use your research to answer the following questions:

1. Do you believe these individuals are, or were ethical leaders? Do they do the right things for both their businesses and their communities?

2. Are these leaders good role models for ethical leadership? Why? Why not?

3. What are the good and bad qualities of these leaders? Make a short list.

A. Steve Jobs
B. Jeffrey Skilling
C. Ann Mulcahy
D. Jeffrey Hollender
E. Melinda Gates
F. Hillary Clinton
G. Charles Schwab
H. Howard Shultz

KEY TERMS

Manager, *p. 7*

Leader, *p. 7*

Managing up, *p. 12*

MyManagementLab

Go to **mymanagementlab.com** for Auto-graded writing questions as well as the following Assisted-graded writing questions:

1-1. Do you think of "leadership" as an active verb or a role some people hold? How would each of these views affect how leaders behave?

1-2. Think of a specific leader that you respect. Who (or what) does this leader follow? Why?

1-3. Mymanagementlab Only — comprehensive writing assignment for this chapter.

1. Why Do Managers Have to Be Leaders? (pp. 4–7)

Objective: Describe why managers must also be leaders.

Summary: It is important for you to know what leadership means to you. In organizations today, everyone must be a leader because globally, many social, political, and economic changes must be faced. You will be called on to make good decisions, act ethically, and inspire others throughout your career.

2. What Is the Difference between a Manager and a Leader? (pp. 7–11)

Objective: Differentiate between managers and leaders.

Summary: Managers and leaders have traditionally been seen as different. The managerial role has traditionally been viewed as one that reduces complexity, whereas leaders are expected to "thrive on chaos." The truth, however, is that everyone needs to develop both managerial and leadership skills. We all need to be able to see the "big picture," as well as be able to plan, organize, and control people and resources.

3. What Is the Other Side of the Leadership Coin? (pp. 11–13)

Objective: Explain what is meant by the "other side" of the leadership coin.

Summary: All leaders need to be able to follow, and all followers need to be able to lead. Indeed, it is hard to imagine any role in work or society that does not include both leading and following in some fashion. Approaching leadership and followership as skills to be developed is a critical challenge for today's managers. Furthermore, the concept of "managing up" reminds us that responsible followership includes the ability to help your boss become a better leader.

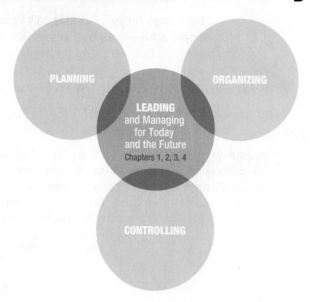

4. What Is HR's Role in Managing and Leading Today? (pp. 13–14)

Objective: Summarize HR's role in managing and leading.

Summary: Human resource management is important to the management and development of an organization's workforce. In particular, HR focuses on handling "people issues" in positive ways that enhance the individual's work experience and the organization's structure and function. HR relies on its expertise in a variety of areas—including recruiting, employee development, and workforce management—to achieve these goals. HR's unique approach to leadership impacts every member of an organization.

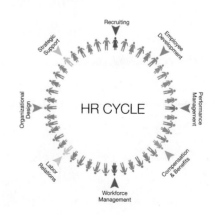

6. **A Final Word: Changing World, Changing Expectations of Managers and Leaders** (pp. 15–16)

Summary: Today's world is calling on all of us—employees, managers, and leaders alike—to take responsibility for our organization's actions. Society is calling on business, and on us, to lead in a socially responsible way.

5. **What Can We All Do to Become Excellent Managers, Leaders, and Followers?** (pp. 14–15)

Objective: Describe what we can do to become excellent managers, leaders, and followers.

Summary: Great leadership is a product of learning, experience, reflection, and strategic planning. To support effective strategic planning, you must develop your capacity for pattern recognition. Pattern recognition is a complex and extremely important competency that allows us to make sense of information today and plan for tomorrow. In addition, developing a personal vision that supports you in planning for the future you desire will make you a better planner and leader.

CHAPTER 2

The Leadership Imperative:

It's Up to You

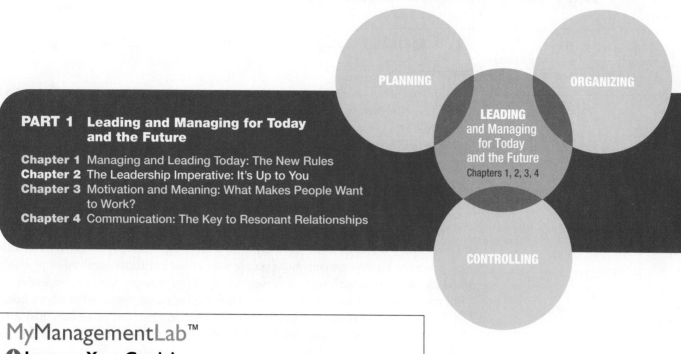

PLANNING

ORGANIZING

LEADING
and Managing
for Today
and the Future
Chapters 1, 2, 3, 4

CONTROLLING

MyManagementLab™

 Improve Your Grade!

Over 10 million students improved their results using the Pearson MyLabs.
Visit **mymanagementlab.com** for simulations, tutorials, and end-of-chapter problems.

Chapter Outline

Chapter Objectives

2.1 Recognize why everyone needs to learn how to lead today.

2.2 Understand the characteristics of effective leadership.

2.3 Understand the characteristics of influential leadership.

2.4 Understand the characteristics of responsible leadership.

2.5 Assess theories and models of management and leadership.

2.6 Determine the necessity of transformational leadership.

2.7 Describe HR's role in supporting and fostering excellent and ethical leadership.

2.8 Describe the steps one must take to become a great leader.

Objective 2.1
Recognize why everyone needs to learn how to lead today.

1. Leadership: Whose Responsibility Is it?

Senior executives in businesses and organizations *should* know how to lead. And many do. However, we don't have to look far to find serious abdication of leadership responsibility. We have seen money laundering at HSBC, a bank that's been respected for over one hundred years for outstanding business practices, Bernie Madoff's Ponzi scheme, and the subprime mortgage debacle—all examples of abuse of power, incompetency magnified by greed, major flaws in character, and a breakdown in values and ethics. These scandals—and the people behind them—ruined lives and tipped entire economies into recession.

It takes more than a few bad apples to do this kind of damage. In most cases, there were only a few architects of fraud and only a few people directly involved in unethical practices. However, many more people were either indirectly involved or probably had an idea that something was gravely wrong. Who is responsible for leadership in our companies? Is it only senior leaders? Or is it all of us, no matter what job we hold?

To answer these questions, let's look at the experiences many of us have had with leaders. Think about the jobs you have held, the teams you have been part of, and the schools you have attended. Chances are, you had opportunities to see leadership up close. How many of your bosses, team leaders, teachers, or counselors were excellent leaders? How many were average or even bad leaders? Most of the time, when we ask people in organizations this question, they remember far more average or bad leaders than good. That simply isn't acceptable today.

The world is faced with great opportunities and even greater challenges. We can't sit around and wait for someone else to step in. We have to get involved. Our businesses, institutions, and communities require all of us to lead—and to lead well. All of us need to learn how to use power responsibly, how to apply our skills, and how to live by our values and ethics. Think about your behavior at work, on teams, and in your community. You have had opportunities to lead people, either formally or informally. How much attention did you pay to learning how to use your power effectively so you could influence others positively? Did you ensure that you lived your values consistently? Did you consciously develop leadership skills? If you are like most people, you had every intention of doing all of the above, and you probably worked hard at being a good leader. However, maybe because of the pressures of the job or because it is difficult to examine your own behavior, you paid less attention to improving your leadership than you wanted. For example, you might have been part of situations that made you feel uncomfortable and were not in line with your values, yet you didn't speak up. This happens to all of us at one time or another. The key to great leadership is recognizing that each of us has the obligation to use power responsibly, study our own leadership behavior, seek to improve, and constantly stand up for the values and ethics that guide us and our organizations.

We Can All Become Great Leaders

In successful organizations, everyone understands the link between their jobs and the company's strategy and mission. And in most organizations today, people have a lot more responsibility than they did in the past. This means that all of us need to know how to motivate others, paint a compelling picture of the future, engage people's passion, build enthusiasm, and direct people's energy.

This isn't easy, because we are constantly faced with new challenges at work and we need to know how to lead, even when the path isn't clear. Change is everywhere in organizations today. People who expect continuity and stability simply will not be effective at work, and certainly won't be good leaders. And people who rely on managers and others to "do the right thing" while they themselves adopt any means to achieve their goals risk making unethical decisions. They also risk treating people badly and creating an unhealthy, dissonant environment that does not support organizational effectiveness. You, however, can choose to explore your values and ethics and rely on them to guide your choices. You can also learn to use your power and to influence people and groups so that *everyone* is better off. If you see change as an opportunity and embrace it with enthusiasm and hope, people will be enthusiastic about following your lead. Most importantly, if you seek to *learn how to lead,* develop leadership competencies, and increase your capacity for self-awareness, you are on the road to becoming a great leader.

Leadership Is Learned

The good news is that you can learn how to be a great leader. *Leaders are not born— they are made.* We learn how to lead as a result of our experiences and by deliberately improving our leadership skills, learning to wield power responsibly, and attending to our values so we can make ethical decisions. Managers and employees can—and must— become better leaders by seeking out experiences that help us learn how to inspire, influence, and support others. Taking responsibility for leadership requires courage. It's always easier to point at "them"—those faraway leaders who can be credited or blamed for everything. In reality, though, there's no such thing as "them." It's just "us."

Today more than ever before, everyone needs to learn how to lead. That's what this chapter is about: How you—as a person, employee, or manager—can become a great leader. To start, you will discover three secrets to becoming an outstanding leader:

- *Emotional and social competence:* The secret to *effective* leadership
- *Power:* The secret to *influential* leadership
- *Ethics:* The secret to *responsible* leadership

You will also study several theories that seek to explain leadership, and you will learn how HR can support excellent leadership. Finally, you will discover what we can all do to ensure that we are great leaders in work and in life.

As you read this book, you will have the opportunity to develop yourself as a leader. To help with this, you may want to reflect on good leaders that you know, or people who we have interviewed for this book. To see what one outstanding leader, Jill Guindon-Nasir, vice president of global business development at Ritz-Carlton, has to say, see the *Leadership Perspective* feature on the following page.

Jill Guindon-Nasir is right: people will follow someone they believe is authentic and real. You will have many opportunities in life to show people who you are. In fact, every action you take, every word you speak, contributes to the picture people have of you. Effective leaders know this, and they make decisions to share who they are—their values, beliefs, thoughts, and feelings—in ways that inspire and motivate others.

Discussion Questions

1. Why does organizational success depend on everyone assuming some leadership responsibilities?

2. Think about bosses, coaches, and teachers you have had. Under the headings "Bad Boss" and "Good Boss," list the names of a few of these people. Now list a few adjectives that describe the people in each group. Do these descriptors reflect responsible use of power, self-awareness, and ethical decision making? Why or why not?

3. Look at the lists of adjectives describing your good and bad bosses. Which of these would people use to describe you?

Leadership Perspective

Jill Guindon-Nasir—Vice President of Global Business Development for the Ritz-Carlton Leadership Center—is involved in training the Ritz's renowned services staff as well as the employees of other companies. She is creative, innovative, and profoundly committed to excellence and her values. In her role, Jill sees firsthand the importance of self-aware leadership and the powerful human connection that is at the heart of great leadership and great followership:

> *Resonant leadership and emotional intelligence are <u>huge</u>. Employees want a real person—genuine, authentic, caring, and able to connect. In order to do this, you have to be it. You need to show them, too. If you tell them to take lunch, then you need to take lunch too. And you can't ever ask them to do something you wouldn't do, either. People will follow you when they see that you are doing what you said you would do, courageously.*
>
> *People can see through you, because they are watching you constantly. You have to know yourself, know your values, and be clear with people about what you stand for. You have to have passion, and people need to see your passion. You need to be clear and honest about what you believe in, and be very open about it. You need a calling and a cause—when you believe in something, nobody can stop you.*
>
> *And you have to be a risk-taker. At times you're going to be standing alone, which can be very uncomfortable and even lonely. That's why it's so important to believe in yourself. You'll fail sometimes, too. But when you do, you need to <u>learn</u>. The definition of insanity is doing the same thing over and over even when it doesn't work. That's the real failure in many businesses. But if you learn, you will do things differently and you will succeed the second time around.*
>
> *In the end, you have to be true to yourself before you can lead others. People follow because of who you are, not what you do. True leadership is not about your title, it's who you are. First, you need to lead yourself. This way, you'll help other people to become leaders, too.*

● **Jill Guindon-Nasir**
Vice President of Global Business Development for the Ritz-Carlton Leadership Center
"Employees want a real person."

Source: Personal interview with Jill Guindon-Nasir conducted by Annie McKee, 2012.

Objective 2.2
Understand the characteristics of effective leadership.

Competencies
Capabilities or abilities that include both intent and action, and that can be directly linked to how well a person performs on a task or in a job.

2. What Is the Secret to *Effective* Leadership?

The secret to effective management and leadership is that we must master competencies related to social and emotional intelligence. **Competencies** are capabilities or abilities that include both intent and action, and that can be directly linked to how well a person performs on a task or in a job.[1] Competencies related to social and emotional intelligence differentiate great leaders from average ones.[2] Social and emotional intelligence are abilities linked to self-awareness, self-management, social awareness, and relationship management. Before exploring social and emotional competencies in depth, let's look at why competencies are important for everyone at work.

Competencies Explained

In an influential article published in 1973, scholar David McClelland argued that we should be more concerned with competencies than with intelligence when attempting to predict the potential success of students and employees.[3] One reason McClelland and his colleagues were looking beyond intelligence for insights into success at work was because, like many standardized tests, intelligence tests tend to have cultural biases built into them that result in inaccurate scores for people outside the majority culture.

In addition, as far back as 1959, research had found that there is little correlation between intelligence test scores and success at work.[4]

When McClelland and well-known scholar Richard Boyatzis sought to determine exactly what *was* related to success on the job, they discovered what they called competencies. Competencies are behaviors that we can see, but there is more to them than that. When a person demonstrates a competency, he or she is *acting intentionally* and behaving in a way that leads to successfully accomplishing a task. For example, if a manager engages an employee in a conversation about performance, the manager is demonstrating a competency called "coach and mentor" if he or she (1) *intended* to guide and direct the employee's behavior toward more effective performance, growth, and development; and (2) provided clear, constructive feedback while sharing positive expectations for the employee's improvement.[5] Let's look at competencies in more detail.

FIVE COMPONENTS OF COMPETENCIES

Competencies also involve personal characteristics that impact intention and action: motives, enduring personal traits, self-concept, knowledge, and skills.[6] *Motives* are needs or drives that fuel action. Motives are closely linked to McClelland's three-needs theory of motivation, which is discussed in Chapter 3. According to McClelland, people are often driven by three needs: to achieve personal goals, have influence, and build positive relationships with others. *Traits* are psychological or physical characteristics and/or consistent ways of responding to situations. For example, race car drivers have good hand-eye coordination and a tendency to remain calm in stressful situations. *Self-concept* includes attitudes, values, and self-image—all powerful drivers of actions. For example, a self-confident person who values honesty will be more likely to take action when he or she sees unethical behavior.

Knowledge is information that a person has at his or her disposal or the ability to find information when needed. For example, when you complete this course, you will have gained information about management and leadership. You should also have gained knowledge about how to evaluate theories of management and leadership, and you should understand how to use research to inform your use of theories in the future.

Finally, *skills* are learned abilities that are needed to perform tasks, such as the ability to type, use the Internet for research, or analyze financial data. Most professions require distinctive knowledge and skills. A surgeon, for example, needs to be skilled in the use of surgical equipment, and he or she must have a knowledge of human anatomy. Similarly, an accountant needs to be skilled in the use of spreadsheet programs and have a knowledge of tax laws.

As you can see in ■ **EXHIBIT 2.1**, knowledge and skills are most easily observed. For this reason, knowledge and skills are often the focus of development in training programs. Motives, traits, and self-concept are "below the water line" and are not as easy to develop. However, in order for people to develop competencies, *all* levels must be attended to. In fact, if the deeper aspects of a competency are not attended to, the likelihood that the competency will be improved is much lower.

THRESHOLD AND DIFFERENTIATING COMPETENCIES

Some competencies are necessary just to do a job (threshold competencies), whereas others support outstanding performance (differentiating competencies). Threshold competencies include basic expertise, experience, and many cognitive abilities.[7] For example, threshold competencies for a project team leader in a technology firm could include electrical engineering, project management, and time

■ **EXHIBIT 2.1**
The iceberg as a metaphor.

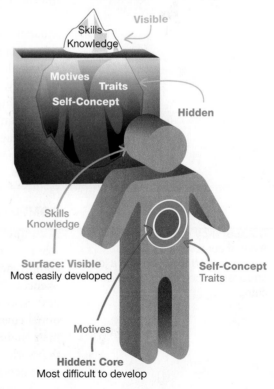

Skills
Knowledge

Visible

Motives
Traits
Self-Concept

Hidden

Skills
Knowledge

Self-Concept
Traits

Surface: Visible
Most easily developed

Motives

Hidden: Core
Most difficult to develop

management skills. These competencies will support average performance as a leader. An outstanding leader, however, will also have competencies related to social and emotional intelligence, pattern recognition, and systems thinking (this will be examined later in the chapter). So, if the project team leader in the tech firm is to be an outstanding leader, he or she will also develop and use competencies such as emotional self-control, adaptability, and positive outlook. These competencies will help him or her manage emotions when things go wrong and to inspire people with a powerful vision.

In recent years, threshold and differentiating competencies that used to be expected of only senior managers have become expected of almost everyone. For example, almost all professionals need to be able to type. As hard as it is to believe, that competency used to be reserved for secretaries and assistants. Everyone also needs to be proficient in common software programs and be able to communicate effectively in writing. Today, most jobs also require some degree of systems thinking and other cognitive competencies that support critical thinking and good decision making. Most roles also require that we manage a wide network of relationships, which means we need to develop competencies such as empathy, organizational awareness, and conflict management. Furthermore, because people often work with less direct supervision than in the past, relational competencies such as self-management and the ability to understand and influence others are essential.

TECHNICAL, COGNITIVE, AND RELATIONAL COMPETENCIES

Early research indicated that competencies fall into one of three categories: technical, cognitive, or relational. People who are adept at technical competencies are proficient in the use of tools and processes related to a specialized field. Technical skills are especially critical in areas such as engineering, finance, and information technology.

Cognitive competencies include the ability to see the "big picture" in groups and organizations. Seeing the big picture means that you recognize that various bits of information are not isolated; they actually form a pattern (this is called pattern recognition). Another example of a cognitive competency is the ability to analyze complex situations and to understand how all things and people relate to one another (this is called systems thinking). These two cognitive competencies—pattern recognition and systems thinking—are crucial in many jobs today.[8]

Finally, relational competencies support the development of strong working relationships with colleagues, direct reports, senior management, and customers. These competencies are often called "people skills," and they include self-awareness, self-management, empathy, and inspirational leadership. Relational competencies support us in building teams, coaching, monitoring performance, and providing feedback.

COMPETENCY MODELS

Competency model
A set of competencies that are directly related to success in a job and are grouped into job-relevant categories.

A **competency model** is a set of competencies directly related to success in a job that are grouped into job-relevant categories. Much of the groundbreaking work on competency models was conducted by scholars Richard Boyatzis and Lyle and Signe Spencer.[9] Thousands of competency models are in use in organizations today. The best ones are well researched and based on the study of people, jobs, and organizational environments. Over the years, Boyatzis and other researchers have extended their studies to include thousands of people performing a wide array of jobs around the world. Their conclusion was that when it comes to leadership, one subset of competencies makes all the difference: competencies related to social and emotional intelligence.[10]

Social and Emotional Competencies and Resonant Leadership

Popularized by Daniel Goleman in 1995, the term *emotional intelligence* and, more recently, the phrase social and emotional intelligence refers to competencies linked to self-awareness, self-management, social awareness, and relationship management (■ **EXHIBIT 2.2**). The shorthand way to describe these competencies is "emotional intelligence." Emotional intelligence competencies enable people to understand and manage their own and others' emotions in social interactions.[11] These abilities are the basis for good leadership and they can be learned.[12]

Emotional intelligence enables people to create resonance in relationships, groups, and organizations. Resonant organizations are characterized by a powerful and positive organizational culture in which people have a shared sense of excitement and commitment to mutual goals. Resonant leaders are emotionally intelligent, visionary people who lead and manage in ways that enable everyone to contribute their very best.[13]

Dan Nowlin, of Sunglass Hut is one of the best resonant leaders we know. Like Dolores Bernardo of Google, Dan knows that leadership is a *profession*. You have to work at it. When you do, the people around you reap great rewards. Dan brings resonant leadership to life, as you can see in the *Leadership Perspective* feature.

Dan's lessons are profound, and they tie directly into the research about social and emotional intelligence. Let's now look at how this research has progressed over the years.

The study of social and emotional intelligence emerged from research about competencies, multiple intelligences (the different ways intelligence can be demonstrated), the study of personality, the psychology of emotion, and neuroscience.[14] This concept has gained tremendous popularity in organizations because research indicates a strong link between emotional and social competence and a person's effectiveness as a leader, manager, and employee.[15] These competencies help us create resonant environments that support people in being their very best.[16]

Social and emotional intelligence
Competencies linked to self-awareness, self-management, social awareness, and relationship management that enable people to understand and manage emotions in social interactions.

Resonant organizations
Organizations characterized by a powerful and positive culture in which people have a shared sense of excitement and commitment to mutual goals.

Resonant leaders
Socially and emotionally intelligent, visionary people who lead and manage in ways that enable everyone to contribute their very best.

■ **EXHIBIT 2.2**
Social and emotional intelligence competencies enable people to understand and manage their own and others' emotions in social interactions.

Source: Based on McKee, Boyatzis and Johnston, Becoming a Resonant Leader, 2008.

Leadership Perspective

Dan Nowlin is senior vice president, North America Store Operations and president, Sunglass Hut Global Culture. Throughout his career, Dan has focused on *people*: who they are, what they need, and how he can help them achieve personal and professional goals. When Dan walks into a store (which he does *all* the time), employees flock to him. He knows their names, when they started with the company, and personal details like their birthdays, their kids' names and whether the employee has decided to pursue a degree (and if not, he encourages them!). As he puts it, "Little things don't mean a lot, they mean *everything*." Here's what else he has to say about leading people:

> As a leader, you have choices to make: how you spend your time, what you say to people, how you communicate your ideas and your vision. How do you know what to do, when everything is complex and changing all the time? You need to be smart—but smart might not mean what you think it does.
>
> There are at least three kinds of intelligence that matter today. You need intellect, of course. We measure intellect with things like SAT tests, final exams, and IQ. These might have their place, but they don't measure the kind of intelligence that is really needed in today's organizations. That's because in most jobs, you don't need to be a genius. You need enough brain power to understand that the world is changing and you have to change with it. You need to think strategically and you need to make sense of what is going on now, so you can have a vision of tomorrow. All of these require keen intellect. But this is only a starting point.
>
> The second kind of intelligence is <u>common sense</u>. This includes the basics: treat people the way you want to be treated; if you're mean, you'll get mean back, and if you're nice, you'll get nice back; if you choose to live a life of giving rather than getting, you will get more than you can possibly imagine. You also need to get out in front—if you want people to do something or act a certain way, do it yourself. You need to value each and every person equally. Diversity and inclusion is a hugely important strategy today. So, you need to learn about other people's views, cultures, and beliefs. You need to value them for who they are, not who you want them to be. These lessons look simple, but they aren't. And they certainly aren't "common" enough in our organizations.
>
> The third kind of intelligence you need is emotional. You need empathy. You need compassion. People work for peo-

> ple—that means that the people who work for you are going to be watching you. They want to know whether you are authentic and real. They will be checking to see if you care about the company, about your work, and especially about them. When they see you care, they care too.
>
> Emotions matter. Your mood affects everyone. I used to work in a big department store, and by the time I got to my office on the third floor, every single person knew what kind of mood I was in. If I was happy, they were more likely to be happy. And if I was in a bad mood, they got there too. When people see their bosses in a bad mood, they can become scared or angry, and they don't focus on their jobs. They try to figure out how to deal with <u>you</u>—a waste of time and energy. But if they see that you are excited to be there, happy and ready to go, they pick up that state of mind and take it into everything they do.
>
> Another thing about emotions: When people live in fear or anger they hold back. This goes for you, too. Your emotions impact what you and others contribute and where you can go in your life and as a leader. There are some things to learn here.
>
> First, love what you do. Find meaning in your company's mission and what it does for the world. We love what we do at Sunglass Hut. We sell sunglasses which are practical and helpful. And sunglasses help people feel good about themselves. We also help the world through OneSight, a nonprofit organization which delivers vision care for people who could never afford it on their own. This program makes all of us feel good about our company.
>
> Finally, no matter how much you love your job, never put it above your family, friends, or your health. When all is said and done, work is a part of life, not the other way around.

● **Dan Nowlin**
Senior Vice President, North American Store Operations and President, Sunglass Hut Global Culture
"Little things don't mean a lot, they mean everything."

Source: Personal interview with Dan Nowlin conducted by Annie McKee, 2012.

Attending to emotional intelligence is critical to leadership because emotions are linked to our ability to think clearly, make good decisions, and focus on tasks. Our brains are complex structures, and there is an important relationship between neurophysiology (how the brain works), psychology (personality, motives, and traits), and values (deeply held beliefs about how to act on our ideals).[17] This relationship is shown in ■ **EXHIBIT 2.3**.

EMOTIONAL INTELLIGENCE AND LIMBIC RESONANCE

Let's look at emotional intelligence in action in a hypothetical—but common—experience. You've just walked into a crowded room and, although no one said anything, you knew something was wrong. You could just feel it. Because you were aware of the uneasiness in the room, you likely behaved differently than if things had felt calm or upbeat.

Some people call this intuition, but it is really a combination of competencies and the fact that emotions are contagious. By closely attending to subtle clues such as people's facial expressions, body language, and who was sitting with whom, you were using the competency called *empathy*.

Catching emotions from other people happens all the time. Limbic resonance is a term used to describe how emotions are both contagious and a powerful driver of our feelings, thoughts, and behaviors.[18] Scholars Annie McKee, Richard Boyatzis, and Frances Johnston put it this way: "Just as [emotions] travel like electricity in our brains and bodies, feelings travel rapidly *between* people. . . . We are constantly tuning in to the emotional state of someone standing next to us, and it affects how we feel, what we think, and what we do."[19] In recent research there is even evidence that there are structures in our brains, called "mirror neurons" that help us to "catch" emotions and experiences from one another.[20] This means that we are "wired" to empathize with one another—couple that with emotional intelligence competencies, and you will be very effective in understanding people.

Back to the example of walking into a charged atmosphere: By employing emotional self-awareness, self-management, and empathy, you increase the likelihood that you (1) can avoid catching people's negative emotions, (2) are prepared to deal with conflict or trouble in the group, and (3) are one step ahead in trying to understand what is happening in the group and what you might do to help solve the group's problems.

SELF-AWARENESS: THE FOUNDATION OF SOCIAL AND EMOTIONAL INTELLIGENCE

Self-awareness is the ability to notice and understand one's emotions and their effects. We have all seen people who *don't* have this competency: the friend yelling at us who says, "I'm not angry!" or the boss with a face like a thundercloud who says, "It's a great day, isn't it?" These kinds of interactions are confusing and can be destructive. The same boss using this competency effectively would recognize that he is angry, maybe as a result of a flat tire on the way to work. He'd know that his mood impacts his employees, so he would take a few minutes to calm down before coming to the office. Or he might say something like, "Sorry, I know I look upset—I just had a flat tire."

■ **EXHIBIT 2.3**
Neurophysiology, personality, motives, traits, and values are all related to competencies.

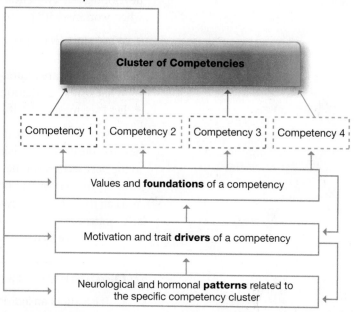

Source: Adapted from Boyatzis, Richard E. 2008. Competencies in the 21st century (Guest Editorial). *Journal of Management Development* 27(1): 9.

Limbic resonance
Refers to the fact that emotions are contagious and a powerful driver of our feelings, thoughts, and behaviors.

Self-awareness is at the heart of emotional intelligence, and emotional intelligence is at the heart of great leadership. So, to become a great leader, you must focus on developing self-awareness. How can you do this? To start, ask yourself these questions when working with people or friends:

- What am I feeling right now and how are my feelings affecting my thoughts and actions?
- What values are important to me, and how do I use them when making decisions?
- What kinds of situations cause me to "lose my cool"?
- Do I see myself as self-confident and powerful? Why or why not?

As you continue to read this chapter, you have the opportunity to develop self-awareness by consciously applying the concepts described in the text to *yourself*. For instance, in the next section you have a chance to reflect on power: How do *you* influence people? How do *you* respond to others' attempts to influence you? Later, we will discuss ethics. You can then reflect on *your* ethics and values. This kind of reflection will improve your self-awareness and your social and emotional intelligence. As a result, you will become a more effective leader.

Discussion Questions

1. Think about an individual you know and respect at school or at work. What technical, cognitive, and relational competencies does the person have that you admire? Why do you admire these competencies?

2. Review the social and emotional competencies in Exhibit 2.2 and consider them in the context of your best leadership experience. Which of these competencies did you demonstrate? How did you demonstrate them?

3. Have you ever "caught" someone else's emotions? If so, how could you have utilized self-awareness and self-control to protect yourself from taking on the negative emotions of others?

Objective 2.3
Understand the characteristics of influential leadership.

Power
Influence over or through others.

3. What Is the Secret to *Influential* Leadership?

Using power effectively is the secret to influential leadership. **Power** is influence over or through others. Power is the ability to get people to do what one desires by changing how those people think, feel, or act.

Because we all need to be leaders at work, we all need to understand how to use our power. It is surprising how often people minimize or misuse their own power and deal poorly with others' power. This is partly because many people are uncomfortable with the idea of wielding power and with the idea that others might use power to influence them. Another reason many people are nervous about power is because the common view of power is that with it come victims. We are constantly on the alert for abuse. People also have difficulty with power at times because it is linked closely to culture, as you will see in Chapter 13. Different cultures view, use, and distribute power differently. In today's multicultural organizations, it is especially important to develop the ability to understand, manage, and use power in ways that are cross-culturally acceptable.[21]

Researchers who study power conclude that it is essential for all of us to understand the sources of power in ourselves and others so we can work effectively and achieve our own and the organization's goals.[22] If you have a clear idea about how to manage your own and others' power, you will be better equipped to make ethical decisions, influence others, and deal well with destructive organizational politics.

Organizational politics involve many things, including internal competition and the pursuit of personal goals at the expense of others or the organization. As distasteful as they are to most people, organizational politics are a reality in most organizations. And if you don't understand organizational politics, you can't help change the situation for the better. Worse, you can become a victim of destructive political dynamics.

Power is a fact of life in organizations, and managers and leaders need to understand how to use it for the benefit of their employees, the organization, and the people and communities that the organization serves. A useful framework for understanding power was developed by scholars French and Raven, as presented in ■ **EXHIBIT 2.4**.[23] This framework describes five sources of power that a person can draw on when trying to influence others: legitimate power, reward power, coercive power, expert power, and referent power.

Sources of Power

Legitimate power is the ability to influence others by right of one's position in an organization, the office held, or formal authority. For example, in your school, numerous people have legitimate power, including the president, deans, and instructors. These individuals have the authority to influence people and processes. As an illustration, instructors may include an attendance policy in the syllabus that requires you to attend all classes.

Reward power is the ability to influence others by giving or withholding rewards such as pay, promotions, time off, attractive projects, and learning experiences. Rewards can also take the form of acknowledgment, praise, attention, and respect. *How* a manager uses reward power affects motivation and group morale. When we feel that rewards are granted in a fair and equitable manner, we tend to be highly motivated. When we believe that managers use rewards unfairly or to control us, we tend to become demoralized, resist our manager's influence, and feel less inclined to do our best on the job.

Coercive power is the ability to influence others through punishment or the threat of punishment. A better term for coercive power may be *corrosive power,* because this source of power can be highly destructive. Punishment is not motivating, and it can have serious negative effects on the individuals punished, the entire group, and the relationship between employees and managers. That said, the use of coercive power and punishment is necessary at times, such as when an employee behaves unethically,

Organizational politics
Involve many things, including internal competition and the pursuit of personal goals at the expense of others or the organization.

Legitimate power
The ability to influence others by right of one's position in an organization, the office held, or formal authority.

Reward power
The ability to influence others by giving or withholding rewards such as pay, promotions, time off, attractive projects, learning experiences, and the like.

Coercive power
The attempt to influence others through punishment.

■ **EXHIBIT 2.4**
There are five sources of power that people can use to influence others.

 Legitimate Power—The ability to influence others by right of one's position in an organization, the office held, or formal authority.

 Reward Power—The ability to influence others by giving or withholding rewards such as pay, promotions, time off, attractive projects, learning experiences, and the like.

 Coercive Power—The attempt to influence others through punishment.

 Expert Power—The ability to influence others through a combination of special knowledge and/or skills.

 Referent Power—Power that comes from personal characteristics that people value and want to emulate and that cause people to feel respect or admiration.

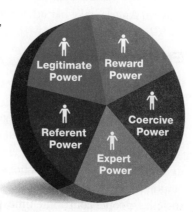

Source: Based on: French, J. R. P., and B. Raven. "The Bases of Social Power." In *Studies of Social Power,* edited by D. Cartwright. 150-67. Ann Arbor, MI: University of Michigan, Institute for Social Research, 1959.

sexually harasses another employee, or is unable to correct serious performance problems. In such serious situations, punishment such as firing or demotion might be a necessary last resort.

In far too many instances, however, managers and leaders rely too heavily on coercive power. Whether managers use coercive power because they are incompetent, insecure, or for some other reason, the result is almost always the same: fearful, angry, or resentful employees who comply only when necessary, and a dissonant environment that saps people's creativity and resilience.[24]

Expert power
The ability to influence others through a combination of special knowledge and/or skills.

Expert power is the ability to influence people through special knowledge and/or skills. For example, Colin Browne is a graduate of the University of Delaware. He is also a master carpenter. For big projects, such as building an addition on a house, he employs architects, electricians, painters, and other carpenters—all of whom are well-respected professionals. Because Colin is known to be an expert carpenter, and because he is also known to be artistic, members of the construction teams gladly accept his advice and leadership. Colin is particularly effective at influencing people because of the way he uses his expert power—he is always respectful of others, never acts as if he is better than his colleagues, and shares his passion for his work in a way that inspires people.

Many people develop expertise over the course of their careers, as Colin has. But expert power is also important to entry-level employees and new managers. Early in one's career it can be difficult to use legitimate, reward, or coercive power. By developing and tapping into expertise you can influence people at any stage of your career.

Referent power
Power that comes from personal characteristics that people value and want to emulate and that cause people to feel respect or admiration.

Referent power comes from personal characteristics that people want to emulate and that they respect and admire. When employees feel that a manager or leader cares for them and will do the right thing even if it means taking personal risks, they often feel a strong sense of loyalty and choose to follow willingly.

Like expert power, referent power is very useful early in your career. Without the benefit of reward, coercive, or legitimate power, new employees and new managers need to rely on their personal characteristics and expertise to get others' attention and respect. Referent power is also important later in your career. Take the example of Angela Scalpello, senior vice president of global human resources at PR Newswire, a global provider of marketing and communications solutions (■ **EXHIBIT 2.5**). As the person responsible for hiring, training and development, and organizational communication, Angela has both legitimate and reward power in the company. Recognized within her company and her field as an outstanding HR professional, Angela also has expert power. What stands out about Angela the most, however, are the characteristics that define her as a person. Her integrity is second to none. She is empathic, but doesn't hesitate to tell the truth. She is trustworthy. She also has a great sense of humor, keen intellect and emotional intelligence. For these reasons and more, Angela has referent power—her personal characteristics draw people to her and command respect. People listen to Angela, take her advice, and are willing to be led by her.[25]

■ **EXHIBIT 2.5**
Angela Scalpello, Senior Vice President of Global Human Resources at PR Newswire

Empowerment
Trusting employees to make decisions and to take responsibility for their decisions and actions.

Empowerment

One of the best ways to wield power is to share it. This is because no single individual has all the answers or can make all the decisions. Effectively running an organization takes everyone's knowledge and good judgment. Good managers find ways to involve everyone, so that everyone's input can be used. This is what is known as empowerment.

Empowerment is trusting employees to make decisions and to take responsibility for their decisions and actions.[26] Noted scholar Gretchen Spreitzer points out that empowerment can be seen as a form of organizational democracy.[27] In democratic societies, people contribute time, talent, energy, and ideas. They engage in the process of governing by voting, expressing concerns, and contributing to their communities. It is much the same in organizations. Democratic participation fueled by empowerment is demonstrated by members' ability to self-govern, voice concerns, and contribute ideas. As you will see in Chapter 3, participation and empowerment are also important to employee motivation.[28]

EMPOWERED EMPLOYEES AND EMPOWERING ORGANIZATIONS

Empowered employees have a say in how things get done—they have a voice at work, and they use it.[29] Because they are encouraged to point out problems without fear, empowered employees can improve work processes. When people have some control over the products or services they create or deliver, they will be motivated to try to improve work design, production processes, and quality. Empowered employees also take responsibility for organizing their work and setting goals. Empowered employees tend to be more engaged and committed, which drives them to surpass average performance.

An empowering organization has systems and processes that encourage employee involvement, such as suggestion programs, ethics hotlines, or quality circles (groups that examine and improve work processes). These organizations may also have programs that enable employees to deal directly with conflicts, such as mediation processes or access to ombudspersons. Empowering organizations often feature compensation programs that support collaboration and quality, such as profit-sharing plans.

Empowering organizations discourage micromanagement. **Micromanagement** is the practice of overcontrolling others and their work, as well as paying too much attention to details and how employees do their work. Micromanagement is widespread and destructive. It is a waste of everyone's time, employees and managers alike. Micromanagement causes employees to feel resentful, discouraged, and disrespected—a recipe for ineffectiveness and dissonance in the work environment.

Empowering organizations support managers and leaders in learning new management skills that focus on excellent communication, accurate assessment of employees' abilities, group and team facilitation, and creating an environment that is marked by trust, commitment, and openness to learning.[30]

Micromanagement
The practice of overcontrolling others and their work, as well as paying far too much attention to details and how employees do their work.

EMPOWERMENT AND THEORIES X, Y, AND Z

Researchers have been concerned with employee involvement and empowerment for several decades. Beginning in the 1960s, Douglas McGregor and then William Ouichi proposed Theories X, Y, and Z to describe three starkly different attitudes about the degree to which people take responsibility for their work.[31]

Theory X states that the average employee is inclined to be lazy, unambitious, and irresponsible. This attitude toward workers can result in micromanagement. Besides being insulting, Theory X results in poor relationships with employees, a dissonant and unpleasant environment, and eventual burnout for the manager. It's simply impossible to guide employees' every move, and stand ready to reward or punish behavior all the time.

Theory Y states that workers are inherently ambitious, responsible, and industrious, and that they will work hard to help an organization reach its goals. This stance fosters an environment that is conducive to employee involvement and empowerment. Most people thrive in such an environment.

Theory Z states that in organizations that have strong, relational cultures, employees can have freedom in local decision making and can be trusted to work autonomously. According to Ouchi, Z organizations have committed employees who are rewarded by the promise of lifetime employment—a promise that is harder to keep in today's fluid employment environment. Z organizations tend to have kind but directive leaders who make the most important decisions.[32] This benevolent and paternalistic approach can generate positive morale and loyalty, because even though managers are very directive, they are genuinely concerned about their employees. Furthermore, research indicates that benevolent paternalism works in many cultures, which is important to know in

Theory X
A belief system that holds that the average employee is inclined to be lazy, without ambition, and irresponsible.

Theory Y
A belief system that holds that workers are inherently ambitious, responsible, and industrious, and that they will work hard to help an organization reach its goals.

Theory Z
A belief system that holds that in organizations with strong, relational cultures, employees have discretionary freedom in local decision making and are trusted to work autonomously.

today's global environment.[33] Of course, there is the other side: When managers make most of the decisions, employees can become overly dependent on their leaders and stop thinking for themselves.

THE EMPOWERMENT MOVEMENT TODAY

The movement to empower people in organizations has been popular for many years for a number of good reasons. First, there aren't as many levels of hierarchy as there used to be in most organizations—organizations are "flatter" today. **Flat organizations** have few levels of hierarchy, which means more people need to make decisions. Second, organizations have become much leaner, meaning that fewer people are doing more work and managers are often extremely busy. It simply is not practical for managers and leaders to make all of the decisions all of the time. When work is well organized, and when employees manage day-to-day activities and are empowered to make certain kinds of decisions, senior managers can spend more time on bigger issues such as spotting industry trends and creating a resonant environment that sparks passion and leads to excellent performance.

The empowerment movement is also taking hold because it has become clear that the person closest to the work can often make better decisions than managers or leaders who are farther removed. Empowerment is also more important today than ever before because the nature of the employment contract is changing. In the past, the employment equation went something like this: "I will come to work and do my best to fulfill the organization's expectations in exchange for respect, reasonable pay, decent working conditions, and a promise of lifetime employment." Today, the equation is more like this: "I will share my talents and expertise with this organization only as long as I am fairly compensated, have opportunities to learn and grow, can be at my best, and feel that my contributions are valued."[34] If these conditions are not met, the best employees can and will leave.

Empowering people at work is good for organizations. When scholars at the Brookings Institution, a well-known think tank, consolidated all major studies on empowerment, they found that "if you sum it all up, employee participation has a positive impact on business success. It is almost never negative or neutral. Research in the role of empowerment over the years has consistently shown a net positive effect of employee empowerment on business performance."[35]

Flat organizations
Organizations that have few levels of hierarchy, which drives a need for more people to make decisions.

Discussion Questions

1. Discuss a situation from your experience in which power was abused. How was it abused, and what were the consequences for you personally and for others?

2. Name a public figure who directly influences you as a leader. What sources of power does this leader draw on? What is the effect of his or her use of power on you? How do you respond emotionally to this person's use of power?

3. Drawing on your own experience at work and in school, discuss the pros and cons of an empowered workforce.

Objective 2.4
Understand the characteristics of responsible leadership.

4. What Is the Secret to *Responsible* Leadership?

The secret to responsible management and leadership is ethics. The relationship between leadership and ethics is simple: How we lead is determined by what we value. The behavior of any individual—in business, politics, medicine, law, or any other field—is determined by the underlying values, principles, and beliefs that contribute to that person's code of ethics.

In this section, we will look at how people develop values and ethics. Then, you will see what happens when individuals lose sight of values and ethics. To further explain how ethics affect us at work, we then examine important aspects of business ethics. Finally, we look at how people rationalize unethical behavior and how you can handle everyday decisions ethically.

Developing Values and Ethics

Ethics is a set of values and principles that guide the behavior of an individual or a group. The word *ethics* comes from the Greek word *ethos,* meaning "moral character" or "custom." Aristotle refers to ethics as being greatly influenced by inner self-control and virtue.[36] Saint Augustine considered it our "inner dwelling place," our heart.[37] That inner dwelling place houses our fundamental orientation toward our lives, including our values.

Values are ideas that a person or a group believes to be right or wrong, good or bad. Values are beliefs about how things should or should not be; they impact how we behave, and they form the basis of our ethical code. An ethical code governs morality and acceptable behavior using a set of ethical principles. When it comes to values and ethics, the example a leader sets is of paramount importance to an organization's reputation and ultimate success.[38] But values and ethics aren't just important for senior leaders. All of us need to understand our own values and ethics and learn how to demonstrate them at work and in life.

The two kinds of values we deal with as leaders are *terminal* and *instrumental.* Terminal values are what we desire for ourselves and others in life, such as freedom, wisdom, love, equality, and a world at peace. Other examples of terminal values include happiness, pleasure, self-respect, inner harmony, and family security.[39]

Instrumental values are preferred behaviors or ways of achieving our terminal values. Examples of instrumental values include ambition, competence, creativity, honesty, integrity, and intellectual ability.

How do we develop and adopt values and ethics? Values are learned, like a language. As children, we quickly learn what our parents and others consider "good" or "bad." This is the beginning of moral development. We learn about values and ethics from our parents, friends, teachers, and spiritual figures, and even from the books we read and the movies we watch. We also learn on the job, often adopting the values and ethics of the organizations we work for, and we emulate the behavior and values of our leaders.

In an era of profound change in almost every aspect of life, what you believe and how you choose to act on your values is more relevant than ever before. The study of personal values and ethics at work is extremely important—maybe the most important topic in this book. Too often, we see blatant ethical transgressions and breaches of trust in every sector of our society. Each of us is responsible for changing this—and to do so, you need to start with yourself. You must identify those values that you will never compromise, no matter what.

Levels of Ethics

According to scholar Edwin Epstein, there are four distinct levels of business ethics: individual, professional, organizational, and societal, as illustrated in (■ **EXHIBIT 2.6**).[40] As we sort out what "the right thing to do" is, we need to understand each of these levels and how they might affect us.

INDIVIDUAL ETHICS

Individual ethics refers to a personal code of conduct when dealing with others. An individual's ethical code is formed and influenced by his or her social environment,

Ethics
A set of values and principles that guide the behavior of an individual or a group.

Values
Ideas that a person or a group believes to be right or wrong, good or bad, attractive or undesirable.

Ethical code
A system of principles governing morality and acceptable conduct.

Terminal values
Personal commitments we make to ourselves in relation to our life's goals.

Instrumental values
Preferred behaviors or ways of achieving our terminal values.

Individual ethics
A personal code of conduct when dealing with others.

 Individual Ethics—A personal code of conduct when dealing with others.

 Professional Ethics—Standards that outline appropriate conduct in a given profession.

 Organizational Ethics—The values and principles that an organization has chosen that guide the behavior of people in the organization and/or what stakeholders expect of the organization.

 Societal Ethics—Principles and standards that guide members of society in day-to-day behavior with one another.

including family, friends, school, and religious organizations. Although individual ethics are derived from personal values, people are also influenced by professional, organizational, and societal ethics.

PROFESSIONAL ETHICS

Professional ethics
Standards that outline appropriate conduct in a given profession.

Professional ethics are standards that outline appropriate conduct in a given profession. Professional ethics are often written and explicit. For example, the American Society for Training and Development, the Financial Accounting Standards Board, the American Medical Association, and various unions are all guided by explicit professional codes of ethics. Some organizations, like the American Institute of Certified Public Accountants (AICPA), have lengthy codes of ethics. One sentence in the AICPA's says it all:

> *The Principles call for an unswerving commitment to honorable behavior, even at the sacrifice of personal advantage.*[41]

Conflicts and differences of opinion often arise when it comes to professional ethics, especially as knowledge advances and societies change. For example, think about the ethics related to the medical field. Not everyone agrees on everything, and some ethical issues, such as assisted suicide, are extremely controversial and present no easy answers.

When you choose to join a profession, you also choose its ethical code. This is an important decision, requiring that you know your values well so that you can choose a profession that fits with what you believe. The same is true when you join an organization.

ORGANIZATIONAL ETHICS

Organizational ethics
The values and principles that an organization has chosen that guide the behavior of people within the organization and/or what stakeholders expect of the organization.

Organizational ethics are the values and principles that an organization has chosen to guide employees' behavior within the organization and/or what stakeholders expect of the organization. Organizational ethics often permeate a company's culture and are expressed in its mission. They usually reflect a company's beliefs and values about how employees, customers, and the environment are to be treated.

For example, it may be less expensive to dump chemical waste illegally than to dispose of it properly, but a company's ethical stance will hopefully drive managers to decide to incur the cost rather than damage the environment. Similarly, a firm may discover a source of cheap labor that could save the company millions of dollars. However, the company's ethics may direct managers to consider matters such as working conditions before making the decision to relocate operations. Ethical situations such as these define an organization and its reputation.

SOCIETAL ETHICS

Societal ethics are principles and standards that guide members of society in day-to-day behavior with one another (▪ **EXHIBIT 2.7**). Societal ethics are related to culture, and they are sometimes supported by laws, social conventions, and even language. Societal ethics can include beliefs, values, and practices related to issues such as justice, individual freedom, equality, equal employment opportunity rights, and how companies should impact the environment.

Societal ethics are at the "macro" end of the ethics spectrum. At this level, values unite the individuals in a society under a particular set of political and cultural ideologies that guide behavior. In some cases, societal ethics are strongly held by everyone. For example, in the United States, Britain, and Germany (among other countries), it is considered unethical to employ children as laborers, and an increasing number of companies refuse to buy products from suppliers who use child labor. Some organizations in certain countries do employ children, but that does not mean everyone in those countries agrees with this practice or finds it ethical.

What happens when certain ethics are not held by everyone within a society? The long-standing argument over access to health care in the United States is one example of such a debate. As far back as 1964, the late Senator Edward Kennedy (▪ **EXHIBIT 2.8**) called for the country to move toward a system that provides health care to everyone, not just people who can afford it. Some members of society—then and now—agree with this position. Others disagree. This is because groups within U.S. society hold differing opinions about who is responsible for the health of a nation's people and whether wealthy people should have access to better health care. These beliefs are based on views about government-influenced social equity versus free-market capitalism—issues that are closely tied to societal values and ethics.

As you will see in Chapter 13, values and ethics are closely tied to culture—and cultures change. In fact, heated public debates are often a sign that changes in values and ethics have *already* occurred. With respect to health care in the United States, programs like Medicare and Medicaid have been in existence for decades (these programs provide payment for health care to help the elderly, the poor, and others). This indicates that societal ethics have already moved toward including government in the financial equation of health care.

So, how are debates about societal ethics resolved? In democratic societies, changes and debates are best dealt with openly and transparently, involving as many people and points of view as possible. People today are involved in discussions and debates about ethics—no matter their government's ideology—largely because of technology. Things that might have been hidden in the past are not as easily concealed—in many cases, this means that minority views can be challenged.

Business Ethics: It's Complicated

Now that we have looked at the individual, professional, organizational, and societal levels of ethics, let's consider how ethics impact business. Business ethics can be complex. For one, different stakeholders often have different beliefs about how a business should enact values and ethics. Stakeholders consist of any organization, group, or person either internal or external to a company who has a stake in the company's success or failure. For example, think about an energy company. One group of stakeholders might believe that the company should provide the cheapest energy to the most people, which could mean using existing energy sources (such as coal) and spending little, if any, money on researching alternative sources of energy (such as biofuels). Another group of stakeholders expects the company to invest in research about alternative energy sources and to seek them out and use them now. Both groups believe their stance is ethical.

Societal ethics
Principles and standards that guide members of society in day-to-day behavior with one another.

▪ **EXHIBIT 2.7**
Why is it considered unethical for people to drink and drive?

Source: Shutterstock

Stakeholders
Any constituent potentially impacted by an organization's actions, either inside or outside the organization.

■ **EXHIBIT 2.8**
What ethical motivations did late Senator Ted Kennedy exhibit in his effort to provide equal access to health care in the United States?

Source: Blackstar/Newscom

Another reason business ethics are complicated is because many companies do business in two, four, or even dozens of countries. It is common to find that the values and ethics of cultures in these countries are in conflict. When we discover "irreducible" differences between cultures, it can be very difficult to find common ground.[42] Take the example of alcohol use. In some cultures, alcohol is a part of daily life—wine with meals in Italy or France, for example. In other cultures, alcohol is forbidden. Sometimes, people can't even be in a room where alcohol is present.

When confronted with this kind of dilemma, we sometimes adopt a relativist approach: We learn to tolerate a wide range of ethical views.[43] In other words, as a manager of a team where some people drink alcohol every day and others never do, we accept both as equally valid, no matter our own views. Putting that into practice can prove difficult, however. For example, how would you organize a team dinner when some members expect wine and others won't be in a room with alcohol?

Alternatively, we may find ourselves faced with conflicting ethical standards, some of which we feel we cannot uphold. For example, when doing business in a country that either allows or turns a blind eye to child labor, what would you do? These examples illustrate the complexity of business ethics in a global society. In the end, we often have to rely on clarity from our company as well as our own values, ethics, and critical-thinking skills when confronted with ethical dilemmas.[44]

ETHICS IN BUSINESS AND THE ROLE OF LAW

Conflicting views regarding ethical and unethical behavior can make it difficult for people and companies to decide on appropriate courses of action in some situations. That's where the law comes in. For example, in some cultures it is not unusual to make "facilitation payments" to officials or workers to move things along. These payments might be small (a few cents to a worker at a hospital to get a death certificate issued quickly) or large (thousands to move goods more quickly from the boat to the docks). Although what is considered unethical differs from country to country, the situation is becoming increasingly complex in business today. This is due in large part to domestic laws that prohibit bribery and other corrupt practices on the part of corporations or their representatives—regardless of the country in which the corrupt actions occur. Similarly, how a company treats its employees or customers is dictated by laws, and there are also laws to protect the environment. All of these laws are in one way or another related to societal values and ethics.

Laws Often Follow Ethical Violations

When situations occur that overstep the bounds of what most people in a society consider fair and just business practices, new legislation typically follows. For example, in 2002, in the wake of the Tyco, Enron, Arthur Andersen, Adelphia, and WorldCom scandals, Congress passed the Sarbanes-Oxley Act (formally known as the Public Company Accounting Reform and Investor Protection Act of 2002).[45] This legislation established new standards and improved on existing ones for all U.S. public company boards, management, and accounting firms. Although no legislation can or will prevent scandals such as Enron or WorldCom from happening again, new laws can establish strict guidelines and oversight to ensure that unethical behavior is less likely to occur.

When Laws Force People to Change

What happens when you need to require that people act in accordance with a company's ethics and your government's laws, even if this requires them to violate their personal ethical codes? This issue is on the top of many multinational companies' agendas as various countries pass increasingly pervasive laws relating to corruption. For example, the U.S. Congress passed the *International Anticorruption and Good Governance Act of 2000* (IAGGA) (Public Law 106-309) "to ensure that United States assistance programs promote good governance by assisting other countries to combat corruption throughout society and to improve transparency and accountability at all levels of government and throughout the private sector."[46]

This goal is complicated by the fact that corruption is defined differently by different countries. For example, the practice of directly influencing lawmakers' decisions by businesses and special interest groups is called lobbying. This practice is legal in the United States, but is an illegal form of corruption in many countries. In other countries, nepotism—or the practice of hiring family members first, regardless of their qualifications—is considered the right thing to do. Then, as suggested by the "facilitation payments" mentioned earlier, there are countries that consider bribery a natural part of business. It is difficult to do business in lands with such different practices, and these very real challenges are not going to go away soon.

The laws governing business ethics apply to both organizations *and* their leaders. Until the 1970s, the study and analysis of business ethics focused only on individuals. Since that time, the focus has shifted toward organizations. Organizations have values, mind-sets, cultures, goals, and objectives, much the same as individuals. Therefore, in terms of ethics, organizations are treated as individuals, both conceptually and legally.

Business ethics are complicated because the world's societies are complicated. What that means is that we have to learn to recognize how to handle ethical dilemmas in life and at work.

DEALING WITH ETHICAL DILEMMAS AT WORK

Acting on values and ethics at work is not always easy, and it's not always clear what to do. Everyone encounters **ethical dilemmas**—situations in which it appears that acting ethically would prevent the achievement of one or more objectives. For example, imagine that you have promised your boss that you will finish a project by the end of the day. You're two days late already and your boss won't tolerate another delay. You don't have a moment to spare. At about 3:00 P.M., your coworker and good friend stops by your desk, upset and scared. His boss has blamed him for something he didn't do, and he is afraid he is going to be fired. He needs you to help him decide what to say to his boss. What should you do?

> **Ethical dilemmas**
> Situations in which it appears that acting ethically would prevent the achievement of an objective.

Consider another example: It is not uncommon for people to request time off to attend religious services and be denied. This was the case for two former AT&T employees, Jose Gonzalez and Glenn Owen. In 2005, they asked for two days off to attend a religious observance that they had attended during their previous years at AT&T. In 2005, however, their request was denied. After suing AT&T for discrimination, a jury awarded the two men $296,000 in back pay and $460,000 in compensatory damages.[47] Supervisors making these decisions are most likely not malicious—they may even think they are being fair to other employees, something they consider to be ethical. They may not be intending to discriminate—but they are. Even good intentions in situations like this (e.g., perceived fairness to other employees) can still result in unethical and even illegal behavior.

In many cases, "right" and "wrong" are hard to determine, especially when situations are clouded by opinions and conflicting points of view. The best solutions to ethical dilemmas can only be determined by people who are in dialogue with one another and thinking deeply about what is best for all. Scholars suggest that ethics are "practiced" when ethical issues are made visible and discussed as complex problems as opposed to absolutes.[48]

ETHICS AND LEADERSHIP

Many companies base their ethical codes on leaders' beliefs. For example, Google's Code of Conduct starts out somewhat provocatively with a one-liner: "Don't be evil."

Cofounders Sergey Brin and Larry Page define what exactly is expected of all employees when they are asked not to be evil:

> "'Don't be evil.' Googlers generally apply those words to how we serve our users. But 'Don't be evil' is much more than that. Yes, it's about providing our users unbiased access to information, focusing on their needs and giving them the best products and services that we can. But it's also about doing the right thing more generally—following the law, acting honorably, and treating each other with respect.
>
> The Google Code of Conduct is one of the ways we put 'Don't be evil' into practice. It's built around the recognition that everything we do in connection with our work at Google will be, and should be, measured against the highest possible standards of ethical business conduct."[49]

Needless to say, "Don't be evil" is harder to do than to talk about, and Google, like any other company, faces its share of ethical dilemmas. In some cases, people disagree violently about whether some actions the company has taken are good or bad. Still, we can see that leaders at Google have set an extremely high standard that they are not afraid to talk about. *Everyone* at Google knows the code, and virtually all decisions are weighed with this code in mind. When leaders have the courage to set a standard this high and then try their very best to adhere to it, the world knows, and employees can feel proud of where they work.

How to Handle Everyday Decisions Ethically

Rules, regulations, and even inspirational codes of conduct can't guide our every move. In the end, it comes down to individual people and the decisions they make. It comes down to you: your values, your code of ethics, your decisions, and your behavior.

Before sharing some tips on how you can handle everyday decisions ethically, let's look at what can happen when we *violate* our ethics, and then rationalize unethical behavior.

WHAT HAPPENS WHEN IT GOES WRONG: THE SLIPPERY SLOPE

If you don't know where your personal "line in the sand" is, you may inadvertently make some very bad decisions or be part of situations that will not make you feel proud of yourself. Let's look at someone who many people believed was a great man, but who stepped way over the ethical line by defrauding people and breaking the law.

Until 2009, Bernie Madoff was a well-known and well-respected financier. But over many years, he deliberately defrauded people by running an elaborate Ponzi scheme.[50] A Ponzi scheme involves taking money from people who believe they are investing it legitimately, then paying dividends from investors' money instead of from profits. Here is what happened: Madoff solicited funds from friends, charities, and everyday people.[51] He told friends and clients that he was investing their money, but he didn't. False financial statements were issued, and although some people suspected something was wrong, the red flags were ignored.[52] Madoff's closely guarded financial records also caused concern for researchers at *Barron's*, but nothing came of that either.[53] Madoff schemed successfully for years, even escaping six botched investigations by the U.S. Securities and Exchange Commission (SEC). He was only caught after admitting his guilt to his two sons, one of whom later committed suicide.[54]

Prosecutors estimated the dollar amount of the fraud at $64.8 billion, including fabricated gains and estimated actual losses of $18 billion, lost by nearly 4,800 investors. Madoff pleaded guilty to 11 felony counts and was sentenced to 150 years in prison.[55] We may never know exactly how all of this happened, or who else was involved, if anyone. What we do know is that Madoff defrauded people for years with dire consequences—not the least of which was the suicide of his own son.

Most people will never compromise their values and ethics the way Madoff did. However, it is likely that at some point in your life, you will be faced with choices that challenge your sense of right and wrong. Most of us don't want to violate our own ethical code, but consider these situations:

- You wrote an outstanding paper for a class, and it fits a new assignment for another class perfectly. Despite your instructor's clear request for original work, you are considering using the old paper.
- You overhear a coworker lying about why he missed class or work. When the instructor or boss asks you to tell her what really happened, you decide not to "rat out your friend."
- You find yourself joining in with a group of friends to make fun of someone. It gets out of control, and you stop saying things about the person, but you don't try to stop what's going on.
- You have found a job that is perfect for you. It requires that you have completed your degree. Knowing you will finish in a few months, you are considering indicating that you *are* done, rather than you *will be* done.

This list shows that living our values and sticking to our ethical code can be difficult because ethics are not always crystal clear, and some of our values can actually be in conflict with other values. And unfortunately, we are also quite clever at finding reasons for violating our own beliefs, values, and ethics.

RATIONALIZING UNETHICAL BEHAVIOR

Enron was a very successful American company involved in energy, among other things. And although the scandal is now over a decade old, it goes down in history as one of the most shameful—and harmful. On the day Andrew Fastow, the former CFO, was indicted by a federal court, some employees at Enron's accounting firm, Arthur Andersen, were busy shredding incriminating documents that amounted to approximately one ton of paper.[56] Enron's fraudulent activity and the attempted cover-up resulted in convictions and also in the demise of Enron and Arthur Andersen, one of the most respected accounting firms of that time. In the end, thousands of people lost their jobs, and thousands more lost money. But how could employees of one of the nation's oldest and most esteemed accounting firms have justified these actions?

What went through the minds of those leaders at Arthur Anderson? "I will be fired if I don't." "I'm not *really* sure what I am shredding." "There's no law against shredding documents." People use all sorts of reasons to justify unethical behavior. One common justification is the belief that once in a while, everyone violates ethics, so it's really no big deal. Or people may believe that they will not get caught, or that it's just a one-time thing and no one will really be hurt. These justifications are often true. But does this make them right? Probably not.

Every genocide in history has involved people violating their ethics and values. For example, at some point in time, soldiers must have questioned themselves when they followed those hideous orders in the concentration camps of Nazi Germany, or when officials of Pol Pot's brutal dictatorship killed millions in Cambodia, or when orders were given to kill protesters in Syria during widespread uprisings beginning in 2011. Surely these people asked themselves questions, but they denied their values and ethical codes by making excuses to justify their actions: "I have to do what I'm told." "They're a threat . . . ungodly . . . evil . . . inhuman." The people who carried out these atrocities found ways to shut themselves off from the truth—and from their feelings.

These massacres might seem far away, but these types of justifications are common at work and in life, too. In organizations, people often use similar excuses: "We won't win unless we do it this way." "The ends justify the means."

Then there's the justification that goes something like, "I know it's wrong, but *they're* doing it, and if I don't, I will lose out." This is called *pluralistic ignorance,* and some scholars believe it is currently a root cause of many corporate ethical scandals.[57] We can learn how this happens from Garrett Hardin's influential essay, "The Tragedy of the Commons," which describes what happens when one party attempts to gain access to resources to maximize personal, organizational, or national benefits, assuming everyone else is trying to get the resources, too.[58] In these situations, a limited communal resource can be quickly depleted. Tragedy of the commons examples abound, such as the behavior and debate around water use in the western United States, or the question about who should "use" the Brazilian rain forest: farmers, loggers, or no one.

Coming even closer to home, consider the following excuses for unethical behaviors: "I only had a couple of beers. It's ok for me to drive." "I called in sick—sure, I'm not really sick, but everyone does it once in a while." "It's just one paper off the Internet. I don't usually do this, but I have to pass this course." Are any of these excuses valid?

Another common justification is that if behavior is not illegal, it is not unethical. This is not the case, of course, because laws generally follow social standards rather than precede them. Maybe the saddest reason for violating ethics is that some people simply don't think about them. These people don't know who they are or what they stand for (■ **EXHIBIT 2.9**).

■ **EXHIBIT 2.9**
What ethical code do you want your doctor to follow?

Source: Vadym Drobot/Shutterstock.com

ETHICAL BEHAVIOR IS UP TO YOU

As you read about some of the ways people justify unethical behavior, you may have recognized yourself. You aren't alone. Most adults have experienced situations in which they have compromised their values and acted outside of their ethical codes. If you want to prevent this in the future, the first step is to become clear about what you believe in. This cannot be overemphasized: If you want to be a good leader, examine your values, create your own personal code of ethics, and challenge yourself to live up to these guidelines at all times.

As you clarify your values and ethics, it helps to also examine the kinds of situations that tempt you to cross the line. Does this happen when there is social pressure? Do you tend to conform, even when you sense it is wrong? What about when you are afraid of failing? Or do you compromise just a little bit when the "prize" is something you really want? If you understand what conditions put you at risk, you can try to avoid them. Better yet, you can try to understand why you feel as you do in these situations and change your reaction.

When it comes to making the ethical decisions that are part of everyday life and work, you can ask yourself a few basic questions. The "golden rule" is a good place to start. How would I feel if I were treated this way? Would I feel confident in telling my boss, my family and friends, or society as a whole about the decision I have made? Can I look at myself in the mirror and know for certain that my conscience is clear and there's no doubt that my decision is ethical and in line with my values? If the answer to any of these questions troubles you, think again. Talk with someone. Reach out to people you trust for advice. Get support. It takes self-awareness, clear thinking, and courage to consistently behave ethically. But, as you know, great leaders make the tough decisions.

Discussion Questions

1. Consider your favorite restaurant. Are the terminal values of this company apparent to the customer? If so, what are they? What instrumental values do the employees use to demonstrate the restaurant's terminal values?

2. Have you ever rationalized unethical behavior (yours or someone else's)? Why and how did you do this?

3. Have you read your school's code of conduct for students and teachers? Why or why not? How does an organization's creation of an official code of conduct influence the behavior of its members? Explain your answer with real or hypothetical examples.

5. How Do Theories and Models Explain Management and Leadership?

Objective 2.5
Assess theories and models of management and leadership.

So far, we have discussed the essentials of outstanding leadership: social and emotional intelligence competencies, effective use of power, and ethics. We now turn our attention to major theories that have informed beliefs about management and leadership during the past 100 years. As a student of management and as a responsible leader in life and work, you must understand and be able to discuss these theories. It is also important that you know their limitations, recognize which models are not well supported by research, and understand which models are most relevant today.

Trait Theories of Leadership

Traits are enduring and distinguishing personal characteristics that may be inherited, learned, or developed. Traits include psychological characteristics such as optimism, pessimism, self-confidence, and sociability, as well as physical characteristics such as energy and stamina. Personal traits also include things like intelligence, maturity, and integrity.

Emerging in the early 1900s, leadership trait theories attempt to link leadership effectiveness to physical, psychological, and social characteristics, as well as abilities, knowledge, and expertise. Most studies focused only on men, one reason why it was often referred to as the "Great Man Approach." Studies paid an inordinate amount of attention to characteristics such as height, bearing (military posture), and neatness.[59] These studies were seriously flawed, and subsequent research did not support a relationship between such traits and leadership success.[60] Another flaw in many of these theories was that they assumed that all traits—physical and psychological—were immutable. In fact, some of what these researchers considered traits can and do change over time.

Despite flaws in the studies, trait theories still impact our beliefs about leadership. In fact, many people still associate good leadership with traits and characteristics that are irrelevant, like height and gender. These beliefs are often tied to outdated cultural stereotypes. For this reason, it is important to understand which traits you associate with good leaders—if these beliefs are inaccurate, you need to change them.

With these cautions in mind, we can also look at several categories of traits or characteristics that do seem to be somewhat related to leadership. These traits and characteristics can be shown in six categories: personality, physical characteristics, intelligence and ability, social background, work-related characteristics, and social characteristics as shown in (■ **EXHIBIT 2.10**).[61]

Some of the characteristics in Exhibit 2.10 are actually traits, while others are more correctly described as knowledge, competencies, or expertise. Although each of these

Traits
Enduring and distinguishing personal characteristics that may be inherited, learned, or developed.

Trait theories
Models that attempt to explain leadership effectiveness by articulation of physical, psychological, and social characteristics, as well as abilities, knowledge, and expertise.

■ **EXHIBIT 2.10**

Leadership Traits Identified in Research[62]

Personality	Physical Characteristics	Intelligence and Abilities	Social Background	Work-Related Characteristics	Social Characteristics
Integrity/honesty	Age	Emotional intelligence	Education	Achievement drive	Ability to influence and persuade
Conscientiousness	Energetic	Emotional control/stability	Social status	Responsibility/power drive	Ability to inspire
Self-monitoring	Appearance/grooming	Empathy	Mobility	Motivation to lead	Charisma
Flexibility/adaptability		Cognitive ability		Vision	Empowerment of others
Open to experience		Intelligence		Stewardship	Ability to delegate
Comfortable with uncertainty/chaos		Knowledge		Task/performance orientation	Administrative expertise
Divergent thinking		Creativity		Entrepreneurial	Trust/credibility
Assertive/aggressive		Comprehension skills		Explicit/tacit knowledge of the business	Diplomatic
Extroverted		Oral and written communication skills		Competence expertise	Shows appreciation
Enthusiastic				Administrative expertise	Desires to serve others
Confident					Team oriented

characteristics affects leadership, rarely do good leaders possess all of them. Moreover, some people who possess many of these characteristics are not effective leaders at all. In the hopes of getting closer to understanding what good leaders actually do, a new wave of research began to focus on how leaders *behaved* rather than the qualities they seemed to possess.

Behavior Models and Approaches to Leadership

The behavioral approach to studying and understanding leadership effectiveness looks at the actual behaviors leaders engage in when guiding and influencing others. The early models drew on disciplines such as sociology, psychology, and anthropology, and they examined human interaction in an organizational environment.

OHIO STATE STUDIES: CONSIDERATION AND INITIATING STRUCTURE

Toward the middle of the twentieth century, researchers at Ohio State University surveyed leaders and found two major dimensions of leadership behaviors: consideration and initiating structure.[63] **Consideration** referred to people-oriented behaviors such as respect, openness to employees' ideas, and concern for employees' well-being. Leaders who emphasized consideration were likely to create trusting, supportive, and amiable environments marked by open communication and teamwork.

Initiating structure included behaviors related to tasks and goals, such as giving clear directions, monitoring employees' performance, planning, and setting work schedules and deadlines. Leaders who emphasized structure were likely to emphasize efficiency and effectiveness and to support employees by identifying what needed to be done so they could succeed at a job or task. The Ohio State studies started a trend that focused on which leadership style was the "best."[64]

Consideration
People-oriented behaviors such as respect, openness to employees' ideas, and concern for employees' well-being.

Initiating structure
Behaviors related to task and goal orientation, such as giving clear directions, monitoring employees' performance, and planning and setting work schedules and deadlines.

UNIVERSITY OF MICHIGAN STUDIES: PRODUCTION- AND EMPLOYEE-ORIENTED BEHAVIOR

Around the same time, researchers at the University of Michigan began studying the behavior of effective supervisors.[65] They identified two dimensions of behavior. The first dimension, *production-oriented behavior,* focused on efficiency, costs, adhering to schedules, and meeting deadlines. These supervisors focused on job tasks and work procedures and regarded employees as a means to the end of achieving work goals.

Supervisors who favored production-oriented behavior tended to be less effective than those who favored *employee-oriented behavior.* Supervisors who favored employee-oriented behavior were supportive of employees, emphasized relationships, and focused on engaging employees through setting and assisting in the attainment of high-performance goals. The study concluded that employees preferred employee-oriented behavior and performed better when supervisors embraced it.

LEADERSHIP GRID

Researchers Robert Blake and Jane Mouton of the University of Texas built on the University of Michigan and Ohio studies. In 1964, they proposed that managerial behaviors could be plotted along horizontal and vertical axes measuring concern for people and concern for production. The researchers concluded that several management styles existed based on the degree to which the manager attended to people and/or task. Although the model focused on the positive attributes of each style, the research team contended that the team management style worked best.[66]

Contingency Approaches to Leadership

Contingency approaches to leadership are models and theories of leadership that call on leaders to adapt their behavior to different situations and/or characteristics of followers. For example, leading a small team of people in an entrepreneurial start-up will call for a different approach than leading a large division of a multinational company. In the start-up, you will rely heavily on interpersonal communication, strong personal relationships, and inspiring people by painting a picture of the future. In a large division, you can't possibly have personal relationships with everyone, so you will need to rely on reaching people in other ways—via webinars, speeches, e-mail, and the like. You will also need to rely on organizational processes and culture to guide people's behavior. In the next four sections, we will look at four contingency approaches to leadership.

FIEDLER'S CONTINGENCY THEORY

Fiedler's contingency theory states that leadership effectiveness is dependent on the characteristics of the leader and the characteristics of the situation.[67] Fiedler proposed that *leader style* is either task oriented or relationship oriented. **Relationship-oriented leaders** emphasize good relationships and being liked by employees. **Task-oriented leaders** focus on accomplishments and ensuring that employees perform well on the job. The theory also states that changing one's leadership style is difficult. Effectiveness, therefore, is dependent on matching a leader's style to the situation.[68]

SITUATIONAL LEADERSHIP THEORY

Situational leadership theory links leader style with followers' readiness for tasks. This model, developed by Paul Hersey and Ken Blanchard, focuses on followers' readiness to do their jobs and leaders' responsibility to notice this and adapt accordingly. The term *readiness* refers to the extent to which employees are capable, confident, and willing to complete an assigned task or perform well on the job. The model suggests that when leaders attend to these factors, they can then vary their level of attention to task and relationship behaviors and choose one of four leadership styles.[69] The *telling style* is appropriate when followers are unable, unwilling, or insecure, and they need

Contingency approaches to leadership
Models and theories of leadership that take into account leader behavior and various aspects of the organizational situation and/or characteristics of followers.

Fiedler's contingency theory
Theory stating that leadership effectiveness is dependent on the characteristics of the leader and the characteristics of the situation.

Relationship-oriented leaders
Leaders who emphasize good relationships and being liked by employees.

Task-oriented leaders
Leaders who focus on accomplishments and seek to ensure that employees perform well on the job.

Situational leadership theory
Contingency model that links leader style with followers' readiness for tasks.

clear direction, close supervision, and guidance. The *selling style* is appropriate when employees are unable to complete tasks, but they are willing and/or confident. The *participating style* can be used when employees are able but unwilling or insecure. Finally, the *delegating style* can be used when employees are able, willing, or confident.

The situational theory is somewhat appealing in that it focuses on *followers* and their competencies and capabilities, or their progress from immaturity to maturity. That said, the model assumes that leaders can accurately read followers' readiness. Unfortunately, that is not always the case. You may have had an experience in which a leader didn't match his or her style to your level of readiness. Maybe you worked on a team, for example, where the leader gave far too many instructions and treated you as if you didn't know what you were doing. This is a common mistake for new managers. They think they have to direct everything, and they ignore the fact that they need to adjust their behavior to people and situations.

PATH-GOAL THEORY

Path-goal theory
A contingency approach to leadership stating that the leader is responsible for motivating employees to attain goals.

Path-goal theory states that a leader is responsible for motivating employees to attain goals.[70] The path-goal theory is based on the expectancy theory of motivation, covered in Chapter 3. In this model, effective leaders boost employee motivation (and presumably effectiveness) by illuminating the path toward organizational and personal goals and linking rewards to goal attainment. Leaders must ensure that the path to the goal is free of obstacles, that goals are meaningful, and that rewards are valued. According to this theory, leaders choose one of four styles. They can be directive, and do things like set clear guidelines and expectations. They can also choose to be supportive and create a warm environment that fosters collaboration. Or, they can emphasize challenging goals, using the achievement-oriented style. Finally, they can choose the participative style and involve employees in making decisions. Path-goal theory assumes that leaders can change their behaviors and styles.[71]

LEADER SUBSTITUTES MODEL

Leader substitutes model
A contingency model of leadership that states that certain characteristics of people or of the situation can make direct leadership unnecessary.

The **leader substitutes model** states that certain characteristics of people or of the situation can make direct leadership unnecessary.[72] For example, when employees are knowledgeable, well trained, and highly motivated, people often don't need close supervision. They will manage themselves and get the job done. Similarly, when goals are clear and the culture is powerful, positive, and resonant, people need less direct guidance.

This theory is quite useful, because it challenges the traditional idea that people *have* to be managed and led, and that if they are not, they will avoid work entirely or not work to their full potential. The belief that people need to be cajoled, told, and controlled colors many theories of management and leadership. The leader substitute model is useful today because most people assume that others are willing and capable.

Contingency approaches to leadership are quite popular today, and many variations and models are used in organizations. For a student of management, probably the most useful lesson is that it is important to attend to one's own leadership behavior as well as the situation, employees' abilities, confidence, self-efficacy, and motivation. Understanding these dimensions can be quite helpful in determining how to influence, engage, and support people.

The Study of Leadership Continues

Each of the theories you have studied in this section has a kernel of wisdom. To utilize the theories, however, you need to discern which aspects of the research apply to work and organizations today. This means you need to be an educated consumer of knowledge. You need to carefully evaluate the models that you hold implicitly and explicitly. You also need to be able to discern which models are operating in the minds of others. Very often, beliefs about leadership are not overt or explicit—they are embedded in organizational culture and systems. This can be dangerous when old, outdated myths about leadership underlie people's beliefs and organizational processes. On the other hand, if leadership is considered to be everyone's responsibility, and organizational systems empower people to lead, organizations can soar.

Discussion Questions

1. Study the common leadership traits in Exhibit 2.10. Which of these traits do you believe are most important to leadership? Why? Which of these traits do you possess? What traits can you adopt to become a more effective leader?

2. Choose two theories of leadership you have studied in this book. Explain why you think they are relevant for today's business environment.

3. Consider a situation where you were expected to lead. Using contingency theories, describe your approach to leadership. Also, explain the reaction of your followers. How did you influence their abilities and willingness to work on the task at hand?

6. Is It Time to Take a Stand for Transformational Leadership?

> **Objective 2.6**
> Determine the necessity of transformational leadership.

Transformational leaders are people who have social and emotional intelligence and who can inspire others to seek an extraordinary vision. In contrast, **transactional leaders** are people who follow a traditional approach to management in which leader and follower behavior is an instrumental exchange (e.g., "You do the work I assign to you, and I will reward you for your effort").[73]

> **Transformational leaders**
> People who have social and emotional intelligence and who can inspire others to seek an extraordinary vision.
>
> **Transactional leaders**
> People who follow a traditional approach to management in which leader and follower behavior is an instrumental exchange.

As you have learned in this chapter, the most effective leaders attend to *people*. Transformational leaders value people and focus on employees' needs for appreciation, inspiration, meaningful work, and personal growth. People find transformational leaders compelling because they are passionate about what they do, and they share their passion with everyone. And most importantly, transformational leaders do the right thing in the right way, as Brad Stevens did with the Butler University men's basketball team.

In 2000, Brad Stevens worked as a marketing associate at pharmaceuticals giant Eli Lilly and Company in Indianapolis. However, the former college basketball player wanted to return to the sport he loved as a coach. He threw caution to the wind and left his job to accept a volunteer position in the Butler University basketball office.[74]

Stevens joined the Butler staff as a coordinator of basketball operations—a largely administrative position. However, he was offered a full-time assistant coaching position during the 2001–02 season. He served as an assistant for six seasons, and he was named head coach in 2007 when his predecessor left for another university.[75] During his first season as the Bulldogs' head coach, he led his team to a school- and league-record 30 wins, became the first coach in school history to post a 30-win season, and secured an NCAA tournament berth. He was only 31 at the time.[76]

In the ensuing seasons, Stevens has continued to show outstanding leadership, earning several coach of the year awards and breaking numerous school and league records. He also became the youngest coach ever to lead his team to back-to-back NCAA tournament championship games.[77] After the team's 2010 appearance, Stevens had offers from larger schools but elected to stay at mid-major Butler and continue building its program rather than pursuing a more high-profile position.[78]

When Stevens arrived, Butler did not have the clout or the recruiting budget to snag big name recruits. But Stevens cultivated the talent he had and started pursuing the hard-working kids who didn't garner the attention of many scouts. He taught these players a defense-centric system—referred to as "the Butler way"—that stresses team above individual.[79]

The positive response of the players to this ideology is clear and is best exemplified by their response to Stevens after a loss to Youngstown State during a rough patch in the 2010–11 season. When Stevens told his team, "I've got to get better," they responded by saying, "No, we've got to get better."[80] Before the season was out, the team made their return trip to the final NCAA tournament game.

Brad is an example of transformational leadership in his work at Butler for several reasons. Transformational leadership almost always starts with the person, as it did with Brad when he connected with his team on a personal, relational level. In this case, Brad's passion led him to take on challenges that others shied away from, and he stayed to see the challenges through even when he had offers from larger, more prestigious schools based on his work at Butler. He sought to live his values, no matter the cost to him, personally. And he took risks. He looked beyond the typical student athletes, bucking both tradition and what some would call common sense. For instance, he devoted attention to hard working players, regardless of their individual name recognition. He knew what he was doing, and it paid off. With dedication and perseverance—other hallmarks of a transformational leader—he built a winning team. And while doing so, he set the stage for the future. This is key: Transformational leaders aren't looking for short-term wins—they build for the long term.

Under the guidance of a transformational leader, followers will enthusiastically accept the organization's vision and goals as a part of their own personal vision.[81] That's because followers of transformational leaders see something bigger than themselves in the leadership vision. They see a vision that is meaningful to them—a vision that inspires them to actively move toward the future.

As you can see in these descriptions, transformational leaders are emotionally intelligent. They are self-aware in that they know how their emotions affect themselves and others, and they use their emotions to create resonance, excitement, and optimism. Transformational leaders are visionary, and they know how to convey their visions in ways that make people feel inspired and committed. Transformational leaders are change agents.

One of the words often associated with transformational leaders is *charisma*. Charismatic leaders are self-confident without being arrogant, honest in their dealings with their employees, and they communicate clearly (■ **EXHIBIT 2.11**). Researchers describe five behavioral attributes of charismatic leaders that define transformational leadership:[82]

■ **EXHIBIT 2.11**
How did Martin Luther King, Jr., demonstrate transformational leadership?

Source: © GL Archive/Alamy

- Vision and articulation
- Sensitivity to the environment
- Sensitivity to people's needs
- Personal risk taking
- Unconventional behavior

Transformational leadership is essential in a world that changes quickly. The best businesses, and organizations of all types, need such leaders. In fact, if we look historically at businesses that have survived and thrived during times of transition and great change, we find that people have been encouraged to be visionary, to take risks, and to rely on skills linked to social awareness. These skills, including empathy and organizational awareness, enable people to stay close to employees' and market needs. Ultimately, environments that support and foster such leadership skills enable organizations to transform themselves.

Unilever, the giant British-Dutch foods, personal, and home care company, is a very good example of a company built on the principles of transformational and ethical leadership. Even its earliest founder-predecessors, such as William Lever of Lever Brothers, took transformational stances regarding the business. For example, former Unilever chairman Niall FitzGerald quotes a visionary Lever: "The truest and highest form of enlightened self-interest requires that we pay the fullest regard to the interest and welfare of those around us, whose well-being we must bind up with our own and with whom we must share our prosperity."[83] This was a revolutionary position in 1901, and it led to revolutionary ways of doing business such as the provision of adequate living quarters for employees and a living wage, as well as the creation of products that had social, as well as monetary, value.

Time and again and decade after decade, the company's employees and leaders have made decisions that enable the company to succeed while also being ahead of the curve when it comes to economic, social, and environmental sustainability. Let's look at this company's approach to transformation in the *Business Case*.

The business case about Unilever demonstrates that transformational leadership is about more than building a strong bottomline; it as about being responsible and

BUSINESS CASE   **Unilever**

Transformation for Sustainability

Unilever's web site proudly states that "160 million times a day, someone somewhere uses a Unilever product."[84] You may be wondering what those products are, as Unilever is not yet a household name. For many years, it was a corporate name behind over 400 extremely well-known brands including household favorites like Axe, Dove, Lipton, Hellman's, Bertolli, Vaseline, Surf, and many more. Over the years, many of these brands have changed, and many haven't—both of which are equally important ingredients for success.

Some companies never change, and some change too much or in the wrong direction. Over the years, Unilever has gotten the equation right. The company's leaders read the local and global markets and respond fast and appropriately. What's as—if not more—impressive is that Unilever listens to more than just what customers and stakeholders want. They have mastered the local-global debate by providing products that local customers want while maximizing efficiency in their research, production, and supply chain processes.

Moreover, the company's leaders and all employees don't just blindly create new products based on fads: They seek to find out *why* customers and other interested parties want something new or different. Then, they go about trying to balance the multiple demands of many stakeholders and do the right thing.

Doing the right thing in business isn't always easy. This is because different constituencies often have different needs and place different demands on a business. For example, investors want growth and profits. Consumers want new, exciting products. And community groups want a business to behave in a responsible manner when it comes to jobs and the environment. These conflicting demands were exactly what Unilever and many other companies have faced in the past two decades. Unlike many other companies, however, Unilever has found a path to success. A path to success in today's complex business environment starts with transformational *thinking*. And transformational thinking starts with refusing to see traditional conflicts in traditional ways. Transformational thinking means looking for solutions in new places and not falling prey to a win-lose mind-set.

In recent years, former chairmen Niall FitzGerald and Antony Burgmans engaged the entire company in transformational thinking as they streamlined their brands in the early 2000s. They also launched a tidal wave of passion and engagement in the company for examining how Unilever was impacting the environment—and making changes. This effort was expanded by the next generation of leaders, as was a complete overhaul of the supply chain. These actions are revolutionary in a business, and they are the outcomes of transformational leadership.

As CEO Paul Polman says, "The great challenge of the twenty-first century is to provide good standards of living for 7 billion people without depleting the earth's resources or running up massive levels of public debt. To achieve this, government and business alike will need to find new models of growth which are in both environmental and economic balance." He goes on to say, "In Unilever we believe that business must be part of the solution. But to be so, business will have to change. It will have to get off the treadmill of quarterly reporting and operate for the long term. It will have to see itself as part of society, not separate from it. And it will have to recognise that the needs of citizens and communities carry the same weight as the demands of shareholders."

This may not seem revolutionary to you, but it is. Many businesses have put the needs of one or two constituencies above all others. Unilever is not doing that. The challenges are not simple, of course. The company, like all responsible companies, is still struggling with answers to the complex questions around sustainability and success; at least they are boldly taking a stand. Unilever is paving a way to the creation of a new way of doing business that, the company's leaders and employees believe, will lead to happy, loyal customers, satisfied investors, safer workplaces, healthier communities, and sustainable environmental practices.

accountable for your actions. It is about understanding the needs of the people whose lives you touch. And it is about remaining true to what you know is right for yourself, for others, and for the world around you.

In this section, we have introduced a way of thinking about leadership that goes to the heart of what is needed today, from everyone at every level. Today, everyone needs to be a leader. To be a great leader, you need to develop your emotional intelligence, understand and live your values and ethics, and manage your power wisely. You also need to understand what research past and present tells us about leadership. This way, you can become an educated consumer of knowledge as you learn to be a better leader.

Discussion Questions

1. Describe the difference between transactional and transformational leadership.

2. How important is it for a leader to be transformational? Why? Use your experience to support your position.

3. Think about your leadership abilities, especially your social and emotional intelligence and your methods for inspiring people. Which emotional intelligence skills do you need to develop in order to become a more effective leader? Why did you choose these skills?

Objective 2.7
Describe HR's role in supporting and fostering excellent and ethical leadership.

7. What Is HR's Role in Supporting Excellent and Ethical Leadership?

During most of the last century, HR professionals were largely relegated to the "back office." Even the most senior HR employees were often not consulted on strategic issues. The HR function (often called "personnel") was expected to provide the technical services necessary to hire, pay, and train professionals, as well as deal with labor unions and the like. HR was not expected to be "at the table" when big decisions were made. That view has changed, and so have the roles that HR professionals need to hold. These roles require that HR professionals revolutionize what their function does and how it is perceived.

HR's Leadership Roles

As you progress in your career, you will deal with HR on many levels, and you may join the profession yourself. As you can see in ■ **EXHIBIT 2.12**, there are several exciting ways that HR professionals can provide leadership in an organization. Today, HR professionals take an active role in creating the architecture for professional development within the organization to ensure that the leadership pipeline is robust. HR professionals are also increasingly taking on coaching and advisory responsibilities to help individuals succeed in their roles. HR leaders are also now more often recognized as strategic business partners, helping to plan the strategies for success in the organization. Finally, HR leaders are respected organizational change agents, designing interventions that help align organizational culture, business processes, and outcomes. These critical roles represent the fresh way that business leaders are looking at the HR function within organizations, which we will address throughout this book.

You will encounter HR professionals as coaches, strategic business partners, change agents, and leadership development architects. Let's look at each one:

Coach: A coach is a person who enables another person to discover answers for themselves. HR coaches help managers solve complex problems related to things like team conflicts, interpersonal problems, issues with a boss, and career choices.

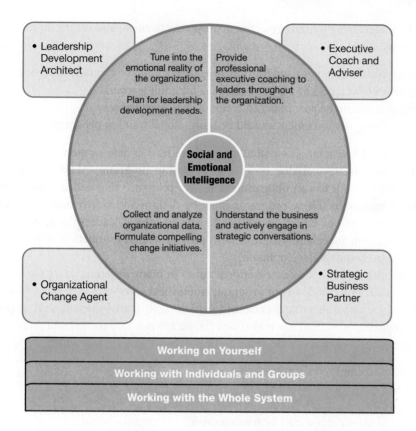

■ **EXHIBIT 2.12**
The four HR leadership roles include social and emotional intelligence at the center.[85]

Source: Annie McKee and Frances Johnston.

Strategic business partner: HR leaders must understand the business they support. How does the business make money? What are the obstacles to efficiency, effectiveness, and quality? What are the ethical dilemmas leaders might face? The HR strategic business partner is informed and able to discuss all questions related to his or her "clients," or managers, with intelligence, conviction, and creativity.

Change agent: All businesses are constantly in flux. In the past, HR has been seen as the keeper of the status quo. That is not true any longer, at least in organizations where the best HR directors take up the role of change agent. HR change agents know how to diagnose complex organizational issues and plan for change. They know how to read the political environment in order to influence key leaders to bring about the right kinds of changes.

Leadership development architect: Many organizations have too many unrelated and poor quality leadership development programs. HR leaders who see their role as an architect of leadership development look across the entire organization, identify learning needs, and create a curriculum that encompasses a set of interrelated programs.

Let's look at one particular program that is built into the best leadership architectures and how to ensure these programs are successful.

Developing Ethical Leaders

According to estimates by the American Society of Training and Development (ASTD), over $171.5 billion was spent by U.S. organizations for training in 2010.[86] While there are no figures for training dollars spent globally, the number may run to well over $1 trillion. With such a large investment in employee development, it is clear that HR leaders have a great responsibility to ensure that training dollars are used effectively and not wasted. Unfortunately, there are no reliable estimates to determine how much capital is wasted on ineffective training. What is clear is that there are things that HR leaders can do to improve the quality, effectiveness, and return on investment in training:

- Leadership development and training programs should be carefully designed around principles of what is known to be effective for adult learners.
- Programs should be part of organizational change processes.
- Post-training reinforcement should be built into all training programs.[87]

Now that you know a bit about what effective leadership development programs look like, let's take the special case of ethical leadership programs. Many people would argue today that HR has an obligation to deliver programs that address issues related to ethical leadership. These programs must be designed to clarify and reinforce the organization's code of ethics, as well as to embed ethical leadership in all levels of the organization. Successful programs also provide a solid foundation of professional ethics and professional development.

Companies can develop organizational ethics in many different ways. For example, within a leadership development program, employees can be provided the opportunity to learn the company's ethical code and explore their own values as well as professional, organizational, and societal ethics. These are not easy topics, and lecture-style programs simply won't work. In order to be successful, these programs need to be:

- Relevant to employees' experiences
- Focused on developing good judgment
- Focused on reflection and dialogue
- Fully and visibly supported by management.

As you progress in your career you will likely have the opportunity to participate in many leadership development programs at work. And, as this section reminds us, HR professionals have a particular role in developing leaders at work. In the end, however, developing yourself as a leader is your responsibility. In the next section, we will look at one foundational competency that you can focus on outside of formal training: developing self-awareness.

Discussion Questions

1. Think of an ethical dilemma in which you stood up for—or failed to stand up for—your beliefs. What are some of the factors that prompted you to respond in this way?
2. What is HR's role in ensuring consistent leadership in the organization? Think of an example from an organization you belong to. How does that organization prepare people for leadership roles?
3. How do you think HR can help build an ethical organizational culture? How does this differ from the traditional "personnel" and "back office" functions HR professionals have filled in the past?

Objective 2.8
Describe the steps one must take to become a great leader.

8. What Can We All Do to Become Great Leaders?

As you learned in this chapter, there are a number of competencies related to social and emotional intelligence that are essential to good leadership. (See Exhibit 2.2.) Throughout this text we will draw your attention to these competencies. In this section we will focus on self-awareness.

When members of the Stanford Graduate School of Business's Advisory Council were asked to identify the most important capability for leaders to develop, their answer was nearly unanimous: self-awareness.[88] If we are to understand how our *view* of the world affects our *place* in that world, we need to be vigilant in understanding all that contributed to who we are. This is one aspect of self-awareness.

As you progress along the path toward deeper self-awareness, you may find that you are more authentic in your relationships and better able to inspire trust. You may even find that deepening your knowledge of yourself enables you to be more confident and to display courage and integrity in the face of challenges. Let's look at how authenticity, trust, integrity, and courage can support you in becoming a better leader.

Self-Aware Leaders Are Authentic

Authenticity is the genuine presentation of one's thoughts and beliefs. This characteristic has been identified as an essential leadership trait by numerous researchers.[89] Authenticity requires a high degree of self-awareness because, after all, how can you be genuine if you don't really know yourself? Authentic leaders are committed to honesty. Because of this emphasis on truth, an authentic leader's behavior and words exhibit a refreshing strength coupled with humility.

Authenticity is often linked with self-esteem: People with low self-esteem are more likely to misinterpret their own feelings, particularly negative ones, due, in part, to fear of rejection or their insecurity.[90] However, high self-esteem allows people to publicly present their thoughts, feelings, and beliefs non-defensively, which others experience as authenticity. So, one powerful step you can take as you develop self-awareness and the capacity for authenticity is to focus on your self-esteem. It is important to recognize that you have special gifts and talents that no one else has, and to know that you can use these gifts for good as a person and as a leader.

Authenticity
Genuine presentation of one's thoughts, feelings, and beliefs.

Authentic Leaders Inspire Trust

Employees trust leaders who act in an ethically justifiable manner, have their best interests at heart, and strive to achieve the organization's goals.[91]

Scholars also propose that a leader's trust in followers and followers' trust in leaders are based on perceptions of ability, benevolence, and integrity in previous encounters. In addition, studies suggest that subordinates' trust in leaders is positively related to such things as job performance and satisfaction, organizational and goal commitment, and belief in the truth of information. One study found that team members' trust was primarily facilitated by three practices: consulting team members on decisions, communicating a group vision, and homogeneity of values.[92] Without trust, people are secretive and serve their own needs first, and they become uncooperative, defensive, and suspicious. If a leader has not earned the trust of the people he or she leads, then this leader is unlikely to be successful.

Authentic Leaders Have Integrity and Courage, and They Live by a Code of Ethics

The ethics of a company are determined in large part by the choices and decisions that employees, managers, and leaders make on a daily basis. It takes integrity to make ethical decisions, and it takes courage to act on these choices. Therefore, integrity is often seen as the starting point for ethical leadership.

But what is integrity when it comes to ethics? Integrity is derived from the Latin word *integrare,* which means "to be whole." A typical dictionary definition of integrity with respect to ethics refers to the quality of steadfastly holding to high moral principles and professional standards. Integrity is related to concepts such as honesty, truthfulness, and reliability, all of which affect ethical decision making and action. In fact, some scholars define *integrity* simply as "principled behavior."[93] Scholars also believe that leadership integrity is essential because today's knowledge economy is

Integrity
The quality of steadfastly holding to high moral principles and professional standards.

fraught with ecological unsustainability and political uncertainty, meaning that our integrity is constantly challenged as we seek to do the right thing.[94]

Finally, some researchers believe that integrity involves consistency between words and actions (the opposite of hypocrisy), and that the outcomes of leadership integrity are trust and reciprocal integrity, as well as satisfaction with leaders and leadership performance.[95]

Leaders with integrity take responsibility for their actions, are principled, are transparent, do what they say they will do, and never compromise their ethics. These leaders are perceived as credible. People believe in them, in what they say, in their vision, and in their commitment to doing the right thing. It's not always easy to act on one's integrity, though, because strong forces can push us toward compromise. What it takes to avoid this situation is courage.

What is courage? Courage isn't the lack of fear; it is the ability to overcome fear.[96] Certainly, fear plays a huge part in whether a person acts or refuses to act on his or her code of ethics. Courage means facing our fears and doing the right thing anyway. But fear isn't the biggest obstacle to courage, conformity is. As commentator Jim Hightower once wrote, "Even a dead fish can go with the flow."[97] Maybe you've had an experience in which the pressure to conform was strong, yet you knew that conforming would be a violation of your personal code of ethics. Courage involves taking risks, including the risk of going against the crowd. Courage, then, can be defined as the willingness and ability to face fear, danger, uncertainty, or pain without giving up whatever course of action you believe is necessary and right.

At one time or another, every great person has to find the courage to step away from the crowd and do the right thing. This can be hard, even painful.[98] But it's worth it. When you come upon injustice, injury, or wrongdoing and make the brave decision to act—to take on the risk of confronting the situation and boldly trying to change it—then you will know you are truly a courageous leader.[99]

Courage
The willingness and ability to face fear, danger, uncertainty, or pain without giving up whatever course of action one believes is necessary and right.

Discussion Questions

1. Sometimes we think about self-awareness as understanding our mind (intellect), body (physical self), heart (emotions), and spirit (values). For each of these areas, discuss two or three things that you believe define who you are as a person.

2. Think of a situation in which you assumed a leadership role. How did you support others socially and emotionally? Were you always authentic in these interactions? How did your self-awareness inspire trust in others?

3. Discuss the role of integrity in college life, both inside the classroom and outside it. How do you maintain your personal integrity? What do you think contributes to the failure to maintain integrity?

---

9. A Final Word on Leadership

Throughout this book, we will emphasize that everyone is a leader—or can become a leader, if he or she chooses. We all influence others every day, and you can too. In this chapter you have had opportunities to reflect on some very important aspects of leadership, such as the social and emotional intelligence competencies you need to develop, how to use your power effectively, and how to ensure that your values and ethics are at the center of your leadership.

You have also learned about several theories of leadership developed during the past few decades. Knowing these theories and *being able to evaluate them* is an important part of being an informed citizen, as well as an informed leader.

As we move into a variety of compelling topics related to leadership and management, you will be well served to turn back to this chapter often, to link what you learn to how you can be an outstanding leader.

EXPERIENCING Leadership

LEADING IN A GLOBAL WORLD
Becoming a News and Media Critic

As you will see in this course, even small companies are affected by the global marketplace. As a leader in an increasingly global business environment, you need to be informed about things like international politics, wars and conflicts, and regional trends. Staying on top of this information is not easy because most news tends to be biased or incomplete. In this assignment, you will develop a way to review world events in such a way that you get "the whole picture."

1. Either alone or with a team, choose a topic of global interest (e.g., oil production and sales) and/or a country/region of the world that you are interested in.
2. Thoroughly investigate various news, media, and other information sources available to you on the Internet, on television, through the movies, etc.
3. Critique several of the media sources you have identified using the following questions:
   A. Whose perspective is most prominently portrayed?
   B. What biases are evident? Why do you think they exist?
   C. What information is missing? Why do you think it is missing?
4. Based on your research, identify a set of at least three sources of information that, if reviewed regularly, will provide a full and balanced portrayal of the topic/issue.

LEADING WITH EMOTIONAL INTELLIGENCE
Developing Self-Awareness by Talking with Others

This chapter has presented research indicating that social and emotional intelligence competencies differentiate outstanding leaders from average ones. Emotional self-awareness is at the heart of emotional intelligence. Many companies help employees develop self-awareness by engaging in 360-degree feedback surveys. You can gain insight into your emotional intelligence by engaging in a similar process with friends and coworkers. Below is a list of statements about your leadership. Fill in your name and copy (or copy and paste) these statements and the scoring code onto several different sheets of paper.

1. Rank yourself on each statement.
2. Ask five trusted friends or coworkers to rank you on the statements. Be sure to choose people who wish you well and whom you can trust. Tell them you are happy to do the survey for them, if they want.

3. Compare your self-ranking with scores others gave you. Ask yourself the following questions:
   A. Do others rank me similarly to the way I rank myself? Why or why not?
   B. Are there any areas that I would like to work on developing? If I strengthen these areas, how will my life and my leadership improve?

Self-Awareness Survey

(Scale: 1–5;
1 = almost never;
2 = sometimes;
3 = often;
4 = most of the time;
5 = almost always)

[your name] is clear about his/her values and shares them appropriately with others
[your name] manages his/her emotions well
[your name] has a vision for him/herself and is also open to new opportunities
[your name] is generally optimistic and has a positive outlook on life
[your name] works well on a team
[your name] is inspiring and motivating
[your name] deals well with conflict
[your name] deals well with change
[your name] helps others develop and learn
[your name] is someone people enjoy following

LEADING WITH CRITICAL THINKING SKILLS
Studying Common Beliefs about Leadership

Leadership is something that almost everyone has an opinion about. In many cases, people's opinions are informed by their cultures, the popular media, and the opinions of friends and family. This is normal; it can also be destructive because these sources perpetuate outdated, unsupported beliefs about what it takes to be a leader.

This assignment is best done individually, then as a research project with a team.

1. Study your implicit theories about leadership.
   A. Write a description of your ideal leader. Be honest with yourself: What qualities and behaviors do you really value (even if you know these qualities and behaviors aren't "right")?
   B. Identify the underlying, unspoken assumptions that draw you to these qualities and behaviors

(e.g., leaders have to be older and/or have a senior management position).

2. Interview six people about the leadership qualities and behaviors they value.

   A. Identify common themes across the interviews.

   B. Identify the underlying, unspoken assumptions shared by your interviewees.

ETHICAL LEADERSHIP
Discovering Differences and the Sources of Dilemmas

Leaders often have to grapple with ethical dilemmas. Your ability to recognize an ethical dilemma, handle your response to it, and help others do the same will greatly impact your effectiveness as a leader. In this exercise, you will explore how to identify ethical dilemmas in the workplace.

1. Choose a company that interests you.

2. Either alone or with a team, identify the groups of people who work in this company. Group people by nationality, ethnicity/culture, religion, gender, and any other groupings that might represent sources of differences in values and/or ethics.

3. Identify noticeably different beliefs and practices of these groups that might create challenges in the workplace.

4. Generate lists of possible ethical dilemmas that may emerge as a result of these differences. Choose one of these dilemmas and come up with at least three ways to address it.

KEY TERMS

Competencies, *p. 26*
Competency model, *p. 28*
Social and emotional intelligence, *p. 29*
Resonant organizations, *p. 29*
Resonant leaders, *p. 29*
Limbic resonance, *p. 31*
Power, *p. 32*
Organizational politics, *p. 33*
Legitimate power, *p. 33*
Reward power, *p. 33*
Coercive power, *p. 33*
Expert power, *p. 34*
Referent power, *p. 34*
Empowerment, *p. 34*
Micromanagement, *p. 35*
Theory X, *p. 35*

Theory Y, *p. 35*
Theory Z, *p. 35*
Flat organizations, *p. 36*
Ethics, *p. 37*
Values, *p. 37*
Ethical code, *p. 37*
Terminal values, *p. 37*
Instrumental values, *p. 37*
Individual ethics, *p. 37*
Professional ethics, *p. 38*
Organizational ethics, *p. 38*
Societal ethics, *p. 39*
Stakeholders, *p. 39*
Ethical dilemmas, *p. 41*
Traits, *p. 45*
Trait theories, *p. 45*

Consideration, *p. 46*
Initiating structure, *p. 46*
Contingency approaches to leadership, *p. 47*
Fiedler's contingency theory, *p. 47*
Relationship-oriented leaders, *p. 47*
Task-oriented leaders, *p. 47*
Situational leadership theory, *p. 47*
Path-goal theory, *p. 48*
Leader substitutes model, *p. 48*
Transformational leaders, *p. 49*
Transactional leaders, *p. 49*
Authenticity, *p. 55*
Integrity, *p. 55*
Courage, *p. 56*

MyManagementLab

Go to **mymanagementlab.com** for Auto-graded writing questions as well as the following Assisted-graded writing questions:

2-1. Consider your most outstanding leadership experience. What did you learn about yourself? How did you learn these lessons?

2-2. How can empowerment support democratic processes? How might participation, empowerment and democratic processes at work have an effect on people's behavior at work and in their communities?

2-3. Mymanagementlab Only — comprehensive writing assignment for this chapter.

1. Leadership: Whose Responsibility Is It? (pp. 24–26)

Objective: Recognize why everyone needs to learn how to lead today.

Summary: In today's organizations, it is important for everyone to learn how to lead with emotional intelligence, use power responsibly, and act ethically. That's because all of us share the responsibility of ensuring that those in power behave fairly and ethically. The good news is that leadership can be learned. Although it can be challenging to step up to leadership, you can do it now—you don't need to wait until you have a senior position at work. It is essential, however, that we learn to create strong relationships with others and powerful, resonant environments in our teams and organizations so everyone can be at their best.

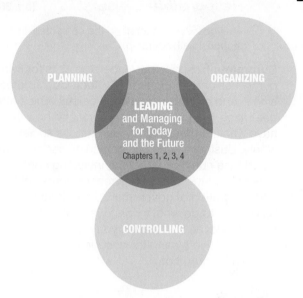

2. What Is the Secret to *Effective* Leadership? (pp. 26–32)

Objective: Understand the characteristics of effective leadership.

Summary: To be an effective leader or manager, mastering social and emotional intelligence competencies—like self-awareness, self-management, social awareness, and relationship management—is essential. Social and emotional intelligence competencies contribute to our effectiveness. All competencies are linked to motives, traits, self-concept, knowledge, and the skills the leader brings to the job. There are two levels of competencies—those that are necessary to do a job and those that support outstanding performance—and three categories that can be used to further subdivide competencies according to technical, cognitive, and relational components. No matter how you classify competencies, however, research suggests that social and emotional intelligence make all the difference in terms of an individual's ability to create resonant relationships, communicate effectively, and be truly aware of the environment. Special attention must be given to self-awareness, the foundation of social and emotional intelligence.

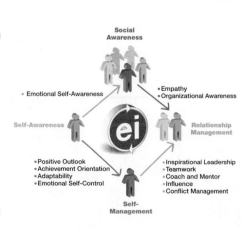

3. What Is the Secret to *Influential* Leadership? (pp. 32–36)

Objective: Understand the characteristics of influential leadership.

Summary: Effective use of power is the key to influential leadership, and power can take several forms—legitimate, reward, coercive, expert, or referent. Each form of power has its place and its uses, and some forms yield more consistently positive long-term results than others. Sharing power by empowering others is one of the most important ways to ensure that you are using your power constructively. Empowerment not only gives employees a sense of ownership of their jobs, but it is essential for the success of organizations today as they become both flatter and leaner and call on their employees to take on more responsibilities.

4. What Is the Secret to *Responsible* Leadership? (pp. 36–45)

Objective: Understand the characteristics of responsible leadership.

Summary: Responsible leadership calls for living our values and acting ethically. Individual, professional, and organizational and societal ethics often determine what we consider moral and how we behave within organizations—and across society as a whole. Business ethics, in particular, can be complicated by a number of factors, including conflict with personal values, ethical differences across cultures, and integration of governmental regulations. It can be difficult to do what's right; when all is said and done, however, as a leader, you must know your values and live by an ethical code of conduct that you can be proud of.

5. How Do Theories and Models Explain Management and Leadership? (pp. 45–49)

Objective: Assess theories and models of management and leadership.

Summary: Theories describing the characteristics of great leaders have been around for many years and are based on a variety of qualities, ranging from immutable physical characteristics, to conscientiousness, to confidence, just to name a few. Despite the reality that many of these theories are not based in fact, many people unfortunately subscribe to them. Behavior models also seek to explain what makes a leader effective, and they come a little closer to hitting the mark through their emphasis on behaviors and approaches to work, colleagues, and subordinates. Contingency theories go even further, emphasizing situational factors and personal abilities. Nevertheless, no single theory or model can explain great leadership in its entirety, and a wise leader draws inspiration from a variety of sources.

7. What Is HR's Role in Supporting Excellent and Ethical Leadership? (pp. 52–54)

Objective: Describe HR's role in supporting and fostering excellent and ethical leadership.

Summary: HR is responsible for supporting leaders in a variety of technical and strategic areas, such as recruiting excellent employees and managing all aspects of the staffing process, maintaining positive relationships with trade groups, providing leadership development and training, and offering strategic support in people-related issues. HR professionals also lead their organizations by taking on the roles of executive coach, strategic business partner, change agent, and leadership development architect. HR can support ethical behavior and leadership through ethics training.

6. Is It Time to Take a Stand for Transformational Leadership? (pp. 49–52)

Objective: Determine the necessity of transformational leadership.

Summary: Transformational leaders are emotionally and socially intelligent and seek to inspire people with vision. This type of leadership tends to foster passion and accountability in employees and create a resonant work environment. It ultimately ties together values, ethics, and responsible use of power in a leadership approach that can be very effective in terms of motivating employees.

8. What Can We All Do to Become Great Leaders? (pp. 54–56)

Objective: Describe the steps one must take to become a great leader.

Summary: Self-awareness is one of the key components of becoming a great leader, because it allows us to understand our place in the world and grants us the courage to act on our core values without compromise. Leaders who possess self-awareness are authentic and inspire trust in their followers. They also show integrity and courage when faced with challenging ethical situations. It can be difficult to develop self-awareness because it requires you to put your ethics and your sense of what is right above what is popular, but the final payoff in terms of living up to your ethics and inspiring others to do the same is worth the effort.

9. A Final Word on Leadership (p. 56)

Summary: We all have the potential to be leaders if we so choose because we all influence the people around us, whether we realize it or not. It is a good idea, therefore, for all of us to develop social and emotional intelligence competencies. Understanding yourself—your values, ethics, and strengths—is one step toward this goal; discerning among theories of leadership is another. As you learn about other important management topics, it is important to keep their relationship to leadership in mind and learn how to continually integrate it into all that you do.

CHAPTER 3

Motivation and Meaning:

What Makes People Want to Work?

PLANNING

ORGANIZING

LEADING
and Managing
for Today
and the Future
Chapters 1, 2, 3, 4

CONTROLLING

PART 1 **Leading and Managing for Today and the Future**

MyManagementLab™

✪ Improve Your Grade!

Over 10 million students improved their results using the Pearson MyLabs.
Visit **mymanagementlab.com** for simulations, tutorials, and end-of-chapter problems.

Chapter Outline

Chapter Objectives

3.1 Define motivation.

3.2 Understand the characteristics of meaningful work.

3.3 Recognize the links between motivation and psychology.

3.4 Learn why it is important to be able to critique theories of motivation.

3.5 Define the basic and higher-order needs theories of motivation.

3.6 Distinguish between the three-needs, equity, expectancy, and goal-setting theories and explain their popularity.

3.7 Describe learning theories that relate to motivation.

3.8 Outline how theories of motivation can be integrated into daily professional and personal life.

3.9 Describe how HR can help motivate employees.

3.10 Describe how you can motivate yourself and others.

Objective 3.1
Define motivation.

1. What Is Motivation?

We spend almost a third of our *lives* working. We work as students, employees, carpenters, dancers, musicians, electricians, small business owners, artists, professional athletes, farmers, consultants, accountants, caregivers—you name it. We all work, and we work a lot. Including school, most of us will spend an astounding 60 years or more working during our lives. That's a good reason to understand what motivates us to do our best and find meaning and satisfaction in work. And if you happen to be a teacher, a parent, a manager, or a leader, it is essential to understand what motivates other people to contribute their very best to their families, teams, or organizations.

What, exactly, is motivation? Motivation is the result of a complex set of psychological and external factors or conditions that cause a person to behave a certain way while maintaining effort and persistence.[1] For example, consider yourself right now—you are reading this chapter and preparing for class. You may be slightly motivated because you have been told you must read. Perhaps you are cramming for a test, and you are motivated by a desire to achieve a good grade. Or, maybe you enjoy the class and are curious about management and leadership. These examples illustrate that you feel motivated to study—or not—based on what you believe others expect of you, your self-image, a desire for certain outcomes and/or because of how you feel about what you are doing.

In this chapter, you will learn that motivation is more than just the drive to get things done or achieve goals. To start, you will learn why finding meaning in life and work is so important to human beings and why work is more than simply a means to an end. You will learn a fundamental truth about motivation: It takes personal commitment, great leadership, and a positive environment to sustain passionate engagement with work. We will then discuss many theories that attempt to explain human motivation. We will also cover HR's role in supporting a motivated workforce through compensation and job design. Finally, we'll examine how self-awareness and empathy can help all of us motivate ourselves and others.

Motivation
The result of a complex set of psychological influences and external forces or conditions that cause a person to behave in a certain way while maintaining a certain level of effort and persistence.

Discussion Questions

1. Make a list of all the jobs you have had, paid and unpaid, including your "job" as a student. What kind of work did you find most meaningful in these jobs, and why?
2. Describe a situation in which you had to motivate other people. How did you do it?

Objective 3.2
Understand the characteristics of meaningful work.

2. What Makes Work Meaningful?

In 1963, Victor Frankl wrote about his life as a prisoner in the Nazi concentration camps.[2] Without minimizing the horrors of the camps, Frankl described how the search for meaning in day-to-day activities and finding a sense of control, if only over his attitude and spirit, were the keys to survival. His powerful reflection helps us see how important it is for people to find meaning in existence, no matter how dreadful life is at the moment. In Frankl's case, doing so was a matter of life and death—finding meaning and a sense of control helped him to survive. (■ **EXHIBIT 3.1**.)

Although most of us are not fighting for survival, we still search for meaning in our work. But what *is* meaningful work? What makes work meaningful to you? We all define meaning a little bit differently, depending on our values, culture, and personality.

What's the same for all of us is this: If you are convinced that you are doing meaningful work, your curiosity, commitment, and passion will soar. You will be energized and enthusiastic, and you will draw on all of your talents. You'll be motivated to work—and work hard.

The Flow Experience

At about the same time that Victor Frankl was writing about meaning, researchers like Mihaly Csikszentmihalyi began studying what it is like to experience deeply satisfying work.[3] When we become truly engrossed in a task that matches our skills and requires full use of our talents, and when the level of challenge is exactly what we want and need, we experience what Csikszentmihalyi calls "**flow**." Sometimes we talk about this as being "in the zone." When in flow, people can work productively for long hours, ignoring hunger, thirst, weariness, and distractions.

Have you ever had a flow experience? You might remember a time when you were writing a paper—you'd done the research, the topic was inherently interesting, and you dove in. Soon, you became completely engrossed, moving back and forth between your writing and your sources, and going to the Internet to check facts. You felt alive and completely in control of the process. At some point, you "woke up" and realized that many hours had passed. You'd missed a meal or two, or maybe you didn't even hear your phone ring. That's flow! Or maybe you've experienced flow while painting, dancing, or playing sports. When in flow, everything works as it should—your mind, body, and emotions are all in synch. The outcome is fantastic: You've written an outstanding paper, danced beautifully, or performed at the top of your game.

Csikszentmihalyi and colleagues associate the following conditions with flow:

- Intense focus
- A sense that one's actions and the task are in synch
- A sense of control over one's actions
- A lack of awareness that time is passing
- A focus on the activity itself, rather than the hoped-for outcome.[4]

When we are passionately engaged in meaningful work, we tend to be more committed, more resilient, even more creative and adaptable. We can work "*smarter*"—more efficiently and more effectively. Wouldn't it be great if we could be in flow more often when we work? That's one objective of this chapter—to help you learn how to motivate yourself so your work is meaningful more often than not.

Motivation: It's Up to You

Motivation is linked to psychology, and many psychological theories attempt to explain what motivates us at work. Before we explore this research, let's consider some of the basics. First, human thoughts, emotions, and behavior are at the center of motivation. This means that you are responsible for motivating yourself. That said, leaders have a tremendous impact on the degree to which employees are motivated at work. The overall work environment—the psychological conditions and the emotional reality of the climate—also impacts people's desire to do well and affects their capabilities and motivation. Let's look at how one very impressive leader, Bonaventure Agata of CSL Behring, has sought and found passion in his work in the *Leadership Perspective* feature.

■ **EXHIBIT 3.1**
How did Victor Frankl find meaning while imprisoned in Auschwitz?

Source: Imagno/Getty Images

Flow
A state of complete engrossment in a task that matches one's skills and requires full use of one's talents.

Leadership Perspective

● **Bonaventure Agata**
General Manager,
Canadat at CSL
Behring
"You have to love what
you do."

Bonaventure Agata—Senior Director of Commercial Development at CSL Behring—is passionate about human health. Bonaventure has lived a fascinating life. Born and educated in Kenya, he grew up in a part of the world where many people have little access to health care. He remembers his father, a physician, recounting how his grandfather could have lived longer with access to the right care. Bonaventure is passionate about ensuring that others receive this type of care, and believes that passion helps leaders find meaning in their work. He says the following about leadership, meaning, and passion at work:

You have to love what you do. Your ideals and your values have to align with the organization's or you shouldn't be there.

This is especially important and challenging during times of change. As things change, it's sometimes hard to know exactly what outcomes you will achieve. You know you want to grow the business and keep costs under control. You have a strategy and plans. But it still takes courage to step out in front and lead people day to day as things change dramatically. It's not that people don't want to go there—they usually do. It's more often the case that they've gotten complacent and are used to doing things a particular way. Complacent people are not motivated people.

As a leader, you need to help your team see that the stretch goals are actually exciting. You need to make sure people understand where you come from—you have to be honest with them. People won't follow you if they don't trust you. And you need to understand where others come from as well—who they are, what motivates them, what drives them.

Once people are aligned around the mission, vision, and goals, you need to hold them accountable: Reward them and appreciate them for success and address performance issues directly and early on. When everyone's singing the same song like this, you've got a motivated team that can achieve even the toughest goals.

Source: Personal interviews with Bonaventure Agata conducted by Annie McKee, 2009 and 2012.
The comments and perspective of Bonaventure Agata are his own personal views and not necessarily those of CSL Behring.

Bonaventure Agata teaches us powerful lessons. First, it is up to each one of us to discover what we are passionate about and to find work that inspires us. There is no perfect job, but if we are clear about what motivates us, we will be more likely to (1) choose the right career and jobs and (2) find aspects of almost any job that engage our passion. This calls for self-awareness—the foundation of emotional intelligence. Self-awareness enables us to make good choices and to discover ways to infuse work with meaning, passion, fun, and great outcomes.

Great Leaders Inspire and Motivate Us

Self-awareness is important when you want to motivate others. When you lead people, you cast a powerful shadow that either encourages or inhibits people's motivation to engage in their work and join together to accomplish goals. This is true for informal leaders as well as people who hold official titles and roles.

If you're leading people, what you do, say, and feel matters to them. People may even adopt your attitudes, beliefs, and behavior—for good or bad. Knowing yourself and understanding how people see you enables you to understand what kind of shadow you cast on the people around you. Being mindful of your leadership shadow allows you to create an environment that motivates people: an environment that is ripe with hope, inspiration, and resonance.

How can you tell what type of shadow you're casting? Companies spend millions of dollars every year hiring consultants and coaches to help people recognize and understand how they affect the work environment and the motivation and commitment of others. Wouldn't it be better if self-awareness became an essential part of the leader's repertoire?

As a leader, you can develop self-awareness. You can also learn how to inspire others. One way to inspire and motivate people is to help them feel hopeful about the future.

Hope is particularly important when it comes to motivation. Hope has been discussed in many ways in spiritual literature, philosophy, and psychology. Hope is a state of mind that includes optimism, an image of a future that is challenging but realistic, and a belief that we can do something to move toward this vision.[5] When people feel hopeful, they are psychologically and physically more resilient, more determined, and better able to envision how to achieve goals.[6] A hopeful state of mind supports people in managing motivation, energy, and effort at work.

As a manager or leader, you can motivate by creating a sense of hope among employees. You can inspire hope by tying work to a clear, compelling vision or by ensuring that employees see how their contributions make a difference. You can also foster hope by helping employees focus on success and what's possible, rather than constantly dwelling on problems. But remember—a vision must be realistic. Attempting to spark hope by painting a picture of an unrealistic future will ultimately backfire.

As a leader, you can also impact people's motivation to work hard and succeed by creating the right kind of "mood" in the environment.[7] You probably know this from your own experience—when working in situations where relationships are good, the mood is upbeat and hopeful, which helps us do our best. Good leaders know they must create such a work environment. They create what we call *resonance* in their relationships, groups, and organizations.[8] A **resonant environment** is characterized by excitement, energy, optimism, efficacy, and hope—positive and powerful emotions when it comes to motivation (■ **EXHIBIT 3.2**). Positive emotions matter because emotions impact our ability to motivate ourselves and others.

In the next section, we look at other psychological conditions that can affect motivation.

Hope
A state of mind that includes optimism, an image of a future that is challenging but realistic, and a belief that we can do something to move toward this vision.

Resonant environment
A work environment characterized by excitement, energy, optimism, efficacy, and hope.

■ **EXHIBIT 3.2**
What qualities characterize a resonant work environment?

Source: © ZUMA Wire Service/Alamy

Discussion Questions

1. What sort of work do you find meaningful? Be specific.
2. Think about a situation in which you were a leader. What sort of shadow did you cast, and how effective were you in motivating people? What led to your success, and what could you have done better?

---

3. What Is the Link between Motivation and Psychology?

Objective 3.3
Recognize the links between motivation and psychology.

To understand motivation, we need to understand people. That's because motivation can be linked to an internal state that is in some way satisfying. This is called *intrinsic motivation*. When we are *extrinsically* motivated, we seek seeking tangible outcomes that can be seen and measured outside ourselves. How does our perception of control over our actions and environment link to motivation? What aspects of personality affect motivation? The following sections address these questions.

Intrinsic Motivation

Csikszentmihalyi's work on flow concentrates largely on **intrinsic motivation**, which is defined as the desire to engage in activities even in the absence of external rewards in order to feel a sense of satisfaction, to use or improve one's abilities, or to learn.[9]

Intrinsic motivation
An internal desire to engage in activities even in the absence of external rewards in order to feel a sense of satisfaction, to use or improve one's abilities, or to learn.

■ **EXHIBIT 3.3**
Intrinsic motivators.

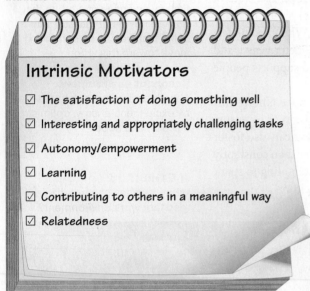

Intrinsic Motivators

☑ The satisfaction of doing something well

☑ Interesting and appropriately challenging tasks

☑ Autonomy/empowerment

☑ Learning

☑ Contributing to others in a meaningful way

☑ Relatedness

When behavior is intrinsically motivated, a person may be very interested in a task, seek a sense of accomplishment, or want to make a worthwhile contribution to other people or the organization. ■ **EXHIBIT 3.3** lists common intrinsic motivators.

Intrinsic motivation is a powerful source of energy, creativity, and enthusiasm for one's job. What intrinsic motivators are important to you? Contributing to something "bigger than ourselves" is a very important source of intrinsic motivation for many people. Mary Ellen Joyce, senior director of Executive Education at the Brookings Institute, is passionate about helping people link what they do every day to an important mission—and not just because it feels good. Mary Ellen knows that this kind of motivation leads to outstanding performance. Her insights can be found in the *Leadership Perspective* feature.

Mary Ellen Joyce of Brookings Executive Education brings the concept of intrinsic motivation to life. She, herself, is passionate about her work and it shows in everything she does and the quality of the programs she offers. She, like other great leaders, knows that one of the most important jobs of all is to help people to be intrinsically motivated.

Leadership Perspective

● **Mary Ellen Joyce**
Senior Director of Executive Education at Brookings Institution
"We all want to feel connected to something bigger than ourselves . . ."

The Brookings Institution is a world-renowned think tank based in Washington, DC. In partnership with Washington University in Saint Louis, Brookings provides outstanding programs for U.S. government employees through their executive education arm. Mary Ellen Joyce, senior director of Executive Education at the Brookings Institutution, is a great leader in her own right, even as she helps others learn to be the best they can be. As director and co-creator of many Brookings Executive Education programs, Mary Ellen truly understands what managers and leaders in the government sector face in jobs that can, at times, feel somewhat thankless and yet are at the heart of a great nation.

The many talented and brilliant individuals who work for the U.S. Federal Government have a lot on their plates: budgets that are cut year after year; serious challenges that must be addressed; complex jobs; and often being part of an organization that people don't understand and criticize. In many cases, these people work for salaries far less than they could earn in the private sector. Why do they do it? Mary Ellen chalks it up to passion and commitment to a higher purpose, which she sees as the keys to motivation and great leadership.

Sometimes I'm asked, 'How important is it to feel that what you do matters?' My answer: 'What could possibly matter more?' We all want to feel connected to something bigger than ourselves—something meaningful, something that makes us proud of what we do and who we are. When we can see that our work matters, we're energized. We're enthusiastic and we get things done. When our work is connected to something that makes a difference, we're passionate.

Someone once told me that "passion" wasn't an appropriate word for the workplace. And I said, 'Are you kidding me?' We spend most of our waking hours working, our entire lives. If you're not passionate about what you do for a living, well, then, you should make every attempt to find something else to do.

Sure, work is not exciting every minute, and sometimes, you have to do things you won't love, or even like very much. That's life. But when it comes right down to it, if you can see that what you do matters, you'll be happier, you'll be more motivated, and you'll be a better leader.

If you can find a job where you feel your work matters, your performance will soar. Why? Because you will care. You'll care enough to give your very best, and more. When you can see that your work—those day to day tasks—connects to the accomplishment of an important and meaningful mission, you'll be motivated to do anything it takes. You'll be passionate about everything you do, every day.

The leaders that I have met are dedicated to their nation and to the world. They've taken an oath to the U.S. Constitution, what can be more enobling? The best leaders help people make the connection from what they do every day to a meaningful mission. Then, people know that no matter what they are doing, their contributions matter and the goals they are working so hard to achieve mean something.

Source: Personal interview with Mary Ellen Joyce conducted by Annie McKee, 2012.

Intrinsic motivation is key to **self-determination theory (SDT)**, developed by Edward Deci and Richard Ryan.[10] Self-determination theory is concerned with people's need for *empowerment* (to feel competent and have a reasonable degree of autonomy) and their need for *relatedness* (to care for and be related to others). Research has shown that when people work for supervisors who foster self-determination, they are positive about their work.[11] Not surprisingly, then, when supervisors are controlling, employees show more negativity. People are more satisfied and motivated when they are allowed and encouraged to take control of their environment, act with autonomy, and actively seek relatedness with others.

The research about self-determination theory supports the idea that intrinsic motivation is a powerful driver of people's behavior and performance at work.[12] On the job, intrinsic motivators include interesting and appropriately challenging work, the opportunity to learn, and a chance to contribute to something that impacts people and society in a positive way. For students, intrinsic motivators may include the chance to share ideas in ways that build good relationships in class and the opportunity to work on a self-directed project as part of a great team.

Self-determination theory suggests that satisfaction of the needs for competence, autonomy, and relatedness has a positive effect on intrinsic motivation. When these factors are present, we may even value *extrinsic* motivation more.[13] But what is extrinsic motivation, and what are some common extrinsic motivators?

Self-determination theory (SDT)
Theory of motivation concerned with people's need for empowerment (to feel competent and have a reasonable degree of autonomy) and their need for relatedness (to care for and be related to others).

Extrinsic Motivation

At work, good leaders work very hard to create the conditions for intrinsic motivation and to use new and innovative extrinsic motivators. Stefano Bertuzzi is a creative, impactful leader who knows just what people need and want, and how to tap into their passion for work. Formerly of the U.S. National Institute of Science (NIH) and now Executive Director of the American Society for Cell Biology, Stefano's ingenuity and genuine respect for people shows in his creative approach to motivation: (■ **EXHIBIT 3.4**). "These are tough times. You don't usually have access to the obvious rewards for good performance that will motivate people to continue to contribute at the highest level. Simply put, you don't always have money to give in bonuses or raises. I've had to get really creative over the years. Sometimes, I ask a well-respected leader to write a personal letter to one of my employees, thanking them for their performance. I try to find the things that mean a lot to people. For example, when with the NIH, I would give people my parking space and I helped to arrange tours that people would enjoy. Above all, I make a point to praise people publicly, talking about details so they know I really understand what they have done. They enjoy the praise, and many people enjoy the conversation about the science even more." Stefano is clearly a very good leader who knows how to create an environment where people feel valued and motivated.

Extrinsic motivation
Motivation that is the result of forces or attractions outside of the self, such as material rewards, social status, or avoidance of unpleasant consequences.

■ **EXHIBIT 3.4**
Stefano Bertuzzi, Executive Director of the American Society for Cell Biology.

Intrinsic and extrinsic motivators are linked to what you find meaningful. Both intrinsic and extrinsic motivators also impact your behavior, effort, and persistence. You may study long and hard for an exam because you want a good grade (extrinsic motivation), or because you enjoy learning (intrinsic motivation). It's the same at work: Both intrinsic and extrinsic motivators are important drivers of behavior.

Extrinsic motivation is the result of forces or attractions outside of the self, such as material rewards, social status, or avoidance of unpleasant consequences. Examples of extrinsic motivators at work include pay, benefits, and job security. For a student, extrinsic motivators might be a good grade

Source: Stefano Bertuzzi

■ **EXHIBIT 3.5**
Extrinsic motivators.

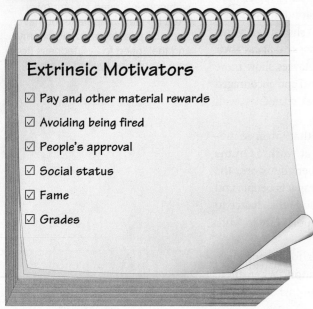

Extrinsic Motivators

☑ Pay and other material rewards

☑ Avoiding being fired

☑ People's approval

☑ Social status

☑ Fame

☑ Grades

Locus of control
Our perception of the degree to which we have control over what happens in our lives.

or the instructor's approval.[14] ■ **EXHIBIT 3.5** illustrates other common extrinsic motivators.

As a manager, team leader, or colleague, it is important to understand how to motivate people so they can be productive individually while also contributing to the achievement of team and organizational goals. This means you need to understand what contributes to both extrinsic and intrinsic motivation. One psychological concept often linked with both intrinsic and extrinsic motivation is *locus of control*, which we explore next.

Locus of Control

Locus of control is a concept developed by psychologist Julian Rotter. As the phrase implies, locus of control refers to our perception of the degree to which we have control over what happens in our lives.[15] The concept allows us to place ourselves (and others) along a continuum of perceived control over our actions, outcomes, and fate. An internal locus of control lies at one end of the continuum, and an external locus of control lies at the other.

If you have a high *internal locus of control,* it means you believe you can impact your environment and your fate. You take personal responsibility for the outcomes of your actions. Conversely, a high *external locus of control* indicates that you believe others and the environment have a great degree of impact on you and what happens to you. If this is the case, you may not take responsibility for your actions, or you may not try hard to achieve results. Why would you try hard if you think that your efforts won't make a difference? Most of us know people who give up too quickly or who are quick to blame others. These people are not positive or inspiring, and they are often difficult to work with.

It is much more gratifying to work with people who have a high internal locus of control. They believe they can get things done, they take responsibility, and they tend to be more positive. The amount of control we feel we have over outcomes impacts our energy and motivation. Other aspects of personality that affect our level of motivation are discussed next.

Motivation and the Big Five Dimensions of Personality

The "Big Five" dimensions of personality were derived from numerous early studies, one of which included 18,000 personality characteristics! Eventually, these personality characteristics were collapsed into the Big Five.[16] These traits are summarized in ■ **EXHIBIT 3.6**.

■ **EXHIBIT 3.6**

The Big Five Dimensions of Personality

- *Openness to experience*: Imaginativeness, openness to new ideas, and curiosity
- *Conscientiousness*: Self-discipline, planning, and achievement
- *Extraversion*: The desire to seek out others and to have a positive, energetic, social attitude and emotions
- *Agreeableness*: Compassion, cooperativeness, and willingness to compromise
- *Emotional stability*: Psychological consistency of mood and emotions

Studies have examined the effects of these dimensions of personality on leadership and motivation, and they suggest that extraversion correlates with inspirational leadership and motivation.[17] In a study of sales representatives, researchers found that extraverts were more likely to be motivated to gain status and power, which helped them to do well as sales representatives. Another study suggested that employees scoring high in conscientiousness were motivated to accomplish tasks, which led to increased job performance.

Now, let's explore several models of motivation that have been developed over the years, starting with an overview. As you read the next few sections, consider carefully which models make the most sense to you.

Discussion Questions

1. What is the difference between intrinsic and extrinsic motivation? How can each type of motivation contribute to a resonant work environment? How can each type of motivation result in dissonance?

2. How does locus of control affect you in college? Explain by using a specific example to illustrate.

4. Which Theories of Motivation Are Important to Know?

Objective 3.4
Learn why it is important to be able to critique theories of motivation.

You have already read about Deci and Ryan's self-determination theory, which is strongly supported by research. In the next few sections, you will learn about several other theories that attempt to explain motivation.

Many theories of motivation emerged during the twentieth century. ■ **EXHIBIT 3.7** shows a timeline of when the theories were introduced, and ■ **EXHIBIT 3.8** summarizes the main focus of each. Some of these theories are strongly supported by research, others are not. Strangely, some of the theories of motivation that are *least* supported by research are the most commonly taught and used in organizations. This needs to change, and as the

■ **EXHIBIT 3.7**

Theories of Motivation: Timeline		
Year	**Theorist**	**Theory**
1953	B. F. Skinner	Operant conditioning theory
1954	Abraham Maslow	Hierarchy of needs theory
1959	Frederick Herzberg	Two-factor theory
1961	David McClelland	Three-needs theory
1963	John Stacey Adams	Equity theory
1964	Victor Vroom	Expectancy theory
1968	Edwin Locke	Goal-setting theory
1969	Clayton Alderfer	ERG theory
1977	Albert Bandura	Social learning theory
1985	Deci and Ryan	Self-determination theory

■ **EXHIBIT 3.8**
Visual summary of theories of motivation.

HIERARCHY OF NEEDS THEORY
Basic and higher-order needs motivate behavior in ascending order

ERG THEORY
Needs for existence, relatedness, and growth can all motivate at once

TWO-FACTOR THEORY
Higher-order factors motivate, and inadequate hygiene factors can lead to dissatisfaction

THREE-NEEDS THEORY
Needs for achievement, affiliation, and power drive thoughts, feelings, and behavior

EQUITY THEORY
Inputs, outputs, and perceived fairness can be used as a formula to determine level of motivation

EXPECTANCY THEORY
Effort affects performance, and performance is moderated by perceived value of outcomes

GOAL-SETTING THEORY
Specific, measurable, achievable, results-based, time-specific goals motivate

SELF-DETERMINATION THEORY
The needs for empowerment and relatedness contribute to motivation

OPERANT-CONDITIONING THEORY
People are motivated by reinforcement

SOCIAL LEARNING THEORY
The motivation to learn and change behaviors is linked to self-efficacy and vicarious learning

next generation of leaders, it will be your job to do so. To help you, we will point out supporting research—or lack thereof—for each theory so that you can form an educated opinion about the extent to which each theory explains motivation and behavior. You do not need to embrace all of the theories described in this chapter—but you should be familiar with them so that you can understand their application at work, in school, and in teams.

Discussion Questions

1. Please review Exhibit 3.8. Which theories of motivation have your heard about? Which seem valid based on these brief summaries? Why?

2. You are about to study nine theories of motivation. This will take effort and persistence. Take a few minutes to list a few intrinsic and extrinsic motivators that will help you stay focused as you read.

Objective 3.5
Define the basic and higher-order needs theories of motivation.

5. What Are Basic and Higher-Order Needs Theories of Motivation?

Needs theories assume that people engage in activities to satisfy certain needs and desires. In this section, we discuss three needs theories:

- Maslow's hierarchy of needs
- Alderfer's ERG theory
- Herzberg's two-factor theory

Each of these theories look at basic human needs, such as what we require to live, and higher-order needs—the things that make life worth living.

Hierarchy of Needs

Abraham Maslow's **hierarchy of needs** is one of the best-known theories of motivation.[18] This theory posits that people are motivated to satisfy human needs, in this order: physiological; safety and security; love and belonging; then self-esteem; and finally self-actualization. Self-actualization describes a state of being in which a person seeks truth, perfection, and meaningfulness. Maslow's theory has not been well supported by research.[19]

In spite of the lack of supporting research, this theory is still taught in many courses and training programs all around the world, possibly because it is simple. An often-criticized aspect of the theory is the assertion that individuals must first satisfy lower-order needs before progressing to higher-level needs. Another element of Maslow's theory that is not supported by research is the idea that once a need is met, it ceases to be a motivator. The theory is also criticized because it states that people will only seek to satisfy self-actualization needs after all other needs have been met.

If you've ever been poor or lived through a natural disaster, you will recognize flaws in Maslow's theory. Even when you were worried about how you would buy food or pay rent, didn't you still care about your friends and loved ones? Even when you felt unsafe and insecure because your community had been ravaged, didn't you still seek to find meaning, truth, and beauty in life? Didn't you look for the "silver lining"? As these situations illustrate, people are complicated, and Maslow's simple hierarchy does not explain everything that motivates us.

Still, the needs that Maslow identified are important to people. As a manager or a team member, you must recognize when these needs are affecting people. Then, you can make decisions about whether satisfying these needs will keep people engaged and committed to their work.

ERG Theory

Basing his theory on the work of Maslow and attempting to deal with some of the criticisms, Clayton Alderfer developed the **ERG theory**, which states that people are motivated to satisfy needs related to Existence, Relatedness, and Growth, and that these needs can all be activated at the same time.[20] Alderfer's research indicated that even when people are compelled to satisfy existence needs, the needs for relatedness and growth can be powerful motivators at the same time (■ **EXHIBIT 3.9**).

Two-Factor Theory

Frederick Herzberg's **two-factor theory**, sometimes called the **motivator-hygiene theory**, states that two distinct sets of factors, called motivators and hygiene factors, affect job satisfaction, motivation, or job dissatisfaction.[21] Until he proposed his theory, most scholars looked at job *satisfaction* and job *dissatisfaction* as two ends of a continuum. Herzberg declared that satisfaction and dissatisfaction with a job are entirely different states and the result of different factors and conditions. (■ **EXHIBIT 3.10**).

Herzberg called the factors that lead to job satisfaction **motivators**. Motivators are higher-order needs, such as the needs for recognition, achievement, and opportunities for growth and development. According to this theory, when these factors are present, people are satisfied and motivated and when these motivators are absent people are neutral about work.

ERG theory
Theory that states that people are motivated to satisfy needs related to Existence, Relatedness, and Growth, and that these needs can all be activated at the same time.

■ **EXHIBIT 3.9**
ERG theory focuses on needs related to existence, relatedness, and growth.

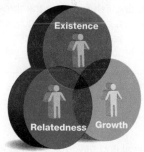

Two-factor theory (motivator-hygiene theory)
Theory that states that two distinct sets of factors, called motivators and hygiene factors, affect job satisfaction, motivation, or job dissatisfaction.

Motivators
Higher-order needs, such as the needs for recognition, responsibility, achievement, and opportunities for growth and development.

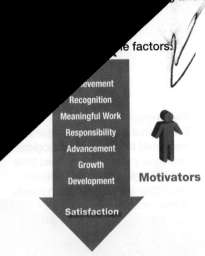

Motivators

Achievement
Recognition
Meaningful Work
Responsibility
Advancement
Growth
Development

Satisfaction

Neither Satisfied Nor Dissatisfied

Dissatisfaction

Supervision
Company Policy
Relationship with Supervisor
Working Conditions
Salary
Relationships with Peers
Personal Life
Relationships with Subordinates
Status

Hygiene Factors

Hygiene factors do not motivate, but they affect the level of *dissatisfaction* with a job. Hygiene factors are both physical and psychological factors that can lead to dissatisfaction. These factors include salary, working conditions, supervision, relationships with coworkers, and level of job security. To illustrate how this works, think about the last time you received a raise. What was the net amount of that raise per week? Was that enough to keep you motivated to get up and go to work, ready to do your best for the next 52 weeks? If you are like most people, a raise would give you a momentary sense of excitement. However, if you found the job boring and didn't feel a sense of accomplishment, even a large raise would not be a powerful motivator for very long.

Like Maslow's hierarchy of needs, Herzberg's two-factor theory is taught in management training programs, despite the fact that research has not, for the most part, supported the theory.[22] The main contribution of this theory is that it encourages us to consider what motivates people and what detracts from motivation. Herzberg's work is also useful because he was one of the first researchers to study white-collar workers and focus on job design and job enrichment.[23] These two topics are discussed later in the chapter.

Discussion Questions

1. Think about a time in your life when physical or safety needs were important. Were other needs, such as the need for friendship and love, or for personal growth, important at the time? Why or why not?

2. Think about a job or a volunteer role where your *hygiene needs* were not met. What was the effect of this on your level of motivation?

Hygiene factors
Physical and psychological aspects of a job that can lead to dissatisfaction, including salary, working conditions, supervision, relationships with coworkers, and level of job security.

Three-needs theory
Theory that states that people are motivated by needs for achievement, affiliation, and power.

6. Why Are the Three-Needs, Equity, Expectancy, and Goal-Setting Theories Useful?

As early research on motivation progressed, several theories began to stand out:

- Three-needs theory
- Equity theory
- Expectancy theory
- Goal-setting theory.

These theories have been studied extensively, are well substantiated by research, and are very useful. Although these theories are quite different from one another, they all focus on linking intention, behavior, effort, and outcomes. This section explores each of these theories and how they apply to you and to work today.

Three-Needs Theory

David McClelland's **three-needs theory** focuses on people's needs for achievement, affiliation, and power.[24] McClelland and others often refer to these needs as motives. McClelland's research on these needs was extensive and has been followed up with numerous studies around the world.[25] Many of these studies have involved managers, making the results particularly important. Let's look at each of these needs individually, and then we'll consider their relevance in the workplace (**EXHIBIT 3.11**).

NEED FOR ACHIEVEMENT

The **need for achievement (nAch)** is the desire to engage in challenging activities, to meet and exceed personal goals, and to seek excellence. The need for achievement can include a desire to do better than others, but people who are high in nAch most often seek to reach a personal standard of excellence. People who are high in nAch also like regular feedback, and they tend to have a relentless desire to succeed in whatever they do. nAch can be a powerful and positive force because it drives people to be and do their very best.

Michael Phelps is a great example of a person whose need for achievement has led him to great heights. As some people put it, he's a "motivation machine." To date, he's accumulated 18 gold, 2 silver, and 2 bronze medals. Born in 1985, Phelps started swimming at the age of 7. By 15 he placed in the 2004 Olympics as the youngest competitor since 1932. In the 2008 Olympics, he astounded the world with his performance. Then, at age 27, he won a spot on the 2012 Olympic team to compete in seven swimming events.

Michael Phelps' accomplishments have not come easily. The sheer number of hours in the pool alone would turn most people off, not to mention the workouts, self-discipline, and missing out on a lot of what other young people enjoy. Why would anyone do this? As he puts it, ". . . once I'm able to accomplish the goals that I have, if I can look back at my career and say I've been successful, that's all that matters to me."[27] That's achievement motivation: challenging goals and competition with *oneself*.

Research indicates that people with high nAch do well early in their careers, when individual contribution is sometimes highly valued.[28] However, few of today's jobs call for individual contribution alone, and even entry-level jobs usually require people to work in teams. Tasks and responsibilities need to be negotiated, and goals and standards have to be agreed on. This can be difficult when team members are motivated by a strong need for achievement.

The need for achievement can really get in the way when managing people. This is because achievement-oriented managers don't always have patience with others' ways of doing things, for people who are learning, or for those who make mistakes. At worst, people who are high in nAch can become micromanagers. **Micromanagers** try to do everything themselves and criticize everyone else's efforts. Clearly, this creates a negative environment and results in people not giving their best effort. So, as valuable as high personal standards and desire for success can be, people with a high need for achievement must take care not to let it harm relationships or teamwork.

NEED FOR AFFILIATION

The **need for affiliation (nAff)** can be described as the desire for warm, fulfilling, and close personal relationships. People who are high in nAff are concerned with others' feelings, care about people's desires and needs, and will expend tremendous time and energy building trusting relationships. These individuals value friendship and camaraderie and will often try to create a sense of team spirit at work. They may avoid conflict and are keen to resolve it in ways that leave relationships intact.

People high in nAff are often great coworkers, as they tend to create environments that are marked by care, empathy, and compassion. Many people thrive in this sort of environment. Problems can arise, however, when a strong nAff drives employees or

■ **EXHIBIT 3.11**
Mcclelland's three-needs theory.[26]

Need for Achievement: Desire to engage in challenging activities, meet and exceed personal goals, and seek excellence.

- Defines success as reaching a personal standard of excellence
- Exhibits a relentless desire to succeed
- Enjoys regular feedback

Need for Affiliation: Desire for warm, fulfilling, and close personal relationships.

- Expends time and energy building relationships
- Concerned with others' feelings, desires, and needs
- Avoids conflict

Need for Power: Desire to have influence, control, and responsibility, either directly or through social status.

- Seeks control and social status
- Gratified by promotion, titles, and symbols of power
- Less susceptible to stress that accompanies power and responsibility

Need for achievement (nAch)
The desire to engage in challenging and complex activities, to meet and exceed personal goals, and to seek excellence.

Micromanagers
People who try to do everything themselves and criticize everyone else's efforts.

Need for affiliation (nAff)
The desire for warm, fulfilling, and close personal relationships.

managers to consistently avoid disrupting relationships. This can result in outcomes that are destructive in the long term. For example, a manager who is high in nAff might avoid giving direct feedback. This can lead to ongoing performance issues. Alternatively, a manager may suppress conflict that is a healthy expression of differing opinions. Another possibility is that a high-nAff manager might build strong friendships with some employees (those with similar needs) and not with others, leading to perceptions of inequity, unhealthy competition, or internal conflict.

NEED FOR POWER

Need for power (nPow)
The desire to have influence, control, and responsibility, either directly or through social status.

The **need for power (nPow)** is the desire to have influence, control, and responsibility, either directly or through social status. Research indicates that the need for power is associated with attaining significant positions of responsibility, such as top leadership jobs. People who are high in nPow seek control and social status and are gratified by promotions, titles, and the like. They can also be motivated by a desire to have positive impact on people, groups, and society. People high in nPow seem to be less susceptible to "power stress"—chronic stress associated with the constant pressure, heavy responsibilities, long hours, and hard work that leaders and managers face today.[29]

So what is the downside of a high need for power? Single-minded ambition for the sake of controlling others is destructive. These kinds of managers and leaders create dissonance, and they wreak havoc on teams and organizations. However, these people can also be strangely attractive, because they exude confidence and strength. We often find ourselves drawn to them, and we may even seek to emulate them. So, it is important to recognize when and how to manage the downside of the need for power both in ourselves and with others.

Personalized versus Socialized Power

Personalized power
A need for power that drives people to seek control through assertive or aggressive behavior, often for personal gain.

Socialized power
An expressed need for power that is based on a desire to support the welfare of others, a group, society, or the common good.

Prosocial behavior
Any behavior that seeks to protect the welfare of society or the common good.

One way to manage a high need for power is to consciously channel it toward the good of the group, rather than simply toward personal gain. In fact, McClelland and colleagues make a distinction between *personalized power* and *socialized power*.[30] Individuals high in **personalized power** seek control through assertive or aggressive behavior, often for personal gain.[31] Individuals high in **socialized power** want to support the welfare of others, a group, society, or the common good. People high in socialized power seek to influence their environments through *prosocial behavior*.[32] **Prosocial behavior** is any behavior that protects the welfare of society or the common good.[33] People motivated by socialized power often experience satisfaction from the accomplishments of others and shy away from notoriety themselves. An example would be a supervisor whose joy comes from watching employees succeed on their own, using skills that he or she has taught them.

Socialized Power, Prosocial Behavior, and Ubuntu

Socialized power and *prosocial behavior* are are important because service, sustainability, and corporate social responsibility are prominent aspects of many organizations' visions and strategies. The terms "socialized power" and "prosocial behavior" are relatively new, but the concepts are not. For example, in some cultures, such as many in sub-Saharan Africa, the good of the group is put ahead of individual needs or desires. This is captured in the word *Ubuntu. Ubuntu* is a Nguni word, but it can also be found in the Zulu and Xhosa cultures, as well as in many others throughout the southern half of the African continent. *Ubuntu* is roughly translated as "I am because you are." Our Zulu and Xhosa colleague, Senzo Mfayela helps us to understand this philosophy of life and relationships in the following phrase: "A person is a person through other people." Zulu—"Umuntu, ngumuntu, ngabantu"; and Xhosa— "Umntu, ngumntu, ngabanye abantu." In 2008, Nelson Mandela (■ **EXHIBIT 3.12**) described *Ubuntu* this way:

Ubuntu does not mean that people should not enrich themselves. The question therefore is: Are you going to [fulfill your needs] in such a way as to enable the community around you to be able to improve? These are the important things in life. And if one can do that, you have done something very important, which will be appreciated.[34]

Ubuntu is a mindset that motivates people to direct their energy toward the good of the group. Today, scholars such as Barbara Nussbaum are applying the concept of *Ubuntu* to business.[35] More recently, following the global economic downturn that began in 2007, several South African multinational corporations have begun implementing Ubuntu-style human resource practices abroad to develop high-potential workplaces.[36] The *Ubuntu* philosophy is an important contribution to people's understanding of how to work well together and how to link what "I" need with what "we" need. Consciously attending to this "I/we" dilemma can help engage socialized power—which can and does impact groups and organizations positively.[37]

MEASURING NEEDS FOR ACHIEVEMENT, AFFILIATION, AND POWER

Because these three motivators are so important at work, McClelland and colleagues also studied how to measure and identify them.[38] For example, they developed a tool called the Thematic Apperception Test (TAT).[39] The TAT is a projective test: Test-takers are asked to look at pictures that show people alone or interacting with others, and they are then asked to write a short story describing what they believe is happening in the pictures. The pictures evoke different ideas for different people, and some of these differences can be linked to each person's needs for achievement, affiliation, and power.[40] Try this for yourself. Look at the picture in ■ **EXHIBIT 3.13** and write a few paragraphs about what you think is going on, how the person feels, and what he might be thinking. As you reread your story, do you see any evidence of achievement, affiliation, or power needs?

This is an interesting exercise, and it can give you some insights about your motives. It is important to note, however, that many projective tests (the TAT included) have low reliability and validity, which means that they don't measure the "truth" about personality or, in this case, needs. Still, these types of tests can give us an idea about what is important to us.

McClelland's and colleagues' research has contributed significantly to our understanding of how our psychological needs influence motivation. Let's now turn to look at equity theory—another well-researched theory that helps us to understand motivation.

■ **EXHIBIT 3.12**
In what ways does Nelson Mandela embody the concept of socialized power?

Source: Geof Daniels/Eye Ubiquitous/Alamy

■ **EXHIBIT 3.13**
What do you think this child is feeling?

Source: © Spencer Grant/PhotoEdit Inc.

Equity Theory

John Stacey Adams's **equity theory** suggests that we are motivated when we feel that our inputs and outcomes at work are fair and just. Equity theory is about our perceptions of fairness: Do my contributions (inputs) and what I receive as a result (outcomes) match what others like me are giving and receiving? Do I get what I believe I deserve? The answer to these questions affects our motivation. In these equations, we compare inputs and outputs with our personal standards of fairness and also with what others give and receive. It's important to note that we each have beliefs about fairness, and hence equity, which differ person to person and are affected by things like values and culture.[41]

Equity theory
Theory that states that we are motivated when we feel that our inputs and outcomes at work are fair and just.

To illustrate equity theory, consider this example: Two recent graduates have accepted jobs as analysts in an accounting firm. Both graduated from good schools with good grades, and both have the same work responsibilities, pay, and titles (analyst). During the first six months on the job, one analyst comes to work at 8:00 A.M. as expected, and leaves at 5:00 P.M., as she was told she could. The other analyst arrives early, and when he feels it it's necessary, he'll stay as late as 9:00 P.M., and he has even worked a few weekends. Initially, he doesn't resent this and even feels good about his commitment and contributions. As time goes on, however, he becomes frustrated by the fact that he still receives the same salary as his colleague and that their manager treats them exactly the same way. He believes things are out of balance and unfair. This perception of inequity causes him to feel anxious and tense, and he feels pressure to restore balance.

Equity theory states that this analyst can respond to this situation in one of four ways:

1. He can ignore the perceived inequity and cope with the stress related to his perception of unfairness.
2. He can decide to stop working so hard (change inputs).
3. He can ask for a raise or try to get his supervisor to recognize his efforts and reward him accordingly (change outcomes).
4. He can attempt to see the situation differently. For example, the analyst may come to see that his colleague is actually doing as much work as he is and the quality is the same. She is just faster.

In this example, the analyst is comparing himself with another individual, called a *referent*. A referent is another individual or a group. A referent can also be oneself in a past or similar situation, or general beliefs about one's worth. In the example, the analyst compared himself with a coworker. He might have also compared his salary to that of analysts in another company. He might have compared his experience in this job to his experience in another job where he was paid more. Here, he would be the referent, because he is comparing his current input-outcome ratio to a ratio from his past. All of these comparisons are informed by a person's beliefs about one's worth and value. This belief can be a result of what a person has learned over the years from family, teachers, and bosses. Hopefully, these beliefs are informed by self-awareness.

You can see why self-awareness is important here: Far too many people have inaccurate pictures of the value of their contributions. If people have inflated pictures of themselves, they may constantly feel as if they aren't getting what they deserve. Such people can be very unpleasant to work with. On the other hand, some people's low self-confidence causes them to see their input as less valuable than it really is. This can be a problem for many reasons, including the fact that it is tiresome to constantly "build people up." And of course, self-confidence is a critical part of working successfully in organizations today.

EQUITY THEORY AND COGNITIVE DISSONANCE

Let's look at another example to further illustrate the choices we have when we perceive inequity, and help us to understand more about the psychology behind the theory. Imagine that you and a colleague have exactly the same job description and title. You accidentally see her pay stub, and you notice that she makes a lot more money than you do. What do you do? It's doubtful that you would just feel happy for her. According to equity theory, you would likely do one of four things to regain your sense of equity and remain motivated: try to ignore it; minimize your own performance so that you feel your effort matches your salary; ask your boss for a raise; or find a reason to change your perception about the fairness of the situation.

Let's reverse the situation to illustrate a psychological concept that is at the heart of trying to restore balance and equity. What if the pay stub indicated you were being paid more than your coworker? Would you go to your boss and ask for a reduction in salary? That's highly unlikely. Still, you might feel very uncomfortable as a result of an inner conflict: you wouldn't want to lower your own salary, of course, but you know your coworker deserves the same. Such an inner conflict is called cognitive dissonance. Cognitive dissonance is a state of psychological stress arising from the attempt to process conflicting ideas, attitudes, or beliefs.[42] To alleviate cognitive dissonance in this example, you might convince yourself that the situation is indeed fair by changing your perception of your input. You might, for example, choose to believe that your contributions are actually more valuable than your coworker's, or that you are in some ways "better" than her, so you deserve to be paid more.

As the example shows, cognitive dissonance can lead to problems. This is because the experience of cognitive dissonance can sometimes lead us to talk ourselves into believing things that just aren't true. Seeing ourselves, other people, and the world accurately is of vital importance to leadership. Some scholars suggest that leaders who are capable of managing cognitive dissonance are more likely to sustain ethical leadership over time.[43] This is in part linked to the social and emotional intelligence competencies of self-awareness, empathy, and organizational awareness. We need to see ourselves and each other accurately. We also need to see situations clearly and accurately in order to set equity expectations accurately.

Equity theory helps us understand the link between people's perceptions and their behavior and how this equation affects motivation. It also gives managers an important road map for motivating employees: Manage the perceived ratio of inputs to outcomes. When people perceive the balance between inputs and outcomes to be fair, they are often motivated to contribute. In contrast, when they perceive the equation to be out of balance, they may change the level or quality of their outcomes, harming team efforts and interfering with the accomplishment of goals. Or, they may experience cognitive dissonance and come to see themselves or others in a distorted way.

IS EQUITY THEORY RELEVANT TODAY?

Attending to equity is important in part because the equity equation is often perceived to be out of balance. "Do more with less" is a common mantra in many organizations. Many companies have downsized numerous times while maintaining the amount of work that needs to be accomplished. In 1990, studies showed that Americans were working fully one month more per year than they were 20 years earlier.[44] Things have only gotten worse since then.[45] People are working early mornings, into the evenings, on weekends, and during their vacations. Even though people are working more, in many cases the rewards have not increased proportionately.

If the equity equation is wrong and you want to fix it, what can you do? Rarely will you say to your manager, "Sorry, this situation isn't fair, so I am not going to work as hard anymore." People attempt to restore balance in more subtle, but destructive, ways. For example, you might justify spending a lot of time texting or on social networking sites because you believe you are not paid enough and have a "right" to spend time this way. Other people might try to resolve perceived inequity by doing only the bare minimum. These employees show up for work, but mentally and psychologically, they are absent.

Emotions are contagious, and the negativity, passivity, and dissonance that accompany widespread perceptions of inequity affect everyone.[46] Even employees who feel that things are fair can become demoralized as a result of working in such an environment. When lots of people feel this way, the work environment can become destructive and not conducive to productivity.

RESTORING EQUITY: WHAT MANAGERS CAN DO

As a manager, you must be alert for perceived inequity—especially in an environment where everyone is working very hard. Look for signs that people are not comfortable

Cognitive dissonance
A state of psychological stress arising from the attempt to process conflicting ideas, attitudes, or beliefs.

with their own or others' contributions and rewards. Talk to people. Find out what they are thinking and feeling. If you discover that your employees perceive inequity, find out exactly why. If they are right, you will need to restore a sense of equity by helping people change inputs and/or outcomes to restore balance.

If equity actually *does exist*, you will need to help people reframe the situation and change perceptions. For example, consider a manager who heard through office gossip that his employees thought he was playing favorites when assigning overtime (something people wanted). The manager wasn't playing favorites, but he realized that perceptions are as powerful as reality. He knew he needed to find a way to prove that he was fair. From then on, he placed all eligible employees' names in a bowl each Friday. During a break, he asked one of the employees to pull names for overtime assignments. The result: the selection process was seen to be fair and the grumbling stopped.

This manager had his eyes and ears open and was able to learn of people's dissatisfaction. It is not enough to rely solely on office gossip, however. To ferret out and understand perceived inequity, managers need to be engaged in honest and authentic communication with their employees. Too many managers shy away from these difficult but ultimately rewarding discussions. The best managers and leaders, however, have the courage to find out the truth and act on it.

It is unrealistic to think that managers can fix everything. Due to economic pressures, most organizations need employees to work hard, and for professionals, the hours are often long. It might also be impossible to pay people more for the work they do. It can be difficult to change the equity equation using rewards like money.

Still, some managers find ways to be creative and try to balance the equation. For example, one leader of a luxury goods company was greatly disturbed that she could not give her valued employees the pay raises they'd asked for and that she believed they deserved. What did she do? First, she told the employees that she valued them tremendously, that they deserved raises, and that she wanted them to stay and be happy. Then, she bought sushi from a fantastic restaurant and invited everyone to the showroom for drinks, food, and fun. She also requested permission to give her best employees more vacation time. She told them, "I can't give you money, and you know how sorry I am about that. But I can give you time. Here's the plan: you can create a buddy system to cover for each other on your birthdays and one Friday afternoon per quarter. Then, you can take that time off, paid. And since it's summer, let's close the offices at 4:00 P.M. on Fridays." This manager used every approach she could to restore a sense of equity: praise and recognition, opportunities for fun, and time off with pay.

Expectancy Theory

Expectancy theory
Theory that states that motivation is affected by the relationship among effort and performance, performance and outcomes, and the perceived value of outcomes.

Expectancy theory goes beyond equity theory in that it looks at the degree to which people *value* the outcomes they receive as a result of their efforts. The theory is attributed to Victor Vroom, who, along with others, engaged in extensive research on the relationship between effort (input), performance, rewards (outcomes), and the perceived value of the outcomes (valence).[47] **Expectancy theory**, then, is a theory stating that motivation is affected by the relationship among effort and performance, performance and outcomes, and the perceived value of outcomes. Let's look at each component of the theory:

Effort
A person's input, which will be affected by the person's perception about whether the effort will lead to an acceptable level of performance.

Performance
The extent to which a task or work is completed successfully.

Instrumentality
A person's belief about the degree to which performance will result in realizing certain outcomes.

Valence
The value placed on outcomes.

- **Effort**: A person's input, which will be affected by the person's perception about whether the effort will lead to an acceptable level of performance.
- **Performance**: The extent to which a task or work is completed successfully.
- **Instrumentality**: A person's belief about the degree to which performance will result in certain outcomes.
- **Valence**: The value placed on outcomes. Outcomes can be extrinsic, such as money, or intrinsic, such as a sense of achievement.[48]

Let's look at an example to see how expectancy theory works in the real world. Say your instructor has given you a team assignment: Select a leader whom you admire; analyze his or her leadership competencies; then write a paper, create a set of slides, and give a presentation to the class. In your first team meeting, you discover that all four people on the team are individually confident that they can do well on the project. You also find out that two of the team members are good writers and two have excellent computer and graphics skills. All of you enjoy giving class presentations and have delivered successful presentations in the past.

You leave the first group meeting confident that if everyone works hard, your group will write a good paper, create a good slide set, and give a great presentation to the class. In other words, you have high *expectations* that your collective *efforts* will result in excellent *performance*. So far, you are motivated to work on this assignment.

But what if you have had this professor before, and you know that he rarely gives As to his students? Everyone on your team wants an A—it is a highly desired *outcome* that has high *valence* for all of you. In this situation, however, your perception of the link between excellent task performance (a great paper and presentation) and the desired outcome (an A) is not positive. You do not believe that your efforts will be *instrumental* in helping you achieve the outcome you desire. Therefore, according to expectancy theory, you will not be highly motivated to work on this assignment.

As another example, picture a consumer goods company in which senior management determined that the company should increase revenue in its beauty products business by 12 percent this year. When rolled down through the divisions, this meant that each brand was expected to increase revenue by anywhere from 8 to 20 percent, depending on the expectations of what could be accomplished in particular geographic areas. The senior executives were excited by this goal. More than a few of them were high in need for achievement, so this stretch goal was exciting and motivating—so much so, in fact, that the executives were blind to the realities in certain geographic areas.

As the plan was rolled out, managers in these areas raised objections, not the least of which was the fact that a recent recession had impacted sales of beauty products negatively. Despite these objections and the fact that sales were going down in many regions, the managers were told by corporate headquarters to hit their targets anyway. Let's follow one manager's thoughts and actions as this plan was implemented.

Bill believed in his company, his products, and his division's capabilities. He truly wanted to achieve the targets for several reasons. He wanted to help the company grow. Bill also expected a promotion, and he knew that his team's compensation was tied directly to achieving the new targets. The *outcomes*, then, had high *valence* for Bill.

For a while, he drove himself and his team as hard as possible. They invested in new marketing plans, engaged a new advertising company, and even changed the packaging on a few of their key products. They worked long hours without complaint. Bill worked weekends and skipped his vacation. In the past, Bill and his team's *efforts* led to excellent results, and they expected a similar outcome.

This time, however, things just weren't turning out the same. No matter how hard the team worked or how many hours people put in, their *performance* constantly fell short of their own and others' expectations. Then, halfway through implementation of the new marketing plan, the budget was cut. Bill was told that the new advertising campaign could only be implemented in two of four regions. Also, the new packaging design took much longer than expected, partly because of mandatory layoffs that left the team understaffed. The situation spiraled downward and Bill came to believe that his team's efforts couldn't possibly lead to reaching the goal. Bill and his team members were not motivated because they no longer believed their efforts would result in achieving their goals.

Although it may seem far-fetched that a company's executives would embark on a strategy with so little chance of success, this scenario is common. Recent years have

...st obsessive focus on short-term (usually quarterly) growth results in pub-
...companies—to please investors, analysts, and the like.[49] In many cases, this
...led managers to try to force their organizations and employees to achieve
...unrealistic goals. Managing companies in such a way is detrimental to both
...term sustainability of the business and the health and welfare of employees.
...mpanies, such as Unilever and Coca-Cola, no longer issue quarterly earnings
...in an effort to break out of short-term profit expectations at the expense of
...rm value.[50]

...is example raises an important question that responsible leaders must ask them-
...s: What are we motivating our employees to do? In this example, if senior man-
...nent had tied the company's strategy more closely to its mission, they may not have
...n so single-minded about growth in a declining market. Instead, they may have
...osen to direct managers' and employees' attention toward creating more recession-
...roof products or finding more effective ways to manufacture their current products.
...n other words, they would have motivated employees to engage in different activities,
with different measures of performance and different outcomes.

Goal-Setting Theory

As illustrated in the previous section, some goals (like unrealistic sales targets) do not
motivate people to achieve excellence—simply because they are the wrong goals! But,
if the right goals *have* been chosen, how can they be used to motivate behavior?

Scholars Edwin Locke, Gary Latham, and colleagues have conducted extensive research that shows a strong relationship between goals and motivation.[51] A goal is an
outcome that a person, group, or organization is attempting to achieve, accomplish, or
attain. Locke and others studied the goal-setting process and subsequently developed
goal-setting theory, which states that people are motivated by the process of identifying and achieving goals, and that the characteristics of these goals will have an impact
on motivation, performance, and results.[52]

SMART GOALS

As we saw in the example about Bill and his sales team, some goals are not motivating.
Other goals, however, focus our attention and our energy and are very motivating. Let's
look at this in practice: Say that two friends want to get in shape. One says to himself,
"I'm going to eat better and exercise." The other decides to lose five pounds and be
able to run three miles easily within eight weeks. Her subgoals include (1) work out
for half an hour every morning, (2) eat a salad every day for lunch, and (3) cook dinner at home except on weekends. Which goal do you think is more likely to help the
person lose weight? The first person's goals are vague. It's not clear what he will do or
how he will measure his success. In contrast, the other person's goals present a specific
set of activities and outcomes. This person has created a **SMART goal**. SMART goals
are specific, measurable, achievable, results-based, and time-specific, as shown in
■ **EXHIBIT 3.14**.[53] Goals that meet the SMART criteria tend to be motivating for many
people, and they are more often achieved than goals that violate one or more of the
SMART criteria.

Once a SMART goal has been determined, commitment, an appropriate level of
complexity, and feedback on our progress are three important factors that influence
the goal's power to motivate us. Feedback tells us where we are in relation to our goals
and how far we have to go to achieve them—it's like a SMART goal GPS. Commitment
is an obvious condition for motivation: We don't work hard to achieve goals we don't
care about. Amazingly, though, many managers don't do anything meaningful to build
commitment to goals. To illustrate this, consider Suzanne, who works at a sports retail
store. She gets an e-mail from her manager telling her that her goal is to sell 10 percent

---

Goal-setting theory
Theory that states that people are
motivated by the process of identifying and achieving goals, and that
the characteristics of these goals
will have an impact on motivation,
performance, and results.

■ **EXHIBIT 3.14**
SMART goals motivate many
people.

Specific

Measurable

Achievable

Results-based

Time-specific

SMART goals
Term describing goals that are
specific, measurable, achievable,
results-oriented, and time-specific.

more running shoes this month than she did last month. No explanation is given for why Suzanne needs to achieve the goal or why it should matter to her personally. The consequences of Suzanne's success or failure are absent. Also, the situation in the department seems to have been ignored: One sales clerk is out on maternity leave, and another is on vacation. Why should she care about this new goal—one that seems to have come out of nowhere? What level of commitment would she have to this goal?

Now, imagine that Suzanne's manager Maria handles the situation differently. Maria sets up a special meeting with Suzanne, maybe over coffee. In a relaxed manner, she praises Suzanne for her work in the shoe department, sharing specific, positive feedback from customers. She indicates that because of Suzanne's performance, management wants her to attend a training session that will prepare her for a promotion. Then, Maria describes some of the initiatives that have been suggested for the store, including improving sales of particular brands of sports apparel and shoes. She asks Suzanne's opinion on this, including what she might need in order to increase sales by 10 percent. Wouldn't Suzanne be more likely to commit to the goal in this scenario?

"DOING" AND "BEING" GOALS

Goal setting as a way to motivate people is embraced by many businesses. However, some scholars argue that many assumptions related to goal setting are based on early twentieth-century manufacturing models that focused on a machine-like equation for achieving results.[54] According to these researchers, the typical goal-setting model works for so-called "doing" goals that are clear-cut (e.g., "Increase sales by 8 percent over the next year"), but it is less appropriate for so-called "being" goals, for which there is no definitive ending (e.g., "Constantly seek to improve leadership practices in our company").

The SMART goal guidelines support "doing" goals. "Being" goals focus on an ongoing transformation.[55] Much attention is given to "doing" goals in organizations, and far less to "being" goals. And yet the latter may ultimately have more impact on long term, sustainable results.

The three-needs, equity, expectancy, and goal-setting theories are well researched and continue to have significant impact on organizations. Despite some drawbacks, they are useful. In the next section, we consider a different but equally well-researched approach: learning theories. Learning theories are especially useful because they focus on learning and change, both of which are essential in today's organizations.

Discussion Questions

1. Which needs do you believe affect your motivation most: achievement, affiliation, or power?

2. Set a SMART goal for yourself—one that you can accomplish by the end of this semester. Discuss how your goal is S-M-A-R-T.

---

7. What Are Learning Theories?

Objective 3.7
Describe learning theories that relate to motivation.

Learning theories help us understand how people can be motivated to learn to change their behavior as a result of experience, consequences, and practice. You may be wondering why we are discussing motivation to learn, in a course on management. The reason: In a knowledge economy, learning and change are constant. As a manager, you will often focus your attention and your employees' efforts on learning to do things in new ways, as well as engaging in entirely different activities. Two theories in particular, operant conditioning theory and social learning theory, provide useful guidelines for motivating people to learn.

Operant Conditioning Theory

Operant conditioning theory
Theory based on the premise that learning and behavior changes occur when behavior is reinforced, and when behavior is not reinforced or is punished, it will cease.

Reinforcement
Consequences associated with behavior.

Operant conditioning theory is based on the premise that learning and behavior changes occur through reinforcement of the desired behavior, and when behavior is not reinforced or is punished, it will cease. **Reinforcement** refers to the consequences associated with behavior.

Behavioral psychologist B. F. Skinner is the scholar most closely associated with this theory.[56] His work continues to have a profound effect on the field of psychology, and the operant conditioning model is seen in numerous organizational processes. The most common applications of operant conditioning at work include positive reinforcement, negative reinforcement, extinction, and punishment. ■ **EXHIBIT 3.15** summarizes each of these methods.

Of these four, positive reinforcement and punishment are of particular importance to managers. They are important because they are used extensively in many organizations and they have a profound effect on people's self-image and motivation.

POSITIVE REINFORCEMENT

Positive reinforcement is a powerful motivator. Think about your own experience: When you are praised or given a bonus or a day off for work done well, don't you feel good about yourself and excited to do well again? You are likely to feel good about your boss and your organization too. That's the other reason positive reinforcement can be a powerful motivator at work: It contributes to a resonant environment, one in which people feel optimistic, energized, and safe.

Take the example of a project team leader—we will call him Marco. Marco is expected to turn in a progress report to his manager, Celeste, every Friday. Until recently, Marco gave the report to Celeste at 5:30 P.M. One week, he finished the report in the morning and gave it to her at noon. Celeste was thrilled. For the first time, she would not have to stay late to review the report. She thanked Marco profusely, praising his time management, thoughtfulness, and professionalism. She even offered to take him to lunch.

Marco truly enjoyed the praise and recognition, and he had a good time at lunch. He and Celeste talked through some of the more difficult aspects of the project and made a plan. They got to know each other better, which both of them enjoyed. These pleasant experiences motivated him to finish the report early the following week. He did so and passed it on to Celeste by 10:00 a.m., again receiving praise and an offer of lunch.

■ **EXHIBIT 3.15**

Operant Conditioning: How It Works		
Type of Reinforcement	**How the Consequence Is Applied**	**Real-World Example**
Positive reinforcement	Addition of a positive consequence following a desired behavior	Bonuses are given to the employee who sells the first car each month
Negative reinforcement	Removal of a negative consequence following a desired behavior	Manager ceases sending harsh reminder e-mails once a report is turned in
Extinction	Withholding of a consequence following a certain behavior	A new employee regularly asks for feedback, and when she gets none, she stops seeking it
Punishment	Addition of a negative consequence following an undesired behavior	A factory worker fails to meet production quotas and her salary is docked

PUNISHMENT

Punishment can be highly destructive to individuals and the organizational environment. Although the threat of punishment might be necessary to stop unlawful, unethical, or harmful behaviors (theft, sexual harassment, and the like), punishment is best used as a "last resort" when trying to change people's behavior. Here are some typical responses to punishment and what a manager can do to minimize the negative effects if punishment is the only option.

"What Did I Do Wrong?"

Unfortunately, people often do things that are unacceptable simply because they don't know the rules or have not been socialized to the organization's work processes, culture, or ethics. It is actually surprising how often people are punished without truly understanding why. This leads to mistrust, suspicion, and confusion—not the optimal circumstances for people to perform at their best. As a manager, if you *have to* use punishment, you *must* link it clearly with the behavior. Make sure an employee understands what he or she did, why it was wrong, and how the consequences relate to the behavior.

"Why Me?"

It is surprising how often managers blame and punish the wrong person or the wrong team. One common example is the "blame the messenger" syndrome. The person who brings bad news to the boss "gets it." When people are blamed and punished for things they didn't do and/or couldn't control, they feel a profound sense of injustice.

In such situations, we learn not to trust our environment or the people in it. We become defensive and self-protective. Needless to say, this kind of environment is not conducive to healthy autonomy, creativity, or positive risk taking—all behaviors that are much needed in many organizations today. So, if you must punish, be *sure* you know who deserves the punishment (if anyone).

"I Must Be an Awful Person."

Punishment damages self-respect and self-image. As a leader, part of your job is to ensure that your people are confident, believe in themselves, and are proud of their contributions. This state of mind is conducive to productivity and commitment to collective goals. So, if you need to stop someone from doing something, and punishment is the *only* way to achieve this, it is important to separate the behavior (what the person is doing that is wrong) from the person (the totality of that individual's humanity: mind, body, heart, and spirit).

Let's say, for example, that an employee has been having outbursts of temper in team meetings, causing serious disruptions. You have spoken to him and have tried rewarding good behavior. Nothing has worked. Finally, you decide to punish him by removing him from the team. You do not talk about the behavior as part of his character or personality (e.g., "You never handle yourself well" or "You just don't fit on this team"). You are careful to share, as objectively as possible, the link between the outbursts and others' ability to work effectively. You are compassionate with him, and you offer help: connection with the HR department, mentoring, coaching.

"I Can't Believe My Manager Did That in Front of Everyone."

Punishment is bad enough. But punishment in front of other people is simply an unacceptable way to address a problem. Why? It almost always fails to accomplish the goal. The shame that most people feel when publicly chastised is profound. Shaming someone poses a threat to that person's identity, which in many cases causes people to fight back.[57] Some people go "underground," hiding everything from the manager. Others may strike back in retaliation or even sabotage the manager, the group, or the organization.

Public punishment affects everyone present—and usually many others who hear about it. Punishing one person in a group is like punishing everyone. Unfortunately, most of us have had the experience of being punished in public. Maybe we've had our faults and shortcomings pointed out to others. Maybe we've been criticized harshly during a team meeting. What was your reaction when you were punished in front of others? There is no right way to punish in public—it's just wrong.

Even when punishment is done "well," it is an extremely risky way to attempt to change behavior or motivate people. As a manager or a team member, you are much better off training for good behavior, rather than having to punish bad.

OPERANT CONDITIONING: DOES IT REALLY WORK?

Operant conditioning is everywhere in organizational life and, in fact, may be at the heart of many assumptions about what motivates people. Think about it: Paychecks, bonuses, incentive programs, the threat of being fired for poor performance, criticism, feedback, and praise—all are examples of operant conditioning at work. But does operant conditioning really motivate people? Is motivation as simple as perfecting the behavior-consequence formulas used in this theory?

Although certain behaviors can be learned and changed through reinforcement, the method can have negative consequences. For example, dozens of studies show that people who expected financial incentives performed at lower levels than those who expected no reward.[58] This could be linked to an argument that extrinsic rewards do not affect emotional or cognitive commitment, especially when intrinsic motivators are absent. This is linked to a potentially serious flaw in the application of operant conditioning at work: the vast majority of rewards are extrinsic.

In fact, the Achilles' heel of many incentive programs is that they rely wholly on extrinsic motivators—and once these motivators are removed, desired behaviors may die out. To ensure that performance continues at a high level, incentives must be kept in place or, very often, increased over time. This is why some organizations seek to transform employees by converting extrinsic motivation to intrinsic motivation, which requires more than a carefully planned operant conditioning program.

These findings should be taken seriously. They indicate that operant conditioning programs at work may not have the desired effect on motivation and behavior change. Let's now look at social learning theory, which addresses some of the concerns associated with operant conditioning.

Social Learning Theory

Social learning theory
Theory that states that people learn new behaviors by observing others, and that self-reinforcement and self-efficacy support learning and behavior change.

Albert Bandura is well known for his work on **social learning theory**.[59] Social learning theory states that people learn new behaviors by observing others, and that self-reinforcement and self-efficacy support learning and behavior change. Social learning theory helps us understand how we can learn by watching others, reinforcing our own behavior, and believing that we can be successful. Let's look at what research says about social learning theory as it applies to motivation at work today.

Early studies showed that people learn from watching others and that employees who were close to supervisors or leaders imitated their behavior.[60] This greatly influenced learning theorists such as Julian Rotter, whose work on locus of control you read about earlier in this chapter. Rotter proposed that an individual's behavior has an impact on the motivation of others to engage in similar behavior.[61] By observing the consequences of others' actions, we can calculate the likelihood of positive or negative outcomes and act accordingly.

VICARIOUS LEARNING: THE BOBO DOLL EXPERIMENT

Bandura built on this early research and conducted fascinating studies. For example, in the famous Bobo doll experiment, he showed how people will replicate the behavior they observe.[62] In this experiment, children in one group witnessed adults behaving aggressively with an inflatable doll (Bobo). Other children witnessed adults calmly engaged in activities without being aggressive. The children exposed to aggressive treatment of the doll were more likely to behave aggressively later. They had "modeled" their behavior on the adults they observed. This is called vicarious learning.

Vicarious learning happens at work all the time. For instance, in many pharmaceutical companies, new hires are paired with experienced sales reps as they make the rounds of doctors' offices and hospitals. The new hires watch, listen, and learn how to build relationships with their customers, how to encourage them to try new drugs, and how to manage their time.

SELF-REINFORCEMENT: DON'T WAIT FOR OTHERS TO REWARD YOU

Bandura's work also indicates that people engage in self-reinforcement to motivate themselves.[63] For example, maybe you've promised yourself an evening out when you finish this chapter. At work, you might reinforce yourself by stopping to feel a sense of accomplishment when you do a good job or by taking your team out for lunch.

Self-reinforcement is not easy at work today, because many people are extremely busy. It takes time and effort to reward ourselves. Self-reinforcement is even more important today because managers simply don't have the time to reinforce us constantly. In our increasingly autonomous jobs, we need to find ways to motivate ourselves.

SELF-EFFICACY: I CAN DO IT

When it comes to motivating people, self-efficacy might be the most important concept in social learning theory. **Self-efficacy** is the degree to which a person believes that he or she is capable of successfully performing a behavior, accomplishing a task, or achieving a goal.[64] Self-efficacy plays a key role in motivation because the stronger a person's belief that he or she is capable of performing a task, the more motivated he or she will be to direct attention, increase efforts, and "stick with it" in order to succeed.[65]

Self-efficacy is important for students and employees alike. Research indicates that "self-efficacious students work harder, persist longer, persevere in the face of adversity, have greater optimism and lower anxiety, and achieve more."[66] At work, it is easy to think of examples where self-efficacy plays a part in success. Imagine, for example, someone who has just been hired to work in the marketing department of a graphic design studio. He's a designer, getting a "foot in the door" by taking this sales job. His duties include finding, calling, and visiting potential clients to interest them in the firm's activities. But say he comes to the job believing that no matter what kind of training he receives, he will never be a good salesman. In college, he tried to raise money for a club and failed. He describes himself as shy with strangers and doesn't think he's very good at small talk. Can you imagine him succeeding as a salesperson?

Is this young professional doomed to fail? Scholars suggest not: Self-efficacy can be improved. What can you do to improve your self-efficacy? First, you can deliberately gain experience with the work you need to do. You can also consciously model your behavior on a successful colleague or friend. It also helps if people around you are supportive and encouraging. Finally, it helps if you are passionately engaged with your work and your vision of the future. When you feel strongly about what you are doing, your energy will be directed and more intense.[67] Try not to feel discouraged as you learn. It is far better to focus on the positive, because this sparks creativity and resilience.[68]

In summary, social learning theory contains powerful messages for how we can improve our own and others' motivation. Many people and companies use the theory explicitly, and many more use it implicitly. As a student of motivation, it will serve you well understand how you can use principles of social learning theory to motivate yourself and others. For example, if you focus explicitly on vicarious learning, you will learn more, faster (or conversely, teach others more, faster). If you learn to reward yourself, and develop your "can do" attitude, you will likely feel more positive about

Self-efficacy
The degree to which a person believes that he or she is capable of successfully performing a behavior, accomplishing a task, or achieving a goal.

what you are doing. Added up, all of these activities and this stance can help you to feel more confident and be more effective.

Discussion Questions

1. Consider rewards and punishments or other reinforcements you have experienced at work. What was the effect on your motivation to learn or change your behavior?

2. Do you feel you have self-efficacy? How did it develop or fail to develop as much as you'd like? Consider your family, school, friends, sports, and other experiences.

Objective 3.8
Outline how theories of motivation can be integrated into daily professional and personal life.

8. How Can We Integrate Theories of Motivation?

Trying to apply so many motivation theories can be overwhelming. So where do you start? First, if you find a theory that is well researched and that you can easily embrace and implement, use it. Don't make the mistake, however, of thinking any one theory has all of the answers or can be applied in every situation. You need to have more than one theory in your toolbox.

To practice integrating theories of motivation, consider a famous company: Google. Working for Google is prestigious, and having the opportunity to create breakthrough technologies and services satisfies many engineers' achievement drives. What's special about Google is that young as the company is, it has managed to institutionalize systems and practices that are explicitly designed to motivate. To illustrate, consider this: Google's pay is competitive and their benefits are better than most companies in the United States. Paternity leave, for example, is granted as is maternity leave. Most companies in the U.S. do not do this. Google's foundation supports innovative projects that support communities, they run part of their operations on solar power, and they stand for freedom of information. Think back on the theories we have presented here: Which support each of these examples?

Now, let's take your review further. The most famous examples of institutionalized motivators include their beautiful campus, free food, volleyball courts, and campus bikes. Another example is the program that allows people to spend work time on new, creative ventures outside of their job responsibilities, as you can see in the *Business Case*. As you read, try to link what Google does to what academic researchers have said is important when it comes to motivation.

BUSINESS CASE   Google

Motivation for Innovation

Google is revered for its focus on innovation. The company has also gained acclaim in another area: motivation in the workplace. What lies beneath Google's success in becoming a company many of us would love to work for?[69]

Google headquarters is second to none. Located in Mountain View, California, it is only a stone's throw from the Shoreline Park wetlands.[70] Bikes are placed all around the campus to help "Googlers" get around. Beach volleyball courts, swimming pools, gyms, numerous cafés, and dozens of micro-kitchens with snacks are just some of the facilities that the company offers its employees.[71] Who wouldn't love to work

for a company that provides opportunities for fun, exercise, and great food?[72] Would these conditions motivate you? Why? For starters, they do more than simply meet basic needs. These conditions make people feel *valued*.

Although comfortable facilities and free meals can help explain

Continued on next page >>

why Google is one of the best places to work, there's more. Google's leaders understand that creating a resonant environment is the key to motivation, innovation, and success. They recognize that morale and innovation are not merely the result of a flashy workplace or progressive bonus structure. At Google, leaders ensure that people are intrinsically motivated, engaged, and passionate.

To motivate high-performing employees and encourage innovation, Google employs a program that is also used at Princeton and 3M. The program is designed to release people's creativity and provide them with a way to contribute their best.[73] In the program, many staff members are encouraged to initiate their own out-of-the-box projects, develop and release them and take some risks. Success is hoped for, of course, but setbacks are also tolerated. That's a big lesson: For people to be truly motivated to take chances on new projects, they have to feel that it is okay to fail. The program, open to high-performing employees and teams, is structured like this:

- Seventy percent of people's time should be dedicated to core business tasks.
- Twenty percent of time can be dedicated to projects related to the core business.
- Ten percent of time can be dedicated to projects *unrelated* to the core business. This is when Googlers can dive into something *new*, something that could be *big*.[74]

Some of Google's most progressive and innovative projects, such as Google Earth, Google News, and Google Local, were a result of this process.[75] These outcomes are notable successes for Google, and for the people involved in them. For these kinds of results to occur, we can assume that (1) employees are actually doing work other than their assigned projects, (2) employees are passionate and creative in these new pursuits, and (3) the company dedicates resources and establishes support structures that allow employees to pursue these projects.

This program has enabled people to focus time on projects that they find deeply meaningful and feel are important to the community and the world. For example, in 2011 the Google workers used their time to build technology to help to deal with the earthquakes and subsequent tsunami in Japan. At the time of the earthquakes and tsunami, Google spokesman Jamie Yodd stated that a lot of Googlers' 20-percent time was being spent on projects for Japan. In fact, according to Yodd, ". . . a group of people at our Tokyo office [was] spending a lot more than 20 percent of their time on this. . . ." These pursuits were supported by the company."[76] As a student of motivation, you can see that socialized power is likely a motivator for Googlers involved in these projects.

This program gives people *time* to innovate and time to spend on work they feel is extremely important, Simple, yes, but something many companies miss entirely. As CEO Eric Schmidt explains, "Innovation always has been driven by a person or a small team that has the luxury of thinking of a new idea and pursuing it. . . . Innovation is something that comes when you're not under the gun."[77] Google's recipe for success is clear: Create an environment that is supportive of people's physical and emotional health; provide a structure that encourages people to share their best ideas and be creative; and engage people's higher selves in the pursuit of doing good work while providing good services. This is what motivation is all about.

Source: Photo Source: nicole waring/iStockphoto.com

Now that you have read the case and considered how Google leaders have used theories of motivation to inform what they do, here are the hardest questions of all: Can you think of other ways to apply theories of motivation to this case? What is Google doing that researchers haven't considered?

Discussion Questions

1. Explain which theory you believe best explains motivation and why.
2. How does Google motivate employees?

9. What Role Does HR Play in Motivation?

Objective 3.9
Describe how HR can help motivate employees.

One of HR's core responsibilities is to ensure that the workforce is energized, committed, and motivated. An important way in which HR affects extrinsic motivation is through creating and administering employee compensation plans. With regard to intrinsic employee motivation, HR leaders are involved in developing the specific characteristics of jobs that lead to satisfaction and in turn, motivation. In this section we will consider each of these HR responsibilities.

Compensation and Reward Programs

Any way you look at it, money is a powerful motivator. Many people value money highly (expectancy theory would say it has high valence), and with good reason. Money enables people to satisfy basic needs (the ERG theories suggest that this is essential for motivation), and pay can be a measure of one's success or status (satisfying the need for achievement or power). Pay also allows people to benchmark their input and output with others, thereby giving them an opportunity to determine equity. Pay can be linked closely with goal attainment, or it can be used as positive reinforcement. Money can even be a factor in social learning theory, because people may have a strong desire to model their behavior on others who receive high salaries.

HR supports managers in determining when, how much, and in what manner people are compensated for work. Pay can be determined by considering an individual's performance, the performance of a group, or the entire organization's performance. Types of compensation plans include the following:

Individual compensation
A compensation plan based on individual performance.

- **Individual compensation:** A compensation plan based on individual performance motivates people the most when the link between performance and compensation is clear, when the compensation is perceived as fair, and when opportunities to learn and improve performance are available to employees.

Group compensation
A compensation plan that bases an individual's compensation on the performance of a group or groups and/or the organization as a whole.

- **Group compensation:** This type of plan bases an individual's compensation on the performance of a group and/or the organization as a whole. Group compensation plans are often used when it is difficult to measure individual performance or when collaboration is required to accomplish goals. These schemes are most effective when the link between individual contribution, group performance, and compensation is clear. They also tend to be more effective when the group functions well and has a shared purpose, constructive norms, and healthy relationships. Some researchers have argued that when applying these schemes, cultural attitudes toward individualism and collectivism need to be considered and reconciled.[78]

Merit-based compensation
A compensation plan in which compensation is determined by the level of performance of an individual or group.

- **Merit-based compensation:** This type of plan is based on the performance level of an individual or group, as opposed to factors such as years with the organization. Very few organizations have "pure" merit-based compensation schemes; most companies balance evaluation of merit and performance with factors such as tenure and role in the organization. Still, many organizations have merit pay schemes that allow managers to offer or increase compensation within a certain range for specific roles.

Compensation package
A plan in which wages, bonuses, and "fringe" benefits (such as health insurance, retirement plans, vacation, tuition reimbursement, and stock options) are all monetized.

Money is not the only component of compensation. HR managers must take into account other benefits that employees may receive. Compensation can include anything that can be monetized. HR is often responsible for creating **compensation packages**, plans in which wages, bonuses, and "fringe" benefits (such as health insurance, retirement plans, vacation, tuition reimbursement, and stock options) are all monetized.

Compensation schedule
A plan defining terms of payment (including regular pay, commissions, and bonuses) and when payment is dispersed to employees.

The way compensation is disbursed is also something HR must consider. **Compensation schedules** define terms of payment (including regular pay, commissions, and bonuses) and when payment is disbursed to employees. Wages and salaries are almost always paid at regular intervals, and in many companies, raises are also given at predictable times. Bonuses and special compensation such as sales commissions may be given at intervals or intermittently, usually determined by individual or collective performance. Compensation, however, is not the only way to motivate people as we will see in the next section.

The Job Characteristics Model

Well-known scholars J. R. Hackman and G. R. Oldham proposed a model that describes the specific conditions that lead to intrinsic motivation in job performance.[79] They identified three types of variables: psychological states contributing to intrinsic motivation, job characteristics that facilitate these psychological states, and personal attributes that determine positive response to job complexity and challenge. The model has come to be known as the **job characteristics model**. According to the model, people need certain qualities in their jobs in order to be intrinsically motivated and satisfied with work. This model includes five core job dimensions that can enhance motivation, job satisfaction, and productivity (■ **EXHIBIT 3.16**). As job designers, HR managers have a responsibility to create jobs that combine the appropriate level of each of the core dimensions of the job characteristics model. Many times, HR professionals design jobs with staff and managers, acting as a partners and advisors. When they do this, it is important that they truly understand the business.

Job characteristics model
Framework that states that people need certain qualities in their jobs to be intrinsically motivated and satisfied with their work.

■ **EXHIBIT 3.16**
Ideal outcomes of the job characteristics model.

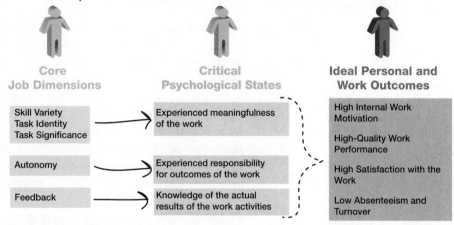

Core Job Dimensions	Critical Psychological States	Ideal Personal and Work Outcomes
Skill Variety Task Identity Task Significance	Experienced meaningfulness of the work	High Internal Work Motivation
Autonomy	Experienced responsibility for outcomes of the work	High-Quality Work Performance
Feedback	Knowledge of the actual results of the work activities	High Satisfaction with the Work
		Low Absenteeism and Turnover

Source: Hackman, J. R./Oldham, G. R., WORK REDESIGN, © 1980, p. 90. Adapted by permission of Pearson Education, Inc., Upper Saddle River, New Jersey.

To enhance the five core job dimensions, HR can use the following types of activities:

- **Job enrichment**: Building intrinsic motivators such as opportunities for learning, more control over how tasks are accomplished, and leadership opportunities, into the structure of a job.
- **Job enlargement**: Combining several simple jobs into one larger job.
- **Job rotation**: Moving employees from one job or job site to another to increase satisfaction and productivity.

Job enrichment
Building intrinsic motivators, such as opportunities for learning, more control over how tasks are accomplished, and leadership opportunities, into the structure of a job.

Job enlargement
Combining several simple jobs into one larger job.

Job rotation
Moving employees from one job or job site to another to increase satisfaction and productivity.

These activities can add to a job's appeal. However, it is important to remember that more is not always "better"; rather, an *appropriate* level of these characteristics can support the right amount of motivation. For example, too much freedom and autonomy can cause employees to feel unsupported and isolated.

Imagine that you've just started a job as a buyer for a retailer. It's your first day. You find your office, say hello to a few people nearby, and start to set up your desk. The people who hired you—your manager and the HR director—are nowhere to be found. You busy yourself, expecting direction from someone, but that direction never comes. A few hours later, the HR director sends you an e-mail with forms to complete. Late that afternoon, your manager shows up and says, "Hi! Great to see you here! Are you settling in okay? Good. See you Friday." Then, he leaves. Most people would agree that's too much autonomy! It is possible to have too much of any one of the other job characteristics identified in this model as well.

Although it is widely used in organizations, the job characteristics model has shortcomings. For example, one study shows that factors other than this model's five characteristics can also lead to increased productivity, happiness, and motivation. Examples of such factors include the needs for respect, growth, and trustworthy leadership, as well as the desire to be a member of the in-crowd and to impact decisions about one's job.[80]

HR Leadership Roles

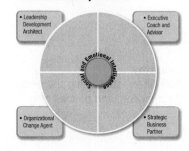

Discussion Questions

1. Pay is often considered a primary motivator. Is it for you? Why or why not? Use theories presented in this chapter to support your stance.

2. Individual, group, and merit-based compensation approaches are intended to motivate workers and enhance organizational performance. What are some potential unintended consequences of each approach?

Objective 3.10
Describe how you can motivate yourself and others.

10. What Can We All Do about Motivation?

What can you do to motivate yourself and others and ensure that everyone's work is meaningful? You can apply various theories and concepts of motivation to people and situations. To do this, you must integrate different theories and viewpoints about motivation. You must also understand what motivates *you* and causes you to perceive work as meaningful. This is self-awareness, a foundational social and emotional intelligence competency. You also need to understand what motivates others, and you must learn how to respond to their needs. This is empathy, another important social and emotional intelligence competency. Both self-awareness and empathy are discussed next. As you read, think about one or two things that you can do to improve your self-awareness and build skills related to empathy.

Self-Awareness and Motivation

Emotional self-awareness is related to social and emotional intelligence.[81] Why do you need to develop a high degree of self-awareness with respect to motivation? For one, you are ultimately responsible for motivating yourself. This means you must understand the conditions that enable you to feel engaged and excited about work. When you are aware of these conditions, you will be better able to make sensible choices about your work and your career. Knowing what motivates you also allows you to support yourself during times when your work isn't as fulfilling as you'd like. Remember Holocaust survivor Victor Frankl from the beginning of the chapter? There wasn't much to motivate him in the prison camps. However, Frankl found ways of looking at life that gave a sense of meaning to his daily activities. If you know yourself, you can do this whenever you are faced with difficult work or life circumstances.

Understanding your own feelings about work, effort, and goals, as well as your own needs, desires, and hopes, can help you understand your own motivation (or lack thereof). With self-awareness, you can monitor your response to work and adjust your stance consciously. You can make decisions about what sort of work is meaningful and motivating to you, and you can seek this kind of work or design features into your job that will enhance your motivation.

Empathy and Motivation

Empathy
Accurately interpreting the emotions, needs, and desires of others.

When we work with, manage, or lead other people, we need to be cognizant of which needs and desires might be affecting them, and how their thoughts and feelings are impacting their behavior. "Reading" others' behavior requires **empathy**. Empathy includes accurately interpreting the emotions, needs, and desires of others.[82] Studies repeatedly show that empathy is a critical component of effective management and leadership.[83] When you empathize, you are better able to connect with people and motivate them to meet their own needs, your needs, and the needs of the organization.

Also, when others believe that you understand them and care about their hopes, desires, and needs, they are motivated to follow your lead.

The capacity for empathy takes on special importance in multicultural settings because different cultures experience work and motivation in different ways. We must be able to read others and their cultures in order to understand which theories are applicable and how they should be applied. In doing so, we must remember that many theories of motivation have a decidedly Western bent.[84] Differences in values and social norms affect expectations about appropriate management behavior, job security, compensation structures, performance evaluation, career development, and motivation strategies. Any person who works in a multicultural or cross-cultural setting must understand how his or her own and others' cultures affect behavior. This requires us to develop abilities related to social awareness, including empathy.

Discussion Questions

1. Think about a relationship with a school or work colleague that you are motivated to improve. Practice self-awareness by examining your role in this relationship: What are you doing to make it better? What have you done to create the current problems? What emotions have driven your behavior?

2. For the same relationship, practice empathy. What do you think is driving the other person's behavior? What motivates him or her to act in certain ways? What emotions is he or she expressing?

11. A Final Word on Motivation and Meaning at Work

As you have seen, there are many theories that attempt to explain motivation and many other factors to consider when trying to keep yourself and others engaged and passionate about work. As you study more about management and leadership, you will likely find that exploring motivation and meaning at work will become more and more important. That is because almost everything we do as employees, managers, or leaders involves harnessing talent and energy in the service of doing something well.

Or, at least it should. We began this chapter by talking about how important it is for people to find meaning in work. Sigmund Freud is widely believed to have said, "Love and work are the cornerstones of our humanness."[85] We'll leave love up to you. As for work, we can't emphasize enough how important it is for you to find ways to use your talents, engage your passion, and bring others along with you on the search for meaningful work. You can start by developing self-awareness and empathy to deepen your understanding of what motivates you, as well as what motivates others.

LEADING IN A GLOBAL WORLD
It's Not Always about the Money

Different cultures are often motivated by different things. Likewise, different generations also find motivation in different rewards, both intrinsic and extrinsic. For some, it's money. For others, it's time off, meaningful work, or the opportunity to advance. A good manager or leader is aware of these differences and motivates accordingly.

Suppose you manage a team of seventy-five individuals. Your team members come from nine different countries in Asia, Europe, and South and Central America, and they are split almost evenly by gender. Ages range from 25 to 61. In the past, you had a very robust rewards and recognition budget to help keep your team motivated, and your team has always been high performing and productive. However, your organization is going through very lean times and your rewards budget has been completely eliminated. Additionally, the company has laid off whole teams based on their lack of productivity. You realize how critically important it is now to keep your team motivated and producing tangible results.

Take on the role of a manager of this organization. Either alone or with a group of 3 to 5 other students, talk about and articulate 10 no-cost motivators. Be detailed and creative with your ideas.

Some critical factors to consider as you create your no-budget program include:

1. What can you do to make the work more meaningful for such a diverse group?
2. Are there basic needs that almost everyone will respond to? If so, what are they? What can you do to motivate for them? Review the variety of needs theories in the text for ideas.
3. What resources might be available to you to help guide your motivation efforts of such an extremely diverse team? Be sure to consider age diversity as well as ethnic diversity.

LEADING WITH EMOTIONAL INTELLIGENCE
A Mandatory Bell Curve for My Management Class?!

When it comes to motivating people, good leaders and managers understand that the messages they send through their actions may be misinterpreted. Empathetic leaders carefully consider the wide variety of possible reactions to sensitive announcements and remember that what motivates some people may completely demotivate others.

Changes in performance review processes (such as grading policies) can be both motivating or demotivating, depending on the employee. Read the scenario below and break into teams to discuss the pros and cons of such a policy. Then, answer the questions that follow.

Hello Everyone:

In an effort to bring more rigor to our course offerings and to help stem grade inflation, the business school executive committee has decided to change the way your instructors grade this course. Specifically, they are not allowed to grant As to anyone who misses any classes, for any reason. Second, As cannot be granted to anyone receiving a B or below on any assignment, regardless of weighting. Third, anyone missing more than three classes, for any reason, will receive a C. Finally, in addition to the normal curve applied at this school, your instructors must eliminate an additional 10 percent from the "A" group.

If you have any questions or concerns, please talk to your professors on the first day of classes.

Thank you.

1. As a student, how do you see this policy affecting your motivation? Why?
2. What are the possible negative consequences of this policy with respect to motivation?
3. What are the possible positive consequences of this policy with respect to motivation?
4. How motivated would you be to collaborate, share notes, or help others in your class under this policy?
5. Who wins with a policy like this?

LEADING WITH CRITICAL THINKING SKILLS
How Have You Been Reinforced?

Understanding learning theories, such as operant conditioning and social learning theory, helps us to understand how people change their behavior. In addition, learning theories help us to understand what motivates people to change.

Operant conditioning is a fact of life in the business environment. Review operant conditioning theory in your text. Think of a situation from your work life, home life, or school life where you were motivated to behave a certain way due to one of the four types of reinforcement: positive reinforcement, negative reinforcement, extinction, and punishment. For each scenario, ask yourself the following questions:

1. What was the desired behavior that was being reinforced?
2. Was the type of reinforcement effective? If so, why? If not, why not?
3. Would another type of reinforcement have been more effective at motivating you to the desired results? Why?

ETHICAL LEADERSHIP
To Paint or Not to Paint?

Managers and leaders must be aware of people's needs, intrinsic and extrinsic motivators, and drivers of behavior. They also must consider tough issues, like whether or not it is ever right to withhold the truth if that truth may demotivate team members.

Suppose that your best friend recently dropped out of school to become an artist. She finds painting intrinsically rewarding and has been doing it for five years, but she has experienced virtually no success with art as a career. She doesn't understand why her work doesn't sell. Knowing that you pursued an undergrad minor in art history, she asks for—and genuinely wants—your opinion about her chances of being successful. You honestly think her art is atrocious and that she has very little chance of a successful art career. You also know that your opinion will hurt her feelings and perhaps demotivate her. Think about what would you do, and answer the following questions:

1. Is lying or withholding the truth justifiable if it prevents someone from becoming demotivated?
2. Have you ever lied to protect someone's feelings or to motivate them to do something? What role does empathy play in this scenario?
3. In situations where you are tasked to motivate others, consider what would happen if your sense of honesty and integrity conflicted with your sense of duty?

KEY TERMS

Motivation, *p. 64*
Flow, *p. 65*
Hope, *p. 67*
Resonant environment, *p. 67*
Intrinsic motivation, *p. 67*
Self-determination theory (SDT), *p. 69*
Extrinsic motivation, *p. 69*
Locus of control, *p. 70*
Hierarchy of needs, *p. 73*
ERG theory, *p. 73*
Two-factor theory (motivator-hygiene theory), *p. 73*
Motivators, *p. 73*
Hygiene factors, *p. 74*
Three-needs theory, *p. 74*

Need for achievement (nAch), *p. 75*
Micromanagers, *p. 75*
Need for affiliation (nAff), *p. 75*
Need for power (nPow), *p. 76*
Personalized power, *p. 76*
Socialized power, *p. 76*
Prosocial behavior, *p. 76*
Equity theory, *p. 77*
Cognitive dissonance, *p. 79*
Expectancy theory, *p. 80*
Effort, *p. 80*
Performance, *p. 80*
Instrumentality, *p. 80*
Valence, *p. 80*
Goal-setting theory, *p. 82*

SMART goals, *p. 82*
Operant conditioning theory, *p. 84*
Reinforcement, *p. 84*
Social learning theory, *p. 86*
Self-efficacy, *p. 87*
Individual compensation, *p. 90*
Group compensation, *p. 90*
Merit-based compensation, *p. 90*
Compensation package, *p. 90*
Compensation schedule, *p. 90*
Job characteristics model, *p. 91*
Job enrichment, *p. 91*
Job enlargement, *p. 91*
Job rotation, *p. 91*
Empathy, *p. 92*

MyManagementLab

Go to **mymanagementlab.com** for Auto-graded writing questions as well as the following Assisted-graded writing questions:

3-1. How can you increase a fellow student's, co-worker's, or employee's sense of intrinsic motivation on a project team? What extrinsic motivators might encourage someone to participate fully on a team?

3-2. Have you ever experienced cognitive dissonance? What were the conflicting ideas, attitudes or beliefs you were trying to reconcile? What did you do about it?

3-3. Mymanagementlab Only — comprehensive writing assignment for this chapter.

1. What Is Motivation? (p. 64)

Objective: Define motivation.

Summary: Almost half of our adult lives is spent working in our careers. That's why it is important to understand what motivates us, as well as how we can make our work meaningful and satisfying. Motivation results from internal psychological influences and external forces. Numerous theories in this chapter attempt to explain where motivation comes from and how it works. Along with understanding these theories, it is important to understand why people need to find meaning in life and work—and why it takes personal effort and leadership to motivate yourself and others.

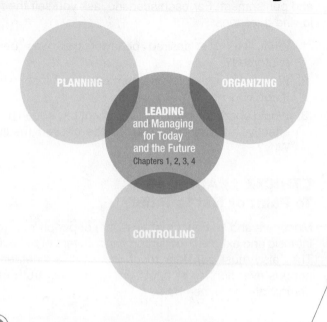

2. What Makes Work Meaningful? (pp. 64–67)

Objective: Understand the characteristics of meaningful work.

Summary: Work is meaningful to different people in different ways, depending on their experiences, their needs, and their goals. When work is meaningful to you, you may find yourself so engrossed in it that you achieve "flow," or a state of being "in the zone." When this happens, you are highly motivated and able to fully meet challenges. Motivation is a psychological state and, ultimately, it is up to you to find what connects you to your work in a meaningful way. This is not to say that leadership is unimportant. On the contrary, organizations choose leaders because of their ability to inspire and motivate. An effective leader does this by instilling hope and creating a resonant work environment.

3. What Is the Link between Motivation and Psychology? (pp. 67–71)

Objective: Recognize the links between motivation and psychology.

Summary: To understand what motivates people, you need to know a bit about psychology. For example, intrinsic motivation is that which we provide for ourselves, while extrinsic motivation refers to what is offered to us by others. Self-determination theory examines the relationship between intrinsic motivation and performance, noting that competence, autonomy, and relatedness are key to motivation. Extrinsic motivators, such as pay and benefits, sometimes also encourage us to do our best. Other factors that contribute to motivation include certain personality characteristics, such as locus of control. A strong internal locus of control means that you believe you have power over your environment. People with a strong internal locus of control are inspiring and enjoyable to work with because they readily take responsibility for their actions.

4. Which Theories of Motivation Are Important to Know? (pp. 71–72)

Objective: Learn why it is important to be able to critique theories of motivation.

Summary: There are several major theories of motivation, and each one says something unique about human behavior. As a manager, it is important for you to familiarize yourself with these theories so you will be better able to understand what motivates both you and the people who work for you. You also need to understand which of these theories are supported by research, as well as how they are used in organizations.

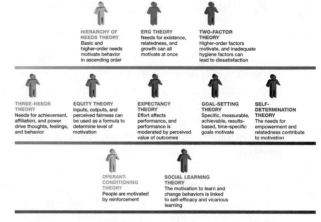

5. What Are Basic and Higher-Order Needs Theories of Motivation? (pp. 72–74)

Objective: Define the basic and higher-order needs theories of motivation.

Summary: Needs theories link motivation with the desire to satisfy various human needs. We all have these needs, from the most basic ones related to survival (e.g., food, water, safety, health) to higher-order needs related to self-fulfillment and a sense of purpose. One popular, but flawed, theory is Maslow's hierarchy of needs, which states that people fulfill their needs in order, starting with the most basic and working toward higher-level needs. This theory is not supported by research. A second influential theory is ERG theory, which stands for needs related to existence, relatedness, and growth. This theory of motivation states that different needs can be activated at the same time. The two-factor theory, argues that people are influenced by motivators and hygiene factors. Motivators, such as the desire for recognition, impact both motivation and job satisfaction, whereas hygiene factors, such as working conditions, do not affect motivation—but do affect job *dis*satisfaction.

6. Why Are the Three-Needs, Equity, Expectancy, and Goal-Setting Theories Useful? (pp. 74–83)

Objective: Distinguish between the three-needs, equity, expectancy, and goal-setting theories and explain their popularity.

Summary: Several theories of motivation—the three-needs, equity, expectancy, and goal-setting theories—are especially useful and well researched. These theories are each unique, but they all focus on the link between intention, behavior, effort, and outcomes.

David McClelland's three-needs theory shows how individuals are motivated through needs for achievement, affiliation, and power. People who are driven by the need for achievement seek new challenges and get a sense of satisfaction from personal excellence; people who have high affiliation needs are motivated by warm relationships with others; and people who are driven by the need for power seek control and influence over others. Need for power can be harnessed to bring about positive change in society and improve the welfare of others; this is called socialized power. For instance, the African concept of *Ubuntu* is a mind-set that motivates people to use power for the good of the group.

Equity theory is based on a mental "accounting" that compares our effort to the rewards we get and/or how our efforts and rewards compare to those of others. According to this theory, people are motivated to the extent that they feel these equations are equitable and fair. When we perceive that our effort is undervalued or overvalued, we may develop cognitive dissonance, in which we experience stress while attempting to process conflicting attitudes, beliefs, or ideas. Expectancy theory holds that in addition to inputs and outcomes, people also consider the degree to which they value these outcomes ("valence"). Outcomes that have a high degree of valence can motivate us to work harder, as long as we believe that our efforts will help us to achieve desired outcomes.

Finally, goal-setting theory tells us that "SMART" (specific, measurable, achievable, results-based, and time-specific) goals motivate many people. To the extent that we can create meaningful, challenging goals, we can improve motivation and outcomes in many cases.

S Specific
M Measurable
A Achievable
R Results-based
T Time-specific

7. What Are Learning Theories? (pp. 83–88)

Objective: Describe learning theories that relate to motivation.

Summary: Operant conditioning holds that we learn and are motivated to change our behavior depending on whether that behavior is reinforced, punished, or ignored. Positive reinforcement is one driver of individual performance, and it also helps create a resonant environment. Punishment may be necessary when laws are broken or when egregious behavior must be addressed, but it is extremely destructive and should be avoided whenever possible. Operant conditioning underlies many organizational incentive programs, but it's too simplistic and relies too much on extrinsic motivation.

Social learning theory tells us that we learn by observing. Vicarious learning allows us to model our behavior on that of others and to make choices based on our observations of the consequences of others' behavior. Both self-reinforcement and self-efficacy—or the belief that we can do something—are important parts of social learning theory.

8. How Can We Integrate Theories of Motivation? (pp. 88–89)

Objective: Outline how theories of motivation can be integrated into daily professional and personal life.

Summary: No one theory of motivation is wholly effective by itself, so it is important to find ways of integrating multiple theories into your personal and professional lives. In order to better understand this concept, think about a leader whom you admire and consider the different theories of motivation that may contribute to his or her behavior.

9. What Role Does HR Play in Motivation? (pp. 89–92)

Objective: Describe how HR can help motivate employees.

Summary: HR plays an important role in motivation at work. For one, HR creates and administers compensation packages, which are motivating for most people. These extrinsic motivators need to be combined and managed appropriately and equitably in order to be motivating. Different forms of compensation can yield different types of motivation—for example, group compensation can motivate teamwork and collaboration. Compensation packages include more than money (e.g., health insurance, status, and opportunities for enrichment). HR also plays a role in establishing conditions for intrinsic motivation. In particular, the job characteristics model helps HR professionals attend aspects of jobs that enrich people's experiences. Of these, job enrichment, enlargement, and job rotation are important areas to attend to.

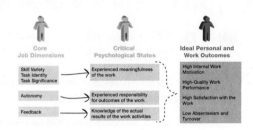

10. What Can We All Do about Motivation? (pp. 92–93)

Objective: Describe how you can motivate yourself and others.

Summary: It is your responsibility to motivate yourself. To accomplish this, you can start by understanding and integrating the different theories of motivation presented in this chapter. You can also develop your social and emotional intelligence, beginning with self-awareness. Self-awareness will help you make sensible decisions about how to choose meaningful work and/or make work more satisfying. You also need to understand how to motivate others, which starts with empathy. Basically, to motivate others, you need to understand them.

11. A Final Word on Motivation and Meaning at Work (p. 93)

Summary: When work is meaningful, people are inspired, motivated, and passionate about what they do. When you study more about management and leadership, you will learn that motivation and the search for meaning are powerful factors that allow us to tap into our energy, skill, and talent and become truly effective at work.

CHAPTER 4

Communication:
The Key to Resonant Relationships

PLANNING

ORGANIZING

LEADING
and Managing
for Today
and the Future
Chapters 1, 2, 3, 4

CONTROLLING

MyManagementLab™

⭐ Improve Your Grade!

Over 10 million students improved their results using the Pearson MyLabs.
Visit **mymanagementlab.com** for simulations, tutorials, and end-of-chapter problems.

Chapter Outline

1. Why Is Communication Central to Effective Relationships at Work? (pp. 102–103)

2. How Do Humans Communicate? (pp. 104–108)

3. How Do We Communicate and Interpret Sophisticated Information? (pp. 108–113)

4. What Is the Interpersonal Communication Process? (pp. 113–117)

5. How Do We Use Information Technology to Communicate at Work? (pp. 117–119)

6. What Are Common Barriers to Effective Communication? (pp. 120–124)

7. Why Is It Challenging to Communicate in a Socially Diverse World? (pp. 124–127)

8. What Is Organizational Communication? (pp. 127–132)

9. What Can HR Do to Ensure Effective Communication and Resonant Relationships in Organizations? (pp. 132–134)

10. What Can We All Do to Improve Communication and Build Resonant Relationships at Work? (pp. 134–137)

11. A Final Word on Communication and Leadership (p. 137)

Chapter Objectives

4.1 Explain why communication is key to fostering effective relationships.

4.2 Explain how humans communicate.

4.3 Analyze how we communicate and interpret sophisticated information.

4.4 Define the interpersonal communication process.

4.5 Describe how people use information technology to communicate at work.

4.6 Define the common barriers to effective communication.

4.7 Analyze the challenges in communicating in a socially diverse society.

4.8 Define organizational communication.

4.9 Outline the steps HR can take to ensure effective communication and resonant relationships.

4.10 Outline the steps you can take to improve communication and build resonant relationships in your workplace.

1. Why Is Communication Central to Effective Relationships at Work?

Success at work is based in part on your ability to share information and to influence others—two main purposes of communication in the workplace (■ **EXHIBIT 4.1**). Effectiveness at work also includes the ability to share one's values, to inspire others, and to create resonance in relationships through positive communication that helps create an environment where everyone can be and do their best.[1]

From your own experiences in school, work, and life, you have learned how to communicate who you are, what you need, and what you think and feel. You've learned to communicate in ways that help you build relationships, manage conflict, influence others, share knowledge, and collaborate with others. Good leaders and successful employees pay a great deal of attention to *what* they communicate. Good communicators also pay attention to *how* they share information, present themselves to others, influence people, and build relationships.

■ EXHIBIT 4.1

How has ineffective communication impacted your work and school experiences?

Source: © Image Source/Alamy

What we communicate through our words and our actions *matters*. If you tell your employees that you are committed to their learning and development and back it up with action, that message will ripple out to others—fast. If you are genuinely passionate about what you do at work, people will know. If your actions contradict what you say, people will know that too.

Commenting on the role of leadership in twenty-first century business, former CEO of Sun Microsystems Jonathan Schwartz noted, "The number one role of a leader is to communicate. And the number one role of a CEO is to be the chief communicator, to make sure that the people inside the organization know what is important, as well as our partner community and our customers and our shareholders."[2] Schwartz embraced this idea through his actions; in fact, he was one of the first CEOs of a major corporation to engage in blogging on a regular basis. No matter the format, when we communicate at work, we inform, persuade, inspire, and motivate. We build—or destroy—relationships based on how and what we communicate.

Resonant relationships
Vibrant and supportive relationships that foster respect, inclusion, openness, and honest dialogue.

In this chapter, we will discuss a number of ways that you can improve your communication skills and your ability to build **resonant relationships**—vibrant and supportive relationships that foster respect, inclusion, openness, and honest dialogue. But what kinds of relationships are important at work? Sometimes, people think that you should not have close friendships at work because it interferes with getting things done. This view is most often held regarding the boss-employee relationship. It's actually more complicated. As a manager, you need to have empathy for people. Meaning, you need to understand what motivates them, what they want and need at work and in their lives.[3] You need to trust them and they need to trust you. You need to show them that you care about them as people, as well as workers. People bring their whole selves to work, not just their professional selves.

On the other hand, you need to be objective about your employees and their performance. If you aren't, you are likely to begin to have favorites, not see performance issues with people you "like," etc. Building effective, resonant relationships at work that are not unhealthy is something many managers spend a lot of time learning how to do. As you start your career, it will be extremely beneficial if you can learn these lessons early. As a start, let's turn to a stellar leader at Eaton Corporation. Annette Rinck is the Vice President of Marketing for the Europe, Middle East, and Africa Regions for Eaton. She has had great successes in her career, and she believes in the ability to inspire people and to build strong relationships with bosses, peers, and employees.

Leadership Perspective

Communication starts with vision. Why is this so important? First, you need to be able to make decisions that are in line with where the business is going. Equally important is using your vision to inspire people. The people you are working with need to understand the goals and objectives, and it's up to you to communicate these in a way that makes them want to achieve. You also need to communicate what's behind the goals and the vision. What do senior managers want and expect for the company? What are we trying to do in the market? For our customers? This vision can seem very far away to people—like climbing Everest. But climbing a mountain involves taking many small steps—it's your job as a leader to encourage people to take these steps.

Second, the best leaders help people to see that the inevitable obstacles they will encounter can be seen as opportunities. Communicating this means that in many ways you become a teacher and a coach. It's not enough to give the answers to people. You need to ask the questions that trigger the right actions. That's what being a good leader/coach really means. You teach people to see situations and issues differently, and you coach them to think outside the box. To be a good coach, you need to recognize their accomplishments, you need to understand people. They need to believe that you really care about them—their problems, their successes, and what's going on in their lives. Remembering things like their sports interest, children's names,

and other personal details are essential. It's the human touch that makes these relationships meaningful and productive, and encourages people to contribute even more.

And third, you need to understand the boundaries. It's important not to be too familiar, too close. This is difficult when you are at the same time building relationships. One way to manage this is to remember that as a leader, you must treat everyone equally and have the same kind of professional relationships with all your employees.

Source: Personal interview with Annette Rinck conducted by Annie McKee, 2012.

● **Annette Rinck**
Vice President of Marketing of Eaton Industries Manufacturing
"... you must treat everyone equally and have the same kind of professional relationships with all your employees."

Annette Rinck is wise: Building resonant relationships that help people to feel inspired by the vision and understand how to learn while achieving goals is important in *all* relationships at work. So, as you read this chapter, think about how you build resonant relationships at work, and how you can manage the complicated boundary between personal and work relationships.

To begin this chapter, we will explore how we use both verbal and nonverbal language to communicate thoughts and emotions. We will introduce interpersonal communication models that demonstrate how we send and receive information. You will also learn how to use communication to manage your image at work and in life. Then, we will discuss technology and communication, followed by tips on overcoming common communication barriers. You will learn about the special challenges of communication in today's socially diverse organizations, how to navigate communication networks effectively, and how to use storytelling as a powerful communication tool. Finally, you will learn what HR can do to improve communication in organizations and what we all can do to communicate effectively and build resonant relationships at work.

Discussion Questions

1. When you begin working with a group or team (on a class project, for example), what strategies do you use to help people get to know each other and build resonant relationships? What are some new ideas for relationship building that you may adopt as a result of this course?

2. Recall a situation in which someone (maybe a boss or teacher) communicated clearly, but in a way that offended you. What happened? Why did it bother you?

Objective 4.2
Explain how humans communicate.

Communication
The act of conveying a message from one person or group to another person or group.

2. How Do Humans Communicate?

Communication comes from the Latin *communicatus/communicare,* meaning "to impart or share."[4] **Communication** is the act of conveying a message from one person or group to another person or group. Human communication is incredibly complex. We share *everything*: our ideas, hopes, dreams, joys, anger, and fears by talking, singing, dancing, painting, writing, smiling, frowning, crying, laughing, kissing, hugging—the list goes on and on. We communicate with words, both spoken and written. We also communicate nonverbally through facial expressions, posture, gestures, and the like. Each of these types of communication is discussed next.

Language: Our Human Specialty

Many animals have communication systems that can be considered language, but none of their languages are as complex as human language, and no animals use language as creatively as we do. Renowned linguist Noam Chomsky points out that the creative function of human language has not been found to exist in animal communication systems.[5] Psychology professor Michael Corballis says that, unlike animals, "Humans use language, not just to signal emotional states or territorial claims, but to shape each other's minds."[6]

Although no one can place an exact date on when humans first began to use spoken language, it seems to have emerged around 50,000 years ago. Scholars believe that language and the ability to reason evolved together, that language is tied to our ability to *think*, and that even the earliest forms of language probably included gestures and sounds associated with both thoughts and feelings.[7]

Language
A systematic form of communication that is composed of a set of sounds and symbols shared by people.

■ **EXHIBIT 4.2**
"I love you" in different languages.

English	I love you
German	Ich liebe dich
Spanish	Te amo
Tagalog	Mahal kita
Japanese	愛しています (aishiteimasu)
Zambian Zambian	Nikukonda Nalikutemwa
Hindi	Females to males: Main tumse pyār kartī hūn Males to females: Main tumse pyār kartā hūn
Russian	Я тебя люблю (ya tebya l'y bk'u)
American Sign Language	

VERBAL AND SIGN LANGUAGE

Language is a systematic form of communication that is composed of a set of sounds and symbols shared by people. Oral language is a combination of sounds that are symbols for our ideas and feelings. For example, the word *table* is a set of sounds that symbolizes what English speakers understand as a four-legged piece of furniture with a flat surface on top. The phrase "I love you" is a set of three sounds that symbolize a complex set of feelings—attraction, respect, commitment, and protectiveness, among others.

You might wonder how words evolve. Do they in some way relate or describe an object, thought, or feeling? In fact they don't. Most words are arbitrary except for the case of onomatopoeia (words that mimic sounds). There is usually no relationship between the combination of sounds and our thoughts, feelings, and ideas. The word *table* could just as easily be the word *horse*. As you can see in ■ **EXHIBIT 4.2**, there are many ways to combine sounds to create words that have meaning for us.

Hand gestures can indicate thoughts and feelings as well. Certain sets of gestures are known as sign language and are used by people who have impaired hearing or speech, as well as their friends, families, and coworkers. Many preschools in the United States routinely teach sign language.

The World Federation of the Deaf estimates that there are about 70 million deaf people in the world and

80 percent of these live in developing countries.[8] Although dozens of sign languages and hundreds of dialects are used throughout the world, only a few are used among large numbers of people. The largest sign language by use is Spanish Sign Language, with 28 million users, followed by 2 million users of Chinese Sign and 1.6 million users of French Sign.[9] British Sign Language is used by about 250,000 people, according to the British Deaf Association.[10] Data posted on Gallaudet University's Web site indicates there are between 500,000 and 2 million users of American Sign Language in the United States; Canada also uses ASL. Estimates vary wildly, and a firm number of ASL users has been elusive.[11]

As you can see in ■ **EXHIBIT 4.3**, even though both Britons and Americans use English as their spoken language, the two countries' sign languages are completely different. Users who know only one of the two languages would not be able to understand each other.[12]

Looking at the vast differences between the American and British Sign Languages, it is easy to understand why an international sign language has been developed. International Sign Language (ISL) has been formally developing since the nineteenth century and arose because of interactions between people who spoke different sign languages, the same way pidgin languages came into being.[13] A **pidgin** is a language that uses signs, words, or phrases from more than one language, allowing people to communicate without learning one another's language.

Along with oral and sign language, people have developed another way to symbolize thoughts and feelings: written language.

Pidgin
A language that uses signs, words, or phrases from more than one language, allowing people to communicate without learning one another's language.

WRITTEN LANGUAGE

It is difficult to say when our ancestors first began using written symbols to communicate. More than 40,000 years ago, our predecessors were drawing on cave walls.

■ **EXHIBIT 4.3**
The American and British sign language alphabets differ.

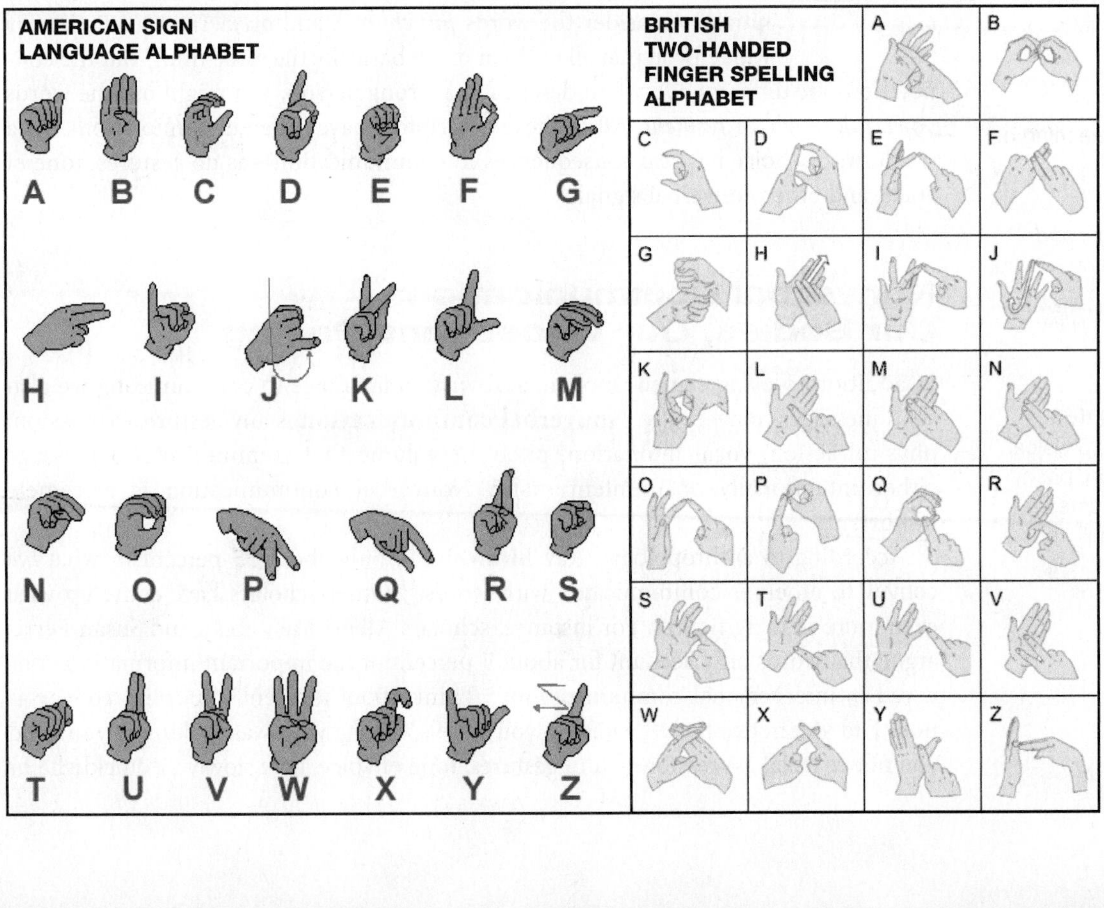

Source: Whitehead Images/Alamy

Denotation
The literal or dictionary meaning of a word.

Connotation
The associations, feelings, and judgments that accompany a word.

Nonverbal communication
Any gesture, expression, physical action, or vocal intonation, pitch, or volume that communicates a message either intentionally or unintentionally.

Were these the first "written" stories? It's hard to tell. But it is clear that for thousands of years, people have used symbols drawn or scratched on stone, wood, and other materials to express and share thoughts and emotions (■ **EXHIBIT 4.4**). Writing probably emerged around 7,000 years ago, although no one knows for sure.

Examples of common forms of written communication used at work include e-mails, text messages, memos, blogs, books, manuals, contracts, and the company newsletter. One significant advantage of written communication is that it produces a permanent record. Why is that important? Written records can be useful when someone needs to refer to an original communication for clarification or to sort out a disagreement. They also allow participants to reproduce the original message and disseminate it easily and accurately.

Written communication is especially helpful for lengthy or detailed ideas. When we craft a message in writing, we often think more deeply about what we are trying to say than when we share a message in conversation. Likewise, when we receive a written message, we can choose to devote more time to thinking about what the message means to us or what the writer intended than we can during a conversation.

DENOTATION AND CONNOTATION

Two concepts are particularly important in all forms of language: denotation and connotation. **Denotation** is the literal or dictionary meaning of a word. It might seem like understanding the literal meaning of words is enough—but many times that is not the case. **Connotation** refers to the associations, feelings, and judgments that accompany words. Understanding the connotation of words is important because communication extends beyond simple definitions to include personal, social, and cultural meanings that cannot be found in dictionary definitions. Consider the words *fat*, *chubby*, and *overweight*. A dictionary will tell you that all of them mean basically the same thing, but the connotations are different. Or, when describing a strong person, you might use the words *powerful*, *tough*, or *resilient*. All of these descriptors have different connotations. As a result, word choice has real consequences in communication—as do gestures, tone of voice, and other nonverbal signals.

Nonverbal Communication: Our Bodies, Our Voices, and Pacing

In addition to using signed, spoken, and written language to communicate, we also send messages nonverbally. **Nonverbal communication** is any gesture, expression, physical action, vocal intonation, pitch, or volume that communicates a message either intentionally or unintentionally. Nonverbal communication is extremely important.

According to anthropologist Ray Birdwhistell, only about 35 percent of what we convey to others is communicated with words.[14] Other scholars have come up with even more striking figures. For instance, scholars Albert Mehrabian and Susan Ferris argue that words only account for about 7 percent of the important information conveyed in interpersonal communication.[15] Think about a recent important conversation. Did you notice how the person you were speaking with was looking at you? Did you notice facial expressions, hand gestures, tone of voice, how slowly or quickly he or she spoke, and how close he or she stood to you? If you're like most people, you didn't attend consciously to many of the person's nonverbal signals. You picked up some nonverbal messages, but missed others.

Learning how to decode others' nonverbal behavior and manage your own might be the most important communication skills you can learn. Our nonverbal messages can be far more nuanced and more accurate than what we convey with words. That is partly because emotions impact our bodies. For example, there are numerous minute facial muscles that respond to our feelings. Others can see and interpret these minute movements and decode our true feelings and messages. Nonverbal communication is linked to a process called limbic resonance. The term limbic resonance describes the complex neurological and psychological processes that enable people to decipher and then mirror one another's emotions.[16] By carefully attending to nonverbal communication, we can manage the limbic resonance process more consciously, and thereby monitor and manage communication and relationships more effectively.

Accurately reading nonverbal signals is linked to your capacity to empathize—a critical social and emotional intelligence competency. Learning to manage your own nonverbal signals involves emotional self-awareness and self-management—two other important competencies for leaders.

The fact that a lot of nonverbal behavior happens naturally is both good and bad—it facilitates fast and accurate communication. However, it can also show others more or different information than you might intend. A good communicator attends carefully and consciously to nonverbal communication. Aspects of nonverbal communication that you should pay special attention to are body language, vocal intonation, volume, and the rate—or pacing—of speech.

BODY LANGUAGE

Body language includes hand gestures, facial expressions, eye contact, physical touch, proximity to others, or any other physical gesture that can convey meaning (■ **EXHIBIT 4.5**). When you want to direct someone's attention to a man entering a room, for example, you might nod in his direction while maintaining eye contact with your conversation partner. You might point or raise your eyebrows in the man's direction. You might use facial expressions or gestures to tell your partner what you think and feel about this man. You could also add to your nonverbal message by varying how obvious your signals are. If, for example, you point and laugh loudly, it may convey that you don't care about his feelings, that you consider yourself more powerful than him, or, depending on your facial expression, that you are friends.

We respond to people's body language with nonverbal feedback. In the example of the man entering the room, for instance, he may communicate that he knows you are drawing your friend's attention to him by waving or joining in the laughter if he interprets your gestures as friendly, or he may tense up and scowl if he senses you are making fun of him.

VOCAL INTONATION, VOLUME, AND PACING IN COMMUNICATION

Vocal intonation is a term that describes using changes in pitch or tone of voice to communicate information. Patterns of pitch and tone help people understand what you really mean. For example, the simple sentence "She's really nice" can mean very different things depending on which words you emphasize and the tone of your voice when you say the sentence. Intonation also signals whether you are making a statement or asking a question, and it can communicate surprise, irony, uncertainty, anger, compassion, sympathy, and many other emotions.

Body language
Hand gestures, facial expressions, eye contact, physical touch, proximity to others, or any other physical gesture that has the capacity to convey meaning.

■ **EXHIBIT 4.5**
What types of body language do *you* use?

Source: © WavebreakMediaMicro/Fotolia

Voice volume also signals what you mean. For example, you may increase the volume of your voice, or lower it, to capture people's attention. In some cultures, softly spoken words indicate deference, shyness, or insecurity. In others, they can indicate power (i.e., you do not have to speak loudly to get attention).

How fast or slowly you talk and how much or little you vary this rate is called pacing. Like intonation and volume, pacing can draw attention to what you are saying and convey your thoughts and feelings. For instance, you might slow down to emphasize the importance of specific instructions.

Variation in how we use our voices is helpful because it holds people's attention. Everyone has struggled to stay focused on a lecture that was delivered in a monotone: The lack of vocal emphasis makes it hard to pay attention. If you learn to speak in a way that captures and keeps people's attention, you will be a more effective communicator.

Body language, vocal intonation, volume, and pacing are all intertwined in communication. Mastering the art of sending and interpreting nonverbal language enables us to be better communicators because we can then share thoughts and emotions more effectively. Good communicators use all aspects of language well. In the next section, we will look at sophisticated communication skills that allow us to interpret complex messages and manage our image.

Discussion Questions

1. How does your use of language change in social settings when meeting new people? In professional settings? How does your use of language affect other people's first impressions of your character, your values, and your code of ethics?

2. Have you ever received feedback on your body language? What was the feedback? How did this affect how you think of yourself as a communicator? How did this affect your awareness of your body language?

Objective 4.3
Analyze how we communicate and interpret sophisticated information.

3. How Do We Communicate and Interpret Sophisticated Information?

In this section, we will discuss four sophisticated topics related to communication: expressing emotions through our nonverbal behavior; interpreting emotions, opinions, and facts; communicating "who we are" and how we want others to see us; and interpreting objective and subjective information.

Expressing Emotions: Nonverbal Behavior Shows the Truth

Expressing and interpreting emotions is an ability that humans are born with, although people differ in their ability to do so effectively. According to noted scholar Paul Ekman, people of all cultures immediately recognize at least six basic emotional expressions: happiness, sadness, fear, anger, disgust, and surprise.[17] Many other emotions are subtly expressed. With the right knowledge and practice, we can effectively learn to read others' feelings and moods more accurately even when communicating with people whose cultures differ from ours.[18] We can also learn how to express our emotions in ways that make it more likely that others will understand what we mean.

At best, managing our expression of emotions is done consciously and the feelings we express nonverbally are in synch with our words. Often, however, our nonverbal language gives "voice" to emotions that we are unaware of or are trying to hide. For a variety of reasons, people often try to mask their emotions.[19] For example, the communication of certain emotional states is not acceptable in some cultures. Nonverbal behavior can also give clues about emotions related to cognitive dissonance or lying.[20] Scholars also note that we sometimes want to communicate our emotions but hold back; when that happens, others often recognize that we are hiding our feelings.[21]

For instance, you may have been in a situation where a decision was being discussed. You disagreed with the direction the conversation was going and were very unhappy about the decision the group was about to make. You hid your feelings because it seemed that everyone else was happy with the choice. It's entirely possible, however, that your nonverbal behavior gave clues about your real feelings. Your nonverbal messages might be interpreted accurately, or not—causing confusion and miscommunication. For example, not knowing why you looked agitated, others may have wondered "What's wrong with her?" or "Is she mad at me?"

Masking, hiding, or denying emotions takes a lot of energy—it is difficult and draining. In fact, the stress that results from hiding our feelings is associated with an assortment of social and psychological problems.[22]

A Sophisticated Skill: Interpreting Emotions at Work

Accurately conveying and reading emotions is essential in life and at work. It is especially important for leaders at all levels in an organization. This is because emotions impact decision making, accomplishment of goals, and the quality of work relationships.[23] Consider this example: A manager is meeting with employees to create a new process to schedule work shifts during the holidays. The business needs to stay open at all times, and employees have made numerous complaints about the demanding hours. Some employees are always asked to work holidays, which they resent. Other employees are rarely asked to work holidays, which means they do not have the opportunity to earn overtime wages.

At the meeting, the manager notices that employees are uncomfortable. She interprets this as people being upset with *her* (she is wrong—they are just frustrated with the situation). She chooses to ignore the nonverbal signals. When someone tries to bring up his or her feelings about the problems, she changes the subject. She is afraid that the employees will verbally attack her and she will be unable to control the meeting. The employees sense her resistance, and several of them become angry: "Doesn't she trust us to have a reasonable conversation?" Others think, "If we can't talk about our problems and feelings, how will we ever find a good solution?" Still others are just confused: "What is her problem?" This meeting is off to a bad start—and it will not end with the best solution. Had the manager been more confident and skilled at reading people's emotions, this would have been a more productive meeting.

This example illustrates several points: emotions are conveyed constantly, reading them accurately is important, and we all need to develop skills to deal with conflicting opinions and different emotions. The example also illustrates another sophisticated topic related to communication: how we communicate to protect our self-image. Part of the reason this manager did not want to address the emotions she saw in her group was that she wanted to maintain her self-image as a manager who doesn't lose control. Let's look at how managing image and identity is an important part of the communication process.

How We Manage Our Image through Communication

In Japan, there is a saying that everybody has two faces—one to keep to yourself and one to present to others. We all choose identities that suit us for the different roles we have in society—leader, manager, student, friend, employee. We support each of our identities by carefully choosing our words and behavior to show and maintain the image we want to present.[24]

Face
The public representation of a part of our identity that we want others to accept.

The identities we create for public view are what are known as *face*. Face is the public representation of a part of our identity that we want others to accept.[25] We want others to agree with how we portray ourselves or, at the very least, not challenge us.[26] For example, you may see yourself as a loyal friend. When someone is in trouble, you will say things like "I'll be there for you." If your friend is really upset, he might say, "No you won't—you're too busy with your own problems." This is a challenge to your identity—the public face you want to present. If this identity is important to you, you'll be upset and want to prove to your friend that you are indeed loyal.

SAVING FACE

When someone challenges the identity you present, you may take steps to "save face" or to avoid "losing face."[27] Maintaining face is especially complicated in the work environment, where people often play many roles. At work, people often expect us to do things that may not fit with our image of ourselves, or that interfere with the identity we are attempting to display. We may have to change our self-presentation, acting in ways that we might not otherwise choose. Some of these challenges to our preferred identity are made as explicit requests (on-record), whereas others are more indirect (off-record).

For example, imagine you've just been hired as an associate at a major telecom company. It's an entry-level job for college graduates, but you will have significant responsibilities. During one of your first team meetings, your manager says to you, "Can you please get coffee for the team?" You don't see yourself as a person who gets others' coffee—your face is challenged by this on-record request. You have a dilemma—swallow your pride and comply, or refuse, risking the consequences. Both choices leave you feeling bad and possibly resenting your manager. This example illustrates why we have to be careful with on-record communication: we can create situations where people lose face.

Off-record requests can be very useful, especially when we are unsure how people see themselves or what face they want to present. Going back to the previous example: The manager could have said, "We take turns getting coffee for meetings." You might then want to present an image of a great team member, saying "Great. Let me do it this time."

A STRATEGY FOR SAVING FACE AND KEEPING RELATIONSHIPS HEALTHY

When an explicit, on-record request is made, it is harder for both parties to maintain face. Someone might have to give in and change how they are presenting themselves. In this case, a strategy may be needed to allow both parties to maintain face. Researchers Penelope Brown and Stephen Levinson created a model that helps us understand how "politeness" can support a strategy for maintaining relationships when either indirect or direct requests are made:[28]

- *Positive politeness* refers to the messages we send that indicate we accept another's face. Positive politeness is a process of reinforcing shared or common values and seeking common ground—the idea that "we are in it together."
- *Negative politeness* is a strategy of recognizing the other person's "territory," independence, time, and resources as private and valuable. For instance, when a direct request for help is required, instead of saying "I need you to help me with this project," you

might say, "I need your help, but I know how busy you are." Your colleague might then respond, "Thanks so much for recognizing how busy I am. Let me see what I can do."

Every interaction is an attempt to show others our preferred self-image while allowing others to do the same. It is amazing that we ever communicate successfully, given how complex this process is. We are able to do so by understanding the rules of polite communication within a society.

Different cultures have different preferences for how people share who they are, and how they express themselves politely. The risk of offending others and endangering important relationships is higher in cross-cultural interactions, even when making the most sincere attempts to be polite. Effective leaders recognize that they must manage this complex social dance and also maintain an image that will enable them to influence others.

Communication is complicated, especially when it comes to emotion and important information such as one's image and identity or cultural rules of interaction. How do we make sense of it all? Let's look at one way to categorize information so we can understand and use it more effectively.

Making Sense of Information

One way to categorize how we understand and share information has been proposed by scholar Ken Wilbur.[29] Wilbur's model allows us to categorize information we encounter in the world as being:

- Related to a single person (*individual*) versus related to a group, organization, or community (*collective*) **and**
- Inside a person or group (*interior*) versus outside a person or group (*exterior*).

As you can see in ■ **EXHIBIT 4.6**, this categorization scheme is clever in that it allows us to more clearly see how information "fits together." This model is complicated, which leads many people to ignore its lessons. Let's try to simplify it by looking first at a real-life example of how one leader understands his institution by looking at several dimensions. Then, we will consider an example of how this can play out in a business.

■ **EXHIBIT 4.6**
Wilbur's model for categorizing how we understand and share information.[30]

Interior (Subjective)		Exterior (Objective)	
Individual	Collective	Individual	Collective
My values	Our culture	My behavior	Our common language

John Fry—president of Drexel University in Philadelphia—emphasizes a leader's responsibility to inspire individuals and create communities that work together to forge strong organizations. To do this, leaders need to understand individuals' and the organization's strengths objectively (that is Wilbur's individual and collective exterior). They also need to strive to understand one another as people with distinct and different viewpoints, as well as understand group cultures (that's Wilbur's individual and collective interior). What does this mean in real life? Let's hear what John has to say in the *Leadership Perspective* feature.

As a student, you have probably experienced the complexity of your own institution. Individual and collective perspectives can be very different. For example, consider one professor's viewpoint about grading versus the institution's policies, or

Leadership Perspective

We have to focus on actually getting things done and measuring our success objectively. We can measure individual students' through things like grades and how many extracurricular activities they participate in. We measure individual faculty through teaching evaluations and publications.

We also need to measure and understand the various groups on campus and their impact. What does each function do? How do academic departments link to HR, Finance, etc.? How many student groups are there compared to the norm? When it comes to groups that have a social mission, how many people do they touch?

These measures are important, but they are not enough. We also need to understand what goes on within and between people and groups. What do individuals believe and care about? For groups, what are their distinct cultures? These things can be measured too, but it is more difficult. In addition to good research, leaders need to constantly hone skills related to social awareness so they can read their environments.

To inspire people to be their very best, we need to read them well and then empathize with them. We need to understand what is important to them, and why. This is true for students, faculty, and staff. At universities, these groups can be very different from one another. They have different goals and even cultures. So, as leaders, we need to decipher these things, so we can help people join together in the service of our shared vision and to work toward an even better future.

All organizations today are faced with the need to change. The job of a leader is to clear the path. You need to focus people on their essential greatness, which allows them to tackle some of the difficult issues. You're not trying to create the aura of a powerful leader; you're trying to create the aura of a powerful community. If this works, long after you are gone the community will carry on successfully and with confidence.

● **John Fry**
President of Drexel University
"To inspire people … we need to empathize with them."

The worst kind of leader is the kind where the place crashes and burns after he or she leaves. To avoid this, you need to manage and lead in a way that people are inspired to learn to work together to get things done.

Source: Personal interviews with John Fry conducted by Annie McKee, 2009 and 2012.

---

the way that objective data (like enrollment figures) and the subjective experience of attending the school are both important to incoming students.

Sometimes, academic models are not useful because they are complicated and/or not relevant in real life in organizations. Wilbur's model is complicated, but it is worth deciphering because it forces people to discipline themselves when communicating information. To illustrate how using this model can improve communication in organizations, consider this example: Senior managers in the sales and marketing division of a company determine that in order to track costs more efficiently and effectively, a more rigorous process for tracking employee expenditures during business trips needs to be used. Managers purchase a software program that allows employees to input expense data on trips, including the specific type of expense (hotel, food, gas, etc.). Employees are trained and expected to use this new program to better track all expenses.

This new process is a big change for employees and for the company. Until the change, expenses had been managed with an honor system—employees could simply write a list of expenses and attach receipts (if they had them) at the end of the month, and they would be reimbursed. Now, they have to enter every last penny for others to monitor.

Six months into the program, the senior management team is meeting to discuss the effectiveness of the new expense-tracking process. Two of the managers are responsible for almost all of the employees who have to use the new system, and they have heard numerous complaints. They are quite sure that the process is doomed to fail, because "all" of the employees hate it. The two other managers on the team are from the finance department. They are delighted with the fact that they now have what they believe to be good information about expenses. It is easy to see how this team could argue endlessly about whether the new process is working or not.

Imagine if this team had organized their conversation by plotting the information they had in Wilbur's four quadrants. ■ **EXHIBIT 4.7** indicates what the information might look like.

Discussing what the management team knew about the employees' subjective experience, as well as the factual data about how well the program was working, would be a very different conversation than the "It's horrible" versus "It's fantastic" debate that might arise without this kind of analysis. For instance, the conversation could be focused on what certain individuals felt about the program (Box 1) and how the program did or did not jive with the culture of the organization (Box 2). The conversation could also include clear and specific information about the *facts* (Boxes 3 and 4): how individuals were actually using the program, and statistics about numbers of people using it, how often, and so forth. This conversation would more likely result in the discovery that there were mixed feelings about the system and that fixing some of the software glitches would help tremendously with the rollout.

So far, we have discussed what communication is and how people share thoughts, feelings, and information. Let's turn now to several models that researchers have developed to understand the interpersonal communication process.

■ **EXHIBIT 4.7**
Applying Wilbur's model to evaluate the new expense tracking system.

	Individual	Collective
Interior (Subjective)	"I do not feel trusted by my manager anymore" *or* "This system could help us, but it is not easy to use." **1**	Mixed feelings about the system: It violates some values (trust and trustworthiness) but supports others (commitment to accurate reporting of data). **2**
Exterior (Objective)	**3** Logs expenses once a month instead of every week as required.	**4** 60% compliance with turning expense reports in weekly; no data regarding how accurate the reports are.

Discussion Questions

1. Recall and explore a recent communication you have had with someone. Describe how you each attempted to maintain face and how you used positive and negative politeness in the interaction.

2. Consider a recent controversial situation at your school or workplace. Use Ken Wilbur's model to "plot" information about the problem, including your individual interior and exterior states (feelings and behavior) and interior and exterior information (culture and actual facts).

4. What Is the Interpersonal Communication Process?

Objective 4.4
Define the interpersonal communication process.

Most interpersonal communication models focus on how people send messages to receivers. In these models, a **sender** is a person who encodes and sends a **message** (information) through a communication channel to a **receiver**, a person who receives and decodes the message. A communication **channel** is the medium through which a message is transmitted from a sender to a receiver.

When communicating, you first choose a message to share with another person. Then, you translate that message into a shared language, some combination of words and nonverbal behavior that the receiver can comprehend. When you convert your thoughts and emotions into a message, you are encoding. **Encoding** is the process of converting information from one format into another before sending it. To illustrate encoding, imagine that you are watching a beautiful sunset and you want to communicate the experience. You have experienced visual stimuli, which you convert into words to describe the colors, the sun, the scenery—you have now *encoded* the message.

Sender
A person who encodes and sends a message.

Message
Information sent through a communication channel to a receiver.

Receiver
A person who receives and decodes a message.

Channel
The medium through which a message is transmitted from a sender to a receiver.

Source: Jose Luis Pelaez Inc/Alamy

Encoding
The process of converting information from one format into another before sending it.

Decoding
The process of converting information from one format into another in order to understand it.

Feedback
The process by which a receiver indicates to a sender through words or nonverbal signals that a message has been received or that more communication is desired.

Feedback loop
The process of sharing information back and forth between sender and receiver.

Noise
Anything that interferes with the transmission or receipt of a message.

Once you have encoded your message, you send it through a channel to a receiver. You (the sender) may choose to send your message about the sunset in a text message (the channel) to a friend (the receiver). When the message reaches the receiver, he or she attempts to interpret what the sender conveyed. This is called *decoding*. Decoding is the process of converting information from one format into another in order to understand it.

Feedback is the next step in the communication process (■ **EXHIBIT 4.8**). Feedback occurs when a receiver indicates to the sender through words or nonverbal signals that the message has been received or that more communication is desired. That message might be a simple confirmation that the original message was received—a nod, "mmhmm," a restatement of the message, or questions. A feedback loop is the process of sharing information back and forth between sender and receiver, and it is complete when both sender and receiver feel that the message has been fully conveyed and accurately interpreted.

Now that you understand the basic components of the communication process, we will explore three models of communication that attempt to explain exactly how the process works.

Models of Communication

The communication process has been studied extensively, and at least three different models are commonly used to help explain how it works. One early model is the Shannon-Weaver mathematical model, which is quite straightforward in that it shows communication to be a linear process.[31] The Schramm model builds on the Shannon-Weaver model by showing how communication is interactive.[32] Finally, Berlo's model includes complex factors, such as culture, as critical components of the communication process.[33] Each of these models is discussed next.

THE SHANNON-WEAVER MODEL OF COMMUNICATION

The Shannon-Weaver model was developed in 1948 and shows how information is encoded by a sender, transmitted through a channel, and decoded by a receiver.[34] The model points out how messages can be misinterpreted due to noise. Noise is anything that interferes with the transmission or receipt of a message (■ **EXHIBIT 4.9**). Noise can be outside sounds; it can also be things like mumbling, poor grammar, or body language that does not fit the spoken words. To lessen the impact of noise, we need to learn how to listen—really listen—to the messages people are trying to share with us.

The original Shannon-Weaver model shows communication flowing in one direction, from sender to receiver. This model has been criticized because it is not representative of the way humans actually communicate, which is not strictly linear and is influenced by many other factors in addition to noise.[35] The model also does not indicate how people distinguish important ideas from those that lack value, or nonsense.[36] Later models attempted to compensate for these shortcomings by showing communication as bidirectional.

THE SCHRAMM MODEL OF COMMUNICATION

In 1954, communication studies pioneer Wilbur Schramm introduced a simple model of communication that emphasized the interactive nature of the communication

■ **EXHIBIT 4.9**
Interpersonal communication is enriched when "noise" is minimized and people can fully express themselves to one another.

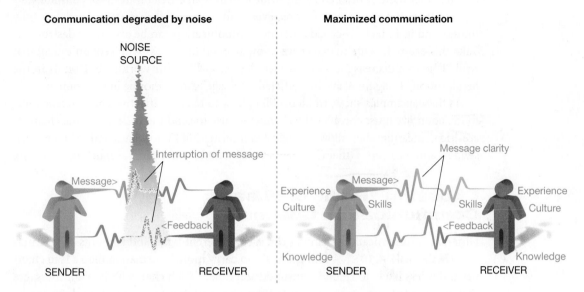

| Communication degraded by noise | Maximized communication |

process. Rather than a simple unidirectional model from sender to receiver, the Schramm model showed communication as a bidirectional (although still linear) process.[37]

THE BERLO MODEL OF COMMUNICATION

In 1960, David Berlo offered a model of communication that elaborated on the process of encoding and decoding messages.[38] The advantage of the Berlo model over the other two is that it recognizes the importance of communication skills, attitudes, knowledge, society, and culture in both encoding and decoding messages.

All three of these models attempt to explain how we send and receive messages, what can get in the way, and how best to understand one another. Let's now look at effective and efficient communication and at how the complexity, or richness, of the message and channel can affect the communication process.

Effective and Efficient Communication

Effective communication is the result of information conveyed accurately by the sender and understood fully by the receiver. When communication is not effective, the consequences can be disastrous. For example, consider the burning of the Quran and other Muslim holy books at a U.S. military base in Afghanistan in February 2012. The books were pulled from the Parwan Detention Facility library because handwritten notes in their margins were presumably used by detainees to exchange messages. The books were boxed up and scheduled for proper disposal. Instead, the boxes were picked up by a garbage detail and taken to a refuse burning pit. Afghan workers noticed the books being placed in the fire and pulled some of them from the flames. Violent protests over the incident led to the deaths of thirty Afghanis and six U.S. soldiers.[39] Investigations of the incident yielded differing accounts that increased tensions between U.S. and Afghan officials. Although ineffective communication does not always lead to such horrific outcomes, it can lead to poor performance, unhappy employees, and disappointed customers. Good communicators make sure their audience understands their messages by soliciting and listening to feedback to ensure full understanding.

Sharing information using the fewest possible resources (time, money, and effort) is considered **efficient communication**. Although we should all endeavor to achieve both, effective communication and efficient communication are often in conflict. For

Effective communication
The result of information conveyed accurately by the sender and understood fully by the receiver.

Efficient communication
Sharing information using the fewest possible resources (time, money, and effort).

example, when managers talk directly and personally with people, the communication is more likely to be effective, but it can be extremely time consuming and inefficient. On the other hand, a brief company-wide e-mail is an efficient means of communicating, but there is no guarantee that receivers will even read the message, much less fully understand it. In fact, so-called efficient communication can be extremely destructive. Take this example: One manager we know worked for a boss who sent an e-mail that read "Due to a decrease in sales, we will lay off 20% of our workforce. Donuts in the break room!" Imagine what this "efficient message" did to morale in the company.

As these examples show, when deciding how to balance effective and efficient communication, we must consider the channel we use to send the message. Some channels are "rich," meaning they allow complicated information to flow back and forth between senders and receivers. Other channels are "lean" and cannot carry as much information.

Choosing "Rich" or "Lean" Communication Channels

Different communication channels can carry different types and amounts of information (■ **EXHIBIT 4.10**).[40] A rich channel can carry more information than a lean channel and is less likely to result in misunderstanding.[41] Rich channels allow for messages that are targeted to a specific receiver, offer opportunities for feedback, and can incorporate a full range of verbal and nonverbal signals, all of which help a receiver achieve full understanding. Rich channels are often used to send messages that are not routine, are emotionally charged, or may be confusing.

EXHIBIT 4.10
Rich and lean communication channels.

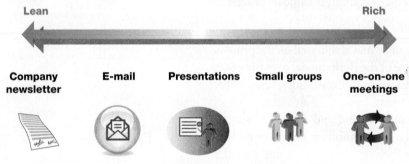

Lean   Rich

Company newsletter   E-mail   Presentations   Small groups   One-on-one meetings

The richest channel is face-to-face communication in pairs or small groups. In such settings, nonverbal communication is possible and feedback can be fluid. There are many good reasons why a manager will choose a one-on-one conversation over other options. Communication about poor work performance, for instance, is a highly personal and sensitive topic that could result in miscommunication or a damaged relationship if handled using a lean channel like a performance-review form. Imagine finding out that your boss is unhappy with your performance by seeing he's rated you a "2" on a five-point scale. Without rich communication, this message can be confusing and very destructive. Sensitive and complex messages are best handled using rich channels like face-to-face discussions, video conferencing, or possibly the telephone.

Videoconferencing and the telephone are fairly rich communication channels. Videoconferences can potentially distort or hide body language, but they can save a company money and time if people are far away from one another. A telephone conversation removes body language from the communication process, but because it allows for intonation and pacing, it retains some of the advantages of the richer face-to-face communication channel. Other types of oral communication slide further along the spectrum from rich to lean. Presentations are less personalized than interactive meetings, and the feedback loop may be somewhat more constrained. On the other hand, presentations allow a sender to reach a wider audience while keeping some of the advantages of face-to-face communication (e.g., the presenter can use body language).

On the leaner end of the spectrum are different forms of written communication. Written personal communication has the advantage that messages can be tailored to specific receivers. However, e-mails, letters, and personalized memos, the most common forms of written personal communication, lack many signals that are associated with oral channels (e.g., nonverbal signals), and feedback can be difficult, slow, or even impossible. Still, the targeted nature of the message and the low resource cost make written personal communication an appropriate channel when we need to efficiently convey simple information to specific individuals.

The leanest of all possible channels is impersonal written communication, such as a company newsletter, which lacks nonverbal signals and a feedback loop, and is tailored for a large audience. It is probably the best way to communicate messages that are fairly straightforward and do not justify the more intensive use of time or other resources.

Communication channels and models are important to understand because they help explain the interpersonal communication process. These concepts were originally developed to explain direct, spoken communication or written communication that was shared on paper. The onset of technology, however, has led to a vast expansion in the various ways we can communicate through writing, video images, and the spoken word. We will explore the role of technology at work in depth in Chapter 11; in the following sections, we will consider how it is affecting communication at work.

Discussion Questions

1. How do you give feedback during a conversation? Do you provide it face-to-face or some other way? Are you aware of how you use body language? Do you ask questions? Do you restate what have you heard? Do you talk about an experience that is similar to what you have heard? How effective are your methods?

2. In general, a rich communication channel is considered superior for accurate communication. Come up with three examples in which a lean channel is more effective for specific purposes. Share the three examples you identify with a classmate and discuss.

---

5. How Do We Use Information Technology to Communicate at Work?

In 1855, the U.S. Congress authorized a study on the use of camels to transport mail from Texas to California. This method didn't work well. Stagecoaches were much better, and they could get mail across the country in less than 30 days, weather permitting. Then came the first rapid communication system in the United States: the Pony Express. The Pony Express was a mail delivery system that used horses to travel the nearly 2,000 miles from Missouri to California in only a few days. A rested horse was used at each 10-mile interval, and riders were changed every 100 miles. It was a marvel of ingenuity that lasted for 18 months, when it was replaced by the transcontinental telegraph.[42]

Advances in technology are constantly changing the way we communicate in our lives and at work. We now communicate with people we may never meet in person, getting to know them professionally and personally. Even language barriers are breaking down with the advent of portable, handheld electronic translation dictionaries and Internet translation services. Technology has also placed pressure on us to develop new rules and conventions for proper communication behavior. For instance, many companies have guidelines for how to use e-mail and social networking, while text messaging has developed its own language system.[43]

E-Mail and Text Messaging

E-mail and text messaging make it possible to quickly communicate in writing over long distances.[44] The benefits are obvious: We can share ideas in real time with people who are far away, who can then provide feedback and build on our ideas. Many people have migrated from communicating with friends and family via e-mail to text

...rk, however, e-mail is still king. Most people use it constantly, and it ...earn how to use it professionally: E-mails should include pleasant and ...al greetings and closures; accurate grammar, sentence structure, and ...n appropriate amount of information.

...e-mail and text messages presents challenges as well:

- ...s in e-mail messages can be hard to interpret and/or inflammatory.
- ...e little tolerance for long e-mails, which means that vital information is often ...itten or not read.
- ...out an immediate response, a sender may jump to conclusions that are ...curate.[45]
- ...nail invites people to be lazy communicators: "Forward" and "cc" are shortcuts ...ople often overuse.
- ...-mail and text messages are not private and can be monitored and retrieved by ...employers or other authorities.[46]

Web Conferencing and Videoconferencing

Web conferencing connects people by phone or video, while simultaneously enabling all participants to view the same documents online and sometimes to work on documents together. Early versions of web and videoconferencing technology required expensive equipment, specialized technicians, and a special location. Today, any individual with a webcam and Internet service can connect with others who have the same tools. Both web and videoconferencing are richer communication channels than e-mail—they allow for more sharing of contextual information and emotion, and more access to nonverbal behavior.

Organizations are using these and other new technologies in ever more creative ways, revolutionizing how people communicate at work. The following *Business Case* shows how IBM was an early adopter of new technologies. They used a "virtual world" to share information and build effective working relationships among employees and technology experts.

The benefits of this type of virtual world communication were revolutionary in 2008. Now, these and other technologies are becoming more common. But what are the risks?

BUSINESS CASE   IBM

IBM and Second Life

In 2008, IBM held a three-day conference for more than 200 participants. This was not a typical conference. The venue was futuristic—almost surreal. There were no drinks or snacks, or even a restroom. The attendees were dressed casually. Most unusual, however, was that there were no "people" at the conference. Instead, IBM employees and others participated in the conference virtually through their avatars in a secure *Second Life* environment.

Second Life, which is a virtual world created by Linden Lab, provided IBM with the virtual space for their conference.[47] The environment allowed people to interact through their avatars, attend keynote speeches and breakout sessions, visit a library, and gather as a community. The format was not entirely new

to IBM—the company had been experimenting with the *Second Life* environment as a way to conduct employee orientation sessions and other events.[48] The size, scope, and complexity of this conference, however, was impressive.[49]

The conference used virtual social networking technology to bring large numbers of leaders together to talk, share information, learn from one another, and build relationships—all from the comfort of their own offices. The conference was an opportunity to gain inspiration and practical knowledge about the impact of virtual reality on communication and relationships between and among people in organizations. There was also a financial benefit—bringing people together without incurring travel expenses represents a significant cost-saving approach to organization-wide communication and collaboration.[50]

Can people communicate fully in such a world? Will individuals who are adept at maneuvering their avatars have richer communication opportunities than those who are not as technically proficient? Is there a hidden time cost in creating "good" avatars that are capable of representing people and employees as they really are? Who controls the environment? HR? Managers? Employees themselves? Are there any rules and, if so, what are they? These questions and many others need to be addressed in order for these technologies to be successfully integrated into the business environment on a large scale.

Let's now look at one technology that most of us are using—social networking.

Social Networking

Social networks such as Facebook and LinkedIn and communication outlets such as Twitter allow us to stay connected and receive real-time updates on a continuous basis. This means that our friends, family, and colleagues, and even our favorite businesses, celebrities, and news are more accessible to us than ever before. It also enables us to share important information about what's going on in our own lives—from promotions to new parenthood—quickly and easily. An amazing 845 million people used Facebook in 2011: That's about one in every 13 people in the world![51]

In spite of the overwhelming popularity and convenience of these outlets, some experts fear that they do not encourage us to develop deep bonds with others or allow us to show our authentic selves. Jaron Lanier, the author of *You Are Not a Gadget*, writes, "I fear that we are beginning to design ourselves to suit digital models of us, and I worry about a leaching of empathy and humanity in that process."[52] Lanier suggests that the carefully curated personas we present in our digital profiles allow us to masquerade as the people who we wish we were—rather than who we actually are—and lead to a preoccupation with ourselves that makes it difficult for us to engage with those around us. One way that this has become a particular—and dangerous—problem is when young children masquerade as being much older. Another problem is that some people use social media as a way to communicate things they don't have the courage to say in person—like breaking up with a boyfriend or girlfriend. And, of course, some people simply masquerade as someone entirely different from themselves, deceiving others and engaging in unethical—even illegal—behavior.

Studies also suggest that while people communicate more often and with more people than ever before through the use of social networks, they are plagued by loneliness. Research indicates that roughly 20 percent of Americans are unhappy with their lives because of loneliness—that's nearly 60 million people.[53] This problem is not unique to the U.S.; health care professionals across the Western world are becoming concerned about the increasing loneliness and isolation of their patients.

Whether a link exists between social networking and loneliness is unclear, as is the nature of that potential link. What is certain is that social networking has become a big part of many of our lives and is changing the way we communicate with one another. Like any other type of communication, social networking can fall victim to common communication barriers. In the next section, we will consider these barriers in detail, look at how they affect our interactions with others, and explore ways to minimize their impact.

Discussion Questions

1. Consider two situations: one in which information technology helped you build a relationship, and one in which it inhibited the development of a relationship. How did technology help in the first instance and get in the way in the second?

2. Many argue that new communication technologies have made social interactions impersonal and that people are not developing enough face-to-face communication skills. What is your opinion on this topic?

Objective 4.6
Define the common barriers
to effective communication.

6. What Are Common Barriers to Effective Communication?

Communication is anything but simple. To be effective, we must try to overcome some of the most common communication barriers. The first barrier we will explore in this section is how language itself can inhibit communication. Then we will examine poor communication skills as well as how misunderstandings occur due to people's biases. We will also consider the role that power and authority play in communication at work.

When Language Gets in the Way of Communication

In many companies today, employees do not share the same native language. Most companies adopt one language as the standard and expect senior-level managers and executives to be fluent in that language. Although this seems reasonable, it is far easier said than done. Even when people are considered fluent in a second language, large differences exist in how well they understand the more nuanced aspects of the language, such as emotional expression or or even stories.

Globalization and migration have produced an increasingly diverse workforce, and language barriers are clearly one potential area of difficulty. Without a shared language, communication can be difficult, even harmful. For example, a pair of researchers describe the following encounter between a Japanese manager and an American employee at an automotive factory. The Japanese manager, noticing that the employee was a very hard worker, attempted to translate a common phrase of encouragement ("gambatte, kudasai"), but what actually came out was "You must work harder." The hard-working American employee was, understandably, quite upset.[54]

In this and countless other situations, literal or near literal translations rarely work or lose a great deal of meaning from one culture to another. This can result in serious misunderstandings. Another source of misunderstanding is the use of humor across cultural boundaries. Humor is tied to culture and not easily translated. People can easily miss jokes and feel left out.

You might be saying to yourself, "Why don't they just get an electronic translator?" That is a good idea, and it can help. But, these devices provide a literal translation and a literal translation rarely works for complex messages. Languages represent cultures, so words translated literally often mean something entirely different in another language. For example, when Kentucky Fried Chicken entered the Chinese market, they discovered that their slogan "finger lickin' good" came out as "eat your fingers off."[55]

Several other common barriers to communication are linked to language. First, it can be challenging for people to get used to one another's accents. Second, native speakers tend to speak their own language quickly and often violate rules of grammar and pronunciation. For example, Americans often drop the "g" in words ending in "ing" and combine the sounds of one word with those of the next (e.g., "going to" becomes "gonna," "should have" becomes "shoulda"). This can make it difficult for nonnative speakers to follow a conversation. Third, it is tiresome for people to speak a second language all day, because doing so takes intense concentration.

DIALECTS

Problems can also arise when people speak the same native language but use different dialects. A dialect can be a form of language spoken in a particular region, such as Southern English in the United States or the variants of English used in the five different boroughs of New York City.[56]

A dialect may also be spoken by people who are from the same socioeconomic background. For example, William Labov studied language differences in a New York department store, showing that different dialects were used, depending in part on the socioeconomic status of the speaker(s).[57] Dialects also exist among racial and ethnic groups.

Besides the dialects that can be found within a country, dialects exist across countries that share the same language. For example, the Spanish spoken in Madrid is different from that spoken in Mexico, and there are significant differences between the English dialects in the United States, England, Australia, India, and South Africa (■ **EXHIBIT 4.11**).

EXHIBIT 4.11
What is the man on the left doing (hint: he is not rowing a boat)? What is the man on the right doing?*

Source: Left: Chris Ballentine/Alamy; Right: Dennis MacDonald/Alamy

*Answer: They are both punting.

JARGON: A SHORTCUT TO COMMUNICATION THAT CAN BACKFIRE

Another language barrier at work is entirely of our own making: Many professions and organizations develop their own sublanguage, called jargon. **Jargon** is terminology that has been specifically defined in relation to certain activities, professions, or groups. Depending on the technicality of the jargon, it may be nearly impossible for a person outside the group or field to understand.[58] Typical examples are the medical jargon that doctors, nurses, and health care workers use; the legal jargon lawyers use; and the financial jargon stock market analysts use.

This textbook is introducing you to managerial jargon, which can be useful in communicating with others in the fields of management, strategy, and leadership. However, you may be greeted with quizzical looks if you try to use the same terms when speaking to friends. Common jargon in business includes the term *sacred cows*, which refers to

Jargon
Terminology that has been specifically defined in relation to certain activities, professions, or groups.

people, products, or processes that cannot be changed, and *C-suite*, which refers to the people who hold the top offices in a company, such as the chief executive officer and the chief financial officer.

In addition to jargon, people in companies often adopt acronyms as shortcuts to describe what they do or how they do it. An acronym is an abbreviation of a phrase that uses the first letter of every word. For example, *ASAP* is an acronym for "as soon as possible," and *JIT* stands for "just in time," which describes a specific type of inventory control process. *SOPs* is an acronym for "standard operating procedures," which are rules for how things must be done. Teams and divisions in organizations are often referred to by acronyms, such as when the senior executive team is called the *EC*, for "Executive Committee," or when human resources is referred to as *HR*.

Language matters at work. As a manager—or an employee, for that matter—it is important to remember that language can foster inclusion or exclusion.[59] Languages that are limited to a small group (such as jargon, dialects, or a language spoken only by executives) can cause company-wide problems. In contrast, language can be a unifying force—when people share the same language and use it well, they can share information smoothly and effectively.

Poor Communication: It Happens Too Often!

Sadly, many people are very poor communicators. Let's look at some reasons why, starting with the basics. Competent communicators know the rules of grammar, express thoughts clearly and concisely, use adequate and situationally appropriate vocabulary, and express emotion appropriately. Competence includes knowledge of the rules of conversation, such as when to talk and how much to say.[60]

Poor communication skills can often hurt an otherwise well-crafted message. Remember that it is the sender's job to encode a message in a way that has meaning for the audience. We need to learn how to express our thoughts, opinions, and feelings in words that others can understand. We also need to organize our ideas in a way that others can follow. Too simple or too complex a vocabulary can be a barrier to communication, depending on the audience. How can you decide what to say and how to say it? That's where empathy comes in: Many barriers to communication can be avoided by simply reading one's audience accurately.

Grammar, spelling, and professional communication are important. An e-mail that is filled with misspellings, errors in grammar, and missing punctuation will hurt the credibility of the writer and force readers to struggle to understand. Speakers who mumble or mispronounce words create similar difficulties for their listeners. People who interrupt others can also harm the communication process and whether written, spoken, or signed, a message that is missing important information or simply does not make sense is highly problematic at work.

It's also up to receivers to ensure that barriers to communication are minimized. In particular, when we are receiving messages, we can avoid all sorts of communication problems if we simply *listen*. People speak at 125 to 175 words per minute, but we can listen intelligently to 400 to 800 words per minute.[61] Because of the difference between how fast we can send information versus how fast we can receive it, it is easy for us to let our minds wander and think about other things when someone is talking. The cure for this is to *pay attention* to the person. Watch for things like nonverbal behavior, cultural information, and emotional expressions.[62]

Good listening is also supported by mentally summarizing the main points, exploring what the person is sharing, generating a few explanations about the message, and determining what other information would be useful.[63] These activities take

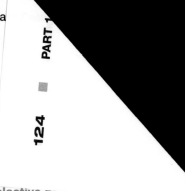

concentration and effort. It's worth it though, because poor listening can be a barrier to understanding a message. So can biases and stereotyping.

Selective Perception and Stereotyping: The Enemies of Communication

Both senders and receivers can hurt communication process by relying on personal biases when encoding or decoding messages. For example, we sometimes pick and choose what to pay attention to. This is called **selective perception**. Selective perception is consciously or unconsciously focusing on certain parts of a message and ignoring others. When people do this, they may only pay attention to the information that they consider most interesting or that supports their beliefs. Or, they may pay more attention to negative or threatening aspects of a message and miss everything else. We all do this—it's related to how we mentally process information. It can be dangerous when it supports biases that interfere with communication and relationships. For example, suppose your manager says, "I really appreciate what you have done this week. You really hit the ball out of the park. There's one small thing I'd like you to fix, though—that last section of the report still isn't quite accurate. I'll need you to take another crack at it." If you are like many people, you will completely ignore the praise and focus on the criticism. This may be a serious misinterpretation of the manager's message. Your inaccurate interpretation is linked to your bias—in this case, to focus on negative feedback.

Selective perception can reinforce stereotypes. **Stereotypes** are rigid and often negative biases used to describe or judge individuals based on their membership in a social group. Selective perception and stereotyping are often linked to **prejudice**, or an irrational, often hostile attitude of hostility based on a person's membership in a particular group. For example, a young manager who believes that older workers are resistant to change might notice each and every time an older person argues about a new idea and completely miss the fact that this happens only about one in ten times. As this situation illustrates, when communication involves stereotypes, valuable information is lost, twisted, or otherwise compromised.

Poor listening, selective perception, stereotyping, and prejudices are somewhat obvious barriers to communication. In organizations, we face another barrier that is less obvious but also a problem: the impact of power dynamics on communication.

The Interaction of Communication and Power

Communication is affected by the amount of power senders and receivers have and the organizational roles they occupy.[64] For example, if a peer whom you like and trust says, "I'm not sure the spreadsheet you showed me was your best work" you are likely to interpret this message as honest and helpful. If your manager says the same thing you may interpret the message very differently. You might interpret it as criticism, as a threat, or as a veiled message about your overall performance. Your interpretations in these examples would be based in part on the power relationships between you and your peer and you and your manager. Going back to the example of the manager's comment, you may feel fearful and become defensive. Conveying this to your manager verbally or nonverbally could cause him to wonder what's wrong with you—and communication spirals downward from there.

Managing your reaction to power in the communication exchange requires self-awareness and self-management. When you understand your visceral response to powerful people, you are more likely to respond so that the relationship remains healthy. Likewise, when you have power, it is wise to remember that "your whisper is

Selective perception
Consciously or unconsciously focusing on certain parts of a message and ignoring others.

Stereotypes
Rigid and often negative biases used to describe or judge individuals based on their membership in a social group.

Prejudice
An irrational attitude of hostility based on a person's membership in a particular group.

heard as a shout." By understanding this, you can consciously manage how you communicate so you are less likely to spark a negative or fearful response.

Power can be used as a means to control different elements of the communication process, including who is allowed to send and receive information. Power is also important because it often determines which communication networks you participate in. For example, senior managers often have access to information that others do not. But power isn't only related to formal roles and hierarchy—power can be linked to social groups as well.

In many organizations, people who are similar to one another along certain demographic lines (e.g., culture, race, gender, or ethnicity) are often members of the same communication networks. These social networks are often seen as more or less powerful, and in turn more or less entitled to have access to certain kinds of information. This means that access to ideas or information can be dependent on being of a particular class, race, gender, or ethnicity.[65] At their worst, these networks are closed—unless you are part of the group, you don't have access to the group's information. This is problematic in organizations, of course, and many companies are doing their utmost to ensure communication flows freely based on organizational needs, not group membership.[66] However, closed networks of powerful people who share the same interests still exist, and business gets done when these people come together to pursue those interests.

Closed networks of powerful people have often been called the "old boys' club." In the past, and even today, women, people of color, and other "outsiders" were not welcome in these networks, which meant these people were excluded from important business conversations. For instance, Catalyst, a well-respected research firm focused on women in the workforce, found that female executives in the twenty-first century are still excluded from powerful informal networks.[67] Additionally, recent research in a study of 1500 top organizations found that in 2009, less than a quarter of the companies had a woman in the top five executive positions. The study also found that when women join boards of directors, more women are seen on senior teams within a very short period of time. This suggests that board membership is a critical first step to increasing the numbers of women in senior executive positions.[68]

Power is one aspect of diversity and inclusion in organizations, but it is by no means the only dimension that affects communication. In the next section, we will explore both the challenges and the opportunities of communication in a socially diverse workplace.

Discussion Questions

1. Do find yourself sometimes engaging in selective perception? What sorts of topics (e.g., politics, religion) or situations (e.g., conflicts, close relationships) cause you to pay more attention to certain things and less to others? While selective perception is usually considered "bad," can you think of some potential benefits?

2. Reflect on powerful people you know personally—either formal leaders or those who have informal power, such as popular people. How would you describe the way that you react to them and to their power and how you communicate with them? How do they communicate with you?

Objective 4.7
Analyze the challenges in communicating in a socially diverse society.

7. Why Is It Challenging to Communicate in a Socially Diverse World?

One of the major challenges to communication arises from one of the greatest *benefits* of a globalized world: diversity in the workforce. Let's look at how better communication can enhance the other inclusion aspect of the diversity equation (■ **EXHIBIT 4.12**).

Communication and Culture

Many aspects of culture affect communication in a diverse workforce. Of these, nonverbal communication, group identity and issues related to gender and age are especially important.

NONVERBAL BEHAVIOR IN CROSS-CULTURAL COMMUNICATION

Acceptable nonverbal behavior differs from one culture to another.[69] A failure to recognize differences in nonverbal cues in cross-cultural communication can produce unfortunate misunderstandings. Something as simple as shaking hands, for example, requires different techniques as one goes from country to country, and it is completely inappropriate in some parts of the world. The "thumbs up" sign and the "OK" sign used in the United States are considered obscene gestures in some countries. Avoiding direct eye contact with strangers is the norm in many countries, such as Japan, while doing so in the United States may result in people viewing you as shifty or untrustworthy.

■ **EXHIBIT 4.12**
What communication challenges do you face in a diverse world?

Source: Pictor International/Alamy

People in different cultures also have varied expectations about personal space. The study of personal space in social interactions was made popular by the anthropologist Edward Hall.[70] People in the United States, England, and other western countries claim a greater amount of personal space and largely avoid touching; this is not the case in countries such as Turkey and India. Cross-cultural training in global business is largely the result of findings in Hall's pioneering work.[71]

Nonverbal behavior has obvious links to culture and needs to be attended to and managed in cross-cultural settings. Other cross-cultural differences may be less obvious, such as the importance of group identity. Now we will turn our attention to a framework that examines how the strength of group identity affects communication styles.

COMMUNICATION IN HIGH-CONTEXT AND LOW-CONTEXT CULTURES

According to Edward Hall, some cultures are "high-context" and others are "low-context."[72] A high-context culture is one in which there is a strong group identity and a relatively closed boundary. High-context cultures rely on shared history and shared views that can be difficult for outsiders to understand. This can make cross-cultural communication difficult. In a low-context culture, it is easier for outsiders to communicate with insiders because there is less emphasis on shared history and identity. But, in a low-context culture a sense of group identity and team spirit can be absent.

There are benefits to each type of culture, of course. Communication can be easy within high-context cultures because everyone understands some basics—values, norms, beliefs. In low-context cultures, new ideas are more readily accepted.

Communication in diverse groups is complex, and it can be difficult. It is essential, however, that we learn how to do it effectively because today's organizations are diverse, as are customers, consumers, and clients. According to David Thomas, Dean and Chair of Georgetown University's McDonough School of Business, diversity will be the core of successful organizational strategies, and it takes dedication and commitment to ensure that people can communicate effectively and succeed in these organizations.[73] We must remember, however, that diversity does not just apply to people of different cultural backgrounds; it also applies to people of different genders and ages.

■ **EXHIBIT 4.13**

What are some ways in which men and women communicate differently?

Source: WavebreakMediaMicro/Fotolia LLC

Yes, Men and Women Communicate Differently

When it comes to communication, it can seem like men and women come from different planets. And, yes, gender does impact communication (■ **EXHIBIT 4.13**). A great deal of research has been done on the differences between men's and women's communication preferences—and even more speculation about it has appeared in popular books, magazines, and the Internet.[74]

Before looking at the research about gender communication, let's remember that communication is *learned*; women and men are not born communicating differently. Let's look at what some research says about common gender-related tendencies.

Men and women often approach the communication process with distinct sets of values and intentions.[75] Generally speaking, men tend to assert independence, and they use communication to define their status relative to others. Women tend to seek connections, and they are more oriented to the types of communication that support relationships.[76]

How do these differences translate into specific communication preferences? Men are more likely to assert ownership and avoid asking questions or offering apologies for fear of admitting weakness or fault. Men may also be more likely to offer candid and direct feedback. Conversely, women are less likely to boast, and they are more likely to admit uncertainty, apologize, and temper their communication with positive feedback.[77] There are pluses and minuses in all of these tendencies.

Robin Lakoff, one of the first scholars to closely examine gender and language, notes that the way women are talked about, as well as the way they are expected to speak, reflect attitudes that marginalize women.[78] Social training in how to use language begins in early childhood, when girls are expected to speak politely—to talk like ladies—rather than use the rough or crude language boys are often allowed to use. Girls are also socialized to use language that expresses uncertainty, such as phrasing statements as questions.[79] Deborah Tannen, another leading scholar, says that girls learn that sounding too sure of themselves may make them unpopular, whereas boys are allowed to use language to promote their status.[80] Boys and girls also learn that girls should not be as aggressive as their male counterparts.

Although women are increasingly taking on top management roles, management scholar Judith Oakley notes that different behaviors are expected of women in "behavioral double binds."[81] A double bind is when we expect something of a person, and then when he or she does it, we criticize him or her. For example, in many industries senior leaders are expected to be assertive, competitive, and aggressive. Yet, women who act this way are often severely criticized by male and female peers, direct reports, and bosses.

Expectations are changing, however, in part because there is a growing realization that the communication strengths associated with women are actually the behaviors most needed in today's organizations. Competencies linked to cooperation, flexibility, empathy, and relationship skills are seen as assets in a global marketplace.[82]

Just as it is important to recognize that there are differences in how men and women communicate, it is also essential to avoid treating these differences as absolutes or unchangeable patterns.[83] Doing so only results in stereotyping, which you will recall undermines our ability to communicate effectively. Your job, no matter if you're a man or a woman, is to learn how to communicate effectively. That may mean going beyond gender-related tendencies and learning new communication skills.

Communication and the Age Factor

Like other cultural barriers, differences related to age and membership in different generations has the potential to interfere with communication in the workplace. A young worker who assumes that an older worker is unwilling to listen to her ideas is as guilty of stereotyping as the older worker who believes that all young people have a sense of entitlement.

To illustrate, let's look at Millenials and Baby Boomers. Baby Boomers are members of the generation born after WWII—between approximately 1945 and 1960. Millennials are members of the generation born between approximately 1981 and 2000.[84] They have entered the workforce in vast numbers—making their mark on work and society in much the same way the Baby Boomers did in the 1960s and 1970s.

According to many scholars, the Baby Boomers and Millennials have some difficulties communicating with one another.[85] Millennials tend to value directness more than previous generations and look for clear, candid communication and more frequent feedback. Millennials also want more flexibility to work and communicate in ways that are comfortable to them, are accustomed to using technology to communicate, and are more likely to favor electronic communication over face-to-face communication.

A frequent complaint Boomers make about Millennials is that Millennials have a sense of entitlement and don't want to work or put in the hours and years it takes to succeed. But a recent study found that despite their ambition and the directness of their communication, Millennial workers are aware of the limits to their competence and are realistic about the qualities that are important in today's workplace.[86]

In this section you have learned about the challenges and opportunities that are inherent in communication within and among socially diverse groups. It is an exciting time to learn how to communicate effectively in our complex and diverse world. Organizations must also adjust for a new world and new ways to share and disseminate information.

Discussion Questions

1. Consider a group that you have worked with that is socially or otherwise diverse. Take a close look: Were there barriers to communication? What were these barriers? How did the group overcome them? How did the group's diversity enrich communication?

2. Have you noticed how your age or gender affects the way you communicate or the way others communicate with you? Describe and explain.

---

8. What Is Organizational Communication?

Objective 4.8
Define organizational communication.

So far in this chapter we have focused largely on interpersonal communication—how thoughts and emotions travel from one person or group to another. In organizations, communication must flow among many people and in many directions using a variety of channels simultaneously. This section we will explore how communication happens within organizations, including direction of communication flow, communication networks, formal versus informal communication, and communication during crises. We will conclude the section with an exploration of a powerful tool for communication within organizations: storytelling.

Downward communication
The flow of information from higher in an organizational hierarchy to lower.

■ **EXHIBIT 4.14**
An example of downward communication is when a manager shares information with her team.

Manager

Employees

Upward communication
The flow of information from lower in an organizational hierarchy to higher.

Filtering
The deliberate miscommunication of information, including changing the information or modifying, eliminating, or enhancing particular parts of a message.

Horizontal communication
The flow of information between individuals at the same or similar levels of an organizational hierarchy.

Internal communication
Communication within the structure of an organization.

External communication
Communication between members of an organization with people on the outside.

Communication network
The pattern of communication among a group of people.

Wheel network (hub-and-spoke network)
A communication network in which one person acts as a central conduit for all information.

Direction of Communication Flow

Communication moves in many directions in an organization: up, down, across, and back again. Consider a manager who directs employees to complete a market research project. The employees divide up the work, complete their tasks, prepare a report, and submit the results to the manager, who may pass it further up in the organization.

In this example, information flows in several directions, accomplishing several goals. The project begins with downward communication (■ **EXHIBIT 4.14**), which is the flow of information from higher in an organizational hierarchy to lower. Downward communication within an organization is often a manager giving direction, providing information, or offering feedback to subordinates.

Upward communication is the flow of information from lower in an organizational hierarchy to higher. In this example the report was given to the manager. Upward communication can be damaged when people filter information as it is shared up the hierarchy.

Filtering is the deliberate miscommunication of information, including changing the information or modifying, eliminating, or enhancing particular parts of a message. Why do people filter information? Filtering information is often done because people are frightened about sharing the whole truth with managers or because they are attempting to further a particular agenda. Sometimes, we filter messages by telling people what we think they want to hear.

People who filter information might fear that the recipient will "shoot the messenger" or that they will have to admit their mistakes. Maybe they want to keep the boss happy. Whatever the reason, filtered messages are almost always inaccurate and often just plain wrong. To discourage filtering, managers and leaders need to create a level of trust between themselves and workers, ensure that communication channels are open and easily accessible, and discourage a culture that allows people to further individual agendas at the expense of others or the organization.

Organizations also depend on horizontal communication, which is the flow of information between individuals at the same or similar levels of an organizational hierarchy. In the example, information would have been shared horizontally within the team (■ **EXHIBIT 4.15**). In the course of their work, people often need to coordinate or collaborate with team members or other colleagues. Horizontal communication is not confined to lower-level employees. Leaders also depend on horizontal communication to coordinate projects, share work, or consult with fellow managers.

Information discussed so far in this section has been about internal communication, or communication within an organization. External communication, which is communication between members of an organization with people on the outside, is also a critical component of effective organizational communication.

■ **EXHIBIT 4.15**
Horizontal communication is the flow of information between people.

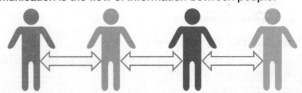

Organizational Communication Networks

Both internal and external communication can be categorized by the pattern, or communication network, through which information flows.

A wheel network is sometimes called a **hub-and-spoke network** (■ **EXHIBIT 4.16**). In this type of network, one person acts as a central conduit for all information. In the previous example, the manager who directed employees was at the center of a wheel network. This arrangement can be very efficient, because one person controls the flow of information. However, it can also hinder collaboration among team members or cause a bottleneck has to pass through the manager.

Another familiar pattern of communication is the **chain network** (▪ **EXHIBIT 4.17**), in which information passes in an organized sequence from one person to the next. Communication in a chain network often moves upward or downward in a specific order according to hierarchical relationships. Because each person has to wait for someone else to do his or her part, it can be an inefficient way to communicate. The clear structure, however, makes the communication process easy to manage because information flows along a clearly defined linear path. Bureaucracies often rely on chain networks.

▪ **EXHIBIT 4.17**
A chain network is one in which information passes in an organized sequence from one person to the next.

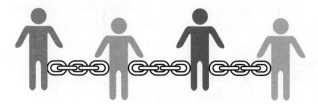

The **all-channel network** is one in which all members of a group communicate with everyone else as needed for maximum flow of information (▪ **EXHIBIT 4.18**). This can be both helpful and challenging. Because many people are involved, the network structure can result in a high level of employee commitment and engagement—people feel that their contributions are valued. If ideas do indeed flow freely, this network can be highly effective and even efficient. However, it is equally likely that this network will be inefficient, because information can flow in a chaotic manner.

Formal vs. Informal Communication

The structure of an organization and its communication network often defines how formal communication should occur—who talks to whom about what, when, where, and how. **Formal communication** is communication governed by known rules about who can communicate with whom and how they should do it. Formal communication is usually linked to the formal power relationships within the hierarchy. Examples of situations in which formal communication often occurs include performance reviews, directives from HR about labor policies, scheduled project updates (meetings or e-mail), and e-mails, memos, or webcasts to all employees about organizational changes.

Informal communication is communication that moves through channels other than those that have been explicitly defined within an organization. Informal communication is usually linked to social networks outside the formal organizational structure. Co-workers sitting in the company cafeteria who casually discuss recent changes in an organization and the manager who runs into an employee in the elevator and asks how a project is going are engaging in informal communication.

▪ **EXHIBIT 4.16**
In a wheel network, also called a hub-and-spoke network, one person acts as a central conduit for all information.

Chain network
A communication network in which information passes in an organized sequence from one person to the next.

All-channel network
A communication network in which all members of a group communicate with everyone else as needed for maximum flow of information.

▪ **EXHIBIT 4.18**
The all-channel network is one in which all members of a group communicate with everyone else as needed for maximum flow of information.

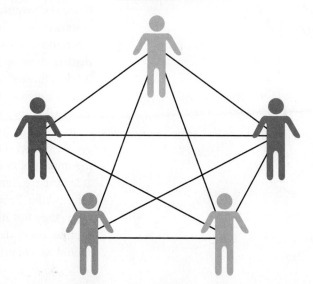

Formal communication
Communication governed by distinct and known rules about who can communicate with whom and how they should do it.

Informal communication
Communication that moves through channels other than those that have been explicitly defined within an organization.

Grapevine
An informal process of sharing information among and between coworkers about what is happening in an organization.

Informal communication is important because it provides an excellent means of gathering and sharing information, and it helps build relationships. Informal communication provides a much-needed social outlet for people. Talking about families, the news, or even the weather are important ways for people to simply connect during the day. Informal communication also provides avenues for people to share information and build relationships outside of the boundaries of the hierarchy. In some cases, this is the best way to gather useful feedback and information that can help the business overall. Another reason informal communication is essential is that formal channels are often unavailable, ineffective, or inefficient means of communicating.

There is nothing inherently good or bad about informal communication. When it benefits an organization, informal communication increases efficiency of information flow, helps workers feel fully informed, and enhances creativity. On the other hand, when it is used inappropriately or maliciously, informal communication can facilitate the rapid spread of inaccurate or incomplete messages. For example, false rumors of an impending downsizing will certainly affect people's mood and performance. "The grapevine" is the term often used to describe informal communication. The **grapevine** is an informal process of sharing information among and between coworkers about what is happening in an organization.

The grapevine is used for topics range from professional (e.g., the status of a big account) to personal (e.g., who the new manager is dating). Whatever the subject, the grapevine is often where people in an organization get much of their information.

The grapevine is not completely reliable, of course, but it often contains surprisingly accurate information. The level of accuracy usually depends on the organization. Organizations whose leaders are more open and frank with their employees are likely to find that the grapevine contains more dependable information.

There is no doubt that informal communication is very important in organizations. One scholar has even gone so far as to suggest that the majority of information is communicated through the grapevine in many organizations.[87] Although it might be hard to quantify exactly how much information is actually shared in this way, it's clearly quite a bit, so it is very important for managers to understand the grapevine's role.[88]

How are leaders and managers supposed to respond to the grapevine? For starters, managers need to accept the grapevine rather than fight it. Attempts to punish people for using the grapevine as a communication channel will backfire. Because it is a highly efficient communication channel, the grapevine can be a good tool for disseminating information quickly. Using it in this way means understanding how it works within one's particular organization: Through whom does most information travel? How exactly is information disseminated?

One way for managers to tap into the grapevine is to spend time engaging in spontaneous conversations with employees in person, on the phone, or via webcam. This is sometimes called *management by walking around*. Informal communication such as this removes some of the barriers that result from status differences, which helps information move up the hierarchy, and it provides a way for employees to share feedback in a less threatening situation. Increased contact between managers and employees also creates a greater level of comfort for employees who might otherwise be more guarded about what they communicate.

In addition to using the grapevine to improve organizational communication, a good manager will increase the accuracy of information in the grapevine and control the impact of negative rumors. How does one do that? Responding with accurate, or at least more complete, information is one measure, as is simply communicating more information. People are less likely to jump to conclusions about management decisions when they feel like leaders are being open and honest. So far, we've been discussing routine, every day communication about work and life in an organization. But how should we communicate in a crisis?

What Every Manager Deals with Sooner or Later: Crisis Communication

Quoting Greek philosopher Aeschylus, President John Kennedy noted: "In war, truth is the first casualty."[89] Similarly, in times of crisis, communication can be the first casualty in organizations. How do managers keep honest, open communication flowing in times of crisis? To start with, managers need to remain calm and gather as much information as possible, communicate information as openly as possible, and respond swiftly.

Common communication errors in a crisis involve jumping to conclusions and trying to calm people down by being overly optimistic. For example, during the aftermath of Hurricane Katrina in New Orleans, President George W. Bush told the head of the Federal Emergency Management Agency (FEMA), Michael Brown, "Brownie, you're doing a heck of a job."[90] In actuality, FEMA's actions were far from effective. In another case, soon after a passenger attempted to ignite a bomb on a Delta flight on December 25, 2009, the then-head of the U. S. Department of Homeland Security, Janet Napolitano said, "The system worked."[91] Most people would not agree, as a man got on a plane with a bomb. Clearly, no one wants to make these kinds of communication errors in a crisis—yet it happens all the time.

Not all of us will have to manage crises like the aftermath of a hurricane or a national security issue. Most people do, however, have to manage crises at work and communicate effectively. Many situations call for the special attention crisis communication deserves: when a layoff is imminent, under way, or just over; when a business grows or shrinks much faster than expected; or when a natural disaster affects people, the company, or business assets. If you need to communicate effectively during a crisis, the trick is to assess the situation and remain calm and coherent so that you can receive and relay the critical information needed to bring the crisis to a satisfactory resolution.

As you have seen in this section, communication in organizations is complicated. But ultimately, organizational communication is simply information flowing among people. Scholar Karl Weick notes that organizational communication is still dominated by people's natural urge to talk with one another, to communicate as fully as possible, and to engage in conversation. In fact, Weick goes so far as to say that conversation is the fundamental activity in organizations.[92]

As complicated as communication is, one simple truth holds: Connection is the beginning of effective communication.[93] One very powerful way to connect with people and to share information is through storytelling. Stories capture people's imagination—and their attention—and are an effective way to convey complex information.

The Power of Storytelling

Storytelling is the art of creating or delivering a narrative—a description of events that people can relate to, learn from, and remember. Stories are powerful tools because they do more than merely convey information: They are a meaningful and enjoyable way to share ideas, lessons, and values. Good stories are persuasive, appealing, and a good way to shape an organization's culture (■ **EXHIBIT 4.19**).[94]

Leaders throughout history have relied on storytelling as an effective means of motivating others, especially during times of uncertainty and rapid change.[95] Stories are far more persuasive and effective than sharing abstract concepts or rules. Stories are a powerful way to present important organizational information,

■ **EXHIBIT 4.19**

Stories Are Persuasive and Effective Leadership Tools	
Stories Are	**Stories Can Be**
• Simple • Enduring • Appealing to people across the organization • A fun way to deliver meaning	• Integral to an organization's culture • A useful form of training • A great method for empowering people • An excellent means to pass on corporate values and traditions

■ **EXHIBIT 4.20**

Seven Rules for Telling Good Stories[96]

1. The story should be about a real person. Using a real person makes the story more credible to your audience.

2. The story should have a strong sense of time and place. This puts the story into a context that people can relate to and will remember: "Two years ago when I was manager of Snuffy's Restaurant in Toledo, Ohio. . . ."

3. The story should be focused, simple, and clear. Too much detail and rambling will cause your audience to lose interest.

4. The story should be told in colorful and animated language. This engages the audience's imagination and captures interest.

5. A good story uses emotions carefully and powerfully. Empathy, surprise, meaningful insight, compassion and even tactful and controlled outrage will engage your audience's attention. It is emotional content that separates raw, boring data from a good illustration of the story's point.

6. Along with emotions, you can also use gestures to add emphasis and a touch of theatre. After all, storytelling is a performance art.

7. Be yourself. Be authentic and sincere. You want people to believe you.

Source: Adapted from Kouzes and Posner 2002, *The Leadership Challenge*, 3rd edition. San Francisco: Jossey-Bass.

engage peoples' imaginations, and stimulate commitment and enthusiasm. This is because stories are emotional, and emotions impact communication. Stories capture our imaginations. They evoke sights, sounds, smells, and other sensory experiences that the presentation of abstract concepts or rules simply cannot.

Storytelling is one of the ways to handle the principal challenges of leadership: sparking action, getting people to work together, and leading people into the future. The right story at the right time can help an organization get ready for a new idea and course of action. Storytelling doesn't replace analytical thinking; it supplements it by enabling us to imagine new perspectives and new worlds.

But just how does one tell a good story? ■ **EXHIBIT 4.20** lists some basic rules that any storyteller can follow to achieve maximum effect with his or her story.

Storytelling, when done right, is truly one of the most powerful and effective tools for engaging and inspiring people to get behind a vision or mission. Stories help create the culture that becomes the heart and soul of the organization.

Discussion Questions

1. Describe a downward communication process used recently in your school or at work. What channels were used? How effective was the communication? How could it be improved?

2. Using the rules of telling a good story, create a story about your success on a difficult school or work project. Make sure that someone hearing the story will learn from your experience.

Objective 4.9
Outline the steps HR can take to ensure effective communication and resonant relationships.

9. What Can HR Do to Ensure Effective Communication and Resonant Relationships in Organizations?

Many people and functions within an organization are responsible for ensuring effective communication. Large organizations often have divisions specifically dedicated to internal and external communication; legal departments also have a role in communication. In most large organizations, HR plays a key role in communication, either alone or in conjunction with other departments. Among other things, HR is often responsible for ensuring that everyone in an organization is fully informed about two key topics:

- *Labor laws:* Local, state, and federal laws that guide processes such as hiring and firing employees, as well as how workers are to be treated on the job
- *Workforce data:* Information that can impact the company's ability to succeed, such as information about the labor pool (both inside and outside the organization), morale, and organizational culture.

Keeping Employees Informed of Their Rights

Labor laws and regulations that guide how employees must be treated at work have proliferated during the past several decades. Two of HR's responsibilities are to be current on all relevant labor laws and regulations, and to be sure that all employees and managers understand how laws impact the way they must do their jobs.

Knowing the laws is only the first step. The real challenge for HR professionals is to communicate information about the laws in a way that people in the organization can understand. For example, simply sending an e-mail with attachments of all the laws wouldn't help people learn how to apply them. Talented HR professionals use a variety of communication channels and techniques to share and teach relevant labor laws, including written communication, workshops, small group seminars, coaching, and directly advising managers on specific issues.

Gathering and Communicating Employee Engagement Information

HR is often responsible for gathering, organizing, and disseminating information about things like the talent pool, compensation, and employees' skills. Data related to the workforce can be difficult to collect and manage, which is why there are many different advanced software applications available.

Information about employee morale and engagement is, in some ways, even harder to collect and use. To be effective in one of the key HR roles—that of strategic business partner—HR professionals must be able to advise managers and leaders by relying on factual information, not just opinions about what is going on in the workforce.

Employee morale is the collective mood or spirit in an organization. Employee morale affects people's ability to do their jobs well and the organization's ability to achieve its goals. High morale is often linked to things like enthusiasm, commitment, trust, belief in the organization's mission and vision, esprit de corps, and faith in leadership. High morale is also linked with employee satisfaction and positive organizational results. Low morale often appears as a general malaise, sense of impending doom, or fear of failure. Typical manifestations of low morale are high employee turnover, absenteeism, and illness, as well as decreased productivity and a dissonant climate.

Collecting information about morale can be complicated. Sometimes, HR professionals gather information through conversations and observation of employees and managers at work. This information can be helpful, of course, but in order for it to be accurate, rigorous methods of data collection are also necessary. In some cases, HR professionals will engage in quantitative research, which is a process of gathering and analyzing subjective data, such as information from conversations and interviews, or answers to open-ended questions on a survey.

Another method that is widely used relies on quantitative research, which is a process of gathering information that can be converted to numbers, then analyzed using statistics and other mathematical tools. To study employee morale this way, HR often administers surveys that ask employees to rank, or otherwise rate, various

HR Leadership Roles

Employee morale
The collective mood or spirit in an organization.

Qualitative research
A process of gathering and analyzing subjective data, such as information from conversations, interviews, or answers to open-ended questions on a survey.

Quantitative research
A process of gathering information that can be converted to numbers, then analyzed using statistics and other mathematical tools.

aspects of morale, such as the degree of trust they have in leaders, the effectiveness of managerial communication, the extent to which teams are effective, and the like. Such surveys are often called *people surveys*, *employee opinion surveys*, *employee engagement surveys*, or *job satisfaction surveys*.

Surveys can be cost effective and efficient because they reach lots of people very quickly. A well-designed survey can give HR professionals a wealth of information, and can help employees feel that their opinions matter. A well-designed survey can also provide benchmark information. Benchmark information allows HR professionals and managers to compare their scores with the average, high, and low scores of similar organizations.

Unfortunately, one major downside of gauging employee morale with surveys is that they only measure what is asked. In other words, if you ask the wrong questions or ask them inappropriately, the data will not be useful. In fact, the information can be harmful if it directs HR and managers' attention to the wrong problems. A second problem associated with surveys is their low return rate. Rarely will everyone—or even close to everyone—respond to a survey, and because only data from those who choose to respond is measured, the resulting information could be skewed. For example, it is not unheard of for only disgruntled employees to respond to surveys, resulting in an inaccurate picture of overall morale. Still, regardless of the shortcomings of the survey method, it is popular and widely used.

Discussion Questions

1. How does your school's HR department disseminate information about job openings, labor laws, and employee policies? What channels do they use to provide people with this information? Are the communication channels effective? Why or why not?

2. Describe a situation in which morale played an important part in the effectiveness of a group or organization to which you belonged. What was the impact of high or low morale? Was anyone responsible for monitoring morale? If so, how did they do it, and how did they communicate their findings to the group?

Objective 4.10
Outline the steps you can take to improve communication and build resonant relationships in your workplace.

10. What Can We All Do to Improve Communication and Build Resonant Relationships at Work?

Despite all the barriers to effective communication at work, we still manage to get our messages across most of the time. How do we accomplish this? It starts with good intentions. Most of us want to be understood and to understand others. Many of us have learned to communicate skillfully and to anticipate potential breakdowns in the communication process before they occur. We all employ social and emotional intelligence when communicating. For example, we tune in to others—that's empathy. We attend to and manage our emotions when communicating—that's self-awareness and self-management. We also track and use communication networks—that's organizational awareness. In this section, we will cover a few tips for ensuring that you communicate well, and we'll also discuss how to improve your ability to engage in fruitful conversations.

A Few Basic Rules for Sending Clear and Powerful Messages

Paying attention to communication basics can go a long way in helping you become an effective communicator. This is particularly true when it comes to sending messages. Your job is to ensure that your intended audience understands your message.

You therefore need to be clear, avoid ambiguity, and be concise. You must also provide just the right level of necessary information—not too much and not too little.

Soliciting and listening to feedback increases the likelihood that your message will be understood. After communicating with a coworker or an employee, a good manager asks tactful questions to test whether his or her message was received. In some cases, people produce this sort of feedback without prompting, or they provide nonverbal signals that demonstrate either understanding (e.g., a nod) or confusion (e.g., a furrowed brow). It is up to you—the sender of a message—to pay attention and tend to these responses to complete the feedback loop. To ensure that you send clear, powerful messages that are likely to be accurately heard, you can follow the guidelines in ■ **EXHIBIT 4.21**. It is worth remembering, however, that the best communicators not only follow the rules, but know when and how to break them.

■ **EXHIBIT 4.21**
Checklist for effective communication.

Checklist for Effective Communication

☑ Be sure you know what message you want to send.

☑ Determine the most appropriate channel for your message.

☑ Adjust your vocabulary to match your audience.

☑ Remember that jargon can hurt communication when it is unfamiliar to the receiver, but it may improve communication when it is familiar.

☑ Create a level of trust that makes people feel comfortable passing bad news up and down the hierarchy.

☑ Be careful about poor or inadvertent use of inappropriate nonverbal signals.

☑ Practice empathy when communicating. Accurately reading others' responses will enable you to help them understand your message.

When to Break the Rules

Influential language philosopher H. Paul Grice devised a set of four maxims—or general rules—to guide effective conversations. Grice's four maxims are as follows:

- *Quality:* Be truthful.
- *Quantity:* Share the right amount of information.
- *Relevance:* Make your contribution relevant to the matter at hand.
- *Manner:* Be clear, and avoid ambiguity or vagueness.[97]

Grice made the point that these four rules are not always observed. Rather, they represent what we try to do when we cooperate in the communication process. When one or more of these rules are violated, the type and manner of the violation carries information about the speaker's values, emotions, and motives. In other words, we make sense of each other by trying to understand how, when, and why the rules are broken.

For example, when we sense that someone is not being completely truthful, we often begin to question why this might be. Is the person pursuing a particular agenda? Is he or she afraid to tell us the truth? Similarly, when someone shares what seems to be too little information, we may question the person's knowledge or capability in addition to wondering about his or her personal agenda. On the other hand, if someone shares too much information, we might speculate about why it is so important to him or her or question his or her communication skills. Finally, if a message is ambiguous or vague, we will often wonder whether a person is trying to hide something, or we might think that the person doesn't know what he or she is talking about. ■ **EXHIBIT 4.22** shows how Grice's maxims might be violated and what communication looks like when violations occur.

Consider a simple example: You are visiting a colleague's office around 1:00 P.M. and you are hungry. If you followed Grice's guidelines, you might simply say, "I want

■ **EXHIBIT 4.22**
Breaking communication rules through indirect requests.[98]

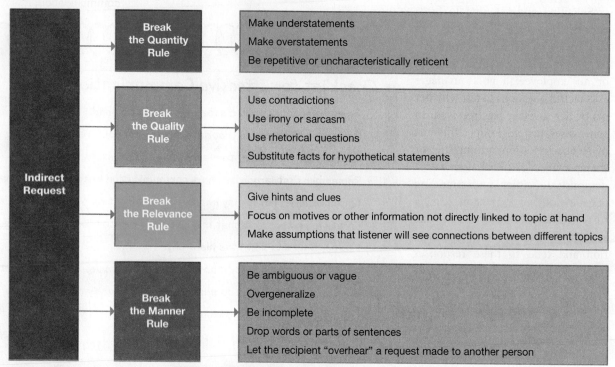

Source: Based on Brown, Penelope, and Stephen C. Levinson. 1987. *Politeness: Some universals in language usage*, p. 214. New York: Cambridge University Press.

something to eat." You tell the truth, giving just enough information. It's relevant in that many people eat lunch at this time of day. You are specific. In some situations, this would be an appropriate way to communicate what you want.

It's also entirely possible, however, that you would decide that following the rules would be rude. So instead, you might ask your colleague if he or she has had lunch, or you might casually mention that you missed breakfast. Neither of these messages will necessarily be interpreted as a request for food, leaving room for your colleague to choose how to respond.

Even though all of Grice's rules were broken, your indirect request was more polite. It made no explicit demands, but you did hint at the real issue in a way that could be understood. This allows your colleague to recognize and take actions to please you. If for some reason your colleague does not want lunch, has already eaten, or does not want to have lunch with you, he or she will not be embarrassed, he or she can save face, and the relationship will remain intact.

This example shows that on some occasions, we will deliberately break communication rules in order to maintain resonant relationships. Successful leaders know how to communicate in ways that build relationships and create resonance among and between people—even if it means breaking some communication rules.

At work, we are all responsible for effective communication. Leaders and managers have a special role, because they are charged with ensuring that employees have the information they need, understand organizational goals and values, and are inspired to do their jobs. For leaders at any level, communication comes with responsibility. When we communicate with others, we can influence, persuade, or inform. What and how we communicate can help others or create obstacles that prevent them from doing their jobs or reaching their goals. As you engage others in communicating about life, work, relationships, or just about anything else, it is worth thinking about what, exactly, you hope to accomplish as you engage them in conversation. Far too many conflicts occur as a result of misguided or poor communication or, even worse, skilled communication used to further personal agendas at the expense of others.

Discussion Questions

1. During the next day or so, consciously monitor your *intentions* when communicating. Then, reflect on these intentions and how they affect both you and others.

2. Think of a situation in your personal or professional life when you specifically used an indirect request to try to get what you wanted. Was it effective? What, in your opinion, is the power of an indirect request that might make it more effective than a direct request? What are some drawbacks?

11. A Final Word on Communication and Leadership

This textbook presents many different theories of leadership, several of which are radically different from one another. However, all of these theories have one thing in common: They all assume that leaders at all levels have the ability to construct or shape the social reality of their organizations through communication.[99] When you think about leadership as *the ability to control communication,* you can see that people who are not traditionally thought of as leaders, such as secretaries and administrative assistants, have an abundance of leadership power by virtue of their positions within the communication networks of an organization.[100] People who are at the center of communication networks usually have numerous positive relationships. They create resonance, they get and share information, and they have tremendous influence, no matter what formal role they hold. In today's diverse and global organizations, well-networked people who understand how to communicate cross-culturally will be the most successful leaders.

LEADING IN A GLOBAL WORLD
Could You Please Repeat That?!

Communication is only effective when the message the sender intended is received with little or no ambiguity or misunderstanding. One of the biggest obstacles to communication is language itself. In a global environment, many international team members may have a good working knowledge of English, but jargon and slang present problems for nonnative speakers.

As such, the best rule of thumb when communicating with an international audience is to use as little jargon and slang as possible.

Break into teams of four. Take a few minutes to write down eight slang and jargon expressions that, if you were a nonnative English speaker, would sound ridiculous or strange (e.g., "It's *raining cats and dogs*"). Then, each group member will take two of the expressions and translate their meaning into plain English for the rest of the group. If your team includes nonnative English speakers, add slang or jargon from their language.

LEADING WITH EMOTIONAL INTELLIGENCE
How Do You Feel about That Thought?

Much of the information we transmit in a message is nonverbal, and this nonverbal behavior reveals our emotional state. Managing our emotions takes conscious effort, particularly in emotionally charged situations. Because our emotions directly impact our decision making and work relationships, all leaders must understand how to accurately read and express emotions when they communicate.

Break into teams of four. One person is the observer/referee while the other three have a *thoughtful* discussion about an emotionally charged topic, such as politics or religion. The discussion should be based on reason and well thought out analysis, and team members should attempt to leave their emotions about the subject out of the discussion.

The observer records instances in which group members betray their emotions through body language, facial expressions, and/or tone of voice. The observer also acts as a referee to remind the group to carry on a thoughtful dialogue when he or she observes emotions gaining the upper hand. After the conversation is complete, the observer shares what he or she has noticed. He or she also shares the personal biases/selective perception that caused him or her to notice certain things and not others.

LEADING WITH CRITICAL THINKING SKILLS
Let Me Be Perfectly Clear

Making sense of information transmitted from sender to receiver is critical to effective communication. Wilbur's model for understanding and sharing information is a useful tool for gaining clarity by categorizing information into individual or collective and interior or exterior.

Break into teams of two or three and apply Wilbur's model to the following scenario:

Your school has decided to go to a new online registration system for spring semester, eliminating half of all undergraduate advisors from the registration process. The administration thinks the advisors give conflicting information to students, creating problems of inconsistency in policy. The new tool is more accurate in tracking course requirements and is faster and more up-to-date on class closings and alternative offerings.

The beta launch of the system received mixed reviews. Some students found it faster and easier to use. Others found it cumbersome and complicated, and they preferred to have an advisor's assistance when using it.

Create a proposal to send to the administration that will gather data for all four quadrants of Wilbur's model. To help administrators understand what information you hope to collect, provide a hypothetical example for each quadrant.

ETHICAL LEADERSHIP
A Stereotypical Response, or Not?

Stereotyping and selective perception are obstacles to communication that sometimes cause us to hear and see only what we *want* to hear and see. Unfortunately, this behavior supports personal biases and makes it impossible to view or interpret information impartially. Many unethical decisions have been based in selective perception and/or stereotyping.

Individually or in teams, read the following scenario and write a short paragraph describing how you would handle the situation.

Richard, a young African American who recently graduated with honors, has joined a prominent consulting firm. He is a brilliant, enthusiastic, highly motivated entry-level associate.

The buzz around the office is that an exciting new client is to be pitched. This project could mean significant revenues, and careers could be made from success on this venture. Richard has been invited to join the team making the presentation to the client in three weeks, and he will have a significant client-facing role in this project if the bid is accepted.

Richard is surprised about this assignment because he is so new to the organization. He speaks to his mentor, a partner in a different division, who explains to Richard that the CIO in the prospective company is an African American man. How do you proceed if you are Richard?

Consider the following questions in your response:

1. Is Richard being stereotyped by his company as someone the client CIO can "relate" to because they are both African American?
2. If you were Richard, would you perceive that your inclusion on the team is a result of your race?
3. How might this translate into an ethical dilemma for Richard and/or his company?

KEY TERMS

Resonant relationships, *p. 102*
Communication, *p. 104*
Language, *p. 104*
Pidgin, *p. 105*
Denotation, *p. 106*
Connotation, *p. 106*
Nonverbal communication, *p. 106*
Body language, *p. 107*
Face, *p. 110*
Sender, *p. 113*
Message, *p. 113*
Receiver, *p. 113*
Channel, *p. 113*
Encoding, *p. 113*

Decoding, *p. 114*
Feedback, *p. 114*
Feedback loop, *p. 114*
Noise, *p. 114*
Effective communication, *p. 115*
Efficient communication, *p. 115*
Jargon, *p. 121*
Selective perception, *p. 123*
Stereotypes, *p. 123*
Prejudice, *p. 123*
Downward communication, *p. 128*
Upward communication, *p. 128*
Filtering, *p. 128*
Horizontal communication, *p. 128*

Internal communication, *p. 128*
External communication, *p. 128*
Communication network, *p. 128*
Wheel network (hub-and-spoke network), *p. 128*
Chain network, *p. 129*
All-channel network, *p. 129*
Formal communication, *p. 129*
Informal communication, *p. 129*
Grapevine, *p. 130*
Employee morale, *p. 133*
Qualitative research, *p. 133*
Quantitative research, *p.133*

MyManagementLab

Go to **mymanagementlab.com** for Auto-graded writing questions as well as the following Assisted-graded writing questions:

4-1. Describe a difficult interpersonal communication experience that you participated in. Identify the sender, receiver, channel used, as well as the encoding, decoding and feedback processes. What happened that caused the breakdown of communication?

4-2. Reflect on your communication skills. Where are you strongest? Where are you weakest? If you could magically improve one communication skill, what would it be? How would this affect your life?

4-3. Mymanagementlab Only — comprehensive writing assignment for this chapter.

1. Why Is Communication Central to Effective Relationships at Work?

(pp. 102–103)

Objective: Explain why communication is key to fostering effective relationships.

Summary: Communication forms the basis for relationships in all aspects of your life and is at the heart of working effectively with other people. Successful leaders and employees understand this and pay attention to what information they share and how they share it. This enables them to build resonant relationships that foster respect and lead to positive resolutions when conflicts arise.

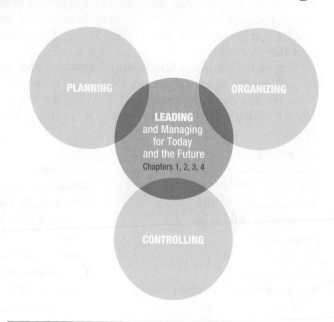

PLANNING

ORGANIZING

LEADING
and Managing
for Today
and the Future
Chapters 1, 2, 3, 4

CONTROLLING

2. How Do Humans Communicate?

(pp. 104–108)

Objective: Explain how humans communicate.

Summary: Communication can take on several different forms. Verbal communication is made up of words and may be spoken, signed, or written. It is affected by both the actual meaning of the words and their connotations. Nonverbal communication is made up of gestures, facial expressions, and voice qualities that are far harder to consciously control and are more nuanced than verbal communication. Learning to control and align verbal and nonverbal communication will make your message more likely to be received correctly and believed.

3. How Do We Communicate and Interpret Sophisticated Information? (pp. 108–113)

Objective: Analyze how we communicate and interpret sophisticated information.

Summary: Much of what is shared between and among people is emotional, and these emotions have a tremendous impact on your communication and your ability to maintain healthy relationships. Good communicators are masters at managing emotion in the communication process, recognize that we are constantly communicating an image to others, and understand that saving face is important in relationships. Good communicators also treat information in a sophisticated manner, categorizing it as relevant to the individual or a group, and recognizing whether it is subjective or objective.

4. What Is the Interpersonal Communication Process? (pp. 113–117)

Objective: Define the interpersonal communication process.

Summary: In its most basic form, communication involves a sender conveying an encoded message via a communication channel to a receiver who decodes it and provides feedback to the sender. Several models have been developed to analyze this process and explain why messages are sometimes misinterpreted, including the Shannon-Weaver model, the Schramm model, and the Berlo model. Regardless of the model used to analyze the process, the effectiveness and efficiency of communication are important factors to consider when crafting messages, and should inform whether a message is sent via a rich or a lean communication channel. The richer the channel, the less likely the message is to be misinterpreted.

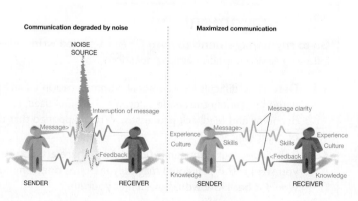

Communication degraded by noise

NOISE SOURCE

Interruption of message

Message>

<Feedback

SENDER   RECEIVER

Maximized communication

Message clarity

Experience   Message>   Experience
Culture   Skills   Skills   Culture

<Feedback

Knowledge   Knowledge
SENDER   RECEIVER

9. What Can HR Do to Ensure Effective Communication and Resonant Relationships? (pp. 132–134)

Objective: Outline the steps HR can take to ensure effective communication and resonant relationships.

Summary: In most organizations, HR plays an important role in communicating important information about labor laws, workforce data, and a variety of other issues related to people. Beyond simply informing people about these issues, HR is responsible for ensuring that people understand and apply the information they receive. HR also is responsible for assessing employee morale and engagement and serves as a research hub for these areas.

8. What Is Organizational Communication? (pp. 127–132)

Objective: Define organizational communication.

Summary: Organizational communication can be top-down, bottom-up, and/or horizontal. Organizational communication involves several types of communication networks, including wheel networks, chain networks, and all-channel networks. Both formal and informal communication regularly take place within an organization, and the grapevine is a powerful communication tool. Storytelling is an effective tool that many leaders and managers are increasingly relying on to share messages within organizations.

7. Why Is It Challenging to Communicate in a Socially Diverse World? (pp. 124–127)

Objective: Analyze the challenges in communicating in a socially diverse society.

Summary: It can be difficult to communicate effectively with individuals different from yourself because each person develops communication skills within his or her own culture. Language can get in the way, as can different expectations about nonverbal behavior. The strength of group identity also affects communication, as do gender and age. All of these factors affect what is communicated and how. With all these differences, however, it's important to recognize that communication is learned, and you can improve your skills.

6. What Are Common Barriers to Effective Communication? (pp. 120–124)

Objective: Define the common barriers to effective communication.

Summary: Even when people have the best intentions there are many barriers to communication. One of these barriers is language; even when speakers all use the same language, they may do so with different dialects, accents, and jargon that create problems. Another common barrier is poor communication skills on the part of the sender and the receiver of a message. Barriers such as selective perception, stereotypes, and prejudice can also harm communication, as can unexamined power relationships.

5. How Do We Use Information Technology to Communicate at Work? (pp. 117–119)

Objective: Describe how people use information technology to communicate at work.

Summary: Technology has expanded the communication channels available to us (e.g., e-mail, text, web or video conferencing). This is good from the perspective that information can be shared more quickly and easily than ever before. However, technology adds complexity because of the challenges it presents when it comes to communicating emotions, providing complete and understandable messages, and managing the volume of messages that come and go via e-mail and other technologies.

10. **What Can We All Do to Improve Communication and Build Resonant Relationships at Work?** (pp. 134–137)

Objective: Outline the steps you can take to improve communication and build resonant relationships in your workplace.

Summary: Paying attention to communication basics is one of the best things you can do to become a more effective communicator—speaking clearly, concisely, and unambiguously are good starters. Knowing the four rules of quality, quantity, relevance, and manner will help too, as will knowing how and when it is appropriate and necessary to break these rules. At work, the way you communicate affects your relationships. One of your most important jobs is to communicate in ways that increase resonance in your relationships.

11. **A Final Word on Communication and Leadership** (p. 137)

Summary: The best leaders, both formal and informal, build strong resonant relationships and powerful social networks. People who can do this in today's diverse organizations will be successful.

CHAPTER 5

Planning and Strategy:
Bringing the Vision to Life

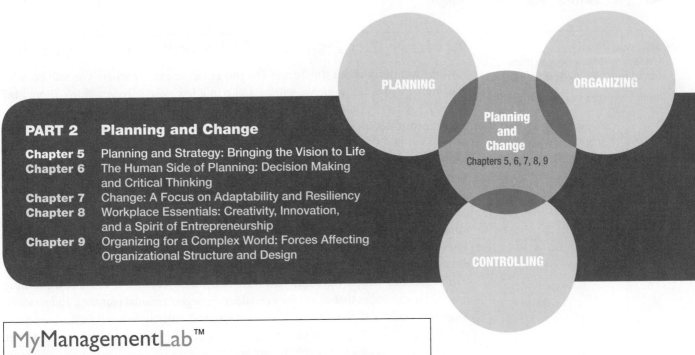

MyManagementLab™

⭐ **Improve Your Grade!**

Over 10 million students improved their results using the Pearson MyLabs. Visit **mymanagementlab.com** for simulations, tutorials, and end-of-chapter problems.

Chapter Outline

Chapter Objectives

5.1   Understand how people think about and plan for the future.

5.2   Describe the planning process in organizations.

5.3   Compare and contrast the typical planning process with the planning process that takes place during periods of uncertainty.

5.4   Define mission and vision and understand why both are important to organizational success.

5.5   Define strategy.

5.6   Understand what needs to be considered during the strategic planning process.

5.7   Know the steps in a typical strategic planning process.

5.8   Describe HR's role in planning and strategy.

5.9   Describe what you can do to support effective strategic planning.

Objective 5.1
Understand how people think
about and plan for the future.

1. How Do People Plan for the Future?

How do *you* think about the future? Do you envision exactly where you will be, who you will be with, and what you will be doing in a few years? Do you think about how you will use your values to guide the choices you make, trusting that you will encounter opportunities along the way and end up with work you love, great relationships, and a good life? Or do you think more about today than tomorrow, concentrating on being in the moment rather than imagining the future?

Some people focus on outcomes: They set goals for themselves and then work diligently and single-mindedly to achieve them. Other people are action oriented: they are content to work hard in the moment, and they spend very little time thinking beyond immediate tasks or projects. Still others focus on direction and a meaningful vision: They think about the future as part of a personally meaningful vision, and they coordinate current activities around less-specific yet compelling images.[1]

The fact that people have different ways of thinking about the future and planning is one of many issues that arise when considering organizational planning and strategy. Most organizational plans and strategies are almost entirely focused on specific goals and objectives, leaving out or underemphasizing how important a vision can be to our sense of meaning and the energy we are willing to expend.

Meaning in life and work is important because *human beings are purposeful creatures.* The Greek word *teleos* captures our stance: We purposefully move toward a future that is better than today, one that we find meaningful, perfect, and complete.[2] This is what we do in our organizations, too. We seek to identify a noble purpose, a mission, and a vision, as well as a way to get there through strategies, plans, goals, and actions. If you can first master how you approach the future and then find ways to inspire others to find meaning in a vision and energy for the work, you will be more successful at creating and implementing plans and strategies.

How do leaders and managers ensure that people plan so that an organization's vision, strategy, and goals, are coordinated? This chapter will answer that question. First, you will learn about planning and types of plans commonly used in organizations. Then, you will look at how an organization's success begins with clarity of purpose, including clarity about why it exists, who it serves, and what it does. For most organizations, this is articulated in a mission statement and brought to life through a powerful vision. You will also learn how an organization's mission and vision can be realized through strategic planning, which will be explained as a six-step process. Finally, you will assess HR's role in the planning process, as well as what we can all do to develop focus and skills around visioning and planning.

Planning Defined

Planning
The cognitive, creative, and behavioral process of developing a
sequence of activities intended to
achieve a goal or move toward an
imagined future state.

Planning is the cognitive, creative, and behavioral process of developing a sequence of activities intended to achieve a goal or move toward an imagined future state. Scholars have looked at organizational planning in many ways. Most agree with scholar Henry Mintzberg, who sees planning as a formal process that includes analysis, creativity, and synthesis of ideas. This process helps people decide on steps and activities that can be integrated to move people—and organizations—toward a desired future state.[3]

Unfortunately, key elements of effective planning are often ignored in organizational planning, such as creativity and synthesis of ideas.[4] This happens in part because many people believe that short-term, visible, and measurable goals are the only way to think about the future and plan, which is not the case. Let's look at how goal setting supports some people in planning for the future, how action orientation supports creativity, and how directional planning ensures that the overall vision doesn't get lost in the process.

Exploring How People Think about and Plan for the Future

The way that humans conceptualize the future is complicated. How we plan depends in part on certain personality traits, including a temperamental disposition toward optimism or pessimism. More importantly, how we think about the future and plan is dependent on what we have learned from family, school, culture, and even the norms and practices in the organizations in which we work.[5] We learn the skills associated with planning from other people and from the social environment around us—including organizations. Let's look at three particular ways in which planning can be described.

GOAL-ORIENTED PLANNING

The goal-setting process is often confused with planning. In reality, goal setting is only one aspect of the planning process—an aspect that focuses on clearly delineated, specific actions and outcomes that will move people toward a clearly defined end point. **Goal-oriented planning** involves determining the activities and steps that will get us from an existing state to a clearly defined end state.

For example, say that the manager of a high-end jewelry store wants to create a new display in the store's front cabinet. The manager will set a goal, such as, "Create a new display that will show our best pieces to advantage by the end of the month." He will then set milestones, such as, "By mid-month, we'll have all materials in stock; by week three, the case will be built." He will assign duties and deadlines and set quality standards.

Goal-oriented planning
The process of determining the activities and steps from an existing state to a clearly defined end state.

DIRECTIONAL PLANNING

Not all planning is goal oriented. Often we choose steps based on the general direction we intend to go. **Directional planning** identifies a domain (general area of activity) and direction (preferred values and activities) rather than specific goals.[6] This means that some people make decisions—even daily decisions—based on personal and organizational values. Such planning involves a different kind of goal focus—a *path goal* as opposed to a *destination goal*. These values rather than specific end-goals help us to choose what activities we should engage in.

For instance, you may be thinking about your career after college. If you are a directional planner, you may have decided you want to work in the management consulting industry because of the variety and travel the work provides. This domain is linked to your values.

Directional planning
The process of identifying a domain (general area of activity) and direction (preferred values and activities) rather than specific goals.

ACTION-ORIENTED PLANNING

Some people avoid goal setting and also avoid identifying a general path toward the future. Instead, their energy is directed toward immediate and short-term actions. Obviously, an overemphasis on immediate tasks could interfere with planning for the future. On the other hand, **action orientation**, or the ability to direct one's full attention to the task at hand, is quite important and can also be fulfilling. For example, you may be the type of person who puts off homework until the last minute. Once you start, though, you become fully engaged in the task. You're not doing it to get an *A*, and you don't even think much about how it relates to success in school. You just love working on the assignment—and you do it well—which moves you toward the future.

These three approaches to planning have value, and you should understand them so that you can create plans that will capture other people's (and your own) interest and commitment. As a manager or team leader, you'll often be helping people plan.

Planning is not something people do once in a while or something only top managers or leaders do. Plans are created and implemented every single day in organizations, by virtually every employee. Managers, of course, plan continuously. They create some plans that will begin and end in a single day and others that will stretch out for years. From planning budgets and meetings to crafting plans for staffing and operations,

Action orientation
Directing one's full attention to the task at hand.

managers juggle many plans all at once. Planning is an essential part of every manager's job. That's why it is important for everyone to learn the various skills involved in planning: visioning, goal setting, and linking actions to goals and vision.

If individual planning is complex, imagine what planning for dozens, or even thousands, of people involves. In the next section, you will discover how plans can be used—and misused—in organizations, and what types of plans are typically developed.

Discussion Questions

1. What approach do you tend to use when planning for the future? Do you focus more on goals, vision, or current activities?

2. Which of the following things do you think you should learn more about and practice: setting goals, envisioning a future that is meaningful to you, or finding ways to be "in the flow" when engaging in work or school activities?

---

2. What Does Planning Look Like in Organizations?

Organizations use many types of plans. Most plans include a process of identifying goals and charting a path to attain them. However, as you have learned, not everyone is goal oriented, and good plans include meaningful vision and engaging activities. Overreliance on goal setting can result in too much attention to short-term objectives. It can also result in overemphasis on the skills associated with goal setting, at the expense of competencies that support visioning and the execution of plans. Given the complexity and constant change in organizations, we need the stability that a meaningful vision provides and we need to know how to create future-oriented activities that engage people's talent and creativity.

Plans: More Than Goals and Metrics

Let's look at an example to illustrate what can happen when people rely too heavily on goal setting and metrics to assess progress when trying to create change. Recently, a large manufacturing company embarked on a new and daring plan to enable people in emerging markets to access their products and services at a reasonable cost. This was driven by a new CEO, who powerfully and publicly set out to redefine the company's mission. People inside the company were inspired, and the market and general public responded favorably.

This kind of change required significant alterations in the organization's culture and leadership practices, so the CEO and his team charged HR leaders with developing a "change program." Over many months, dozens of people explored what aspects of the company's leadership practices, culture, and even values needed to change. The talented HR team and thoughtful executive sponsors focused on exploring some of the less obvious strengths and weaknesses in leadership practices and organizational culture.

Six months into the change project, it fell apart. Some leaders (including the CEO and his team) simply couldn't tolerate the ambiguity that a robust change plan requires. They wanted clear, short-term goals and a quick fix. In the change program's place, a more typical change process was selected that focused on operational efficiency. (The process the company finally adopted is called lean management, which you will learn about in Chapter 12.)

The change program that was ultimately chosen in this organization looked good—there were clear goals, objectives, milestones, and action steps. Project managers toiled endlessly to create spreadsheets outlining actions and due dates. Tasks and roles were clearly assigned. Outcomes were linked to metrics so goal attainment could be measured. All of this activity was fine, and even could have been useful *if* it had addressed the right things. This plan failed in that it did not do what was required: It did not change leadership practices or organizational culture, and it did not result in shifting the organization so that it could fulfill the new mission in emerging markets. This failure was due in part to the fact that the company's leaders took a simplistic view of how to change the organization. In particular, they confused goals and metrics with a *real* change plan. As a result, four years from the CEO's brave new vision, the company has changed very little.

The sheer complexity of planning inside multifaceted organizations is daunting. To move and change organizations, plans must be both rational and creative, and they must link mission and purpose with goals and activities. A good plan helps people focus on an overarching vision, goals, *and* activities. The plan in the previous example focused largely on short-term goals. Purpose and vision alone are not enough, and neither are goals and metrics. Even seemingly small changes usually require careful planning. Take, for example, the addition of a new entrée to a restaurant's menu—say, a new type of burger. Managers may plan market research activities to find out if the entrée is something customers will order. They also oversee the wording in the menu so that the entrée will sound appetizing. Kitchen staff will learn when and how to order ingredients and how to prepare the entrée. These are just a few activities that must be planned.

Why go through all this trouble? Wouldn't it be easier to simply add a new double bacon cheeseburger to the menu? The problem with this approach is that adding the wrong menu item could be a costly decision. If the new burger is not something patrons will order, stocking the ingredients, training staff to prepare the dish, changing the menu, and so forth will ultimately be a waste of money. Even if customers like and order the new dish, the restaurant may not see profit if adequate planning hasn't gone into marketing, advertising, and training employees.

In addition to all the steps involved in planning for a new dish, there are bigger issues to consider. Say the restaurant's mission is to provide healthy, fresh food. When a new item that doesn't fit the restaurant's image is added (such as a double bacon cheeseburger), this can cause customers to feel let down or confused. Employees may also wonder if the restaurant's mission is changing, and they may feel discouraged by having to offer an item that customers do not want.

If we were to examine this example in more depth, we would discover that adding a new entrée actually requires the creation of several different types of plans. For example, the new entrée may fit into a larger, long-term plan to broaden the restaurant's appeal and attract new customers. There would also likely be a short-term marketing plan, as well as a plan for the day the entrée is first introduced. In the next section, we will look at the types of plans that are typically used in organizations.

Types of Plans Used in Organizations

Distinct differences exist in the types of plans used in organizations, as seen in ■ **EXHIBIT 5.1**. To illustrate these different types of plans, let's look at the fictitious example of a clothing store called Classic Style. As you can see in the table, Classic Style's plans differ in terms of scope, time frame, and how often they are used.

Organizations have many different types of plans operating at all times. Many plans fall apart during implementation because various parts of the organization lose sight of how their piece of the plan fits into the whole. It is important for the management team to ensure that the goals of the various plans are not in conflict with one another. The plans need to be carefully coordinated as they are created—and as they change.

■ **EXHIBIT 5.1**

Types of Planning Used by Classic Style Clothing Store

Type of Plan	Definition	Example
Short-term plan	Typically created for a period of one year or less; has a definite endpoint	Plan for hiring two employees over a three-month period
Long-term plan	Often in place for three or more years; endpoint not always determined; can be complex and require substantial resources	Plan for doubling the number of retail stores in four years
Single-use plan	Used once for a unique situation	Plan for issuing stock on publicly traded markets
Standing plan	Designed for repeated, ongoing activities	Plan for preparing monthly budget reports
Operational plan	Detailed outline of how goals are to be achieved	Plan for managers' and clerks' sales training, customer service training, and sales targets
Strategic plan	A far-reaching plan that articulates and synthesizes mission-driven, strategic goals for a business	Plan for moving from in-store sales to sales over the Internet only
Financial plan	Plan for providing financial resources to support an organization's activities	Plan for financing start-up costs of the new Internet business
Contingency plan	Designed to respond to a crisis or a failed plan; a "backup plan"	Plan for getting stock to stores in the event of a transportation strike
Project plan	Outlines specific actions, time frames, roles, responsibilities, objectives, and outcomes for particular work projects to be *done by one or more employees*	Plan for helping managers understand employees' attitudes about leadership practices; in this instance, the team outlines the steps necessary to collect information, analyze data, create reports, and share results with managers and employees

Discussion Questions

1. Think about a sports team, club, or committee to which you belong. What types of plans does your group use? Give two examples.

2. Choose one organization and describe its planning process using this sentence as a guide: "A good plan focuses on overarching vision, goals, *and* activities."

Objective 5.3
Compare and contrast the typical planning process with the planning process that takes place during periods of uncertainty.

3. How Do You Plan in Uncertain Times?

The word "plan" was adapted from a fifteenth-century word "plane," meaning a level or flat surface. Later, the word came to mean "scheme of action" or "design." First recorded in 1706, the word and its origins bring to mind a linear process—a clear, two-dimensional image of something, possibly moving from one state to another.[7] But that's not how life works, and it's not what planning is really like either. Most plans in organizations are complex, coordinated with other plans, and often nonlinear. Plans aren't static. The minute a plan becomes rigid, it becomes irrelevant. That's because things change, and if the plan can't change too, it's likely to fail. Sure, it's important to keep overarching goals, purpose, and vision in mind. However, as individuals, groups, and organizations move toward any vision, plans and goals almost always need adjustment.

Creating Plans That Can Change: A Modular Approach

The best course of action to ensure that plans are dynamic and can be adapted is to (1) clearly link plans to mission and vision and (2) include multiple subgoals that are discrete and individually planned.[8] We will discuss mission and vision later in the chapter. First, let's focus on how to create goals, subgoals, milestones, and action steps that can be adapted and changed.

GOALS, SUBGOALS, MILESTONES, AND ACTION STEPS: MAPPING THE JOURNEY TO YOUR DESTINATION

As Confucius reminds us, "A journey of a thousand miles begins with a single step." A journey is a metaphor for what plans allow us to do: move from here to there.[9] Assuming your vision is clear, you can then set destinations (goals and subgoals), take steps to get there (action steps), and mark your progress (milestones). Let's consider the definitions of goals, subgoals, milestones, and action steps and explore how to map the journey to your destination:

- *Goals:* According to the *American Heritage Dictionary*, a goal is "[t]he purpose toward which an endeavor is directed; an objective."[10] The word *goal* originally meant "end point of a race," and it was possibly derived from the Old English *gal*, meaning "obstacle."[11] Goals (and especially subgoals) that are "SMART" are specific, measurable, achievable, results oriented, and time specific.[12] For example, you may have set a goal to achieve a 3.6 GPA this semester.
- *Subgoals:* A subgoal is a goal that is created to help attain a larger and often more complex goal. A larger goal can have several smaller subgoals, which are easier to attain and often more concrete than the larger goal.[13] Returning to the previous example, you may set a subgoal of earning an *A* in this course.
- *Milestones:* The term *milestone* comes from the practice of marking distance on ancient highways by placing stones at periodic intervals ("miles"). Today, the term *milestone* refers to a marker that indicates how far we've come. Milestones help us mark progress toward a goal or subgoal. For example, in your effort to earn that *A*, a milestone marking your progress toward your subgoal may come at the end of week seven, when you achieve perfect class attendance. Sometimes, the terms milestones and subgoals are used interchangeably.
- *Action steps:* As the term implies, action steps are individual actions that support goal or subgoal attainment. The word *steps* implies a linear process over time. Action steps, however, are not always organized to follow a time sequence, nor are they always linear. For your goal of achieving a 3.6 GPA for the semester, you might have identified action steps related to the subgoal of getting an *A* in this class that include eating nutritious food all semester, partying with friends only on weekend nights, and completing your reading assignments two days before class. These things happen at various times and in various ways, not in any specific sequence. It's good to practice this type of nonlinear planning because it is a form of logic that is highly prized and extremely useful in leadership.

Useful plans include macro goals that can be broken down into modular subgoals. These subgoals should be designed in a way that allows for continual evaluation, flexibility, and adaptation of subgoals and action steps. This is a modular approach to planning: After each subgoal is achieved, we recalculate the actions needed to achieve the next subgoal or reach the next milestone.[14]

MODULAR PLANNING: WHAT WE CAN LEARN FROM BLACKJACK

We can learn a little bit about modular planning from mathematician Andrey Markov, who showed us that analyzing what *might* happen next can help us adapt our plans.[15] For instance, expert blackjack players plan how to win—and card counting in blackjack is a Markov process (■ **EXHIBIT 5.2**). Each card value from 2 through 9 has a 1/13 probability of appearing, a 10 or a face card has a 4/13 probability of appearing, and an ace has a 1/13 probability in a complete deck of cards. Each turn of a card, however, changes the probability of what card can appear next because there is one less card in the deck. Expert blackjack players mentally calculate this change and adapt their plans accordingly.[16]

■ **EXHIBIT 5.2**
Should counting cards be against the rules in casinos?

Source: Tony French/Alamy

If card sharks can adapt plans, managers can too. Effective managers realize that change is inevitable—and it's not even as predictable as in blackjack. The last decade saw global economic woes, double-digit unemployment, very low interest rates, and the collapse of iconic, century-old companies. Constant and dramatic change is the environment for twenty-first-century managers. The ability to adapt to change in a timely manner sets the successful employees, managers, and leaders apart. Therefore, although plans, goals, and subgoals are important guides, we must all recognize that changes in plans are almost inevitable.

For example, suppose a sales manager plans to support the North Carolina region, where sales are increasing rapidly. Her goal is to hire two new sales representatives for territories in that state. Subgoals include articulation of the following:

- The products the reps will sell
- The clients the reps will serve
- The recruiting and hiring process
- A training plan

Just before hiring the reps, however, the manager is shown reports that clearly reveal a much stronger growth trend in Texas than in North Carolina. The manager has limited resources and can't hire for both regions. She now has at least two choices: She can continue with her staffing plan in North Carolina while going through the long and risky process of requesting a budget increase, or she can revise her plan. The best decision seems straightforward and logical—she'll probably be better off changing her plan. Many people, however, have difficulty changing plans. Maybe they're emotionally attached to the first course of action, or they feel frustrated about all the work that has led to nothing. Some people are even blind to the need for change. As employees, managers, and leaders, it serves us well to get used to the idea that plans almost always change. Better yet, we can prepare for change.

Scenario Planning

Scenario planning
A dynamic, systematic process in which people envision all of the "what if" scenarios for given situations and plan for several likely possibilities.

In the previous example, the manager and her team could have gathered as much information as possible about the regions and developed several scenarios for staffing should one or another region begin to grow unexpectedly. This is called scenario planning. **Scenario planning** is a dynamic, systematic process where people envision all of the "what if" scenarios for given situations and plan for several likely possibilities.[17] A classic example of scenario planning is the constant work done by the World Health Organization (WHO) and the U.S. Centers for Disease Control (CDC) with regard to influenza, potentially deadly types of related viruses that constantly mutate. The WHO and CDC collect and compile information throughout the year and make projections regarding which strains of influenza will cause the most illness during the upcoming flu season. It is these strains that vaccinations are designed seasonally to prevent.[18]

Managers, leaders, and employees who are nimble and proactive in how they approach planning are more likely to achieve personal and organizational success than those who long for stability and hold on to the status quo. Still, most people and most organizations need something they can be sure of—a north star or guiding light. This comes in the form of an organization's mission and vision, as discussed in the next section of the chapter.

Discussion Questions

1. Why is it important to learn to plan—and to change plans—in today's world and work environment? Give examples from your experience.

2. Write out three goals and subgoals that you hope to attain within the next year. What milestones can you define for each goal and subgoal? What action steps can you take to accomplish your goals, subgoals, and milestones?

---

4. What Is a Mission? Why Does Vision Matter?

> **Objective 5.4**
> Define mission and vision and understand why both are important to organizational success.

An organization's mission articulates its fundamental purpose. A **mission statement** describes what an organization is, what it does, and what it stands for. One scholar who has studied hundreds of mission statements from American businesses says, "A mission statement is an enduring statement of purpose for an organization that identifies its scope of operations in product and market terms, and reflects its values and priorities."[19] Clear mission statements are not just created to make people feel proud of their

> **Mission statement**
> A statement that describes what an organization is, what it does, and what it stands for.

Leadership Perspective

● **Dr. Luis Ottley**
Head of School at Marin Horizon School in Mill Valley, California
". . . you have to have a clear sense of the purpose that will guide how you make decisions."

Dr. Luis Ottley—Head of School at Marin Horizon School in Mill Valley, CA—is driven to help students love school. He has served as an educational leader of several prestigious schools across the country, and was drawn to Marin Horizon because its educational mission and his own are closely aligned. Luis believes this shared sense of purpose is an important tool for building relationships and achieving goals:

*To be a great leader today, you have to have a clear sense of the purpose that will guide how you make decisions. When you have a purpose and that purpose is clear, you can create a win-win situation. A clear sense of purpose also opens the door to collaboration—all of a sudden, we're not talking about what you do, or what I do. We are talking about **what we can do together** to achieve the same goals.*

Now, you don't have to love the people you work with, but you do have to be in relationships with them. That means you have to understand and respect them, and they you. Relatedness allows you to enroll people, to bring them along, to engage them with the mission. It allows you to tap into passion. So, when you invest time and energy in relationships, you will get so much more from people. When they know we are all in it together, and that we all care a lot, you get much more robust decisions, stronger commitment, and people will give their all.

Source: Personal interviews with Luis Ottley conducted by Annie McKee, 2009 and 2012.

Competitive advantage
Anything that positively distinguishes one organization from others.

Vision
A description of what an organization wants to become—its future identity—which can be realized through the successful accomplishment of its mission.

Vision statement
An articulation of a company's vision.

organization (although they do that too). Mission statements are concrete: They guide what people *do* at work. Let's look at what Dr. Luis Ottley, Head of School at Marin Horizon School, has to say about this in the *Leadership Perspective* feature.

As Dr. Luis Ottley shows us, a clear sense of purpose plus positive relationships helps Marin Horizon School be at its best. The same is true for businesses. In strategic terms, an organization's mission is what sets it apart by articulating its **competitive advantage**, or anything that positively distinguishes one organization from others. For instance, an organization's competitive advantage might be the quality of the products or services offered, the speed of delivery, or the caliber of employees.

A mission also creates a rationale for working that unifies employees. A powerful mission helps managers and leaders make decisions, motivate employees, create unity, and integrate short- and long-term goals. In a similar way, an organization's vision serves to inspire employees and customers alike. A **vision** describes what the organization wants to become—its future identity—which can be realized through the successful accomplishment of its mission. An organization's vision is often articulated in a **vision statement**. ■ **EXHIBIT 5.3** illustrates a couple mission and vision statements that will give you an idea of what these particular organizations aspire to.

■ **EXHIBIT 5.3**

Examples of Mission and Vision Statements		
	Mission Statement	**Vision Statement**
Big Brothers Big Sisters[20]	The Big Brothers Big Sisters mission is to help children reach their potential through professionally supported, one-to-one relationships with mentors that have a measurable impact on youth.	The Big Brothers Big Sisters vision is successful mentoring relationships for all children who need and want them, contributing to brighter futures, better schools, and stronger communities for all.
Toyota Motor Sales[21]	To attract and attain customers with high-valued products and services and the most satisfying ownership experience in America.	To be the most successful and respected car company in America.

Source: Big Brothers Big Sisters mission and vision statements; Toyota Motor Sales mission and vision statements.

Mission Clarity Leads to Better Choices

Without a well-established mission, an organization may lose focus. For example, suppose an entrepreneur decided to start a small coffee shop in her hometown. She has some money and finds a few friends to invest in the shop. After renting a store, she purchases equipment, buys nice tables and chairs, contracts with suppliers to provide high-end ingredients for her coffees, and hires three employees. She distributes flyers at the local supermarket and advertises online.

Sales are good from the start. So good, in fact, that she decides to offer ice cream. Sales continue to improve and after a year in business, she's flush with cash and decides to add a deli. She signs more contracts with suppliers, buys more equipment, and hires more employees. The little coffee shop has now become a full-fledged restaurant. The owner is delighted—she feels like she's made it. But now, the environment in the restaurant is bustling and noisy, when it used to be quiet and serene. Gone are the comfortable chairs and calming music. The owner thinks this change is the price of growth.

Customers notice the change, too—and they don't like it. Sales begin to plateau. Accounts payable increase faster than revenue. The owner must take action, so she lets a couple of her employees go. Customers now find themselves waiting longer for their orders, and the remaining employees feel overworked. Sales begin a steep decline and creditors request immediate payment. The business is on a slippery slope from which it will be difficult to recover.

What went wrong? Isn't growth the goal of any business? Not necessarily, and certainly not this way. This entrepreneur lost her focus—or maybe she never had one. If she had been clear that the purpose of her business was to make and sell excellent coffee drinks in a relaxing environment, her mission statement may have read, "We provide top-of-the-line coffee and coffee drinks to local community members in a beautiful, relaxing environment." With this mission to guide her when she was flush with cash, she might have chosen to open another coffee shop rather than entering into three totally different businesses. Or, she could have upgraded her equipment or supported her star employees through tuition assistance so they would be ready to manage new shops.

As this example shows, leaders have many choices. Without a well-defined mission and vision for guidance, a company is a ship without a rudder.[22] Clarity about the organization's mission, its fundamental purpose, and how it is different from its competitors can help make choices easier, more logical, and more likely to lead to success.

Vision: Our Highest Aspiration

Once leaders are clear about an organization's mission, they need to tie that mission to a clear, compelling, and accessible vision. A vision is both aspirational and inspirational. It describes a future that an organization has not yet attained, but one that can be accomplished with the right planning and strategies. Employees and customers alike can be inspired by an organization's vision, which can result in a committed workforce and loyal customers.

A company's mission and vision are the umbrella under which all of the activities of the organization happen. All the strategies, plans, projects, initiatives, and work must ultimately connect to the organization's purpose. What this means in practice is that managers and leaders need to help people understand where they fit—how their work is tied to the mission and vision. Managers and leaders also need to create visions of their own, specific to what they and their teams need to accomplish.

Mark McCord-Amasis is the Head of Global Strategy, Planning, and Workplace for GlaxoSmithKlein (GSK), and he helps bring the company's mission and vision to fruition. His responsibilities include oversight of the design, planning and building of facilities, plants, and office buildings all over the world. Included in this is the design of space *inside* buildings generally referred to as Workplace. GSK wisely recognizes the importance the physical environment has on performance, productivity, and innovation. As Mark puts it, "The layout of a workplace is instrumental in fostering interaction, collaboration, trust, accountability, teamwork, and innovation."[23] These competencies, along with outstanding leadership and management, are what enable companies like GSK to thrive in challenging times. In the *Leadership Perspective* feature, Mark McCord-Amasis, a great leader himself, helps us to see how vision is an important component of every single project, large and small.

Leadership Perspective

Mark McCord-Amasis is a creative and dedicated leader. He leads a full and exciting life, and he's inspiring. He has a unique perspective on his work—one not often found in the real estate and facilities industry. Mark sees one of his primary responsibilities as creating "inspiring workplaces where people can do their very best work."[24] A robust change management process is critical to driving behavioral changes required to deliver maximum benefit from these innovative work spaces. That's why vision and change go hand in hand. Mark relies on strong and talented

people in teams all around the world to help bring a vision, and the accompanying changes, to life. Here's what he has to say about vision and leading change:

> *The essential act of leadership is to envision the preferred future you want to create for your business or organization and put that into words—and then lead people in translating words into actions. But you can't do this alone. It's essential to involve people in the visioning process because a new*

Continued on next page >>

Perspectives Continued

● **Mark McCord-Amasis**
Head of Global Facility Strategy for GSK
"The essential act of leadership is to envision the preferred future you want for your business or organization and put that into words. . . ."

vision means a new path, and it means new ways of working. That means people will need to change.

To get people behind change, you need to make sure people understand the vision for the project—in my case, new workspaces. They must also see how where we're going connects with the company's mission and vision. You need to help them feel excited about the future. Just as you need to feel inspired and optimistic about where you are going, so does every single person who will be involved in the hard work of implementing change.

My approach is not to tell people what to think or do, but to facilitate an interactive visioning and strategic planning session with key leaders and managers. I don't take this process lightly; I prepare. I make sure that I have really thought about where we need to go, what the issues are, what our vision is, what changes must occur. Then, together, we discuss and brainstorm the key issues. We come to real agreement about what matters most in terms of our goals and objectives. We understand critical success factors and barriers and develop strategies to address them. As people go through this process, there is a sense of engagement and ownership of the vision, the strategic plan, and the change process. Everything is transparent. We are excited and committed.

We're now ready to go to the next step: planning how to implement our strategy. We're ready to reach out to others—the managers and staff who are closest to the workspace, the business operations, and logistics. We're ready to get them as excited and engaged as we are. This process isn't necessarily easy, and it takes time. But it's worth it. As we move into the hard work of implementation, we have a single, coherent vision and strategy that we have all contributed to, feel good about, and buy into. We also believe in and are committed to the change plan.

By taking this approach, people take ownership of the vision, strategy, and the change process, and they are ready and willing to do the hard work that follows. Too often, leaders get people behind the vision, and maybe the strategy, but not the changes required to realize that vision. That's a mistake. People need to get behind all three—vision, strategy, and the change plan.

Clarity and commitment to both vision and the changes that need to happen are very important, because people are much more able to choose the right activities and jettison the rest. Most of us have too much to do—a clear vision and strategy, alongside an agreed-upon change process, allows us all to say "no" to unnecessary activities or work that fit the old model, but not the new.

Source: Personal interviews with Mark McCord-Amasis conducted by Annie McKee, 2009 and 2012.

As Mark McCord-Amasis shows us, the best leaders are capable of clearly imagining an organizational future that is inspiring. But they go much further—they involve people at every step, they link vision to planning, and they include change management in everything they do. How do good leaders do this?

Scholars note that the creation of a concrete and meaningful vision is partly the result of systems thinking. Systems thinking involves taking in as much information as possible about people, the organization, and its environment, and then using that information to understand complex cause-and-effect relationships and to predict what could happen in the future.[25]

As we saw in the *Leadership Perspective* feature, visioning is best done by a combination of people: leaders, managers, and employees. Someone, however, usually starts this process and brings ideas to the table. In small, entrepreneurial start-ups, it is often the founder (or founders) of the company who begin to define the mission and vision. In larger organizations, it is often the top leaders, including the president or CEO, vice presidents of business divisions, finance and HR leaders, and possibly others who explore important aspects of mission and vision. In many companies, HR leaders drive this process by doing research and creating opportunities for the executives to engage in conversations about the vision. They also engage employees in dialogue, debating and fine-tuning the vision and mission to make them come alive in the business.

Sometimes employees drive the process more directly, with the support of leadership and HR. This is popular because effective leaders understand the importance of getting buy-in from employees, especially on things as central as an organization's mission and vision.

Some companies, such as Johnson & Johnson, set their mission many years ago. This mission is a pillar on which the organization is built, and the company is (rightly) proud of it. Sometimes, though, fundamental changes in mission and vision are necessary. Technology, globalization, and the advent of new industries can drive profound change in an organization's central purpose.[26]

A company's mission and vision therefore need to be carefully tended to, communicated, and *used* to guide choices. Mission and vision direct the organization's choices about plans, goals, and activities, and they facilitate the strategic planning process, as you will see in the next section.

Discussion Questions

1. Take a look at your college's mission statement. What does it tell you about the institution? Do you feel it accurately describes what your college is and does?

2. Write a personal mission statement that captures who you are. You might start with answering these big questions: What do you stand for? What's your purpose in life and in work?

---

5. What Is Strategy?

Objective 5.5
Define strategy.

Imagine a football team running onto the field to play the first game of the season. All of a sudden it becomes clear that the players on the field are unprepared and have no sense of how they are going to win the game. These players probably will not be successful, even if their mission (play football) and vision (win the division championship) are clear. It's the same with organizations. Mission and vision alone, as critical as they are, are not enough. Just as teams and players need strategies, so do organizations, leaders, and employees.

But what, exactly, is strategy? The history of the word is telling. From Greek to French, and then to English in 1810, *strategy* meant "the art of a general." Indeed, the Greek word *strategia* meant "office or command of a general," and it was composed of *stratos* ("that which is spread out") and *agos* ("leader"). So, historically, the word meant to spread leadership beyond a leader's direct reach. Today strategy is an organization's overarching plan that articulates its direction, approach, major areas of focus, and major goals.

Strategy
An organization's overarching plan that articulates its direction, approach, major areas of focus, and major goals.

Tom Malnight is a professor of strategy at IMD, a leading international business school in Switzerland. He believes that strategy begins with answering questions such as: What value does the company add? How are we making money? How will we grow or maintain our position? In addition, it is important to honestly assess the competition with questions like: Why or how is our strategy better than our competitors? Why might some customers prefer their company to our company?[27]

Creating a strategy means assessing the current reality, challenging assumptions, seeing things from multiple perspectives, and creating alternatives.[28] This in turn means taking some risks, because challenging assumptions invariably means leaving a comfort zone. Malnight advocates stepping up to risk by thinking in terms of "what must we do" as opposed to "what can we do." By defining what we must do to achieve our mission or long-term goals, a path to achievement can be developed by choosing actions that are necessary, as opposed to actions that are easy or convenient.

Strategy Links Mission, Vision, Goals, and Actions

A strategy helps an organization realize its mission and brings its vision to life. Whether it is a collegiate soccer team, a small local start-up, or a huge multinational corporation, every organization needs a strategy to guide decisions, direct behavior, and organize activities. In this section we will explore a number of important concepts related to strategy. First, though, let's look at what one well-known company did to create and sustain innovation through its strategy.

BUSINESS CASE   **3M**

Investing in the Future

3M is a successful company, and its products—including Post-it Notes, Buf-Puf facial sponges, and Scotch Tape—are well known. 3M is renowned for its innovation, and many people are familiar with the story of the invention of the Post-it Note. Arthur Fry, a 3M employee, was a church choir member who got annoyed that his bookmark wouldn't stay in place. "It was during the sermon that Sunday morning that I thought, 'What I really need is a little bookmark that will stick to the paper but will not tear the paper when I remove it.'"[29] After this realization, Fry did some experimenting and his efforts ultimately generated the adhesive behind the hugely popular Post-it Note.[30]

Innovations like this keep companies relevant. And to stay relevant, businesses like 3M must constantly shift goals and strategies.[31] During the 1990s, 3M's management decided to take a very new approach to the changing market: They banked on innovation. Leaders planned for a 30 percent growth in revenue from *new* products, and they intended to keep revenue coming from new products going forward.[32] But how did 3M plan for, create, and sustain innovation? Let's look at two of their approaches to strategy and change.

Lesson 1: Strategy Is a Navigation of Future and Current Realities

3M decided that strategy must be a living process happening throughout the organization at all times. The new role of strategy, as understood by 3M, was to support the organization's need to deliver results today while simultaneously adapting for the future.[33]

In order to make this change, 3M redefined its decision-making processes to allow for fluidity and timeliness. For example, it streamlined vendor and human resources management processes so typical activities (such as hiring people) could be completed within an average of three weeks.[34] Moreover, it understood that none of the efforts to change would work without quality leaders. 3M accordingly developed leaders who not only manage processes but also lead through vision, mission, and inspiration.[35]

Lesson 2: Get into Other People's Shoes: Your Customers, Competitors, and Employees

The challenges 3M's leaders faced were the usual ones associated with change management: tension among groups, fear of change, and complacency. Most challenging, though, was the realization that the company couldn't find the solution to these problems alone. What followed was a bold step to open up dialogue both inside and outside the organization.[36] 3M started by asking itself about its stakeholders: Who were the ones who could critically influence the company's path to sustained success? The answer was customers, competitors, and employees.

3M realized that "lead users" (or customers who use a product frequently) were ahead of the product development curve and were likely to start thinking up the next solution before the developers.[37] In response, 3M developed the *lead customers methodology*, which is built on the notion that innovation is driven by customers. As part of this process, 3M managers conduct regular focus group interviews, and they invest in relationship building between developers and lead customers.[38]

3M also got into its competitor's shoes and increased its focus on competitor information.[39] 3M now uses competitor data at the core of its planning process, ensuring that key data is timely and available to all decision makers within the organization.[40]

Finally, 3M walked in its employees' shoes. To help foster innovation, 3M employees now have 15 percent of their time free to invest in special projects.[41] This framework enables them to experiment with outside-the-box ideas: "Most of the inventions that 3M depends on today came out of that kind of individual initiative," says Bill Coyne, retired senior vice president of research and development.[42]

3M has succeeded in making innovation a central driving force in the company. But change is a constant process, and perhaps 3M's biggest success has been making change a constant factor in its strategic planning processes.

We can learn many things from 3M's long-term strategic focus on innovation. Not the least of these lessons is that strategy and strategic planning are not one-time events. At its best, strategy is a living, breathing process that includes multiple activities, frameworks, and linkages.

Most strategies, even for small businesses, are complex. For large, multidivision and/or multinational companies, this complexity is multiplied exponentially. ■ **EXHIBIT 5.4** shows a simplified view of the components of most strategies. You can imagine that the full picture for any of these institutions would be extensive and complex.

■ **EXHIBIT 5.4**

Components of Strategies

Example	Mission	Vision	Long-Term Strategic Goals	Short-Term Goals and Subgoals	Tactics and Actions
College Women's Soccer Team	Engage players, students, faculty, staff, and alumni in the noble game of soccer.	Become the top women's college soccer team in the United States.	1. Create and maintain an exemplary training program. 2. Build the bench for the next three years.	1. Win the season. 2. Create and implement this year's recruiting program.	1. Assess each player for training needs. 2. Identify top high schools from which to recruit.
Start-Up Coffee Shop	Provide the best coffee in the city in an atmosphere that both customers and staff enjoy.	Become *the* place in our city where local people enjoy coffee and friends.	1. Open two more coffee shops within three years. 2. Buy the shop we now rent.	1. Identify and select suppliers. 2. Provide technical training for all baristas. 3. Provide customer service training for all employees.	1. Conduct a taste test during a local street fair. 2. Test and buy comfortable furniture.
Large Multidivision Food Corporation	Provide healthy, tasty food for the people of the world.	Become the company of choice when it comes to good food all over the world.	Snacks Division: 1. Streamline and reduce number of brands. 2. Expand research and development to support creation of products that are desirable and that meet caloric and fat restrictions.	1. Evaluate each brand in major markets. 2. Implement testing to ensure that all snacks meet caloric and fat restrictions.	1. Examine financial reports by brand for the past three years; create a forecast by market. 2. Conduct analysis of research and development operations to determine HR and technical needs.

Types of Strategies

One of the ways leaders and managers attempt to handle the complexity of strategic planning in large organizations is by categorizing types of strategies. One way to categorize strategies is by describing them in terms of the part of the organization they support. Corporate strategies are designed for the entire organization. Business strategies are designed for particular divisions or lines of business. Functional strategies guide key areas of the business, such as human resources, finance, and marketing. Within each major category of strategies, there can be other types of strategies that support achievement of organizational, business, or functional goals.

CORPORATE STRATEGIES

As can be seen in ■ **EXHIBIT 5.5**, a company has several options for strategies at the corporate level. For instance, companies can decide to follow a growth strategy to expand operations and/or increase market share. A growth strategy might include plans for projects like enhanced and innovative marketing, soliciting capital to expand into new territories, or plans to improve productivity.

Growth strategy
A corporate strategy that involves expansion of operations and/or an increase in market share.

■ **EXHIBIT 5.5**

Corporate Strategies

Corporate Strategy	Focus	Example
Growth	Expansion into new market(s) and/or increasing market share. May be accomplished through expanding business, acquiring or merging with other businesses, or joint ventures.	Annick Goutal is a French fragrance company that created a growth strategy in 2009. The strategy called for expansion: creation of new products, doing business in new territories, and increasing the number of stores that sell the company's products from 11 to 40. By 2012, the company's products were sold in 110 stores in France.[43] In comparison, the largest wine company in the world, Constellation Brands, grew through acquisition. In 2004, Constellation acquired Robert Mondavi for just over $1 billion in cash.[44] Later, in 2007, Constellation purchased Fortune Brands, makers of Clos du Bois, Geyser Peak, and Wild Horse wines, for $885 million.[45]
Stability	Maintaining current market position.	In the early 1990s, Powell Flute Company of New England was known for making the best handcrafted flutes in the world. So, when the company learned of a new technology for hole placement on the flute body, there was a great deal of debate as to whether the company could adopt this method and still retain its identity as Powell Flutes, as well as maintain existing sales levels. Balancing the need for change and retaining a stable market image and identity required that company leaders focus carefully on maintaining certain aspects of the artisans' craft and the organizational culture, while simultaneously learning and changing.[46]
Retrenchment	Defensive posture to hold off threats while turning a company around.	Bank of America has focused since 2009 on transforming the company, primarily by strengthening its foundation, which the CEO identified as its balance sheet. The company focused on selling non-core assets and reducing its workforce, improving its capital ratios, building up liquidity, and reducing exposure to risk. In its 2011 Annual Report, the bank claimed to have achieved "a stronger, leaner company better prepared to handle economic uncertainty."[47]
Divestiture	Selling off or folding a particular division.	In 1998, German automaker Daimler purchased American carmaker Chrysler for $35 billion. Within fewer than 10 years, dramatic financial losses led Daimler to essentially pay Cerberus Capital Management more than $600 million to take Chrysler off its hands.[48]

Acquisition strategy
A corporate strategy that involves joining with other businesses by buying, merging with, or taking over other companies.

Joint venture
A formal arrangement between two or more entities to engage in activities together and to share risk.

There are several ways a company can implement a growth strategy. One way is to employ an **acquisition strategy**, which involves joining with other businesses by buying, merging with, or taking over other companies. This might include acquiring companies in the same industry or in industries that support the core business. It may also require purchasing altogether different businesses.

Although acquisitions seem like a great way to grow, the phrase "buyer beware" can apply. Noted scholar Harbir Singh and colleagues studied acquisitions of technology firms and argue that sometimes integration can decrease innovation in an acquired firm, particularly for firms that have not launched products prior to being acquired.[49] Of course, acquisition-related problems are not limited to tech firms. Factors such as the differing languages and cultures of two organizations can slow down the integration process in any strategic merger or acquisition.[50] Such complications exist regardless of whether the organizations' employees actually speak different languages, because each organization has its own culture and its own way of using words.[51]

Strategic alliances, which are often called **joint ventures**, are another way for organizations to implement a growth strategy. A joint venture is a formal arrangement between two or more entities to engage in activities together and to share risk. For example, the San Francisco Bay Joint Venture was created under the Migratory Bird

Treaty Act. Public and private organizations such as conservation and land development groups came together in this joint venture with a common mission to preserve and restore wetlands in and around the San Francisco Bay.[52]

Another example of a joint business venture is Walmart's partnership with Bharti Enterprises, an Indian company. In 2009, Walmart started doing business in India for the first time. However, the Indian Walmart is not the typical Walmart you see in cities across America. Rather, the retail giant had formed a joint venture in 2006 with Bharti, one of India's leading business groups, to plan for and ultimately conduct business in India while complying with strict government restrictions on foreign competition with India's domestic businesses. The Indian Walmart is a wholesale business catering to the specific needs of vegetable vendors, hospitals, restaurants, and hotels, operating under the name BestPrice Modern Wholesale (■ **EXHIBIT 5.6**).[53] As of 2012, BestPrice Modern Wholesale has 17 stores and continues to expand.[54] This is despite highly politicized populist criticism of foreign direct investment in retail.[55]

When companies contemplate a joint venture, they must consider whether, how quickly, and to what degree to integrate. Professor Harbir Singh notes that costs of coordination can be high, and they must be monitored and moderated.[56] Often, organizations attempt to manage coordination by developing bureaucracies with lots of rules, which often slow things down. Interestingly, however, trust tends to decrease the need to rely on rules and bureaucracy. This means that in complex joint ventures where the cost of coordination may be high, it is well worth leaders' time and effort to build trusting relationships and an environment that fosters confidence and collaboration.

A choice to remain relatively static would call for a **stability strategy**. This strategy is intended to maintain a company's current position. Perhaps due to a struggling economy or to disruptive societal or technological changes, a company's top managers might decide that the best approach is to simply maintain the current position. This is not a strategy of doing nothing, however. In fact, during crises or challenging times, a company might have to adopt dramatic measures to ensure stability, such as restructuring, closing plants, or initiating layoffs in order to maintain its current position in the market.

Stability strategy
A corporate strategy that is intended to maintain a company's current position.

■ **EXHIBIT 5.6**
What benefits and drawbacks might be involved in a joint venture?

Source: David Pearson/Alamy

Retrenchment strategy
A corporate strategy that is adopted when a company needs to regroup and defend itself while turning the business around.

A third type of corporate strategy is a **retrenchment strategy**. This kind of strategy is adopted when a company needs to regroup and defend itself while turning the business around. An example of this would be General Motors in 2009, after the company was purchased, in part, by the U.S. government. At that time, CEO Rick Wagoner was either fired or pressured to resign and a new CEO, Fritz Henderson, took his place. Henderson sought to create a strategy to turn General Motors around and restore it to the successful company it once had been.

Divestiture strategy
A corporate strategy in which a company sells off or folds a particular division, business, brand, product, or service line.

Finally, a **divestiture strategy** is one in which a company sells off or folds a particular division, business, brand, product, or service line. Sometimes companies do this so they can focus on their core businesses. Daimler, for example, essentially paid a capital management firm to take control of Chrysler less than a decade after purchasing the American automaker for a sum of $35 billion.

BUSINESS STRATEGIES

Differentiation
A business strategy of providing a product or service that is perceived as unique by customers.

At the business level, companies craft strategies that support a particular division of the business, brand, product, or service line to remain or become successful in the marketplace. As you can see in ■ **EXHIBIT 5.7**, one business-level strategy is **differentiation**, which involves providing a product or service that is perceived as unique by customers. Swedish-based retailer IKEA has differentiated itself with the layout of its stores. Apple's iPhone was also instantly perceived as unique. *Time* magazine even declared the iPhone the "Invention of the Year."[57] Unique products and services are often related to an organization's core competencies. A **core competency** is an activity that an organization does very well. These sets of skills or knowledge are those that customers readily identify with the company, as well as those that set the company apart from its competitors.[58]

Core competency
An activity that an organization does very well.

Cost leadership
A business strategy of providing the lowest prices in the industry for a particular product, product line, or service.

Cost leadership is a strategy of providing the lowest prices in the industry for a particular product, product line, or service. In grocery retailers, the "store brand" is typically the lowest-priced item in each category. The grocer is utilizing a cost leadership strategy by pricing common goods such as canned vegetables, cookies, and pasta lower than their name-brand competitors.

Niche strategy
A business strategy that caters to a narrow segment of the market.

A **niche strategy** caters to a narrow segment of the market. Companies such as Rolex, Bulgari, and Lamborghini Gallardo all cater to a specific niche in the market—upper-income customers. These luxury goods are marketed in entirely different ways than mainstream products. One is not likely to see a commercial for them during the evening news.

■ **EXHIBIT 5.7**

Business-Level Strategies		
Business Strategy	**Focus**	**Example**
Differentiation	Providing unique products, services, or features	Apple iPhone (when released) IKEA store design
Cost leadership	Being most competitive (lowest priced) in terms of the cost of a product or service	Grocery store brand products, which are lower-priced than other items on the store's shelves Trader Joe's store brand products
Niche	Catering to a particular segment of the market or a particular demand	Rolex watches and Gucci bags (high-price status symbols) Richforth Limited (school uniform manufacturer)
Vertical integration	Seeking cost savings and efficiency through operating businesses along the supply chain	Delta Airlines: purchased oil refinery to make the jet fuel to power their planes Heroin cartel: own and operate poppy farms, heroin manufacturing plants, shipping fleet; manage sales force on the ground

Finally, **vertical integration** is a strategy of acquiring or developing businesses along the **supply chain**. A supply chain includes all of the resources, products, services, and operations that contribute to producing and selling goods or services. An example of vertical integration would be a pasta manufacturer that elects to buy farms that produce semolina wheat, a key ingredient in pasta. Owning the farms may cut costs and help the company control quality.

Vertical integration
A business strategy of acquiring or developing businesses along the supply chain.

Supply chain
All of the resources, products, services, and operations that contribute to producing and selling goods or services.

FUNCTIONAL STRATEGIES

Examples of functions include human resources, finance, marketing, sales, information technology, facilities, health and safety, risk management, and legal services. Many large businesses have divisions or departments for these functions. In smaller companies, services are often assigned to individuals or provided by consultants or specialized businesses.

Functional strategies are departmental strategies that are developed to help an organization achieve its goals. For example, if a differentiation strategy was selected, the marketing team might develop a strategy to enhance advertising, focusing on the unique features of the business or products. This strategy could include plans for brochures, videos, television ads, or an online ad campaign to show customers the unique features and benefits of new products. Meanwhile, the operations team might retool a manufacturing facility to prepare for an increase in production demands.

Functional strategies
Departmental strategies that are developed to help an organization achieve its goals.

As you can see, strategy and strategic planning are multifaceted and complex. How are these strategies developed? Where do managers and strategists start, and what steps do they follow? In the next section, you will learn about strategic planning—how it is typically done, as well as some guidelines for avoiding common problems.

Discussion Questions

1. Consider a product you see advertised on television, on the Internet, or in magazines. What business strategy do you think the company is employing with regard to the product?

2. Using the Internet, review facts about a company you know well. What is the company's corporate strategy? What are its business strategies? Functional strategies?

6. What Needs to Be Considered in a Strategic Planning Process?

Objective 5.6
Understand what needs to be considered during the strategic planning process.

Strategic planning is the process of examining an organization's internal and external environments and determining major goals that will help the company realize its mission and move toward its vision. The strategic planning process addresses the following questions: What is the state of the business, both internally and in the market? What are the goals that will enable the business to achieve its mission? What activities and tasks will the business need to engage in to achieve these goals?

Strategic planning
The process of examining an organization's internal and external environments and determining major goals that will help the company realize its mission and move toward its vision.

Strategic planning is a complex and multilayered process that often begins with an examination of the competitive landscape; the social, technological, and natural environment; and stakeholders' needs and expectations. Each of these is discussed in the following sections.

Environmental Scanning

Environmental forces and conditions can have a profound impact on strategic planning and an organization's success or failure.[59] **Environmental scanning** is the

Environmental scanning
The process of assessing social and natural conditions that have the potential to affect an organization.

process of assessing social and natural conditions that have the potential to affect an organization. Let's look at this process in practice.

Today, many people are concerned about the cost of oil and gas, as well as the negative impact of burning fossil fuels. In response, people in many countries are increasingly concerned about the fuel efficiency of their cars. These conditions affect the automobile industry. For example, when the U.S. government began funding the creation of hybrids in the American auto market, Japanese automakers noticed. Moving quickly, they invested heavily in the creation of hybrid vehicles and beat the American automakers in introducing products to the market. The result? The Toyota Prius hybrid has been the highest selling hybrid in the United States every year since its introduction, and U.S. Prius sales surpassed one million vehicles in April 2011.[60]

It's only fair to note, however, that when massive innovations occur, such as changes to the gas-powered engine, there will be numerous problems, as well as starts and stops. The hybrid vehicle is no exception. There are numerous consumer complaints about hybrids, they are expensive to buy and maintain, and some have even had safety issues.

When planning revolutionary changes, successful companies pay careful attention to aspects of the economic, sociocultural, legal, tax, political, technological, natural, and industrial environments when formulating strategies. Then, they listen to feedback from customers.

ECONOMIC ENVIRONMENT

The economic environment encompasses the local, regional, national, and global economic conditions that affect an organization's ability to achieve its mission and attain its goals. Economic conditions will determine how easy or difficult it is for a company to access capital to invest, whether the company has access to credit, and, if so, how much it will cost. For example, the economic crisis in the Eurozone began in 2009 and caused a widespread loss of confidence that is, according to *The Economist* (in 2011), "as much political as economic."[61] As this example shows, business leaders examine the current climate, but they also try to predict the state of the economy in the coming months and years.

SOCIOCULTURAL ENVIRONMENT

As social changes occur, managers must attempt to understand how these trends will help or hurt a business. For example, gluten-free diets have increased in popularity. Originally designed for celiac patients who cannot tolerate gluten protein, the diets have been adopted by people wishing to treat other conditions and lose weight. In 2012, an estimated $7 billion was spent by millions of U.S. consumers on food products labeled gluten-free.[62] Similarly, social networking tools such as Facebook and Twitter have dramatically changed how people communicate.[63] Social networking has affected music, news, education, and book publishing firms. Sociocultural evolutions—and revolutions—will continue, and leaders must stay abreast of these changes and adapt their strategies quickly.

LEGAL AND TAX ENVIRONMENT

Laws are powerful guidelines that inform what an organization can and cannot do. Larger companies often have an entire legal team to keep abreast of new and pending laws, as well as to ensure that the firm complies with existing laws. Smaller organizations are more likely to retain legal assistance only when needed. In either case, knowing and abiding by international, federal, state, and local legislation is important. The price of acting outside the law can be high—in many ways.

For example, in December, 2011, Pelican Refining Company LLC, a Texas concern, agreed to pay $12 million for a slew of violations against the U.S. government's Clean Air Act, constituting the largest criminal fine ever paid in Louisiana for air pollution.[64] On a smaller scale, countless businesses have felt the pinch when county and local governments have assessed fees for legal violations related to things as varied as zoning, chemical emissions, and fair labor practices, to name just a few.

Consider the effects of tax laws. States, counties, and cities can all adopt taxation policies that either support businesses or do not. The geographic variation in tax laws is profoundly important for businesses to consider when deciding where to locate headquarters, manufacturing plants, and field offices. It is also important for entrepreneurs: Many people are aware of major taxes, like federal and state, and include these in their business plans. They often forget city taxes, however, which can be significant.

POLITICAL ENVIRONMENT

The United States has a stable political environment. However, this is not the case in other parts of the world, so keeping tabs on the political climate is a necessity when doing business globally. For example, following the Arab Spring in 2011, Egypt's tourism business saw 32 percent less revenue than the previous year.[65] Companies that want to do business in politically volatile countries need to be highly attuned to the special circumstances, conditions, and costs associated with manufacturing goods or providing services in these nations. In addition, politically negotiated international trade agreements can help or hinder a business. (We will explore trade agreements in Chapter 14.)

TECHNOLOGICAL ENVIRONMENT

When formulating strategies, leaders need to recognize that technologies will change, resulting in both opportunities and potentially more competition. The information revolution has changed business practices profoundly. Some businesses, such as Facebook and Yahoo!, exist solely because of the advent of the Internet. Other companies have used the Internet to enhance their sales by permitting customers to purchase products online. Additional technological advances exist as well. For example, in 2012 UPS leveraged its logistics system to set up a new service designed to eliminate missed deliveries by sending a text, phone, or e-mail message to the recipient the day before delivery. Recipients can provide signatures and authorizations online. The company also offers additional services such as a delivery planner, a two-hour delivery window, detailed delivery instructions (for example, on the back porch), choice of address, and the ability to redirect deliveries while on vacation.[66]

NATURAL ENVIRONMENT

The natural environment is a focal point for many businesses today because of the threat and impact of global warming, the realization that the supply of fossil fuels is finite, and the widespread attention paid to land use and threats to biodiversity. Companies such as IBM, Infosys, and Toyota Motor Sales are all taking steps to become more energy efficient.[67] They are likely doing this to save costs, but they are probably also responding to the rising awareness that use of alternative energy sources will set companies apart from their competitors.

Of course, there are a number of other ways in which the natural environment might affect strategy and strategic planning (■ **EXHIBIT 5.8**).

Nature is unpredictable (witness the 9.0 magnitude earthquake and subsequent tsunami in Japan in 2011, which crippled the country's energy supply and destroyed or seriously damaged nearly 200,000 buildings, including five nuclear reactors). The best strategies include contingency plans and risk management strategies to guide actions when unpredictable events occur.

LAST BUT NOT LEAST: THE INDUSTRY ENVIRONMENT

An **industry** is a collective group of companies that provide the same or similar products and services. For example, Domino's, Papa John's, and your local pizzeria are all specific companies in the pizza industry. The five forces model was developed by

Industry
A collective group of companies that provide the same or similar products and services.

■ **EXHIBIT 5.8**

How the Natural Environment Can Affect Strategy and Strategic Planning

Natural Environment	Examples
Weather patterns can influence choice of business location and business services.	Knowledge that an area is prone to tornadoes would factor into site selection and construction plans.
Terrain may affect decisions about the distribution of goods	A company that is selling ice cream in Indonesia would need to have a plan for distribution to hundreds of islands.
Vegetation and wildlife often need to be taken into account	Consider the Brazilian rain forest: Millions of acres have been burned or developed in recent years, raising questions about land use and development.

Harvard professor Michael Porter in 1979 as a framework to analyze the industry in which a company resides and competes.[68] Each of the five forces is presented below, along with questions managers might ask to determine where a company fits within its industry. The five forces model—and the answers to the questions this model provokes—can contribute to an evaluation of a company's competitive position in the market.

- *Competitive rivalry within the industry:* Within the industry, how intense is the rivalry? Are competitors "cutthroat" or more laissez-faire?
- *Threat of new entrants:* What is the likelihood that a new competitor will enter the industry? Do barriers currently exist to keep new competitors at bay?
- *Threat of substitutes:* How easy is it for customers to substitute something similar? Can the products or services in the industry be substituted?
- *Bargaining power of suppliers:* Are suppliers and vendors to the industry powerful enough to hold a great deal of bargaining power? Is it difficult to negotiate with suppliers?
- *Bargaining power of customers:* Do customers have strong bargaining power? Can they demand lower prices or more services because of their position?[69]

The five forces model has been adapted over the years. For example, a sixth force called *complementors* is sometimes added to help evaluate strategic alliances.[70] To explain this force by way of a metaphor, remember that complementary colors make each other brighter. Similarly, businesses that serve as complementors to one another enhance each other's potential.

Stakeholder Analysis

When scanning the environment, one of the most important arenas to explore is what people want from a business. FreshDirect, an online grocer in the New York metropolitan market, illustrates this concept quite clearly.

FreshDirect has been in business since 1999 and specializes in delivering fresh foods to the doorsteps of its online shoppers. Since that time, the company has relied on Internet-savvy leaders to bolster its stakeholder and online sales knowledge and improve its customer service. This, in turn, has helped the company thrive in a particularly challenging industry.

Based on customer feedback, FreshDirect has developed initiatives to increase customer value and build relationships.[71] These initiatives include utilizing socially responsible packaging, creating a system that tracks shoppers' purchase history and prompts them if they forget historically common items, and developing a product rating system so shoppers can grade their purchases.[72]

In all of these activities, FreshDirect focuses on one group of stakeholders—customers. A **stakeholder** is any constituent potentially impacted by an organization's actions, either inside or outside the organization. One way to look at stakeholders is to see them as individuals, groups, or organizations that have an interest in a particular outcome. This includes all those who have an *effect* on the outcome of a plan, project, or policy, as well as any person or any group *affected by* the outcome.[73]

Some stakeholders, such as customers and employees, have a greater deal of influence on an organization, but other stakeholders who wield less influence can still be important. For example, the local community where a firm is based may have little interaction with the company, but maintaining a positive image in the community and in the local press is vital.

■ **EXHIBIT 5.9** shows a stakeholder map—a visual representation of people and groups that can impact and/or will be impacted by an organization's actions.[74] In a typical analysis, stakeholders can be placed into one of three groups:

- *Key stakeholders:* Those who have significant influence or importance
- *Primary stakeholders:* Those who are directly affected by an organization's actions
- *Secondary stakeholders:* Those who are indirectly affected by an organization's actions.[75]

Sometimes, a list of stakeholders can be quite extensive, and it is often difficult to determine which stakeholders are key, primary, or secondary. For this reason, stakeholder analysis is an important part of strategic planning. A **stakeholder analysis** includes an audit of all stakeholders and an analysis of how each stakeholder will be affected by an organization's decisions, and/or how the stakeholder can affect the organization. Stakeholder analysis was publicly debated in 2008 and 2009 when the U.S. government was deciding whether to bail out Ford, Chrysler, and General Motors, the country's three largest domestic automakers. Although it seemed unfair to bail out companies whose strategies over many years had left them unable to compete in the world market, other stakeholders far removed from these companies would have been dramatically affected by their demise. One widely publicized estimate was that nearly 2 million jobs in the United States were in some way directly connected with the U.S. auto manufacturing industry. Clearly this stakeholder analysis was an important part of the government's decision-making process.[76] Ultimately, large portions of the debt were paid off early. While some of the money may never be recouped given the ways in which some of this debt has been restructured, all of the major automakers have experienced a turnaround and are doing well. Treasury Secretary Timothy Geithner stated in 2011, "We didn't do this to maximize return. We did it to save jobs."[77] In that respect, this decision was successful for that set of stakeholders.

Stakeholder
Any constituent potentially impacted by an organization's actions, either inside or outside the organization.

■ **EXHIBIT 5.9**
The stakeholder map shows all the groups and people who are affected by an organization's actions.

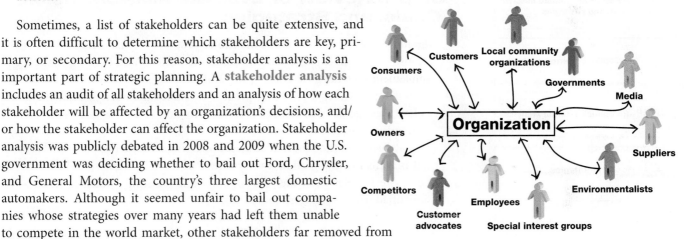

Stakeholder analysis
An audit of all stakeholders and an analysis of how each stakeholder will be affected by an organization's decisions, and/or how the stakeholder can affect the organization.

Discussion Questions

1. Think of an organization to which you belong (school, work, community group, social, or sports club). Does this group have a strategic plan? Who developed it? Who is aware of it and who is not? How has the plan's development and dissemination impacted the organization?

2. Think about a big decision in your life. Draw a stakeholder map to include the people or groups who will be affected by your decision. Code them as *key, primary,* or *secondary* stakeholders. Reflect on how this map can help you in stakeholder management.

7. What Are the Steps in the Strategic Planning Process?

To illustrate how important strategic planning is, and how often plans need to change, consider what happened when the entertainment service Netflix attempted to split itself into two separate companies with two separate Web sites: The Netflix name was slated to remain with the streaming video service, while the company's DVD-by-mail service would take on the name Qwikster. Subscribers were angered by this move, which came on the heels of a 60 percent price increase, and roughly 25 million people cancelled their service. This record number of cancellations and a wealth of negative subscriber feedback led Netflix to abandon this plan.[78]

As this scenario demonstrates, when big, unexpected changes occur, strategic plans often need to change.[79] So how do managers develop a new strategic plan? The strategic planning process can be seen as a series of sequential steps (▪ **EXHIBIT 5.10**).[80] In the next few sections, we will use this stepwise model to discuss how leaders can develop and implement strategic plans.

▪ **EXHIBIT 5.10**
The strategic planning process involves six steps.

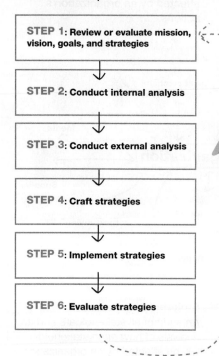

STEP 1: **Review or evaluate mission, vision, goals, and strategies**

STEP 2: **Conduct internal analysis**

STEP 3: **Conduct external analysis**

STEP 4: **Craft strategies**

STEP 5: **Implement strategies**

STEP 6: **Evaluate strategies**

Step 1: Review or Evaluate Mission, Vision, Goals, and Strategies

Mission and vision should guide the choice of strategic goals. Mission and vision are also critical in engaging employees in the difficult and exciting challenge of implementing strategies. Once vision and mission are reviewed and agreed on, an effective strategic planning process examines the current strategic goals. Have these goals been achieved? If not, why not? Are these goals still relevant in today's business environment?

Remember, though, that strategic planning is more than just goal setting. It is a creative integration and synthesis of decisions, goals, and actions. To evaluate the current state, the organization's existing strategies need to be identified. Here, managers should ask:

- What strategies have we been using?
- Why did we choose these strategies in the past?
- Which strategies are providing us with measurable success?
- Are these the strategies that we should be using?
- Which strategies did not work? Why?

The answers to these questions provide insight into what the current strategic goals are and which strategies have been successful or unsuccessful.

Steps 2 and 3: Conduct Internal and External Analyses

Clarity about mission, vision, goals, and current strategies provides a big picture of the existing situation. Once this situation has been reviewed, strategists can begin a deeper, systematic analysis of the business and the environment within which the business operates. To start, managers and leaders examine what is happening inside the organization: internal strengths, core competencies, and weaknesses, as well as internal stakeholders' needs, desires, and demands.

Factors outside the organization such as opportunities, threats, and external stakeholders' needs can also impact a company. For example, rising fuel prices may hurt a trucking company but help oil companies. A decline in new and existing home sales and inventory, as occurred in the United States from 2008 through 2011, can affect realtors, construction companies, lumber suppliers, and the banks that provide home loans both during and long after the change seen in the market.[81] These examples point to why strategists also examine what's happening *outside* the organization, including opportunities and threats, and external stakeholders' needs, desires, and demands.

SWOT ANALYSIS: ONE APPROACH TO INTERNAL AND EXTERNAL ANALYSIS

One way to look at what is going on inside and outside an organization is to conduct a **SWOT analysis**.[82] SWOT is an acronym for strengths, weaknesses, opportunities, and threats: factors that may affect the achievement of mission, vision, strategies, and business objectives.[83] SWOT analysis is a popular tool for strategic planning because it can help managers examine what is potentially helpful or harmful to the process of attaining strategic goals, as illustrated in ■ **EXHIBIT 5.11**.

A **strength** is any positive characteristic or activity that an organization possesses that can have a positive impact on the organization. For instance, home improvement chain Lowe's can count a recognizable name and reliable customer service among its strengths. One type of strength that is often the focus of SWOT analysis is an organization's core competencies. German-based chemical giant BASF's core competency is innovation.[84] This sets it apart from competitors, and BASF's customers easily recognize the difference.

A **weakness** is any characteristic or activity that an organization possesses that can have a negative impact on the organization. A food company who has had to recall meat, for instance, might discover cleanliness issues—clearly a dangerous weakness.

The other half of SWOT analysis is the identification of opportunities and threats that could impact the organization. An **opportunity** is any situation, condition, or event that is favorable to the organization. For example, an airline's management may have identified an opportunity if research indicates that routes between major cities are crowded and the airports can handle more flights.

In contrast, a **threat** is any situation, condition, or event that can negatively impact an organization. For example, leaders at Starbucks likely perceived a threat to their high-end coffee drinks when Dunkin' Donuts began to advertise less expensive, tasty coffee and customers began to respond. Customers responded for many reasons including the downturn in the economy and Starbucks' reputation for being expensive. Some threats aren't as obvious, such as slowly growing consumer trends. Many organizations have systems in place to monitor potential threats.

DRAWBACKS OF SWOT ANALYSIS

SWOT analysis can be helpful, but it has some drawbacks. First, even SWOT proponents note that simply filling in the four boxes with brainstormed lists isn't enough—long lists of unevaluated information are just "garbage in, garbage out." As a result, scholars have attempted to evaluate the SWOT technique by asking users questions such as:

- Are strengths, weaknesses, opportunities, and threats described clearly and specifically?
- Were the items weighted or prioritized? If so, how?
- Was the information used in decision making? If so, how?[85]

The researchers found that information from typical SWOT analyses was almost never prioritized, weighted, or organized beyond the general categories. The study revealed that items were brief, clarification was rarely sought, and independent verification was rarely if ever conducted. Another problem that affects the quality of SWOT analysis is that many people have only vague ideas about their organizations' real strengths.[86] Additionally, the

SWOT analysis
A technique that examines strengths, weaknesses, opportunities, and threats that may affect achievement of strategic mission and vision.

Strength
Any positive characteristic or activity that an organization possesses that can have a positive impact on the organization.

Weakness
Any negative characteristic or activity that an organization possesses that can have a negative impact on the organization.

Opportunity
Any situation, condition, or event that is favorable to an organization.

Threat
Any situation, condition, or event that can negatively impact an organization.

■ **EXHIBIT 5.11**
A SWOT analysis examines an organization's strengths, weaknesses, opportunities, and threats.

	Strengths: Any positive characteristic or activity that an organization possesses that can have a positive impact on the organization.	**Weaknesses**: Any characteristic or activity that an organization possesses that can have a negative impact on the organization.
(Internal)		
(External)	**Opportunities**: Any situation, condition, or event that is favorable to the organization.	**Threats**: Any situation, condition, or event that can negatively impact an organization.
	(Maximize)	**(Minimize)**

researchers found that in making SWOT lists, the distinction between internal and external factors was frequently confused. Finally, completed SWOT analyses were rarely utilized as input in subsequent strategic planning.[87]

Taken as a whole, scholars' critiques indicate that the SWOT technique can be useful, but only if it is conducted as a true analysis and not simple list making. A good SWOT analysis requires the time and attention of people who are willing to *think* about the current state of the company.

Step 4: Craft Strategies

As you can see, a great deal of work takes place prior to formulating a strategy. Steps 1 through 3 ensure that the right strategy is selected. Then, in step 4, managers take all the information they have collected and analyzed and formulate strategic goals and plans for the organization.

But crafting strategy is more than simply saying "Let's do this." Even though a great quantity of information has been amassed about the company, its competitors, and the various environments, strategists still need to grapple with prioritizing where to expend resources within the organization. The BCG matrix is one method for understanding how and where to invest, especially in a diversified company.

THE BCG MATRIX: ONE WAY TO VIEW A BUSINESS

A **diversified company** is a company that has two or more distinct divisions that produce different products or services. General Electric (GE), for example, makes everything from appliances and jet engines to light bulbs. For diversified companies such as GE, Procter & Gamble, and Newell Rubbermaid, strategy does not take a one-size-fits-all approach. Different divisions of these companies perform better than others and have varying needs.

For this reason, large corporations often use an analysis tool developed by the Boston Consulting Group (BCG). This tool is called the **BCG matrix**, and it illustrates how a business unit, product, service, brand, or product portfolio is performing in terms of market share and market growth.[88] Managers can use the BCG matrix to categorize businesses or products by how much market share they have and their growth potential. As you can see in ■ **EXHIBIT 5.12**, the resulting categories are called stars, question marks, cows, and dogs.

Let's look at how the BCG matrix works. As shown in Exhibit 5.12, the horizontal axis illustrates market share. **Market share** describes the percentage of the market that a product, service, or business unit has captured. For example, there is fierce competition for market share of paid search advertising on the Internet, which is tied to market share of search engine browsing. These statistics are monitored closely by Google, Microsoft, Yahoo!, and many other companies.

Plotted on the vertical axis, **market growth rate** is a measure of growth in the market for given products or services. The top of the vertical axis represents high market growth rate, whereas the bottom of the axis represents low market growth rate. Take, for example, the market for Apple's iPhone, which is categorized as a smart phone. The market for smart phones is growing, and estimates suggest that the market will grow by more than 18 percent per year through 2016. This marks a bit of a slowdown in the smart phone market, largely due to the fact that the market is becoming increasingly flooded with high-quality products. Consequently, iPhone is expected to lose a portion of its market share to competitors; however, even with these losses, iPhone's market share would remain higher than some companies ever have.[89]

Diversified company
A company that has two or more distinct divisions that produce different products or services.

BCG matrix
An analysis tool used to illustrate how a business unit, product, service, brand, or product portfolio is performing in terms of market share and market growth.

Market share
The percentage of the market that a product, service, or business unit has captured.

Market growth rate
A measure of growth in the market for given products or services.

■ **EXHIBIT 5.12**
The BCG matrix helps companies analyze products and businesses.

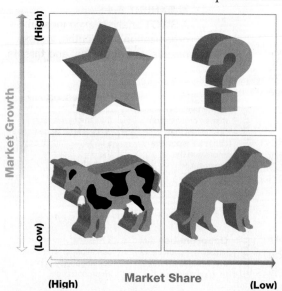

Market Growth (High) / (Low)

Market Share (High) / (Low)

Source: The BCG Portfolio Matrix from *The Product Portfolio*, © 1970. The Boston Consulting Group.

By using the BCG matrix, a company can make decisions about how to support certain parts of the business or products. For instance, dogs can be liquidated, whereas investing in stars could turn them into cash cows. Question marks are the most difficult. They may have the potential to generate a lot of income if they capture market share, but they can also be a drain on financial resources. For large companies, the challenge is to craft strategies that support a good balance among products and business lines.

DRAWBACKS OF THE BCG MATRIX

The BCG matrix has its drawbacks. First, the matrix is most useful for large conglomerates with a variety of different units, a business model that was more common in the 1980s than it is today.[90] Another problem is that the BCG matrix oversimplifies the relationship between market share and income generation. Market share is not a reliable indicator of future profitability in a rapidly shifting technological landscape. In fact, no matter how elegant the model, there is no single reliable indicator that can replace human interpretation and good analysis.[91]

Steps 5 and 6: Implement and Evaluate Strategies

A good strategic plan puts form and substance around information gathering, analysis, and business decision making. However, even a perfect strategic plan is useless if it is never enacted. Imagine spending time in meetings, working long hours over the weekend, and exchanging countless e-mails in order to develop a strategic plan. Everyone agrees that it is a fine plan, but it gets filed away with no action taken. Unfortunately, this occurs in companies of all sizes. Without implementation, the strategic plan is nothing more than a good idea.

IMPLEMENTING A PLAN IS SOMETIMES CALLED "EXECUTION"

Consultant Ram Charan has dedicated a good deal of his work to examining how leaders implement plans. Charan and his colleagues have found that a crucial element of strategy that is often overlooked is execution—getting the job done. According to Charan, the discipline of executing plans requires leaders to do the following:[92]

- Make assumptions about the business environment
- Assess organizational capability
- Link strategies to operations and identify the people to carry out the strategies
- Coordinate the efforts of people in charge of carrying out the strategies
- Create a clear and explicit reward system based on outcomes
- Develop the mechanisms for challenging and changing assumptions as the business environment changes

Charan suggests that most of the time, a CEO fails not because of ideas, but rather because of failure to follow through on commitments.[93] Other scholars take a broader view, suggesting that high-performing companies are successful because of their focus on both planning *and* execution.[94]

EVALUATION AND "MUST-WINS"

Evaluation of strategies is and should be a continual process. Professor and scholar Tom Malnight believes that strategy implementation and evaluation is a process of constantly determining which strategies are the "must-win battles."[95] Must-wins are the business priorities that are most likely to support the success of the strategy. Malnight argues that the average organization can only wage a few must-win battles at any given time, which may mean refocusing the organization to do fewer things better.

This process needs to be continual and timely. In today's fast-paced environment, constant attention to change—and changing priorities—can give a company the edge it needs.

Discussion Questions

1. Discuss how each step of the strategic planning process could be used to support launching a small business on campus.

2. Conduct a SWOT analysis on yourself as a student. Be candid with yourself when it comes to your strengths, weaknesses, opportunities, and threats. How can you capitalize on your strengths and opportunities while downplaying your weaknesses and avoiding threats?

Objective 5.8
Describe HR's role in planning and strategy.

HR Leadership Roles

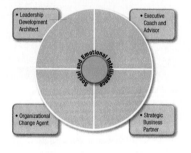

8. What Is HR's Role in Planning and Strategy?

In decades past, the human resources department was relegated to the back corners of the corporate office, being viewed primarily as the "compensation and benefits" staff. In recent years, however, this philosophy has evolved to one of inclusion of—and reliance on—HR for advice and support around workforce planning. Forward-thinking CEOs now see partnering with HR as an opportunity to work with business experts and consultants who can impact an organization's strategy in a positive manner.[96] In fact, linking HR activities to workforce planning is essential, especially when it comes to the "people strategy." HR ensures that employees are supported to maximally allow them to realize the organization's mission, vision, and strategy.

In this section, we will focus on how HR can support workforce planning by ensuring that the right kinds and right numbers of people are in the right places. Workforce planning includes recruiting, selection, and succession planning, as well as overall plans for workforce growth or reductions.

Workforce Growth and Reductions

When an organization's strategy calls for growth, HR is often responsible for workforce expansion. When supporting a growth strategy, recruiting can be both demanding and rewarding. It's a chance to truly reshape a business. And, when done in close conjunction with managers, the results can be outstanding.

Unfortunately, not all workforce planning is positive or fun. The flipside to a growth period is a downturn, and HR managers are often the architects of downsizing plans, and they support managers in terminating employees. Perhaps the toughest part of any manager's job is the task of terminating an employee. When a job is taken away through a termination, a person's livelihood is affected—and so is the person's self-image. That's because an individual's job is an integral part of that person's identity.

There are several types of termination situations. A reduction in force is the dismissal of employees due to economic reasons, technological advancements, or redundancy of work. The United States, Europe, and many other parts of the world saw drastic and devastating reductions in force due to the extended global recession that began in 2007.

Imagine sitting in a meeting with a list of 100 or more employees, most of whom you know well and most of whom are doing a great job. Your responsibility is to decide which 20 people you need to lay off. A **layoff** is a termination with the

Layoff
A termination with the possibility of rehire once conditions improve.

possibility of rehire once conditions improve. When conditions that require layoffs are in place for a long time, rehiring is usually a distant dream. What makes these situations so difficult is that employees who did nothing wrong have to be let go. In addition, companies can be left with too few people to do the work that is needed, and individuals and families suffer tremendously. An effective HR manager is one who handles these situations with professionalism and treats the people who are losing their jobs with dignity.

Another type of workforce reduction is firing people. This is called for-cause termination, and it involves the dismissal of an employee for breaking a company policy, failing to perform, or failing to adjust to company values, norms, or culture.

Terminations—whether for cause or workforce reductions—are important factors in strategic planning. Obviously, fewer workers can impact a company's productivity. In many cases, fewer workers means that remaining employees have to take on additional responsibilities—sometimes to the point that people burn out. Workforce reductions also affect morale profoundly. Those who remain can feel guilty, angry, or fearful—feelings that don't support effectiveness on the job.

For-cause termination
The dismissal of an employee for breaking a company policy, failing to perform, or failing to adjust to company values, norms, or culture.

Succession Planning

On September 11, 2001, two planes slammed into the twin towers of the World Trade Center in New York, and more than 2,700 people lost their lives in the two buildings—a tragedy for families, friends, and the world. It was also a tragedy for many businesses, and the event became an important wake-up call for companies: In a situation in which a large percentage of the staff is suddenly gone, what can you do? For example, the Port Authority of New York and New Jersey had 2,000 employees in the World Trade Center, and lost 84 of them that day—including the executive director. Financial services firm Cantor Fitzgerald lost 658 people—two-thirds of its total workforce and all of the employees in its headquarters offices at the time.[97] The New York City Fire Department lost 343 of its 11,000 firefighters in a matter of moments.[98]

Beyond the tragic loss of numerous employees, attrition also creates a constant need for a well-developed succession plan. A succession plan is a plan for filling management positions in the event those positions are vacated. Succession planning is an important part of HR professionals' overall workforce planning process. This is particularly important today in some countries because of demographics. For example, as Baby Boomers retire, other people will need to be developed to fill management vacancies.

So far, we have discussed specific processes related to the size and shape of the workforce. In order for these processes to truly support the workforce, HR professionals must understand how to recruit and select the right employees.

Succession plan
A plan for filling management positions in the event those positions are vacated.

RECRUITING EMPLOYEES

How do companies find individuals who have the necessary qualifications for a job? The process of attracting qualified candidates for jobs is known as recruiting. Today, companies compete to find "stars" in the labor pool, and they use a variety of ways to locate these candidates. The first place many HR professionals look is within their own organizations. Internal recruiting includes two primary approaches. The least expensive and easiest method is to post the job on the company's intranet or bulletin boards, in company newsletters, and so forth. A second method of internal recruiting is through the use of an HR inventory. An HR inventory is an internal system that maintains information about people within an organization. It tracks relevant skills, training needs, career plans, and other information about employees.[99] These systems are used to identify talent in the organization. As positions open up, the HR inventory can provide a list of qualified candidates.

Recruiting
The process of attracting qualified candidates for jobs.

Of course, HR recruiters may have to look outside the company for talent. It may be that no one within the organization is qualified, or there may be a need to bring in fresh ideas and approaches. External recruiting methods are numerous and include such things as visits to colleges, career fairs, use of online recruiting and placement companies (such as Monster.com), postings on the company Web site, social networking, and the like.[100] HR will also often tap employment agencies, professional recruiters (sometimes called "headhunters"), and competitors. Some of these methods are quite expensive; for instance, professional recruiters can earn 100 percent or more of a candidate's first-year salary for their services.

SELECTING THE RIGHT EMPLOYEES

Selection
The act of choosing whom to hire from among a group of qualified applicants.

Selection is the act of choosing whom to hire from among a group of qualified applicants. But what does "qualified" mean? This is where the HR professional must make some important determinations. Obviously, the right kind of experience for the job is necessary, as are the appropriate number of years of experience. In addition, college degrees, certifications, and specific skills are often considered. But, other criteria are also weighed. Will a candidate fit with an organization's culture? Can he or she get along with others? Is he or she the type of candidate who can be promoted into other positions in the company in the future? Questions such as these help the recruiter assess a candidate's "fit" with the company. From a workforce planning perspective, HR professionals must ensure that they are hiring individuals who will achieve the organization's goals while adhering to the mission and vision of the firm.

Discussion Questions

1. Do you know anyone who has been fired or laid off from a job? How was it done? What was the impact on the person? How would you handle firing or laying off an employee?

2. Describe a selection process in which you have participated (either at work, at school, or in a social club). Was the selection process strategic? In what ways? Was it tied to the mission, vision, or strategic goals of the organization? If so, in what ways?

Objective 5.9
Describe what you can do to support effective strategic planning.

9. What Can We All Do to Support Effective Strategic Planning?

Plans are great, and good plans are even better. But good plans don't happen by accident. Solid plans are the result of critical thinking and research, and they rely on pattern recognition. Being able to recognize patterns enables you to analyze situations—both internal and external to an organization—thereby allowing you to engage in strategic planning more effectively.

Pattern recognition is a higher order competency that is important to analytical thought.[101] Pattern recognition is the process of taking in raw information and mentally organizing it into a model that helps explain a situation. This is a critical skill because leaders must be able to make connections when information is not perfectly clear (which is quite often the case).

Recognition of patterns is a central aspect of social awareness, which is the ability to quickly identify relevant patterns, integrate them into decision-making processes, and act accordingly.[102] Decision making and planning in real-world situations often rely on the use of "fuzzy logic."[103] This means that patterns encountered in the real world are rarely exactly the same as those held in memory, so we need to be able to recognize vague, or "fuzzy," patterns and make them more clear.

How can you develop pattern recognition? You probably already have. Our educational processes are geared toward developing this skill; from learning to read, to solving math problems, to writing term papers, we have been taught to look for patterns in information. Beyond what you have already been taught, you can enhance your pattern recognition capacity by becoming more aware of your automatic thought processes. This is called *mindfulness*. Esteemed scholar Ellen Langer explains it this way: "When we are mindless, we are like programmed automatons, treating information in a single-minded and rigid way, as though it were true regardless of the circumstances. When we are mindful, we are open to surprise, oriented in the present moment, sensitive to context, and above all, liberated from the tyranny of old mindsets."[104] So, the single most important thing you can do to develop your capacity for pattern recognition is to pay attention—really pay attention—to what you encounter in the world. Then, ask questions, challenge yourself to see things differently than you normally would, and come up with more than one explanation for what you see, think, or experience.

Once you are sure that you have challenged beliefs and gotten input from lots of people and lots of sources, try to link various bits of information together in unique and novel ways. This calls for a certain amount of playfulness, as well as good-natured willingness to be wrong. In the end, mindfully attending to the information in your environment will give you more access to the right answers, and it will permit you greater success as you plan for the future.

Discussion Questions

1. How have you developed your ability to recognize patterns?
2. To practice pattern recognition, think about your group of friends. What similarities exist among them? What are some differences? How is your "group" different from other groups on campus or at work?

10. A Final Word on Planning and Strategy

We started this chapter by considering the different ways people envision and plan for the future. As you have seen, managers and leaders have different options in terms of planning methods, and many different kinds of plans can be created and adopted by organizations. Planning is a complex and multifaceted process that any manager will tell you doesn't always work. There is much for us to learn about planning and strategy from the models and theories presented in this chapter. On the other hand, it is important to know that many plans and strategies are compromised because of inattention to certain aspects of the planning process or its implementation. Henry Mintzberg, mentioned earlier in the chapter, and other scholars have criticized strategy formulation because it often devolves to a formal planning process that creates a stepwise, primarily quantifiable process. This essentially reduces strategy to an algorithm—an impossible oversimplification in today's businesses.

In the next chapter, we will address these problems directly, by considering what is really needed to create and implement a successful plan: decision making and critical thinking—the human side of planning.

EXPERIENCING Leadership

LEADING IN A GLOBAL WORLD
Modular Planning on a Global Scale

These days, few companies don't have some kind of global presence. Planning and setting global strategy in uncertain times takes insight, coordination, and flexibility. In a highly competitive global marketplace, an organization must be able to change its strategy, or components of its strategy, quickly and effectively.

Today, there is much political, economic, and environmental instability that directly affects an organization's profitability and survival. For example, consider the problems Japanese businesses encountered following the 2011 earthquake and tsunami. How quickly these businesses recovered and resumed operations was partially determined by their disaster plans and the degree to which plans were modularized.

Select one of the global companies below and discuss how they can benefit from employing a modular planning approach to assist in quick strategic adjustments or changes. Be sure to include scenario planning as a key strategic element in identifying what a company can do to be prepared for natural disasters or political upheaval.

- Toyota
- GE
- Facebook
- Philips
- Siemens
- LG Corp

LEADING WITH EMOTIONAL INTELLIGENCE
SWOT You

A SWOT analysis is a useful tool for assessing what is going on both inside and outside an organization. Internally, a company can evaluate its strengths, such as excellent customer service, and its weaknesses, such as backlogged inventory. Externally, there may be opportunities, such as untapped markets, as well as threats, such as strong competition. If done thoroughly, a SWOT analysis can provide useful data for guiding a company's mission and vision toward success.

You, too, can be viewed as an organization: YOU, Inc. Your success as a student depends on both internal and external forces. For instance, if your strengths include self-awareness and self-management skills, the pressures of a rigorous course load may have little effect on you. If your weaknesses include relationship management, for example, you may find it difficult working with others on collaborative projects. External forces, such as a teaching assistantship or scholarship opportunities can benefit you nicely. Threats, such as a tuition hike or a student loan rejection, might slow down your advance toward early graduation.

Do a SWOT analysis on YOU, Inc. When complete, answer the following questions:

1. What was the most difficult part of the SWOT analysis?
2. What was the easiest part of it?
3. How can your emotions work as both a strength and a weakness for YOU?

LEADING WITH CRITICAL THINKING SKILLS
Stereotypes and Sustainability

As sustainability movements gain momentum worldwide, more companies are revising their mission and vision statements to address environmental and social issues. Some companies are "going green" because it is fashionable *and* profitable to care about the environment and social injustice.

When it comes to sustainability and strategic planning, some industries face a bigger challenge than others. Chemical companies, for instance, tend to be associated with pollution, poison, and profits. Modern chemical companies may engage in safe, responsible practices, but the industry's checkered past has led to this negative stereotyping. So how do companies like DuPont or Dow Chemical strategically position themselves in a world that demands increasing accountability from businesses?

In a group or individually, choose two of the four major chemical companies (Dow, DuPont, BASF, and Union Carbide) and research their current market strategy. As you conduct your research, be sure to do the following:

1. Identify the mission, vision, stakeholders, and long-term and short-term strategic goals of the companies.
2. Determine how the companies address environmental sustainability in their mission and vision.
3. Describe any social components of the companies' strategies.
4. Outline any particular areas that these companies should focus on when doing environmental scanning as part of the strategic planning process.

ETHICAL LEADERSHIP
Planning for Disaster

What does a company do when it is involved in a major environmental and public relations catastrophe? When the Deepwater Horizon oil platform exploded in 2010 killing 11 men and injuring 17 others, BP found itself in this situation.

Over the course of three months, five million barrels of crude oil gushed from the ruptured pipe in the Gulf of Mexico. A government commission determined that BP and its partners were to blame for cost-cutting decisions that impacted well safety. After the spill, BP did major damage control of its image and revised its strategic plan.

Review
cess and thi
build its strat
the global co
Consider thes

1. What does
   vision, goal
   reputation?

2. What informa
   gards to its ir
   going partners

3. What strategie
   pany forward a
   problems?

KEY TERMS

Planning, *p. 146*

Goal-oriented planning, *p. 147*

Directional planning, *p. 147*

Action orientation, *p. 147*

Scenario planning, *p. 152*

Mission statement, *p. 153*

Competitive advantage, *p. 154*

Vision, *p. 154*

Vision statement, *p. 154*

Strategy, *p. 157*

Growth strategy, *p. 159*

Acquisition strategy, *p. 160*

Joint ventures, *p. 160*

Stability strategy, *p. 161*

Retrenchment strategy, *p. 162*

Divestiture strategy, *p. 162*

Differentiation, *p. 162*

Core competency, *p. 162*

Cost leadership, *p. 162*

Niche strategy, *p. 162*

Vertical integration, *p. 163*

Supply chain, *p. 163*

Functional strategies, *p. 163*

Strategic planning, *p. 163*

Environmental scanning, *p. 163*

Industry, *p. 165*

Stakeholder, *p. 167*

Stakeholder analysis, *p. 167*

SWOT analysis, *p. 169*

Strength, *p. 169*

Weakness, *p. 169*

Opportunity, *p. 169*

Threat, *p. 169*

Diversified company, *p. 170*

BCG matrix, *p. 170*

Market share, *p. 170*

Market growth rate, *p. 170*

Layoff, *p. 172*

For-cause termination, *p. 173*

Succession plan, *p. 173*

Recruiting, *p. 173*

Selection, *p. 174*

MyManagementLab

Go to **mymanagementlab.com** for Auto-graded writing questions as well as the following Assisted-graded writing questions:

5-1. Choose a company that you respect. Perhaps it is one you buy from repeatedly or one whose products you have always dreamed of buying. What do you see as that company's competitive advantage?

5-2. How often do you think an organization should develop a strategic plan? What might cause an organization to change strategies?

5-3. Mymanagementlab Only — comprehensive writing assignment for this chapter.

1. Do People Plan for the Future? (pp. 146–148)

Objective: Understand how people think about and plan for the future.

Summary: People plan for the future in different ways; some are goal oriented, others are driven by direction and vision, and still others are action oriented. A good planning process reflects these different preferences.

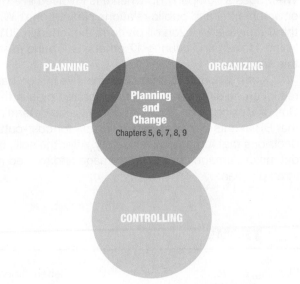

2. What Does Planning Look Like in Organizations? (pp. 148–150)

Objective: Describe the planning process in organizations.

Summary: When engaging in organizational planning, leaders must not focus solely on goals and metrics; rather, they must link the organization's mission and vision to particular goals and activities. Often, this means crafting many types of plans—such as short-term, long-term, single-use, standing, operational, strategic, financial, contingency, and project plans. All of these must be coordinated with one another.

3. How Do You Plan in Uncertain Times? (pp. 150–153)

Objective: Compare and contrast the typical planning process with the planning process that takes place during periods of uncertainty.

Summary: A good plan is flexible so that it can adapt to changing environments and conditions. To ensure adaptability, it's helpful to employ a modular approach to planning because it's easier to change individual goals, subgoals, milestones, and action steps than to adjust an entire plan. It's also a good idea to envision various "what if" scenarios for given situations and prepare for several likely possibilities.

4. What Is a Mission? Why Does Vision Matter? (pp. 153–157)

Objective: Define mission and vision and understand why both are important to organizational success.

Summary: When crafting a plan, leaders and managers must carefully create and/or adapt their organization's mission and vision. A clear mission articulates an organization's purpose and competitive advantage. It also unifies employees. A good vision inspires people both within and beyond the organization because it focuses on a better future. Together, a strong, well-communicated mission and vision can help a company make better choices.

5. What Is Strategy? (pp. 157–163)

Objective: Define strategy.

Summary: A strategy helps an organization realize its mission and bring its vision to life. Many strategies are complex, and they exist in a variety of forms. The three primary categories of strategies are corporate strategies, which are designed for an entire organization; business strategies, which are designed for particular divisions or lines of business; and functional strategies, which guide how different support services within an organization can help the entire organization achieve its goals.

10. A Final Word on Planning and Strategy (p. 175)

Summary: Although the models and theories presented in this chapter can greatly assist leaders, managers, and others in crafting effective plans, it's important to remember that strategy formulation is ultimately a human process.

9. What Can We All Do to Support Effective Strategic Planning? (pp. 174–175)

Objective: Describe what you can do to support effective strategic planning.

Summary: To support effective strategic planning, you should develop your capacity for pattern recognition. Pattern recognition is a complex and extremely important competency that allows us to make sense of information today and plan for tomorrow.

8. What Is HR's Role in Planning and Strategy? (pp. 172–174)

Objective: Describe HR's role in planning and strategy.

Summary: Human resources are heavily engaged in workforce planning. This process involves managing periods of workforce growth and reduction; creating succession plans; recruiting qualified job candidates; and selecting candidates who will support the organization's vision, mission, and goals.

7. What Are the Steps in the Strategic Planning Process? (pp. 168–172)

Objective: Know the steps in a typical strategic planning process.

Summary: Strategic planning consists of a series of steps. First, the organization must evaluate its mission, vision, goals, and existing strategies. After that, all internal and external factors that might affect the organization's ability to achieve its objectives should be analyzed. Following analysis, the organization can craft specific strategies and put them into place. Finally, the organization must evaluate the strategies it has chosen to determine whether they have been effective.

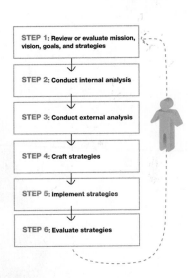

6. What Needs to Be Considered in a Strategic Planning Process? (pp. 163–167)

Objective: Understand what needs to be considered during the strategic planning process.

Summary: Strategic planning is a complex and multilayered process. Before beginning this process, it's important to examine the various forces at work in an organization's economic, sociocultural, legal, political, technological, natural, and industrial environments. In addition, the needs and expectations of the organization's stakeholders must be taken into consideration.

CHAPTER 6

The Human Side of Planning:
Decision Making and Critical Thinking

PLANNING

Planning and Change
Chapters 5, 6, 7, 8, 9

CONTROLLING

MyManagementLab™

⭐ Improve Your Grade!

Over 10 million students improved their results using the Pearson MyLabs. Visit **mymanagementlab.com** for simulations, tutorials, and end-of-chapter problems.

Chapter Outline

1. What Is Decision Making? (pp. 182–185)

2. How Do Cognitive and Emotional Processes Affect Decision Making? (pp. 185–190)

3. How Can You Apply a Systematic Approach to Making Decisions? (pp. 191–196)

4. How Can People Make Good Decisions with Incomplete Information? (pp. 196–199)

5. How Can You Improve Your Critical Thinking Skills and Make Better Decisions? (pp. 199–204)

6. What Can HR Do to Support Good Decision Making and Critical Thinking? (pp. 204–205)

7. What Can We All Do to Improve Critical Thinking and Decision Making? (pp. 205–208)

8. A Final Word on Decision Making and Critical Thinking (p. 208)

Chapter Objectives

6.1   Define decision making.

6.2   Compare and contrast how cognitive and emotional processes affect decision making.

6.3   Learn to apply a systematic approach to decision making.

6.4   Understand how to make sound decisions with incomplete information.

6.5   Improve your critical thinking skills.

6.6   Describe what HR can do to support critical thinking and sound decision making.

6.7   Describe what you can do to improve critical thinking and sound decision making.

hat Is Decision Making?

e only as good as the decisions that go into them. Even the most detailed,
plan will not be helpful if the people who created the plan failed to analyze
:heck and double-check their assumptions, and avoid common errors, such as
g information that does not fit with their beliefs. To help you avoid these pit-
is chapter addresses the human side of planning: decision making and critical
ig. Both processes are essential to effective management and leadership—and
nvolve a variety of factors, including emotion, intuition, logic, and perception.
factors affect your decisions in the workplace, and your decisions in *all* aspects

s difficult to engage in effective decision making and critical thinking without
rstanding what each process entails. Developing such an understanding is the
ose of this chapter. We begin with a brief definition of decision making, along
with a look at different types of decisions. We also discuss the role of logic, emotion, and intuition and explore ways in which perception and bias can either help
or hinder the decision-making process. In the next section, we turn to a simple
model that can help when making decisions. We also share research about how to
make decisions when information is incomplete (which is common). Next, we shift
our focus to critical thinking, examining what it involves and how you can improve
your skills in order to make better decisions. You'll also learn about several common errors that impede decision making. Finally, we conclude with an examination
of what HR can do to support managers and leaders in effective decision making
and critical thinking, as well as what we can all do to develop our capabilities in
these areas.

Decision Making Defined

Decision making A cognitive, emotional, and neuropsychological process involving thoughts, feelings, and neurological functioning that results in making a judgment or choosing from alternatives.

Decision making is a cognitive, emotional, and neuropsychological process involving
thoughts, feelings, and neurological functioning that results in making a judgment or
choosing from alternatives. Making decisions includes the following tasks:

- Collecting information related to a dilemma, problem, or opportunity
- Reacting to and considering this information
- Incorporating emotional responses to possible choices with other information about
  those choices
- Evaluating alternatives using logic, reasoning, emotion, and intuition
- Reacting and responding to risk and uncertainty
- Making a judgment or choosing a course of action

This definition may be broader than those you have encountered in the past, because it includes emotion and intuition. Decision making is often taught as a purely
rational process involving *only* cognitive assessment of problems, rational consideration of alternatives, analysis of costs and benefits, and selection of a course of action.
We now know, however, that decision making is *not* a purely cognitive process. It also
involves neurological activity linked to emotions and biases that can cause us to pay
more or less attention to certain information while making choices.[1] Decision making
involves also becoming aware of and using intuition and emotion to guide how we
evaluate information and make choices.[2]

Types of Decisions

Every single day, you make decisions that require little thought, such as whether to
brush your teeth, what to have for breakfast, or whether to say hello to your manager.

These and many other daily decisions are quick and easy, so we may not think about them for more than a moment or two.

At other times, we agonize over which direction to choose, which alternative to select, or which solution to try. Think about some of the major decisions you have made in life. When you were young, you might have been faced with the decision about which sport to pursue, what instrument to play, or which kids to be friends with. Later, you may have had to choose whether to take a part-time job, weighing financial need and a desire for experience against the job's potential impact on your grades or social life. Other important decisions—such as whom to date, what career to pursue, and where to live—can also be very difficult. These types of decisions require you to think about what you want now, *and* they require you to consider your future. You'll need to consider the kind of life you want, the kind of people you want to surround yourself with, your financial needs or desires, and the kind of work you want to do for the next several years or perhaps your whole life.

Just as in life, decisions at work can be easy and automatic, or they can be complicated and difficult. For example, you may make simple decisions every day about how to complete routine tasks. Other decisions, such as whom to hire or whether to open a new manufacturing plant, are much more complicated and have far-reaching consequences. They usually involve any number of facts and opinions, not to mention people. As a manager and leader, you'll need to learn how to tell the difference between simple, routine decisions and those that are more complicated. Surprisingly, people often confuse these two types of decisions.

Decisions can be classified depending on how often and how easily they are made. Decisions that are routine in nature and occur with some frequency are known as **programmed decisions** (■ **EXHIBIT 6.1**). For instance, the selection of a classroom for this course was most likely a programmed decision. Selecting a classroom is a choice that occurs with regularity and is based on known factors such as instructor preference, number of students, and available classrooms. Within a business setting, programmed decisions include things like ordering office supplies, choosing where to hold weekly staff meetings, and determining whether a customer can return an item without a receipt. When things are working well within an organization, programmed decisions are easy, seamless, and cost effective.[3] Thus, many organizations dedicate a great deal of attention to making decisions as routine—or programmed—as possible.

Programmed decisions
Decisions that are routine in nature and occur with some frequency.

■ **EXHIBIT 6.1**
Which of these activities involves a programmed decision?

Source: Bill Lyons/Alamy; AVAVA/iStockphoto.com

Nonprogrammed decisions
Decisions that are not routine and/or involve unique information or circumstances.

Decisions that are not routine are called **nonprogrammed decisions** because they are novel and involve unique information or circumstances. Nonprogrammed decisions occur infrequently, take more time to evaluate, can involve numerous people and stakeholders, and have significant implications in terms of personnel, time, and money. Two examples of nonprogrammed decisions that you have likely faced are choosing which college to attend and which major to select.

As in personal life, employees and managers also face many nonprogrammed decisions. Recognizing nonprogrammed decisions when you encounter them is critical, as is how you then go about making them. This chapter will help you in this area. As a way to start, let's hear what Ivor D'Souza, at the National Institute of Health (NIH) has to say about involving people in complex decisions.

Leadership Perspective

● **Ivor D'Souza**
Director, Information Systems, National Library of Medicine, NIH
"Innovation starts at the very top."

Ivor D'Souza, Director of Information Systems of the NIH, is a brilliant young leader with a unique perspective on the link between innovation, people, and good decisions. His background in leading mission-focused change has prepared him well to join the ranks of outstanding leaders in an organization that is second to none in research. His values include serving others, a focus on excellence, and democratic inclusion of people in making decisions that affect them. All of these contribute to his outstanding leadership. Ivor says this about how to approach complex decisions:

Innovation starts at the very top. And, it starts with a leader seeing the need for change, and recognizing that his people can take him there. He states the outcome he is seeking in simple terms, in ways that his people can relate to the organization's mission. The

outcome does not specify how the work gets done. It just sets the standard by which the end product will be judged. So, it fosters innovation and empowers individuals to creatively determine the best approach to achieve the stated outcome.

A leader with an eye for innovation tends to value his people resources. He sees his staff as not just regular grunt workers—but as innovators. Such a leader believes that he can stimulate innovation more by asking questions than by making statements (telling people what to do). Further, he doesn't ask just any question. He asks questions that are open-ended and least restrictive—questions that state the outcome of WHAT needs to be achieved, but are not restrictive in HOW things get done. It's no secret then that most of his questions begin with WHAT, and not HOW. By giving his people the freedom to choose a path forward, the leader has given his people a front seat in their collective journey, and so they all own the decisions they make along the way.

Source: Personal interview with Ivor D'Souza conducted by Annie McKee, 2012.

Ivor D'Souza is right: Innovation and good decisions require people's best thinking, and the people involved need to own the outcomes. That is especially true—though not easy—when leaders face changes that might occur only once in an organization's history. Think, for example, about the conversations and decisions that were made by Facebook leader Mark Zuckerberg and his team as they moved toward taking the company public. Or, consider other common nonprogrammed and strategic organizational decisions:

● Choosing to expand the business geographically
● Choosing to invest in a new product line
● Choosing to eliminate or dramatically reduce an entire class of jobs
● Choosing to institute a wage freeze
● Choosing to change the company's logo or Web site
● Choosing to relocate the company's headquarters

These are nonprogrammed strategic decisions that are likely made by senior managers. Managers, however, are not the only ones who have to make tough decisions. For instance, what do you do if a more senior employee wants to go out on a date with you?

He or she is not your manager and you'd really like to go, but this person leads some of your project teams. Or what do you do if you feel someone in your work group is behaving in an unethical manner, such as by spending three to four hours a day at work on the Internet? Or what if someone is selling goods that "fell off of the truck" (i.e., have been taken from the loading dock)? Or at school, what if someone in your class obtains a copy of a midterm before the exam? The answers to these dilemmas may seem pretty obvious on the surface. In actuality, however, they involve making very difficult decisions. For instance, you might think: "Will I get in trouble if I go out on this date?" or "What if my manager doesn't believe me about what people are doing?" Your feelings will also affect your decision. You might be afraid, for example, or outraged. Your cognitive assessment of situations like these and your feelings can be complex. That's why it's important to understand how cognition and emotion affect decision making.

Discussion Questions

1. Why, in your opinion, does decision making include thoughts *and* feelings? Name some ways that feelings can help effective decision making. Name some ways that feelings can hinder effective decision making.

2. Identify three nonprogrammed decisions that you need to make this year. Describe what is unique about each of these decisions. What information will you need in order to make these choices?

---

2. How Do Cognitive and Emotional Processes Affect Decision Making?

Objective 6.2
Compare and contrast how cognitive and emotional processes affect decision making.

Many people believe that decision making is a purely rational process, and that if we analyze a situation carefully enough, a perfect decision will emerge. Making decisions includes reason and logic, of course. Good decisions are also the result of *how* we apply reason and logic. For instance, people process information differently, so it is important to understand certain aspects of cognitive processing. And, emotion affects our thoughts about the problems we are trying to solve, the information we gather, and the choices we identify. Intuition also has an important impact on many decisions, so we need to understand what it is—and what it is not.

Reason and Logic in Decision Making

Organizational scholars James March and Chip Heath note that people commonly describe decision making as a process of rational choice and that the term *rational* is used synonymously with *intelligent*.[4] Rational decision making follows the logic of consequences: If I do X, then Y will happen. Rational decision making is the foundation of decisions in realms such as computer programming and mathematics.[5] A computer follows an algorithm of pure logic, which means that given the same set of inputs, the output will be identical each time. In other words, it is *deterministic*: outcomes are determined by inputs.

Most decisions are more complicated than that because rarely are life's choices and outcomes purely logical or deterministic.[6] Reasoning is a "psycho-logic" process in which we seek out evidence and different alternatives to support existing beliefs when faced with a decision.[7] This means that pure, or formal, logic is rarely the only input to human decision making.

Cognitive Processing: Perceptions Impact How We Understand Information

People's decision-making abilities often differ based on how well they understand and manage their emotions and thought processes. In this section, we will explore several aspects of cognitive processing that can either help—or greatly harm—our decision-making abilities.

SCHEMAS: THE BRAIN'S FILING SYSTEM FOR INFORMATION

To understand how we process and interpret information, it helps to understand what cognitive psychologists refer to as *schemas*. Schemas are conceptual maps in our minds that allow us to understand and mentally categorize information as we receive it.[8] To simplify this with a metaphor, think about a massive filing system that we have created over our entire lives. The system has billions of files, each carefully labeled with an idea, an experience, or an emotion. Most of the files are very complex and include numerous subfolders. For example, you might have a file for "Management Course." Within that file will be everything you have ever heard about, experienced, thought, or felt about this course.

When new information comes to us, the first thing we try to do cognitively is file the information. If we have a file into which the new information easily fits, we store it there. If we don't, we either try to force the information to fit into our filing system or we create a new file. To illustrate this, consider Lucas Johnston-Peck, a very bright boy. When Lucas was young, his parents read stories to him every evening. One of the stories was about animals, and Lucas began to link the pictures in the book with words. He learned that a small furry animal with pointy ears and whiskers that said "meow" was a cat. He learned that a larger animal that said "woof" was a dog, and that an even larger brown animal with round ears that said "grrr" was a bear. Lucas was developing schemas—new files—that enabled him to quickly file information about certain animals.

Once, when Lucas was learning about animals, his aunt visited—with a *dog* named *Bear*. At first, Lucas insisted that this was impossible and refused to call the dog by name. Very quickly, however, Lucas adjusted his filing system to include the concept that dogs could be named Bear. Lucas didn't know it, but he was engaging in a sophisticated cognitive process called accommodation: Lucas was adapting his existing filing system to include new information. This is one sign of an intelligent human being.

Lucas was engaging in a process psychologists call accommodation, which was initially proposed by the famous developmental psychologist Jean Piaget. **Accommodation** is the process of adapting one's cognitive categorization system to allow for new information, new schemas, and new ways of understanding information.[9] Small children learn to accommodate new information quite naturally. As we age, it can become more difficult, especially if we do not have new and different experiences that challenge our beliefs. An important competency related to accommodation is self-awareness. If you know your biases, you guard against them.

According to Piaget, another way to deal with new information is through assimilation. **Assimilation** is the process of integrating or forcing new information to fit existing cognitive categorization systems.[10] This is when cognitive schemas get us into trouble: If we are forcing information to fit what we believe to be true, we are not seeing information clearly and we will likely make poor decisions as a result.

To illustrate how assimilation happens at work, consider two brothers in a family business. As a child and during high school and college, the older brother, Greg, saw himself as the serious, scholarly one. His younger brother Marty was involved in lots of activities, had a busy social life, and was considered the "life of the party." When Greg later hired Marty to make his parents happy, he refused to give Marty any

Self-Awareness   Social Awareness
Self-Management   Relationship Management

Accommodation
The process of adapting one's cognitive categorization system to allow for new information, new schemas, and new ways of understanding information.

Assimilation
The process of integrating or forcing new information to fit existing cognitive categorization systems.

serious responsibilities. Greg continued to shoulder the burden of the business without sharing it with Marty because he did not believe that his brother *could* contribute. Marty—who was actually a very good manager, well-liked by employees, and adept at motivating people—became fed up after a few years of this and left the family business to start a competitor, thereby creating a schism in the family.

The problem in this situation wasn't Marty; it was Greg's inability to change the way he *saw* Marty. Greg could not change his habitual way of judging his brother. He literally could not understand that Marty was actually more competent than he gave him credit for. Underlying this example are common problems related to cognitive processing that often get in the way of good decision making at work: stereotypes and the halo effect.

STEREOTYPES

As you remember from Chapter 4, stereotypes are simplistic generalizations about members of a social group that are rigid, difficult to change, and often negative. Unfortunately, stereotypes often affect decisions. Many stereotypes are extremely destructive because they cause us to misjudge people and situations. When stereotypes about a person or group are based on incorrect or derogatory assumptions they are extremely destructive. For example, stereotypes linked to race, gender, politics, religion, sexual preference, and other aspects of people's identities often lead to discrimination and the denial of rights, liberties, or resources. In the end, many stereotypes fuel hatred and inequity.

We often assume that damaging stereotypes are no longer present in the workplace. Unfortunately, this is not the case. For instance, a female executive recently flew into Cleveland on business and her company arranged for a driver to pick her up at the airport. Upon arrival, the executive saw the driver waiting, holding a sign with her name—Dr. Auld—written on it. When she introduced herself, he looked at her blankly and said, "Oh, I was expecting a man. They told me it was *Doctor* Auld." When the executive expressed surprise and jokingly said something about the stereotype, the man said, "It's not a stereotype; it's common sense." This particular situation is a perfect example of a rigid stereotype that resulted in the driver making two very bad decisions: looking for a man (hence, missing his customer) and expressing discriminatory views (only men can be doctors).

In this case, the executive made sure that her company never used that chauffeur business again. Often the effects are more serious: People are misjudged, overlooked, or treated unfairly; contract negotiations break down; or groups are pitted against one another.

Although the egregious use of stereotypes in the previous example was easy to recognize, sometimes the use of stereotypes is more subtle. For instance, a manager who is originally from New York may believe that people from her home state are more cosmopolitan than employees from other states and are better suited for travel assignments. She may also believe that graduates from her alma mater are better educated than graduates of other colleges and therefore a better fit for certain assignments. This might look like simple favoritism, but it is actually poor decision making based on stereotypes.

Here's the dilemma: Whether obvious or subtle, everyone has stereotypes. You might say we should strive to eliminate all stereotypes, and that is quite true when they are based on negative and untrue biases. However, stereotypes can facilitate easy decisions about how to behave if they are based on accurate and non-harmful assumptions. That's because stereotypes reduce people's cognitive processing load: They are automatic and do not require conscious effort.[11] For example, when we talk to the pharmacist at the local drug store, we have certain stereotypes about the profession and the kind of information he can share with us. Pharmacists, in turn, have certain stereotypes about customers, such as that they may be ill or worried about a family member. These stereotypes facilitate smooth interactions.

That said, uses of stereotypes like this need to be constantly scrutinized: Do the underlying assumptions still apply? Do they apply in *this* situation? Should I let go of preconceived notions and view this situation as new and different? In all cases, we must continually examine our own stereotypes in order to improve the way we make decisions. Stereotypes that are harmful to individual members of groups are simply destructive and, as responsible leaders, we cannot tolerate them in ourselves or in others. Nor can we allow them to influence the decisions we make. Other stereotypes are more reasonable and perhaps worth using, such as our assumptions about the pharmacist–customer interaction.

THE HALO EFFECT

Halo effect
The phenomenon in which we judge something or someone positively based on a previous positive experience or association with someone or something we admire.

The halo effect is a kind of stereotype that can also affect decisions. The halo effect occurs when we judge something or someone positively based on a previous positive experience or association with someone or something we admire.[12] Every good student has learned this lesson: If you are enthusiastic and engaged in the first few classes, do extremely well on the first test or paper, and seek out the instructor for a chat, the professor just might go easy on you for the rest of the semester. In this example, the halo effect may be interfering with the professor's objectivity and maybe even decisions about grades. This happens at work, too, and can result in favoritism—or the opposite.

According to personality theory, judgments regarding an individual's first-noticed trait or behavior can have a cascading effect on interpretations of other characteristics.[13] One characteristic in particular seems to draw forth the halo effect: attractiveness. That's one reason why people pay so much attention to how they look, and it's also why the halo effect is the bread and butter of marketing. For instance, brand marketers use the halo effect when they try to make us like a product simply by linking it to something we already like. Celebrities are used in marketing because the positive feelings people have for them are projected onto the things the celebrities endorse.

Similarly, a negative halo effect, or "devil effect," can be seen when a negative judgment is made based on first-noticed characteristics or an association with someone or something that we do not like. For example, the student who cracks jokes and seems to be ignoring the professor may, unfortunately, be graded more harshly than someone who is quiet and looks studious. It is the same at work—the employee who misses a deadline soon after starting a job may be judged more negatively and harshly by unthinking managers long after the incident is over. Or, returning to marketing campaigns, we often see "guilt by association"—when a celebrity suddenly falls out of the public graces and the products he or she endorses become less popular (■ **EXHIBIT 6.2**).

Cognitive processing, stereotypes, and the halo effect are powerful because they often operate at a subconscious level. Some researchers have demonstrated that even when confronted with evidence that our judgments are biased, we may still be completely unable to see how our thoughts are affecting our behavior and our decisions.[14] To make the best decision possible, therefore, we need to become more aware of some of our habitual thought processes and learn to examine them. That's true with emotions, too.

Emotions: A Legitimate and Important Part of Decision Making

Emotions have a profound effect on decision making, yet common decision-making models have largely ignored this fact. How do we know emotions have an effect on decision making? For one thing, patients who have experienced damage to sections of the brain that process emotions but no damage to their cognitive centers (the "thinking brain") have tremendous difficulty making even the simplest decisions.[15] Second, neuroscientists now recognize that powerful emotions like fear, love, and anger are

■ **EXHIBIT 6.2**
How should companies cope with scandals involving celebrities who endorse their products?

Source: AP Photo/Eric Gay

processed through centers in the brain that can trigger what is called the sympathetic nervous system. This is a part of our nervous system that activates things like heart rate, blood pressure, and large muscle contraction and also tells us what to focus on and what to screen out.[16] This is likely a survival mechanism that helps us realize when we are in danger (fight-or-flight situations) or when we might be able to connect with others (comfort, nurture, make friends, or mate). Our emotions, then, affect what we take in, what we ignore, and our perceptions of people and situations. Clearly this will affect decision making.[17]

Emotions guide us as we sift through the vast amount of information we face on a daily basis.[18] This is because emotions direct our attention to certain things and not others, and are also tied to our beliefs, attitudes, and preferences. All of these impact our choices. Many times, emotions are extremely helpful because they point us in the right direction. At other times, however, they can get us into trouble. When emotions simply "flood" our brains, for example, we can be completely unaware of anything else. Here is a common example: You've fallen in love. Your new partner is (in your view) the most perfect human being on the planet. You want to spend every minute of every day with him or her. Nothing else is important—not school, work, friends, or family. You make some questionable decisions in these areas, while also totally ignoring those little signs that he or she isn't perfect—that short temper, chronic lateness, or texting constantly while with you. A few months down the path, when the flood of emotions recedes, you'll see your partner more clearly and realize you've made bad decisions in other areas of life.

Another way that emotions affect decision making is related to whether a problem, situation, or choice is framed in a negative or positive way. When a choice is framed in negative terms, people may steer away from it. One famous example involves a research decision that was framed in two different ways, but where the outcomes were identical. The research subjects were leaders faced with a decision about how to proceed during an epidemic. One choice was framed as, "400 people will live," the other as, "200 people will die." They were told it was inevitable that 400 would live and 200 would die. Subjects consistently chose the approach that focused on how many would live. The researchers believed this happened because the research subjects experienced more positive emotions when thinking about people surviving.[19]

Intuition in Decision Making

The power of intuitive understanding will protect you from harm until the end of your days.

> —**Lao Tzu,** ancient Chinese philosopher[20]

There is no logical way to the discovery of these elemental laws. There is only the way of intuition, which is helped by a feeling for the order lying behind the appearance.

> —**Albert Einstein,** genius known for developing the theory of relativity[21]

Intuition is not born purely of rational thought. But if intuition does not come from logic, is it also "illogical"? Some people view intuition as a sort of mystical knowledge. Others talk about intuition as if it were instinct—something encoded in our DNA like a baby's natural ability to develop language. It is also something often attributed to women rather than men, as suggested by the common phrase "woman's intuition."

Intuition is not a mystical power, it's not encoded in DNA, and it's not just for women. **Intuition** is tacit knowledge, or knowledge that we have access to at an unconscious level. Intuition is that sense of knowing something while not being able to explain how you know. Intuition is a result of memory that links past experiences and emotions with complex processing of a current situation.[22] Intuition often plays a role

Intuition
Tacit knowledge, or knowledge that we have access to at an unconscious level.

in the big decisions in life: who to date or marry, which job to take, even which car to buy. But, how do we know when intuition is at play?

Many people experience intuition as a "gut feeling." You may have had these kinds of feelings when deciding to go somewhere, do something, or try something new. For some reason, you just knew the right decision. If someone asked you to explain it, you couldn't. That is another clue: If you can't explain your thoughts or feelings about a decision you want to make, it could be that you are drawing on unconscious experiences and emotions and applying them to the situation at hand. Another way we can determine whether a decision is intuitively based is to consider whether it is accompanied by memories of past experiences and emotions.[23]

Herbert Simon studied the role of intuition in expert chess players' decision making.[24] Chess is an intensely cerebral game of strategy that relies heavily on logic and intellect. However, top chess experts intuitively single out the move they will make from hundreds of potential moves within the first few seconds. Even when they take a long time to make a move, most of that time is spent examining the chosen move for potential weaknesses.

Experts, Simon argues, see information holistically, rather than in bits. Each pattern is linked to similar patterns stored in memory at an unconscious level. Simon suggests that this intuitive processing of expert knowledge is the same for all people, whether they are chess masters, physicians, or managers.[25]

Intuition is an unconscious process that is automatic and often below the level of awareness. This process operates at a subconscious level of cognition, and it filters out information that is not relevant and organizes what is left into holistic patterns. People process information and make decisions both intuitively *and* rationally, often engaging in below-the-surface and deliberate processes at the same time.[26] Many researchers agree that the type of activity a person is engaged in has a strong influence on whether tacit (intuitive), explicit (analytical), or both cognitive systems are used when making decisions.[27]

Taking intuition into the realm of leadership, scholars Daniel Goleman and Richard Boyatzis note that intuition is a powerful tool that leaders can learn to use to make decisions. Their research indicates that intuition can be found in the brain—in particular, the cells that regulate emotion are wired to other cells that notice patterns and make judgments. They conclude that leaders should not fear acting on intuition, provided they are correctly attuned to other people, the situation, and the experiences from which they are drawing conclusions.[28]

Experiences help build the repertoire from which intuition draws. The value of experiences can become limited, however, when feedback is poor or incorrect. These can create work environments that are inhospitable to the development of intuitive skills that can be used to make effective decisions.[29]

You now have a deeper understanding of the many processes that affect decision making: logic, cognitive processing, bias, emotion, and intuition. Let's look at a model that can help you organize all of this as you take steps toward making a decision.

Discussion Questions

1. Describe a moment when you had an incredible insight at school or at work. How did you react emotionally? What logical process did you employ to explain the new information? Was this insight intuition? Explain.

2. In this section, we noted that taking in new information can require accommodation—that is, adapting your cognitive filing system to include new ways of understanding people and situations. Have you ever consciously done this? What was the situation? Was this easy or hard for you? How did accommodation help you?

3. How Can You Apply a Systematic Approach to Making Decisions?

Objective 6.3
Learn to apply a systematic approach to decision making.

A **decision-making process** refers to the steps taken when choosing a course of action. The type of decision-making process selected depends on the nature of the problem, the availability of information, and the alternatives being considered. A person's values also play a role in the type of decision-making process that is chosen. The complexity of the decision, the number of people who need to be involved, and the extent of the consequences are also factors that need to be considered when selecting or creating a decision-making process.

Decision-making process
The steps taken when choosing a course of action.

Some problems are simple, and the consequences of a bad decision are not serious. These decisions are straightforward and present themselves along with sufficient information. In comparison, complex decisions often need a structured and elaborate decision-making process. This is the case for a number of reasons. First, identifying a problem (i.e., what needs to be decided) can be challenging and confusing. Second, decision makers frequently lack the information they require. For instance, several alternative choices may exist, and you may not be able to predict the outcome of these choices. Take the example of choosing a major in college. You can't know everything— or even very much—about how a particular course of study will affect your career or your life. Emotions play a part in a decision like this, as do intuition and your habitual way of processing information. Plus, you have so many available alternatives. You must make a decision—but how? This is when it helps to have a model or a structured process to follow to begin organizing your thoughts and feelings about a decision, the information available, and your choices.

One decision-making model emerged from research about how customers choose what products to buy (■ **EXHIBIT 6.3**).[30] While it has limitations, this model can help us to rationally identify a problem and then choose and implement a specific alternative. The following sections take a closer look at each of the distinct steps in this process.

Step 1: Identify the Problem

The first step in any good decision-making process is to properly identify the problem.[31] A problem exists whenever a desired state is not in line with the actual state. For example, say that in a department store, the desired state is for sales to increase by 6 percent this year, but sales declined by 10 percent in the first quarter of the year. What is the problem? The obvious problem is that sales are dropping. But why? One possible factor is that the department store has a high rate of absenteeism. At any given time, at least one out of every ten employees is home sick. When so many people are out, other employees can't provide excellent service. If this is determined to be the primary problem causing low sales, managers might decide to hire new employees.

■ **EXHIBIT 6.3**

Eight Steps to Better Decision Making
Step 1: Identify the problem.
Step 2: Establish the decision criteria.
Step 3: Allocate weights to decision criteria.
Step 4: List alternatives.
Step 5: Analyze alternatives.
Step 6: Choose an alternative.
Step 7: Implement the decision.
Step 8: Evaluate the decision.

However, absenteeism could also be a symptom of a larger problem. The real problem might be that the store's supervisors are ineffective and difficult to get along with. They are not motivating employees. In fact, supervisors are causing employees to experience a great deal of stress—hence, the higher rate of absenteeism and the drop in sales. If managers correctly identify the supervisors' leadership abilities as the root problem, they will realize that simply hiring new employees isn't the right decision. Instead, the managers might decide to provide the supervisors with opportunities to develop their leadership skills.

Too often in organizations (and in life, for that matter), people derail the decision-making process in its very first step by incorrectly identifying the real problem. For that reason, it is important to carefully consider exactly what underlying issues contribute to more obvious problems.

Let's look at another example related to problem identification that you can probably relate to. During the first or second year of college, most students are required to select a major. This can be a difficult decision, often because a student has many interests or because he or she isn't sure which career to pursue. However, the real problem may be even deeper.

Take the example of Jason (■ **EXHIBIT 6.4**). Jason is under pressure from his parents to pursue a degree in accounting, but he is not sure that he wants to be an accountant. Regardless of how thoroughly he weighs his alternatives and imagines his career, he still can't make a decision. That's because Jason is actually faced with a bigger problem than simply choosing a major—in effect, he is deciding whether to follow his desires or to pursue his parents' plan. This situation is very emotional for Jason, but he knows he must find the courage to decide for himself. Jason will have to talk honestly with his parents about what he wants, and what they want as well.

Step 2: Establish the Decision Criteria

In the second step of this decision-making process, decision criteria are established. For instance, if the problem is that a manager must hire a new employee, he will create job-relevant criteria such as level of education, past experience, and ability to handle stress. These criteria will help him evaluate such candidates.

Let's return to the example of choosing a major. Jason has realized that the real problem is that he wants to start a business, but his parents want him to Jason's father is especially insistent about this because he is a successful accountant, and he believes a similar career path will provide Jason with a satisfying job and a good salary. To help himself better understand the alternatives, Jason brainstorms a set of decision criteria. He then phrases each criterion as a question:

- Which major will allow me to follow my dream of becoming a business owner?
- Which major will ensure that I am prepared to get a job after college if I can't start my own business right away?
- Which major will help me obtain a broad education in business and management?
- Which major will accept the elective credits I already have?
- Which major will allow me to finish college in four years?
- Which major will ensure that my parents aren't worried about me or my career opportunities?
- Which major will permit me to take classes with my girlfriend?

Jason may continue brainstorming decision criteria until he comes up with a fairly long list. Obviously, some of the criteria will be more important to him than others—and that's where the next step in this decision-making process comes into play.

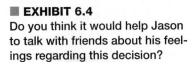

■ **EXHIBIT 6.4**
Do you think it would help Jason to talk with friends about his feelings regarding this decision?

Source: VikramRaghuvanshi/iStockphoto.com

Step 3: Allocate Weights to Decision Criteria

The third step in the decision-making process involves prioritizing the decision criteria and assigning weights to them based on their relative importance. This may sound complicated, but people prioritize decision criteria all the time. For example, whether you realize it or not, you probably assign weights to your criteria when choosing where to go for lunch. In this situation, your decision criteria might be quantity of food, price, flavor, healthiness, and convenience, and you may place the greatest weight on price and the lowest on convenience, or perhaps the greatest on healthiness and the lowest on price. The way you prioritize your criteria will affect your ultimate decision.

But what about Jason's decision criteria? After much soul searching, Jason has decided that he must follow his own path. However, he also wants to please his parents and relieve their fears regarding his future job security. Accordingly, Jason prioritizes his decision criteria as follows, beginning with the most important criterion and moving toward the least important:

1. Which major will allow me to follow my dream of becoming a business owner?
2. Which major will allow me to finish college in four years?
3. Which major will help me obtain a broad education in business and management?
4. Which major will ensure that I am prepared to get a job after college if I can't start my own business right away?
5. Which major will ensure that my parents aren't worried about me or my career opportunities?
6. Which major will accept the elective credits I already have?
7. Which major will permit me to take classes with my girlfriend?

Jason is passionate about following his dream of being a business owner—that's why he gives this criterion the most weight in his decision-making process. He also knows that he must finish college within four years for financial reasons. Jason is aware that the job market is tight, and it's important to him to be prepared to support himself before starting his own business. In addition, Jason understands that by preparing himself for a job and finishing college in four years, he can alleviate his parents' anxiety and please them as well as himself. Finally, as he assigns weights to his list of criteria, Jason realizes that he doesn't mind taking more electives and that taking classes with his girlfriend is really not that important in the grand scheme of things.

Assigning weights to decision criteria is obviously subjective and includes thoughts, emotions, and intuition. That's why you must carefully consider the logic behind your prioritization and also be honest with yourself. In Jason's case, it was hard for him to admit that his parents' wishes were lower on his list, but he had to be honest about this situation in order to arrange his criteria in a way that most accurately represented his own wants and needs.

Step 4: List Alternatives

During the fourth step of this decision-making process, a list of alternatives is generated. This is the part of the process in which the decision maker outlines all of the possible choices that can be made. Consider the example of a restaurant that is facing the problem of declining sales. The restaurant owner's initial list of alternatives might include cutting prices, having a sales contest among servers, changing the menu offerings, offering lunch specials, offering free drinks, increasing advertising, and sending press releases to local newspapers about the restaurant. As this wide and varied list demonstrates, outside-the-box thinking can play a critical role when facing a complex decision.

How might this step progress for Jason? At first glance, Jason's list of possible alternatives seems simple:

1. Choose to major in management.
2. Choose to major in accounting.

As Jason examines his choices more creatively, he realizes that he has at least three other choices as well:

3. Choose a dual major in both management and accounting.
4. Choose to major in management and minor in accounting.
5. Choose to major in accounting and minor in management.

Thanks to creative thinking, Jason now has five alternatives. Jason is not making any effort to "qualify" or compare his alternatives—that comes during the next step in the decision-making process.

Step 5: Analyze Alternatives

In step 5 of this decision-making process, each alternative is evaluated. Here, the decision maker must ask whether each alternative is truly a viable option. This step is made easier by the decision criteria that were established in step 2, and also by the weights that were assigned in step 3. The decision maker takes an objective look at each alternative and determines which one (or ones) can realistically be implemented. For instance, in the restaurant example, the owner may elect to throw out the alternative of changing menu offerings because this can't be done without the high costs associated with reprinting menus, ordering ingredients from different suppliers, and training the kitchen staff to cook new items.

What should Jason do (■ **EXHIBIT 6.5**)? When he analyzes the alternatives more closely, Jason comes to the conclusion that majoring in accounting is out of the question. For one, majoring in accounting will not prepare Jason to run his own business. (Remember, this is Jason's most important decision criteria.) Even if he pairs accounting with a minor in management, Jason still doesn't think this will be enough. He also knows that he cannot complete a dual major within four years (his second most important criteria), so he takes that option off his list. Hence, Jason is left with only two alternatives:

1. Choose to major in management.
2. Choose to major in management and minor in accounting.

Jason believes that he can make a case for either of these two alternatives that will satisfy his decision criteria and possibly help his parents feel less anxiety about his future.

Step 6: Choose an Alternative

Step 6 in this decision-making process involves choosing one alternative from the list. Based on the evaluation conducted in step 5, one alternative may emerge as the best choice. In Jason's case, for instance, a clear choice has emerged: major in management and minor in accounting. This choice meets all of Jason's most important criteria—it allows him to pursue his dream, finish school in four years, obtain a broad education, and prepare himself to get a job. Because of the minor in accounting, Jason feels his parents will be less anxious. As an added bonus, he knows his father will be pleased that he has some interest in the accounting field.

In many cases, choices are not as clear as Jason's; there may be several good options, for example, or none that are perfect. Similarly, time and other constraints might make it impossible to carry out a full and thorough investigation during each step in the

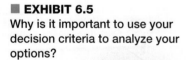

■ **EXHIBIT 6.5**
Why is it important to use your decision criteria to analyze your options?

Source: VikramRaghuvanshi/iStockphoto.com

decision-making process. In such instances, **satisficing** may be necessary.[32] Satisficing means choosing an alternative that is adequate but not perfect. For example, when you are deciding where to go for lunch, the best decision based on price and the quality of the food might be the $4.99 pizza buffet on the other side of campus. You are satisficing if you go to the cafeteria because it is "good enough" for a quick lunch.

Step 7: Implement the Decision

The seventh step in this decision-making process is implementing the decision. Here, you put things into action. For the chosen alternative to be successful, the right amount of time, money, and resources must be dedicated to carrying out the decision. Returning to the restaurant example, if the owner decides that the best option is to offer lunch specials, several actions must accompany this decision. Promotional materials need to be created and servers must be trained. The kitchen staff has to be alerted that certain entrées may be ordered in greater numbers than normal. Last but not least, a break-even point will need to be determined so that the restaurant owner knows how many more lunches he must sell at the reduced price to begin making a profit.

Let's go back to Jason's decision and see how he implements it. Jason first contacts his adviser and fills out the appropriate forms. He then finds out what the management department expects of him by meeting with the chair of the department, signing up for an orientation session, and so on. As he plans his courses, Jason also begins thinking about his senior project. Lastly, Jason makes plans to talk with his parents, which is a difficult yet vitally important step in implementing his decision.

Step 8: Evaluate the Decision

In the eighth and final step of this decision-making process, the decision is evaluated. Although this step is often forgotten and ignored, it is one of the most important parts of the entire process. After all, how can you know whether the decision was correct if you don't evaluate the outcomes? In our restaurant scenario, for example, suppose that the owner decided to try offering lower-priced lunch specials to boost sales. If no evaluation takes place, the owner will not know how the reduced price lunches affected sales. What if sales continue to decline? What if the cut in prices was so severe that the restaurant is now losing money on certain entrées? Is this difference being made up somewhere else? Evaluation of decisions is essential in organizations and an important part of managing a business.

Of course, it is difficult (if not impossible) to evaluate many decisions immediately. In the restaurant, for instance, initial sales figures might be misleading. There could be an increase in sales the first week when customers first notice the cut in prices, but this might do little to offset the restaurant's overall drop in revenue. Alternatively, there could be a gradual increase in sales that slowly helps the restaurant get back on track.

Decisions that are emotionally charged and that involve several people are often even harder to evaluate. Let's go back to Jason (■ **EXHIBIT 6.6**). Immediately upon making his decision, Jason may feel a huge sense of relief. He may feel proud of himself and convinced that he made the right decision. Therefore, at this point, his evaluation of his decision would be very positive. One year into his major, however, when faced with a semester full of difficult courses, he may have second thoughts. At times like this, it often helps to revisit the decision criteria, because remembering why you did something in the first place can help you evaluate your decision over time.

In summary, the eight-step process presented in this section is a useful tool when making decisions. It forces us to consider each aspect of decision making, from identifying the "real" problem (as opposed to symptoms) to carefully considering the available alternatives and making an informed choice. The model is rational and easy to follow. The problem, however, is that most decisions are not made under conditions

■ **EXHIBIT 6.6**
Do you evaluate your decisions after you make them, as Jason did?

that are purely rational. This is because "perfect" rational decisions require that we have access to all necessary information and use this information in a perfectly logical manner. In reality, neither condition ever occurs. For this reason, scholars have looked at how we can make decisions when conditions are not perfect, such as when we do not have access to all the information we'd like.

Discussion Questions

1. Apply the eight-step process discussed in this section to a decision you are currently grappling with. Now, ask yourself some tough questions: Are you being realistic and honest with yourself about the decision criteria, the weights you assigned to them, and even your alternatives? Are you "too close" to the problem to decide on an effective course of action? Why? What can you do to change that?

2. Do you evaluate your big decisions regularly? How? Name a few reasons that might cause you to reevaluate one of these big decisions.

Objective 6.4
Understand how to make sound decisions with incomplete information.

4. How Can People Make Good Decisions with Incomplete Information?

Rarely, if ever, can we make use of *all* the information potentially available to us when making a decision. Doing so simply isn't practical. Try this: Imagine that your professor has asked you to learn everything you can about decision making and summarize it in a paper. To begin the assignment, you search "decision making" on the Internet—and you immediately realize you can't possibly attend to all the information available. Indeed, at the time of this writing, there are nearly 397 million sites dealing with the topic![33]

In organizational life today, there is an almost unlimited amount of information available to us, and we just can't use it all. When it comes to almost all complex decisions, we simply cannot know everything about our problems, the alternatives, or the consequences of our decisions. Let's look at two ways we can deal with these problems: working with bounded rationality and remembering the 80/20 rule.

Bounded Rationality

From Aristotle to Kant, philosophers have implored people to rely on reason and logic when approaching life's choices.[34] It may be true that if all the information needed to make a decision were available, accessible, and accurate, and if all humans were perfectly rational all the time, then decisions would be universally logical and perfect as well. In reality, however, even the simplest decisions can involve an amount of information that is literally impossible to process in an efficient and effective manner. Also, for most decisions, no matter how extensively we research the problems and alternatives, it is unlikely that we will discover *everything*. Finally, even if we could access all the information we need, what we do with that data is not always logical. As influential social scientist Herbert Simon points out, humans are far from perfect rational beings.[35]

In the real world, decisions are often rushed and irrational. There will always be either too little, too much, or flawed information to consider; as humans, we usually won't be able to take in or evaluate all the information available; and there is never enough time to evaluate all information or all possible choices. Rather than fight this, we can simply accept that our decision-making process is constrained. Herbert Simon and colleague James March call this bounded rationality.[36] **Bounded rationality** is an approach to decision making that accepts that all decisions are made under conditions or constraints that limit rationality. Such conditions include the following:[37]

Bounded rationality
An approach to decision making that accepts that all decisions are made under conditions or constraints that limit rationality.

- Information will never be complete or completely accurate.
- We cannot always evaluate the quality of the information we get.
- People are not purely rational: Emotions, intuition, biases, and the like are always present.
- We simply don't have the time to implement the rational decision-making process in its purest form.

Many studies show that there are limitations to the amount and quality of information people can and do use when making decisions.[38] Daniel Kahneman, who received the Nobel Prize in 2002 for his work on bounded rationality, notes that although we are not poor reasoners, we frequently act without full consideration of information, suggesting that the cognitive costs of getting and processing information are very important factors in how we make decisions.[39]

What this means is that it is hard work to contemplate and analyze information, we will never be purely objective and rational, and we make trade-offs. We mentally balance the "cost" of gathering and processing information, and at some point we are willing to run the risk that something is potentially eliminated from framing a problem, considering alternatives, or selecting a solution.[40] But, as you've seen, we need to avoid destructive judgments based on biases and stereotypes.

So, to make any decision at all, we need to understand how much and what type of information to seek, how much time we can actually allot to the decision-making process, and how to best manage given the limitations and the people involved. Under these conditions, we can arrive at satisfactory (but possibly not optimal) solutions—in other words, we can satisfice.[41]

All leaders constantly grapple with the fact that decisions must be made under imperfect conditions. Truly outstanding leaders, though, understand how to make the best decisions possible, and how to implement these decisions with everyone's full support. Gavin Patterson, Director of British Telecom (BT) Group PLC and Chief Executive of BT Retail, is one such leader. Gavin is an outstanding forerunner in his field, and also contributes widely to other organizations and his community. He's a Non-executive Director of British Airlines PLC and is a Trustee of the British Museum, as well as being President of the Advertising Association. In all of these roles, Gavin brings a unique perspective on how leaders can handle the challenges of uncertainty in our changing world.

Leadership Perspective

- **Gavin Patterson**
  Director of BT Group PLC,
  Chief executive BT Retail;
  "Living with uncertainty is the new norm."

Gavin Patterson is a dynamic, engaging leader at British Telecom (BT), Britain's premier telecommunications company. Gavin is quite young to be a CEO, but his success is no accident. He knows the business inside and out—and he is passionate about it and about the people he serves. He is smart, hardworking, and emotionally intelligent. Also, when it comes to making tough decisions and ensuring that people are with him, Gavin has some good advice:

First, you have to truly understand what you are trying to accomplish and where you are going. That's not always as easy as it sounds, because the environment is shifting so quickly—you have to be clear about your general direction and focus on your values and principles. You can't wait until you have every single piece of information, or for all the alternatives to become clear. There's just too much information, things are changing too fast, and many of the decisions we make are too complex for this kind of clarity.

Waiting for absolute clarity, for the markets to become stable and predictable, is just not going to happen—certainly not in the next few years. Living with uncertainty is the new

Continued on next page >>

norm. *Agility and the ability to maintain a number of positions and options while driving your business forward is the art that is setting the winners apart from the laggards. To be one of those winners, you must learn how to make decisions that place bets on what your customers will need and want in the future, even if they can't afford or are otherwise too distracted to take up today.*

What it comes down to is that you'll need to be ruthless in terms of what input you take and what you discard, so you can make the right bets. And you need to do this in a way that engages people, rather than pushing them away—you need their input, and you need them to be with you.

Once you make a decision, you need to simplify it for people—make it as clear as you possibly can what was decided, why, and what needs to be done. You need to give

people confidence that they can achieve the goals. You need to let them know that you believe in them. More than anything, it's important to create the right atmosphere—one that is filled with passion and commitment. You want an environment that is marked by positive and powerful competitiveness around delivery, and that balances supportiveness with challenge and excitement. People need to feel that they can be themselves and bring the best of themselves to the work that has to be done. They need time to laugh, have fun—and work hard. In this kind of atmosphere, people are willing to debate the hard decisions, come to a conclusion, and move forward.

Source: Personal interviews with Gavin Patterson conducted by Annie McKee, 2009 and 2012.

As Gavin Patterson knows, most decisions have to be made in the midst of uncertainty, without complete or perfect information, by people who are also not perfect or purely rational. Another complicating factor when it comes to decision making at work is related to which issues or problems we should focus on. One rule of thumb that seems to have caught on is called the 80/20 rule.

80/20 Rule

In the early 1900s, economist Vilfredo Pareto noted that 80 percent of the land in Italy was owned by 20 percent of the population. Then, a few decades later, management theorist Joseph Juran came to the conclusion that in manufacturing, 20 percent of the problems in a production process cause 80 percent of the quality issues.[42] Juran called this effect the Pareto principle, in honor of Vilfredo Pareto. Also known as the 80/20 rule, this principle is commonly used as a rule of thumb to quickly see possible causal relationships, such as that 80 percent of sales come from 20 percent of clients or that 80 percent of a company's work is done by 20 percent of its employees. Other examples might be that 80 percent of disciplinary write-ups are given to only 20 percent of your employees, or that 80 percent of a restaurant's sales come from just 20 percent of the patrons—the "regulars."

What does the 80/20 rule have to do with decision making? We often have to make decisions about *what* to focus on. The 80/20 rule tells us that 20 percent of what we do each day results in 80 percent of our output, suggesting that it can be productive to focus on the 20 percent.

Obviously, the 80/20 rule isn't 100 percent accurate (especially if you don't identify the 20 percent correctly!). Rather, it's a guideline that many people find useful because it helps them determine what to focus on at work. If you approach problems assuming that the 80/20 rule is in effect, then you are likely to consider causes, alternatives, and decisions differently than if no rule of thumb applies. For example, managers who want to leverage their success might focus more attention on a vital few clients, their star employees, or their regular patrons. Alternatively, they might focus on the 20 percent causing problems—underperforming employees, for example.

Sometimes, when making decisions about how to solve problems, focusing on the 20 percent is wise. In other cases, however, it is not. The assumptions underlying the 80/20 rule are helpful in guiding our attention when we attempt to understand a challenge or a problem. However, it is critical to always remember that this rule is merely a guideline.

In this section, we've reviewed how the paradox of always having too much information—but never really having it all—is a major factor in most decisions. This problem, coupled with our inherent irrationality, can impact our ability to make good choices. To deal with these problems, we must learn to make decisions under conditions of bounded rationality and to use rules of thumb such as the 80/20 rule to help guide our thought processes. In the next section, we will discuss critical thinking—yet another way of understanding and using the information we have available to us to improve our decision-making ability.

Discussion **Questions**

1. Use the concept of bounded rationality to explain how you made the decision to choose your major.

2. Do you believe the 80/20 rule is a useful model for attempting to understand organizational strengths and weaknesses? Why or why not? Give one example in which the model would be helpful and one in which it could result in a bad decision.

5. How Can You Improve Your Critical Thinking Skills and Make Better Decisions?

Objective 6.5
Improve your critical thinking skills.

When it comes right down to it, *people* make decisions and the ultimate quality of any decision depends on the quality of the thinking that goes into it. In this section, we will consider how you can hone your critical thinking skills so you can make better decisions.

Critical Thinking Defined

For many people, the word *critical* has negative connotations—it may bring to mind judging others or their ideas. However, critical thinking is *not* about criticizing. Rather, **critical thinking** is the disciplined intellectual process of evaluating situations or ideas and making appropriate judgments. It is a structured intellectual process that we can use to objectively examine ideas, assumptions, knowledge, and reasoning in order to evaluate their logic and validity and to determine a course of thought or action.[43]

Critical thinking
The disciplined intellectual process of evaluating situations or ideas and making appropriate judgments or taking certain actions.

Scholars Goodwin Watson and Edwin Glaser have studied critical thinking in depth, and they have devised categories of skills along with a well-known self-assessment instrument for measuring these skills. Their test, the Watson-Glaser Critical Thinking Appraisal, is composed of five skill sets that these researchers have linked to critical thinking skills: inference, recognition of assumptions, deduction, interpretation, and evaluation of arguments.[44] ■ **EXHIBIT 6.7** provides a definition for each of these skill sets.

Critical thinking is *very* important in most jobs today. In most industries, people have to make more decisions than in the past, there is less direct supervision, and there are more opportunities to access and weigh information as a normal part of work. Employees who can take the vast amount of information they will encounter during

■ **EXHIBIT 6.7**

Critical Thinking Skills and Definitions	
Critical Thinking Skill	**Definition**
Inference	Drawing conclusions from evidence or known information
Recognition of assumptions	Recognizing underlying beliefs, biases, etc., in information
Deduction	Reasoning that moves from generalities to specific conclusions
Interpretation	Articulating the meaning of a collection of facts
Evaluation of arguments	Judging an argument based on logical criteria

the day—reports, e-mails, meeting notes, budgets, and so on—and form appropriate assumptions about that data before making key decisions are incredibly valuable to organizations.

To better understand the importance of critical thinking, consider how much information is now shared through social networking. Information is generated at an ever-faster pace and available to more and more people. But how do we know that what we read is accurate? We need to understand how to think critically about what we read. For companies like Wikipedia, whose mission is to involve as many people as possible in the creation and generation of knowledge, contributors' critical thinking skills will be a main factor in success or failure. Let's look at Wikipedia in some depth in the following *Business Case* feature. As you read through it, consider how critical thinking impacts Wikipedia's information at all steps in the creation and delivery process.

BUSINESS CASE   **Wikipedia**

Critical Thinking Required

American inventor Ward Cunningham pioneered the idea of the *wiki*—a collaborative, computer-based environment that enables people in different locations to work simultaneously on shared files. However, businessman Jimmy Wales and philosopher Larry Sanger used this idea to revolutionize how knowledge is compiled and shared through the creation of Wikipedia.[45]

The "big idea" behind Wikipedia sounds simpler than it really is: Allow people to compile knowledge and enable individuals everywhere to access this knowledge for free.[46] On Wikipedia, *everyone* can write and edit articles and the final product is the result of mass collaboration. Its 4 million English-language entries alone make Wikipedia far larger than the online edition of the *Encyclopaedia Britannica*, which contains only 120,000 articles.[47]

The immense popularity of Wikipedia has impacted popular culture, and the word *wiki* has become an official part of the English language.[48] People all over the world turn to Wikipedia every day for information about a wide variety of subjects, and many large organizations and corporations use the site as a simple way to share information about themselves with a global audience.[49] Despite this generally positive reception, several serious objections have arisen regarding Wikipedia and similar sites that allow unlimited access to information. For one, some companies see this movement as a threat to their intellectual

property.[50] If everything goes "open source," how will companies sell "their" ideas, their patents, and their copyrighted material?

Also, the open nature of Wikipedia's system makes it easy for people to deface entries, delete others' opinions, or push one-sided views. Sometimes, extreme measures must be taken to prevent this from happening. For example, in 2004, entries about U.S. presidential candidates John Kerry and George W. Bush had to be locked for most of the year.[51] Still, thanks to Wikipedia's corps of devoted editors, obscenity and other problems are usually quickly recognized and corrected. In fact, according to one MIT study, any obscenity randomly inserted on Wikipedia is removed in an average of 1.7 minutes.[52]

Still, at the core of these criticisms is the fact that many people believe that Wikipedia is an unreliable source of information. This is why many teachers forbid students from using the site when doing papers and projects. For example, an entry on well-known journalist John Seigenthaler was edited to falsely state that he was under suspicion for both the John F. Kennedy and Robert Kennedy assassinations. This particular incident led Wikipedia to tighten their standards and increase their self-monitoring.[53]

Despite such concerns, it's obvious that Wikipedia is here to stay, and that it continues to change how people gather, think about, create, and share information. In this information-sharing environment, critical thinking skills—along with ethics and

Continued on next page >>

BUSINESS CASE Continued

personal responsibility—are more important than ever before. Not only do Wikipedia's contributors need to think carefully about what they add to the site, but its editors must make rapid judgments and move quickly when they discover something amiss.

Perhaps most importantly, because Wikipedia's users can never be 100 percent sure that everything they find on the site is accurate, they must continually use their critical thinking capabilities to determine the validity of what they read on the screen.

As this case demonstrates, many factors play a role in Wikipedia's success—with one primary factor being contributors', editors', and users' capacity for critical thinking. Indeed, people's ability to understand existing knowledge, examine assumptions, deduce specific conclusions, interpret complex ideas, and evaluate arguments are key when it comes to generating and managing knowledge in all environments. Whether you're receiving information from Wikipedia or from a newspaper, a network news program, or a faithful friend or coworker, it's essential that you evaluate that information critically. Each and every bit of information we receive represents the work of some person somewhere who has his or her own opinion, agenda, experience, and worldview—and these things ultimately influence that person's message, whether intentionally or not.

Critical thinking is especially important in a global organization. A tremendous number of organizations do business in countries outside their own and/or recruit talented people from around the world. In such companies, you will be called on to reflect on your assumptions and your beliefs about people, cultures, and business practices. Critical thinking skills are a must, or you will be left on the sidelines of leadership. Connie Wayne, Director of Leadership Development at Eaton Corporation, has spent her career helping leaders to develop critical thinking and other leadership skills. Eaton is a leading technology company that provides products, services, and solutions in the power industry. The company is based in the United States, and does business in countries all over the world. In the *Leadership Perspective* feature, Connie Wayne has unique and powerful advice on building critical thinking skills as you learn to lead today.

Leadership Perspective

● **Connie Wayne**
Director of Leadership Development, Eaton Corporation
". . . you need to challenge your assumptions constantly."

In a global business you need to challenge your assumptions constantly. You need to ask yourself whether your line of thinking, your views, experiences, and knowledge are valid in new situations. If your perspective seems to be valid, how and to what extent? You need to be open. One way to challenge yourself to stay open is to think about the first time you went to a country other than your own, or maybe a city in a region of the country that is very different. Remember how you felt—curious, excited, maybe a bit overwhelmed. Once you've had the experience of being challenged in a totally new environment, you never think the same again.

You need to hold on to this attitude and mind-set in business and at

work—seek new experiences, talk to people who come from different backgrounds than yours. Learn what it means to do business in different countries—chances are, it's not at all the same as doing business in your home country. There will be different laws and regulations that you have to understand and obey. There will be different norms and different cultural preferences. You need to be able to evaluate these, compare them with what you (think you) know, and make reasoned decisions about how to operate. Every aspect of business is included in this. For example, sometimes people make the mistake of thinking that financial management is the same all over the world. It's not—and it's no longer as simple as profit and loss. How money can be invested, spent, and used differs from country to country. This requires you to be knowledgeable and to have critical thinking skills as you make financial decisions.

At Eaton, we've decided that it is better to give senior leaders the chance to experience some of these things firsthand, before they move into the most senior jobs. Our leadership program, which we call "The Zone," does just that. While

Continued on next page >>

most training programs are "just in time" learning, we provide learning experiences before people need them. This enables them to make a leap conceptually and in how they lead in their current jobs, while being fully prepared for the next one. The Zone focuses on all aspects of leadership. When it comes to critical thinking, we

- *Provide a deep dive into strategy. People have the experience of critically evaluating how their job, function, or business fits into the organization's strategy.*
- *Give people the chance to expand their thinking and mental models. A broader view of the global business, our multicultural people, and our customers helps our leaders to learn how to tailor products, services, and solutions.*

- *Enable people from all over the world to come together in the same room. Over many months, they rejoin their group, learning from each other on a very deep level about cultures and beliefs about business and about life.*

The Zone is a program that exposes participants to how they will need to think and what they'll need to focus on as they move to even more senior roles in the company. We're lucky to have such a program, but you can learn some of these things on your own. What you need to do is to first open your mind. Then, seek people out who come from different places and backgrounds. Then, learn from them.

Source: Personal interview with Connie Wayne conducted by Annie McKee, 2012.

As Connie Wayne of Eaton so eloquently points out, you must have critical thinking skills to succeed in global business. Your point of view is just that—your own point of view. You need to be able to evaluate it objectively, while taking in information and perspectives very different from your own.

Another reason that critical thinking is important today is that people have to make more decisions than in the past, there is less direct supervision, and there are more opportunities to access and weigh information as a normal part of work.

As organizations move to empower employees to make more—and more important—decisions, the need to analyze situations (and people) has become part of everyday work at all organizational levels. To be a successful manager, you will need to master critical thinking. Much of this comes from experience: The more complex situations you face in your career, the better your critical thinking skills become. You don't have to wait until you are older, however; you can improve your critical thinking now by learning to avoid common thinking errors.

Critical Thinking Errors and How to Avoid Thinking Traps

Critical thinking is a dynamic process with many opportunities for making mistakes. *One common mistake people often make is jumping too quickly to a conclusion.* For example, maybe a manager has seen countless employees complain about their hours. Because of this experience, when a new employee asks why he is scheduled to work on a Saturday morning, the manager might jump to the conclusion that the employee doesn't like working weekends and is trying to find a way out of it. However, the employee might actually want to know whether he can work all day Saturday, or whether he can work both Saturday and Sunday mornings. This particular employee may not have any problem at all with the Saturday morning shift.

Second, *critical thinking errors frequently occur because people don't have the courage to carry out the entire critical thinking process, especially when it means confronting others with new ways of looking at things.* By nature, we often want to "fit in" and not go against the crowd, which can make critical thinking difficult in a group setting. If our urge to conform is greater than our need to make effective choices, we are in danger of shortchanging the critical thinking process. Taking a position that is not popular may feel uncomfortable. It's not easy to be the one who is different from the rest of the team. When you do speak up, however, you may discover that others were thinking the same things you were. Good leaders have the courage to see things as they are, speak up, work through problems completely, and act on solid decisions.

Finally, *critical thinking errors occur when we assume from the outset th* *right.* Do you know anyone who is convinced that they are never wrong? Thes self-proclaimed perfection is often a sign that they are unable to engage i thinking. These people assume from the start that they are right, when in re may only be partially correct or even entirely wrong. Being open to suggesti others and taking time to learn more about a situation facilitates critical which contributes to good decisions.

Scholars John Hammond, Ralph Keeney, and Howard Raiffa have provid useful guideline to add to the critical thinking errors discussed so far. Th which you can see in ■ **EXHIBIT 6.8**, allows us to see specifically where "trapped" when trying to make decisions and what we can do about it.[54]

Let's take two of these thinking traps and look at how they played situations:

Supporting the status quo: Supporting the status quo affects decisions both inside and outside an organization. Take this example: Within two months of taking the job, a prominent medical services firm's CEO realized that her CFO and the finance division

■ **EXHIBIT 6.8**

Thinking Traps in Decision Making		
"Thinking Trap"	**Explanation**	**Avoidance Strategy**
Anchoring Bias	Giving too much value to the first piece of information you. The result is that you might prematurely stop gathering information, or the overvalued information may bias your perception of new information. The information is an "anchor" that restricts thinking.	Seek out diverse perspectives that challenge your views. Recognize the natural tendency to orient toward the first piece of information. Generate more than one hypothesis to explain information you encounter. Pursue multiple lines of analysis.
Status Quo Bias	Favoring new choices that are similar to the current situation.	Question the value of the current situation: Is it really good/right/the only way? Ask yourself whether you are choosing something just because it is "normal". Try completely redefining the key concepts of an idea. Don't be afraid of the effort or cost of change.
Sunk Cost Bias	Continuing to make choices that justify past decisions or expenses, even though they are no longer relevant to the current situation.	Know when to quit. Consider the perspectives of individuals who weren't involved in the earlier decisions. Avoid encouraging fear of failure.
Confirming Evidence Bias	Selectively seeking out information that supports your point of view.	Question whether you are seeking all relevant information or whether you are favoring only information that supports your point of view. Seek out voices that argue against you. Avoid "yes men."
Estimating and Forecasting Bias	Being unduly influenced by memories of powerful examples.	Consider whether examples in memory on which you base estimates are extremes. Obtain actual data rather than relying on impressions.
Framing Bias	Being overly influenced by how a problem is explained or seen.	Consider alternative ways to see and articulate a problem. Consider whether the problem has been articulated with a sufficient amount of detail.

Source: Adapted from John S. Hammond, Ralph L. Keeney, and Howard Raiffa. 1998. The hidden traps in decision making. *Harvard Business Review* 76(5): 47–58.

were not up to par. First, the division was far too large. Comparable firms' finance teams were about 50 people; this one was 120. Second, there were numerous errors in financial reports, even some that went to the board. Third, the CFO was known to be an abrasive, unpleasant manager—employees had been complaining about him for years.

It seems obvious what the CEO needed to do, right? It was time for a new CFO and extensive restructuring of the finance division. The new CEO, however, felt that for at least a year, she needed to keep the team in place. Why? First of all, the chairman of the board wanted her to: He had been involved in hiring the CFO and wanted him to stay. Second, the CEO had just come from a job where in her first six months, she completely changed her top team. This action had resulted in her being despised and mistrusted during her entire term as senior vice president. She did not want that experience again! She decided that the status quo would do for a while.

Unfortunately, during the year that the CEO gave herself before making changes, serious discrepancies were found in the finance area. Money was missing, reports had been doctored, and the like. The CEO was in big trouble.

Sunk costs: This is a common problem in many organizations. For example, in one company we know, managers had decided to invest heavily in a particular type of diet food. They spent millions, and the project was the "one to be on" because of the visibility and hype around how popular the product would be when it hit the market. Ultimately, the product flopped—badly. Consumers didn't like the taste, didn't like the ingredients (lots of chemicals), and felt it was too expensive. Rather than scrapping the product, this company launched a massive ad campaign—spending many more hundreds of thousands of dollars. The result: Product sales went up minimally. Consumer feedback was still exactly the same: Taste, ingredients, and cost were still huge problems. What did the company do? Another marketing campaign! And all because they were trapped by the "We've come this far, we just need to keep going" mentality. They did not know when to quit.

As you have gathered throughout this chapter, decision making and critical thinking are complicated. There are many things to consider, from accurate diagnosis of a problem, to dealing with imperfect information, to understanding how your own emotions and thought processes can help or harm your ability to make good decisions. In the next section, we will look at how HR can help employees make good decisions.

Discussion Questions

1. Consider three common critical thinking errors mentioned in this section. Reflect on an example of each error from your own experiences. Based on these outcomes, what could you have done better?

2. Review Exhibit 6.8 about "thinking traps." Consider a decision you need to make in the near future, and imagine what would happen if you fell into one of the thinking traps. Now, review the avoidance strategies and apply a few to your reflection about the decision.

Objective 6.6
Describe what HR can do to support critical thinking and sound decision making.

6. What Can HR Do to Support Good Decision Making and Critical Thinking?

Effective human resource leaders help employees, managers, and leaders make good decisions. They also often teach skills and processes to help others make good decisions. In fact, as the function that often supports leaders in solving problems, HR is well placed to implement techniques that help people make better decisions. In this section, we will concentrate on two such methods: brainstorming and the Delphi technique.

Brainstorming

Brainstorming is the process of generating a list of ideas within a group at any point during a decision-making process. The process involves bringing together individuals and asking them for ideas about an issue, decision, criterion, alternative, etc. Each person offers ideas without any critique—good or bad—from other participants.[55] The process continues until everyone is out of ideas. Once you have a good list of ideas, you will next need to push people to prioritize. This can and usually will result in conflict, so a team leader needs to be ready to facilitate disagreements. After priorities are clear, it is important for the group to determine what to do with the ideas, who is responsible, and so forth.

Brainstorming is common and sometimes helpful, too. However, brainstorming has been challenged as a useful method for a few reasons. First, people often don't really brainstorm. They simply list the most obvious answers, and/or the ones they think the boss wants to hear. Related to this, collective brainstorming may not be as effective as individual brainstorming because groups have a tendency to narrow focus and converge quickly on a smaller number and less diverse set of ideas. Third, people sometimes attempt to use brainstorming *in place of* decision making. Brainstorming is a tool for idea generation, not for decision making.

> **Brainstorming**
> The process of generating a list of ideas within a group.

The Delphi Technique

Brainstorming often includes non-expert participants. Sometimes, however, companies need expert opinions and input. One way to gather this type of advice is through use of the **Delphi technique.** This method was designed at the RAND Corporation, a think tank, during the Cold War as a method for forecasting military technology developments, but it has useful applications in all types of business.[56] The process is based on the assumption that with complex issues and decision-making processes, group consensus and informed expert opinions support good decisions. In practice, the Delphi technique is a focus group or panel of experts, each of whom comes up with ideas regarding a topic and provides justifications for those ideas.[57] The process often begins with asking the experts to consider certain specific questions. The ideas and justifications are then synthesized and summarized before moving to the next round of questions.

> **Delphi technique**
> A technique in which a panel of experts is asked to reach agreement after responding to a series of questions.

HR professionals are often called on to assist managers and leaders in solving problems and making decisions. The techniques discussed here are two that help to ensure that HR business professionals can be outstanding strategic business partners—not because they know the business inside and out, but because they can facilitate employees and experts in finding the best solutions and making the best decisions.

HR Leadership Roles

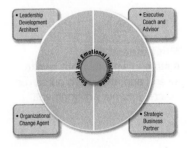

Discussion Questions

1. Consider a problem you are facing. Brainstorm reasons for the problem. Now brainstorm solutions. How does brainstorming reasons *before* solutions impact your choices?

2. Think of an example that you have participated in, seen, or read about in which brainstorming or the Delphi technique was used to solve a problem. What were the benefits to using the approach? Under what situations would you not use these techniques?

7. What Can We All Do to Improve Critical Thinking and Decision Making?

> **Objective 6.7**
> Describe what you can do to improve critical thinking and sound decision making.

We all make hundreds of decisions every single day. Most are small and of little consequence, some are important, and some are life changing. It serves us well to be able to learn how to make good decisions. It also serves us well to learn from our experiences, so we can apply all that we learn today to the decisions we will make tomorrow. In this section, we will look at how practicing mindfulness will help us attend to the problems and opportunities we face, as well as reflect consciously on the process of making decisions. Then, we will look at how a method called double-loop learning can help us learn from our experience.

Mindfulness: The Secret to Conscious Decision Making

One of the most important ways to improve your ability to make good decisions is to make the process as conscious as possible. Although this might seem obvious, the fact is that most decisions are extremely complicated and involve dozens—if not hundreds or thousands—of factors. Because our brains are extremely efficient machines when it comes to processing data, a good deal of this information is processed automatically and unconsciously.

Let's think about ordering lunch to illustrate this point. Imagine yourself standing in line, waiting to order your meal. You've consciously noticed the two choices that appeal to you—the salad and the burger. You've noticed the nutrition information, and you're remembering eating both of these items before with pleasure. You have weighed how hungry you are, and you've decided that either option would be fine. While all this is happening more or less consciously, many other factors are operating beyond your awareness. For example, the picture of the burger on the menu board is brighter and more colorful, so it captures your attention. You *always* have the burger—it's a habit—and you've told your friends that the burger is the best thing on the menu. You *love* pickles, which come on the burger but not the salad. The door opens and a cold wind blows in, making a hot lunch more attractive. Meanwhile, someone walks by with the salad and you unconsciously register how small it is. Also, you didn't sleep much last night and your body is craving the quick energy fats and sugars would provide—and on and on.

Obviously, this example does not represent the many more complex decisions all of us face, such as where to live, what career to pursue, or how to motivate our teams or manage resource allocation in our departments at work. Still, this simple scenario does illustrate what often happens when making small and large decisions: Much of the process happens mindlessly. It doesn't have to be this way.

Scholars Ellen Langer and Jon Kabat-Zinn believe that we can greatly improve our capacity to take in information, learn, and make decisions by developing the capacity for mindfulness.[58] **Mindfulness** is a state in which we are awake, aware, and attuned to ourselves, others, and our environment. Mindfulness enables us to be more fully aware of all that is happening inside us—physically, psychologically, and cognitively—while also being tuned in to what is going on around us.[59] Mindfully attending to your lunch decision, for example, might mean recognizing that your habit of ordering the burger causes you to select it without thinking; if you were more mindful, you might notice that what you really need is sleep, not fats and sugar. Alternatively, mindfully attending to this decision might cause you to notice that the door blew open for an instant, but you quickly warmed up when the door closed. You might also consciously recognize that the brightly colored, appealing picture is an advertising ploy—the real burgers don't look like the picture at all.

What would it be like if you were living more mindfully? Would you examine your choices more carefully and make better decisions? Might you be healthier, choose a better diet, get more exercise, or even engage in different social activities? Would you be less stressed? Would you have an easier time dealing with information and choices? Research suggests that the answers to all these questions is yes.[60]

But how do you develop mindfulness? Some people believe that practicing mindfulness means you have to meditate every day or examine yourself constantly. Neither is the case, although reflective practices like meditation can help. For

Mindfulness
A state in which we are awake, aware, and attuned to ourselves, others, and our environment.

example, you might decide that for 10 minutes a few times a week, you will focus on a few good things you have done or been part of recently. Or, you might commit to walking to class more often, running again, or enjoying some other individual physical activity. While doing this, you don't think about all the issues, problems, and stress you have—you simply pay attention to yourself and your environment. Or, you can adopt the simplest practice of them all: Just pay more attention to what you think, feel, and do. For most of us, developing mindfulness involves a few simple—but profound—changes.

Mindfulness can impact many areas of your life, including what and how you learn. Let's look at one process that does not talk specifically about mindfulness, but that does call on us to be more conscious of how we learn: double-loop learning.

Double-Loop Learning

There are two ways to slide easily through life: to believe everything or to doubt everything. Both ways save us from thinking.

—**Alfred Korzybski**[61]

In this chapter, we have stressed that it is important to examine your thought processes, feelings, and approaches to decision making. If you want to go one step further, you can also focus on improving your capacity for learning from experience. Why should you do this? Doing so will help ensure that you get better at understanding common problems, generating more solutions, and charting a course for implementing decisions that work.

Surprisingly, many people don't pay much attention to learning from experience until a huge wake-up call occurs, like being caught driving while under the influence of alcohol. Even in serious learning situations like this, some people simply never learn how bad decisions can lead to devastating consequences. For example, a person will have the experience (drinking too much, driving, and getting caught). Then he will ultimately suffer the subsequent experiences that come along with that bad decision, including court appearances, fines, driving school, and even jail. The person knows that what he did was risky, so in the future, he does not drink and drive—unless he is "sure" he won't get caught or he thinks he is under the legal limit. He has changed his behavior, but not the underlying beliefs that allowed him to drink and drive in the first place, such as "The law has no right to control my behavior" or "I am an excellent driver and alcohol doesn't compromise my abilities."

This is an example of **single-loop learning**, a process that results in taking in feedback and changing behavior, but not changing underlying beliefs about one's self, others, or the environment. People use these underlying beliefs to explain what happens and why, as well as what to do in certain situations.

The process of **double-loop learning** focuses on changing underlying beliefs as well as behavior.[62] In the example about driving drunk, the person could have examined his belief that his needs and desires were more important than people's safety, or he may have come to realize that alcohol does indeed impair his driving skills. With these new mental models in place, he won't *ever* drive while under the influence.

Consider this scenario at work: Suppose a manager has an underlying belief that goes something like this: "Once an employee starts questioning my decisions, we're on a path that will end in me having to fire her. Such behavior is insubordination, and that is not allowed at work, and especially not on my watch." With this belief in place, the manager may start paying more attention to the employee's behavior in general and taking notes on any apparent questioning of authority. If single-loop learning is in operation here, the employee is very likely to be fired, even if the questions she brought to her manager were intended to be helpful.

Single-loop learning
A process that results in taking in feedback and changing behavior, but not changing underlying beliefs about one's self, others, or the environment.

Double-loop learning
A process that focuses on changing underlying beliefs as well as behavior.

If, however, this manager challenges his own assumptions and beliefs as this scenario plays out, he has a chance to truly learn from the experience. Say that he notices that the employee's questions are always raised respectfully, politely, and in private. He starts attending more carefully to the content of the questions (safety of the group of employees, a few good ideas about improving quality). As he does this, he begins to see that questioning one's manager isn't always bad, and it can indeed be helpful. He is changing his underlying beliefs and his behavior. That's double-loop learning.

We can reinforce double-loop learning by deliberately challenging or testing our assumptions on a regular basis. This requires a conscious effort to overcome our natural tendency to retain the beliefs that guide our actions.[63]

Discussion Questions

1. Do you have a daily practice that allows you to reflect, calm down, and become more mindful? Brainstorm several other things you can do to foster mindfulness.

2. Consider a situation where you believe you made a bad decision. Did you apply single-loop or double-loop learning to the situation? How could you have changed your approach to make a better decision?

---

8. A Final Word on Decision Making and Critical Thinking

Of the skills essential to effective management and leadership, decision making and critical thinking are among the most important. Although many of the decisions you face on a daily basis are simple and perhaps even routine, others are far more complex. To make the best choices possible when confronted with complex decisions, you need to understand the many inputs to the decision-making process: logic, cognitive processes, emotion, and intuition.

It is also important to use a systematic approach to support decision making, such as identifying the problem; establishing the decision criteria; allocating weights to these criteria; listing, analyzing, choosing, and implementing alternatives; and evaluating your decision. Furthermore, you must be aware of the strategies to employ when faced with either too little or too much information about the situation at hand.

Of course, none of the aforementioned actions is possible without the ability to engage in critical thinking. Unlike decision making, critical thinking is not a stepwise endeavor; rather, it is a dynamic process. You can improve your decision-making and critical thinking skills by practicing mindfulness, remembering that pure rationality isn't always possible, and understanding how unexamined biases may be hindering your ability to think clearly.

LEADING IN A GLOBAL WORLD
Logical Celebrations

As we have already seen, reason and emotions are an integral part of decision making. Cognitive processing—or the way we understand and acquire information—is also important to this process. But where does culture fit into the equation? For example, do people in Asian countries use the same logic when making a decision as people in Europe or the United States? What influence do religious differences have over a person's ethical approach to solving a problem?

Imagine you are a manager of a very diverse, multicultural team and describe the team in detail. Include information about the number of men and women on the team, where they come from, the religions they practice, etc. Be sure to give each team member a name. Now, imagine that you have to decide which holidays your team members will be paid for and which holidays they will not be paid for.

1. List all possible holidays.
2. Think of the issues you may encounter in making this decision.
   - Give examples of how accommodation and assimilation could play a role.
   - Give an example of how stereotyping could be involved.
   - Discuss potential differences of culture, gender, and religion and the impact these differences will have on team members' opinions.
3. Create a guide for facilitating the discussion so the decision will be made to the satisfaction of all or most people.

LEADING WITH EMOTIONAL INTELLIGENCE
The Joys of the Open Road

A decision-making process uses systematic steps to determine a course of action. The size and complexity of a problem determine how much time and effort go into the process. However, no matter how analytical or systematic the process may be, it also includes a profound emotional component that needs to be acknowledged.

Think back to a first and important adult decision-maybe purchasing your first car. It was an exciting purchase that came with a great deal of responsibility and a great deal of freedom. There were probably many different emotions involved in your experience. Maybe you envisioned the places you'd go and the things you'd see on your own or with your friends. You may have even been a little fearful about the debt you were taking on or impatient with the car sales people.

1. Review the eight-step decision-making model. For each step, identify the emotion (or emotions) you recall experiencing. For instance, in step 1 you may have experienced frustration about which make and style of car to buy. Try to list the emotion that had the greatest impact on you. Be honest with yourself.
2. Once you have identified the emotion, try to analyze the source of that emotion. For example, why were you frustrated over the choice between a Ford Mustang and a Toyota Prius? Identify at least one emotion and its source for all eight steps.

LEADING WITH CRITICAL THINKING SKILLS
Thinking Traps

The great nineteenth century psychologist and spiritual philosopher William James observed, "A great many people think they are thinking when they are merely rearranging their prejudices."[64] Unfortunately, this is true in many instances of decision making and problem solving.

The quality of your decision making depends on your ability to evaluate ideas and situations and make informed, appropriate judgments. In this way, critical thinking is a key component of decision making. The critical thinking skills identified by Watson and Glaser are very useful in helping you hone your decision-making abilities.

Review the five critical thinking skills and the six thinking traps in the text. Alone or in teams, go to http://www.etalkinghead.com/, an online political news magazine. Pick two articles or blogs, one that is liberal and one that is conservative. Use the five critical thinking skills to analyze and assess the writers' viewpoint. In addition, pay attention to any of the traps you may fall into in regards to your personal political leanings. As you do this exercise, keep in mind William James' observation and mindfully attend to whether you are rearranging your prejudices or thinking critically.

ETHICAL LEADERSHIP
To Cheat, or Not to Cheat?

In management, ethical dilemmas are common. In these situations, good managers rely on their values *and* the company's code of ethics in order to decide what is best, fair, and honest. Read the following scenario and respond using your sense of right and wrong as a guide.

Your best friend has gotten the answers to your management midterm exam from someone in the earlier section. You haven't done very well on the homework and the quizzes up to this point. At best, you are holding a low C. You think you know the information for the exam fairly well, but sometimes you have an issue with test anxiety. You are already on probation at school and this semester can make or break you. You are holding a B average in your other classes. Your best friend has

prepared a cheat sheet for the exam just for you. She hands it to you an hour before the exam.

Write a thoughtful response to this situation that reflects on the following questions:

1. What are all the consequences of your decision, both negative and positive?

2. How are your emotions, such as fear or gratitude, influencing your decision to use the cheat sheet?

3. Are there just two choices to make here, or are there others you haven't considered?

KEY TERMS

Decision making, *p. 182*

Programmed decisions, *p. 183*

Nonprogrammed decisions, *p. 184*

Accommodation, *p. 186*

Assimilation, *p. 186*

Halo effect, *p. 188*

Intuition, *p. 189*

Decision-making process, *p. 191*

Satisficing, *p. 195*

Bounded rationality, *p. 196*

Critical thinking, *p. 199*

Brainstorming, *p. 205*

Delphi technique, *p. 205*

Mindfulness, *p. 206*

Single-loop learning, *p. 207*

Double-loop learning, *p. 207*

MyManagementLab

Go to **mymanagementlab.com** for Auto-graded writing questions as well as the following Assisted-graded writing questions:

6-1. How do your emotions impact you when making important decisions? Are there certain kinds of situations or decisions that trigger your emotions more than others? Why is this so?

6-2. Consider a decision you have made this year—one for which you did not have all the information. Why was it difficult to gather all the information? How did you know when you had enough information to proceed? How did you feel about not having all the facts, and how did your feelings impact your behavior?

6-3. Mymanagementlab Only — comprehensive writing assignment for this chapter.

CHAPTER 6 Visual Summary

1. What Is Decision Making?

(pp. 182–185)

Objective: Define decision making.

Summary: Decision making is complex; it involves cognitive, neuropsychological, and emotional processes. When making judgments or choices, we need to consider the information available to us *and* how we react to it. This is especially true when making nonprogrammed decisions—decisions that are not routine.

2. How Do Cognitive and Emotional Processes Affect Decision Making? (pp. 185–190)

Objective: Compare and contrast how cognitive and emotional processes affect decision making.

Summary: Decision making is commonly understood to be a rational process, but reasoning and logic are only two of the tools a decision maker should use. We need to also understand how our cognitive processes affect our judgments, watching out for misunderstandings and stereotypes. In addition, we need to examine our emotions and intuition, two legitimate sources of information that can affect decision making.

3. How Can You Apply a Systematic Approach to Making Decisions?

(pp. 191–196)

Objective: Learn to apply a systematic approach to decision making.

Summary: The eight steps of decision making include accurately identifying the problem and establishing and prioritizing decision criteria. Once you know what you're trying to do, and what's most important to you in how you do it, you can move on to listing, analyzing, choosing, and then implementing an alternative. The final step, and the one that is most often overlooked, is evaluating the decision and recognizing whether the problem was solved appropriately and completely.

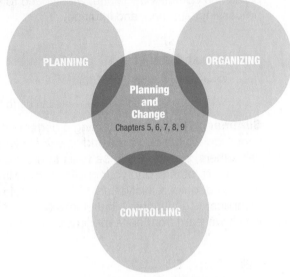

Eight Steps to Better Decision Making

Step 1: Identify the problem.
Step 2: Establish the decision criteria.
Step 3: Allocate weights to decision criteria.
Step 4: List alternatives.
Step 5: Analyze alternatives.
Step 6: Choose an alternative.
Step 7: Implement the decision.
Step 8: Evaluate the decision.

4. How Can People Make Good Decisions with Incomplete Information? (pp. 196–199)

Objective: Understand how to make sound decisions with incomplete information.

Summary: We are navigating the information age with this paradox: We have both too much and not enough information when making decisions. We must make decisions under conditions of bounded rationality, meaning that we will always be constrained by time, the amount and quality of information available, and our own inability to be perfectly rational. One tool that is helpful under these conditions is the 80/20 rule, which helps us see causal relationships.

5. How Can You Improve Your Critical Thinking Skills and Make Better Decisions? (pp. 199–204)

Objective: Improve your critical thinking skills.

Summary: Developing and using our critical thinking skills is paramount at work and elsewhere in our lives. Do you draw accurate conclusions from evidence? Can you recognize the assumptions you're making and their validity? Can you understand specific issues by analyzing general information? Are you able to evaluate arguments using logical criteria? Do you work hard to interpret a collection of facts? If so, you're applying critical thinking skills.

Critical Thinking Skills and Definitions

Critical Thinking Skill	Definition
Inference	Drawing conclusions from evidence or known information
Recognition of assumptions	Recognizing underlying beliefs, biases, etc., in information
Deduction	Reasoning that moves from generalities to specific conclusions
Interpretation	Articulating the meaning of a collection of facts
Evaluation of arguments	Judging an argument based on logical criteria

8. **A Final Word on Decision Making and Critical Thinking** (p. 208)

Summary: Critical thinking skills are essential to long-term success in any endeavor. When approaching complex decisions, we all need to recognize and rely on reason, conscious cognitive processing, emotion, and intuition.

7. **What Can We All Do to Improve Critical Thinking and Decision Making?** (pp. 205–208)

Objective: Describe what you can do to improve critical thinking and sound decision making.

Summary: The key to becoming a better decision maker is clearly understanding your emotions, knowledge, intuition, and worldview (including biases and beliefs). One way to understand yourself, others, and the world better is to practice mindfulness—that is, being aware of and attuned to yourself, others, and your environment. Mindfulness practices, which can be as simple as a few minutes of quiet reflection each day, can help us to understand ourselves and others, as well as complicated situations. Mindfulness can lead to the deeper process of double-loop learning, in which we learn from our experiences and change our underlying beliefs as well as our behavior.

6. **What Can HR Do to Support Good Decision Making and Critical Thinking?** (pp. 204–205)

Objective: Describe what HR can do to support critical thinking and sound decision making.

Summary: HR can guide employees and managers to make the best decisions by ensuring that groups allow different informed viewpoints to be heard. Two techniques that help groups identify new ideas are brainstorming and the Delphi technique. When facilitated well, brainstorming allows your group to overcome the fear of criticism that can shut down promising ideas. The Delphi technique allows you to use a group of experts to generate informed answers to complex questions—a positive input into decision making.

Change:

A Focus on Adaptability and Resiliency

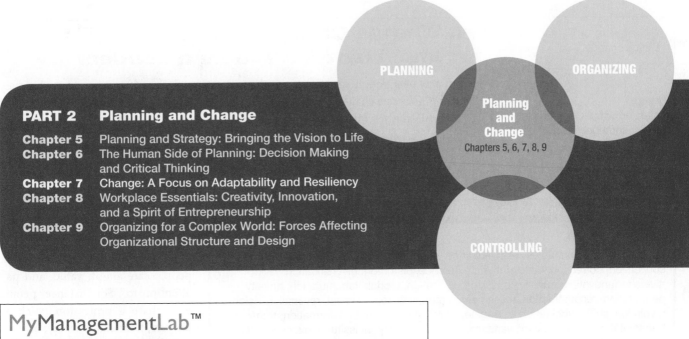

PLANNING

ORGANIZING

Planning and Change
Chapters 5, 6, 7, 8, 9

CONTROLLING

MyManagementLab™

✪ Improve Your Grade!

Over 10 million students improved their results using the Pearson MyLabs.
Visit **mymanagementlab.com** for simulations, tutorials, and end-of-chapter
problems.

Chapter Outline

Chapter Objectives

7.1   Define change.

7.2   Learn how you and other people
change.

7.3   Recognize drivers of change in
organizations.

7.4   Identify the difference between
incremental and transformational
change.

7.5   List and describe models that
assist in understanding change.

7.6   Describe which practical models
are useful tools for managing
change in organizations.

7.7   Learn how HR can foster effective
change.

7.8   Understand how you can change
and develop yourself.

Objective 7.1
Define change.

1. What Is Change and Why Is It So Important for You as a Leader?

You may hear people say "Change is the new normal," and you may wonder what they mean. How can change be normal? This seems like a contradiction, if you think of "normal" as a state that is familiar and predictable. However, change is so widespread in our lives and at work that it has truly become commonplace. What do we mean by change? **Change** means to alter, adjust, modify, or transform yourself, someone else, or something. As you can see in ■ **EXHIBIT 7.1**, the word *change* can be used as either a noun or a verb, and many words and phrases in English are synonymous with the word change.

Change
To alter, adjust, modify, or transform yourself, someone else, or something.

Scholars note that the richness of vocabulary indicates what people care about, value, and pay attention to.[1] For instance, people who share a profession (such as lawyers, financial advisors, or doctors) or a social organization (such as members of a political party, union, or community of practice), often use special words to talk about things that are important to them.[2] So, given the rate and pace of change during the past two hundred years or so, it's not surprising that we have many ways to describe change. In businesses and organizations we talk about change a lot, and we have many ways to describe change because it happens almost every day.

■ **EXHIBIT 7.1**

The Many Ways We Say "Change"

Change Is a Noun

about-face, addition, adjustment, advance, break, compression, contraction, conversion, correction, development, difference, distortion, diversification, diversity, innovation, metamorphosis, modification, modulation, mutation, novelty, permutation, reconstruction, refinement, remodeling, replacement, reversal, revision, revolution, shift, substitution, surrogate, switch, tempering, transformation, transition, transmutation, turn, turnover, variance, variation, variety, vicissitude, exchange, flip-flop, interchange, swap, trade, turnabout, turnaround.

Change Is a Verb

accommodate, adapt, adjust, alter, alternate, commute, convert, diminish, diverge, diversify, evolve, fluctuate, make innovations, make over, merge, metamorphose, moderate, modify, modulate, mutate, naturalize, recondition, redo, reduce, reform, regenerate, remake, remodel, renovate, reorganize, replace, resolve, restyle, revolutionize, shape, shift, substitute, tamper with, temper, transfigure, transform, translate, transmute, transpose, turn, vacillate, vary, veer, warp, barter, displace, exchange, interchange, invert, remove, reverse, supplant, swap, switch around, trade, transmit.

■ **EXHIBIT 7.2**
Why is change as certain as "death and taxes" today?

Source: Pictorial Press/Alamy

Change Is Constant

At the age of 83, Benjamin Franklin said, "Everything appears to promise that it will last; but in this world nothing is certain but death and taxes."[3] Today, we can say "nothing is certain but death, taxes, and *change*" (■ **EXHIBIT 7.2**).

Change is constant in life and at work, but this has not always been the case. During most of human history, the way we lived and worked remained more or less the same from generation to generation. Changes such as migration, marriage, birth, and death occurred, but these were normal and somewhat predictable. Customs and traditions about behavior surrounding weddings, deaths, and births helped people deal with the anxiety and excitement that accompany change. When rapid, unpredicted changes occurred, such as natural disasters, many societies had religious rituals to help deal with stress and to normalize disruptions.

Our ancestors experienced significant changes, such as the domestication of animals, the taming and riding of horses, and the production of iron and tool forging. Interestingly, neuroscientists, such as Vilayanur Ramachandran, believe that relatively rapid and widespread changes, such as the use of fire, are linked to the development of "mirror neurons"—structures in our brains that help us to empathize with others and share knowledge.[4]

Although some changes in our history happened quickly, people still had centuries to adjust to them. This is not true anymore. Change happens very fast today and we need to understand how to work, manage, and lead when the future is not predictable.

The reason it is so important for *you* to understand how to deal with change is twofold: First, you'll change personally and professionally all throughout your life. Second, the environment within which today's organizations operate is becoming increasingly dynamic and competitive—things change all the time at work. Change is constant at work and in life due to factors such as advancing technology and social, economic, and political shifts around the world. These shifts are happening at an unprecedented pace and are affecting billions of people. Old ways of life are being replaced by radical new ways of approaching basic human activities: communication, health, lifestyles, birth, and death.

Is constant change a good or bad thing? Imagine living in a world that did not change. Tomorrow would be the same as today (which would be boring). Technology would stay the same (there would be no new computers, phones, cars, or energy sources). Social norms, such as how people relate to one another, who's on top, and who's not, would stay the same. This would mean hopelessness for some people, such as the poor or those who experience discrimination. With no new services, products, or markets, competition would be static, and the world's economy would be flat. This sounds awful, doesn't it? Yet, people complain about change all the time and have trouble understanding it, coping with it, and managing it. To be successful in our dynamic organizations today, you need to understand change on a personal level, and also how to support others as they face change in how they work and live.

Change: What It Means to You

How do you feel about change? When you started college, you probably had to change a lot of things, such as your lifestyle, how you spend your time, and maybe where you live. What were your emotional responses? How did you cope? Chances are you felt exhilaration about starting college and excitement about the future. Maybe you felt scared or uncertain about how to organize your time, handle the workload, or make new friends. Or, you might have felt sad about what you were leaving behind.

People react to change in many ways. For some, a move across town or a change in jobs is experienced as difficult, even when it means a better life. Others aren't bothered at all. When faced with making a big change, like starting college, taking a new job, getting married, or having a child, most people experience emotions as varied as joy, fear, resentment, excitement, and hope. Most people also experience willingness to change as well as resistance. That's part of the reason change is so complicated: It forces us to deal with conflicting emotions and give up habits while also learning how to think about or do things differently. *The ability to deal with change is one of the most important things you can learn.*

Joan Snyder Kuhl, Associate Director of Training and Development at Forest Laboratories, is a young leader who has taken this lesson to heart early. She is adaptable and resilient—two key competencies in today's workplace. She is a great leader, and it shows in what she's done only a few years out of college. Her wisdom shines in the *Leadership Perspective* feature on the next page.

Joan's advice is important because all of us deal with so much personal and professional change throughout our lives. For example, people change careers an average of three times over the 40 years most of us will be in the workforce, and these statistics don't reflect how often we change *jobs*, as opposed to careers.[5] The U.S. Bureau of Labor Statistics (BLS) found that in 2010, the median length of time employees had worked for their current employer was only 4.4 years.[6] Among major occupations, managers had the longest tenure, at 5.1 years, with engineering and architecture managers in particular having the longest tenure at 6.4 years.[7] If you act according to these numbers, you are likely to change jobs *ten times* over the course of your working life.

Given the rate and pace of change in life and at work, the ability to adapt and change personally and to inspire others to change is at the center of great leadership and management. It is also a big part of being an effective employee today.

Leadership Perspective

● **Joan Snyder Kuhl**

Associate Director of Training and Development, Forest Laboratories; Board Member, The Frances Hesselbein Leadership Institute "Prioritize people. It's as simple as that."

Joan Snyder Kuhl is soaring in her career, both inside her company and in her other endeavors. She has tremendous responsibility at work, and is seen as a go-to person when changes are occurring and people need to be engaged and motivated. Outside of work, Joan is on the board of the Frances Hesselbein Leadership Institute, a not-for-profit focusing on leadership in the public sector and bridging the gap between the public, private, and government sectors. Joan also mentors young people in the U.S. and around the world. She shares these insights with all the people she touches:

It's evident right now that we're all faced with change every single day at work and in life. This is partly because of the economy and the wild ups and downs. Part of it is technology and part of it is just the world we live in. Things just aren't the way they were when our parents, most of our professors, or our managers were young.

We pay a lot of attention to changes that affect our customers—we have to, and we want to. Lots of managers pay far less attention to how changes affect employees. I see this in many organizations, and I hear about it from the young leaders I mentor. Despite all the research about the importance of communication, consultation, and involvement, lots of managers simply don't engage employees in the change process.

The leaders who have had an impact on me are those who do pay attention to people. They don't let ego get in the way, they don't work in silos, and they truly listen to people at all levels. Especially when dealing with change (which is all the time), you need to manage yourself so that insecurity doesn't drive you to shut people out. Everyone is scared when big changes are on the horizon—it's a given and it's ok. But, if fear, insecurity, or ego get in the way, you won't make the best decisions, and people will "catch" your negative emotions. Then, they'll begin to lose trust in you while also becoming demotivated. This is exactly what you don't want to happen when you are leading change. So, here's what you can do:

1. *Recognize that ego is always at play, fear is natural, and pretty much everyone feels insecure at one time or another. You need to understand this about yourself, so you can reach for the high road—don't let yourself be governed by these negative states of mind.*
2. *The most successful leaders of change are people who don't work in silos. No one person holds the key to success. Reach out to people, talk and listen deeply. You'll learn a lot and both you and others will get the support you need.*
3. *Prioritize people. It's as simple as that.*

Source: Personal interview with Joan Snyder Kuhl conducted by Annie McKee, 2012.

In this chapter, we will first look at how people change and how we can foster enthusiasm for change in groups, organizations, and communities. Then, we will turn our attention to why organizations need to change, and the difference between incremental and transformational change. Then, we will explore models that explain the forces for and against change, and how change is constant in today's organizations. We will also look at practical approaches to organizational change, followed by HR's role in organizational change, and what we all can do to embrace change and help others do the same.

Discussion Questions

1. List a few major changes you have experienced in life (such as moving, divorce in the family, illness, starting college, or starting or ending a relationship). Now, using the synonyms for change in Exhibit 7.1, list some words that describe each of these changes. Can you see any patterns in the words you chose? What do those patterns suggest to you?

2. List several major changes that you have experienced. Now, organize them into two categories: "Changes I Initiated and Wanted" and "Changes That Were Forced on Me." Some of your life experiences may fall in the middle of these two extremes, but try to put them in the category that fits best. How do you feel about each of these lists? What were the differences in how you dealt with changes in the two categories?

2. How Do People Change?

Objective 7.2
Learn how you and other people change.

Organizations change when people change. That's why we have to understand how people respond psychologically to positive change and changes that are not welcome. With a deeper understanding about how people deal with change, we can turn our attention to a model that helps us create a change process that actually works for individuals.

Change: It Is Not Always Easy for People

For many adults, change can be painful. It makes us feel uncomfortable. Part of the reason is that when things remain the same, our minds can function efficiently along well laid out neural pathways—conscious attention is not needed. However, as changes occur, our working memory is limited, and memory overload can lead quickly to fatigue. The act of simply paying attention corresponds to real chemical and physical changes that occur in the brain as we form new neural pathways. This takes effort. As we pay more attention and practice new ways of thinking, these pathways become stronger and more efficient.[8] So, how we change is linked to how our brains work.

For example, the process of taking in information from our five senses and processing the information is complicated. One of the first things we do with information is process it in a part of our brains called the limbic system. Parts of our limbic system (such as the amygdala and the thalamus) process information before messages are sent to our prefrontal lobe—where decisions are made and actions are planned. This complicated system holds our emotional memories, and these help us determine whether or not what we see, hear, or experience is a threat, and whether what we encounter is a call to nurture others, care for them, and pursue relationships.

This emotional response serves a purpose: It focuses our attention on both threats and opportunities. In fact, emotions are primal drivers of attention, focus, and ultimately behavior.

We need to cultivate and develop emotional intelligence competencies, such as self-awareness and self-management, to ensure that emotions *guide* our thoughts and behaviors, rather than *hijacking* our brains.[9] When our brains are hijacked, we often act before we think. We can be hijacked by anxieties or fears that have little to do with survival; in addition, things like attraction to another person can also hijack us.[10] In either case, we often do things that we would not have done if we'd thought about it—even for a moment. Let's take this a bit further and look at exactly how some emotions affect our capacity for learning, change, and resilience.

The Psychology and Neuropsychology of Individual Change

Emotions matter when dealing with change because emotions impact our ability to stay focused and succeed at whatever we are doing. Environments that are characterized by positive emotions, challenge, and excitement can be highly motivating and results-oriented. If we look to psychology to explain why, we find that when people experience what scientists call positive emotional attractors, they are resilient, creative, and open to change.[11] A **positive emotional attractor** is a psychological state of well-being and hope that engages the parasympathetic nervous system and can counter the effects of stress. The concept of emotional attractors is derived from chaos theory, a recent and popular approach to understanding human behavior.[12]

Not surprisingly, a negative emotional attractor has the opposite effect. A **negative emotional attractor** is a psychological state characterized by negative emotions that is linked to the sympathetic nervous system and that can cause people to feel defensive,

Positive emotional attractor
A psychological state of well-being and hope that engages the parasympathetic nervous system and can counter the effects of stress.

Negative emotional attractor
A psychological state characterized by negative emotions that is linked to the sympathetic nervous system and that can cause people to feel defensive, threatened, and stressed.

threatened, and stressed. When such emotions are pervasive in our organizations and teams, the climate becomes dissonant and people shut down, avoid risks, and generally sub optimize their performance. That's not the best state to be in when approaching change. Negative emotional attractors can be activated by factors such as a fear of doing things differently, being forced to change against one's will, or a lack of clarity about what the changes entail or how they affect us personally.

How we deal with and manage emotion has a strong effect on how we approach change—both around us and in ourselves. ■ **EXHIBIT 7.3** lists some positive and negative emotional attractors. You can see how these states of mind affect how you feel and perform. Let's look at how leaders put this into action, paying special attention to a model that can help us *use* emotions proactively to engage in change.

Intentional Change

Most approaches to individual change focus people's attention first on their deficiencies. However, what research tells us quite conclusively is that, for most people, sustainable change starts with an inspiring vision of the future.[13] People need a compelling personal vision as a starting point for the change. People need *hope*.

Hope is a state of mind that includes optimism, a realistic vision, and a belief that you can do something to move toward this vision.[14] **Optimism** is a positive outlook on life, coupled with the belief that good things will come and that bad things are only temporary and can be overcome.[15] Optimists typically perceive bad situations as welcome challenges and opportunities for learning. Both hope and optimism change the way you perceive the world, which has an effect on health, decision making, and productive change.[16] Encouraging hope, optimism, and other positive emotions helps us deal with the stress inherent in change and cultivate the resiliency needed to focus on attaining our change goals.[17]

Intentional change theory was developed by Richard Boyatzis to show exactly how this works.[18] This model was developed after many years of research into how people actually change behavior and competencies.[19] The model includes several distinct and yet interrelated steps, as you can see in ■ **EXHIBIT 7.4**. The model is different from other individual change models in a significant way: It starts with a positive vision of one's future, rather than focusing on deficiencies.

Take an example from your personal life. Imagine that you believe you have gained too much weight as a result of studying (and partying) too much. You might say, "I look terrible, and I need to lose weight." You plan to eat less and exercise more. However, after a few days, you are back to fast food and sodas. If you follow a process of intentional change, however, you might first identify a future state that is important to you. For example, you might know of a race two months in the future. You know that if you run the race, you can raise money for cancer research, which is something that is important to you. You know that at the moment, you cannot run the race, so you plan a training schedule that includes eating well and walking, running, and cross training four days a week. You are energized and motivated to continue with the program because you consider the goal to be noble and worthy. In the process, you lose weight.[20]

■ **EXHIBIT 7.3**

Positive and Negative Emotional Attractors	
Positive Emotional Attractors	**Negative Emotional Attractors**
Hope	Fear
Joy	Despair
Compassion	Anger
Excitement	Resentment
Challenge	Jealousy
Serenity	Mistrust
Growth and learning	Forced compliance
Love	Hate
Respect	Disdain

Hope
A state of mind that includes optimism, a realistic vision, and a belief that you can do something to move toward this vision.

Optimism
A positive outlook on life, coupled with the belief that good things will come and that bad things are only temporary and can be overcome.

This happens because a vision of one's *ideal self* sparks a psychological state that supports the hard work of learning, whereas focusing on shortcomings is actually demotivating.[21] Intentional change encourages you to identify your *ideal self*, examine your current state (your *real self*), identify gaps, and then create a personal learning plan that actually works. By following this process and actively seeking and accepting the support of others, we can all learn and develop complex competencies, change long-held patterns of behavior, and become better leaders.[22]

Now that you know a bit about how to mobilize your own energy for change, let's look at a model that helps us understand what comes next for us—and how we can help others mobilize their energy.

Motivating and Sustaining Energy for Change

One of the primary tasks of employees, managers, and leaders is ensuring that people join change processes rather than resist them. This is not as easy as saying "You have to" or "Trust me, this is good for you." Oftentimes, these approaches spark more resistance. In this section, we will explore the **Gestalt cycle of experience**, a model that helps us understand how to mobilize and sustain energy, direct our attention, and choose actions that result in change in ourselves and in groups.

GESTALT CYCLE OF EXPERIENCE EXPLAINED

To engage people in a change process, you must find ways to engage their hearts and minds, help them get over resistance, and prepare them to share their ideas, energy, and commitment. One of the best ways to ensure that people are ready to support change is to focus on their awareness of the need for change, then help them manage their energy and enthusiasm throughout the change process. The Gestalt cycle of experience explains this.

The Gestalt cycle of experience cannot be traced to any one particular source, but some scholars credit Fritz and Laura Perls during the 1950s as two key drivers of many of the ideas that the model is based on.[23] This model shows that there are actually a number of steps that help people become aware of the need for change, mobilize their energy, act, and evaluate the change process.[24] Others, including Gestalt therapist Elaine Kepner, contributed to the creation of the model in ■ **EXHIBIT 7.5**. In addition, scholars, such as David Kolb, combined ideas of other scholars, including educational philosopher John Dewey, sociologist Kurt Lewin, and Gestalt practitioners, to help us better understand how adults learn—an important form of change.[25]

This model illustrates that what we do and feel *before* changing actually impacts how ready we are to engage in change and stick with it. Let's use a simple example created by scholar-practitioner Frances Johnston to explain each step and then apply it to an organizational situation.[26]

Imagine a lioness, just waking from a long and restful sleep. It's dusk, and she sniffs the air and scans the environment—she *senses* something. Slowly, she becomes aware that she is uncomfortable. Is there danger? She sniffs again and decides all is well. Is she still tired? Lying down again, she feels restless. It's not sleepiness. Her cubs sense her uneasiness, and they become restless because they, too, begin to feel anxious and uncomfortable.

■ **EXHIBIT 7.4**
The intentional change model.

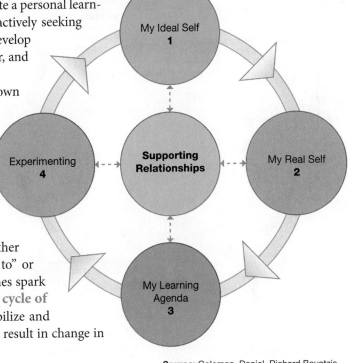

Source: Goleman, Daniel, Richard Boyatzis, and Annie McKee. 2002. *Primal leadership.* Boston: Harvard Business School Press, p. 110. © 2002 Daniel Goleman. For more information on Intentional Change Theory, see Boyatzis, Richard E. 2006. Intentional change theory from a complexity perspective. *Journal of Management Development* 25(7): 607–623.

Gestalt cycle of experience
A model that helps us understand how to mobilize and sustain energy, direct our attention, and choose actions that result in change in ourselves and in groups.

■ **EXHIBIT 7.5**
The Gestalt cycle of experience.

The Beginning–Sensation: Feeling, introspection, reflection, review

Awareness: Seeking information, questioning, uncertainty

Resolution, closure, and assessment: Completions, withdrawal of attention, evaluation

Energy: Mobilizing and gathering resources

Contact: Facing change head on

Action: Experimenting, taking risks

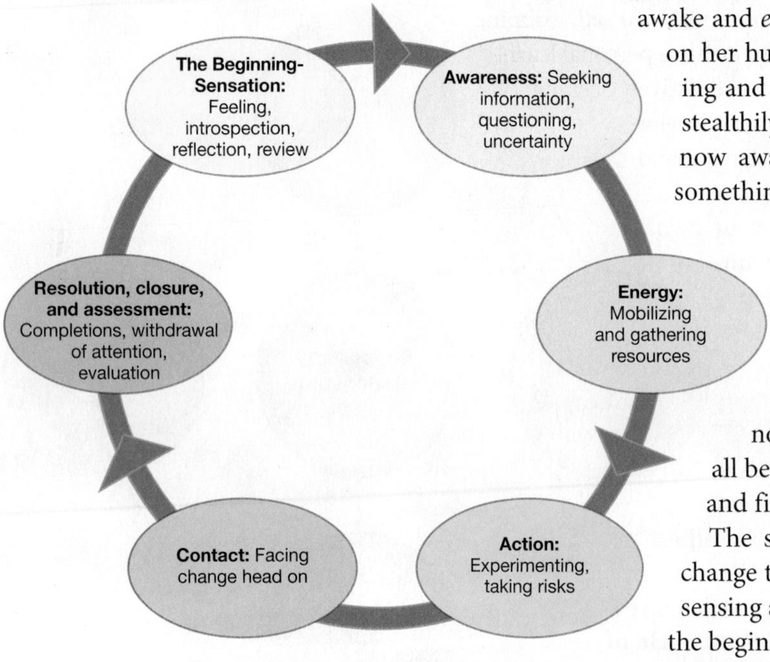

The lioness gets up, stretches, and becomes *aware* that she is hungry. Aha! That's it—and if she's hungry, she knows her cubs are too. All of a sudden, she feels more awake and *energized*: She is ready to *move*. The lioness is focused on her hunger, and she *acts* on her desire to get rid of this feeling and to feed her cubs. She gracefully leaves the forest and stealthily walks to a favorite watering hole. The cubs follow, now aware that they are hungry and that they need to *do* something.

Then it happens: The lioness sees her prey, tenses, prepares, and pounces! She's made *contact* with what she desires—a way to alleviate her hunger and a way to feed her cubs. They eat, totally focused, until their hunger is gone. After a while, the lioness and her cubs sense *resolution* and *closure*—there's nothing driving them to search for food anymore. They all become bored with their meal, *withdraw their attention*, and find another good spot for a nap.

The story of the lioness and her cubs shows us that for change to occur, we need to first pay attention to what we are sensing and what we are aware of. This directs our attention—the beginning of mobilizing our energy for action—for making contact with what we need to address or change. Once action is taken, we can then reflect on and evaluate what has occurred—likely sparking a new cycle of experience.

THE GESTALT CYCLE OF EXPERIENCE AND CHANGE IN GROUPS, ORGANIZATIONS, AND COMMUNITIES

Now, let's look at how this works in an organization and what can happen if steps in this change model are skipped, which they often are. Take the example of a company that manufactures food products. It was a successful and steadily growing company until, inexplicably, they had a bad year, then two. The top leaders spent countless hours exploring the problem, finally coming to *awareness* and collective agreement that many of the company's products were outdated—too high in fats, sugars, and preservatives, to which people were beginning to object. This conclusion *energized* them. They believed they understood the problem and they *acted* on a massive process to change products, brand images, ingredients, and formulas.

So far, so good—or so they thought. The top executives moved past the bad feelings (sensation) that arose during the downturn. They believed they understood what was wrong (awareness). They were energized, and they acted. Their actions were reasonable considering the issue. As they began to roll out the change plan, however, they met huge resistance from other senior leaders, managers, and employees. How could this be? From the top leaders' point of view, it was obvious that the change plan was the way to go.

What they missed was that outside their small group of about eight people, no one else truly sensed a need for change, nor was anyone else aware of the real problems. Therefore, most managers and employees were not energized or motivated to act. Instead, they were resistant—they argued and interfered with change activities at every turn.

Luckily, this organization was led by a person who recognized what was happening. He slowed the process down—stopped it, in fact. Then, he began a series of "cascade" events that enabled ever-larger groups of people from the senior executives down to first-level employees to personally engage in activities that heightened sensation and awareness of the issues. The process also helped people see how the change would benefit them personally and enable them to reach for their dreams.

It worked: People became highly energized, and they mobilized for action. When the change process resumed, more people were ready to act and change age-old company formulas and practices. During the next two years, people and the company made great strides as they tackled and truly made contact with some of the most difficult and expensive problems related to changing products and brand image. They made tremendous headway, and success led to a feeling of resolution. The market responded well and growth figures began to improve. Over time, executives and managers evaluated progress. They were free to withdraw their attention from this change process and focus on other important issues.

As this example shows, conscious and uninterrupted movement throughout the Gestalt cycle produces optimal change.

Many managers and leaders don't pay enough attention to mobilizing and sustaining energy for change. Common mistakes, such as skipping steps, lead to problems. One technology organization we know, for example, has an HR department that has the tendency to jump to solutions long before anyone is really clear on what the problems or opportunities are. This means that lots of people waste lots of time resisting whatever comes from the HR department. In fact, the department has become a joke. No one wants to engage in anything the department is involved in (even though some programs are necessary and quite good).

Another type of blockage occurs when an individual or organization becomes stuck in one stage. For example, it's not uncommon for people and organizations to be stuck in sensation or awareness. Signs that this is happening include an obsessive focus on analyzing problems (sometimes called *analysis paralysis*) or endless complaining and a general sense of hopelessness about organizational challenges.

To conclude this section, consider the *Business Case* about change in Cambodia. This case shows how conscientious use of models such as the Gestalt cycle of experience and intentional change can help bring about massive change for good. In this case, leadership scholar-practitioners Frances Johnston and Eddy Mwelwa point out the relevance of involving everyone in change and add that the cycle of experience does not begin and then end. Instead, it is continuous because change occurs in cycles that overlap. Energy flows from awareness to action in recurring sequences that allow for the possibility for change. This requires leadership.[27] Let's look at how skilled change agents Johnston and Mwelwa used this model to lead a large-scale social change initiative.

Now that you know quite a bit about how people change, let's turn our attention to why organizations need to change today. In the next section, we will explore economic and social drivers of change. As you read, bear in mind what it will take to ensure that people change in ways that help their organizations and the people who work in them to succeed.

Discussion Questions

1. Think about a situation that caused you to feel hopeless about changing something in your life. What was the impact of this emotion on your behavior? Now, think about a situation that caused you to feel inspired and hopeful about changes in your life. What aspects of the situation caused you to feel this way? How did these emotions impact what you actually did in your life?

2. In a few sentences describe your ideal self. How you can make a future where your real self is your ideal self? Use the intentional change model to give an example of one thing that needs to change in order for this to be a reality.

BUSINESS CASE

Combating the Spread of HIV and AIDS in Cambodia

Frances Johnston and Eddy Mwelwa of the Teleos Leadership Institute partnered with a talented team of change agents from the United Nations Development Program (UNDP) and other organizations to help stem the spread of HIV and AIDS in Cambodia. The program was designed by Teleos with the support of Monica Sharma and other leaders at the UNDP. It had been successfully launched in South Africa and Swaziland, where program faculty sought to support the development of leadership for people from all walks of life as they addressed the growing problem of HIV and AIDS. The program also included "capacity development": preparing leaders in South Africa, Swaziland, Cambodia, and later other countries to teach the program themselves, without outsiders. Let's see how it worked in Cambodia.

In 2001, UNAIDS estimated that 170,000 people (about 1.3 percent) were living with HIV/AIDS in Cambodia. Over the course of the team's work—which concluded in 2005—awareness about how the disease spreads grew while the rate of infection steadily and continuously dropped, and continues to drop today. By 2009, adult HIV was measured at 0.09 percent—down nearly 60 percent from 2001. HIV infections in women decreased from a high of 2.1 percent in 1999 to nearly half that by 2006, shortly after the end of the initiative. Additionally, 78 percent of HIV-infected people were receiving antiretroviral therapy and the Ministry of Education had included HIV/AIDS education in the national curriculum.[28]

Of course, there were many initiatives working to combat the spread of HIV during this time period in Cambodia. The program designed by the Teleos Leadership Institute was, however, part of the success and was designed to take into account how individuals, leaders, communities, and cultures change.

The change team's first step was to build their own awareness of the challenges facing the country, including the prevalence and spread of the virus and the primary methods of transmission. In Cambodia, as is true in most of the world, HIV is spread primarily through heterosexual practices and/or needles used to inject illicit drugs.

It was also essential to learn about the cultural, social, and emotional realities of Cambodian life. This information was gathered through communication and observation, interviews with dozens of people, and building trust with key stakeholders. Through this information-gathering process, the researchers were able to identify gender inequality as a key contributing factor in the spread of the disease. This was not an easy topic to discuss, nor would an intellectual understanding of it lead to the necessary changes. The team members realized that they needed to ensure that the people they were working with *sensed* the issue, and became informed and more *aware* of it. They had to create a situation in which people became energized through an open dialogue between men and women that empowered everyone to consider the decisions they made about their relationships and sexual practices.[29]

How did they foster this kind of dialogue? Johnston and Mwelwa explain it like this:

- *We created activities that helped people talk about the issues openly and to appreciate that the most common spread of infection was through individual sexual behavior, which was under personal control.*

- *We raised awareness and mobilized energy through giving people experiences that caused them to feel deep empathy and compassion. For example, we arranged visits to families living with HIV/AIDS, orphanages, clinics, hospitals, and brothels to experience the realities of what was happening and the very real emotional impact on people. Visiting places like these (which were often in the center of towns and villages but largely ignored), we were able to heighten awareness of the implications of the disease and its impact on organizations and the country.*

- *We also supported raising awareness and energy mobilization by including people living with HIV and AIDS in the group. That was particularly powerful in terms of reducing stigma and prejudices. For most of the participants, it was the first time they had actually been in close contact with anyone living with the virus. Having people living with the virus in the group ensured that the issues regarding HIV and AIDS were faced head on rather than avoided.*

- *To really prepare people for change, we started with a powerful vision. We had group members envision a different and desired Cambodia without the stigma associated with the disease. What would it look like if men's and women's relationships supported respect and good health? What could the country look like as it entered a new era?*

Under the Khmer Rouge, Cambodian citizens were tortured, murdered, and brutalized until the dictator Pol Pot and his regime were driven out of power. It is estimated that between one and two million people were killed—14 to 27 percent of the population at the time.[30] As the country began to rebuild families, communities, and a democratic government, people struggled to find a new identity, new pride. To help spark a powerful vision of the future, we arranged a visit to Angkor Wat, a group of twelfth-century temples in the jungle rediscovered in the 1860s. It was built during a time when Cambodia, then part of Siam, was a power in the region. The temples are some of the greatest works of art and architecture on earth.

These experiences were deeply meaningful to people— they were touched and inspired—they wanted the vision they saw. They were ready to act.

Continued on next page >>

The Cambodians took charge of the issues. Teams from the group crafted plans to work in their communities on every issue imaginable: education for children and adults about how HIV and AIDS is spread; work with prostitutes to help them (and their clients) remain virus-free; work with men about their feelings and treatment of their wives and other women; anti-discrimination laws were passed in the Senate; education and support for women as they took on a new, more empowered way of dealing with life.

By taking a pragmatic and multidisciplinary approach to change that included activities at every level of society and involved emotional, legal, educational, and multi-sectorial interventions, Cambodia has been able to reverse a very dangerous trend. Local leaders learned how to collaborate, mobilize energy for change, and craft change projects that resulted in increased awareness and action in order to achieve the Cambodia they desired.

3. How Do Societal Shifts Lead to Organizational Changes?

> **Objective 7.3**
> Recognize drivers of change in organizations.

Why do organizations change? Organizations change because they must remain relevant, productive, and profitable. Organizations that do not change quickly enough risk becoming obsolete.

Organizations choose to change—or are forced to change—for many reasons. In this section, we will briefly review four major trends that are causing organizations to change dramatically: technology, globalization, major social changes, and the movement toward environmental sustainability. Each of these topics is addressed in depth in other chapters. Following this overview, we will focus on two profoundly important social changes that are affecting organizations everywhere: shifts in the balance of economic power and the diversity and inclusion imperative.

Four Trends That Will Affect Organizations for Decades to Come

There are many forces affecting businesses today. At the top of everyone's lists are the following:

- Technology, especially information and communications technologies, affects what organizations and people can do at work and how they do it. Changes in technology affect almost every aspect of organizational life and work, including communication; advertising; manufacturing processes; how goods are transported, bought, and sold; and the increased capability of organizations of all sizes to produce and distribute goods and services globally. For example, with the advent of dramatically less expensive videoconferencing technology (e.g., Skype), many meetings are no longer held in person. This means that people have to learn how to build strong relationships with people they may never meet face-to-face.

- Globalization has been fueled by advances in transportation, information, and communications technologies. Different patterns of social interaction, enhanced competition, shifts in world politics, and expanded markets all accompany globalization.[31] Globalization also makes international educational opportunities more affordable and, in turn, produces an international talent pool of skilled, well-educated workers that companies can access more easily than ever before.[32]

- Social and political revolutions are taking hold and spreading rapidly and very publicly around the world. In our well-connected global world, uprisings like the revolutions in parts of North Africa and the Middle East—collectively known as the Arab Spring—can arise. These revolutions are possible because one nation's quest for freedom can spread to and inspire other nations in real time. This is due in part to the Internet and social media. Whereas in the past it was possible to hide abuses against citizens—or employees—this is no longer quite as easy. People are demanding rights as never before in history. For example, a 2011 report by CNN warned of an "epidemic" of worker deaths in Asia.[33] This occurrence will not go unnoticed as it might have in days gone by. The organizations linked to these deaths will take note—and have to change.

- Environmentalism and the need to ensure a sustainable world are impacting many aspects of organizational life.[34] The "Green Revolution" has been under way for a long time and is having profound effects on organizations and businesses because there are now more laws regulating things like carbon emissions—not to mention the fact that sustainability is a worldwide social movement.[35] Many business people's commitment to supporting environmental sustainability—while making a profit—has driven them to search for new and better ways to manage their businesses. For example, Patagonia, the outdoor clothing and supply company, is entirely designed around sustainable business practices.[36] These include initiatives to audit and decrease products' waste streams, recycle worn out gear, and create sustainable business buildings. In fact, as of 2011, two of Patagonia's three headquarters buildings relied on solar panels to provide half or more of their power; that same year, the company brought in $414 million in sales.[37]

In the next sections, we will explore changes in the world that have a profound impact on organizations: a shift in the world's economic balance and the diversity and inclusion imperative.

Shifts in the World's Economies

The economies of the West and North (particularly Europe, the United Kingdom, and the United States) have held sway in most of the world for several hundred years. Today, however, a distinct shift in the balance of power is under way. Economies in the East and South, such as those of China and India, are quickly overtaking the traditional powers in terms of economic growth. To illustrate this, consider the 2012 Brookings Institution report on GDP and employment trends for 2010–2011 in 200 of the world's largest metropolitan economies. The report found that 90 percent of the fastest growing metropolitan economies were not in the United States or Western Europe, while the majority of slow-growing economies could be found in those countries and tsunami-ravaged Japan.

Compare this to what the U.S. economy has seen in recent years (see ■ **EXHIBIT 7.6**). This picture is partly the result of the worst recession in many years, and, growth rates did begin to improve in 2010. However, the trend remains that strong economies such as India, China, and others are growing much faster than the United States, United Kingdom, and other Western economies.

Long-term growth rates in countries such as the United States are projected to be around 2 to 3 percent, although the economic conditions since 2007 have resulted in remarkable volatility in short-term growth rates. Fast-growing economies such as India have been seeing upwards of 7 percent annual growth, as has China. These high rates of growth are not likely to be sustained indefinitely. In fact, there is evidence that a slowdown may be inevitable in both Indiaand China. However, such a "slowdown" still represents significant growth of these economies.[39]

■ **EXHIBIT 7.6**
United states GDP growth rate, adjusted for inflation, 2008–2012.*[38]

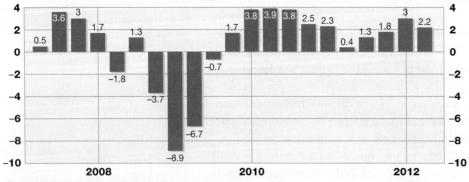

*Figures that go into calculating GDP are constantly changing, and adjustments are made retroactively.

These trends mean that the world's businesses have to shift strategies quite dramatically. Social and global trends can have a profound effect on organizations and businesses. Business and organization leaders need to understand change and how to respond to it. Accordingly, in the next two sections, we look at how change happens (incrementally or radically) and how we can respond to it (adaptation or transformation). Then, we look at models that can help us understand how to manage change in organizations, groups, and individuals (including ourselves).

The Diversity and Inclusion Imperative

One social change that is linked directly to changes in organizations is increased diversity among the employee base, customers, and consumer markets.[40] Diversity is good for business.[41] Consider the following:

1. Recognition of consumer diversity opens up many new opportunities for businesses to sell in multiple niche markets (■ **EXHIBIT 7.7**). For instance, Amazon, eBay, and Facebook are prime examples of companies that have tapped diverse niche markets.

2. Acknowledging cultural diversity in global markets by tailoring products and services to local needs offers companies a competitive advantage. For example, KFC menus around the world feature different dishes designed specifically for local populations.[42] Flipping the equation around, the "Korean Wave" refers to the dramatic increase of people in the West who watch Korean TV dramas. While these programs are not tailored for the West, Western viewers now like this "new" type of show. The best media companies will take note.

3. Educational and skills diversity offers companies new and potentially revolutionary opportunities to access people with a wide base of relevant knowledge. For example, Walt Disney Imagineering taps experts from 140 disciplines.[43]

4. Diversity in the workplace—including, among other factors, skills, background, gender, race, ethnicity, religion, and sexual orientation—can improve decision-making quality and facilitate strategic organizational change as a result of multiple perspectives.[44]

5. Valuing diversity in the workplace pays off in terms of employee satisfaction and can lead to significant savings in terms of employee engagement and productivity.[45]

6. Countries and regions throughout the world have a wide range of laws that enforce cultural, racial, gender, and linguistic diversity in the workplace, and these laws are becoming more stringent.[46]

To illustrate diversity's impact on niche marketing (point one on the list), Amazon and eBay showed the world how to capitalize on the "long tail" of the market.[47] The concept of the long tail refers to diversity in consumer interests and geographic distribution, resulting in small, widely dispersed potential customers. For instance, you might have only a small handful of customers in a given region who want books on farming in a far-northern climate. No bricks-and-mortar store would ever survive selling these books alone, or maybe even all gardening/farming books combined. If you had access to all the customers in all the different regions in the nation, however, you could have a booming business. This is what Amazon.com does—and does well. In 2009, Amazon stock more than doubled in value, although it was the worst year for many businesses since the Great Depression.[48]

Even education is getting into the business of marketing to the long tail. With increasingly sophisticated online courses, it is now possible for smaller schools to diversify their educational offerings, even if the physical location of the school only has one or two students interested in a particular subject. By aggregating students nationally or globally, schools can create larger class sizes and quality interactions.

■ **EXHIBIT 7.7**
How does Amazon.com's business model enable the company to tap niche markets?

Source: Gary Lucken/Alamy

Diversity
The varied perspectives and approaches to work that members of different groups bring.

The case for diverse employees in the workplace is a bit more complicated. Part of the problem, David Thomas, Dean of Georgetown University's McDonough School of Business, notes, is that we have been trained to confuse issues of racial, gender, and ethnic equity with issues of diversity. Dean Thomas argues that when **diversity** is understood as "the varied perspectives and approaches to work that members of different groups bring," you can more easily see how diversity can improve decision making, as well as approaches to complex things like organizational change and organizational change processes.[49]

Of course, demographic differences are also important aspects of diversity, and there continues to be a need to foster positive relationships, effective communication, and employment equity across the many ethnic, racial, class, gender, and other boundaries in our societies. Many businesses grapple with serious problems in their attempts to change their organizational cultures to be more inclusive so that people from all backgrounds and with diverse demographic characteristics can work together effectively. Some companies, like Cisco, are far ahead of their competitors and others when it comes to inclusion as a business imperative that adds value. For example, Marilyn Nagel, former Chief Diversity Officer, points out that diversity and inclusion needs to be positioned as central to the company's key business goals rather than as an addition whose costs and value must constantly be justified: "When [diversity and inclusion] is seen as an add-on, it's really hard to sustain." Nagel built diversity and inclusion into every level across the organization chart and achieved commitment at the most senior levels of the organization—the C-Suite.[50] Although Nagel has left Cisco, she has left a strong impact as the company continues to be a leader in the field. In 2011, the company was ranked number 6 among the world's best multinational workplaces.[51]

Despite the many improvements and advances led by companies like Cisco, as well as more stringent laws in many countries, a host of problems still exist that result in serious inequities. These problems run the gamut from what psychologists call "unconscious bias" to pay differentials. Unconscious biases are deeply held beliefs and prejudices that cause us to do things like ignore certain people and/or their contributions, assume that only "our" group can be successful, or heighten our awareness about the faults and shortcomings of members of groups we believe are not as good as certain other groups.[52] Unconscious biases are often at the heart of organizational cultures. Many times, unconscious bias is at the heart of other serious problems as well, like paying certain people less than others for the same work or job. Practices like these are still very much in use, as you will see in the next section.

Each of the topics discussed in the following sections involves important and pressing issues that organizations must address. These issues include changing cultures to be more inclusive and responsive to diversity and changing organizational systems (such as pay and benefits) to foster equity.

ETHNICITY, GENDER, AND PAY: SOME CHANGE, BUT MORE IS NEEDED

As of 2010, the most recent year for which the Bureau of Labor Statistics (BLS) has data, in the United States, Asians (as a group) working full time earn more on average across occupations than whites (11 percent), African Americans (40 percent), and Latinos (60 percent). Whites earn 25 percent more than African Americans and 43 percent more than Latinos. African Americans earn 14 percent more than Latinos. The lowest paid of these groups is Latinas, who earn about 5 percent less than their male counterparts.

Women make up just under 42 percent of the full-time white workforce. African American women make up about 53 percent of the full-time African American workforce, while among Latinos, women account for about 38 percent. Among Asians, women make up over 44 percent of the full-time Asian workforce.[53]

Full-time female workers, as a whole, earned 81 cents for every dollar men earned. The pay gap is smaller for African Americans and Latinos, where women earned 94 cents and 91 cents for every dollar their male counterparts earned, respectively. Asian women earned only 83 cents for every dollar Asian men earned, while white women only earned 80 cents for every dollar white men earned.

In the United States, women now make up more than half of the full-time management, professional, and related occupations, and they earn about 26 percent less than their male counterparts nationally. In management occupations alone, women earn 28 percent less, while about 40 percent of the jobs are occupied by women. When it comes to executive management positions, the story has been improving: 26 percent of chief executive positions are held by women. However, they receive just 72 percent of the pay of their male counterparts.[54]

Fortune magazine, which tracks the progress of women in the top 1,000 corporations in the United States, reported that in the Fortune 500, there were 15 women CEOs, or just 3 percent.[55] The story is even worse for the Fortune 1000, where there were only 28, or 2.8 percent.[56] This picture is better when medium and small businesses are considered across all sectors. The BLS reported that in 2011, just under 25 percent of all chief executives were women.[57] Although this number is better than those for top corporations, it is still quite small considering the fact that in 2008, women made up 46.7 percent of the workforce.[58]

These statistics reflect some improvements over past years in terms of pay equity and the representation of certain groups in the workplace. However, we have a long way to go in this change process: In the United States and in most countries around the world, women earn less than men for the same work and they are not proportionately represented in professional managerial and leadership jobs.

AGE DEMOGRAPHICS AND CHANGE

Another aspect of diversity that drives change in businesses and organizations is the changing average age of populations around the world. ■ **EXHIBIT 7.8** lists examples of averages for various countries worldwide.

Populations are shrinking and getting older on average in the North and West (the United States, Europe, and the United Kingdom, for example). The number of people under age 25 in the United States in 2012 was about 106 million, or about 34 percent of the population.[60] In Western Europe, the number was 52 million, or a little over a fourth of the population.[61] Populations in the South and East are much younger. For example, in Latin America and the Caribbean, the number of people under age 25 was 270 million, or about 45 percent of the population.[62] In India, there were 572 million people under age 25, or about 48 percent of the population.[63]

■ **EXHIBIT 7.8**

Approximate Number of People under Age 25 in 2012[59]		
Country	Number of People under Age 25	Percentage of Population under Age 25
United States	106 million	34%
India	572 million	48%
Brazil	87 million	43%
Germany	20 million	24%
United Kingdom	19 million	30%
Russia	39 million	28%
China	449 million	33%
Latin America and the Caribbean	270 million	45%
Western Europe	52 million	27%
Sub-Saharan Africa	543 million	63%

In this section, you have learned about a few very important reasons that organizations need to change. Many of the changes we have discussed are quite radical, considering where the world was economically and socially even just a few decades ago. So, how do organizations address these forces? Do they change overnight, or is it a longer, more deliberate process? To begin to answer these questions, let's consider incremental and transformational change.

Discussion Questions

1. What do you think today's workers, managers, and leaders need to do *on a personal level* to cope with technological, social, and economic changes?

2. What are some reasons other than discrimination that might account for differences in pay for men and women doing the same type of work? Do men and woman value various benefits (like vacation time, flexibility of schedule, insurance, and bonuses) the same way? Explain your answers.

Objective 7.4
Identify the difference between incremental and transformational change.

Top-down changes
Changes that are introduced by leaders and managers who identify the necessary changes and create a change plan.

Bottom-up changes
Changes that occur when employees or managers at various levels spark a movement for change, influence one another and leaders, and contribute to the planning and implementation of change.

■ **EXHIBIT 7.9**
This model shows four ways to approach change in organizations.

Source: Adapted from Nadler, David A., and Michael Tushman. 1989. Organizational frame bending: Principles for managing reorientation. *Academy of Management Executive* 3: 196.

4. What Is the Difference between Incremental and Transformational Change?

In an organization, change can be viewed as any shift in the work environment, including how it is organized, perceived, created, or maintained. Change can be anticipated or it can happen unexpectedly. Organizational change can happen as a result of forces inside the organization, such as the development of a new product or service or employee morale becoming more positive or negative. Change can also happen as a result of forces outside the organization, such as the social changes discussed in the previous section. In addition, change can be "top down" or "bottom up."

Top-down changes are introduced by leaders and managers who identify the necessary changes and, hopefully, create a change plan.[64] The company's business and functional managers and employees then implement changes. **Bottom-up changes** occur when employees or managers at various levels spark a movement for change, influence one another and leaders, and contribute to the planning and implementation of change.

Whatever the reasons for change or wherever it originates, change can be either incremental or sudden. According to scholars David Nadler and Michael Tushman, there are four approaches to organizational change, as you can see in ■ **EXHIBIT 7.9**.

According to this model, leaders and organization members can either anticipate the need for change or react to change that occurs in the organization or the environment. Change can be incremental, occurring in small steps over a long time, or it can involve dramatic shifts in strategy or ways of working or doing business.[65]

In this model, the four ways of dealing with change are called *tuning, adaptation, reorientation,* and *re-creation*. Tuning and adaptation are incremental approaches that involve limited, gradual changes. Tuning is an anticipatory approach (what we now call *proactive*) that is adopted in response to expected changes in the internal or external environment. For example, an organization might choose not to fill empty positions if leaders anticipate a decrease in sales.

Adaptation is another incremental approach but it is made in response to an event or series of events. Adaptation is *reactive* in the sense that changes are planned after unforeseen changes in the environment or organization have occurred. For example, adaptation occurs when you develop new packaging or advertising after the development of new products.

Strategic approaches to change include reorientation and re-creation. Both of these approaches involve completely changing ways of working and doing business, shaking things up. Reorientation is anticipatory, whereas re-creation is reactive. Reorientation refers to large scale organization-wide strategic change made in anticipation of a future occurrence. These changes involve a basic redirection of the organization, such as changing a business model or shifting from a storefront to a primarily online presence due to anticipated changes in consumer shopping preferences. Re-creation is large scale or strategic change brought about by (often unexpected) external events.

General Electric, one of the oldest companies in the United States, underwent dramatic strategic change in the 1990s that involved both reactive and anticipatory approaches. Senior leadership decided to shift the company's strategy and began moving more of GE's operations overseas. They did this because being centered primarily in the United States was already hurting the company in an era of increasing globalization.[66] This was a reactive approach. At around the same time, GE invested heavily in research on environmentally friendly technology long before such concerns were proven to be profitable. This was a reorientation. Today, GE is a major supplier of efficient energy-producing wind turbines and other innovative green products.[67] GE's proactive reorientation in research and a move into uncharted territory in the 1990s is just now beginning to reap bigger rewards. Many of its competitors are way behind.

Many people argue that the American auto industry missed opportunities to anticipate changes in recent years (for example, they did not adequately forecast the need for hybrid vehicles). Failing to anticipate business and social changes and act accordingly meant that U.S. automakers, including Ford Motor Co., had to react to changes later—an expensive and difficult situation. General Motors and Chrysler were forced into bankruptcy during the economic recession that began in late 2007. While Ford managed to stay afloat, the company also faced problems: The price of Ford stock dropped dramatically in 2008, and the company borrowed heavily against its assets to finance the research and development needed to revamp its vehicles, amassing a huge amount of debt along the way. Ford stock prices have since recovered, and the company is in the process of paying off its debt. While this payoff is happening faster than anticipated, had the company been better prepared for change to begin with, it might have avoided this situation altogether.[68]

Revolutionary and Evolutionary Change: Slow Is Not Always Better

Nadler and Tushman suggest that leaders, managers, and employees should try to anticipate change and then engage in change more strategically. They also suggest that incremental change is easier to manage. Although this is partially true, there are at least two counterpoints. First, we simply cannot anticipate everything that might happen. Changes can result from unpredictable natural forces, such as the tsunami in Japan in 2011. This catastrophic event caused the world to react with an outpouring of compassion as well as fear. The entire nuclear energy sector was called into question, as noted in a 2012 article in *The Economist*, which stated, "The need to keep questioning things—from the details of maintenance procedures to one's sense of the worst that could go wrong—is at the heart of a successful safety culture."[69] Second, how can we rely on slow, predictable changes during a time when many aspects of technology, society, and our world's economies are changing at warp speed? When Nadler and Tushman wrote about their model in 1989, the world was very different. It was pre-Internet, pre-globalization as we know it today, and before many of the social and economic models that had been in place for decades were called into question. In other words, the model was built for a world where things did not change as fast or as unpredictably as they do today.

Another reason that incremental change might not always be best is linked to what some consider to be its benefits: It happens subtly over time and is sometimes hard to detect. In many cases, this allows leaders to plan for change, adapt these plans as they go, and engage in an orderly change process, but the metaphor of the boiling frog shows the downside:

They say that if you put a frog into a pot of boiling water, it will leap out right away to escape the danger. But, if you put a frog in a kettle that is filled with water that is cool and pleasant, and then gradually heat the kettle until it starts boiling, the frog will not become aware of the threat until it is too late. The frog's survival instincts are geared towards detecting sudden changes.[70]

Like frogs, people are hardwired to notice dramatic changes and *do* something. We often take incremental changes in stride, sometimes not examining them too carefully. However, we (and our companies) must pay attention to slowly changing trends in the environment and not just devote our attention to sudden changes. Consider what happened to the world's financial institutions in the years leading up to the recession that began in 2007.

■ **EXHIBIT 7.10**
What incremental changes led to the economic recession that began in 2007?

Source: Nik Wheeler/Alamy

Investment banks
Institutions that raise capital, trade securities, and assist with mergers and acquisitions.

Net capital rule
Rule that guides how much debt an institution can hold.

Leveraging money
A practice that allows financial institutions to increase the amount of debt they handle in proportion to the amount of money they hold.

Incremental Changes That Led to the Great Recession

The financial crisis that exploded in late 2007 has been called the worst economic crisis since the Great Depression. How did it occur? What went wrong? Well, many things went wrong, and the wheels were set in motion decades ago. Incremental changes over many years in financial policies, lending policies, the commodities market, and consumerism among other things, created a "perfect storm" that resulted in the Great Recession.

THE LONG STORY LEADING TO A GLOBAL RECESSION

The story of the events that contributed to the Great Recession began more than three decades ago. A number of incremental changes in both U.S. Federal Reserve policy and financial services institutions were adopted over the course of nearly 30 years prior to the recession. Many of these changes did not seem radical and, in fact, some were not even noticed by many people—to our collective detriment. Let's look at how some of these changes happened.

In 1982, President Ronald Reagan's administration took steps toward federal deregulation of the U.S. banking industry (with the help of Congress, of course).[71] This meant that banks had more freedom of choice about the terms and conditions of their financial products, such as loan structures and the like (■ **EXHIBIT 7.10**). Then, when President Clinton's administration tore down the walls between commercial banks and investment banks in 1999, more potential problems loomed. That's because **investment banks**, which are institutions that raise capital, trade securities, and assist with mergers and acquisitions, tend to take far more risks than commercial banks. With deregulation, commercial banks were allowed to take even more risks than before, which they did. More and more financial institutions subsequently moved toward a culture of risk taking that proved entirely unsafe.[72]

At the same time, many banks were moving from being privately owned to publicly traded, and shareholders were demanding short-term gains. The U.S. Securities and Exchange Commission's relaxation of the **net capital rule**, which guided how much debt an institution could hold, also had a profound effect because banks could drastically increase the practice of **leveraging money**, which allowed them to increase the amount of debt they handled in proportion to the amount of money they held.[73] The result was a dramatic increase in debt. As we neared the year 2000, countries such as China increased exports to the United States dramatically and underwrote U.S. debt, while Presidents Bill Clinton and George W. Bush encouraged home ownership through their support of lower interest rates and similar measures.[74]

MAYBE NO ONE NOTICED THERE WAS A PROBLEM

Those of us who have looked to the self-interest of lending institutions to protect shareholders' equity, myself included, are in a state of shocked disbelief.

–Former chairman of the U.S. Federal Reserve Alan Greenspan to Congress in its 2008 investigation of the financial crisis (■ **EXHIBIT 7.11**).[75]

When President Reagan removed Paul Volcker and appointed Alan Greenspan as chairman of the U.S. Federal Reserve in 1987, no one imagined that Greenspan would become the most revered chairman of the "Fed" in decades and then fall so far off this pedestal that he probably will have to explain himself for the rest of his life.[76] Following the September 11, 2001, terrorist attacks and a series of high-visibility corporate scandals, Greenspan sought to keep the economy going (and the president and U.S. citizens happy) by cutting federal interest rates to 1 percent by 2003. This meant that money was cheap and easy to borrow.

The low interest rates held for a long time, which helped fuel a housing boom in 2002 and 2003. A **housing boom** is a way to describe a high level of activity in the housing market, resulting in rapidly increasing home values.[77] From 1997 to the peak of the housing bubble in 2006, median home sale prices increased 124 percent.[78] Because of low interest rates and a variety of other factors, more and more people were able to buy houses. In many cases, they were buying houses that were extremely expensive and more than they could actually afford. Easy credit, predatory lending, and subprime lending led to an unsustainable housing boom, which quickly inflated housing prices. **Predatory lending** is a term used to describe deceptive or unfair practices, such as not disclosing the legal or financial terms of a mortgage or charging exorbitant fees when a mortgage is originated. **Subprime lending** is a term describing the practice of lending money to people who normally would not qualify for a mortgage because they have maxed-out credit cards, a poor debt-to-income ratio, or bad credit. By 2005, subprime lending had jumped from approximately 8 percent to 20 percent.[79]

During this time, investors were buying up U.S. cash at historically low prices and using the money to invest in high-interest markets overseas.[80] Globally, there was roughly $70 trillion seeking higher yields than U.S. treasury bonds were paying. This led to the development of financial innovations, such as mortgage-backed securities and collateralized debt obligations that were considered "safe" investments. These were based on the supply chain of mortgages, and they further fueled the bubble.[81]

These factors, when taken together, meant banks were carrying far too much debt. They also meant that much of this debt would never be paid back because people had been encouraged to take on loans they could not afford and because the terms of their mortgages changed dramatically after a few years in ways that caused them to suffer financially and even declare bankruptcy. It's not as if no one noticed what was happening. As Paul Volcker predicted in 2005, "I don't know whether change will come with a bang or a whimper, whether sooner or later. But as things stand, it is more likely than not that it will be financial crises rather than foreign policy foresight that will force the change."[82]

■ **EXHIBIT 7.11**
Why was Alan Greenspan shocked by the recession?

Source: Scott J. Ferrell/Congressional Quarterly/Alamy

Housing boom
A high level activity in the housing market resulting in rapidly increasing home values.

Predatory lending
Deceptive or unfair lending practices such as not disclosing the legal or financial terms of a mortgage or charging exorbitant fees when a mortgage is originated.

Subprime lending
The practice of lending money to people who normally would not qualify for a mortgage because they have maxed-out credit cards, a poor debt-to-income ratio, or bad credit.

Despite a few outcries, the situation continued to heat up. New ways of commoditizing debt, such as the expanding derivatives market, also contributed to the growing problem. Derivatives are extremely complicated financial instruments that are very difficult to measure and value because they represent the anticipated future value of underlying financial products such as bonds or currency. Financial genius Warren Buffett famously called derivatives "financial weapons of mass destruction," and argued that although they generate reportable earnings, those earnings are based on "wildly overstated" estimates "whose inaccuracy may not be exposed for many years."[83] In fact, the incorrect pricing of risk in loans, especially subprime loans, led to the overnight collapse of some of the world's largest financial institutions, including AIG, Lehman Brothers, and Bear Stearns.[84]

The road from recession to recovery has been slow and extremely difficult for countries like the United States, the United Kingdom, and most countries in Europe. While many other economies continue to grow (e.g., China and India) some of the world's most powerful countries have almost been brought to their knees. This continues to have a profound effect on businesses, governments, and people. When you read this in a textbook or hear it on the news, these issues can seem very far away. However, for many people, the facts and figures associated with the recession have translated into lost homes, lost jobs, and underemployment. **Underemployment** is a term used to describe a situation in which people are working at a lesser, or insufficient level. This can include working part time when you want a full time job, or working in a job for which you are overqualified. So, for example, let's say you will graduate college and can expect to earn $40,000 per year as an entry-level employee in your field. However, you find you can't get a job in your field and have to take a job waiting tables or working in a retail store. That's underemployment. In 2012, *USA Today* reported that fully half of college grads are either unemployed or underemployed.[85] What this means for people, businesses, and organizations of all types is that they will continue to deal with a great deal of uncertainty—and more change.

Let's translate this into facts that matter:

- In the United States, in April 2012, over 5 million people who had lost their jobs during the recession—more than 41 percent of the unemployed—had been unemployed for more than two and a quarter years.[86]
- Small business failures in the United States increased 40 percent between 2007 and 2010.[87]
- In Greece, GDP growth plummeted 6 percent in 2011, and the country has seen negative GDP growth since 2008.[88]
- In Germany, a country that by all accounts remained relatively strong despite the recession, GDP decreased by 5.1 percent in 2009 and unemployment experienced a moderate increase.[89]
- During the first quarter of 2012, bank profits were over $35 billion—their highest since 2007—while lending decreased by $56 billion. Furthermore, some banks continue to engage in risky deals. For example, JP Morgan announced in 2012 that they lost two billion in six weeks in hedge bets.[90]

Behind every one of the facts listed above are men, women, and children—most of whom had nothing to do with the decisions that led to the recession.

Back to the topic of incremental change: Although any one of the many changes that occurred between 1982 and 2007 probably would not have led to global recession on its own, together, these incremental changes were disastrous. Somehow the world's leaders and financial wizards didn't see the problem coming. In the next section, we will discuss some approaches that can help leaders pay more attention to change processes and also help people cope with the change process itself.

Underemployment
A term used to describe a situation in which people are working at a lesser, or insufficient level.

Discussion Questions

1. How has the recession that began in 2007 affected you, your family and/or friends? How do you think it will affect your future? What changes might you need to make in your life to deal with this?

2. What revolutionary changes have you seen in a business or institution you are familiar with? What caused this organization to change radically? What was the effect on the organization's individual consumers? How did this change affect your perception of the organization?

5. Which Models Can Help Us Understand the Dynamics of Change?

Objective 7.5
List and describe models that assist in understanding change.

There are many different views of how change occurs and how individuals react to the process of change. In this section, we look at one popular and useful model created by social scientist Kurt Lewin that examines how forces for and against change affect what happens. Then, we look at a metaphor that helps us explain and understand the idea that change is a constant in modern life, work, and organizations.

Lewin's Force Field Analysis Model of Change

In 1951, social scientist Kurt Lewin proposed that change involves forces in people and the environment.[91] The model that bears his name is still widely used today because it remains relevant for complex modern organizations. Lewin's change model, called *force field analysis*, can help us to understand change in individuals, groups, organizations, and larger human systems such as communities and even nations.

As you can see in ■ **EXHIBIT 7.12**, Lewin's model views change as having three distinct phases. Prior to the beginning of a change process, a system is seen as frozen, and the status quo is firmly in place. Later, in the first stage of the change process, the system begins to "unfreeze." Then, in the second phase, change occurs. Finally, in the third stage, the system refreezes, settling into a new status quo. The model as originally presented argues that social habits are fixed, or frozen. To initiate change, these social habits have to "unfreeze," which requires "[breaking] open the shell of complacency . . . by causing] an emotional stir-up" to bring these habits into consciousness, where they can be worked on.[92] After desired changes are activated, the refreezing process locks in new ways of feeling, thinking, and behaving.

In each of Lewin's stages, dynamic forces are at work that are both driving change and preventing it. When these forces are balanced, no change occurs and the status quo remains in place. In contrast, when driving forces become more powerful than restraining forces, the system begins to un-freeze—old habits are questioned, old patterns of behavior don't seem to work as well, and people feel anxious and uncertain. If the

■ **EXHIBIT 7.12**
Lewin's force field analysis model of change helps us look at forces for and against change.

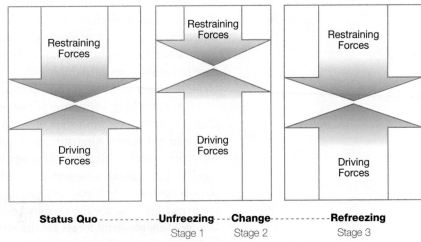

Status Quo ---------- **Unfreezing** --- **Change** ---------- **Refreezing**
Stage 1   Stage 2   Stage 3

Source: Based on Lewin, Kurt. 1952. Group decision and social change. In *Readings in social psychology*, ed. E. Maccoby, T. Newcomb, and E. Hartley, 459–73. New York: Holt, Rinehart, & Winston.

driving forces continue to be powerful enough, change can occur. Then, in the third stage, the forces for and against change are once again balanced, which allows people and the organization to settle into new ways of feeling, thinking, and behaving.

Lewin's approach to change has many of the right elements, though some of them are not obvious in the model.[93] Namely, Lewin emphasized that change can be effectively implemented only if the entire context is considered. For example, in organizations, culture and values must be addressed overtly, as well as goals, mission, business practices, and the like.

CONSIDER THE CONTEXT: THE WHOLE PICTURE

Lewin believed that change at any level of a system has to include a deep understanding of the context in which beliefs, behaviors, and habits have developed.[94] This means that it's not enough to simply look at a person, group, or organization—you have to look at the entire picture and how each part of a system is linked to and related to the other parts.

Considering the context for organizational change is extremely important. Take, for example, what Apple's founder, the late Steve Jobs, had to say about the context—the market environment—that existed at the time the iPod Nano was introduced. The iPod was already dominating the market when Jobs challenged his top executives and engineers to develop a product to replace it. "Playing it safe is the most dangerous thing we can do," Jobs warned.[95] At the time, iPod claimed 74 percent of the market, which might convince some people and companies to relax. Jobs, however, didn't want to give the competition any time to catch up, and that meant ensuring that the only company to make the iPod obsolete would be Apple. The result of this was the very successful iPod Nano. Steve Jobs and Apple didn't follow the rules of the industry, and as a result, they kept the competition off balance and inspired the company's team of creative workers.[96]

CONSIDER THE POWER OF CULTURE

Lewin believed that change only occurs when group and cultural norms, values, and dynamics are addressed. It isn't enough to simply try to change individuals, because the power of culture almost always trumps a person's desire to change—even when it is sincere. That's because culture is a powerful restraining force that helps maintain the status quo. In Chapter 13, you will learn about culture. For now, consider aspects such as shared values and beliefs and accepted behaviors—that is, "the way we do things around here."

Think about culture from your own experience. It's likely that when you started college, you learned new things about how to behave with people, build new friendships, and communicate. Maybe you were a bit shy before college or perhaps you were one of the "stars" back home. Upon entering this new "system"—college—you realized that you would have to learn new behaviors. You may have also found that some of your beliefs and values were challenged as a result of meeting people whose cultures were very different from your own. You might have become more outgoing so you could meet new friends. You might have realized that there were many "stars" in college, and you'd have to behave somewhat differently than you did before. You likely made a number of changes to how you behave, how you perceive others, and even how you see yourself.

Then something very strange happened. On your first visit home, after having changed some of your old ways of behaving and thinking, you found yourself slipping into your old habits. Almost immediately, you took up the roles you had always held with your parents, siblings, and friends, behaving in much the same way you did before you left. If you didn't return to these old behaviors, you might have found that people were not particularly happy with you and tried to push you back to your old ways. This happens a lot—and for the reasons Lewin pointed out. The cultures of the groups we belong to are powerful forces for the status quo.

When trying to change a situation, *you need to understand the situation as it is before trying to change it.* Change must start with a significant examination of what currently exists, such as forces for and against change; culture, beliefs, and values; and behaviors, processes, and structures—which brings us to Lewin's third point about change: you need to understand the system as it currently is. Social scientist Edgar Schein agrees with Lewin, noting that you cannot understand how to change a system unless you know what the system is changing *from*.[97] Also, because all systems are in a constant state of change, it is important to identify and locate those elements that are already at work to produce change. In essence, you need to continually find ways to take a snapshot of where the organization is at the moment and use that information to spark the desire for change.

STUDYING A SYSTEM *CHANGES* THE SYSTEM

According to Lewin, the very act of studying a system changes it.[98] Lewin proposed a process for studying human systems while simultaneously changing them, called action research, that we will discuss later in the chapter. Action research assumes that the act of studying a group, organization, or community results in change—regardless of whether the researchers intend this or not. That means that while we study human systems, we need to understand and manage the changes that occur *because* of our research. For example, say you're part of a team that is experiencing lots of conflict. You want to understand this, so you "study" the group by asking each team member questions such as, "Why do you think we fight so often?" Simply by asking these questions, you draw people's attention to how they're acting. Increased attention will most likely cause people to monitor their behavior more carefully, which might result in less conflict.

Change Is Constant: The Permanent White-Water Metaphor

Although Lewin's model is extremely useful when considering change in human systems, it has drawbacks. The most notable drawback is this model appears to indicate that a system starts in a fixed or static place and ends that way—static, albeit different.

Peter Vaill is a well-known organizational change theorist who coined the term *permanent white water*. **Permanent white water** is a metaphor that refers to the fact that organizational systems face unrelenting turbulence and constant change.[99] As a result, managers have to accept that they have limited control over their environments.

However, in *real* white-water rapids, expert rafters know how to use paddles, body weight, posture, currents, and the quiet water near the shore to help them deal with the dangers of navigation. Managers and leaders everywhere must learn the equivalent skills for dealing with fast-paced and constant organizational and environmental change.[100] In fact, whatever role you have today, you will need to be a creative lifelong learner, steering yourself toward new skills and the information you'll need to deal with constant change.[101]

Kurt Lewin's force field analysis model is helpful in understanding change, and the permanent white-water metaphor helps us see that change is constant and must be managed. Now, let's look at some practical ways to implement change in organizations.

Permanent white water
Metaphor that refers to the fact that organizational systems face unrelenting turbulence and constant change.

Discussion Questions

1. Think about a change you attempted this year in school (such as a change in study habits, your social life, or your extracurricular activities). Identify the status quo before you made the change. Identify the forces *for* this change (those that helped you) and the forces *against* this change (those that interfered) during the unfreezing process. What could you have done to capitalize on the forces that helped you while minimizing those that did not?

2. How does the permanent white water metaphor apply to your life?

Objective 7.6
Describe which practical models
are useful tools for managing
change in organizations.

6. What Practical Models Can Help Us Manage Change in Organizations?

Scholar-practitioners John Kotter and Gregory Shea help us consider what to pay attention to and do when implementing change. Both Kotter's and Shea's models help us focus our efforts when attempting to bring about organizational change.

Kotter's Eight-Stage Change Model

As you can see in ▉ **EXHIBIT 7.13**, Harvard Business School professor John Kotter's well-known approach to organizational change involves eight clearly defined steps.[102]

KOTTER STAGES 1 THROUGH 5: PREPARING FOR CHANGE

Kotter Stage 1: John Kotter, like Kurt Lewin, believes that in order for a change process to actually begin (with any hope of continuing), the first stage of any change process in an organization must *ensure that people feel an urgent need for change.* Everyone involved, or potentially involved, needs to have both a cognitive understanding of why change is necessary and an emotional investment in what needs to be done and why.

To see how Kotter's first stage plays out in reality, consider the pharmaceutical industry. In this industry, the business model revolves around research, development, and marketing of "blockbuster" drugs. Blockbuster drugs tend to be company "jewels." Developing these drugs requires a huge investment of money and time, but if the drugs are taken up by the market, they provide huge amounts of revenue to the company for the entire time the company holds the patent. Examples of 2011 blockbuster drugs include Lipitor, Plavix, and Nexium (see ▉ **EXHIBIT 7.14**).[103] As you can see, these medications made a *lot* of money.

In spite of the power of this business model, many market analysts and pharmaceutical executives believe that it is on the way out. The pressures related to the costs and time needed to develop these drugs, the inevitable loss of patents, the public's growing impatience with marketing strategies that foster a perceived need for a particular drug, and the call for pharmaceutical companies to behave in a socially responsible manner add up to one thing: Change is coming. Wise industry leaders in the drug industry are paying attention.

Kotter Stage 2: According to Kotter, the second stage of any change process involves *getting the right people involved to lead change.* This can include people at all levels, but it

▉ **EXHIBIT 7.13**

John Kotter's Stages of Effective Organizational Change

Stage 1: Ensure that people feel an urgent need for change.

Stage 2: Get the right people involved to lead change.

Stage 3: Create a new strategic vision.

Stage 4: Make sure the new vision is effectively communicated.

Stage 5: Empower a broad group of change agents.

Stage 6: Successfully pull off short-term victories.

Stage 7: Consolidate the victories and go after more changes.

Stage 8: Solidify the change in the organizational culture.

■ **EXHIBIT 7.14**

Top Three Blockbuster Drugs in 2011

1. Lipitor
   a. Treats: High blood pressure
   b. Annual Sales: $9.6 billion
   c. Annual Growth: 11%
   d. Manufacturer: Pfizer
   e. Approved: September 2005
   f. Patent Expiration: November 30, 2011[104]
2. Plavix
   a. Treats: Heart disease
   b. Annual Sales: $7 billion
   c. Annual Growth: 6%
   d. Manufacturer: Bristol-Myers Squibb and Sanofi Pharmaceuticals
   e. Approved: November 1997
   f. Patent Expiration: May 17, 2012[105]
3. Nexium
   a. Treats: heartburn and gastroesophageal reflux disease
   b. Annual Sales: $4.4 billion
   c. Annual Growth: 11%
   d. Manufacturer: AstraZeneca
   e. Approved: February 2001
   f. Patent Expiration: May 27, 2014[106]

must include senior leaders. Without senior leadership involved, most change efforts will fail. Sometimes this takes the form of a "change council" that is composed of senior leaders, people from all levels of the organization, representatives of all major functions, and expert advisers who understand change and/or the issues the organization is facing.

Kotter Stage 3: Kotter's third stage involves the *creation of a new strategic vision* for the organization. A new strategy is often created at the top of the organization by the senior team and/or the board of directors. However, when preparing for large-scale change, it is important to gather information and to involve key people from throughout the organization.

Kotter Stage 4: In fourth stage, steps must be taken to *make sure the new vision is effectively communicated* throughout the organization. If people know what's going on and why, they are far more likely to be willing to make changes—even difficult ones. When it comes to this kind of communication, it is important to note that impersonal forms of communication (such as company-wide e-mails) rarely work. Leaders have to find ways to inspire and excite people, and they need to help people understand how the new organizational vision supports *individuals'* hopes and dreams.

Kotter Stage 5: After people understand the new vision, it is time to *empower a broad group of change agents.* This means finding, training, and creating a plan for a group of people to actively support the change process. Change agents work to inspire, and they mobilize people to engage in new behaviors and even adopt new attitudes and values. They must, of course, have the skills to help people be enthusiastic about the change and to deal with the details of change implementation.

Although empowering change agents is an important part of the model, it is a stage that often fails in organizations. Part of the reason for this failure is that change agent skills, such as managing resistance, engaging in inspirational leadership, and displaying personal resilience, are not necessarily what people learn at work. In fact, in many organizations, skills related to sponsoring and encouraging change are discouraged.

KOTTER STAGES 6 THROUGH 8: CHANGE

Kotter Stage 6: Kotter says that, in the sixth stage, leaders should *successfully pull off short-term victories*. In other words, they should set their sights on identifying opportunities for small victories that give confidence about the direction of the change process, rather than going after one big, splashy, noticeable change.

Kotter Stage 7: The seventh stage of Kotter's model involves *consolidating the smaller victories and going after more and bigger changes.* By this time, people's hearts and minds will have shifted, and they will be inspired and motivated to continue and to take on even bigger, more significant change efforts.

Kotter Stage 8: Finally, in the last stage of Kotter's change process, the *new ways of thinking and doing must be solidified in the organizational culture.* This can take the form of changing some of the "symbols" of the culture (such as the mission statement), emphasizing and capitalizing on the "good stories" that have emerged about the new organization, or embedding the new ways of being and doing into organizational systems and processes.

Kotter argues that organizational change often fails because leaders ignore or overlook one or more steps in this model. For instance, without selecting and empowering change agents to implement change, obstacles become barriers. Overconfidence after accomplishing small gains might make leaders believe that they have achieved success. Even when the vision of change is successfully accomplished, the failure to embed the change into the organizational culture can lead to long-term failure.

Kotter's model has been and continues to be used extensively as a framework for implementing change in organizations. Let's now look at another practical model that, when coupled with Lewin's force field analysis and Kotter's approach, further improves the chances of successfully implementing change in an organization.

■ **EXHIBIT 7.15**
Gregory Shea's work systems model shows the complexity of change in organizations.

Source: Adapted from Shea, Gregory P. 2001. Leading change. In *Medicine and business: Bridging the gap*, ed. S. Rovin, p. 47. Gaithersburg, MD: Aspen Publishers. Used with permission of Shea & Associates, Inc. © Shea & Associates, Inc.

Gregory Shea's Work Systems Model

Gregory Shea, an expert on organizational transformation at Wharton, sees today's businesses and institutions as complex, dynamic systems that are constantly undergoing change. Shea has developed a model called the work systems model (shown in ■ **EXHIBIT 7.15**) that shows the levers in an organization that must be considered when trying to bring about change.[107] A *lever* is an aspect of an organizational system or subsystem that can be studied, attended to, emphasized, or ignored during the change process.

In this model, change efforts are directed toward a new and better way of doing things, a more effective and efficient organization, and an overall context that is more likely to result in success, employee satisfaction, and resonance. As Gregory Shea puts it:

Change involves creating a different workplace reality. People do things differently. To get that to happen, you must first figure out the workplace reality that you want. 'What will be happening in this office setting, that production area, or within that cross-national, continental, or global virtual team?' If you can't see it, then you can't design for it. If you can't design for it, then you just dramatically cut your chances of getting and sustaining it. So, first things first: What constellation of behaviors or scenes or film clips are you trying to bring to life?[108]

SHEA'S LEVERS OF CHANGE IN THE WORK SYSTEMS MODEL

Let's look at Shea's model in more detail. According to Shea, there are eight levers of change in an organization:

- Basic structure of the *Organization*
- Physical and virtual *Workplace Design*
- Business processes, pathways, and protocols that make up *Tasks*
- Human resources in the form of *People and Skills*
- The offering and allocation of *Rewards*
- Data collection in the form of *Measurements*
- Modes and types of *Information Distribution*
- Who makes what decisions, or *Decision Allocation*

For example, Children's Medical Center of Dallas used the people, rewards, and task levers in a change process to ensure that doctors and Spanish-speaking patients could communicate better. The hospital was increasingly facing problems because many of its doctors were not fluent in Spanish and many of its patients were not fluent in English. The hospital first tried hiring several dozen professional medical translators, but doing so was costly, and the translators were hard to manage.

Then, the hospital system turned to its own population. Many of the employees who were working as receptionists and in other areas of the hospital were bilingual, but they were not familiar with medical language. The hospital's leaders thus decided to offer volunteers free training in both English and Spanish medical language. They awarded bonuses and a pay raise to people who successfully passed the training, along with the additional title of "language liaison." Now, when translation service is needed, doctors can tap a staff member in the immediate vicinity with confidence.[109]

In this example, leadership first tried to fix the situation by changing the organization (hiring outside translators). This didn't work, partly because they were only shifting one lever—the structure of the organization. Then leadership addressed several more levers. By asking for volunteers and providing training, they influenced the *people* lever, and by evaluating people's success in the training program, they influenced the *measurement* lever. By adding new duties and responsibilities, the *task* lever was influenced. And finally, bonuses and pay raises influenced the *reward* lever.

This situation shows us that it is important to pick the right levers, as well as to choose enough levers on which to focus. Shea cautions that paying attention to just one or two levers is a mistake. He notes, "In my experience working with organizations on change initiatives, one has to hit at least four of these drivers at the same time to make change happen . . . one doesn't have to use all these levers of change, but you can't use just use one and expect to succeed."[110]

Shea goes on to say that constant change requires constant choices and the development of new skills—along with constant attention to the environment within which the organization exists. Shea's advice: "I have seen very talented managers and executives chewed up and spit out by this environment. They thrash about and even drown in change. The environment is relentless."[111]

SHEA ON HOW TO CHOOSE *WHAT* TO CHANGE—AND WHAT *NOT TO*

The selection of which levers to study and influence is extremely important. Depending on the type of change needed or desired, this decision can make or break the change process. Each of the levers is a potential contributor to or inhibitor of successfully introducing change to the whole system. This is the case because change in any one part of the system has an impact on the *entire* system.

You need to focus on things that are important. To determine what's really important, however, you have to know whether the issues are real and require immediate attention. According to Shea, there are three other ways to categorize situations to help you decide what to do (or not). Some things truly are unimportant, and you should ignore them. Some things are a *waste of time*. They capture your attention and tempt you to spend time on them. But, some things don't seem important, but in fact they are. Shea calls these *bombs*.

So, what happens when something does not capture your attention but is, in fact, a bomb that's ready to explode? The now-defunct financial services firm Lehman Brothers found out the hard way—the company's leaders seemed to ignore a bomb that blew up in a big way. There were numerous important clues that Lehman Brothers's banking practices could lead to difficulties. For example, at least one individual claims to have brought transgressions to management's attention, and he was fired. Presumably, no one paid attention or realized how important these clues were. Too many people inside and outside the organization ignored these clues and a century-old company went out of business, taking with it thousands of jobs and many people's life savings.

Or take the example of the financial services firm Merrill Lynch (now part of Bank of America, or BofA). Late in 2008, in the middle of one of the biggest financial meltdowns in history, a decision was made to remodel the new CEO's office to the tune of $1.2 million.[112] This is a classic example of *wasting time* while a ticking *bomb* (public opinion) was being ignored. Surely people had better things to worry about than the new furniture or, worse yet, the toilet in the new CEO's office. Somehow, though, and maybe due to a combination of tradition, policy, and possibly the CEO's and other peoples' desires, the remodeling went ahead. Needless to say, the press got hold of this information and the bomb exploded. The company's reputation was badly damaged and employees all over the company were embarrassed. From a business perspective, the time and effort spent on defending, explaining, and apologizing for these actions surely took leaders away from the financial crisis—and the sale of the then 100-year old institution to BofA.

Merrill has made the transition into Bank of America quite successfully and is even part of BofA's attempt to regain financial health and public favor.[113] It's possible that the "bomb" that exploded during the financial crisis is a lesson that the company's current leaders have taken to heart.

A less disastrous but more common example of a bomb at work is ignoring people's feelings about factors such as working conditions. For instance, within organizations, it is common to hear about people's pleasure or displeasure with their offices, cubicles, or workspaces. As a manager, you may decide to ignore this (which might be the right decision in some cases). However, when workspace affects people's status or physical comfort, emotions can run very high. People care about their spaces, and managers must decide when it is important to pay attention to this.

How can you tell the difference between something that is unimportant and a bomb that might explode? It's not easy to decide what to pay attention to. That's part of the reason why people waste countless hours on things that simply aren't important. For example, many people spend a lot of time dealing with e-mails that should never have been sent to them in the first place. One reason people receive unnecessary and distracting e-mails is because others are trying to protect themselves by copying *everyone*. They want to be sure that no one can come back and say "I didn't know," or "Why didn't you ask me?" You're not going to be able to change this situation all by yourself, because this kind of behavior is often a part of an organization's culture. However, you can choose not to be part of the problem.

Sometimes, people waste a lot of time on things like complaining about their bosses or colleagues without trying very hard to change anything. This is a tremendous waste of time—but again, you can't stop it just by telling people it's not acceptable. You can, however, consider this kind of behavior to be a symptom of a bigger problem, and try to discover the source of the real problem. Maybe, for example, the culture encourages this kind of behavior—in such an environment, the person who complains loudest has the most power. Or maybe there are one or two troublemakers—"bad apples" so to speak. Only by getting to the source of this behavior can you begin to change it.

To understand where to focus your time and attention, especially when it comes to change management, questions such as "Should we consider if this is important *now*?" and "Will it be important later?" should be asked regularly. That's because in today's volatile world, things are changing all the time—and priorities need to change too.

In the preceding two sections, you learned about models of organizational change. Kurt Lewin's change model explains that there are both forces for and forces against change. Peter Vaill and others say that change is constant in society, the economy, and organizations. John Kotter helps you see that there are stages in the organizational change model, and each one is crucial. Finally, Gregory Shea's model helps you understand where you can focus your efforts to change organizations and how to constantly evaluate your choices. All of these models assist you in understanding what change is and how it can be integrated into organizations.

In the next section, we will look at how HR can guide planned change through organization development practices, including action research and action learning. This, in turn, necessitates that HR professionals help prepare leaders for changes by developing key leader competencies.

Discussion Questions

1. Consider a change that you encouraged in your family, a group, or a team at school or work. What did you do to ensure that people were ready for change? Did it work? Why or why not?

2. What are some of the small victories that you have had in your school career? How did these victories contribute to changes in your behavior or aspirations?

---

7. What Can HR Do to Foster Effective Change?

Objective 7.7
Learn how HR can foster effective change.

Change does not occur magically. It requires individual energy, effort, and support. Good HR leaders know that change is supported by organization development and continual learning. To start this section, we will review *organization development*, a set of change activities that HR often leads. Then, because HR departments and professionals need to understand how to engage the organization's members in improvement processes that help identify an organization's strengths and challenges, we will discuss *action learning* and action research.

Finally, because HR professionals are responsible for teaching others the skills and competencies needed to manage change, we will conclude with how they can create *leadership development programs that work*.

Organization Development Defined

Organization development (OD) refers to a systematic, scientific, and research-based approach to change in organizations.[114] The goals of OD are often to improve the organization's competitive advantage through changing the organization's culture and leadership practices and to improve problem-solving and change management skills.[115] According to the *NTL Handbook of Organization Development and Change*, Kurt Lewin is considered by many to be the father of both action learning and organization development because he links two important ideas, which are the study and effective use of group dynamics and the application of an action learning methodology.[116]

There are many different approaches to OD, but all of them essentially focus on *planned* change at the organizational level—structures, processes, culture, and so forth. Planned change starts with the view that the organization is a complex system composed of many elements, each influencing and being influenced by the other elements of the system.[117] The process starts with examination of the organization, followed by "diagnosis" and then strategic change management, which engages the organization at different levels of the system.[118]

Because so much of an organization is people, HR plays a huge role in collaborating with employees and leaders. Unfortunately, in too many cases, HR departments and professionals do not see this as a priority. Douglas McGregor and Joel Cutcher-Gershenfeld, authors of *The Human Side of Enterprise*, note that limits to collaborative and OD work in organizations are not a result of *human* limits but rather a failure of HR creativity and leadership.[119] Another problem is that some OD interventions are not linked to strategy and reap poor results because HR leaders are not well integrated into organizational strategy.[120] To avoid this and to be able to conceptualize changes and change processes that work, HR professionals can learn new ways to study their own organizations by using processes such as action learning.

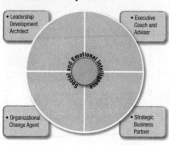

HR Leadership Roles

Action Research and Action Learning

Kurt Lewin first coined the term *action research* in 1946 in a paper discussing research to address issues concerning minorities in society.[121] Action learning is closely related to action research in that they are both reflective processes involving learning and problem solving.[122] Action research and action learning are also change processes that engage people in the experiences of action, reflection, review, and planning. The main difference between the two is that action learning is more of an educational process used to help people improve performance, while action research is more of a deliberate problem-solving process or process of leveraging an organization's strengths. These approaches have been used and expanded on by a number of scholars and practitioners in fields as varied as organizational development, education, race relations, environmental sustainability, and social justice.[123] They were at the heart of the powerful work done by educational scholar Paolo Freire, who was concerned with the issues of social justice and empowerment. Action research and action learning have also been used successfully in communities and organizations around the world.[124] Let's look at how action research differs from more traditional research and how it can support learning and change.

Action research, like all research, is done to further knowledge and understanding.[125] Traditionally, change tends to be what you do *after* research is concluded. This is not the case for action research. Action research assumes that the very act of studying a group, organization, or community results in change—regardless of whether the researchers intend this or not. That means that while we study organizations, we need to understand and manage the changes that occur because of our research. Another difference between traditional research and action research is that traditional research separates the researcher from the problem that is being examined. Action research makes no such artificial separation, placing the researcher in a role of both researcher and participant in the situation.

Action research starts with a research plan to explore an issue, a concern, or an opportunity. Many different approaches can be taken in action research, but all of these methods focus on understanding interrelationships through hands-on participation in your research. In other words, you are a participant and a researcher at the same time: a participant-researcher.[126] In most cases, HR professionals or external experts join with organization members to conduct this research, which includes conversations, reflection, and activities involving many people beyond the research team.

As research continues, results are continually reevaluated, and new research is conducted, observed, reflected on, and acted on. This is a continual spiral. In other words, action research is an iterative process designed to shift people and perspectives and to affect the problem or opportunity until it is resolved or leveraged.[127] The use of a feedback loop to engage constant improvement has also been called *organizational cybernetics* and can be found, among other places, in the practices of total quality management an organizational control process that will be covered in Chapter 12.[128]

Leadership Competency Development and Change

The process of developing leadership competencies as one way to support complex organizational change has been greatly expanded in recent years. Such an approach can be supportive of individual and organizational effectiveness in change processes *only* when the competencies that are developed are the *right* competencies.

However, in many companies, the popularity of the competency model approach has led HR professionals and others to cobble together models that are ineffective for people and jobs in today's organizations. For example, so-called "competencies" observed in some organizational models often include a mixture of observable behaviors, personal values, vague terms more related to personality, and even allusions to organizational values. Although all of these might be valuable in certain situations, they are not competencies, and it is hard to link these confusing mixtures directly to performance—or to effective change management.

So, if HR professionals take on the responsibilities related to teaching employees, managers, and leaders, the first thing they need to do is to create an architecture for leadership development that enables employees to learn the right competencies at the right time. When it comes to change, many of the right competencies relate to emotional intelligence. For example, to understand and manage change, it is essential to develop one's capacity for social awareness by building *empathy* and *organizational awareness*. To create and implement change initiatives you need to read people's needs and desires accurately and understand how various factors (such as culture and politics) affect the organization.

In addition to discovering *what* to teach, HR professionals need to reflect on *how* to teach. What kinds of leadership development processes actually work? Many HR professionals and others struggle with this question. In fact, research indicates that far too many leadership development programs and processes are simply a waste of time. Often, the competencies and models that are taught do not lead to more effective leadership, and the learning methods that are employed do not support learning or retention of knowledge.

Researchers are stepping in to help resolve this problem. For example, Richard Boyatzis and colleagues have been engaged for years in what are called *outcome studies*.[129] These studies involve the creation of learning and development programs that focus on competencies, such as those related to social and emotional intelligence, that are shown to improve leadership development.[130] These leadership development programs, particularly those that employ the intentional change model, enhance learning and retention of knowledge.

A final note on leadership development in support of effective change in organizations: Although the development of programs focused on leadership development is one of the most common interventions used to improve performance and provide people with the tools to address change, it is certainly not the only approach that is needed. Some scholars believe that training is a much overused approach to fixing organizational problems and that a large portion of the hundreds of billions of dollars spent yearly on these programs is wasted.[131]

Discussion Questions

1. Draft a plan to interview people about a group or organization to which you belong. Now, generate a list of things that might happen to the group or organization as a *result* of your interviews (e.g., people would be curious about what you are doing or they might talk to each other about your questions).

2. Have you ever participated in a leadership development program at work or school? What competencies did you work on? Did the program help you change? Why or why not?

Objective 7.8
Understand how you can change and develop yourself.

8. What Can We All Do to Support Change?

In most organizations everyone is involved in change. Just like leadership, change is up to all of us, no matter what role we hold. In this section, we explore two very practical approaches to contributing positively to change processes: becoming a change agent and learning how to care for others during a change process. Then we look at one last important issue: how to face changes that are truly unwelcome.

Becoming a Change Agent

Much has been written about the role of individuals in organizations who act as agents of change—people who are able to make an impact on organizational goals, processes, and resources. We have noted in this book that HR professionals must be change agents, but that's not enough. Given the rate and pace of change in most organizations today, everyone needs to know how to spark, manage, and lead change. Change agents need to have good interpersonal skills related to social and emotional intelligence, and good networking skills that enable them to access and control the flow of information.[132]

At a more fundamental level, change agents need to have an understanding of and the ability to manage politics and power as influential levers of change within the organization.[133] Scholars have identified three power-related skills that change agents need[134]:

- The power to enlist organizational resources. This can be difficult, especially if you don't have formal authority. However, it is possible. You just need to learn how to influence those who *do* control resources.
- The power to affect the agenda and participate in decision making. This is easier in organizations that empower people. However, even in those that do not, it is often possible to "get your voice heard" by identifying the people who listen, talking to them (this takes courage), and mobilizing others to use systems (such as employee surveys) to make a point (this takes inspirational leadership).
- The power to use the current culture and "the way we do things around here" to enlist people and to begin seeing new ways of being and working. This has been referred to as *management of meaning*.[135]

Effectively accessing and mobilizing different forms of power, managing politics, and utilizing interpersonal communication skills to further a change agenda are all skills related to emotional intelligence.[136] In fact, some scholars even proclaim that the essential role of a leader is that of a change agent, and the ability to be effective in that role comes through the development of the skills of emotional intelligence.[137] Emotionally intelligent change agents are able to demonstrate resilience in the face of uncertainty, partly because they see the big picture—they take a systems perspective. A systems perspective helps us to recognize that current problems can be overcome and to understand and address others' reservations regarding new endeavors.[138]

Caring for Others during Change: Empathy, Inspiration, and Managing Resistance

Through any organizational change, people expect and deserve care and attention from leadership. As you can see in ■ **EXHIBIT 7.16**, emotional and behavioral responses to change range from acceptance to active resistance. Resistance can be obvious or subtle and can occur immediately or be delayed by days or even months.

Exhibit 7.16 covers a wide range of behaviors. The first tip for managing resistance to change is to stop assuming that resistance will be people's automatic response. This is a common assumption and is in fact not true. If you assume the people will resist, you might actually be the one who adopts an approach that is forceful, negative, or manipulative.

There are many ways people respond to change, as you can see in ■ **EXHIBIT 7.17**. People do not, however, like being forced to change. They want to choose. You need to give people as much freedom of choice as possible (and that's usually more than most managers give). People can handle change, and they often have good ideas about the specifics of change and how to implement it. Let people contribute. Don't feel you have to control everything, because that in itself sparks resistance.

You can do a number of things personally to help others respond to change (see Exhibit 7.17). How people respond to change is partly dependent on how *you* respond. Again, start with emotional intelligence: self-awareness and self-management. If you are enthusiastic and committed, people are more likely to "catch" your emotions and contribute positively. Similarly, if you are secretly resentful or fearful, people know it—no matter how much you try to hide it. In times of turmoil or when we feel threatened, we take emotional cues from others, especially formal and informal leaders.

■ **EXHIBIT 7.16**
How people may respond to change.

Acceptance
- Cooperation
- Support
- Resignation

Indifference
- Apathy
- Ambivalence
- Minimal compliance

Passive Resistance
- Strict compliance to unproductive rules or procedures
- Minimizing work output
- Failing to develop new skills or knowledge
- Overlooking or failing to correct errors

Active Resistance
- Overt rudeness
- Disobedience
- Sabotage

Source: Based on A. S. Judson. 1991. *Changing behavior in organizations: Minimizing resistance to change*, p. 48. Cambridge, MA: Basil Blackwell.

■ **EXHIBIT 7.17**

The Smart Way to Lead Change

1. Become aware of and manage your own emotional response to change first.
2. Don't assume people will resist change; it's only one of many possible responses.
3. Don't force people to change (unless it's life or death).
4. Don't try to control everything (or everyone).
5. Be empathetic. Change is hard sometimes.
6. Inspire people with a vision that is meaningful to them.
7. Face real resistance with hope, resolve, and courage.
8. Negotiate where and when you must; do it respectfully and in good faith.
9. Tell the truth.
10. Be a role model.

As we mentioned, if you don't assume people will always resist change, you don't need to force people. Forcing things on people or over-controlling everything sparks resistance. You should be empathetic with people as they go through change. Change is hard sometimes, even when it is welcome. Truly seeking to understand people's experiences and being supportive can go a long way toward minimizing potential resistance. In practice, this might mean providing emotional support, giving time off after a demanding period, or providing training in new skills.

You can work on being inspirational: Paint a vision of where the group is going and make sure it links to people's individual dreams. To do this, you have to *know* what people's dreams are. When you face real resistance, don't despair. Face the difficulties with optimism, hope, resolve, and courage. Negotiate where and when you must, and do it respectfully and in good faith. Tell the truth. Be a role model.

Facing Change with Courage

In this chapter, you have learned many ways to deal with change, manage change, and lead change. These skills will serve you well at work and in life. There's one more thing we need to address, however: What do we do when the changes we face are unwelcome? What about when something really bad happens—how do we face this kind of change? What happens when the changes that occur are things that we would never, ever have chosen?

Throughout our lives, we all have to deal with changes that we do not want to face. Natural disasters destroy homes and communities, wars break out, and people engage in crimes that hurt innocent people. Relationships break up, people get sick, and loved ones die. No one welcomes these changes—we don't want things like this to happen. So how can we deal with changes that aren't welcome and that hurt rather than help us?

The answer to this question is complicated—so complicated that most of the world's religions and many of its great philosophers have tried to discover the secret. In the end, there's no easy answer. However, there are some things that you can do to help yourself when change is hard.

First, remember what neuroscience teaches us: When we feel hopeful, we are more open to learning, more able to solve problems creatively, and more resilient.[139] So, in whatever situation you find yourself, try as hard as you can to find something to be hopeful about. It might be small—like knowing you are a strong person and have faced difficult times before. Or, maybe you can find hope in the learning that comes from surviving a difficult experience. Alternatively, if things are really bad, you may just hold on to the belief that at some point, things will work out and get better.

Second, cultivate practices of mindfulness as discussed in Chapter 6. When we are mindful, we are awake, aware, and attuned to ourselves and others. As tempting as it might be to hide from changes we don't like—to deny what's happened and our feelings about it—doing this just postpones the inevitable. Ultimately, we all have to deal with what life brings us. When we live life mindfully, taking time to reflect and to build our resilience and our capacity for awareness, we are more prepared to stay calm and grounded when things are tough.

Finally, get help. People aren't meant to deal with problems or sadness alone. We need other people, especially when facing difficulties in our lives. What you can do now to help yourself prepare for the inevitable ups and downs of life is to make sure you build strong relationships with people who care for you—people who will do anything for you. Then, you can be there for each other.

Hope, mindfulness, and the help of others are a few of the keys to living through hard times, when changes are unwelcome or even tragic. Approaching life's most difficult times in this way will help you be a better person—and be ready to help others when they need it.

Discussion Questions

1. Look at Exhibit 7.17. For each of the 10 tips on managing resistance and leading change, note some concrete actions you can take to help bring about change in a group at work or at school.

2. When you encounter change that you do not like, do you face it head on or tend to hide from it? Do you take time to reflect on issues and emotions during unwanted change? How do you spend that time? Have you built strong relationships to help support you through difficult times?

9. A Final Word on Change

Regardless of whether people resist change or thrive on it, change is never easy. Even the word "change" evokes different reactions from people and organizations because each person and every organization defines "change" in a different way. Those who do thrive on change see change as an opportunity to grow and learn. To manage change with others, you must first seek to understand people: What do they need? How will the proposed changes help them or hurt them? How can you make them want change? If you understand these things, you will have more success in change efforts, large and small. Inspiring people with a vision of a better tomorrow, even if it means hard work in the short term, is how the world's best companies continue to be competitive.

EXPERIENCING Leadership

LEADING IN A GLOBAL WORLD
Gender Diversity

A large, multinational oil and gas company, Giant Oil, has recently recognized that it has no women in senior management or leadership positions. The organization wants to change that situation. The executive team has decided to institute a Women's Leadership Program that focuses specifically on developing female employees to take on more senior level management and leadership roles. The executive team wants to roll out this program globally; however, they recognize that there may be cultural resistance in some of the Asian, European, and African offices. Additionally, some of the candidates for the program expressed concern that they may not be taken seriously by their male colleagues. These same women have also stated that they don't want to be "token" women in Giant's management structure.

Using Shea's Levers of Change in the work system, answer the following questions.

1. Which levers of change should Giant focus on? Why?
2. Shea claims that it is as important to identify what *not* to do as it is to identify what to do. What do you think Giant can afford to ignore? Conversely, what should be their top three priorities?

LEADING WITH EMOTIONAL INTELLIGENCE
Change, Then and Now

In organizations, families, and life, change is inevitable and constant. The way we handle change—by adjusting to it, resisting it, or embracing it—depends in part on our degree of emotional intelligence. Organizations change to remain relevant, productive, and profitable. The same can be said about you—you change to remain relevant, productive, and profitable—and your education should be a transformative experience that guides you in this direction.

Review the Gestalt cycle of experience. Now, think back on yourself when you were in high school. Consider the ways you have changed in that relatively short span of time.

1. Make a brief list of the type of person you were back then—shy, outgoing, humble, geeky, etc. Be honest with yourself. How have you changed in terms of self-awareness and managing your emotions? How do you handle relationships differently now?
2. Choose one obvious and powerful change that you have experienced since that time. It may be the beginning or ending of a relationship, deciding to go

or not go to college, or deciding on a profession or major.

3. Apply the Gestalt cycle of experience to that change. Identify when you first became aware that a change was needed. How did you energize yourself to make a move? What action(s) did you take? Pay particular attention to the way you felt during the course of the change. Were you excited, afraid, or confused? Compare your feelings with where you are now relative to where you were before, during, and after the change. Are you more mature? Are you a better person for the change?

LEADING WITH CRITICAL THINKING SKILLS
Eight Stages for Participation

Change in organizations can be slow, time-consuming, and sometimes counter-productive. Unless it is done right, organizational change can be a nightmare for the management team and employees. Practical models can help organizations make smooth transitions from old to new. John Kotter's Eight-Stage Change Model, for instance, is useful in focusing the energy of the organizational change process on desired goals and objectives.

Break into teams. Imagine it is Jan 2, 2025, and that your team is the student government organization. Since the start of the fall semester, you have been struggling with indifference and low participation in your sponsored events and activities. You continually lose money on the events and the dean has threatened to cut your budget by 50 percent if attendance doesn't increase by 25 percent by the end of the summer. Using Kotter's Eight-Stage Change Model, create a plan to change participation and interest in your events.

1. How will you create a sense of urgency among the student body? How will you engage them logically and emotionally?
2. Do you have the right people onboard? Who else might you need?
3. What is your vision for the student body?
4. Do you have a robust communication plan?
5. Have you engaged a team of advocates outside of your team?
6. What small gains can you achieve to build momentum?
7. How will you continue the momentum?
8. What does success, or change, look like for your team? For your school?

ETHICAL LEADERSHIP
Foreclosuregate

The incremental changes that led to the worldwide financial crisis of the last decade have had a far-reaching effects for consumers, particularly homeowners. For instance, when subprime lending changed the traditional rules for mortgage qualification, people who would not previously have qualified for a mortgage were given loans and home sales skyrocketed. Then, when the economic crisis burst the housing bubble, foreclosures skyrocketed.

In small groups, research the robo-signing mortgage foreclosure debacle, or "Foreclosuregate," of the last few years. Robo-signing is a term used by consumer advocates to describe the robotic process involved in the mass production of false and forged execution of mortgage foreclosures and other legal documents related to foreclosures. Too often, for example, mortgage company employees would sign off on these foreclosures when the notaries and witnesses required were not present. Once you have identified the issue(s), answer the following questions:

1. Do employees of banks and mortgage companies have an ethical obligation to question the process of mass robo-signing? Who has ultimate responsibility for the mistreatment of hundreds of thousands of homeowners by banks and lenders?

2. Is it OK to change the rules (by not having notaries and witnesses present at foreclosure signings) in an attempt to remedy an issue that began when lending rules changed (with subprime lending)?

3. What ethical issues are apparent in the practice of robo-signing?

4. Identify whether actual laws were broken and where the line between unethical and illegal may have been crossed.

5. It is easy to assume that all responsibility for this debacle lies with banks and their employees. What about customers? How can/should customers attempt to gather information about a loan before they sign? What if there are roadblocks to getting information? What if customers realize they don't understand the "fine print"?

6. Identify some of the changes that need to occur to prevent this from happening again.

KEY TERMS

Change, *p. 216*

Positive emotional attractor, *p. 219*

Negative emotional attractor, *p. 219*

Hope, *p. 220*

Optimism, *p. 220*

Gestalt cycle of experience, *p. 221*

Diversity, *p. 228*

Top-down changes, *p. 230*

Bottom-up changes, *p. 230*

Investment banks, *p. 232*

Net capital rule, *p. 232*

Leveraging money, *p. 232*

Housing Boom, *p. 233*

Predatory lending, *p. 233*

Subprime lending, *p. 233*

Underemployment, *p. 234*

Permanent white water, *p. 237*

MyManagementLab

Go to **mymanagementlab.com** for Auto-graded writing questions as well as the following Assisted-graded writing questions:

7-1. In recent years, businesses have become more global, and populations have become more diverse. In addition, sustainability has become more important than ever to many businesses. What kinds of changes might an organization choose to begin in order to deal with these societal shifts?

7-2. Choose a simple example of a situation in which you wanted others to change. Apply the Gestalt cycle of experience to the situation, noting the actions you could take at each point.

7-2. Mymanagementlab Only — comprehensive writing assignment for this chapter.

1. What Is Change and Why Is It So Important for You as a Leader? (pp. 216–218)

Objective: Define change.

Summary: Change is all around us, and it's quite important to us, as evidenced by, the many words we use to describe it. Both employees and managers need to be aware of how pervasive change is today. We must also understand our personal attitudes to change, and how to support change in individuals, groups, organizations, and communities. We need to adapt and change ourselves to meet the different and ever-changing demands of the world around us.

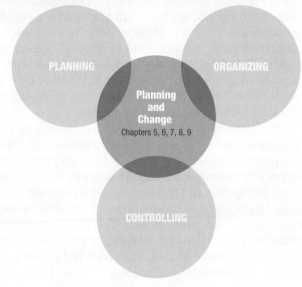

PLANNING

ORGANIZING

Planning and Change
Chapters 5, 6, 7, 8, 9

CONTROLLING

2. How Do People Change? (pp. 219–225)

Objective: Learn how you and other people change.

Summary: We know from our own experience that individual change is difficult and exciting, but it can be stressful, too. One way to support personal change is to imagine a compelling vision of the future. Hope and optimism will focus your attention and give you energy to change. This is the first step in intentional change—a model that includes focusing on a positive view of the future *first*, then on the reality of your current situation, then on planning. When leading change in an organization or community, it also helps to think about the Gestalt cycle of experience, which focuses on mobilizing energy before engaging in actions.

3. How Do Societal Shifts Lead to Organizational Changes? (pp. 225–230)

Objective: Recognize drivers of change in organizations.

Summary: Technology, globalization, social shifts, and changes in our desire to preserve the natural environment are four trends driving profound changes in businesses and societies today. Technology affects just about everything at work and it's constantly changing. Globalization brings about different ways for people and companies to interact, enhances competition, and has contributed to shifts in economic power. Social changes occur rapidly and transparently, as evidenced by the Arab Spring, and this transparency is prompting more and more people to call for changes in human rights and access to education and other services. Finally, increased attention to sustainability and the environment has become a way for companies to improve our world and their businesses at the same time. These four trends—along with important changes in the world economy and the diversity and inclusion imperative—are fueling rapid changes across the globe.

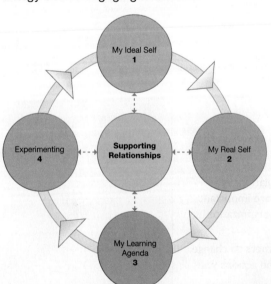

My Ideal Self
1

Experimenting
4

Supporting Relationships

My Real Self
2

My Learning Agenda
3

6. What Practical Models Can Help Us Manage Change in Organizations? (pp. 238–243)

Objective: Describe which practical models are useful tools for managing change in organizations.

Summary: John Kotter created an eight-stage model for approaching organizational change, beginning with "Ensure that people feel an urgent need for change" and ending with "Solidify the change in the organizational culture." He argued that each step must be attended to in order to ensure that change does not fail. Gregory Shea created a work systems model identifying organizational levers that can be attended to during change processes. Multiple levers must be engaged simultaneously for change to be effective. Additionally, because change is constant, we have to determine what to pay attention to, what to change, and what to ignore.

> **John Kotter's Stages of Effective Organizational Change**
>
> Stage 1: Ensure that people feel an urgent need for change.
> Stage 2: Get the right people involved to lead change.
> Stage 3: Create a new strategic vision.
> Stage 4: Make sure the new vision is effectively communicated.
> Stage 5: Empower a broad group of change agents.
> Stage 6: Successfully pull off short-term victories.
> Stage 7: Consolidate the victories and go after more changes.
> Stage 8: Solidify the change in the organizational culture.

5. Which Models Can Help Us Understand the Dynamics of Change? (pp. 235–237)

Objective: List and describe models that assist in understanding change.

Summary: Kurt Lewin's force field analysis model is useful when considering change in an organization. Lewin presented change as occurring in three steps: status quo, an unfreezing or changing phase, and a refreezing phase that sets the new status quo. Peter Vaill suggested that, instead of existing in either frozen or changing phases, organizations instead are in permanent white water—or a constant state of change.

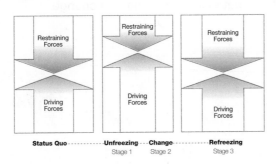

4. What Is the Difference between Incremental and Transformational Change? (pp. 230–235)

Objective: Identify the difference between incremental and transformational change.

Summary: Tuning, adaptation, reorientation, and re-creation describe four approaches to change. Tuning and adaptation are incremental approaches to change. Reorientation and re-creation are transformational approaches. Traditionally, incremental change has been seen as easier to manage. However, even slow changes can be difficult to manage and even dangerous if ignored: Witness the recent recession and global financial industry meltdown, which was the result of decades of incremental changes.

9. A Final Word on Change (p. 249)

Summary: Change is a difficult process that elicits a broad range of reactions from people. To be successful in a changing world, it helps to understand what people need and how changes will help them or hurt them. If you understand others, you will be more likely to help them to see how the organization's new vision can be meaningful and beneficial to them, too.

8. What Can We All Do to Support Change? (pp. 246–249)

Objective: Understand how you can change and develop yourself.

Summary: There are two useful approaches to becoming a positive contributor to change in your organization: First, you can see yourself as a change agent, no matter what job you hold. A change agent needs to be able to access, or know how to access, organizational resources, decision-making opportunities, and the current culture in the organization, and have the emotional intelligence and people skills to move that culture toward the path of change. Second, you can use empathy and inspiration to help deal with resistance during a change process. Being positive and committed to change can help manage the resistance of those around you. It will also help you face unwelcome change in your organization or personal life. No matter what type of change you face, it helps to remember that change can be hard and that you must face it with courage.

7. What Can HR Do to Foster Effective Change? (pp. 243–246)

Objective: Learn how HR can foster effective change.

Summary: HR often leads change by engaging in organizational development—systematic processes to improve organizational systems, culture, and leadership practices. One tool that is very helpful in diagnosing groups and organizations is called action research. Action research furthers knowledge but sees a researcher as a participant in a situation, not just an observer. This can lead to better and more precise knowledge of what aspects of an organization must be changed and how to do it, and can facilitate HR leaders, ability to teach organizational leaders and employees important competencies for managing change.

CHAPTER 8

Workplace Essentials:

Creativity, Innovation, and a Spirit of Entrepreneurship

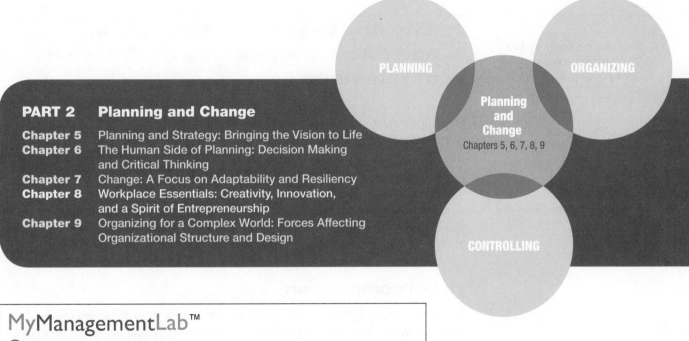

PLANNING

ORGANIZING

Planning
and
Change
Chapters 5, 6, 7, 8, 9

CONTROLLING

MyManagementLab™

⭐ **Improve Your Grade!**

Over 10 million students improved their results using the Pearson MyLabs.
Visit **mymanagementlab.com** for simulations, tutorials, and end-of-chapter
problems.

Chapter Outline

1. Why Are Creativity, Innovation, and Entrepreneurship
   at the Heart of Business? (pp. 258–259)

2. What Is Creativity? (pp. 259–262)

3. How Can We Encourage Creativity at Work?
   (pp. 262–264)

4. What Is Innovation and Why Is It Important?
   (pp. 264–268)

5. How Can We Foster Innovation in People and Companies?
   (pp. 268–271)

6. What Is Entrepreneurship? (pp. 271–275)

7. What Is Intrepreneurship? (pp. 275–276)

8. How Does a New Business Get Started? (pp. 276–282)

9. What Is HR's Role in Supporting Creativity, Innovation,
   and Entrepreneurship? (pp. 282–284)

10. What Can We All Do to Be More Creative, Innovative,
    and Entrepreneurial? (pp. 284–285)

11. A Final Word on Creativity, Innovation,
    and Entrepreneurship (p. 286)

Chapter Objectives

8.1 Explain why creativity,
     innovation, and entrepreneurship
     are critical to business.

8.2 Define creativity.

8.3 Learn how to encourage
     creativity at work.

8.4 Define innovation and describe
     its importance.

8.5 Understand how to foster
     innovation.

8.6 Define entrepreneurship.

8.7 Learn about intrepreneurship.

8.8 Describe how a new business
     gets started.

8.9 Outline HR's role in supporting
     creativity, innovation, and
     entrepreneurship.

8.10 List ways you can be more
     creative, innovative, and
     entrepreneurial.

Hypercompetition
A state of constant and escalating
competition.

1. Why Are Creativity, Innovation, and Entrepreneurship at the Heart of Business?

To stay relevant in an ever-changing world, leaders must foster an environment that encourages creativity, innovation, and an organization-wide spirit of entrepreneur-ship. As you have learned, organizational leaders also need to avoid defensive reactions to change. Leaders need to focus on sustainable success and avoid over-focusing on short-term results. The new rules for success in business include learning how to excel in an environment of **hypercompetition**—a state of constant and escalating competition. All of this means we need to be creative, to bring our ideas to life in innovative products and services, and to approach our work with the attitude of an entrepreneur—empowered, energized, and totally committed to our mission.

Hypercompetition

Professor Richard D'Aveni is credited with coining the term *hypercompetition*. In his book, he argues that hypercompetition is characterized by a rapid escalation of competition in pricing, quality, and development of new technologies and processes, as well as competition to enter new global markets.[1] Hypercompetition has become the norm in many industries.[2]

Bold and aggressive actions result in constant changes in the market, which can be seen in the shortening of product life cycles (how long a product is viable) and product design cycles (how long it takes to design new products), as well as the rush to develop new technologies. Think about smartphones—new ones are in development constantly (■ **EXHIBIT 8.1**). Is this the case because companies think you really need a new phone? Or is it because these companies will be left behind if they don't innovate as fast as their competitors?

Another source of hypercompetition is the frequent entry of new competitors onto the scene, which makes competitive advantages difficult to maintain. This leads companies to compete on price or quality, or to increase efficiencies in the production of goods or delivery of services, and to rely on innovation.[3]

Hypercompetition increases uncertainty. Scholars have argued that due to the constant change present in hypercompetitive environments, managers cannot rely on traditional frameworks for making sense of the competitive landscape (such as SWOT analysis and the BCG matrix).[4] Today's competitive environment calls for constant attention to creativity, innovation, and entrepreneurship. Simply put: We need to learn how to do things differently.

Adopt a Long-Term Outlook and Embrace Innovation

Sometimes, the response to uncertainty is to react defensively and slip into crisis management. Too often in business, this means focusing on short-term results or overcontrolling people and processes. When a company puts too much emphasis on short-term financial results while cutting corners on investments in new products and services, it can find itself unable to compete, out of date, or even out of business within a few years. And when people are micromanaged, good ideas that can solve problems dry up.

Another common misconception is that when in crisis, leaders should become more autocratic. In some situations this may be true, such as when there is a fire in the building and people aren't leaving the building. However, in most cases, allowing

■ **EXHIBIT 8.1**

How does the iPhone remain in-novative in the hypercompetitive smartphone market?

Source: Oleksiy Maksymenko/Alamy

people closest to the work to make decisions will yield better results, in part because these very people are the ones who can generate new knowledge, creativity, and innovation.[5]

Controlling employees too tightly or focusing on short-term financial results rarely supports creativity, innovation, or an entrepreneurial mind-set. Yet, we see such short-term and over-controlling mind-sets in many companies, even after the onset of the Great Recession.[6] In this chapter, we will help you to learn how you can move away from such dysfunctional ways of operating. You will learn how to create environments that support entrepreneurship, creativity, and innovation. You will also examine how we can all think and behave in ways that help people and companies rise to the top in our exciting—but challenging and turbulent—environments. Specifically, we will explore the art and science of creativity and innovation, and we will look at how to foster a spirit of entrepreneurship at work.

In this chapter, you will also explore how creative ideas can be turned into innovations that support businesses, organizations, and communities. You will learn what it takes to be an entrepreneur and what you can do to be successful. Finally, you will consider some of the things you will need to understand about HR in small businesses, as well as what we can all do to develop our own creativity.

Discussion Questions

1. Have you ever been in a situation where a manager, teacher, or another authority figure was controlling your actions too much? What did that do to your desire to be creative and to help that person achieve his or her goals?

2. Have you ever dreamed of owning your own business? Which aspects of this idea are attractive to you? Which are daunting or frightening, and which don't you understand very well yet?

---

2. What Is Creativity?

Objective 8.2
Define creativity.

Creativity is the process of imagining and developing something new. We often associate creativity with artists and writers, but it is at the heart of all work. Creativity can be the source of an idea that explains something (like gravity or the theory of relativity), or it can be something tangible (such as a work of art, a product, or a new process). For example, the marketing professional who devises a new slogan is using his or her creativity. Likewise, the factory worker who continually encounters a bottleneck (an area where production slows due to limits of equipment, supplies, or other resources) and thinks of ways to relieve it is also being creative.

Why is creativity so important today? There's a simple answer: The way we work, manage, and lead organizations has changed because the environment has changed. We need to find new ways to build, organize, and position businesses for success; new ways to engage and motivate employees at all levels; and new ways to face even more changes. We need curiosity and courage, and we need new ideas. All of these require creativity.

Are you creative? Do you know friends or family who are? Many people do not see themselves as very creative. They reserve the term for musicians, artists, dancers, and the like, as well as the special few, such as Facebook founder Mark Zuckerberg or Microsoft founder Bill Gates. In actuality, we can all be creative. As you can see in

■ **EXHIBIT 8.2**, many factors affect creativity, all of which are available to you and many of which can be developed.

Creativity
The process of imagining and developing something new.

■ **EXHIBIT 8.2**

Factors Affecting Creativity

Factor	Explanation
Knowledge	Creativity always involves a combination of new ideas and existing knowledge.[7]
Age	The prefrontal cortex, which is an important area of the brain for creativity and memory, does not fully mature until we reach our early 20s, and may also be one of the first to deteriorate as we get older.[8]
Positive outlook	Research has connected positive emotions to performance on cognitive tests.[9] There is also a connection between positive emotions and the ability to take in new information.[10]
Cognitive flexibility	Cognitive flexibility is a person's ability to break out of traditional or conventional patterns of thought, as well as to identify more abstract concepts and principles.[11] Replacing the language of "certainty" with the language of "possibility" removes mental barriers and allows for more cognitive flexibility.[12] Cognitive flexibility can also include the ability to embrace paradoxical ideas.[13]
Working memory and sustained attention	Working memory can help us use existing knowledge and generate new ideas. Sustained attention can be limited by how much information can be held in working memory.[14]
Self-esteem	People who have high self-esteem are able to engage in independent thought and action despite criticism.[15] They also tend to have a more positive outlook, which affects their ability to learn and to stay motivated.[16]
"Rogue" behavior and avoiding conformity	People who defy the status quo are less inclined to slip into traditional mind-sets and more inclined to challenge assumptions that never were or no longer are valid.[17]
Mindfulness	Mindfulness is a state in which we are awake, aware, and attuned to ourselves, others, and our environment. This enables us to be more fully aware of all that is happening inside as while also being tuned in to what is going on around us.[18]

Our brains are literally wired for creativity—we just need to cultivate our abilities and use them more often. In the following sections, we will look at some common ways of talking about and explaining creativity, and then we will discuss research about how our brains support creative thinking and actions.

Convergent and Divergent Thinking

It is not easy to describe creativity. Part of the reason for this is that creativity happens inside an individual or among individuals as they work together. Because creativity is so hard to see, people often take shortcuts to explain it. For example, it is commonly thought that outcome-oriented, or convergent thinking, is not creative, whereas more open divergent thought processes are creative. This is an oversimplification and not entirely accurate.

Convergent thinking is an analytical thought process that follows the steps and rules of logic.[19] **Divergent thinking** is a thought process that relies on the generation of many ideas, random connections, observations, and interpretations. Divergent thinking is often spontaneous and relies more on pattern recognition than on isolated facts and logic to work out problems.

The confusion about how creativity links to convergent and divergent thinking has existed for years.[20] Specifically, it has been argued that creativity is linked most directly to divergent thinking.[21] This view would mean that logic and creativity are in opposition to each other—that somehow, logic is the absence of creativity, and vice versa. The innovative researcher Arne Dietrich wants to destroy the myth that creativity and divergent thinking are synonymous, and that convergent thinking is not involved in creative thinking.[22] For instance, convergent thinking involves examining identified patterns and developing meanings by exploring and understanding the complex relationships among diverse pieces of information. Such processes are inherently creative.[23]

Convergent thinking
An analytical thought process that follows the steps and rules of logic.

Divergent thinking
A thought process that relies on the generation of many ideas, random connections, observations, and interpretations.

Creativity is a complicated process that involves many parts of the brain, not just those that link to divergent thought. As long as we continue to promote the myth that only divergent thinking involves creativity, we are less likely to recognize creativity in ourselves or to help others develop creativity in themselves. Another common myth that we need to examine (and do away with) is that creativity is linked to one half of the brain and not the other.

The Left versus Right Brain Myth

Dr. Arne Dietrich also attacks another myth about creativity: the idea that creative thought occurs only in the right brain, and logical thought occurs only in the left brain. There is no evidence that creativity is controlled by the right brain.[24] Many regions, processes, and types of neurological activities are involved in creativity (■ **EXHIBIT 8.3**). Depending on the type of creative work being done, these activities can be both profoundly different and located in different parts of the brain.[25]

The idea that there are right-brained and left-brained people is a popular myth. Michael Corballis, an early pioneer of split brain research, warned in 1980 that thinking of creativity in terms of right versus left brain could not be supported by actual research.[26] So why does this myth continue? Political economist Catherine Weaver calls the left-brain/right-brain hype "dichotomania," and suggests that the myth says more about society's need to classify and categorize than it does about logic or creativity.[27] Let's examine some of the more recent research about the neuroscience of creativity.

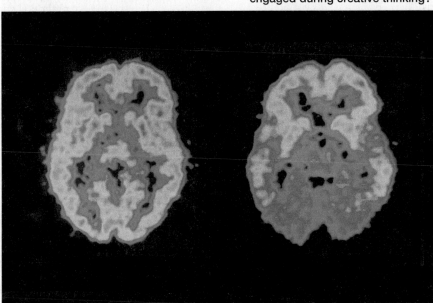

Source: Medical-on-line/Mediscan/Alamy

■ **EXHIBIT 8.3**
What parts of the brain are engaged during creative thinking?

The Neuroscience of Creativity: Thinking *and* Feeling

Neurological activities related to creativity are difficult to isolate.[28] According to Dr. Dietrich, two streams of neurological activity seem to be related to creativity. One is the *knowledge domain*, which includes both thoughts and feelings. The other is the *processing mode*, which includes sustained, deliberate effort and spontaneous generation of creative thoughts.[29] Research has also shown that during focused creative activity, the brain actually shuts down certain regions, blocking unnecessary information in order to preserve cognitive resources for the creative effort.[30] In other words, specific parts of the brain slow down the processing of some kinds of information so that the conscious mind can focus on a creative task. However, when the task involves using language, this slowed-down processing state is not activated, suggesting that there is a difference between verbal and nonverbal creativity in how the brain functions.[31]

Based on information learned about the knowledge domains and processing modes of creativity, Dietrich proposes that there are *four different domains of creativity*, depending on whether the brain processes information through its emotional centers or through its cognitive centers, and whether the process is deliberate or spontaneous.[32] These four types of creativity are shown in ■ **EXHIBIT 8.4**, which is adapted from Dietrich's work.

■ **EXHIBIT 8.4**

Four Types of Creativity			
		Knowledge Domain	
		Emotional	**Cognitive**
Processing Mode	**Deliberate**	Insights start in the prefrontal cortex, which recruits attention processes to locate and access emotional memories, which are stored in emotional structures. Example: Insight during therapy or coaching	Insights start in the prefrontal cortex, which recruits attention processes to enhance perception and to direct the search in long-term memory for relevant information. Example: Thomas Edison's inventing style, which was systematic and exhaustive
	Spontaneous	Insights begin in the limbic system, and then higher-level emotional processing is continued in other parts of the brain, such as areas of the prefrontal cortex.[33] Example: Artistic inspirations, epiphanies, revelations	Insights originate in the areas that process perceptions (possibly where unconscious learning and automatic behavior occur and originate). These unconscious thoughts "break into" the working memory of the prefrontal cortex, where they can then be consciously processed. Example: The "Eureka!" moment

Source: Adapted from Dietrich, Arne. 2004. The cognitive neuroscience of creativity. *Psychonomic Bulletin and Review, 11*(6): 1011–1026.

Creativity is complicated. Yet, it is a process that is natural for human beings and one that we can all enjoy and benefit from. Thoughts, feelings, knowledge, experience, age, and several other factors affect our creativity, as do conditions in our workplaces. In the next section we will explore how creativity can be enhanced at work.

Discussion Questions

1. Review the factors affecting creativity in Exhibit 8.2. For each of these factors, identify a situation in which the factor helped you to be creative. Which factor do you find has the greatest influence on your creativity? In which of these factors do you feel you excel when it comes to creativity?

2. Do you consider yourself a predominantly convergent or divergent thinker? Explain and give examples.

Objective 8.3
Learn how to encourage creativity at work.

3. How Can We Encourage Creativity at Work?

The first step to more creativity at work is establishing an environment where it is valued and rewarded. Surprisingly, far too many of our organizations do a lot to kill creativity rather than encourage it. Take, for example, a manager we know who is often described by his employees as "grumpy" and "old school." This man is quite talented and has years of experience, which means he could be quite valuable to the organization. However, people hate to work with him. He first ridicules and then kills any idea he doesn't personally come up with. He wants things to remain exactly as they were in the past. In addition, even when projects come in under budget and are very high quality, he complains and criticizes his employees. The result: Every single member of his team has stopped offering ideas. This manager is a liability to his organization.

The reason this manager is a liability is because he is killing the creativity that is needed today to meet all kinds of challenges, such as unexpected opportunities, falling sales, rising costs, unsafe working conditions, and so on. The ability to approach these challenges in new ways is important to both short- and long-term success. How can leaders develop an organizational culture where creativity is viewed as valuable?[34] Let's look at five steps leaders can take to foster creativity: challenging the status quo, encouraging challenging debate, ensuring that the workforce is diverse, supporting people in taking risks, and providing a work environment that supports relaxation and conversation.

Developing a Culture Where Creativity Is Valued

Leaders can create a culture that supports creativity by engaging in certain behaviors themselves, and encouraging others to do the same. Let's look at five ways to do this:

1. *Challenge the status quo:* Some companies struggle with creativity because policies and procedures remain as they have been for decades. Companies where challenging the status quo is encouraged will be competitive because doing things the same way as in the past does not work in the twenty-first century. An example of a company that breaks the status quo barrier is Procter & Gamble (P&G). Creative P&G employees are supported in questioning the unquestionable. One result is that the common household mop was completely redesigned. The Swiffer is P&G's twenty-first-century mop, and it uses electrostatic attraction rather than water to remove dirt.[35]

2. *Encourage challenging debate:* Brainstorming conventions often discourage criticism of ideas based on the assumption that a safe space is needed for people to feel comfortable generating ideas.[36] While brainstorming can help people generate ideas, it is not enough because it isn't a good process for making a determination of their quality.[37] Creativity is encouraged in settings where groups challenge and defend ideas through debate. This is because dissent stimulates divergent thinking by challenging assumptions that get in the way of novelty.[38] Additionally, researchers have found that debate, itself, sparks idea generation.[39]

3. *Build a diverse workforce:* Creativity among employees occurs more often when groups and the entire workforce are composed of people with different perspectives. Companies who continually hire the same types of people end up with "cookie-cutter" employees who all think alike. This is not how innovation and creativity happen. Creativity and innovation emerge when varying perspectives are applied to problems. Different perspectives come from people who have different cultures, backgrounds, experience, training, education, and careers. Unilever, the multinational company with brands including Dove, Axe, Vaseline, and Lipton, believes strongly in diversity as a foundation for creativity and innovation. For Unilever, diversity means everything from age, nationality, and gender to level of expertise and years with the company. For this firm, the broad diversity in its research and development function has resulted in highly creative products and marketing.[40]

4. *Encourage risk-taking:* Employees should feel comfortable taking risks and making mistakes. One roadblock to creativity occurs when people feel that offering up a suggestion will result in humiliation or even just being ignored. People will simply not make their ideas known if they believe they won't be heard. They surely won't share creative ideas if they fear being punished for taking risks.

5. *Provide a comfortable, thought-provoking work environment:* Managers can foster creativity by providing physical spaces for groups to meet and thoughts to flow. Designating spaces for talking and quiet places for reflection are just a few examples of how this can be done. For instance, employees working for the American Industrial Hygiene Association in Virginia decided to create their own space for creative thoughts. They worked together to choose color schemes, furniture, and so on, and for a small budget they crafted a creativity room for employee use.[41]

The suggestions in this section are useful guidelines for promoting creativity. Can you suggest a few more radical guidelines?

Discussion Questions

1. Consultants and HR professionals use a wide variety of role-plays, games, and other experiential exercises to foster creativity in training sessions. One such exercise involves presenting a mundane object to participants, who must generate a list of all possible uses for this object. With two or three of your friends or classmates, see how many uses you can think of for a nail, leaf, penny, and spoon.

2. Why would you want to avoid working on a problem with people who have solved similar problems in the past? Explain.

Objective 8.4
Define innovation and describe its importance.

Innovation
The process of implementing new ideas.

4. What Is Innovation and Why Is It Important?

The word *innovation* is everywhere in the business press. Scholars study it, consultants and advisers promise to foster it, and leaders obsess about it. But why? What is it? **Innovation** is the process of implementing new ideas. Businesses, organizations, and communities of all kinds have reasons to focus on innovation, starting with the fact that our social, economic, political, technological, and environmental conditions have changed tremendously in recent years.

Innovation is happening everywhere, at every level of society and in business. For example, let's look at one innovative business practice that helps people, communities, and a company called Comcast. Comcast is a media giant. Founded in 1963 as American Cable Systems, the company grew rapidly within the cable TV and broadband services industries. More recently, they have expanded to include phone services, quickly expanding to be one of the nation's largest providers.[42] In 2011, they joined forces with NBC Universal—a solid move into the media environment.[43]

Throughout its history, Comcast has supported the communities where it does business. Recently the company devised a very innovative program to address the technology gap between the poor and those who are more financially secure. The Comcast program offered nationwide in the United States is called *Internet Essentials*, and it is designed for low-income families with school-aged children for up to three full school years. Internet service is provided at an affordable monthly fee, and at the time of signing up, families have the opportunity to purchase a low-cost netbook-style laptop for a very low price.[44] One benefit that Comcast leaders no doubt are betting on: new, loyal customers.

Throughout this textbook we have emphasized the fundamental changes in the world of technology, economics, and society in general. Every aspect of life and society is touched by such changes. In the best cases, this leads to innovation in all sectors: business, health care, and education, to name just a few.

Worldwide, education is changing dramatically. New technologies have enabled people to access information and research while learning in the comfort of their own homes and offices. This isn't entirely new, obviously. Distance learning (formal education and training via the Internet) and open educational resources (free access to research and other information) have been around for well more than a decade. More innovation is needed, however. Many educators are grappling with how to change professors' and academia's approach to teaching and learning to bring education into the new era. Fortunately for students, with each year we see many more outstanding examples of innovation in this realm.

Innovation: What It Looks Like in the Business World

In 1993, organizational scholar Peter Drucker proclaimed that knowledge was "the only meaningful resource."[45] However true this may be, knowledge itself does not lead to innovation. Rather, it is knowledge applied by groups of people in new, meaningful, and creative ways that results in innovation. Take the example of Netflix, an online movie-rental company. Netflix revolutionized the video rental industry, but is being replaced by more—and more flexible—companies. Founded in 1997, Netflix went public in 2002.[46] By 2010, it had 12 million active subscribers.[47] The company had no physical stores to contend with, while its main competitor at the time, Blockbuster, had stores all over the United States and beyond. Although Blockbuster eventually moved toward a Netflix-type model, it was reluctant to let go of its physical presence, and by 2010, it was faced with the forced closure of a thousand stores and filed for bankruptcy. This is a clear warning: Innovation that comes late in the game is not innovation at all.

Netflix tried to overcome other limitations, starting with a time delay of several days between customers' selection of a video and getting it in the mail. People didn't like waiting and they didn't like late fees. When streaming video became feasible for movies, some of these problems were solved as Netflix offered instant access to videos through its Web site (■ **EXHIBIT 8.5**).[48]

The company tried to continue to innovate and include the involvement of people outside the company in problem solving. For example, they launched the Netflix Prize, which is an award of $1 million to anyone who could help to improve services.[49] To the company's credit, they awarded the prize in 2009 to BellKor's Pragmatic Chaos team, which beat Netflix's own algorithm for predicting ratings by 10 percent.

Despite all of this, the market in this particular industry requires constant innovation and instantaneous implementation of new ideas. Today, Netflix is in disfavor due to dramatically increasing costs over a short period of time and botching the rollout of their online streaming services.[50] As innovative as this company was, it seems to have lost its edge—something that is not at all uncommon in the technology and media

Source: NetPics/Alamy

sectors. Companies such as Hulu, an Internet service that offers thousands of television shows and movies, are honing in on the market. Hulu allows people to use the service for free, but with programs such as Hulu+, paying customers have access to a wider variety of movies and television shows, as well as earlier access to the most popular shows.[51]

Some companies have gone beyond innovating just their products and services to looking at ways to engage in business that supports profits *and* the environment.[52] These companies consider not only what people want and need, but how the product should "fit" into the overall environment (both business and natural). For many companies, this makes good business sense while also doing the right thing for a wide range of stakeholders. Consider the following *Business Case* on Seventh Generation, a company that produces green cleaning products.

Most Innovative Companies and Products

Innovative companies like Seventh Generation and Netflix are not alone in focusing an incredible amount of energy, time, and money on finding new and better ways

Seventh Generation

Innovation and a Long-Term View

Many breakthroughs in human history were driven by challenges to long-held assumptions and beliefs. One prominent challenge facing the world today is this: Can organizations sell environmentally friendly products and still make a profit? Many people see sustainability and profitability as incompatible. Others, however, have tested the waters and found that there is no contradiction, and that producing and selling sustainable products can actually be highly profitable.

In 2009, Vermont-based Seventh Generation was the largest American wholesale distributor dedicated to environmentally friendly household products, from diapers to cleaning and laundry products and paper solutions.[53] In 2008, the company recorded sales of more than $150 million.[54] Given Seventh Generation's two decades of success, many say they were the first company to understand the potential value of green products in the U.S. market even before "going green" became a key competitive advantage.[55]

Clearly, Seventh Generation's product line is innovative (although more and more companies are getting into the business of green products). The company's business model is also innovative. To start, the name "Seventh Generation" comes from the teachings of the Native American Iroquois Confederacy: "In our every deliberation, we must consider the impact of our decisions on the next seven generations."[56] Seventh Generation takes a strong stand that, for a business to succeed, it must take this long-term view in everything it does: from the type of products

it manufactures, to relationships it builds with customers and suppliers, to the way employees work.[57] This company's belief is that economic, environmental, and social systems are actually influenced by each individual activity of an organization, so the organization is responsible for attending to its actions at all levels of the value chain, even including vendors and suppliers outside the company.[58]

For example, Seventh Generation has adopted a truly innovative way to think about what products *really* cost. Their approach goes beyond consideration of the costs of raw materials, production, people, and transportation of goods to market. Instead, the company also considers the costs of resource utilization and production in terms of their impact on the environment.[59] Here's what this looks like: At this time, organic and green products tend to cost more because they can be more expensive to produce. Seventh Generation's point of view, however, is that if you tally the *real* costs, *nongreen products are more expensive in the long term* because of their negative impact on the environment, so they *should* cost more than green products.[60] This new approach promotes an organization's responsibility to cover the cost of producing goods, *and* things like the cost of replacing raw materials, disposal, and potential reuse of goods.[61] This is a truly innovative approach.

Innovators like Seventh Generation discover new ground and make us think differently about what we are doing, buying, and selling. As Co-Founder and former President and CEO Jeff Hollender puts it: "Seventh Generation is really in the business of helping people make more thoughtful and conscientious choices about how they lead their lives. Raising consciousness is a large part of why we are in business."[62]

---

to position themselves and their products in the marketplace. In fact, this issue is so important that a number of prominent business magazines track the most innovative companies and the most innovative products. For example, an interesting list of innovative companies and products can be found on *Fast Company*'s Web site (■ **EXHIBIT 8.6**).[63] *Fast Company*'s list is creative because it looks at many more issues than financial performance or short-term impact on the market. *Fast Company* tries to choose innovative companies and institutions that matter to real people. For comparison, take a look at ■ **EXHIBIT 8.7** to see what some 20-somethings think were the most innovative products of the past decade or so.

Innovation is a key long-term strategy for business. So, while we might assume that a few geniuses are coming up with the products and services, most innovations in products and services take years of collective effort and tremendous investment. But, when it pays off, a product or service can pay off big and take the market by storm—as the iPad did, for example.

So far in this chapter, we have looked at what innovation looks like in businesses. This can include a wide range of types of innovations, such as offering better services, more advanced products, increased efficiency, more effective marketing, decreased cost, or innovations that support communities and the environment. Today, innovation needs to be central to most business plans or companies risk becoming obsolete quickly.[64] So how do businesses ensure that they are innovative? We will explore that next.

■ **EXHIBIT 8.6**

Fast Company's Top 10 Most Innovative Companies of 2012

1. Apple: With new CEO Tim Cook at the helm, Apple continues its legacy of tech industry domination. The iPad controls the tablet market and with Siri, the iPhone 4S personal assistant, Apple introduced a premier technology that left Google and Amazon scrambling to compete.

2. Facebook: By exposing an ever-expanding global membership base to display advertising, the social network is poised to reap astronomical profits.

3. Google: Moving forward in what some consider a plan for total Web domination, the search engine superpower added YouTube to its family and burst into the Android scene, amassing a fortune in mobile revenues via its partnership with Apple iPhones.

4. Amazon: By claiming the number two tablet spot with the Kindle Fire and acquiring e-commerce company Quidsi (a conglomerate of Web-based merchants offering products ranging from diapers to household essentials), Amazon continues to expand its reach into the online marketplace.

5. Square: With an idea once considered "naive" by the financial world, Square founder and CEO (and Twitter cofounder) Jack Dorsey combined a simple credit card reader with an iPhone and opened the doors for nearly anyone to accept credit card payments.

6. Twitter: Using a maximum of 140 characters per tweet, Twitter sparked a worldwide conversation and created a platform for sharing international current events in real time.

7. Occupy Movement: Harnessing the power of the Web, Occupy Movement united an international network of protesters dedicated to opposing businesses and organizations that promote social and economic inequality.

8. Tencent: With earnings of $1 billion per quarter, Tencent—China's most popular instant messaging computer program—now offers an assortment of products, including games and apps. Tencent has emerged as the world's third-largest publicly traded Internet company.

9. Life Technologies: Among other services, this innovative global biotechnology corporation has the means to quickly identify genetic strains of infectious diseases (e.g., *E. coli*) and to create tests for use in identifying the source of the outbreak.

10. Solar City: While other solar companies are collapsing, Solar City is building its client list. In large part, its success can be attributed to offering a full range of customer care; the company maintains and finances each solar system after installation.

■ **EXHIBIT 8.7**

A Group of 20-Somethings Love These Innovative Products and Services

According to a diverse group of young people, the most innovative gadgets range from entertainment products to specific technologies, including GPS systems and mobile phones. The following top-innovative product list was created by this group of 20-somethings. As they put it, "It's not scientific, but we had a lot of fun putting it together!!"

1. Phone apps! GPS, games, restaurant listings, etc.—everything is so accessible!

2. Online learning—college students don't even have to attend class anymore.

3. 4G—speed of the Internet and communication at the tips of your fingers.

4. Ever-evolving Apple products—iPad 3 is amazing! And iPhone 4's Siri is saving people time from thinking. Can't forget the MacBook Pro!!

5. Car share—i.e., Zipcar . . . saves 20-somethings the hassle of car payments, insurance, etc.

6. Online dating—OkCupid is the new bar minus the awkward small talk and saves you a few bucks—no buying drinks, either!

7. The cloud—unlimited space to store all of your music, photos, info, everything, online.

8. Video conferencing—Skype, Facetime, etc., —the new way to stay in touch with family and friends and still feel the one-to-one connection.

9. Kindle Fire—the newest way to read books without all the weight.

10. Online couponing—Groupon and Social Living help you get the best deals on activities in your city.

Discussion Questions

1. Do you think innovation in business is done primarily for market competitiveness and profit? Why else might a business engage in innovation?

2. Is innovation always good? When and where has innovation had a negative impact? What are some of the ethical dilemmas associated with innovation in the music and communication industries?

Objective 8.5
Understand how to foster innovation.

5. How Can We Foster Innovation in People and Companies?

The lists in the previous section point to several companies that can teach us about innovation. However, these lists also spark a question: Are *companies* themselves innovative, or are the *people* in companies innovative? The answer is both. For a company to be innovative, it must have creative people who can take their own ideas and work with others to turn them into innovative products and services. Innovation may come from a flash of genius, but it most often comes from a conscious search for opportunity. This can be hard work, take a long time, and require skills that have not necessarily been taught to us in school or in our first jobs.

Many of us have simply not been taught how to transform our creativity and good ideas into something that can be developed for use. There is growing awareness that teaching creativity and innovation and linking both to leadership helps companies succeed.

Leaders everywhere are beginning to see that we need to foster innovation in people so they, in turn, can foster it in their organizations and communities. In addition, the best leaders know that innovation is not a one-time event. Innovation has to be at the top of everyone's list if companies are going to evolve to meet the needs of a world that is constantly changing. This isn't easy, and there is no formula. Take AOL, the media and Internet giant that has been around since 1983, when it was called Control Video Corporation. The company officially became AOL in 1991, just one of the many tremendous evolutions over its three decade history.[65] It can rightly claim a place with the pioneers who transformed Internet and telecommunications technologies into commercial businesses. Today, AOL runs the Huffington Post, a well-respected Internet site for original news, blog, and editorial pieces. The company has shifted from its initial role as the gateway to the Internet to a new role as provider of premier quality Internet content and improved online experience.[66]

John Reid-Dodick is a leader that we can look to for wisdom, creativity, humor, and an incredible capacity for building strong, positive relationships at work. John's career has been divergent and fascinating: lawyer, business executive, and country and western singer. He's found innovative ways to live his life, as well as to contribute to the companies he has worked for, including AOL.

As you will see in the *Leadership Perspective* on the next page, John Reid-Dodick understands that when it comes to creativity, innovation, and leadership we are talking about *people*. So what can you do to spark your own creativity and your capacity for innovation? How can you lead in a world where innovation must be the norm, rather than the exception? Once again, it starts with you. How you tap your talents, your creativity, and your passion will help you to be successful as a leader and an innovator.

Innovation doesn't happen in a vacuum. The best companies provide structures that help people to be creative and protect them from some of the forces inside organizations (like bureaucracy) that kill innovation. Let's look at how this works.

Leadership Perspective

● **John Reid-Dodick**
Chief People Officer, AOL
"You need an always-on openness to what is happening in the world."

I believe there are four dimensions to great leadership today. We live in a world that is changing so fast and so completely, it is a challenge to stay current with everything that is happening and to still engage meaningfully with people.

1. *Curiosity*—You need an always-on openness to what is happening in the world. This means that you actively have to seek out new ways of looking at things, listening to people, questioning what is going on around you. Take advantage of new devices and emerging media to gather as much information as you can. Pay attention to whom you talk to—are they new and different, or the same people you always speak with? Be in listening mode so you truly understand other points of view. Be planful about how and where you travel, particularly when you have opportunities to travel globally. The world is so complex and so fast-paced you can't function without complete openness and curiosity.

2. *Vision*—All of these inputs can be overwhelming. You need to know how to make sense of them—looking for patterns, understanding the trends, developing a point of view. You'll need to try to look around the corner and see what's coming so you can begin to envision the future in a way that makes sense to you and to everyone around you.

3. *Empathy*—You need to be attuned to others at a fundamental and emotional level. Do you understand how people feel? Do you know what they need? What do they want? What is their context? What's happening in their lives, and how does it affect them as people? Empathy with everyone is the key—with your colleagues, your boss, your customers, everyone. And sometimes, you have to think creatively about how to understand people. Take customers, for example: Of course you want to understand them, and what they need and want. But do you also think about them as having their own customers, so you can figure out how to help them be better at what they do and truly have their best interests at heart? Empathy, a willingness to help, and generosity will take you a long way toward becoming a leader people will be loyal to no matter what.

4. *Resilience*—At a personal level, you need to take care of yourself. This can mean simple, common sense things like eating well, drinking enough water, sleeping enough (even taking naps!). You will want to find the things that renew you—reading, working outside, laughter—and make these a part of your life, every single day no matter how much pressure you're experiencing. Be active—whether it's finding a workout you enjoy and doing it, or just making time to walk for a half hour every day. Have fun. Make sure that you have time with friends and people you love. Looking after yourself isn't being selfish. It's like they say on the airplane—"Put your oxygen mask on first"—you can't help others until you help yourself.

Source: Personal interview with John Reid-Dodick conducted by Annie McKee, 2012.

Structures That Promote Innovation

Promoting innovation isn't a new trend; it's been important to the best companies for many years. But, bureaucracy and slow, traditional decision-making processes can seriously hinder the development of new technologies and designs.[67] So, the best companies help people be innovative by providing organizational structures that protect people from the day-to-day grind. From customer focus groups to new venture teams to formalized innovation teams, the intent is the same: Get new ideas and then get them up and running. Today, some common structures that promote innovation include Skunk Works® and idea incubators.

SKUNK WORKS®

Skunk Works® is a term used in business to describe a group within an organization that is relatively autonomous and is unhampered by bureaucracy. Entrepreneurial research teams and divisions designed as Skunk Works® provide highly creative people the time and freedom to focus on breakthrough ideas. The work within such teams is often secretive.

The term Skunk Works® is trademarked by Lockheed Martin, where it was first used as the official nickname of an entrepreneurial branch of the company that is

Skunk Works®
A term used in business to describe a group within an organization that is given a high degree of autonomy and is unhampered by bureaucracy. The term is trademarked by Lockheed Martin.

actually called Advanced Development Programs. This structure was created in the mid-twentieth century and continues today. Skunk Works® teams developed such legendary craft as the U2 spy plane, the SR-71, and the stealth bomber. The division was created because Lockheed Martin realized that the creativity and innovation the company needed was hampered tremendously by its bureaucracy.[68] People needed time, and they needed to be able to break some bureaucratic rules.

Many companies honor the trademark and have chosen different names for their own innovation groups. For example, Boeing has its "Phantom Works," while the U.S. Air Force has Area 51. Similarly, in 2006, Ford Motor Company's chief diesel engineer, Adam Gryglak, called his innovation and development team "Project Scorpion." This group fast-tracked innovation and helped bring competitive advantage back to Ford.[69]

IDEA INCUBATORS

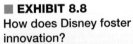

Idea incubator
Part of the research and development (R&D) branch of an organization that focuses on the development of entrepreneurial ideas.

An idea incubator is another way to facilitate innovation. An idea incubator is usually part of the research and development (R&D) branch of an organization that focuses on the development of new ideas. The metaphor is not accidental. An incubator protects and nurtures an idea until it is viable and healthy, just as an incubator protects and nurtures premature infants. New ideas require supportive challenge while they grow and change. Plans for innovations must also include involvement of key stakeholders—often a difficult task. All of this needs to be done in a safe environment.

For example, the U.S. Army has an idea incubator called the Army Suggestion Program. This program offers cash awards for military personnel or civilians who develop ideas that result in tangible savings for the army. On average, several thousand suggestions are submitted per year, of which only about 10 to 12 percent can be acted upon. Each year, these suggestions save the army millions of dollars.[70] Universities have idea incubators as well.

Innovative Divisions outside an Organization's Bureaucratic Hierarchy

One interesting example of an innovation structure is Disney's Imagineering, a permanent division of the organization whose purpose is to dream up wild ideas about new things a guest at Disneyland might experience. Walt Disney Imagineering is the branch of Disney that is involved in creative development and planning of major projects, as well as research and development.[71] To support innovation, the group draws on more than 150 different disciplines in the creation of new resorts, theme parks, real estate projects, and media. The name *Imagineering* is a play on *imagination* and *engineering*, as the group blends advanced technology and creativity to develop innovative and distinct storytelling. The company owns more than 100 patents in ride systems, fiber optics, audio, special effects, and interactive technologies.[72]

Imagineering has been an integral part of the Disney franchise since 1952, when it was formed as an independent company to help create Disneyland.[73] Recently completed projects include the 2008 *Spaceship Earth* attraction at Orlando's Disneyworld (■ **EXHIBIT 8.8**), the 2009 *Turtle Talk with Crush* in Tokyo DisneySea Park, the 2012 *Cars Land* attraction at

■ **EXHIBIT 8.8**
How does Disney foster innovation?

Source: © Mervyn Rees/Alamy

Disney California Adventure, the 2012 *Toy Story Midway Mania* at Tokyo DisneySea, and the 2012 *Grizzly Gulch* at Hong Kong Disneyland.

Another innovation that supports people in sharing new ideas is Disney ImagiNations. Disney ImagiNations is a Walt Disney Imagineering-sponsored design competition that promotes diversity and allows students to develop their talents and knowledge in creative design. Finalists in the competition receive an all-expenses-paid trip to present their work to Imagineering executives, and many are chosen for internships.[74]

So far in this chapter, you have learned about creativity and innovation. We have examined how creativity and innovation are important for you as an employee, manager, or leader. We have also looked at how creativity and innovation support existing organizations in continuing to be successful. Now, we will turn our attention to *new* organizations where creativity and innovation are a must. As we look at entrepreneurships and new businesses, you might want to imagine yourself as an entrepreneur.

Discussion Questions

1. In this chapter you have learned that innovation is not just about new products or services. Innovation is also about how businesses and organizations are structured and managed. Brainstorm a list of ways a small business, such as a coffee shop, local restaurant, or auto repair garage might, change the way it does business to more effectively meet the needs of its clientele.

2. Brainstorm a list of innovations that would help you be more efficient or have more fun in your daily life. Which of your ideas could become a product or service?

6. What Is Entrepreneurship?

Objective 8.6
Define entrepreneurship.

Entrepreneurship is the process of identifying an opportunity, developing resources, and assuming the risks associated with starting a new business. An **entrepreneur** is a person who starts a new business. The word *entrepreneur* is borrowed from French. Although we attach a number of meanings to this term, its original and fundamental meaning is "one who undertakes or manages."[75] Entrepreneurship is about creating and taking ownership of new ideas, plans, business activities, or responsibilities.[76] This view of entrepreneurship includes being creative and innovative—that is, having an "entrepreneurial spirit."[77] Many people argue that the opportunities and challenges we face today require all of us to develop an entrepreneurial approach to work and life, and even world leaders are talking about the need for an entrepreneurial spirit.

For example, consider the World Economic Forum's interest in social entrepreneurship. The Forum—which brings together business, political, social, and intellectual leaders from around the world—tapped 30 social entrepreneurs to participate in their annual meeting in January 2012. The entrepreneurs were chosen because of their work in finance, nutrition, renewable energy, health care, housing, and education.[78] We'll learn more about social entrepreneurs later in this section, but for now the important thing to understand about these individuals is that they use their creativity and innovation to improve their communities and the world, and efforts such as theirs are greatly needed today (■ **EXHIBIT 8.9**).

We often think about entrepreneurs as individual people whose creative genius results in a technological breakthrough or an invention that results in hugely profitable or popular businesses. Bill Gates of Microsoft, the late Steve Jobs of Apple, and Craig Newman of Craigslist are examples of this type of entrepreneur. Most entrepreneurs,

Entrepreneurship
The process of identifying an opportunity, developing resources, and assuming the risks associated with starting a new business.

Entrepreneur
A person who starts a new business.

■ **EXHIBIT 8.9**
Why do all societies need
entrepreneurs?

Source: © Guido Vrola/Fotolia

however, are everyday people in your neighborhood or city who are providing products and services to their customers while earning a living.

Despite the fact that many small entrepreneurial businesses have been swallowed up in recent years by "giants" such as Walmart, most communities have small grocery stores, coffee shops, dry cleaners, and landscape companies, among other entrepreneurial businesses. In office parks and office buildings you will find entrepreneurs specializing in fields such as research, technology, fashion design, consulting, and manufacturing. Entrepreneurship is alive and well in almost every single industry in both the private (business) and public (non-for-profit) sectors in all communities.

The Importance of Small Businesses in Our Economies

All businesses and organizations started as entrepreneurial ventures, and most started *small*. A small business is often defined as one that employs fewer than fifty people, but some definitions include businesses up to 500 people. Oftentimes in the study of management, we don't pay much attention to small businesses. That's a big mistake. In the United States and many other countries, small businesses are the backbone of the economy. For example, in the U.S. Small Business Administration's "Frequently Asked Questions" publication, one of the questions is "How important are small businesses to the U.S. economy?" The question is answered in this way:

"Small businesses in the United States:[79]

- *Represent 99.7 percent of all employer firms.*
- *Employ just over half of all private sector employees.*
- *Pay 43 percent of total U.S. private payroll.*
- *Have generated 65 percent of net new jobs since 1994.*
- *Create more than half of the nonfarm private gross domestic product (GDP).*
- *Hire 43 percent of high-tech workers (such as scientists, engineers, and computer programmers).*
- *Are 52 percent home-based and 2 percent franchise.*
- *Made up 97.5 percent of all identified exporters and produced 31 percent of the known export value in FY 2008.*
- *Produce 16.5 times more patents per employee than large patenting firms; these patents are twice as likely as large firm patents to be among the one percent most cited."*

Just think about it: 99.7 percent of companies that employ people are small businesses. More than half of all private-sector employees work for small businesses.

Small businesses are important all over the world, and they do not always look the way we might expect. For example, in some countries, many entrepreneurial ventures are not the typical one-person owner, employing a few people to provide services or sell goods. Instead, they are owned and operated by entire communities.

Entrepreneurs can also be found in the world of music and television. As you can see below, a lot of celebrities you know are entrepreneurs:[80]

1. Kim Kardashian's career took off in 2007 with the unauthorized release of a sex tape, followed by a successful reality television show featuring her family. In 2009, Kardashian began endorsing an Internet shoe company called ShoeDazzle, which she co-founded and for which she is the chief stylist. Kardashian also co-owns a clothing boutique along with her sisters Khloe and Kourtney. Additionally, Kardashian has launched numerous clothing lines.[81]

2. Rapper Shawn JAY-Z Carter overcame a difficult childhood to develop a career as a hip-hop artist and entrepreneur. His efforts to build a business empire through a

record label, to own a stake in an NBA team, and to pursue other business ventures brought him to the attention of Berkshire Hathaway CEO Warren Buffet, who has become a friend.[82]

3. Tyra Banks became a successful talk-show host and created "America's Next Top Model," a popular reality TV show, after forging her reputation as a model and actress. A graduate of Harvard Business School's Owner/President Management Program, she urges fans to "be the CEO of your own life" and provides professional and career-oriented advice on her Web site.[83]

4. Comedian and actor Steve Carell bought Marshfield Hills General Store in Marshfield, Massachusetts—his hometown. The store is run by family members.

5. Academy Award-winning actor Robert De Niro translated his on-screen success to the restaurant industry when he opened Nobu, an upscale sushi restaurant with locations around the world. He's also involved in another restaurant concept, Ago, as a part owner.[84]

Similarly, many celebrities have used their fame and fortune to help spur efforts for social change. Consider the examples listed below:

- *Oprah Winfrey:* The world renowned celebrity founded the Oprah Winfrey Leadership Academy in 2007, a school for girls in South Africa who could not otherwise obtain an education because of poverty or because they live in remote rural areas. As Oprah puts it, "The school will teach girls to be the best human beings they can ever be; it will train them to become decision-makers and leaders; it will be a model school for the rest of the world."[85]

- *Sean Penn:* A two-time Oscar-winning actor, Penn was so moved by the images of destruction following the January 2010 earthquake in Haiti that he stays on the island for long stretches to personally oversee ongoing relief and recovery efforts through J/P Haitian Relief Organization, a not-for-profit that he cofounded.[86]

- *Brad Pitt:* A popular actor who has been involved in numerous causes over the years, Pitt's effort to help rebuild a sense of community in New Orleans' Lower Ninth Ward is notable because it stems from his twin interests in architectural design and green technology. Pitt's Make It Right Foundation aims to build 150 safe, affordable, and energy-efficient homes and be a catalyst for change in the building industry. In the spring of 2012, Make It Right announced it would extend its reach by converting an abandoned public school into affordable apartments in Kansas City, Missouri.[87]

People start businesses for many reasons. Some see it as an opportunity to make a fortune. Others want the freedom to make their own decisions and not have to deal with cumbersome bureaucracies. Still others just want to know if they can do it. They want and enjoy the challenge. Other people want to contribute to their communities in a different way, and they cannot find a way to do it in more traditional organizations. But who becomes an entrepreneur? Does it take a special kind of person?

Profile of an Entrepreneur

Are there characteristics and competencies we can point to and say, "That person would make a good entrepreneur"? In reality, too many factors influence the success of any entrepreneurial venture to be able to sum up the profile of an entrepreneur in a simple list. Every demographic characteristic you can imagine—race, gender, age, national origin, education, and so on—is represented among successful entrepreneurs. There are, however, a few similarities that make entrepreneurs different from their peers in society.

For one, entrepreneurs *embrace risk*.[88] Deciding to start a business is not easy and requires courage. Entrepreneurs enjoy challenge and take calculated risk. This can be scary—but the biggest risk is to watch the world change around you without doing anything to make sure you can contribute in a meaningful way.

Entrepreneurs also *take initiative*.[89] They are *self-starters*. Entrepreneurs have a strong need for achievement. When they see something that can be done better, they do it. Along with achievement drive, entrepreneurs have high *self-esteem*, and they may even be a bit self-centered.[90] Additionally, entrepreneurs can *see the big picture* while taking care of the details of the business as well. They have to. A new business rarely has the resources of a large organization, so an entrepreneur must have a hand in a wide variety of tasks. An entrepreneur's day can include work as varied as dealing with investors and sweeping the floor. Many entrepreneurs are also *engaged and passionate learners*.[91] They spend evening hours on the Internet looking for best practices and attend trade shows to learn about the latest trends in their industry. Finally—and not surprisingly when you consider all the other characteristics on this list—entrepreneurs tend to be *energetic*.

Entrepreneurs can be found throughout society—in business, of course, but also in education, medicine, law, agriculture, psychology, and consulting. Literally every field lends itself to entrepreneurship. To conclude this section, we will look at entrepreneurs who work to support societies and communities while also building businesses. Then, in the next section, we will look at entrepreneurs inside organizations.

Social Entrepreneurship

Social entrepreneurship
The activity of identifying opportunities to help society in some way, with financial gain taking a secondary position if it factors in at all.

Social entrepreneurship is the activity of identifying opportunities to help society in some way, with financial gain taking a secondary position if it factors in at all. Social entrepreneurs promote social change. Their work is neither charity nor business in any strict sense, although it can improve the effectiveness of both.[92]

For example, Josh Nesbit, a Stanford University student, became a social entrepreneur when he took 100 reconditioned cell phones and a laptop to doctors in Malawi.[93] Using open-source software, health care providers in this African country are now able to keep in touch through text messages about patient conditions and emergencies.[94] The text messaging platform—provided by FrontlineSMS—enables Nesbit and others, including Ken Banks who founded kiwanja.net, to create organizations that improve life for people in Malawi and other places in Africa.[95] Josh Nesbit has moved on (as entrepreneurs do) to found and run Medic Mobile, which is similar to the organization in Malawai and to kiwanja.net, but is based in San Francisco.[96]

Another well-known example of social entrepreneurship is the solar cooker known as the Kyoto Box. This solar cooker was developed by Norwegian inventor Jon Bohmerin 2009 to meet the needs of the rural poor in an environmentally friendly way.[97] This cooker, which is a modern adaptation of a 1767 invention, was developed for the HP-sponsored *Forum for the Future Climate Change Challenge*.[98] The 15-euro machine won the top prize of $75,000, which is being used to fund large-scale trials in 10 countries.[99] The cooker derives all its energy from the sun, produces no smoke, and requires no other resources to operate. It can cook, bake, clean water, and dry food while at the same time reducing environmental damage caused by CO_2, deforestation, and electricity production.[100] Innovations like this often die long before they reach their potential: not so the Kyoto Box.[101] It is still around and the design has been improved. Solar cookers in general are rising in popularity and hundreds of thousands of people are using them today. The company, Kyoto Energy, has expanded beyond the basic Kyoto Box to include a variety of solar projects based on similar concepts and values.[102]

Let's look at social entrepreneurship in action through the company Ashoka. Ashoka was founded in 1980 by Bill Drayton. It began with the premise that "the most effective way to promote positive social change is to invest in social entrepreneurs who have innovative solutions to society's problems that are sustainable and replicable, both nationally and globally."[103] A social entrepreneur is a person who identifies social issues and organizes people, resources, and networks to address these problems. When Ashoka locates such individuals, it chooses some of them to be "fellows." The company then supports each fellow with guidance, expertise, and funding as he or she launches and grows a business.

James Nguo, an Ashoka fellow from Kenya, was awarded the UNESCO-IPDC Prize for Rural Communication based on his development of a network of community-based Maarifa, or knowledge centers. With Ashoka's help, Nguo founded the Arid Lands Information Network, an organization that helps connect remote villages to the rest of the world.[104] The United Nations Educational, Scientific and Cultural Organization (UNESCO) recognized Nguo for his work in creating knowledge-based communities that exemplify how technology can play a role in raising living standards via customized agricultural and environmental information.[105]

As the examples here illustrate, social entrepreneurs have many of the same characteristics as entrepreneurs, but they have a greater desire to pursue opportunities that help others. They are intrinsically motivated by their work, which sustains them, encourages them to work hard, and inspires them to think creatively.

Discussion Questions

1. Would you like to own your own business one day? Why? What specifically attracts you to the idea of becoming an entrepreneur?

2. Think about a social issue that is important to you. Brainstorm a few ideas for social entrepreneurship. Pick one of your ideas and explore in some detail what it would take to launch your social entrepreneurship venture.

---

7. What Is Intrepreneurship?

Objective 8.7
Learn about intrapreneurship.

Researchers have adopted the term *intrepreneurship* to describe creative and innovative talent and the spirit of entrepreneurship within organizations.[106] The term **intrepreneur** was coined in 1976 to describe an employee who behaves like an entrepreneur inside his or her own organization.[107] Intrepreneurship is the process of identifying an opportunity, developing resources, and assuming some of the risk associated with a new idea, all while being employed by an organization.[108] Intrepreneurship is a compelling topic today because of the need for creativity and innovation in organizations.

In our organizations and businesses it can be very difficult to launch new products or services. Bureaucratic rules, competition for resources, and even organizational culture often inhibit people and companies from starting something new—and yet that is just what most businesses need. Because of this, intrepreneurs need to have some of the same characteristics as entrepreneurs. They especially need to be creative, innovative risk takers.

Because less than 10 percent of Americans own their own business, and likely far more would like to, intrepreneurship is one way for everyone to win.[109] What, then, can you do to ensure that your good ideas are used? One of the keys to successful intrepreneurship is making sure ideas surface and are taken up by an organization.

Intrepreneur
An employee who behaves like an entrepreneur inside his or her own organization.

Building Support for Ideas

Creative ideas—ones that truly stand out—can help to improve products or services, enhance marketing efforts, make the workplace safer, or cut costs. All of these are areas where companies like to see their employees and managers taking an interest and offering suggestions. But once you have a great idea, what do you do with it? How do you get others in the company to buy into it?

First, you should constantly be on the lookout for new ideas. Anything that makes the company better, faster, less costly, or safer is fair game. Do you see cables stretched across common areas that could be dangerous hazards? Have you been thinking about a great new ad campaign for your company's products? Do you see a wasteful practice in the company's warehouse area? Have you identified a way to reduce paper in the office that will also speed up communications? The first step in getting support for good ideas like these is to focus your attention and creativity on problems and opportunities.

You also need to talk about your ideas. Share them with others. Also, be patient and make sure you don't fall into the "I can't do it" trap. If you engage in self-defeating thoughts like "This will never work" or "We don't have the money to do this," your ideas will lay dormant.

It is one thing to come up with ideas; it's another entirely to implement those ideas. Thus, another way to build support for your ideas is to clearly articulate how they can be implemented and demonstrate this to the right people. But who are the right people? That's where the emotional intelligence competency called organizational awareness comes in. To build the right kind of support, you must accurately scan your environment. You need to understand who you must bring on board (e.g., your boss), who will be strong supporters, and who will resist. You also need to know who has funds to support the implementation of your idea. With this understanding, you will be able to craft an approach for who, where, how, and when to share your ideas. Crafting an action plan that shows in step-by-step fashion how the idea is put into effect will give more credibility to your idea and illustrate its feasibility.

Finally, don't become frustrated. Some ideas simply won't get the support you expected. Due to budget, time, or staffing constraints, suggestions may have to be placed on the back burner until those resources are available. Don't stop. Just keep generating new ideas.

Today, more and more companies are creating systems that support intrepreneurship tangibly. For example, the best leaders build cultures that tolerate risk. When this works, intrepreneurs have the advantage of a steady, relatively secure income from their employer, and in most cases, they will not lose their jobs if an idea fails or does not live up to expectations.[110] Most organizations truly want employees who have an intrepreneurial spirit.[111] They encourage and reward those employees who think creatively, solve problems, and are innovative.

Discussion Questions

1. Think of yourself as an intrepreneur in your school. What opportunities for innovation can you see? List five areas where you could apply your creativity and innovation to make changes that would support students, faculty, staff, or the community. What support and resources would you need to start this new venture? Who would you need to include in the stakeholder group to take this forward?

2. What obstacles might you run into if you attempted to act as an intrepreneur in your school? List as many of these obstacles as you can think of from the example in question 1. What are some comprehensive ways of overcoming these obstacles? How would you deal with them individually?

Objective 8.8
Describe how a new business gets started.

8. How Does a New Business Get Started?

Suppose you have an idea for a business. It's new. It's unique. You think you can really make it work. Many people cannot seem to take the next step: going from idea to reality. They tell themselves that their idea will never work, or that they don't have enough money or business experience. Sometimes, they simply don't know how to ta[...] idea forward.

If you want to overcome these obstacles, there are a few things you can do:

- Know the right questions to ask
- Learn how to write a business plan
- Determine how to secure funding
- Understand the life cycle of a business
- Learn how to avoid common pitfalls
- Lead and manage for success

In the next few sections, we will explore each of these very important topics so yo[...] be a successful entrepreneur if you choose.

Questions to Ask When Starting a Business

Say you have a good idea for a business. You can't wait to start. You know, however, that many, many new businesses fail within the first two years.[112] You'd like to be one of the businesses that makes it and is around for a long time. So, you do some soul searching. You ask yourself some tough questions, such as:

- How much will it really cost me to get this business off the ground? You need to count every possible expense from supplies to cell phones to securing office space to buying insurance and more.
- What taxes must I pay? Many entrepreneurs fail to realize that taxes can be substantial. If you plan on hiring employees, you will have payroll taxes. You will also have to pay taxes: city, state, and federal taxes on revenue, income, property, and the like. Depending on what your business does, you may also need to collect sales tax from customers. If your business will buy and/or sell internationally, taxes can be even more complicated.
- What is my break-even point? A **break-even point** is the point at which expenses equal income. For example, let's say you add up all the costs associated with running your new business for a year (payroll, supplies, taxes—everything). Your yearly costs add up to $120,000 (including paying yourself). Let's assume the revenue you bring in each month from the sales of your products or service is about $15,000 per month. Since $15 \times 8 = 120$, it will be eight months into the year before you cover the costs of doing business. Knowing your break-even point is vital because it shows you the importance of budgeting.
- What will be my personal income? What if I need to forego an income for some period of time? Many start-ups require personal financial sacrifices. You must have a candid discussion with your family and be realistic with yourself to determine whether you can afford to live without any personal income for many months or even a year or two. How will your lifestyle be impacted if it takes over a year to finally bring a paycheck home? How will you pay for things like health care costs and insurance (home, renter, office, business inventory, car, etc.)?
- Are you and your family up for the 24/7 work that most start-ups require? How will you take care of yourself and your relationships?
- Who can advise you? Paying for advice is costly. Are there people in your social network who might help?

Break-even point
The point at which expenses equal income.

These are just a few of the questions you will need to explore. Depending on the type of business you are opening and your needs as a person, there may be many more. It is more than worth the time and effort to think through these questions so you can understand what you are getting into and what you need to do to prepare yourself and your family. In addition, asking these questions will help you get to the next step: writing a business plan.

Writing a Business Plan

an

document that states the of a business and its goals outlines how the business will succeed.

The formal outline of a business venture is often captured in a business plan. A **business plan** is a formal document that states the nature of a business and its goals and outlines how the business will succeed. Many business plans also include other information, such as the background of the entrepreneur, financial statements, and an analysis of the industry. ■ **EXHIBIT 8.10** illustrates typical elements of a business plan to give you a better idea of how to write one.

A business plan is important for several reasons. First, if an entrepreneur is seeking a loan from a third-party, such as a bank, the lender will want to review the business plan to ensure it is realistic.

Second, even if you are not attempting to secure outside funds, having a business plan helps structure the idea behind the business. In other words, outlining how success will be measured will keep you on track. The very characteristics that make entrepreneurs successful—creativity, risk taking, and action orientation—can cause them to fail because they lose sight of where they are going.

■ **EXHIBIT 8.10**

The Elements of a Business Plan[113]

I. Cover sheet
II. Statement of purpose
III. Table of contents

- **A. The business**
  1. Description of business
  2. Marketing
  3. Competition
  4. Operating procedures
  5. Personnel
  6. Business insurance
- **B. Financial data**
  1. Loan applications
  2. Capital equipment and supply list
  3. Balance sheet
  4. Break-even analysis
  5. Pro forma income projections (profit and loss statements)
  6. Three-year summary
  7. Detail by month, first year
  8. Detail by quarters, second and third years
  9. Assumptions on which projections were based
  10. Pro forma cash flow
- **C. Supporting documents**
  1. Tax returns of principals for last three years
  2. Personal financial statement (most banks have these forms)
  3. For franchised businesses, a copy of franchise contract and all supporting documents provided by the franchisor
  4. Copy of proposed lease or purchase agreement for building space
  5. Copy of licenses and other legal documents
  6. Copy of resumes of all principals
  7. Copies of letters of intent from suppliers, etc.

Where Does the Money Come From?

Most entrepreneurs quickly discover that starting a new business is expensive. Some people use their personal savings to finance the venture. Others use credit cards to pay for the startup costs—obviously, this is a potentially dangerous solution. Many entrepreneurs seek funding from a third party, such as venture capitalist firms and/or banks or other financial institutions.

Other entrepreneurs look to family and friends as investors. An **investor** is someone who provides money as a loan and is, in return, paid back with interest. Investors can also be people you don't know. Or, perhaps you know of someone who wants to invest in something other than the stock market. These investors are sometimes referred to as angels. An **angel investor** is a person or a small group of people who offer money to start-ups in exchange for a stake in the business. **Venture capitalist firms** seek to earn a profit through investments in start-up firms or companies that are undergoing change.[114] When venture capitalists get involved in an entrepreneurial venture, they often enter into a financial partnership with the entrepreneur. Though the entrepreneur may have operating control of the business, a venture capitalist retains some, most, or in some cases all the legal ownership of the company. Venture capitalists tend to be very selective, choosing to invest in only about six of every thousand business plans they review.[115] That said, it is estimated that venture capitalists invest nearly $30 billion each year in the United States alone.[116]

Perhaps the most common source of third-party funds is financial institutions. Financial institutions are organizations such as banks and credit unions that receive, hold, invest, and lend money. With a well-crafted business plan in hand, an entrepreneur may seek a business loan from a financial institution. He or she may have to show proof of collateral or personal investment in the business. In addition, a payment schedule is determined and, in most cases, repayment begins immediately. Some financial institutions have been designated as Small Business Investment Companies (SBICs). An **SBIC** is a financial institution that makes loans to entrepreneurs under the auspices of the Small Business Administration, a U.S. federal government agency.

Investor
Someone who provides money as a loan and is, in return, paid back with interest.

Angel investor
A person or a small group of people who offer money to a start-up in exchange for a stake in the business.

Venture capitalist firm
A company that seeks to earn a profit through investments in start-up firms or companies that are undergoing dramatic change.

SBIC
Small Business Investment Company; a financial institution that makes loans to entrepreneurs under the auspices of the Small Business Administration, a U.S. federal government agency.

The Life Cycle of a Business

As an entrepreneur starts a business, he or she is setting forth on a journey of exploration and discovery. It is exciting and frightening at the same time because of the unknowns that lie ahead. There will be successes and challenges. As a business matures, it goes through four stages: start-up, growth, maturity, and decline/renewal.[117]

STAGE 1: START-UP

This is the first stage in launching a business. It is here that the first steps are taken to transform a dream into reality. Early on, it is critical for the entrepreneur to have a good grasp of the business's financials. It is easy to become overextended if expenses are not understood. A name must be chosen, physical or virtual locations secured, all legal issues associated with setting up the venture must be addressed, and the initial marketing of products or services must be carried out. Organizational scholars have also referred to this stage as "birth" and note that successful leaders in this stage develop their systems of operation and successfully manage the inevitable crises that occur.[118] Scholars also note that what works for a mature organization just doesn't cut it for a start-up.[119] For instance, in a start up, sales structures have to be tactical and quickly evolving, job descriptions are often vague, and HR and management practices are often informal.

STAGE 2: GROWTH

If a venture survives the start-up stage and begins showing a profit, it may then enter the growth stage. As revenue and profits increase, more employees might need to be hired, and operations become more firmly established. Issues such as planned growth, specialization, marketing, customer service, and strategic human resources become more important.[120] The business is now viable, as long as it is managed well.

Entrepreneurs have choices about how much to grow, and these decisions need to be made consciously. A successful business need not grow. Many owners are perfectly content to see their businesses remain small rather than pursue continual growth.[121]

STAGE 3: MATURITY

When an organization reaches maturity, growth slows down. Rather than capturing market share or customers, organizations think more about maintaining stability.[122] A great deal of focus, then, goes into cultivating a long-term strategy through effective marketing and good customer service. Another way of protecting long-term viability at the maturity stage is to invest more time and energy in technical efficiency and quality control.[123] Enhancing production methods, improving marketing efforts, exceeding customers' expectations, and training employees are all important at this stage.

STAGE 4: DECLINE OR RENEWAL

An organization that is over-focused on stability may be more at risk of decline than one that is more adaptable. Scholars have argued that organizational decline is often due to too much bureaucracy. This prevents the organization from responding to changing market conditions.[124] Changes such as a tough economy or societal transformations can threaten a mature organization and cause it to go into decline. As the environment changes, organizations need to change too. If they don't, they can become obsolete.

For example, Napster, an online music distribution channel, started out as a free site where people could exchange music files. The company was hailed as revolutionary, but it also faced huge threats from the more traditional music industry. In fact, the company was shut down because courts found that Napster was violating copyright laws.[125] Let's look at what happened.

Napster was founded in 1999 by Shawn Fanning and Sean Parker, and it became an instant success. By December of that year, the Recording Industry Association of America filed a lawsuit against the company, followed by another lawsuit brought by music group Metallica. Within a few months, the courts ruled that Napster was not protected by the Digital Millennium Copyright Act. Two months later, an injunction against the company was granted.

In 2002, Bertelsmann, a music company in Germany, agreed to buy the struggling company's assets for $8 million. After Napster filed for bankruptcy, a judge blocked the sale. The bankruptcy court allowed Roxio to buy the bankrupt company for $5.3 million at the end of 2002, and Napster reopened the next year under Roxio's ownership with a different model that did not allow free file sharing. Napster continued to struggle for many years, but was eventually bought by Best Buy for $121 million.[126] In 2011, the company merged with Rhapsody, a large on-demand music service based in the United States, in exchange for Best Buy taking a minority stake in the company.[127]

We can see from the example of Napster that its birth and growth were dynamic and rapid, but the company was challenged early and beset by many obstacles. It never reached the maturity stage before decline set in. However, after coming out of bankruptcy, Napster was rejuvenated, found stability, and went through a five-year process of growth before being bought by Best Buy.

This case illustrates how a company might face rapid decline without going out of business. Massive changes in strategy, business operations, and even ownership were necessary as the organization renewed itself and survived.

How to Avoid Common Pitfalls and Succeed as an Entrepreneur

In 2005, the U.S. Bureau of Labor Statistics determined that about two-thirds of all new businesses lasted at least two years and that after four years, 44 percent were still in existence.[128] Said another way, one-third of new businesses fail in the first two years, and 56 percent fail within four years. This failure rate is significant and keeps many people from even attempting to start their own business. From 2007 to 2010, small business failure rates rose 40 percent. California had the worst small business failure rate at 69 percent.[129] We will now explore what you can do to ensure that your business succeeds.

GOOD LEADERSHIP AND MANAGEMENT SUPPORT SUCCESS

As you might suspect, being able to lead and manage effectively is a must for an entrepreneurial venture.[130] Very often, entrepreneurs are highly achievement oriented, under a lot of pressure, and somewhat individualistic. This often results in micromanaging—overcontrolling employees, processes, and everything else related to the business. This usually backfires. Even entrepreneurs who do manage well often skip the leadership part. Don't forget that people need inspiration. They need you to create a culture that focuses on effectiveness and innovation, as well as a climate that is ripe with optimism, excitement, and a feeling of "we're all in it together."

DEVELOP YOUR EMPLOYEES

Training and development of employees is not only for large businesses. Even if you have only one other employee besides yourself, that person deserves to be sufficiently trained in what he or she does. Local community colleges and other educational institutions often have low-cost seminars and classes in all aspects of business. Building your employees' skills helps them to improve while helping your business as well.

REMEMBER YOUR BUSINESS PLAN AND UNDERSTAND YOUR FINANCES

Drafting a comprehensive business plan is a must.[131] Too many entrepreneurs jump right in with little if any planning, resulting in failure. Many entrepreneurs believe that their ideas are so good and the business opportunity so compelling that a detailed plan isn't necessary, and writing a plan can be daunting. Whatever the reason, skipping this step is risky. Your business plan provides guidance and keeps you focused on your mission and vision for your company. You simply need to do it.

In addition, many entrepreneurs have the technical expertise and the passion to start a business, but they do not understand finance.[132] Get the advice and help you need regarding financial matters.

STAY FLEXIBLE

Change is inevitable. Something unexpected *will* occur in a new business (that's part of the fun). The advantage of a small business is that you can be nimble and move quickly—more quickly than your larger competitors. You can decide to change and then do it—you'll have less need to secure permissions, approvals, and the like. So, avoid setting up too much bureaucracy, and be ready to adapt.

MANAGE GROWTH AND MEASURE SUCCESS

Controlled growth should be your entrepreneurial mantra. As profits begin to increase and you find yourself with more cash, the temptation is to grow the business as fast as you can. However, uncontrolled growth can result in overextension to the point that you and your employees can't keep up and quality slips.

Be sure to measure your success. There is an old axiom in business: "What gets measured gets done." This speaks to the notion that those activities that are monitored for progress on a regular basis are the ones that are typically more successful.

MARKETING MATTERS

Effective marketing is a must. Many entrepreneurs fail to realize how important marketing is to their business. You may believe that your products or services are fabulous and assume that others will automatically recognize this. Unfortunately, that is rarely the case. You have to let your potential customers know that you exist.[133] As with financial planning, if you don't know how to market your company, get advice. Marketing is a professional field—it is not nearly as easy as it looks.

FOCUS ON CUSTOMER SERVICE

One way to ensure repeat business is through outstanding customer service. What is the formula for great customer service? First, you truly need to care about your customers. You need to listen to what they really want from your business.[134] You also need to let them know you have heard them, that you value their input, and that you will do whatever it takes to make them happy. As a leader, you need to model this kind of behavior. You also need to provide motivation, inspiration, and training for employees who face your customers.

BE A GOOD COMMUNITY MEMBER

Successful entrepreneurs recognize that they are part of larger communities and networks—both physical and online. You should become involved in community events, get to know other business owners, and take pride in the town or county where you work.

Discussion Questions

1. Review the questions in this section that you should ask yourself before starting a business. Brainstorm five more questions that relate specifically to your knowledge and expertise, personality, and desired lifestyle.

2. Do you know someone who has started a business? If it is successful, what factors do you think contributed to its success? If it is failing or has failed, what caused its demise?

Objective 8.9
Outline HR's role in supporting creativity, innovation, and entrepreneurship.

HR Leadership Roles

9. What Is HR's Role In Supporting Creativity, Innovation, and Entrepreneurship?

As an entrepreneur in your business, you might end up as both the leader *and* the worker. You may be the CEO, CFO, director of marketing, and vice president of HR while doing whatever you need to do to bring business in, sell products, etc. By virtue of necessity, you become your own HR business partner. For this reason, we will use this section of the chapter to present two very important aspects of the HR role: knowing and communicating laws regarding your intellectual property and minimizing bureaucracy.

Protecting Your Creative Ideas

As an entrepreneur, becoming familiar with and communicating the laws that protect your (and others') creative ideas and intellectual property is essential. Simply put, the concept of intellectual property is one that you must understand. **Intellectual property** refers to the ownership of a creative thought or idea and legal control over the representation of that thought or idea. Ownership is usually established in the form of a patent, copyright, or trademark.

A **patent** is a legal grant given by the U.S. Patent and Trademark Office that prevents anyone other than the grant holder from manufacturing, selling, or utilizing a particular invention. Typically, a patent is applied for when someone wants to ensure that no one copies their idea, product, or service. In 2008, nearly half a million patents were applied for in the United States; this is up from only 150,000 in 1988.[135] In the United States, most patents are granted for 20 years. For ornamental design—or design elements that have nothing to do with an invention's functionality—patents typically last for 14 years. During this time, the patent holder has a virtual monopoly over the use of the product. However, after the patent expires and assuming there are no enhancements or design changes to the original patent, the protection ends, and others can legally copy the product, process, or ornamental design.

A **copyright** is the exclusive rights granted to the creator of an original work, which includes the rights to copy, distribute, and adapt. These rights can be licensed or transferred. Copyright is granted for things like books, articles, music, lyrics, and art. A copyright can be secured through the U.S. Copyright Office and is designated by the symbol ©. It lasts the entire lifetime of the creator of the work, plus 70 years.[136]

A **trademark** is any distinctive sign, image, slogan, etc., used to identify a product or service as originating from a particular individual, business, or legal entity. This can include symbols (such as the Nike "swoosh"), names (Starbucks), logos (Intel's name in its distinctive circle), designs (Coca-Cola's bottle), or words, phrases, and slogans (Magic™ tape). In other words, a trademark must be truly distinctive. Unlike patents and copyrights, though, a trademark remains in the originator's possession as long as it is continually used—there is no expiration. It is represented by the symbols ™ and ®. ™ signifies an unregistered trademark, while ® represents a trademark that has been officially registered with the U.S. Patent and Trademark Office. Both types of trademark offer certain legal protections, but officially registering a trademark makes legal action much smoother in the event of a violation of the entrepreneur's intellectual property.

Laws are an important part of any business. They provide boundaries that a company must honor. This can sometimes feel constraining, but in the long run, laws are often very helpful. Other rules that are put in place may not be as necessary or as helpful—for example, bureaucratic policies and procedures that interfere with creativity and innovation or that waste time.

Don't Let Bureaucracy Get in the Way of Creativity

One way HR managers can foster entrepreneurship in their organizations is to reduce bureaucratic constraints. Policies and procedures that get in the way of new ideas become major roadblocks for employees and may eventually get in the way of creativity and innovation. As you will see in Chapter 12, controlling for effectiveness, quality, and efficiency is important. However, far too many bureaucratic policies and procedures are unnecessary.

HR professionals are in a unique position to influence all levels of management in an organization. That influence can be a powerful force for removing bureaucratic obstacles. Note that as many as 42 percent of professionals have considered

---

Intellectual property
The ownership of a creative thought or idea and legal control over the representation of the thought or idea.

Patent
A legal grant given by the U.S. Patent and Trademark Office that prevents anyone other than the grant holder from manufacturing, selling, or utilizing a particular invention.

Copyright
The exclusive rights granted to the creator of an original work, which includes the rights to copy, distribute, and adapt. These rights can be licensed or transferred.

Trademark
Any distinctive sign, image, slogan, etc., used to identify a product or service as originating from a particular individual, business, or legal entity.

quitting their job solely because of creativity-stifling bureaucracies that exist in their companies.[137] As an entrepreneur, you simply can't afford this loss of creative talent.

Discussion Questions

1. What is your opinion about companies and individuals who violate copyright laws? Justify your for, against, or situational opinion.

2. Have you worked or been a student in a highly bureaucratic organization? How did the many rules and regulations impact you? In your opinion, how do layers of bureaucracy emerge in businesses?

Objective 8.10
List ways you can be more creative, innovative, and entrepreneurial.

10. What Can We All Do to Be More Creative, Innovative, and Entrepreneurial?

Luckily, we can all learn to be more creative. In this section, we will focus on how you can develop your creativity. Creativity supports both innovation and entrepreneurship. Let's look at some simple rules you can adopt relatively easily. Then, you will learn about a specific technique to support creative thinking called mind mapping.

Becoming More Creative

How can you support yourself in being more creative in life and at work? Scholar Mihaly Csikszentmihalyi has spent a lifetime exploring how to find fulfillment in creative work. His advice, shown in ■ **EXHIBIT 8.11**, is useful—and profound.

Thinking Outside the Box

Another tip on how to be more creative is to adopt practices and to use tools that cause you to think "outside the box." For example, whether taking down information, strategizing a problem, or developing a concept, you can use a creative tool called *mind mapping*, which is illustrated on the next page in ■ **EXHIBIT 8.12**.[138]

As you can see, mind maps are diagrams with a central idea from which other concepts branch off, with more important concepts nearer the idea and lesser ones

■ **EXHIBIT 8.11**

Mihaly Csikszentmihalyi's Suggestions for Enhancing Creativity and Happiness

- Try to be surprised by something every day.
- Try to surprise at least one person every day.
- Write down each day what surprised you and how you surprised others.
- When something strikes a spark of interest, follow it.
- Recognize that if you do anything well, it becomes enjoyable.
- To keep enjoying something, increase its complexity.

- Make time for reflection and relaxation.
- Find out what you like and what you hate about life.
- Start doing more of what you love and less of what you hate.
- Find a way to express what moves you.
- Look at problems from as many viewpoints as possible.
- Produce as many ideas as possible.
- Have as many different ideas as possible.
- Try to produce unlikely ideas.

Source: Csikszentmihalyi, M. 1997. Happiness and creativity. *The Futurist*: 31(5).

■ **EXHIBIT 8.12**
Mind map

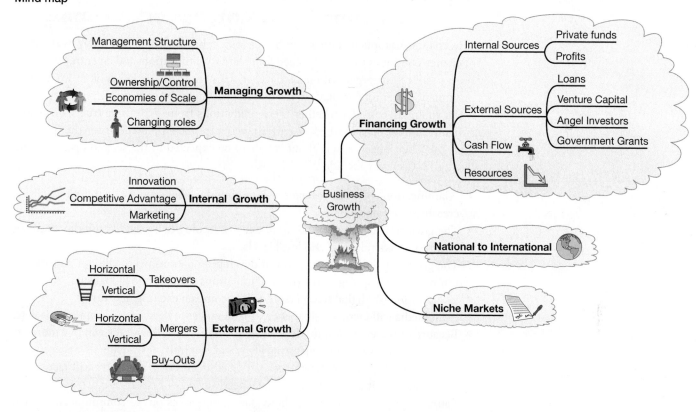

further away. These branches show relationships between concepts.[139] Mind mapping
allows us to take notes or to capture our ideas as they occur, and to link our thoughts
and information in ways that support creative thinking.

The reason this process sparks creativity is that it encourages us to think in a nonlinear fashion and allows us to indicate emphases and relationships between ideas.
Taking notes is a linear process in which we capture ideas and information as it is
presented to us, or as it occurs to us—in a chronological order. Mind mapping, on the
other hand, starts with a central image or idea and radiates out, using colors, visual
imagery, and key words. Lines connecting concepts are used, and these lines can also
represent the level of importance (through thickness, color, solid or dashed, etc.). They
can also represent the directionality of influence using such things as loops and arrows.

Images can also be used to represent the emotional content associated with ideas,
concepts, problems, and so forth. The important thing is to come up with a code that
makes sense—both cognitively and emotionally.[140] You can use mind mapping in the
traditional way—pen and paper—or find one of the wonderful computer programs
that are available.

Discussion Questions

1. Have you ever met people who follow the rules no matter what? How do these
   people impact your and other people's abilities to be creative?

2. Use the process of mind mapping to create a plan for your next paper. You may
   consider your study methods, environment, motivation, preparedness, etc., when
   developing branches for your mind map. Make this map as detailed as possible
   and include positive imagery, color, and line thickness to differentiate importance
   at each level. Give a brief description of this map after its completion.

11. A Final Word on Creativity, Innovation, and Entrepreneurship

This chapter has touched on a number of topics that are important today as the pace of change continues to drive the need for creativity, innovation, and an entrepreneurial spirit in all of our organizations. So, rather than ending here, let's look at what some prominent entrepreneurs have to say about what might be coming in the future.

As you read, consider whether these predictions from 2010 came true. The *Global Human Capital Journal* asked 17 entrepreneurs to make predictions for the future of Web 2.0. Their observations about trends to be expected in the second decade of the twenty-first century include:[141]

- "Gamification" of work means that the boundary between work and play will increasingly become blurred.
- The government will respond to modern technologies by shedding old patterns of business at federal, state, and local levels.
- The green revolution will take off in developing nations, who will look to extreme innovation to leapfrog infrastructure limitations straight into globalism.
- The position of "digital salesperson" will become an exciting new career.
- Print media will increasingly seek creative alliances to keep from becoming obsolete.
- Because of the explosion in ideas and information, organizations will pay more attention to finding ways of nurturing ideas and maximizing individuals' engagement.
- Enterprise 2.0 (social network software used in business contexts) will face many challenges, but it will continue to make headway.
- Latin American countries that hold state monopolies on telecommunications will founder in developing the next generation of network infrastructure.
- More focus will be given to developing trusted relationships and improving the quality of interpersonal interactions to quantify and add value to social networks.

Our economies, the rapid pace of change, and technological advances require us to think ahead and to think differently. As such, creativity, innovation, and a spirit of entrepreneurship are increasingly prevalent in our organizations. The best part about this is that it is *fun*.

LEADING IN A GLOBAL WORLD
Microloans to Help Developing Nations

Part One: Understanding Microfinance

In 2006, Muhammad Yunus was awarded the Nobel Peace Prize for his innovation in the microloan arena by creating a new category of banking known as microcredit for the poor. Microcredit involves granting small loans to people who would not qualify for conventional bank loans. Microcredit enables even very poor people to become successful entrepreneurs.

Research three different international entrepreneurial projects that have been financed through microloans. Then, answer the following questions:

1. What was the community need that each entrepreneur fulfilled?
2. What were the social and economic conditions of the entrepreneur prior to the microloan?
3. Describe the success each entrepreneur has had—were their goals met or exceeded?

Part Two: Being a Social Entrepreneur

Imagine you live in a poor, rural village in India. Clean water and sanitation are problematic. Most of the huts in the village are in disrepair. Farming is the primary occupation of the villagers, but fertilizer and farming tools are expensive. You have an entrepreneurial streak in you. You would like to help your fellow villagers and still make a small profit. Pick a village project for which you would like to get a loan. Write a short and compelling description of your new business. Assume that this description will determine whether or not you get a microloan to start the business. Be sure to Include the following in your description:

- What is the personal/community need you wish to fill?
- How much money will you need? How will you repay the initial loan with interest?
- Will you partner with others?

LEADING WITH EMOTIONAL INTELLIGENCE
Entrepreneurs Are a Special Breed

Do you believe that entrepreneurs need better emotional intelligence skills than your ordinary non-entrepreneurial person? How critical are self-awareness and relationship management to a successful entrepreneur?

1. Interview someone you know who has started, or has attempted to start, his/her own business (it may even be you!).

2. Use these questions to get your interview off to a successful start:
    A. In your opinion, what are the essential characteristics or qualities of an entrepreneur?
    B. How important was it to be aware of and manage your emotions as you planned and launched your business? Please explain why this was important.
    C. What role, if any, did fear, risk-taking, hope, or self-confidence play in your effort?
    D. What role did innovation and creativity play in your entrepreneurial experience?
    E. Do you think emotional intelligence is critical for entrepreneurial success? Explain your answer.

LEADING WITH CRITICAL THINKING SKILLS
Hypercompetition

Hypercompetition has had a lasting impact on our world. Think back to 10 years ago. You may not even have been in high school, but chances are you had a cell phone and/or an MP3 player. Now, fast forward to today. Rapid technological advances in innovation and creative design and fierce competition in the global market have placed smartphones and tablet computers in your hands at an affordable price.

Go online to research three smartphones and three tablets. Be sure you choose three different companies and do not choose two smartphone or tablet models from the same company. You may, however, choose one smartphone and one tablet from the same manufacturer. Once you have chosen your smartphones and tablets, answer the following questions either in teams or individually:

1. Which smartphone/tablet has the most appealing design? Why?
2. Which smartphone/tablet has the most innovative features and functionality? What are those features/functionality and how do they stand out from competitors' features?
3. Which product stands out as the best choice in value, creative design, and innovative features?

Once you have answered these questions, choose your favorite smartphone or tablet based on creativity and innovation. Then, create a short list of additional innovative features or suggest a more creative design for your chosen device—YourSmartphone 1.0 or YourPad 1.0. Use your own creativity to enhance the product.

ETHICAL LEADERSHIP
Copyright Infringement

Imagine that you have a 10-page management paper due at the end of the semester. You are swamped with schoolwork and your job waiting tables at a restaurant. You copy large chunks of text from a Website that addresses the issue you have chosen as your topic. You turn it in as your own. Of course, this is unethical.

Infringement of copyright is a fairly common practice. In the Internet age, it is all too easy to download and use something that we legally and ethically have no right to use without first seeking permission. It is possible that, at one time or another, you've unknowingly infringed on a copyright. But how do you know when you have broken copyright laws?

Break into teams and research copyright on the Web. Take notes on what is permissible and what is not. Then, review the following scenarios and determine whether each situation involves copyright infringement (assume you have not asked permission in any of the scenarios):

1. You have added a short audio introduction to your Website that includes the beginning of Beethoven's 5th symphony. Infringement or not?

2. You copy an album cover online from your favorite CD and post it to your Facebook page. Infringement or not?

3. You copy 10 lines of dialogue from Shakespeare's *Midsummer Night's Dream* and post it as an introduction to your blog site. Infringement or not?

4. You find the perfect chart on climate change at a U.S. Federal Website and use it in your midterm report on Global Climate Change. Infringement or not?

5. You go to the PirateBay Website and download your favorite artist's new CD, burn it to a disc, and give it to your best friend for her birthday. Infringement or not?

6. You find a great article on copyright infringement online for your management presentation that costs $3. You pay for it, download it, and make 25 copies for your classmates as a part of your presentation. Infringement or not?

7. You find several very cool graphics online from an artist who has been dead for 15 years. You copy the graphics to post on your online business Website. Infringement or not?

8. You just bought a new laptop and need the latest version of Microsoft Office. Your friend, who bought the software six months ago, lends you his copy to download onto your computer. Infringement or not?

KEY TERMS

Hypercompetition, *p. 258*

Creativity, *p. 259*

Convergent thinking, *p. 260*

Divergent thinking, *p. 260*

Innovation, *p. 264*

Skunk Works®, *p. 269*

Idea incubator, *p. 270*

Entrepreneurship, *p. 271*

Entrepreneur, *p. 271*

Social entrepreneurship, *p. 274*

Intrepreneur, *p. 275*

Break-even point, *p. 277*

Business plan, *p. 278*

Investor, *p. 279*

Angel investor, *p. 279*

Venture capitalist firm, *p. 279*

SBIC, *p. 279*

Intellectual property, *p. 283*

Patent, *p. 283*

Copyright, *p. 283*

Trademark, *p. 283*

MyManagementLab

Go to **mymanagementlab.com** for Auto-graded writing questions as well as the following Assisted-graded writing questions:

8-1. Think about a group that you participated in that included people with differing backgrounds, experiences, and points of view. When managed effectively, diverse groups like this can be much more creative than homogeneous groups. How did diversity affect your group's creativity?

8-2. Which stage of the business life cycle would be most exciting for you? Why? Which stage is least exciting? Why?

8-3. Mymanagementlab Only – comprehensive writing assignment for this chapter.

1. Why Are Creativity, Innovation, and Entrepreneurship at the Heart of Business? (pp. 258–259).

Objective: Explain why creativity, innovation, and entrepreneurship are critical to business.

Summary: In the constantly changing climate of modern organizations, relevancy is based on the ability of leaders to encourage creativity, innovation, and entrepreneurship. Good leaders shift their focus from short-term outcomes and employee overcontrol to fostering creativity. In the long run, this gives rise to innovations that support businesses and communities.

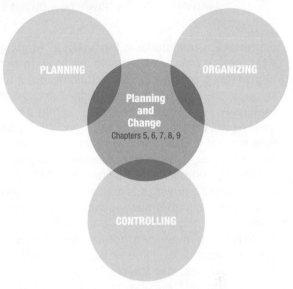

2. What Is Creativity? (pp. 259–262)

Objective: Define creativity.

Summary: Creativity is the process of imagining and developing something new. People can be creative at all levels of organizations—from the factory floor to the boardroom—and creativity should not be limited to people who are considered artistic. Unfortunately, some of us don't realize our full creative potential because we've been taught that logical thinking and creativity are mutually exclusive. In fact, creativity involves both divergent and convergent thinking, and involves many parts of the brain.

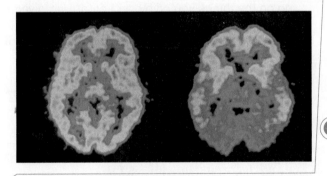

3. How Can We Encourage Creativity at Work? (pp. 262–264)

Objective: Learn how to encourage creativity at work.

Summary: Managers need to develop organizational cultures in which creativity is viewed as valuable, the status quo is challenged, the workforce is diverse, employee risk taking is supported, and creative spaces are provided. This enables organizations to embrace new, more competitive ways of doing things and developing goods. Encouraging this kind of creativity requires a rethinking of traditional rules.

4. What Is Innovation and Why Is It Important? (pp. 264–268)

Objective: Define innovation and describe its importance.

Summary: Innovation is the process of implementing new ideas, and it is a central component of modern organizations because it prevents obsolescence. In the business world, innovation does not just apply to the application of technological advances; it applies to new ways of providing service, employing sustainable practices, and increasing efficiency. Innovation is a long-term strategy for organizations of all types today. Despite the huge investments of time, effort, and money it requires, in the long run, innovation pays off for individuals, organizations, and communities.

5. How Can We Foster Innovation in People and Companies? (pp. 268–271)

Objective: Understand how to foster innovation.

Summary: In order for a company to be innovative, it must employ people with the creativity and drive to turn ideas into products and services that will help the company and its stakeholders. Innovation is often difficult in bureaucratic organizations and/or when the demands of day to day business are stifling. Some organizations have combated this by adopting business structures that promote innovation, including Skunk Works® and idea incubators. Regardless of how it is encouraged, innovation supports organizations in the quest for continued success.

8. How Does a New Business Get Started? (pp. 276–282)

Objective: Describe how a new business gets started.

Summary: Understanding the basics of starting a business—which questions to ask, how to write a business plan, how to secure funding, what the business life cycle is, and how to lead and manage for success—increases the likelihood that a new venture will be successful. Even if you think your idea is great and believe that other people will feel the same way, there is no substitute for preparing yourself emotionally and financially before you launch your business. It is also important to understand that, no matter how well prepared you are, unexpected things will crop up that will require you to rethink your strategies. You will weather these storms successfully if you lead as well as manage your employees, stay flexible, focus on customer service, and seek outside help when you need it.

7. What Is Intrepreneurship? (pp. 275–276)

Objective: Learn about intrepreneurship.

Summary: Intrepreneurship is the process of engaging employees in entrepreneurial activities inside an organization. Intrepreneurship tends to thrive in organizations that actively support innovative ideas and provide a safe environment for creative thinking. Most organizations are on the lookout for intrepreneurial employees, even if their structure is not entirely conducive to the process.

6. What Is Entrepreneurship? (pp. 271–275)

Objective: Define entrepreneurship.

Summary: Entrepreneurship is the process of identifying an opportunity, developing resources, and assuming the risks associated with a new venture. Even though many of us think of entrepreneurs as creative geniuses, most entrepreneurs are average people who own small companies in local communities that all of us do business with on a regular basis. These small businesses are an important component of national and global economies. Entrepreneurs are innovative, energetic risk takers who love to learn. There are many types of entrepreneurial ventures. One category worth noting is social entrepreneurship: the process of seeking to improve a social condition while also building a sustainable business.

9. What Is HR's Role in Supporting Creativity, Innovation, and Entrepreneurship? (pp. 282–284)

Objective: Outline HR's role in supporting creativity, innovation, and entrepreneurship.

Summary: Many entrepreneurs must assume the HR roles within their own businesses. Entrepreneurs who act as HR professionals must understand two of the most common HR functions these individuals are faced with involve understanding laws and regulations related to intellectual property and minimizing bureaucracy to foster creativity. HR professionals and entrepreneurs need to understand how to protect their intellectual property through patents, copyrights, and trademarks. Entrepreneurs should also learn how to structure policies and procedures within their organizations in such a way that they do not hinder employees' creativity.

10. What Can We All Do to Be More Creative, Innovative, and Entrepreneurial? (pp. 284–285)

Objective: List ways you can be more creative, innovative, and entrepreneurial.

Summary: Developing your creative skills will help you be more innovative in all aspects of your life and more entrepreneurial in your work. Noted scholar Mihaly Csikszentmihalyi offers many suggestions for enhancing creativity—and happiness—by taking joy in the surprises life offers, recognizing and reflecting on the things you enjoy, and producing diverse ideas. Mind maps can also help you in your efforts by enabling you to create visual representations of your ideas and their conceptual connections.

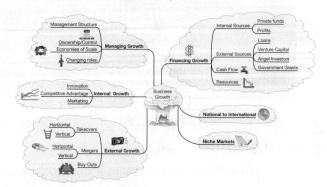

11. A Final Word on Creativity, Innovation, and Entrepreneurship (p. 286)

Summary: Creativity, innovation, and entrepreneurial spirit are driven by the pace of change in organizations today. Each of these concepts is important to organizational survival and will continue to be so well into the future. As we move into the future, innovation in several key sectors will change the way we do business.

Organizing for a Complex World: Forces Affecting Organizational Structure and Design

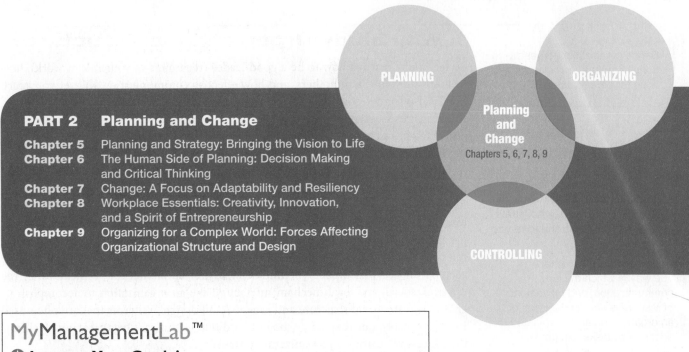

PLANNING

ORGANIZING

Planning
and
Change
Chapters 5, 6, 7, 8, 9

CONTROLLING

PART 2   Planning and Change

Chapter 5   Planning and Strategy: Bringing the Vision to Life
Chapter 6   The Human Side of Planning: Decision Making
             and Critical Thinking
Chapter 7   Change: A Focus on Adaptability and Resiliency
Chapter 8   Workplace Essentials: Creativity, Innovation,
             and a Spirit of Entrepreneurship
Chapter 9   Organizing for a Complex World: Forces Affecting
             Organizational Structure and Design

MyManagementLab™

⭐ Improve Your Grade!

Over 10 million students improved their results using the Pearson MyLabs. Visit **mymanagementlab.com** for simulations, tutorials, and end-of-chapter problems.

Chapter Outline

Chapter Objectives

9.1   Define organization, organizational structure, and classifications for organizations.

9.2   Understand how work is structured.

9.3   Describe how traditional concepts affect current views of organizational structure.

9.4   Assess how we can view organizational structures in nontraditional ways.

9.5   List and define common contemporary organizational structures.

9.6   Describe the factors that affect the design of organizational structures.

9.7   Learn how organizations are legally structured and classified.

9.8   Define HR's role in organizational design and structure.

9.9   Learn how you can work more effectively within an organizational structure.

293

Organization
A group of people assembled to perform activities that will allow the entity to accomplish a set of strategic and tactical goals and to realize its mission.

Organizational structure
The way in which the labor, communication, and movement of resources among the parts of an organization are coordinated to accomplish tasks and goals.

Organization design
The process of creating an organizational structure.

1. Why Study Organizational Structure?

So far, you've learned how to be a good leader (regardless of your role at work), how to motivate yourself and others, and how effective communication will set you apart. You've also learned that excellent planning, strategizing, decision making, and critical thinking are essential for your success. You now know how to deal with change in life and at work, and how creativity, innovation, and a spirit of entrepreneurship are exciting and important aspects of work today.

Good leadership is not completely dependent on you as a person—many external conditions impact how effectively you lead and work. This includes the organization itself and how the organization is structured. An **organization** is a group of people assembled to perform activities that will allow the entity to accomplish a set of strategic and tactical goals and to realize its mission. The phrase **organizational structure** refers to the way labor, communication, authority, and resources are coordinated to accomplish goals. A broader definition of organizational structure includes all the physical, social, and legal mechanisms that enable an organization to accomplish its goals. Organizational structure and organization design are terms that are often used interchangeably, but they really mean two different things. **Organization design** is the process of creating an organizational structure.

Organizational Structure and Design in Real Life: Your School

To illustrate these three concepts, consider your school. Your school is an organization. Within its geographic and virtual structure, groups of people work independently and together to advance and share knowledge, among other things. Your school's mission includes educating students, and it has a strategy to fulfill that mission. The strategy likely includes processes for identifying students who fit the mission, enrolling them, and ensuring that they receive a good education. All of these activities require that work, communication, and resources be coordinated.

Over the years, your school's employees have designed an organizational structure that can support the school in implementing its strategy through finding, enrolling, and educating students. For instance, it is likely that your school has an admissions department. Within this part of the organizational structure, employees select potential students who meet the school's standards for admission to the institution. In many schools, selecting students is a process conducted by an admissions committee. This committee is a team structure within a departmental structure. Imagine if the admissions department did not exist: How would the school select students who fit the school's mission? Would the president select students? Would students have to write to an instructor and ask to be admitted?

Or, imagine the chaos if there were no registration or finance departments. How would students enroll in classes? How would class sizes be controlled? What if 500 students wanted to attend a particular course and the room could only hold 30? Whose problem would that be? Would each instructor have to collect tuition and fees from every student each semester? How would employees get paid? How would financial aid be dispersed?

Finally, your school has academic departments. Academic departments foster ease of communication among faculty whose jobs and interests are similar. These departments are structured to provide a sense of identity for both students and faculty. They house classes, study groups, and research projects that enable faculty members to advance and share knowledge and support students in furthering their education.

In this example, you can see how your school—an organization—has been structured in ways that allow people to simplify, divide, and coordinate work. Your school is a particular type of organization—one that is most likely a not-for-profit. Many other types of organizations exist, as you will see next.

Common Classifications for Organizations

Think about the businesses and organizations in your hometown. You probably have restaurants, retail stores, manufacturers, and banks. You may also have theaters, charitable organizations, churches, local government offices, and so forth. All of these organizations can be classified in many ways, as you can see in ■ **EXHIBIT 9.1**. Organizations can also be classified by whether they provide goods or services, how large

■ **EXHIBIT 9.1**

Common Types of Organizations

Type of Organization	Definition	Examples
For-profit organization	Any business whose mission includes making profit for owners	Williams-Sonoma, Inc. (headquarters in San Francisco); Sanrio Co. Ltd (Tokyo)
Not-for-profit organization	An organization that provides goods or services and that invests profits in pursuit of organizational goals as opposed to sharing profit among owners	The Conference Board (New York); National Association for the Advancement of Colored People (NAACP; Baltimore, Maryland)
Governmental organization	An organization that leads, manages, and controls a nation, state, province, town, etc.	U.S. Senate (Washington, DC); Parliament of the United Kingdom of Great Britain and Northern Ireland (London)
Nongovernmental organization (NGO)	An organization that is not directly or solely linked to government(s) and that seeks to support human or social issues; NGOs are usually not-for-profit	World Wildlife Fund (Headquarters in Gland, Switzerland); Amnesty International (London), Human Rights Watch (Headquarters in New York)
Small business	Any organization that is organized for profit, independently owned, and not dominant in its market	WilliamsTown Communications (Indianapolis, Indiana); Couens CMBH (Munich, Germany)
Local organization	Any organization that operates in a defined geographic area	Hal's Delicatessen and Sandwich (Ithaca, New York); Simi Valley Chamber of Commerce (Simi Valley, California)
International organization	Any organization that has substantial operations in multiple countries	African Development Bank (headquarters in Tunis-Belvedère, Tunisia); Teleos Leadership Institute (headquarters in Elkins Park, Pennsylvania)
Multinational corporation	Any for-profit business that has formalized operations in many countries	Google (headquarters in Mountain View, California); Nestle S.A. (headquarters in Vevey, Switzerland)
Importer	Any organization that specializes in importing goods or services from another country or countries	Atlas Coffee Importers, LLC (Seattle, Washington); Vanilla, Saffron Imports (San Francisco)
Exporter	Any organization that specializes in exporting goods or services to another country or countries	Future Generation Company Ltd. (Hanoi, Vietnam); DeBeers Diamonds (Jaipur, India)
Public charity	A type of not-for-profit organization that is organized for purposes beneficial to the public	International Federation of Red Cross/Red Crescent Societies (Geneva, Switzerland); Save the Children (Westport, Connecticut); Lance Armstrong Foundation (Austin, Texas)
Private foundation	A type of organization set up by an individual, family, or group of individuals for philanthropic purposes; although not public charities, they are often an important source of funding for charities through grants	Bill and Melinda Gates Foundation (Seattle, Washington); Carnegie Foundation (San Francisco)
Virtual organization	Any organization that provides some or all of its products or services via information and telecommunications technologies, particularly the Internet	Amazon.com (headquarters in Seattle, Washington); eBay Inc. (headquarters in San Jose, California); Facebook (headquarters in Palo Alto, CA)

or small they are, or by industry (e.g. can also be categorized by industry: consumer goods, electronics, telecommunications, apparel, luxury goods, and so forth). In addition, organizations may be classified by where they do business: locally, nationally, or globally.

Classifications are helpful when talking about organizations. However, they can be confusing because many organizations can be described by more than one classification. For example, an international organization can also be a small business and a local organization (such as a food bank) can also be not-for-profit. Organizations may even be set up and funded by the government but not owned or managed by that government, such as state schools, hospitals, or universities.[1] In the not-for-profit category, there are laws and governmental regulations affecting not-for-profits, even though the government doesn't "run" these entities. For example, in the United States, one type of legal entity is called a "501(c)(3)," which can be a corporation, community chest, fund, or foundation run for educational, scientific, religious, charitable, literary, or other purposes.

Understanding how organizations are structured—who does what; how people, groups, and divisions work together; and how jobs are designed—will help you be a better leader, manager, and employee. In the following sections, we will define the basic concepts related to work, jobs, tasks, and roles. We will then look at several concepts that are traditionally important in organizational structure and design. Then we will analyze several intriguing, nontraditional, and modern concepts related to organizational structure. Following this, we will explore the most common contemporary organizational structures. We will then study the factors that managers and leaders consider when designing an organizational structure, such as the organization's strategy; the environment in which the organization operates; and its technology, size, and geographic dispersion. We will follow this with another important factor: legal designations in the United States Finally, the chapter will conclude with a look at what HR and all of us can do to create and sustain a healthy organizational structure.

Discussion Questions

1. Think about your family as an organization. Who is/are the leader(s)? Who makes major decisions? How does your family organize household work?

2. Does your family structure help create a resonant and supportive environment within which family members can communicate openly, share roles, and cooperate? How can you encourage this type of environment within your existing family structure?

Objective 9.2
Understand how work is structured.

2. How Is Work Structured?

Students (and some faculty and managers) consider organizational structure boring and unrelated to what really happens at work. The topic doesn't have to be boring and irrelevant, and you can bring it to life by thinking about a place you have worked or one of your schools. As you read, apply the concepts in this chapter to that organization, and think about how the structure affected the ways people behaved—including you. Ask yourself the question: Was behavior partly a result of the forces linked to organizational structure? Could you or those around you have behaved differently? Should you have? Often, structure is an invisible force that drives people to behave in ways that don't make sense. To start this (hopefully) more interesting discussion of structure, let's begin with the basics that we are most familiar with: jobs, tasks, and roles.

Jobs, Tasks, and Roles

A job is defined as a group of tasks and responsibilities related to accomplishing organizational objectives. Jobs can be classified in many ways. For example, jobs can be classified by profession or industry, type of workplace, associated tasks, grade or pay level, union or nonunion status, public or private sector status, or paid or unpaid status. What jobs have you had, paid and unpaid? It's important to recognize that unpaid jobs, such as working for a nonprofit, taking on an internship, or being a stay-at-home parent are *jobs*. They often aren't recognized as such, are dismissed as unimportant, or are even maligned. Let's stop making that mistake. If you have had a job that wasn't paid, consider it a legitimate part of your experience and learn how to present it as such. This author did, and it helped pave the way for a meaningful and rich career. If you are hiring someone, look beyond their paid jobs and consider what they have done in other jobs in their lives.

Whether paid or unpaid, you need to understand the tasks associated with jobs. Tasks are smaller units of work—activities that people do as part of their jobs. So, if you want to impress future employers with work you did in an internship, an unpaid job, or work in the home, you need to learn how to break down the tasks associated with those jobs and express them in a way that is meaningful to an employer.

Another concept that is important to decouple from the idea of a job is *role*. When talking about organizational structure, a role is the description, or title, linked to a job. The easiest way to show the distinctions between jobs, tasks, and roles is by example:

An administrative assistant (role) answers his boss's phone (task) as part of his job, which is to provide support to his boss in a variety of ways, including managing his boss's calendar, editing written materials, arranging travel, and preparing speech and presentation materials. A sales representative (role) completes her monthly expense report because it is a task for which she is responsible. Her job is to sell products to customers within a geographic region.

Understanding how to delineate roles and organize tasks is an important and much-ignored rule of good management, leadership, and followership. Take for example two people on a team who have very different jobs and roles, but who are expected to work on joint projects. Who does which tasks is an important negotiation that can help avoid redundancy and—maybe more importantly—friction and bad feelings between the individuals (and those who line up behind them). You may have had this experience. The other reason tasks are important is because they are what we *do* every day. Tasks make our jobs exciting, interesting, and fun—or boring and mind-numbing.

Some jobs are narrowly focused, some more broad. For example, on Henry Ford's assembly line in the early twentieth century, workers were assigned very few tasks—sometimes just one, which they did over and over. This is efficient, perhaps, but also mind-numbing.[2] Let's look at this concept of specialization more closely and consider its impact on workers' interest in tasks.

Job Specialization

Job specialization is an old topic. Plato discussed it extensively in his famous work *The Republic*.[3] Centuries later, famed economist Adam Smith explained that specialization increased production output and wealth.[4] In the twentieth century, job specialization was explained as a core concept of scientific management by industrial researcher Frederick Taylor.[5] Job specialization has been linked to **division of labor**, which is the process of reducing work to the smallest, simplest, and most easily repeated tasks possible.

Some jobs are highly specialized while many others are broader and include more tasks and activities. For example, the HR director in a manufacturing facility may

Job
A group of tasks and responsibilities related to accomplishing organizational objectives.

Division of labor
The process of reducing work to the smallest, simplest, and most easily repeated tasks possible.

perform most tasks associated with that position. She may coordinate all the recruiting, hiring, pay practices, benefits administration, training, employee relations, and safety practices, and she may even craft policies and procedures.

A person who performs a wide variety of tasks is known as a generalist. A specialist, on the other hand, is someone who has a very narrowly focused set of job tasks. Using the HR analogy, in a large corporate center you may have one person responsible for benefits, several people responsible for payroll, a team of training program facilitators, and so forth. These are specialists.

Job flexibility is very important in many organizations today. This is true because technologies are emerging constantly, customer demands change quite often, and, as you will learn later in this chapter, people often have less well-defined jobs in certain types of organizational structures. This means that people need to be able to "flex"—to change what they are doing based on what the market demands and the environment allows. In a manufacturing environment, scholars have recommended that functional specialization can give way to "flexible specialization," or the ability to quickly and efficiently manufacture customized products in smaller quantities.[6] In this model, employees are given the opportunity to vary the types of tasks and their order.[7] This basic idea can be applied to jobs other than manufacturing as well.

Now that you understand some basics of work structure, let's look at a few traditional concepts that impact our beliefs about organizational structure.

Discussion Questions

1. Have you ever done a highly specialized job? What was it? What did you like and what did you dislike about it?
2. Would you prefer to be a generalist or a specialist? Why?

Objective 9.3
Describe how traditional concepts affect current views of organizational structure.

3. What Traditional Concepts Impact Organizational Structures Today?

In this section we will discuss traditional concepts that are very important to our understanding of organizational structure. We will first look at hierarchy, span of control, and centralized vs. decentralized decision making. Then, we will conclude by considering a traditional way of depicting organizational structure—the organizational chart.

Hierarchy in Organizational Structures

Hierarchy
A way of organizing people and groups according to formal authority.

In an organization, a **hierarchy** is a way of organizing people and groups according to formal authority. A simple organizational hierarchy looks like a pyramid, with one person on the top (e.g., the president), a few below him or her (vice presidents), several beneath each of them (managers), and on down until you get to first-level employees at the bottom.

Organizational hierarchies can be "tall" or "flat." Tall organizational structures have many layers of management, whereas flat organizations have few. We will discuss the implications of how tall or flat a structure is later in the chapter.

A hierarchy includes reporting relationships—who reports to whom. This is sometimes called the *chain of command*. Three concepts related to hierarchies and reporting relationships are important when it comes to how people behave within a hierarchical structure: authority, responsibility, and accountability.

AUTHORITY

The first traditional concept in hierarchy is authority. Authority in an organization is defined as the legitimate right of a person in a role to make certain decisions, allocate resources, and direct certain other people's activities. Note that in this definition, we mention roles—that is because in the traditional sense, authority is associated with roles and jobs, not individuals. If, for example, you were called by the university president today and told you'd been hired to teach this course, you would, by virtue of your role, have the authority to ask students to complete assignments and grade them. This example shows why it is important to understand the person–job fit, which we will discuss later in the chapter.

Within a traditional organizational hierarchy, the job at the top of the structure has the most authority, and the jobs at the bottom have the least. Everyone within the hierarchy accepts his or her level of authority and honors others' levels of authority both above and below their own. For instance, in this management class, your professor is at the top of the hierarchy. Maybe there is a teaching assistant (TA) who is one step below the professor in the hierarchy. Then there is you (and the other students), located below the TA. If this is a typical and well-functioning hierarchy, you will know exactly what level of authority the TA has compared to your professor. This knowledge allows you to honor the hierarchy by, for example, approaching the TA with certain questions, rather than your professor.

Authority
The legitimate right of a person in a particular role to make certain decisions, allocate resources, and direct certain other people's activities.

RESPONSIBILITY

A second important traditional concept related to organizational hierarchy is responsibility. In an organization, responsibility is defined as the obligation to satisfactorily accomplish the tasks associated with a job. As a student, you are likely responsible for reading the assignments and preparing for and attending class. Your professor is responsible for sharing information with you in a manner that will enable you to learn.

Responsibility
The obligation to satisfactorily accomplish the tasks associated with a job.

ACCOUNTABILITY

Along with authority and responsibility comes accountability. Accountability is an individual's willingness to report success or failure regarding expected job outcomes to his or her manager or other superiors in the chain of command.[8] For example, say you are a manager in a bookstore. You are responsible for managing the daily finances of the shop, which in turn means overseeing the cashiers and ensuring that they balance their registers correctly every evening. If one of the cashiers is short or over, *you* are accountable for the situation and must report it to your manager.

Accountability has received a great deal of attention recently in terms of one particular aspect of work: ethical conduct on the job. Many senior-level jobs explicitly include ethical guidelines, and many organizations have explicit ethical codes of conduct as well. Partly as a result of gross ethical transgressions in some businesses in recent years, employees, managers, and leaders are being held more accountable for transparent and ethical behavior. Companies are under much greater scrutiny than in the past.

In addition to the mistrust felt for many companies, especially in the financial sector, there is the simple fact that information about what company employees do on the job is increasingly available to the public. Examples of claims that went public almost immediately abound, including the JP Morgan trading practices in 2012 that led to a multibillion dollar loss of investors' money, Asian workers' suicide pacts, and claims of money laundering at HSBC, a large international bank. In some cases, even if the claims are later found to be groundless, the damage to the company's reputation has already been done.

Accountability
An individual's willingness to report job success or failure regarding expected job outcomes to his or her manager or other superiors in the chain of command.

Span of Control in Organizational Structures

Span of control
The number of jobs that report to a position at the next higher level in a hierarchy.

The second key traditional consideration in organizational structure is span of control. The term **span of control** refers to the number of jobs that report to a position at the next higher level in a hierarchy. Let's go back to the college classroom example: In a very large class, a professor might have five TAs reporting to him or her. This means that the professor's span of control is five. Similarly, if each TA is responsible for twenty students, each TA's span of control is twenty.

But does the professor *really* control the TAs? Do the TAs control the students? In both cases, this is unlikely. A more realistic way of describing this concept might be span of management, or even better, span of leadership. **Span of leadership** refers to the number of jobs reporting to a person who is responsible for influencing, inspiring, and developing the people who hold those jobs.

Span of leadership
The number of jobs reporting to a person who is responsible for influencing, inspiring, and developing the people who hold those jobs.

A key question related to span of leadership is how many jobs/people should report to any one job/individual. The practical consideration is clear: How many individuals can one leader actually influence, inspire, and develop? Twenty employees? One hundred? One thousand? Most research indicates that when aspects of the leader's responsibility include direct in-person supervision in a traditional hierarchy, a reasonable expectation for span of leadership is probably around ten jobs/people.

Although this formula might hold true in many cases, today's organizational designers must address at least two serious issues when considering span of leadership. First, in many organizations, maintaining a small span of leadership is simply too expensive. Second, in recent years, the trend has been to move away from many layers of hierarchy, to fewer levels and more empowered employees. By definition, this means that span of leadership is much larger than in the past.

These changes lead to several conclusions:

- Organizations will need to provide managers with the skills to lead more people.
- Organizational structures will need to be created that support individuals and groups working autonomously.
- People at all levels will need to use critical thinking skills to make more and better decisions on their own.

Whereas in the past, many of the most important decisions were made at the top of an organization, in many cases, this is no longer true in organizations today. This means we need to understand yet another traditional concept—the degree to which decision making is centralized in an organization.

Centralized and Decentralized Decision Making

Centralized decision making
Structural model in which the vast majority of decision-making power is concentrated, typically among those at the top of the organizational hierarchy.

Centralized decision making refers to a structural model in which the vast majority of decision-making power is concentrated, typically among those at the top of the organizational hierarchy. One advantage of this model is that responsibility and accountability are very clear—everyone knows who can decide what. Another advantage is greater consistency within an organization around key processes. For example, if leadership development is centralized in the senior HR group, it is more likely that the organization will have one leadership model, one set of training programs, and so forth. A downside of centralized decision making is that it can be extremely inefficient, slow, and unresponsive to internal organizational needs or to changes in the external environment. For this reason, many organizations adapt a decentralized decision-making approach.

Decentralized decision making
Structural model in which decision-making power is distributed among the people closest to the relevant information, those who will be affected by the decision, or those who will have to implement the decision.

Decentralized decision making is a structural model in which decision-making power is distributed among the people closest to the relevant information, those who will be affected by the decision, or those who will have to implement the decision. In an organizational structure, then, decentralizing decision making can mean that people lower in the hierarchy and most directly involved in a given situation are empowered to make decisions. Decentralization is characterized by a more dispersed and shared decision-making process—a "leaderless" or distributed leadership model.

Decentralized decision making offers many advantages. First, most people enjoy having some control over their actions and decisions. Empowered employees are more committed, engaged, and creative. Second, employees closest to the problems and opportunities often have the best solutions and ideas. For example, say the chairs in your classroom are extremely uncomfortable. Who would make a better decision about criteria for new chairs—students, or administrators who never sit in these chairs?

A third advantage of decentralized decision making is that things can happen *fast*. This is important in many organizations today because the environment changes rapidly. Decentralized decision making can help an organization respond to customers' needs in a timely manner, rather than waiting for far-away research teams to collect data, analyze trends, and begin the process of adjusting products or services.

Decentralized decision making also has disadvantages. First, the quality of such decisions is wholly dependent on the individuals making them. This means that these employees must have excellent critical thinking skills and highly developed competencies such as pattern recognition, systems thinking, empathy, and social awareness. They need to be able to see the big picture to understand how their decisions fit into the organization.

Second, decentralized decision making can result in the development of practices at the local level that should be—but are not—consistent with organization-wide systems, such as ethics policies, financial management processes, human resource processes, customer service and leadership models, and so forth. For this reason, and to ensure that decision-making models fit the organization's strategy, leaders need to pay careful attention to which kinds of decisions are centralized and which are decentralized.

Employees, managers, and leaders can be more effective in their jobs if they understand and learn how to navigate an organization's structure. In the next section, we will examine a visual tool that helps us simplify this structure in order to study it.

The Organizational Chart

An **organizational chart** depicts how roles, jobs, authority, and responsibility are distributed within an organization. ■ **EXHIBIT 9.2** shows the organizational chart for the U.S. Department of Homeland Security. This organizational chart includes Homeland Security's mission statement at the top. Each of the boxes represents a job that includes certain responsibilities and is granted a certain level of authority. The people doing these jobs hold roles that are distinct and different. For example, the Secretary of Homeland Security is charged with the administration and enforcement of laws relating to immigration and naturalization. In addition, the secretary is responsible for the control, direction, and supervision of all employees and all the files and records of the department. The secretary has the power and duty to oversee and guard the borders of the United States against the entry of people without appropriate visas.[9]

Organizational charts are helpful because they show hierarchy, jobs, and roles. However, the picture painted by an organizational chart doesn't tell even half the story about how an organization is really structured. For example, considering what the U.S. Department of Homeland Security does, do you think this chart represents the way things actually work? What about when the director of the Domestic Nuclear Detection Office needs to put together a team with people in the Coast Guard? Can that director call the commandant? Or does the director ask his or her boss—the secretary or deputy secretary? Who is her boss, anyway? You can see that a line from the secretary goes all the way through each level. In a flat organizational structure like this, all the positions technically report to the secretary. How can the secretary manage the

Organizational chart
A visual representation of how roles, jobs, authority, and responsibility are distributed within an organization.

■ **EXHIBIT 9.2**

An abbreviated organizational chart for the U.S. Department of Homeland Security (the complete one is 25 pages long).

Mission Statement: "This Department of Homeland Security's overriding and urgent mission is to lead the unified national effort to secure the country and preserve our freedoms. While the Department was created to secure our country against those who seek to disrupt the American way of life, our charter also includes preparation for and response to all hazards and disasters. The citizens of the United States must have the utmost confidence that the Department can execute both of these missions."

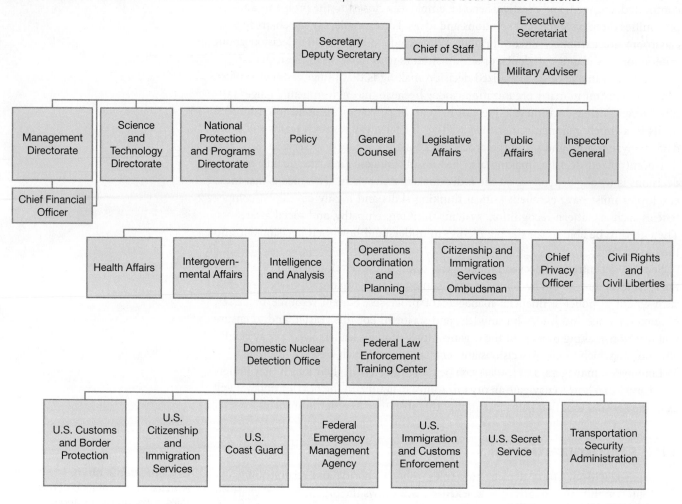

27 people who report to him or her? Or, what if one of the directors is close to the president of the United States? Would that affect this director's power in the organization? Or, say two individuals worked their way "up" in the government and have had interpersonal problems. Would this get in the way of interdivisional coordination?

The questions one could ask about the Department of Homeland Security illustrate that reporting relationships are only one determinant of how people work and coordinate tasks. Formal and informal communication, power relationships, and even physical proximity are examples of some of the complex factors that affect how work is coordinated and accomplished. An organizational chart can help us talk about some aspects of structure, but in the end, it is only a two-dimensional picture of jobs, roles, and hierarchical reporting relationships—nothing more, nothing less.

In this section, we have covered important concepts that claim a rightful place in the study of how organizations are designed. As helpful as these ideas are, however, they don't tell the whole story. Organizations are groups of *people*, and people are complicated. Accordingly, in the next section, we will explore several models and metaphors that allow us to consider organizational structure in more sophisticated and creative ways.

Discussion Questions

1. Have you ever worked in an environment that used centralized decision making? If so, what did you like and dislike about it? Similarly, have you ever worked in an environment in which decision making was decentralized? If so, what did you like and dislike about it?

2. Draw an organizational chart for your family. In what ways does this chart demonstrate "how things really work" in the family? In what ways does it not capture things like communication, power relationships, and coordination of work and chores?

4. What Are Some Important and Nontraditional Ways to View Organizations?

Objective 9.4
Assess how we can view organizational structures in nontraditional ways.

Although organizational charts and topics such as hierarchy are very important to understanding organizations, we also need to be more creative when we think about organizations and their structures. That's because organizations are full of *people*—and people make choices about what to do based on how they perceive their relationships with others and with the organization, the organizational culture, and internal and external pressures. In addition, organizations and their structures are becoming even more complex as the external environment changes and as technologies become central to the workplace.

In this section, we'll look at four innovative ways of seeing organizations: organizations as open systems, mechanistic versus organic structures, metaphors describing organizations, and organizations as "spiders" and "starfish."[10]

Open Systems Theory: No Organization Is an Island

Open systems theory states that any human system is constantly influenced by and is influencing its environment.[11] Organizations are open systems, as seen in ▪ **EXHIBIT 9.3**. Both an organization and its environment are constantly changing each other.[12]

Borrowed from the natural sciences, open systems theory is the idea that a system is made up of individual parts that create a whole system, and it is also part of the environment within which it exists. The organizational environment includes factors such as economic and social systems (such as capitalism and national cultures), educational systems that prepare employees, raw materials, and customers. Within the boundaries of an organization are elements such as employees, technology, organizational culture, work and communication processes, and leadership practices. All of these serve to link various organizational subsystems, creating a complex whole that has the capacity to manage internal work and processes and also interact with the environment.[13]

To understand open systems theory, think of the organization as a living being. It receives inputs from the environment, processes those inputs (sometimes called throughputs), and shares outputs with the environment. For example, British Petroleum (BP), a huge multinational corporation headquartered in the United Kingdom, has operations in dozens of countries. As one of the largest corporations in the world and extremely important in the United Kingdom, BP can exert a great deal of influence on aspects of its environment such as the British economy, the economies of the different oil-producing countries in which it operates, and so forth. However, BP is still powerfully influenced by its environment in terms of the demand for and price of oil;

Open systems theory
A theory stating that any human system, such as an organization, is constantly influenced by and is influencing its environment.

■ **EXHIBIT 9.3**

Organizations function as open systems and are affected by the environment in which they operate.

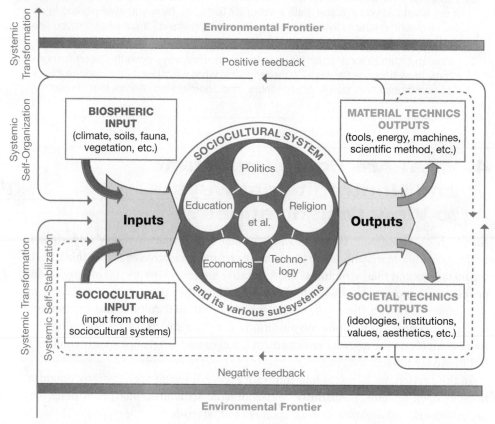

the stability of governments throughout the world; the local cultures of its employees and customers; international conflicts; piracy; and local, national, and international laws, to name a few factors.

BP affects the physical environment, especially the earth and its atmosphere, through the operations of extracting oil, refining it, and selling it. Companies like BP are well aware of their impact on the natural environment. They are both mandated by law and voluntarily driven to take responsibility for how their operations affect the air, water, land, plants, and animals in areas in which they do business. BP's relationship to the natural environment became painfully clear in 2010, when an explosion destroyed BP's deep-water oil platform in the Gulf of Mexico that was owned and operated by a company named Transocean. Another company, Halliburton, had been contracted to apply a special cement to cap the bore hole that tapped the sub-sea oil reservoir. Tragically, the explosion killed 11 workers and injured several others. Another tragedy involved the oil itself, which flowed nearly unrestricted out of the uncapped well 5,000 feet below the surface for months after the explosion, endangering the ocean, all kinds of sea life, and the livelihoods of thousands of people who depend on the ocean.[14] By April 2011, BP had filed $40 billion in lawsuits against Transocean, Halliburton, and Cameron, the manufacturer of the blowout preventer.[15] By 2012, plaintiffs suing BP agreed to settle roughly 100,000 claims against the company totaling nearly $8 billion, pending a judge's approval.[16] This example, while tragic and extreme, points out that no organization can ever be separate from the environment within which it operates.

The physical environment has an impact on companies such as BP through things like weather patterns and geological formations. To understand BP, then, means also being able to understand something about a great many different factors and how they interact—geology, politics, culture, meteorology, economics[,] trade, for example. Both the organization and its environment are constantly prov[iding] feedback to each other, and the organization adapts to the environment as appro[priate.] This output-as-feedback indicates the degree to which the environment or the o[rgani-]zation is healthy.

Organizational structure is complicated. That's why it's important for us to [study] the topic carefully and not oversimplify it. Let's turn to a few other viewpoints t[hat] help us understand how organizational structure works.

Mechanistic and Organic Organizations

Many theories put forth in the last century were based on the idea that stabilit[y is a] goal in organizations. But, most organizations *must* be flexible or they will not su[rvive] today. To understand this better, let's look at what is meant by the terms *mechanistic* and *organic* when applied to organizations and their level of flexibility.

A **mechanistic organization** is characterized by routine, specialized jobs. It is usually hierarchical and bureaucratic, with routine processes and standard operating procedures.[17] **Standard operating procedures, or SOPs,** are detailed and specific instructions for carrying out routine tasks. A mechanistic organization is inflexible and formal, and it often has centralized decision-making processes.

In comparison, an **organic organization** is characterized by a high degree of flexibility, low levels of specialization, less formality, and decentralized decision-making processes. The greatest strength of an organic organization is its flexibility. It can change and adapt, depending on internal and external conditions and demands.

Organic organizations are adaptable and open to the environment and to change.[18] As organizational scholar Gareth Morgan puts it, there is a constant "exchange with their environment," but different parts have different degrees of openness in this exchange so the organization can function well internally while also adapting to the environment.[19] This means that parts of the organization are structured differently depending on the specific functions and purposes of each subsystem, like specialized organs within the human body. For example, we would expect to see manufacturing structured differently than marketing, because manufacturing tends to have more routine functions and marketing requires more creativity. Additionally, processes in manufacturing have to be stable and predictable in order to ensure quality in production. This is not the case in marketing, which adapts to different technologies, venues, and customer populations based on a number of environmental factors, such as what is currently popular, who the competition is and what they are doing, and what venues are currently available for marketing programs. By enabling different parts of the organization to be more or less open to the environment, the organization can maintain what is called homeostasis—an internal self-regulation that keeps it healthy, in balance, and distinct from its environment.

Because environments change, organizations have to change with them: They need to evolve and adapt to stay competitive and to function properly.[20] Organic organizations are also adaptive organizations. An **adaptive organization** is one that is very flexible and readily responds to feedback—to internal and external changes in conditions and the overall environment.[21] In an adaptive organization, leadership and management practices, organizational culture, and structure are designed to ensure that people can respond to threats and opportunities quickly and effectively.

Organizational scholar Karl Weick describes adaptive organizations as "loosely coupled." A loosely-coupled organization is one in which there is less centralized control and greater flexibility within and among parts of the organization.[22] Because of this flexibility, there is a greater ability to adapt to changing environmental conditions.

Mechanistic organization
An organization that is typically hierarchical, bureaucratic, and characterized by routine, specialized jobs and standard operating procedures.

Standard operating procedures (SOPs)
Detailed and specific instructions for carrying out routine tasks.

Organic organization
An organization characterized by a high degree of flexibility, low levels of specialization, less formality, and decentralized decision-making processes.

Adaptive organization
An organization that is very flexible and readily responds to feedback—to internal and external changes in conditions and the overall environment.

Examples of the importance of loosely coupled but coordinated activity lies in the case of natural and man-made crises. Researchers have studied the global crisis network that was put in place to respond to the threat of a deadly pandemic of severe acute respiratory syndrome (SARS) in 2002 and 2003. SARS had a high mortality rate (9.6 percent) and had spread globally before being identified.[23] Luckily, even though the disease was highly contagious and had spread to dozens of countries, the global crisis network was able to contain it and fewer than a thousand people died.[24] The researchers found that the combination of loosely-coupled, decoupled, and tightly coupled (highly coordinated and centrally controlled) interactions gave the global crisis network the amount of flexibility it needed to respond effectively to the crisis while at the same time averting chaos.[25]

Researchers Dessein Wouter and Tano Santos argue that adaptive organizations may empower employees to structure their work processes to meet the needs, opportunities, and demands of the local environment.[26] This approach requires a great amount of coordination in a geographically dispersed organization. These researchers also make the case that adaptive organizations need to rely less on specialization because this can lead to ignoring "local knowledge."[27] Examples of this problem are abundant in multinational organizations that apply company-wide standards to regions around the world where the context is quite different.

For instance, environmental hazards in the workplace are strictly regulated in the United States by the Occupational Safety and Health Administration (OSHA), but such standards are not internationally adopted, and the processes outlined in the United States may not even be appropriate in another country. The United Kingdom has its own standards as well, which differ from those of the rest of the European Union. So, a compliance measure that was crafted at a company's U.S. headquarters may be difficult to implement in other countries; or worse, it may make no sense because the laws don't match or because the needs of the foreign subsidiary might be completely different. For example, lean, finely textured beef—also known as "pink slime"—is a low-cost ground beef filler made primarily from connective tissue (■ **EXHIBIT 9.4**). Because the tissue is sterilized with ammonium before being added to ground beef, many countries and economic zones do not allow the filler to be used. These include the European Union (EU), Canada, and the United Kingdom. Although pink slime is not banned in the United States, in 2012 many companies and restaurants voluntarily banned its use in the products they sell.[28]

Characteristics of an organization—such as its flexibility—are important to understanding its structure. Ideas and beliefs about organizations are also important and warrant our examination too. Let's look at how metaphors can help us interpret these ideas and beliefs.

Gareth Morgan's Metaphors for Organizations

We see organizations differently depending on the lens through which we view people and systems. Researchers such as Gareth Morgan use metaphors to help us understand our beliefs about how organizations should function. Metaphors allow us to describe organizational structures and how they function in familiar and simple ways. A few useful metaphors or images of organizations are listed in ■ **EXHIBIT 9.5**.[29]

Metaphors help us think creatively. Different images come to mind when we think of organizations as "machines," "organisms," and "brains." These different images help us see the different ways

■ **EXHIBIT 9.4**
Should companies and restaurants ban "pink slime"?

Source: AP Photo/Nati Hamik

■ **EXHIBIT 9.5**

Our Metaphors for Organizations Affect What We Notice and Do		
Metaphor	**How We See the Organization**	**What We Do**
The organization as a machine	How do the "parts" fit together? Are the "gears" well oiled (e.g., effective and efficient supply chain, intake, and output)?	Manage for efficiency; attend to flow of inputs and outputs; reduce jobs to their simplest form.
The organization as an organism	What does the organization need in order to be healthy? How can we ensure that the entity has the "food" it needs (e.g., raw materials, committed people)?	Commit to employee health and welfare; scan the environment for changes; adapt to those changes.
The organization as a brain	How does the "brain" control the organization? Are our leaders smart enough? Are our employees high in IQ and emotional intelligence?	Develop excellent knowledge management systems; focus on leadership development.
The organization as a culture	How do our values and beliefs affect our actions inside and outside the organization? Is our sense of identity, commitment, and purpose clear and shared among all of us?	Focus on ethical conduct inside and outside the organization; show customers how we live our values through our business practices.
The organization as an instrument of power and domination	Do we exploit our people and our customers? Are we focused on winning at *any* cost? Or, are we focused on empowerment and activities that support ourselves and others in our external environment?	Consciously manage personalized and socialized power; consider ethical implications of actions.

in which organizations function and can be structured. They also show us different ways organizations can interact with the environment. The metaphors of organizations as "spiders" or "starfish" show us yet another way to look at organizations today.

Organizations as Spiders and Starfish

Authors Ori Brafman and Rod Beckstrom believe that given the changes of the twenty-first century, we must look at our organizations in radically different ways. Brafman and Beckstrom use the metaphors of "spiders" and "starfish" to describe traditional and adaptive organizations, respectively.[30]

Spider organizations are traditional, hierarchical, and mechanistic. Decisions are made higher up and then pushed down the chain of command. The information required to make these decisions must pass through numerous bureaucratic barriers before it can reach people with the authority to make decisions, so response to change is slow, inefficient, and often ineffective.

Power is centrally organized at the top of spider organizations. The head and brain of the spider represent centralized power and control in the organization, and the legs are the collective actions of divisions, departments, and groups (■ **EXHIBIT 9.6**). The legs do what the head tells them—nothing more and nothing less. They only work together with the support of the head, and if one of the legs dies, the others have to find a way to walk without it—out of balance and overburdened. If two legs die, the problem becomes worse, and if more die, the spider will be unable to function and it will die, too. If the head dies, the whole organism dies with it.

Starfish are very different from spiders. First, the legs of a starfish act independently of one another, smoothly and gracefully moving over and around obstacles. Also, the starfish's brain isn't making all the decisions or controlling all the action: All the knowledge for the activities needed to stay healthy, adapt, and change is self-contained

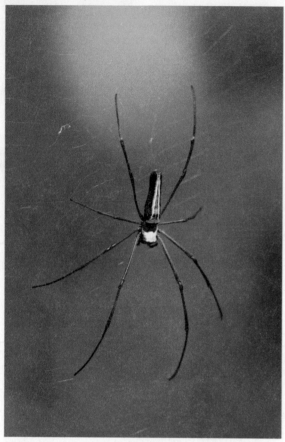

Source: Nachiketa Bajaj/Shutterstock.com

in various parts of the starfish. If you cut off one of the creature's legs, a new leg will grow back. In fact, in some species of starfish, each piece will regenerate into a whole new organism. This animal is built to adapt, to survive threats, and to thrive in the face of adversity (■ **EXHIBIT 9.7**).

The decentralized starfish organization has appeared many times in human history, and each time it has thrived and in some cases brought about significant social change. A twentieth-century example is Alcoholics Anonymous. This organization gets its power from the fact that each group is locally autonomous; members hear about it by word of mouth and stay because it is beneficial rather than because someone tells them to. There is no supreme owner of the organization. Rather, there is local, collective ownership. Each meeting and each group is different, yet all of them function with the common goal of sobriety.

In the twenty-first century, many examples of decentralized, networked organizations have appeared. Brafman and Beckstrom cite Al Qaeda as a powerful starfish organization that is changing how nations defend themselves.[31] In 2011, the head of this organization, Osama bin Laden, was killed. Scholars—not to mention national leaders—are waiting to see if this organization is indeed a starfish capable of functioning with its head gone.[32]

Brafman and Beckstrom also point out that a number of organizations and structures, including Wikipedia, Craigslist, peer-to-peer (P2P) networks, and open-source software, rely on participatory membership, collective ownership, and commitment to a new and different way of interacting.[33] The authors describe starfish organizations as powerful social networks that guide people's values and behavior. These networks often include inspiring individuals, called "catalysts", who mobilize others to act. They also have "champions", people who do a lot of the hard work. Finally, people in starfish organizations share ideology, such as sobriety in Alcoholics Anonymous.[34]

You've now learned about new and innovative ways to view organizations and their structures. This is important because in many parts of the world, and in many industries, traditional models are not a perfect fit for what needs to be done, how cultures function, which resources are scarce or abundant, etc. This is definitely the case in many parts of the developing world where people seek to do business in creative ways. Cooperatives are one organizational structure that blends some traditional (e.g., spider) models with some nontraditional (e.g., starfish) models. Let's see how the Chaisa Multipurpose Cooperative is doing this for the people of Zambia in the *Business Case*.

The Chaisa Multipurpose Cooperative is inspiring, especially when you consider the ways in which it seamlessly folds together the tenets of both traditional and nontraditional organizational structures. The cooperative format meets the needs and culture of the people it serves, and it enables these individuals to exercise their passion, commitment, and talents in meaningful and profitable ways.

In this section, you have learned how to view organizations in many different ways. This knowledge allows you to consider basic information about organizational

Source: WILDLIFE GmbH/Alamy Images

The Chaisa Multipurpose Cooperative

Population increase is a major problem that affects many developing nations, such as Zambia. Zambia's population grew about 33 percent between 2002 and 2012.[35] Amazingly, the median age in Zambia is just 16.5 years old! With the right policies in place, a large population can positively influence economic development and growth through its large labor force and consumer base. However, population increase can make it difficult for an economy to sustain the large number of people, as has been the case in Zambia. In that country, there just aren't enough jobs and the unemployment rate is very, very. In a quest to reduce unemployment levels, the Zambian government has been encouraging skills development and entrepreneurship—both of which come alive through the formation of cooperatives.

A cooperative (or co-op for short) is an organization made up of a group of people who come together voluntarily to meet common economic, social, and cultural needs through a jointly owned and democratically controlled enterprise. Chaisa Multipurpose Cooperative is one of the oldest in Zambia, situated about 5 kilometers away from the central business district of the capital city, Lusaka. Formed in 1982, this co-op has a membership of 150 people and is involved in several different business activities, including selling a variety of consumer goods, carpentry, and metalworking.

Mr. Dube, the chairperson of the co-op, has been a member for over 15 years. In 2008, Dube and six other members were elected to the board of directors. This leadership structure helps the cooperative have a path through which it can achieve its goals. It is the duty of the chairperson together with the board of directors to see that the cooperative's objectives are carried out.

Benefits of the Cooperative to the Members and the Community

- The joint ownership of the cooperative creates a sense of belonging and brings about unity in the society.
- There are over 400 people who use the facilities of the cooperative. These people get to help each other, especially in the event of bereavement.
- The co-op is a huge source of income for the members and creates employment for the people in the surrounding community. This means that many people are able to earn income through the co-op's activities and through the dividends from the cooperative.
- All economic benefits are kept within the cooperative.
- Because cooperatives are legal entities, it is far easier for members to borrow money than if a single individual was starting a business.
- Cooperatives help create employment and help improve the standard of living of their members and the surrounding communities.

People who decide to form a cooperative are entrepreneurs, because they take risks by investing in the cooperative, developing businesses, and taking their products and services to the marketplace. One of the most important aspects of this type of entrepreneurial venture is that it empowers people. As the co-op becomes more successful, both members and employees become better equipped and more empowered to open their own businesses. In other words, co-ops start a cycle of entrepreneurship, which is necessary and inspiring in Zambia and around the world.

Source: Adapted from a case by Chikasha Muyembe.

---

structures in a more sophisticated manner. We will now turn our attention to common types of organizational structures and ownership models. As you read about these, continue to think creatively about how you can seek to understand the ways in which organizational structure affects individual behavior and overall organizational success.

Cooperative
An organization made up of a group of people who come together voluntarily to meet common economic, social, and cultural needs through a jointly owned and democratically controlled enterprise.

Discussion Questions

1. In what ways does the external environment influence the structure of your school as an organization?

2. Think about your class as an organization that is part of an open system, including your school and the outside environment. What external factors affect what you do in class? How does your class process these factors internally (i.e., discussions, assignments, or lectures)? Do the conclusions drawn from your internal class processes cycle back into the external environment? How so (i.e., projects, presentations, academic clubs, volunteer groups, or social advocacy groups)?

Objective 9.5
List and define common contemporary organizational structures.

5. What Are the Most Common Contemporary Organizational Structures?

In this section, we will look at several common organizational structures in use today. One reason we focus on specific structures is that at some point in your career, you are likely going to need to weigh in on how to structure your organization, or at least the part of the organization in which you work. In fact, employees at all levels are more and more likely to be asked to weigh in on decisions like these—especially in flatter organizations, which we will explain later in this section.

Another reason why it is important to recognize typical organizational structures is that you will probably feel more or less comfortable working within some organizational structures than others. For example, you may prefer more or less guidance, autonomy, certainty, ambiguity, or change. You might prefer very clear lines of authority, or you might like more networked and informal authority. Recognizing which kinds of organizational structures foster the kind of conditions you enjoy and where you can be at your best will help you make better choices about the organizations you join and the jobs you accept.

We will start this section by looking more deeply at the differences between "tall" and "flat" organizational structures. Then we will discuss departmentalization and how structures differ when jobs are grouped by division, function, product, process, customer, and geography. Finally, we'll conclude by looking at several structures that have emerged in recent years to support organizations in dealing with today's complex environment: matrix, hybrid, and networked structures.

"Tall" and "Flat" Organizational Structures

A vertical organizational structure can be "tall" with many levels of hierarchy, or it can be "flat" with few levels of hierarchy. In theory, tall vertical structures support fluid movement of information and resources up and down the hierarchy, whereas flatter structures facilitate faster and more effective communication horizontally across and among groups in the organization.

Tall vertical structures involve a chain of command that forms a pyramid-type organizational chart, extending from boards of directors and the most senior leaders at or near the top, to managers, supervisors, and then lower-level employees at the bottom. Tall structures can be understood purely in terms of hierarchy, as in the rank system of the U.S. Army. As you can see in ■ **EXHIBIT 9.8**, enlisted soldiers are classified into 13 hierarchical ranks, 9 of which represent the category of "non-commissioned officers" (NCOs). The hierarchy of "commissioned officers" (the lowest of which technically outranks the highest ranking enlisted soldier) has 11 different ranks, for a total of 24 hierarchical levels.

A major benefit of clear vertical structures is that information sharing up and down the chain of command can be efficient.[36] One drawback is that different vertical structures within an organization (e.g., marketing, finance, manufacturing) can develop a "silo mentality." The term *silos* is often used to describe parts of an organization that are isolated from and interact less with other parts of the organization.[37]

Many organizations try to minimize the negative impact of silos by creating cross-functional teams for important organization-wide projects. Cross-functional teams consist of individuals from many parts of an organization who are brought together to provide different points of view and skills in the service of organization-wide challenges and opportunities, innovations, and special projects.

Another potential problem in a tall vertical structure is that more managers and executives are needed to make decisions, allocate resources, and the like. This is expensive and can be highly inefficient. That is why in recent decades, many organizations have reorganized their hierarchies so that fewer managers are needed to oversee

Cross-functional teams
Teams that consist of individuals from many parts of an organization who are brought together to provide different points of view and skills in the service of organization-wide challenges and opportunities, innovations, and special projects.

■ **EXHIBIT 9.8**

The U.S. Army uses 24 rank designations for enlisted soldiers and officers.

Enlisted Soldiers*			Commissioned Officers		
Insignia	Rank	Designation	Insignia	Rank	Designation
	Sergeant Major of the Army	E–9		General of the Army (GOA)	0–11
	Command Sgt Major (CSM)	E–9		General (GEN)	0–10
	Sergeant Major (SGM)	E–9		Lieutenant General (LTG)	0–9
	First Sergeant (1SG)	E–8		Major General (MG)	0–8
	Master Sergeant (MSG)	E–8		Brigadier General (BG)	0–7
	Sergeant First Class (SFC)	E–7		Colonel (COL)	0–6
	Staff Sergeant (SSG)	E–6		Lieutenant Colonel (LTC)	0–5
	Sergeant (SGT)	E–5		Major (MAJ)	0–4
	Corporal (CPL)	E–4		Captain (CPT)	0–3
	Specialist (SPC)	E–4		First Lieutenant (1LT)	0–2
	Private-First Class (PFC)	E–3		Second Lieutenant (2LT)	0–1
	Private (PVT2)	E–2			
NO INSIGNIA	Private (PVT)	E–1			

*Among enlisted soldiers, corporal and above are referred to as non-commissioned officers.

operations. In other words, organizations are becoming "flatter." Think of a pyramid that is very wide at its base and not very high, and you have the basic concept of what a flat organization looks like (■ **EXHIBIT 9.9**).

In flat organizations, communication can be more effective horizontally across teams, work groups, and departments. Theoretically, resources can flow more easily across the organization. To this end, flat organizations often have team-based structures, less specialization, and wider spans of control and leadership.[38] A flat structure can potentially result in decreased costs and increased speed because there are fewer layers of management.

A truly flat structure is rare. Many people have a hard time imagining what it would be like to work in a flat organization. People want to move "up." In addition, metrics, planning, and budgeting all continue to support the vertical, hierarchical organization.[39]

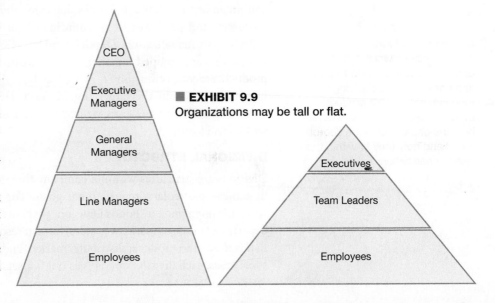

■ **EXHIBIT 9.9**
Organizations may be tall or flat.

IDEO

Empowering Employees

Companies are not limited to traditional organizational structures. Innovative firms often bypass these structures and create new configurations that allow more freedom for creativity, innovation, and teamwork. Consider the example of IDEO, a global design consultancy firm with over 500 employees worldwide. The word "ideo" is Greek for idea, and one of the company's founders, David Kelley, has become well known as an innovator. His inventive style in designing products and services can also be seen in IDEO's unique organizational structure. Kelley recalls working for large corporations early in his career and finding them oppressive. In his words, "You could feel the weight of the organizational chart. My boss was a person I didn't know, who was making decisions about my life." Therefore, when he later started his own company, Kelley wanted to do something different—something he refers to as "employee empowerment."[40]

The result of Kelley's innovative thinking was IDEO's current structure. Although the firm's employees can be described as a flat team, they also form "studios" and multidisciplinary "hot teams." Studios are departments that vary in size from 15 to 25 people, with each studio head responsible for the profit and loss of his or her particular group. Studio heads are not hired from the outside but are instead groomed from within IDEO.

Hot teams are groups of people with multidisciplinary backgrounds who work together for a certain period of time. The leaders of the hot teams come from within the teams and are not hired to be leaders; rather, these individuals have worked at IDEO for some time and have come to be respected by their colleagues.

Clients and thinkers from outside IDEO are also vital participants in the company's hot teams. This cross-disciplinary approach has contributed to IDEO's success in the completion of design projects such as the Palm V, the Apple mouse, and the Crest Neat-Squeeze Tube for toothpaste. In fact, IDEO has won more Business Week/IDSA Industrial Design Excellence Awards than any other firm and has been ranked among the 25 most innovative companies by both Fast Company and Boston Consulting Group.[41] David Kelley attributes his company's success partly to its use of teams: "We have the advantage of working in multiple industries. Let's say we are working on a chair, but we've learned something in the automobile industry before. Maybe we learned about a certain kind of spring in the automobile industry. We just cross-pollinate that into the chair, and now we have an innovation in the furniture industry."[42]

Source: Case written by Laura Town, WilliamsTown Communications.

When a flat structure is implemented, the changes in employee attitudes and organizational culture can be both beneficial and challenging. For instance, researchers have found that when a firm flattens, employees feel empowered but often get less feedback. Additionally, involvement increases, but identification with the organization can suffer. Finally, intrinsic motivation tends to rise dramatically, but this can be at the cost of decreased satisfaction in important extrinsic motivators such as pay and job security.[43]

Departmentalization and Organizational Structure

Departmentalization
The process by which individuals or activities are grouped together into departments according to function, geography, product, process, or customer, as well as how the departments are coordinated and how they fit within the larger organization.

Within an organizational hierarchy, jobs are often grouped in ways that allow people, resources, and processes to be coordinated for efficiency and effectiveness. This is called departmentalization. **Departmentalization** is the process by which individuals or activities are grouped together into departments according to function, geography, product, process, or customer, as well as how the departments are coordinated and how they fit within the larger organization. Departmentalization can also support matrix, hybrid, and network structures. Let's examine each of these departmental structures in turn.

DIVISIONAL STRUCTURES

Divisions are structures within a company that include all the departments necessary to achieve particular organizational goals. For example, a global consumer goods company might have a "Foods Division" that is a self-contained organization including departments such as marketing, sales, human resources, and supply chain—everything that is needed to produce, distribute, market, and sell the company's food products. In some cases, each division operates as if it is a separate business with its own hierarchy,

■ **EXHIBIT 9.10**
General Electric's organizational chart illustrates its divisional structure.

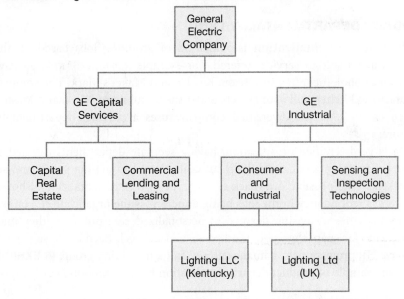

top leaders, and even board of directors.[44] As you can see in the example of General Electric (■ **EXHIBIT 9.10**), a company chooses a divisional structure to support separate and self-contained structures for the production of certain products or service lines. In Exhibit 9.10, the top two structures of the company, GE Capital Services and GE Industrial, are divisions. Within each division are departments necessary to manage the entire production-to-market cycle.

"Pure" divisional structures would not need or have any hierarchical or reporting relationships with the parent company, except through the division's leader. In practice, however, it is more common for certain business units and functional groups, such as HR and finance, to have secondary "dotted line" reporting relationships into the central organization to ensure consistency in vital organizational processes.[45]

FUNCTIONAL DEPARTMENTALIZATION

Functional departmentalization is a method of grouping jobs based on the nature of the work being performed. Most organizations have five functional areas: operations (all the jobs related to what the organization does, produces, or provides), marketing, sales, human resources, and finance. Information technology (IT) is also a key function. ■ **EXHIBIT 9.11** illustrates functional departmentalization at the executive level of an organization, showing the president at the top of the organization and five vice presidents (VPs) of each functional area.

One benefit of functional departmentalization is that each functional area works as a cohesive whole, and information sharing within each function can be efficient.[46]

Functional departmentalization
Method of grouping jobs based on the nature of the work being performed.

■ **EXHIBIT 9.11**
Functional departmentalization groups jobs based on the type of work being performed.

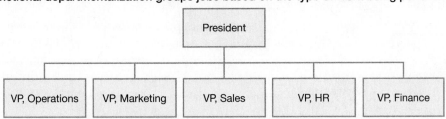

A drawback is that the different functions can develop the "silo mentality" mentioned earlier because they may interact less with other functions of the organization.[47]

PRODUCT DEPARTMENTALIZATION

Product departmentalization A method of grouping jobs based on the products made or services offered.

Product departmentalization is a method of grouping jobs based on the specific products made or services offered. For example, Fortune Brands owns various brands of alcohol, including Jim Beam, Kessler, and Maker's Mark. The company also manufactures kitchen and bath faucets under the brand name Moen and Masterbrand kitchen cabinets.[48] This diversified company uses a product departmentalization structure.

In a large diversified organization, having separate departments devoted to particular products or services can help cut costs related to getting goods and services to market.[49] One possible drawback to this type of departmentalization, however, is that there is redundancy in the jobs being done across the organization. For example, if a company has a division devoted to personalized care products, they may have departments for soap, shampoo, toothpaste, and hair gel. Each of those departments may have HR professionals, a finance group, and a marketing group. ■ **EXHIBIT 9.12** shows an example of product departmentalization for a frozen food company.

■ **EXHIBIT 9.12**
Product departmentalization groups jobs based on the products or services offered.

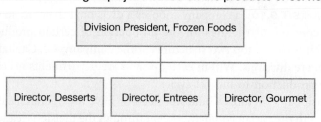

PROCESS DEPARTMENTALIZATION

Process departmentalization A method of grouping jobs based on the sequential steps of the work people do to produce products or services or engage in other business activities.

Process departmentalization is a method of grouping jobs based on the sequential steps of the work people do to produce products or services or engage in other business activities. Let's say you work in a manufacturing plant where soda is produced, bottled, and prepared for market. Using process departmentalization, one department would have all the jobs associated with mixing the soda. Another department would be involved in manufacturing the glass bottles and metal caps. A third would be involved in pouring the soda into individual bottles and capping those bottles. The fourth department would include all jobs related to labeling the bottles, and the fifth department would be responsible for inspection and quality control. Finally, one department would be responsible for packing the bottles into boxes and shipping them out. ■ **EXHIBIT 9.13** illustrates the process departmentalization structure.

■ **EXHIBIT 9.13**
Process departmentalization groups jobs based on the sequential steps required to create a good or provide a service.

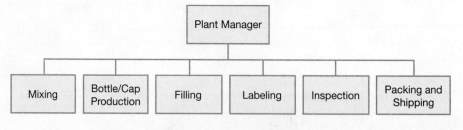

CUSTOMER DEPARTMENTALIZATION

Customer departmentalization is a method of grouping jobs based on the needs of customers, consumers, or clients. Focusing attention on the specific customers who purchase products or services can enhance customer satisfaction because it often means a team of individuals—or an entire division—is devoted to certain customers. For example, Newell Rubbermaid has teams of sales representatives dedicated to their largest customers, such as Home Depot and Lowe's. As with some other types of departmentalization, however, this structure suffers from job redundancy. ■ **EXHIBIT 9.14** shows an example of customer departmentalization for a management consulting firm.

Customer departmentalization
A method of grouping jobs based on the needs of customers, consumers, or clients.

■ **EXHIBIT 9.14**
Customer departmentalization is a structure that groups jobs based on the needs of customers, consumers, or clients.

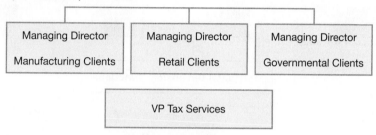

GEOGRAPHIC DEPARTMENTALIZATION

Geographic departmentalization is a method of grouping jobs based on their physical location. This is often seen within sales divisions of large organizations (■ **EXHIBIT 9.15**).

Departmentalization structures are complex, no matter what form they take, because it is challenging to coordinate complex vertical structures (e.g., the hierarchy) and even more daunting to coordinate horizontally among departments, because they often have inherent walls between them. Nevertheless, several popular new structures have been developed to eliminate some of the problems inherent in structures that hamper communication, creativity, and speed. We look at three of these structures next: matrix, hybrid, and networked structures.

Geographic departmentalization
A method of grouping jobs based on their physical location.

■ **EXHIBIT 9.15**
Geographic departmentalization groups jobs based on their physical location.

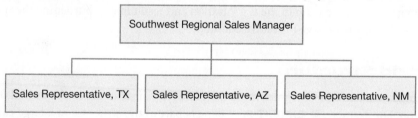

Matrix Structure

A **matrix** is a structure in which departments within an organization are linked directly to one unit in the vertical organization and to one or more units in the horizontal organization. The purpose of a matrix structure is to maximize the positive attributes of vertical structures while also supporting effective coordination, communication, and agility across the organization. A common type of matrix is organized by function and geography, as shown in ■ **EXHIBIT 9.16**.

Matrix
A structure in which departments within an organization are linked directly to one unit in the vertical organization and to another unit in the horizontal organization.

■ **EXHIBIT 9.16**
A basic matrix structure combines vertical and horizontal structures.

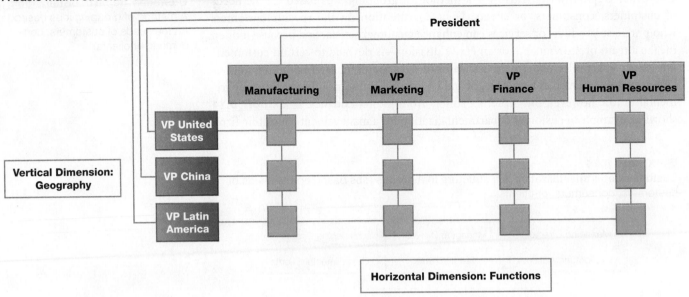

The horizontal and vertical dimensions of a matrix structure can be any of the structures studied so far: divisional, functional, product, process, customer, or geographic. Sometimes, organizations will create a matrix structure for special projects, innovation teams, or any group that needs the support and control inherent in a vertical chain of command as well as the expertise from a department in the horizontal organization.

A matrix structure often helps shift the organizational culture away from a silo mentality in which each department or division is isolated from the rest of the organization. At its best, this type of structure allows for optimal control in the hierarchical organization while also ensuring maximum efficiency and effective coordination of the horizontal organization.

The downside of the matrix structure is that it can be very confusing. Most people are used to working within a single hierarchy. In a basic matrix structure, people often report formally to two bosses. Even if the structure does not have everyone reporting formally to two bosses, the department itself is responsible for the outcomes required by two distinct and different parts of the organization—each of which has its own goals. Sometimes, the required outcomes can be in conflict with one another. This can cause a great deal of tension in the organization and result in overburdening the senior leader or leaders who have to resolve conflicts.

Hybrid Structure

Hybrid structure
A structure that incorporates more than one type of structure in the overall organization.

A **hybrid structure** incorporates more than one type of structure in the overall organization. For example, ■ **EXHIBIT 9.17** depicts part of the structure of a large cancer center. The structure is divisional, but it also includes flat team structures within the clinical investigations and clinical affairs divisions.

Many variations of hybrid structures exist. One hybrid structure that is worth mentioning because it hardly ever shows up on an organizational chart is the vertical structure that often emerges in teams. As mentioned earlier in the chapter, many people have been socialized to view hierarchy as the most important aspect of organizational structure. We tend to be most comfortable with the rules of hierarchies, even if we don't like them. For this and other reasons, people often gravitate toward implementing a hierarchy, yet often resist being led.

■ **EXHIBIT 9.17**
The hybrid nature of this cancer center incorporates more than one type of structure.

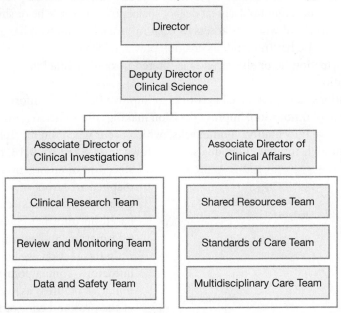

You may have experienced this on a project team. When you started to work together, members were equal. As a team, you decided who the team leader would be, and what his or her responsibilities were. Maybe your leader was busy or unavailable and suddenly (it seemed to you), one of the other members was now the "project manager." He or she was planning, delegating tasks, and reporting back to the team leader. Not everyone on the team appreciated this, so two people designated themselves as "committee leaders." They began organizing the work of the remaining members. At this point, you had a team of eight people, four of whom were organizing and delegating, and four of whom were actually doing the work. This obviously makes no sense—especially for the four people doing the work!

It is surprising how often this hybrid structure emerges in real settings at work. This team structure may arise in part because some people resist being led and need to learn the art of followership. It may also arise because of poor team leadership—flat structures such as teams are not easy to lead, as you will see in Chapter 10. It takes special skills and a high level of self-confidence to let people work collaboratively without micromanagement.

As more and more organizations adopt flat and hybrid structures, it will serve you well to learn to recognize the signs that a flat structure is turning into a dysfunctional hierarchy. It will also serve you well to learn how to manage and lead groups without the benefit of a formal hierarchical structure. This is particularly true when it comes to flat, networked structures—in which power dynamics are an important part of the overall structure that must be understood and tracked.

Networked Organizational Structures and Power Dynamics

All the structures we have looked at so far have been described primarily in terms of formal authority, responsibility, and accountability. As important as these are, however, they don't tell the whole story. An organization is a social network. People are linked in many ways, such as similarity in jobs, level of authority, personal relationships, common interests, and access to information and power. Typically, we think of people in higher-level jobs as having access to more organizational knowledge and resources. This can be true, but take the example of an executive assistant. This person has little position power but might hold a great deal of social power because he or she constantly makes decisions about who gets access to what information and who has access to the boss. The boss, who has tremendous position power, may have little power in the sense that the information he or she receives is filtered through a small group of people in the organization.[50]

Organizations can tailor social networks to improve the flow of information, facilitate the spread of innovation, improve decision making, strengthen organizational culture, and remove information "bottlenecks," which occur when too much information is passing through too few individuals.[51] As shown in ■ **EXHIBIT 9.18**, the network structure of an organization can be mapped in terms of which groups connect. Networks can also be based on informal power, access to information, and even friendships.

In this section, we have described numerous contemporary organizational structures, as well as a few of the pros and cons of these structures. One form of organization we have not yet discussed is the virtual organization. Because of advances in information and communication technologies, a vast number of organizations are now at least partially virtual. For this reason, Chapter 11 is entirely dedicated to this topic. Now, let's turn our attention to factors that need to be considered when designing an organizational structure.

■ **EXHIBIT 9.18**
The network structure at Indymedia.

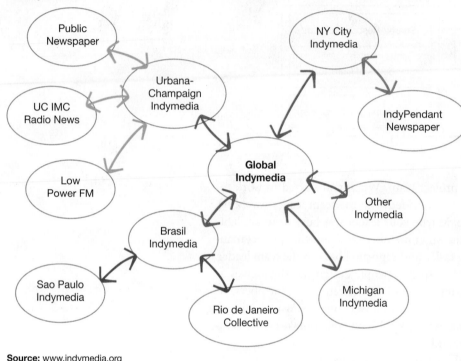

Source: www.indymedia.org

Discussion Questions

1. Does a traditionally tall organizational structure appeal to you? Why or why not? What is the purpose of establishing a cross-functional team within these types of structures?

2. In a matrix organization, you could have two bosses. What problems might arise in this situation? How would you deal with these problems?

Objective 9.6
Describe the factors that affect the design of organizational structures.

6. What Factors Affect the Design of Organizational Structures?

We have been discussing structure as if it is something that already exists, something you can see and evaluate—which of course you can. But how is an organizational structure created? When the organizational design process is deliberate, leaders and HR professionals consider several important factors when creating a structure: the organization's strategy, the external environment, technology, size, and geography.

The Relationship between Structure and Strategy

Over the years, scholars have debated the relationship between structure and strategy. You will often hear people in organizations say "Structure follows strategy," as if it is a known and unquestionable fact. It's a little more complicated than that, however.

STRUCTURE FOLLOWS STRATEGY

Organizational scholar Alfred Chandler was one of the first to propose that structure must follow strategy. The argument is pretty straightforward: An organization exists in a particular environment from which it draws its resources and within which it provides products or services. The decisions about how to position the organization in the environment are part of the organization's strategy. To implement that strategy, the organization makes certain choices about structure. In other words, the organization's structure is part of the outcome of the strategic decision-making process. Hence, structure follows strategy.[52]

STRATEGY CAN BE DETERMINED BY STRUCTURE

Others have argued just the opposite—that structure *determines* strategy. This argument states that the benefits and limitations of the structure will determine what types of strategies are viable. Because structures can limit the implementation of certain strategies, it is important for organizations to develop a proactive approach to strategy formation. In a proactive organization, strategy and structure are constantly influencing each other. When this is not the case, the strategy is in danger of becoming "the lackey of the structure."[53]

STRUCTURE AND STRATEGY: AN ITERATIVE PROCESS

Now, let's consider the issue from another perspective. Tactics are actions tied to specific objectives, which are in turn tied to strategy. The problem is that strategies can be far removed from on-the-ground actions, and these same actions can be impossible to implement if the structure does not support them. For example, resources cannot be used by one part of the organization if they are tightly controlled by another in a tall, siloed organization.

On the other side, tactics can be chosen deliberately because they will force changes in the organizational structure. Take the same example: A strategy might call for greater attention to customers' needs. To implement this strategy, managers in marketing, customer service, and manufacturing are required to coordinate their touch points with customers. In a tall, siloed functional organization this just would not happen naturally. So, leaders require the creation of "customer groups"—a tactic that in effect changes the structure of the organization. If this change in structure works, different tactical choices become possible down the road.

More scholars are coming to recognize the importance of putting strategy and structure in an iterative relationship—a relationship in which strategy influences structure, structure influences strategy, and both are constantly improving.[54] And it's not only scholars who are paying attention—organizational leaders are as well. This is especially true in new, fast moving organizations that are responding to new needs in the market. Creative Commons, led by CEO Cathy Casserly, is one such organization. According to its website,

> *Creative Commons is a nonprofit organization that enables the sharing and use of creativity and knowledge through free legal tools.*
>
> *Our free, easy-to-use copyright licenses provide a simple, standardized way to give the public permission to share and use your creative work—on conditions of your*

choice. CC licenses let you easily change your copyright terms from the default of "all rights reserved" to "some rights reserved."

Creative Commons licenses are not an alternative to copyright. They work alongside copyright and enable you to modify your copyright terms to best suit your needs.[55]

Creative Commons is part of the movement to simplify information sharing around the world, improving public access while also honoring the originators of knowledge, art, music, and other creative works. Creative Commons is taking on one of the biggest challenges of our time: the consideration of, and changes to, ownership models and dissemination of knowledge and artistic works. In the traditional model, research reports, books, music, and art are created and then published in one form or another by someone or some entity like a publishing house, music company, journal, or individual. Typically, the publisher has full control over how the material is used and disseminated, while the author, artist, or composer receives a royalty, which is often no more than 10% of revenue. In the case of scholarly articles there is usually no royalty at all. The cost of accessing the work, or of getting the publisher's permission to use it in another work, may be prohibitive for many people.

On the Internet, there are no barriers to publishing one's own works, and authors are free to choose whether to retain all the rights the Copyright Law gives them by default, or give up the ones they don't need or want to keep. Founded in 2001 by a group of scholars, lawyers, and people passionate about open educational resources, Creative Commons exists to make it easy for creators of copyrightable material to grant rights to the public with the goal of making more creative works more accessible to everyone. The organization's primary tool is a suite of licenses that are easy to apply to any work published on the Internet. The licenses explain the ways in which the author has permitted use of the work; anybody can take advantage of the license without having to hire a lawyer or create a separate agreement. In the early days the organization was managed by its board of directors—many of whom were experts in the field of copyright law and helped to create the original set of licenses. As Creative Commons matured and its functions increased, it became clear that more of its management and direction had to come from a full-time, in-house Chief Executive.

Creative Commons is a very good example of an organization that is both strong and fluid: the mission and vision are clear, while strategy and structure have flexed to meet the needs of this exciting and growing organization. CEO Cathy Casserly has held several roles with respect to the company: funder, when she worked for the Hewlett Foundation; board member; and since 2011, CEO. Let's hear what this highly intelligent, resonant leader has to say about the interface of leadership, structure, and strategy in the *Leadership Perspective* feature.

Cathy Casserly's advice (on the next page) is sound, and leads us to the next important input to structure (and strategy): the external environment.

The External Environment

The external environment in which an organization operates also plays a key role in the structure of the organization. For example, Chrysler was an American icon for decades. Known in the 1950s and 1960s as a solid and dependable car, sales were good and customers were happy. Over time, however, Chrysler lost its edge. This was in part because the company didn't keep up with external market demands for stylish, fuel efficient cars. In addition, this company, like many American companies, has to pay much higher wages than do many non-American competitors. This resulted in expensive cars that people didn't want to buy.

By 2007, the company's financial picture was disastrous and it faced bankruptcy. The U.S. government stepped in with loans, largely because bankruptcy of this and

Leadership Perspective

● **Cathy Casserly**
CEO of Creative Commons
"We have to be nimble."

Organizations like ours have to be flexible so we can adapt to rapid and constant changes: technology, laws, beliefs about how information should be disseminated and paid for—all of these are changing dramatically, technology almost daily. We are constantly looking for the latest innovation, the gap, the needs that no one is meeting. That's how we stay relevant.

We have to be nimble. When you're hit by a wave of change, or public opin- ion in either direction, you can easily go off course. So, we deal with ambiguity—we can't change our entire strategy or our organization each time something in the world changes. If we did, we would never get anything done. We'd be constantly focusing internally, rather than externally. What's important is to be comfortable staying in ambiguity long enough to decide which opportunities to chase, which to leave alone for the time being. We have to stay in a place where things aren't clear long enough to make the right choices. This can be uncomfortable, but it's a must.

The impact of this reality is that our strategy needs to be living and dynamic. We have to have that blueprint—a well-crafted picture of where we are going, where we are placing our bets, and how we get and use resources. But, it can't be set in stone. We can't have a "rigid five year plan" mentality.

This approach to strategy requires a flat organization. Each individual needs to put his or her ideas out there and the group has to listen respectfully. If not, individuals will pull back, hold onto their resources, and try to operate alone. This doesn't work in an organization like ours. Even small organizations are not immune to silos.

"A Mosaic of People and Ideas"

When we are at our best, Creative Commons is a mosaic of people and ideas. Each unique piece fits with the others, and each contributes significantly to the whole. The whole mosaic is far more stunning and clever than any one piece. The organizational structure gives meaning and order to the pieces allowing contributions of talent and ideas to shine. As strategy and opportunities shift, the structure adapts by reordering the pieces to create the new mosaic. This movement depends on a collective that owns the process.

"20 Degrees Off"

To myself, I often note when things are "20 degrees off"— when the plan or the implementation of the plan is not quite right and needs to change. Those 20 degrees are critically important and signal to me that something in the environment needs to shift—and accordingly that the strategy likely needs to adjust as well.

So, you need a flat organization where the best ideas can be generated, discussed, and acted upon. Everyone in the organization needs to be clear about what they are responsible for and how that contributes to the overall mission of the organization. And they need to be held accountable for their piece of the mosaic. It's critical that filters don't preclude ideas from reaching the leaders, or vice versa. An organization needs both vertical and horizontal alignment.

For leaders of this kind of organization—everyone, actually— there are a few behaviors and abilities that are a must. Listening is the first and most important. Neither strategy nor structure will shift in the right direction if leaders aren't listening to team members and the wider environment. You need to intentionally create a culture of inclusion to get people with new, different, and fresh ideas at the table. You need to create a culture where people support one another's new ideas, even if they're not fully formed. The culture also has to encourage people to help each other. That sounds simple and obvious, but it's easier said than done. Finally, you need to have your finger on the pulse of everything that's going on in your industry. Just because you are the leader doesn't mean you can stop learning about your field. You need to read widely—blogs, books, newspapers, twitter feeds, TV, everything. You need to be smart and informed.

Source: Personal interview with Cathy Casserly conducted by Annie McKee, 2012.

---

other auto manufacturers would result in job losses in the tens of thousands, including job losses outside the company itself.

On June 10, 2009, the Italian carmaker Fiat stepped in, paid off some of the company's debt and took partial ownership of Chrysler. Over the next year, after purchasing equity held by the U.S. treasury and Canada, Fiat owned nearly 60 percent of Chrysler.[56] The American icon is now owned by an Italian firm. In 2011, Chrysler began a new marketing campaign called "Imported from Detroit" to bring new focus on Detroit as a re-emerging manufacturing center.[57] Fiat's five-year plan is to sell seven of its models in the United States and for Chrysler to sell nine of its models in Europe by 2014.[58]

As this example shows, how well an organization adapts to the environment is very important. For example, companies are taking a variety of approaches to addressing higher fuel costs beyond simply raising their prices.[59] Contingency clauses are increasingly being used to stipulate the right for a transportation company to add a fuel surcharge should prices rise rapidly. Many companies are moving toward leaner models and improving their logistics to improve routes and decrease fuel usage. No idling policies are in place in an increasing number of organizations that maintain fleets of vehicles—a policy that saves money and is better for the environment. Fuel is increasingly being bought wholesale and stored in larger volumes by companies, as well.

Changes in the external environment happen *fast*. Positive changes such as advances in technology and the emergence of new markets are the norm, and companies need to be ready to take advantage of these changes. The global environment is volatile and uncertain. Major changes can and do happen very quickly.

Environmental uncertainty
A situation in which market conditions are changing rapidly or are unclear.

Environmental uncertainty refers to a situation in which market conditions are changing rapidly or are unclear. Environmental uncertainty can be the result of many things, including political instability or changes such as elections or regime changes in influential countries. For example, when resources are controlled for political reasons (as happens with oil), entire industries can be forced to change what they are doing overnight.

Social changes, such as how people use technology to share information, can also cause environmental uncertainty. For example, only a few years ago news reporters were usually the ones to find and report stories. Now, anyone with a cell phone camera can do this work. This means that the news industry has changed dramatically. And because of our increasingly interconnected world, other environmental conditions such as wars, conflicts or potential conflicts, regional environmental regulations, and even local laws can cause environmental uncertainty in places far from an organization's activities.

Competition on a global scale can also create environmental uncertainty. The recession in the late 2000s combined with increased international competition in the auto industry hit U.S. automotive companies especially hard. Since 1990, the 30,000 companies involved in supplying the auto industry have consolidated into 10,000 as a result of failures, mergers, and acquisitions.[60] In the auto industry and many others, environmental uncertainty will continue to affect business profoundly, in turn affecting how businesses and organizations structure people and operations.

Technology

We will discuss the effects of technology on individuals and organizations in depth in Chapter 11. For now, let us simply say that technologies in an organization impact both structure and strategy. As early as the 1950s, British researcher Joan Woodward found that the structure of an organization is influenced by the technology that it uses. For example, if a manufacturing company uses technologies associated with mass production, the structure might be one in which managers supervise more employees than in a custom manufacturing environment in which there may be fewer employees reporting to each manager.[61] In more modern times, computer technologies have greatly influenced the structure of organizations.

Organizational Size and Geography

In addition to strategy, the environment, and technology, numerous other factors can affect how leaders design or redesign an organization. Two that we will mention here are the organization's size and geography.

ORGANIZATIONAL SIZE

An organization's size affects its structure in obvious ways. If your company has 20 people, you would not have 20 departments—you probably wouldn't even want four departments. If you differentiated that much, you would certainly be wasting resources. Similarly, if your organization has 20,000 people, you wouldn't organize them all in one department. Doing so would be chaotic and unmanageable.

There are no rules that dictate how leaders should design organizations of various sizes. However, in traditional vertical organizations, there seem to be some trends as organizations grow: power becomes less concentrated; there are increasingly more levels of management, but this levels off as the organization becomes quite large; and more formal policies tend to emerge.

Most research on how size affects structure has concentrated on traditional organizations in which the people counted are employees. Considering the fact that there has been a rapid increase in different employment relationships (such as contractors and temporary workers), we now need to look at the relationship of size to structure differently. As social networking continues to affect the virtual size of an organization, more research will be conducted as to what actually constitutes a small, medium, or large business, and how the various internal and external groups work together to impact structure—and vice versa.

GEOGRAPHY

Geographically dispersed employees and customers have an impact on organizational design. For example, national clothing store chains have hundreds of locations, and thousands of employees are needed to staff the individual store sites. Each store has a manager, but each manager also reports to a district manager. The reason why these district managers are responsible for specific geographic areas is because it would be too difficult to manage thousands of staff from one central corporate office. It would be challenging to maintain consistency, and controls on operations could be very limited.

In addition to the geographic dispersion of employees, geographic distribution of customers also affects structure. For example, U.S. companies like the drugstores CVS and Walgreen's often determine number and locations of stores based on population density and potential customers' socioeconomic status.

All the topics presented so far in this section have an effect on organizational design. One would imagine, then, that leaders would always consider such factors before deciding to design, or redesign, an organization. That is not always the case, however, as we will see next.

Organizational Design: It's Not Always Deliberate!

As organizations grow, strategies change, or technology changes, organizational structures often emerge without much conscious planning or design. Individual managers and business leaders often make structure decisions for their parts of the organization, resulting in something of a hodgepodge over time. This emergent process can support adaptability. On the other hand, it can also result in chaos and redundancy of tasks and functions.

For example, in one very large company we know, the HR function was decentralized in the late 1990s. What this meant was that HR leaders were empowered within each division to make decisions that suited their particular needs with regard to leadership development, hiring practices, and the like. About five years later, the organization bought another large company that had to be integrated into the current organization. Numerous problems were discovered, including the fact that there was no consistency in technology or software. This meant, among other things, that it was not easy to track hiring or salaries from one part of the organization to the other.

Second, the acquiring organization wisely wanted to ensure that this new entity's managers and leaders would share a common approach to leadership, values, and culture. As the central HR team began investigating the leadership models that were in use around the business, they found that over the five years of decentralization, no less than 187 new leadership models had been adopted and taught in as many regions and divisions! Imagine trying to coordinate communication about leadership and culture under those circumstances.

As much as empowerment and adaptability are key to success, so is ensuring that the structure used across the organization is coherent. In most organizations, this is accomplished through centralized planning around key issues related to the environment and technology, as well as a host of factors like the organization's size, geographic dispersion, degree of specialization, and the like.

Discussion Questions

1. Organizational structure is not always easy to see when we interact with a company, but it is important to understand when taking a job. Brainstorm a list of questions you could ask an interviewer about the company's organizational structure that would help you to determine if it is a place you would like to work. Note: "What is this organization's structure?" is a given. See what else you can come up with.

2. Describe how technology and environmental uncertainty have affected your school in the past four years.

Objective 9.7
Learn how organizations are legally structured and classified.

7. What Are Common Business Ownership Models and Legal Designations in the United States?

Business ownership models affect many aspects of organizational life, including leadership behavior, organizational culture, and structure. To the casual observer, ownership may not be apparent, other than indications on a company's letterhead such as "Inc." or "LLC." Each form of ownership is based on a number of factors and comes with its own set of pros and cons for the owner(s) related to taxes, legal restrictions, and governance models. ■ **EXHIBIT 9.19** shows several common forms of business ownership in the United States, each of which is discussed in the following sections.

SOLE PROPRIETORSHIP

Sole proprietorship
An ownership model in which a single individual owns a business.

As the name implies, a **sole proprietorship** is an ownership model in which a single individual owns a business. Legal requirements for setting up a sole proprietorship vary from town to town and state to state in the United States. A good source of information on starting and running a sole proprietorship in the United States is the Small Business Administration, a governmental organization that provides guidance and support to small business owners.[62] The simplicity of this type of ownership (at least in the United States) is a distinct advantage. There are fewer legal restrictions on how an owner operates his or her business, especially if there are less than 50 employees. However, while there are fewer restrictions on small business operations, the regulations that do exist impact small businesses more than large companies. In fact, the cost of complying with regulations was found by the U.S. Small Business Administration to be more than 200 percent higher for small businesses.[63]

A sole proprietor is personally responsible for all financial assets and debts. This means the owner can do as he or she sees fit with profits. But, all money earned by

■ **EXHIBIT 9.19**

Common Forms of Ownership

Form of Ownership	Definition	Examples
Sole proprietorship	A business that is owned by an individual and has not been registered as a corporation or partnership. A sole proprietorship can be a limited liability company if the owner elects not to treat it as a legal corporation or partnership.[64]	figureplant (San Francisco); Creative English.net (United Kingdom)
Partnership	A legal structure for a business with two or more people is called a general partnership when qualifiers such as "limited" or "limited liability" are not used. Partners share profits and are each personally liable for all business debts, and each partner also claims a portion of the business income (or losses) on his or her individual tax return.	Smock Sterling (Lake Bluff, Illinois); Community Orthopedic Medical Group Partnership (Mission Viejo, California)
Corporation	A corporation is a legal entity and is treated as such by the government. The corporation owns the business, whereas individuals, called shareholders, own a percentage of the corporation. Publicly owned corporations have ownership shares traded on a stock exchange.	DryShips, Inc. (Athens, Greece); First Solar, Inc. (Tempe, Arizona)
Limited liability company (LLC; in some countries, this is referred to as a public limited corporation or PLC)	Relatively new to the United States, this is a hybrid form of ownership that combines elements of a partnership and a corporation. As a partnership, the liability of owners is "limited," and partners may also take ownership of corporate losses to offset taxes. Member-owners can be people, corporations, other LLCs, and/or foreign entities.[65]	3H Technology, LLC (Reston, Virginia); 51 Minds Entertainment, LLC (Los Angeles)

a sole proprietor (after expenses) is taxed as personal income, all loans are personal loans (which are often difficult to obtain), and all debts incurred by the business are personal debts.

Similarly, a sole proprietor is liable for any and all events that occur on his or her property or as a result of business-related activities. For example, if a customer falls and is hurt on business property, or is harmed by a business product, practice, or service, the business owner is personally liable for damages. Although a primary home or primary vehicle is exempt from seizure, any other possessions can be seized by the courts to pay for unpaid debts associated with the business in the United States.

PARTNERSHIP

A **partnership** is an ownership model in which two or more individuals share the ownership of a business. Ownership of the business can be split 50/50 or any other way, as long as all partners are in agreement. Whatever is decided, the partners should have a legally binding partnership agreement. This document states agreements such as ownership shares, how profits are to be distributed, resolution of disputes, and how a partner can leave the partnership. In the event that the business is sold or goes out of business, the partnership agreement also specifies how the profits or debts are to be divided among the partners.

The advantages to this form of ownership revolve primarily around the saying "Two heads are better than one," as well as the fact that there may be more capital for startup and growth activities than in a sole proprietorship. The drawback is that personal liability is still an issue. Also, if the business depends on one partner more than another, and if that person becomes ill, dies, or simply no longer has an interest in the business, the business will likely suffer.

CORPORATION

In 1819, U.S. Supreme Court Justice John Marshall declared that a corporation is "an artificial being, invisible, intangible, and existing only in contemplation of law . . . and

Partnership
An ownership model in which two or more individuals share the ownership of a business.

Corporation
An organization that is legally recognized as a unique entity, pays taxes, and can be sued.

may act as a single individual . . . to manage its own affairs, and to hold property . . . "[66] We define a corporation, then, as an organization that is legally recognized as a unique entity, pays taxes, and can be sued. Corporations do not have the personal liability issues of sole proprietorships and partnerships. Like other forms of ownership, specific laws governing corporations differ from state to state in the United States.[67]

Ownership of a corporation is usually distributed among many people or groups. Individuals or groups buy stock (shares) in the corporation. They buy shares of the business in hopes that the value of the corporation will go up, and that the value of their stock will also increase. Profits, called dividends, are distributed among shareholders. The more shares that an owner purchases, the more money that owner stands to gain—or lose. So, if a corporation fails or goes into debt, the shareholder may lose the money he or she invested initially, but no more than that.

One possible disadvantage of the corporation, especially for very small businesses, concerns taxes. The business is taxed as a separate entity, and shareholders who draw a salary are also taxed on their personal income. Another possible disadvantage is that setting up a corporation is a more complex and expensive process than setting up other forms of ownership.

How Corporations, Not-for-Profits and Partnerships Can Be Structured Legally: S Corporation and LLC

S corporation
A type of corporation that has 100 or fewer shareholders and does not pay federal income taxes.

An S corporation is a type of corporation that has 100 or fewer shareholders and does not pay federal income taxes. Instead, income, losses, deductions, and credit are passed on to the shareholders for federal tax purposes.[68] S corporations have only one class of stock.[69] With this type of setup, the owner(s) avoids double taxation because the corporation is *not* taxed on earnings and losses, which pass directly to the shareholders.[70] The S corporation is a very common form of ownership, with about 4.5 million S corporations in the United States, according to the S Corporation Association.[71]

LLC
A hybrid form of ownership that provides limited personal liability to the owners of a business.

An LLC is a hybrid form of ownership that provides limited personal liability to the owners of a business. It combines characteristics of a corporation with characteristics of a sole proprietorship or partnership.[72] The greatest advantage of an LLC in the United States is that it can be taxed according to what the owners or members of the LLC designate as most appropriate—either as a corporation, S corporation, partnership, or sole proprietorship. This is because the U.S. federal government does not recognize an LLC classification for tax purposes.[73] In addition, the owners are protected from many of the personal liabilities associated with the business.

In the next section, we will expand our discussion of ownership models to include structures that allow organizations to expand their reach through agreements with individuals or other organizations.

Structural and Legal Relationships between Organizations

In addition to the forms of ownership we have discussed so far, other relationships may exist between businesses. These include cooperative contracts, licensing agreements, franchises, strategic alliances, and wholly owned affiliates.

COOPERATIVE CONTRACTS

Cooperative contracts
Friendly business agreements that result from equity joint ventures, which are also known as equity alliances.

Cooperative contracts are friendly business agreements that can be linked to many forms of joint economic activities, such as equity joint ventures, also known as equity alliances.[74] Equity alliances come in two forms. In the case of partial acquisitions, a company takes a minority stake (less than 50 percent ownership) in the other company. In contrast, cross-equity alliances occur when each company takes a stake in the other, essentially exchanging shares.[75]

Equity alliances carry less risk than either buying or building a company, which makes them attractive. A company can focus on its core business while at the same time exploring other options. This can be especially helpful when expanding into overseas markets, where a company may not have the cultural knowledge, expertise, or resources to operate or manage operations.

One highly successful international cross-equity alliance has been Fuji Xerox in Japan, with equal equity ownership by both companies. Although Fuji and Xerox hold equal equity, nearly all members of the executive board are Japanese, and one of the members also sits on the board of Xerox International. When Xerox suffered contraction in the United States, the alliance served as an important source of revenue.[76]

LICENSING AGREEMENTS

A **licensing agreement** is a business agreement in which the owner of trademarked material authorizes an individual or company to use that material to sell or market products or services in exchange for a fee. Licensing is a popular method by which companies can expand their business by granting other entities the right to use trademarked material.[77] For example, an artist and his or her producer might license a film studio to use a song in a movie. Trademarked, copyrighted and other creative works, products or services are sometimes referred to as intellectual property (IP), and the owner(s) of the IP is the licensor. The licensor, in effect, rents his or her IP to a licensee, who is then allowed to create products based on the IP in exchange for fees or royalties.[78] Some licensing agreements require the licensee to submit products bearing the IP to the licensor for final approval prior to sale and distribution. This helps the licensor ensure that the IP is being used in a suitable fashion and that the quality is acceptable.[79]

A familiar example of this model involves clothing bearing a sports team logo. Typically, the team's owner(s) grants a license for the logo's use to a clothing manufacturer. The manufacturer produces clothing bearing the logo and pays an agreed-on percentage of sales to the owner.[80]

Licensing agreements can be beneficial to both parties involved. In the previous example, the manufacturer may increase revenue by selling popular apparel, while every individual wearing a sweatshirt bearing the licensor's IP is a walking advertisement.

Licensing agreements have disadvantages too. For licensors, these are primarily associated with the quality of licensed products and the way in which the trademark is portrayed in those products. For licensees, these are primarily monetary, because some agreements include guaranteed fees that must be paid regardless of how well a licensed product sells.[81]

FRANCHISING

A **franchise** is an agreement in which the owner of a business grants an individual or group of individuals the right to sell or market products or services under that business name in exchange for a fee. In this type of agreement, a franchisor owns a particular business and grants the second party, known as the franchisee, the right to market products or services under that business name. In return for this right, the franchisee pays a fee to the franchisor.

The two primary types of franchises are business format franchises and product distribution franchises. Business format franchises are more common, and they dictate the marketing plan and operations procedures the franchisee will use to sell products

Licensing agreement
A business agreement in which the owner of trademarked material authorizes an individual or company to use that material to sell or market products or services in exchange for a fee.

Franchise
An agreement in which the owner of a business grants an individual or group of individuals the right to sell or market products or services under that business name in exchange for a fee.

or services. The majority of fast-food restaurant franchises are business format franchises. Product distribution franchises, on the other hand, do not specify the way in which the franchisee is expected to sell products or services. Car dealerships are often an example of a product distribution franchise because automobile makers may not specify how individual dealerships must market their products.

When it comes to these types of agreements, one benefit to the franchisor is monetary; franchisees pay fees and royalties to the franchisor. A second benefit is the possibility for wide distribution of products or services and increased name recognition. The primary benefit for the franchisee is that they are marketing services or products that customers may already be familiar with, so they do not have to spend a great deal of time generating customer awareness.

The disadvantages of franchise agreements are most strongly felt by franchisees who are not given the freedom to establish their own standards for marketing and pricing.[82] For example, in 2009 Burger King ran a $1 double cheeseburger promotion nationwide, forcing franchisees to adopt the pricing despite resultant losses. The franchisees sued Burger King over the promotion. Franchisees eventually dismissed the lawsuit in 2011 after forging an agreement with Burger King that gives them more input into pricing in future promotions.[83]

WHOLLY OWNED AFFILIATES

Wholly owned affiliate or subsidiary
A company whose stock is completely owned by a second company, referred to as a parent or holding company.

A **wholly owned affiliate or subsidiary** is a company whose stock is completely owned by a second company, referred to as a parent or holding company.[84] The parent company often seeks to control, but not dissolve, the internal structure of the affiliate. This arrangement is beneficial from a legal standpoint because it enables the parent and affiliate to remain separate entities, and in most situations, it protects the parent company in the event that the affiliate is sued.[85]

The wholly owned affiliate ownership form is also advantageous because it provides the parent company with the technical expertise of another company without having to share any of its own expertise with a competitor, as sometimes happens with joint ventures.[86] Multinational parent companies may also receive more favorable treatment in terms of taxation when they adopt a wholly owned affiliate structure within certain countries.[87] Another important benefit of the wholly owned affiliate model is that the parent company may be able to capitalize on name recognition and marketing associated with the affiliate and utilize existing distribution channels already established by the affiliate.[88] Companies interested in international expansion often explore this model.[89]

For instance, cosmetics giant Estée Lauder acquired Aveda, a manufacturer of plant-based and natural beauty products, as a wholly owned affiliate in 1997 for approximately $300 million.[90] This purchase enabled Estée Lauder to enter the hair care market and acquire a private salon distribution channel. At the time of the purchase, Aveda was experiencing pains associated with its rapid growth and welcomed Estée Lauder's centralized purchasing power and policy structure. Aveda has maintained its own manufacturing facility, which uses organic products and sustainable practices, as well as its own executive structure, while Estée Lauder has been reaping the financial benefits of the affiliation.[91]

Of course, wholly owned affiliates do pose several disadvantages to parent companies. Chief among these is that the parent company bears the full cost and risk of business operations should the objective for which it acquired the affiliate fail.[92] Additionally, the parent company must be careful to maintain the affiliate as a separate entity with its own interests and operational procedures.[93] This separation is important when it comes to a range of issues, including taxes and liability. These two issues are chief among the reasons why some companies seeking international expansion opt to pursue joint ventures rather than wholly owned affiliates.[94]

STRATEGIC ALLIANCES

Strategic alliances are agreements between two or more parties to work together to achieve a common goal. These agreements may or may not be legally binding, but in either case, creating an alliance contract is pivotal to enabling both parties to protect their assets, engage in amiable and beneficial business interactions, and delineate how and under what circumstances the alliance will end.[95] Formation of any alliance, regardless of the strength of the contract, is risky, but many businesses explore strategic alliances to drive growth.[96] Many companies around the world have decided that the benefits in terms of global capabilities, marketplace adaptation, and formation of economies of scale are worth the risk.[97]

Strategic alliances are similar to partnerships or joint ventures in which two companies team up for their mutual benefit in creating or distributing a product. Unlike partnerships and joint ventures, however, strategic alliances can be more limited in scope and timeframe. For instance, strategic alliances may be set up around one or two products or lines for a defined period of time.[98]

For example, two companies may team up temporarily through a strategic alliance because one has the technical expertise to develop a new video gaming system and the other has the resources to build and distribute it.[99] Strategic alliances are especially important in today's economy because they may yield greater economic benefits to companies faster than would be possible if companies pursued certain projects on their own. Research and development, licensing, advertising, and distribution costs are shared among the two parties in the alliance, and innovative products and technologies can be made available to the public more quickly across broader market segments.[100]

Strategic alliances often result in strong business networks. Sometimes, these networks are vertical and bring together a vendor company and a customer company. Other times, they are horizontal and bring together two vendor companies.[101] In the latter case, the networks created occasionally bring together rival companies. Rival-based alliances are complex because of the vulnerability each company assumes by engaging in information sharing with a competitor, but they can be successful too.

One strategic alliance success story involves a joint venture between PepsiCo and Unilever, the company that produces Lipton tea. The two companies came together to bring bottled teas to stores around the United States in 1991.[102] Lipton, a name long associated with tea, brought brand recognition and manufacturing capabilities to the alliance, whereas PepsiCo brought an established distribution network.[103] By 2003, the bottled beverages produced through this alliance were the leading ready-to-drink teas in the U.S. and Canadian markets, which prompted PepsiCo and Unilever to expand their agreement to include international distribution in 60 additional countries.[104] The alliance continues to be successful and innovative. In 2008, it partnered with Starbucks to manufacture, market, and distribute Tazo Ready to Drink tea.[105] It also launched its first-ever sparkling tea beverage in 2009 (■ **EXHIBIT 9.20**).[106] In 2012, the partnership expanded its scope to include social projects, and teamed up with Grammy winning trio Lady Antebellum in a charity benefit to raise money for victims of tornadoes in Indiana.[107]

Now that you know about organizational classification systems and ownership structures, let's turn our attention to the people aspects of a healthy organizational structure. We'll begin by looking at how HR works with labor unions and ensures that the division of labor is clear and that employees understand the responsibilities of their jobs. Then, we'll look at what we all can do to be effective within the structure of the organizations in which we work.

Strategic alliances
Agreements between two or more parties to work together to achieve a common goal.

■ **EXHIBIT 9.20**
What makes the strategic alliance between PepsiCo and Unilever successful?

Source: vario images GmbH & Co.KG/Alamy

Discussion Questions

1. Interview a small business owner to find out what form of ownership model he or she utilizes. Why did the business owner choose that particular form of ownership? What are the pros and cons of the model he or she chose? How did this business owner become educated about how to make this decision?

2. Briefly describe a small business you would like to start. If you were setting up this business, what form of ownership would you choose and why?

Objective 9.8
Define HR's role in organizational design and structure.

8. What Is HR's Role in Organizational Design and Structure?

The HR function is heavily involved in organizational design. Organizational design, however, is not a one-time job—our hypercompetitive, changing environment results in constant pressure on organizations to change quickly and often. In many cases, these changes are structural, and HR must be ready to provide leaders with advice and counsel, and to anticipate, plan for, and implement structural changes that enable the organization to keep up with—or stay ahead of—the environment. These structural changes may require HR to deal with labor unions and job design.

Labor Unions

Labor unions, for better or worse, are part of the reality of many organizations in the twenty-first century. The topic itself tends to conjure up strong feelings and opinions among employees, managers, and leaders. It is important for HR leaders to understand these opinions in order to contribute to the effective organization of labor unions and maintenance of positive labor relations.

Unions are one structure that emerged during the Industrial Revolution to protect workers against poor treatment and low wages and to serve as a way for employees to pool their collective power. They began forming in the middle of the nineteenth century in the United States and Europe. One of the largest and most well-known of these unions in the United States, the American Federation of Labor (AFL), was formed in 1886 and was led by Samuel Gompers, leader of the Journeymen Cigar Makers' International Union of America.[108] Another large union, the Congress of Industrial Organizations (CIO) was formed in 1938 and was strongly guided by a communist ideology. Both the AFL and the CIO grew in power and significance in the United States during World War II. The communist elements of the CIO were eventually purged and, in 1955, the AFL and CIO joined forces to create the largest U.S.-based labor union. The AFL-CIO is still in existence today, and membership exceeded 12 million workers in 2012.[109] The AFL-CIO is affiliated with the International Trade Union Confederation (ITUC), a globe-spanning network based in Brussels, Belgium, that represents 175 million workers.[110]

Today, the United States is seeing a significant shift in union representation of employees. In the 1940s, less than 10 percent of public (government-paid) employees were members of unions, while over one-third of private, non-agricultural employees had union representation. In the twenty-first century, this has literally flipped, with 37 percent of public employees belonging to unions, while just 7 percent of private sector employees are union members. In total, just under 12 percent of U.S. workers belonged to unions in 2011.[111]

In other parts of the world, the picture is dramatically different. Seventy-four percent of Finland's workers are in unions, and 71 percent of Sweden's workers are as well.

The European Union as a whole has twice as many union members as the United States at 23 percent, though some nations—including France with only 8 percent—have fewer union members than the United States.[112] About 65 percent of the labor force in South Africa—or over 11 million workers—were formal union members in 2012.[113]

The collective bargaining power of unions has influenced nearly every aspect of labor relations between employers and employees, and it has been credited with spurring the growth of the global middle class. As you can see, unions can have a significant impact on organizational structure. Negotiations with employers can include issues involving scope of responsibility and accountability, employee-manager relations, how many bosses an employee can have, and span of control/leadership. Unions can also impact job analysis and job design.

As alluded to above, part of the collective bargaining process involves conducting job analyses to determine the requisite skills and competencies associated with different roles in the organization. When done correctly, such analyses ensure that compensation and incentives are appropriate, effectively motivate employees, and ensure long-term sustainability of the organization. Analyses should also seek ways to enrich jobs for the benefit of both employers and employees. We turn our attention to job analysis and job design next.

Job Analysis and Job Design

Job analysis is the systematic process of gathering and analyzing information about jobs and the knowledge, skills, and competencies needed to perform these jobs. Two products emerge from the job analysis process: job descriptions and job specifications. A **job description** is a written document that lists the major tasks and responsibilities of a particular job. A **job specification** is a written document that lists all the necessary knowledge, skills, and abilities that a person must possess in order to perform a particular job.

Job analysis is important for effective utilization of employees. It becomes the foundation for HR practices such as labor relations, compensation, employee training and development, recruiting, safety programs, and job design.

The process of job analysis involves seven steps. These are outlined in ■ **EXHIBIT 9.21**.[114] In the first step, a review of all pertinent and current information about jobs throughout the company is done. HR professionals determine what documentation is already in existence and how relevant and accurate the current job descriptions and job specifications are. Step 2 entails choosing a specific job analysis method. Job analysis methods include surveys, interviews, observations, or any combination of these methods.

Job analysis
The systematic process of gathering and analyzing information about jobs and the knowledge, skills, and competencies needed to perform these jobs.

Job description
A written document that lists the major tasks and responsibilities of a particular job.

Job specification
A written document that lists all the necessary knowledge, skills, and abilities that a person must possess in order to perform a particular job.

■ **EXHIBIT 9.21**

Job Analysis Process

Step 1: Review current information about the job or jobs.

Step 2: Choose a job analysis method.

Step 3: Collect data about the job or jobs through surveys, observation, interviews, focus groups, or by studying benchmark jobs.

Step 4: Compile and analyze the data, then create job description and job specification documents.

Step 5: Have employees verify or provide final input to the job description and job specification documents.

Step 6: Seek supervisory approval of the job description and job specification documents.

Step 7: Maintain and update the job descriptions and job specifications as needed.

In the third step, the data about the jobs is collected. Obviously, this takes a great deal of time and effort. If surveys are used, it takes time out of employees' busy schedules to complete these instruments. In large companies, vast amounts of data can be generated that then need to be analyzed—which is also time consuming and complex. To deal with these issues, job analyses may focus on collecting data about benchmark jobs, rather than every job throughout the firm. A **benchmark job** is one that is representative of other similar jobs. For example, rather than surveying every person in the operations department, an HR manager may only send questionnaires to a few randomly selected front-line supervisors, warehouse managers, logistics coordinators, and plant managers.

Benchmark job
A job that is representative of other jobs that are similar in nature.

Step 4 consists of compiling and analyzing the data. As the surveys are returned or observations collected, the HR manager begins to have enough information to craft job descriptions and job specifications. Then, in the fifth step, these documents are sent out to people in those jobs for review and correction.

In the sixth step, input is sought from the job holders' supervisors. Occasionally, people tend to inflate their level of responsibility or the importance of their positions. Having others examine these documents facilitates a more accurate portrayal. The seventh and final step is one of the most critical, but also one that is most often forgotten or ignored. Maintaining these records and updating them as necessary keeps these documents fresh. The use of new technology can render a job description or job specification obsolete very quickly. Additionally, restructuring and process improvements can rapidly cause job descriptions to become outdated.

Discussion Questions

1. Find a job search site on the Internet and review job descriptions for several jobs you might like to do at some point in your life. Discuss what is appealing about these jobs, and what you would have to do to qualify for them. From this exercise briefly write a job description of a job that you would like to attain in the future.

2. Consider a job you have held, whether paid or unpaid. What aspects of the job and its responsibilities did you like? Now consider what you could do to make enhancements to that job. How would the job have appealed to you more with these enhancements?

Objective 9.9
Learn how you can work more effectively within an organizational structure.

9. What Can We All Do to Work Effectively within Our Organizations' Structures?

Given the amount of time you will spend working in your life, you should make the most of it. To do so, you must learn how to function effectively within your organization's structure. You will need to know how to communicate, get and share resources, and learn and innovate within certain constraints—even if you work in a "flat" organization. In this section, we will explore two ways to work effectively within an organizational structure. The first topic we will cover seems contradictory: We will explore how to work effectively *outside* the formal structure. This is an essential skill because no matter how perfect a formal organizational structure is, there is always an informal structure within which people build relationships, manage power dynamics, and get things done.

Next, we will discuss an important skill that you will need to work within a hierarchy: managing "up." Most people think of a hierarchy as a structure in which people above manage people below. But it goes both ways, and it takes special skills to manage your boss.

Managing and Leading the Informal Organization

A formal organization is one in which all departments, jobs, reporting relationships, rules, policies, and procedures are standardized. As an example, consider a company that has many layers of management, each with a clear division of responsibilities and tasks. In this company, people follow rules, policies, and procedures. In fact, the policy manual is a large book, divided into sections, covering everything from how to conduct meetings to what personal items are permitted on your desk. In this company, all employees have a set of duties that are dictated by their job description and by their manager. Most major decisions require the approval of at least one senior manager, and employees have very little actual authority over how they approach their work. This describes a formal organization.

This imaginary company and its large rule book are not necessarily bad. In fact, this is fairly typical of large organizations. However, rules and policies just can't dictate everything, for every situation, every time. It is also not unusual for a formal organization and the structure that goes with it to be somewhat out of synch with how people really communicate and what it takes to make things happen. That is one of the reasons why people find ways around the formal organization, sometimes by creating what is called an "informal organization."

An informal organization includes the organization's social structure, social networks, and culture. You won't find the rules for your informal organization written anywhere, but they exist. For example, in many organizations leaders have an "open door" policy—anyone can contact them at any time (this is an informal structure). In one organization we know where managers and leaders adhere to this informal policy, the CEO abides by different rules. She has a chief of staff who vets all communications, all e-mails, and all meetings. Knowing this, you won't naively send an e-mail to her—you will build a relationship with the chief of staff to the point that he begins to trust you. That's the way to get to your CEO in this particular organization.

Working effectively within an informal organization requires a high degree of social awareness. Understanding how to maneuver within your informal organization is one of the most powerful skill sets you can have at work, so it's worth developing early in your career.

When you are trying to mobilize people, to get them interested and involved, you can't rely on position power or even rewards. In the informal, networked organization, people get things done by joining rather than forcing, by inspiring rather than telling, and by encouraging rather than criticizing.

One place you *do* need to consider position in most organizations is when you are dealing with your boss and other leaders. This is a special situation that requires special influencing skills, as you can see in the next section.

Managing Up

Despite the fact that organizations are becoming flatter, and that traditional hierarchies don't always meet organizations' or their environments' needs, traditional structures are still firmly in place in most organizations. Most organizations in the world have some type of hierarchy, and most people who work in organizations have a boss. It is likely that you will too.

So what can you do to effectively negotiate your relationship with those who are in leadership positions over you? For one, you can remember that your boss probably knows less about your job than you do. He or she has many responsibilities and is not intimate with the day-to-day context of your work. This is why it is important to manage up (or lead up) when and where you can.[115] As career coach Janet Bickel explains, managing up is creating a working partnership with your boss.[116]

A first step is to size up your boss—to understand him or her and to identify needs and values. This takes mindfulness and emotional intelligence as you try to uncover the thinking behind important decisions and read verbal and nonverbal cues.[117] For example, if you know your boss resists changes, but you want to use a more efficient or more effective way to accomplish something, you can add your idea in a request for directions: "Would you like me to . . . ?"

Another way of managing up is to learn your boss's preferred style of communication and present information in the format he or she is most likely to respond favorably. These ways of managing up also require you to look at yourself and to understand who you are through the eyes of your boss.[118] Knowing how others see you can become a strong motivation to work on changing those perceptions through modifying your own behaviors in a positive way.

Discussion Questions

1. Think about a department in your school or place of work that you do business with or that you belong to (the finance department or the management department, for example). Draw an organizational chart depicting the hierarchy, formal groups, and so forth. Now, draw another chart that reflects the informal organization. The person(s) at the top should be the ones that have the most information about what is really going on in the department—people who can get things done. Discuss the implications of this chart, along with the formal chart, for your engagement with this department.

2. What informal lines of communication are used in this class among you, your peers, your teaching assistant, and your professor? How do you utilize these lines of communication to be successful in this class?

10. A Final Word on Organizational Structure

Learning about organizational structure while you are still in school might seem like preparing for a race that you will run in 10 years. Hopefully this chapter has shown you otherwise. First, as we have mentioned many times in this book, our organizations are changing in response to the many economic, social, and technological changes that are occurring. This means that organizational structures will need to change, too. If you can be one of the "thinkers," one of the people who imagines new and better ways to organize people to work in this new age, you will be way ahead of the game. The world's businesses, institutions, and even governments need people like you, who have learned about the many traditional concepts related to organizational design but are creative and can craft new and better ways to coordinate people, processes, products, and services.

EXPERIENCING Leadership

LEADING IN A GLOBAL WORLD
A Union Made in Heaven?

Governments are among the most difficult organizations to run effectively for a number of reasons. The governing body of a nation creates its organizational structure around its particular form of government, whether democratic, socialist, or communist. However, no matter the type of structure the government adopts, it still has the almost impossible goal of trying to please most of the people most of the time. Now, imagine how difficult it would be to please a collection of numerous countries that are trying to organize themselves into a unified whole. That is what the European Union has attempted to do since 1993.

1. In a group or on your own, research the EU's organizational design.

   - Does the EU have a single governing body or is it a collection of different bodies all contributing their input to a central body? Is the decision making centralized or decentralized? Please explain your answer.
   - How does the EU reach decisions on major issues, such as the debt crises in Greece, Portugal, Ireland, and Spain?
   - Is the EU a typical mechanistic bureaucracy—a spider organization—or is it an adaptive starfish organization?
   - What are some of the major structural strengths of the EU? What are some of its weaknesses?
   - Identify the span of leadership within the EU's governing body. Who or what is ultimately accountable for the successes and challenges of the EU?

2. Create an organizational chart for the EU. Start from the top governing body down to individual country representation. Is it a departmentalized structure? If so, how would you break it down into different departments?

LEADING WITH EMOTIONAL INTELLIGENCE
Managing Up, Not Sucking Up

Managing up is a highly effective way for you to negotiate a healthy relationship with your boss. It helps you create a working partnership between the two of you that requires you to be emotionally intelligent and mindful.

The professor of your class is, for the semester, your manager. He or she will assign you tasks and projects to help you to meet the goals and objectives of the course—your job. He or she will also determine your performance in this job at the end of the class with your final performance review—your grade. How can you create an effective partnership with your professor?

1. Make a list of the different ways you can manage up in this class. Going beyond the obvious "job description" stated in the syllabus, seek to understand what he or she may be looking for you to do in order to enhance your learning experience and his or her teaching experience. For example, how would knowing the professor's personal academic interests or specialization be useful when deciding on a topic for a paper? How would turning in assignments ahead of schedule possibly make his or her job easier? How could you effectively use office hours to your benefit and the professor's benefit? How would anticipating certain of your professor's administrative needs work to your mutual advantage?

2. Once you have developed four or five managing up insights, make a to-do list of behaviors that you will employ to manage up. For example, turning in assignments two days early may allow your professor to stagger his or her grading, rather than grading all assignments at once.

LEADING WITH CRITICAL THINKING SKILLS
Government for and by the People

Governments, as mechanistic organizations, tend to be very bureaucratic and centralized in their decision making and power structure. Organic organizations, in contrast, are more decentralized in their decision making and power structure, and they are designed to be highly responsive to threats and opportunities. Many governments are spider organizations. However, some governing bodies are starfish organizations that are more organic in their structure and operate with less formality, allowing more flexibility in decision making.

1. Research your hometown government. Determine if it is a spider or a starfish organization. Make a short list of organizational qualities that qualifies it as either a spider or starfish.

2. Interview your parents about the efficiency and effectiveness of your hometown government. Do they see it as bureaucratic or organic? Are decisions made centrally or are decisions made by soliciting input from the town's inhabitants? Ask your parents what works well and what could be different. Ask them what changes they would suggest to the town's organizational design.

ETHICAL LEADERSHIP
Friends in High Places

When organizations restructure themselves, they typically combine some business units to reduce the complexity of reporting structures, merge skills and competencies, and eliminate duplication in jobs and work tasks. This effort may begin with layoffs. Imagine that you're a midlevel manager. Your manager calls you into his office to share the company's plans to begin restructuring your business unit, which will include layoffs. Eight people from your 40-member team have to be selected and laid off. Your manager asks you to try to exclude four people that he hired three months ago from your list. You know that these four people are his friends. Two of the four are not very productive or eager to learn and are very vocal about their friendship with your manager. The other two have assimilated well and are doing good work. Half of the other team members have been with the company for a minimum of 10 years and the other half have been with the company for 20 years or more. Each group has two or three people who are minimally productive. What do you do?

1. In a group or on your own, decide the hierarchy of the layoff list. Will seniority be a consideration, opening you up to the old motto "Last in first out"? How will performance be evaluated?

2. How do you explain your decision to your manager if you choose to include at least two of his friends on your list? Do you have a reason to fear for your own job if you don't protect your manager's friends? What alternatives do you have? How can HR help you in your dilemma?

KEY TERMS

Organization, *p. 294*
Organization design, *p. 294*
Organizational structure, *p. 294*
Job, *p. 297*
Division of labor, *p. 297*
Hierarchy, *p. 298*
Authority, *p. 299*
Responsibility, *p. 299*
Accountability, *p. 299*
Span of control, *p. 300*
Span of leadership, *p. 300*
Centralized decision making, *p. 300*

Decentralized decision making, *p. 300*
Organizational chart, *p. 301*
Open systems theory, *p. 303*
Mechanistic organization, *p. 305*
Standard operating procedures, or SOPs, *p. 305*
Organic organization, *p. 305*
Adaptive organization, *p. 305*
Cross-functional teams, *p. 310*
Departmentalization, *p. 312*
Functional departmentalization, *p. 313*

Product departmentalization, *p. 314*
Process departmentalization, *p. 314*
Customer departmentalization, *p. 315*
Geographic departmentalization, *p. 315*
Matrix, *p. 315*
Hybrid structure, *p. 316*
Environmental uncertainty, *p. 322*
Sole proprietorship, *p. 324*
Partnership, *p. 325*

Corporation, *p. 326*
S corporation, *p. 326*
LLC, *p. 326*
Cooperative contracts, *p. 326*
Licensing agreement, *p. 327*
Franchise, *p. 327*
Wholly owned affiliate or subsidiary, *p. 328*
Strategic alliances, *p. 329*
Job analysis, *p. 331*
Job description, *p. 331*
Job specification, *p. 331*
Benchmark job, *p. 332*

MyManagementLab

Go to **mymanagementlab.com** for Auto-graded writing questions as well as the following Assisted-graded writing questions:

9-1. Have you experienced any reporting relationships at work or school where a formally equal peer or colleague was granted more authority than you due to his or her informal relationship with someone above you in the organization's hierarchy? Do you feel this relationship was justified or did this cause concern for you?

9-2. People often feel comfortable with hierarchical structures and will create a mini-hierarchy around themselves, even if the formal structure does not call for it. Why do you think people do this? Briefly describe a situation where you have encountered this in the past, and how you dealt with it.

9-3. Mymanagementlab Only — comprehensive writing assignment for this chapter.

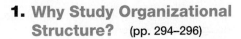

1. Why Study Organizational Structure? (pp. 294–296)

Objective: Define organization, organizational structure, and classifications for organizations.

Summary: The structure of an organization has a major impact on your success because it affects the way you behave and think about work. It also dictates the efficiency and agility of your organization. Understanding who does what, how people and groups interact, and how jobs are designed in your organization are key to helping you do your best in your role as an employee, a manager, and a leader.

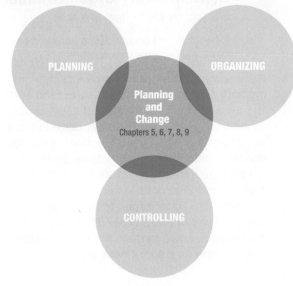

2. How Is Work Structured? (pp. 296–298)

Objective: Understand how work is structured.

Summary: Work is structured around jobs and tasks. Tasks are the individual activities that, when taken together, form a job. A job, then, is a grouping of tasks that enable an individual to accomplish an objective. Some jobs are specialized, allowing for a high degree of division of labor. These jobs may involve very few tasks, which may be repeated over and over. Other jobs are broader and require people to engage in many and diverse tasks.

4. What Are Some Important and Nontraditional Ways to View Organizations? (pp. 303–309)

Objective: Assess how we can view organizational structures in nontraditional ways.

Summary: Open systems theory states that an organization is constantly influenced by and is influencing its environment. Organizations can be described as mechanistic or organic. These terms refer to the degree of flexibility, specialization, formality, and centralized/decentralized decision making within an organization. Metaphors allow us to imagine how an organization functions. The spider and starfish metaphors present the spider as a hierarchical organization reliant on centralized decision making and the starfish as a flat organization that is decentralized.

3. What Traditional Concepts Impact Organizational Structure Today? (pp. 298–303)

Objective: Describe how traditional concepts affect current views of organizational structure.

Summary: Organizational structure is the way in which labor, communication, and resources are coordinated in order to accomplish organizational goals. Structure helps simplify the complexities inherent in most organizations. Traditionally, hierarchy has been an important component of structure because it outlines the relationships among managers and employees, and the authority, responsibility, and accountability afforded to each. Span of control and span of leadership are closely related to hierarchy; they refer to the number of jobs that report to a specific job and the number of people a leader needs to inspire and motivate. Finally, the degree of centralization of decision making impacts the speed with which organizational decisions are made and the quality of those decisions. The relationships that are built on these concepts may be visually represented using an organizational chart.

5. What Are the Most Common Contemporary Organizational Structures? (pp. 310–318)

Objective: List and define common contemporary organizational structures.

Summary: Contemporary organizations are becoming flatter as cost-cutting measures lead companies to turn away from traditional, tall hierarchies. A common structure called departmentalization is often used to group jobs by job functions, products, processes, customers, or geography. Some organizations utilize a matrix structure that links the vertical and horizontal structures in an organization. Other organizations have turned to hybrid structures that combine two or more types of structures. Still others utilize a networked structure, approaching the organization as a social network.

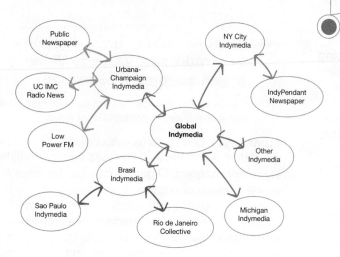

6. What Factors Affect the Design of Organizational Structures? (pp. 318–324)

Objective: Describe the factors that affect the design of organizational structures.

Summary: Although it is commonly held that structure should follow strategy, it is more accurate to say that the two have a symbiotic relationship. The external environment exerts a strong influence over organizational design, often necessitating rapid changes in order for a business to adapt to changing conditions. Technology, company size, and geography also impact the way an organization is designed. Surprisingly, adequate attention is not always given to organizational design, resulting in structures that emerge without much conscious planning. This can be both ineffective and inefficient.

7. What Are Common Business Ownership Models and Legal Designations in the United States? (pp. 324–330)

Objective: Learn how organizations are legally structured and classified.

Summary: Organizations can be classified by size, industry, and location, and most organizations can be classified in multiple ways. From a legal and taxation standpoint, the form of ownership a business has is important because it dictates many aspects of the business, including its income structure, tax, and reporting procedures. Forms familiar to most of us include sole proprietorships, partnerships, corporations, and LLCs. Less familiar and more complex relationships also exist between businesses that coordinate efforts to expand their markets and product lines through cooperative contracts, licensing or franchising agreements, wholly owned affiliates, and strategic alliances.

10. A Final Word on Organizational Structure (p. 334)

Summary: Organizations change as the world changes economically, socially, and technologically. As a result, organizational structures also need to change. Understanding traditional organizational structures is a first step in developing the skills to creatively improve them.

9. What Can We All Do to Work Effectively within Our Organizations' Structures? (pp. 332–334)

Objective: Learn how you can work more effectively within an organizational structure.

Summary: Learning to work effectively within the informal structure of your organization helps you be more effective at work. It is also important that you learn to work effectively with, or manage, your boss. Being able to identify his or her needs, preferred communication style, and opinions of you will allow you to be more effective and efficient.

8. What Is HR's Role in Organizational Design and Structure? (pp. 330–332)

Objective: Define HR's role in organizational design and structure.

Summary: HR is responsible for many aspects of organizational design, including negotiating with labor unions and performing job analyses. Labor unions can impact organizational structure and job design, and it is important for HR professionals to understand the attitudes and issues of both managers and employees when it comes to these unions. Job analysis is another particularly important responsibility of HR because it enables the organization to understand job specifications and requirements. A rigorous analysis of jobs can result in a better fit between people and jobs.

CHAPTER 1

Teams and Team Building:

How to Work Effectively with Others

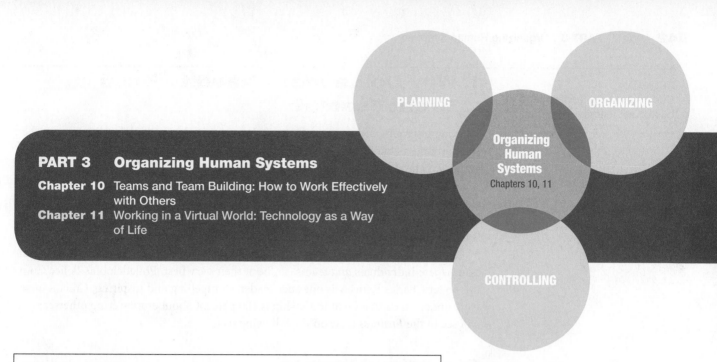

PLANNING

ORGANIZING

Organizing
Human
Systems
Chapters 10, 11

CONTROLLING

MyManagementLab™

✪ Improve Your Grade!

Over 10 million students improved their results using the Pearson MyLabs.
Visit **mymanagementlab.com** for simulations, tutorials, and end-of-chapter
problems.

Chapter Outline

Chapter Objectives

10.1 Understand why leaders need to build great teams.

10.2 Explore and understand group dynamics.

10.3 Explain the reasons groups change over time.

10.4 Describe how group dynamics impact team effectiveness.

10.5 Explain how teams function at work.

10.6 Explain how to handle the challenges of working in groups.

10.7 Define the role conflict plays in groups.

10.8 Describe how HR can support effective team performance.

10.9 Describe how we can create and sustain resonant teams.

1. Why Do Leaders Need to Build Great Teams?

Working in groups comes naturally to us. We are wired to empathize with one another, align around a shared purpose, and collaborate to achieve common goals. Working in groups is natural and it's also necessary—but it's not always easy. This is true for many reasons. For one, people often don't understand the dynamics that impact groups. You will learn about that in this chapter. Another reason is linked to our (often misguided) view of leadership. We often see it as a solitary act, and link results with one person's actions. But rarely, if ever, can one individual succeed without others' input, help, and support.

Good leaders understand that success and effectiveness are linked to creating conditions where individuals *and* teams can be at their very best. Philadelphia's Police Commissioner Charles Ramsey is one such leader. Compelling and inspiring, Chief Ramsey truly understands that great leadership is 100 percent about empowering others, as you will see in the *Business Case* on the following page.

Groups and Teams: Where We Learn, Live, and Work

As Commissioner Ramsey knows, much of what happens at work is done in groups and teams. Generally, a small group is defined as any structure that includes three to approximately 15 people. A **team** is a small group (ideally 6 to 10 individuals) whose members share a common purpose, hold themselves individually and collectively responsible for goals, and have complementary skills and agreed-on processes for working together.[1] In this chapter, we will use both the word *group* and the word *team*, because the chapter is about groups at work, which are usually called teams.

Within organizations, teams can be structured in many different ways. Some teams always meet in person; others interact virtually. Some teams have formal leaders; others do not. Some teams stay together for a very long time; others form for specific purposes and then disband when the job is done. Some teams stay in place even when all of their members change. For example, a senior team in an organization will still exist after one CEO resigns and another takes over. The team will also continue to exist even if the new CEO hires new people and lets the old members go. In this example, the team members will have changed, and perhaps individual members' roles will be somewhat different, but the governance structure called the senior team still exists.

We need to learn about teams because they are the structures within which most of an organization's work is accomplished. We also study teams because they provide a "home" for us at work: Belonging to a team provides us with a sense of personal identity, and contributing to a team enables us to fulfill our desire to achieve important goals that we could not achieve alone. Groups and teams are the places in which our most important social interactions occur at work. We laugh and learn in our work groups. We build solid collegial relationships and even friendships in our groups at work. We fight and learn how to deal with conflict in groups, and it is in groups and teams that we learn how to respect people who are different from us.

Groups Are Mysterious

Have you ever wondered about the feelings and behaviors that swirled around you as you worked in a group? Have you ever considered why some groups are great at getting things done while others struggle? Have you thought about why you feel motivated to work harder in some groups than in others? Groups are complex and mysterious. That's

Team
A small group (ideally 6 to 10 individuals) whose members share a common purpose, hold themselves individually and collectively responsible for goals, and have complementary skills and agreed-on processes for working together.

Philadelphia Police Commissioner Charles H. Ramsey on Leadership

Commissioner Charles H. Ramsey of the Philadelphia Police Department grew up in Chicago at a time when becoming a police officer was hardly the thing to do. As a child, Chuck (as he was called then) never imagined joining the police force, even for a minute. Then, after high school, he started on a pre-med course, working his way through college. Along the way, he got to know a couple of police officers who often came to the store where he worked. These officers were friendly and interesting, and when one of them asked Chuck whether he had ever thought about becoming a cadet, the young man gave the question some serious thought. When Chuck learned that Chicago had a tuition reimbursement program for police cadets, his decision was made.

Ramsey joined the Chicago Police Department in 1968. He loved his job. He was helping people and making a difference in the city he cared so much about. He was working with great people on great teams, and he could see a future that made *sense* for him. This vision crystallized one cold night when Officer Ramsey and a few others were dealing with a homicide. In those days, old-timers were assigned to ambulance detail. While watching the veteran officers, Ramsey had a blinding insight: If his life continued on the path he was on, that would be *him* in thirty years, struggling to carry a body down icy stairs. The very next day, Ramsey signed up for the sergeant exam.

Ramsey passed, of course, and this marked the beginning of a fulfilling journey packed with great experiences, tough situations, and fascinating people. Although Ramsey started out with the right stuff, it was along the way that he *learned* to be a great leader. These leadership abilities didn't go unnoticed, and when the call eventually came for Ramsey to interview for the top police job in Washington, DC, he was ready for the challenge. And what a challenge! Washington had been suffering for years under poor leadership and a host of social and economic problems, and the city's police force had been beaten down, battered, criticized, and disrespected. As the newly appointed chief of police, Ramsey certainly had his work cut out for him.

Person by person and group by group, Chief Ramsey soon learned just what Washington had to offer—and it offered a lot. He found great people, tons of talent, and profound commitment to the city and its police force. Ramsey also learned everything he could about the strengths of the individuals on his team and on the force. Some needed just a bit more attention; some needed guidance; and some needed him to keep distractions at bay. With his team and other groups within the city, Ramsey faced up to Washington's problems. When things didn't work out as planned, he was the first to step up and say that a different direction was needed. Ramsey didn't cast shame or blame anyone; rather, he simply expressed his commitment to making things work.

And make it work they did. For example, when protesters made their way to Washington, DC, in 2002, many people feared there would be riots, as had occurred the year before in Seattle during the World Trade Organization meetings. Ramsey and the police force had to help the city avoid this fate while maneuvering through complex political dynamics and ensuring that people could gather and speak freely, as is their constitutional right. On the whole, the force acted with restraint and respect. People were able to protest and voice their concerns, but no buildings or property were damaged and no people were harmed.

When planes toppled the World Trade Center and crashed into the Pentagon on September 11, 2001, Ramsey and his strong and renewed force were ready as well. Throughout that dark day and the weeks that followed, the force functioned like a well-oiled machine, protecting not just the citizens of Washington, DC, but the interests of the country as a whole. In fact, over the eight years that Ramsey served in Washington, DC, the city's crime rate dropped by 40 percent, and its force earned the reputation of being one of the best urban police forces in the country.[2] Chief Ramsey remembers the moment that he considers his best reward—when an officer walked up to him in a crowd and said, "Chief, you have given us back our pride."

In 2008, Charles Ramsey was appointed Commissioner of the Philadelphia Police Department, where he immediately began tackling some of the most difficult social and economic issues ever faced in an urban area. The way Ramsey looks at the situation goes something like this: "*I* won't be able to 'fix' these issues in Philadelphia, but *we will*. When the community—all of us—pull together and say, 'No more crime; we want our city to be better than it is now,' that's when change will happen."

Later in the chapter, we'll hear more from Commissioner Ramsey. For now, let's start studying groups by considering some of Ramsey's words of wisdom:

It's great to talk about individual leaders as if they do it all. But that's not what it's all about. Success is about a group of people coming together to do something. If you can be the person to draw people together, that's great. And if you can be part of the group that does something fantastic together, that's great too.[3]

partly because people are complicated, and it's also partly because it is hard to understand what is going on between and among people in a group. For instance, you can't really see how people's emotions and moods impact one another, or how people feel when they are included, excluded, looked up to, or ignored in a group. You can't see people's psychological reactions to power—their own or others'—and you can't see the inner satisfaction or struggles people experience when their ideas are accepted or rejected by a group. You can only see people's behavior. This can be confusing, and you may find that you're constantly trying to interpret why people behave the way they do in groups.

This chapter is dedicated to helping you demystify what happens in groups and teams and to giving you another lens through which to view leadership and human behavior at work. There are several streams of knowledge and skills that can help you and the groups you belong to become more effective. We will begin by exploring early studies of the impact of leadership behavior on group dynamics, followed by interesting research about how groups develop over time. After that, we will focus on key aspects of group dynamics, including roles, norms, status, power, and diversity. Once you have a solid grounding in how groups develop and function, we will study work teams, paying special attention to various factors that enable high performance. We will discuss the challenges involved in working in groups, as well as the benefits and drawbacks of the conflict that inevitably arises in group settings. Finally, we'll conclude the chapter with a look at how HR can support effective teamwork in organizations and what we can all do to be more effective group members and team leaders.

Discussion Questions

1. Think about the best and worst groups you have ever led or been a part of. For each group, describe the members, the group's purpose, and what the group achieved. In your opinion, why was one group "best" and one "worst"?

2. Success is rarely, if ever, dependent on one person, no matter how good a leader that individual is. Do you agree with this idea? Why or why not? Support your response using examples from your own experience.

Objective 10.2
Explore and understand group dynamics.

2. How Does Leadership Behavior Affect Group Dynamics?

Scholar Kurt Lewin's time in Nazi Germany left him with an enduring interest in the positive and negative influence of groups. Lewin's work set the stage for a great deal of research about people in work settings, including how people behave in groups (■ **EXHIBIT 10.1**).

At the time, most studies of human behavior focused solely on individuals—personality, intelligence, capability, and other personal characteristics. Lewin turned the nature of inquiry into human behavior upside down by moving away from this singular focus on individual characteristics, emphasizing that groups have a profound influence on what people think, feel, and do. He proposed an intriguing formula that you can see in ■ **EXHIBIT 10.2**. In this formula, *behavior* (B) is a *function* (f) of the interaction of the *person* (P) and the *environment* (E).[4]

This formula points out that how a person behaves is linked to both personal characteristics (intelligence, social and emotional intelligence, personality, etc.) and the conditions of the environment. A group's environment can include things like the group leader's behavior, the physical conditions in which the group works, the society and organization in which the group operates, the outside pressures on the group, the size of the group, and so on.

Lewin and his colleagues created an experiment to test the effects of different styles of leadership on small groups.[5] Their subjects were boys working on projects in voluntary teams. Each team was randomly assigned an adult leader who demonstrated one of three styles of leadership: autocratic, democratic, or laissez-faire. An **autocratic leader** tends to make decisions without input from others, whereas a **democratic leader** will seek input and then either make a decision or engage the group in collective decision making. A **laissez-faire leader** remains at a distance from the decision-making process, allowing the group to make decisions without leadership intervention.

In this study, the groups were observed as they worked, and their productivity and aggression were analyzed. The researchers found that the autocratic group spent more time working than the democratic group. Both the autocratic and democratic groups were more productive than the laissez-faire group. Autocratic leadership had negative effects on group stability, and hostility and aggression were highest within the autocratic group. Frequently, the boys in the autocratic group destroyed their work after the work session ended.[6] These findings began a long tradition of research that showed that autocratic leadership has negative consequences over the long term, whereas involving people in a democratic manner increases commitment to both the task and the leader.[7]

For example, one recent study found that group members were less willing to work hard in groups where leaders took an autocratic approach.[8] Another interesting study of people on juries found that jurors' satisfaction with a verdict was in part dependent on how their fellow jurors treated them and listened to them. This supports the idea that a democratic approach to making decisions in groups results in a higher level of satisfaction with the outcomes of a group's work.[9]

In a follow-up to the findings about laissez-faire leadership, research has shown that the style is a "common, but unrealistic and immature" way to manage teams.[10] This is an important lesson because many people adopt a passive approach to team leadership, thinking they are empowering team members. Unfortunately, delegation of authority to team members is often more about avoiding responsibility than about empowerment. In these cases, productivity, relationships, and innovation tend to suffer.[11] Good leaders don't take a hands-off approach with their teams, even when team members are empowered to make decisions and do their jobs. It takes effort and action to lead teams and to create an atmosphere in which people can give their best.

Over the years, thousands of studies of groups and teams have been conducted in laboratories and in real-world settings, resulting in a wealth of knowledge about what happens in small groups and teams. Many of these studies have focused on leadership and leader–member relationships. Other studies have focused on how and why groups included or excluded people, how patterns of behavior developed, and how conflict emerged and was dealt with in groups. Some studies also looked at how and why groups changed over time.

The 1980s and 1990s saw increased interest and research about group development and group dynamics within many disciplines, including political theory, family systems theory, communication, and organizational development. Today, emerging research on the impact of neuropsychology, emotions, and social networking is adding depth and richness to the research of the previous century. In the next several sections, we will look at how this research can help us understand group development, group dynamics, and how to lead and manage teams today.

■ **EXHIBIT 10.1**

How might psychologist Kurt Lewin's experience in Nazi Germany have fueled his curiosity about how people behave in groups?

Source: INTERFOTO/Alamy

■ **EXHIBIT 10.2**

Lewin's Formula

$$B = f(P, E)$$

Autocratic leader
A leader who tends to make decisions without input from others.

Democratic leader
A leader who seeks input and then either makes a decision or engages the group in collective decision making.

Laissez-faire leader
A leader who remains at a distance from the decision-making process, allowing the group to make decisions without leadership intervention.

Discussion Questions

1. Have you ever been part of a group that was led by an autocratic leader? How did you react to this person? What was the impact on your group's performance?

2. Why do you think people often adopt a laissez-faire approach to leading groups?

3. How Do Groups Change over Time?

Think about a group you have been a member of from the beginning—maybe an athletic team for an entire season or a study group during a whole semester. If your group was like most, the way people interacted in the beginning was very different from later on, the way conflict was dealt with changed, and the group's effectiveness probably improved over time.

Beginning with landmark research by scholars Warren Bennis and Herb Shepard about how groups deal with authority, structure, intimacy, and interdependence, a long tradition of research has examined how groups develop over time and the extent to which member and leader behavior can be predicted based on a group's stage of development.[12] In this section, we will look at two models of group development devised by researchers Bruce Tuckman, Mary Ann Jensen, and Susan Wheelan.

Bruce Tuckman and Mary Ann Jensen: A Five Stage Model of Group Development

In the mid-1960s, researcher Bruce Tuckman synthesized the results of numerous studies and created a model of group development that initially included four sequential stages: *forming, storming, norming,* and *performing.*[13] He and scholar Mary Ann Jensen later added a fifth stage, *adjourning.*[14] This five-stage model suggests that groups mature over time and that during each stage, there are specific ways in which people deal with interpersonal relationships and task behaviors.

STAGE 1: FORMING

Forming is the first stage of group development, in which members start to get to know one another, are polite and friendly, and avoid conflict. During this stage, people work to build a group, and they avoid any topics or interactions that might harm relationships or the development of common ground.

STAGE 2: STORMING

Storming is the second stage of group development. It is characterized by disagreements about how to work together, bids for power, and conflict with leaders. In this stage, people are more apt to speak up, disagree, and attempt to influence others and the group. It is not uncommon for group members to fight openly with one another and with the leader in this stage.

STAGE 3: NORMING

Norming is the third stage of group development, when the group agrees on rules of behavior (**group norms**), who does what (**group roles**), and how best to work together. Group norms are informal but powerful standards that guide group members' behavior. For example, many work groups will establish norms about timeliness, adhering to deadlines, how people should treat one another, and group member roles.

Group member roles are shared expectations about who does what. For example, during the norming stage, people might discuss and agree that a particular member will take on the role of meeting agenda planner, while another will take the role of note taker.

STAGE 4: PERFORMING

Performing is the fourth stage of group development, during which the group channels energy into tasks rather than into building relationships, resolving conflicts, or deciding how to work together. Interpersonal relationships now support the group in accomplishing tasks, and roles are more fluid (e.g., anyone can step into the leadership role as the task requires).

Forming
The first stage of group development, during which members start to get to know one another, are polite and friendly, and avoid conflict.

Storming
The second stage of group development, which is characterized by disagreements about how to work together, bids for power, and conflict with leaders.

Norming
The third stage of group development, when the group agrees on common rules of behavior for members (group norms), who does what (group roles), and how best to work together.

Group norms
Informal but powerful standards that guide group members' behavior.

Group roles
Shared expectations among members about who does what.

Performing
The fourth stage of group development, during which the group channels energy into tasks rather than into building relationships, resolving conflicts, or deciding how to work together.

STAGE 5: ADJOURNING

Adjourning is the stage during which the group finishes its tasks and decides or is forced to dissolve membership. This stage can cause people to feel sad and to try to hold on to the group even though it no longer serves a purpose. Sometimes at work, groups actually do stay together after their tasks are completed. This can be a source of confusion, contention, and wasted resources. One important group skill, then, is knowing when to let go.

Tuckman and Jensen's model of group development became popular over the years, partly because it is so simple. The model's simplicity has been criticized, however, and in recent years, scholars such as Susan Wheelan have attempted to look at group development in more depth.

Adjourning
The fifth stage of group development during which the group finishes its tasks and decides or is forced to dissolve membership.

Susan Wheelan's Integrated Model of Group Development

By the 1990s, more powerful computers allowed for more sophisticated analyses of people's behavior in groups and how groups develop. Based on such research, Susan Wheelan proposed a model of group development that is similar to other models in that it is linear and outlines the stages through which a group progresses.[15] Like other models of group development, Wheelan's model associates certain kinds of behavior with each stage of group development (■ **EXHIBIT 10.3**). What is different about this model is that Wheelan reasons that time is not the only factor that influences group development. She proposes that people's experience with one another is also an important factor, and that experience is not always time dependent. Let's look at an overview of stages of group development and the behaviors we tend to see as a group evolve.

STAGE 1: DEPENDENCY AND INCLUSION

In the first stage of group development, members are dependent on the leader to tell them what to do.[16] If there is no formal leader, then a powerful member usually takes charge. Members are concerned about emotional safety and issues of inclusion. They ask themselves questions like "How do I fit in?" and "Is it safe here?"

In work teams, the dependency and inclusion stage can be awkward because no one knows exactly how to behave or what to do, even if the task is clear. This stage can be frustrating because there is an expectation from team members and managers alike that the team will be productive immediately, which is very hard to do. People usually can't focus their energy on tasks and goals because of the uncertainty surrounding norms and roles. Oftentimes we make the mistake of ignoring the real needs people have during this stage, such as the need to find their place on the team, to feel included, and to feel accepted for who they are and the contributions they can bring.

On the other hand, Stage 1 can be exhilarating at first because it seems that everyone gets along, and with direction from a member or leader, things go well for a while. It's fine to enjoy this part of Stage 1, but don't let it fool you. Things almost always change in Stage 2.

■ **EXHIBIT 10.3**
Time and experiences influence group development.

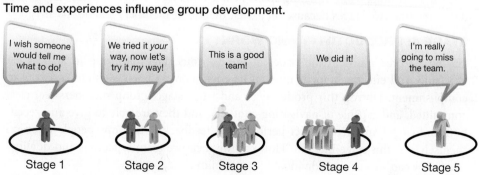

| Stage 1 | Stage 2 | Stage 3 | Stage 4 | Stage 5 |

STAGE 2: CONFLICT AND COUNTERDEPENDENCE

Counterdependence
Attitudes and behaviors related to resisting leadership or direction from others.

The group's task during Stage 2 is to develop a unified set of goals, values, and operational procedures. These negotiations inevitably generate conflict. Many times, this conflict is directed at the leader and/or powerful group members, which is a dynamic that is called counterdependence. **Counterdependence** refers to attitudes and behaviors related to resisting leadership or direction from others.[17] Questions people often ask themselves at this stage include "Do I have power in this group?", "Must I fight to be heard?", and "Do I respect the leader?"

During the conflict and counterdependence stage, people argue, form power coalitions with other members to get their plans implemented, or even sabotage the leader or other powerful group members. This can be a nasty and unproductive period, especially when conflict becomes personalized or has nothing to do with helping the group learn how to work together or achieve its goals. In these situations, groups often get stuck or blow up.

In order for conflict to be dealt with in a constructive manner, both members and the group leader need to be clear about and committed to the group's purpose. When this is the case, people need to learn that it is possible to disagree without destroying the team. At this stage, it's important to remember that conflict in groups is healthy because it is necessary to establish a climate in which members feel free to disagree. Having individuals who are willing to disagree is great insurance against thoughtless conformity.

As the group survives conflicts, people begin to feel safer and more willing to share different viewpoints. As members try out their independence and differentiate from one another, they gain confidence and are more willing to take on roles and responsibilities. There is more positive relational and emotional engagement among members and more commitment to the group as a whole. What emerges from this process is a broader range of ways to negotiate differences, make decisions, communicate, and lead.

STAGE 3: TRUST AND STRUCTURE

If the group emerges from Stage 2, it is ready to enter Stage 3, the trust and structure stage. In this stage, norms and roles are more clear, and the group is not as dependent on a leader. Members welcome guidance from the leader, and they are more open to being led by other members as well. Members understand that structures such as roles and decision processes are helpful, and they use them. They also adjust group norms and roles if needed, rather than rigidly holding on to "the way it is" as sometimes happens in earlier stages. People trust each other more and can more maturely negotiate roles and stay organized, allowing the group to maintain positive working relationships. Questions people often ask themselves at this stage include "What role can I take on that will help the group?", "What subgroups will help us achieve our goals?", and "What systems should we create to manage our time, work flow, etc.?"

In the trust and structure stage, people often feel a sense of relief. They know where they fit and how people relate to one another, and they feel confident that the group can handle conflict without falling apart. People don't take things as personally as they did in the first two stages because they trust that other members' intentions are good.

STAGE 4: PRODUCTIVITY AND WORK

Having resolved many of the issues of the previous stages, a group in Stage 4 can efficiently and effectively focus most of its energy on goal achievement and task accomplishment. During this productivity and work stage, group members feel clear, committed, and capable of navigating conflicts, and they are able to give and receive both individual and group-level performance feedback. Questions people often ask themselves at this stage include "How can we measure team outcomes and quality?" and "How can we ensure individual accountability?"

STAGE 5: TERMINATION

Wheelan's model speaks to the termination stage of a group's life as a time when members reflect on task accomplishment and relational memories. Sometimes when a group stays together for a long time, "eras" of the group's life can be tracked by paying attention to what members become nostalgic about. Questions people often ask themselves at this stage include "How will we know we are "done"?", "How can we mark the end of our work together?", and "How should we say goodbye?"

Group Development: A Useful but Limited Way to Explain What Happens in Groups

Models of group development are useful in that they help members and leaders understand some of what occurs at different times in a group's life. Group development models do not, however, tell the whole story. First, most group development research has focused on groups that worked together in person in the laboratory. Today, however, many work groups rarely, if ever, meet in person. They rely on electronic communication and meet more often in subgroups than as a whole (we will discuss virtual teams in more depth in Chapter 11.) For now, it is important to note that it is not clear whether the same developmental progression occurs in virtual groups as in groups whose members meet in person.

Second, developmental models are difficult to apply in a fast-paced organizational environment in which projects and teams change all the time. Third, group development models do not take into account the fact that, in many cases, teams are responsible for significant joint outcomes yet members spend little time working *together*—in such situations, work looks more like a series of hand-offs than a collective effort. Let's look at some practical considerations that must be considered when applying models of group development to teams in organizations today:

- Groups cycle through the developmental processes over and over, engaging with each stage in a different manner depending on why they need to revisit it. For example, people join and leave groups at work often. When a new group forms, group members may revert to a stage-one level of dependency, but they can cycle through it very quickly by bringing the new member up to speed on norms, roles, and so forth. Similarly, if a new leader is assigned, a group could easily slip back into stage one or even stage two behavior. If you have a really effective team, you are able to adjust quickly to changes that affect the group's stage of development so that the group does not blindly slip into old or dysfunctional patterns.
- Groups in organizations are often extremely short lived, yet they need to accomplish very sophisticated tasks. Group development models assume that goals will never be achieved or results will be compromised if people do not have enough time or enough experience working with each other. Practical experience in organizations today tells us otherwise. Stages of group development are not as discrete as the models we've studied suggest, and in many groups at work, it can be difficult to tell where one stage ends and another begins.[18] This means that either people are learning to speed through the stages of group development, or they are adapting to new ways of building relationships more quickly and resolving conflicts more effectively even before they really know each other. The need to work this way could be linked to the growing importance of social and emotional skills in the workplace today.
- Globalization means more diversity in many groups. This means that the amount and types of conflict are greater and more varied than in the past. The upside: Team results can be and often are better.

Group development models will continue to be studied, and it is likely that new research will inform how these models can better support groups today. For a practical tool to help

■ **EXHIBIT 10.4**
What you need to consider when building a resonant team.

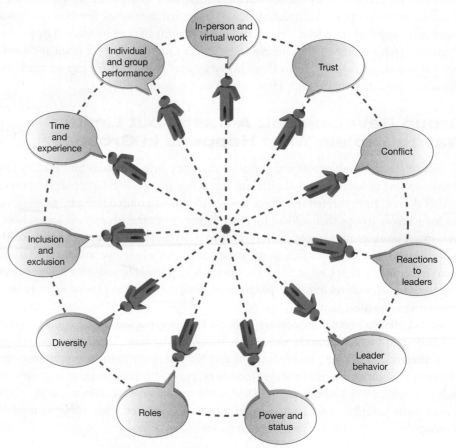

you think about the aspects of groups you should consider when building or working in a team, see ■ **EXHIBIT 10.4**. This model illustrates that some of the early work on group dynamics is still valid (e.g., all groups must deal with leader behavior and conflict). It also includes a few new things, like considering whether the team works in person or virtually, what roles team members play, how power and status are distributed, and how the team handles diversity. In the next section, we will explore these group dynamics more deeply.

Discussion Questions

1. Think about a group that you have belonged to for a long time. What stage of development do you think this group is in? Explain your answer in terms of member–leader relationships, conflict, and communication.

2. Review the things to consider when building a resonant team in Exhibit 10.4. Now, think about a work or school team you belong to (or a group of friends). Which of these factors are most important for you to work on in this group? Why?

Objective 10.4
Describe how group dynamics impact team effectiveness.

4. How Do Group Dynamics Impact Team Effectiveness?

In this section, we will explore four aspects of group dynamics that affect people's behavior and group effectiveness: roles, norms, status and power, and diverse interaction and learning styles. We will then conclude the section by considering the paradoxes we need to resolve in ourselves and with others in order for our groups to function well.

Group Roles

A role in a group includes expectations about who does what and who is responsible for what. Roles can be formal and assigned (e.g., official leader, project manager) or informal (e.g., meeting organizer, snackbringer) (■ **EXHIBIT 10.5**). Roles help members because they define responsibilities associated with the work the group needs to do and relationships among members.

Early group theorists pointed out that roles can be associated with *task functions* and *group maintenance functions*.[19] The roles that accompany these functions are important and deserving of effort and energy on the part of members and leaders.[20]

People who take on task roles engage in behaviors and activities that help the group accomplish tasks and achieve goals. Examples of task roles include:[21]

■ **EXHIBIT 10.5**
How do formal roles in a group differ from informal roles?

Source: © Eddie Gerald/Alamy

- *Information provider:* One who offers facts and research.
- *Diagnoser:* One who points out the obstacles to successful group work.
- *Evaluator:* One who measures the accomplishments of the group against set criteria.

Group maintenance roles include activities that are important to relationships and to the morale of the group, such as:[22]

- *Tension reliever:* One who relieves the group's stress.
- *Encourager:* One who asks for and encourages participation and ideas.
- *Trust builder:* One who inspires others to take emotional risks.

These roles are people oriented and create an atmosphere that enables each member to contribute maximally.

People often pay more attention to task roles than group maintenance roles. This may be because it is easier to focus on a task than on relationships or because there is often extreme pressure to perform at work and in school. Whatever the reason, ignoring roles and activities that support relationships is foolhardy. Groups fail when attention is not given to human beings.

HOW ROLES DEVELOP IN GROUPS

Sometimes people choose a role in a group, such as when someone volunteers to be the person to schedule meetings. Other times, roles are assigned. For example, your instructor might ask you to lead a study group. In still other instances, a role can emerge over time—no one asks for it and no one assigns it. For example, after a few meetings of a study group, you may realize that you are the one who always asks the group to set deadlines. The group has come to depend on you for this service. They begin to *expect* this from you, and "deadline setter" is now your role. This might be fine if you also see yourself in this role. If, on the other hand, you set deadlines a few times to help the group but believe that others should do so as well, you may find that your group will have to deal with conflict. Conflict about group roles also emerges when members have not fully outlined the work associated with each role.

Roles are a powerful social force: They dictate our behavior, sometimes far more than they should. We've all encountered the person who, when given the role of group leader, becomes a tyrant. We have also all taken on roles and found ourselves acting in ways that didn't really represent who we are. This was made painfully clear in a study done at Stanford University in 1971, famously called the *Stanford prison experiment*.

Source: Photos 12/Alamy

STANFORD PRISON EXPERIMENT

The Stanford prison experiment was conducted in 1971 at Stanford University in Palo Alto, California (■ **EXHIBIT 10.6**). In the experiment, volunteers from the university participated in a mock prison, where some volunteers played guards and others played prisoners. The researchers wanted to know things like "What happens when you put good people in an evil place? Does humanity win over evil, or does evil triumph?"[23] Only people who were considered psychologically stable were chosen to participate in the experiment.

To re-create prison conditions, guards were given uniforms, wooden batons, and mirrored sunglasses to prevent eye contact with prisoners. The prisoners were given poorly fitting outfits and were called by the numbers assigned to them, which were sewn onto their prison outfits. They also wore chains around their ankles. Guards were explicitly told not to physically harm prisoners, but they were encouraged to find ways to create boredom, fear, and hopelessness.[24]

Over the course of the experiment, the participants adapted to their roles far beyond researchers' expectations. Within a short period of time, guards became cruel and even sadistic. They humiliated and degraded the prisoners. At first, the prisoners revolted, but as their treatment worsened, they began to show signs of extreme emotional disturbance. The situation became so dire that the experiment had to be stopped after six days, more than a week earlier than planned.[25]

The Stanford prison experiment gained considerable attention in recent years as a result of the abuse of prisoners (many of whom had not been convicted of any crime) in Abu Ghraib, a prison run by U.S. military personnel in Iraq.[26] The lesson for us is that roles *do* affect how we see ourselves and others and how we behave. It is very important, then, to be highly self-aware whenever we take on a role, especially a leadership role.

Group Norms

Remember your first day in college or your first day on the job? Chances are you paid careful attention to the behavior of the people around you to get some sense of what was expected of you. What you were searching for, even if you didn't realize it, were norms. Group norms are informal standards for behavior that guide group members' behavior. Norms are the "way we do things" and how we expect one another to behave. Norms help us predict social interaction—they tell us what we are supposed to do and what we are not allowed to do in certain situations.

For instance, norms guide your behavior in school: You arrive on time, take a seat, and behave as if you are attentive to the lecture. Some instructors set other norms, such as "ask questions" or "participate in class discussions." Societal norms also dictate our behavior. For example, societal norms guide what sort of swimwear we wear and what we wear to bed or to a funeral. If we switched things around and wore pajamas to a funeral or a swimsuit to work, people would be offended. That's a lesson about norms: The surest way to identify a norm is to violate it—people will let you know.

Norms are a very important aspect of group dynamics. As in society, they become the informal rule book that guides individual behavior in groups. Group norms differ depending on things such as the society in which the group is operating, the group's purpose, members' social and cultural backgrounds, and the actual work that the group is expected to perform.

GROUP NORMS NEED TO BE EXPLICIT

Norms may be clear to all group members (explicit), be sensed by a few members (implicit), or be operating completely below the level of awareness. Many groups adopt implicit norms based on their backgrounds and prior experiences, without discussion or explicit agreement. Sometimes implicit norms provide enough guidance, particularly if the group members belong to the same or similar cultures, the same organization, and have worked together in the past.

Most of the time, however, implicit norms are not sufficient to support members in all necessary interaction, and they can even interfere with group effectiveness. For that reason, it is helpful for work groups to agree on norms when they begin to work together. Common norms that groups might agree to are listed in ■ **EXHIBIT 10.7**.

Let's now look at norms related to social and emotional competencies that can support group effectiveness.

■ **EXHIBIT 10.7**

EMOTIONAL INTELLIGENCE AND GROUP NORMS

Effective groups translate social and emotional intelligence into group norms. At the beginning of the chapter, you read about Commissioner Ramsey of the Philadelphia Police Department, an outstanding leader who knows how to build great teams. Let's see what he has to say about what kind of norms we can adopt to work successfully with others in teams in the following *Leadership Perspective* feature.

Our Group Norms

1. Everyone has the responsibility to lead this group when his or her area of expertise is needed.
2. Everyone in this group is responsible for making sure we perform at our very best individually and as a group.
3. We are committed to open dialogue: Everyone *can* speak, and everyone *must*.
4. We respect one another at all times.
5. We put group needs in front of our individual needs.

Leadership Perspective

● **Charles Ramsey**
Police Commissioner for Philadelphia
"You need to know yourself."

"You need to know yourself. And you need to be true to yourself. You're not John Kennedy or Frances Hesselbein or Barack Obama— you are first and foremost yourself. What makes you tick? You've got to do the self-assessment, over and over. Take inventory. Until you do this, you're not going to get very far. You've got to know what triggers you, so you can back away or change a situation before you do something you will regret. You can't influence anyone else if you can't control yourself.

And you need to really listen to people—even people you don't like. Their criticism may not be what you want to hear, and most of it might be wrong, but I've found that when you really listen, even to these people, you're likely to find out that one thing that you really need to know. You can learn so much just by watching others. You'll learn the good and the bad—what you want to do as a leader, and what you'll never do to people.

And finally, learn to be a good follower. Even the best leaders have to be followers sometimes. When I go to a crime scene, I'm not going to step in and take over. I let the experts do it—the homicide squad or the narcotics officers. My role is to follow them, and to get obstacles out of their way."[27]

Source: Personal interview with Commissioner Charles H. Ramsey conducted by Annie McKee, 2010.

Commissioner Ramsey could write a book on emotional intelligence competencies and leadership; he truly understands the impact of self-awareness, self-management, and social awareness on a leader's effectiveness and his or her impact on individuals and groups. As a leader, he sets the stage for those around him to adopt norms that support group and institutional effectiveness.

To help a group be emotionally intelligent, leaders like Commissioner Ramsey create explicit norms that encourage members to draw on their emotional intelligence competencies. The creation of norms that are grounded in emotional intelligence supports the development of trust, group identity, and a belief in group efficacy. In fact, scholars Vanessa Druskat and Steven Wolff argue that developing group emotional intelligence is a necessary condition for maximizing effectiveness in groups.[28]

In addition, the group's culture—underlying values, beliefs, and language—should also support emotionally intelligent behavior. If culture and norms support emotional intelligence, members will more naturally adhere to these guidelines. Then, if a member crosses the line and engages in behavior that violates these norms, the group will likely feel more comfortable calling attention to the behavior because it violates the group's identity.

You can see an example of an expanded set of group norms that focuses on emotional intelligence in ■ **EXHIBIT 10.8**. Working in groups that adhere to emotionally intelligent norms can be satisfying and fun. That does not mean, however, that these groups don't experience conflicts. Emotional intelligence in groups is not just about group harmony, tight friendships, and the absence of tension. Rather, it is about the ability of members to deal with the pressures, stress, and conflict in ways that do not destroy individuals or the group.

Group norms and group roles are usually linked to another set of group dynamics related to status and power, which we will now explore.

Status and Power in Groups

Meritocracy
A system in which people are granted power, responsibilities, and roles because of superior intellect, talent, emotional intelligence, and other leadership competencies.

In organizations, team leadership should be based on **meritocracy**. A meritocracy is a system in which people are granted power, responsibilities, and roles because of superior intellect, talent, emotional intelligence, and other leadership competencies. Unfortunately, this does not always happen. People are often granted the right to influence others for reasons that have little to do with

■ **EXHIBIT 10.8**

Our Emotionally Intelligent Group Norms

1. Each one of us is to be aware of our impact on others and seek to ensure that our ideas, actions, and emotions support other members and the group as a whole.

2. Each of us is responsible for understanding and managing our own emotions in ways that support the group and its members.

3. Each of us is responsible for being attuned to and empathetic with other members.

4. We will collectively notice and monitor group dynamics for the purpose of managing our team in the most effective way possible.

5. Everyone has the responsibility to lead this group toward achieving our goals and becoming and remaining a healthy and resonant group.

6. Everyone in this group is responsible for making sure we perform at our very best individually and as a group.

7. We put group needs in front of our individual needs.

8. We are committed to open dialogue: Everyone *can* speak, and everyone *must*.

9. We support one another personally even when we are in conflict.

10. We respect one another at all times.

meritocracy. For example, group leaders are often chosen for the wrong reasons, such as their social status or a power base unrelated to the group's tasks, goals, or mission.

SOCIAL STATUS

The *Merriam-Webster Dictionary* defines status as "a position or rank in relation to others; relative rank in a hierarchy of prestige."[29] **Social status** is the relative standing or prestige you have compared with others in groups to which you belong. Social status can be formal, such as a rank or a position within a hierarchy. It can also be formally recognized through membership in a social class or a caste. We have all been in situations where people with high social status are granted special rights or roles. Even people close to high-status individuals sometimes benefit. It happens in school, when the popular students are given leadership roles on sports teams and their friends are allowed to join certain groups. It happens at work when "friends of the boss" are given special assignments or when we treat them more gingerly or with more respect than others. It happens in life when we meet someone who knows a celebrity and we think the fame has rubbed off on us.

Social status
The relative standing or prestige you have compared with others in groups to which you belong.

HOW WE "GET" SOCIAL STATUS

Different factors affect social status in society. For instance, socioeconomic status—your wealth, education, and occupational history compared to others—is a big determinant of whom you can meet and how you are able to interact with them. Gender, religion, race, and other factors also contribute to social status. One contributor to social status that has dramatically changed during the past 20 years is the richness of your social network.[30] Richness here refers to the number of people you know and interact with, as well as the variety of their experiences and social positions. This has been changing due to the rise of social networking as an activity available throughout society. Blogs, Twitter, Instagram, and Facebook are just a few tools that allow people to increase the range of social groups to which they belong, which provides opportunities for increasing social status (■ **EXHIBIT 10.9**).[31]

Social status has a powerful effect on how we see ourselves, whom we interact with, and how we are expected to behave. This is why people who join high-status groups often employ coaches to help them learn new ways of behaving or image consultants to help them learn how to dress to fit in. Our behavior, our mannerisms in speech and gesture, our clothing, our jewelry, and many other things communicate information about who we are. All of these things become symbols of our membership in different groups.[32] The more exclusive a group is, the more difficult it is to coordinate all these different symbols in ways that convince others we truly belong.

■ **EXHIBIT 10.9**
How do social networks break down the traditional barriers between social groups?

Source: Kevin Britland/Alamy

STATUS AND INFLUENCE IN GROUPS

Research has found that high-status members can more directly influence the outcome of group activities and group processes, such as communication and conflict. Low-status members have less influence on the group, and their attempts to influence the group are weaker, less direct, and often less effective.[33] This means that status is very important when it comes to leading groups.

A topic that is related yet different from social status is power. Your sources of power are also linked to how easily people accept your leadership in a group. A person's power in a group can be linked to factors other than social status, providing the person with different avenues through which to influence groups.

POWER IN GROUPS

Power is related to the ability to influence others, and there are several sources of power. These include:[34]

- The *legitimate* position you hold; for example, you are the official team leader.
- The extent to which people believe you can *reward* them; for example, you manage the project finances.
- The extent to which people believe you can *coerce* or *punish* them; for example, you have a special relationship with the boss and have been known to talk badly about other team members.
- Your degree of *expertise*; for example, you are the only one on the team who understands accounting, a skill needed to complete the project.
- Your personal characteristics that people admire (*referent* power); for example, you are inspiring and hopeful, even when the work is difficult.

Each of these sources of power can be useful in group settings, and each is potentially available to you. Let's say you find yourself designated by an instructor or a manager as a team's leader. You now have legitimate power, which makes influencing others easier, although you will find you still have to earn people's respect before they will follow you. You can also use reward power. You may not be able to reward people with money, but you can praise them and draw the group's attention to their contributions. You could also punish people in a group through shaming them or pointing out flaws. If you want long-lasting power in a group, however, don't even think about doing this. It will backfire on you.

When it comes to expertise, most groups at work require a wide variety of skills. Surely you have some of them. You just need the confidence to offer your services. Another hallmark of a good group leader is that he or she can inspire people. Literally anyone can do this. It takes effort, of course, as well as self-confidence and a commitment to using and developing your social and emotional intelligence.

POWER AND INFLUENCE IN SELF-DIRECTED TEAMS

Self-directed teams
Teams in which there is no formally designated leader and members organize their own activities.

Self-directed teams are becoming more common in organizations. In self-directed teams, there is no formally designated leader and members organize their own activities. Self-directed teams grew in favor and number during the implementation of total quality management (TQM; see Chapter 12). TQM relies on the initiative and insight of employees to solve problems and improve processes in the areas with which they are intimately familiar. The key characteristic is that the teams themselves take responsibility for their work, finding solutions to problems they identify, providing performance feedback, meeting goals, and monitoring performance.

Self-directed teams can be effective, but usually only when members are skilled at managing group dynamics, equally committed to the team's success, and willing to share leadership as the task requires. These conditions are most often seen in mature teams.

Many teams at work are not mature. So, if you find yourself a member of a self-directed team that is not ready to work without a leader, one solution is for the team to designate an individual as the leader for a period of time. This can be difficult if more than one person wants this role, or if no one does. Despite the challenge of choosing a leader, it is often worth doing at the beginning to get things going. Most groups have a difficult time working together in the beginning and, therefore, need a temporary leader. Most managers at work or instructors have little tolerance for delayed projects as a result of dysfunctional team dynamics, so it is important for you to take steps to organize the team for performance as soon as you can.

Even if it is only temporary, taking on leadership of a self-directed team requires skill and humility. It also requires presence—a quality that includes things like self-confidence, the ability to speak up in groups, and an authenticity that is palpable. Scholars Mary Ann Rainey Tolbert and Jonno Hanafin work with leaders all over the world. In their view, presence includes being able to consistently align personal assumptions, values, beliefs, and behaviors so that others experience you as honorable and trustworthy. People with presence are also willing to take a stand on meaningful issues and go against the flow when it is necessary. Tolbert and Hanafin state that presence can also help leaders guide others through change because these leaders are curious and willing to experiment. Maybe most importantly, people with presence show a genuine interest in others. In return, people are willing to follow.[35]

Although self-directed teams often need the safety net of a leader, especially in the beginning, it is also likely that members will resent this (and possibly you, no matter how much presence you have). To avoid this or at least minimize it, you should draw on other sources of power, such as your expertise, to gain the team's respect. You will also need to watch team dynamics carefully, using empathy and social awareness competencies to track the team members' responses to you and the team's development.

As a designated team leader, you also need to monitor yourself. It is easy to become "drunk on power" because (1) at first, the team really needs you; (2) people will praise you a lot—sometimes genuinely, and other times to get your attention; and (3) at some point, people will resent being dependent on you and will begin to fight with you, at which point, it's natural to try to hold on to your position. Self-awareness and self-management are key in these situations. You need to be able to see clearly how power is affecting you, manage your reactions, and always remember that you are there to serve the team as long as it needs you, not vice versa.

We have now discussed several topics that are commonly associated with group dynamics. There are, of course, other topics such as communication and decision making, which you have learned about already. A topic that hasn't always been considered but is increasingly critical to understand is the relationship between member diversity and group effectiveness.

Diverse Personality Types and Learning Styles Impact Team Dynamics

If we are to achieve a richer culture, rich in contrasting values, we must recognize the whole gamut of human potentialities, and so weave a less arbitrary social fabric, one in which each diverse human gift will find a fitting place.

—**Margaret Mead,** Sex and Temperament in Three Primitive Societies (1935)[36]

Everyone knows that working with people who are different from ourselves is a fact of life. Gone are the days when people debated about how to "manage" diversity in the workplace, as if it were something we need to control. In fact, in most companies it's not even called "diversity" anymore; it's called "diversity and inclusion" because, after all, diversity is a means to an end—the inclusion of people, perspectives, and ideas.

We need to learn how to make the most of the rich and varied viewpoints and talents of everyone in our teams. Elsewhere in this text, we discuss how aspects of human diversity, such as race, gender, age, and culture, impact people in the workplace. In this section, we will focus on several other types of diversity that impact group functioning. We will start with an aspect of diversity associated with personality type as measured by the Myers-Briggs® Type Indicator and the Golden™ Personality Type Profiler Test. Then we will look at another issue that impacts groups called learning style, as measured by David Kolb's Learning Style Inventory.

■ **EXHIBIT 10.10**
Why are Carl Jung's ideas about information processing important to groups today?

Source: Mary Evans Picture Library/Alamy

WE DIFFER IN HOW WE TAKE IN AND PROCESS INFORMATION

Psychologist Carl Jung proposed that we all have preferences about how we gather and evaluate information, and we all have rational and nonrational ways of organizing this information (■ **EXHIBIT 10.10**).

No one way of gathering or processing information is inherently better.[37] In fact, diverse ways of understanding and using information support better group outcomes. Over the years, two interesting tests have been developed to help us understand how we process information. These tests are often used in teams at work as ways for members to understand group dynamics.

PERSONALITY TESTS CAN HELP US UNDERSTAND DIVERSITY

The Myers-Briggs® Type Indicator (MBTI) and the Golden™ Personality Type Profiler tests are useful tools for helping team members understand group dynamics because they identify specific differences in individuals' ways of processing information and their approaches to making decisions. There are three dimensions that are similar in both tests:

Intuiting-sensing: Intuitive-type people tend to like abstract concepts, value insight and hunches, and begin with the big picture and work down from there. These are positive attributes, of course, yet intuitives can run into trouble because turning abstract goals into realizable tasks can be difficult. In comparison, sensing-type people are more pragmatic, rely on facts and examples, and prefer to work with data and details. Their problem might be that they are unable to see the "big picture."[38]

Thinking-feeling: Thinking-type people analyze data dispassionately—they tend to be more objective and are ordered and logical in their interpretation of information. This is a positive attribute in many workplace settings, but it can limit creativity. In contrast, feeling-type people use emotions as an important input to their interpretations and see information as subjective. While a subjective worldview can get in the way of fast, pragmatic decision making, these people have a lot to offer a group because they communicate powerfully with others, look deeply into relationships and follow their hearts.[39]

Introversion-extraversion: Introverts are energized when they are alone with their thoughts and feelings, which can make them ideally suited for working alone, but they may run into problems when working as part of a highly interactive team. In contrast, extraverts are energized by being around people and have little difficulty being vocal when necessary. Extraverts may run into difficulty working on their own because their energy and many of their ideas come from interaction with others. Most teams require people to work together *and* alone.[40]

The MBTI® also measures *judging-perceiving*. Judging-type people tend to make decisions based on the data at hand and generally prefer closure. They are plan- and process-oriented individuals who like to have a course of action mapped out—good qualities in general, but these people can run aground by rushing to judgment too quickly and failing to consider information once an opinion has been formed. Perceiving-type people are comfortable with ambiguity and change, which is an excellent skill when an organization's environment is uncertain, as during organizational changes. These people play things by ear, preferring matters to remain open ended, and they may change a decision several times before making it final, which can cause some problems when a decisive course of action is called for.[41]

The Golden™ Personality Type Profiler also measures *organizing-adapting* and *tense-calm*. Organizing is linked with planning and reliability, while adapting is linked to tendencies like being open ended and spontaneous. Tense-calm is the dimension that measures being uneasy and insecure versus being optimistic and confident.[42]

The dimensions that the MBTI® and Golden™ tests measure are popular topics in training programs in organizations. Part of the reason for this is that most people can see themselves in these dimensions. Another reason is that the tests categorize people in a nonthreatening way, making it easier to talk about differences in approaches and perspectives. Finally, by using tests such as the MBTI® and the Golden™ Personality Type Profiler, an organization can create teams with complementary members.

Another way to look at diversity in teams is to consider how people learn and adapt. One tool used widely for this purpose was developed by well-known scholar David Kolb.

DIVERSE LEARNING STYLES ARE IMPORTANT TO TEAMS

Educational researcher David Kolb is known for his work on learning styles. Kolb's model illustrates four styles of learning: converger, diverger, assimilator, and accommodator. *Convergers* are people who like working with abstract concepts and devising experiments to test these concepts. They are the applied scientists of the world. *Divergers* tend to focus on concrete experiences and to reflect deeply and generate lots of possibilities. They come up with ideas and look at them through different lenses. These are the artists of the world. *Assimilators* live in the world of abstract ideas, which they create through observation and reflection. They are the theoreticians of the world. Finally *accommodators* are "doers." They live in the world of concrete experience and experimentation. They are practitioners.[43] All of these styles are measured by the Learning Style Inventory, a test developed by David Kolb that is widely used around the world.[44]

When people learn differently, they tend to pay more or less attention to certain kinds of information and make decisions differently. Different learning styles can be a barrier to communication in groups, simply because people don't understand one another's approach to discovering new ways of doing things. For example, when faced with a problem to solve, a diverger will want to seek as much information as possible and to think out of the box—he will resist coming to a conclusion. This can be frustrating for a converger, who will have identified what she thinks is the most relevant information quickly and is ready to make a decision. People with different learning styles can get very irritated with one another. On the other hand, the diversity in styles on a team can, when well managed, ensure that the group balances creativity with closure, research with experimentation, and reflection with action.[45]

You now have a solid understanding of several important aspects of group dynamics: roles, norms, status and power, personality and learning styles, and how certain aspects of personality and learning styles can affect diversity of perspective. Understanding these dynamics should help you decipher what happens in the groups you work with, as well as social groups. We will conclude this section by looking at how certain conflicts, or paradoxes, affect individuals and group effectiveness.

Paradoxes of Group Life

A paradox is a statement that seems contradictory on the surface. For example, "I am hungry but I don't want to eat." Or, in physics, quantum mechanics states that light is a particle and is also a wave.[46] By definition, if something is a wave it cannot be a particle, and vice versa. But light is both a particle and a wave. That is a paradox.

According to scholars Kenwyn Smith and David Berg, what happens to us in groups can be paradoxical as well.[47] For example, we have a deep and abiding desire to be independent, and we have an equally strong, almost primal, drive to be accepted by others and to be part of groups—family, friends, school, work teams, and society. We feel tension when this paradox is activated, such as when our group requires us to give up our independence.

We also want to be unique, to be different, but our personal differences are almost always tied to our membership in certain groups. For example, take a moment to describe yourself as a unique human being. Perhaps you love dogs, or autumn is your favorite season, or the 1965 Mustang is your favorite car. You are male, female, American, Korean, British, athletic, friendly, passionate, quick to anger. You love baseball, hate football, have an IQ of 120. You are gracious, shy, funny, pretty, tall, Asian, Hispanic, Black, White. As you can see, how you describe your uniqueness also describes what groups you belong to. Even describing yourself as a "non-joiner" puts you in a certain group: people who don't like to join groups. This exercise illustrates what Smith and Berg call the paradox of identity: How we define ourselves as individuals is linked to membership in groups, yet membership in groups means that we are not unique individuals.[48]

Smith and Berg point out that another paradox we experience in groups is related to trust. This paradox is very interesting in that it takes a leap of faith to resolve. Here's how it works: Group members need to trust one another for people to feel safe sharing themselves, their ideas, and their talents. Where does that trust come from? You have to give trust in order to have trust.[49]

Another paradox involves authority. People in authority have power over others, yet only if others accept their authority. In other words, your power over others comes from people's willingness to follow—their power over you is that they can decide to follow or not. As Smith and Berg put it, "one develops power as one empowers others."[50]

The last paradox we will discuss here is the paradox of courage. Smith and Berg note that to really *belong* to a group demands a great deal of courage.[51] It takes courage to submit to the will of a group, trusting the group to meet our needs.[52]

These paradoxes and others that Smith and Berg write about affect us deeply when we work in groups, but we rarely talk about them. As you learn to manage group dynamics, you may want to explore some of these complicated but fascinating paradoxes to see how they affect you, other group members, and the dynamics of the group as a whole.

Discussion Questions

1. Describe a situation in which you realized an implicit norm was in place because you broke the unspoken rule of how to behave. How did you feel? What did other people do or say? How did this scenario affect your self-awareness and your empathy toward other group members?

2. How does your social status affect how you interact in groups? What sources of power do you use most effectively? What sources of power do you respond to in the most positive way? Please explain your answer.

Objective 10.5
Explain how teams function at work.

5. What Is a High-Performing Team?

As long as human beings have lived and worked together, we have organized ourselves to get things done in groups. Flash forward thousands of years, and here we are today, getting things done in teams at work and in school. Teams are one of the most important structures in most modern organizations because they are where ideas are generated, decisions get made, and work gets done. As well-known authors Jon Katzenbach and Douglas Smith said in their influential book on teams, "a real team—appropriately focused and rigorously disciplined—is the most versatile unit organizations have for meeting both performance and change challenges in today's complex world."[53]

Authors Katzenbach and Smith believe that teams, as opposed to working groups, have shared leadership roles, mutual accountability, and collective work products.[54]

These scholars encourage the use of teams as a way of improving performance by circumventing organizational hierarchies and boundaries. Hierarchy and boundaries get in the way of organizational and team performance, which is why Katzenbach and Smith argue that team members, especially those in leadership positions, should be carefully selected for their skills and not because of status or seniority.[55] Katzenbach and Smith's research on teams has uncovered numerous findings, such as the following:[56]

- Teams are the most efficient method of integrating ideas and performance across hierarchical and structural organization boundaries.
- High-performance teams are the exception, not the rule.
- Real teams are more frequently found in organizations with high-performance standards.
- A real team naturally integrates learning and performance.

It's hard to generalize, of course, but it is safe to say that in many organizations, too little attention is paid to the development, dynamics, or support that teams need in order to be effective. During the past two decades, this has begun to change as researchers have helped us see how effective work teams can be structured and managed for maximum use of individuals' talents and to support the collective energy, knowledge, and wisdom of the team. These teams can be highly effective and are sometimes referred to as high-performance teams.

A **high-performance team** is a team that exceeds expectations and performs better than other teams in similar situations.[57] According to Katzenbach and Smith, attributes of high-performance teams include the following:[58]

1. Small (fewer than 12 members)
2. Members have complementary skills
3. Members are united under a common purpose
4. Members have a mutually agreed-on set of performance goals
5. Members agree on an approach to the work
6. Members share accountability for performance and work products.[59]

Other researchers have also focused on what can be done to ensure that teams are effective. Researcher Richard Hackman concludes that groups, like people, need the support of organizational systems in order to be most effective.[60] For example, he suggests that reward systems, systems that help people learn how to do the expected task(s), information management systems, and clear project timelines are structures that support group effectiveness.

How do you lead a team so it—and each member—can perform at the highest level? Ninan Chacko has sound advice for leaders of teams everywhere. Ninan is the CEO of PR Newswire, a news and multimedia distributer whose parent company is UBM, based in London. You can read Ninan's wise advice about leadership, building relationships, and creating strong and effective teams in the *Leadership Perspective* feature on the following page.

Ninan Chacko's advice to us is worthy of serious consideration. Most of us will lead teams at some point in our lives, and everyone will be a member. Ninan goes beyond the rules that academics have given us to bring high performing teams to life.

High-performance team
A high-performance team is a team that exceeds expectations and performs better than other teams in similar situations.

Discussion Questions

1. Imagine you have to assemble a self-directed, diverse team to assess the current environmental sustainability efforts on your campus. How would you go about selecting team members? How many team members would you need? Who would you *want* on this team? How would you establish goals and norms?

2. Using Katzenbach and Smith's six points about high-performance teams, analyze a team with which you are currently involved.

Leadership Perspective

● **Ninan Chacko**
CEO, PR Newswire
"Trust is the foundation of all good relationships at work and on teams."

Ninan Chacko's background is fascinating. Born in Malaysia and educated there, India, the UK, and the US, he knows first hand what it means to live with people of many nationalities, ethnicities, and religions. These diverse multi—ethnic societies have worked hard to bring harmony to their communities and businesses—increasingly successfully. Valuing diversity of thought, then, is something that comes naturally to Ninan. So is integrity. And so is passion. Ninan's personal coda includes all of these, as well as a profound value around applying one's innate intelligence toward the greater good. Here is what this outstanding leader has to say about building strong, powerful relationships:

If we are to lead others, we must first look inside ourselves and understand truly what is most important to us. I have no interest in being one person in one situation, and another in a different situation. What this means is that with people—whether they are your team members or others at work, you need to be utterly authentic. You don't want to try to be someone you're not—it simply doesn't work. This doesn't mean that people need to know everything about you. But, they do need to know that "what you see is what you get" and that you will be yourself. They need to understand your strengths, and your weaknesses. Why? Because we all have weaknesses, and if we are constantly trying to cover up, people will know and they will simply not trust you. So, to build trust and strong teams, you need to be yourself.

People need to be able to say "I know this person, and I trust him or her."

Trust is the foundation of all good relationships at work and on teams. Authenticity—yours, as a leader, and others, as team members—is the key to trust and the basis for strong, powerful teams.

After authenticity and trust, the next most important thing in building a strong team is a vision. As a leader, you need to have the ability to see patterns, to understand how things fit together and to clearly define where you are headed. I believe pattern recognition is one of the most important competencies for leaders—right behind self-awareness. When you can create a vision that people can be passionate about, you inspire them to want to follow you. And if this vision is challenging, people see the opportunity to be something bigger than themselves. Finally, if the vision evokes just a little bit of fear, that's ok. Fear keeps us out of the comfort zone.

Finally, to build a great team you need to be sure to invite people who are very different from you, and different from one another. This can be challenging, because people who have different perspectives disagree. But, that's what great teams do: They grapple with questions, look at things from different vantage points, and manage the dialectic tension that is inherent in diversity.

So, how do you manage such tensions, and even conflict? As a team leader, you try to focus on the chemistry—you build strong bonds through focusing people on their respect for one another's integrity, yet still creating an environment where they can challenge each other in a respectful way. You also constantly remind people that even if they have different roles and individual goals, on the team, there is one goal—whatever the enterprise calls on them to do together.

No one works alone in organizations today. So, our challenge is to learn to lead—and to follow—on teams. If we can focus on authenticity, trust, passion, vision, and integrity, we will come closer to living a life that is meaningful. Life is too short to live without passion, or to try to be someone we aren't. Find yourself, and your passion, and you can live the life you want to live.

Source: Personal interview with Ninan Chacko conducted by Annie McKee, 2012.

Objective 10.6
Explain how to handle the challenges of working in groups.

6. How Can We Deal with the Challenges of Working in Groups?

In this section, we will address challenges that almost every team deals with: membership, participation, communication, influence, social loafing, and emotions. Then we will look at how dangerous conformity can be in teams.

The Big Six Challenges We Face in Teams

As you have read this chapter, you have probably had some insights about how the teams you have been part of developed, the dynamics that affected you and the team, and how your teams might have been more effective. To take the next step, you can learn more about six challenges that everyone faces when working in groups: membership, participation, communication, influence, social loafing, and emotions. These are issues *you* can do something about right away. For each team challenge, we've provided a checklist you can use with the teams you belong to.

MEMBERSHIP

How people behave can provide clues to the degree and kind of membership each person wants and needs. By tracking these patterns and taking corrective action, you can ensure that group members feel appropriately welcomed and included. For example, you might ask yourself the following questions:

- Do some people seem to be "outside" the group? Do some members seem to be "in"? How are the outsiders treated?
- Are there subgroups? Sometimes two or three members may consistently agree and support each other, or they may consistently disagree and oppose one another. This causes an in-group/out-group dynamic that can be destructive.
- Do some members physically move in and out of the group, for example, leaning forward or backward in their chairs or not talking on a teleconference? Under what conditions do they join in or not? The physical setup of a group, and/or who talks and who does not on a conference call can indicate who feels "in" and who feels "out." Similarly, if people are consistently late for meetings or do not respond to e-mails regularly, these could be signs that these individuals feel as if they are on the outside of the group.

PARTICIPATION

The most effective groups enable everyone to share their best ideas. If you notice that participation in your group is uneven or that certain members dominate, you have an issue to address. To better diagnose what is going on, you might ask:

- Who are the high and low participators?
- Has there been any shift in participation? For example, have high participators become quiet? Have low participators suddenly become talkative?
- Do you see any possible reason for changes in the group's interaction pattern?
- How are the silent people treated? Is silence interpreted as consent? Disagreement? Lack of interest? Fear?
- Who talks to whom? Why might certain people talk, or not talk, to certain other people?
- Who keeps the ball rolling?

COMMUNICATION

In any team, constructive communication is crucial to effective performance. Communication problems can manifest in many ways. Some typical communication problems to watch out for include:

- Are some people silent? Although some silence is good, members may avoid speaking up even when their thoughts can benefit the group. Members can encourage each other to communicate through appropriate verbal and nonverbal signals, as well as through directly soliciting opinions from less talkative members. Making communication more democratic—for instance, by using a round-table technique—can be a useful way to encourage participation.
- Are some people cynical? Anger and resentment are often communicated through cynicism. Cynicism kills team spirit. Rather than shutting down members when they express cynicism, you need to find out the source of these feelings and deal with

it. Often, when participants' views are calmly listened to, their anger dissipates and they feel more involved in the group.

- Do people interrupt each other in ways that are hurtful or shut others down? In most conversations, speakers tend to overlap one another's comments to some degree. There is a difference, however, between talking at the same time as another person and actively seeking to interrupt him or her. Interruptions that silence the voice of others should not be tolerated.
- Is rambling on or talking too much allowed? Some people take longer to get to the point than others, so there should be some tolerance for rambling. Additionally, different cultures have different tolerance for directness when attempting to make a point. However, if people in your group habitually go off point, a lot of time can be wasted. Points should be periodically summarized and compared to the group's goals. If talk meanders away from those goals, then effort to bring the conversation back into focus is needed.
- Is there so much arguing that nothing gets done? Disagreements can be healthy when they challenge assumptions and biases that lead to poor group performance. However, some arguments are personal and lead to unhealthy relationships. In addition, some arguments are the result of not taking the time to understand each other. Effective teams monitor conflict carefully. They stop it if it gets personal or when people are fighting because they simply don't understand one another. A good practice is to make sure that people are actually talking about the same thing when they are arguing.

INFLUENCE

Influence, participation, and communication are related, but they are not the same. Some people may speak rarely, yet they capture the attention of the whole group. Others may talk a lot but are not listened to by other group members. Effective groups manage influence so the person with the most relevant experience and knowledge can influence the group when needed. To track how well your group is managing influence, ask yourself:

- Do certain members always have more influence than others? Which members are high in influence, and which are low in influence? Why do these people have influence on the group?
- Are there any shifts in influence patterns? What has shifted and why?
- Do you see any rivalry in the group? Is there a struggle for leadership?

SOCIAL LOAFING

Social loafing is exactly what it sounds like: Someone decides to take a free ride and let the rest of the group do the work. Sometimes it is hard to tell at first that someone is taking advantage of the team. Social loafers are clever. They have a million and one excuses, most of which are plausible. Some indications that you are dealing with social loafing and not legitimate excuses for missing work and deadlines include the following:

- Leaving group meetings before assignments are handed out
- Pairing up with another member because it will be "fun" or "better" even when a task is obviously suited to one person
- Bragging to others outside the group about how little work he or she has to do
- Stepping up and getting involved only when authorities are around.

One extensive study found that social loafing is common, but it does not happen as much when team members feel that the task or the team itself is important.[61] Therefore, one way to minimize social loafing is to organize teams and groups around tasks that are important to members, and to build commitment to the team. One thing you don't want to do with social loafers is to protect them from being caught by managers, instructors, and so forth. You're just hurting yourself and your team if you do that.

EMOTIONS

During any group discussion, interactions will frequently generate emotions among members that are not discussed openly. You may have to make guesses about what people are feeling based on tone of voice, facial expressions, gestures, and many other forms of nonverbal cues. If you are aware of people's feelings, you will be better able to deal with them in a way that is helpful, rather than harmful, to the individuals and the group. To diagnose feelings, you might ask questions such as:

- What feelings seem to be allowed in the group? What purpose do these feelings serve in the group?
- Who expresses which emotions in the group? Is there a pattern?
- What emotions are not allowed in the group or remain unexpressed?
- What do you commonly notice in people's body language?
- Do you see any attempts by group members to block the expression of feelings, particularly negative feelings? How is this done? Does anyone do this consistently?

In this section, we have provided you with some tips for diagnosing what is happening in groups. This skill is tremendously helpful in just about any career: If you can figure out what is happening in groups, you can usually help them be more effective. Let's now turn to yet another problem that you can help groups avoid: too much conformity.

Conformity and Groupthink

Between 1951 and 1956, psychologist Solomon Asch published a series of studies that examined independence and conformity among individuals. The work, collectively known as the *Asch conformity studies*, typically conducted tests on groups of students, in which only one student was actually the subject. The other group members were secretly working for the experimenter. The question was how the student-subject would respond when all other group members seemed to agree and he or she alone had a different opinion.

In these studies, the researchers asked group members to compare the lengths of lines that were written on cards and to choose the ones that were the same. After making the real subject comfortable, the research assistants posing as group members started giving wrong answers. They gave their answers first, and they always agreed with each other. The majority answer was clearly wrong, but surprisingly, test subjects wound up answering all questions incorrectly 32 percent of the time, and 74 percent of test participants answered at least one question wrong.[62]

Why did the student-subjects do this? They felt pressure to conform. The experimenters knew that conformity was a factor because in other experimental conditions in which there was no pressure to conform, only 3 percent of test participants ever offered an incorrect answer.[63]

However, some recent researchers have been reexamining the Asch studies and suggest the answer may not be as simple as first explained. When faced with a situation such as that in Asch's experiment, participants must make a number of decisions that balance the importance of many different values and relationships, and it is the negotiation of these inner conflicts that can result in conformity. In particular, group decisions are frequently linked to people's beliefs that consensus is the most important group goal.[64] Because there was little opportunity to reach consensus in other ways, the lone participant in Asch's studies was forced to demonstrate consensus by conforming to the majority opinion of the single task of the group within which he found himself a member.

ormity can lead to groupthink. So, **groupthink** is a situation in a group that
cterized by strong pressure to arrive at consensus, a high degree of agreement
nformity, and/or defense of group decision even in the face of evidence proving
lecisions to be wrong or senseless.[65] What Janis meant by this is that when there is
, pressure to arrive at a consensus in groups, members may come to hold the same
and then vigorously defend this consensus as consistent with their own opinion.
pthink has been blamed in a number of incidents including the Bay of Pigs inva-
the Space Shuttle *Challenger* disaster, and even some activities in financial services
panies that contributed to the recession that began in 2007 (■ **EXHIBIT 10.11**).[66]

IDING DYSFUNCTIONAL CONFORMITY
GROUPS

nformity and groupthink are significant problems in business teams. When group-
ink occurs, team members may truly shut down because they do not want to go
against the group. Team leaders can ameliorate this by ensuring
that everyone gets a turn to speak, that one individual does not
dominate the discussion, and that more dominant members avoid
providing their opinions too early in the decision-making process.

Another way of combating conformity is to bring outsiders
into the group to evaluate the group's work and offer contrasting opinions and new information. Another tactic is for groups
to create a norm in which someone is formally designated the
"devil's advocate" to question group opinions and decisions.

Yet another way to avoid the negative effects of conformity in
groups is to implement processes that encourage teams to revisit
and reexamine decisions and their effects.[67] In Solomon Asch's
studies, for example, if there was even one other person in the
group who supported his or her answer, the subject would not
simply go along with the secret researchers who knowingly chose
the wrong answer.[68]

This finding has important implications for understanding
how to mitigate group pressure on individuals. For instance, you
should ensure that group norms are set up that encourage everyone to voice their opinions. That way, the best answer is likely
to be voiced *and* supported, and individuals are more likely to
stand by their opinions even when others disagree.[69]

Perhaps the best way of avoiding conformity is to ensure that
group norms support differing opinions. Selecting individuals
for membership in a group because of their different views—as
in international or cross-functional teams—can also help if proper team building is
done to build trust among members.[70]

In this section we have discussed what happens when people go along with each
other too much. But what if the opposite is true? What if people can't agree on anything? Let's look at both the upsides and the downsides of conflict in groups.

... ...
to disasters like the ~~~
Challenger explosion?

Source: Horizon International Images
Limited/Alamy

Discussion Questions

1. Consider the "big six" common challenges in groups. Of the six, which are *you* most
   likely to have problems with? Why do you think you do this? Can you think of some
   strategies to overcome this problem?

2. How could you serve the role as "devil's advocate" in a group without being destructive or hostile toward other group members and their opinions?

7. What Role Does Conflict Play in Teams?

Objective 10.7
Define the role conflict plays
in groups.

Many people shy away from conflict, most likely because of bad experiences. And, if we look across history, conflict and wars have and continue to do immeasurable damage. That may be why we try to control conflict and channel our desire for competition and conflict into safe activities. Some researchers believe that ritual conflict—like what we see in some sports—has evolved to take the place of and lessen the likelihood that groups will engage in real fights.[71] In fact, ritualized conflicts are common in our societies. Many cities and countries have team sports, where conflict and competition play out. In many places huge buildings and tracts of land have been dedicated to these sports so thousands of fans can watch their teams play games that involve competition and conflict.

When it comes to ritual conflict in groups at work, things like sales competitions can be fun and motivating. Unfortunately, conflict often has negative consequences at work.[72] Researcher Karen Jehn conducted a study in organizations and found that conflict involving relationships had negative consequences for both performance and satisfaction with the organization.[73] In high-performance teams, relationship conflicts were almost nonexistent except when projects neared deadlines, when this type of conflict suddenly rose.[74] So how can we determine when conflict is necessary—and even healthy—and when it is destructive?

Functional and Dysfunctional Conflict

Conflict can be either functional or dysfunctional. **Functional conflict**, sometimes called constructive conflict, involves allowing or encouraging differences of opinions among team members in order to yield better group outcomes. A moderate amount of conflict has been indicated as good for group creativity and group problem solving.[75] Organizational research has shown that the absence of functional conflict among team members can lead to complacency and the loss of a competitive edge. On the other hand, dysfunctional conflict, sometimes called destructive conflict, is counterproductive and results in poor performance and poor team cohesion. **Dysfunctional conflict** can involve aggression, personal attacks, or ways of expressing differences that undermine group success.

Functional conflict
Involves allowing or encouraging
differences of opinions among team
members in order to yield better
group outcomes.

Dysfunctional conflict
Involves aggression, personal attacks, or ways of expressing differences that undermine group
success.

Sources of Conflict

Where does conflict come from? At one level, we can say that all conflict arises out of attempts to access or maintain position and/or resources, either personally or for a group.[76] This is certainly true of political conflicts, border disputes between countries, and competition for market share of a product. Conflict in groups within organizations can also be the result of a number of other factors, as shown in ■ **EXHIBIT 10.12**.

Conflict can be examined at three different levels: intrapersonal, interpersonal, and group. At the intrapersonal level, conflict is experienced inside a person. For example, sometimes we experience clashes between our values and what we are expected to do, or we might be exposed to facts that challenge our way of seeing the world.

Interpersonal conflict occurs between people, often as the result of challenges to identity, bids for power, protecting one's "turf," and other such situations.

At the group level, there is always a dynamic tension between the identity of the individuals and the identity of the group. Conflict can result when individuals challenge group values and processes, or when group norms are inconsistent with members' beliefs and behaviors. It can also arise when the group becomes too focused on and involved in one member's life and contributions, or when members get caught up

■ **EXHIBIT 10.12**

Sources of Conflict in Groups	
Sources of Conflict	**Explanation**
Resource conflict	Conflicts of interest within a group frequently happen when resources are scarce and each group member desires more rather than less of those resources.[77]
Cognitive conflict	Conflict can occur when group members share the same group goals but disagree on how to best achieve the desired result.[78]
Relationship conflict	Relationship conflict has to do with personal conflict among members of the team. This kind of conflict has been seen to negatively impact group performance.[79]
Process conflict	Process conflict refers to conflict within teams about who should be doing what and how the group should operate.[80]
Task interdependency conflict	Task interdependency is another source of conflict, and one to which you can probably relate. As you may have experienced when working on group projects, your entire team depends on each individual member to complete his or her tasks. When one person misses a deadline, everyone is affected. Naturally, conflict results in this situation because the project is not complete until all participants have accomplished their respective tasks.[81]
Overlapping authority conflict	Overlapping authority is also a source of conflict when two or more people claim authority for the same tasks or functions. In many instances, redundant work by two different business, political, or legal units results in an overlap of managerial authority and employee scheduling.[82]
Reward conflict	Finally, different evaluation and reward systems can cause conflict among departments and divisions. If one division is evaluated by how low they keep their overhead while another division in the same organization is evaluated on how much they sell despite overhead costs, conflict can result from opposing systems of evaluation and rewards for work effort.[83]

too heavily in group life.[84] Conflict may arise when an individual member's needs and interests are served by the group at the expense of other members' needs and interests. For instance, if a person feels she is not getting enough support or recognition from the group, she may develop anger or resentment toward the group in general.

An individual can get too caught up in the needs of the group, as well, and this can lead to conflict. For instance, when the demands of a group at work are high, this may leave little time for fulfillment in family life, leading to conflict within the individual.[85] These feelings can affect how the person relates to groups at work and at home.[86] Another source of conflict is when power is not equally distributed in groups. When some people accumulate a disproportionate amount of power, the group may serve those people more than other members.

Trust: The Basis for All Conflict Resolution Strategies

A cohesive group requires a great deal of trust among its members. If that trust never fully develops or if it is threatened, individuals may feel that they are not accepted by the group, and people may not be willing to fully contribute.[87] This can result in conflict. For these reasons, there are often ritualized processes of induction in groups where trust is a must (such as elite military units, secret societies, and sororities and fraternities). Many people consider such rituals to be harmless, but in this age of transparency, it has become clear that these rituals are often far from harmless. Many are humiliating and painful; some are deadly, such as the tragic and unnecessary death of drummer Robert Champion in a hazing ritual at Florida A&M University. Twenty-six band members of the Marching 100 were suspended because of their involvement in the hazing activities that led to Champion's death, while eleven members were charged with felony hazing and two more with misdemeanor counts. The entire band has been banned from performing at the University's football games through at least 2013.[88]

Hazing and other rituals are meant to test people to see if they are worthy of membership and can be trusted. Trust is particularly important when a group is experiencing conflict and/or when the stakes are high. No one can (or should) argue that tests that put people at risk physically or emotionally have any place in a healthy group.

But, if people need to rely on one another to resolve conflict, how can people be sure that trust should be granted? This is where relationships come in. Trust is in part a belief that people take one another's interest seriously and can be relied on to be consistent. These things are learned in relationships. So, if you want to build a team that can deal with conflict, build trusting relationships. Trust is at the heart of conflict resolution, no matter what approach is chosen.[89]

Several conflict resolution strategies involving trust and trustworthiness are typically employed when a team is faced with strife. One of these strategies is compromise. Compromise involves a give-and-take approach that may require concessions by both parties. Collaboration, on the other hand, requires that the parties work together to solve problems or achieve goals.

Other conflict management strategies include accommodation, which occurs when the party with less power defers to the other, more powerful party, and avoidance, which occurs when both parties ignore a problem, hoping the conflict will disappear. This strategy often doesn't work because conflicts fester and spread rather than simply disappearing. Finally, competition can often occur when each party tries to best the other by maximizing its own position of power without considering the other party's needs or goals.

One of the best *practical* conflict management strategies is to call a group meeting and get the various perspectives about relationships, processes, and issues out in the open.[90] The team leader, or a strong group member, needs to take responsibility for structuring the conversation and facilitating the group to reevaluate its norms and procedures, or simply support appropriate expressions of "I am sorry."

Conflict Management: Negotiating to Find the Win–Win

Successful conflict management strategies rely on negotiation, a conflict resolution method in which both parties give, take, and make concessions, to achieve an agreeable solution to a conflict. Several different scenarios are possible when negotiation tactics are used. In a lose–lose scenario, neither party gets what it desires or needs from the negotiation. The distributive negotiation approach creates a win–lose scenario (also popularly referred to as a *zero-sum* negotiation), in which one party reaches its desired goal in the negotiation while the other party does not.[91] In another approach, integrative bargaining, a win–win scenario results. In this scenario, both parties maximize their desired goals by finding common ground to integrate their interests, and the conflict is resolved.[92] This approach requires cooperation by both parties and uses a win–win frame of mind to achieve the best possible outcome for all and to preserve relationships.

Objective 10.8
Describe how HR can support effective team performance.

8. How Can HR Support Effective Team Performance?

HR can take on many important responsibilities when it comes to training, evaluating, promoting, and rewarding teams. In this section we will discuss how HR can help employees and managers build and sustain resonant teams. To start, we will summarize some of the activities HR professionals often lead in support of effective teams. Then, we will share some tips on how you can build a more resonant, effective team.

HR Leadership Roles

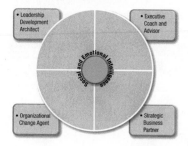

How HR Can Help with Team Building

The following is a list of helpful things HR can do to support the groups and teams:

- Provide training and development to team leaders about how to set up and lead teams.
- Pay attention to the personal transitions in and out of teams, especially at the leadership level.
- Provide high-quality team building workshops, especially in the important formation phase.
- Develop processes to evaluate team performance that include the level of team effectiveness in addition to goal achievement.
- Recognize outstanding teams—teams that get results and that people are happy to join. Highlight their best practices so other teams can learn from them.
- Develop team-based incentive programs.
- Model all of the above and establish high-performance HR teams.

These are just a few ideas about how HR professionals can design systems and processes to support team effectiveness and enable teams to grapple with the inevitable challenges inherent in working in groups. You don't have to wait for HR, however. There are many things you can do personally, such as starting, designing, and organizing a team retreat.

Resonant Team Building: You Can Do It!

Team retreats can be used to build, sustain, and improve the effectiveness of teams. Retreats are often led by HR professionals, but you can do it too.[93] Let's see how it's done.

RESONANT TEAM BUILDING: GETTING STARTED

If you can, plan to take people out of the office or classroom. Find a location that is really different and preferably close to nature. Maybe you can find a lodge in the mountains. Maybe you will simply go to someone's backyard. Wherever you go, plan carefully. Make sure you will have privacy, relative comfort, and safety. Make sure the environment doesn't inadvertently single people out—for example, if there are people in your group who are not physically fit, make sure they can participate safely and without shame.

Ahead of time, you should select a few discussion topics and activities that will enable people to get to know each other. Ensure that the flow of conversation moves from light and safe to more intense and just a bit risky. Set ground rules; for example, be respectful, don't violate one another's privacy, and keep people's confidences. Think about how you will move people through actually doing the activities, how you will address what comes up, and how you will prepare members for the future direction the team or organization will take.

One way to build or reinforce a team's identity is to give people the chance to engage in—and then talk about—activities that will help them reflect on and share their personal visions and life stories. For this to work, you need to create resonance by establishing an environment that is optimistic, energized, and focused on building constructive relationships. People need to be open to possibilities, and your leadership presence in this phase is critical. You need to consciously manage yourself so that you can help people feel comfortable, engaged, and ready to work on becoming a better team.

RESONANT TEAM BUILDING: VISIONING

How do you help a group work together to create a collective vision? First, you need to find out what personal visions are shared among the members. It is more than likely that different team members' personal visions have a few commonalities—hopes for families, lifestyle, professional success, team achievements, ways of working together, and so forth. Don't let these similarities go unnoticed. When conversations about people's personal hopes are authentic and respectful, openness to a shared vision grows. A parallel and linked process can unfold as people consider their team's vision and connect it to their own dreams.

RESONANT TEAM BUILDING: SETTING NORMS AND ROLES

Once people have shared personal visions, you can go back to your team's mission, purpose, and current challenges. Review together the reason the team exists, the organization's strategy, and how the team's work supports the organization's goals. Consider your team's emotional reality in terms of whether your norms, habits, and culture will support you in attaining your vision: Do your patterns of interaction support you in working effectively? What is your team's explicit charge? The implicit charge? Are you all on the same page? Will you get in your own way? A clear picture of your team's objective and emotional realities provides you with a platform to build a full picture of what your group can be and do in the future.

Then, for each member, clearly work through accountabilities: What are our expectations of each other? Who will be responsible for leading the different elements of our work together? What is the plan to take the process forward? How will energy be sustained? How will each individual continue to grow and develop along the way?

SUSTAINING RESONANT TEAMS

An occasional team retreat can dramatically renew a tired team. Every so often teams need to be refreshed; they need to revisit their purpose and renew their relationships. When we get into deep, authentic, emotional contact with each other, our mood almost always elevates and we feel renewed hope and connection.

To strengthen this process, you should try to come away with team members' commitments to engage in group processes that support people in working more effectively together. This might be as simple as reserving 15 minutes at the end of each team meeting to ask, "How are we doing?" The process can also be much more complex—maybe you need to change your performance management and incentive systems to encourage people to work toward group goals. However simple or complex your support systems need to be, the most important thing is that you *continually* take actions to support your team's effectiveness. The stress and pressure of work are enemies of effective teams. Make sure you attend to your group's health through occasional team renewal sessions. Regular process "checkups" can make all the difference in your overall effectiveness.

Discussion Questions

1. Have you ever participated in a retreat with fellow workers, a school group, or another organization? Where did you go? What happened? How did the experience impact the relationships of the group members? If you had planned the retreat, would you have done the same thing or something different?

2. Imagine yourself as an HR professional. How can you set an example when it comes to team building?

Objective 10.9
Describe how we can create and sustain resonant teams.

9. What Can We All Do to Create and Sustain Resonant Teams?

You now understand what happens as teams develop, how group dynamics affect people and teams, what a high-performance team looks like, and how to help teams be more effective. All of these theories and models are useful and have their place. When it comes right down to it, however, *people* make or break teams. What each one of us says, does, and believes affects whether our teams will be great or miserable. In this section, we will share a few practical tips about one skill that is crucial to team leadership: listening. We will zero in on skills related to listening because many problems arise in teams when people simply don't listen to one another. Then, we will share tips about how to lead a resonant team.

Listening to What People Actually Say

Listening is a foundational skill on which other communication and team skills are built, including the abilities to ask relevant questions, be attentive, offer appropriate feedback, and negotiate effectively, among other skills.[94] It is important to appreciate that listening and hearing are not the same thing. Hearing is the passive reception of incoming messages, whereas listening requires full engagement with another person. Effective listening requires that you attend to people's words and feelings—which, by the way, takes more energy than speaking. Some tips for better listening include the following:

- *Concentrate:* Do not be distracted. Focus your attention fully on the person (what is being said, what is *not* being said, body language, *everything*).
- *Listen empathetically:* Empathy is crucial to effective listening. By focusing on the person and the emotions that underlie his or her message, you are more likely to receive the full message, including that which is not said directly. Also, when the other person experiences you as empathetic, he or she is much more likely to trust you and expand and extend the message as necessary.
- *Listen for facts and feelings:* Remember that what someone says contains facts, opinions, beliefs, values, and emotions. You need to be able to tell the difference between the many messages people send when they are expressing themselves.
- *Avoid jumping to conclusions:* Always wait until you have heard everything before assuming you know what that person means. This sounds obvious, but poor listeners are often impatient and will interpret a message prematurely. Some people even jump in and interrupt the other person, wasting time and confusing the process as they provide what turns out to be inappropriate interpretations.
- *Judge content, not delivery:* If someone has poor communication skills, this does not excuse you from being a good listener. Your job remains to seek to understand and respond to the other person.
- *Provide feedback:* Remember that feedback is part of what makes communication meaningful. Eye contact, nods, note-taking, and other nonverbal responses

let people know that you are paying attention and that you understand what they are saying, as do brief verbal responses. Asking clarifying questions or restating the message can also help ensure that you understand the message completely.

This last point—providing feedback as part of the listening process—is particularly important because it allows you and the person you are communicating with to come to a much deeper understanding. Learning a technique called "active listening" will help you hone this skill.

Active Listening

Active listening is the process of attending and responding to what people say more deeply and consciously in order to really understand what they mean. At the heart of active listening is an interest in both the person and in what is being said, as well as respect and authenticity.[95]

Active listening involves listening fully to what is being expressed. Instead of interpreting, commenting on, or even building on what is said, an active listener will reflect back to the speaker what he or she heard, including both facts and feelings.

Active listening is a process that involves a number of distinct skills that are used simultaneously, as listed in ■ **EXHIBIT 10.13**.[96] Active listening involves cultivating a frame of mind that allows you to mindfully focus on the person speaking. Emotional intelligence and empathy are required to withhold judgment until you have heard all of what the person has to say. An active listener should try to understand what is being said from the speaker's perspective or point of view. This is a process that involves empathy, and it is closely related to social and emotional intelligence.

To understand someone else's perspective, you must listen for total meaning, including both the objective and the subjective content of what is being said. The objective content involves the meaning of what is actually said, whereas the subjective content includes details about the speaker's feelings or attitudes about the information. Scholars refer to this information as the speaker's stance.[97] An active listener will respond to feelings and pay attention to all communication cues, both verbal and nonverbal.[98]

Active listening helps us avoid common traps such as listening with the goal of influencing the speaker toward your point of view. People also routinely send out signals that request or challenge the listener to agree or to disagree with what they have said. Responding to requests for advice, information, and judgments can result

■ **EXHIBIT 10.13**

Tips for Active Listening

- Pay attention *mindfully.*
- Let the other person know you are listening: Body language is key. Use eye contact and facial expressions; don't fidget.
- Empathize with what the person thinks and feels.
- Listen for what is *not* said, as well as what is.
- Paraphrase what the person said and ask: "Is this right?"
- Summarize facts and feelings you think you heard, and check in with your listener: "Is this right?"

Source: Based on Hoppe, Michael H. 2006. *Active listening: improve your ability to listen and lead.* Greensboro, NC: Center for Creative Leadership.

in a conversation that closes prematurely—the speaker hasn't expressed him or herself fully, and the listener hasn't expressed him or herself at all.

As an active listener, of course, you cannot just listen. Eventually, you must share your own thoughts and questions and also give feedback.

Leading a Resonant Team

Have you ever had the experience of being in or leading a truly resonant team—a team in which you and a few other people acted, thought, and felt as one? When a group is at its best, it is able to accomplish amazing feats. Resonant teams create an experience, a condition—together—that transcends the boundaries of individual human beings. This state is elusive, yet if you have had such an experience, it remains a touch point for you about what is possible for teams.

If you follow the tips listed in ■ **EXHIBIT 10.14**, you can create and sustain a resonant team. As you build a resonant team, pay attention to the emotional life of the team members, to establishing and reinforcing trust in the group, and to making sure you have clarity about team goals. Be sure that the team feels excited by the challenge. Add in the use of humor, loving feedback, and having fun while pursuing your goals, and you've got a resonant team.

■ **EXHIBIT 10.14**

Leading a Resonant Team

1. *Start with yourself:* All the rules, roles, and guidelines for creating and sustaining resonance in a team start with you. As Commissioner Ramsey said earlier in the chapter, it all starts with knowing yourself.

2. *Build resonance with people around you:* Resonance doesn't happen by accident. You need to reach out to people, connect with them, show them a vision of what the team can be, and demonstrate how the team can help them achieve their personal goals and dreams.

3. *Seek to understand the emotional reality of your team:* It's not always easy to see the "emotional reality" of a group—the feelings that swirl around and the team's stance and attitudes about certain things. But you need to know these things. Watch group dynamics carefully, and take the time to talk with people more deeply about what they are thinking and how they feel about the team.

4. *Engage people's hearts and minds:* It's easy to get caught up in the pressure of deadlines and deliverables. To create resonance on a team, however, you need to slow down enough to engage your own and others' imagination and passion around the work and the team itself.

5. *Capture the dream:* People need a dream to hold on to, especially when work is hard and the team is facing obstacles. Find ways to remind yourself and others about why you're working so hard. Remember the noble purpose of your work.

Source: Adapted from McKee, Annie, Richard Boyatzis, and Frances Johnston. 2008. *Becoming a Resonant Leader: Develop your emotional intelligence, renew your relationships, sustain your effectiveness.* Boston: HBP.

Discussion Questions

1. The next time you're with a group, consciously monitor your listening habits. Do you concentrate? Jump to conclusions? Judge people? Do you really empathize? Review the sections on listening and active listening, and note one or two areas where you can improve your listening skills.

2. Think of your favorite musical group. Explain how they function (or fail to function) as a resonant team during a live performance or music video.

10. A Final Word on Teams and Team Building

One foundation of democracy is the idea that concentrating decision-making power in the hands of too few individuals can lead to injustice in society. For this reason, we have instituted collective decision-making bodies throughout society. We have juries to judge guilt or innocence, branches of governments within which officials elected by people work in groups to create laws and policies, and boards of directors to guide organizations. As the saying goes, two heads are better than one.

Researchers have compared group performance to individual performance on a number of different tasks and found that groups indeed tend to outperform individuals.[99] Groups can pool resources and have more opportunities to identify and correct errors. Additionally, when a group member works with another member who has better skills, the less-skilled individual tends to perform at a higher level. That's why we spend so much time and energy trying to understand groups and how to use them effectively at work: You can get better results when people work together and collaborate on tasks—at least when these teams are functioning effectively.

When team dynamics are dysfunctional, or even when we underattend to our team's norms, roles, and leadership, it's a very different story. In these groups, decision making and collective work can take an inordinate amount of time, the most competent individuals' contributions can be ignored, the morale of the entire team can suffer, and results can be compromised.[100] In some situations like this, it's impossible for a group to come together around a shared purpose. In others, just the opposite often happens: People fall prey to groupthink.[101]

What all of this means for us at work is that we must pay attention to how teams function. Great teams don't just happen; they are created and sustained by people who understand group dynamics. In every single team you work with, you have the chance to create an environment in which people can share their talents and ideas, have fun, and create outstanding results.

You will probably lead many teams during your career. As you do, it will help to think about some of the guidance shared with us by prominent businessman and well-known leader Niall FitzGerald. FitzGerald, chairman of the board of directors of the British Museum and Hakluyt, an international security firm, puts it this way:

Leaders are defined by the actions of their followers. The very few really great leaders I have encountered have had:

> *CLARITY (of vision)*
> *COURAGE (to take risks and be unpopular)*
> *EMPATHY (for those they lead)*
> *HUMILITY (which is real)*
> *INSPIRATION (which all followers need)*
> *SIMPLICITY (of expression)*
> *SELF-AWARENESS (of themselves and their impact on others)*
> *TRUST (which they give to others)*
> *WILLPOWER (which drives people and process)*

The best leaders also understand that they will only sustain success if they gather around them people who are more talented than themselves and give these people the freedom to act and grow. Ultimately leaders will be defined by their willingness to live by the credo that "there are few limits to achievement providing we have no concern for who gets the credit."

The kind of leaders that Niall FitzGerald is talking about get things done and help each of us grow as citizens and human beings.

LEADING IN A GLOBAL WORLD
Building a Global Management Team

Organizations worldwide are recognizing that their workforces are becoming more multicultural every day as they hire people of every race, nationality, religious background, and age group. For instance, more than 200 nationalities currently live and work in the United Arab Emirates, so organizations within the country are learning to adapt to this diversity. Organizations are beginning to realize that diverse multicultural teams require multicultural leadership.

Imagine you are the newly appointed human resources director of a major global organization. You have been tasked with designing a program to develop and train multicultural team leaders—people who can lead teams of people from many backgrounds. As you plan your program, craft an outline of the different components that may be involved: What resources will you need? Who will you need on your planning team? How do you propose to launch the program?

Once you have an outline, answer the following questions:

1. What are the qualities of a typical multicultural team?
2. What demographic and other aspects of diversity should impact your choice of candidates? What leadership qualities are you looking for in your candidates?
3. What are some of the major obstacles on the path to success?

LEADING WITH EMOTIONAL INTELLIGENCE
Do You Believe in Miracles?

What does it take to create a high performance, resonant sports team? One of the key ingredients is emotional intelligence. Without self-awareness, self-management, social awareness, and relationship management, players often compete against each other in addition to opposing teams.

The 1980 U.S. Olympic Hockey Team was a high-performing, resonant team. Against overwhelming odds, the U.S. defeated the USSR 4–3 to win the gold medal. However, they didn't start out as a strong team. Their coach, Herb Brooks, selected players from two rival schools, the University of Minnesota and Boston University. There was conflict among some of the players, many were young, and many had not yet developed self-awareness and self-management skills. Managing these players was a demanding challenge.

Statistically, the odds were against the U.S. team in their gold medal match. The average age of the Soviet team was 29 years to the U.S. team's 22 years. The Soviet team had also won four gold medals in a row and was coming off a 21-game winning streak. Additionally, many members of the Soviet team played professional hockey in the USSR. Despite the odds, Herb Brooks managed to create a high-performance team that achieved what is considered to this day a sports miracle.

On your own or with a small team, research the 1980 U.S. Olympic Hockey team. The 2004 Disney film *Miracle* re-creates the team-building events and how Coach Brooks led the team. Many excerpts from the film can be found on YouTube. Assemble a "playbook" of best practices that helped shape this high-performance, resonant team. When building this playbook, consider the following questions:

1. What did Coach Brooks do to manage the relationships of a group of young, non-professional players?
2. What were some of the lessons Coach Brooks taught the team about self-awareness and self-management? What group norms did he establish to encourage these competencies?
3. What were three sources of conflict or three of the "big six" challenges on the team and how were these resolved?
4. What role do emotions like loyalty, pride, and passion play in creating a highly effective team? How did Coach Brooks leverage these emotions in his players?
5. Are Coach Brooks' results repeatable? If so, what elements of his coaching style or methods would be useful for other coaches?

LEADING WITH CRITICAL THINKING SKILLS
Calendar Challenge

Our emotions, the ways we communicate, and our level of participation can have a positive—or challenging—effect on a group. If we know what to look for we can become better team players and/or help others to improve their team skills.

1. Individually, create a calendar of colors for the months. Assign a color to each month and provide a justification for that color. For example, "July is Red because it is the hottest month."
2. Break into teams of 4–6 people. Have one team member agree to act as an observer who will take notes about the challenges individuals and the team experience: membership, participation, communication, influence, social loafing, and emotions.

3. Ask team members to share their color calendar choices and their justifications. As a team, reach consensus on a color and the corresponding justification for each month. The color and the justification can be a single team member's suggestion or one that integrates ideas from team members.

4. Debrief the exercise by having the observer share input about where communication broke down, who participated and who didn't, which emotions were displayed, and how influence was managed.

ETHICAL LEADERSHIP
Is All Fair in Business and War?

Conformity and groupthink are major challenges for teams, particularly in situations that may present themselves as ethical dilemmas. Sometimes, the easiest solution is to conform or to justify a questionable decision.

In small groups, read the following scenario. Discuss and come to a consensus about your decision.

You work for a company that provides baggage handling equipment to the major airlines. Your company is competing in a bid for the nation's largest airline. The bid has come down to your company and your toughest competitor. Your team is preparing the bid. One of your team members arrives to your last preparation meeting, an all-nighter, with a large, sealed envelope. The team member tells your group that he has all the competition's bid numbers in the envelope. When asked how he got them, he refuses to reveal his source. He assures the team that the numbers inside are very legitimate. Your company can certainly use this contract. What does your team decide to do with the envelope? When consensus is reached, discuss the following questions:

1. Did the team find itself conforming at any point in the discussion? Did the team find it easier to conform because of the difficulty of the dilemma?

2. How easy was it to lean toward groupthink in the decision-making process?

3. Did any team member take on a leadership role? If so, how did he or she take control of the discussion?

4. Was there conflict in the group? If yes, was it functional or dysfunctional? Was the issue of using the competition's bid numbers resolved to all team members' satisfaction? If not, why not?

KEY TERMS

Team, *p. 342*
Autocratic leader, *p. 345*
Democratic leader, *p. 345*
Laissez-faire leader, *p. 345*
Forming, *p. 346*

Storming, *p. 346*
Norming, *p. 346*
Group norms, *p. 346*
Group roles, *p. 346*
Performing, *p. 346*

Adjourning, *p. 347*
Counterdependence, *p. 348*
Meritocracy, *p. 354*
Social status, *p. 355*
Self-directed teams, *p. 356*

High-performance team, *p. 361*
Groupthink, *p. 366*
Functional conflict, *p. 367*
Dysfunctional conflict, *p. 367*

MyManagementLab

Go to **mymanagementlab.com** for Auto-graded writing questions as well as the following Assisted-graded writing questions:

10-1. Name a political leader who led, or is leading, a democratic country other than the United States. Describe how his or her approach to leadership supported democracy. What did he or she do to seek input from followers? How did he or she engage followers in the process of decision making?

10-2. Do you believe that conflict in groups results in hurt feelings? Why or why not?

10-3. Mymanagementlab Only — comprehensive writing assignment for this chapter.

CHAPTER 10 Visual Summary

1. Why Do Leaders Need to Build Great Teams? (pp. 342–344)

Objective: Understand why leaders need to build great teams.

Summary: Working in groups is natural and necessary for humans. It is difficult for an individual to be successful without the ideas, help, and support of others—and this includes leaders. Understanding team structures is important because most work in organizations is completed in teams and teams function as work families that support and uplift us.

2. How Does Leadership Behavior Affect Group Dynamics? (pp. 344–345)

Objective: Explore and understand group dynamics.

Summary: Scholar Kurt Lewin and colleagues started a long tradition of research that looked beyond the individual to groups to help us understand why people behave as they do. In particular, this research focused on how behavior is a function of the person and the environment. Research in this area looked at leadership as one important aspect of the environment. Both early and more recent studies have looked at the effects of autocratic, democratic, and laissez-faire leadership on group members' behavior. Democratic leadership has proven helpful to groups because it provides sufficient structure and support to individuals without dictating what they should do. Autocratic leadership breeds hostility in group members and laissez-faire leadership is actually not leadership at all—it's an abdication of responsibility.

Lewin's Formula

$$B = f(P, E)$$

3. How Do Groups Change over Time? (pp. 346–350)

Objective: Explain the reasons groups change over time.

Summary: Researchers inlcuding Bruce Tuckman, Mary Ann Jensen, and Susan Wheelan have developed widely accepted group development models that describe the group formation, learning how to work together, trust building, performance, and dissolution phases. During each stage, some aspects of member and leader behavior are typical, such as politeness in the beginning and conflict when learning how to work together. Stages are not as discrete as the models suggest, especially as the world and organizations change with new technologies and globalization.

4. How Do Group Dynamics Impact Team Effectiveness? (pp. 350–360)

Objective: Describe how group dynamics impact team effectiveness.

Summary: Group roles can be divided into task roles that focus on task performance and maintenance roles that focus on supporting group members emotionally. Norms are important to groups because they help group members know how to behave. Member status and power strongly impact group functioning in either positive or negative ways. Diversity is a group dynamic that extends beyond the culture, race, or nationality of group members to also include personality types and how people learn. Group must also resolve paradoxes, such as how to place one's trust in a group before the group has had time to prove that trust is deserved.

5. What Is a High-Performing Team? (pp. 360–362)

Objective: Explain how teams function at work.

Summary: Work teams can be defined in many ways—by function/purpose, structure, participant type, or assignment. Self-directed work teams are becoming increasingly common and they rely on employees to take responsibility for identifying and correcting problems themselves. High-performance teams utilize members' talents and skills in complementary ways that enable the team to function at an optimal level. This, in turn, allows the team to be self-motivated and makes membership its own reward.

10. A Final Word on Teams and Team Building (p. 375)

Summary: Knowing the basics of team dynamics and understanding the decades of research on the topic will prepare you for your working life. Even as organizations change in our modern world, the basic skills of being a good teammate and leader—clarity, courage, and empathy, to name a few—will help you sustain success no matter the changes you face. Understanding that you can't do everything alone and that you need the support of your team will also enable you to grow as a leader and a person.

9. What Can We All Do to Create and Sustain Resonant Teams? (pp. 372–374)

Objective: Describe how we can create and sustain resonant teams.

Summary: One of the most important things you can do to improve team dynamics is develop your listening skills. Active listening enables you to accurately interpret what is being said and shows respect for the person speaking by reflecting back to the speaker what you have heard. To build and lead truly resonant teams, you can start with yourself: Build resonance with people, understand your team's emotional reality, engage people's hearts and minds, and capture the dream.

> **Leading a Resonant Team**
>
> 1. *Start with yourself:* All the rules, roles, and guidelines for creating and sustaining resonance in a team start with you. As Commissioner Ramsey said earlier in the chapter, it all starts with knowing yourself.
> 2. *Build resonance with people around you:* Resonance doesn't happen by accident. You need to reach out to people, connect with them, show them a vision of what the team can be, and demonstrate how the team can help them achieve their personal goals and dreams.
> 3. *Seek to understand the emotional reality of your team:* It's not always easy to see the "emotional reality" of a group—the feelings that swirl around and the team's stance and attitudes about certain things. But you need to know these things. Watch group dynamics carefully, and take the time to talk with people more deeply about what they are thinking and how they feel about the team.
> 4. *Engage people's hearts and minds:* It's easy to get caught up in the pressure of deadlines and deliverables. To create resonance on a team, however, you need to slow down enough to engage your own and others' imagination and passion around the work and the team itself.
> 5. *Capture the dream:* People need a dream to hold on to, especially when work is hard and the team is facing obstacles. Find ways to remind yourself and others about why you're working so hard. Remember the noble purpose of your work.

8. How Can HR Support Effective Team Performance? (pp. 370–372)

Objective: Describe how HR can support effective team performance.

Summary: HR contributes to teams by ensuring that people are trained, supported, and rewarded for effective group performance. Additionally, HR professionals can facilitate resonant team-building by helping team members understand one another, build a shared vision and set expectations.

7. What Role Does Conflict Play in Teams? (pp. 367–370)

Objective: Define the role conflict plays in groups.

Summary: Conflict in groups is not inherently bad and, in many situations, promotes creativity, improved processes, and problem solving. Unfortunately, if not handled properly, the advantages of conflict are lost. Understanding the various sources of conflict and how to resolve it is a good first step to ensuring positive results. When resolving conflict, trust is the starting point. Allowing group members to explain their positions and utilizing appropriate, win–win negotiation strategies also enables conflict to be constructive.

6. How Can We Deal with the Challenges of Working in Groups? (pp. 362–366)

Objective: Explain how to handle the challenges of working in groups.

Summary: Every team is faced with challenges that threaten its ability to perform—membership and inclusion needs, participation, communication, influence, social loafing, and emotions all require thoughtful attention. These issues need to be diagnosed and dealt with by leaders and group members. Conformity and groupthink are two other group challenges that must also be addressed.

Working in a Virtual World:

Technology as a Way of Life

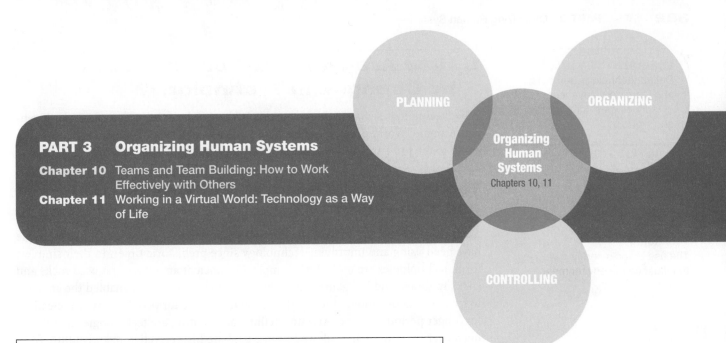

PLANNING

ORGANIZING

Organizing Human Systems
Chapters 10, 11

CONTROLLING

MyManagementLab™

⭐ **Improve Your Grade!**

Over 10 million students improved their results using the Pearson MyLabs. Visit **mymanagementlab.com** for simulations, tutorials, and end-of-chapter problems.

Chapter Outline

Chapter 11 Objectives

11.1 Define technology and ICTs, and learn how advances in technologies change life and work.

11.2 Learn about sociotechnical systems theory.

11.3 Explain how technology impacted people during the Industrial Revolutions.

11.4 Understand how computing and telecommunication technologies have evolved.

11.5 Describe how people use ICTs at work.

11.6 Learn where and how virtual work is conducted.

11.7 Learn about virtual organizations.

11.8 Understand the challenges of working in a virtual world.

11.9 List steps HR can take to support virtual work.

11.10 Describe how to work effectively in a virtual world.

Objective 11.1
Define technology and ICTs, and learn how advances in technologies change life and work.

1. How Are Life and Work Affected by Changes in Technology?

When technologies change, work changes. In the words of the respected scholar Krishnan Kumar, "Work, play, education, family relationships . . . gradually adapt or succumb to the pressures and opportunities of the new technological forces."[1]

Technological Changes, Our Brains, and Human History

Technology
The use of tools and knowledge to influence the environment.

Technology is the use of tools and knowledge to influence the environment. People have been using and improving technology since prehistoric times. In their simplest form, technologies are tools. For example, our ancient ancestors first used rocks and sticks to forage and kill game. Later, the invention of the wheel enabled the ancients to transport goods more efficiently, making it possible for people to live in one place for longer periods of time. Art, storytelling, and writing are technologies that developed over time too—they allowed people to share history, religion, and culture from one generation to the next. Scholars believe that at one point in our history—about 100,000 years ago, our brains developed in ways that allowed us to both develop these tools and learn rapidly from one another. This advancement was related to what we call "mirror neurons—" Brain cells activate when we perform an action ourselves (for example, using a tool) or observe acts performed by others. These cells help us learn from each other and they support empathy and learning.[2]

These developments in our brains are significant because for more than 90 percent of our history, changes in how our species lived and worked were gradual. People lived in small groups of 30 to 150 people, foraging, gathering, and hunting food in order to survive.[3] Scholars such as Vilayanur Ramachandran believe that the rapid spread of technology among humans, which began about 75,000 years ago, can be directly attributed to mirror neurons, which help people to "imitate and emulate" what they observe. Ramachandran contends, "There is no real independent self, aloof from other human beings, inspecting the world, inspecting other people. You are, in fact, connected not just via Facebook and [the] Internet, you're actually quite literally connected by your neurons."[4]

Still, because technologies evolved over many generations and with a few rare inventions (such as gunpowder and the printing press), most advances caused people to *adjust* their lifestyles rather than fundamentally change the way they lived or worked. This remained the case until the onset of the First Industrial Revolution, which marked the beginning of rapid technological advances.

Technologies of all sorts have dramatically changed every field imaginable, and the convergence of two vital technologies, computers and telecommunications, has had the greatest impact on work life of any innovation in human history. Almost every aspect of our lives is now inexorably linked to **information and communication technologies (ICTs)**—the hardware and software related to electronic communication and information sharing.

Information and communication technologies (ICTs)
All of the hardware and software related to electronic communication and information sharing.

ICTs now help us with virtually everything: how we meet our partners and mates, where and how we work, how we create and enjoy music and the arts, and how religions are shared and disseminated. ICTs and other technologies have launched us into a new era—one that is unparalleled in human history. And, the dawn of this social and technological revolution is destined to continue to bring massive changes in political, economic, and social structures all over the world.[5]

ICTs and Unrivaled Social Changes

During the past few decades, changes in many of the social structures that developed alongside advances in technologies have begun to shift, often in unpredictable ways.

Let's look at just a few of the social changes related to ICTs that are occurring today, as well as their far-reaching consequences:

- The nation-state is now rivaled by social structures (such as Al Qaeda) that are not located in one geographic area or centered in a single nation, yet wield tremendous power on the international stage. Groups like these can create and support sophisticated governance and communication structures, all as a result of ICTs.
- News and information can now be shared around the world in a matter of milliseconds.
- Access to information is currently less dependent on wealth or social class than it was in previous decades, and unprecedented numbers of people have access to communication networks.
- Developing nations are often leapfrogging certain aspects of industrialization (e.g., many countries are not making massive investments in land-line telephone technology) because newer, more advanced (and often cheaper) alternatives are already available.[6]

ICTs are increasingly at the center of how people learn and work, as well.[7] The spread of computer networks has made communication across long distances possible and affordable. As a result, today's workers can collaborate, share, and access information more efficiently and easily than ever before, and managers have a vast array of technological tools for coordinating and monitoring work. In today's work environment, even employees who never leave their local sites often interact with people from a range of cultures, nationalities, and ethnicities on a regular basis.[8]

Tech-Savvy Competencies

Today's business environment is characterized by rapid, discontinuous, often unpredictable change. Also, partly as a result of ICTs and other technologies, the global market has become hypercompetitive. Slow-moving companies are at a major disadvantage, especially if they continue to organize work, ICTs, and people as they did in the past.

Tech savvy communication competencies, delegation skills, and the ability to participate in and manage virtual teams are only a few of the skills people will need to develop to be successful at work today. Social and emotional intelligence competencies are also important because the use of ICTs adds a dimension of complexity to building and maintaining effective relationships. To deal with this complexity, we all need to be highly self-aware and self-managing and able to practice empathy, positive influencing skills, and coaching and mentoring skills—even with people we never meet face to face.[9] To this list, former U.S. Secretary of Labor Robert Reich adds four additional capabilities: abstract reasoning, systems thinking, collaboration, and the ability to experiment.[10]

Let's take these ideas into the real world. Mukul Pandya is the executive director and editor-in-chief of Knowledge@Wharton. Knowledge@Wharton is run by the Wharton School of the University of Pennsylvania. It is a subscription website that provides information—knowledge—to over two million subscribers *for free*. If you add in Time.com and other publications, which republish material from Knowledge@Wharton, the audience includes millions more. And what do these subscribers get? As Mukul puts it, "They have access to academic knowledge and research, published in ways that are useful to people in business and organizations." This is not to say, of course, that research published in academic journals is not useful. But, it is experts talking with experts—which frankly leaves most people out of the conversation. Let's hear what Mukul Pandya has to say about Knowledge@Wharton and leadership in our unprecedented times.

Leadership Perspective

● **Mukul Pandya**
Executive Director and Editor-in-Chief, Knowledge@Wharton
"Good leadership starts with the desire to make a difference."

Mukul is a humble and powerful leader. Many would say he is brilliant. The reason for this: along with a supportive group of faculty and administrators at Wharton, Mukul was able to drive the creation of Knowldge@Wharton way back in the 90s—long before most business schools were providing information this way. What's more, it's free—unheard of more than a decade ago. In his role over the past fourteen-plus years, Mukul has met some of the most impressive leaders of our time. He's also read and participated in their research and published their work. Because of this, and more importantly because of his own beliefs and principles, Mukul has lessons for us all about leadership in the digital age.

I am honored to be a part of Knowledge@Wharton, and to work with the brilliant people from the Wharton faculty, our corporate sponsors, and our advisory board. I learn so much from them. Learning is a quest that never ends. When I was growing up, it was not easy to have big dreams, like being part of an institution like Wharton. But learning, and life, have conspired to help me to be here, and it continues to be an amazing journey.

Good leadership starts with the desire to make a difference. It all has to do with seeing something that needs to change, or people that need help, and deciding to do something about it. You can choose to do nothing. Many people go through life that way. Leaders don't. Leadership is an act of choice. Good leaders are people for whom doing something matters more than not doing something. Let's take an example we can all understand. If you see a child crying on the side of the street, it's likely that not doing anything at all will be harder than approaching the child and helping her. That's how it is for leaders with the challenges we find today in our businesses.

For example, when I first came to Wharton, I realized we were sitting on a goldmine of knowledge. But, by and large, it was only available to professors and researchers. It was a true paradox—all this information on business, and business people couldn't use it. I saw that we could mine, mint, and circulate this information in an entirely new way. This was long ago, and the search engines weren't what they are now, but I saw what could be as the Internet gained speed and power.

But that brings me to another principle of leadership: You've got to be passionate about your ideas, but never, ever

think they are yours alone. To succeed, "your" ideas need to be completely owned by others. This can mean an almost complete absence of ego. And yet, as a leader, you still need to drive things forward.

Driving things forward almost always starts with consensus. This is very true in academic institutions, partnerships, consulting firms, and professional services of all sorts. It's also increasingly true in our era because so many people have access to information about problems and opportunities and they want a voice. And, in organizations that aren't as hierarchical as in the past—which is most of them—people behave in a much more collegial manner. This means that lateral communication is extremely important. In the end, good ideas are not the prerogative of one person, and they get much, much better when others get involved. In my case, I knew I had to build consensus and that the Knowledge@Wharton dream needed to be others' dream, not mine. So, I connected with over forty faculty members at Wharton, sharing a small proposal. They were excited and they had ideas. I took every single one of those good ideas and built it into the initiative. And, here we sit, many years later, with key faculty fully owning Knowledge@Wharton.

I've thought a lot about where the desire to do something comes from, and how people learn to lead in an "egoless" way. I believe it is connected to our humanity, and the values we grew up with. It is human to want to help others. The best leaders do this more, and more often, than others. For me, and I think many people, there are a few values that contribute to this. First, there's kindness and compassion. How can you build consensus if you don't view others with respect, and a desire to help their ideas become part of the whole? That is an act of kindness. But it's more than that.

If you are angry, or selfishly holding on to negative emotions, the person who is hurt the most is you. Let's say you are angry at a colleague and you lash out. You might feel better for a short time, but in the end, the damage that is done will hurt you more than anyone else. But if you are compassionate, quick to forgive, and kind, you, more than anyone, will benefit. I learned this from my grandparents. They were exceptionally kind people, and as a child I saw how much they benefited from this.

Another value that is incredibly important today is about learning and education. Our world revolves around change—and then learning—today. If you are curious, and interested in seeing things done differently, and open to new ideas, you will succeed. This is especially true for leaders. I learned this from my parents. They were both college professors in India, and our house was full of books and thoughtful conversations.

I have been asked many times what advice I would give to leaders today. I would say it starts with kindness, compassion, and learning. Then, there is this. When my daughter, Tara, was born, I wrote a poem. The last two lines go like this:

'…Above all, measure yourself by who you are and can be, Never by what you have.'

Source: Personal interview with Mukul Pandya conducted by Annie McKee, 2012.

Mukul Pandya's wisdom is profound. His beliefs about leadership are based on personal experience, of course, but they are also based on sound science. We know today that the best leaders are emotionally intelligent—as Mukul is. We also know that they are able to flex, learn, and change. Mukul Pandya's wise advice helps us to learn how to lead today—in a world that is vastly different from the world in which many theories of leadership were developed.

In this chapter, we encourage you to consider your leadership and your ability to deal with change as you learn to work effectively in an increasingly virtual world. To help you, we first consider why both technology *and* people need to be considered as organizations change, focusing on sociotechnical systems theory. We will also consider what you need to learn to be successful in a world where technologies are changing at warp speed. Then, we explore some of the recent technological innovations that have revolutionized how people communicate and work, including the Internet and Web 2.0. After that, we look at how ICTs are used at work, virtual work structures such as telecommuting and virtual teams, and virtual organizations. Lastly, we examine what HR can do to support effective virtual work and workers, as well as what we can all do to be as effective as possible in an increasingly virtual world.

Discussion Questions

1. List the ICTs you use each day, beginning with the most important device and ending with the least important. Consider the top three items on the list. Why are they so important to you?

2. Access to ICTs is not equal across the globe. On the Internet, find one country where ICTs are widely used and one that you believe has less access (e.g., in the developing world). What social and economic outcomes could occur if imbalances like these continue?

2. Why Must We Consider Technology *and* People When Working in a Virtual World?

Objective 11.2
Learn about sociotechnical systems theory.

ICTs are special, certainly, and many of us are enamored of technology. However, ICTs—like any technology—are merely *tools* that *people* use to get things done. ICTs are part of the equation when it comes to working in a virtual world, but people are still the most important factor. In this section, we will demonstrate the profound effect of ICTs on work and discuss a theory that explains how technology and people need to be considered equally as organizations change.

Technology, Students, and Dinosaurs

To illustrate how important it is to consider both technology and people in organizations, let's consider an example that many students will recognize. Imagine that your school has introduced a new application that allows you to communicate with your professors and other students more effectively via e-mail, webinars, and social networking sites. You and other students like the new program and adapt quickly—but your professor does not. He or she likes the old program, is under pressure to do research, and does not believe taking the time to learn the new one is worth it. So, your professor refuses to use the new program and forces you to stick with the old one. You think he or she is a dinosaur.

Now, say that this is a widespread problem at your school, and the administration gets involved. They recognize that professors are not using the new system, and they jump to the conclusion that professors don't know how to use the technology. The administration distributes instruction manuals and "tip sheets" and even offers classes. Few professors take advantage of these services.

Next, the administration decides the new technology must be too complicated, so they eliminate some of what students consider the best features. Still nothing changes, because the problem is that professors aren't rewarded for learning new technologies—they are rewarded for research and publishing. Taking time to learn and use the new system isn't worth it to them. In addition, now the students don't like the program either. Both professors and students are frustrated, and relationships have begun to deteriorate among the three groups—students, professors, and the administration. The school now has an even bigger problem.

Of course, there are many professors and administrators who are far more sophisticated than those in this example, and some students who won't use new technologies. Still, this example shows that an improvement in technology does not necessarily result in improvement overall unless the people side of the equation is addressed. In this case, the administration would have needed to recognize and deal with the professors' belief that they should not waste time learning new technologies. When it comes to ICTs and innovation at work, we need to pay attention to the *interaction* between technology and people.

Sociotechnical Systems Theory

The dilemma and problems described in the previous example are not new. As new technologies have appeared on the scene, people have had to change individual behavior, work processes, and organizational cultures. One especially useful theory for understanding how to support people and organizations in linking people and technology is called sociotechnical systems theory, or *sociotech*. As its name implies, sociotechnical systems theory examines both social and technical characteristics of tasks and how work is organized, focusing on the interaction between people and technologies. The two primary principles of this theory are:[11]

Sociotechnical systems theory
Theory that examines both social and technical characteristics of tasks and how work is organized, focusing on the interaction between people and technologies.

1. Organizational performance is tied to the interaction of social *and* technical factors. Technological advances alone do not necessarily lead to organizational success. Social factors—what people choose to do, how they feel about it, and the culture of the organization—are equally, if not more, important.
2. Optimization of either social or technical elements alone increases the unpredictability of relationships and can lead to less effective performance. Therefore, a coordinated optimization of both elements is needed.

Sociotechnical systems theory can be traced back to 1951, when scholars Eric Trist and Ken W. Bamforth presented a case study of an organization that had suffered from decreased productivity even though it had improved its technology. Despite human resource interventions such as increased pay and benefits, employee absenteeism and mutual scapegoating rose following the technological changes. Trist and Bamforth found that these changes had the unpredicted effect of increasing the bureaucratic structure of the organization, which in turn had a negative effect on employee productivity.[12]

Sociotechnical systems theory was further developed by scholars Fred Emery and Eric Trist during the 1960s, with many others following through to the present time.[13] In the 1980s, after reviewing more than 130 studies, noted sociotech scholar William Pasmore concluded that the research made a strong and valid point: More attention should be paid to the effects of technological changes on people's behavior.[14] The best technology in the world is worthless if people won't use it, and organizations can actually be harmed rather than helped if the people side of the equation is ignored. As you read this chapter keep in mind that people are still at the heart of an organization's success. It's up to managers and leaders to support people in changing behaviors, values, and norms as technologies are introduced. Attention to the people side of the equation is even more important in our world today, because technologies are changing constantly. As a way to understand where we are now, it helps to understand the history of technological changes made during the Industrial Revolutions.

Discussion Questions

1. Review the two points listed in the section on sociotech. Describe your school as a sociotechnical system and explain how the people and technologies in this system work well together and how they do not.

2. Visit three shops in your community and observe how people work. What could be done to improve the link between people, the physical space, and technology?

3. How Did Technology Affect Life and Work during the Industrial Revolutions?

Objective 11.3
Explain how technology impacted people during the Industrial Revolutions.

Many people think of the Industrial Revolution as an event, or series of events, that occurred in Europe and the United States during the seventeenth and eighteenth centuries. This, as you will see, is only partially accurate and refers to the first Industrial Revolution. Most scholars agree that there have actually been three industrial revolutions, with some overlap in time and geographies. What is true for all of them is that technology has been, and continues to be, a major driver of social, political, and economic changes.

Technology and the First Industrial Revolution

The **Industrial Revolution** refers to the period in the eighteenth and nineteenth centuries during which major advances in technology, manufacturing, and transportation changed people's way of life, mainly in England, the United States, and parts of continental Europe. This revolution occurred over time.[15] Key events that took place during this period included the shift from manual and animal labor to the use of machinery in manufacturing, the harnessing of steam power, and the improvement of older technologies such as water power.[16]

Throughout the Industrial Revolution, changes in technology drove widespread changes in society. For example, as factories were built to produce textiles and other goods, massive numbers of people moved from rural areas into cities. People whose families had farmed or worked as craftsmen for generations were now living in crowded cities, earning wages, and buying things they had always made themselves. Ways of life that had been in place for hundreds of years disappeared in a short period of time.

During much of this time, a philosophical transformation was also sweeping through the Western world. This movement, now known as the **Age of Enlightenment**, fueled radical new ideas about government, science, economic systems, and wealth across Europe and parts of North America.[17] This philosophy inspired Western

Industrial Revolution
The period in the eighteenth and nineteenth centuries during which major advances in technology, manufacturing, and transportation changed people's way of life, mainly in England, the United States, and parts of continental Europe.

Age of Enlightenment
Primarily eighteenth-century movement that fueled radical new ideas about government, science, economic systems, and wealth across Europe and parts of North America.

◼ **EXHIBIT 11.1**
How do the ideas presented by Adam Smith in *The Wealth of Nations* apply to modern society?

Source: Classic Image/Alamy

Second Industrial Revolution
The period from the mid-nineteenth century through approximately 1915 that was marked by the development of several life-altering technologies, including electricity, motors, synthetics, internal combustion, and mass production techniques.

society to see logic and reason as the greatest of human gifts and to believe that self-interest is a primary driver of human behavior.

The Scottish philosopher Adam Smith was one of the leading figures of the Enlightenment. His writings addressed the relationship between reason, the production of goods in a free-market economy, self-interest, and wealth (◼ **EXHIBIT 11.1**). One of Smith's transformative ideas was his belief that self-interest is a primary source of both action and innovation. Smith also believed that self-interested behavior ultimately serves the larger society, an idea he elaborated most famously in his book *The Wealth of Nations*:

> It is not from the benevolence of the butcher, the brewer, or the baker that we expect our dinner, but from their regard to their own self-interest. We address ourselves, not to their humanity, but to their self-love, and never talk to them of our own necessities but of their advantages.[18]

Smith's second transformative idea related to how wealth is created.[19] He believed that a free market creates order in an economic environment by guiding the amount of goods produced (what people want) and the price the market will bear for those goods (what people will pay), resulting in the optimum use of society's resources. This stance, coupled with the belief that self-interested behavior is beneficial for individuals and societies, helped to legitimize the power and high social status of the new owner class—the individuals who owned and operated the means of production. During this period of time, wealth became more concentrated in the hands of this new class of people and the divide between the owner class and the worker class grew.

Later, influential thinkers such as Karl Marx sought to expose inherent problems in the world of "haves" (capitalist owners) and "have nots" (workers).[20] For instance, Marx believed that a society in which workers had little or no access to the wealth they produced would ultimately result in an unsustainable social and economic system.

During the time the philosophies represented by the writings of Adam Smith and Karl Marx were taking hold, a new manufacturing and goods-consuming society and shifts in the concentration of wealth dramatically altered life in England, the United States, and parts of Europe. This was just the beginning: Continuing technological advances catapulted even more of the world's people into a new era.

Technology and the Second Industrial Revolution

Sometimes referred to as the Second Industrial Revolution, the period from the mid-nineteenth century through approximately 1915 was marked by the development of several life-altering technologies, including electricity, motors, synthetics, internal combustion, and mass production techniques.[21] This period witnessed Henry Ford's creation of the assembly line, which allowed for scientific precision in the division of labor and created new possibilities for mass production. As a result of assembly lines, traditional forms of labor-intensive work were automated and eliminated, and in many cases, workers began to specialize in only one or two of the thousands of functions involved in complex manufacturing processes.[22]

New means of communication such as the telegraph and the telephone also transformed life during the Second Industrial Revolution. Organizations could now be managed more efficiently, even when work sites and workers were geographically dispersed. At the same time, wealth-sharing structures such as wider access to stock ownership, increases in manufacturing wages, and the slow transition of landowners from lenders to borrowers began emerging. Together, these developments allowed more people to be involved in the growing industrialized economy and helped to spread the wealth that had formerly been concentrated in the hands of the elite owner class.[23]

Industrialization brought about fundamental shifts in societies and work in several countries in the Western world. These countries' experiences during the Industrial Revolutions helped shape societies and businesses. But what was happening elsewhere during this period? To better understand global dynamics today, it's important to understand what was happening in the rest of the world during the 200-plus years that saw England, the United States, and much of Europe become industrialized nations. In the seventeenth and eighteenth centuries, as countries and industrializing regions developed free labor systems and democratic ideologies, they often did so by utilizing slavery, imperialistic approaches, and unfair trade practices.[24]

Africa, India, South America, and China during the Era of Western Industrialization

Why is it so important to study how other parts of the world were developing during this period? First, many countries and regions that used to be uninvolved in the global economy are not only players today—they are leaders. In addition, people everywhere now have an opportunity to be vitally involved in global economic and social changes that can provide a better quality of life. Finally, because many parts of the world—most of it, in fact—did not industrialize in the same way or at the same time that England, parts of Europe, and the United States did, we face vast differences in the experiences people and entire countries have had with respect to business and work. To get a better picture of these differences, let's consider what was happening in Africa, India, South America, and China during the era of industrialization.

AFRICA DURING THE ERA OF INDUSTRIALIZATION

Despite its proximity to Europe, much of Africa remained largely closed to the outside world until after the end of World War II. While Africa's eastern coastline was part of an important trade route between India and Europe as early as the 1500s, most ships did little more than stop to replenish supplies, wait out harsh weather, or purchase slaves and raw materials. Europe's imperialist powers penetrated Africa's interior very little other than along the coastal ports and near a few large rivers.

Throughout this period, all of Africa remained relatively isolated. There was little to no interest in exploring the interior or setting up ongoing trade, which meant that there was little development of larger cities or industrialization. The reasons for this were many—Portuguese and other Western traders found few centralized tribal governments, the terrain was harsh, and there were tropical diseases to contend with, among others. Also, much of Africa was densely populated with tribes whose members were well armed and hostile toward outsiders. There was, therefore, little contact between most of Africa and the West, with one major exception: traders who found easy access to gold, ivory, gum, wax, and especially slaves.[25]

Since at least the seventh century and continuing through the twentieth century, Arab traders enslaved some 18 million Africans. The Atlantic slave trade, which began several centuries later and ended a century earlier, enslaved 7 to 12 million Africans, most of whom ended up in the Americas (■ **EXHIBIT 11.2**).[26] The slave trade was largely one-sided, as was the trading of raw materials like gold and diamonds. In other words, traders took out much more than they brought in. There was also little spread of technological innovations that might have fostered industrialization. Even after European colonialism began in earnest in Africa during the nineteenth century, there was little change in Western nations' unbalanced and oppressive relationship with African communities.

■ **EXHIBIT 11.2**

What were some of the lasting effects of the Atlantic slave trade?

Source: Friedrich Stark/Alamy

Another horrific reason why the continent was not part of the Industrial Revolution was the widespread belief among white Europeans and North Americans that African cultures were primitive and could not adapt to a modern way of life. Multicultural consultant Paula Rothenberg notes that racist attitudes led many to perceive the failure of modernization in Africa as evidence of Africans' inferiority, rather than the result of trade practices and colonialist systems. These biases, inequities, and brutal systems kept many Africans in menial and labor-intensive jobs, often accompanied by repressive and even brutal treatment (as was the case in the Americas as well).[27]

INDIA DURING THE ERA OF INDUSTRIALIZATION

By the sixteenth century, several European powers had established trading ports in India, which developed into colonies over time. As the British expanded their political power in India, a system emerged that included a class of wealthy landlords who heavily taxed the peasantry.[28] Although Indians attempted to rebel in 1857, the uprising resulted in a harsh crackdown on Indian citizens by the British-run regime.[29]

During the many years of British rule, Indian craftsmanship became virtually worthless, primarily because the country's residents were required to buy products that were imported from England. Indian soldiers and administrators were kept in low-level jobs, while the best jobs were reserved for the British.[30] Meanwhile, the textile industry, which fueled the Industrial Revolution in England and other Western countries, was virtually destroyed in India through high taxes and a British embargo on Indian exports. Subsequently, many industrial towns fell into decline.[31] In short, British colonial rule effectively and systematically compartmentalized labor and destroyed any opportunity for industrialization in India during Colonial rule.

SOUTH AMERICA DURING THE ERA OF INDUSTRIALIZATION

Although South America had been the target of European interest since the days of the conquistadors, it too remained relatively unaffected by industrialization. The continent's "discovery" by European powers during the late 1400s and early 1500s first brought the conquistadors, whose sole purpose was to lay waste to wealthy indigenous civilizations such as the Aztecs and the Incas and bring treasure back to Europe. As a result, highly sophisticated agrarian societies were destroyed.[32] Soon after the early conquistadors, missionaries arrived with the goal of converting local populations to Christianity. This too resulted in fundamental changes to local societies, including replacing local governance structures with church and/or foreign leaders.[33] Over time, several European nations—primarily Spain and Portugal—established colonial governments throughout South America, and they continued to rule until the 1800s when many South American colonies won their independence.[34] Still, despite (or perhaps because of) years of colonization, the continent remained somewhat isolated and trade was mainly in the form of raw materials and cash crops produced by cheap labor on large plantations.

From the mid-1800s up through the first few decades of the twentieth century, economic growth remained slow in the region, partially as a result of many South American nations' unwillingness to be dependent on foreign powers as a more global economy emerged.[35] During this period and continuing through most of the 1980s, many South American countries industrialized to some extent and produced goods locally. Weak ties with industrialized nations for so many years caused problems in some ways, but there was a pronounced upside: Isolation helped much of the continent escape the worst effects of the Great Depression and World War II.[36] By the late 1980s, however, social unrest, wars, political intervention by world superpowers, collapsing South American economies, and widespread debt pushed many countries away from their isolationist policies and toward a more open economic stance.[37]

CHINA DURING THE ERA OF INDUSTRIALIZATION

China was not a major contributor to the Industrial Revolutions of the eighteenth and nineteenth centuries. It is somewhat surprising that China was so late to industrialize. Chinese society in the seventeenth and eighteenth centuries had the infrastructure, the technological means, and the labor to do so. So, why didn't industrialization happen earlier? Some reasons include:

- Despite established relations with the West, the nation's military empire severely restricted trade, accepting only precious metals from the West in exchange for Chinese goods such as silks and ceramics.[38]
- China imposed severe restriction of information and repression of writers, known as the "literary inquisition," during the eighteenth century.[39] This meant that some of the philosophies and ideas that supported industrialization and subsequent social changes in the West were not widely disseminated in China.
- China had severe restrictions on women working outside the home.[40] Particularly in England and the United States, women were a major part of the labor force in factories. In China women were not only prohibited from working outside the home, but the practice of binding their feet (which continued until the late nineteenth century) ensured that they had limited mobility—and limited capacity to work.[41]
- Among the working poor, there were severe restrictions on Chinese men's access to females: Widows were not allowed to remarry, and wealthy households kept several female concubines, so many poor men had no wives. As a result, poor farming families often had few children. This meant that for several generations, offspring would often stay on and work a family's small plot of land.[42] The trend was different in Europe, where high birth rates and the decline of feudal systems caused young people from the lower classes to move to the growing cities to seek work.

A final word on Chinese industrialization: The rise of Communism after World War II resulted in widespread destruction in the countryside, which was already decimated by war. Much of the infrastructure and industrial means of production that had been developed during the early twentieth century was compromised, as was much of the infrastructure in large cities. As Mao Zedong claimed power, private farms were obliterated and replaced by collectives. The idea was that the money generated by farm collectives would finance industrialization and the building/rebuilding of the country's economic and industrial infrastructure. During this period, there was widespread famine, violence, and repression, as well as almost complete isolation from Western economies.

THE WORLD ECONOMIC STAGE AS WESTERN INDUSTRIALIZATION WANED

Africa, India, South America, and China changed a great deal during the two to three centuries of Western industrialization. They did not, however, develop either the technological infrastructure or socioeconomic structures that governed many Western nations' politics, economies, and cultures by the mid-twentieth century. By the early to mid-twentieth century, technological changes, increased global trade, decline of political structures such as colonialism, and the rise of the working middle class had resulted in vastly different social and economic systems around the world. The stage was set for the next, even more radical (and faster) social and technological revolution. This time, the revolution has the potential to include everyone, even the most remote and isolated countries.

The Post-Industrial Society and the Third Industrial Revolution

By the 1960s, it was becoming clear that another massive change was under way in many parts of the world. The technological innovations that had previously shifted work from farms to factories in industrialized societies were once again poised to shift many people's work from mass production to the generation and dissemination of knowledge and services.[43] In 1973, futurist Daniel Bell described this post-industrial society as one in which the manufacturing workforce would be replaced by a workforce of professionals and service providers.[44] Whereas during the First and Second Industrial Revolutions, wealth was linked to the means of production, during the latter half of the twentieth century, wealth became more and more linked to the ability to create, acquire, and share knowledge.

As the twenty-first century neared, the Third Industrial Revolution began to emerge. The Third Industrial Revolution describes a period of time beginning in the mid- to late-twentieth century through today in which economic activities are marked by an increased focus on ICTs along with greater attention to issues of environmental sustainability and economic competition. According to social thinker Jeremy Rifkin, the convergence of ICTs, a focus on environmental sustainability, and economic competition will, "require a wholesale reconfiguration of the transport, construction, and electricity sectors, creating new goods and services, spawning new businesses, and providing millions of new jobs."[45]

These massive changes, along with the need to move away from reliance on fossil fuels and to respond to climate change, will bring about great transformations in how energy is created and used, as well as in manufacturing processes. In the words of writer Kurt Anderson, this new era can therefore be thought of as the "reset economy"—an opportunity to correct the wrongs of past business practices, promote clean energy, clean up the environment, and invest in social goods and services such as health care and education.[46] Let's look at some of the changes we are seeing that impact business and work today.

ICTs AND GLOBALIZATION

ICTs have helped foster rapid movement toward globalization and interconnectedness in business, which we will discuss thoroughly in Chapter 14. For example, transportation technologies have made it possible to move goods (and people) more quickly and easily, allowing for organizational models such as "just-in-time" inventory management to be used more efficiently and effectively. A vast number of products are not produced in one location anymore. Intel, for example, has manufacturing and assembly facilities in China, Costa Rica, Ireland, Israel, Malaysia, the Philippines, and Vietnam.[47] Similarly, the raw materials required to create a single product often come from numerous parts of the world. For example, the gold used in a computer's circuit board could have come from mines in Africa, the silicon may have been mined in Brazil, and the plastics may have been created from oil that was pumped out of the ground in the Middle East but processed in the United States. To manage the complex supply chains that are necessary for this kind of production process, businesses use highly sophisticated ICTs and workflow management systems.[48]

JOB MIGRATION AND GLOBAL LOGISTICS

To better illustrate the interconnectedness of these sorts of changes in ICTs, society, and work, let's look at two examples of major shifts that are currently under way in the modern workplace: job migration and global logistics.

Third Industrial Revolution
The period beginning in the mid- to late-twentieth century through today in which economic activities are marked by an increased focus on information and communication technologies, along with greater attention to issues of environmental sustainability and economic competition.

Job Migration

Given the desire to maximize profits—and the abundance of lower-priced labor in less-developed countries—many companies move some of their operations far from home. This has been especially true in the manufacturing sector in countries that industrialized early on. For example, in the United States the number of manufacturing jobs declined by 23 percent between February 2002 and February 2012.[49] This drop and others like it are due in large part to jobs and operations moving elsewhere. This is far more possible now than in the past because of ICTs.[50] We will look at this issue in greater depth in Chapter 14.

Global Logistics

The term *global logistics* refers to how goods are processed, transported, and stored along a supply chain. Advanced global logistics processes are made possible in part by satellite tracking technologies, an advanced form of ICTs. Given that so many products are manufactured in one place and sold in another, and/or include parts made in various places around the world, global logistics is an increasingly complicated and important part of how goods are made and sold. Advances in global logistics have allowed for business integration, streamlined operations, and leaner organizations. Companies such as UPS have been able to perfect certain aspects of the process and now sell their services to other organizations.[51]

Consider how technology has changed one aspect of global logistics: the docks where ships load and unload cargo (■ **EXHIBIT 11.3**). Since 1968, the amount of cargo flowing through U.S. docks has increased by about 500 percent, while the number of employees has decreased by nearly half.[52] In the face of advancing technology, dock workers were understandably worried about the future of their jobs and their industry.

For example, in 2002, after a three-month failure to renegotiate a union contract and an alleged work slowdown (a type of strike), the Pacific Maritime Association instituted a 10-day lockout of International Longshore and Warehouse Union (ILWU) employees, costing billions of dollars.[53] The dispute was settled with an agreement between the Pacific Maritime Association and the ILWU regarding the role of technology. Ultimately, the union accepted the use of new technologies and the related loss of 400 jobs, with the guarantee that the 400 employees would be retrained and put to work elsewhere on the docks. In addition, the union negotiated for a large wage and benefits increase.[54]

■ **EXHIBIT 11.3**
How do you think global logistics has changed international trade?

Source: © dipego/Fotolia

In a more recent example, in 2011, the state of Wisconsin was an ideological battleground regarding the issue of collective bargaining for unions representing government-paid employees. The dispute began with the flight of key democratic lawmakers from the state in an effort to stop passage of legislation. Republican lawmakers then folded the measure into a budget law, which required fewer lawmakers present to achieve a quorum for voting. They could do this because virtual presence and voting are now possible. As many as 100,000 union members and public workers flooded the state capitol for a weeks-long sit-in protest.[55] After the state supreme court upheld the bill, the protests dwindled to about one thousand people; however, the protests had some effect. A similar bill in nearby Ohio lost the support it needed for passage.[56]

As you can see, many of the changes under way in the world during the past 200 to 300 years are the result of shifts in technology, especially ICTs. In the next section, we will take a closer look at the development of the World Wide Web and telecommunications technology, as well as how these things support us on a daily basis as we work.

Discussion Questions

1. Search the Internet to find out what parts of the world are currently industrializing. How is this wave of industrialization different from the Industrial Revolution of the eighteenth and nineteenth centuries? How might this new wave of industrialization affect global business? Has it affected you? If so, how?

2. Through social networking, connect with a college student in Africa, India, South America, or China. Discuss how industrialization has affected your respective countries, and how more recent advances in ICTs have affected each of you personally.

Objective 11.4
Understand how computing and telecommunication technologies have evolved.

4. How Have Computing and Telecommunication Technologies Evolved?

ICTs are important drivers of new ways of working. In this section, we'll explore how the Internet, intranets, extranets, and the cloud facilitate information sharing and collaboration among and between people at work.

Computing Technology: From a U.S. Defense Strategy to Web 2.0

Internet
A global system of interlinked, hypertext documents contained within an electronic network that connects computers and computer networks around the world.

■ **EXHIBIT 11.4**
What characteristics of the Internet made it revolutionary?

Source: Alex Segre/Alamy

The birth of the Internet can be traced back to 1962, when MIT computer scientist Joseph Licklider first began working for the Advanced Research Projects Agency (ARPA), a Cold War agency of the U.S. Department of Defense.[57] By 1968, a plan for the creation of an information-sharing network called ARPANET was approved. Within months, a link was established between two computers at UCLA and Stanford Research Institute. Electronic mail was now possible, and in 1971, the first e-mail message was sent between two ARPANET-linked computers that sat side by side.[58]

This technology was used by only a handful of individuals for almost two decades, and most people weren't even aware of its existence.[59] This all began to change in 1989, when British researcher and MIT professor Tim Berners-Lee used the idea of interlinked hypertext documents (Web pages) to develop the "WorldWideWeb" (one word).[60] Later, the term "World Wide Web" (WWW or "the Web") became interchangeable with the term "Internet." The **Internet** is a global system of interlinked, hypertext documents contained within an electronic network that connects computers and computer networks around the world (■ **EXHIBIT 11.4**).[61] In 1993, the code for developing Web pages was released to the public. At the time, there were only 130 Web pages—but that wouldn't be the case for long.

Indeed, by 2004, Google had indexed approximately 8 billion pages, and by 2008, that number had hit the 1 trillion mark.[62] Since then, and According to Google, the number of individual Web pages was growing by billions per day by 2008.

Innovation has continued. Web 2.0 is often described as the second generation of Web technology and software development that allows for increased interactivity, user design and control, and collaboration. Web 2.0 applications permit faster sharing of greater quantities of information, greater ease of use, and more opportunities for people to interact with the technology and with one another.

Specific examples of technologies associated with Web 2.0 include social networking sites, virtual worlds in which "real" activities can occur, multiperson gaming, wikis, interactive blogs, and peer-to-peer networks. One particular benefit of many of these applications is that they are not dependent on a single brand or manufacturer of hardware (e.g., PC or Mac). This allows organizations and individuals greater control of their own data and has expanded the types of applications available to many people at work.[63]

For businesses that sell products and services, Web 2.0 has facilitated far more communication and interaction with customers and among organizations than ever before. For example, online user reviews of products and services can lead to more informed buying and increased power for the consumer. In addition, according to author Amy Shuen, the real benefit of bigger, faster, more interactive information-sharing networks is increased traffic—which means that more people can access businesses, and businesses can market to more people faster.[64] Shuen cites Google, eBay, Skype, and Wikipedia as prime examples of networks benefiting from the positive impact of network traffic.[65]

One popular example of the networks Shuen describes is Craigslist. Craigslist is essentially a classified advertisement for a connected world. Started in 1995 by Craig Newmark, the site runs separately in major cities throughout the world, with a concentration in the United States. It is a marketplace for sellers and buyers of goods and services. While most advertisements are free, some postings are sold, which generates the majority of the company's revenue. With only a handful of employees, the site essentially runs itself, which gives users a great deal of power. However, the freedom of Craigslist's marketplace has led the company into controversies as a result of users advertising illegal products and services and, in the case of Phillip Markoff, stalking victims. Still, the site remains a popular online destination and averages roughly 30 billion page views per month.[66]

Another network that takes a more conservative approach to the libertarian market of Craigslist is Angie's List. Angie's List was founded in 1995 by William Oesterle and Angie Hicks, and the site promises a great deal of oversight when connecting consumers to products and services. The site is restricted to paid members—including consumers. It offers verified consumer reports and evaluations of products from unbiased sources. The site has 1.5 million subscribers and a growing yearly revenue that reached $90 million in 2011.[67]

The Internet, Intranets, Extranets, and the "Cloud"

Some of the technology at the heart of the Internet is also used by companies to manage their own internal communication through the creation of an intranet. An intranet is an internal company network that is usually accessible only to employees. To keep company information secure, intranets have firewalls and other security features that prevent outsiders from gaining access. An extranet is a computer network designed for an organization to communicate in a secure environment with certain external stakeholders, such as customers.

Web 2.0
The second generation of Web technology and software development that allows for increased interactivity, user design and control, and collaboration.

Intranet
An internal company network that is usually accessible only to employees.

Extranet
A computer network designed for an organization to communicate in a secure environment with certain external stakeholders, such as customers.

Cloud computing
Hosted services offered via the Internet that are available on demand, are highly flexible in terms of the amount of service users have access to, and are fully managed by the provider.

In the past two decades, many companies have built huge and expensive equipment, including servers, to manage information flow and storage. In the past few years, however, processes for working electronically have been increasingly shifting away from company-maintained computing centers to vast data structures located in third-party run computing centers.[68] This is referred to as **cloud computing**. Cloud services are different from traditional local hosting services in that they are offered on demand, are highly flexible in terms of the amount of service users have access to, and are fully managed by the service provider.[69]

Cloud computing is not a new concept. Early computers operated on a "hub-and-spoke" structure that provided users access to data services for a fee. Computing was a somewhat centralized technology. When personal computers arrived on the scene in the 1980s, people were thrilled that they no longer had to buy time on a network, but could manage and store documents and applications themselves. We still value this benefit, but even the most powerful personal computers cannot keep up with people's needs for massive storage capacity.

One current example of cloud computing is Google Docs. With this online word-processing and spreadsheet application, documents are stored on a server run by Google, and they are instantly accessible via the Internet to any invited collaborator. Because the document is centrally located, it no longer has to be passed around from person to person by e-mail for multiple rounds of editing.[70] Another example is the Amazon Elastic Compute Cloud (Amazon EC2), which offers virtual IT services.[71] Also, Apple's MobileMe offers application hosting and data storage, along with applications integration.[72] These cloud technologies create new IT economies of scale, which we will explore in Chapter 14.

Work in many organizations today depends on the ability to communicate effectively and rapidly across distance and time. Computers, networks, and the cloud allow us to transmit a wide variety of information digitally. Of course, this capability is greatly enhanced by advances in telecommunications technology.

The Evolution of Telecommunications

During the Cold War, technology did not allow for much "traffic" over the airways due to political tensions.[73] As new digital technologies emerged and the Cold War ended, all of this began to change. The digital cell phone revolution began in 1991, when Finland launched the world's first 2G public network. The phrase *2G* refers to the second generation of cellular phone technology, which used digital rather than analog technology. We're now in 4G, and the fifth generation of these technologies is in development.

The new cellular technology was a tremendous success, and it soon spread very quickly across the planet. The International Telecommunication Union (ITU) reported that by December 2008, the number of mobile phone subscribers worldwide had passed 4 billion, up from 3 billion just 18 months earlier. By mid-2009, there were more than 276 million cell phone subscribers in the United States alone, and the world's two most populous countries, China and India, surpassed 700 million and 500 million subscribers, respectively.[74] By 2012, China registered 1.03 billion cell phone users.[75] In addition to these cell phone figures, there were also a reported 1.27 billion fixed lines, 1.54 billion Internet users, and close to 800 million broadband subscribers, including 430 million mobile broadband users. As you can see in ■ **EXHIBIT 11.5**, the trend toward cellular technology and broadband is steadily increasing at a very rapid pace.

What that means is that people can connect in ways unimaginable a few decades ago. This has changed people's lives, and it has certainly changed work. Your cell phone or smart phone probably has more and better computing power than large desktop computers of the past.

■ **EXHIBIT 11.5**

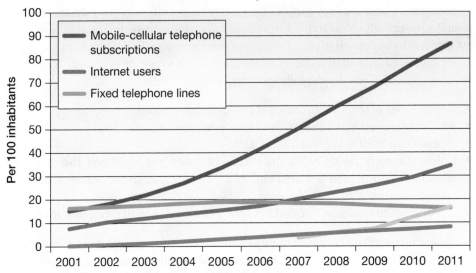

Global ICT developments, 2001–2011

Per 100 inhabitants

- Mobile-cellular telephone subscriptions
- Internet users
- Fixed telephone lines

Source: Adapted from: Global ICT Developments 2001–2011. International Telecommunication Union. Retrieved May 24, 2012, from www.itu.int/ITU-D/ict/statistics/.../Global_ICT_Dev_01-11.xls.

Information and communication technologies have paved the way for entirely new modes of working. In the next section, we will look at the many ways people can work and communicate via electronic technologies.

Discussion Questions

1. Some of the technologies that ultimately supported the development of mobile phones existed early in the last century. Develop a list of reasons that might explain why it took so long for cell phones to be commercially available.

2. Explain why recent advances in ICTs are contributing to changes in social structures such as economics and politics. Begin your discussion by focusing on how people's lives and work have changed in your community. Then, consider how ICTs are driving changes in parts of the world far from your home.

5. How Do People Use ICTs at Work?

Objective 11.5
Describe how people use ICTs at work.

In many jobs, ICTs are the basis upon which work is planned, conducted, shared, and evaluated. We use computers to capture and share ideas, plan projects, evaluate performance, and calculate costs, expenditures, revenues, profits, and debt. We track inventory, create graphics, market our products and services, conduct research—the list goes on and on. In this section, we will focus on certain types of ICTs that enable communication, learning, and knowledge sharing at work: e-mail, texting, teleconferencing, videoconferencing, Web conferencing, and social networking. The reason we are focusing on these few is that no matter what job you have, what school you attend, or what type of work you do, you will need to use these applications effectively and professionally.

E-mail

The high speed and low cost of e-mail make it a highly efficient and often effective channel for both internal and external communication at work. E-mail has all the value of traditional written communication, but with a number of added benefits. E-mail is fast—almost immediate—and it provides for a quick feedback loop if all parties are on-line and actively reading and responding. E-mail also allows us to communicate with any number of people in any part of the world with one efficient message. In addition, e-mail is essentially democratic, theoretically allowing anyone to communicate with anyone else in an organization, regardless of their positions in the hierarchy.

Of course, despite all of its benefits, e-mail is also a source of numerous communication problems. Consider the following examples:

- E-mail is one of the leading causes of information overload.
- Much of the e-mail sent and received is a complete waste of time.
- E-mail lends itself to lazy communication.
- Unless the users are skilled, e-mail tends to lessen the likelihood that the right amount of information is shared and that the content of the information includes enough context.
- It is difficult to communicate and interpret emotion in e-mail communication.

Mastering e-mail is an important way to improve your communication effectiveness in the world of virtual work. You have likely used e-mail for years and are quite proficient, as are many (if not most) of the people you interact with. Nonetheless, misuse of e-mail is prevalent in organizations today. Given these potentially negative effects, it is critical that you learn to use e-mail responsibly at work. Several methods for using e-mail more effectively are outlined in ■ **EXHIBIT 11.6**.

Sometimes, no matter how skilled the users are, e-mail is simply not the right way to communicate certain messages. We've heard of people firing employees, demanding salary increases, and criticizing colleagues via e-mail. Needless to say, these were not very effective messages, and harmed relationships tremendously. E-mail is not a good way to convey sensitive messages or messages that can be easily misunderstood. For example, if someone has made a mistake, it's not a good idea to offer criticism by e-mail; pick up the phone, use video conferencing, or meet face to face for difficult conversations. And don't forget that e-mail is a permanent and public form of communication: *Nothing is confidential in an e-mail message.* Even when messages are deleted, they exist on record and are retrievable.

■ **EXHIBIT 11.6**

Tips for Using E-mail Effectively at Work

Sending E-mail

- Use clear, informative subject lines.
- Avoid mass e-mails. Be judicious with the "Reply All" button and include only those people who need to see the message.
- Assume that management will read your e-mail.
- Assume that your e-mail will be seen by people outside of your organization.
- Do not send inappropriate or critical messages.

Receiving and Interpreting E-mail

- Look at subject lines to see whether you want to open an e-mail.
- If your organization has not already installed them, use e-mail filters to avoid spending time deleting spam.
- If you receive an e-mail that causes you to have a strong emotional reaction, do not respond immediately. Calm down, reflect on the message, and then respond appropriately—which may or may not be via e-mail.
- Don't let e-mail pile up: Answer it, move it to an appropriate folder, or delete it.
- Purge your inbox folder regularly.

Another potential problem is that transmitting emotion via e-mail is a tricky process. The first mistake many people make is to assume that e-mail communications are emotionless. Communication *always* includes emotion, so we must seek ways to appropriately express our emotions even when we communicate via technology.[76]

Not understanding how emotion comes across in e-mail affects more than our personal relationships—it can also result in problems at work. Frequent mistakes include the following:

- Assuming that your reader understands your intended emotions
- Overstating emotions in e-mail to make sure receivers get the point
- Assuming that all readers will interpret the emotions expressed in an e-mail in the same way
- Failing to recognize that emotion can be magnified when interpreted and received in e-mail communications—especially negative emotions.

To overcome some of the drawbacks of sending and interpreting emotion in e-mail and texts, we sometimes use emoticons. The word *emoticon* is a combination of *emotion* and *icon*. **Emoticons** are letters and symbols combined to represent emotions—a clever way to indicate feelings. There are now hundreds, if not thousands, of well-known emoticons, some of which are illustrated in ■ **EXHIBIT 11.7**. The use of emoticons in work-related e-mail is still generally unacceptable, but this is rapidly changing,

Emoticons
Letters and symbols combined to represent emotions.

■ **EXHIBIT 11.7**

Emoticons Communicate Emotions via Written Communications		
Facial Expression	**Emoticon Text**	**Emotion**
1.	:-)	Happy
2.	:-(	Sad
3.	>:-<	Angry
4.	:-|	Disappointed
5.	:-$	Embarrassed
6.	:-P	Joking with tongue sticking out
7.	:-D	Laughing
8.	:~/	Mixed up
9.	:->	Sarcastic
10.	:-O	Surprised

especially in less formal communications. Before using shortcuts like these, you should be sure that these methods are acceptable to the group or organization with which you need to communicate.

It is also important to remember that in contrast to face-to-face or video communication, where people can help one another regulate their emotions, people are on their own in managing their emotions when writing or receiving e-mail. This can result in communication that is confusing or lacking empathy—even when the sender intended otherwise.

Text Messages

Text messaging can take the form of instant messaging (IM) via the Internet or transmission of text (or SMS) messages via cell phone. Texting involves real-time communication in short bits. It is immediate and lends itself to conversation. But, text messaging also has drawbacks:

- Text messages are short and often incomplete.
- They include acronyms and codes for certain words that some people do not understand.
- They can be a huge distraction.
- It is difficult to accurately send and interpret emotions in texts.

Constant attention to text messages also hinders—and can harm—communication and relationships. Consider how you would feel if you were interviewing for your dream job and your interviewer, the vice president of the company, was texting during the entire interview! This is exactly what happened to our colleague recently.

Microblogging, such as Twitter, can also be done via cell phones. Microblog messages can reach wide audiences very efficiently, and the technology has become exceptionally useful in situations where information is hard to get or is changing rapidly, such as during natural disasters.

Teleconferences, Videoconferences, and Web Conferencing

Together, teleconferencing, videoconferencing, and Web conferencing have greatly increased our ability to link people who are geographically distant from one another. Teleconferences can include just a few people, or they might involve hundreds. Teleconferencing allows for better feedback and potentially more accurate interpretation of messages and emotion. It also permits interaction among participants, which can increase people's sense of belonging and allow for more complete information sharing. Videoconferencing has all of the qualities of teleconferencing, with the added benefit of video images that allow people to convey other communication-enhancing forms of body language, such as gestures and facial expressions.

Web conferencing enables participants to view the same information on their computers at the same time, usually while on a tele- or videoconference. This enables workers to complete interdependent tasks that used to require people to be in the same room or same building.

All of these technologies, of course, have limitations. Teleconferences become less interactive as more and more people are involved, as do video- and Web conferences. None of these methods allows for full use of nonverbal communication, and it is often difficult for people to join the conversation because normal social cues are not easy to give or interpret. This can mean that certain people may dominate interactions, some people may not get a chance to talk, or participants may find it awkward to interrupt a speaker. Finally, teleconferences, videoconferences, and Web conferences can be tedious if the meetings are long.

Tools to Help Us Work and Communicate Using ICTs

Groupware is a term that encompasses a wide variety of software and technological applications that enable people to work collaboratively via ICTs. We've already introduced Web conferences as one way for people to work together via electronic communication. Other common groupware includes wikis, blogs, and additional applications that allow users to share documents with ease.

Wikis are inexpensive and effective applications that allow users to create and edit documents without passing them back and forth via e-mail. Wikis can be highly efficient—indeed, the name comes from *wikiwiki*, the Hawaiian word for "fast"— because they permit real-time collaboration while archiving the history of what the participants create together.

Blogs are another example of groupware. The word *blog* is shorthand for "Web log," or an online site that allows people to share ideas. Blogs originally served as a way to post one's observations, ideas, and commentary on the Web. Today, however, most blogs provide a comments section so people can respond. The result is that blogs can contain a public, recorded feedback loop. Blogs are a popular way for companies to share new ideas and policies with employees, to solicit feedback, and to market products (either by setting up their own blogs or by asking popular bloggers to review their products). Leaders of organizations also use blogs to enhance internal communication and reinforce organizational culture. Externally, blogs are sometimes used to gauge or increase interest, gather consumer information and feedback, and educate the general public.

Groupware
A wide variety of software and technological applications that enable people to work collaboratively via information and communication technologies.

Social Networks

Social networks such as Facebook, YouTube, Flickr, LinkedIn, and Friendster have exploded across the technological landscape, as have "closed" social networks such as Ning. Social networking sites provide an interactive forum in which people can share information and take advantage of professional and personal networks. Within the workplace, social networking sites are often an electronic manifestation of the grapevine, enabling workers to connect with one another even in large or geographically dispersed organizations. Organizations can also communicate with current customers and potential new ones through social networks, and they sometimes use these networks to share information with shareholders, financial analysts, and other stakeholders.

As useful as social networks can be, some organizations have banned their use at work, fearing that employees will spend too much of their time tending to personal communication instead of working. Also, the public nature of social networks presents a challenge to the security of an organization's proprietary information, and there is the additional danger that employees will communicate sensitive information via these networks. Many organizations have reduced such security risks by using software and Internet applications that are specifically designed for business use. Applications such as Yammer and Socialtext, for example, are well suited to business because they maintain security behind a firewall, are more easily integrated into e-mail systems, and are more amenable to archiving and searching functions.

Putting It All Together: When Business Goes Multimedia

Today's organizations need an integrated approach to business that harnesses as many of the benefits of ICTs as possible. Given the rapid pace of innovation, the most

Leadership Perspective

● **Sheila Robinson**
Founder and Publisher of
Diversity Woman
"We are looking forward, to a
world with fewer borders and
more opportunities."

The Information Age has brought great changes to the publishing world. Sheila Robinson, Founder and Publisher of *Diversity Woman*, has managed to take challenges and turn them into opportunities by using technology to connect with readers. She is a true entrepreneur, and sees opportunities where others see closed doors. She is always ahead of the curve. For example, when other magazines were struggling to stay alive in traditional print, or were ditching print completely for Web-based distribution channels, she took her fledgling magazine online—without killing her print business. Why did it work? It worked partly because of Sheila herself, and her team. They approach everything they do with an attitude of "If not us, who?" and "What are others in our industry missing?" As an example of this, many publications online or otherwise that focus on diversity and inclusion are actually quite exclusive—meaning they are for one group or another. Sheila sees the value in that, but it's a crowded market. So, her magazine and conferences are open to and inclusive of women from all walks of life, all races, creeds, ages, and ethnicities. Sheila is a great leader—a business woman who understands our times. Here's what she says about leading in the digital age:

My industry is filled with challenges—the environment, the economy, constant changes. We thought the economic challenges, great as they were, would begin to settle down after a year or two. But, the challenges continue. This situation can be very difficult for a magazine, especially for one that is focused on the leadership advancement of women and the needs of women entrepreneurs. Why? During hard times, people's attention goes to the basics—keep my job, put food on the table. Exploring new ideas and learning can go to the bottom of the list.

But, this is exactly the time when we should be learning more and developing ourselves. That's why we are even more committed to getting our messages out there. Diversity Woman is an Internet magazine as well as a traditional one. We're also on Twitter, Facebook, LinkedIn, and we have an RSS feed. We use every single medium we can, and explore what's on the horizon. We jumped on Twitter early, and

have over 10,000 followers. We've expanded our business globally, when competitors thought our business model was U.S.-specific. Now, we have more readers outside the U.S. borders than within.

We're not doing all of these things because they are fads. We are looking forward, to a world with fewer borders and more opportunities. We need to be ahead of the curve, to serve the many women out there who need and want support and good ideas about how to succeed. We are passionate about leadership and executive development for women. And if we are to move ahead, instead of lose ground, we have to get the information out there to support a more diverse workforce.

The workforce is changing. You have four or five different generations all in the workforce at the same time, and each one has its preferred way of getting and delivering information. You need diversity in how you deliver the content, and if we are going to support that, we have to embrace not just traditional conceptions of diversity, but also all these different types of technology available to us. That's why we call ourselves a multimedia company.

Success is not just about technology, however. It's not even just about vision. Success comes with building relationships. That means building strong, trusting relationships with everyone. This takes time. You don't just walk into someone's office and say "Hi, I have a good idea and I want your company to sponsor it." People support your business because they trust you. And it's the same with people who work with you or for you: They will give their best and commit to the dream if they know you and trust you. This is even more important when people are working virtually, far from the buzz of an office. In business, sometimes you build relationships for years before you ever see your first dollar. Relationships come first. The money follows. That takes patience, commitment, and staying true to your values. You have to care about your customers as people.

Why do you have to stay true to your values? Why care about people? Isn't business just a transaction? Hardly. People know it when you just want their efforts, their business, or their money. And they don't like it. No one likes to be used. Sure, you both want something from each other, and that's fine. But if you are going to sell and keep your customers, people want to know beyond a doubt that you understand them, their business, and what matters most to them. You can't just be in it for yourself—that's short-term thinking.

We are a media business, and technology is at the core of what we do. What's more important, though, is who we are.

Source: Personal interviews conducted with Sheila Robinson by Annie McKee, 2009 and 2012.

successful organizations will be those that remain flexible in the face of constant change—ones that adapt their business processes as they integrate these evolving ICTs. As an example, let's look at how one thoughtful and insightful leader has managed to keep her entrepreneurial business ahead of the curve. Sheila Robinson is the founder and publisher of *Diversity Woman* magazine and organizer of a signature conference. In part because of her outstanding leadership and networking skills, she is known to— and sponsored by—many well-respected business leaders. Let's look at how Sheila has, and continues to, transform her business as ICTs and society evolve.

Doing business today requires flexibility, adaptability, and openness toward constantly evolving ICTs. Sheila Robinson has taken her magazine company in the direction it needs to go to fulfill its mission. But in the case of many other companies, the task can seem daunting. Further, though ICTs encourage efficient virtual approaches to work, human relations and face-to-face communication are still important and cannot be replaced completely—a topic we will return to throughout later sections.

In this section we have focused on a few ways in which people use ICTs at work and to redefine the work that their organizations do. Next, we will look at a few of the ways that people can work "virtually."

Discussion Questions

1. Imagine that you are managing a team of six people—all of whom live in different countries (e.g., the United States, England, Italy, and South Africa). Taking into consideration time zone differences and the need for effective collaboration, create a three-month communication plan. (Assume the team will have two face-to-face meetings during the three-month project, with regular telecommunication occurring between meetings.)

2. The next time you need to write an e-mail related to work or school, experiment with communicating your thoughts and emotions as fully as possible while still remaining concise and professional. After sending your e-mail, ask for feedback from the receiver.

6. How Is Virtual Work Conducted?

Objective 11.6
Learn where and how virtual work is conducted.

Unlike traditional work that is conducted in one physical location among a group of people, virtual work depends on ICTs as the primary vehicles for interaction, creativity, collaboration, and doing business. Of course, even virtual work is done in a physical setting—somewhere, someone is using a computer, on the phone, etc. Virtual work also requires a social setting—a psychological and relational "space" where people connect. Scholar Matti Vartiainen points out that even the most virtual of all jobs takes place in *physical, mental/social,* and *virtual spaces.*[77]

To show how this works in real life, consider the example of Steven, a telemarketer who has been hired to conduct surveys about consumers' preferences. He will use the telephone and videoconferencing technology like Skype when possible. These provide virtual work spaces. Steven, along with several other new telemarketers, has been briefed by his manager about the company, its goals for the project, and the manner in which the phone interviews are to be conducted. This particular company places high value on professionalism, friendliness, and respect—all of which are translated into norms of communication, which in turn have been translated into performance measures that Steven and the others must seek to achieve. The company also has specific metrics—for instance, how many calls must be made each day, how long they should last, and what data the telemarketers must collect. This kind of training gives Steven a clear picture of what is expected of him and information about the company's values. As a result, he feels that he is part of a team whose members all *share the same mental and social space*.

When Steven makes calls or Skypes, he relies on *virtual spaces* such as the telephone and video. He is also connected to several networked computer applications that allow him to enter the data he gathers into a shared database. Steven's *physical space* is the dining room of his home, which is off-limits to his two small children so it will be quiet while he is on the phone. All three spaces—shared mental and social space, virtual settings, and physical space—are essential for Steven to do his job well.

Telecommuting

In the previous example, Steven was an example of a telecommuter—someone who works for a company in a different location than the company's offices. The trend toward telecommuting first emerged about 20 years ago, as people began to see the possibilities of using technology to work from home. In addition, as travel became more common for employees at all levels in the global business environment, more people needed to work "on the road."

Examples of telecommuting abound. For instance, many catalog operations have employees who work from their homes using special phones connected to an 800 number. Cruiser, an experimental system at Bell Communications Research, uses small video cameras, a central computer, and an onscreen window to allow users to visit colleagues' offices without ever leaving their desks.[78] The U.S. federal government even got involved in telecommuting with the passage of the Telecommuting Act in 2010. This act requires the heads of executive agencies within the government to establish and implement telework policies for their agencies with regard to which employees are authorized to telecommute and under what conditions.[79] Still other people routinely work in coffee shops, on trains, and on airplanes. Indeed, many jobs today are so knowledge centered that wherever a computer and/or phone can be used, work can be done.

In the United States, the number of people reporting that they have telecommuted grew steadily from 1996 to 2006, from a total of 9 to 32 percent.[80] Also, telecommuting seems to be a perk that is reserved for the upper middle class, with those people earning more than $75,000 being twice as likely as those earning between $30,000 and $75,000 to have telecommuted. In addition, telecommuting was about 20 percent more likely to occur outside regular business hours (another indication that the boundary between home and work is becoming more blurred).[81]

According to the Telework Research Network's annual report, the greatest and by far most significant barrier to telework continues to be mistrust of employees' work ethic while away from the office. The 2011 report also found that 45 percent of U.S. workers held jobs that were compatible with at least part-time telework. The number of regular telecommuters is expected to continue growing through 2016. While in 2005, more than four-fifths of telecommuters worked in private sector jobs, the number has dropped to 76 percent as more government workers have begun to telecommute.

Despite all the benefits of telecommuting, many employees simply seem to prefer going to work. There may be many reasons for this, such as the enjoyment and effectiveness of face-to-face interaction, distractions at home, or even fears about being left out or overlooked by management. For these and many other reasons, new forms of hybrid structures are developing, in which people work some of the time in their company's physical setting and some of the time elsewhere.

The Hybrid Worker

More and more people work part of the time in an office setting and part of the time elsewhere. So, many organizations are creating work spaces specifically designed for temporary use. Instead of having their own offices or cubicles, people reserve or share space that is not designated for any one person. The spaces are mobile ready: electronic connections, wireless networks, Internet cables, conference phones, and video technology all await the user.

This practice, sometimes called *hoteling*, allows for hybrid workers to reserve a station to plug into the network and conduct in-office work whenever they are in the facility.[82] For example, PricewaterhouseCoopers (PwC) is a global accounting firm with offices in 158 countries around the world. Currently, the organization serves 16 industries, including governments, educational institutions, financial firms, and non-profit organizations. PwC is a leading proponent of global workforce mobility. Web conferencing is a standard form of team communication, and PwC has invested in the development of extensive online databases to allow for rapid creation, sharing, and retrieval of information.[83]

Virtual Teams

It is fast becoming the norm for organizations to rely on virtual, cross-functional, and culturally diverse teams to promote stability, increase efficient use of resources, and keep up with changing markets.[84] A **virtual team** is a group of individuals who collaborate on work projects while operating from different locations and using ICTs to establish shared goals, coordinate work, manage work processes and outcomes, and build effective relationships and team norms.[85] Virtual teams often exist in an extremely dynamic, changing state.[86] Such teams are typically project based or task focused and can be stable in membership or quite fluid. The task itself usually provides the initial motivation to work together across time and space.[87]

Today, many teams within organizations (including schools) combine traditional face-to-face work with virtual work. One approach to describing virtual teams has been to view the "virtualness" of the team as based on the amount of face-to-face time: the lower the time spent in face-to-face interactions, the more virtual the team is.[88]

> **Virtual team**
> A group of individuals who collaborate on work projects while operating from different locations, and using ICTs to establish shared goals, coordinate work, manage work processes and outcomes, and build effective relationships and team norms.

MAKING VIRTUAL TEAMS MORE EFFECTIVE

Given how hard it can be for conventional teams to maintain effective working relationships, why would organizations choose to create geographically dispersed teams that may never meet face to face? Virtual teams offer several benefits that are not available with conventional teams. These include cost savings, increased ability for employees to accommodate their personal and professional lives, and the possibility of assigning individuals to multiple teams or projects regardless of physical location. Also, virtual teams may lead to higher levels of creativity as a result of their greater openness, flexibility, diversity, and access to information.[89]

Research has identified a number of strategies for maximizing the effectiveness of virtual teams:

1. Explicit and detailed communication about roles and relationships and how to use ICTs
2. Agreement on team norms
3. Agreement on which ICTs to use, how to use them, and when to use them
4. Agreement on how to share, store, and manage knowledge and information
5. Clarity regarding members' responsibilities and contributions to the team
6. Shared, explicit understanding of problems and challenges[90]

Members of virtual teams also need to find ways to deal with and manage conflict and minimize uncertainty. This means that team norms must in some way deal with how to manage differences of opinion and how to bring conflicts into the open to discuss and resolve them. Virtual teams can also manage conflict by actively engaging in the development of standard practices, which help reduce ambiguity. This includes collectively deciding on the mix of communication technologies and when they will be used; selecting proper processes for documenting interactions; defining and clarifying the roles and responsibilities of all team members; coming up with an explicit description of problems to be addressed by the team; and keeping a log of past activities and ways to solve problems.[91]

TRUST AND ACCOUNTABILITY IN VIRTUAL TEAMS

Two additional dimensions must be considered to ensure that virtual teams are truly effective: trust and accountability. Trust in virtual relationships is important for several reasons. First, virtual work has to be based on trust and minimal supervision because it is very difficult to supervise and control people and activities from a distance.[92] In traditional organizations, managers oversee how employees spend their time and what they do. In a virtual workplace, managers must rely heavily on trust and processes that aid in monitoring output. To be most effective with virtual teams, managers need to shift their focus from overseeing how employees spend their time to evaluating team results. They must also develop supervisory skills that include building and managing relationships virtually.

Moving from a "face time" orientation to a results orientation is essential within virtual teams, too. People simply have to trust one another to do what is expected and to carry out their tasks. We do not yet know how trust develops in virtual teams, but we do know that the process is not the same as in face-to-face groups. In fact, a team of researchers investigating trust in virtual and face-to-face teams found that virtual team members started out with a lower level of trust, but after a few weeks they caught up with their face-to-face counterparts. These researchers also noted that people were more likely to make inflammatory remarks at the outset of virtual team work when members had never met each other, and they attributed the slower development of trust to this.[93] What this means is that virtual teams might have to pay more attention to building trust explicitly in the early stages of team development in order for members to be able to hold one another accountable from the start.

In any team, trust is a critical factor that influences the ability to achieve productive results. Trust is key to results. In virtual teams, trust is an even more important factor. This is because virtual teams often do not have the advantage of face-to-face contact, which facilitates the development of meaningful working relationships.[94] When possible, bringing members of a virtual team together, even briefly, can help develop a team identity. When this is not possible, reliance on Internet and communication technologies (ICTs) such as videoconferences can help to develop critical interpersonal relationships—and trust.[95]

Leadership is an important factor in how trust develops in virtual teams.[96] Clearly recognizable leadership significantly contributes to team trust and cohesion. However, a facilitative approach to leadership has additional advantages because it leads to greater adaptability with regard to which ICTs are used, as well as how they are used. Research has shown that the ability to adapt to technology by adopting, modifying, or discontinuing the use of ICTs is strongly associated with team trust and cooperation.[97]

Trust and accountability go hand-in-hand. Scholars Gina Hinrichs, Jane Seiling, and Jackie Stavros describe what you can do to create constructive accountability in virtual teams.[98] Behaviors focused on explicit communication and relationship-building help virtual teams work effectively. Therefore, to increase virtual team performance, build a shared understanding of information, tasks, and relationships, and you will build shared accountability (■ **EXHIBIT 11.8**).

Good communication, role clarity, effective norms, trust, and accountability are at the heart of a virtual team's success. They are also essential within any virtual work structure. Telecommuting, hybrid work, and hoteling all require people to connect and

■ **EXHIBIT 11.8**

Scholars Offer Tips for Building Accountability and Trust in Virtual Teams

- Organize extra virtual meetings to get to know each other and discuss new issues.
- Build meaningful relationships by encouraging full participation and contribution in meetings and conversations in both face-to-face and virtual spaces.
- A virtual relationship is a relationship. Engage in casual communication by swapping stories and sharing some personal information.
- Make clear and explicit time commitments, and communicate with others immediately when these commitments cannot be met.
- Openly share information and resources you have available that would support team goals.
- Mindfully engage in critical thinking by listening for differences and similarities in the views of others, asking for clarifications, and challenging assumptions—your own, as well as others'.
- Advocate for the team or individual team members.
- Actively engage in collective virtual brainstorming.
- Communicate with all key stakeholders, solicit feedback, and make others feel that they are part of a collaborative effort.

Source: Based on Hinrichs, Gina, Jane Seiling, and Jackie Stavros. 2008. Sensemaking to create high-performing virtual teams, in *Handbook of high-performance virtual teams: A toolkit for collaborating across boundaries*, ed. Jill Nemiro, Michael M. Beyerlein, Lori Bradley, and Susan Beyerlein, 131–52. San Francisco: Jossey-Bass.

collaborate with few or no face-to-face meetings and often with limited, indirect, or no formal supervision. In order for people to work effectively under these conditions, we all need to take responsibility for paying attention to our interactions, our roles, and our responsibility for contributing to building healthy virtual work relationships. In the next section we will go beyond looking at what people need to do and be in order to work virtually, and look instead at the virtual workplace itself.

Discussion Questions

1. Consider groupthink and social loafing, which you studied in Chapter 10. Can these things happen in a virtual team? Why or why not? If you believe it can happen, how might you prevent it?

2. Consider a virtual work project or school team that you have been part of (even if it was only partially virtual). What did you do to help the team build effective relationships and esprit de corps?

7. What Is a Virtual Organization?

Objective 11.7
Learn about virtual organizations.

Organizations have traditionally been structured around hierarchies that dictate responsibility for work output and accountability for results. This basic design emerged from the Confucian civil service model in ancient China, early models of military organizations, and the Catholic Church, which, for centuries, was the most powerful organization in Europe.[99] When companies that relied on few leaders and many workers began to emerge during the early part of the Industrial Revolution, these companies were typically modeled after those earlier organizations. The hierarchical model continues to shape many businesses today.

However, there has been a shift in organizational design as we adapt to our increasingly virtual world. Companies are moving away from vertical hierarchies to flatter, more networked structures in order to take advantage of rapidly flowing information and to adapt to a constantly changing global environment. Today, "[t]he network is the

Virtual organizations
Organizations that consist of diverse people, groups, and networks that are geographically dispersed and that rely on information and communication technologies for communication and coordination of activities.

paradigm, not the Catholic Church or the military," according to former president of PepsiCo and former CEO of Apple Computer, John Sculley.[100] **Virtual organizations** consist of diverse people, groups, and networks that are geographically dispersed and that rely on ICTs for communication and coordination of activities.[101]

Virtual organizations have defined and shared goals, limited physical presence (e.g., distribution sites rather than office buildings), and rely on ICTs for the coordination of employees, suppliers, and customers as they produce, distribute, or provide goods or services. Although it is true that the trend toward virtual organizations is greatly magnified today, this trend is not entirely new. In fact, organizations like Mary Kay and Tupperware have successfully used hybrid virtual structures for many years.

During the first decade of this century, we have experienced dramatic increases in the number and types of organizations that are adopting networked and virtual structures, or expanding the use of ICTs in existing networks. Let's take a closer look at some of these characteristics that distinguish virtual organizations from more traditional organizational models.

Components of Virtual Organizations

Virtual organizations differ from traditional models in that employees are often not located in the same place, customers may never visit a physical store, information is shared digitally, and money is transferred electronically. According to scholars Geraldine DeSanctis and Peter Monge, all virtual organizations are characterized by the four key components listed in ■ **EXHIBIT 11.9**.

DeSanctis and Monge's early work on virtual organizations is helpful in that it permits us to see general characteristics that are found in most virtual organizations. In the years since this study, there has been a tremendous amount of additional research conducted on virtual organizations, and scholars are now able to identify several specific models of virtual organizations, as described in the following section.

■ **EXHIBIT 11.9**

Four Key Components of Virtual Organizations

1. Structures that allow for swift adaptation to meet the needs of the marketplace.

2. Permeable boundaries, meaning a customer may directly order a product from a company's online catalog, but in reality, five distinct and separate organizations are involved in the process of designing, creating, managing, and delivering the product.

3. Contractual relationships among entities, including temporary or short-term partnerships or collaborations with "experts" for the duration of a project or task. A virtual organization that manufactures a product, for instance, may partner with an outside marketing firm to handle all of its sales instead of hiring its own sales staff.

4. Dynamic processes, such as rapid, customized, relationship-based communication (e.g., e-mail, Web conferencing), along with a high degree of collaboration using wikis, social networking, and groupware.

Source: Adapted from DeSanctis, Geraldine, and Peter Monge. 1998. Communication process for virtual organizations. *Journal of Computer-Mediated Communication*, p. 6.

Models of Virtual Organizations

Models of virtual organizations can be understood in a number of ways, depending on how the organization interfaces with its clients and how its network is structured. For example, researchers Janice Burn, Peter Marshall, and Martin Barnett classify virtual organizations into four functional and seven structural models.[102]

- *Destination sites:* This category consists of online storefronts, advertising sites, and content sites that offer services such as searchable databases for a fee, either to the user or to sponsors who advertise on the site. Questia is one example of a destination site model; Angie's List is another.
- *Traffic control sites:* This category consists of virtual malls, "incentive sites" (e.g., free e-mail and free Web page hosting sites), and free Internet service providers. NetZero is an example of a traffic control model.
- *Business portals:* This category consists of sites that are shared by businesses within a particular industry. For example, travel planning sites such as Expedia.com use the business portal model.
- *Auction sites:* These are sites where sellers and customers join together to buy, sell, or trade goods and services. eBay is perhaps the best-known auction site company.

Burn, Marshall, and Barnett have identified seven common structural models, which are described in ■ **EXHIBIT 11.10**.

The seventh structural model (virtual space), if taken literally, does not exist. Somewhere, people are in a physical space creating, maintaining, and managing the services. PayPal, for example, is dependent on virtual interaction, but it also has a very large building in California where employees work together physically.

An eighth structure known as a peer-to-peer (P2P) network can also be added to this list. P2P networks are common in virtual project work because they allow all members of a network to be directly linked and to have direct access to one another.[103] This model differs from the star alliance/hub-and-spokes model described in Exhibit 11.10 in that members do not have to rely on the central organization for transfer of information or resources among themselves. P2Ps flourish on the Internet, where users can access each other through a service and swap information, files, programs, and so on. Skype is a P2P communication network. Bitcoin is an ingenious P2P digital

■ **EXHIBIT 11.10**

Seven Structural Models of Virtual Organizations

Model	Description	Examples
Virtual face model	An online store as an extension of a physical store; a "clicks-and-bricks" model	Target.com
Co-alliance model	A structure linking two organizations that offer complementary services	Netflix and Xbox[104]
Star alliance model	A "hub-and-spokes" model linking several member organizations through a central, core organization[105]	Airline companies united under Star Alliance
Value alliance model	Operates on a supply chain principle to link "a range of products, services, and facilities based on the value or supply chain";[106] has been described elsewhere simply as a supply chain model[107]	Travel booking companies that link transportation plans, rentals, hotels, and tours in a single package
Market alliance model	A highly networked supply chain that offers a range of products and services, although only one core organization might serve as the virtual face for the entire network	Amazon.com
Virtual broker model	Model in which one core organization "provides structure around specific business information services"[108]	eBay
Virtual space	Model that is completely dependent on virtual interaction	Some cloud computing services

Source: Adapted from Burn, Janice, Peter Marshall, and Martin Barnett. 2002. *E-business strategies for virtual organizations.* Woodburn, MA: Butterworth-Heinemann.

currency with a very stable exchange rate of over $5 per Bitcoin. The total number of Bitcoins in circulation cannot exceed 21 million, which means that, at the current exchange rate, their value could be a little over $105 million.[109]

Today, a wide variety of organizations conduct all or part of their operations virtually—this includes everything from public schools, such as the kindergarten through grade 12 Agora Cyber Charter School in Pennsylvania, to virtual stores such as eBay, to stock-trading organizations such as eTrade. Virtual organizations are sometimes called e-businesses. For example, Amazon.com and Craigslist are two examples of real companies that interface with customers and sellers by way of a virtual marketplace. In e-businesses and virtual organizations like these, people can engage in certain activities that would normally—or that used to—occur in a physical location. Let's take a closer look at how several specific industries have evolved to include virtual organizations.

Traditional Organizations Are Evolving to Better Use and Offer Virtual Services

To illustrate how traditional organizational forms have evolved to include more and more aspects of virtual organizations, consider what has occurred in banking, the consumer goods industry, and education and training.

THE EVOLUTION OF VIRTUAL BANKING

One of the earliest virtual banking services was the credit card, which has been around since the early twentieth century. These cards were originally made of paper and issued by oil companies and department stores.[110] The first nonproprietary credit card not issued by a company was issued in 1966, and by 1970 only 6 percent of households used credit cards. By 1995 it was 65 percent, and in 2002 the Gallup organization reported that only one in six Americans had no access to a credit card, while 81 percent of adults had their own card.[111] This dramatic rise in credit card usage is linked to the increasingly widespread use of computing technologies, which allow merchants to plug into the central banking companies that manage credit.[112] However, according to a 2010 poll, as the Recession took its toll there was a 10 percent decrease in credit card ownership between 2009 and 2010.[113] In 2011, credit cards amounted to 3 percent less of all consumer purchases than in 2010.[114]

During the second half of the twentieth century, cash also began flowing through electronic funds transfer networks, first through the use of ATMs and debit cards, and later through fully online banking systems that are accessible via the Internet.[115] The first ATM was actually installed at Rockefeller Center in Manhattan in 1969, but it was part of an offline network.[116] This machine read cards with a magnetically encoded strip that contained enough bank account information for limited cash withdrawals, but it could not perform other teller services.[117] It wasn't until the early 1980s that computerization allowed for online banking and widespread distribution of ATMs at grocery and convenience stores, along with point-of-sale use of debit cards.

A 2002 research report found that institutions that offered Internet banking were more profitable than those that did not.[118] At that point, even the laggards joined in. Now, it would be almost impossible to succeed in the industry without an online presence (■ **EXHIBIT 11.11**). Some banks have even gone completely virtual. ING Direct (owned by Internationale Nederlanden Groep) was a leader in this movement when it opened in Canada in 1997. Shortly thereafter, it began operating in Spain and the United States.[119] Although ING Direct is no longer wholly online, it continues to operate cafes in some major cities that provide customers with access to computer terminals and agents

■ **EXHIBIT 11.11**
What benefits and risks accompany the increased popularity of Internet banking?

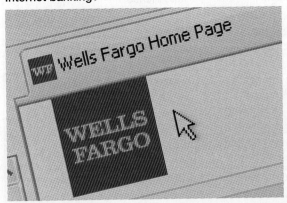

Source: © NetPics/Alamy

for support.[120] Other Internet-only banks have sprung up as well, including Ally Bank and FNBO Direct. It is worth mentioning that these institutions were spun off from GMAC Financial Services and First National Bank of Omaha respectively.[121]

More innovations are occurring in the financial services industry as information technology advances. For example, eBay-owned PayPal is an online service that acts as an intermediary between buyers and sellers in Internet purchasing arrangements. The service acts as a buffer that protects individuals from disclosing financial information.[122]

Now, consider **microfinancing**, which is the practice of providing financial services, such as loans, on an extremely small scale. Microfinance loans can be as small as $25 or, in some cases, even less. Microfinancing has been used all over the world to support local entrepreneurs in developing countries start their businesses, especially where small amounts of money can have a big impact.

Consider as an example Kiva, a virtual company that manages small P2P loans. This microlending Web site specializes in loans as small as a few dollars to people in developing nations, who usually pay back their debt in 6 to 12 months.[123] As you can see in the *Business Case*, Kiva is fascinating in that it is on the cutting edge of microfinance and it is truly changing people's lives.

This case shows us beyond a shadow of a doubt that the Internet is indeed changing societies all over the world. It's not just that banking is more convenient with ATMs everywhere, that you can pay for goods with a click, or that you can transfer money and pay bills on your phone. The Internet, combined with brilliant ideas like microfinancing, is helping people to survive and thrive economically. Equally important, people

Microfinance
The practice of providing financial services on an extremely small scale.

Using the Internet to Change Lives, One Entrepreneur at a Time

With Kiva.org, microfinancing went global in a big way, bringing ordinary people together with entrepreneurs around the world. Kiva works by doing two things. First, it enlists the support of volunteer lenders through its Web site, which also showcases entrepreneurs. Second, Kiva partners with microlending institutions in countries around the world that manage the loans locally. Member microlending institutions post profiles of entrepreneurs on Kiva's website, and lenders can browse these profiles and then make loans free of charge through PayPal. Because Kiva is a not-for-profit organization, lenders do not receive interest on their loans, but it doesn't matter because the experience of doing this service is highly rewarding. Kiva's story is interesting and inspiring.

It all started in 2003 at Stanford, when then-student Jessica Flannery was fortunate enough to listen to a speech by Nobel Laureate Muhammad Yunus about microlending. The talk affected her profoundly and as a result Jessica joined a nonprofit organization called the Village Enterprise Fund and went to Africa to help people start businesses.

When Jessica's soon-to-be husband Matt visited her in Africa, the two started exploring how to use the Internet to help

people access microloans. The couple founded Kiva in October 2005 as a nonprofit organization with the mission of fighting global poverty by "enabling people to connect with and make personal loans to low-income entrepreneurs in the developing world."[124]

As of June 2012, the total value of loans through Kiva exceeded $320 million, provided by 770,417 lenders to 794,274 entrepreneurs in 61 countries, with a reported repayment rate of 98.94 percent. More than 82 percent of Kiva's funded entrepreneurs in the developing world have been women.[125] Kiva operates in 54 countries and partners with 111 regional microfinance institutions, and has made 178,143 loans. The average loan size is just under $400, with many loans at amounts much less than that.[126] To put the power of microlending into perspective, a $400 loan is significantly less than 1 percent of the 2011 per capita Gross Domestic Product (GDP) of the United States, while it is 31 percent of Uganda's per capita GDP and 133 percent of Congo's per capita GDP for the same time period.[127] So, what we consider a very small loan in the United States can be a lifeline for a business entrepreneur in another country. Just a little effort on our part can change the lives of hundreds of people and reduce global poverty—through the Internet, one person (and one click) at a time.

Source: Case written by Chris Allen Thomas

are able to use their brilliance and creativity in their own businesses—and the dignity and self worth that comes along with this are beyond measure.

Now, let's turn to the history of another innovation—Internet sales. This, too, is changing the world.

THE EVOLUTION OF VIRTUAL CONSUMER SALES

As far back as when the Silk Road was filled with traders, people have been placing orders for goods from remote and distant places. When we look at the evolution of virtual sales in more modern times, a good starting point is catalog shopping in the United States, which began in the nineteenth century and became especially popular in the early part of the twentieth century. During this period, the Sears and Roebuck catalog sold everything from medicines to dry goods, clothing, tools, and even houses. In isolated rural towns in the United States, catalogs were the only way people could shop for many goods.

In the United Kingdom and other parts of Europe during the nineteenth century, fashion was as important as it is today. France, and in particular Paris, was the fashion capital of the world. In certain elite circles, women waited with great anticipation for publications from France that contained pictures of the newest dresses. Although not a typical catalogue, the fashion plates in these magazines most certainly impacted the European fashion industry.[128]

Later, the United Kingdom had a small but thriving mail-order catalog industry, but it ran aground due to wartime and post-war austerity in the late 1930s. It was not until about 1950 that the catalog industry came back in full force in the United Kingdom due to a booming middle class.[129]

Today, all large department stores and thousands of specialty stores have Web sites to complement their physical businesses and/or catalogs. Some companies have no storefront at all. For example, Amazon.com is heralded as one of the most successful virtual shopping sites. Founded in 1994 and launched the following year, Amazon is a virtual store that began by selling books and later diversified to offer many other products. Amazon has an advantage over many brick-and-mortar stores in that its offerings are not limited by physical space; similarly, unlike mail-order retailers, Amazon is not limited by the size of its catalog.[130] In recent years, Amazon has implemented a model that incorporates third-party sellers into its vast online sales network, effectively linking its Web site to sellers and resellers around the world who hold accounts with Amazon.[131] A similar model of networked third-party sellers is used by eBay. However, eBay acts only as a virtual marketplace and does not sell products at all except through third parties that set up their own auctions and online stores.[132]

THE EVOLUTION OF VIRTUAL EDUCATION AND TRAINING

Distance learning has been around for a long time in the form of correspondence courses, in which assignments were completed without supervision and submitted to an instructor via mail. Most courses were quite basic and did not allow for much, if any, teacher–student or student–student interaction. The introduction of the Internet, however, changed all of this. Computers allowed for much more complexity in the information shared, more engaging instructional materials, and more meaningful online interaction between and among teachers and students.

The first e-learning course was introduced in 1995.[133] Since then, Internet-based learning has expanded to include K-12 education, higher education, corporate universities, and various types of training programs. Virtual education and training programs have moved far beyond the traditional classroom model and now include services to support faculty in designing and preparing courses, multimedia to support learning and interaction, and a variety of groupware processes that encourage collaboration.

One big advantage of virtual learning is that it has begun to level the playing field in terms of people's access to education and training. For companies, training can now be delivered to any employee, wherever they are and whenever they need it. Similarly, when it comes to general education, populations that are far from brick-and-mortar institutions now have access to learning as more computers find their way to remote corners of the world. In addition, educational institutions can offer a greater variety of niche programs because they can aggregate learners nationally or even globally.

As these examples suggest, virtual learning comes in a variety of forms. Adult learning scholars Bob Zemsky and William Massey have identified four distinct cycles of evolution in virtual learning, as listed in ■ **EXHIBIT 11.12**.[134]

Clearly, organizations have been and are continuing to change dramatically in the virtual age. This has implications for all of us: employees, managers, and leaders alike. The technological revolution brings tremendous opportunities, yet it also means we must learn new ways of interacting with our work and with peers, managers, and networked colleagues. In the next section of the chapter, we will explore virtual work even further by looking at how people can face challenges associated with virtual work so that they can be most effective.

■ **EXHIBIT 11.12**

The Evolution of Virtual Learning Technologies

- *Cycle 1:* The first cycle enhances the existing traditional course structure through the use of online materials, e-mail communication, multimedia materials, and pre-packaged software.
- *Cycle 2:* The second cycle involves the use of course management systems such as Blackboard, a virtual platform for both blended and fully online courses.
- *Cycle 3:* The third cycle involves the importation of course objects by instructors and facilitators, such as compressed video and interactive simulations.
- *Cycle 4:* The last cycle involves re-engineering the learning structure, fully integrating learning systems, and developing configurations that blend synchronous, asynchronous, and face-to-face interaction in effective and innovative ways.

Source: Adapted from Zemsky, R., and W. Massey. June 2004. *Thwarted innovation: A Learning Alliance report*, p. 11. West Chester, PA: Learning Alliance.

Discussion Questions

1. Do you know of any business that does *not* have a virtual component? Should it? Why or why not?

2. What are the advantages and disadvantages of online learning programs? Give examples from your own experience with each of the four cycles discussed in Exhibit 11.12. Do you feel more empowered by in-class or virtual learning environments?

8. What Are the Challenges of Working in a Virtual World?

Objective 11.8
Understand the challenges of working in a virtual world.

Technology has improved our lives and made many aspects of work easier, faster, cheaper, and more fun. That said, there are some definite downsides to living and working in a virtual world, which we will now explore. First, we will consider the challenges individuals face in the 24/7 world of virtual work. Then, we will look at the impact of information overload. Finally, we will examine problems related to knowledge management.

The Challenges of the 24/7 Virtual Work World

Working virtually offers several benefits to employees and organizations alike. For one, business continuity can be maintained 24 hours a day if people are working in different time zones around the world, or when a workplace has been lost or temporarily closed due to catastrophe.[135] A company and its employees might also experience cost

Carbon footprint
The amount of carbon dioxide emitted as a result of a person's or organization's consumption of fossil fuels.

savings due to a decrease in real estate costs and expenses such as meals and transportation. Working from home can also decrease employees' and organizations' **carbon footprint**, or the amount of carbon dioxide emitted as a result of the consumption of fossil fuels. Sometimes, this term is used to describe our individual impact on the environment. Used this way, things like how much gas we use, how and where we fly, and how many dedicated office spaces we use would go into the equation. Working virtually can help workers develop skills that are useful for being part of diverse teams and virtual collaboration.[136]

Still, virtual work has several notable downsides. First, people can feel like they are on-call all the time. Advances in ICTs have blurred the lines between personal and professional time, making it easier for work to reach us once we have left the office, and making it harder for us to disengage from our work when we should be enjoying free time. We can feel like we are *always* working. On the other hand, many people now find it easier to use organizational time and resources for personal activities. That said, the blurred separation between home and work can cause stress, as can the feelings of isolation that can result from working alone.[137]

When it comes to virtual relationships, conflict may become more problematic if communication and work norms are not clear and agreed on.[138] Also, because virtual work requires independence and less oversight, problems can arise when role clarity and responsibilities are not firmly established. Additionally, there is the potential for loss of quality and efficiency due to some reduction of direct control and oversight, as well as a decrease in face-to-face communication.[139]

Other challenges relate to the sheer amount of information we receive every day in the form of e-mails, texts, downloads to our computers, and the like—taken together, we can easily find ourselves drowning in information.

Technology and Information Overload

Information overload is a problem for many people at work. People have turned to e-mail as a primary communication channel, our cell phones are with us constantly, and any time we log on to a computer, others can find us. You could probably spend most of your time reading and responding to e-mails, texts, and social media messages, but is that the best use of your time?

According to a survey in 2011, more than half of U.S. employees lose between one and three hours to all types of workplace distractions, while over one third more admit to losing at least thirty minutes.[140] Assuming an average one hour of productivity lost due to distractions, for a workforce of 150 million at an average full time yearly income of approximately $43 thousand, this translates to over three-quarters of a trillion dollars in productivity cost due to distractions. Think about your own experience as you have read this chapter: How many e-mails, text messages, phone calls, or social networking alerts have you received? As welcome as these distractions may have been, they most likely haven't helped you study productively.

Information overload comes with a high price. First, the sheer volume of communication at work can take up a huge amount of time—time needed to do other kinds of work. Second, when we are barraged with information, it becomes difficult to prioritize work tasks—typically, the most immediate bit of information gets our attention while more important tasks are left for later. Third, more communication doesn't necessarily mean better communication—too often, the information shared via e-mail, texts, and social networks is peripheral (at best) to the task at hand.

Microsoft, Google, Intel, and IBM are among the organizations that formed the Information Overload Research Group in 2008 to examine and address the problem of too much information.[141] In a 2011 media release, the organization announced the financial cost of productivity lost to too much information:

"According to research published by Basex, a knowledge economy research firm and IORG member, information overload cost the U.S. economy at least $997 billion per year in reduced productivity and innovation as of 2010, reflecting a loss of 25 percent of the working day for most knowledge workers."[142]

These companies are also trying to devise remedies for information overload within their own organizations. Intel, for instance, started the Next Generation Solutions program specifically with the purpose of reducing information overload. The company began by encouraging a team of employees to limit both electronic and in-person communication just one morning a week so they could focus on their other work. They also experimented with a program called Zero E-Mail Fridays, in which people were asked to avoid e-mail as much as possible on Fridays. The program met with limited success; most employees continued using e-mail on Fridays because they found it essential. Still, 60 percent of the employees recommended the program for wider use following certain modifications.[143] What this example illustrates is that simply going back to how we worked before e-mail isn't an option—yet we must do something.

In the next section, we will look at some of the challenges managers and employees face in trying to manage the huge volume of information that is generated at work today.

The Challenge of Knowledge Management

Managing the vast amount of constantly changing information that is traveling at light speed into, around, and out of organizations is profoundly challenging for people. Even more challenging is organizing this information so that multiple people can access and use it.

Organizations and people need systems to capture, store, and disseminate information and knowledge. A deadly example of how difficult this can be is found in the stories of information that was available prior to the Christmas day bombing attempt in the United States in 2009. In this case, different individuals or groups held different pieces of information about the situation, but these pieces were not shared among the parties in ways that allowed the information to be pieced together. For example, the suspect's father had reported concern over his son's "radicalization and associations" to the U.S. Embassy in Nigeria in 2007, and his name was added to a terrorist-related activities database in November 2009.[144] However, this and other small pieces of information were not wholly available to certain key authorities such as government security bodies, embassy officials, and airline personnel. In the end, nobody could see the entire picture. As a result, the United States suffered a frightening breach of security.

The consequences of inadequate knowledge management systems at work aren't usually so dire, but they still matter. For example, when a sales employee in Malaysia learns something important about a customer, competitor, or supplier, you need to have a structure in place for getting that information back to the organization, as well as a process for disseminating critical data to the right employees. Or what about the vast amount of time wasted when people "re-create the wheel," designing presentations, proposals, or reports that have been done many times before?

All of these examples point to the fact that organizations must create systems to capture, organize, and disseminate knowledge so it can be easily accessed by those who need it. This is a huge challenge—one that cannot be addressed until leaders understand the limitations of knowledge management systems. Accordingly, some common myths about knowledge management systems must be debunked, as summarized in ■ **EXHIBIT 11.13**.

Ultimately, knowledge management technologies do not take the place of human beings. *People* must ensure that the knowledge generated and stored makes sense. This requires repetitive questioning, critical thinking, and revision of the assumptions underlying information.[145]

■ **EXHIBIT 11.13**

Common Myths about Knowledge Management Technologies

- **Myth Number 1: Knowledge management technologies can deliver the right information to the right person at the right time.** Businesses can no longer predict what will be needed when, where, or in what form, so automated or static knowledge management systems do not always work. Nor can businesses predict who will need what information at any given time. Knowledge management systems now need to be designed to anticipate change, to include processes for quickly updating information, and to anticipate how to share it across the organization.

- **Myth Number 2: Knowledge management technologies can store human intelligence and experience.** Technologies such as databases and groupware applications store bits and pixels of data, but they can't store the rich schemas that people possess for making sense of this data. Information is context sensitive—meaning the same data can evoke different responses from different people. ICTs don't think. People do. Storing a static representation of some aspects of a person's knowledge is not tantamount to storing human intelligence and experience.

- **Myth Number 3: Knowledge management systems should replicate traditional filing systems.** Data archived in computer files is often irrelevant to any situation other than the one for which it was created. Such systems do not account for renewal of existing knowledge and creation of new knowledge. The best knowledge management systems enable people to find what they need quickly—even when information related to a "new" situation is housed in many places and in many ways. Organizations need knowledge management systems that allow people to quickly sort through irrelevant data and to interpret relevant information in order to find gaps in the information, patterns, surprises, and anomalies.

Source: Adapted from Malhotra, Yogesh. 2000. *Knowledge management and new organization forms: A framework for business model innovation*, pp. 7–8. Hershey, PA: Idea Group Publishing.

Discussion Questions

1. In your life at school or work today, is there ever a time when you "unplug" from ICTs? Why or why not? How connected do you need to be in order to be effective at school and at work? What impact does it have on your quality of life and health?

2. Examine the knowledge management system you have in place for organizing e-mail, texts, schoolwork, work-related projects, and so on. Is your technology up to the task? Are you using it to full advantage? What can you do to improve your system?

Objective 11.9
List steps HR can take to support virtual work.

HR Leadership Roles

9. What Can HR Do to Support Virtual Work?

Managing virtual work is everyone's job in organizations today. By focusing on how virtual team members are trained and how they work together, HR leaders can help managers and leaders while making virtual work safe, rewarding, and productive for all employees. HR professionals contribute to this process in particularly important ways. First, HR is often responsible for understanding and applying emerging laws and regulations that affect virtual work, such as those related to workplace privacy. Second, HR is responsible for creating guidelines that support workers and managers in using technology (such as social networks) in an appropriate manner at work.

The Privacy Question: HR's Role in Monitoring Employee Electronic Communications

In addition to tracking and ensuring compliance with laws involving e-commerce and related topics, HR is at the center of a growing debate about the privacy of communication in the workplace. Today, employers can easily access and monitor employees' e-mails, Internet searches, phone calls, and text messages. The debate over these practices is complex and heated. In many countries, individual privacy is a deeply held cultural value—one that is backed by the power of the law. When an employee is using company property (computers, cell phones, or even the network that connects employees to the Internet) or company time to engage in personal communication, who actually "owns" the information that is communicated? Also, does an employer have the right to ensure that employees are working, as opposed to engaging in personal communication or surfing the Web?

It appears to be only a matter of time before legal precedents will be set to either further protect employee privacy or erode it, at least to some degree. Indeed, an increasing number of employees are bringing their own devices into the workplace, at least in part as protection against workplace security rules. The practice, called Bring Your Own Device (BYOD), presents some new challenges to employers and HR professionals who are responsible not only for directing how employee time is used but also for how information is used in the workplace.[146] In the meantime, it is often HR's responsibility to create and enforce policies that both protect employees from privacy violations and ensure that communication within the organization serves its stated goals.

Some employers, including schools, government institutions, and private companies, have started requesting access to applicants' social media websites, such as Facebook and LinkedIn, as part of the application or employee review process. Employees and applicants have been required to "friend" their employer, login in the presence of HR professionals, or submit their passwords so employers can access their accounts and private information. The practice has been widely criticized and, as of 2012, a dozen state legislatures and the U.S. Congress have proposed or passed measures to limit such actions. Unfortunately, most of these laws provide few—if any—mechanisms for enforcement. For instance, the federal Password Protection Act of 2012, if passed in its current form, would allow agencies in the executive government to exempt any position that involved access to classified information. Classified is a loose word, and over 4 million federal employees and contractors with security clearances could be forced to give up their passwords to their government employers.[147]

Establishing Guidelines for On-the-Job Social Networking

Laws can't do it all, and HR is also often responsible for creating and enforcing guidelines and policies related to social networking. Interactive applications such as Facebook, LinkedIn, and Pinterest, as well as applications such as Twitter, have given rise to mass networking for both personal and professional purposes. To date, there have been few studies about how much time employees spend on social networking. However, the perception is that as the number of people or groups in an individual's network increases, the more time that individual will spend during the workday reading postings and updates that have nothing to do with work. Some organizations have banned access to these tools at work because of violations of trust in the working relationship (e.g., spending time with friends on the network instead of working).

The vast majority of social networking sites were originally designed with a focus on *personal* (rather than professional) social networks. LinkedIn is slightly different in that it began as a professional tool, but there is no regulation for how individuals use this site. Thus, there are often as many personal notices posted on LinkedIn as there are professional ones. Given these observations, organizations must carefully weigh the advantages and disadvantages of engaging social media for business use. As with any technology, clear communication about company rules and guidelines and the provision of appropriate training will lend itself to the effective use of social networking applications.

Discussion Questions

1. Imagine that your instructor has organized your class to work in teams to plan a fundraiser for a local not-for-profit group. There are four teams of six to eight people, and you are all expected to work virtually. Given what you have learned in this chapter, design a virtual organization within which all teams and their individual members can accomplish this task.

2. Try to find out information about the policies for employees use of social networking sites at a familiar virtual organization. If you were charged with creating guidelines for the use of social networking sites at work in this organization, would you make any changes in these rules to empower or restrict social networking at work? In general, what would your top five rules for use of social networking sites at work be?

Objective 11.10
Describe how to work effectively in a virtual world.

10. What Can We All Do to Work Most Effectively in a Virtual World?

Communication and relationships are at the heart of virtual work. Some people even say that effective communication should be the primary focus when it comes to understanding and designing virtual work processes. All relationships require effort to build and maintain, and virtual relationships are no exception. This means you have to consciously attend to how you relate to people and they to you in the virtual work space. In this section we will look at how you can build healthy relationships virtually and how you can help virtual teams be successful.

Virtual Relationships Are *Real* Relationships

Factors that are critical when working in an office, store, or factory are just as important when working virtually: mutual trust, respect, morale, constructive influencing behaviors skills, and dealing with conflict effectively. This can be tricky in the virtual world, however, because face-to-face meetings where we have the benefit of nonverbal communication and social cues are often missing. Media that allow for visualization, such as Web conferencing and videoconferencing, address some of these issues, but not completely.

To be most effective when working virtually, you must focus on the development of skills that allow you to build effective working relationships—often with people you rarely see or may not ever meet. It is important to develop communication norms that create a common way of signaling and interpreting relational information, such as emotions.

Humans are emotional beings. Our brains are physically wired to pick up subtle cues that help us interpret others' emotions.[148] Emotions are key to communicating, collaborating, accomplishing goals, and creating an environment in which people can be at their best. In short, emotions are central to building effective relationships at work. So is good communication—virtual or face-to-face. It helps to make communication norms explicit in advance and to establish procedures for reconciling differences in communication practices that emerge as you work across personal, cultural, and professional boundaries. Some of these can be quite simple and straightforward. For example, an agreement about what sort of information can be shared over e-mail (e.g., project planning documents, factual information, meeting details) versus what should be communicated either over the phone or in person (e.g., serious difficulties with the project, interpersonal conflicts, or misunderstandings about who is responsible, accountable, and so forth) can be extremely helpful.

Some norms that need to be discussed are more sensitive and difficult to agree on than others. For example, when people are in different time zones, whose schedule dictates when meetings will be held? Whose schedule is most important and who has to accommodate? Finally, since virtual teams do not have a designated formal leader, all team members therefore need to understand and agree on who is leading what, when, and how.

Whether your leadership is formal or informal, you need to understand how to lead virtual teams. This process draws on your communication competencies in different ways than leading more traditional work teams.

Taking Charge of Virtual Teams

The very nature of virtual work and virtual teams means that more of us will have to take on leadership more often, and in many cases without a formal role or designation. You need to be well versed in the variety of communication tools, strategies, and techniques that are needed for virtual collaboration. However, technological mastery is only one factor in providing leadership or even being a member of a virtual team. Other critical factors involve the same kind of leadership competencies that are important in face-to-face interactions.[149]

Virtual teams need good leaders. They need members to be open to feedback, willing to adapt their usual approach to work, and able to manage the stress and frustration that sometimes go along with virtual work. You can lead virtual teams more effectively if you actively create explicit norms for communication, attempt to decrease ambiguity, encourage interaction, and help the team collectively develop goals.[150] In fact, some scholars have found a strong relationship between team members' perceptions of the quality of the goal-setting process and project managers' perception of team effectiveness.[151]

You can also help a virtual team be more effective by empowering people and delegating management functions.[152] This approach casts the leader more in the role of a facilitator than that of the traditional manager.[153] One study that examined 35 virtual teams found that the less face-to-face contact there was among team members, the more crucial empowerment was to team effectiveness.[154]

Managers of virtual teams will find that self-management, influence, and inspirational leadership are critical competencies for team members. So, what can you do to encourage development of these behaviors? First, you can help team members create a connection both interpersonally and with the task at hand. For example, one study of 29 global virtual teams that communicated strictly by e-mail for six weeks indicated that three factors were central to the teams' success: (1) initial messages that were social and allowed members to get to know one another well, (2) establishment of clear roles for each member, and (3) establishment of the norm that all communications during the project should be positive and action oriented.[155]

Working virtually is fun and exciting. The rewards that come from focusing on one's own skills as a leader while simultaneously empowering others are huge—not just for you, but also for the team members and the organization.

Discussion Questions

1. From your own experiences, create a list of "dos and don'ts" for how to manage relationships virtually.

2. Compare the leadership skills needed in face-to-face versus virtual teams. What similarities or differences can you identify? How can you make virtual team members feel empowered, connected, and grounded by well-defined norms?

11. A Final Word on Working in a Virtual World

ICTs have changed how we work and live. These technologies are also changing our world's societies. Thomas Friedman's popular book *The World Is Flat* addresses how people across the globe are dramatically more interconnected now than ever before, which has, in turn, resulted in greater opportunities for intense cooperation and competition.

The metaphor of the "flat world" centers on the idea that computers and telecommunications have vastly increased the competitive advantage for people in developing nations while simultaneously decreasing the competitive advantage for people in developed nations. This "flattening" marks the beginning of a global revolution. Many believe that these changes will occur so quickly and have such far-reaching effects that the world in the twenty-first century will look nothing like the world we knew in the twentieth century.[156]

However, while more people around the world have the potential to participate and contribute, we can also see a disturbing sociological trend emerging. The term **digital divide** refers to the lack of access to, and lack of skill in using, Internet and communication technologies among various underprivileged groups and residents of lesser developed countries. In Cambodia, for instance, there is only one Internet user per 200 people, whereas in Canada, more than 75 out of every 100 people use the Internet, indicating a strong digital divide that leaves Cambodians potentially unprepared for work opportunities that require skill in modern technologies.[157] Even in industrialized countries that are quick to embrace digital technologies, older employees may find it difficult to develop competitive skills in these technologies. Other groups that face socioeconomic and educational challenges may also find it challenging, if not impossible, to develop the critical computer-based skills required for many jobs in an information society.[158]

The changes we are seeing in our societies can either support the development of a more just and equitable world—or not. It's up to us. Human beings—and their knowledge, creativity, and passion—are still, and always will be, at the heart of personal, organizational, and societal success.

Digital divide
The lack of access to and lack of skill in using Internet communication technologies among various underprivileged groups and residents of lesser developed countries.

EXPERIENCING Leadership

LEADING IN A GLOBAL WORLD
The ICT Revolution

Millions of people now have access to communication networks that were unheard of 40 years ago. In fact, these networks made the revolution known as The Arab Spring possible. By using social networking sites, activists organized and publicized the unprecedented protests that gave rise to this movement, which has seen governments in Egypt, Libya, Yemen, and Tunisia fall; regimes in Syria and Bahrain clash with the opposition; and leaders in Jordan, Saudi Arabia, and the United Arab Emirates offer more benefits to their people. Social media has unquestionably played a critical role in mobilizing, empowering, and influencing change.

1. In a group or on your own, research how social media and ICTs are enabling sweeping social changes. Organizations like Witness.org, Wiser.org, SierraClub.org, and the GlobalOneness Project are good starting points.
2. What future changes or revolutions can you envision happening as a result of ICTs such as social media and IT networks?
3. How do you think ICTs and social media have affected an "awareness revolution" in unethical and irresponsible business practices and environmental and social issues?

LEADING WITH EMOTIONAL INTELLIGENCE
I Can't Live without My Smartphone

Sociotechnical systems theory helps us to see that both technology *and* people must be considered in relationships and at work. Organizations need to recognize that if strong, healthy work relationships are to be built and maintained, development of emotional intelligence competencies in their people is critical. This is especially important in light of the argument that the rise of technology leads to the decline of face-to-face interpersonal experiences and skills.

1. Make a list of the five to eight ICTs that you rely on the most in order of importance to your day-to-day functioning.
2. Identify three ways that each ICT helps promote emotional intelligence.
3. Next, make a list of three ways that each of those same ICTs hinder or inhibit emotional intelligence. As you make your lists, consider the following:
   - What value does this communication technology add to my life?

- If I were not using this particular ICT, how else could I send and receive information?
- What can I do to improve self-awareness and relationship management through ICTs?
- What do I gain in interpersonal communication from ICTs and what do I lose?

LEADING WITH CRITICAL THINKING SKILLS
Becoming a Cyber Sleuth

Ever since the Internet has become a global tool for sharing information and data, countless organizations have gone virtual. They rely on ICTs to coordinate employees and customers as they produce, distribute, or provide goods or services. As the virtual world of business and personal data has expanded, so, too, has cybercrime.

According to a 2011 Symantec study, hackers and cybercriminals have cost the global economy an estimated $114 billion annually.[159] Whether from malware (malicious software), phishing scams, network downtime, or identity theft, the virtual world of retail sales, banking, and finance is exposed to many of the same criminal threats apparent in the real world. Still, there is tremendous confusion about what should be regulated, how it should be regulated, and by whom.

1. Become your own cyber sleuth. Research the top five cybercrimes or scams that are currently a threat to business and personal security. Write a short description of each threat and what, if anything, is being done to address it.
2. Next research the group Anonymous, the Internet "hacktivist" group whose unofficial slogan is "The corrupt fear us, the honest support us." How are groups like Anonymous forcing governments to rethink their own security?
3. How is Anonymous forcing businesses, like the recording and film industries, to rethink their online strategies in terms of serving their own business interests while, at the same time, respecting the rights of the public?
4. Discuss the following:
   - What is your own personal view of hacktivism?
   - Does it provide the same service as a consumer watchdog organization, or is it just another cybercriminal movement?

ETHICAL LEADERSHIP
Your Password, Please

Some employers and schools have made it standard practice to review potential applicants' Facebook profiles. In some cases, they have gone even further: They demand that applicants hand over their passwords so they can view individuals' restricted profiles. Currently, the federal government is reviewing the legality of the practice because a person's age, sexual orientation, religion, and political affiliation may be just some of the private information disclosed. Whatever the outcome of this investigation in the United States, it is worth noting that this practice also exists elsewhere in the world.

1. Suppose your best friend has applied for a job with your employer. She has a very strong chance of getting the job. However, HR is requesting that she hand over her personal Facebook password as a part of the hiring process. You know there are several playful yet unflattering posts on her page from you that are about your manager and your business

unit. Your best friend really wants and needs this job. You are afraid that if HR reads your posts, you will lose your job. What do you do?

2. In a group or on your own, research the issue and discuss the consequences of schools and employers seeking applicants and new hires' personal passwords.

3. In the above scenario, discuss what your options are. Do you tell HR? Do you say nothing, hoping not to draw attention to the posts? Do you research your legal rights?

4. Discuss whether the practice is ethical. Do some basic social media legal rights research. Does this practice violate the first, fourth, and fifth amendments to the Constitution?

KEY TERMS

Technology, *p. 382*

Information and communication technologies (ICTs), *p. 382*

Sociotechnical systems theory, *p. 386*

Industrial Revolution, *p. 387*

Age of Enlightenment, *p. 387*

Second Industrial Revolution, *p. 388*

Third Industrial Revolution, *p. 392*

Internet, *p. 394*

Web 2.0, *p. 395*

Intranet, *p. 395*

Extranet, *p. 395*

Cloud computing, *p. 396*

Emoticons, *p. 399*

Groupware, *p. 401*

Virtual team, *p. 405*

Virtual organizations, *p. 408*

Microfinance, *p. 411*

Carbon footprint, *p. 414*

Digital divide, *p. 420*

MyManagementLab

Go to **mymanagementlab.com** for Auto-graded writing questions as well as the following Assisted-graded writing questions:

11-1. Do you believe that people have become overly dependent on ICTs for interpersonal communication or teamwork? Explain your answer in terms of how the use of ICTs impacts people's effectiveness.

11-2. How are cell phones and internet technologies influencing children currently in elementary school? How will this affect their education and their ways of communicating with one another? Are all children affected equally? Why or why not?

11-3. Mymanagementlab Only — comprehensive writing assignment for this chapter.

1. How Are Life and Work Affected by Changes in Technology?

(pp. 382–385)

Objective: Define technology and ICTs, and learn how advances in technologies change life and work.

Summary: Information and communication technologies (ICTs) have changed the way we communicate and live. They have also led to major changes in social structures, in the availability and dissemination of information, and in the way nations develop and industrialize. ICTs dramatically impact business and employees, where tech savvy communication competencies mean the difference between effective and ineffective employees, teams, and leaders. However, technological ability is not the only thing needed for success. Social and emotional intelligence must be employed to help overcome the challenges that ICTs pose.

PLANNING

ORGANIZING

Organizing Human Systems
Chapters 10, 11

CONTROLLING

2. Why Must We Consider Technology *and* People When Working in a Virtual World?

(pp. 385–387)

Objective: Learn about sociotechnical systems theory.

Summary: ICTs are productivity tools; as such, they are only part of an equation in which people are the most important factor. Therefore, both the social and technical characteristics of work must be considered in the effectiveness equation. This is captured in sociotechnical systems theory. According to this theory, if the human side of virtual work is not considered, even the most amazing technology may not help—and could, in fact, harm—an organization's results.

3. How Did Technology Affect Life and Work during the Industrial Revolutions? (pp. 387–394)

Objective: Explain how technology impacted people during the Industrial Revolutions.

Summary: Technological developments have been a key to social progression since prehistoric times. Advances in technology during the First Industrial Revolution dramatically changed work and life for people in England, the United States, and portions of continental Europe. The Second Industrial Revolution brought electricity, automobiles, and mass production and further moved some Western societies away from their rural, cottage-industry roots to an urban consumer culture. It is important to note that many non-Western regions that are important players in the modern world were largely left out of these revolutions, for reasons that impact how they are industrializing and progressing today. The current Third Industrial Revolution is gradually replacing manufacturing jobs with professional and service jobs, is generating international business networks, and is creating a kind of alternate route to industrialization for those regions that were not involved in the previous revolutions.

4. How Have Computing and Telecommunication Technologies Evolved? (pp. 394–397)

Objective: Understand how computing and telecommunication technologies have evolved.

Summary: Computing as we know it today started out small—with just two computers linked to each other via the earliest form of the Internet. Today, technology is paving the way for continuous and rapid development and new ways to communicate, live, and work. Modern telecommunications have also seen rapid changes that have led to new ways of working.

5. How Do People Use ICTs at Work? (pp. 397–403)

Objective: Describe how people use ICTs at work.

Summary: Most people use ICTs in both their personal and work lives. Conferencing hardware and software, groupware, and social networks are examples of ICTs that promote collaborative working relationships between individuals and groups in remote locations. It is important to remember, however, that communication via ICTs is more limited than face-to-face communication and can open the door for misinterpretation of emotion and intent.

Tips for Using E-mail Effectively at Work

Sending E-mail
- Use clear, informative subject lines.
- Avoid mass e-mails. Be judicious with the "Reply All" button and include only those people who need to see the message.
- Assume that management will read your e-mail.
- Assume that your e-mail will be seen by people outside of your organization.
- Do not send inappropriate or critical messages.

Receiving and Interpreting E-mail
- Look at subject lines to see whether you want to open an e-mail.
- If your organization has not already installed them, use e-mail filters to avoid spending time deleting spam.
- If you receive an e-mail that causes you to have a strong emotional reaction, do not respond immediately. Calm down, reflect on the message, and then respond appropriately—which may or may not be via e-mail.
- Don't let e-mail pile up: Answer it, move it to an appropriate folder, or delete it.
- Purge your inbox folder regularly.

6. How Is Virtual Work Conducted? (pp. 403–407)

Objective: Learn where and how virtual work is conducted.

Summary: All virtual work is conducted in three spaces—shared mental and social space, virtual settings, and physical space. Telecommuting is one example of a virtual work structure that involves performance of essential work functions outside of traditional offices via ICTs. Hybrid work involves individuals who use traditional physical spaces, like offices, and also work virtually. Finally, virtual teams connect individuals in different locations with one another using an agreed-on mix of ICTs to complete project- and task-based work, and must pay special attention to building trust and accountability among team members.

Emoticons Communicate Emotions via Written Communications

	Facial Expression	Emoticon Text	Emotion
1.		:-)	Happy
2.		:-(	Sad
3.		>:-<	Angry
4.		:-|	Disappointed
5.		:-$	Embarrassed
6.		:-P	Joking with tongue sticking out
7.		:-D	Laughing
8.		:-/	Mixed up
9.		:->	Sarcastic
10.		:-O	Surprised

7. What Is a Virtual Organization? (pp. 407–413)

Objective: Learn about virtual organizations.

Summary: Virtual organizations are made up of diverse people and networks that are geographically dispersed and rely on ICTs to share information and coordinate activities. Many virtual organizations tend to be flatter than traditional organizations in order to maximize the rapid exchange of information. Some virtual organizations have only a small physical presence and complete a majority of their business transactions online. Online storefronts, auction sites, and business portals are a few common examples of virtual organizations. Many industries have been increasing their virtual activities for many years, as can be seen in the banking industry, consumer sales, and education.

8. What Are the Challenges of Working in a Virtual World? (pp. 413–416)

Objective: Understand the challenges of working in a virtual world.

Summary: Some aspects of the virtual world make our work faster and simpler; other aspects introduce stress and complications that must be managed. One of these is the constant accessibility of workers and managers through laptops and smart phones at the expense of their personal time. Another challenge is information overload. Finally, we must manage knowledge effectively and appreciate that people generate knowledge and determine the flow of information through ICTs.

10. What Can We All Do to Work Most Effectively in a Virtual World?
(pp. 418–419)

Objective: Describe how to work effectively in a virtual world.

Summary: Working in the virtual world requires you to build relationship skills that help you forge bonds with people you may never meet. An important first step in this process is appreciating the fact that virtual relationships are real relationships that involve real people with real emotions that must be attended to. You also must establish communication norms in advance that clarify the types of information you will share via particular communication channels. Finally, you must be prepared to lead your virtual team and be mindful of the ways in which virtual communication requires you to alter your approach to leadership and collaboration.

9. What Can HR Do to Support Virtual Workers? (pp. 416–418)

Objective: List steps HR can take to support virtual work.

Summary: HR professionals in many organizations are involved in two key aspects of controlling virtual communication: understanding personal privacy laws and creating guidelines that support organizational members' use of technology. Privacy is often difficult to balance in the workplace as individuals may use company property—computers and cell phones specifically—to stay in contact with friends outside of the office and take care of personal needs. A related issue that HR often has to manage is the creation of rules for the use of social networking and other non-business Web sites during work hours. Both of these issues require HR professionals to carefully weigh employees' rights and the importance of such communication to employees and the organization as a whole.

11. A Final Word on Working in a Virtual World (p. 420)

Summary: Computers and telecommunications have impacted modern work more than any other innovation, and have led to great competitive and cooperative opportunities. However, you must remember that ICTs are not a substitute for human knowledge, creativity, or passion. Additionally, some nations, socioeconomic groups, and age groups experience a digital divide, or knowledge gap, when it comes to using ICTs. As a society, it is important to be mindful of this divide and strive to overcome socioeconomic, educational, and age-related challenges in the virtual world.

CHAPTER 12

Organizational Controls:

People, Processes, Quality, and Results

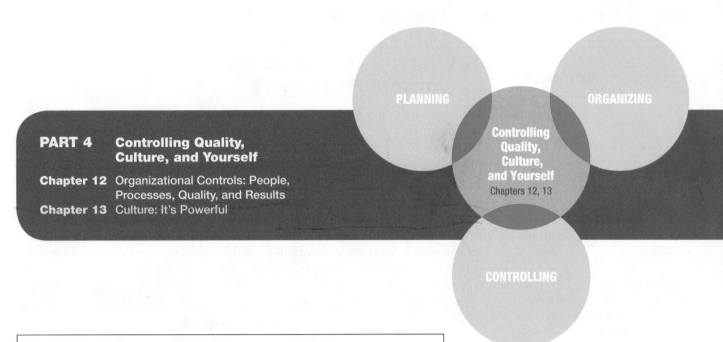

Controlling
Quality,
Culture,
and Yourself
Chapters 12, 13

PLANNING

ORGANIZING

CONTROLLING

MyManagementLab™

⭐ **Improve Your Grade!**

Over 10 million students improved their results using the Pearson MyLabs. Visit **mymanagementlab.com** for simulations, tutorials, and end-of-chapter problems.

Chapter Outline

Chapter Objectives

12.1 Define organizational control.

12.2 Understand which historical perspectives help us understand control in organizations.

12.3 Describe common control systems.

12.4 Understand conventions and forces that guide the organizational control processes.

12.5 List the typical steps in the control process.

12.6 Assess what companies should control.

12.7 Learn what HR can do to help control for effectiveness and efficiency.

12.8 Learn what we can all do to be effective and efficient at work.

Customer relationship management (CRM)
A customer-centric approach to business with the aim of implementing a customer intimacy strategy or establishing a customer-friendly brand image—or both.

Control process
An organization's systems for establishing standards to achieve goals, monitoring and measuring performance, comparing performance to standards, and taking corrective action as necessary.

1. What Is the Organizational Control Process?

When you walk into a store, you may be greeted by an employee and asked if you need help. This isn't just politeness; it's an organizational control process known as **customer relationship management**, or CRM. This customer-centric approach to business aims to create customer intimacy or establish a customer-friendly brand image—or both. Maybe there's also a security guard at the door—an obvious part of the inventory control process. The cash register, which likely records inventory as it is sold, is another control mechanism. If you're in a shoe store, associates may carry devices that signal to stockroom staff which shoes you'd like to try on. This isn't just a convenience; it helps manage stock. Behind the scenes, there are job descriptions, accountants, rules, and a code of ethics. These are all parts of the store's organizational control processes. A **control process** includes systems for establishing standards to achieve goals, monitoring and measuring performance, comparing performance to standards, and taking corrective action as necessary.

Controls are created and used to monitor and regulate how an organization performs in relation to its strategic goals and objectives. Controls are also put in place to ensure that people behave in an ethical manner and obey the law. Controls are typically applied to employee behaviors, financial processes, resource allocation and use, customer experience, risk management, and quality.

Control systems protect and help companies, their customers, and communities. Companies often pay particular attention to risk management and risk analysis. Unfortunately, risk analysis control systems can fail, resulting in the destruction of a great deal of wealth. In 2008, this happened at Société Générale, a major European bank and financial services provider, when "rogue" hedge-fund trader Jérôme Kerviel lost billions of dollars investing in derivatives.[1] As a hedger, buying opposite more senior partners, trading limits should have been applied, but Kerviel had invested many billions of dollars, which he had hidden by making fake trade orders that balanced each of the real orders that he had placed. Whenever the fake trades were questioned, Kerviel would just say it was a mistake and then cancel the trade, which he would replace with another transaction. He avoided detection for years. Kerviel's activity finally became known when one of his trading positions was flagged by the company's control system as going over his trading limit. The company uncovered nearly $50 billion in exposure, more than the entire market capitalization of the bank. Over the next several days, Société Générale attempted to recoup its losses as quickly as it could, ultimately contributing to the financial panic that gripped Europe during the stock market crash of 2008. Société Générale has been eager to describe the losses as nothing more than isolated and exceptional, but such descriptions do little to explain why control systems failed to detect the rogue activity sooner (■ **EXHIBIT 12.1**).

Several years later, in 2012, the U.S.-based financial services company JP Morgan reported a loss due to bad trades of an estimated $2 billion. This amount was soon revised upward to $4 billion, and later to $5.8 billion, with some observers estimating that the losses could reach billions higher.[2] All of these losses have been attributed to the trading of credit default swaps, the derivatives that were at the heart of the implosion at Bear Stearns and AIG. The trader in this instance, nicknamed "The London Whale," operated out of the company's London office and made gigantic trades that went horribly wrong. Similar to Société Générale, JP Morgan attempted to downplay the significance of the losses by describing media reports as a "tempest in a teapot."[3] However, JP Morgan's CEO soon publicly reported that the company's Chief Investment Office would no longer trade derivatives.

■ **EXHIBIT 12.1**
What would you do if you found an easy—but possibly unethical—way to make money for your clients?

Source: Visions of America, LLC/Alamy

You now have an idea about what can happen when controls fail. In most situations, controls are used to prevent disasters *and* improve performance. In this chapter, you will learn about the historical perspectives that influence the control processes currently used in organizations, as well as the kinds of things organizations tend to control today. We will give special attention to several popular quality control processes, including business process reengineering, Total Quality Management, Six Sigma, and Lean Management. You will also learn about several common models of organizational control, including one that is very familiar: bureaucratic control. Next, you'll investigate typical steps in the control process, as well as the way quality and quantity of goods and services are typically controlled in organizations. We will also explore a very important topic: how organizational structures, processes, and legislation support controls and ethics. Finally, the chapter concludes with a discussion of how HR can support control processes in organizations, along with a look at what we all can do to ensure that our performance—and others' contributions—are outstanding. Throughout this chapter, we will explore how people can and must behave ethically, even when controls aren't present.

Discussion Questions

1. Think of an organization you know well, such as a club, a team, or your workplace. How does this organization control behavior? Resources? Finances?

2. Have you ever been part of a workplace that lacked sufficient controls? How did this impact the organization? How did you and other team members respond?

---

2. Which Historical Perspectives Help Us Understand Control in Organizations?

> **Objective 12.2**
> Understand which historical perspectives help us understand control in organizations.

Many early theorists and practitioners can help us understand management and control systems today. This section will focus on several of these individuals. It will also take a look at best practice in a compelling *Leadership Perspective*.

In his *Economic and Philosophic Manuscripts,* written in 1844, German philosopher Karl Marx first elaborated his theory of alienation, arguing that laborers do not have any control over their work and that they lose control of their lives in a capitalistic system that forces them to produce goods and services for others (■ **EXHIBIT 12.2**). Marx asserted that in such situations, work is meaningless because the worker has no say in how to accomplish the owner's objectives. Therefore, according to Marx, workers do not gain any personal satisfaction from their accomplishments.[4]

Thinking back to the horrid factory conditions prevalent during the mid-nineteenth century, it's easy to see how Marx came to these conclusions. In Marx's view, management really *did* control workers' lives. Little or no attention was paid to workers' physical needs beyond what was minimally necessary for them to get the job done, and virtually no attention was given to their feelings, goals, or aspirations. It is not surprising that concerns about the relationship between workers and factory owners swept across the industrialized world, with the study of management emerging as one of the results. Indeed, during this period, several early management theorists—notably Frederick Taylor, Elton Mayo, and Mary Parker Follett—played particularly prominent roles in setting the stage for how work and workers would be managed in organizations for years to come.

Source: North Wind Picture Archives/Alamy

Scientific management
An approach that involves organizing work for maximum efficiency.

Frederick Taylor and Scientific Management

Frederick W. Taylor (1856–1915) was an engineer who made a case for redesigning work processes for greater efficiency by studying the relationship between people and the tasks they performed. Known as the "Father of Scientific Management," Taylor also promoted the idea that management should be viewed as an academic discipline. **Scientific management** is an approach that involves organizing work for maximum efficiency.

Taylor argued that all aspects of society were riddled with waste and inefficiency, and that organizations could be improved if experts studied and determined the best way to carry out work. Accordingly, he focused on how work could be broken down into manageable tasks, and how these tasks could be broken down into discrete actions, so that both time and motion could be managed more efficiently. Operating from this point of view, Taylor proposed four principles of scientific management:[5]

1. Develop a science for each element of work.
2. Scientifically select and train all workers.
3. Ensure that all work is being done in accordance with the scientific method (i.e., that techniques are developed to maximize efficiency based on observation and experimentation).
4. Divide work between managers and workers. Managers must scientifically plan the work, and workers must carry it out.

Stories about how Taylor applied these principles are legendary. For example, when studying how men shoveled coal, Taylor noticed that if the shovel blade was designed to hold what an "average" worker could lift, that worker could be more efficient and move more coal each day. Taylor drew many such conclusions as he consulted to many organizations about workplace efficiency. However, because Taylor's clients were company owners and managers, it is not surprising that his findings tended to support management's desires to find ways for people to do more with less.[6]

Despite questionable research and findings, the efficiency movement caught on and even came to be called "Taylorism." Some say that the efficiency movement went far beyond organizations and has affected countless aspects of the way we live. Kitchens, for example, are designed so that minimum steps and effort are required as the cook moves between the stove, sink, and refrigerator.

Although it is true that Taylor's work has had a profound impact on how we work and live, it is important to mention that even during his lifetime, Taylor was at the center of a number of controversies. Most of these controversies centered on many people's belief that Taylor's approach to work design focused on efficiency at any cost—even when the cost involved harming workers. With regard to Taylor's coal-shoveling observation, for instance, many people suspected that few human beings could actually lift the amount of weight Taylor recommended for very long.

Although Taylor certainly has an important place in the history of management, his theories aren't necessarily a good fit for the twenty-first-century workplace. Present-day workplaces and employees are profoundly different from the factories and manual laborers of the late 1800s and early 1900s. In today's knowledge economy, efficiency equations rarely involve something as simple as changing the shape of a shovel. Also, in the current service economy, efficiency is only part of the effectiveness equation.

Scientific management is not nearly robust enough a theory for today's organizations. However, it is still the basis for many of the control processes seen in modern companies. Total Quality Management, Six Sigma, and Lean Management are just a few examples of current methods that incorporate aspects of Taylor's principles. Each of these methods will be discussed in depth later in the chapter. But first, let's explore two other early approaches to the relationship between management, employees, and work processes: those proposed by Elton Mayo and Mary Parker Follett.

Elton Mayo and the Hawthorne Studies

In comparison to Taylor, Elton Mayo championed a different approach to management that focused less on tasks and work processes and more on the relationship between managers and workers. Mayo is considered to be one of the founders of the human relations movement, which started around the beginning of the twentieth century and emphasized placing people, interpersonal relationships, and group behavior at the center of workplace studies.

Mayo is best known for a series of experiments conducted at the Western Electric Company between 1924 and 1932, commonly called the Hawthorne Studies. These studies involved a series of research projects demonstrating that when workers perceived that management cared about them and/or when they felt they were getting special treatment, both morale and productivity improved. In the earliest of the Hawthorne Studies, certain physical conditions (e.g., lighting) were altered and changes in employee productivity were monitored. The results revealed that lighting itself actually had very little effect on productivity, unless it became too dark for the workers to see at all. What did have an effect on productivity and morale was the workers' belief that management cared about them and their working conditions, and that they were somehow special. Subsequent studies found that an employee's work group also had an effect on productivity, because social pressure and group norms dictated acceptable levels of productivity and even people's attitudes about work and management.[7]

These findings are relevant today, and the term *Hawthorne effect* is still used to describe the improvement in productivity and morale that occurs when management pays attention to people. The Hawthorne Studies put the relationship between employees and managers firmly at the center of the organizational success equation. In the wake of these studies, more and more scholars began to make the case that to increase productivity, managers and leaders must be educated about how to motivate people and create environments that make employees feel special and cared for. Scholars also began to focus on how managers could become more adept at creating work groups with behavioral norms that support productivity and positive attitudes. The Hawthorne Studies legitimized common sense: It makes good business sense to attend to workers' feelings and factors that affect how they think about their work. It also makes good sense to support the development of group norms that encourage productivity and high morale.

Mary Parker Follett: Control Is More Than Telling People What to Do

As the Hawthorne Studies suggested, controlling people's behavior involves far more than simply telling people what to do or enhancing physical conditions in the workplace. This perspective is closely linked to the work of yet another highly influential theorist: Mary Parker Follett.

Follett is considered by many management experts to be a visionary in the fields of human relations, democratic organization, and management. Her work focused on the important relationship between leaders and employees, the impact of groups on people's behavior, conflict management, and the role of informal leadership in the workplace. Her outstanding contributions in the 1920s were ahead of their time. Decades later, famous management author Peter Drucker called Follett his guru.[8] Her work continues to receive widespread attention and acclaim.

Follett's writings explored the interdependent relationships between employees, leaders, and organizations. She believed that organizational results are an outcome of the interplay between people, systems, processes, and organizational culture. Follett also believed that the best people to solve problems are those closest to and most familiar with the issues.

Human relations movement
A movement that started around the beginning of the twentieth century and emphasized placing people, interpersonal relationships, and group behavior at the center of workplace studies.

Hawthorne Studies
A series of research projects demonstrating that when workers perceived that management cared about them and/or when they felt they were getting special treatment, both morale and productivity increased.

While Follett's work was largely ignored by the organizational researchers of her time, its importance is no longer overlooked. Follett paved the way for some of the most important theories and models of *our* time, including employee participation, engagement, and decentralized decision making. These processes are now used in many organizational control systems that focus on quality, which we will discuss later in the chapter.

Although the importance of employee participation is obvious, many managers still make most decisions and try to force people to do their jobs. We know, however, that Follett's position holds merit: Power and decision making should be fluid and should go to the people who have the most knowledge and ability, not necessarily the most senior people in the hierarchy. When it came to control in the workplace, Follett suggested what must have been a revolutionary way of looking at power: Managers should emphasize "power with" as opposed to "power over" people, thus empowering people at all levels of an organization. Further, Follett believed that empowerment would both enable and motivate the employees closest to a problem to find the best solution possible.[9]

The Human Touch

Mary Parker Follett set the stage for modern theories of leadership and organizational behavior. Many other theorists followed her lead, and one clear finding from their decades of research is that leaders, managers, and employees have interdependent relationships that benefit from certain types of controls. Specifically, the best types of controls are those that focus on people *and* processes *and* results. As you will see in this chapter, the best controls can take the form of rules, guidelines, and measurement systems, and they always consider people and behavior.

Many effective forms of organizational control are linked to the field of psychology. For example, the command and control approach to managing people has been studied and critiqued as an ineffective way to build organizational climates that foster high performance. The phrase "command and control" is often used to describe an approach to management that relies on powerful managers who dictate what needs to be done and obedient employees who do what they are told. Research has shown that outside of life-threatening situations (e.g., when a fire breaks out), this approach is not useful because it does not result in maximum performance over time. In fact, organizations that employ this approach tend to breed dissonance and dissent. Negativity permeates the walls, and employees feel guarded and even despondent—which means they don't perform at their best.[10]

Beginning with the works of Elton Mayo and Mary Parker Follett and continuing through today, research shows that organizational climate and culture (sometimes referred to as the "environment") also a profound effect on people and organizational results.[11] In particular, resonant environments that employees and customers experience as positive, inclusive, and focused on excellence have been found to be powerful drivers of people's behavior and effectiveness. These kinds of environments are often empowering, which means that people are vitally involved in how work gets done, as well as in how effectiveness and efficiency are monitored and controlled.[12] These environments tend to be places in which people feel supported, valued, and recognized for their contributions.[13]

Resonant work climates and cultures that embody the "spirit" of an organization and support empowerment significantly impact productivity in a positive direction. In cultures that support positive attitudes and productivity, the people who do the actual work are often the ones to create appropriate controls to improve work processes and systems.[14] Leaders have a special role when it comes to creating resonant environments—especially when times are tough. It isn't as hard as one might think to create an environment in which everyone can be at their best, solve problems together,

and jointly control quality. As you learned in Chapter 2, leaders who are self-aware and who know how to engage their own and others' emotions can create environments where people can be at their best. And being at our best means doing what is needed for our teams and the organization—without violating ethics or the law.

Jane Luciano, Vice President of Global Learning and Organizational Development at Bristol-Meyers Squibb (BMS), is a leader who makes it her primary focus to create a resonant environment in her global team. Bristol-Myers Squibb is a leader in the pharmaceutical industry—one that experienced a very difficult period some years back. The company began remaking itself as a leader in biopharma, leaving behind aspects of the more traditional pharmaceutical company model. They tightened everything: decision making processes, research and development programs, and people's job scopes and responsibilities. These moves, which began a few years before major competitors made similar ones, were not easy. But, taking a radically new approach to the market, and developing a strong research pipeline will enable the company to weather the storm that the industry is currently facing in the United States and worldwide.

Leadership Perspective

● **Jane Luciano**
Vice President of Global Learning and Organizational Development for Bristol-Myers Squibb
"Face the unknown with courage"

Jane Luciano is a principled person who cares deeply about others, and when all is said and done, this may be the highest praise of all. She works very hard to do the right thing by her team, her colleagues, the company, the environment and the patients Bristol-Myers Squibb serves, including the poor and disadvantaged who often cannot access drugs and treatment. Jane has a *systems perspective*—she sees everything in the context of the bigger picture. That's one of the competencies that makes a big difference when it comes to making ethical decisions. Jane says this about principled and resonant leadership:

It's a fascinating time to be alive. Everything changes constantly—it's almost as if we have a new generation every five years or so. We're working with people from different countries, cultures, religions, everything. Wave after wave of technology revolutionizes our industry and how we work. Markets are moving from developed countries to developing

countries. And while you might still be making most of your money in your traditional, Western markets, the tide is most definitely turning.

There is so much unknown! Many people are so caught up in the present that they simply don't see the future. Or they are truly closed. But you, as a leader, <u>have</u> to think about what the future will bring—and the future isn't far off. It's essentially the day after tomorrow. Ask yourself, "Where's the world going? Where do I fit in? Where will our business fit? How can I prepare myself as a leader? What is the right thing to do?"

Nothing is totally clear and in this kind of environment it's easy to make mistakes. Asking the questions is a good start. Then, you need to be open and curious about the answers. Be prepared to ask for feedback on your opinions and your actions. Seek it out. Find those people who are connectors and integrators. They are an underutilized resource in most organizations, and you can learn a lot from them about the <u>right</u> course of action.

You also need to lead up, down, and across. It's no longer enough to just lead your team. You need to influence in every direction, so everyone has the information they need to make the <u>right</u> decisions. Sometimes, this means you will have to say what's unpopular. You have to speak truth to power. You need to share patterns that you see, that others don't. For example, "How will one small decision affect our patients? People and parts of the business far away? The environment?" Bringing this level of consciousness—systems thinking—helps all of us do the right thing.

All of this takes courage, which might be the most important thing of all. There are a lot of risks when you lead from the front. But, you have to walk on the edge. If you do, and if you ask yourself, "What's the right thing to do, from all possible angles?" you will be the kind of leader we need today. The added benefit of thinking this way and doing the right thing: people will trust you and follow.

Source: Personal interview with Jane Luciano conducted by Annie McKee, 2012.

What's interesting about Bristol-Myers Squibb is that during the period of fundamentally rethinking the company and making big changes, ethics and sustainability moved to the top of the list, rather than becoming an afterthought as they often do in times of strife. Senior executives and talented, passionate leaders like Jane Luciano added "doing the right thing" for the company *and* for the world into the equation for every single decision. Jane has excellent advice for all of us about what it takes to be a strong, ethical leader in our competitive business environment.

As you can clearly see in Jane Luciano's words, when it comes to organizational controls, people matter most of all. The best control systems in the world can be completely ineffective if people and organizational cultures drive toward parochial thinking or unethical choices. In Chapter 13, you will learn more about organizational culture and its role in the control process. For now, as you read about what organizations try to control and the sometimes complex systems that have been designed to control people and processes, remember that people are at the center of it all. Ultimately, no matter the rules, processes, or possible sanctions, people decide what to do, how to do it, and whether they will do what is best for the organization—and/or what is ethical.

Discussion Questions

1. Have you ever experienced the Hawthorne effect at work or at school? If so, what happened, and how did your manager's or teacher's attention affect your morale and productivity?

2. According to Mary Parker Follett, what is the difference between using "power over" people and "power with" people? Describe a situation in which the "power with" strategy would be more effective.

Objective 12.3
Describe common control systems.

3. What Do Companies Try to Control Today?

Now that you understand what organizational control is and its historical perspectives, it's time to consider what organizations often try to control today. Some things are obvious, like financial performance, employee productivity, and ethical behavior. But how is this done? And what about things like quality and service excellence? As you will see in this section, some controls are actually in conflict with one another—like cost and quality. It costs money to provide quality goods and services, and cutting costs can harm quality.

As this typical conflict demonstrates, all areas of a business are interrelated. An improvement in performance in one area can have a detrimental effect in another area. In 2008, for example, Hershey decided to control costs by replacing cocoa butter with vegetable oil in some of its candy bars. Sales of Almond Joy subsequently dropped, and customers complained. So, in trying to control costs, sales and profitability were lost. After months of declining sales and increasing complaints, Hershey went back to its original recipe for the Almond Joy bar.[15]

Finances, Customer Service, and Quality

In this section, we will examine how businesses often control three important areas: finance, customer service, and quality. To illustrate important points in each section, we'll use the fictitious example of small business owner Tameka Jenkins and her company LearnIT, which creates online educational courses for information technology professionals (■ **EXHIBIT 12.3**). Following this discussion, we will turn to two other areas that leaders can seek to control—ethical behavior and ensuring that their organizations achieve results.

CONTROLLING FINANCIAL PERFORMANCE

Part of what makes a company financially healthy is its managers' and leaders' ability to control expenses and produce profit. To measure how a company is performing financially, there must be financial plans (budgets) and ways of analyzing how money is being earned and spent (profit and loss statements and cash flow analyses). Each of these controls, as well as an interesting and more recent process called *Beyond Budgeting*, is discussed in the following sections.

Financial Controls

Financial controls are used to plan how money is earned and spent, to track financial activities such as costs and revenues, and to provide guidelines to manage expenditures. When considering financial controls, what is most commonly thought of first are things like budgets, which we will discuss next. However, an often-missed topic relates to revenue generation. Many companies have processes in place for tracking, monitoring, and improving revenue-generation activities. For example, there is essentially a whole industry built around software programs that enable employees and companies to track their business development activities. Many programs are available on smartphones and tablets, enabling people to easily monitor interactions with potential and existing customers. Collectively known as Customer Relationship Management (CRM) software, these tools can facilitate client relationships, track progress through customized workflows, and aggregate data for analyzing business development across the organization to identify important patterns that can provide critical insights for strategic decisions.[16]

As previously mentioned, one of the most common financial controls is a budget. A budget is a document that outlines when and how money is spent within a company and who is spending it. In many organizations, budgets are created for the entire company for a specific period of time. Within the company's overall budget, various divisions and departments have their own budgets. For example, a company's HR department will have its own budget that outlines the amount of money it will receive for a given period of time and what it must do with that money. Each departmental budget may be broken down even further to reflect the allocation of funds to specific departmental projects and activities. For example, within the HR department's budget, training and development initiatives may have their own budget, and this will determine how much and what sort of learning activities can be provided to employees.

Accounting professor David Otley argues that budget development should be based on the organization's underlying strategic plan.[17] Assuming that this plan clearly enumerates organizational expectations and objectives, the resulting budget should do the following:

1. Provide a set of expectations for managers.
2. Motivate managers and employees.
3. Promote communication among people and units.[18]

Source: Rommel Canlas/Shutterstock.com

Financial controls
Controls that are used to plan how money is earned and spent, to track financial activities such as costs and revenues, and to provide guidelines to manage expenditures.

Budget
A document that outlines when and how money is spent within a company and who is spending it.

If budgets are well thought out, they can be powerful financial control mechanisms. Of course, managers must sometimes revisit budgets and adapt them in response to unforeseen circumstances, such as changes in the business environment, the emergence of a new competitor, variations in the cost of raw materials, or changes in customer demand.

So, how might Tameka approach the budgeting process at LearnIT? When Tameka started LearnIT, she had a certain amount of money. She had to project what her expenses would be, so she created a budget that defined her expectations for research and development, marketing, office space and utilities, taxes and start-up fees, salaries, and benefits. Tameka thought she would be able to hire the right people for her company at a certain salary level, which was represented in her budget. However, once she began interviewing and offering jobs, she recognized that she would have to pay more than she had anticipated in order to hire the best people. So, Tameka had to revisit her budget to see whether she could decrease the amount of money allocated to another area in order to increase the amount of money allocated to salaries and benefits. Alternatively, Tameka could have chosen to hire fewer employees than originally planned until she had more revenue coming in.

Accounting Controls

In addition to budgets, there are a number of accounting controls that provide documentation of what an organization owes and is owed, as well as its assets and liabilities. Three of the most common accounting controls are the cash flow analysis, the balance sheet, and the profit and loss statement.

A cash flow analysis looks at the money coming in and going out of an organization in a given time frame, either current or projected. The cash flow analysis from LearnIT is depicted in ■ **EXHIBIT 12.4**. This table shows that the company will have

Accounting controls
Controls that provide documentation of what an organization owes and is owed, as well as its assets and liabilities.

Cash flow analysis
A document that looks at the money coming in and going out of an organization in a given time frame, either current or projected.

■ **EXHIBIT 12.4**

Cash Flows for LearnIT		
Cash Flows from (Used in) Operating Activities		
	Line Item	**Totals**
Cash receipts from customers	$250,000	
Cash paid to suppliers and employees	($122,217)	
Cash generated from operations (sum)	$50,000	
Interest paid	($2,000)	
Income taxes paid	($60,000)	
Net cash flows from operating activities		$115,783
Cash Flows from (Used in) Investing Activities		
Proceeds from the sale of equipment	$500	
Loans received	$10,000	
Net cash flows from investing activities		$10,500
Cash Flows from (Used in) Financing Activities		
Dividends paid	($10,000)	
Net cash flows used in financing activities		($10,000)
Cash Flow Totals for the Year		
Net increase in cash and cash equivalents		$116,283
Cash and cash equivalents, beginning of the year		$20,000
Cash and cash equivalents, end of the year		$136,283

■ **EXHIBIT 12.5**

Balance Sheet for LearnIT			
Assets		**Liabilities and Owner's Equity**	
Cash	$136,283	**Liabilities**	
Accounts receivable	$6,200	Notes payable	$36,400
Tools and equipment	$5,000	Accounts payable	$3,994
		Owner's Equity	
		Capital stock	$88,289
		Retained earnings	$18,800
Total Assets	$147,483	*Total Liabilities and Equity*	$147,483

$136,283 in cash on hand at the end of the year. It also shows that LearnIT's largest cash outflow is the money paid to suppliers and employees, and that the company has paid out less money than it has taken in from sales.

A balance sheet provides a snapshot of a company at a particular moment in time, highlighting both its assets and its liabilities. For instance, LearnIT's balance sheet, as depicted in ■ **EXHIBIT 12.5**, shows that the company has an equal amount of assets and liabilities.

Balance sheet
A document that provides a snapshot of a company at a particular moment in time, highlighting both its assets and its liabilities.

■ **EXHIBIT 12.6**

Profit and Loss Statement for LearnIT, Year Ending December 31, 2012		
Revenues		
Gross profit		$300,000
Interest*		$2000
Net revenue		$302,000
Expenses		
Advertising	$6,300	
Bank and credit card fees	$ 244	
Bookkeeping	$3,350	
Employees	$90,000	
Entertainment	$3,550	
Insurance	$1,750	
Legal and professional services	$1,575	
Licenses	$632	
Printing, postage, and stationery	$325	
Rent	$13,000	
Utilities	$1,491	
Taxes	$60,000	
Total Expenses		($182,217)
Net Income		$119,783

*Some companies use profit and loss statements that do not capture interest and taxes.

Profit and loss statement
Also called a P&L or an income statement, this document itemizes revenues and expenses and provides insight into what can be done to improve a company's results.

A **profit and loss statement** (also called a P&L or an income statement) itemizes revenues and expenses and provides insight into what can be done to improve a company's results. P&Ls use the fundamental accounting equation (profit equals revenues minus expenses) to show the profitability of an organization and whether owner/stakeholder equity is going up or down. Together, the cash flow analysis, the balance sheet, and the P&L are often used by senior management and business leaders to assess how well a company's current strategy is working and what, if anything, needs to be adjusted. In larger companies, these three tools may be used at the departmental or divisional levels as well.

LearnIT's profit and loss statement for 2011 is shown in ■ **EXHIBIT 12.6**. Looking at this statement, Tameka wonders where she can make adjustments in order to increase her profit. She is considering trying to renegotiate her office rent, because she sees that rent is her highest category of expenses after employee salaries, benefits, and taxes.

Like any type of financial reporting, these three accounting statements are only indicators, and they do not tell the whole story of an organization. Often, companies take short-term losses in order to make important long-term investments that will improve their market position. So expanding the view beyond monthly and annual financial data to include mission, environmental impact, and other indicators is important.

Beyond Budgeting

Beyond Budgeting
A control model that is intended to support more adaptive, decentralized, responsive, and ethical organizations.

Beyond Budgeting is a control model that is intended to support more adaptive, decentralized, responsive, and ethical organizations. This method has emerged in response to the growing belief that centralized financial management of organizations can be both inefficient and insufficient. Proponents of the Beyond Budgeting model believe that its benefits include faster response to issues, greater innovation, and lower costs through local negotiations with vendors, all of which can result in more loyal customers.

Beyond Budgeting is based on 12 major principles.[19] Six are classified as *adaptability* principles:

1. Outperform the competition.
2. Reward teams for their successes.
3. Continually focus on strategy, making it an inclusive process.
4. Use resources as needed.
5. Develop highly coordinated cross-company interactions through forces that are essentially the same as market forces.
6. Offer fast and relevant information built around multiple levels of the organizational system.

The remaining six principles are classified as *decentralization* or *devolution* principles:

1. Develop a climate of performance that is based on sustained competitive success.
2. Build committed teams that are united under a shared purpose, values, and rewards.
3. "Devolve strategy" by a process of decentralization that gives teams local decision-making power.
4. Be financially conservative, and question the value that all resources are believed to add to the organization.
5. Create a dynamic network that allows teams to serve customers more efficiently.
6. Support transparency and open availability of information.

CONTROLLING SERVICE: CUSTOMER RELATIONSHIP MANAGEMENT

Although the financial perspective is critical to the success of a business, without satisfied customers or clients, the company will die (■ **EXHIBIT 12.7**). This is obvious, of course, but creating processes to ensure customer satisfaction is not necessarily easy.

CRM focuses on customers with the aim of implementing a customer intimacy strategy and/or establishing a customer-friendly brand image. CRM evolved in the 1990s, as many businesses moved away from transactional customer interactions toward more relational customer interactions.[20] CRM focuses on building and maintaining a loyal customer base over the long term, rather than simply maximizing the number of transactions in the short term.

A CRM focus includes control mechanisms to measure customer data, but it can go far beyond simply collecting information through surveys and the like. When a real CRM strategy is adopted, the focus is evident in the organization's mission statement and values, as well as in its leadership behaviors and culture. Indeed, attention to the customer is obvious in almost everything anyone in the organization does.

The success of CRM strategies is measured in both financial terms and the degree of customer loyalty and retention. Although technology plays an important supportive role in tracking and managing relationships and things like customer loyalty, if relationships with customers are poor, technology often hurts rather than improves customer relations.[21] That is because communication via technology is often impersonal, and the feedback channel is relatively weak. This can make customers feel even more dissatisfied. For example, they may not be able to communicate directly or they may not feel "heard" if they respond to a survey and never see the results.

QUALITY CONTROL

So far in this section we have discussed financial controls and ways to manage and monitor the customer experience. Financial success and customer loyalty are almost always tied to both quality of products and services and efficiency of business operations. Thus, over the past several decades, a number of processes have been developed to help organizations attain quality results while operating efficiently. Let's take a look at some of those methods.

Operations management is the term that refers to the transformation of inputs—materials, labor, and ideas—into outputs, such as products or services. A number of approaches are used to design and measure operations management processes while controlling for quality. These include quality initiatives such as business process reengineering, Total Quality Management, Six Sigma, and Lean Management. Each of these approaches is described in the following sections, followed by a discussion of ISO 9000 and 14000—well-known management systems for ensuring quality and adhering to environmental standards. The section concludes with a discussion of the Baldrige Award, an honor bestowed on companies in recognition of outstanding quality.

Business Process Reengineering

Business process reengineering (BPR) is a management approach that utilizes technology and management science to redesign business processes, products, and systems to increase efficiency and focus attention on customer needs. According to BPR experts Thomas Davenport and James Short, reengineering is a process that starts from scratch. Rather than simply modifying the design of existing processes, the goal is to redesign from the ground up, even if the result is a radical reconceptualization of the organization.[22] Whereas other approaches such as Total Quality Management (discussed next) offer incremental improvements, BPR seeks improvements through a fundamental rethinking and redesign of the business. Davenport notes, "Today firms must seek not fractional, but multiplicative levels of improvement—10X rather than 10%."[23]

Scholars Michael Hammer and James Champy argue that BPR must include employees in the decision-making process because it is "the fundamental rethinking

■ **EXHIBIT 12.7**
What could this Moroccan pastry shop do to earn customers' loyalty?

Source: Anne-Marie Palmer/Alamy

Operations management
The transformation of inputs—materials, labor, and ideas—into outputs, such as products or services.

Business process reengineering (BPR)
A management approach that utilizes available technology and management science to redesign business processes, products, and systems to increase efficiency and focus attention on customer needs.

and radical redesign of business processes to achieve dramatic improvements in critical, contemporary measures of performance, such as cost, quality, service, and speed."[24] BPR includes the customer as well: It is a process that is customer-centric, not technology-centric.[25]

The twentieth century was dominated by the notion of a mass market, and the response was mass production for an abstract mass customer. In contrast, in BPR, the notion of "*the* customer" is replaced by "*this* customer," resulting in a refocus on individual customer needs.[26] Information technology is often at the center of the redesign, with the intended outcome being creation of added value for the customer.

Davenport and Short suggest that BPR be incorporated into an organization by way of a five-step approach, as described below:[27]

1. Define the business vision and objectives.
2. Identify which business processes need to be reengineered and which changes will make the biggest impact.
3. Understand what is and what isn't working.
4. Determine which IT systems and functions should influence the business process reengineering.
5. Design the new process and build a pilot project or prototype based on the new design.

Although critics have pointed out that BPR has led to downsizing and a more stifling workplace environment, the approach was quickly adopted by many companies in the early 1990s. In fact, it is estimated that by 1993, more than 80 percent of large companies in North America had adopted BPR.[28] It's important to note, however, that if BPR is not conducted carefully, the results can have a strong negative impact on the business, especially for small- and medium-sized enterprises, which are more fragile than large, stable organizations. Research suggests that for such businesses, owners and managers can facilitate success by having enough knowledge of and support for the BPR process to implement methods of streamlining and automating processes to enhance efficiency.[29]

Total Quality Management

Total Quality Management
(TQM)
A quality control philosophy that supports the elimination of deficiencies and removes variation in output quality through employee involvement in decision making, continuous improvement in processes, and a strong focus on the customer.

Total Quality Management (TQM) is a quality control philosophy that supports the elimination of deficiencies and removes variation in output quality through employee involvement in decision making, continuous improvement in processes, and a strong focus on the customer. TQM revolves around the idea that, rather than wiping a slate clean, life and organizations should be incrementally and constantly improved. The central principles of this approach are described in ■ **EXHIBIT 12.8**.[30]

Although TQM has been widely employed in manufacturing industries, it is important to note that this process is also being used in other types of organizations. Banks, call centers, and technical fields such as aerospace are also reaping the benefits of the TQM philosophy. The same is true of the Six Sigma strategy.

Six Sigma

Six Sigma
A management strategy that employs quality management methods in a specific sequence to either reduce costs or increase profits.

Originally developed by Motorola in an effort to eliminate defects in their manufacturing processes, Six Sigma is a management strategy that employs quality management methods in a specific sequence to either reduce costs or increase profits. Over time, it has evolved into a business management strategy that is used to improve a wide array of manufacturing and business processes.[31] People trained in Six Sigma are placed into a hierarchical infrastructure with "Champions" at the top. After "Champions," the descending levels of expertise are termed as follows: Master Black Belts, Black Belts, Green Belts, and Yellow Belts.[32]

Companies such as GE, Boeing, Caterpillar, and Raytheon have implemented Six Sigma. It is worth noting that these companies are among the largest in the world.

All do ALOT of welding

▪ **EXHIBIT 12.8**

Fundamental Principles of TQM

1. *Kaizen:* A focus on continuous process improvement, often through incremental changes. Kaizen involves the following five elements that facilitate the elimination of waste:[33]

   - Teamwork
   - Personal discipline
   - Improved morale
   - Quality circles (employee groups that seek solutions for quality problems)
   - Suggestions for improvement.

2. *Atarimae hinshitsu:* The idea that "things" will work according to their function and purpose (e.g., a pen will write).

3. *Kansei:* The idea that understanding the way people use products leads to the improvement of these products.

4. *Miryokuteki hinshitsu:* The idea that manufactured products should have an aesthetic quality.

Large companies have the expansive financial resources required for implementation of Six Sigma, whereas smaller companies may not. Training one person to attain Yellow Belt status, for example, can cost more than $1,000.[34] In larger organizations, hundreds if not thousands of employees receive Six Sigma training, making it a significant investment of time and money.

The goal of Six Sigma is to limit defects through a process of incremental adjustments and attention to even the smallest details of the manufacturing process. Two common uses of the Six Sigma method are for process improvement and for new product or service development. These two situations require different approaches, as seen in ▪ **EXHIBITS 12.9** and **12.10**.

The results of Six Sigma implementation have been mixed. GE, for example, boasts of a $10 billion gain through cost reduction and/or increased profits over the initial five-year period following implementation.[35] Similarly, research done at Samsung that was published in 2012 established a link between Six Sigma management processes and improved quality and innovation that ultimately led to enhanced corporate competitiveness.[36] 3M, however, found that the implementation of Six Sigma dampened creativity and innovation.[37] This conflict between innovation and the efficiency improvements from Six Sigma has been explored by author Stephen Ruffa, who points to data that show the Six Sigma program did little to help Ford Motor Company.[38] Despite widespread critiques, Six Sigma initiatives are still widely pursued by companies today.

▪ **EXHIBIT 12.9**

Six Sigma for Process Improvement: Define, Measure, Analyze, Improve, and Control

- *Define* high-level project goals and the current process.
- *Measure* key aspects of the current process and collect relevant data.
- *Analyze* the data to verify cause-and-effect relationships.
- *Improve* or optimize the process based on data analysis.
- *Control* to ensure that any deviations from the target are corrected before they result in defects.

■ **EXHIBIT 12.10**

Six Sigma for New Product and Service Development: Define, Measure, Analyze, Design, and Verify

- *Define* design goals that are consistent with customer demands and the enterprise strategy.
- *Measure* and identify *CTQs* (characteristics that are *Critical To Quality*), product capabilities, production process capability, and risks.
- *Analyze* to develop and design alternatives, create a high-level design, and evaluate design capability to select the best design.
- *Design* details, optimize the design, and plan for design verification.
- *Verify* the design, set up pilot runs, implement the production process, and hand it over to the process owners.[39]

Lean Management
A management approach that organizes manufacturing and logistics to maximize efficiency and eliminate waste by reducing variation in every process.

Lean Management

Lean Management is a management approach that organizes manufacturing and logistics to maximize efficiency and eliminate waste by reducing variation in every process. Although the term Lean Management has appeared sporadically in various contexts in Europe since the 1980s, it was popularized in a 1990 book on Japanese lean production systems.[40] Currently, one of the best-known lean production methodologies is the Toyota Production System, which relies on the following Lean Management goals to eliminate waste and maximize efficiency:[41]

1. *Improve quality:* To be competitive, a company must have a quality product that exceeds customers' expectations.
2. *Eliminate waste:* There are several different types of waste, including overproduction, downtime, defects, and rework. All such waste must be eliminated to stay lean and profitable.
3. *Reduce time:* Time from the beginning of the manufacturing process to the end must be reduced in order to stay competitive.
4. *Reduce total costs:* Any extra costs, such as those that come from keeping an unnecessary inventory of parts or finished projects, hinder a company's profitability and should be reduced.

Lean Management improves efficiency primarily by reducing wasted time, space, effort, materials, and so forth. This can be done, for instance, by identifying and removing redundancies.[42] Although many Lean Management principles are common sense and can result in greater efficiency, when taken to the extreme and/or when efficiency trumps effectiveness and quality, results can be catastrophic. Therefore, when processes like Lean Management are employed, it is important to ensure that processes are not so lean that they can't adapt or that human errors become more likely.[43]

ISO 9000 and 14000

The ISO 9000 and 14000 families of management system standards are some of the best known in the world, and they have been implemented by more than 1 million organizations in approximately 175 countries.[44] The ISO (International Organization for Standardization) is an international standards-setting body composed of national-level representatives. ISO 9000 and 14000 address quality management and environmental management, respectively. Although widely used in the automotive and industrial sectors, these standards are not specific to any one industry.[45] In fact, the ISO strongly encourages small- and medium-sized enterprises across all industries to consider adoption of these standards, particularly ISO 14000, so that they can reap the economic benefits they offer.[46]

The ISO 9000 standards are auditable international standards that have guided quality control since 1987, when they were first published.[47] Revised repeatedly since then, the standards are rooted in eight quality management principles that are designed to enable companies to exceed the quality requirements of their customers and enhance customer satisfaction while at the same time meeting regulatory requirements.[48] These principles include:

- Focusing on the customer,
- Providing leadership,
- Involving people,
- Utilizing a process approach,
- Employing a systems approach to management,
- Striving for continual improvement,
- Implementing a factual approach to decision making,
- Developing mutually beneficial supplier relationships.[49]

In support of these eight principles, ISO 9000 requires that any company using the system produce documentation in support of quality management, such as quality manuals and procedural instructions.[50] Companies can also seek independent certification, or registration, of their quality management system that recognizes successful maintenance of standard requirements. This certification is not required of companies that implement ISO 9000, but it is often beneficial in terms of marketing and securing customers that require certification.[51]

ISO 9001 has been widely adopted. As of 2010, the most recent year in which global adoption of ISO 9001 has been tracked, the top 10 countries for certificates are:[52]

1. China
2. Italy
3. Russian Federation
4. Spain
5. Japan
6. Germany
7. United Kingdom
8. India
9. United States
10. Republic of Korea.

Furthermore, the BRIC countries China, Russia, and Brazil are three of the four fastest-growing nations with regard to adoption of ISO 9001 standards, while the United States does not even appear on the top ten list for ISO 9001 growth.[53]

ISO 14000 was developed in 1992.[54] The goal of this set of standards is to encourage environmental responsibility within the business community by helping companies reduce their environmental impact and increase their long-term sustainability.[55] The key points of ISO 14000 are identifying the ways in which companies impact the environment, improving environmental product labeling, promoting company life cycle analyses, and evaluating environmental performance on an ongoing basis.[56] Ultimately, this will lead companies to get more out of their inputs and develop positive relationships with their stakeholders.[57] Companies may pursue ISO 14000 certification via an independent audit, in much the same manner that they seek ISO 9000 certification. This certification signals that the company is going above and beyond minimum government regulations regarding waste disposal and pollution control.[58]

Interestingly, there is a competitor to the ISO 14000 standards: the Eco-Management and Audit Scheme (EMAS), which is used by the European Commission. Developed in 1993 for the European Union, EMAS registers sites, rather than entire companies. Sites that are granted EMAS registration have proven that they run an effective environmental management system. These sites must also report their environmental performance via an independently verified environmental statement.[59]

ISO 9000 and ISO 14000 standards are not intended to dictate specific quality or environmental practices. Rather, they are designed to provide a framework and a systematic approach to evaluating processes.[60] Both systems take time and money to implement, but both lead to improved profits by way of more effective management. Moreover, they also enable companies to be more ethically responsible to their customers and the environment.[61] Perhaps that is why so many companies worldwide have adopted these standards as part of their day-to-day operations.

Baldrige Award

The need for quality assurance and improvement in industry is not solely a concern of the private sector; it is a governmental concern as well, as evidenced by the Malcolm Baldrige National Quality Award. This award was established by U.S. Public Law 100-107 in 1987, and it was first given out in 1988. It is named for Malcolm Baldrige, U.S. Secretary of Commerce from 1981 through 1987.[62] During his tenure as secretary, Baldrige espoused the idea that long-term economic improvement in the United States was closely tied to quality management, and he put these concepts into practice within the Commerce Department. Under his leadership, the department's budget and administrative overhead were drastically reduced, and its effectiveness and efficiency greatly improved.[63]

The Baldrige Award is presented each year by the President of the United States to manufacturing and service businesses, educational institutions, health care enterprises, and nonprofit organizations of all sizes. Companies apply for the award themselves and are judged on their performance in seven specific areas: leadership; strategic planning; customer and market focus; measurement, analysis, and knowledge management; workforce focus; process management; and results. Award winners typically exercise good citizenship and public responsibility as well as superior relationships with customers and employees. In addition, they exhibit outstanding production and delivery processes that are aligned with organizational objectives.[64] Far from simply recognizing exceptional companies, however, the Baldrige criteria have become a "way of organizational life" for many businesses that have introduced them into their daily operating standards.

When applied to business operations as a whole, the Baldrige principles assist organizations in focusing on strategy-driven performance, and they promote organizational sustainability.[65] To that end, Baldrige Award winners are asked to share their performance strategies with others in order to perpetuate a culture of excellence in industry.[66] It is this culture of excellence that helps keep U.S. companies vital to the world economy and keeps the Malcolm Baldrige National Quality Award relevant in our ever-changing business climate.

Discussion Questions

1. Consider a group or organization you work with that has a budget. How could this group or organization institute Beyond Budgeting principles into its organizational control systems? What impact might this approach to budgeting have on the group or organization's management of its money?

2. Imagine that your school or workplace plans to implement TQM, Six Sigma, or Lean Management. What changes might you see in how resources are used? In how people are managed?

4. What Are Common Control Systems?

Objective 12.4
Understand conventions and forces that guide the organizational control processes.

Now that we've explored some of the control processes that employees typically see, let's explore overarching models of organizational control. The first is common and seen in most, if not all organizations: bureaucracy. In the language of organizational control, this is called bureaucratic control. We will also look at a similar model called objective control. These models are often implicit, meaning that they are so much a part of how we think about organizations that we don't always see them as control mechanisms. Partly for this reason, these models are accepted without question, which of course means it is hard to improve them. As a way to overcome this, some researchers are considering a new model known as the levers of control system.

Bureaucratic Control Systems

Bureaucratic control systems are control processes that use specific rules, standards, and hierarchical authority to achieve planned and desired organizational outcomes. Sometimes referred to as a "compliance" model, the bureaucratic system mandates that employees abide by established rules, policies, and standards. This type of control system focuses on roles rather than individuals. In other words, responsibilities and duties are linked to jobs and roles, and people who hold certain roles are expected to behave in a prescribed manner.[67]

Managing a bureaucratic control system involves comparison of performance to established standard operating procedures (SOPs) and metrics to determine whether people and/or the organization are meeting strategic goals. In the bureaucratic system, if standards are not adhered to or metrics are not met, corrective action is taken. Bureaucratic control systems are designed to ensure that output is predictable. Organizations that employ this system are managed in a highly structured fashion and rely heavily on hierarchy and authority to influence behaviors.

Bureaucratic controls are widespread in organizations of all types. They include such things as safety protocols, signing in and out of work, tracking vacation and sick time, the procedures managers must use to request raises for their employees, systems that track and monitor goods when they are shipped—and on and on. You have probably experienced bureaucratic control in schools and organizations. For example, it is likely that you had to fill out a form asking for personal information before you could receive your student identification card (■ **EXHIBIT 12.11**). This is part of a bureaucratic control system that ensures only students can obtain such cards. Later on, you likely used your ID in yet another bureaucratic control system when you either showed your card to someone or slid it through an electronic reader. This process enables the school to control who enters which building, as well as to monitor people's comings and goings.

In a bureaucratic control system, policies and rules are valued above using one's own judgment. Let's see what this means by returning to the example of your school ID card. Most likely, you are fully capable of determining which building you should enter for class on your own—you personally don't *need* a card that provides or limits access. However, at some point, the school's leaders determined that they needed to control student behavior so they could gather information, protect students, or make sure all students did certain things in the same way. It's the same in many businesses—rather than leaving matters up to the individual, businesses rely on standard processes that ensure that behavior can be monitored at the organizational level and that all employees complete specific tasks in the same manner.

Bureaucratic control systems
Control processes that use specific rules, standards, and hierarchical authority to achieve planned and desired organizational outcomes.

■ **EXHIBIT 12.11**
How many different ID cards or badges have you had at work or school?

Source: David Adamson/Alamy

THE INFORMAL RULES OF BUREAUCRACY

Besides actual rules and policies, bureaucratic control systems also rely on social control mechanisms to create common value systems, understandings, and expectations among employees. In many instances, aspects of the bureaucratic control system become inseparable from an organization's culture.[68] The social rules associated with this bureaucracy may not be written down or even articulated—but they are nevertheless powerful. For example, in the hierarchical system of reporting relationships, employees are often expected to deal directly with their own managers when problems arise. There may be no rule that prohibits going to a manager in another division or to your boss's boss about a problem. Still, the social pressure that prohibits such actions can be extreme, and in some cases, people may even be fired for violating rules in this less formal part of the bureaucratic control system.

BUREAUCRATIC CONTROLS ARE EVERYWHERE—AND ARE SOMETIMES PROBLEMATIC

Bureaucratic control systems are everywhere, and their rules and regulations are often robust and effective. These systems, however, can inhibit innovation and honest communication. They can breed an environment in which good judgment is suspended in favor of following the rules. For many of us, the idea of being discouraged from using our own common sense paints a picture of a repressive work environment. In fact, when taken to the extreme, such formal, rules-bound organizations can become dissonant and even toxic.[69]

Furthermore, too much bureaucracy can introduce layers of administrative activity and radically slow down decision making. (Anyone who has dealt with governments will understand this.) The trick to leveraging bureaucratic control systems is to use them in settings in which they promote ethical behavior and better performance and safety, such as in manufacturing facilities and certain financial functions. However, even in these cases, steps should be taken to limit the detrimental effect that excessive regulation can have on the positive climate needed to bring out the best in an organization's people.[70]

Objective Controls Go Beyond Rules

In traditional bureaucracies, following the rules can actually become more important than the quality of work that gets done. When quality is truly valued, however, behavior and work outputs are considered in addition to whether rules are adhered to. The bureaucratic control system is pervasive in our organizations, however. Within or in addition to bureaucratic systems, then, scholars suggest that there are several other control processes that can add to the benefits and limit the downsides of a bureaucracy. These types of controls are "objective" because they focus on observables—what managers can see and measure related to work outputs and employee behavior. As discussed next, these control processes include output, behavior, and normative controls. A modern take on all of this is discussed in the last section—levers of control.

OUTPUT CONTROL

Output control
Type of control in which outcomes are measured against financial performance and other clearly articulated metrics, such as customer retention.

Two important aspects of objective control are output control and behavior control. In **output control**, outcomes are measured against financial performance and other clearly articulated metrics, such as customer retention. With this system, incentives and rewards are tied to meeting or surpassing a set of predetermined metrics; thus, clarity of expectations, measurable and achievable targets, and transparency around measurement and evaluation of goals are essential. Output control can allow managers and employees a relative amount of freedom when determining how to best meet goals, without too much direct supervision.[71]

BEHAVIOR CONTROL

Behavior control focuses on what employees actually do in order to attain desired outcomes. When an organization focuses on behavior control, managers closely monitor and evaluate employee behavior, addressing any deviations from expectations.[72] The most obvious form of behavior control is seen in the supervisor–employee relationship. Here, supervisors watch over employees, assist them in developing the skills required to perform their duties, and monitor their effectiveness and efficiency to ensure they are acting in accordance with expectations. In this system, incentives are often given to those individuals who exhibit the desired behaviors. In other words, employees are rewarded for behaving in accordance with expectations, and they are also punished for deviations from expectations.

Objective control systems involve the development and implementation of mechanisms such as measurement processes.[73] Behavior and outputs are often controlled and measured through standards and procedures. Once these standards and procedures are in place, objective control operates through the use of hierarchical controls, chains of command, and communication.[74]

NORMATIVE CONTROL

Normative control is about sharing and embedding an organization's values and beliefs so they act as a guide for employees' behavior. When normative control is effective, organizations typically have fewer formal rules and standard operating procedures. Rather, employees are encouraged to use their best judgment and the organization's values to guide their judgment. With this type of system, new employees often look to more seasoned colleagues (rather than a policy manual) for clues and cues about acceptable behaviors.

Normative control is most often enforced through an organization's culture (discussed in Chapter 13), and it works well when the fit between employees and the organization is good—in other words, when individual employees' values, beliefs, and expectations about work behavior are aligned with those of the organization. This means that organizations that rely on normative control need to be very selective in their hiring process, looking for people who have compatible attitudes and values. Taking this a step further, one scholar who studies control systems notes that the most important (and often underutilized) form of control is retaining the best employees.[75]

Levers of Control

One of the more recent and innovative control systems in use today is the levers of control model proposed by Harvard professor Robert Simons.[76] A lever is a simple machine that gives the user an advantage. Imagine prying a large rock out of the ground with a bar—when you push down on one end, less effort is needed to lift the heavy weight than if you tried with your bare hands. Levers work the same way when it comes to controls in an organization. Thus, the more levers you use, the more likely you are to change and control aspects of work and outcomes.

The levers of control model expands our understanding of the factors that contribute to organizational performance, allowing us to pay close attention to the people- and process-oriented, relational aspect of getting things done. Levers of control are about creating and maintaining a cultural mind-set that contributes to behaviors within an organization in addition to putting systems and processes into place. This model attempts to integrate some of the best aspects of other models. It includes belief systems, boundary systems, diagnostic control systems, and interactive control systems, as illustrated in ■ **EXHIBIT 12.12**. The same control mechanism can be used in more than one of the levers of control. Simons' model examines how control mechanisms are used, rather than examining the control mechanisms themselves.[77] Researchers have found interactions

Behavior control
Type of control in which an organization focuses on what employees actually do in order to attain desired outcomes.

Normative control
A control system that involves sharing and embedding an organization's values and beliefs so they act as a guide for employees' behavior.

Levers of control
A control system that relies on various levers such as organizational values, rules, feedback systems, and focused involvement in decision making.

■ **EXHIBIT 12.12**

Simons' Levers of Control[78]		
Lever	**How It Works**	**Examples**
Belief Systems	Defines the core values of an organization and its members	Credos, mission statements, and values statements
Boundary Systems	Defines territory or span of control for people within the organization	Rules, proscriptions, and regulations of the organization
Diagnostic Control Systems	Feedback system that allows the organization to monitor standards	Systems to measure output, as well as incentives and goals
Interactive Control Systems	Allows managers to plan how to regularly involve themselves personally in their subordinates' decision-making activities	Project management systems, knowledge management systems, and scheduling systems

among the four levers of control in terms of interdependencies and complementarity.[79] Within control systems, employees may have various levels of input and involvement. In some organizations, control systems are a top-down set of rules that cannot be changed and must be obeyed. In other organizations, control systems are more participative, and people have opportunities to be involved in the creation and implementation of the control process. In the latter case, people are seen as an asset whose cooperation and input is essential to full realization of the organization's goals and potential.

When considering control systems in organizations, it is important to consider the steps in the control process as well as the various forces that organizations choose to—or must—incorporate in their control processes, including corporate governance, audits, laws, and customers. These concepts will be examined in greater detail in the following sections.

Discussion Questions

1. Brainstorm a list of some of the bureaucratic controls that guide your behavior as a student. Which of these do you believe are necessary or helpful, and which do you believe are unnecessary or harmful? Explain.

2. What control systems do you believe are linked to productivity and effectiveness of workers in Japan, the United States, Russia and South Africa? Please support your answer with Internet or other research and avoid assumptions and biases.

Objective 12.5
List the typical steps in the control process.

5. What Are the Typical Steps in the Control Process?

As you can see in ■ **EXHIBIT 12.13**, control systems can be applied at any point in the business process, from input (e.g., monitoring the quality and price of raw materials), to throughput (e.g., measuring the efficiency of manufacturing processes or employee behavior), to output (e.g., applying quality standards to the finished product). At all of these stages, an organization's goals can be transformed into specific quality, efficiency, and ethical standards and metrics, such as baselines for cost and quality of raw materials, expectations for internal production processes, standards for employee performance, product quality specifications, timelines for getting products to market, adherence to ethical principles, and so on. Indeed, almost any aspect of the business and work process can be measured and monitored as an organization attempts to meet its goals and objectives.

Creating Standards and Metrics

Standards and metrics are measures established to define quality and efficiency. They also act as important indicators of an organization's ethical environment. Standards and metrics can come from internal analyses of behaviors and systems that lead to desired outcomes. Alternatively, they can be determined by talking to customers about their preferences. In addition, they may be established by benchmarking an organization's results against those of other companies in the same industry.

Standards can be either quantitative (e.g., "A retail clerk is to sell 25 pieces of clothing per shift") or qualitative (e.g., "A retail clerk is to treat customers in a friendly, respectful manner"). The logic behind standards and metrics is as follows: If the right standards and metrics are created, and if all standards and metrics are met or exceeded, then the organization should meet its goals. Standards and metrics also serve as a basis for comparison, giving employees and managers guidelines for performance.

To see how standards affect workers' daily tasks, let's consider two fictitious workers: Tiffany and Will. Tiffany works in a factory. She must ensure that 60 smartphones are produced per hour (■ **EXHIBIT 12.14**). In addition, these phones must conform to the specific dimensions defined in the product specifications (five inches tall by three inches wide). Thus, Tiffany's controls are quantitative.

In comparison, Will works in a call center, where he must make five outbound calls per hour and answer an additional five inbound calls per hour. He is expected to keep each call to five minutes and then document each call in a period of one minute. These are quantitative measures. When on a call, Will is also expected to be helpful and engaging. These are qualitative measures. Thus, the standards that Will must meet are both quantitative and qualitative.

Measuring Performance

After determining standards and metrics, another important step in the control process is measuring the extent to which organizational performance is meeting, falling short of, or exceeding expectations. Answering this question might include looking at levels of production, safety records, customer retention rates, or monthly revenues. Measurements are then recorded for use in the next phase of the control process as a benchmark for determining what, if any, corrective action needs to be taken.

To illustrate how this works, let's look at the differences in how Tiffany's and Will's performances are measured. Tiffany's performance is measured by the quantity of smartphones produced per hour and by the dimensions of what is produced. Tiffany, therefore, has two quantitative controls that are used to judge her performance. Quantitative controls like this are common in manufacturing environments. Will's managers have a more difficult job because his performance is not only measured quantitatively (by how many calls he makes and receives), but also qualitatively

■ **EXHIBIT 12.13**
Controls can be applied at any point in the business process.

External Environment

People, Materials, Money, Information → Inputs → Throughputs → Outputs → Goods and Services Delivered to Market

Feedback

Standards and metrics
Measures established to define quality and efficiency criteria.

■ **EXHIBIT 12.14**
If Tiffany's company can accurately predict the number of phones produced per hour, what other metrics can they create?

Source: pumkinpie/Alamy

(by the tone of his voice and his friendliness as he talks to customers). This is typical in a customer service or sales environment.

Comparing Performance to Standards

The next step in the control process is to compare an organization's actual performance with desired standards. The clearer and more precise these standards are, the easier it is to make this comparison. For instance, emergency rooms often have standards regarding the average amount of time patients must wait before seeing a doctor. According to data from the U.S. Centers for Disease Control and Prevention, in 2004, patients spent an average of about 3.3 hours in the emergency department from arrival to discharge.[80] By 2007, two-thirds of emergency room visitors waited for up to four hours to be treated.[81] According to a Press Ganey report, by 2009, average wait times for emergency departments varied considerably from state to state, averaging as low as over three hours in Iowa to more than nine hours in Utah.[82] These figures provide benchmarks that a hospital can use to gauge its own performance. For example, if a hospital's goal is to improve the patient experience or to become the local hospital of choice for emergency treatment, then that hospital might implement a standard that is significantly less than the benchmark—say, two hours or less.

So, how do Tiffany's and Will's performances compare to the standards set by their managers? Tiffany needs to produce 60 smartphones per hour, and these devices need to meet certain size specifications. Say that from 2:00 P.M. to 3:00 P.M. on October 25, Tiffany produces 51 smartphones with the correct dimensions. This is nine fewer than the standard calls for, and it represents a downward deviation of 15 percent. This is a control loss: a downward deviation from the benchmark.

Meanwhile, Will made five outbound calls but only answered four inbound calls during the same hour-long period on October 25. This represents a control loss of 20 percent against the standard for incoming calls, and a loss of 10 percent against his overall requirements for calls of all types. On these nine calls, Will's attitude was helpful and engaging in seven of them, but in the remaining two calls, the manager who reviewed Will's audiotapes thought he sounded unhelpful and irritated.

Taking Corrective Action

After comparing actual performance to standards, the next phase in the control process involves reconciling the gap. In the event that standards were exceeded, this may mean that performance was stellar or that the standard was set too low. If performance was low and standards were not met, then managers must decide whether and how to address the situation through corrective action.

Before taking action, however, it is important to understand the reasons why standards were not met. In some cases, it's simple to see cause and effect—for instance, employees were late for work; therefore customers could not get into the store until after the scheduled opening time and sales were down. However, many other reasons for failing to meet standards are not as easy to understand.

Let's look at the reasons behind Tiffany's and Will's failures to meet standards. Tiffany's manager interviewed her and her coworkers to determine why they were all 15 percent below their production targets. Through these interviews, the manager determined that Tiffany's team was taking extraordinarily long breaks. Tiffany's production team was issued a verbal warning and informed that they would receive a written warning if this production shortfall occurred again within the next 30 days.

Meanwhile, at the call center, Will's manager reviewed the notes Will made about each call and determined that he was only able to take four inbound calls (instead of the standard five) because two of the other calls were with customers who required extra attention and help. Because these customers had special needs, the manager did not take corrective action. However, the manager issued a warning to Will about his tone of voice and lack of helpfulness with customers. Will did not believe his tone was inappropriate, but he promised to try to improve nonetheless.

This example points to what can be a big problem when managers take action to correct an employee's behavior: They need to have judged that behavior accurately, and they also need to help the employee see the situation the same way. In this case, Will's manager judged him to be unhelpful and irritated. If this manager is highly skilled and emotionally intelligent, he will have read Will's behavior accurately, and he will have correctly judged the impact that Will had on customers. But what if this manager isn't skilled in reading human behavior? Or what if he was in a rush, and he didn't take the time to listen to the entire audiotape? These sorts of problems are extremely common when it comes to making judgments about employee behavior—yet another reason why employees and managers need to develop skills that will enable them to build strong, positive relationships and accurately assess behavior.

Feedback Processes

Without feedback, the control process does not work (■ **EXHIBIT 12.15**). Usually, when people hear the word *feedback*, they automatically think about getting information after the fact—which is often the case in organizations. Feedback of this kind is discussed first. Then, we will review two additional types of information and input that affect many control systems: feed-forward control and concurrent control.

FEEDBACK CONTROL

Feedback control is a type of control in which information about performance is gathered and shared after the fact. This is often necessary and can be done in such a way that people and organizations can improve. However, after-the-fact feedback can be costly to an organization, and/or the feedback can come too late so the damage can't be undone. For instance, when safety standards in a factory are ignored, feedback in the form of an injured employee is not something that can be rectified for that individual. Or, if ethics standards were breached but not noticed until afterward, the damage will have already been done.

■ **EXHIBIT 12.15**
Why is feedback an essential part of the control process?

Source: The Stock Asylum, LLC/Alamy

How might feedback control operate in Tiffany's situation? If Tiffany's boss hears from an electronics retailer that red smartphones are outselling blue smartphones, then he will want to increase production of red smartphones. However, it takes time to switch the production process so that more red phones can be manufactured. Here, the retailer's feedback may have been communicated too late, resulting in a missed opportunity.

FEED-FORWARD CONTROL

In contrast to feedback control, feed-forward control is a type of control system that anticipates potential issues or problems before they arise. It is an educated guess approach that proactively sets a course to control for potential problems and opportunities early on, rather than waiting for the problems or missed opportunities to occur. For example, Tiffany's employer might actually research production machinery and

Feedback control
Type of control in which information about performance is gathered and shared after the fact.

Feed-forward control
Type of control system that anticipates potential issues or problems before they arise.

buy the most stable equipment before the factory starts producing the phones. This feed-forward control is meant to prevent problems from happening in the first place, or at least to reduce the number of equipment repairs required later.

CONCURRENT CONTROL

Concurrent control
The process of collecting real-time information to decrease the lag time between performance deficiencies and corrective action.

Finally, concurrent control is the process of collecting real-time information to decrease the lag time between performance deficiencies and corrective action. For instance, with the introduction of software that performs real-time tracking, an entertainment venue's managers could see, at any time, how many tickets have sold for an upcoming concert without having to wait for monthly or weekly sales reports. If sales are down, the managers will know immediately, and they can take corrective action such as more advertising. Some airline reservation systems use this type of control to determine cost per seat as the plane fills up. Here, prices can be increased or decreased to maximize revenue and capacity usage.

Let's consider how concurrent control might work at Will's call center. Say the center is constantly monitored by managers through the use of real-time audio monitoring, report generation, and software that tracks numbers of calls and time spent on each call. Will and his manager are provided with this information at frequent intervals, which allows them to immediately take corrective action if standards are not being met.

Integrating Feedback

The feedback that employees receive can affect them either positively or negatively. If feedback is delivered and perceived in a positive way, then employees are more likely to use this feedback and to integrate it so their performance improves. In contrast, if feedback is seen as unrealistic, or if it is delivered in a caustic or demeaning manner, employees are less likely to improve.

In the cases of Tiffany and Will, Tiffany's manager delivers his feedback in a positive way. He always begins by telling Tiffany what she did right and lets her know how to improve. Will's manager is different. He is capricious—it's hard to know how he will react to things. He tends to be dismissive and disrespectful, and he doesn't always have his facts straight. So, although in this case Will assured his manager that he would try to do better, he was angry and unmotivated.

Of course, employees are ultimately accountable for their own behavior. The control process is one manifestation of an organization's values, and it communicates to employees what the organization's leaders deem most important. The responsibility for using the steps in the control process to support and motivate workers falls squarely on the shoulders of managers and leaders—and this is no easy task! The best leaders and managers keep a balanced perspective on how controls affect the quality of products and services and on how those same controls act to motivate and support employees to perform their jobs. When employees feel supported and processes are aligned with values and objectives, organizations perform better over time.

Discussion Questions

1. Think about the last time you wrote a paper or report for school. Consider how to create standards, how to measure your performance, how to compare your performance to standards, and how to take corrective action to create a control process that will enable you to get an A on the next paper you write.

2. We've all worked for organizations with bosses who we believed judged our performance unfairly or gave us inaccurate feedback. Think back to one of those times, and consider how it affected your behavior. If you had been your manager back then, what would you have done to make sure this feedback was delivered more effectively?

6. How Do Corporate Governance, Audits, and Legislation Support Ethical Behavior?

Objective 12.6
Assess what companies should control.

In this section, you'll learn about two conventional structures organizations often use as part of their control processes: corporate governance and audits. You'll also explore how legislation impacts the control process and how today's most innovative organizations seek to involve customers in their control systems. These systems have always been important, but today, their significance cannot be underestimated. In the past fifteen years, there have been legal and ethical transgressions large and small in organizations all over the world. These actions—many of which have been criminal—include fraud, deception, and stealing, to name just a few. Individual leaders, teams, and entire organizations have been complicit, and many innocent people have lost money, and in some cases their dreams. For these reasons, corporate governance is increasingly taking up a traditional role that may have been less important in the past: upholder of the law and the organization's ethical code. Managers, leaders, and others involved in corporate governance often employ audits to help them in their quest to support ethics and uphold laws. These laws have become much more stringent in recent years, which we will also discuss.

Corporate Governance

Corporate governance refers to the way in which an organization is controlled, administered, or directed as prescribed by laws and the processes, policies, regulations, ethical code, and customs of that organization. Corporate governance can also be described as the set of rules, policies, and procedures for managing an organization and ensuring that the organization's behavior and practices are aligned with laws, market forces, internal control structures, and ethics as defined by that organization.[83] For example, corporate governance is the method by which suppliers of capital ensure returns on their investment in the company.[84] Corporate governance is also involved in reviewing major changes management is considering, to ensure that these changes will be financially responsible, in line with the organization's mission, and of course, legal and ethical.

Corporate governance is frequently spelled out in a corporate charter. A **corporate charter** is an articulation of policies, rules, and procedures that address a variety of governance issues, such as the legal name, location, mission, rules relating to its board of directors, and classes of securities (stocks) that are issued if it is a publicly traded company. Many corporate charters include an explicit ethical code of conduct.

Corporate governance involves three primary sets of players: the board of directors, management, and selected stakeholders. Together, these parties are responsible for ensuring that the company's mission, values, and legal obligations are upheld.

The **board of directors** usually includes individuals who are not employed by the company and who may have expertise that will be helpful to management. These individuals are called "independent directors," and they are often paid a stipend for their service (which can be quite a lot of money in some cases). The board of directors also usually includes representatives from the top of the organization, such as the CEO, CFO, and general counsel. The board helps guide the organization's strategy and ensures that the organization is meeting both its own objectives and the expectations of stakeholders. In many companies, the board of directors has ultimate fiduciary and legal accountability for the organization.

The second major player in the corporate governance equation is management, which, of course, is responsible for ensuring that the organization is governed according to its charter and that the organization and all its employees uphold all applicable laws. Management is charged with making sure that all stakeholders are satisfied.

Corporate governance
The way in which an organization is controlled, administered, or directed as described by laws and the processes, policies, regulations, ethical code, and customs of that organization.

Corporate charter
An articulation of policies, rules, and procedures that address a variety of governance issues, such as the legal name and location of the business, along with the business's mission, rules relating to its board of directors, and classes of securities (stocks) that are issued.

Board of directors
Usually includes indivduals who are not employed by the company and who may have expertise that will be helpful to management.

Privately held company
A company that is wholly owned by an individual or group of individuals and does not sell shares of ownership on the open market.

Publicly traded company
A company that issues shares of ownership, or stocks, that are traded on the open market.

Shareholders
The individuals or groups that own shares of a company.

Selected stakeholders are the third major party involved in corporate governance. The selection of which stakeholders to include in corporate governance differs depending on whether a company is privately held or publicly traded. A **privately held company** is a company that is wholly owned by an individual or a group of individuals and does not sell shares of ownership on the open market. In privately held companies, special stakeholders can include advisers, experts in areas such as finance or community relations, and even friends and family. A **publicly traded company** is a company that issues shares of ownership, or stocks, that are traded on the open market. In publicly traded companies, stakeholders can include experts in various functional areas (finance, accounting, etc.), as well as senior-level advisers such as ex-CEOs or sitting senior members of other companies. They also include a company's **shareholders**, or the individuals or groups that own shares of the company. These individuals and/or groups may have purchased shares on the open market or they may have acquired stock through reward or as a result of an IPO. "IPO" stands for initial public offering and is what it sounds like—the first time shares of ownership in a company are offered to the public.

Other stakeholders that may have a say in governing an organization include community representatives, founders, and employees, to name just a few. Responsible companies are very keen to understand both stake- and shareholders' views and incorporate them into the control process.

A last word on governance: Regardless of how a board is structured, its members need to share an understanding of the company's mission, vision, and goals. Furthermore, members must offer positive and constructive advice to management. The relationship between external board members and management is extremely important and must be designed to support open communication, mutual respect, and effective governance. As obvious as this seems, the governance process is often complicated and even undermined because not everyone is on the same page.

Audits

Audit
A formal review to make sure that certain processes have been fully and accurately managed and reported.

Corporate governance is the umbrella control mechanism under which an organization functions. Beneath that umbrella, audits are one of several means for ensuring that people and the organization as a whole are doing what they are supposed to be doing. An **audit** is a formal review to make sure that certain processes have been fully and accurately managed and reported. For example, an audit might be conducted to check that a financial statement has been completed accurately. Although audits are usually associated with accounting tasks like this one, they can actually be performed on a wide range of processes. For instance, an audit could be conducted to ensure that environmental protection laws are being followed; human resources might conduct an audit to ensure that the company is complying with labor laws; or a company may carry out an audit of its safety practices.

Audits are sometimes internal and conducted by employees such as accountants, specialists, or HR professionals.[85] External audits employ independent professionals or firms. One especially common practice for medium-to-large businesses is to hire outside accountants to audit the finances of the company. These auditors ensure that financial records are accurate, complete, and prepared according to GAAP (generally accepted accounting principles), as well as state and federal regulations.

Legislation and Sarbanes-Oxley

All businesses and industries are controlled to some extent by government regulations. Let's first look at how laws affect businesses in general, then consider a special piece of important legislation (Sarbanes-Oxley) that has been instituted in recent years.

LEGISLATION AND CONTROLS

Regulations can be local, such as zoning laws that dictate what kind of business can be conducted where. State or provincial laws also control how business is carried out, how employees are treated, and the like. Businesses must additionally abide by applicable national or federal laws, such as the Civil Rights Act in the United States, which protects rights of employees in the workplace.[86] In many cases, these laws are supported and upheld by regulatory agencies, such as the U.S. Food and Drug Administration (FDA) and the Environmental Protection Agency (EPA). Through legislation and agencies such as these, the government exerts control over a wide range of business practices. For example, the government regulates how products are labeled and advertised, including whether they can be called "certified organic" or "fair trade."

All countries have these sorts of laws and regulatory bodies, and they greatly impact how, when, and where a company can do business. In addition, international organizations that govern trade and business practices, such as the World Trade Organization (WTO), can have an impact on issues such as pricing, what goods are sold by whom, and where goods are sold.

Many of these laws and regulations have been implemented to ensure that businesses act in a fair and responsible manner with respect to the communities and the people they serve. Often, they are intended to provide balance to the profit-seeking imperative of market economies. This could mean looking out for the interests of workers, consumers, or society, and it may involve local, national, or international regulating bodies or agencies.

SARBANES-OXLEY AND CONTROLS

In recent years, one set of regulations in particular has been instituted to ensure that businesses operate in a fair and ethical manner. These regulations and standards are the result of the Sarbanes-Oxley Act of 2002, commonly abbreviated as SOX and formally known as the Public Company Accounting Reform and Investor Protection Act. SOX is essential to all publicly traded companies in the United States because it sets new or enhanced standards for these companies' boards, managers, and public accounting firms. SOX applies only to public companies, not to privately held companies.

SOX was enacted as a result of several major corporate and accounting scandals in the early 2000s, including those at Enron, Arthur Andersen, Tyco International, Adelphia, Peregrine Systems, and WorldCom. These scandals caused the companies' financial infrastructures to collapse, which cost employees and investors billions of dollars. The fraud involved in these scandals, and the government's inability to detect and stop the fraud, shook public confidence in previously prominent companies and in government regulators.

The act contains 11 sections that cover topics ranging from additional corporate board responsibilities to criminal penalties for violation of standards, and it required the U.S. Securities and Exchange Commission (SEC) to implement rulings regarding compliance with the new laws. The act also created a new agency called the Public Company Accounting Oversight Board, which is charged with overseeing, regulating, inspecting, and disciplining accounting firms (■ **EXHIBIT 12.16**). The act additionally covers issues such

Sarbanes-Oxley Act of 2002
Formally known as the Public Company Accounting Reform and Investor Protection Act, this act sets new or enhanced standards for publicly traded companies' boards, managers, and public accounting firms.

■ **EXHIBIT 12.16**

The Public Company Accounting Oversight Board shall:[87]

1. Register public accounting firms;
2. Establish or adopt, by rule, auditing, quality control, ethics, independence, and other standards relating to the preparation of audit reports for issuers;
3. Conduct inspections of accounting firms;
4. Conduct investigations and disciplinary proceedings, and impose appropriate sanctions;
5. Perform such other duties or functions as necessary or appropriate;
6. Enforce compliance with the Act, the rules of the Board, professional standards, and the securities laws relating to the preparation and issuance of audit reports and the obligations and liabilities of accountants with respect thereto;
7. Set the budget and manage the operations of the Board and the staff of the Board.

as auditor independence, corporate governance, internal control assessment, and enhanced financial disclosure.

Debate continues about the perceived benefits and costs of SOX. Supporters contend that the act was necessary and that it has restored public confidence in U.S. businesses and oversight procedures by strengthening corporate accounting controls. Opponents of SOX claim that it has reduced America's international competitive edge by introducing an overly complex regulatory environment.[88] Critics of the act have blamed the complex regulatory environment and the added expense for prolonging economic recovery following the global recession that began in 2007.[89] They point to the decreased numbers of IPOs as well as the increased likelihood of new small companies choosing to list on foreign exchanges as indicators that SOX stifles economic development.

So far, we have discussed how companies set standards to ensure adherence to both internal governance criteria and laws originating outside the organization. In the next section, we will look at a third, more innovative approach to control—letting customers in on the processes of product design and marketing.

When Customers Control

Often, companies *must* comply with certain controls, such as those created by government legislation and the ethical standards that they will not violate. Some companies, however, start at the other end of the spectrum: They *seek* to be controlled. This is the case in the growing number of organizations that strive to involve customers in product design and quality control. Consider the example of Threadless in the *Business Case* feature on the following page.

As described in the case study, Threadless challenges the traditional approach to controlling business practices and marketing. Although every business is intuitively aware of the importance of consumer loyalty and brand trust, Threadless is proof that consumer-controlled product design and marketing can be a company's core competence and its most important asset. Threadless is clearly employing a very different business model; though not yet that common, it will doubtless be explored by more organizations as technology and social networking take on ever-greater importance in our day-to-day lives.

You have now read about several common control systems, as well as some new and innovative ways of looking at the control process. In the next section, you'll get a better idea of how these systems operate as you learn about the typical steps in control processes.

Discussion Questions

1. Do you believe that laws such as SOX were a reasonable or effective response to the corporate accounting scandals of the time? Why or why not?

2. Have you ever worked for—or been served by—an organization in which the customer really was the center of all decisions? How was this organization different from others you have experienced?

Objective 12.7
Learn what HR can do to help control for effectiveness and efficiency.

7. What Can HR Do to Help Control for Effectiveness and Efficiency at Work?

Human resources management has a central role in developing and enforcing controls within an organization. It can be a challenging yet ultimately rewarding task for HR leaders to develop, implement, and provide quality feedback about effective measures of performance—and then partner with managers to implement them. Sometimes it's

Customer Control

Threadless Customers: Masters of Design

Jake Nickell, founder of online T-shirt retailer threadless, had no intention of creating a revolution in management or rewriting books on organizational design. As a 20-year-old part-time student, he spent much of his time browsing design sites, interacting on forums, and designing Web pages.[90] The trigger event that eventually caused him to launch threadless came when Nickell won a competition at the New Media Underground festival for a T-shirt logo he designed. There was no prize money—not even a copy of the shirt he designed—but it was validation.

Together with his friend Jacob DeHart, Nickell decided to host an online T-shirt design contest. The first contest was held in November 2000, and the response was just under 100 submissions. The prize? Two free shirts and a promise from the company that all proceeds would go to funding the next competition. Two dozen copies of the five most popular designs were printed up as T-shirts and priced at $12 each. They sold out very quickly.

By 2002, with over $100,000 worth of T-shirt stock and over 100,000 site members, Nickell and DeHart realized that they had much more than a hobby on their hands. They formed a company, named it threadless, and brought more people on board. Just four years later, in 2006, threadless's sales hit $16 million, with a profit of roughly $6 million, and the company had a member base of around 700,000.[91] By 2009, threadless was selling 100,000 T-shirts every month and was regularly approached by venture capitalists.[92]

As these figures demonstrate, threadless is a tremendous success both financially and in terms of customer loyalty.

Today, there is even an unofficial threadless fan blog (www .lovesthreadless.com), a threadless Facebook site with nearly 500,000 followers and a threadless Twitter account with nearly 2 million followers in mid-2012, along with competitions to spot celebrities wearing threadless T-shirts.

Part of threadless's popularity is due to the fact that instead of restricting customers to the role of buyer, the company takes every opportunity to encourage their participation in designing products, voting, or just spreading the word. Nickell and his crew spend much of their time discussing and participating with members on their forums, and members seem to relish the openness of the company, as shown by the exponential growth in the company's customer base and sales.

When it came to building the threadless brand, the company didn't spend a cent—not in real money, anyway. What they did spend was *time*. So far, threadless's primary marketing channel has been straightforward, simple word of mouth. In fact, fans of the company were responsible for setting up the company's Facebook page and other fan sites. Although Nickell and DeHart briefly experimented with advertising, they soon abandoned the idea because it didn't produce the desired effect and elicited a negative reaction from their existing customer base. In Nickell's own words:

With our company, it's all about trust and honesty, and we just don't like the idea of pushing our brand on people who otherwise wouldn't hear about it . . . organically, naturally. It's not that we don't market; we just don't advertise.[93]

When it comes to employee selection at threadless, the topic of trust plays a major role. "It's pretty much the only thing we talk about when we interview," Nickell says.[94] The idea is to find people who can work on their own, without supervision. Many of the employees are designers themselves or have art degrees. In fact, 75 percent of the company's employees were threadless Web site members before ever working for the company.[95]

Threadless has big plans. The company has already opened a retail store in Chicago, initially as a flagship marketing channel with only a few products. The majority of the space is dedicated to displaying the work of emerging artists. Although the store was opened with the expectation of losing money, it became profitable within six months, and it currently attracts customers from all over the country. threadless is also considering expansions and opening regional warehouses, which would enable European customers to get their T-shirts faster.[96] threadless has also extended the range of community design products to children's apparel, clothing accessories, and even dishware. The opportunities are truly unlimited.

Photo Source: Handout/MCT/Newscom.

a highly enviable job: developing top performers and preparing them for increasing opportunity and responsibility. Other times, it is the toughest job in the organization and requires a tremendous amount of emotional sensitivity and compassion. In this section, we will focus on performance management—a powerful control mechanism in the workplace.

HR Leadership Roles

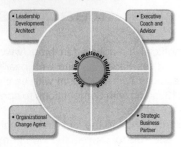

The Performance Management Process

Performance management is a tremendous responsibility that is entrusted to managers and HR professionals within organizations. By directly working with employees or supporting managers who are tracking the performance of people in their groups, HR has a significant role in creating processes that enable employees to improve performance and help the organization track employee strengths and developmental needs.

Performance management processes set standards, monitor performance, and help people leverage strengths and overcome deficiencies. When performance management systems work well, they focus less on simple monitoring of behavior and more on measuring contributions and accomplishments that lead to organizational success, as shown in ■ **EXHIBIT 12.17**.[97]

HR professionals can be instrumental in the development of robust performance management systems that follow all the steps in Exhibit 12.17, and they can go beyond this to help leaders, managers, and employees link performance management to virtually everything they do.

■ **EXHIBIT 12.17**

Five Steps in the Performance Management Process
1. Planning work and setting expectations
2. Continually monitoring performance
3. Developing people's capacity to perform
4. Completing periodic performance reviews
5. Rewarding good performance and correcting underperformance.

Gathering Information about Employee Performance

To evaluate performance and help employees develop, managers need to collect accurate information about employees' behavior on the job. Performance data can consist of the manager's observations, data collected and measured through metrics (e.g., how much revenue a sales representative generated), self-appraisal (in which the employee reflects on his or her own performance), feedback gathered from people who work with the employee, customer feedback, or a combination of all or some of these things.

There are many ways to gather information about employees' performance. HR is often responsible for crafting the process by which robust data about employees' performance is gathered and for teaching managers how to use and share this information. Some methods are straightforward, such as those used for performance that can be easily quantified (e.g., did the employee meet targets for revenue generation through sales, meet with the agreed-on number of customers, or hit production targets?). Other aspects of performance are harder to quantify but are nevertheless essential. These can include demonstration of job-specific and emotional intelligence competencies, all of which are key to individual and group success.

One form of data collection that has become very popular in recent years is called a 360-degree review. A **360-degree review** is a process in which a picture of an employee's or manager's impact and performance is created through self-assessment along with feedback from peers, managers, customers, and other relevant stakeholders. This information can be gathered via an anonymous questionnaire about competencies. The data can then be tabulated to provide the employee with a report that shows how the groups of supervisors, colleagues, and subordinates view him or her. The second way 360-degree data can be

360-degree review
A review process in which a picture of an employee or manager is created through self-assessment along with feedback from peers, managers, customers, and other relevant stakeholders.

gathered is for a manager, HR professional, or an outside consultant to conduct structured, confidential conversations about the employee with relevant individuals. This data is then analyzed to discover themes, which are subsequently presented to the employee (without divulging who said what, of course). This offers the employee a more well-rounded perspective with a wider range of information about how others perceive him or her.

A 360-degree review is a powerful tool because it offers a robust perspective of an employee's effectiveness. However, like any process that involves people's opinions of others, it must be used carefully. First of all, a 360-degree review is far more effective when used for development as opposed to identifying weaknesses. Second, how the feedback is shared is almost as important as what the data says.

Performance Review

Once performance data has been collected, managers and HR professionals often share it with employees in what is called a performance appraisal. A **performance appraisal** is the process of sharing an evaluation of an employee's performance in (ideally) a face-to-face meeting that usually takes place between an employee and his or her manager, although in some organizations, this appraisal is delivered by a human resources manager. Of course, even pristine performance data is useless unless it is shared with employees in a positive way.

Unfortunately, performance appraisal processes are often highly ineffective. Rather than engaging employees in healthy conversations, managers and HR professionals often share feedback in ways that spark resistance, defensiveness, anger, and hurt feelings.[98] It's HR's job to ensure that performance appraisals are positive and helpful, as opposed to negative and destructive.

To do this, HR professionals can develop a performance appraisal process that supports managers and employees during these conversations. This process can include creating a timeline for such conversations: Do they happen once a year or more often? How long should each conversation last? Simple guidelines like these can make a big difference because both managers and employees know what to expect.

HR professionals can also craft a process to follow before, during, and after the performance appraisal conversation. Robust processes include preparation for both the manager and the employee (e.g., structured data collection that includes self-reflection and self-appraisal). Such processes also include a structured way to have the conversation, often using a written document created by the manager that includes relevant data about performance as well as how it was measured. This document provides the guideline for the conversation. One example of such a process is the Balanced Scorecard.

The **Balanced Scorecard** was developed by scholars at Harvard Business School in the 1990s, and it is considered a significant move beyond the traditional concept of performance measurement, which often focuses a tremendous amount of attention on financial measures of success. The Balanced Scorecard takes a more holistic view of success and measures several factors related to performance.[99] With the Balanced Scorecard, four areas are usually measured: financial performance, customers, business processes, and learning and growth. Each of these may be further broken down into subcategories of measurement. When used in performance management, a scorecard can be developed in different ways for different levels and functions within the organization. The scorecard, then, can link employees' performance with the organization's goals and priorities.

The third way in which HR professionals can support effective performance appraisal processes is by training managers to engage in conversations that are meaningful, nonthreatening, and honest. This is harder than it sounds. Having direct, supportive, honest, and caring conversations with employees requires a high degree of emotional intelligence. In order for these conversations to be perceived as helpful, employees need to believe that managers' assessments are accurate, unbiased, and fair.

Performance appraisal
Process of sharing an evaluation of an employee's performance in (ideally) a face-to-face meeting that usually takes place between an employee and his or her manager, although in some organizations, this appraisal is delivered by a human resources manager.

Balanced Scorecard
A review process that takes a holistic view of success and measures several factors related to performance.

Employees also need to experience managers as empathetic: Do they really understand the employees' jobs, working conditions, goals, and hopes? Employees are most likely to respond well to feedback if they believe managers care about them. In addition, research strongly suggests that the most effective appraisals take into consideration employees' lives and personal goals and dreams for themselves and their loved ones. The art and science of establishing developmental goals during appraisals involves finding meaningful intersections between the employee's life and his or her professional aspirations and the needs of the organization.[100]

Management by Objectives: Use with Caution

One common—but not necessarily helpful—performance management approach is called management by objectives.[101] Let's begin by looking at some pros and cons of this method. Management by objectives (MBO) is a performance tool used to help people set goals for themselves in the context of an organization's goals. MBO is often thought to be passé, but it is still adapted for use in organizations today. The method is based on the notion that employees can participate in setting meaningful goals for themselves to help accomplish the organization's goals. The process is based on the idea that if employees receive regular feedback, and are then properly rewarded, they will be motivated, satisfied, and successful. The idea behind this philosophy is to focus employees'—and managers'—attention on outcomes rather than just activities.[102]

Some companies do it right, but more often than not, the MBO process withers on the vine. That's because without open communication, trust, and excellent facilitation of an MBO program, employees can be very reluctant to be involved in the planning and goal-setting processes.[103] Numerous problems can get in the way, such as lack of training for managers or a hostile culture that makes it unsafe for employees to be open about shortcomings. Or, the process becomes just that: a process. Everyone fills in the blanks on the form once a year, but the form is never looked at again. These problems point out how important it is that a performance review process includes robust ways to gather and share information about employee performance.

Discussion Questions

1. Form a group of three to four people from your class. Use your combined knowledge of HR's role in an organization to create a bulleted list of ways to fulfill each one of the five steps in the performance management process given in Exhibit 12.17.

2. Have you ever had a formal performance appraisal with a supervisor? Describe the interaction, and consider how it made you feel before, during, and after. Have you ever discussed your performance in an informal setting with a supervisor? How did this differ from the appraisal?

Objective 12.8
Learn what we can all do to be effective and efficient at work.

8. What Can We All Do to Enhance Effectiveness and Efficiency at Work?

Many people believe that they are not responsible for the control processes you have learned about in this chapter. To the contrary, there are many ways in which you can contribute to an effective control system in your organization. From involvement in the creation of products and services, to measurements of results, to constant attention to improvements, to being personally committed—all of these matter tremendously. In this section, we will focus on two ways that you can become an effective part of an organization's control process: bringing controls to the forefront of your attention and making the right choices in support of a well-managed organization and ethics.

Bringing Financial, Customer, and Quality Controls to Your Attention

As you have learned in this chapter, of particular importance in the control process are three arenas: financial controls, customer service and customer relationship management, and quality control. Virtually every employee is involved in all three of these—but they might not focus on them explicitly (a problem) or ignore them (an even bigger problem). In the *Leadership Perspective*, Rafidah Mohamad Noor of the Ministry of Education in Malaysia weaves a focus on controls in everything she does. Rafidah is the Assistant Director, Management Services Division, Department of Community Colleges, Ministry of Higher Education Malaysia. As she eloquently writes about leadership in the *Leadership Perspective* feature, see if you can identify how she is focusing on controls—as all of us must.

Rafidah Mohamad Noor's words are interesting in that she mentions controls and quality at every possible turn. This is how it should be: No matter where you sit or what you do, the outcomes that your organization achieves are your responsibility. So, what can you do to make sure you pay attention and do the right thing? In the next section, we will look at two things that only you can do: self-management and emotional self-control.

Emotional Self-Awareness and Emotional Self-Control

Emotional Self-awareness and emotional self-control are probably the most important control mechanisms we have at work. Ultimately, we all choose what to do and what not to do. External control measures such as rules, regulations, and culture have a powerful effect on our attitudes, values, and behavior—but when it comes right down to it, we make choices about how we work, which rules we obey, and how we impact others. In order to make choices about what we want and what we do, we need to understand ourselves. Self-awareness is the foundation of emotional intelligence—and self-control. You can't control yourself if you don't understand yourself.

No matter what the organization dictates, we have choices about setting goals for ourselves related to personal or professional development, such as learning a second language, completing our assigned tasks, or supporting the development of new members of our teams. This is self-management—and only you can do it. Interestingly, effective self-management is often seen in organizations that set a tone of positivity, trust, and high expectations for their people.[104] This may be because empowering organizations actually create a positive loop: Trust engenders self-management and effectiveness, which, in turn, engenders more trust, and so on.

In addition to managing our behavior at work, we have choices about how to manage our emotions when we are under pressure, when we are challenged by having to learn new ways of doing things, or when we have the chance to share optimism and excitement about our work. This is called emotional self-control—a fundamental emotional intelligence competency that is at the core of good leadership.[105] When others look to us for guidance—whether as a formal leader, a mentor, or someone they look up to—they pay a lot of attention to our emotions. In fact, a leader's emotions are part of what people use to determine how effective that leader is—and whether to follow him or her.

As we have stressed throughout this book, everyone is a leader in one way or another in today's organizations. As a result, it is important for you to understand how your emotions can affect others. In one study, researchers investigated the effect of the emotional displays of leaders on the emotional states of observers. This study found that the display of negative emotions had a significant, detrimental effect on others' assessments of the leader's effectiveness.[106]

Leadership Perspective

● **Rafidah Mohamad Noor**
Assistant Director, Ministry
of Higher Education Malaysia
"A transformational leader enhances the motivation, morale, and performance of all employees."

Rafidah Mohamad Noor is the Assistant Director, Management Services Division, Department of Community Colleges, Ministry of Higher Education Malaysia. Rafidah is a well-respected professional and leader, young as she is in her career. Her insights are very useful, as they help us see how quality and controls are important in *all* jobs, all around the world. As Rafidah describes in the following overview of her job and what she does to support education in Malaysia, transformational leadership is at the heart of quality services in any organization. Here is what Rafidah would like to share with us:

I am an Assistant Director attached to Management Services Division, Department of Community Colleges in Malaysia. My specific job in the division is the Head of the Human Resources Unit. My job includes, among other things, managing human resources performance, planning and managing training programs, managing staffing, managing job rotation, and serving as a supervisor for six subordinates. Together, we are responsible for all staffing needs for the entire community college system other than the faculty.

The Department of Community Colleges has an inspiring tagline: 'Leading a Knowledgeable and Skilled Community'. The College Community vision is to be a centre for educational development with the commitment to build a knowledgeable and skilled community in line with the National Education Philosophy. The mission is to expand access to education, improving the socio-economic well-being and welfare of the community through education and skill training programs as well as lifelong learning.

Community colleges are a big part of Malaysia's future, as they are in many places around the world. And yet, this type of higher education is not necessarily accepted. This is a very big challenge, but we must change this perception. One of the ways that we will do this is to ensure that every aspect of the community college system is outstanding. We will know we have succeeded when our students feel truly proud to be attending community colleges.

Another challenge that we face in this department is to serve the human resource needs of the entire system, with our small team. We are charged with ensuring the correct placement of employees in all 80 community colleges and the headquarters. This starts with fairly evaluating the candidates and determining where they fit best. Then, we need to manage and monitor their performance so they provide excellent service and improve their skills.

In order to ensure the quality of programs the colleges offer to the community, all the divisions in the department together with the community colleges' management always work hand in hand in planning and executing the programs for the staff and the community. It is crucial that we provide the community colleges with enough budget and quality, skilled, and knowledgeable people in the administration as well as experts.

One of the ways that I direct employees' attention to quality issues is to ensure that they understand the organization's vision and mission and why we need to perform to a certain level. I listen to them and always encourage them to provide ideas to improve our productivity. In managing the routine tasks, we work together in a team to produce the standard operating processes and procedures and revise them together through brainstorming and post mortem. And, to ensure employees can be productive and provide quality services, I understand the need to go through their job scopes frequently to ensure their workloads are reasonable and their goals achievable.

When faced with the challenge of changing the perception of community college education, while educating our students very well along the way, we must ensure quality at every step. This means that no matter what role each employee holds, they must think of themselves as the upholder of the highest standards. It cannot only be the leader who does so—we all need to. And, we need exceptional leadership too.

I admire transformational leaders. A transformational leader enhances the motivation, morale, and performance of all employees. They do so by connecting the employees' sense of identity and self to the mission and the collective identity of the organization. Transformational leaders know their employees: they understand each one's strengths and weaknesses, and they then align each employee with jobs and tasks that optimize their performance.

Transformational leaders are inspiring role models. They challenge employees to take greater ownership for their work, which enables all of us to provide the best, highest quality services possible.

Source: Personal interview and written correspondence with Annie McKee, 2012.

Emotions are also contagious.[107] This means that if you are angry, upset, or stressed, others around you will probably feel this way as well—or be anxious about your state of mind. We know from research in cognitive psychology that when people experience extreme or chronic negative emotions, they are not as effective, do not make the best decisions, and are less creative.[108] On the other hand, when you are appropriately challenged, excited, and optimistic, others will catch this, too, and their performance can soar.

This means that you, as a leader, can have an impact on others' performance simply by managing your emotions. This starts, of course, with recognizing your emotions (that is, with emotional self-awareness). You can improve your ability to recognize and interpret your own emotions by more consciously monitoring your feelings during everyday activities. Then, as you notice how you feel, you can extend your awareness to track how others are responding to you. This simple—but profound—practice can dramatically improve your capacity for self-awareness and self-management.

Discussion Questions

1. Considering a group, team, or organization you belong to, reflect on the ways in which you take personal responsibility for controlling your own—and others'—effectiveness and efficiency. What do you do? What could you do more or less of to improve your contribution to the control process?

2. Think about a group situation in which you are a leader (formal or informal). Now, think about a challenge this group has faced and your emotional response to this challenge. How do you think your emotions impacted other people, the situation, and the outcomes?

9. A Final Word on Organizational Control

Frederick Taylor and other early scholars set the stage for nearly 100 years of research about how to increase efficiency in organizations. This focus continues today, and with the advent of technologies, we have a number of complex and powerful tools we can use to help us be more efficient and improve the quality of our products and services. Still, as positive as these tools and the efficiency/quality movement have been and despite our fascination with this stream of research, these practices have led to some problems.

First, in some organizations, efficiency and cost savings have become primary goals. When this happens, the mission of an organization can be obliterated—noble goals such as providing safe vehicles, safe workplaces, and contributing to society take a backseat to maximizing human and organizational output and financial results. Second, when controls become the goal rather than an enabler of organizational success, organizational cultures can become toxic. In companies where people are constantly under pressure and stressed, it is difficult to sustain creativity and innovation, and people are often not able to do and be their best.

Having said all this, we *need* controls in our organizations. We welcome ways to work more efficiently, and all leaders want to produce quality products and services. So the question isn't whether we need controls at work; it is "How can we use control processes to help us realize all aspects of our organization's mission and create a workplace that is inspired and inspiring?" Luckily, researchers have been pursuing this stream of thought.

Throughout this book, you have been reading about scholars, managers, and leaders who seek to understand how to empower people at work and how to create an environment that supports people in making good decisions about how they work and solve problems. Empowerment is at the heart of positive and powerful organizational controls systems. You've also read about leaders who put ethics first rather than cutting corners, which can foster even more success in the long term. Ethical behavior and cultures that support all of us in making the right choices are key to healthy organizational controls. Finally, you've also learned that when we develop social and emotional intelligence competencies, we can all be great leaders. When we see ourselves as leaders, we take responsibility for guiding people to work in the most effective ways. This, too, is at the heart of the best organizational control systems.

LEADING IN A GLOBAL WORLD
Poor Quality for Sale

One way many organizations have increased efficiency and productivity while lowering costs is offshoring or outsourcing. With China being one of the primary providers of cheap labor and materials to these organizations, the issue of quality control has come into the spotlight many times. Over the last few years, the FDA has issued warnings about poisoned pet food, tainted fish, contaminated food and drugs, and toys tainted by lead paint—all made in China.

1. Research companies that have had quality issues linked to their outsourcing or offshoring practices and their suppliers, vendors, or joint venture partners. How has substandard quality from outsourcing or offshoring partners affected those companies' reputations? Their profitability? What steps did the companies take to remedy the problem? How did they respond to government and public outcry?

2. In small groups, discuss how much influence the government—through agencies such as the FDA in the United States, for example—should have over organizational control processes. What do you think organizations can do to control the standards of the products they buy to resell under their own name?

LEADING WITH EMOTIONAL INTELLIGENCE
Try Being a Little More Human

The human relations movement was spearheaded by people like Elton Mayo and Mary Parker Follett. Their focus on the interdependence of employees, management, and the organization set the pace for people-oriented management control processes. Frederick Taylor, on the other hand, is known as the father of scientific management. Taylor's focus was on efficiency.

1. Research some a few organizations within an industry (e.g. the garment industry), where tasks and efficiency are still the focus and scientific management seems to be a viable philosophy. What type of control processes do they employ to maintain high productivity and efficiency? Where do people fit into the organizational equation? Do you think that scientific management is a legitimate framework in these companies? Why or why not?

2. Research some organizations that make people the primary focus. Many of these organizations refer to their employees as internal customers. How does treating employees like customers change the control process from task-focused to human

relations-focused? Discuss how treating employees with respect and empathy can actually increase productivity and efficiency.

LEADING WITH CRITICAL THINKING SKILLS
Making the Grade—or Not

Control processes take many different forms in organizations. Some organizations define their vision and mission, set goals and objectives related to the vision/mission, and then, literally, "go about their business" in order to meet those stated goals and objectives. At any point in the business process, control systems can be applied to measure quality, efficiency, and profitability.

In addition to being an educational facility, your school is a business. Therefore, it controls and measures, among other things, the quality of the faculty it hires and of the students it admits by setting performance standards for both.

1. Identify the various control processes your school has implemented to ensure quality, efficiency, and profitability. For instance, research the metrics and standards of your school. What is the minimum GPA needed for graduation? The minimum GPA for your major? What other metrics does your school use to control students' academic outcomes? Social outcomes? Ethics? Other?

2. Now, think of a past class. Plot the typical "performance measurement" points through a semester—the number of tests, exams, homework, projects, etc. How was your performance compared to standards? Other than grades, what are some of the other forms of feedback you typically received for your performance? Do you think the standards and measurement methods were fair? Why or why not?

3. Interview a faculty member about how he or she is measured on performance. Describe the evaluation process for faculty. How often are they reviewed for their performance? What different points are faculty evaluated on? Do faculty members think the performance measurement process is fair and/or right for the students—one of their primary "customers"? Why or why not?

ETHICAL LEADERSHIP
Ranking and Yanking

Organizations are expected to encourage ethical behavior among their employees. Most companies do; unfortunately, some do not. Imagine that you work as a salesperson for one of these unethical companies. Your fictitious employer not only encourages unethical behavior, but bases your review and compensation upon your compliance with these practices through a system commonly referred to as "rank-and-yank." Your manager has made it clear that neither poor performance nor questions about the company's business practices will be tolerated. You know the manager isn't bluffing; you've seen a friend and coworker who openly disagreed with company policy be bullied and intimidated by management before being fired. In other words, you know you have to play by the company's rules if you want to get ahead keep your job—even if that means going against what you know is right.

1. If you are like most people, losing your job will cause extreme hardship. So, you might be tempted to rationalize behavior you would not otherwise accept in yourself or others. How might you rationalize your behavior if you worked for this company? Make a list of specific justifications you might use to rationalize the unethical behavior your company expects.

2. Pretend that your company's unethical practices have been uncovered by CNN. Break into pairs and with your partner prepare for an interview with CNN. In the interview, you will discuss how your job, pay increases, and bonuses are based on clearly unethical practices. While preparing for the interview, compare your list of rationalization points with your partner. Also be sure to discuss the following points:

- Does it matter if you're a single parent with two children in college or a new hire fresh out of college in your first job?
- Would it matter if these practices were being investigated for their legality?
- Who, ultimately, holds accountability for your actions as an employee?

If you need to, refer back to Chapter 2 for information about handling ethical dilemmas.

KEY TERMS

Customer relationship management (CRM), p. 428

Control process, p. 428

Scientific management, p. 430

Human relations movement, p. 431

Hawthorne Studies, p. 431

Financial controls, p. 435

Budget, p. 435

Accounting controls, p. 436

Cash flow analysis, p. 436

Balance sheet, p. 437

Profit and loss statement, p. 437

Beyond Budgeting, p. 437

Operations management, p. 439

Business process reengineering (BPR), p. 439

Total Quality Management (TQM), p. 440

Six Sigma, p. 440

Lean Management, p. 442

Bureaucratic control systems, p. 445

Output control, p. 446

Behavior control, p. 447

Normative control, p. 447

Levers of control, p. 447

Standards and metrics, p. 449

Feedback control, p. 451

Feed-forward control, p. 451

Concurrent control, p. 452

Corporate governance, p. 453

Corporate charter, p. 453

Board of directors, p. 453

Privately held company, p. 454

Publicly traded company, p. 454

Shareholders, p. 454

Audit, p. 454

Sarbanes-Oxley Act of 2002, p. 455

360-degree review, p. 458

Performance appraisal, p. 459

Balanced Scorecard, p. 459

MyManagementLab

Go to **mymanagementlab.com** for Auto-graded writing questions as well as the following Assisted-graded writing questions:

12-1. Consider a process that you see implemented at school or at work every day, such as cleaning the classrooms or offices. What controls seem to be in place to ensure effectiveness and efficiency? Are the employees who perform these jobs involved in controlling their work output? If so, how?

12-2. Research some companies that involve their customers in product design via the Internet. What is your opinion about involving customers in design and other control processes? What are the benefits? What are the drawbacks?

12-3. Mymanagementlab Only — comprehensive writing assignment for this chapter.

1. What Is the Organizational Control Process? (p. 428–429)

Objective: Define organizational control.

Summary: The control process includes systems for establishing standards, monitoring and measuring performance, comparing performance to standards, and taking corrective action when needed. These systems apply to a variety of areas, from employee behavior to product quality. In most situations, control processes are designed to prevent disasters problems and improve performance.

2. Which Historical Perspectives Help Us Understand Control in Organizations? (pp. 429–434)

Objective: Understand which historical perspectives help us understand control in organizations.

Summary: Three theorists figured prominently in the early study of management and organizational control: Frederick Taylor, Elton Mayo, and Mary Parker Follett. Taylor, with his concept of scientific management, was primarily concerned with reducing waste and inefficiency in production processes, often with little regard for the individuals performing work tasks. Mayo and Follett, on the other hand, were particularly interested in the people aspects of management, including how employees and managers interact, how power is used, and how the personal and production aspects of work interact. These people-centric theories, particularly those developed by Follett, are largely responsible for the modern movement toward empowerment and resonant leadership.

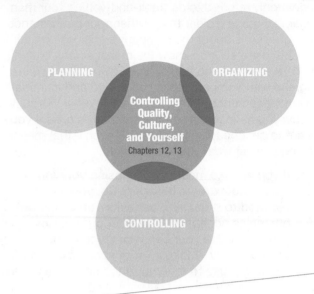

3. What Do Companies Try to Control Today? (pp. 434–444)

Objective: Describe common control systems.

Summary: Companies typically seek to control finances, customer service, and quality, and activities in one area impact the other two. A budget is one of the most basic financial controls. Accounting controls include cash flow analyses, balance sheets, and P&L statements. Customer service controls are directed toward monitoring and improving customer service, with the goal of building and maintaining a loyal customer base. Finally, quality controls strive to ensure that inputs are being transformed into ideal outputs through systems like TQM, Six Sigma, Lean Management, and the ISO family of standards.

4. What Are Common Control Systems? (pp. 445–448)

Objective: Understand conventions and forces that guide the organizational control processes.

Summary: Bureaucratic control systems use rules, standards, and hierarchical authority to achieve desired outcomes in ways that involve little individual judgment. Objective controls can enhance and/or replace bureaucratic controls as they focus on what is actually done or accomplished and less on formal rules and policies. Output, behavior and normative controls are examples of systems that can augment bureaucratic controls. Finally, the levers of control model combines the best aspects of several control systems to ensure a people- and process-oriented control system.

Simons' Levers of Control[78]

Lever	How It Works	Examples
Belief Systems	Defines the core values of an organization and its members	Credos, mission statements, and values statements
Boundary Systems	Defines territory or span of control for people within the organization	Rules, proscriptions, and regulations of the organization
Diagnostic Control Systems	Feedback system that allows the organization to monitor standards	Systems to measure output, as well as incentives and goals
Interactive Control Systems	Allows managers to plan how to regularly involve themselves personally in their subordinates' decision-making activities	Project management systems, knowledge management systems, and scheduling systems

5. What Are the Typical Steps in the Control Process? (pp. 448–452)

Objective: List the typical steps in the control process.

Summary: Control systems can be engaged during any stage in the organizational process and are typically used to determine the efficiency and quality of business processes and/or the goods or services produced or provided. Both quantitative and qualitative measurements can be used to measure performance against goals. Corrective action must be taken when specifications aren't met or opportunities are being missed.

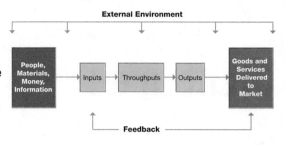

6. How Do Corporate Governance, Audits, and Legislation Support Ethical Behavior? (pp. 453–456)

Objective: Assess what companies should control.

Summary: Corporate governance is an important control process, as it dictates the ways in which the company is administered based on internal policies and external laws. To ensure that people and the organization as a whole are doing what they should, a formal review or audit may be used as an evaluation tool. Both of these structures are increasingly important for ensuring that a company's legal obligations are met, particularly since the passage of the Sarbanes-Oxley Act (SOX) and in the United States and subsequently, and increased oversight of publicly held companies. Recently, some companies are shifting from a compliance mentality to inviting guidance from key stakeholders, such as customers. This concept is likely to gain popularity in the future thanks to social networking and the desire of consumers to have a hand in making decisions about the things they purchase.

7. What Can HR Do to Help Control for Effectiveness and Efficiency at Work? (pp. 456–460)

Objective: Learn what HR can do to help control for effectiveness and efficiency.

Summary: Performance management as a control mechanism is often the responsibility of the HR professionals within an organization. In order for performance management systems to be effective, we need adequate structures and processes for gathering data about people's performance and sharing it with them. It is essential for feedback to be delivered in a constructive, compassionate way to ensure positive employee response. Appraisals should also help employees set goals for their careers that strike a meaningful balance between their professional and personal aspirations and the goals of the organization.

8. What Can We All Do to Enhance Effectiveness and Efficiency at Work? (pp. 460–463)

Objective: Learn what we can all do to be effective and efficient at work.

Summary: Emotional self-awareness and emotional self-control are two things that all of us can develop as powerful organizational control processes. Emotional self-control is important because negative emotions can interfere with one's effectiveness. Emotions are also contagious, so a leader's emotions, both positive and negative, can impact others' performance. Before we can control ourselves, of course, we have to understand ourselves. That's why emotional self-awareness is key to emotional intelligence and self management.

9. A Final Word on Organizational Control (p. 463)

Summary: Organizational control processes need to strike a balance between financial goals, customer goals, and the overall mission of the organization. We need to be careful not to rely too much on tools and processes that foster efficiency, and to balance this with empowerment, ethics, and resonant leadership—three keys to truly effective control systems in organizations.

CHAPTER 13

Culture:

It's Powerful

PLANNING

ORGANIZING

Controlling
Quality,
Culture,
and Yourself
Chapters 12, 13

CONTROLLING

MyManagementLab™

⭐ Improve Your Grade!

Over 10 million students improved their results using the Pearson MyLabs.
Visit **mymanagementlab.com** for simulations, tutorials, and end-of-chapter
problems.

Chapter Outline

Chapter Objectives

13.1 Define culture.

13.2 Understand the importance of
culture at work.

13.3 Describe the dimensions of
national and organizational
culture.

13.4 Explain various types of
organizational cultures.

13.5 Learn how to study organizational
culture.

13.6 Assess the important aspects of
organizational culture.

13.7 Learn how HR can support
the development of positive
organizational cultures.

13.8 Learn ways we can create
positive and powerful
organizational cultures.

Objective 13.1
Define culture.

Culture
Everything that the people in a society have learned and share through traditions, pass on to children, and teach new members; this includes religion, beliefs, political ideologies, values, customs, foods, language, gender roles, sexuality, and many other aspects of everyday life.

■ **EXHIBIT 13.1**
What lessons about our own culture can we learn from Margaret Mead's study of Samoan culture?

Source: Pictorial Press/Alamy

1. What Is Culture?

The famous anthropologist Margaret Mead defined **culture** as everything that people in a society have learned and share through traditions, pass on to children, and teach new members (■ **EXHIBIT 13.1**). According to this view, culture includes religion, beliefs, political ideologies, values, customs, foods, language, gender roles, sexuality, and many other aspects of everyday life.[1]

Culture is a powerful force in our lives because it guides our beliefs, our values, and almost everything we do at home, in our communities, and at work. We learn about culture from the moment we are born. The language we learn is part of our culture. The food we eat is part of our culture. Our manners and how we behave are part of our culture. Culture and cultural expectations affect how we think, feel, and act. Culture is often invisible and so much a part of us that we may not realize we are following its "rules." Rather, these "rules" are simply the way things are supposed to be. As organizational scholar Geert Hofstede puts it, culture is the "collective programming of the mind."[2]

To be an effective leader, manager, or employee, you must appreciate how culture affects people, influences relationships, and impacts organizations. In this chapter, you will study aspects of culture that affect people at work and in other relationships. You will also learn about models of culture in organizations. In addition, you will evaluate the types of organizational cultures that are important today, HR's role in creating and maintaining healthy cultures, and what we can all do to create powerful organizational cultures. Let's start by developing a deeper understanding of the ways in which values, attitudes, and commonly held expectations of behavior relate to culture.

Values: The Heart of Culture

Values are ideas that a person or a group believes to be right or wrong, good or bad, attractive or undesirable.[3] Values linked to a society's culture often include ideas about principles like freedom, democracy, truth, and justice. Values also include beliefs about things such as sex, marriage, and raising children. For example, you might have certain values associated with family life: Should you be married before having children? Should adult children care for elderly parents at home, rather than moving them to a nursing facility? Should family members be loyal no matter what someone does? You may have strong opinions about these questions. That's because values aren't just abstract ideas—they often help define who we are and can therefore produce very strong emotions.

Deeply held values are profound drivers of our behavior at work and in life. People will fight and even die for values that are important to them, such as justice, freedom, or those linked with religious beliefs. Do you know which values are most important to you and why? Do you know how your values affect you at work? Understanding your values will help you both in life and at work.

One example of a personal value that often impacts how people feel and behave in the workplace is "fairness." People who place a high value on fairness often act in ways that enhance justice and equality. Individuals who hold this value typically favor use of the merit system, and they believe that employees should be rewarded for their performance. In addition, these people are generally on the alert for any signs of injustice. If such signs are detected, people who value fairness may become angry, frustrated, and demoralized at work.

Organizations often promote values that guide behavior among employees, customers, and stakeholders and describe how to treat property and the natural environment. One example of an organizational value that is commonly espoused in many companies goes something like this: "People are our greatest asset." Companies that hold this value tend to place special emphasis on supporting people's learning, development, health, and well-being.

In companies that put a high value on people, you might expect that managers who mistreat employees would be chastised and maybe even let go. Indeed, this was recently the case in one U.S. law firm. This firm was a partnership—meaning that the senior lawyers owned the business together. In this sort of business structure, it is very difficult to fire people. Nevertheless, this particular company decided that some of its partners were not living up to the firm's values about how to treat people. These partners were not supporting the young attorneys' development, they often communicated in harsh and unprofessional ways, and they were causing employees to burn out. The firm's leadership felt that this violation of values was serious—and they fired several partners as a result.

Attitudes: A Collection of Beliefs and Feelings

Sometimes we hear people say things like "He has a bad attitude" or "Her attitude is so positive!" These types of statements are often shorthand for any number of beliefs, values, and behaviors that relate to how someone treats others and/or how he or she is seen at work. When we hear statements like these, it is important for us to go beyond the shorthand and find out exactly what is meant.

Attitudes are interrelated ideas, values, beliefs, and feelings that predispose a person to react to a thing, a situation, another person, or a group in a certain way.[4] What is your attitude toward school? Do you value learning and feel generally positive about your classes, and do you usually see the benefits of attending school? Or do you resent having to go to school? How does your attitude about school affect your study habits?

Attitudes matter when it comes to how we perceive situations and judge people, and in turn, how those people see and judge us. Strongly held attitudes evoke strong emotions in people in much the same way that values do. Many people don't spend much time thinking about their values or attitudes, or about which of these are most important and which are less so. That's because values and attitudes are so much a part of who we are that they often go unexamined.

Good leaders, however, do not leave values or attitudes unexamined. They constantly push themselves to understand what is driving them, which values are sacrosanct, and which attitudes may need to change. Understanding our own values and attitudes—and the emotions we attach to them—is critical, because this kind of self-awareness helps us understand our behavior and develop a personal code of ethics. Knowing our values also helps us better understand other people's values, and it permits us to examine the values that our organizations ask us to uphold. Values and attitudes are also important because they affect behaviors and norms.

Attitudes
Interrelated ideas, values, beliefs, and feelings that predispose a person to react to a thing, a situation, another person, or a group in a certain way.

Norms: We're Supposed to Do What?

Norms are internalized standards for behavior that support agreed-upon ways of doing things and what people expect of one another within a cultural group. For example, norms guide how we dress and behave at a formal dinner, how we greet one another, and how we behave with friends versus family versus coworkers.

Norms are often unspoken, and in some cases, people may not even recognize them until they are violated. For instance, in the United States, people go to the end of the line at a counter in a store and wait until it is their turn to pay for their merchandise.

Norms
Internalized standards for behavior that support agreed-upon ways of doing things and what people expect of one another within a cultural group.

No one has to tell us to do that—it's just what happens. Now, imagine what you would think and feel if someone violated this norm and walked to the front of the line. You'd probably be irritated. Or, imagine how you would feel if someone joined you on an elevator and stood several inches closer than normal. What would you do? What would you think of the person? Your thoughts and feelings would be in part related to the fact that the person was violating norms about personal space.

Some norms function like guidelines, whereas others are more like social rules. Accordingly, scholars have identified two distinct categories of norms: folkways, which are like guidelines, and mores (pronounced "morays"), which are stricter social rules. Folkways are the routine conventions of everyday life. They include aspects of culture such as appropriate dress and good manners. People who violate folkways may be perceived as odd or weird, but not necessarily as evil or bad (■ **EXHIBIT 13.2**). For example, if you jumped fully dressed into a crowded pool, others would view you as an oddball. Folkways also exist at work, and they might include such things as how you greet senior managers, how you are expected to behave at an office party (e.g., don't drink too much), or how carefully you attend to the start and end times of meetings.

As opposed to folkways, mores are norms that are central to the functioning of society or a group. Closer to rules than guidelines, mores might include a society's stance on murder, rape, sexuality, or childrearing practices. When people violate mores, they can face serious reprisals, often because many of our mores are codified into laws. For example, in many societies, people face trial and possible jail time for theft, murder, or incest.

Societies differ, of course, and mores are not universal from one culture to the next. For instance, several countries, including the United States, have laws that prohibit polygamy. The nation of Senegal, however, does not have mores prohibiting polygamy. Thus, in Senegal, polygamy is allowed and practiced alongside marriages between one man and one woman. Indeed, one researcher found that 15 percent of Christian men and 28 percent of Muslim men in Senegal reported having polygamous marriages in the year 2000. This equaled close to 29 percent of the country's population.[5] This data is, predictably, hard to track. Mores can change over time. And, as globalization takes hold, traditional values are being challenged around the world. For example, there are indications that polygamy is being questioned in many countries in which it is practiced.

Within the work environment, mores often revolve around core business practices and ethics. For example, many businesses expect their employees to refuse to take or offer bribes for any reason or in any situation. Another example of a more might relate to the protection of corporate secrets, such as the formulas involved in preparing products like Kentucky Fried Chicken or Coca-Cola.

Understanding how values and norms differ in cultures is critical in business today. That's because so many businesses conduct operations outside their home countries and/or employ people whose cultures differ. To work together effectively, people need to understand and respect one another's norms and values. For example, it is often said that the failure of the auto industry merger between Daimler-Benz (maker of Mercedes-Benz) and Chrysler was linked to irreconcilable differences in culture and the inability of company leaders to bridge these gaps.[6] In the next section, we will look at other aspects of culture and how they affect us at work.

Folkways
The routine conventions of everyday life.

Mores
Norms that are central to the functioning of a society or group.

■ **EXHIBIT 13.2**
Why are unusual hairstyles often seen as a violation of folkways?

Source: blickwinkel/Alamy

Discussion Questions

1. What are your core values—those values that define who you are as a person and guide you in some of the most important areas of your life, including family, relationships, and work?

2. Have you ever experienced a new and different culture? If so, how did you learn about the norms of that culture?

2. Why Is Culture Important at Work?

Objective 13.2
Understand the importance of culture at work.

Culture is important at work because it guides people's behavior. Today's organizations often consist of individuals from many countries, and these individuals' cultures are different. This impacts how people work with and relate to others. Within many countries, numerous cultures exist—and need to coexist—in organizations. Diversity is therefore a fact of life in modern organizations.

Culture and Diversity in a Global World

People from different cultures often have different ways of expressing their values, different ways of building and maintaining relationships, and diverse needs and habits. In today's organizations, we can't even assume that people will speak the same native language. These differences can be tricky to navigate in a workplace, so we need to find a way to build bridges across our differences. People must understand their own and others' cultures in order to work together effectively.

Many leaders and companies today take culture and diversity seriously. They focus time and attention on helping leaders build the skills necessary to navigate the differences inherent in working globally. Take, for example, CSL Behring, a global plasma-based pharmaceutical company that specializes in protein biotherapeutics—making life-saving drugs from the proteins found in human plasma.[7] Let's see what one of the company's leaders, Michael Gaines, has to say about working in a multicultural organization in the *Leadership Perspective* feature on the following page.

Like CSL Behring, many organizations employ a multicultural workforce and also do business outside their home countries. For example, Unilever, a large consumer goods company based in London and Rotterdam, has operations in about 50 countries and does business in 190. ExxonMobil lists 45 countries in which it operates, and it sells gas and other products in 100 countries. Similarly, Nike is based in Beaverton, Oregon, but employs people in Europe, the Middle East, Africa, Asia, and the Americas.[8] Global business isn't just for large companies, either. Consider the case of a small leadership consulting firm called the Teleos Leadership Institute. Teleos is based in Philadelphia and has less than 20 full-time employees, but the company provides services in over a dozen countries. It also employs full-time and associate staff from several nations.[9]

Organizational Culture

Yet another reason why it is important to study culture is that culture is an incredibly powerful force in organizations. Each and every organization develops its own culture that is related to—but distinct from—the national and regional cultures from which it emerged. Organizational cultures are powerful drivers of behavior and results. Organizational culture is a set of shared values, norms, and assumptions that guide peoples' behavior within a group, business, or institution.[10] Organizational culture contributes significantly to the effectiveness of an organization.[11] Each organization has its own unique blend of values, customs, habits, traditions, and beliefs. Moreover, culture is a form of control in organizations, and it can have a tremendous impact on individual behavior and, ultimately, on an organization's success or failure. Organizational culture regulates behavior both implicitly and explicitly, and it can direct people's actions more effectively than standard control systems.[12] This is the case because, unlike rules and directives that come from outside an individual, culture tends to be internalized—it is part of who we are.

Organizational culture
A set of shared values, norms, and assumptions that guide peoples' behavior within a group, business, or institution.

We will dedicate a good portion of this chapter to issues related to both diversity and organizational culture. First, though, it's important to understand how scholars understand dimensions of national and organizational culture.

Leadership Perspective

● **Michael Gaines**
Director of Global Commercial Development, CSL Behring
"Your feelings about your work and other people show—it's a universal language that affects the morale of everyone . . . "

Michael Gaines, director of Global Commercial Development at CSL Behring, is a dynamic and powerful leader. Michael's team is co-located in the United States and in Switzerland, and his company does business all over the world. Michael's keen intelligence and, in particular, his emotional intelligence are evident in the way he builds great relationships and gets immense results when working in a global, multicultural environment:

First, you need to have patience. It takes a while for people to trust each other across cultures. You need to spend time on projects, at dinner, over lunch. People need to feel that you understand them, and that you have some idea of who they are outside of work. It takes a lot of time, but it's worth it.

And simple things aren't as simple as they may seem. Take language—precision in language is essential. Things can be misunderstood when people are working in a language that is not their native tongue.

And this next one is hard—you have to understand that everyone holds certain beliefs about cultures that may or may not be true—including ourselves. We don't like admitting that such perceptions exist, but they do. If you know them, you can either leverage them or break them down.

All of these guidelines matter a lot when working in a multicultural environment. But what matters most of all is who you are. When you have genuine interest in what you do and the people you work with, that's positive and it's contagious. When you take pride in what you do, what your team has accomplished, others will as well, no matter how different your cultures are. Your feelings about your work and other people show—it's a universal language that affects the morale of everyone, as well as organizational results.

Michael goes on to describe how learning to work successfully in a multicultural environment can help people become great leaders:

If you approach working in a multicultural environment openly with intense focus on maintaining your self-awareness, you will have the ability to connect with people even if their point of view is in opposition to your perspective on a project. People will sense that you are seeking, "What can I learn from you?" They will feel more inclined to learn from you as well. You will be seen as approachable—someone who looks at things from different points of view. You will be seen as a person with a high level of integrity—one who treats people fairly and someone people can trust.

Source: Personal interviews with Michael Gaines conducted by Annie McKee, 2009 and 2012.

Discussion Questions

1. Have you ever experienced a misunderstanding as the result of a cultural difference between you and someone else? If so, describe that experience.

2. In what ways do you think you may have benefited from being in a culturally diverse workplace, school, or group? How has the experience affected your people skills, your adaptability to new environments, and your understanding of other ways of doing things?

Objective 13.3
Describe the dimensions of national and organizational culture.

3. What Are the Dimensions of National and Organizational Culture?

In this portion of the chapter, you'll learn about various dimensions of culture that are found in national or ethnic groups and in organizations. Much of this information can be traced to the groundbreaking research conducted by psychologist Geert

Hofstede in the 1960s and 1970s.[13] More recently, research by the Global Leadership and Organizational Behavior Effectiveness (GLOBE) project has extended Hofstede's work by identifying nine dimensions in which cultures differ. Dimensions of culture are important to understand, in part because they give us simple ways to describe how cultures and subcultures affect us at work.

Hofstede's Dimensions of Culture

During the late 1960s and early 1970s, Geert Hofstede studied the attitudes and values of over 70,000 IBM employees working in 40 countries. This was the beginning of decades of studies involving many more people and countries. In his research, Hofstede identified four dimensions that he proposed represent differences across cultures: power distance, uncertainty avoidance, individualism/collectivism, and masculinity/femininity (■ **EXHIBIT 13.3**). Several years later, Hofstede added a fifth dimension, long- versus short-term orientation.[14]

Power distance
The degree to which members of a society accept/expect an unequal distribution of power.

■ **EXHIBIT 13.3**
Hofstede's five dimensions of culture.[15]

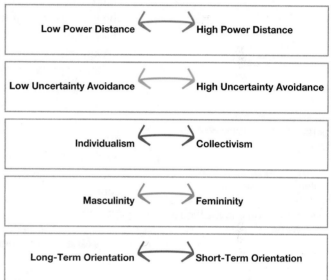

Let's look at each dimension in turn. **Power distance** is the degree to which members of a society accept/expect an unequal distribution of power. In high power distance cultures, people accept wide variance in the amount of power possessed by different individuals and groups. Titles, rank, and status are important in these societies. Within organizations in high power distance cultures, employees show great respect for individuals in positions of authority. In low power distance cultures, however, people downplay power and authority and do not see these characteristics as legitimate ways to differentiate people. For example, in a low power distance society, people might be focused on minimizing the difference between the rich and poor. In organizations with low power distance, employees might feel they have the right to disagree with their managers, and managers might be more inclined to involve employees in making decisions. Moreover, managers may be empowered to make decisions and take risks even when they are farther down in the leadership hierarchy.

Uncertainty avoidance reflects the degree to which people tolerate unpredictable, ambiguous, or uncertain situations. In high uncertainty avoidance cultures, people feel threatened by ambiguity and change, and they may be less tolerant of new ideas. In such cultures, we often see high need for written rules and regulations. In organizations characterized by the tendency to avoid uncertainty, managers are often closely involved with details and activities tend to be highly structured. In comparison, managers in cultures that accept uncertainty are more comfortable with taking risks: Uncertainty and change are a way of life and are easily accepted.

Uncertainty avoidance
The degree to which people can tolerate unpredictable, ambiguous, or uncertain situations.

Individualism/collectivism refers to different orientations toward self-interest versus group interest. Individualism refers to the degree to which people prefer to act in their own self-interest instead of acting on what is best for the group as a whole. High individualism cultures tend to place importance on personal time, freedom, autonomy, and challenge. Accordingly, people from individualist cultures are expected to look after their own interests and those of their immediate families, and individual decisions are frequently considered better than group decisions. In contrast, collectivism is the degree to which people prefer to act as members of a group (rather than as individuals) in exchange for loyalty and the benefits of membership. Collectivists expect people in their group to look after and protect them, just as they look after and protect others. In cultures high in collectivism, group decisions are viewed as better than individual decisions, and employees are often very loyal to their companies.

Individualism
The degree to which people prefer to act in their own self-interest instead of acting on what is best for the group as a whole.

Collectivism
The degree to which people prefer to act as members of a group (rather than as individuals) in exchange for loyalty and the benefits of membership.

Masculinity/femininity
The extent to which society values achieving (masculine) versus nurturing (feminine).

The masculinity/femininity dimension focuses on the extent to which a society values achieving (masculine) versus nurturing (feminine). It is important to note that this does *not* necessarily mean that certain traditional roles, behaviors, or emotions are the sole responsibility of one gender or the other.

Masculinity refers to the preference for achievement, assertiveness, and/or the acquisition of money and material goods. In masculine cultures, the dominant approach can be summarized as "live to work," and emphasis is placed on independence and decisiveness. In cultures that are high in masculinity, women must adopt certain behaviors associated with stereotypical masculinity in order to succeed. The same would be true for men who don't naturally tend toward the cultural traits that Hofstede termed masculine.

Within Hofstede's model, femininity refers to a preference for relationships, cooperation, and quality of life. Accordingly, in cultures that are high in femininity, the dominant approach can be described as "work to live," and there is an emphasis on interdependence. In organizations that embody this trait, women and men high on the feminine side of the equation would not have to adopt more masculine behaviors in order to be successful. Rather, everyone would be required to exhibit behaviors that strengthen relationships or place quality over quantity.

Long-term orientation
Refers to a greater concern for the future and for values such as thrift, perseverance, and avoidance of shame.

Short-term orientation
Refers to a desire for gratification of personal needs, as well as a focus on tradition and meeting social obligations.

Long- versus short-term orientation refers to people's concerns for the future versus immediate gratification. Long-term orientation refers to a greater concern for the future and for values such as thrift, perseverance, and avoidance of shame. In cultures with a long-term orientation, people focus on the future and value persistence. On the other hand, short-term orientation refers to a desire for gratification of personal needs, as well as a focus on tradition and meeting social obligations.[16] Hofstede added the long- versus short-term orientation dimension as a result of additional studies conducted both at IBM and in China. Interestingly, this dimension was first called Confucian dynamism because it called attention to traditional Confucian values.[17]

In the years since its initial publication in 1980, Hofstede's work has formed the basis for a vast number of studies about organizational culture. One of these efforts has gained traction with both researchers and managers because it supports and extends Hofstede's work. This study is known as the GLOBE project.

The GLOBE Project Value Dimensions

Using data from 18,000 managers in 62 countries, the research team behind the GLOBE project proposed nine dimensions of culture in 2004 (■ **EXHIBIT 13.4**).[18] Two of the GLOBE value dimensions are similar to Hofstede's dimensions: power distance and uncertainty avoidance. Also, GLOBE's future orientation is much like Hofstede's long- versus short-term orientation, and its institutional collectivism is akin to Hofstede's individualism/collectivism dimension. The five remaining GLOBE dimensions offer additional insights into culture. These five dimensions are assertiveness, gender differentiation, in-group collectivism, performance orientation, and humane orientation.

As a leader, it's important for you to understand how cultures differ. In seeking to bridge gaps related to cultural differences, you can begin by studying the dimensions presented in both the Hofstede and the GLOBE models. For example, say that you are an American manager who has been asked to manage a subsidiary in Sweden. Based on your knowledge of the GLOBE model, you might be prepared for differences in how you and the people in the subsidiary approach assertiveness. Partly because of the influence of American culture and partly because of your own personal style of interaction, you tend to be highly assertive at work. You are often the first to propose or push an idea at a meeting, for instance, and when you notice that people are not participating in a discussion, you tend to publicly draw them out. However, because

■ **EXHIBIT 13.4**

GLOBE Project Value Dimensions[19]

GLOBE Project Dimension	Description	Country Examples	
Power Distance The strength of social norms regarding inequality in the distribution of power.	Societies high on power distance focus on status and power, and leaders expect deference from their subordinates. Societies low on power distance favor participative decision making and egalitarian relationships.	**HIGH:**	Russia Spain Thailand
		MED:	England France Brazil
		LOW:	Denmark Netherlands South Africa
Uncertainty Avoidance The degree of importance members of a society place on social norms, rules, and procedures to diminish unpredictability.	Societies high on this dimension value structure and clear expectations. Societies low on this dimension do not value rules and procedures and accept ambiguity.	**HIGH:**	Austria Denmark Sweden
		MED:	Israel United States Mexico
		LOW:	Russia Greece Venezuela
Future Orientation The importance that members of a society place on long-term goals and rewards relative to short-term goals and rewards.	Societies high on future orientation plan for the future and delay gratification. Societies low on this dimension focus on short-term results and instant gratification.	**HIGH:**	Denmark Canada (English speaking) Singapore
		MED:	Slovenia Ireland India
		LOW:	Russia Argentina Italy
Institutional Collectivism The extent to which the members of a society are encouraged and take pride in being part of collective actions.	An institutional emphasis on collectivism allocates resources so that all members can participate in economic, social, and political processes. A greater emphasis is placed on group goals than individual goals. Low emphasis on collectivism encourages self-interest. Here, rewards are based on individual performance.	**HIGH:**	Denmark Japan Sweden
		MED:	United States Poland Egypt
		LOW:	Argentina Greece Italy
Assertiveness The value a society places on being direct, assertive, and competitive.	A high value for assertiveness represents a society that encourages and rewards toughness, a certain degree of forcefulness, and competitiveness. A low value for assertiveness refers to a society that values gentleness and modesty.	**HIGH:**	Spain United States Austria
		MED:	Egypt France Ireland
		LOW:	Sweden Switzerland Japan

(continued)

■ **EXHIBIT 13.4** *(continued)*

GLOBE Project Value Dimensions

GLOBE Project Dimension	Description	Country Examples	
Gender Differentiation The degree to which a society differentiates "masculine" and "feminine" qualities, and how much status and decision making responsibilities are given to women.	Societies high on this dimension grant one gender higher status. Societies that score low on gender differentiation grant more equal status to men and women.	**HIGH:**	South Korea Egypt China
		MED:	Italy Brazil Venezuela
		LOW:	Sweden Denmark Poland
In-Group Collectivism The importance societies place on close-knit social networks, such as family, small groups, close circles of friends, and teams.	Societies high on this dimension will likely provide benefits for families or have structures encouraging groups to get together to socialize. Societies low on this dimension might place less emphasis on the importance of the nuclear family and more on allegiance to country.	**HIGH*:**	China India Egypt
		MED:	Japan Italy Israel
		LOW:	Denmark Sweden Finland
Performance Orientation The degree of value societies place on performance and achievement as significant goals.	Societies high on this dimension value training and development and believe in taking initiative. People who live in societies that are low on this dimension may feel uncomfortable with feedback.	**HIGH:**	United States Taiwan Singapore
		MED:	Sweden Japan England
		LOW:	Russia Greece Italy
Humane Orientation The degree of value societies place on altruistic behavior, empathetic concern for others, and generosity.	Societies high on this dimension focus on human relations and sympathy. Societies low on this dimension are motivated by material possessions.	**HIGH:**	Indonesia Egypt Ireland
		MED:	Sweden United States Hong Kong
		LOW:	Germany (Former West) France Spain

*A high score corresponds to collectivism and a low score corresponds to individualism.[20]

Source: Based on Robert House, Paul J. Hanges, Mansour Javidan, and Peter W. Dorfman (eds.), *Culture, Leadership, and Organizations: The GLOBE Study of 62 societies* (Thousand Oaks, CA: Sage Publications, 2004).

you are aware that people in Sweden generally score low on assertiveness, you decide that it would be wise to adjust your usual approach. Otherwise, you are likely to offend people, or at the very least confuse them. In this situation, you must also work to understand what your Swedish employees value and how this affects their behavior.

Culture: It's Complicated!

As you can see, considering the most effective ways to bridge cultural differences can be complicated. After all, it's extremely difficult to account for all of the many values, norms, and other dimensions of a culture. That is partly because dimensions and values are by no means pure or truly shared by every member of a society. Why is this? First, multiple strong subcultures always exist within a society's dominant culture, and second, culture is always changing.

SUBCULTURES

Rarely (if ever) do all members of a broader culture share all of the same values, attitudes, beliefs, and norms. This is the case because every culture functions much like an umbrella under which many smaller subcultures exist. Examples of subcultures abound, including religious, age, political, or regional groups, among many others. Consider, for instance, some of the regional subcultures found in the United States, including those associated with the South, the Northeast, the Midwest, New York City, and California. Or, consider regional subcultures in China: Three important Chinese subcultures include those in Tibet, Cantonese-speaking Guangzhou province, and the Xinjiang Uyghur Region. Different values, attitudes, and norms exist in each of these different subcultures, although all of these subcultures still reflect elements of the broader national culture.

Have you ever had roommates? Chances are they came from different subcultures than you. What differences in culture were most obvious to you? How did these similarities and differences affect your relationships? Which were easiest to get used to? Which were the most difficult to understand and/or accept?

Subcultures are important to understand for the same reasons culture is: The values and norms of subcultures affect our behavior in life and at work. Another reason why subcultures are important is that they are often where changes that affect the larger culture begin.

CULTURE CHANGE

Every culture is dynamic and constantly changing. Consider the current controversy in the United States regarding who can and cannot marry. Values have influenced laws, and until relatively recently, only heterosexual couples could legally marry. Today, however, many people believe that same-sex couples should have the legal right to marry. This is a sign that American subcultures and the overarching culture are changing. These changing values and the resulting attempts to change the laws didn't arise overnight—they've actually been brewing for over four decades.

The battle over same-sex marriage dates back to at least 1970, when Jack Baker and James Michael McConnell requested a marriage license in Minnesota and were refused. For Baker and McConnell to even reach the point where they could make this request, values and culture must have already been changing. The couple subsequently sued, and the resulting case was won by the State of Minnesota.[21] A later appeal to the U.S. Supreme Court was dismissed without being heard.

Fifteen years later, two California cities (Berkeley and West Hollywood) granted benefits for and recognition of same-sex domestic partnerships, but this fell short of an official recognition of marriage. Currently, same-sex marriages are performed in a number of states, and a few other states recognize such marriages granted by other countries or states.[22] Still, as of 2012, 38 states had either defined marriage as between a man and a woman or had enacted explicit bans of same-sex marriage.[23] These numbers are in

■ **EXHIBIT 13.5**
How does the debate about same-sex marriage reflect changes in values and culture in the United States and elsewhere?

Source: © Diana Pappas/Alamy

constant flux, however. For example, California briefly allowed same-sex marriages to be performed (June 16 to November 4, 2008). Although the law permitting such marriages was rescinded by popular vote, all marriages performed during that time are still recognized (■ **EXHIBIT 13.5**). Several years later, on May 9, 2012, U.S. President Barack Obama became the first president to openly support same-sex marriage.[24]

Debates about same-sex marriage continue to rage across the United States and other countries around the world. Views about this culture change seem to split along traditional conservative/liberal lines (these too are subcultures). To illustrate this, when President Obama spoke out in favor of same-sex marriage, people on both sides of the issue rose up once again. Others joined the discussion, but felt that this issue has taken far too much time and energy away from the real issues of jobs and economic hardships in the United States. Still, even in the midst of extremely important issues such as war, the fight against terrorism, serious problems with health care, and looming economic problems, the issue of same-sex marriage often takes center stage.[25]

As this heated debate illustrates, cultural changes often cause a great deal of internal conflict for people as they begin to question the values they have learned and adopted, or as their values are threatened. This happens in organizations as well. For example, in the early 1990s, Powell Flute Company of New England was known for making the best handcrafted flutes in the world. So, when the company's leaders learned of a new technology related to the placement of holes on the flute body, there was a great deal of debate as to whether Powell could adopt the so-called "Cooper scale" and still retain its identity. After all, making this change meant more than just adopting a new methodology—for the craftsmen, it meant taking in and accommodating something new and very different, something foreign to their practice that challenged their identity, their ideas about how flutes should be made, and the company's organizational culture.[26]

Research has helped us understand the dimensions of culture that impact organizations. In the next section, we will look at how scholars and practitioners classify organizational cultures.

Discussion Questions

1. Use the Hofstede and GLOBE models to describe your national culture and one other culture you know well. How do the two cultures compare? What implications do the similarities and differences between these cultures have for work relationships?

2. Generate a list of values and norms in your primary culture that have changed or are in the process of changing. Why do you think they are changing?

4. How Can We Link Organizational Culture with Business Issues?

Objective 13.4
Explain various types of organizational cultures.

In this section, we turn our attention to how scholars have classified organizational cultures to help us understand how cultures impact business. First, we will explore a categorization scheme called the competing values model. Then, we will look at cultures in another way—by considering the degree to which they are strong or weak and examining how this difference in intensity affects people's behavior.

The Competing Values Model of Organizational Culture

One model that helps explain the relationship between organizational culture and organizational performance is the **competing values framework**. This model shows how organizational cultures can be measured along two axes—structure (stability versus flexibility) and focus (internal versus external)—as depicted in ▪ **EXHIBIT 13.6**.[27]

The focus dimension of the competing values framework includes internal focus and external focus. An organization with a high internal focus dedicates most of its attention to factors inside the organization, such as employee satisfaction or internal controls. An organization with a high external focus directs attention to factors outside the organization, such as how the organization fits into and/or affects its environment. The structure dimension of the framework measures the degree of flexibility an organization has versus its need for stability. An organization with high flexibility has a tolerance for self-directed behavior, whereas an organization with high stability has more systems to regulate employees' behavior. Using this framework as a starting point, researchers have identified four distinct types of organizational cultures: clan culture, hierarchy culture, adhocracy culture, and market culture.[29]

A **clan culture** has an internal focus and encourages flexibility. This culture values collaboration among organizational members and promotes cohesion by focusing on things such as agreement and employee satisfaction. Clan cultures often devote significant resources to recruitment, selection, and employee development.

A **hierarchy culture** has an internal focus and encourages stability and control. In general, organizations with this type of culture have structured work environments and numerous control mechanisms to ensure reliability and efficiency.

An **adhocracy culture** has an external focus and encourages flexibility. In adhocracy cultures, organizations concentrate on innovation and creativity, and they are adaptable and respond well to changes in the environment. This type of culture supports members who seek new ways of doing things.

Competing values framework
A model that shows how cultures can be measured along two axes: structure (stability versus flexibility) and focus (internal versus external).

Clan culture
A culture that has an internal focus and encourages flexibility.

Hierarchy culture
A culture that has an internal focus and encourages stability and control.

Adhocracy culture
A culture that has an external focus and encourages flexibility.

▪ **EXHIBIT 13.6**
The competing values framework.[28]

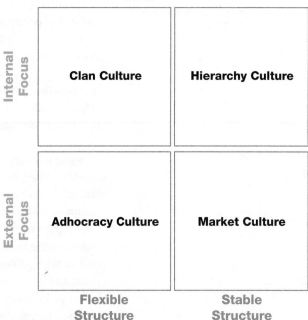

	Flexible Structure	Stable Structure
Internal Focus	Clan Culture	Hierarchy Culture
External Focus	Adhocracy Culture	Market Culture

Market culture
A culture that has an external focus and encourages stability and control.

Balanced culture
A culture that has values linked to each of the culture domains of the competing values framework, and all of these values are perceived to be important and are held by organization members quite strongly.

Strong culture
A culture in which central values and norms are shared and strongly upheld by most members of the organization.

Weak culture
A culture in which the values and norms are shared by a limited group of people and employees' goals may not be in line with management's goals.

A market culture has an external focus and encourages stability and control. Organizations with market cultures emphasize competition and are driven by results and profitability. Members of such organizations are therefore expected to deliver timely, quality products.

In other research, a fifth type of culture is added: the balanced culture.[30]

A balanced culture has values linked to each of the culture domains of the competing values framework, and all of these values are perceived to be important and are held by organization members quite strongly. In such cultures, organization members are supported in adapting their behavior to specific situations.

Although all types of cultures can support organizational effectiveness in certain circumstances, the clan and balanced cultures seem to have the most positive effects on effectiveness and outcomes.[31] This is because these two cultures provide the most support for their members and are most adaptable to environmental changes.

Strong and Weak Cultures

Organizational cultures differ in the *degree to which* they impact people's values, attitudes, and behavior. For instance, in a strong culture, central values and norms are shared and strongly upheld by most members of the organization. In addition, most managers also share a set of business practices.[32] Strong cultures empower employees to perform at a higher level because they are committed and self-confident.[33] Companies with strong cultures are also more likely to be successful in the short term and to produce a return on investment for investors.[34] Many researchers support the idea that strong cultures lead to enhanced commitment and increased productivity and performance.[35]

Sometimes, a culture may be so strong that it continues to affect people even after they have left the group. As illustrated in the *Business Case*, McKinsey and Company (a global business consulting firm) is one company for which this holds true.

Strong cultures are often found in partnership organizations like McKinsey. Entrepreneurial start-ups and family-owned firms also tend to have strong cultures. One of the benefits of a strong culture is that shared values and commitment to a common vision can hold people together during the challenging early days.

In contrast to strong cultures like McKinsey's, a weak culture is one in which the values and norms are shared by a limited group of people. In an organization, this can mean that employees' goals may not be in line with management's goals.

It would seem natural to conclude that strong cultures are better than weak cultures, but strong cultures are not necessarily always best. As it turns out, strong cultures can inhibit an organization's ability to adapt to environmental changes because they control people's beliefs and behavior so tightly. Scholars refer to this phenomenon as "value engineering."[36] A strong culture may also regulate and control behavior so strictly that it limits the possibility of innovation, and this in turn can decrease organizational effectiveness.[37] Thus, in stable environments, strong cultures enhance performance, but when the environment changes, the benefits of this type of culture decrease dramatically.[38]

Some scholars have concluded that diverse and/or international companies might be able to perform better when they do not have strong overarching organizational cultures, but rather have distinct, strong subcultures within each of their business units.[39] In these companies, employees must embrace uncertainty and rely on the combined expertise of the diverse components of the overall organization.[40] The central underlying value that organizes the firm, then, is a strong orientation to learning and adaptation.

You have probably had experiences with both strong and weak organizational cultures, and you can probably describe various types of organizational cultures in simple language based on your observations of people's values and how they behave. In the next section, we will explore how you can get better at "diagnosing" organizational

They Get You for Life

The desire to belong to a group is a basic human need. When asked to talk about ourselves, most people start by talking about the groups they belong to, such as professions, organizations, and schools. The Japanese language includes important words defining "in-groups" (*uchi*) and "out-groups" (*soto*).[41] The groups that we belong to determine who we are. They also define who we are *not*.

You would think, then, that once you leave a group, you are no longer "in." That's not true of former McKinsey employees. They belong to a very strong in-group, and the personal network connecting them is one of the most admired in the business world. McKinsey has produced more CEOs for large-scale corporations than any other company. Alumni include Bobby Jindal, the Governor of Louisiana; Roberto Nicastro, General Manager of UniCredit; Vittorio Colao, CEO of Vodaphone; and Stephen Green, trade minister of the United Kingdom.[42]

McKinsey is an "up or out" company.[43] This means that employees must climb the company's career ladder toward partnership, and if they cannot meet the standards, they must leave. Not everyone makes it. In addition to those who *have* to leave, a good number of McKinsey employees *choose* to leave—often to join

one of McKinsey's client organizations at very senior positions. In fact, some of the best leaders, like those mentioned above, left McKinsey to pursue significant and important careers in business and government.

To some, this seems like a brutal system that would result in resentment among employees who are pushed out and disappointment among teammates when a "star" employee departs. McKinsey, however, has learned how to capitalize on this process.

When people leave—or have to leave—McKinsey supports them in finding good jobs, very often with clients.[44] In the long run, this is advantageous for both the employees and the firm. Many ex-McKinsey stars end up in powerful positions. They stay close to their McKinsey colleagues personally and professionally, and often bring the firm in to consult to their "new" companies.[45]

Although some people don't like the exclusive nature of the club (they call it the "McKinsey mob"), the fact is that this network is powerful.[46] McKinsey's culture places great value on loyalty to the company, and there is a lasting feeling that past and present employees are part of an in-group that shares values about work standards, loyalty, and business practices.[47] These beliefs and behaviors are part of McKinsey's culture—a culture that is strong enough to guide people even when they no longer work for the company.

cultures. Knowing how to study cultures will help you choose the right organization when accepting a job. It will also help you support the development of healthy cultures wherever you work.

Discussion Questions

1. Using the competing values framework, discuss McKinsey. Is the company's culture likely to be more flexible or more stable? Is it likely more internally or more externally focused? Of the four types of culture, which do you think McKinsey practices, and why?

2. Is the culture of your school or workplace strong or weak? What evidence do you have to support your opinion? How does the strength of the culture impact students? Faculty? Staff?

5. How Can We Study Organizational Culture?

Objective 13.5
Learn how to study organizational culture.

Culture is often difficult to understand. However, it's critical to learn how to study organizational culture because it has such a powerful effect on people's values, attitudes, and behaviors. Culture also affects organizational results. In this section, you'll begin by considering two ways to look at culture. The first method enables you to see three levels of culture—from more obvious to less. The second method draws your attention to stories, traditions, taboos, and the way in which language is used in

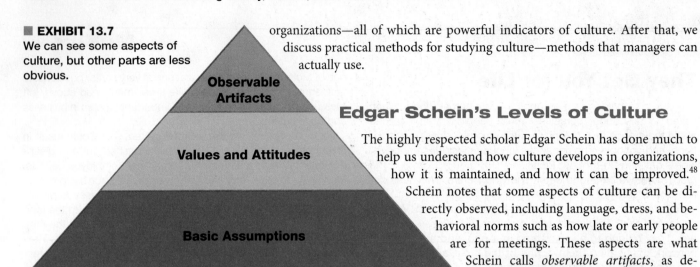

Observable Artifacts

Values and Attitudes

Basic Assumptions

organizations—all of which are powerful indicators of culture. After that, we discuss practical methods for studying culture—methods that managers can actually use.

Edgar Schein's Levels of Culture

The highly respected scholar Edgar Schein has done much to help us understand how culture develops in organizations, how it is maintained, and how it can be improved.[48] Schein notes that some aspects of culture can be directly observed, including language, dress, and behavioral norms such as how late or early people are for meetings. These aspects are what Schein calls *observable artifacts*, as depicted in ■ **EXHIBIT 13.7**. Other aspects of culture—values, for example—are not as easy to see, and even less visible are what Schein calls *basic assumptions*.[49] Let's look at each of these levels of culture and how they might play out in an organization.

OBSERVABLE ARTIFACTS: THE TOP LEVEL OF SCHEIN'S ORGANIZATIONAL CULTURE MODEL

Observable artifacts are those aspects of a culture that can be seen, heard, or experienced by an organization's members. Observable artifacts can often be easily determined just by asking questions. Some common examples of observable artifacts include the following:

- *Dress code:* An organization's dress code may be written or unwritten, but in either case, most organizations have a clear expectation of how employees should dress for work. To determine a company's dress code, try asking yourself: Do people wear jeans to work? Do men wear ties? Do people pay a lot of attention to things like polished shoes? Do some people wear uniforms but other people wear their own clothes?

- *Language and jargon:* Language and jargon are clues to what people value and pay attention to in a culture. When studying language and jargon, ask yourself the following questions: Do people use words that have meaning only to organization members? Are acronyms frequently used? Is slang used? By whom and how? In a multicultural organization, is one language the norm for senior leaders? We'll discuss language in more depth in the next section.

- *Interpersonal relationships:* Organizations have cultural rules about how people relate to one another. When determining these norms, you can start by asking: Do people know much about one another's personal lives? Do people do things together outside of work? Do people treat each other with respect and consideration?

- *Technology:* How people use technology is linked to beliefs and norms about how work should be done. To explore how technology relates to people's beliefs, ask the following sorts of questions: Are Macs or PCs used? Do employees communicate mainly through e-mail, or do they talk to each other directly? Is travel common to enable face-to-face meetings?

- *Workspace:* Where people do their work is an indication of communication norms, power dynamics, and the like. You can study this aspect of a company's culture by asking: Do the big bosses have special offices? Is management close to staff or far away? Does everyone have a desk in an open space? If it's a virtual organization, does technology support group work?

- *Ceremonies, rituals, and awards:* Ceremonies, rituals, and awards indicate what is valued in a culture. To explore this area, you can ask: Are there events that can't be missed and that people will cancel vacations to attend? Do managers always bring food to early morning meetings? Are there "prizes" for certain outcomes, such as hitting sales targets?

There are many observable indicators of culture. Learning how to question what you see will enable you to draw conclusions about some of the less visible yet still very powerful aspects of organizational culture, such as values.

VALUES AND ATTITUDES: THE MIDDLE LEVEL OF SCHEIN'S ORGANIZATIONAL CULTURE MODEL

The espoused values of an organization are explicit values that are preferred by the organization and communicated deliberately to the organization's members. Founders and leaders have an important role in shaping these values, which are often listed in the company's marketing materials, mission statement, and employee training materials. Note, however, that the term *espoused values* refers only to what is said, and not necessarily to what is actually done. For example, a company can communicate to its employees and customers that one of its core values is quality, but if the organization does not evaluate the quality of products or services, then these values are merely espoused, not enacted.

Enacted values are the values that are actually exhibited in an organization. These values can be seen, and they may or may not be the same as the organization's espoused values. It can be very confusing when espoused and enacted values are not the same. This often happens during times of profound change and/or around issues that are controversial. For example, most companies espouse equality. If these values were truly enacted, women would receive equal pay for equal work. However, in the United States, women currently earn only 81 cents for every dollar that men earn.[50] Enacted values may also be different from espoused values in areas related to ethics, in policies regarding sustainability, and in the behaviors for which employees are rewarded.

BASIC ASSUMPTIONS: THE DEEPEST LEVEL OF SCHEIN'S ORGANIZATIONAL CULTURE MODEL

In Schein's system, the deepest level of organizational culture consists of basic assumptions, or the *core* beliefs that are deeply embedded in people's minds and the organizational culture. These beliefs are largely invisible and often taken for granted. Many times, these basic assumptions explain the difference between espoused and enacted values. Organization members are usually unaware of these assumptions or how they guide behavior. For example, a basic assumption may be that people are opportunists and will steal when given the opportunity. In this situation, you may never hear anyone say that people are untrustworthy, and if asked, people might not admit to this basic assumption. You would see, however, that managers are highly vigilant, inventory is checked regularly, security is tight, and monitoring cameras are used throughout the organization's facilities. Another example of a common basic assumption is that only leaders can fix organizational problems. Again, people would not say this directly and if asked would not necessarily agree. But this basic assumption would be evident in things like the number of small decisions made at senior meetings.

This brings us back to the importance of carefully observing and interpreting observable artifacts. The basic assumptions that truly explain these, and espoused and enacted values, are the clues to "what's really going on around here." To deepen your understanding, you can also look at other indicators of culture: organizational myths and heroes, taboos, sacred symbols, and language.

Espoused values
Explicit values that are preferred by an organization and communicated deliberately to the organization's members.

Enacted values
The values that are actually exhibited in an organization.

Myths, Heroes, Taboos, Sacred Symbols, and Language

Culture is rarely communicated directly. More often, it is conveyed through the stories people tell, through what is considered good or evil, and through the ways in which language is used. Therefore, when seeking to learn about an organization's culture, it is especially helpful to consider the organization's myths, heroes, taboos, sacred symbols, and language. These expressions of culture are linked to values and basic assumptions, and they drive members' behavior because they are part of what people look to when they make decisions about what to think, believe, and do.[51] Understandably, these expressions of culture are important because they support socialization, or the process of teaching new members about a culture. They also provide a way to explain current practices and shape the future.[52]

MYTHS AND HEROES

In anthropology, myths are stories that describe ideologies.[53] In the business world, an organization's myths are exaggerated stories that are told and retold to communicate values and promote norms. These stories usually involve important events or people, such as the founder of the organization, setbacks that occurred long ago, heroes who overcame problems, or even examples of "perfect" or "evil" behavior.[54] Myths point to what an organization values, and they communicate which behaviors are desirable and which are considered taboo. Because they bind people together around a common vision of good and bad behavior, myths demonstrate what it takes to succeed in a company.

Myths often center on the actions of a hero. Here, a hero is defined as a legendary person who embodies the highest values of a culture. He or she defends the organization against external or internal forces that threaten values, beliefs, or the organization's viability. For example, author William Rogers relates a story about a low-level IBM employee who refused to admit the chairman of the board to a secure area without proper identification. When others in the group verbally assaulted the employee, the chairman rewarded his behavior by silencing the critics and obtaining the requested identification.[55] This particular story communicates the cultural belief that rule breaking is unacceptable, even for the highest status members of IBM.[56] The employee who challenged the chairman was elevated to the status of folk hero through the telling and retelling of the story. Stories like this show how heroes uphold organizational values even when facing danger. Heroes are courageous and bigger than life.

How can you recognize a hero story? Chances are, you'll hear the story a lot, and the hero will be talked about frequently. In addition, people tend to use strong language when talking about heroes, using words like *amazing, incredible, brilliant, unbelievably creative,* and *charismatic.* He or she will be referred to with respect and perhaps even reverence.

TABOOS

Hero stories describe what people *should* do while taboos tell people what *not* to do. Taboos are strong prohibitions against certain activities, and they are often associated with what a group considers sacred or profane.[57] Taboos act as unwritten laws that forbid various activities, thoughts, and even feelings. In many societies' cultures, they involve such things as food, sexuality, religious practice, and death. Violating taboos can lead to severe sanctions, such as shaming, ostracism, or, in some societies, losing one's life.

Every culture has taboos, and this includes organizational cultures. For instance, some organizational cultures include an unspoken rule that you should never get mad at your boss. Other common examples include taboos around whom employees can date—sometimes, other employees are off limits, and oftentimes, clients are as well. In addition, some scholars who study conflict between men and women believe that

Socialization
The process of teaching new members about a culture.

Myths
Exaggerated stories that are told and retold to communicate values and to promote norms.

Hero
A legendary person who embodies the highest values of a culture.

Taboos
Strong prohibitions against certain activities.

many cultures have strong taboos against men and women arguing or disagreeing with one another.[58] You can see how this would not be helpful in organizations, because disagreement often leads to better solutions.

Other researchers have focused specifically on taboos related to an organization's willingness to engage in socially responsible behavior. One scholar has identified three taboos that inhibit corporate social responsibility: the taboo against seeing business as having moral responsibility; the taboo against questioning the goal of continuous economic growth; and the taboo against becoming involved in the debate around social responsibility.[59] Of the three, the taboo against interfering with continuous economic growth is perhaps strongest. For most of the twentieth century, growth was the "Holy Grail" and anything that interfered with it seemed to be taboo.[60]

SACRED SYMBOLS

A culture's **sacred symbols** are the things, people, and events that are untouchable and unquestionable. Consider how people sometimes feel about their nation's flag: It's just a piece of cloth, really, but it holds such special meaning that it is often protected from harm by laws and taboos (■ **EXHIBIT 13.8**). Thus, to some people in some cultures, the flag is sacred.

The same sort of thing happens in organizations. Certain objects, people, or events take on such special meaning that they cannot be harmed, removed, or changed. In some organizations, status and power come with sacred trappings like the corner office, or perhaps a private washroom or a special cafeteria. These privileges are viewed as sacred symbols of having made it in the organization.

When something becomes sacred, it is extremely difficult to change. This can even apply to products, such as Coca-Cola. The Coca-Cola Company's management found out the hard way that consumers weren't going to tolerate any changes to their beloved drink. When "New Coke" was introduced in the mid-1980s, consumers rebelled. In fact, some people actually stockpiled "real" Coke before the change, and many people felt betrayed by the company.

Sacred symbols
Things, people, and events that are untouchable and unquestionable within a culture.

■ EXHIBIT 13.8
Is addition to burning, what are some other taboos associated with handling a nation's flag?

Source: Sergey Kamshylin/Shutterstock

What's especially interesting about the "New Coke" example is that the Coca-Cola Company had changed Coke's recipe numerous times since the product was first introduced in the mid-1880s. Back then, the drink was known as "Cocawine," and its recipe included both alcohol and derivatives of coca leaves, which are used in the production of cocaine. By the 1930s, however, the company had phased out these ingredients, eventually arriving at the formula we know today.

Few people complained when the company adjusted its recipe between 1880 and 1930, yet when Coke's formula was changed in the mid-1980s, customers rebelled. Maybe it was because the recipe had been the same for more than 50 years, and two or three generations had grown up with the "old" taste, logo, bottles, and packaging. Or maybe it was because Coke had become a symbol of something much bigger than a sweetened drink—it had become an American icon, and for some, a symbol of freedom. Indeed, before the end of the Cold War in the late 1980s, whenever Coke's advertising appeared on the streets of a Communist country, some people believed that progress was being made toward establishment of a less restrictive society.[61]

Whatever the reason, one thing remained certain: New Coke wasn't Coke, and it really didn't matter if the updated version was better or not. Ultimately, this public outcry convinced the Coca-Cola Company to switch back to the previous formula.[62] In doing so, the company had to take on the cost and time burdens associated with two major changes in production and marketing within a short time frame.

Sometimes events unfold in the opposite direction of the New Coke debacle. In such cases, companies refuse to change their products or services or wait too long to do so because their products or services have historically been part of the company's image. These products and services are therefore viewed by the company as sacred and untouchable, even when the market no longer wants or needs them. For example, for some years now there has been more awareness that fast-food restaurants often serve foods that are high in fats, sugar, and the like, and that these are not good for you. One would think that these restaurants would have paid attention to the trend. In fact, they appeared to do so when, in the late 1990s, we started seeing things like "chicken Caesar salads" appear on menus. Customers soon discovered, however, that these salads often had more fat and more calories than burgers! It is only recently that truly healthy foods have begun to show up on fast-food menus.

LANGUAGE

The way people use words, the prevalence of one native language over others, and even the types of body language people use are powerful indicators of culture. An organization's culture can therefore be studied by looking at how language and symbols relate to ideologies and practices that unify the organization.[63]

Because spoken language is a key form of communication, familiarity with the sayings, slang, jargon, and/or acronyms specific to an organization is useful when seeking to understand that organization's culture. Consider the following expression: *"I can't believe the butterbar went VFR direct to the Old Man!"*[64] Can you translate this? Unless you belong or have belonged to a military subculture that uses this language, you probably won't have a clue what this sentence means. In this case, a butterbar is a second lieutenant, the lowest officer rank in the army. The derogatory term refers to the yellow color of the single bar insignia. VFR is an acronym for "visual flight rules" and means to take the most visually direct path. Here, VFR becomes a metaphor for circumventing the chain of command to reach the top officer (the "Old Man"), a taboo in the military and many other cultures.

This example illustrates problems related to the use of slang, jargon, and the like: Although this language tends to unify members inside an organization, it also serves to keep other people out. In addition, unique language can establish a barrier between an organization and its customers, consumers, and vendors. In today's flat, complex, international organizations, this can be destructive.

Many companies have a much bigger problem than simply controlling the use of jargon and acronyms: Today, members of many organizations speak different native languages. Consider the example of a large European company with senior managers whose native languages are Italian, German, and English. Several managers prefer using their native Italian, several others prefer doing business in German, and one or two prefer English. Also, in company subsidiaries around the world, many employees speak only the local language. Situations like this are common today. Thus, many organizations have had to develop "language policies" to guide which language(s) are used on the job and what language(s) employees must learn in order to be promoted.[65]

The inseparable relationship between language and culture means that a choice of one language over others has an organization-wide impact on how power is perceived and who has access to it. To return to the previous example, the company's leaders eventually decided that English was the preferred language for business. This decision caused a great deal of conflict and disagreement, because it was seen as a sign that the company was going to adopt more British and/or American ways of doing business. Many of the Italian and German managers were highly displeased with the decision and the implications for the organization's culture.

Nonverbal communication provides us with another means for understanding a culture. By examining people's facial expressions, body language, posture, tone of voice, and so forth, you can gain a significant amount of information. For example, if you notice that people tend to lower their eyes and speak softly when talking with senior managers, this might indicate high power distance—or a large status differentiation between lower level employees and upper management.

Language, nonverbal communication, and the stories people tell about their cultures are powerful in that they can help maintain and strengthen that culture. This is fine when the culture supports the goals of the organization—but that isn't always the case, especially in today's rapidly changing world. For instance, when myths are really just questionable beliefs that are protected by taboos, or when heroes' behavior is actually harmful, myths and hero stories can be destructive.[66] Similarly, when things that are sacred really need to be changed, or when taboos prevent people from doing the right things, culture becomes a barrier to success. Accordingly, one powerful way to begin to change a culture is to examine the various aspects of that culture, then consciously use those aspects that support positive outcomes and change those that don't. In the next section of the chapter, you'll learn how to study culture to better understand which aspects of culture help an organization and which get in the way.

Leaders and Managers as Ethnographers

Observing myths, heroes, taboos, sacred symbols, and language can help tremendously in understanding a culture. Sometimes, however, you need to go beyond simple observation and interpretation. You also need to find out about a culture from the people who are part of it. Most of the time you can't simply ask questions because peoples' culture is so deeply buried that they don't consciously recognize it. For that reason, students of organizational culture—and good managers and leaders—must become ethnographers.

Ethnography is the systematic study of human cultures. An ethnographic approach includes observation and co-inquiry. In a co-inquiry process, people observe and collaborate with one another to truly understand what is happening within their group or organization. This is sometimes called *participant observation*, and it isn't necessarily easy.[67] It's hard to really look at your culture. That's because when we co-inquire into an organization's culture, we attempt to explore the unspoken aspects of the culture—things

Ethnography
The systematic study of human cultures.

that are a part of "who we are" but that might need to change. When faced with this challenge, good leaders can remember a quote widely attributed to Plato: "We can easily forgive a child who is afraid of the dark. The real tragedy of life is when men are afraid of the light."[68]

Through observation and inquiry, we can literally shine a light on an organization's culture. Dynamic inquiry is a co-inquiry approach developed by scholar Annie McKee with support from colleagues Cecilia McMillen, Chris Thomas, and many others. This process enables organization members to uncover cultural values and the basic assumptions that drive people's behavior, as well as how leadership practices affect people and the organization.[69] Authors Daniel Goleman, Richard Boyatzis, and Annie McKee describe the process this way:

> *Many large companies have processes in place for systematically evaluating employee attitudes, values, and beliefs—a kind of proxy for the emotional reality. These processes can be very helpful, but the problem is that surveys measure only what they set out to measure—and they rarely tap the more subtle layer of . . . complex norms that flow through an organization. This blind spot can result in simply measuring what people want to know, but not what they don't want known . . . .*
>
> *Dynamic inquiry offset[s] the "find what you look for" effect of most surveys and enable[s] leaders to begin to address the underlying cultural issues that are getting in their way. . . . Through the process of discovering the truth about their organization, people begin to create a shared language about what's really going on as well as what they'd like to see—their ideal vision of the company.*
>
> *Dynamic inquiry involves focused conversations and open-ended questions intended to get at people's feelings. . . . It is only when people talk about their feelings that they begin to uncover root causes of problems in the culture and the true sources of inspiration around them. . . . They create a language that captures the real truth about the forces that affect people's day-to-day lives in the organization as well as their hopes for the future. . . . Once people are engaged in this kind of open dialogue about their culture and their dreams, it is very difficult to put the lid back on the box. . . . The creation of a shared language that is based on feelings as well as facts is a powerful driver of change. This shared language provides a sense of unity and resonance, and the resulting momentum helps people to move from talk to action. They feel inspired and empowered, willing to work together to address their collective concerns.[70]*

Another ethnographic method often used to discover the underlying attributes of culture focuses exclusively on what's working in a group or organization. Developed by David Cooperrider, *appreciative inquiry* is a process that explores people's and the organization's strengths—in other words, everything that stimulates both people and the organization to become healthy and productive.[71] Appreciative inquiry is a form of ethnographic research that often includes interviews and large-group meetings where people can identify cultural and organizational strengths and opportunities and then explore these together. This method can be particularly powerful when a company's employees have lost sight of what their unique contributions are, or when morale is so low that people need to build psychological strength to face challenges.

Methods such as dynamic inquiry and appreciative inquiry are built on the assumption that as a study of an organization is conducted, *change will begin to occur.* In other words, these methods are forms of action research, or research that seeks to effect organizational change as part of the study process.[72] With this type of research, all people who are involved in the interviews are also viewed as active participants in the change process.[73]

Studying culture isn't reserved for experts or consultants. We all need to learn how to do it—employees, managers, and leaders alike. Understanding an organization's culture can help us make the right choice about joining a company. Equally important is the fact that understanding culture can help us be effective in a company. In the next section, we will look at what kinds of cultures leaders are attempting to create and foster in order to help their companies be successful in today's complex environment.

Discussion Questions

1. How do things like dress, language, spatial arrangement, technology, relationships, and rituals reflect the cultural values of your school or place of work?

2. Articulate several core values for a group to which you belong. Now, try to determine the underlying basic assumptions that drive these values. Think about some taboos in your family, workplace, or at school. How do these taboos affect how people interact and/or how effective the group is?

---

6. Organizational Culture: What's Important Today?

Objective 13.6
Assess the important aspects of organizational culture.

Today's managers and leaders often struggle with issues related to organizational culture. One reason for this is that many organizational cultures have developed with very little guidance. Indeed, for much of the last century, managers and leaders paid little attention to the "people issues" in their organizations, including culture. Many organizational cultures, therefore, have been developed in haphazard ways. Many current cultures are also problematic in that they feature norms, values, and attitudes that support simpler ways of doing business that worked a few decades ago but do not adequately support the complexity of today's business environment.

For these and other reasons, many leaders are trying to change their organizational cultures to better support long-term organizational sustainability, excellence, and success in today's environment. The next few sections explore organizational cultures that focus in turn on customer service, diversity and inclusion, ethics, innovation, sustainability, and supporting employees in becoming the best they can be.

Customer Service Cultures

One way companies can distinguish themselves from their competitors is by providing superior service to their customers. For example, the Ritz-Carlton Hotel Company's credo includes the following statement: "We are ladies and gentlemen serving ladies and gentlemen"[74] This philosophy highlights that Ritz-Carlton's goal is to excel at providing service with a high degree of professionalism.

In a study of best practices in the U.S. lodging industry, one common characteristic shared by all of the leading companies was that their hotels created a service culture. Consider the Four Seasons & Regent Hotel and Resorts, for instance.[75] This company has a comprehensive orientation and training program designed to teach its employees the value of personalized service. Then, to support employees in delivering such service, the company keeps a higher than normal ratio of employees to guests. Finally, senior management collects data from focus groups, guests, and managers to ensure that a service culture is not just created, but successfully maintained.

Many organizations far removed from the lodging industry also focus on creating cultures that support excellent customer service. In businesses ranging from banks to clothing stores to software companies, service has become a priority. Interestingly, researchers note that successful customer and market orientation—and the cultures that support these characteristics—are highly dependent on good leadership.[76]

Diversity and Inclusion Cultures

To achieve lasting success, people must be able to work together effectively inside the organization—and one potential challenge to this ability lies in the area of demographics. The demographics in many business organizations have changed rapidly in recent years, and they continue to change today. For example, according to the research organization Catalyst, in 2008, more than half of management and professional occupations were held by women.[77] However, only 6.2 percent of top earners at Fortune 500 companies were women and only 3 percent of Fortune 500 CEO positions were held by females. Still, in 2011, women held 16.1 percent of Fortune 500 board seats, compared to only 11.7 percent in 2000.[78] Another issue that is impacting worker diversity is that Baby Boomers are working longer, partly because people are healthier and want to work longer and partly because the economy has made retirement difficult. The impact of this shift is that there is not enough room at the top for GenXers, which in turn means less room in the middle and so on.

Companies are becoming increasingly diverse in terms of ethnicity and race. According to U.S. Bureau of Labor Statistics (BLS) projections, 68.3 percent of entrants into the U.S. labor force from 2006 to 2016 will be people of color or women, and 22.3 percent of this total will be Hispanic.[79] It is expected that the fastest rate of growth will be among Asian and Hispanic employees.[80] Also, many modern organizations—even small- and medium-sized companies—are international and have employees, suppliers, and vendors from more than one country, as well as customers and consumers all over the world. Finally, diversity in the work place also includes differences in sexual orientation, religion, and physical abilities.[81]

Research indicates that diverse perspectives lead to better decisions, and they help companies attract the best employees. Nonetheless, diversity can also be a source of conflict—when people have different ways of engaging with each other, different ways of working, or different cultures, clashes sometimes ensue. Thus, diversity is more likely to produce benefits if an organization focuses on integration and learning, which can help people better understand these sorts of differences.[82]

Some companies already know how to leverage diversity in the workforce to ensure that both employees and the company thrive. For one example of a culture that promotes diversity, consider the efforts of Johnson & Johnson, a global pharmaceutical company based in the United States. Chairman and CEO William C. Weldon and his management team believe that diversity increases competitive advantage, and their efforts kept Johnson & Johnson in the number-one spot on Diversity Inc.'s list of the Top 50 Most Diverse Companies of 2009.[83] Since then, the company has remained high on the list.[84]

Weldon and his team are vitally involved in the company's many concrete efforts to build a culture that supports diversity, as depicted in ■ **EXHIBIT 13.9**. For example, Weldon meets regularly with employees to discuss diversity initiatives. These types of meetings between the CEO and rank-and-file employees are rare in most companies. Another notable example of the company's diversity efforts is that Johnson & Johnson offers benefits to employees' same-sex partners.

Companies like Johnson & Johnson aren't leaving the development of a diverse workforce to chance. Rather, they are actively engaged in building cultures that support everyone in contributing their best, and they also help employees develop the skills necessary to work effectively across cultural boundaries. In today's global business environment, this isn't just a "nice-to-have" characteristic—it's a must.

Ethical Cultures

Yet another attribute that distinguishes companies from one another is their commitment to ethics. Social pressure for people and companies to act in an ethical manner has been increasing steadily for years, and recent high-profile cases of business leaders

■ **EXHIBIT 13.9**

Johnson & Johnson's Diversity Efforts[85]	
Diversity Area	**Johnson & Johnson's Efforts**
CEO commitment	Chairman and CEO William Weldon regularly meets with employee-resource groups.
	Weldon has the company's chief diversity officer as a direct report.
	More than 6 percent of the bonuses for Weldon's direct reports are tied to meeting the diversity targets set forth in their goals and strategies.
	Johnson & Johnson has a diverse board of directors: Among the 11 directors, African Americans, Latinos, and women are well-represented.
Company-wide commitment	Johnson & Johnson is a pioneer in work/life benefits and in the benefits it offers to employees' same-sex domestic partners.
	Both the company's overall workforce and its management populations reflect the demographics of the communities Johnson & Johnson serves in the United States.
	Thirty-one percent of the most senior-level executives (CEO and direct reports) and nearly half of the company's top 10 percent of highest paid employees were women.
	All of the top three levels of management engage in formal mentoring with a cross-cultural component. Both mentors and mentees receive training in cross-cultural competence.
	Johnson & Johnson has excellent employee-resource groups, including a group for employees of Middle Eastern and North African heritage.
Supplier diversity	Johnson & Johnson sponsors business school programs for key diverse suppliers.
	The company also sponsors memberships and other professional development for diverse suppliers, such as participation in the National Minority Manufacturing Institute.
	More than 10 percent of the company's top contractors are minority-owned or woman-owned.

acting unethically have caused this movement to gain momentum. Beyond this pressure, more and more people all over the world are deciding that doing the right thing is the right thing to do. But doing the right thing can be difficult, especially when working in a multicultural, fast-changing world. What this means is that much of the time, choosing to act in an ethical manner means grappling with ethical dilemmas—situations in which the right thing is quite different depending on factors like cultural and religious values.

Employees today are faced with numerous dilemmas. What helps in these situations is a set of clear organizational guidelines. For example, most multinational companies support the hiring and promotion of women. This practice is not necessarily approved of or even done in some countries. However, if the value and ethics around this issue are clearly communicated to employees, then managers have more support when hiring and promoting women. For many employees who want a meritocracy, this kind of support is necessary, especially when going against a cultural practice or habit. For these individuals, working in an organization that rewards ethical decisions is important. And it's not just rules: Having an ethical culture is also extremely important. When values and norms support ethical behavior, there is pressure for employees throughout a company to behave ethically in all circumstances.[86]

Research suggests that it is important for ethics to be institutionalized—but what does this mean? For some organizations, the process of institutionalizing ethics means explicitly encoding ethics in rules and guidelines. For example, companies may prohibit bribery, have rules about how to dispose of toxic waste, or set policies for investing employees' retirement funds. These rules protect the companies' ethical stance on a variety of social issues. However, explicit institutionalization of ethics is not enough. If an organization adopts guidelines that support ethical decision making but its managers don't follow these guidelines or some people aren't expected to observe them, then the organization's employees are bound to receive mixed signals.

This is why implicit institutionalization of ethics is important. Implicit institutionalization is the integration of ethics into the organizational culture. This process must include having management make a commitment to ethical leadership, as well as promoting a culture of personal responsibility when making ethical choices.

Scholars have found that when ethics are not mandated but are instead internalized, they have a much more powerful effect on employees' belief that the workplace is ethical.[87] This is linked to another reason to focus on implicit institutionalization of an ethical culture: Research suggests that implicit institutionalization leads to job satisfaction and high morale, whereas explicit institutionalization alone does not.[88]

How, then, can companies build an ethical culture? Luis Ramos, CEO of The Network, a company that provides ethics and compliance services, suggests the following:[89]

- A company's ethical code should be thought of as a living document—historical, yet modern. The code of ethics should therefore be an accessible resource which can easily be read by others.
- Ethics is a way of doing business; it is not a "program," which means it is a dynamic and continuous process.
- Ethics training is always relevant and, with the right attitude, it can be fun. If a company's ethics training is relevant, employees will more likely be interested in participating.
- Make sure that employees are actively engaged members of the organization and are aligned with the company's culture.

These actions support both ethical values and ethical behavior, two key aspects of an ethical culture.[90]

So, what types of companies carry out these activities successfully? One example is Cisco Systems, a firm that creates and supplies network management products for the Internet. Cisco wants its more than 65,000 employees to know that ethics are at the core of its business practices. In support of this goal, Cisco rewrote its code of ethics to make it more user-friendly, and the company helps promote ethics and two-way communication by having monthly meetings for employees.

When a culture does not support ethical behavior, people can get away with bad behavior. Consider Bernie Madoff, former non-executive chairman of the NASDAQ stock exchange, who was exposed for defrauding thousands of investors out of more than $60 billion. Although Madoff claimed that he was solely responsible for this scheme, authorities questioned whether he could have conducted such a vast fraud on his own. On August 11, 2009, Frank DiPascali, Jr., a former Madoff deputy, was taken into custody after admitting guilt to 10 felony counts of fraud. DiPascali was a cooperating witness in the Madoff trial, and he was the second insider to admit criminal responsibility in Madoff's scheme. Although Madoff insisted that he acted by himself, DiPascali implicated others in the criminal enterprise.[91]

Managing the details of a fraud of this magnitude would have been a monumental job, and it is not likely that one person, or even two or three, could have done it alone. So, it is possible that Madoff's company had developed a culture that supported actions that ultimately resulted in fraud. One can easily imagine some of the unspoken norms and beliefs in such a culture—perhaps "Don't ask questions," "Do as you are told," or "The founder can do no wrong."

Innovative Cultures

Organizations must be innovative to remain competitive in today's global marketplace. An innovative culture can support employees in creative problem solving, formulating breakthrough ideas, developing new products and services, and finding more effective and efficient ways to work. Research demonstrates that when a culture has little bureaucracy, gives people autonomy, and allows them to take risks, then innovation flourishes.[92] Furthermore, when employees perceive their work environments to support originality and imagination, there is an increased level of creativity in their own work.[93] Of course, an innovative culture must be supported by management and organizational reward systems, and employees must not be burdened by excessive workloads and pressures, because these can inhibit development of this type of culture.[94]

Cultures That Support Sustainability and Service

Today, companies of all types are choosing—or being forced—to reduce their negative impact on the environment and to do business in a socially responsible manner. Many companies are finding that in order to become responsible stewards of the environment and to be socially responsible, they need to change their cultures. What might such a culture look like? Unilever, the British/Dutch manufacturer of consumer goods including Lipton tea and Dove soap, is an example of a company that infuses its business projects with a focus on sustainability. One Unilever project that reflects this commitment is the company's Cleaner Planet Plan. As a result of this plan, since 1995, Unilever claims to have reduced energy-related greenhouse gas emissions from its laundry product factories by 44 percent, disposal waste by 70 percent, and water consumption by 76 percent per metric ton of production.[95] Indeed, Unilever is currently ranked by the "Global 100" organization as one of the top 100 global companies with regard to sustainability."[96]

Yet another Unilever project highlights the corporation's focus on a socially responsible approach to marketing. Specifically, in its "Campaign for Real Beauty," Unilever has deliberately moved away from traditional stereotypes of women and attractiveness. One element in this campaign is the now-famous "Dove Evolution," a short documentary film produced by the Dove Self-Esteem Fund.[97] This short film and the marketing campaign for Dove soaps and beauty products depict women of all ages, races, and sizes as beautiful and strong—which is markedly different from some of the more typical marketing images that limit beauty to the young and slender.

The movement toward sustainable business practices and social responsibility requires significant cultural changes. Instead of viewing the world as "us and them," people must come to visualize the entire planet as "us." Also, the practice of seeking individual success at any cost must end. To thrive, an organization's culture must support both success *and* acceptable practices, especially with respect to the natural environment and the wider communities within which an organization exists.

Cultures That Support the Whole Person: Mind, Body, Heart, and Spirit

In recent years, the amount of attention paid to employees' health, psychological well-being, work/life balance, and even spirituality has increased dramatically. The idea that companies should support employees in reaching their full potential as both workers and unique individuals has been embraced by a wide variety of organizations. One primary reason behind this focus on the whole person is that our society is changing, and people now have different expectations about what work—and the culture of the workplace—can and should provide. Also, during the past 50 years, women have entered the workforce in unprecedented numbers. This means that work is now a family affair. In addition, people are living longer than ever before in many parts in the world. Today, individuals frequently work well into their seventies, so being employed is no longer something to do while you wait to retire.

Moreover, technology has made it possible to work around the clock from almost anywhere. This is both good and bad—theoretically more can be done, but people can easily burn out, too. Finally, the global workforce is far more mobile now than in the past. People move more often, change jobs more often, and even change careers more often than in the past. One of the outcomes of these changes is that people don't have to stay in organizations that treat them poorly.

When employees feel satisfied, fulfilled, physically resilient, and committed to their work and the organization, results can soar. Thus, it makes good business sense for leaders to create cultures that focus on the mind, body, heart, and spirit. In practical terms, focusing on "the mind" might mean creating a culture that enables people to learn and grow and to develop their intellect and their talents. Similarly, focusing on "the body" might mean ensuring that the culture supports physical health.

But what about focusing on "the heart" and "the spirit"? A culture that supports people's "hearts" is one that values productive relationships, positive and effective communication, respect, and compassion. Recent research in psychology and neuroscience indicates that when people are excited, appropriately challenged, and experiencing positive emotions, they are more creative, flexible, and resilient.[98] In comparison, a culture that supports spirituality is one that focuses on ensuring that work is meaningful and that people feel connected when working together toward an important mission.[99] People naturally seek meaning in life, so a sense of meaningfulness in the workplace can be highly motivating. More and more businesses have recognized this fact, and the term *workforce spirituality* has become increasingly popular in recent years. An important note: The term workforce spirituality refers to meaningfulness in work and the organization's goals, *not* religion. At the time of this writing, searching Google for "workforce spirituality" resulted in more than 222,000 links.[100] But why is workplace spirituality important? Scholars highlight the following points:[101]

1. Workplace spirituality can facilitate organizational effectiveness and productivity. For instance, one study revealed that employees who experienced workplace spirituality were more likely to increase their work unit performance.[102]

2. Workplace spirituality may facilitate ethical behavior. When employees are focused on connectedness as opposed to individual self-interest, they may be more likely to think about how their decisions influence others and whether they are ethical.[103]

3. The incorporation of spirituality in the workplace can be important in providing employees with feelings of connectedness, empowerment, and work/family balance. These conditions are becoming increasingly important to people today.[104]

Research therefore proves that people seek meaning in their work, and leadership that seeks to integrate ways for people to feel deeply fulfilled in the workplace can have a significant impact on employee motivation.[105] Creating a culture that supports people in finding meaning in their work will support positive organizational performance.

Leading Powerful, Positive Cultures

As you have learned in this chapter, culture is not something magical—it is created by real people. You will have a role in the creation and maintenance of your organization's culture, and you will probably be involved in changing the culture of some of the organizations in which you will work. As a leader, this will probably be one of your most important jobs.

Some leaders make culture top priority—to the benefit of their organizations and customers. Fred Hassan, Chair of the Board of Bausch and Lomb, has had a long and distinguished career and is known to many, many people as an outstanding leader. Fred began his career in Pakistan in fertilizer sales, then joined Swiss pharmaceutical

Leadership Perspective

● **Fred Hassan**
Chair of the Board, Bausch and Lomb
"When principles are at the heart of all actions, you will make the right decisions..."

"Depending on the leader's span of influence, large groups of people, possibly the entire organization, may carefully emulate the leader's thoughts, beliefs, emotions, and the overall mood." In other words, the leader has a huge impact on culture, which Fred Hassan knows very well. Fred's "Rules for Resonance" include:

● *"Don't accept life's scripts": Your background is where you start from, not who you are.*

● *"It's not about being nice": Creating a resonant culture means managing your own and others' emotions so people can change and do the right thing.*

● *"Stay open, but let values drive all your choices": When principles are at the heart of all actions, you will make the right decisions in new situations. As a result, people will trust and follow you.*

Fred goes on to say more about the role of trust in leadership and building a great team and culture:

You must earn people's trust. This is especially true when you are attempting to bring about changes. Whether this be changes in the culture, team, or business, people need to know that they can depend on you. Earning trust has at least three components—each important but not enough alone. It's like compound interest—adding one to the other yields much bigger returns.

First, you need to be competent. This means you need to know your stuff—understand the environment, the industry, your strategy. Then you need to be authentic. You need to be a real person who people can relate to in a very human way. Finally, you need to care about people. True caring unleashes people's passion and commitment like nothing else.

A lot of leaders leave a lot on the table because they do not have trust. Building a great team, culture, and organization is very hard work, requiring people to change and to make great sacrifices. Trust, and trustworthiness, starts with you. As you look in the mirror every single day, you need to ask yourself, 'Am I honest with myself? Do I have the right motives? Am I the right person for this job?' If you can answer yes, then you have taken the first step toward earning the trust of the people who will create a great organization.

Sources: McKee, Annie, Richard Boyatzis, and Frances Johnston. 2008. *Becoming a resonant leader.* Boston: Harvard Business School Press; Personal interview with Fred Hassan conducted by Annie McKee, 2012.

giant Sandoz Pharmaceuticals. He ended up leading the company's U.S. operations, and went on to take leadership roles in companies such as Pharmacia & Upjohn and Monsanto, and was CEO of Schering Plough during the merger with Merck. Fred's business ventures have been successful for the companies he has served, his people, and stakeholders. Today, in addition to chairing the Bausch and Lomb board, Fred sits on the boards of Avon and Time Warner. His leadership style is unique in that he discovered long before many of his contemporaries that teams and culture matter a lot. His advice to us is in the *Leadership Perspective* feature.

Fred Hassan reminds us that it is the *interaction* between leaders, people, and culture that yields great results in our organizations—and in our communities. As you learn more about culture, remember that you have a role in this equation.

Discussion Questions

1. Of the types of cultures discussed in this section which is the most appealing to you? Why?

2. Consider a team with which you have worked in recent months. Examine the cultures and backgrounds of each team member. What was the nature of the diversity on this team? How did the team deal with diversity?

7. How Can HR Support the Development of Positive Organizational Cultures?

The human resource function—and human resource professionals themselves—can have a profound effect on an organization's culture. One way that HR can support the development and maintenance of a healthy organizational culture is through a "push strategy"—compelling people to comply with rules and regulations that support the kind of culture the organization's leaders want and need. Conversely, HR can also use a "pull strategy"—guiding people in positive ways to adopt cultural values and engage in behaviors that support organizational effectiveness.

HR's Role in Creating an Inclusive Culture: A "Push" Strategy

HR engages in push strategies to control employee behavior when it codifies and enforces culture via organizational policies and rules. Policies, rules, and laws all reinforce "how we do things around here." These things may be based on the values and basic assumptions that form the culture, or they may reinforce an ideal culture that the organization's leaders are striving to create.

PROMOTING DIVERSITY AND INCLUSION IN THE WORKPLACE AND THE EEOC

To illustrate how HR pushes culture in the right direction, consider the issue of diversity in the workplace. For example, many companies strive to hire and promote talented individuals without consideration of gender, race, national origin, religion, sexual orientation, age, or disability status. That's because these companies and their leaders understand that they are doing business in an environment where talent is essential, and that the characteristics listed above have nothing to do with talent.

HR SUPPORTS EQUAL OPPORTUNITY

Equal Employment Opportunity Commission (EEOC)
A federal commission created as part of the Civil Rights Act of 1964 that handles complaints of discrimination against organizations.

Equal opportunity laws
Federal regulations that ensure that organizations provide equal opportunities for all people.

Unfortunately, not all individuals or all companies are this smart. Discrimination still occurs, and people are often denied access to jobs, training, and equal pay because of gender, race, national origin, religion, sexual orientation, age, or disability. Similarly, employees are still victims of sexual harassment and other forms of discrimination. Because discriminatory practices like these continue to be problematic, laws have been necessary to support cultural change in the United States. In 1965, the **Equal Employment Opportunity Commission (EEOC)** was created as part of the Civil Rights Act of 1964. The EEOC is a division of the U.S. Department of Justice. It deals with complaints about discrimination and can punish organizations for engaging in discriminatory practices. An organization's leaders, managers, and employees must take steps to comply with all federal anti-discrimination laws. If they don't, serious consequences can and do occur.

■ **EXHIBIT 13.10** shows a number of the equal opportunity laws that have been passed by the U.S. government during the past 45 years to ensure that organizations provide equal opportunities for all people. These laws "push" organizations to change their cultures and practices.

HR is responsible for ensuring that the laws listed in Exhibit 13.10 are known to employees—and supported and enforced by managers. Although all of these laws are extremely important, we would like to discuss more fully the prohibitions against sexual harassment.

PREVENTING SEXUAL HARASSMENT IN THE WORKPLACE

One form of discrimination that is covered in these laws is sexual harassment, and HR is often responsible for preventing this from happening at work.

■ **EXHIBIT 13.10**

Equal Opportunity Laws

Law	Year Passed	Coverage
Executive Order 11246	1965	Prohibits covered federal contractors and subcontractors from discriminating on the basis of race, color, religion, sex, or national origin, and requires affirmative action to ensure equal employment opportunity without regard to those factors.
Age Discrimination in Employment Act	1967	Protects the rights of employees 40 years of age or older from discrimination on the basis of age in hiring, promotion, discharge, compensation, or terms, conditions, and privileges of employment.
Title IX Sex Discrimination in Educational Programs and Federally Funded Activities	1972	Prohibits discrimination on the basis of sex in educational programs and activities that receive federal financial assistance.
Rehabilitation Act	1973	Protects qualified individuals with disabilities in federally funded activities and contracts.
Vietnam Era Veterans' Readjustment Assistance Act, amended (Disabled Veterans Act)	1974	Protects qualified veterans with disabilities in federally funded activities and contracts. Requires affirmative action in projects that cost more than $25,000.
Employee Retirement Income Security Act (ERISA)	1974	Sets minimum standards for most voluntary pension and health plans in private industry to protect individuals in these plans.
Age Discrimination Act	1975	Prohibits discrimination on the basis of age in federally assisted programs.
The Migrant and Seasonal Agricultural Worker Protection Act (MSPA)	1983	Protects migrant laborers in their dealings with contractors, agricultural employers, and migrant housing providers.
The Consolidated Omnibus Budget Reconciliation Act (COBRA)	1985	Protects workers and their families who lose health benefits due to job loss or reduction in hours by giving them the right to choose to continue group health insurance for a limited time.
The Americans with Disabilities Act (ADA)	1990	Title I prohibits employers of 15 or more workers, employment agencies, and labor organizations of 15 or more workers from discriminating against qualified individuals with disabilities. Title II prohibits state and local governments from discriminating against qualified individuals with disabilities in programs, activities, and services.
Family and Medical Leave Act (FMLA)	1993	Protects workers' rights to family and medical leave under certain circumstances; grants eligible workers the right to take up to 12 or 26 weeks of unpaid military family leave.
Uniformed Services Employment and Reemployment Rights Act (USERRA)	1994	Protects the jobs of employees who have been called to active duty.
Health Insurance Portability and Accountability Act (HIPAA)	1996	Provides rights and protections for participants and beneficiaries in group health plans; protects against exclusions for preexisting conditions; prohibits discrimination against employees and dependents based on health status; and allows a right to purchase individual coverage for those who have no group health plan coverage available and have exhausted COBRA or other continuation coverage.
Workforce Investment Act	1998	Section 188 protects qualified individuals with disabilities in all WIA Title I financially assisted programs or activities.
Veterans Employment Opportunities Act	1998	Requires an agency to allow eligible veterans to apply for government jobs when the agency will accept applications from individuals outside its own workforce; allows preference in certain circumstances.

(continued)

▪ **EXHIBIT 13.10** *(continued)*

Equal Opportunity Laws

Law	Year Passed	Coverage
Veterans Benefits and Health Care Improvement Act (VBHCIA)	2000	Protects veterans with regard to health care and educational benefits. Title III protects jobs during redeployment and provides protections for veterans with disabilities.
Executive Order 13166	2000	Protects limited-English speakers' rights to access federally conducted or federally assisted services.
Jobs for Veterans Act	2002	The final rule expands the coverage of veterans with disabilities; expands Disabled Veterans Act to cover veterans of wars other than the Vietnam Conflict.
Fair Minimum Wage Act	2007	Increases federal minimum wage standards in increments.
Lilly Ledbetter Fair Pay Act	2009	Eases statute of limitations restrictions to make it easier for employees who have been discriminated against to file lawsuits.

Sexual harassment
"Unwelcome sexual advances, requests for sexual favors, and other verbal or physical conduct of a sexual nature such that submission to or rejection of this conduct explicitly or implicitly affects an individual's employment, unreasonably interferes with an individual's work performance, or creates an intimidating, hostile, or offensive work environment." —EEOC

According to the EEOC, **sexual harassment** is defined as "unwelcome sexual advances, requests for sexual favors, and other verbal or physical conduct of a sexual nature such that submission to or rejection of this conduct explicitly or implicitly affects an individual's employment, unreasonably interferes with an individual's work performance, or creates an intimidating, hostile, or offensive work environment."[106]

Sexual harassment does not necessarily have to cause economic suffering or include threats. In the United States, the behavior of the harasser must only be unwelcome. Although most sexual harassment cases consist of a man harassing a woman, sexual harassment can come from men or women and can be directed toward members of the same sex or the opposite sex. In fact, in recent years, the percentage of sexual harassment charges filed by men rose from 11.6 percent to 16.3 percent between 1997 and 2011.[107] The harasser can be a supervisor, a subordinate, a coworker, a client, or a nonemployee. The victim does not even need to be the person to whom offensive behavior was directed; *anyone* affected by the offensive behavior has the right to report it.[108] By 1998, 95 percent of large employers in the United States had harassment grievance policies, and 70 percent of U.S. companies provided training related to sexual harassment.[109] Unfortunately, however, most people who experience sexual harassment do not report it.[110]

It can be difficult to measure the cost of sexual harassment. There are litigation costs, settlement costs, and productivity costs. The EEOC keeps track of the monetary settlements paid out for sexual harassment charges. Between 1997 and 2009, the total average yearly monetary cost was $48 million in non-litigation settlements alone.[111] However, the highest costs may come from loss of productivity. A survey of U.S. federal government employees estimated that sexual harassment cost the U.S. government $327 million between 1992 and 1994 alone due to issues such as those listed in ▪ **EX-HIBIT 13.11**.[112] A study of organizational productivity costs for same-sex harassment in the U.S. Army in 1999 found these costs to exceed $95 million.[113] These costs likely are much higher now. According to the Pentagon, sexual assault reports had jumped by nearly 40 percent in 2005 and another 24 percent in 2006 before decreasing in 2007.[114]

HR's Role in Preventing Sexual Harassment

So, what can HR do about sexual harassment? Basically, there are two streams of activities that HR professionals can direct when it comes to preventing sexual harassment in the workplace. The first stream of activity is related to education and awareness. HR is responsible for ensuring that employees understand what sexual harassment is, what

■ **EXHIBIT 13.11**

Sexual Harassment Is Costly to Employees and Employers

Costs for the Employee

Increase in sick leave and time away from work

Decrease in individual productivity of individual victims of sexual harassment

Lost productivity of work groups in which harassment occurs

Job turnover, including job transfers, firings, and resignations

Stress, depression, and other emotional and physical consequences, including alcohol-, sleep-, and weight-related problems.

Costs for the Employer

Decrease in overall employee productivity

Higher staff turnover

Increase in sick leave and other types of leave, as well as higher medical payouts

Damaged company reputation (leading to difficulties associated with retention and attraction of employees)

Decrease in teamwork

Poor staff morale

Possible legal and consultant costs.

the law says about it, and what the company's policies are. Education and awareness activities include (but are not limited to) training programs, company-wide communication via the Web, brochures, statements by company leaders, one-on-one coaching sessions with managers, and small group discussions with employees.

A second area of activity that HR must support with respect to sexual harassment relates to compliance and consequences. This set of activities often includes creating processes for reporting sexual harassment and investigating the reported incidents. This is obviously a complex and sensitive process. Oftentimes, employees are hesitant to report sexual harassment for fear of reprisals. This means that HR and other managers must provide safe and confidential processes that encourage employees to come forward. On the other hand, claims must be investigated and proven true or false—false claims are extremely damaging as well.

One would hope that at some point, laws won't be required to ensure a fair and equitable workplace. For now, however, they are necessary—and HR is responsible for ensuring that these laws are enforced. Meanwhile, HR professionals are also responsible for exploring and developing an organization's culture via "pull" strategies.

How HR Can Help Diagnose and Develop Culture: A "Pull" Strategy

In addition to pushing employees, leaders, and managers to create and maintain a healthy organizational culture, HR professionals can lead people, or pull them, in the right direction. First of all, HR can be strategic business partners with the organization's leaders and managers, helping them determine what kind of culture would best fit the mission, vision, and goals of the organization.

Then, HR leaders can develop skills and competencies that enable them to diagnose culture and help change it. Skills that support such a diagnosis include selecting appropriate measurement tools (such as surveys) and correctly interpreting the collected information in order to identify key cultural issues. As mentioned earlier in this chapter, however, surveys tend to result in finding little other than what you were expecting to find in the first place.[115] Thus, HR professionals must also hone the skills and competencies that enable them to conduct dynamic inquiry and other ethnographic research. These methods will help uncover an organization's deeper norms, values, and basic assumptions.

For example, HR professionals can be trained to conduct interviews and to analyze the information obtained in these interviews for themes related to culture. This is a process called *thematic analysis*, and it results in identifying patterns in the values, norms, and assumptions that drive employee behavior.[116] By dealing with patterns as opposed to isolated situations, feelings, or behavior, HR professionals and organization management can more effectively deal with both the culture's strengths and its problems.

Recently, this process was effective with employees inside a large financial services company. In this situation, certain HR professionals were selected to participate in a program aimed at enhancing their abilities to be executive coaches and advisers, leadership development and facilitation experts, strategic business partners, and change agents—four key roles for HR today. As part of this program, the HR team was trained in dynamic inquiry and thematic analysis. Then, team members interviewed approximately 75 HR professionals and 75 business professionals throughout the company. The interviews were analyzed, and the themes were presented to management. Key cultural drivers of effectiveness were identified, as were aspects of the culture that were hindering the organization.

Armed with this information, leaders, managers, and their HR business partners were much more prepared to create plans designed to change those aspects of the culture that were harmful and to support those aspects that were helpful. These are just a few examples of how HR can help develop, maintain, and enhance a powerful and positive organizational culture. Businesses today recognize how important HR's role is in these critical "pull" activities, and many forward-thinking organizations are investing in the skills and competencies of their HR professionals.

HR Leadership Roles

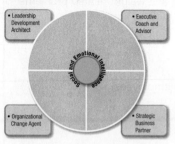

Discussion Questions

1. Have you ever attended diversity training or sexual harassment awareness and education programs? What was the impact of the training on you? What do you think the impact of such training was on the culture of the organization to which you belonged during the training?

2. How does your university or workplace create and promote an inclusive culture? Try to come up with five examples.

Objective 13.8
Learn ways we can create positive and powerful organizational cultures.

8. What Can We All Do to Create Positive and Powerful Organizational Cultures?

Leaders and managers have a powerful effect on culture, and you, as a member of an organization, can have impact, too. Powerful, positive cultures foster resonance. In such cultures, emotional intelligence enables people to create and sustain relationships and an environment where positive values drive behaviors. Emotional intelligence competencies support what's called cultural intelligence, and these competencies also enable us to lead cultural change.

People who use the emotional competency called empathy to understand an organization's culture can be leaders within the organization.[117] That's because people who can manage culture well are able to use self-awareness, self-management, and empathy to bridge differences. Researcher Daniel Goleman emphasizes the importance of empathy in social interactions. "Fast . . . empathy" involves complex connections in our brains, allowing us to read others' emotions and even catch their moods very quickly.

He also emphasizes that a slower form of empathy involves our thinking brain to a greater degree. When we use this form of empathy we imagine ourselves in the situation of the other person and think about how it would feel to be in that position. This allows us to truly examine and understand another individual, or a group, along with the accompanying cultural values and norms.[118]

Develop Your Cultural Intelligence

Employees and managers who are most successful in managing and leading across cultures are adaptable, patient, and flexible—in other words, they exhibit the behaviors associated with cultural intelligence. *Cultural intelligence* is a term that some scholars use to describe a set of behaviors that are related to emotional intelligence that focus specifically on a person's ability to interpret values and behavior.[119] Important aspects of cultural intelligence include the use of reasoning and observational skills to interpret unfamiliar behavior and situations (cognitive abilities), willingness to "stick with it" when encountering a new culture (emotional/motivational abilities), and a willingness to adopt body languages and gestures (physical abilities). These three sources of cultural intelligence can be described this way:[120]

- *Cognitive cultural intelligence* encompasses a person's observational and learning skills. It's the ability to pick up factual information about important values and norms of behavior.
- *Emotional cultural intelligence* deals with a person's self-confidence and motivation. Adapting to a new culture is not always easy, and it may involve setbacks and obstacles. Thus, it's important that people have self-efficacy—they need to believe in themselves, avoid becoming discouraged, and not give up.
- *Physical cultural intelligence* is a person's ability to adapt his or her speech patterns, expressions, and body language to those of another culture. By adopting these patterns and mannerisms, a person can better understand what it's like to be part of that culture.

Note that there are two complementary types of cultural intelligence.[121] The first involves the ability to understand values, norms, and the like within one's own culture. The other, often called cross-cultural intelligence, involves the ability to adjust quickly and with little stress to the mores of cultures other than one's own when and where needed.

Leading Culture Change

What we hear most often about culture from leaders today is: "Our culture needs to change. We need to change the mind-set of our people. We need to preserve our most precious values, and change—or get rid of—some of the beliefs that just don't serve us anymore."

But how can leaders and managers address this challenge? Scholars Daniel Goleman, Richard Boyatzis, and Annie McKee have compiled guidelines for leading cultural change based on their research and work in organizations. The following guidelines can support examination and the subsequent transformation of an organization's culture:[122]

- *"Respect the group's values and the organization's integrity.* Vision changes, but as the vision evolves, the leader needs to be sure that the 'sacred center'—what everyone holds as paramount—remains intact. That's the first challenge: Knowing what the sacred center actually is—from the perspective of others, not just oneself. The second challenge is seeing clearly what *must* change, even when it is held dear, and getting other people to see it too."[123]

- *"**Slow down in order to speed up.** A target-shooting coach we know tells his students, 'If you're in a combat situation, you can't miss fast enough to save your life.' So too with building resonance and an emotionally intelligent organization—the shotgun approach to change doesn't work. The process of slowing down and bringing people into the conversation about their systems and their culture is one we don't see enough in organizations but that nevertheless is critical. Processes such as dynamic inquiry require a supportive, coaching approach and democratic style: The leader must really listen to what people have to say"—and this takes time.[124]

- *"**Start at the top with a bottom-up strategy.** Top leadership *must* be committed to facing the truth about the emotional reality of the organization, and they must be committed to creating resonance around a vision of the ideal. But that's not enough: A bottom-up strategy is needed as well, because powerful resonance only develops when everyone is attuned to the change. This means engaging formal and informal leaders from all over the organization in conversations about what is working, what is not, and how exciting it would be if the organization could move more in the direction of what *is* working. Taking time out to discuss these kinds of issues is a powerful intervention. It gets people thinking and talking, and it shows them the way. Once the excitement and buy-in builds, it's more possible to move from talk to action. The enthusiasm provides momentum. But the movement needs to be directed: toward the dream, toward collective values, and toward new ways of working together. Transparent goals, an open change process, involvement of as many people as possible, and modeling new behaviors provide a top-down, bottom-up jump-start for resonance."[125]

Leadership today means embracing all members within the larger culture of an organization, taking the time to engage all stakeholders in the process of culture change, and carefully negotiating the right balance between core values and new demands. Creating and maintaining a positive organizational culture takes work. Cultural intelligence, and the ability to lead change effectively and empathically, are critical skills that can facilitate that work.

Discussion Questions

1. Do you think you use cultural intelligence in your interactions with people at school or at work? If so, how and where?

2. Consider a group or an organization you belong to that would benefit from examining its culture. Choose one of the guidelines from the "Leading Culture Change" sections and describe how you would use this advice to help the group or organization.

---

9. A Final Note on the Power of Culture

In this chapter, you have explored culture at several levels—what it means for you, how it affects nations and communities, and how it impacts organizations. You've learned how to study culture, and how we can shift organizational culture to make our groups and organizations more effective.

Maybe the most important lesson to take from this chapter is that when it comes to personal, group, or organizational culture and effectiveness, *it's not all about individual behavior.* Culture is a powerful force in our lives, and it affects virtually everything we do. If we want to be successful personally, or in our organizations or even our nations and communities, we must focus on ensuring that our cultural "rules" are in synch with our visions and goals.

LEADING IN A GLOBAL WORLD
Walking the Diversity Talk

In a global economy, diversity is a fact in businesses. People from diverse backgrounds, ethnicities, races, religions, sexual orientatons, ages, physical abilities, and of course genders make up the modern organization. Research indicates that the diverse perspectives these individuals offer lead to better decisions and help attract the best employees.

1. Research some of the largest multinational companies in the United States. Pick one and, using the information on its Web site, assemble a report card for the company's diversity efforts using the Johnson & Johnson example in your text as a model.

   A. From the company's organizational chart, identify senior management and leadership who are women or people of color.

   B. Does the company have a diversity policy? If yes, briefly summarize the policy.

   C. Do the company's diversity efforts mention religious and/or sexual orientation? What about age?

2. Draw a map of the countries where the company has offices and/or where it does a majority of its business. Does the company seem U.S. focused from its Web site, or does it appear inclusive and multicultural? Try to determine if the company offshores any of its work. If yes, to what countries?

LEADING WITH EMOTIONAL INTELLIGENCE
Firms of Endearment

A culture that focuses on heart and spirit is one that values productive relationships, positive and effective communication, respect, compassion, and a sense of meaningfulness in the workplace. Organizational cultures that support their workers' spiritual and emotional well-being can see dramatic improvement in employee performance.[126]

In 2007, three marketing professors wrote a book about world-class companies that profit from passion and purpose. The book, *Firms of Endearment*, identifies the most humane companies; they are also some of the most successful. These companies focus on the heart, spirit, intellect, and emotions of their internal and external customers while returning tidy profits to their shareholders.

1. In a group or on your own, research the companies that made the *Firms of Endearment* cut.

2. Choose three and identify what they are doing, how they are doing it, and what the results have been in regards to building a "whole person" culture. Be sure to investigate the following:

   A. What is unique about the cultures of these companies?

   B. What are the companies doing to make employees' work meaningful and significant?

   C. How do the cultures affect customer relations?

   D. If you have patronized some of these companies, what was your experience with the culture?

   E. Has anything changed since the authors wrote this book? If so, what and why?

LEADING WITH CRITICAL THINKING SKILLS
Zappos: Heart and Sole

In Edgar Shein's Levels of Culture model, observable artifacts are at the top of the pyramid, values and attitudes are in the middle, and basic assumptions are at the bottom.[127] You can tell a lot about an organization's culture by paying attention to how these three levels are expressed in the organization's day-to-day activity. Some companies are fairly transparent; others are hard to distinguish.

Zappos.com—the online shoe, clothing, and accessory store—has a highly unusual and successful culture. Tony Hsieh, its founder and CEO, authored a book called *Delivering Happiness*.[128] Hsieh discusses the thriving culture at Zappos and how his sole motivation to be a business owner is to deliver happiness to both his employees and his customers. Hsieh says that Zappos "is not a company, it's a mission." Many business scholars point to Zappos as a role model for how to build and sustain a highly successful business based on culture.

1. In a group or on your own, research Zappos's culture. Create a culture profile of the company. Be sure to include the following:

   A. Observable artifacts, values, and basic assumptions. For example, what are the dress and cubicle codes for Zappos? What drives interpersonal relationships between management and employees and between employees and customers? Considering that Zappos is an online retailer/call center, what role does technology play in Zappos's culture? What ceremonies, rituals, and awards are important to the Zappos's family? What are Zappos's espoused and enacted values?

B. Where does Zappos fall on the competing values model? Is it easy to place it in the framework?

C. What and who are the myths and heroes of Zappos? What are some of its taboos and sacred symbols? What does happiness have to do with selling shoes and other items online?

2. After you have created a culture profile, call the company's 800 number and speak very briefly to a Zappos employee about the culture. (Remember, it is a business, so keep the call short.) They will be delighted to tell you how much they love their job.

ETHICAL LEADERSHIP
Do Muppets Have Financial Portfolios?

Today more than ever, social pressure for people and organizations to act in an ethical manner is great. Employees at all levels in an organization are faced with numerous dilemmas that require sound, values-based judgments. Therefore, all organizations should encourage ethical behavior through their cultural values and norms.

In March of 2012, the executive director and head of Goldman Sachs United States equity derivatives business in Europe, the Middle East, and Africa resigned in an open letter published in *The New York Times*. Greg Smith's letter, entitled "Why I Am Leaving Goldman Sachs," is frank and brutal in its portrayal of Goldman Sachs' culture of the vulture—doing whatever it takes

to make money for the firm, referring to customers as "muppets," and making references to "ripping customers' eyeballs out" to make a buck.[129]

1. Read Greg Smith's letter (or his book on the subject) with a critical eye:[130] http://www.nytimes.com/2012/03/14/opinion/why-i-am-leaving-goldman-sachs.html?pagewanted=all

2. Research Goldman Sachs' espoused values in their mission and vision statements on their Web site. Next, research their enacted values. Smith's letter reveals a lot of information about his opinion about these, but be sure to look at other sources, too. It may be helpful to begin by looking into any past ethical transgressions, such as Goldman Sachs' involvement in the subprime mortgage crisis. You can also research positive press abou the company.

3. Write a response, your own open letter, to Smith's letter for the fictional newspaper *The Ethical Times*. Smith has been called a "hero," "whistleblower," and "traitor."[131] Ask yourself why a relatively young, very successful person would resign so publically, knowing full well there would be repercussions? In your opinion, what does Smith stand to gain by blowing the whistle on Goldman Sachs' culture? What did—or does—he stand to lose? Considering the meltdown of Wall Street in 2008 for unethical and potentially illegal activities around mortgage lending, hedge funds, and derivatives, how objective can you be in judging Goldman Sachs?

KEY TERMS

MyManagementLab

Go to **mymanagementlab.com** for Auto-graded writing questions as well as the following Assisted-graded writing questions:

13-1. How would you describe the culture of your school? How does your school's culture impact your behavior?

13-2. When you are in a situation with people from another culture, how do you use empathy? How could you do this better?

13-3. Mymanagementlab Only — comprehensive writing assignment for this chapter.

1. What Is Culture? (pp. 470–472)

Objective: Define culture.

Summary: Culture is an important force that affects all aspects of life. Culture includes values, traditions, language, and all that a group or society shares. Values and attitudes refer specifically to the ideas or groups of ideas that people hold dear and that predispose them to react to certain things in certain ways. Norms are standards of behavior held by a culture that are based on the values and attitudes of its people.

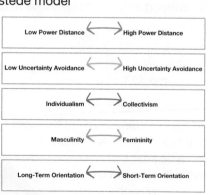

2. Why Is Culture Important at Work? (pp. 473–474)

Objective: Understand the importance of culture at work.

Summary: Understanding culture is important because culture is a powerful driver of people's behavior and organizational results. Many organizations do business in multiple countries and employ a workforce with diverse cultural backgrounds. In order for these cultures to peacefully coexist, respect for and understanding of differences must be developed.

4. How Can We Link Organizational Culture with Business Issues? (pp. 481–483)

Objective: Explain various types of organizational cultures.

Summary: Scholars have attempted to categorize cultures to show their impact on business. One such scheme is called the competing values framework, which looks at whether cultures tend to be focused internally or externally and whether they are flexible or stable. Within this framework, scholars have classified cultures as clan, hierarchy, adhocracy, market, and balanced cultures. Cultures can also be described as strong or weak, depending on the degree to which culture impacts members' values, attitudes, and behaviors.

3. What Are the Dimensions of National and Organizational Culture? (pp. 474–481)

Objective: Describe the dimensions of national and organizational culture.

Summary: Organizational culture is commonly studied using two models: the Hofstede model and the GLOBE model. Each of these models rates cultures as either high or low on dimensions, including the importance placed on power, the way uncertainty is handled, whether assertive (masculine) or relational (feminine) behaviors are favored, whether forward-looking activities are pursued, and whether individual or collective achievement is valued. The study of culture is complex because of the many factors that must be considered, including the subcultures that exist within larger cultures and the constantly changing nature of culture.

| Low Power Distance ⟷ High Power Distance |
| Low Uncertainty Avoidance ⟷ High Uncertainty Avoidance |
| Individualism ⟷ Collectivism |
| Masculinity ⟷ Femininity |
| Long-Term Orientation ⟷ Short-Term Orientation |

9. A Final Note on the Power of Culture (p. 504)

Summary: The study of organizational culture is important because it points out that the forces affecting our behavior and our success at work are not linked to just individual talents or even leadership. Instead, culture is a collective phenomenon that profoundly affects people.

8. What Can We All Do to Create Positive and Powerful Organizational Cultures? (pp. 502–504)

Objective: Learn ways we can create positive and powerful organizational cultures.

Summary: Creating powerful, positive cultures is the responsibility of everyone in an organization. Social, emotional, and cultural intelligence skills enable you to understand your own culture and to adapt quickly and easily to other cultures and to changes within your own culture. Cultural change is sometimes necessary and can be difficult to achieve, but you can support change by respecting the values and integrity of the organization as it changes, and learning how to slow down, study your culture carefully, and choose shifts in values and behavior that will help the organization and its people.

7. How Can HR Support the Development of Positive Organizational Cultures? (pp. 498–502)

Objective: Learn how HR can support the development of positive organizational cultures.

Summary: HR professionals in many organizations are responsible for and have a profound effect on culture. HR uses "push" strategies to ensure that an organization's culture and employee behavior are in line with important societal rules and laws (such as those related to the EEOC and sexual harassment). HR can also use "pull" strategies to help leaders and employees study, evaluate, and change their organization's culture when necessary. Together, these strategies create a more positive and productive work environment for employees.

6. Organizational Culture: What's Important Today?
(pp. 491–497)

Objective: Assess the important aspects of organizational culture.

Summary: Some organizations struggle with issues related to their culture because, for many years, the people issues at the heart of culture have been ignored, and hence, cultures often develop organically in ways that do not support employees or organizational results. In recent years, some business leaders have made a point of supporting innovative, customer service-oriented, diversity and inclusion, and ethical cultures with great success. Leaders are also focusing more deliberately on developing cultures that support sustainability, social responsibility, and whole-person well-being at work.

5. How Can We Study Organizational Culture? (pp. 483–491)

Objective: Learn how to study organizational culture.

Summary: Understanding culture in organizations is key to knowing how to maintain and improve it. Edgar Schein proposes that we can study culture by looking at observable artifacts, values, and basic assumptions. These reveal both the obvious and the deeply embedded elements of an organization's culture. We can deepen our study of culture by looking at myths, heroes, taboos, sacred symbols, and language. To study culture more formally, managers can take an

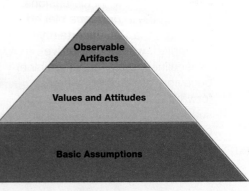

ethnographic approach, combining observation with co-inquiry to understand people's own sense of their own culture. This approach allows employees and leaders to create a collective, dynamic picture of an organization's culture.

Globalization:

Managing Effectively in a Global Economic Environment

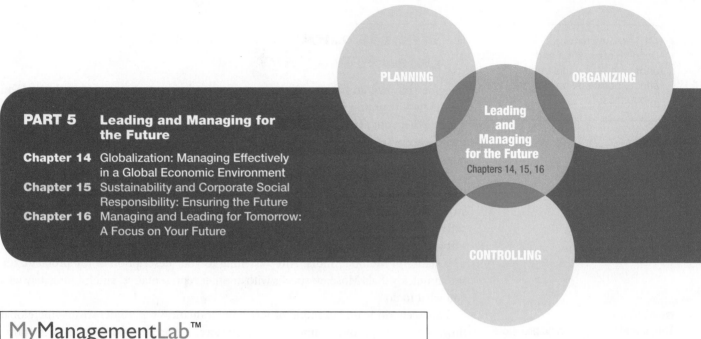

MyManagementLab™

⭐ **Improve Your Grade!**

Over 10 million students improved their results using the Pearson MyLabs. Visit **mymanagementlab.com** for simulations, tutorials, and end-of-chapter problems.

Chapter Outline

Chapter Objectives

14.1 Define globalization and understand how this trend affects business, politics, and economics.

14.2 Understand how technology plus political and economic changes fostered globalization.

14.3 Define the key economic factors that are affecting global business.

14.4 List factors that must be considered when developing a global business strategy.

14.5 Define and assess the opportunities and risks in a global business environment.

14.6 Learn about the opportunities that exist in emerging markets.

14.7 Define HR's role in supporting global business.

14.8 List steps we can take to succeed in a global environment.

1. What Is Globalization and Why Does It Matter?

Imagine you own an interior design company and operate it out of your home. You need new accounting software, so you visit a small computer store located down the street. When you arrive, the store's owner asks about your business, and they recommend a software package. You purchase the software, confident that you've bought a quality product. You also feel good about supporting a local business.

A few hours later you begin the software installation process, and you notice the disc was made in China. You insert the CD into your computer and follow the instructions that appear on screen. Soon, a problem arises—you cannot install the new software because it conflicts with another program on your computer. You dial the software manufacturer's toll-free customer assistance hotline and your call is answered by a staffer in Mumbai, India. After listening to your description of the problem, the staffer quickly dials Moscow, speaks with another representative, and immediately tells you what to do.

Globalization
The global flow of money, products,
information, services, expertise,
and people.

This scenario is one example of just how dramatically globalization—the global flow of money, products, information, services, expertise, and people—has transformed both the business environment and society in recent years. Some scholars think of globalization as the dismantling of trade barriers between nations and the changes that this will bring to people and cultures.[1] Of course, nations have traded with one another for centuries, and ideas have been passed among different groups of people forever. Within the past few decades, however, globalization has come to permeate every aspect of our lives. Products we use are designed and manufactured far from home, news from distant and remote areas reaches us instantaneously, and trends in one part of the world catch on in others overnight.

Globalization Matters Because It Is Changing Our Lives

Globalization is changing all of our lives. It changes how we think about college, how we choose a career, and how we move up the career ladder. For example, in 1970, if you wanted a career in aerospace with Boeing, you might be competing with 100 aerospace engineers who wanted to work in Seattle, Washington. Now, you are competing with people from all over the world for positions all over the globe. The most successful professionals today are people who are willing to learn new skills, work in diverse organizations, and even move their homes and families.

Globalization has done a tremendous amount of good around the world. Individuals in many parts of the world have more choices. The goods we can purchase, where we can work, and what types of jobs we can have are just a few examples of these changes. Globalization has helped entire groups of people in many societies, such as the worldwide middle class, which continues to expand.[2] Supporters of globalization argue that the end result will be increased prosperity for many of the world's poor, as corporations and governments invest in undeveloped regions.[3] It has also been argued that increased integration of economies and technologies will make war less likely—or at least more costly.[4] This perspective is based on the idea that when all of the world's countries are potential markets, and when people are more interconnected, going to war anywhere affects individuals everywhere.

THE LOCAL-GLOBAL DEBATE

Some people oppose globalization. Anti-globalization advocates have been vocal and occasionally violent in their protests (■ **EXHIBIT 14.1**). They see progress toward globalism as a capitalist movement with built-in inequities that are designed to hurt the average citizen and destroy the autonomy of the developing world and indigenous cultures.[5] Unfortunately, these people have good reason to be concerned. For example, a report prepared for the United Nations (UN) found that millions of farmers in both developing and developed countries were losing their farms and their livelihoods in the name of progress and globalization.[6] Water rights are also a concern, as rivers are dammed or diverted, underwater aquifers disappear, and weather patterns change as a result of global warming.

These issues are contentious. In a global economic environment, whose needs are more important? Farmers? Developers? Businesses? What about when jobs migrate en masse away from certain countries (such as the United States) to other countries (like China and India)? Whose well-being should be considered? In light of these issues, many people now advocate a form of responsible globalization that incorporates democratic freedoms and representation, as well as protection of the environment and human rights through fair trade and development.[7]

Another factor affecting the movement toward globalization has emerged since the onset of the recession in 2008: the movement back toward *localization*.[8] What this means in practice is that some companies are choosing to hire people, use local resources, and sell goods locally. This trend is emerging because business are carefully evaluating the obvious and hidden costs of producing goods far from the markets they serve. In addition, many more consumers are more conscious of "buying local" in order to help ensure that jobs remain in the community. This movement can be seen in decisions made in boardrooms and HR departments in companies large and small.

In addition to the movement toward hiring and selling locally the local movement is also apparent in communities. Take for instance American Express: In the United States, the credit card company supports a program called "Small Business Saturday." Advertisements and incentives encourage customers to buy from their local businesses on the Saturday after Thanksgiving, as well as all year round.[9] A benefit of this program is that more small businesses may come to accept the American Express credit card, which tends to be expensive for merchants to use. An offshoot of the local movement in the United States is the "Grow Local" movement, which has gained tremendous ground in recent years. Farmer's markets can be found in places as varied as the streets of New York, city parks everywhere, and even the parking lot of the local shopping center in Kailua, Hawaii.

The financial pressures of the recession have brought some of these decisions and the movement toward localization to the forefront of businesses and communities everywhere.

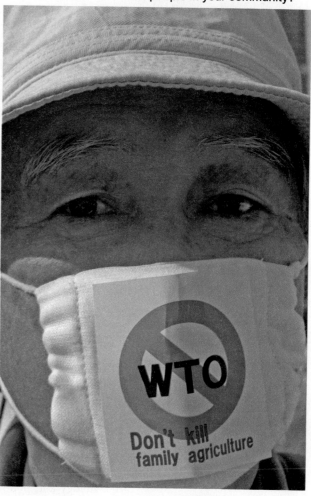

■ **EXHIBIT 14.1**
What are the risks and benefits of globalization for the businesses and people in your community?

Source: Islemount Images/Alamy

GLOBALIZATION IS HERE TO STAY

Despite the movement toward localization, globalization is undoubtedly here to stay. Changes in the way we think, do business, and interact culturally and interpersonally have begun and will not be turned around. Countries that will be successful in the era of globalization are those that are open to change. It is the same for businesses, people, and cultures. Consider the following advice from Jerry Rao, CEO of the IT firm MphasiS and head of the Indian high-tech trade association:

> *Cultures that are open and willing to change have a huge advantage in this world. My great-grandmother was illiterate. My grandmother went to grade two. My mother did not go to college. My sister has a master's degree in economics, and my daughter is at*

the University of Chicago. We have done all this in living memory, but we have been willing to change. . . . You have to have a strong culture, but also the openness to adapt and adopt from others. The cultural exclusivists have a real disadvantage.[10]

In this chapter, we will examine some critical political and economic events that have helped foster globalization. We will also consider how trade agreements and international regulatory bodies affect worldwide business relationships. After that, we will explore key aspects of global business and how organizations develop and implement a global strategy. We'll also look at some of the major opportunities and risks associated with global business, paying special attention to four key emerging markets: Brazil, Russia, India, and China. Finally, to conclude the chapter, we'll explore HR's role in supporting an organization's global strategy, as well as what we can all do to be successful in an increasingly interconnected world.

Discussion Questions

1. How has globalization affected the community in which you grew up?
2. Do you think globalization is here to stay? Why or why not? What will slow progress toward seamless global business (e.g, specific cultural, political or economic issues)?

Objective 14.2
Understand how international political and economic changes fostered globalization.

2. How Do Changes in Technology, World Politics, and Economics Foster Globalization?

Globalization didn't just happen: It is the result of a number of factors that have come together during the past few decades. Chief among these are massive changes in technology and political and economic shifts that have led people around the world to demand more say in how they are governed, how their economies are managed, and which products are available to them.

Technology's Role in Fostering Rapid Globalization

Globalization means that businesses and people everywhere are more closely connected—and more reliant on one another—than ever before. This is due, in part, to advances in technology, especially information and communication technologies (ICTs). Former U.S. Secretary of Labor Robert Reich points out that the technologies that drive globalization surfaced several decades ago.

[Starting in] the 1970s . . . large firms became far more competitive, global, and innovative. . . . The shift began when technologies developed by government to fight the Cold War were incorporated into new products and services. This created possibilities for new competitors, beginning in transportation, communications, manufacturing, and finance.[11]

Since the period described by Reich, there have been rapid advances in ICTs. People now know more about what is going on outside their communities, which has resulted in global demand for access to products and services as varied as automobiles, food, music, and movies. For example, moviegoers from all areas of the world want to see the latest films from Hollywood and Bollywood, and many movies are now made with the international audience in mind. Similarly, global demand for Big Macs and fries has resulted in tens of thousands of McDonald's restaurants in over one hundred countries worldwide (■ **EXHIBIT 14.2**).[12]

New demands and new technologies for producing and disseminating goods and services are at the heart of globalization. ICTs that have become commonplace in our lives—like the Internet, smartphones, and social networking sites—are important drivers of globalization that have changed the way we live and work, and the way our social structures operate. They are also changing the way that countries develop, particularly when it comes to industrialization. Advances in ICTs have been rapid, which means that within a few generations global citizens have become more connected with their friends, neighbors, and coworkers. For example, at work you are increasingly likely to find yourself e-mailing, texting, or videoconferencing with coworkers who are separated from you by a diverse culture and thousands of miles, and you may regard these colleagues as friends even though you've never met face-to-face.

ICTs and Global Business

Technology has also enabled a host of changes in how businesses are created, managed, and run. For example, technological changes related to transportation and manufacturing enable goods to be distributed in new and cheaper ways, leading to revolutionary changes in the way business is conducted in many industries. These and other changes allow companies to arrange for the production, marketing, distribution, and sale of goods and services far from home more cheaply and more efficiently than ever before.

To put this into perspective, consider a fictitious company located in St. Paul, Minnesota, that produces handcrafted watches. The company has been in business since the 1890s and has a long-established clientele among wealthy Europeans who consider the handmade timepieces a status symbol. During the first hundred years of the company's existence, the process of ordering and obtaining a watch was onerous. First, a letter describing the customer's wishes had to be written and sent to St. Paul, and could take months to arrive. Then, if the watchmaker had additional questions about the customer's wishes, more months would pass as letters went back and forth. Once the details were in order, it took another month to craft the timepiece and then several more to ship it to the customer. By the time all was said and done, more than a year would have passed since the original request.

Today, the company has a Web site through which customers submit their orders and special requests. Watchmakers can e-mail any questions and quickly receive feedback. The company's process for handcrafting the watches has changed little and the watch still takes a month to produce, but customers can e-mail asking for status updates and the watchmakers often send pictures to their customers and solicit their feedback as they work. Once the watch is completed, it is shipped and is received by the customer in a few days. Payment is made via credit card or bank transfer, and the transaction clears quickly. Thanks to advances in ICTs and shipping, the process of purchasing a custom watch from the company has gone from taking about a year to taking a little over a month. And thanks to the company's Internet presence, their customer base has expanded to include people across the globe.

As this example shows, advances in ICTs and other key technologies have changed global business in a big way, but they are not the only important pieces of the puzzle. Factors such as world politics and shifts in economic models are also important.

■ **EXHIBIT 14.2**
Besides McDonald's, what are some other well-known global brands?

Source: Dennis Cox/Alamy

Changing Global Politics and Economic Shifts after the Cold War

Many political and social events have impacted globalization, and educated managers and leaders appreciate this. In this section, we'll start with a review of Cold War politics, then move on to more recent political and social shifts that are important to your understanding of globalization.

THE COLD WAR: A POLITICAL *AND* ECONOMIC CONFLICT

Cold War
A political and ideological conflict between the former Soviet Union (USSR) and the United States.

The Cold War was a political and ideological conflict between the former Soviet Union (USSR) and the United States. These countries were known as "superpowers." The Cold War lasted from the end of World War II until the early 1990s. It was characterized by military antagonism, economic competition, and ideological warfare between the superpowers. This warfare often took the form of proxy wars, or wars started or encouraged by one of the superpowers, that allowed the superpowers to fight each other indirectly without declaring war. The Korean War, the Vietnam War, and conflicts in Afghanistan are examples of proxy wars. Another tactic used by both sides to influence people and countries was propaganda. Propaganda is biased and/or untrue information that is communicated to further a specific agenda and/or weaken the position of a competing party. Propaganda often includes derogatory and/or untrue depictions of people, cultures, and values. It is still used today.

Propaganda
Biased and/or untrue information that is communicated to further a specific agenda and/or weaken the position of a competing party.

During the Cold War period, the United State. and the Soviet Union sought to either spread democracy or communism, with the corresponding political and economic models. The divide between these two ideologies was most obvious in Germany: The country was divided into West Germany and East Germany after World War II, with control given to the United States and the Soviet Union, respectively. The city of Berlin was physically split by the Berlin Wall, which became symbolic of the Iron Curtain, a seemingly impenetrable physical and political boundary that separated democracy-favoring Western Europe from Communism-favoring Eastern Europe and the Soviet Union (■ **EXHIBIT 14.3**).

Iron Curtain
The seemingly impenetrable physical and political boundary that separated democracy-favoring Western Europe from Communism-favoring Eastern Europe and the Soviet Union.

During this period, most major countries chose sides—or were forced to. The Soviet Union widened its sphere of political and economic influence through military occupation of areas such as Hungary, the Baltic States, Czechoslovakia, Romania, and Afghanistan. Meanwhile, the United States sought to protect democracy and the worldwide balance of power by providing military and economic aid to countries fighting communism.

■ **EXHIBIT 14.3**
Why was the Berlin Wall a powerful symbol of the divide between democracy and communism during the Cold War?

China was involved in the Cold War, although not controlled by either power. As political scientists Andrew Nathan and Robert Ross put it, "During the Cold War, China was the only major country that stood at the intersection of the two super power camps, a target of influence and enmity for both."[13] During this time, China played a central role in two wars that presented major difficulties for the United States: the Korean War and the Vietnam War.

Source: Norbert Michalke/Alamy

Sadly, the events of the Cold War brought great harm to all parties involved. For example, during the Vietnam War, hundreds of thousands of American soldiers were killed or injured, as were far more North and South Vietnamese soldiers and civilians.[14] Later, in Afghanistan, the United States provided arms and money to local guerrillas in an attempt to assist them in driving out the Soviets. Some of the people who received this top-notch American weaponry and training would later become terrorists. Finally, the economies of the USSR and most of Eastern Europe suffered profound negative effects as a result of the Cold War. Poverty; inability to access information, goods, and services; and a system that stifled innovation left many countries in shambles.

After many years of diplomacy and weakening economies in Eastern Europe, the Berlin Wall came down in November 1989, and East and West Germany were reunified. Other Communist governments behind the Iron Curtain fell rapidly—including those in Hungary, Czechoslovakia, and Romania—and were replaced with more democratic or socialist regimes. By 1991, the Soviet Union itself was no longer a Communist nation. As the Cold War concluded, the tenuous balance of power that had existed since the end of World War II shifted dramatically.

The demise of the Soviet empire discredited top-down totalitarian Communism as a legitimate form of government in almost every corner of the globe. At the same time, countries including Brazil, India, and even China began to open their economies to outsiders. With this openness came more interaction among people, businesses, and governments. As Nobel Prize–winning economist Amartya Sen once said,

> *The Berlin Wall was not only a symbol of keeping people inside East Germany—it was a way of preventing a kind of global view of our future. We could not think globally about the world when the Berlin Wall was there. We could not think about the world as a whole.*[15]

Emerging cooperation among nations was not the only change on the horizon, however. A new world order was on the rise—one that had the production and use of oil at the center of the conflicts.

OIL, WEALTH, AND INTERNATIONAL RELATIONS

Several countries in the Middle East and elsewhere grew very wealthy very quickly as oil reserves were discovered and exploited during the latter half of the twentieth century. The wealth of these countries, and the fact that they control vast quantities of oil, has had significant impact on the world's businesses and governments.

This shift in power became apparent in 1973 when countries belonging to the Organization of Petroleum Exporting Countries (OPEC) proclaimed an oil embargo. The limited supply of higher-priced oil impacted businesses and people dramatically.[16] The increased price per barrel of oil resulted in rising consumer costs worldwide and introduced the potential for economic collapse in less stable economies. Additionally, it negatively impacted political ties among some Western nations.[17]

Today, certain nations—including the United States—are particularly affected by the price of oil. The United States is by far the largest consumer of oil in the world, and oil products, such as gas, are much cheaper in the United State than in other countries. For example, a gallon of gas ranges from $2.80 to $4.50 in the United State. In the United Kingdom, a gallon may run as much as $10.00 to $12.00. To see just how important the price of oil is, consider recent U.S. presidential elections: The price of gas is an important campaign issue, and in some cases, races are won or lost on whether voters believe a candidate will be able to get the price down.

The price of oil also affects many exporting nations significantly. Some oil-rich countries have accumulated vast amounts of wealth. Some of this income has been used to create infrastructures within their countries and to provide for their citizens. Brunei, for example, is an oil-rich country on the island of Borneo. The population is about two-thirds Malay, but it is a sovereign state separate from Malaysia. Brunei has one of the highest per capita incomes in Southeast Asia, due in part to oil exports. The government, which is a constitutional sultanate, pays all medical care, subsidizes housing and certain staple foods, and provides education for all its citizens, up to and including college.[18]

Many wealthy oil exporters have also provided a good deal of aid to underdeveloped nations affected by high oil prices. On the other hand, much of the wealth in some exporting countries has been used to reinforce the power and privilege of the elite classes, or to solidify power in certain regions—the Middle East and South America, for example. Key regional issues have remained unresolved as leaders of some of these nations have built up their own regimes. Some governments have even become corrupt, exploitative police-states.[19]

RELIGION, POLITICS, AND INTERNATIONAL RELATIONS

Some newly oil-rich governments have done more than just alienate their neighbors; they have alienated their own citizens, particularly youth. In countries such as Libya under the late Muammar Gadaffi, the majority of citizens lived in abject poverty for decades, despite the wealth of the nation. In addition, in many countries, like Libya forms of government have prevented people from voicing concerns, voting on leaders, and so on.

In recent years, some citizens sought refuge from the realities of poverty and the other inequities of their daily lives in religion—in some cases, fundamentalist forms of Islam.[20] The rise in religious fundamentalism has affected both national politics and international relations. In some cases—at the present time and in recent history—fundamentalist religion, notably in Saudi Arabia, Iran, Iraq, and Afghanistan, has resulted in violence and repression of citizens by their governments. Widespread attention has been given to one particular aspect of this: repression of and denial of rights to women.[21]

Over time, some fundamentalist groups have come to be associated with causes more than individual nations. For example, Al Qaeda emerged as a force to be reckoned with even though it was not officially sponsored by or part of any one government. Groups like Al Qaeda began to fight ideological (and very real) wars, largely against Western powers. Some of these wars were manifested in terrorist activities like the bombing of the World Trade Center in 1993; the September 11, 2001, terrorist attacks on the United States; and the 2004 and 2005 attacks on the transport systems of Madrid and London.[22]

Fundamentalist religious groups are not only found in the Islamic world. For instance, fundamentalist Christian groups have built strong, wealthy, and powerful lobbying groups that have greatly impacted politics and laws in the United States. The conflicts surrounding social issues important to some religious groups (e.g., abortion and homosexuality) have at times taken top billing in congressional and presidential races—even when serious economic and other problems plagued the nation.

World politics, conflicts over oil, and social issues linked to religion have played and continue to play a very large role in international relations and business. These issues are not dying down; in fact, as the world becomes smaller and more citizens get involved in the debates, these issues are becoming even more important. This is especially true when it comes to citizens' demands for more say and control over their governments and economies. These demands have resulted in the toppling of decades-old governments. At times, the ensuing conflicts have been violent and destabilizing, though the millions of people fighting for a voice in the governments and economic systems involved believe these dangers are worth it. Nowhere was this more apparent than in the 2011 revolts known as the Arab Spring. These revolts and the events that followed have heralded profound changes in politics, which in turn affect global businesses.

CITIZEN RIGHTS AND THE ARAB SPRING

The Arab Spring involved uprisings against dictatorships and restrictions of freedoms in several countries in the Middle East and North Africa. The movement began in Tunisia on December 17, 2010, when a street vendor named Mohamed Bouazizi immolated himself outside the municipal government building after the police confiscated his vegetable cart.[23] His suicide galvanized the people of his community, who began protesting in the streets the next day. News of the protests went viral, and the first "Day of Rage" protest was organized; further protests ensued and within weeks the Tunisian government was overthrown. Emboldened by the events in Tunisia, activists across North Africa and the Middle East organized their own Day of Rage protests using Facebook, Twitter, and other social media.

By January 2011, citizens in Algeria, Lebanon, Jordan, Mauritania, Sudan, Oman, Saudi Arabia, Egypt, and Yemen had all participated in similar protests. Protests also spread to Iraq, Bahrain, Libya, Kuwait, Morocco, Western Sahara, Syria, and the border regions of Israel.[24] By the end of 2011, the political landscape of North Africa had changed dramatically with the overthrow of the Tunisian, Egyptian, and Libyan governments. Middle Eastern governments also saw shakeups that included resignations, parliamentary changes, and revolution that continued into 2012.[25] Also during this period, a brutal conflict between citizens and government forces exploded on the scene in Syria, and crackdowns on protests resulted in injuries and deaths in a number of countries whose governments remained in power.[26] On the positive and hopeful side, Egypt held the first democratic election in its 6000 year history.

As these examples illustrate, when information about other people and places becomes more accessible, cultures begin to change. The result? Businesses change and respond as well. And, business is a powerful force in the world—it can bring about even more social changes. For example, when Coca-Cola began to distribute its products in China, it was more than a brand.[27] To some, it meant freedom. To others, it was a sign of the decadent West invading society. In either case, it meant change. The same was true of the introduction of Levi's jeans to Russia. Partly because business can have profound impact on societies, many countries in the international community have decided to join forces to guide and regulate business activities, as you will see in the next section.

Discussion Questions

1. Explain why educated students of management and business need to understand world politics. Give at least two examples of current events that are important to today's business environment and explain how they impact the business, the people in the organization(s), and consumers.

2. How has technology—particularly ICTs—contributed to the Arab Spring? Do you think social and political revolutions like the Arab Spring will continue to spread globally? If so, where to, and why?

3. How Do Trade Agreements and International Finance Affect Business and Economies?

Objective 14.3
Define the key economic factors that are affecting global business.

Now that you understand a bit about changing global politics, let's look at how nations work to manage trade and business practices. The concept of globalization is fairly new, but trade between peoples and countries has existed since the Stone Age, when obsidian was first exchanged for flint. If we fast-forward to the twenty-first century, we see that international trade has become complicated by countries' competing desires to attain goods and to protect homegrown industries. This tension has led to various forms of protectionism and agreements between nations to attempt to create a fair and equitable system.

In this section, we will look first at global regulatory groups, then several powerful trade alliances, followed by discussions of international investment, finance, and debt. We will conclude with an in-depth look at the European Union, which illustrates the impact of economic interconnections around the world.

Global Forums for Debate, Oversight, and Regulation

Business and government leaders often come together with experts in economic policy to discuss economic issues that affect the entire world. Some of these forums are meant to enable leaders from different sectors (e.g., business and government) to share information and perspectives. Other bodies directly influence national policies and/or international agreements. Five such groups are summarized in ■ **EXHIBIT 14.4**.

Four of the bodies in Exhibit 14.4—the Group of Eight (G8), Group of Twenty (G-20), World Economic Forum, and the United Nations Economic and Social Council (ECOSOC) influence things like monetary policies and trade agreements. The G8 includes the heads of state of eight major economic powers who aim to promote globalization through international trade and improved relations with developing countries. The G-20 consists of leaders from 20 economies, the International Monetary Fund, and the World Bank who work on initiatives related to economic cooperation. The World Economic Forum brings together social and political leaders on projects related to international and humanitarian issues. Lastly, ECOSOC is a division of the UN that focuses on improving the standard of living within UN member states. Each of these organizations approaches international issues differently and each draws its strength from different sources. However, all of these bodies tend to focus on the growth of underdeveloped nations, the protection of world citizens, and the development of peaceful and productive economic alliances.

The World Trade Organization (WTO) has a more specific oversight role than the others. Its two main functions are to oversee international trade and to provide a more objective forum to settle trade disputes. Tenets that guide decisions made by members of the WTO include:

- Nondiscrimination, meaning that all member nations must receive equal treatment from other member nations
- Exclusion of reciprocity, meaning deals cannot be struck in one contract to gain favor in another
- Strive for legally binding contracts, as opposed to informal "handshake" agreements
- Transparency, meaning members must make trade policies public
- The ability to restrict trade when necessary.

The WTO is the largest trade organization in the world in terms of number of members, so it wields enormous influence. Today, more than 95 percent of the world's trade is conducted among WTO nations.[28]

Global Trade Alliances

For many years in the last century, North America, Western Europe, and Japan were responsible for more than 70 percent of the world's manufactured exports. As the Cold War ended, however, technology advanced rapidly and governments began deregulating international trade.[29] The end result was a rapid increase in global business in terms of **exporting** (the transportation and sale of domestic goods to foreign markets) and **importing** (the transportation and sale of foreign goods to a domestic market), as well as a rise in the production of goods far from a company's home base.

Deregulation of trade is particularly beneficial to developing and newly industrialized countries because it simplifies the process of exporting goods, thereby enabling them to

Exporting
The transportation and sale of domestic goods to foreign markets.

Importing
The transportation and sale of foreign goods to a domestic market.

■ **EXHIBIT 14.4**

Important International Regulatory Bodies

Organization	Who They Are	What They Do
World Trade Organization (WTO)[30]	Representatives from over 150 nations	• Oversee international trade and enhance the transparency of laws, policies and agreements among member states • Provide a forum for settling disputes • Seek to liberalize trade by enabling member states to agree to policies that minimize barriers while judiciously managing barriers that members agree need to exist
Group of Eight (G8)[31]	The heads of state of eight major economic powers	• Promote globalization • Focus on economic issues like international trade and employment • Address political issues such as relations with developing countries and global security • Launch aid initiatives and development programs tied to debt- and disease-relief
Group of Twenty (G-20)[32]	Representatives of 20 major economies, the International Monetary Fund (IMF), and the World Bank,	• Encourage economic cooperation for the collective good • Develop an action plan that is implemented by various working groups • Promote five major tenets: global trade and investment; financial supervision and regulation; international financial institution funding and reform; inclusive, sustainable market building; and confidence, growth, and job building
World Economic Forum (often called "Davos")[33]	A prestigious forum that brings together business, political, social, and intellectual leaders from around the world	• Engage in ongoing projects to address the major challenges facing the world today • Focus on sustainable food production, disaster recovery, global education, and humanitarian relief in addition to business, management, and economic issues • Promote responsible governance among 1,200 corporate members as a means of generating stability within the global economy.
United Nations Economic and Social Council[34]	Division of the UN that coordinates the economic and social work of 14 different UN agencies and their commissions.	• Promote higher standards of living within UN member states • Support people and nations through programs tied to international relations

better compete with larger, well-established nations.[35] As a result, the end of the twentieth century marked the beginning of a dramatic shift in the balance of international trade. For example, newly industrialized economies entered and eventually dominated the textiles and manufacturing export markets while the United States and other industrialized nations moved away from these markets and toward technology and service sectors.[36]

The economic benefits realized by countries involved in exporting goods are numerous. For one, the development of stable foreign markets insulates the economies of individual nations from internal booms and busts. Free trade also stabilizes world markets.[37] In fact, because private sector exports have such an important effect on national economies, many governments help companies get started in foreign markets, and nations the world over have formed free-trade agreements designed to reduce trade barriers.[38]

Of course, there is another side: Shifts in the balance of trade also mean that some countries and companies lose market share, which translates into lost jobs. This has been the case for many U.S.-based manufacturing companies for many decades. This shift is tied to economic indicators. For example, in 2011, industrial output in the United States grew at a 2.5 percent rate over the previous year, but it ranked 118 out of 166 countries and regions across the globe.[39]

Some business people (and citizens) favor trade alliances. Others do not. Informed opinions require an understanding of what these trade agreements are and how they are enacted. Several of the major international trade agreements are summarized in ■ **EXHIBIT 14.5**.

As you can see in Exhibit 14.5, most trade alliances have the goal of increasing trade within a particular region. When trade alliances are successful, the economic fortunes of the member nations as a whole improve, making the region more powerful within the global economy. On the other hand, trade alliances can be risky. Let's see how they work by taking a close look at the European Union in the next section.

■ **EXHIBIT 14.5**

Worldwide Trade Alliances

Alliance	Who Is Involved	What It Does
The European Union (EU)[40]	27 nations across Europe	• Provides economic power and protection • Handles treaty negotiations, foreign relations, legal matters, energy programs, and coordination of development • Eliminates trade and immigration barriers among members with a standard passport (for full members) • Operates a standard currency for all member states meeting currency criteria except for the United Kingdom and Denmark
North American Free Trade Agreement (NAFTA)[41]	The United States, Canada, and Mexico	• Lifts tariffs and other trade barriers among nations • Addresses collaboration to improve environmental and labor practices across the continent • Helps integrate the three economies
United States-Dominican Republic-Central America Free Trade Agreement (CAFTA)[42]	The United States, the Dominican Republic, Costa Rica, El Salvador, Guatemala, Honduras, and Nicaragua	• Removes tariffs and other trade barriers among signatory nations • Promotes agricultural and rural development • Improves environmental management and labor practices
Union of South American Nations (UNASUR)[43]	All independent South American countries	• Strives to create a single market system • Aims to phase out tariffs over a five-year period from 2014–2019 • Promotes cooperation on infrastructure construction and environmental initiatives
Association of Southeast Asian Nations (ASEAN)[44]	Indonesia, Malaysia, the Philippines, Singapore, Thailand, Brunei, Myanmar, Cambodia, Laos, and Vietnam	• Promotes political security, economic growth, and cultural development • Allows free trade among members • Negotiates agreements with non-ASEAN countries
Asia-Pacific Economic Cooperations (APEC)[45]	The Asia-Pacific region	• Aims to free up trade and investment, simplify member business relations, and increase cooperation on economic and technical ventures • Seeks to lift tariffs on industrialized and developing countries

The European Union

During the twentieth century, many European countries struggled to compete with the United States and Russia, which led them to experiment with trade alliances. This experimentation ultimately resulted in the formation of the European Union (EU). You can read about the history of the EU and the challenges it currently faces in the *Business Case*.

Founded in 1993, the EU is an economic and political union of 27 member states as of 2012. In 2013, Croatia will enter the EU, and Turkey, Macedonia, Iceland Montenegro, Serbia other candidates for entry—Turkey, Iceland, Montenegro, Serbia and Macedonia—are under review.[46] The EU is an example of supranationalism, a structure in which members transfer a portion of their power to the union in exchange for certain benefits. With supranationalism, nations lose part of their individual identities but gain the power and protection of a large economic bloc. The EU governing bodies deal with treaty negotiation, foreign relations, legal matters, energy programs, coordination of development, and several other arenas.[47]

The formation of the EU has impacted trade on many levels. Barriers to trade and immigration have been virtually eliminated among member nations. Additionally, most member nations use a common currency call the Euro, though a few, including the United Kingdom, sparked controversy by deciding to keep their own currency. By 2011, the EU had the largest economy in the world with an estimated GDP of $15.465 trillion. This is especially impressive when you consider that the population of the EU makes up only about 7 percent of the global population, but it accounts for nearly 20 percent of total world trade.[48]

For all the strengths of such a union, there are definitely drawbacks as well. This was brought into stark relief in a situation that became apparent in 2010 when one member nation—Greece—faced economic disaster partly as a result of poorly structured debt. The EU had to step in, costing member nations a great deal of money and further destabilizing economies still reeling from recession. This is discussed in more depth in the *Business Case* later in this section. For now, let's consider other factors that impact businesses and economies significantly in the global era: global investment, finance, debt, and inflation.

Global Investment, Finance, Debt, and Inflation

Global investment is generally a positive force because it helps countries finance their infrastructure. It can, however, also have negative effects. For example, global investors own trillions of dollars' worth of U.S. stocks, bonds, and other securities. Some economists have suggested that the vast amount of money funneled into the U.S. market by foreign investors allowed American financiers to engage in sloppy credit practices in the first few years of the twenty-first century simply because there was so much money that the risks seemed smaller than they actually were. As economist Robert Samuelson put it, "Too much money chased too few good investment opportunities."[49]

Global finance is the supply and demand of money on a worldwide stage. Today our businesses are so interconnected that financial difficulties in one country have the potential for global impact. For example, during the recession that began in 2007, the United State tightened the flow of money. This had a ripple effect around the world.

National debt can also have a ripple effect. For example, by 2012, China had financed the public and private debt of the United States to the tune of nearly $2 trillion, leaving the United States economically exposed globally and facing domestic political strife.[50] Another example: In 2011, China was the largest holder of foreign debt in the world. For this and other reasons, the country was asked by European leaders to play a large role in financing EU debt in order to help stabilize the EU's fiscal crisis.[51] Support can come with a price, however. Because of Chinese financing, U.S. and EU leaders

European Union (EU)
An economic and political union of 27 European nations (as of 2012).

Supranationalism
A structure in which members transfer a portion of their power to the union in exchange for certain benefits.

The European Union's Growing Pains

The EU traces its history to the European Coal and Steel Community (ECSC), which was established by the Treaty of Paris in 1951. The ECSC had six members: France, Italy, Belgium, The Netherlands, Luxembourg, and West Germany. The European Economic Community (EEC) was established in 1958, following what was known as the 1957 Treaties of Rome, which established a union in terms of customs and nuclear energy development. This group eventually became known as the European Communities (EC) in the late 1960s, following another treaty.

The EC began growing in the 1970s with the inclusion of Denmark, Ireland, and the United Kingdom, and it continued to grow in the 1980s with the inclusion of Greece, Portugal, and Spain. In 1985, passport controls were removed among member states as well as some other countries in Europe. This was followed in 1986 by the adoption of the European flag.

In the 1990s, following the fall of the Soviet Union, East Germany joined the EC as part of the newly unified Germany. Former communist countries Cyprus and Malta also took interest in joining, although their membership would not come for another decade. Following the Maastricht Treaty, which went into effect on November 1, 1993, the European Union (EU) was born. Austria, Finland, and Sweden joined the EU in 1995. A new currency, the Euro (€) was created and replaced the currency of 12 member states establishing what came to be known as the Eurozone. The EU again grew in 2004, with the admission of Latvia, Lithuania, Malta, Poland, Slovakia, Slovenia, the Czech Republic, Cyprus, Estonia, and Hungary. Over the next few years, Romania, Bulgaria, and Iceland also joined. By 2012, the Eurozone had spread to include 17 nations, and the EU had expanded to 27 member states.

Today, the EU is recognized as a supranational organization, and it has the largest economy in the world.[53] At 228 million, it also has the third largest workforce, exceeded only by China and India.

European Union and Eurozone Members[54]

EU Member States (2012)		EU Candidate Countries (2012)	The Eurozone (2012)
Austria	Latvia	Croatia	Austria
Belgium	Lithuania	Iceland	Belgium
Bulgaria	Luxembourg	Macedonia	Cyprus
Cyprus	Malta	Montenegro	Estonia
Czech	Netherlands	Turkey	Finland
Republic	Poland	Serbia	France
Denmark	Portugal		Germany
Estonia	Romania		Greece
Finland	Slovakia		Ireland
France	Slovenia		Italy
Germany	Spain		Luxembourg
Greece	Sweden		Malta
Hungary	United		Netherlands
Ireland	Kingdom		Portugal
Italy			Slovakia
			Slovenia
			Spain

The Eurozone

Not all members of the European Union are members of the Eurozone, the economic and monetary union officially named the Euro Area. Only member states of the EU that have adopted the Euro as their currency are part of the Eurozone. To be considered for inclusion to the Eurozone, a member state must meet what are known as Euro Convergence Criteria. These criteria include strict control of inflation, government debt, government deficit, and long-term interest rates.

Most EU member states are obliged to adopt the Euro once they have met the criteria. As of 2012, 17 member states have adopted the Euro. The United Kingdom and Denmark have maintained their membership in the EU while opting out of joining the Eurozone, and Sweden's citizenry voted against joining the EU's two-year exchange-rate mechanism, which is a prerequisite to adopting the Euro. The remaining seven member states are scheduled to enter the Eurozone by 2017, contingent on their meeting inclusion criteria.

The European Sovereign Debt Crisis

The recession that began in 2007 was a key driver of the ensuing financial crises in the EU. It's not as simple as that, however: The causes and solutions for what has come to be known as the European sovereign debt crisis are many, complex, and interrelated. The crisis began with fears in late 2009 related to the economic stability of certain EU countries and the effects on the federation as a whole as well as on the Euro.

Because of the interrelationships, both financially and otherwise, a crisis in one EU state is a crisis for all. So, in May, 2010, the EU as a body realized it needed to step in, finance ministers approved a rescue fund of €750 million to help maintain economic stability. By late 2011 this was raised to about €1 trillion. Countries in the EU that were hardest hit have been Greece, Ireland, Portugal, and Spain.

Bailouts put together by the EU, the International Monetary Fund (IMF), and other cooperating countries have come at a steep political and societal cost in terms of required austerity measures, which in economic language refers to deficit-cutting, spending decreases, and reduction in benefits and services. In February, 2012, Greek citizens responded to austerity measures by rioting across the country, setting historic buildings ablaze, looting stores, and defacing the central bank.[55]

The EU, IMF, and European Central Bank have already forced private bondholders to reduce their claims against Greece by 53.5 percent; unfortunately, it appears that this may not be enough. As of July 2012, downward projections for global economic recovery indicate that financial aid to Greece will be $36 billion less than needed. In other words, Greece's creditors will need to reduce their claims by at least $36 billion more.[56] Furthermore, an additional $9 trillion is expected to be withdrawn from support of sovereign debt globally by 2016.[57]

What we can learn from the EU situation is that sovereign debt crises remain very real, and that bailout money is proving hard to come by.[58] Additionally, the debt crisis also has an impact felt far beyond the borders of EU member states—a state of affairs that is increasingly likely as the world's economies globalize. These impacts are especially clear when you consider that the IMF's projections for global economic growth in 2013 are predicated in part on the assumptions that the Eurozone crisis has reached its peak and that EU leaders will continue their commitment to support struggling peripheral economies.[59] Whether these assumptions are true and what they mean for the world economy remains to be seen.

may be compromised and unable to make demands on topics such as the environment, human rights, or intellectual property rights, fearing that the Chinese might demand immediate repayment of loans. Such actions could cause currencies to plummet, adversely affecting the lives of many people and harming economies around the world. And, financing debt gives the debt holder legitimate right to expect fiscal responsibility. Chinese Premier Wen Jinbao gave strict advice:

> *China's willingness to support Europe to cope with sovereign debt problems is sincere and firm . . . [but China also expects] those highly indebted countries to strengthen fiscal consolidation, cut deficits and reduce debt risks in light of their national conditions . . .* [60]

Another topic that affects global business is **inflation**. Inflation is the rise in prices for goods and services over a period of time and the decrease in the relative purchasing power of a currency. Inflation can be caused by a number of factors related to a weakened economy. It is also a financial tool used by governments for a number of reasons.[61] Inflation can be sparked by increasing interest rates, selling government bonds, or simply by printing money. Inflation is often painful for consumers, and can destabilize an economy on the world stage. It can, on the other hand, support manageable growth in an economy, which is a plus in the longer term.

You now understand some of the key factors that affect global business. As you have seen in this section, there are many factors to consider in our global business environment. What does this mean for managers and leaders on the ground, working every day to make the right decisions about people, resources, plans, and problems? In the next section, we will answer this question in part by looking at globalization from a practical standpoint, focusing on those things business leaders must consider when planning and implementing a global strategy.

inflation
The rise in prices for goods and services over a period of time and the decrease in the relative purchasing power of currency.

Discussion Questions

1. Check the label on your clothes, phone, television, computer, or bedding. Where were these items made? What kind of oversight or regulations do you think were followed to ensure you are using a safe product that is produced in conditions that are aw-abiding and ethical (e.g. without the use of child labor, safe working conditions, etc)?

2. Within the EU, people can move freely between countries and can work in any member country without a visa. What are the benefits and potential problems that arise from such policies?

---

4. What Must Be Considered When Developing a Global Strategy?

Objective 14.4
List factors that must be considered when developing a global strategy.

Numerous factors need to be explored and understood when developing and implementing a global business strategy, including market needs and quality control measures. Other issues are also important, such as trade regulations, laws, organizational structure, and cultural considerations—not to mention myriad technical issues around such things as availability of raw materials, environmental impact of your business, transportation, and the like. In this section, we'll take a closer look at legal and organizational structure issues and also explore the interaction of global business and international differences, such as those related to culture.

Reviewing Legal and Organizational Structure Issues

Leaders of a company that want to do business in one or more countries beyond their own national borders have many options in terms of legal and organizational structure. For example, and as you remember from Chapter 9, cooperative contracts are friendly business agreements linked to joint economic activities like equity ventures, and strategic alliances are agreements that involve two companies temporarily joining forces to achieve a common goal such as creating or distributing a product.[62] Both of these processes lend themselves to international business, under certain circumstances. Licensing agreements, in which one company pays for the right to use trademarked material owned by another company, are also common ways to expand one's geographic reach.[63] Franchising is still another example, and involves one company paying for the right to use another company's name and market its products.

In other cases, a company may purchase all of another company's common stock; the purchaser is known as a parent company and the purchasee as a wholly owned affiliate.[64] Finally, a company may choose to pursue the **global new venture** start-up model. This model calls for infant companies to go global before securing domestic market share, thereby securing resources and marketing channels in multiple countries simultaneously.[65]

It is important to create and implement a global strategy thoughtfully, carefully, and attentively. Let's look at some of the other major issues that should be considered with respect to culture and how to position an organization on the global stage.

Global new ventures
Start-up model that calls for infant companies to open globally before securing domestic market share.

Global Strategy and Cultures

In a seminal 1993 article in *Foreign Affairs*, Samuel Huntington argued that world politics had entered a phase in which the predominant sources of conflict would revolve less around differences in political or economic ideologies than around cultural ones.[66] According to Huntington, this scenario might play out through so-called "McDonaldization" or, alternatively, through hybridization.[67]

"McDonaldization" refers to the homogenization of business products and services with a focus on standardization and efficiency.[68] What this means in practice is that things like products, services, music, art, and so on are transferred around the globe without adaptation. These become part of local cultures, and ultimately, cultures look very much the same from one place to the next. This is disturbing to many people.

It's also notable that pure "McDonaldization" is proving very difficult because when it comes to some goods and services (like food and care of the elderly, for example), cultures are very powerful and resist homogenization. In fact, the term itself is erroneous: McDonald's adapts its menu in many of its markets.[69] For example, in Hawaii, you can buy Saimin noodles, a local favorite, at many McDonald's restaurants, and in Thailand, you can buy marinated pork burgers or pepper chicken burgers. That said, it is true that many goods and products linked to trends move quickly around the world. Take fashion, for example. While in a remote, rural part of South Africa recently, this author noticed that teenage girls were wearing exactly the same fashionable clothing as their peers in England and the United States.

Hybridization is a term reflecting the viewpoint that interconnectedness will not destroy individual cultures. This viewpoint holds that as globalization continues, we will see the development of a hybrid culture that brings together the best of many cultures without losing distinctiveness.[70] Let's look at an example that illustrates the importance of thoughtfully considering cultures when developing and implementing a global strategy.

EXPORTING DISNEY

Exporting can be an important part of a global growth strategy. To be successful, companies need to evaluate the attractiveness of particular products in foreign markets, shipping methods, and government regulations both at home and abroad.[71] Companies also need to understand the cultures of the foreign markets they hope to serve. Let's look at an important example from the past about that still has lessons for us today about paying attention to local culture in the global business environment.

EuroDisney theme park opened in Paris in 1992 and lost approximately $1 billion during its first 18 months (■ **EXHIBIT 14.6**).[72] A recession in Europe was partially responsible for these losses, but Disney's failure to understand the differences between French, European, and American cultures was a major reason why the park faced so many problems.[73]

Some of these cultural differences led to problems in the park's operations, such as the fact that designers failed to account for the European tradition of dining after 8 P.M. As a result, dinner time at EuroDisney involved long lines and overcrowded dining facilities not seen at the American parks, where the dinner hour is earlier and more fluid.[74] Cultural differences also contributed to difficulties with staffing and labor relations because workers were unaccustomed to company-dictated dress codes and the American management style.[75] Other Disney policies struck at long-held traditions—especially a ban on alcohol at a theme park located in the heart of Europe's wine-making region.[76]

As the park's debt mounted, executives had to learn how to make EuroDisney succeed in a decidedly non-American environment. Sweeping changes were enacted to help the park fit into the local and regional culture. In addition, a massive marketing campaign was launched that included renaming the park Disneyland Paris, lowering ticket prices, adding new attractions, and carefully targeting marketing efforts to individual countries within Europe. Although EuroDisney had a rough start due to cultural issues, it eventually became the biggest tourist attraction on the continent, attracting over 15 million visitors in 2011.[77] What's more, the company remained successful during the recent recession. Some critics note that this may be the result of an aggressive marketing campaign and deeply discounted tickets, which, while impacting revenue, may also have contributed to more traffic in the park. In support of this position,[78] record ticket sales in 2011 appeared to be linked to increased tourism in the region.[79]

■ **EXHIBIT 14.6**
What national and organizational culture issues may have caused Disney to decide not to serve wine with meals when they first opened EuroDisney?

Source: Lourens Smak/Alamy

CRAFTING AN *INTERNATIONAL* STRATEGY

Disney started its venture in Europe by trying to share its distinctive organizational culture, along with American culture. Like many companies that do business outside their home country, this is a legitimate strategy: Build organizational cohesiveness by building a common culture everywhere—regardless of differences in local cultures. Other companies, however, have found that in order to focus on local customer needs, it is important to have both foundational, shared business practices and an understanding of local culture. That is precisely the policy of global telecommunications company Vodafone, as discussed in the *Leadership Perspective* feature.

As you can see in this section, a company's formal business model is important, but it takes more than a good structure, good lawyers, and good accountants to succeed in a business that serves customers around the world. It takes a sound philosophy. For Vodafone's CEO Vittorio Colao and all of Vodafone's leaders, managers, and employees, this philosophy involves respect and the celebration of distinctive cultures around the world.

Leadership Perspective

● **Vittorio Colao**
CEO of Vodaphone
"People in each country, each region of the world are proud of their own distinctiveness."

Vittorio Colao, CEO of Vodafone, is one of the world's best leaders when it comes to crafting a global strategy that enables a company to succeed—*no matter where it is operating*. As of 2011, Vodafone operated in more than 30 countries and had 440 million subscribers.[80]

One structure in particular, called Partner Market Agreements, is interesting in that it enables this global business to operate in a truly international fashion, honoring the local culture while allowing everyone in the company to share the same basic set of values. According to Vodafone's Web site, Partner Market Agreements "[enable] Vodafone and its partner operators [to] co-operate in the marketing of global products and services with varying levels of brand association. This strategy enables Vodafone to implement services in new territories and to create additional value to their partners' customers and to Vodafone's travelling customers."[81]

But, as Colao and Vodafone's other leaders understand very well, it isn't just the company's structure that makes it work—rather, it's how the business is led and managed, and how its leaders and managers create an environment based on the foundational values of speed, simplicity, and trust; focus on customers; and servant leadership.

Colao is a brilliant and dynamic leader—a powerful man who sees himself serving his customers and his company above all. As he puts it:

You serve as a leader. For a period of time, you are empowered to bring about changes and to build the company. People trust you to see that your employees are part of changes and that they feel as if they are doing something meaningful. And you are trusted to understand your customers. For me, that means being totally in tune with who our customers are, wherever they are in the world.

There is no such thing as a "global culture." People in each country, each region of the world are proud of their own distinctiveness. Today of course, many people do the same things: They use mobile phones, text, and Facebook. They listen to the same music and even share some values. But the way people do things and the way they express their values is different from one part of the world to another.

A simple example: I recently visited some of our companies and stores. In every single one, people were proud of our company values, but they expressed them in different ways. In Ghana, they created a song about who and what we are; in Portugal, they created a painting. Somewhere else, it might be a formal plaque on the wall: "Speed, Simplicity, Trust." At Vodafone, we encourage this kind of difference. The expression of our values is different, but we all share core values and agree on core business practices.

We are committed to being close to our customers. And we do something about it. We have begun to dedicate one day a month solely to our customers. We simply call it "Customer Day." On this day, there are no internal meetings. Everyone focuses directly on customers. Everyone. Even me and my executive team. This symbolic and very real commitment to staying close to our customers is reshaping the way we do business.

Source: Personal interview with Vittorio Colao conducted by Annie McKee, 2009.

Discussion Questions

1. Do an online search to identify examples of organizations representing the following global business structures: cooperative contracts, licensing, franchising, strategic alliances, wholly owned affiliates, global new ventures, and outsourcing.

2. On the Internet, find two or three stores that you patronize regularly that have international operations. Based on what you read on the Web, discuss aspects of the companies' values, ethics, and cultures that you believe the companies want visible in their stores everywhere. Can you see any indication that the Web sites you reviewed are tailored specifically to one culture? If so, which culture, and what is your evidence? Be wary of your own cultural biases and stereotypes, which might cause you to pay attention to some things more than others.

5. What Are the Opportunities and Risks in a Global Business Environment?

Objective 14.5
Define and assess the opportunities and risks in a global business environment.

Globalization offers opportunities and risks for societies and for businesses. Businesses that want to compete internationally are usually enticed by the potential of improved sales, improved quality, improved costs, and improved lead time. When expanding internationally, however, many companies run up against the dangers of uncertainty, rapid growth, poor partnerships, and political and popular resistance. Each of these opportunities and risks is explored in the following sections.

Opportunity: Expand Sales in Developing Markets

Selling products in new markets can open up new revenue streams. Considering just the populations of India and China (each has well over 1 billion people), it's staggering to think of how much buying power these countries alone will possess as their middle classes grow. At the present time, it seems very possible that within the next 50 years, Indian and Chinese consumers could be driving the world economy. Overall, the world's population is increasing, as are the number of people with income to spend on products and services. Much of this growth in markets will be seen in what is now the developing world. Companies that reach these markets with the right products and services will prosper.

Opportunity: Access to Expertise While Saving Money

Sometimes, outsourcing or offshoring work can result in a business being able to capitalize on greater expertise and less costly labor. **Outsourcing** is the process by which companies subcontract specific jobs or work functions to non-employees or other companies.[82] **Offshoring** is a form of outsourcing in which companies transfer jobs to countries other than their own to reduce labor and other expenses.

A qualification to the opportunities inherent in outsourcing and offshoring is that with these practices, someone usually loses. For example, Infosys, an Indian global technology services provider, became a financial powerhouse as its clients in the United States moved jobs to companies and regions that had access to less expensive labor and overhead.[83] One controversial example of taking advantage of expertise and low wages overseas can be found in the tuna industry. Samoa Packing Company (makers of Chicken of the Sea brand canned and packaged tuna) and StarKist have used workers in American Samoa to clean and prepare tuna since the first Samoan cannery opened in 1954.[84] Until recently, these companies have been exempted from U.S. minimum wage standards. As a result, it was common for cannery workers to receive as little as $3.60 an hour. In light of this situation, Congress passed the Fair Minimum Wage Act of 2007, which stated that these canneries and other businesses have to raise their wages by $0.50 per year until the minimum wage in Samoa equals that in the 50 states. In response to this act, Samoa Packing left the island altogether to seek cheaper labor, and 2,041 employees were laid off. This meant that almost half of all Samoan cannery workers were out of work.[85] Later legislation delayed additional minimum wage increases in American Samoa, but the damage was already done and many (albeit low-paying) jobs were lost.[86] Many blamed the rise in the minimum wage, but noted that other factors—such as the cost of goods and utilities compared with other countries, such as Thailand—made American Samoa less attractive to business than it had been in the past.[87]

Outsourcing
The process by which companies subcontract specific jobs or work functions to non-employees or other companies.

Offshoring
A form of outsourcing in which companies transfer jobs to countries other than their own to reduce labor and other expenses.

Opportunity: Take Advantage of Time Zones and Round-the-Clock Business

More countries are creating friendly climates for global businesses. This means that companies can, if they choose, work and sell around the clock. Media companies, such as Thomson Reuters, utilize this approach to maintain a 24-hour news cycle.

Opportunity: Economies of Scale

Economy of scale
The process of using increased production to lower per-unit production costs.

One issue that is both a positive and negative factor in business expansion is called **economy of scale**. Economy of scale is the process of using increased production to lower per-unit production costs. Many times when a company grows too fast (or is simply disorganized), managers and leaders miss opportunities to capitalize on economies of scale. This is an easy mistake to make in the global environment, as it is sometimes difficult to determine what should be centralized and what should be left to local operations.

Many companies, however, have overcome this risk and manage economies of scale well in the global environment. For example, United Parcel Service (UPS) is an example of a company that relies on an economy of scale as it delivers over 15 million packages per day.[88] Cloud computing is also based on an economy of scale.[89]

The term cloud refers to the Internet, and it seems to have been adopted through the stylized drawings of clouds populated with applications, services, and hardware to depict them as a communal resource. Cloud services may focus on infrastructure as service (for example, Google Compute Engine or Amazon CloudFormation), operating platform as service (for example, Google App Engine or Microsoft Azure), and software as a service (for example, Quickbooks Online or Salesforce.com).[90]

In these examples, businesses can reap the benefits of economies of scale as the cost of space, support, etc., goes down as the number of buyers goes up. There are many benefits to users, too. For example, it can be far cheaper for a company to rely on the infrastructure of a cloud solution than to invest in software, hardware, services, and human capital within the organization. On the other hand, relying on an external cloud can have implications for security and control over sensitive information.

Risk: Uncertainty Due to Government Involvement and Political Instability

Depending on a country's political climate, the business environment can change quickly. For example, the 2011 Egyptian revolution had significant implications for doing business in the country. According to the Central Bank of Egypt, in one year foreign investment went down significantly. This, in addition to revenue lost because businesses could not open, transportation was disrupted, and tourists did not come because it was deemed unsafe, resulted in huge financial losses for the country—and the global businesses that have operations there.[91] Other government related problems are more routine, but also problematic. For instance, again in Egypt, bureaucratic processes caused such a delay in obtaining legal title to a vacant piece of land that the average amount of wait time was ten years, according to noted economist Hernando de Soto. The result? More than 90 percent of Egyptians lack legal title to the land they hold, which in turn can stop them from being able to obtain business licenses.[92]

This problem is not limited to Egypt, by any means. In his now famous work, de Soto notes that in dozens of countries around the world—including Haiti, Mexico, Peru, Indonesia, Malaysia, Sweden, and South Africa to name a few—doing business is incredibly difficult because of archaic, difficult laws and processes.[93] For these reasons, many developing countries are trying very hard to create processes that are easier, smoother, and can withstand political turmoil.

Despite the recession that began in 2007, the American economy remains one of the most stable in the world. Among several reasons for this, a few stand out. First, the

United States controls its own currency and financial policies. That means that adjustments can be made that help to stabilize the economy during tough times. Second, the United States has a predictable political system in which elections are held on a routine basis. In addition, America's government does not interfere in businesses to the degree that some other governments do. Unfortunately, even this strong and stable business climate is risky—and the risk comes from inside the business environment itself. The many scandals, ethical violations, and illegal activities of recent years have caused a different kind of crisis: a crisis of trust.

Risk: Growing Too Fast

During periods of global expansion, companies can be tempted to grow too fast. When this sort of growth occurs, leaders often take shortcuts and compromise on quality, which can lead to a business's downfall. In addition, a rapid increase in the number of employees is difficult to manage. Recruiting and hiring at a rapid pace can be time consuming and risky, and the chance of hiring the wrong people is present when the pressure to simply fill positions is high. Similarly, in times of rapid growth, it can be difficult to ensure that the organization's culture develops as leaders want it to.

Risk: Global Partnerships Can Increase Exposure

When one partner in a business has a problem, others may as well. For example, Toyota's bulk purchase of auto parts from its suppliers led to a massive recall of vehicles in 2009 and 2010 when one of these parts turned out to be faulty. Unfortunately, Toyota was not the only company affected by the recall. French automaker Peugeot had to join the recall as well, because its Peugeot 107 and Citroen C1 cars were made in a Czech plant that operated as part of a joint venture with Toyota.[94] Pontiac also had to recall its Vibe cars because they were built with parts similar to those used in Toyota vehicles.[95]

The fortunes or misfortunes of one global company can affect that company's consumers, and the partner business and its consumers as well.

Risk: Political and Popular Disapproval

Job migration is part of globalization. In the United States and many other nations, job migration has been going on for quite some time. This has been and continues to be controversial. According to some estimates, more than 5 million manufacturing jobs were lost in the United States during the 25-year period from 1979 to 2004, with more than half of these losses occurring since 2000.[96] Indeed, in 1950, about 30 percent of all American jobs were in the area of manufacturing; by 2012, only a little over 8 percent of working Americans had jobs in manufacturing.[97]

Jobs are shipped overseas for several reasons, including lower labor costs and increased availability of skilled labor.[98] Ironically, education is one of the United States' and other developed countries' most prominent exports. According to a 2010 Brookings Institution report, education was the eighth-largest export to Brazil, India, and China.[99]

As you can imagine from these examples, what is considered a risk in one context can be an opportunity in another, as is the case of job migration from one country to another. One set of risks and opportunities must be considered wherever you go and whatever business you are in: These relate to leadership. Sandy Cutler is the CEO of Eaton Corporation. "Eaton is a global technology leader in diversified power management solutions that make electrical, hydraulic and mechanical power operate more efficiently, effectively, and safely."[100] Let's learn more about Eaton in the *Leadership Perspective*, and about how they focus on leadership as an opportunity in their global business.

Leadership Perspective

● **Sandy Cutler**
CEO of Eaton Corporation
"The best global leaders today are the people who can facilitate different points of view, reconcile different perspectives to capture the best ideas, build alignment, and get people excited about the future."

Eaton Corporation has been mentioned by Thomson Reuters as one of 2011's top innovators and also noted as an exemplar when building a socially responsible stock.[101] Eaton's business is complicated and the company does business all over the world. Its managers and employees are technically brilliant and, in an unusual combination, outstanding leaders as well. CEO Sandy Cutler tells us how Eaton's leaders help the company to thrive in the global environment:

The greatest failures in leading a global business come from flat thinking. Flat thinking is two dimensional—you see the world the way you've always seen it and your point of view is the only point of view. When you're stuck in flat thinking, you don't see your organization as part of a larger system that includes different cultures, perspectives, assumptions about business, and beliefs about right and wrong. With this mindset, when faced with a dilemma, you'll tend to look up at your boss and other leaders and say, "They don't have a clue." Or, you'll look "down" at the people who work for you, or people in a different division, and think, "It's their fault we're having this problem."

Our leaders aren't stuck in flat thinking. To the contrary—they think in three dimensions;

1. *Three dimensional thinkers consider personal experiences and filters as one aspect of the "truth." It's hard to see ourselves, but you need to know how your experiences, cultures, and beliefs affect how you see people, business and the world. If you know this about yourself, you are in a better position to choose which of your perspectives are valid, and which are simply wrong.*

2. *Related to self awareness, you need to seek to understand others. You need to understand how people literally see things differently, depending on country, region, gender, religion, culture—a host of factors goes into this. As a leader, it's your job to understand others, not their job to make themselves understood.*

3. *Once you understand the first two dimensions—self and others—you can turn to the organizational dimension. People often see the world from the perspective of their job, role, or function. In a global business, this is simply too narrow. You need to see the world as if you sit in different jobs, roles, or functions. That's the only way you will be able to understand the resistance to change and to working as a unified team. This resistance does exist, and it's your job to understand it, first, then deal with it in a way that helps people to grow, to adopt three dimensional thinking themselves.*

Each of these dimensions helps us to get out of our own way, to see the world through other people's eyes, to take in different ideas, to consider the organizational point of view. Of course, three dimensional thinking starts with common sense. For example, if you are planning something with your diverse, global team, learn about the cultures of the team members. Plan meetings and team building events during the workday. Know religious holidays. Don't plan things around food and most definitely don't plan around alcohol.

Learning to take a systems perspective in business does not happen by accident. In any global business, there are fundamental differences based on differing social, religious, and other cultural norms. If you leave it to chance, you may or may not learn to approach these differences in a nonjudgmental way. What can you do? Think inclusively, rather than excluding information and facts that don't fit your worldview. Strive for as much breadth as possible in your career—take that new assignment, move away from your home. If you haven't had certain experiences and are faced with new situations, get help. Call someone. Ask for advice. This isn't a sign of weakness, it's a sign of strength and intelligence.

The best global leaders today are the people who can facilitate different points of view, reconcile different perspectives to capture the best ideas, build alignment, and get people excited about the future.

Source: Personal interview with Sandy Cutler conducted by Annie McKee, 2012.

Flat thinking
Two dimensional thinking in which people see the world in the same way they've always seen it and consider their point of view to be the only point of view.

Sandy Cutler has put his finger on exactly how leadership can be an opportunity, not a risk in a global business. Developing yourself as a "three dimensional thinker" is extremely important. In addition, it becomes more important the further from your home culture you go—or your business goes. This has been a challenge for many, particularly when working in emerging markets. Therefore, in the next section, we'll explore quite a lot about key emerging markets, including those in Brazil, Russia, India, and China.

Discussion Questions

1. Imagine you have been asked to transfer abroad to work for an indefinite period of time. What opportunities might this provide for you as a person and a professional? What concerns would you have, and how might you address them?

2. Higher education has been one of developed nations' most prominent exports. This has resulted in cheaper or more skilled labor abroad. What are other pros and cons of exporting higher education?

6. What Opportunities Exist in Emerging Markets?

Objective 14.6
Learn about the opportunities that exist in emerging markets.

The acronym BRIC is commonly used to describe four large emerging markets: Brazil, Russia, India, and China. At the time the acronym was coined in 2001, a prediction was made that these countries' collective GDP would constitute more than 10 percent of global output by 2009. The BRIC economies actually surpassed this prediction, reaching 15 percent of global output by the end of 2008.[102] World Bank figures show that in 2010 the BRIC countries contributed a whopping 17.7 percent of the world GDP (■ **EXHIBIT 14.7**).[103]

To better understand why the BRIC nations have had so much success in recent years, take a look at ■ **EXHIBIT 14.8**. As you can see, India and China dwarf the other countries in the table (and indeed, all other countries in the world) in terms of population—a potential advantage in terms of number of available workers and consumer potential. Also, note that U.S. government spending has far outpaced the spending rate in most other developed countries, as evidenced by America's immense national debt, which is measured as a percentage of GDP. Finally, notice that all of the countries in the table import and export billions, even trillions of dollars' worth of goods, which creates opportunities for the global economy—especially in countries with growing middle classes such as the BRIC nations. For a more thorough understanding of the emerging BRIC markets, let's look at each country individually, beginning with Brazil.

■ **EXHIBIT 14.7**
Brazil, Russia, India, and China are the world's four largest emerging markets.

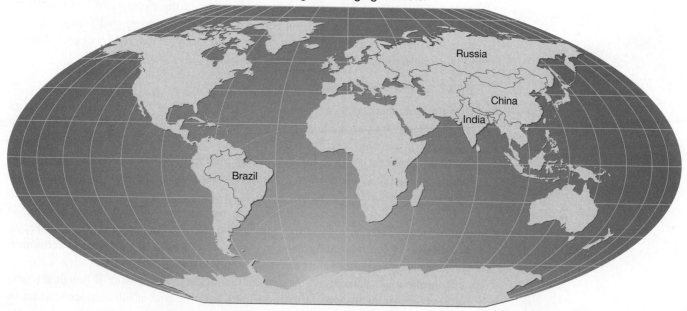

■ **EXHIBIT 14.8**

Comparing the United States and the BRIC Nations, 2010–2012

	United States	Brazil	Russia	India	China
Population (2012 est.)[104]	313.8 million	205.7 million	138.1 million	1.205 billion	1.343 billion
Total GDP (2010, nominal*)[105]	$14.58 trillion	$2.09 trillion	$1.48 trillion	$1.73 trillion	$5.88 trillion
Total GDP (PPP**, 2011 est.)[106]	$15.04 trillion	$2.38 trillion	$2.27 trillion	$4.46 trillion	$11.29 trillion
GDP per Capita (PPP, 2011, est.)[107]	$48,100	$11,600	$16,700	$3,700	$8,400
Birth Rate (per 1,000 people, 2012 est.)[108]	13.68	17.48	10.94	20.60	12.31
Death Rate (per 1,000 people, 2012 est.)[109]	8.39	6.38	16.03	7.43	7.17
Life Expectancy at Birth (2011 est.)[110]	78.49 years	72.79 years	66.46 years	67.14 years	74.84 years
Number of Internet Users (2010 estimate)[111]	244 million	82 million	60 million	88 million	456 million
Literacy Rate (2010)[112]	99%	90%	100%	63%	94%
Value of Imports (2011 est.)[113]	$2.31 trillion	$220 billion	$310 billion	$451 billion	$1.74 trillion
Value of Exports (2011 est.)[114]	$1.51 trillion	$251 billion	$499 billion	$298 billion	$1.90 trillion
Public Debt (amount owed by national government, expressed in % of GDP, 2011 est.)[115]	69.4%	54.4%	8.7%	51.6%	43.5%
External Debt total amount owed to creditors outside the country, 2011 est.[116]	$14.71 trillion	$410 billion	$519 billion	$267 billion	$697 billion

*Nominal GDP measures a country's overall economic output

**"PPP" or "purchasing power parity" amounts are calculated using rates that equate the price of a set amount of goods in a particular country to the price of the same set of goods in the United States. This method attempts to compensate for the weakness of various national currencies.

Brazil

Although it has enjoyed positive growth for most of the twenty-first century, Brazil has not been known for long-term economic stability or widespread prosperity. This lack of economic strength is primarily the result of a past marked by drastic shifts in political ideology and ineffective economic policy.

BRAZIL: THE PAST (1889–1985)

Brazil was established as a Portuguese colony in 1534. From then until the end of the eighteenth century, slave-supported sugar plantations brought some prosperity. This wealth, however, was controlled by plantation owners, who spent much of it on imported goods rather than local products. Similarly, the discovery of gold and diamonds during the 1700s profited some individuals but contributed little to the overall domestic economy.[117]

Brazil's fortunes began to improve when the Portuguese royal family fled to Rio de Janeiro in 1808 to escape the Napoleonic Wars in Europe. As you can see in ■ **EXHIBIT 14.9**, this resulted in some progress as well as a great deal of economic, political, and social uncertainty during the next 170 years.

From the mid-1970s until 1985, Brazil was under military rule, although the government was gradually becoming more open, with the goal of full democratization by

■ **EXHIBIT 14.9**

Key Events in Brazil's History, 1808–1975	
Year and Event	**Effects on Brazil's People and Economy**
1808: The Portuguese royal family arrives in Rio de Janeiro.[118]	Colonial shipping restrictions are relaxed.
1822: Brazil gains independence from Portugal and establishes a constitutional monarchy under Dom Pedro I.[119]	The country enters a period of relative peace and prosperity, and the size of its middle class increases.
1889: Dom Pedro II is overthrown. Brazil becomes a constitutional democracy, although the government remains under the control of wealthy planters and the military.[120]	Ordinary citizens lose many of their freedoms and coffee becomes Brazil's primary cash crop. European immigration increases and is followed by industrialization.
1930:[121] A military coup results in suspension of Brazil's national legislature and constitution. Demand for coffee decreases due to the Great Depression.	The drop in coffee demand weakens the economy, and the government establishes social security benefits and wage regulations. These efforts improve the status of the lower classes and overall national prosperity.
1935: After an attempted Communist coup, the president seizes dictatorial power. Society and the economy are subsequently organized into "corporations," each of which represents a major interest group.[122]	Many industries are nationalized, and state-owned iron and steel production facilities are developed using foreign funding. Labor organizations are formed to oversee these enterprises, although they are largely ineffective.
Post–World War II:[123] The government continues to develop state-owned monopolies and expand protectionist trade policies.	Inflation skyrockets and the working-class standard of living declines. As the deficit increases, the government prints more money.
1954–1964: A new military regime arises that attempts to promote economic growth and borrows heavily from foreign governments. This regime evolves into a dictatorship.[124]	Although oppressive, the new government ushers in an era of political stability and economic growth.
Mid-1970s: The existing regime moves toward democratization of Brazil's political system and eases its repressive policies. The world economy begins to slow down.[125]	Hyperinflation sets in, and the national deficit grows significantly as financial markets and exchange rates collapse. Brazil finds itself unable to repay its large foreign debt.

1985. Throughout this period, the country's protectionist stance allowed little importation of goods and kept Brazil largely removed from the world's economies.

BRAZIL: THE PRESENT

In 1985, military rule came to an end when Brazil's parliament elected Tancredo Neves president. Neves died several weeks later, and Vice President José Sarney became president. During Sarney's presidency, a new constitution that extended civil rights to all citizens and gave state and local governments greater authority was adopted. Still, Sarney's time in office was plagued by inflation and little economic development.[126]

Succeeding Sarney in 1989 via the first direct election in 29 years, Fernando Collor de Mello was unsuccessful at curbing Brazil's rapidly rising inflation. Corruption and political scandal forced him to resign in 1992, and he was succeeded by Vice President Itamar Franco.[127] Franco, along with his appointed minister of the treasury, Fernando Cardoso, attempted to address the crippling hyperinflation with a set of reforms called the Plano Real.[128] Under this plan, the government issued a new currency called the *real* and initially linked its value to the U.S. dollar. This plan helped Brazil's inflation rate drop into the single digits within just one year.[129]

Cardoso's economic "miracle" made him popular, and he was elected president in 1994. As president, he continued to push financial reforms, including privatization of government-owned telecommunications, mining, and energy enterprises.[130] In 1998,

Source: Dida Sampaio/ZUMA Press/Newscom

Cardoso led Brazil out of another financial crisis, this one related to a burgeoning deficit, climbing interest rates, and devaluation of the real.[131]

When Luiz Inacio Lula da Silva became president in 2002, Brazil was in a period of relative stability. During Lula's administration, the country's economy grew rapidly, performed comparatively well during the 2007–2008 world financial crisis, and experienced a strong, early recovery from the crisis.[132] In fact, Brazil weathered the storm better than many emerging economies, largely due to proactive government efforts that led Brazil's economy to show multiple indicators of growth, including decreased unemployment, increased export levels, and increased inflow of foreign investments.[133]

In 2011, Dilma Roussef— Lula da Silva's Chief of Staff and hand-picked successor— became the first female president of Brazil (■ **EXHIBIT 14.10**). Roussef has indicated her intent to continue Lula da Silva's macroeconomic policies and, during her tenure, Brazil's long-term sustainable growth rate has exceeded 4 percent.[134] Division of the UN that coordinates the economic and social work of 14 different UN agencies and their commissions.[135]

BRAZIL: THE FUTURE

In the years to come, Brazil is likely to experience continued economic growth and greater recognition on the world stage. The government is dedicated to strengthening the country's economy and combating poverty.[136] If these efforts are successful, Brazil's middle class will continue to expand, and the demand for consumer products will continue to rise.[137]

But where will the money for growth come from? Most likely, much of it will involve agricultural exports. Brazil is already the world's largest grower of coffee, sugarcane, and tropical fruits, and a leading exporter of soybeans, corn, livestock (especially beef cattle and poultry), rice, and forest products.[138] Brazil is also expected to profit from global interest in plant-based biofuels. By 2008, Brazil was already the world's largest producer of biofuels—much of it in the form of sugarcane-derived ethanol.[139] This may serve Brazil well, as demand for plant-based fuels will likely grow as concern about the use of fossil fuels and global warming intensifies.[140]

Brazil can also benefit from its natural resources, including large reserves of potassium, tin, copper, uranium, phosphate, tungsten, lead, graphite, chrome, and iron ore.[141] In addition, the nation is already one of the world's top 15 oil producers, and the recent discovery of vast offshore reserves means that it could become a top 10 producer within the next two decades.[142] These valuable mineral and oil deposits have led to the development of extensive mining and refining operations, as well as the growth of manufacturing industries that rely on these substances. For instance, Brazil is a global leader in steel production, which contributes to its thriving aircraft, machinery, motor, and auto parts industries.[143] Brazil also houses large reserves of niobium and tantalite, both of which are used in superconductors and electronic components.[144] As worldwide demand for electronics grows, Brazil stands to profit, and its emerging tech industry will no doubt grow as well.

Brazil has also spearheaded diplomatic and trade efforts within the Western Hemisphere, and it is a founding member of the Union of South American Nations (UNASUR), Mercosur, and the Latin American Integration Association (ALADI). Globally, Brazil has played a leading role in World Trade Organization negotiations, sent troops to United Nations peacekeeping efforts, and signed several prominent nuclear nonproliferation treaties. In addition, Brazil is a member of the G-20 group of nations, and in 2009, it became one of several countries that contribute to the International Monetary Fund in order to help poorer nations bolster their economies.[145]

ADVANTAGES AND DISADVANTAGES OF DOING BUSINESS WITH BRAZIL

Brazil is becoming increasingly attractive to international firms. As shown in ■ **EXHIBIT 14.11**, Brazil offers many advantages beyond the factors mentioned earlier,

■ **EXHIBIT 14.11**

Advantages and Disadvantages of Doing Business with Brazil	
Advantages	**Disadvantages**
Economic Stability:[146] Brazil's economy has grown at an average annual rate of 3 percent since 1993. Recently, the government has enacted policies to increase the liquidity of the economy, reduce interest rates, and cut taxes in the manufacturing sector.	**Aversion to Imports:**[147] In its trade negotiations, Brazil pushes an agenda of liberalization for its exports and protectionism from foreign imports. As a result, its tariffs tend to be high. Brazil has better import relationships with other South American countries than with the United States.
Openness to Foreign Investment:[148] Brazil's government welcomes foreign investment, particularly by U.S. companies. Public–private partnerships are strongly encouraged, especially in the area of infrastructure improvements.	**Potential for Political Upheaval:**[149] Radical changes aren't expected as a result of future presidential elections, but these contests still bring some uncertainty. Changes in governments can be more disruptive in developing countries than in developed countries.
Engagement in Global Exports:[150] Brazil is heavily engaged in the export market, with its products being sent to the United States, the European Union, Asia, and Latin America. The country's exports reflect a wide mix of raw, semi-manufactured, and manufactured goods.	**Differing Standards for Meat:**[151] Brazil is the global leader in meat exports, but the prevalence of foot-and-mouth disease prevents the sale of beef and chicken in the United States. These factors also limit access to markets worldwide and contribute to lowered export values.

including economic stability, openness to foreign investment, and engagement in the global export market. Potential disadvantages to conducting business in Brazil include continued aversion to imports, the potential for political instability, and health concerns related to meat exports.

Russia

Although a fast-growing economy, Russia faces significant obstacles to becoming a true economic powerhouse. Most of these obstacles can be traced to Russia's authoritarian roots and its lack of economic sophistication due to years of participating in a **centrally planned socialist economy**. Centrally planned socialist economies have a variety of characteristics that make them different than **capitalist economies**. The most important difference is that the government dictates every aspect of the economic system in a centrally planned economy, including what goods are produced by whom, how much these goods cost, and how much people are paid for their work. In contrast, in a capitalist economy, the market determines what is produced and sold, how much goods and services cost, and what workers are paid.

RUSSIA: THE PAST (1917–1989)

Russia's history reflects a combination of outward aggression and inward oppression. Through conquest, annexation of other lands, and exploration, a series of tsars built the Russian Empire of the eighteenth century into the second-largest contiguous empire in the history of the world. This empire existed from 1721 until the Bolshevik Revolution of 1917. During the reign of the tsars and of the Bolsheviks, citizens had few rights or civil liberties. Freedom of speech, freedom of religion, freedom of press, and even the freedom to earn a living in the manner one desired were often denied. This repressive internal environment, combined with a desire to promote the spread of Communism after the Bolshevik Revolution, triggered a series of events that shaped Russia and its economy during the next seventy years, as outlined in ■ **EXHIBIT 14.12**.

Centrally planned socialist economy
An economy in which the government dictates every aspect of the economic system, including what goods are produced by whom, how much these goods cost, and how much people are paid for their work.

Capitalist economy
An economy in which what is produced and sold, how much goods and services cost, and what workers are paid is determined by the market.

■ **EXHIBIT 14.12**

Key Events in Russia's History, 1917–1989

Year and Event	Impact on Russia's People and Economy
1917:[152] The Bolsheviks, a group of Marxist revolutionaries led by Vladimir Lenin, overthrow the tsarist autocracy and establish a centralized government that tightly controls all aspects of Russia's economy, politics, and culture.	Citizens are subject to repression, including imprisonment or death for anti-Bolshevik activities. Private property is confiscated and the government takes control of industry and business. Incomes are redistributed and the state assumes responsibility for social services. These events mark the rise of Communism.
1922–1927:[153] Communist Russia merges with several surrounding states to form the Union of Soviet Socialist Republics (USSR). Lenin's death results in a power struggle, with Josef Stalin eventually emerging as supreme leader.	Existing restrictions on political, economic, and religious freedoms are tightened. During the next 10 years, Soviet intelligence agencies are granted increased authority; political dissidents are purged; millions of citizens are deported or relocated; farms are collectivized; and government policies contribute to widespread famine.
1939–1945:[154] The USSR joins with the United States and the United Kingdom to help defeat Germany in World War II.	Following Nazi surrender, the Cold War begins as the USSR and the United States attempt to gain influence over lands previously held by Germany. Stalin's government takes over many Eastern European countries. People within the Soviet sphere of influence are subject to political and cultural oppression and increasing economic distress due to government policy, trade embargoes, and geographic isolation.
1953–1985:[155] After Stalin's death in 1953, the USSR is controlled by a series of Communist leaders (Nikita Khrushchev, Leonid Brezhnev, Yuri Andropov, and Konstantin Chernenko), each of whom differs in his approach to domestic policies and relations with the West.	Under Stalin's successors, residents of the USSR and its satellite countries are subject to alternately relaxed and tightened restrictions on basic civil liberties. The nation devotes massive sums to aeronautics, the military, the sciences, and creation of an educational system that identifies "future stars" deemed worthy of development. The vast majority of citizens suffer under increasing poverty and heavily rationed goods and services. The country engages in a series of wars with satellite countries and other nations.
1985–1989:[156] Mikhail Gorbachev is elected premier in 1985. Soon thereafter, he spearheads a series of landmark reforms, including *glasnost* (openness), *perestroika* (restructuring), *demokratizatsiya* (democratization), and *uskoreniye* (acceleration of economic development).	Gradually, the economies of the USSR and its satellite nations begin to open. The movement in support of democracy and capitalism gains ground as more and more citizens demand greater freedoms and access to international products. The United States and other Western nations increase the amount and visibility of the pressure they place on the Soviet government.

RUSSIA: THE PRESENT

Although the Soviet Union began to institute reforms as early as 1985, the fall of the Berlin Wall in 1989 was the most dramatic indicator that the Cold War era was drawing to a close. By this time, many satellite countries and republics that had once been part of the Soviet Union were breaking away and forming their own governments, leaving Russia less powerful.

Throughout this period, great changes were happening inside Russia. Most notably, the Russian people held a democratic election for the first time in their history, and Boris Yeltsin was elected president. Upon taking office, Yeltsin immediately set about transitioning Russia's economy from command and control to one that embraced free trade. This was no simple task, and numerous growing pains in this process led to a severe downturn in the Russian economy. During the 1990s, Russia's GDP fell by 50 percent, and the country sank into a serious economic depression.

Yeltsin resigned at the end of 1999, stating, "I want to beg forgiveness for your dreams that never came true. And I would also like to beg forgiveness not to have justified your hopes."[157]

Following Yeltsin's resignation, Prime Minister Vladimir Putin served as acting president until the 2000 presidential election, which he won. In his role as president, Putin governed Russia in a more authoritarian manner than Yeltsin. He also oversaw a period of economic recovery in which the country's GDP increased by 72 percent and the number of Russians living in poverty was cut in half.[158] Thanks in part to these statistics, Putin was reelected President in 2004. Although the global economic recession that began in 2007 hit Russia particularly hard, Russia's continual rise in economic prowess led to his reelection as Premier in 2008 and as President in 2012.

Throughout his first two terms as president, Putin approached the West with an attitude that some viewed as antagonistic. Rarely supporting the United States or Western Europe in international endeavors, he blamed the West for many of Russia's ills while promoting an attitude of Russian nationalism and anti-Americanism.[159] By law, Putin could not run for a third term as president in 2008, and President Dmitry Medvedev was elected in March of that year. Although Medvedev had never before held elected office, his ascension was not surprising: Medvedev faced no serious competition at the polls and was Putin's hand-picked successor. Before the election even took place, Medvedev declared his intention to appoint Putin prime minister. Analysts believe that this combination of factors accounted for Medvedev winning 70 percent of all votes cast.[160]

Putin was a visible, powerful prime minister, and many critics viewed the Medvedev administration as little more than a continuation of the Putin administration. Medvedev was aware of these criticisms, and repeatedly declared his intentions to employ a "softer style" than his predecessor while pushing for needed economic, political, and judicial reforms.[161] However, few reforms materialized. When Medvedev's term as President came to an end, he supported Putin's bid for a third, nonconsecutive term in the 2012 election, which Putin won handily despite widespread anti-Kremlin protests during the preceding winter.[162]

RUSSIA: THE FUTURE

Russia is considered to be at a political and economic crossroads. Relations between the Russian government and others continue to be strained. Russia's continued heavy dependence on oil and gas exports does not bode well because the country lacks economic diversification, leading some economists, such as Nobel Laureate Paul Krugman, to question whether Russia belongs in the BRIC countries.[163] According to Krugman:

> *Russia really doesn't belong in the group, it's a petro-economy in terms of world trade . . . There's China and India, which in important ways belong together—labor-abundant rapid-growth economies . . . Brazil is a middle-income, not a lower-income country and still more than half of its exports are raw-material oriented. But it does have a strong manufacturing sector . . . Russia doesn't fit at all.*[164]

On the positive side, Russia has a GDP of $1.5 trillion, and as of 2010, its economy was the eleventh largest in the world. Moreover, Russia's middle class—nonexistent before the 1990s—made up 25 percent of the population in 2010.[165] Russia therefore has an economy that is poised for growth, as well as a population that can support it.

ADVANTAGES AND DISADVANTAGES OF DOING BUSINESS WITH RUSSIA

While it simply wasn't possible to do business in Russia during much of the twentieth century, international companies now look to Russia as a place to outsource work and establish operations. This is due in large part to Russians' high level of education and expertise and their low wages in comparison to Western workers.

In spite of the record growth in Russia's economy between 2000 and 2011, Russia's financial sector remains weak. This and other areas of weakness, along with several advantages of doing business in Russia, are summarized in ■ **EXHIBIT 14.13**.

■ **EXHIBIT 14.13**

Advantages and Disadvantages of Doing Business with Russia

Advantages	Disadvantages
Education and Expertise:[166] Russia has a highly educated and technologically savvy population. The nation's literacy rate is deemed to be 99 percent, and more than half of the adult population has a university-level education.	**Population Decline:**[167] In recent years, Russia's population has declined at an annual rate of about 0.5 percent, due to a combination of poverty, poor health, and a death rate that significantly exceeds the birth rate. In 2008, the country had nearly as many yearly abortions as live births, a decrease from previous years when abortions were more common than live births. The country also has one of the world's highest suicide rates, more than double the global average.
Cultural Proximity to the West:[168] Cultural conventions in Russia are similar to those in Europe and North America, which makes Russia attractive to Western companies. A strong work ethic is an important part of the Russian identity, and after years of oppression, many Russians have a pent-up desire for more variety in their career choices.	**Weak Economy:**[169] Russia's per capita GDP is lower than the GDPs of most of its former satellites. Output and employment are back on the rise, but the ruble lost more than a quarter of its value against the U.S. dollar since the recession that began in 2007. In addition, a large portion of Russian business and industry remains under the control of the inefficient central government and unscrupulous politicians or business owners/leaders.
Geographic Proximity to the West:[170] Russia's relative proximity to most European countries means that time differences and travel concerns are negligible. Also, the latter part of the Russian business day coincides with the beginning of the business day in most American offices, and it has become increasingly easy to get a direct flight to Moscow from many major U.S. cities.	**Weak Banking Sector:**[171] Russia's financial sector is plagued by well-capitalized banks. As more and more money flowed into the country's economy during the past 15-plus years, a handful of large, powerful banks were able to consolidate their control of the market. Of the 1,178 banks operating in Russia in March 2007, 30 controlled roughly 70 percent of all assets. Of the remaining banks, 60 percent operated with a capital base of less than €5 million (about U.S. $7 million).
Low Wages:[172] By the end of 2011, the average Russian wage earner brought in approximately $933 per month. Accordingly, many Russian professionals (including engineers and IT professionals) receive approximately one-fourth the wages of their American counterparts.	**Weak Rule of Law:**[173] Within Russia, there is no firm guarantee that citizens' rights will be upheld or that legal matters will be decided fairly and uniformly. This is the result of a poorly paid, poorly trained judiciary; a legal system that does not operate on the principle of precedent; and widespread corruption and strong-arm tactics undertaken by various criminal factions.

India

Since 1991, India has been in the midst of a financial boom fueled by liberalization of its economic policies and improved political relations with the West. According to many current scholars, India's unique approach to management and leadership is a distinct and powerful advantage on the global scene.[174] Today, India offers opportunities to foreign investors and businesses, but it must overcome significant hurdles before it can regain the economic prestige it enjoyed in centuries past (see ■ **EXHIBIT 14.14**).

INDIA: THE PAST (2500 B.C.E. TO 1990)

India is home to one of the oldest continuous civilizations on Earth, and for much of its history, the country was a center for global trade. For instance, the Indo-Aryan culture of

■ **EXHIBIT 14.14**

Key Events in India's History, 1757–1990

Year and Event	Impact on India's People and Economy
1757–1857:[175] The British East India Company assumes control of a large portion of India in 1757, ousting both the French and the Mughals. The company gradually takes over the areas that make up present-day Pakistan, Bangladesh, and Sri Lanka.	The Indian people lose control of their government, their economy, and to some extent, their way of life. India remains one of the largest economies in the world, although an increasing percentage of its products are sent directly to Britain.
1857:[176] Control of India is transferred from the East India Company to the British crown. The British government assumes direct authority over the region and grants some measure of self-government to its Indian subjects.	The British government establishes provincial councils and appoints Indian advisers to the British viceroys governing the country. These moves are meant to appease India's middle class but do not quell the call for an end to British rule.
1858–1919:[177] India's self-rule movement intensifies, reaching a fever pitch by the end of World War I. Although India's economy still remains among the world's largest, the country loses ground to other nations, including the United States and Germany.	After sacrificing on behalf of the British war effort, many Indians feel it is time to demand independence. The spread of industrialization means that India's handicraft-based economy disappears in favor of an economy based on mass production.
1920:[178] Mohandas Gandhi rallies people against British rule. His message of nonviolent resistance and noncooperation with the colonial government garners millions of followers and makes it difficult for Britain to fight the movement (■ **Exhibit 14.15**).	More and more Indians refuse to cooperate with the British government. Meanwhile, industrialization continues to spread across India. Rapid population growth means that India must begin widespread importation of food products for the first time.
1947:[179] Britain decides to abandon its control of India. Independence is finally realized on August 15, 1947, when India becomes a dominion within the British Commonwealth and Jawaharlal Nehru is named the country's first prime minister (Exhibit 14.15).	India faces a devastating array of problems. The country's population is nearly 360 million, and its infrastructure and social services cannot support so many people. Hostilities with Pakistan result in ongoing tensions and full-scale war. Without Britain as a primary trade partner, India has no market for its products, and British exploitation has left the country without the industry necessary for self-sufficiency. As a result, India's share of the world income drops. Crippling poverty sets in.
1950s to early 1980s:[180] India's leaders feel that industrialization will cure the country's financial woes, specifically championing a form of this process inspired by the USSR. Consequently, they launch a centralized planning program in which nearly every aspect of the country's industrial sector is either owned or heavily regulated by the national government.	India's GDP grows at an average rate of just below 4 percent, which is significantly less than that of surrounding nations. The country's inefficient bureaucracy and business licensing processes consume a large portion of the national budget, make it difficult for people to run businesses, and make foreign investment in India almost impossible. Between 40 and 50 percent of the population suffers from extreme poverty and high unemployment, especially in rural areas.
Mid- to Late 1980s:[181] India's leaders acknowledge that the socialist system of the previous 40 years has failed to build the economy or improve the plight of the population. The fall of the Soviet Union, the phenomenal growth of other Asian economies, and India's near financial collapse due to an inability to pay for imports illustrate that a new approach is needed.	The stage is set for widespread economic reform.

the Indus River valley developed heavily traveled trade routes that unified the Indian sub-continent.[182] This extensive trade system fostered the development of textile weaving and metal smithing industries, as well as a flourishing market for Indian-grown teas and spices.

India's commercial wealth and vast supply of spices attracted the attention of many foreigners over the years. Among the best known was Alexander the Great, who took control of much of the subcontinent during the fourth century B.C.E. Alexander was

■ **EXHIBIT 14.15**
Do you think Jawaharlal Nehru and Mohandas Gandhi's vision for India has been fulfilled?

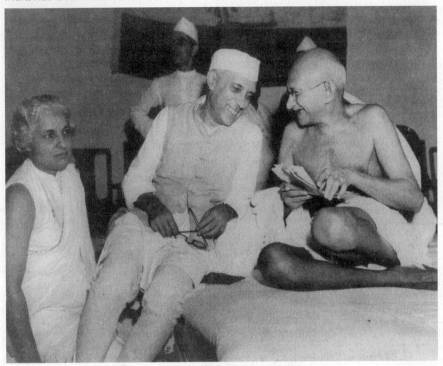

Source: Dinodia Photos/Alamy

followed by Roman traders, Turkish and Afghan invaders, and Mongol conquerors over several centuries.[183] By the time Portuguese explorers landed in 1498, the Indian population had already been exposed to a wide range of foreign influences.[184]

During the 1500s and 1600s, the Portuguese, French, Dutch, and British all sought a foothold in India in order to obtain spices, tea, silk, and other goods. The British East India Company soon became the dominant Western presence in the country, maintaining a peaceful relationship with India's ruling Mughal Empire for over a century. When regional clashes and wars erupted in the country in the mid-1700s, however, Great Britain and France began to battle each other for a greater share of control in India. Great Britain won this battle, and the long British Colonial period continues to impact India today, more than half a century after Independence.

INDIA: THE PRESENT

India began taking major steps toward liberalization of its economic policies in 1991, thanks to the leadership of Finance Minister Manmohan Singh. Under Singh, the business licensing process was dramatically simplified.[185] The Indian government also reduced tax rates, opened the economy to more foreign and large-business investment, decreased tariffs on incoming goods, and overhauled the nation's banking system.[186]

The results of this market liberalization were rapid and astounding. By 1993, India's GDP was increasing at a rate of 5.1 percent per year, and since 2000, that rate has risen to an annual average of about 7 percent. Moreover, foreign direct investment jumped from $165 million in 1991 to over $225 billion in 2010.[187] India is now the world's fourth-largest economy, and it accounts for nearly 3 percent of the overall world GDP.[188]

Even with this phenomenal growth, India's economy is not problem free. For one, as much as 55.6 percent of the nation's GDP is based on the provision of services, and a full 34 percent of the country's laborers are employed in service-related occupations.[189] This is no surprise to most observers, as India is widely recognized as a world leader in technical support and computer services. This sector has promoted an economic boom and contributed to the emergence of the middle class. The dominance of this sector, however, means that the country has a feeble industrial sector, with only 14 percent of Indians employed in industry. Another problem is that the majority of the wealth obtained through the provision of services remains in the hands of the middle class, most of whom reside in urban or suburban areas. India's many poor are not faring anywhere near as well, and the nation has a 37 percent poverty rate. This concentration of wealth is the result of vast inequities in the Indian educational system and lingering class divisions linked to the traditional Hindu caste system. The net result is that millions of Indians, especially those in rural areas, continue to live in abject poverty.

Finally, lingering political conflicts with neighboring countries, especially Pakistan and China, continue to make some foreigners hesitant to invest in India. In fact, as the country began to acquire and test nuclear weapons as part of escalating tensions with Pakistan in the 1980s and 1990s, the United States and other Western countries enacted various sanctions against India. By the early 2000s, the U.S. government recognized India as a valuable strategic and financial partner and lifted many of these restrictions, thereby permitting vast amounts of American capital to flow into the now-flourishing Indian economy.[190]

INDIA: THE FUTURE

The Indian government is dedicated to continued economic growth and estimates GDP growth for 2012 will be 6.5 percent.[191] Liberal approval of foreign business projects is expected to continue, with emphasis on the telecommunications and services sectors and infrastructure development.[192] In addition, India's biotechnology sector has become particularly attractive to investors due to the large domestic talent pool. According to the European Business and Technology Center, the sector grew to $3 billion U.S. dollars in 2009–2010, a 17 percent growth, and was projected to continue growing rapidly through 2015.[193]

Foreign investments are a primary driver of India's growing middle class. In turn, expansion of the middle class has increased disposable income and created shifts in spending that are leading to even more industrial growth. The processed food, paper, and mobile broadband industries in particular are experiencing rapid expansion and are expected to continue growing through 2015.[194] Industrial growth is also expected to come from privatization of government-owned industries as a means of offsetting the national deficit.[195] These efforts, coupled with vast reserves of coal, iron ore, and bauxite, could lead India to become one of the top five suppliers of steel in the world during the next decade.[196] Privatization efforts are also likely to benefit the electricity industry, partially through increased access to coal reserves and partially through improved delivery systems.[197]

Current industrial growth has led to a steady decline in the share of GDP held by India's agricultural sector, and this decline is likely to continue. This is a positive signal for India's economy because it will reduce the impact of agrarian crises on the national economy.[198] Still, during the past few years, natural disasters and poorly managed food distribution chains have led to rapid increases in inflation.[199] The target inflation rate set by Indian authorities was between 5 and 5.5 percent; during 2010, however, this rate was 12 percent, although it dropped to 8.6 percent in 2011 according to the International Monetary Fund. Rates are expected to continue dropping through 2017.[200] The Reserve Bank of India is taking steps to fight inflation, but it is having difficulty reconciling its aims with those of the Indian government.[201] The effects of inflation on the Indian economy, therefore, are difficult to predict.

The current population of India is dedicated to economic progress. This is due in large part to the relative youth of the Indian population, with more than 50 percent of citizens under age 25 in 2010. The median age is expected to continue to rise as India continues to develop during the twenty-first century.[202] This youthful generation was raised in a globally driven economy rather than a socialist economy and is interested in using their talents and education for the betterment of their lives, their families, and their communities.[203]

Finally, scholars believe that India's management and leadership practices, which are quite different from American or other Western approaches, are at the heart of the country's current and future growth and economic development. Wharton professors Peter Cappelli, Harbir Singh, Jitendra Singh, and Michael Useem point out that greater attention paid to people and culture, more adaptability and creativity, a long-term focus, and a commitment to values, mission, purpose, and community set India's businesses apart.[204] Many of these attributes are in stark contrast to the short-term profit orientation of Western businesses.

ADVANTAGES AND DISADVANTAGES OF DOING BUSINESS WITH INDIA

India offers a number of advantages to international companies, including a large pool of educated workers, a growing middle class, and widespread fluency in English. The most prominent disadvantages of doing business with India include the extreme poverty of certain portions of the population, insufficient infrastructure, and social prejudices held over from the days of the caste system. These advantages and disadvantages are summarized in ■ **EXHIBIT 14.16.**

■ **EXHIBIT 14.16**

Advantages and Disadvantages of Doing Business with India

Advantages	Disadvantages
Large Pool of Educated Workers:[205] In India, strong emphasis is placed on education—but only for those who can afford it. The public education system is in need of reform, but the private system provides a very good education to millions of students. Many Indians receive higher education; in fact, India ranks second only to China in the number of students it sends to the United States for college.	**Poverty:**[206] As much as 25 percent of India's population (nearly 300 million people) lives in poverty. Just a decade ago, as many as 130 million people lacked even basic health care, and up to 226 million had no access to safe drinking water. This far-reaching poverty is reflected in the nation's average per capita GDP, which, at about $3,700 in 2011, gives India the rank of 163rd in the world.
Growing Middle Class:[207] India already has a large middle class, estimated at roughly 50 million people. This population is growing rapidly and is expected to reach 583 million by 2025, accounting for more than 40 percent of the country's residents. India's middle class had a discretionary income of 55 percent by the end of 2009, while the overall population of India had a discretionary income of 25 percent.	**Poor Infrastructure:**[208] India's infrastructure is inadequate to support the nation's population—let alone business expansion. Roads are too small to accommodate high volumes of traffic in urban areas, and in rural areas, many roadways have deteriorated. Other infrastructure problems include inadequate airports and bridges, too little clean water, and unreliable electricity.
Fluency in English:[209] India has the second-largest English-speaking population in the world after the United States. With 21.09 percent of the country's population conversant in English, 226,449 people in India speak English as a first language, 132 million speak it as a second language, and 100 million speak it as a third language.	**Social Prejudices:**[210] Caste-based discrimination is illegal in India, and in many urban areas, members of different castes apparently mingle freely. In rural communities, however, caste discrimination is a problem. Economic development may improve conditions for the lower castes, but the social divisions are unlikely to disappear.

China

Breaking free from a centrally planned economy in the 1990s, China quickly became an economic powerhouse thanks to the sheer size of its population and its commitment of tremendous resources to modernization and economic growth. Today, a mix of authoritarian controls and free-market practices creates both opportunities and obstacles for companies that want to do business in China.

CHINA: THE PAST (1912–1989)

China is one of the world's oldest civilizations. It was ruled by a series of powerful dynasties from 2100 B.C.E. until 1912, when Sun Yat-sen of the Nationalist Party was proclaimed president of the new Chinese republic. By the late 1920s, the party and the country were unified under Chiang Kai-shek for an extremely brief period. Beginning in 1927, the Western-supported Nationalists went to war with the Soviet-supported Communists for control of China. The war was fought intermittently and continued in parallel with China's second modern war with Japan.[211] These and other important events between 1925 and 1989 dramatically transformed many aspects of China's economy, government, and culture, as depicted in ■ **EXHIBIT 14.17.**

■ **EXHIBIT 14.17**

Key Events in China's History, 1925–1989

Year and Event	Impact on China's People and Economy
1925:[212] Following the death of Sun Yat-sen, the Nationalist party is united under Chiang Kai-shek, beginning a period of one-party rule.	Despite political instability, China dramatically increases its trade with the Soviet Union (■ **Exhibit 14.18**). Still, high unemployment affects nearly 128 million Chinese citizens, many of whom are farmers.
1927:[213] The Western-supported Nationalist Party and the Soviet-supported Communist Party engage in intermittent warfare for control of China; meanwhile, the country battles Japan in the Second Sino-Japanese War.	The ruling Nationalist Party launches a forced purge of Communists and other dissidents, resulting in the death of nearly 12,000 people in Shanghai. Many Communists flee to rural areas, where they work to consolidate their power. The country begins to see modernization, especially in military-related industries.
1935:[214] Chiang Kai-shek's attempted final purge of the Chinese Communist movement chases Mao Zedong and 200,000 of his followers across China in what becomes known as the Long March.	Not many Communists survive the Long March, but they form the core of a successful Communist Party. Ongoing warfare and efforts to defeat the Communists drain Chiang Kai-shek's resources, leaving him vulnerable to both Japanese and Russian influence.
1937:[215] The Second Sino-Japanese War continues, leading to an uneasy alliance between China's Nationalist and Communist parties.	The Nationalists are forced to accept Mao Zedong's assistance in fighting the Japanese, their common enemy. Meanwhile, Japan enters an alliance with Germany's Adolf Hitler and Italy's Benito Mussolini, forming what would become the Axis powers of World War II. The Second Sino-Japanese War begins to wind down after nearly 20 million Chinese have died and the country's industries have been crushed. Following Japan's surrender, China's civil war resumes.
1949:[216] China's civil war ends. Mao Zedong takes control of mainland China (now known as the People's Republic of China). Chiang Kai-shek and his Nationalist followers retreat to Taiwan. Both call themselves the "true China."[221]	Mainland China undergoes a period of economic restoration from 1949 to 1952. The banking system is nationalized, and the monetary system is unified with the government's guarantee to back all currency. By the end of 1952, nearly all of China's industries have been similarly nationalized.
1958:[217] The Great Leap Forward, an ambitious economic and social restructuring plan, is implemented.	The Chinese government rejects the Soviet model of industrialization, instead placing emphasis on agricultural reform and rural industrialization, as well as establishment of farm collectives. Economic disaster and famine result, leading to 30 million deaths.
1966:[218] Mao Zedong launches the Cultural Revolution in response to the disaster of the Great Leap Forward. In doing so, he seeks to purge all Western and "old" Chinese influence. Red Guards (a cadre of 11 million youths) terrorize the country. Red Guards nearly undermine the Chinese Communist Party and are subsequently dismantled. Many members of the group are sent to the countryside.	Temples and churches are destroyed throughout China. In Shanghai, municipal power is undermined and links to the West are severed. Chinese "intellectuals" are sent to the countryside. Red Guard activity leads to production decreases throughout the country. Later, the country's universities reopen and the most extreme phase of Chinese isolationism ends. As a result, foreign investment resumes, and China's industrial output grows by 8 percent per year.
1978:[219] Deng Xiaoping becomes leader, ushering in an era of post-Maoist economic reforms.	The introduction of market mechanisms leads to increased efficiency. Centralized control of China's economy is scaled back, and the country begins to experiment with merit pay and free enterprise. Most communes are dissolved, and the Chinese standard of living rises. Special economic trade zones are established.
1989:[220] Protestors in Tiananmen Square are chased away, imprisoned, or killed by the Chinese military.	The events in Tiananmen Square impact China's relationships with the rest of the world into the present era (see following section).

CHINA: THE PRESENT

Near the time that the West was preparing to tear down the Berlin Wall, Chinese dissidents staged a protest of their own, centered in the heart of China: Beijing's Tiananmen Square. Led primarily by students and intellectuals, the protestors lacked a unified cause, but were all disillusioned by China's Communist Party and its

Source: Photos 12/Oasis/Alamy

■ **EXHIBIT 14.19**
How do the events that unfolded in Tiananmen Square continue to impact China today?

Source: The Photolibrary Wales/Alamy

continuing authoritarian rule. The protests, some of which involved 100,000 people at a time, lasted seven weeks before the government took action. At that point, tanks were dispatched to Tiananmen Square, and the military chased away, imprisoned, and killed untold numbers of protestors. Even high-ranking members of the Communist Party who voiced support for the protesters were put under house arrest. It is not known exactly how many people died, although the Chinese Red Cross initially estimated 2,600 before retracting the statement due to objections of the Chinese government.[221]

Known in many parts of the world as the Tiananmen Square massacre, this event unfolded on television news, and it greatly affected how people across the globe viewed (and continue to view) China. China experienced significant economic losses as a result of the incident and its impact on world opinion. For example, the World Bank and governments around the world suspended loans to China. Tourism revenue from the United States decreased to half its previous level, and the European Union and the United States enacted an embargo on weapons sales that remains in place today. As late as 2008, the United Nations Committee Against Torture urged China to apologize for the massacre, conduct an investigation of what happened, and release any protesters still held in prison. Discussion of the event is still taboo in China, and any press mention of it is censored inside the country (■ **EXHIBIT 14.19**). Still, the protesters were not entirely defeated, and many continue to speak out to this day, although they risk their lives in doing so.

Despite ongoing and nearly universal condemnation of the Tiananmen Square incident, China was successful in joining the WTO in 2001. Many critics felt that China should be kept out of the organization due to the government's repression of free speech. Others, however, argued that making China a global partner would help promote increased freedom. By becoming part of the WTO, the international business community began to believe that China would not return to a centrally planned economy. This inspired confidence and by November 2001, 400 of the companies in the Fortune 500 had invested in more than 2,000 projects in mainland China.[222] Similarly, a 2006 report by the Organization for Economic Cooperation and Development states that China had become a leading destination for foreign direct investment.[223] In fact, by 2011 the amount of foreign direct investment in China and Hong Kong was second only to the United States.[224]

CHINA: THE FUTURE

On the global stage, China remains powerful, both in terms of its economy and its military. In 2005, China was the world's largest producer of coal, steel, and cement, as well as the third-largest importer of oil.[225] In fact, China has consistently been the world's largest producer of coal since 1985 and has dominated steel production throughout the first decade of the twenty-first century, despite ongoing criticisms of the quality of the steel.[226] In addition, it owns trillions of dollars in U.S. treasury securities, which puts the United States at a disadvantage in negotiations. China will likely continue to be a powerful economic force as the United States and EU continue to find support for their recovering economies.

Still, China faces several major obstacles as it continues to improve its economy. For one, as the country's standard of living continues to rise, its laborers will likely demand higher salaries. In light of these demands, many companies are choosing to leave China in search of cheaper labor. Another prominent obstacle relates to China's educational system, which does not yet fully compete with those of the United States, India, or Russia. Of course, the issue of human rights also looms: Businesses and governments routinely need to address issues such as unfair labor practices and censorship.

ADVANTAGES AND DISADVANTAGES OF DOING BUSINESS WITH CHINA

Many businesses already have operations in China, and still others are poised to enter the country in the near future. From a purely financial perspective, it makes sense to do business in China because of its population size, the rapid growth of the middle class, and the relatively low wages and benefits paid to the average worker.

The disadvantages in working with China are very complicated. Many drawbacks stem from the country's authoritarian government, its lack of regard for human rights, and its repression of political activists.[227] The Chinese government, however, is well aware of the downsides of many of its policies. On occasion, such as when the blind activist Chen Guangcheng was released and allowed to leave the country, concessions are made to avoid sanctions and worldwide outcries. You can explore these and other prominent advantages and disadvantages of working with China in ■ **EXHIBIT 14.20**.

■ **EXHIBIT 14.20**

Advantages and Disadvantages of Doing Business with China	
Advantages	**Disadvantages**
Population:[228] With roughly 1.343 billion people, China has the largest population in the world. More than 160 Chinese cities have populations of 1 million or greater.	**Human Rights Violations:**[229] Widespread reports of child laborers in Chinese factories have drawn worldwide condemnation. In addition, freedom of speech is greatly curtailed in China. Citizens are prohibited from studying subjects like Tibet, the Dali Lama, and Tiananmen Square, and access to print- and Web-based information is strictly limited.
Growing Middle Class:[230] China's middle class is growing, and the members of this group have more discretionary income and buy more goods and services than ever before. This growth is the result of globalization and an influx of jobs into the cities. Currently, more than 80 million people are part of China's middle class, and this number is expected to reach 700 million by 2020.	**One-Child Policy:**[231] Since the late 1970s, the Chinese government has allowed most couples to have only one child. This has led to higher adoption and abortion rates and even the murder of babies after birth. Many parents prefer sons, which means that the proportion of females in the population is shrinking. Some estimates predict that by 2020, nearly 30 million Chinese men will be unable to find a wife.
Wages and Benefits:[232] Wages are projected to rise in China, but they will continue to be low by American standards. The average wage for a factory worker is $150 per month, or less than one-tenth of what an American factory worker earns over the same period.	**Environmental Sustainability:**[233] China's rapid industrialization has led to high levels of pollution, smog, and degradation of natural resources. The world's 10 most polluted cities are in China. The country is also the world's largest emitter of carbon dioxide.

(continued)

■ **EXHIBIT 14.20** (*continued*)

Advantages and Disadvantages of Doing Business with China

Advantages	Disadvantages
Low Health Care Costs:[234] Health care costs remain low in China for several reasons, including the absence of a legal system that tolerates medical malpractice lawsuits, as well as a lack of expensive equipment and facilities that need to be maintained. Also, China's low wages mean that health care providers must keep their prices down if they wish to stay in business.	**Software Piracy and Counterfeiting:**[235] The software piracy rate in China is one of the highest in the world. Every year, U.S. companies lose over $1 billion as a result of this piracy. When China joined the WTO in 2001, one of its provisions for acceptance was strengthening of the country's intellectual property laws. However, enforcement of these measures has been inadequate because of corruption and a lack of training among officials, dedication of only limited resources to the problem, and a complicated system for handling complaints.
	Lax Safety Standards:[236] Chinese manufacturers do not always adhere to the same safety standards that American and EU companies do. In recent years, this has been evidenced by massive recalls in pet food and children's toys that contained Chinese components. In addition, many pharmaceutical products that are manufactured in China contain unregulated and impure chemical ingredients.

A Final Word on Emerging Markets

In this section, we've focused on the BRIC countries because of the allure they hold for countless organizations around the world. All of these countries are significantly industrialized and are already global players. Numerous other countries are not as far along the path to industrialization and modernization, yet they too are globalizing, often as a result of tourism, as is the case with Zambia. According to student Mwitwa Muyembe, Zambia is a beautiful country with many natural resources, including abundant wildlife: Lions, elephants, giraffes, zebras, and a host of other indigenous animals roam huge, pristine game reserves. The country has been seen as politically stable since independence in 1963, and has not faced some of the human rights challenges neighboring Zimbabwe or Congo have. Still, as a developing nation, Zambia struggles with poverty and an infrastructure that makes it difficult for companies to do business (e.g., unreliable telecommunciation technologies, poor roads in the rural areas, etc.). While tourism has helped the country in its progress toward globalizing, additional growth will require focusing on improving access to education as well as eliminating external threats to Zambia's economy such as removing barriers to international trade. As Mwitwa puts it, "If Zambia improves our telecoms and physical infrastructure, we will be more attractive to tourist *and* able to develop our farms and agriculture businesses. This will improve life for all Zambians. We invite tourists to come to view our wonderful animals and land, and we also hope that businesses that can support the improvement of telecommunications and our infrastructure will also join us as we develop our nation."[237]

Discussion Questions

1. Review the advantages and disadvantages of working and doing business in Brazil, Russia, India, and China. Which advantages are most appealing to you and why? Which disadvantages concern you the most and why?

2. How would you need to prepare yourself to live and work in Brazil, Russia, India, or China? Consider all aspects of life, not just work.

7. What Is HR's Role in Supporting Global Business?

Objective 14.7
Define HR's role in supporting global business.

HR leaders prepare employees to be part of the global workforce. To prepare people for this exciting and challenging experience, HR is often charged with creating and supporting workforce development programs to help people succeed in countries other than their own. An important aspect of this preparation is training in the form of coaching to help managers and employees prepare for the unique challenges of working across cultures, languages, and societal norms. In this section, we will examine the role of coaching for a global workforce. Then, we will consider training specifically targeted at expatriate (expat) employees. Finally, we will present a case study to see how teams can be used to help a company understand its global market.

Coaching for Success: Helping Employees and Managers Adjust to Globalization

Preparation for even a brief period of working abroad is important. But what about when people are sent to another country for an extended period of time? How can HR support employees in dealing with the many personal and professional challenges that come with long-term living and working abroad? One important way HR can help in this situation is to provide expat employees with coaches. Trained coaches can provide much-needed guidance on the complex issues related to working outside one's home country.

Executive coaching has become very popular in recent years. In the early days of the profession, many coaches were retired employees coming back to give advice, while others were psychologists. As the field of coaching began to mature, many more people entered the field: therapists, consultants, even people with little or no training in organizational behavior, leadership, or management. This resulted in many problems because untrained coaches can do a great deal of harm. In addition, the popularity of coaching has resulted in some organizations hiring dozens—even hundreds—of coaches, many of whom may not be aligned in approach and values. Because of these problems, organizations are formally training HR professionals to be coaches. The best training programs, such as those certified by the International Coach Federation, include training in coaching ethics and coaching competencies (e.g., active listening, establishing trust, and self-awareness).[238]

HR Leadership Roles

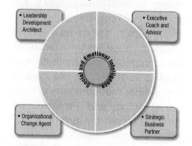

Coach training is important in any setting, and it is absolutely essential to prepare people for working in a cross-cultural environment because of the added complexity. Tips for coaching success in such an environment include the following:

- Understand your client's culture and the host country culture.
- Deliberately build a strong, trusting, and confidential relationship.
- Have a plan for the overall coaching engagement (e.g., what will be worked on for the first third of the time period, the second third, and the final period).
- Ensure that you help your client focus on the future and his or her dreams, not just the problems he or she faces at the present time.
- Avoid prolonging the coaching relationship beyond the time you are needed.

We are fortunate to have the opportunity to live and work abroad or to work with people who come from places far from our homes. We have many choices about how to make these interactions and our cross-cultural workplaces most effective. Our HR departments can help tremendously. In addition, we can also help a great deal ourselves, as we will see in the next section.

The Expat Experience: HR Designs Programs That Matter

Expat employees work outside their home country, sometimes for extended periods of time. Multinational organizations and governments rely on expats to act as knowledge transfer agents and representatives of the company's culture, ethics and business practices.[239] These jobs are important and challenging. First, conducting business in a foreign country, even one where people speak the same language, requires a deep understanding of the local cultural, business, and legal environments, as well as the culture of the organization in that country.[240] When it comes to finding the best way to develop talented employees and prepare them for an international assignment, we can learn some lessons from FedEx, as discussed in the *Business Case*.

BUSINESS CASE

FedEx

FedEx is well known for delivering packages around the globe; in fact, the company delivers more than 9 million packages in 220 countries and territories each day. It also boasts a global workforce of more than 300,000 employees and made nearly $43 billion in revenue during the 2012 fiscal year.[241] In addition, *Fortune* magazine honored FedEx as one of the "25 Best Global Companies to Work For" in 2011 (it ranked fifth).[242]

What is the secret to FedEx's success? It is most certainly linked to in the company's approach to employee development, which traces its roots to FedEx's Leadership Development Institute. The Institute was started in 1984 with the goal of promoting the company's People, Service, and Profits (PSP) culture. Today, the program emphasizes the importance these three areas in that specific order.

Judith Edge, FedEx's Vice President of human resources, says The company adopted a global worldview that was intended to strengthen its culture of global citizenship, a factor that contributes to FedEx's reputation as one of the world's most admired companies. To that end, expat assignments are carefully planned, and a solid global training program is in place. U.S.-based expats are used at the beginning of any new startup to ensure that FedEx's culture is established. After that,

the startup is handed over to locals to operate. Edge credits this model for the increasing diversity of the company's global executives.[243]

FedEx also develops employee leadership skills through international corporate volunteerism programs, including the FedEx Global Leadership Corps (GLC), which was launched in Summer 2011. The first GLC program involved FedEx employees traveling to Salvador Bahia, Brazil, along with employees from IBM, to spend a month living and working with the people in the local community. In Brazil, GLC members worked with the Instituto Cultural Steve Biko, a local organization that serves Bahia's Afro descendant populations. GLC and IBM developed an IT training program and professional development plan for the organization. According to Tess Smith, an HR manager and GLC participant, "International corporate volunteer experiences like this have a ripple effect, deepening the capacity of not only social mission organizations, but of businesses as well."[244]

GLC is continuing its work, and in 2012 it sent a team to Bangalore, India. While in India, the team worked on a variety projects, ranging from eye care to IT solutions to energy.[245]

Photo Source: Accent Alaska.com/Alamy

What FedEx did with these programs is an excellent example of effective workforce development. The company clearly identified the need to prepare people and give them the experience of working internationally. Then, HR and others fostered a very visible and important company-wide initiative to promote individual employees' knowledge and understanding of other countries and cultures.

Discussion Questions

1. Think about an experience you have had working or living in a community and culture not your own. If you haven't had an international experience, consider a time when you joined a new organization at your school or when you took a new job. How did you learn about the business practices and culture in the new setting?

2. When you visit a country or a region that has a different culture than your own, what do you do to try to "fit in"? Are there some occasions where it might not be important or even a good idea to fit in? Why or why not?

8. What Can We All Do to Succeed in a Global Environment?

Objective 14.8
List steps we can take to succeed in a global environment.

Globalization requires us to learn and change. Often, our attitudes, values, and even ethics will be challenged when working abroad or working with people from other cultures. In this section, we'll look at two key areas that you will need to attend to in order to be successful in our global work environment: values and ethics, and your emotional intelligence competencies.

The Intersection between Personal Ethics, Societal Ethics, and Company Ethics

Professor Ronald Sims argues that ethical failures at the organizational level are failures of leadership to integrate the values and ethics of key stakeholders.[246] What that means for you is that you need to be clear about your own values and ethics, as well as those of your society and your organization. You need to be able to see where differences lie and seek to resolve them, as shown in ■ **EXHIBIT 14.21**.

Understanding values and ethics this way requires thoughtfulness, openness, and critical thinking. That is partly because it is easy to underestimate or ignore differences between cultures when it comes to ethics and values. If you can't see differences, you are unlikely to resolve them. In addition, it's easy to assume that people will always follow an organization's code of ethics. However, this simply doesn't happen all the time. People don't always defer to an organization's code of ethics, in part because personal values may be a more powerful driver of behavior.

Another potential problem is that external codes of ethics (like an organization's ethical code) can be seen to constrain behavior, which many people resist. Values, on the other hand, are motivating because they are deeply held beliefs about right and wrong, good and bad. In other words, ethics act as a kind of legal code that tells us what not to do and reminds us of the consequences, whereas values propel us toward what we want to obtain or achieve.[247]

So, whose values and ethics win? That is one of today's biggest leadership challenges. The resolution starts with each of us examining what we believe and finding ways to craft codes of ethics that work for us, our societies, and our companies—even when it means changing some of our values and ethics in support of healthy businesses and healthy societies.

■ **EXHIBIT 14.21**
Knowing where the intersection between personal ethics, societal ethics, and company ethics lies is key to operating successfully in a country other than your own.

Competencies That Support Working Abroad

International managers report that communication is a very important skill to consider when choosing employees for expatriate assignments.[248] For example, international business communication researcher Lena Zander conducted a study of leadership preferences in 16 countries and among 15,000 employees. She found that even when the languages were similar, leaders differed in their communication preferences in important areas, such as general and personal communication, achievement reviews, and feedback.[249]

In addition to communication, other competencies are central to success when you work abroad, such as many of the emotional intelligence competencies you have learned about in this book.

For example, exploring your emotions is important because working in a culture other than your own tends to provoke strong emotions such as excitement, confusion, and anxiety. If you know what you are feeling, you are much more likely to engage in self-management and not say or do things that are inappropriate. Organizational awareness will support you in assessing both the organizational environment and the culture within which your organization operates—again, helping you behave in an appropriate and even inspiring manner. Of course, adaptability is essential. You simply can't do or say many things the way you do at home. You need to be willing to adjust your approach to teamwork, management, and social relationships.

To develop your competencies, you'll want to start with a vision of why this learning is important to you. Maybe you envision yourself working abroad, or you want to be considered a global citizen. Or, maybe you want a life that includes travel. Whatever your dream, being clear about it will give you energy for the learning process as you develop your social and emotional competencies.

Discussion Questions

1. Choose a company that does business in the United States and in several countries that have different values and ethics when it comes to things like nepotism, bribery, and negotiating the price of goods. What dilemmas might employees face? How would you deal with these ethical dilemmas?

2. Which emotional intelligence competencies and personal strengths do you have that would help you work in a country other than your own? In addition to your emotional intelligence competencies, consider personal resiliency, and your experience with other cultures.

9. A Final Word on Globalization

Globalization touches virtually every aspect of our lives, from what we can and want to buy, to the music we listen to, to the culture we live in, to the work we do every day. Although this trend has emerged over several centuries of social, political, and economic change, it is now moving fast, and the effects are rippling across the planet.

Looking back 50 years from now, people may say that the technological, environmental, and social changes we are currently experiencing were the beginning of a "new world order." As you engage in this exciting and challenging time of globalization, you have a chance to impact the world in ways unimaginable to your grandparents. What will you do to help your friends, family, community, nation, and world adopt practices that will enable us all to connect positively and effectively across the globe? What will you do at work to ensure that your company benefits from globalization while also supporting places and people far from home?

Today's global environment offers tremendous opportunity. Take advantage of it!

EXPERIENCING Leadership

LEADING IN A GLOBAL WORLD
On Global Economic Assignment

Global economic issues, such as the global recession that began in 2007, are impacted in part by international organizations like the WTO, G8, G-20, and the World Economic Forum. These bodies typically meet once a year to discuss economic issues in the global arena and what member nations can do to resolve those issues jointly.

1. Imagine you are a journalist for the international newspaper the *Global Economic Observer*. You have been assigned to cover the most recent G-20 meeting. Research this year's meeting and focus on gathering data about the following five points:
   - Global trade and investment
   - Financial supervision and regulation
   - International financial institution funding and reform
   - Inclusive, sustainable market building
   - Confidence, growth, and job building
2. Once you have gathered data, write a brief article for your paper about the discussions and outcomes of the G-20 meetings. Be sure to consider which of the five above points received the most focus and which received the least. What working groups were established and who is responsible for them? What was the primary theme of the summit? How was this summit different from the previous one in its scope and focus?

LEADING WITH EMOTIONAL INTELLIGENCE
A Crib Sheet for Cultural Sensitivity

Working in and among other cultures can be an awesome learning experience. Another culture's ethics, values, beliefs, and social norms can be both enlightening and challenging, depending on the circumstances. In these situations, our emotional intelligence competencies are put to the test.

Imagine you are going to start a business in another country. You want to get your business off on the right foot, so you decide to research the culture. Pick a country for your business headquarters. Interview three people from that country or people who are very familiar with that culture. They can be international classmates, business owners from that country, or members of the university's administration or faculty. In the interview, you will want to keep the following questions in mind:

- What are some of the most important values and social norms of the culture?
- What are some of the easiest and most effective ways to build and sustain strong work relationships in the culture?
- What are some of the social dos and don'ts?
- What kind of ethical issues may you encounter? Are things nepotism or bribery an everyday fact of life? If so, find out how people in the country tend to view these practices, and how they are dealt with in international business settings.
- How easy or hard was it for the interviewee to adjust to U.S. culture and business practices?

LEADING WITH CRITICAL THINKING SKILLS
Emerging or Submerging Markets

The BRIC countries are large emerging markets that are poised for major growth; however, in our networked global economy, global recession affects every country in the network. For example, China may continue to produce massive quantities of goods, but their customer countries may reduce the amount of goods they purchase because of the global recession.

1. Review the table of statistics in Exhibit 14.8 and research any changes to the stats of the five countries. You can use the CIA World Factbook, the IMF, or the World Bank as online resources for gathering your numbers. Be sure to check statistics such as:
   - Public debt
   - External debt
   - Value of imports
   - Value of exports
   - Total GDP
   - GDP per capita
2. Next, identify some new opportunities and risks currently faced by BRIC countries. Have opportunities and risks changed dramatically? Have new opportunities and new risks arisen? If yes, what are they?

3. South Africa and Indonesia are also important emerging markets. Using the CIA World Factbook, the IMF, or the World Bank as online resources, gather data related to the public and external debts, value of imports and exports, total GDP, and GDP per capita of these nations. How do they compare to the BRIC countries in terms of these statistics and in terms of the risks and opportunities they present?

ETHICAL LEADERSHIP
Who You Know, Not What You Know

Globalization places a burden on all of us to learn and to understand how our values and ethics will be challenged when working abroad or with people from other cultures.

In many countries, bribery is a very common business practice. When bidding for competitive contracts in these countries, more often than not it isn't what you know or what you can provide, but who you know and how much the deal "costs." For example, in 2011, eight former executives and contractors of the Siemens Corporation were charged with conspiring to bribe government officials in Argentina.[250]

1. On your own, research just how extensive business corruption is worldwide. Organizations like Transparency International and the Organization for Economic Co-Operation and Development (OECD) will prove useful resources in your research. What are these groups doing to curb corruption? Which countries are the worst offenders and which are the most ethical?

2. In a group, identify three major corruption cases in the last five years. Who was involved? What are the details of the cases? Has a resolution been reached? What were the repercussions of these cases?

KEY TERMS

Globalization, *p. 512*

Cold War, *p. 516*

Propaganda, *p. 516*

Iron Curtain, *p. 516*

Exporting, *p. 520*

Importing, *p. 520*

European Union (EU), *p. 523*

Supranationalism, *p. 523*

Inflation, *p. 525*

Global new ventures, *p. 526*

Outsourcing, *p. 529*

Offshoring, *p. 529*

Economy of scale, *p. 530*

Flat thinking, *p. 532*

Centrally planned socialist economy, *p. 537*

Capitalist economy, *p. 537*

MyManagementLab

Go to **mymanagementlab.com** for Auto-graded writing questions as well as the following Assisted-graded writing questions:

14-1. What are some of the things we must be mindful of with regard to globalization? Why is it important to be mindful of your impact on the local environment, culture, and politics as you travel? How can you encourage others to be responsible for their global impact?

14-2. Have you experienced "culture shock" before? What was the cause of the culture shock? What did you learn from the experience?

14-3. Mymanagementlab Only — comprehensive writing assignment for this chapter.

CHAPTER 14 Visual Summary

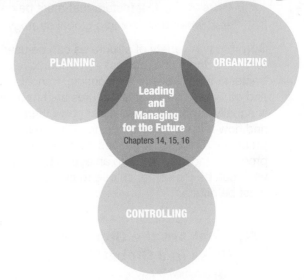

1. What Is Globalization and Why Does It Matter? (pp. 512–514)

Objective: Define globalization and understand how this trend affects business, politics, and economics.

Summary: Globalization is the global flow of money, products, information, services, expertise, and people around the world. The rapid and widespread move toward globalization is due in large part to technologies that enable us to connect with other nations and people. Some people favor globalization for the benefits it can bring to people; others oppose globalization and fear its impact on individuals and the world. Globalization is a transformational force that is changing the way we think about school, work, and life today.

2. How Do Changes in Technology, World Politics, and Economics Foster Globalization? (pp. 514–519)

Objective: Understand how international political and economic changes fostered globalization.

Summary: Changes in technology and political and economic shifts are important forces in our global world. ICTs are the most obvious drivers of change in global business, but politics also exert a great deal of influence. For example, the conclusion of the Cold War ended decades of conflict between Communist and capitalist nations and brought about new opportunities for growth. Conflicts over oil and both social and political issues also affect economies and businesses. Citizens' demands for a say in government and the economy is increasing as the world globalizes, as evidenced by the Arab Spring. Together, these changes suggest that globalization is about more than just business; it is about societies and economies, too.

3. How Do Trade Agreements and International Finance Affect Businesses and Economies? (pp. 519–525)

Objective: Define the key economic factors that are affecting global business.

Summary: Global trade is a prominent factor affecting global business. Regulatory organizations promote ethical trade policies and social improvements among member nations. Each of these organizations takes a different approach to the common goals of growth for underdeveloped nations and global economic stability. The WTO is particularly important among these organizations due to its role in overseeing trade and settling trade disputes on a global level.

Trade alliances are also important in business today, and can be as simple as regional alliances or as complex as supranational federations like the EU. These alliances have a general goal of improving trade for the benefit of member nations. Ultimately, increased international trade has led to an interconnectedness of world economies that has given rise to investment and financial opportunities on a global scale. The unfortunate drawback to this is that when one nation in an alliance suffers, the others may feel the effects as well.

4. What Must Be Considered When Developing a Global Strategy? (pp. 525–528)

Objective: List factors that must be considered when developing a global strategy.

Summary: A variety of structures can be used for organizing global business—cooperative contracts, strategic alliances, licensing, franchising, and others. While these structures are important, it is equally important to consider how cultures differ, and how this will impact business and management practices. The best strategies consider business products and services with an eye to balancing what can be the same, culture to culture, and what must be different.

5. What Are the Opportunities and Risks in a Global Business Environment? (pp. 529–533)

Objective: Define and assess the opportunities and risks in a global business environment.

Summary: Globalization presents both opportunities and risks that must be carefully weighed. Expanding markets and improving sales by reaching untapped markets, improving quality by incorporating new knowledge, and lowering costs by accessing cheaper labor are some of the opportunities presented by globalization. On the other hand, economic and political uncertainty in some countries, growth that outpaces the ability to expand, risky partnerships, and popular disapproval of certain globalization policies all represent risks. Opportunities and risks will differ by company and environment and, in some cases, a risk for one company will represent an opportunity for another.

7. What Is HR's Role in Supporting Global Business? (pp. 549–551)

Objective: Define HR's role in supporting global business.

Summary: As more and more businesses become involved in globalization, HR is increasingly asked to prepare employees for working abroad through workforce development initiatives. HR professionals can help expatriate employees succeed by providing one-on-one support in the form of executive coaching. Additionally, the best HR teams contribute to the creation of leadership development programs that help people learn to work in cultures that differ from their own.

6. What Opportunities Exist in Emerging Markets? (pp. 533–548)

Objective: Learn about the opportunities that exist in emerging markets.

Summary: Four emerging markets—Brazil, Russia, India, and China—are collectively known as the BRIC countries. They have been identified as extremely important to the world economy. The first of these markets, Brazil, is enjoying its newfound prosperity as a result of increased political and economic stability, a growing agriculture and alternative-fuel industry, and its wealth of mineral reserves. Russia's well-educated populace and low wages have contributed to its growth. Like Russia, India's educated masses have proved advantageous to the economy, as has the overall English proficiency of its people and its growing middle class. Finally, China's low wages and benefit structure, low health care costs, and sheer population size have contributed to its success. Along with the positive changes these countries will bring to global business, they also bring a number of potential and very real challenges such as poverty, corruption, and problems with human rights.

8. **What Can We All Do to Succeed in a Global Environment?** (pp. 551–552)

Objective: List steps we can take to succeed in a global environment.

Summary: Knowing where personal, societal, and company ethics intersect with one another is one key to success in a global business environment. This knowledge makes it possible for you to perform your job in a way that does not compromise you or your company and does not clash with the culture in which you find yourself. It also provides you with a way to identify what might need to change—even with respect to your own values and ethics. It is also important to have strong emotional and social competencies—self-management, organizational awareness, and adaptability—when working as an expatriate.

9. **A Final Word on Globalization** (p. 552)

Summary: Globalization impacts both the personal and professional aspects of our lives, and is changing our needs, wants, and culture. The skills you learn today will help you lead in the global environment now and in the future.

CHAPTER 15

Sustainability and Corporate Social Responsibility:

Ensuring the Future

Karel Gallas/Shutterstock.com

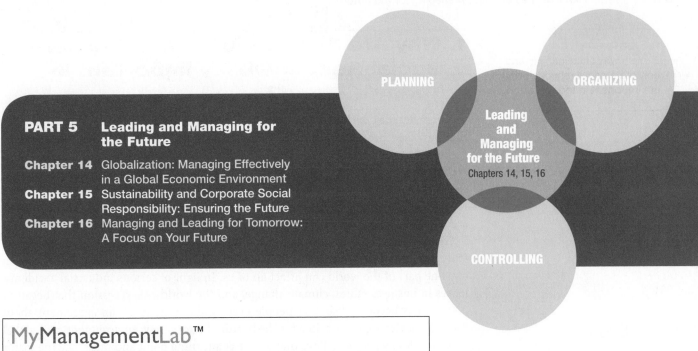

PLANNING

ORGANIZING

Leading
and
Managing
for the Future
Chapters 14, 15, 16

CONTROLLING

MyManagementLab™

⭐ Improve Your Grade!

Over 10 million students improved their results using the Pearson MyLabs.
Visit **mymanagementlab.com** for simulations, tutorials, and end-of-chapter
problems.

Chapter Outline

Chapter Objectives

15.1 Explain why sustainability and
corporate social responsibility
are important in today's world.

15.2 Define sustainability.

15.3 List and describe the three
pillars of sustainability.

15.4 Define environmental
sustainability.

15.5 Define social sustainability.

15.6 Define economic sustainability.

15.7 Define corporate social
responsibility.

15.8 List steps companies can take
to be socially responsible.

15.9 Define HR's role in sustainability
and corporate social
responsibility.

15.10 Describe steps you can take
to support sustainability and
corporate social responsibility.

559

Objective 15.1
Explain why sustainability and corporate social responsibility are important in today's world.

1. Why Are Sustainability and Corporate Social Responsibility Important in Today's World?

In recent decades, we have witnessed environmental, technological, and social changes that have had profound effects on individuals, families, communities, and governments. These changes have affected the ways in which businesses and organizations are designed, organized, managed, and led—as well as the ways in which people do their jobs and relate to one another at work. Technology has sparked a communication revolution, economies have become global, and previously underdeveloped countries are industrializing at an incredible pace.

Massive social changes continue, and one thing has become crystal clear: We are truly interconnected and the actions of individuals, institutions, and businesses in any one part of the world can affect all of us. In light of serious industrial accidents, lapses in business ethics, climate change, and the worldwide recession that began in 2007, it has become clear that people everywhere must reach an agreement about how businesses are responsible for the health of our society, environment, and global economy. Many people believe that we are at a turning point and must face the major challenges of our day head-on—especially the threats of climate change and global warming. The call for increased social responsibility designed to support the health and well-being of the natural environment, people and societies, and businesses is greater now than ever before. So, although we often derive great benefit from the products and services businesses provide, we must also figure out how businesses can support sustainability and social responsibility.

In this chapter, we explore how organizations and individuals are approaching the closely related topics of sustainability and social responsibility. Sustainability is a word associated with practices that support the future, as well as the present. Social responsibility is the phrase used to describe the role businesses, institutions, and people can have in creating and maintaining the health and well-being of communities. The chapter begins with a more substantial definition of sustainability, followed by a brief look at the history of this practice and the primary reasons why sustainability is important today. Next, we introduce and examine the three "pillars of sustainability"—environmental, social, and economic sustainability.[1] After that, our focus turns to corporate social responsibility, including ways that organizations have integrated this idea into their daily operations. Finally, the chapter concludes with a look at what HR can do to support sustainability and social responsibility at work, as well as what we all can do to ensure that our organizations and communities are positioned for success both today *and* tomorrow.

Discussion Questions

1. List some of the major environmental, technological, and social changes that have occurred in the past five years. Focus on changes that have implications for issues of sustainability and corporate social responsibility. How do they affect your school or workplace?

2. Research a recent environmental disaster that resulted from a lapse in ethical decision making by the leaders of a large organization. What were the repercussions of the leaders' actions? How did the disaster affect the local people? How did the organization respond to the crisis? What could the leaders of the organization have done differently to avoid this catastrophe?

2. What Is Sustainability?

Objective 15.2
Define sustainability.

Sustainability means different things to different people. In fact, there are more than 350 documented definitions of *sustainability* and *sustainable development*.[2] One of the most popular definitions comes from the United Nations (UN), which describes sustainability as "the process of meeting present needs without compromising the ability of future generations to meet their needs."[3] Notice that this definition includes a focus on time. Looking at sustainability in this way allows us to consider how our current activities impact the health of our social and ecological systems in the short term and in the more distant future.

Sustainability
As defined by the United Nations, the process of meeting present needs without compromising the ability of future generations to meet their needs.

People Have Been Practicing Sustainability for Generations

Although it's become a hot topic in recent years, sustainability is hardly a new idea. The concept can be traced back to prehistoric times, when our ancient ancestors recognized that biodiversity had to be maintained and the consumption and replenishment of resources had to be balanced if humans were to survive.

Before the rise of agriculture, our ancestors were hunters and gatherers. Whenever resources became scarce, perhaps because of too much foraging or hunting, tribes might move to prevent starvation and to preserve the area for the future. Some early peoples were nomadic, following the migratory routes of their animal prey or traveling in search of better weather, water supplies, and grazing lands. When these nomadic bands became too large for the available resources, members often splintered off to form new groups.

Then, about 10,000 years ago, the development of agriculture led to the gradual development of population-dense cities, as well as increases in the overall population.[4] As resources became more scarce, competing tribes sometimes fought wars so they could lay claim to particularly desirable pieces of land. Sometimes, multiple tribes formed loose confederations in an attempt to work out territorial rights and join together to fight off outside invaders.[5]

We know these things because artifacts from that time have been discovered, and because some tribes and nomadic bands still exist today, using technologies that have remained relatively unchanged for hundreds or even thousands of years.[6] For instance, not many years ago the Dani tribes of New Guinea engaged in warfare to help the tribe to maintain control over available resources. Today, aspects of these warlike practices still exist, although they are now ritualistic. Similarly, the semi-nomadic Maasai people, who inhabit regions of the Rift Valley in present-day Kenya and Tanzania, were historically known as fierce warriors. Partly to maintain balance with natural resources, they often displaced other groups through warfare.[7] Today, however, the Maasai are pastoral and live off their cattle, while also maintaining ceremonies and traditions that celebrate values related to balancing their human needs with the needs of their environment.[8]

The Maasai have developed an incredibly fine-tuned, symbiotic relationship with their animals, although in times of drought or disease, they have had to turn to hunting or agriculture to survive.[9] In part because of their ability to manage themselves and their environment, the Maasai have been able to maintain their sustainable way of life, despite two centuries of some of the most intense imperialist pressures of any region in the world.[10] Still, even this healthy balance is threatened today. Increasing reliance on trade with the outside world has made the future of the Maasai culture uncertain, largely because this reliance threatens the precarious balance between people, neighboring tribes, and the environment.[11]

Four Key Reasons Why Sustainability Is Important Today

Today, of course, sustainability means more than simply ensuring that we have adequate food and water or that our populations can be supported by the immediate environment. The question of sustainability has been brought into stark relief by at least four major issues that have captured our attention in recent years:

1. Climate change and the potential effects of this change on people, businesses, communities, and countries
2. A profound shift in economic power as countries and regions industrialize and join the world economy
3. Massive lapses of judgment and unethical business practices that have ruined many people's lives and brought formerly great companies to their knees
4. A global economic crisis that became obvious by about 2007. This happened, in part, because changes in key financial policies in certain parts of the world.

The following sections examine each of these factors in greater detail.

1. CLIMATE CHANGE, GLOBAL WARMING, AND SUSTAINABILITY

Changes in Earth's climate affect the planet's entire ecosystem. When temperatures rise or fall by even a degree or two, water levels change and weather patterns are altered, resulting in stress on the ecosystem. Thousands of species struggle, while only a handful tend to thrive during such times. Therefore, the threat of climate change—and global warming in particular—represents a potential challenge to humankind's ability to live and thrive on planet Earth.

But what is global warming, and how might it affect us and our planet's ecosystem? The term **global warming** is used to describe a fairly recent increase in the temperature of Earth's lower atmosphere (the air we breathe) and the land and water that make up Earth's surface. The causes and effects of global warming are matters of heated international debate. To better understand this debate, let's first consider several elements of the controversy.

One position holds that the gradual warming and cooling of the global climate is a regular and natural occurrence. Throughout human history, there have been many significant changes in global climate, such as the Ice Age and the thaw that followed it. Notable changes also happened during the "little ice age," which began around 1300 and lasted into the nineteenth century, ending around the same time that the Industrial Revolution went into high gear.[12] Those who argue that current warming of our atmosphere is natural cite solar changes and orbital cycles as the primary reasons behind the rise in temperatures.[13] However, many experts believe that these natural cycles would support a period of significant cooling today, as opposed to warming.[14] In addition, some proponents of this position point out that the results of global warming may not be as adverse as claimed by many media reports. People who support the solar change theory argue that humans have little or no impact on Earth's temperatures—and accordingly, they believe that government measures aimed at imposing stricter requirements on emissions, manufacturing practices, and waste control are unnecessary and even unfair to businesses.

On the other side of the global warming debate are those who argue that humans have indeed been responsible for much of the increase in Earth's temperatures (■ **EXHIBIT 15.1**). For example, the United Nations Intergovernmental Panel on Climate Change (IPCC) has published reports stating that current levels of global warming are the direct result of human activity.[15] Similarly, many scientists support the finding that human activity is contributing to "enhanced" greenhouse effect.[16] The **greenhouse effect** is a phrase that describes how air, water, and land temperatures are affected by

Global warming
Term used to describe a fairly recent increase in the temperature of Earth's lower atmosphere (the air we breathe) and the land and water that make up Earth's surface.

Greenhouse effect
Term used to describe how air, water, and land temperatures are affected by certain gases in Earth's atmosphere. These gases trap infrared energy, which leads to an increase in the planet's atmospheric and surface temperatures.

certain gases in Earth's atmosphere. These gases trap infrared energy, which leads to an increase in the planet's atmospheric and surface temperatures. Greenhouse gases include water vapor (the most prevalent), carbon dioxide, ozone, nitrous oxide, and methane, all of which occur naturally, to a certain extent. The greenhouse effect has occurred for eons, and we should all be grateful for it. Scientists estimate that without the greenhouse effect, vastly lower temperatures would render much of our planet uninhabitable.[17] Although it appears likely that the greenhouse effect contributes to global warming, just how much these trapped gases are affecting our climate is a point of debate.

Today, few people dispute that average temperatures are rising all across the planet. In fact, several agencies keep track of global temperatures, including NASA, whose data show that the five-year mean global surface air temperature has risen about 0.53°C since 1970. This increase is more than triple the temperature rise that occurred between 1900 and 1970.[18] Therefore, it's not the increase in temperatures but rather the *reasons* for and the *relative speed* of this increase that are a source of controversy.

■ **EXHIBIT 15.1**
Why is global warming such a hotly contested topic in the United States and across the globe?

Source: blickwinkel/Alamy

Whatever the cause of this rise in temperature, one fact remains: Our climate is getting warmer, and this will likely affect people's lives in numerous ways. This fact is quite obvious at this point, so the argument about how it happened is now accompanied by debates about what to do about it.

Potential Effects of Climate Change and Global Warming

How might climate change and global warming affect life in the years to come? In 2007, the IPCC identified a variety of current and potential impacts of global warming, as outlined in ■ **EXHIBIT 15.2**.[19]

Changes like the ones listed in Exhibit 15.2 may have already begun, and if so, they will have a profound effect on individuals, communities, and nations, not to mention businesses and other organizations. In addition, even if these sorts of changes don't happen in the near future, widespread public concern about their eventual possibility means that companies and government officials are wise to consider climate issues when making long-term decisions. But thinking about these topics is not the responsibility of business and political leaders alone.

Facing the Threat of Climate Change and Global Warming: It's Up to All of Us

Who is responsible for dealing with the threat of climate change? Scientists? The United Nations? Government leaders? Businesses and organizations? Most likely, the answer is "all of the above"—plus each one of us. That's because it will take all of us to find solutions for the many challenges we face.

For example, the human population is increasing rapidly, which means there are more people cutting down trees for farmland and burning fuel to cook and heat their homes. A growing population means there is increased demand for energy—more electricity for homes and businesses, more oil and gas for cars and machines, and so on. In turn, as energy consumption rises and developing nations industrialize, greenhouse gases will likely be produced at an alarming rate.

■ **EXHIBIT 15.2**

Current and Potential Effects of Global Warming

Effects on the Ecosystem

- Climate change could potentially alter many ecosystems, and some researchers predict that it will bring disturbances such as floods, droughts, fires, insect overpopulation, and acidic oceans.

- An estimated 20 to 30 percent of plant and animal species may face the threat of extinction if global average temperature increases exceed 1.5° to 2.5°C.

- Global warming may trigger changes in water quality that will likely have an adverse effect on many freshwater species and their ecosystems.

Effects on Food Supplies

- In mid- and higher-latitude regions, crop yields will likely increase with a rise in average temperature. However, in lower-latitude regions, this yield will likely decrease, especially in drier and more tropical climates. In turn, decreased crop outputs in these areas may increase the risk of famine.

- Overall food production is predicted to rise with an increase in temperature of 1° to 3°C but decrease at temperatures in excess of this amount.

Effects on Coastlines

- Many researchers estimate that global warming will increase rates of coastal erosion due to rising sea levels. Human land use may exacerbate this phenomenon.

- By the late twenty-first century, yearly floods are predicted to affect millions more people, particularly in densely populated river deltas and on small islands.

Effects on Industry and Associated Populations

- According to many researchers, coastal industries and populations, as well as areas of rapid urban development, will likely be most vulnerable to the negative effects of climate change. This seems particularly true for industries and societies that are economically dependent on resources that are sensitive to disruptions caused by global warming.

- Impoverished communities in high-risk areas are predicted to be most vulnerable overall.

Effects on Health

- Increased malnutrition, diseases, injuries, and deaths may occur as a result of extreme weather events. Higher concentrations of ground-level ozone might increase the prevalence of cardiorespiratory diseases. Diarrheal diseases may also become more common.

- Should Earth's climate become warmer, the range and infectiousness of some diseases (e.g., malaria) are expected to increase, in part because warmer temperatures provide a more hospitable environment for many insects and pathogens.

- Fewer deaths and injuries due to exposure to extreme cold are expected.

Effects on Water Supplies

- Should climate change, population growth, and urbanization continue, water resources will likely be increasingly stressed.

- Water resources in the form of mountain snowpacks and glaciers have already been reduced, and this reduction is predicted to accelerate, which could lead to a drop in freshwater availability.

- Changes in rainfall and temperature patterns could result in a 10 to 40 percent increase in runoff in high latitudes and wet tropical regions, whereas a 10 to 30 percent decrease is expected in dry, mid-latitude regions and the dry tropics. Semi-arid regions will likely lose water resources, which could adversely affect farming, energy, and health.

- Up to 20 percent of Earth's population could live in areas with high flood potential by the end of twenty-first century.

- Water quality and drinkability are predicted to decrease. Groundwater is predicted to rise in salinity.

Source: Adapted from IPCC's *Climate Change 2007.*

2. THE RISE OF NEW ECONOMIES, SHIFTS IN ECONOMIC POWER, AND SUSTAINABILITY

Economic growth in newly and rapidly developing nations is, of course, profoundly good for the world and its people and can lead to more sustainable societies everywhere. Economic growth leads to better quality of life for countless people. On the other hand, the massive growth in emerging nations increases the already substantial strain on forests, waterways, land, air, and fossil fuels. While it is not impossible for new economies to adopt a sustainable approach from the start, it can be extremely expensive. This cost eats into the profits generated by these economies, which in turn slows the growth process.[20]

There are quite heated debates on the international stage about how much developing nations should strive to meet the same standards that many developed nations have agreed to vis-a-vis reducing things like pollution from fossil fuels. One side of the argument: Global warming and pollution of all sorts are a threat to us all, and we now have some ways to alleviate the problems, so all nations should do their utmost. On the other side of the argument: Many Western nations industrialized with no constraints whatsoever, and are still primary users of fossil fuels and major polluters—why should developing nations pay for past mistakes and not have the same opportunities to grow?[21]

To help alleviate these growing pains and accelerate sustainable development, the United Nations champions the concept of development cooperation. Development cooperation aims to engage nations, policymakers, philanthropic groups, and the private sector in efforts to make sustainable development more accessible and more affordable to new economies.[22] The goal of development cooperation is to empower developing nations and their citizens to achieve their economic goals while simultaneously building policies that address important social and environmental issues. Many initiatives exist that support this goal; however, most of these fall short of their natural resource preservation and poverty alleviation targets.[23]

There are a number of reasons why development cooperation initiatives aren't reaching their goals, two of which are particularly problematic: Governments of developing nations have a hard time changing the status quo and many of the world's developed economies have not adopted many principles and policies that lead to economic, social, or environmental sustainability.

The Status Quo: Business as Usual

Indonesia offers a good example of the difficulty associated with changing the status quo when it comes to monitoring and curbing practices that harm the environment and overall sustainability efforts. Indonesia has been aggressively pursuing development for decades, resulting in nearly half of Indonesia's forests being stripped since the 1970s. The logging industry is the nation's largest producer of greenhouse gases.[24] What is the right course of action: stopping deforestation or supporting logging (and the economic development it has supported?). Indonesia is currently facing pressure from the United Nations to decrease its greenhouse gas emissions, and national leaders want to make that happen. However, these same leaders face pressure to maintain Indonesia's six percent growth rate and continue to expand its workforce.

The United Nation climate control program—known as Reducing Emissions from Deforestation and Forest Degradation (REDD)—aims to cut greenhouse gas emissions by slowing deforestation and channeling aid money to participating governments. Indonesian officials are attempting to enact REDD, but face problems associated with illegal logging. This long-standing problem is difficult to regulate, and there are simply not enough enforcement agents to stem the tide.[25]

Leaders of developing nations are keenly aware of these types of problems and understand the uphill battle involved with changing business as usual in their nations. African leaders face some of the same problems as Indonesian leaders, and Liberian President Ellen Johnson Sirleaf has described it as necessary "to conceptualize new approaches on how to account for, how to integrate every aspect of our national development policies. Increasingly, one of the imperatives of any sustainable development is to strike the right balance between our current needs and our global future."[26]

Greening the World and Building Sustainable Societies Everywhere

Sustainability is a concern for all economies—not just newly developing economies. Unfortunately, as much as world leaders agree that sustainable initiatives are essential in today's global environment, they cannot reach consensus on how best to enact new programs and practices on a global scale. Everyone agrees that change is needed, but the potential impacts of those changes on citizens and industry make many leaders hesitate before committing their countries to change. So, heated debates continue about whether developed or developing nations should shoulder more of the sustainability burden.

Caroline Spelman, UK Secretary of State for the Environment, Food and Natural Affairs succinctly summed up this situation: "Sustainability is not fully integrated into economic decision-making. The world's economy needs to be greened."[27] Spelman believes that the best way for governments—no matter their stage of development—to truly engage in this process is for the business community to prioritize sustainability. Ideally, this move by business leaders will show that sustainability is what industry wants and needs. This, in turn, will prompt governments to enact the right laws and pursue the right sustainability initiatives.[28] Given the global nature of many businesses, this could lead to better integration of sustainability practices around the world.

Beyond pursuing sustainability, companies—regardless of the economies in which they exist—face another change that relates directly to how they operate: Business practices today are instantaneously visible to millions of people—each of whom has an opinion about right and wrong.

3. THE CALL FOR BUSINESS ETHICS AND SOCIAL RESPONSIBILITY

In recent years, the public has learned of countless scandals in companies that once seemed to be positive contributors to the economy and to society in general. The list of such companies and the people who led them astray is lengthy: Enron, Tyco, Arthur Andersen, Parmalat, Bernie Madoff, News of the World, and J.P. Morgan Stanley are just a few examples. The list goes on and on—as does the list of companies whose practices have been questioned in recent years, even when no criminal activities took place. For instance, the public questioned Apple as to whether children were working in Chinese factories owned by its suppliers. Unfortunately, in 2011, the answer to this question was yes.[29] Businesses and institutions of all kinds rise and fall based on the moral, ethical, and legal actions of individuals. More importantly, untold human suffering is the result of these transgressions, as was made painfully clear when formerly idolized Penn State coach Jerry Sandusky was convicted of sexually abusing young boys.

Unfortunately, we don't need to look very hard to find examples of practices that are illegal, unethical, or both. For example, Walmart's labor practices and compensation scheme have come under public scrutiny over the years. In 2004, a report outlining several unethical and illegal labor practices in Walmart's stores in California was published by the United States House of Representatives Committee on Education and the Workforce. The report included assertions that employees were forced to skip breaks, paid wages that kept them below the poverty level, encouraged to seek welfare, and denied health insurance. In addition, there was strong evidence that Walmart's unfair labor practices targeted women, who were paid significantly less than men and underrepresented in management positions. The report concluded that a 200-employee Walmart store actually cost the government more than $420,000 a year in subsidized housing, health care, utilities, low-income tax credits, and meals.[30] As of 2012, Walmart stores in 17 U.S. states led the private sector in the number of employees on welfare. Walmart, along with many other organizations, has struggled to find ways to provide health insurance to workers. To date, this has resulted in changes in policies such that full-time employees have access to more flexible benefits than in the past.[31]

Yet another recent controversy involved the question of whether Yahoo! revealed to the Chinese government the identity of its Chinese users, including dissidents, while they were residing outside mainland China. Again, this really did happen, which caused human rights groups to question the company's role in supporting government censorship.[32]

One particularly devastating controversy involved subprime mortgage lending in the United States. Subprime mortgages are loans to people who may have difficulty repaying them. Prior to 2007, many U.S. banks engaged in this kind of lending; unfortunately, when issues with these loans came to a head, they created problems that were felt around the world. Not only did the American housing market collapse, but markets, funds, and banks around the world were impacted by widespread investments in bonds that were backed by these loans.[33] The end result was financial turmoil and recession that had devastating impacts on individuals, businesses, and economies across the globe. This topic will be explored in more depth in the next section.

Questionable practices and scandals like these have soured many individuals on business. More and more often, stakeholders do not want to support companies that pollute rivers, steal from investors, or fail to give back to the community in meaningful ways. Likewise, employees do not want to work for companies that are engaged in unethical or unsustainable business practices. Most of us would cringe if we found out, for example, that our company is actively destroying the Brazilian rain forest, dumping waste, or hiring children to work in its factories.

Some debate surrounds the topic of whether companies and their leaders are engaging in a greater number of unethical or questionable practices now than in the past. The answer to this question is unclear. What is clear is that almost everything a company does can be discovered and shared around the world within a matter of seconds. In the past, workers (and perhaps their unions) were often the only groups directly challenging businesses' practices. Today, however, millions of people are involved in discussions about companies' labor policies, working conditions, environmental impact, and executive compensation.

People care what companies do, and they care a lot. Individuals far removed from businesses can and do weigh in with opinions and demands for practices that result in long-term sustainability. This has become increasingly apparent in recent years, as business leaders have been called on to take responsibility for the conditions that resulted in the recession that began in 2007—a global economic crisis of a magnitude not seen since the Great Depression. Let's take a closer look at what happened.

4. THE GREAT RECESSION

The global economic crisis that began in 2007 exploded in 2008, causing an untold amount of damage to individuals, families, businesses, not-for-profit organizations, governments, communities, and countries. This crisis was caused by many factors, including the widespread financial industry practice of approving subprime mortgages. There is no doubt that the economic crisis was and continues to be harmful—devastating, in fact, for the many people who lost their jobs, homes, and life savings. However, there might be a silver lining of sorts. In particular, the crisis was so bad, and business's role in it was so clear, that it is now apparent that companies must adopt a different outlook on their role in society.

Niall FitzGerald is a world-renowned leader who understands how important it is for individuals—and for businesses—to recognize how interconnected we all are, and what this means in terms of leadership and responsibility. Among his many accomplishments, FitzGerald was chairman of Unilever, a global consumer goods company, from 1996 through 2004. During this period, the company fundamentally remade itself—reducing its number of brands, changing its marketing strategy, and focusing explicitly on environmental sustainability and corporate social responsibility.

In 2006, FitzGerald spearheaded the Investment Climate Facility for Africa, a not-for-profit organization that supports economic development in that continent.[34] Today, FitzGerald serves as chairman of the board of Hakluyt, a security company of the British Museum. FitzGerald understands business and finance, and he also knows what it means to work in today's interconnected world. This is an example of what he has to say about rebuilding trust in business:

> I believe the economic events [related to the recession that began in 2007] have brought the business world to a crossroads. If business is to recover, it is vital that we choose the right turn. . . . [This crisis] invites us to create a business world in which the world can have future trust and confidence, to rebuild our business institutions on stronger and sustainable foundations. . . . I believe that social responsibility has to become a core value of the business, a central tenet that affects the way it works. . . . Businesses should be explicit about these values and ensure that all employees understand that they will be judged on their contribution to this core value of social responsibility as much as they are judged on such things as production and sales.[35]

As FitzGerald points out, companies can no longer justify their performance based solely on financial figures. Today's best leaders know that the decisions they make can have far-reaching effects—and that their actions impact people, communities, and ecosystems far beyond the walls of their corporate offices. Sustainability and corporate social responsibility are therefore much more than faddish buzzwords: They are philosophies that are here to stay, and they will increasingly impact how we conduct business. Warren Buffet, one of the most brilliant leaders in the world, argues that what's bad for the environment is bad for the bottom line.[36] In the following sections, we will discuss sustainability in greater depth, focusing on the "three pillars" of this practice: environmental sustainability, social sustainability, and economic sustainability.

Discussion Questions

1. Choose a major global business and analyze global warming's effects on it to date, considering social, political, and financial factors. Next, consider how climate change may affect this company or industry during the next five years.

2. Conduct a five-minute search on the Internet of business ethics issues in the news recently. How many can you find? Are there any similarities shared across the group? For example, are concerns focused largely on one industry? Are the complaints similar in any way?

Objective 15.3
List and describe the three pillars of sustainability.

Environmental sustainability
Term that refers to the preservation of environmental resources and biodiversity, creation of sustainable access to safe drinking water, and enhancement of quality of life among the most impoverished.

3. What Are the Three Pillars of Sustainability?

The United Nations describes "three pillars of sustainability": environmental sustainability, social sustainability, and economic sustainability.[37] In this model, **environmental sustainability** means preservation of environmental resources and biodiversity, creation of sustainable access to safe drinking water, and enhancement of quality of life among the most impoverished.[38] **Social sustainability** refers to the improvement of daily life for the greatest number of people through improving fair income distribution; promoting gender equality; ensuring equal access to land ownership, employment, and education; investing in basic health and education; and enlisting the participation of beneficiaries.[39] Finally, **economic sustainability** is "an economy's capacity to regularly produce outcomes consistent with long-term [economic development]."[40] The UN model, illustrated in
■ **EXHIBIT 15.3**, is extremely valuable when considering how businesses and

organizations must think about sustainability.[41] As a way to introduce you to these three topics, consider the following examples:

1. **Environmental Sustainability and the Deepwater Horizon Oil Spill in the Gulf of Mexico**

   During the spring of 2010, an explosion on an offshore oil drilling platform owned and operated by British Petroleum (BP) in the Gulf of Mexico killed 11 people and injured 17 others. The environmental impacts of what's now called the Deepwater Horizon oil spill have been tremendous. The spill, which released around 5 million barrels of oil, found its way ashore from Texas to Florida. Birds as far away as Minnesota showed signs of being contaminated with oil two years after the spill.[43] The potential revenue from the estimated 50–100 million barrels of oil in the Macondo Prospect, where the spill occurred, would only make up a fraction of the costs of repairing the environmental damage.[44] By mid-2012, BP had already spent more as a result of the spill than the value of the entire field.

2. **Social Sustainability and Social Security Program Karnataka (SSPK)**

   One province in India, Karnataka is tackling poverty directly through a bold program called Social Security Program Karnataka (SSPK). SSPK is supported by the national government, local governments and the Deutsche Gesellschaft für Internationale Zusammenarbeit. This program is led by Hans-Christoph Ammon of GIZ and supported by capacity development specialist Jalajakshi Krishnappa, and socio-economic researcher Jochen Lohmeier. SSPK seeks to inform citizens about existing social sustainability programs which many people do not know about or have difficulty applying for. SSPK facilitators:

   - Reach out and build trusting relationships with citizens so that information can be shared and collected about peoples' needs and existing government programs
   - Assist people in applying for programs and assistance
   - Follow up on applications with officials so that the public can claim social services.

   In summary, SSPK supports social sustainability by focusing on people's needs today, while also focusing on the future. According to Jochen Lohmeier, "Sustainability does not mean everything stays the same. It means doing things today that avoid short term gains at the expense of the future. Social sustainability relates to the sustainability of social dynamics and relations. Different groups of a society have different needs and require specifically adjusted schemes. And many societies have different cultures, the change of which may be unavoidable but needs to be managed with respect and care for ownership."[45]

3. **Economic Sustainability and Norwegian Policies**

   Norway has remained incredibly resilient through the global economic recession and the subsequent economic crises confronting the Eurozone and most of the rest of Europe. Norway has been addressing economic sustainability on a number of fronts. The country established an institutional framework that includes rules for regulating its huge oil and gas revenues. While the country is dependent on oil and gas revenues, Norway is also working on the development and use of Carbon Capture and Storage (CCS) technology and investing in new renewable energies to ensure long-term economic sustainability.[46]

At no time in history has the topic of sustainability been taken up as globally and as powerfully as today, and business is a leader in this conversation. That's because there is growing recognition that no company is an island and that the social, economic, and environmental spheres are indelibly linked. Negative effects to the environment can adversely affect economic stability, and these events can cause social upheaval if they are harmful enough. For example, imagine what would happen if a natural disaster destroyed many oil production facilities. Certainly, gas prices would be sky-high, people

■ **EXHIBIT 15.3**
The Intersection of Social, Environmental and Economic Sustainability Results in Optimal Conditions.[42]

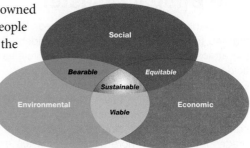

Source: Based on a report from the United Nations World Summit on Sustainable Development, August 26–September 4, 2002. Retrieved May 27, 2010, from http://www.un.org/events/wssdsummaries/envdevj8.htm.

Social sustainability
Term that refers to the improvement of daily life for the greatest number of people through improving fair income distribution; promoting gender equality; ensuring equal access to land ownership, employment, and education; investing in basic health and education; and enlisting the participation of beneficiaries.

Economic sustainability
Term that refers to an economy's capacity to regularly produce outcomes consistent with long-term economic development.

The Bhopal Disaster

On the night of December 3, 1984, near Bhopal, India, more than 40 tons of deadly toxins were accidentally released into the atmosphere. These chemicals were released from a pesticide plant owned by the American company Union Carbide Corporation and operated by Union Carbide India Limited, its Indian subsidiary.[47] The nearly half-million people who lived in Bhopal at the time were immediately exposed to a variety of harmful chemicals, including methyl isocyanate gas, which degrades into an even more deadly gas when exposed to high temperatures like those present in the plant.

In the aftermath of the disaster, many Bhopal residents suffered from cyanide poisoning.[48] Officials put the death toll at fewer than 4,000 people, but other estimates suggest that roughly 25,000 eventually died.[49] Those victims who died first were the poor who lived in the slums adjacent to the plant. Of course, the cyanide gas that was released from the factory didn't just kill humans; pets, wildlife, and livestock, including cattle—which are sacred to Hindu people—also died.[50]

The Bhopal disaster precipitated a number of long-term actions. In the spring of 1985, India passed the Bhopal Gas Leak Disaster Act, making the government the "sole representative of the victims in legal proceedings both within and outside India," and it eventually had all claims filed in the United States transferred to India.[51] The court-recognized official death toll was only around 3,000, so the settlement of $470 million did not include many of the people who died later, and it recognized only 102,000 victims who had permanent disabilities. More recent estimates suggest that the long-term injury total is over 500,000.[52] Even today, the long-term effects of the disaster result in an estimated 4,000 daily visits to health clinics in the Bhopal region. In June 2010, more than 25 years after the Bhopal disaster, former officials were convicted of criminal negligence, leading the Prime Minister of India to set up a new Bhopal panel to examine the fairness of the settlement.[53]

Union Carbide's Bhopal factory was closed in 1985 and 1986, and some of the facility's equipment was subsequently cleaned and sold. However, many toxic materials were left on site, where they continue to infiltrate the soil and water. Because the area around the plant was used as a toxic dumping ground, the water there is toxic to fish, and there is evidence that the groundwater supply has been contaminated by a long list of chemicals. Lead, mercury, and organochlorines have been detected in the breast milk of nursing mothers.[54]

In addition, some of the many poisons found in and around the former factory cause mutations, which means they have affected subsequent generations of humans and animals with various diseases and deformities.[55] Some 30 years after the incident, the region's high court finally ruled to have the more than 350 metric tons of toxic waste removed through incineration.[56] This is a promising development, but it comes far too late for the thousands of people and animals who suffered, as well as the land, water, and vegetation that won't recover for many years.

---

would suffer economically, and this could cause social unrest. Or, consider the short- and long-term effects of the BP oil well disaster in the Gulf of Mexico in 2010. This situation has and will continue to affect water, sea life, coastal biodiversity, and people's livelihoods. The disaster also sparked heated social debate about oil companies' responsibility for preventing such catastrophes. Similarly, the tsunami in Sendai in northern Japan destabilized the Fukushima Daiichi Nuclear Power Plant in the neighboring Fukushima Prefecture. The result was dangerously high levels of radiation, widespread criticism of the nuclear power industry, and questions about the Japanese government's involvement in withholding key information about the disaster from the public. Closer to home, in 2012 hurricane Sandy devastated parts of the east coast of the U.S., leaving people without power, homes destroyed, and many businesses unable to engage in trade or the provision of services.[57] Let's look at the *Business Case* to explore another far-reaching disaster: what happened in Bhopal, India, where an accident and lax standards resulted in devastation for the natural environment and for thousands of people.

As the Bhopal example shows, sustainability is not just about avoiding disasters. It is also about business practices that attend to environmental, social, and economic concerns while simultaneously maintaining the profitability and viability of the organizations to which they belong. Without these kinds of business practices, great and devastating consequences can occur.

Tracking Companies That Focus on Sustainability

The Global 100 Most Sustainable Corporations in the World is a project that attempts to track and measure business activities and identify those companies whose approach to sustainability is outstanding. According to Global 100's Web site, this tracking is reflective of the organization's belief structure:

> We believe that a company's ability to manage its extra-financial aspects, such as those related to environmental, labour, and human rights, is a powerful proxy and a leading indicator for its overall management quality. Management quality, in turn, is the single greatest determinant of companies' financial performance. The aim of this initiative is thus to promote better managed and better performing corporations regarding sustainability issues.[58]

In 2012, the Global 100 list included companies such as Novo Nordisk, Intel, Adidas, L'Oreal, Unilever, and GlaxoSmithKline. Sixteen companies based in the United Kingdom made the list, followed by twelve companies from Japan and eight companies each from the United State and France. The Global 100 is not the only group that tracks companies' sustainability records, however. The Dow Jones also has an index, and *Newsweek* tracks companies headquartered in the United States. *Newsweek*'s top-five green companies for 2011 are listed in ■ **EXHIBIT 15.4**.

In the following sections, we will explore each of the three pillars of sustainability in some depth to see how people, communities, and companies alike can join the movement to promote environmental, social, and economic sustainability.

■ **EXHIBIT 15.4**

Newsweek's 2011 Top-Five Green U.S. Companies

1. *IBM* began supporting environmental policies in the early 1970s. With a strong focus on reducing carbon waste, the company has been awarded the EPA's Climate Protection Award twice and received a Climate Leadership Award in 2012. The company has also established corporate responsibility and environmental management guidelines for its suppliers.

2. *Hewlett-Packard* has created programs to help reduce greenhouse gas emissions throughout its entire supply chain. The company has also worked to decrease the number of harmful toxins in its products and, in 2009, launched an initiative to make its facilities more sustainable.

3. *Sprint Nextel* has launched four environmentally responsible mobile devices since 2009 and has developed an eco-logo to help customers identify such devices. Additionally, the company's manufacturing processes focus on emission reductions. Sprint is devoted to a further 15 percent reduction by 2017 as well as a 90 percent phone-collection recycling rate.

4. *Baxter* is a health care manufacturer that reduced its emissions by 7 percent during 2010 and kept increases in its energy use low. In fact, the company's energy consumption has only gone up by only 4 percent since 2005, even though Baxter's sales increased by 30 percent during that timeframe.

5. *Dell* launched a 2010 initiative to track and reduce the carbon footprint of its products and, in 2011, its manufacturing processes maintained a recycle and reuse rate of 95.7 percent. In addition, Dell has started using mushroom and bamboo packaging when shipping its products. This packaging is biodegradable and can be used as compost.

Source: Newsweek. October 16, 2011. America's Greenest Companies. Retrieved June 5, 2012, from http://www.thedailybeast.com/newsweek/2011/10/16/green-rankings-2011-america-s-greenest-companies-photos.html.

Discussion Questions

1. How does your school or company approach the three pillars of sustainability? Research and compile relevant data, such as information about mission statements, environmental programs, and community-service activities.

2. Do you think your school or company is doing enough in the area of social sustainability? Why or why not?

Objective 15.4
Define environmental
sustainability.

4. What Is Environmental Sustainability?

Many people believe that unless we find a way to ensure environmental sustainability, both social and economic sustainability are impossible. For that reason, we will explore the environmental aspect of sustainability in some depth. First, we will look at the history of the conservation and ecology movements in the United States—precursors to today's environmental movement—and we'll consider international agreements and some of the methods nations are currently using to curb greenhouse gas emissions. Then, we'll look at an *unsustainable* source of energy: fossil fuels. We will then discuss an economic model that is predicated on the exploration and use of alternative energy sources. Finally, we'll conclude the section with an exploration of how to deal with waste and pollution, sustainable practices that support animal and plant life, and some of the other ways that U.S. businesses and government are working to promote greater environmental sustainability.

The History of the Conservation and Ecology Movements in the United States

For well over a century, America's citizens, leaders, and philanthropists have recognized that land, water, and clean air are precious and need to be protected. From the 1800s through the present, numerous acts of Congress, as well as state and local ordinances, have been passed with the goal of protecting the country's land, timber, plants, animals, and waterways.

Land conservation in particular has a robust history in the United States. Yellowstone became the first protected national park in 1872.[59] Later, in 1897, the federal government set aside many areas as national forests, and in 1903, President Theodore Roosevelt created the United States' first wildlife refuge. Just over a decade later, the National Park Service was formed on August 25, 1916. Today, with a budget of just under $3 billion, the agency manages 84.4 million acres, including nearly 400 units of nationally protected land, 59 of which are national parks.[60]

U.S. citizens and governmental agencies did not stop their conservation efforts with the creation of parklands, however. By the middle of the twentieth century, it became clear that industrial pollution was seriously harming land, water, air, and people. Attention to pollution issues grew, partly because the growing number of televisions in American homes allowed people to see what was happening to natural resources all over the country. Thus, in 1970, the U.S. Environmental Protection Agency (EPA) was established in response to enormous public sentiment in favor of a cleaner environment.

Since its creation, the EPA has been charged with defining and enforcing specific controls and standards for industries and individual polluters. These controls are loosely based on "the best available and best achievable technology for each source of pollution in each industry."[61]

As you can see in ■ **EXHIBIT 15.5**, tremendous progress has been made in the years since 1970, with Americans currently focusing more attention and resources on protecting the environment than ever before.[62]

Among the EPA's efforts, one especially notable success has been the reduction of sulfur dioxide emissions from electric utility plants. This reduction was spurred in large part by the Clean Air Act Amendments of 1990, which set a cap on total sulfur dioxide emissions. Under the amendments, instead of requiring all power plants to meet a technology-based standard, the EPA allocated electric utilities a share of the maximum allowable national emissions amount. The utilities could then buy or sell emission allowances among themselves, depending on their individual needs. This program has worked well, reducing total control costs by an estimated $750 million

■ **EXHIBIT 15.5**

Timeline of the Environmental Movement in the United States Since 1970[63]

1970s

1970: Following celebration of the first Earth Day, the EPA is created. Congress amends the Clean Air Act so that air quality, automobile emission, and antipollution standards can be set and enforced.

1972: The EPA bans use of DDT, a dangerous pesticide that was implicated in the near extinction of the American bald eagle. The United States and Canada agree to improve water quality in the Great Lakes. The Clean Water Act is passed, thereby limiting the release of pollutants into U.S. waterways.

1973: Lead begins to be phased out of gasoline.

1974: The Safe Drinking Water Act is passed, and the EPA is charged with its regulation.

1975: Congress sets fuel economy and emissions standards for automobiles.

1976: Congress passes the Resource Conservation and Recovery Act, which regulates hazardous waste production and disposal. President Ford signs the Toxic Substances Control Act. The EPA begins to phase out production of PCB (a cancer-causing liquid used in numerous applications).

1977: President Carter signs an amendment strengthening the Clean Air Act.

1978: The federal government bans use of chlorofluorocarbons as propellants in aerosol sprays.

1979: The EPA bans PCB manufacture and begins to phase out use of these substances.

1980s

1980: Congress establishes Superfund, a federal program to clean up toxic sites. The program is operated by the EPA.

1982: Congress passes laws to clean asbestos from schools.

1983: Cleanup of the Chesapeake Bay gets under way. The EPA publicizes the dangers of radioactive radon gas and encourages testing.

1985: The EPA sets new limits on the use of lead in gasoline.

1986: Congress passes amendments to the Safe Drinking Water Act.

1987: The EPA mandates sanctions against individual states that fail to meet air quality standards.

1988: After medical and other waste begins washing up on shore in New York and New Jersey, Congress bans the dumping of industrial waste into the ocean.

1989: The accidental spill of 11 million gallons of oil in Alaskan waters leads to a public outcry.

1990s

1990: Congress passes more Clean Air Act amendments that require states to demonstrate progress in improving air quality. The EPA creates a Toxic Release Inventory that makes public which pollutants are being released into which communities. President Bush signs the Pollution Prevention Act.

1991: Federal agencies begin to use products that contain recycled components. The EPA launches a voluntary industry partnership to promote energy efficiency.

1993: The EPA begins a campaign against secondhand smoke. President Clinton orders the federal government to buy more recycled and environmentally friendly products.

1994: The EPA issues new emissions standards to reduce air pollution by over 500,000 tons per year.

1995: The EPA offers incentives to reduce sulfur dioxide emissions, which are a primary cause of acid rain.

1996: Suppliers of public drinking water are required to provide information about chemicals and microbes in the water they supply. President Clinton signs the Food Quality Protection Act, which tightens standards for pesticide content on food that is brought to market.

1997: The EPA implements the Food Quality Protection Act.

1998: President Clinton signs the Clean Water Action Plan to protect American waterways.

1999: New standards require auto emissions to be at least 77 percent cleaner. The EPA increases air quality standards for national parks and wilderness areas.

(continued)

■ **EXHIBIT 15.5** *(continued)*

Timeline of the Environmental Movement in the United States Since 1970

2000s

2000: The EPA establishes new regulations that require 90 percent cleaner diesel fuel engines.

2003: The EPA proposes regulation of mercury emissions for power plants.

2004: New ozone and fine particulate standards become effective across the country. Construction and farm engines are required to use cleaner fuels.

2005: The EPA establishes the Clean Air Interstate Rule.

2006: The EPA is the first federal agency to buy 100 percent of its energy from green power sources.

2008: The EPA drastically cuts locomotive and marine diesel pollution.

2009: The EPA officially finds that greenhouse gases endanger public health, which gives it authority to regulate emissions of these gases.

to $1.5 billion per year, while simultaneously meeting or exceeding goals for sulfur dioxide reduction. In recent years, similar programs have been proposed for various fluorocarbons, methane, and carbon emissions.[64]

The EPA is responsible for administering numerous laws, a few of which are described in ■ **EXHIBIT 15.6**. As the laws illustrate, supporting environmental sustainability means everything from addressing global warming to preventing accidents that harm the ecosystem—and innumerable other things that touch every aspect of business and daily life. Of particular interest to global leaders, businesses, and organizations are activities related to the reduction of greenhouse gas emissions.

■ **EXHIBIT 15.6**

Laws Administered Either Wholly or in Part by the EPA[65]

Law	EPA's Role in Administration
Atomic Energy Act (1946)	The EPA offers guidance for federal and state agencies that set radiation protection requirements. It also works with states to establish and administer radiation protection programs.
Clean Air Act (1970)	The EPA establishes and reviews emission standards for hazardous air pollutants.
Occupational Safety and Health Act (1970)	The EPA establishes standards for workplace health and safety and enforces compliance in all 50 states.
Clean Water Act (1972)	The EPA implements programs to control water pollution, including industry wastewater standards.
Superfund (1980)	The EPA cleans up toxic waste sites in all states and territories when the culprit cannot be identified or compelled to act.
Emergency Planning and Community Right-to-Know Act (1986)	The EPA oversees the emergency planning and notification activities of local governments and facilities. It also enforces community right-to-know rules regarding hazardous chemicals through the use of publicly available Material Safety Data Sheets (MSDS).
Executive Order 13045: Protection of Children from Environmental Health Risks and Safety Risks (1997)	The EPA evaluates the effectiveness of planned regulations related to environmental health or safety risks to children and recommends alternative approaches when necessary.
Executive Order 13211: Actions Concerning Regulations That Significantly Affect Energy Supply, Distribution, or Use (2001)	The EPA determines whether a regulatory action or activity is likely to significantly and adversely impact the supply, distribution, or use of energy.
Federal Food, Drug, and Cosmetic Act (2002)	The EPA is authorized to set maximum limits for the presence of pesticide residues on foods. Foods that exceed these limits are subject to seizure.

Reducing Greenhouse Gas Emissions: World Leaders Try to Agree on a Course of Action

Although among many of the world's leaders there is general consensus that regulating air, water, and ground pollution is in the best interests of the world's people, precisely what to regulate and how to regulate it has long been an area of controversy. This controversy has played out very publicly in meetings organized by the United Nations and other international bodies in an attempt to get world leaders to agree on a course of action for curbing the effects of greenhouse gases. Perhaps the most famous of these meetings was held in Kyoto, Japan, in 1997. More recent meetings have been organized almost every year.

THE KYOTO PROTOCOL

The Kyoto Protocol is an international agreement drafted during the 1997 United Nations Framework Convention on Climate Change for the purpose of supporting and enforcing the reduction of greenhouse gas emissions. Although the Kyoto Protocol recognizes that all nations must engage in activities to support this initiative, it places a heavier burden on developed nations. The rationale behind this decision was that developed nations are largely the cause of the current situation, and developing nations should not be prevented from advancing because of the financial burdens associated with greenhouse gas reduction.

Kyoto Protocol
An international agreement drafted during the 1997 United Nations Framework Convention on Climate Change for the purpose of supporting and enforcing the reduction of greenhouse gas emissions.

THE KYOTO TREATY: A SUMMARY OF MAJOR INITIATIVES

Under the Kyoto Protocol, a three-pronged approach to addressing global warming has been developed:[66]

1. Emissions trading (often called carbon trading or the carbon market), may be the best known outcome of the Kyoto Treaty (KT). Carbon trading includes limiting the amount of greenhouse gases (most notably, carbon) member countries can release into the atmosphere in a given period. If a country is producing more airborne carbon than it is allotted, it can buy emission credits from other countries that are producing less than their allotment. Within countries, businesses and industries can also participate in buying, selling, and trading emissions credits.

   During the past several years, the carbon trading model has been expanded to include what is commonly called cap and trade. Under the cap-and-trade plan, companies purchase annual emissions credits, and fewer credits are available each year.[67] The reduced supply drives up the cost of the credits, which encourages companies to create new business methods that do not result in the release of as many greenhouse gases. Cap-and-trade legislation is one component of a comprehensive bill passed by the U.S. House of Representatives in June 2009. In the United States, national limits for mercury and toxic air pollution from power plants have also been established, new fuel economy standards for cars and light trucks have been proposed, and the Climate and Clean Air Coalition to Reduce Short-Lived Climate Pollution has been launched as a global initiative.[68]

2. The Kyoto Protocol also created the clean development mechanism (CDM). Under the CDM, countries that are actively involved in an emission reduction or limitation commitment may start projects in developing countries to help those countries reduce emissions while also developing their industries and economies. The goal is to encourage sustainable development yet permit industrialized countries flexibility in how they meet their emission targets.[69]

3. Joint implementation (JI) projects are also an outcome of the KT. These projects were designed to allow Kyoto Protocol member countries to earn credits for helping reduce or remove emissions in another member nation—even a developed one.[70]

According to the Kyoto Protocol, developed nations were expected to monitor, report, and reduce their greenhouse gas emissions by 2012 relative to a 1990 baseline, or else they would face significant financial penalties. Reduction amounts varied by country, but the overall goal was a reduction of 5.2 percent. The total target reduction for the European Community, for example, was 8 percent; Japan's target was 6 percent; and the United States' was 7 percent.[71] The United States never ratified the KT, and by 2009 had increased carbon emissions from fossil fuels; similarly, Japan has seen an increase rather than a reduction in emissions. The European Community no longer exists as an organized body, but some former members—including the United Kingdom and Germany—met their individual emissions targets.[72]

RATIFICATION OF THE KYOTO TREATY

In 2009, 187 governing entities had signed and ratified the Kyoto Protocol, including 36 developed nations. Several countries had not signed the agreement, while others had signed but not ratified it. The United States was the only developed nation to fall into the latter category—in fact, the U.S. Congress has never even been asked to ratify the Kyoto Protocol. Why? The principal argument is that complying with the Kyoto Protocol would cripple the American economy, which other nations depend on. Also, there is tremendous debate about the heavier burden of responsibility placed on developed nations. For instance, 4 of the top 10 emitters—Brazil, Russia, India, and China (the BRIC nations)—are exempt from any emissions reductions under the protocol.[73] Many people consider this a significant problem, especially because China and India have the world's fastest rates of emissions growth.[74]

Another problem, some say, is that the protocol delays the impact of global warming by only a few years, yet it costs trillions to implement.[75] For these and other reasons, the U.S. Senate unanimously passed a resolution in 1997 stating that the United States should not sign a binding agreement that did not address emissions by developing nations.[76] Also, it's important to note that even though the United States has not ratified the Kyoto Protocol and Congress has not passed legislation on emissions reduction, many U.S. states have stringent guidelines and effective enforcement policies and practices. In fact, more than half the states have existing climate legislation, and California, the world's eighth-largest economy since 2008, has some of the most stringent legislation in the world.[77]

Although debate continues as to what each country, community, and business must do to curb global warming, the problem of climate change is becoming more pronounced. Thus, in 2009, the world's leaders and scientists have met numerous times to try to iron out a new agreement and further the cause of reducing greenhouse gas emissions.

THE UNITED NATIONS CLIMATE CHANGE CONFERENCES POST-KYOTO

Many important climate change conferences have been sponsored by the UN since Kyoto. For example, in 2009, world leaders met in Copenhagen to produce a framework for mitigating the effects of climate change beyond the year 2012.[78]

The fact that the U.S. federal government had not passed legislation on emissions reduction or ratified the Kyoto Protocol weighed against the United States as discussions began. In fact, China and other developing countries started the summit by strongly criticizing wealthy developed countries, including the United States, the European Union, and Japan, for setting themselves low targets for emissions reduction. In response, the EU proposed a 20 percent cut, and Japan proposed a 25 percent cut but made it contingent on legally binding cuts from developing nations.[79]

Meanwhile, President Obama expressed U.S. commitment to reduce emissions 17 percent from 2005 levels by 2020. While even these aggressive targets were not met with enthusiasm, especially from developing countries, other news was seen as extremely promising.[80] In particular, the United States announced that the EPA now officially recognizes six greenhouse gases, including carbon dioxide, as dangerous pollutants and hazards to human health. The official identification of these gases as dangerous to health allows the EPA to develop emissions standards for industry and automobiles, bypassing Congress in the process.[81]

Despite some progress, by the end of the conference, international media had concluded that the summit faced significant problems.[82] Much of the trouble resulted from strenuous opposition from developing countries to the efforts and promises of developed nations, as well as their fear that the Kyoto Protocol would be abandoned in favor of more stringent demands on countries that were exempt from its requirements.[83]

When talks broke down, the United States, China, India, South Africa, and Brazil met privately and developed an agreement known as the Copenhagen Accord, which recognizes the importance of keeping temperature increases below 2°C without outlining what commitments are required to meet that goal. This agreement also contains a pledge of U.S. $30 billion to developing nations over three years.[84] The accord has been widely criticized, including by some of the countries that signed it. Critics say one major flaw is the nonbinding nature of the agreement.[85] In other words, it is not enforceable.

Following the Copenhagen talks, France withdrew from the Kyoto Protocol. In 2011, Canada renounced the protocol. Japan and Russia stated that they would not take on further Kyoto targets.[86] The Kyoto Protocol, scheduled to end in 2012, was negotiated in 2011 at the South African climate talks and again in Qatar in 2012, extending it to 2015. However, the May 2012 climate talks in Bonn ended without a clear path forward and many unresolved issues. In particular, the goal of the Bonn talks was to work out plans to negotiate a new global climate treaty to succeed the Kyoto Protocol in 2015 and to be fully enacted by 2020.[87]

As you can see, reducing greenhouse gases is difficult, complicated, and controversial. Ultimately, regulations can only do so much. For that reason, we must also look at a major source of greenhouse gas emissions that people use all the time—fossil fuels. Since the onset of the Industrial Revolution, people have relied heavily on these fuels. The problem with fossil fuels is that they help create greenhouse gases and the supply will eventually be depleted.

Reliance on Fossil Fuels: It Can't Last Forever

Underneath many of the environmental issues linked to global warming is the use of fossil fuels for energy. According to the *CIA World Factbook*, the United States is the world's largest consumer of oil at close to 20 million barrels per day, which is about 25 percent more than the entire European Union, even though it has 200 million more people than the United States. China, the world's most populous country, uses about 50 percent of the oil that the United States uses, and India, which has four times as many people as the United States, uses only 16 percent.[88] The United States produces less than half of the oil it consumes, which means that it is dependent on other countries.

In part because of this imbalance in production and use, and in part because of the political agendas of some countries that produce much of the oil used in the United States, American dependence on fossil fuels is considered an environmental issue *and* a security issue. Of course, oil use and production represent an important economic issue as well. When oil prices rise, gas and other fuels do as well. This impacts businesses and households. For example, the oil embargo against the United States in 1973 in response to American policies in the Middle East caused oil prices to quadruple in less than a year.[89] In this situation, control of oil output was effectively used as an economic weapon. Similarly, after the Iranian Revolution of 1979, loss of that country's oil on the world market caused widespread panic, and oil reached its highest ever price (adjusted for inflation) until March 2008.[90] More recently, indirect reports of oil production among members of the Organization of the Petroleum Exporting Countries (OPEC) indicate that Iran decreased production by about 12 percent in the first three months of 2012. U.S. news agencies attribute the decrease in oil production in Iran to the effect of heavy U.S. sanctions against that country in response to its continued progress toward the development of nuclear energy and possible nuclear weapons. In OPEC's report, however, Iran has actually indicated that it has *increased* oil production during the same period of time.[91]

As more countries industrialize, demand for oil is rising, and with this jump in demand comes higher prices. The situation is only going to get worse if warnings that the world has already passed its peak oil-production capabilities are true.[92] This doesn't mean, of course, that it is possible to simply stop using fossil fuels. As U.S. Secretary of the Interior Ken Salazar put it in 2009, "We must recognize that we will likely be dependent on conventional sources—oil, gas, and coal—for a significant portion of our energy for many years to come."[93] To this end, the U.S. government has sold leases for lands for offshore drilling, and it has also proposed some new ideas about how to reduce the country's dependence on foreign oil.

One of these ideas includes the practice of hydraulic fracturing, or "fracking." Fracking is a process used to increase production of gas and oil by introducing heated water, chemicals, and sand into the rock layer to create vertical fissures, or cracks, thus allowing for enhanced release of the gas and oil, that can then be pumped to the surface.[94] Fracking relies on deep vertical wells and channels that are drilled horizontally through thousands of feet in rock layers that may be only one to two hundred feet thick.

Fracking has been practiced since the middle of the nineteenth century. However, it was not until late in the twentieth century that hydraulic fracturing was developed and used in Texas. Today, it is being introduced in the Northeastern United States and many other places. Fracking is controversial because it has been blamed for air and groundwater pollution. It is even thought to be linked to a 4.0 magnitude earthquake in Ohio.[95]

Many U.S. administrations have aggressively pursued policies to help the United States become less dependent on fossil fuels through an array of initiatives to promote and fund improvements in solar energy, wind energy, hydropower, and hybrid and electric vehicles. Some of these policies have been geared toward businesses. Others have been geared toward consumers, such as the "green button" program introduced in 2012 to help individual households track and understand their energy consumption and explore their options for becoming more energy efficient.[96] Ideally, these activities will help move the nation toward economic and social conditions that are less dependent on fossil fuels."

Most lawmakers agree that the United States needs to become more energy independent, but not all of them agree that pursuing initiatives that promote or increase the use of alternative sources of energy is the way to accomplish independence. Some support continued expansion of domestic fossil fuel extraction—including increased mining of domestic coal, fracking, and offshore drilling—as a way to become less dependent on foreign oil. Regulations aimed at improving the environmental safety of these procedures are being considered, and it is likely that a combination of green and traditional energies will continue to power the United States moving forward.[97]

The Green Economy and Green Jobs

Green economy
An economic model that focuses on development and use of renewable energies such as wind, biofuels, and so on to displace traditional fossil fuels and move businesses and communities toward environmental sustainability.

Green-collar jobs
Jobs related to providing environmentally friendly products or services.

As previously discussed, overdependence on fossil fuels is both risky and ultimately unsustainable. A truly sustainable way of living would consider human interdependence with the natural world and a focus on renewable energy sources such as solar power, wind energy, biofuels, to name just a few (■ **EXHIBIT 15.7**). Use of alternative energy sources is part of what is called the **green economy**. The green economy is a term used to describe an economic model that focuses on development and use of renewable energies such as wind, biofuels, and so on to displace traditional fossil fuels and move businesses and communities toward environmental sustainability.

With the emergence of the green economy, several other new terms have entered the business vocabulary as well. For example, **green-collar jobs** are jobs related to providing

■ **EXHIBIT 15.7**
How important is the green economy to meeting our future energy needs?

Source: Goodluz/Shutterstock.com

environmentally friendly products or services.[98] Green-collar jobs often pay more than blue-collar jobs and have been promoted as a way to help the lower and middle classes while simultaneously helping the economy.[99] The list of green-collar jobs includes positions such as organic farmers, environmental consultants and trainers, solar-power engineers, architects, recycling experts, and compliance officers. In 2010, the Bureau of Labor Statistics estimated there were approximately 3.1 million green-collar jobs in the United States, which accounted for roughly 2.4 percent of all jobs in the United States.[100]

Another aspect of the green economy is the growth of construction practices that have fewer negative effects on the environment. Today, as organizations build new facilities, greater attention is being paid to addressing environmental concerns. For example, in 2011 Apogee Stadium at the University of North Texas was the first college football stadium in the United States to attain a Platinum-Level Leadership in Energy and Environmental Design (LEED) designation. This designation considers everything from the materials used in construction to how the building is heated and cooled. Key features of the stadium include the wind turbines that provide its power and the mechanical and lighting system designed to reduce carbon emissions. Additionally, more than 80 percent of the waste generated by the building project was able to be reused or recycled. Finally, the finishing touches on the stadium include permeable paving and drought-tolerant native plants intended to help beat the Texas heat. In addition to all of these environmental touches, the new stadium addressed many shortcomings of the old stadium—including too few restrooms and concession stands.[101]

In addition to climate change and fossil fuels, businesses and organizations also need to attend to other issues related to environmental sustainability, such as pollution, waste, and biodiversity. Let's look at these topics next.

Pollution, Waste, and Environmental Sustainability

The United States has been regulating pollution for decades. The nation's current set of pollution control laws regulates the use of numerous materials that are potentially harmful to both human health and the environment. One of these statutes—the

Comprehensive Environmental Response, Compensation, and Liability Act, commonly called "Superfund"—is of particular note. According to the EPA Web site, "Superfund is the federal government's program to clean up the nation's uncontrolled hazardous waste sites."[102] Superfund is operated by the EPA, which is authorized to identify those parties responsible for toxic pollution and compel them to clean up hazardous sites. As of May 2012, approximately 1,305 Superfund sites were operating had been identified across the country.[103]

Issues about how to deal with waste are not just related to toxins and big businesses. Household waste is also a huge issue. Although problems remain, the United States and other countries have made great headway in developing and promoting technologies and people's habits related to recycling. Currently, most communities in the United States provide the services necessary for recycling aluminum, plastic, and paper. In fact, in today's world, just about anything can be recycled—not only paper, metal, and plastic, but also oil, batteries, and even nuclear waste.

France is currently the world leader in the recycling of nuclear waste, in part because the French (unlike many Americans) embrace nuclear energy.[104] In fact, more than 75 percent of France's electricity came from nuclear sources in 2012.[105] France first became heavily involved in nuclear recycling in the 1970s, when it modernized its recycling plant in La Hague.[106] Since then, the plant has never had a serious accident, although it does release tiny amounts (below legal limits) of radioactive substances into the atmosphere and into the water of the English Channel.[107] The facility is able to recycle 1,700 tonnes of nuclear waste per year, extracting up to 99.9 percent of the plutonium and uranium from the waste. The uranium is stockpiled so that it can be reused at a later date, and the plutonium can be blended with fresh uranium for fresh fuel.[108]

Compare this situation with that at Yucca Mountain, a facility located in the middle of the Mojave Desert about 100 miles northwest of Las Vegas. In 1987, with stockpiles of nuclear waste accumulating across the country, the U.S. government decided to convert the mountain into a dump where this waste could be buried deep underground.[109] This plan has generated a great deal of controversy because no one wants a nuclear waste facility in their backyard—not even 100 miles away. To the relief of many Nevada residents, funding for this plan was revoked in 2011. However, since then, no new plan for nuclear disposal in the United States has emerged and lawmakers are beginning to take another look at Yucca Mountain as a disposal site.[110]

In the years to come, we are likely to see more efforts aimed at managing waste products in a manner that supports environmental sustainability. This will include complex and controversial plans for disposing of dangerous materials such as nuclear waste. It will also include how to deal with more mundane things like household trash. Indeed, one of the most promising streams of technology emerging in today's green economy is the push to find ways to turn trash into energy—a movement that will result in new technologies, new jobs, and a cleaner environment.

Plants, Animals, and Environmental Sustainability

Within the United States, endangered species are protected by the U.S. Fish and Wildlife Service per the terms of the Endangered Species Act of 1973.[111] As of June 2012, this agency classifies 1,201 species as endangered or threatened, and 597 of these species have important habitats in the United States.[112] The Fish and Wildlife Service also acts as a consultant on a wide range of environmental safety and sustainability issues, and it actively works to plan habitat conservation and recover damaged habitats. In addition, the agency operates fisheries to replenish threatened fish populations, as well as "conservation banks"—parcels of land that are set aside for the conservation of various species.[113]

The leading cause of species loss worldwide is destruction of natural habitats.[114] The most species-rich habitats such as rain forests are often the most threatened.[115] According to some scholars' estimates, rain-forest loss and other habitat destruction could result in the extinction of as many as 12 percent of plants and 11 percent of birds in the medium-range future.[116]

Another prominent threat to biodiversity is species invasion. This refers to the transplantation of species to new habitats, which frequently occurs as a result of global trade. In a new environment, a species may have no natural predators, which means it can easily overpopulate. Also, the introduction of nonnative species may threaten native plants and animals to the point that they become endangered or are driven to extinction.[117]

The introduction of nonnative species to islands is especially harmful because of the delicate balance that must be maintained in a limited space.[118] A particularly salient example took place on the big island of Hawai'i. Early shipping introduced rats to the island, and these rats threatened the large bird populations by eating their eggs. To get rid of the rats, the mongoose was introduced to the island, but no one accounted for the fact that rats are nocturnal and the mongoose hunts by day. The two species rarely meet, so of course, the mongooses have not eliminated the rats. Worse yet, mongooses also eat bird's eggs, so the island's native bird species were even more threatened.[119]

Although protection of native species is clearly required to protect biodiversity, problems arise when efforts to prevent habitat loss come into conflict with business interests and the need for jobs. Another example, also in Hawai'i, involves the billion-dollar 30-meter telescope (which will be the largest telescope on Earth) to be constructed at an observatory atop Mauna Kea. Of all the arguments community members and groups like the Sierra Club put forth, the one that almost won the day was that a small insect lives among the cinder cones where the telescope is to be built. Because the mountaintop is this insect's sole habitat, the land is protected.[120] This points out the very difficult choices that must be made as we try to balance environmental sustainability with social and economic sustainability.

What Else Are We Doing to Foster Environmental Sustainability?

Everyone who is involved in producing and consuming goods and services has a role in environmental sustainability. This includes customers, suppliers, manufacturers, and service providers. Manufacturers are sometimes among the most visible proponents of adopting sustainable practices and marketing the resulting products to consumers. Ford Motor Company, for example, has developed a "blueprint for sustainability" that outlines ways to get more power out of more efficient engines, such as by building cars that perform like they have an eight-cylinder engine when they have only six cylinders.[121]

Many firms incorporate this sort of strong commitment to the environment into their marketing efforts. In 2009, for instance, Toyota ran a series of commercials for its hybrid automobile, Prius, which featured the tag line "Where man's wants and nature's needs agree" (■ **EXHIBIT 15.8**).[122] Since that time, Toyota has expanded the Prius line into a family of four different vehicles, including a plug-in hybrid.

Despite some progress, laws and policies that do not promote environmental sustainability continue to exist. In the United States, for example, even though businesses have received tax credits for purchasing hybrid vehicles, until recently, they also received tax credits for buying gas-guzzling Hummers. This was the result of a law passed in the 1970s with the original intent of allowing small farmers and self-employed workers to buy trucks without being subject to the luxury car tax that was in place at the time. Laws or loopholes such as these do not automatically change with the

Source: David Hancock/Alamy

times, so Congress must intervene when necessary. Until Congress takes action, outdated laws can and often do reward behavior that does not promote sustainability.[123]

Even new laws and programs crafted by proponents of environmental sustainability are not without controversy. For instance, in response to the economic recession that began in 2007, Congress passed a "Cash for Clunkers" program that gave Americans a tax credit of $3,500 to $4,500 for each old, inefficient car they got rid of. The Cash for Clunkers program was intended to get inefficient cars off the road and replace them with cars with better gas mileage, while also supporting the auto industry. The program was deemed a success, because approximately 700,000 cars were traded in over the span of a few weeks.[124] But did the program really reflect sound principles of sustainability? To answer this question, let's consider some of the arguments against the program:

- Those consumers who received a $3,500 rebate had to improve their mileage by only four miles per gallon. This is not much of an improvement, and it makes little difference in the long run.[125]
- Consumers could use their rebates toward new cars only; used cars weren't eligible, even if they had better gas mileage than new cars. This triggered a demand for certain models (e.g., hybrids) that could not be met. As a result, auto companies resumed production of several high-demand models. However, by producing more new cars, these companies also used more resources and fossil fuels and thereby contributed to existing environmental problems.
- All of the "clunkers" turned in through the program were destroyed, save for a few exotic cars with historical or financial value. The destruction of these assets left fewer cars to be donated to charities that rely on such donations.

On the other side of the debate, people disagreed with the criticisms. For example, once the Cash for Clunkers program ended, the federal government reported that the cars purchased under the program averaged a 58 percent improvement in miles per gallon (from 15.8 to 24.9 miles per gallon).[126] This means that buyers went far beyond the mandated 4 miles per gallon improvement. In light of all arguments, would you say that the program promoted environmental sustainability? What about economic sustainability?

As technologies advance and research continues, your role as a manager and leader will become increasingly focused on supporting your company in providing goods and services while supporting environmental sustainability. That's not the whole story, however. Partly because of our increasingly interconnected world, there is also a growing awareness of the importance of fostering social sustainability—which, of course, is linked to environmental sustainability. In the next section, we will explore a few aspects of social sustainability that are particularly critical to organizations, businesses, and responsible leaders.

Discussion Questions

1. Using the Internet, research a company that supports environmental sustainability. Would you want to work for this company? Why or why not?
2. What renewable energies have given rise to green-collar jobs in your region of the United States or the world?

---

5. What Is Social Sustainability?

Objective 15.5
Define social sustainability.

As you saw earlier in the chapter, social sustainability focuses on improving people's lives through equity, equality, and access to health care and education. Social sustainability examines the ways in which natural resources, education, skills, and social institutions help to improve the quality of life for all people. Similar to other sustainability concepts, social sustainability is concerned with meeting the social needs of the present population while ensuring that healthy conditions are put in place for future generations. At the heart of social sustainability is the recognition that equality, equity, education, opportunity, and protection of all basic human rights are pivotal to the creation of a truly sustainable global society.[127]

There are numerous ways to look at social sustainability. Three particularly important issues are poverty, access to education, and global health. One organization that addresses the issue of poverty is Novica, which you can read about in the *Business Case*.

BUSINESS CASE

Novica.com

Founded in association with National Geographic in 1998, Novica.com began as a way for artists in developing and undeveloped countries around the world to showcase their art. The site offers these craftsmen and women an opportunity to sell their products in a global marketplace they would not otherwise have access to. In fact, this ideology forms the basis of Novica's mission statement:

> *We want to give artists and artisans around the world a global platform to express their true artistic talents and to spur their creativity. And, we want to provide you with access to unique, hard-to-find items at great values that only the Internet infrastructure can allow.*
>
> *At the deepest essence of our philosophy, we want to create a bridge between you and the many talented artisans across the globe. We want you to know about who you're buying from. We want you to feel that attachment to the product and*

to the hands that created it. In the spirit of the Internet, let us bring you together.[128]

Courtesy of Novica. www.novica.com

Each artist provides a personal message and personal vision on the Web site, and shoppers can use this information to learn about the artist and the craft they are buying. In addition, customers often receive a handwritten note from the artist along with their purchase.

Novica was co-founded by Roberto and Andy Milk. It is a fair-trade company, and prices for the artists' work are set by the artists themselves based on their interpretation of what the market will bear. A percentage of the proceeds goes directly to the artist and the community, and Novica does not charge its artists a fee.

In addition, Novica helps some artists expand their business by helping them access microloans through its Web site. Customers can also directly lend money to artists through Novica.

Most of the company's 30 to 50 full-time employees are spread throughout the world in a dispersed network, though the company is headquartered in Los Angeles, California. Novica's last reported revenue was about $3.2 million.

Novica supports social sustainability by allowing artists to expand their market and their opportunity to earn fair wages for their work. These conditions are part of fair trade, which is considered a key contribution to social sustainability. Other key issues related to social sustainability that we will discuss in this section are child labor, slavery, and workplace safety.

Child Labor

There is little doubt that most leaders today would object to the use of child labor—so why does this practice continue to exist? To answer this question, let's consider a bit of history. First, throughout history, children have always worked alongside family members on farms and in small businesses. How children were treated varied widely. While in many cases these situations were likely quite brutal, many others were likely fair, just, and even loving ways for families and children to grow and get by. Today, in most of the world, children continue to contribute to their families and communities by working. So, children working is not necessarily the problem. What *is* a problem, however, is when children are subject to brutality, denied education, and forced into poor working conditions without legal or other protections. This sort of exploitation of child workers first came to public attention in the United States and Great Britain during the Industrial Revolution. What followed was a movement in which many societies recognized the evils of forcing children to work in dangerous factories and sweatshops, and this movement eventually resulted in the eradication of child labor in many countries around the world.[129]

Unfortunately, global statistics show that exploitation of children is far from gone. A 2011 report by the U.S. Department of Labor estimated that 215 million children were working in hazardous conditions worldwide.[130] The Department of Labor believes this number has likely increased as a result of the global economic crisis.[131]

The problem of child labor can be more complicated than it seems, especially when cultural differences and economic inequities collide on a global scale. For example, in 2006, after it was revealed that Nike products were made with child labor, the company severed its ties with Pakistani supplier Saga in order to repair its public image in the United States and other countries. Saga was severely affected by this loss, and it estimated that as many as 20,000 Pakistani families may have been impacted as well.[132] Nasir Dogar, chief executive of the Independent Monitoring Association for Child Labor, notes that although Saga was in the wrong, Nike may have intensified the damage to society by relying on child labor and then suddenly cutting ties as soon as public pressure mounted.[133]

Most companies intend to act in a responsible manner, especially when it comes to issues such as child labor. But then there's the issue of global competition. When countries allow child labor or companies find ways to exploit children illegally, costs of doing business are lower. Indeed, if companies in some parts of the world can hire child workers and pay them very little to work in a dangerous environment, then these companies can make a cheaper product that other nations will likely buy. Nevertheless, lower costs and higher profits do not justify exploitation of children—or anyone else for that matter. One way to stop it is to hit businesses where it hurts: We can stop doing business with companies that exploit children. To do so, we need to be informed, and we need to make choices based on values and ethics—not just the cost of doing business or the price of goods.

Today, ever more people are rejecting companies that exploit people for the sake of profit. The Fair Trade Federation, whose stamp of approval began appearing on coffee years ago, is one of several watchdog organizations that ensure the products they endorse are not linked to exploitation and that they create opportunities for economically disadvantaged regions. Products that bear the Fair Trade seal are produced by businesses that participate in transparent trade, offer reasonable pay for labor and materials in developing countries, and protect children and other workers from exploitation.[134]

Today, the Fair Trade label can be found on clothing, chocolate, and a wide variety of other products whose manufacture has traditionally involved labor exploitation. Equal Exchange is another organization similar to the Fair Trade Federation, and it too issues a stamp of approval for certain products. Lots of consumers now look for things like the Equal Exchange and the Fair Trade stamps of approval to help them make informed choices about what they buy. Both of these labels are growing quickly in popularity, and they are a symbol for how people are changing the way they think about corporate social responsibility.[135]

Slavery in the World Today

When we think about slavery, we often focus only on that shameful period of history when millions of Africans were taken from their homes and sold as slaves in places like the Caribbean, South America, and the United States. The practice of enslaving people and forcing them to work in plantations, ships, homes, and other businesses during the sixteenth through nineteenth centuries left a lasting and terrible mark on many communities around the world. However, that period was not the only time in which people enslaved others, robbing them of freedom and dignity in order to foster personal (usually economic) interests. As shown in ■ **EXHIBIT 15.9**, slavery has existed for an incredibly long time.

The term *slavery* refers to a type of forced labor in which people are owned by others as if they were property. According to the United Nations Educational, Scientific, and Cultural Organization (UNESCO), most definitions of slavery focus on the practice as a legal institution; however, slavery today is largely illegal.[136] Nevertheless, slavery is rampant today. Women and children tend to be the victims—as sex slaves, child soldiers, and sweatshop workers (■ **EXHIBIT 15.10**).

For example, Joseph Rao Kony is leader of the Lord's Resistance Army (LRA), a guerilla group in Uganda known for its violence and its exploitation of 66,000 or more children as sex slaves and as soldiers.[137] A massive Internet campaign spurred by a short film called *Kony 2012* exposed the fugitive leader as a perpetrator of child slavery, telling the story of how he and his henchmen have stolen children from villages and towns.[138] Once enslaved, the children are forced into work—including sex work—or forced to become soldiers. The film, created by an organization called Invisible Children, Inc., was intended to create global awareness of Kony's crimes. The campaign

■ **EXHIBIT 15.9**

Less Well-Known Examples of Slavery throughout History			
Masters	**Time Frame**	**Sources of Slaves**	**Types of Work**
Ancient Greeks[139]	Roughly 6th to 3rd century B.C.E.	Primarily war, but also piracy and trade	Agricultural laborers, domestic servants, tradesmen, mine workers
Han Dynasty of China[140]	206 B.C.E to 220 C.E.	Penal enslavement, children born of illegal unions, children of slave parents, darker-skinned border people	Laborers, servants, concubines
Aztecs[141]	Roughly 14th to 16th century C.E.	War prisoners from neighboring tribes	Human sacrifices for religious ceremonies, among other things
Buganda[142] (present-day Uganda)	Probably before 19th century B.C.E. until well into the 20th century	Captives of war, primarily women and children	Domestic servants, laborers, concubines

Source: Alamy/Trinity Mirror/Mirrorpix

quickly went viral, causing both the United States and the African Union to act. According to reports, the LRA sharply increased its abduction of children in the weeks following the release of the film. Activists increased their efforts. Now, with millions more people aware of what was happening, there was huge pressure on the world's governments to try to put a stop to Kony's regime and its practices.[143]

Not everyone agrees how many people are enslaved today. According to Kevin Bales, renowned researcher and founder of the organization Free the Slaves, there were an estimated 27 million slaves in the world in 2010. While Bales acknowledges that it is difficult to pin down a figure given the illegality and underground nature of the slave trade, his years of research and his work with the UN have made him confident that this figure represents "the right kind of shape of problem."[144] This estimate is more than double the number of Africans who were sent to the Americas during the 400 years of the African slave trade.[145]

According to the International Labour Office (ILO), at the turn of the twenty-first century, 8.4 million children between the ages of 5 and 17 were victims of human trafficking, forced/bonded labor, armed conflict, prostitution, pornography, and other illegal activities.[146] A later report by the ILO calculates that, at a minimum, 12.3 million people worldwide are victims of forced labor, with 2.4 million of these cases involving human trafficking.[147] Although these estimates differ, they have one thing in common: The number of people who are likely enslaved today is huge. In addition, lest you think slavery is hidden, it's often not. This author, for example, has on at least two occasions met women whose "work contracts" were nothing short of slavery. Both were forced to work in substandard conditions, forced to live in a certain place, and had documents (especially passports) confiscated so they could not leave. One such institution was in Dubai, and the other in London, England.

Sex trafficking is one of the most pervasive and hardest to eliminate forms of modern slavery. In January 2010, the Indian Supreme Court issued a demand that the country's government do more to stop sex tourism in the country, which has been a source of international embarrassment. Some experts estimate that more than 70 percent of Indian sex workers are children under the age of 18.[148] Sex slavery exists in all corners of the world, even in the United States. For instance, in 2010, both MSNBC and the *Today* show featured the story of a Honduran girl and her friends who had been forced to work in a Texas brothel after coming to the United States. The girls left their village with what appeared to be legitimate businessmen who promised them jobs in an

American textile factory.[149] In addition, many women have been tricked into slavery in Eastern Europe as well, often with enticements of legitimate work offers.[150]

Slavery—sex slavery in particular—is active in all parts of the world, including the United States. Data related to the number of actual victims is difficult to come by and estimates vary widely; however, the U.S Department of State confirms that in 2010 individuals from 47 different foreign countries and from the United States itself were illegally enslaved in America. The majority of foreign victims came from Thailand, India, Mexico, Honduras, the Philippines, Haiti, El Salvador, and the Dominican Republic.[151] Data from the Department of Justice suggests that the majority of suspected slavery incidents in the United States from 2008 to 2010 were for sex slavery. The majority of these sex slaves—many of whom were women and children—were U.S. citizens, while the majority of labor slavery victims came from other countries.[152] Department of State data from 2011 indicates that most enslaved persons in the United States are engaged in commercial sex work, domestic service, agriculture, manufacturing, janitorial work, hotel and hospitality services, construction, health and elder care, and strip club dancing.[153] In 2011 the Department of Justice convicted a total of 151 human traffickers on a combination of forced labor, adult sex trafficking, and minor sex trafficking charges.[154]

The stories and statistics are nothing less than shocking—and it's even more shocking to imagine what these statistics actually *mean*. The concept of social sustainability is meaningless if we allow practices like this to continue.

So why does slavery exist? Obviously there are many reasons, but when it comes to business, globalization and increasing consumer demand for cheap products have led to the perpetuation of practices that decrease costs, such as exploitation of children and slave labor. In 2009, the U.S. Department of Labor released a list of countries that engage in slave and child labor along with the following statement:

> As a nation and as members of the global community, we reject the proposition that it is acceptable to pursue economic gain through the forced labor of other human beings or the exploitation of children in the workplace. However, we are aware that these problems remain widespread in today's global economy. Indeed, we face these problems in our own country.[155]

Excepting sex work and pornography, the industries identified by the Department of Labor are all in the agricultural, mining, and manufacturing sectors. Goods identified as having especially high concentrations of child and forced labor are cotton, sugarcane, coffee, cattle, bricks, and gold.[156] The Department of Labor periodically releases updates to this list, and particular instances of slave labor cited in the 2009 report and its subsequent updates include the examples in ■ **EXHIBIT 15.11**.[157]

One reason this report was initially released and continues to be updated is to help American companies and consumers make informed buying decisions based on information about how and under what conditions goods are produced.

■ **EXHIBIT 15.11**

Slave Labor Throughout the World

- Brick making workers in Afghanistan
- Garment manufacturers in Argentina
- Cotton farmers in Benin
- Agricultural workers in Bolivia and Brazil
- Cotton farmers and gold miners in Burkina Faso
- Cassava and tobacco farmers in Cambodia
- Workers in a host of industries in China

(continued)

◼ **EXHIBIT 15.11** *(continued)*

Slave Labor Throughout the World

- Toy and drug manufacturers in Colombia For Colombia—Coca harvesting
- Cassiterite and coltan miners in the Democratic Republic of Congo
- Sugarcane farmers in the Dominican Republic
- Gold miners in Ethiopia
- Fishery workers in Ghana
- Garment, textile, quarry, incense, and agricultural laborers in India
- Garment workers in Jordan
- Cotton and tobacco farmers in Kazakhstan
- Tobacco workers in Malawi
- Garment manufacturers in Malaysia
- Rice farmers in Mali
- Textile and quarry workers in Nepal
- Cocoa growers and quarry workers in Nigeria
- Mine laborers in North Korea
- Agricultural workers in Pakistan
- Cattle workers in Paraguay
- Mining and agricultural laborers in Peru
- Pornography workers in Russia
- Diamond miners in Sierra Leone
- Cotton growers in Tajikistan
- Garment and fishery workers in Thailand
- Cotton growers in Turkmenistan and Uzbekistan

What can you do to help? First, you need to become informed by reading reports such as the one released by the Department of Labor. Then, you need to investigate. Are any of the organizations, businesses, or groups that you typically engage with involved in such practices? It may seem unlikely, but during the past 10 years or so, a number of well-respected manufacturers, hotels, farms, and other businesses have been revealed to use people in a way that is essentially slavery. If we are to claim that we support social sustainability, then we each have a responsibility to find out where our money is going and to refuse to do business with companies that use these horrific practices.

Safety and Risk at Work

While the social and human costs of slavery and child labor are devastating, it is also true that in some cases, work itself can be dangerous or even deadly. For example, one of the worst workplace accidents in U.S. history occurred in 1947, when a harbor explosion in Texas City, Texas, claimed the lives of 576 people both on land and at sea.[158] Sadly, Texas City also experienced an explosion in 2005 that claimed 15 lives and injured 170 people.[159] In China, there are reports of lead poisoning from industrial facilities affecting hundreds of factory workers and thousands of children, and many families have been forced to relocate because of pollution.[160] In Thailand, a 1993 fire in a toy factory claimed the lives of 188 workers, mostly young females, and seriously injured 500 more.[161]

While these dramatic incidents capture our attention, there are many less obvious safety risks at work. According to the Bureau of Labor Statistics in the United States, "In 2010 [the year for which most recent data is available] a total of 4,690 workers died from injuries they suffered at work. That works out to one U.S. worker dying every 2 hours from a work-related injury."[162] Sales organizations face car accidents; manufacturing plants deal with machine accidents; chemicals spill or are used inappropriately. The list goes on and on. And it's not just company conditions or policies that are problematic—employees often make very bad decisions: Sales people don't use seat belts and die in crashes; machine operators try to fix equipment while it's running and lose hands; employees walk through hazardous chemical spills. Why would people do such stupid things? There are many reasons, including inadequate safety standards and/or compliance processes, bad habits, organizational cultures that encourage speed or results even when safety is compromised, overtiredness, and stress. Whatever the reasons, organizations that want to support social sustainability within their boundaries need to attend to creating conditions where people can be, and choose to be, safe.

In an age of globalization, workplace safety is no longer just a concern for individual employees, their companies, or their immediate communities. Global trade means that dangerous materials used in a factory in one country can poison and even kill humans and animals in other countries worldwide. Pollution does not respect national boundaries—for instance, nuclear waste from the Chernobyl nuclear reactor disaster in the former Soviet Union (now Ukraine) traveled halfway across the globe.[163] More recently, leaks of radioactive water from the damaged Fukushima Daiichi nuclear reactors into the Pacific Ocean have raised concerns about the disaster's impact on sea life. Scientists believe that shellfish and other creatures living in sea beds nearest the plant will suffer the worst effects, and that migratory fish moving through the water will experience minimal exposure. Concrete evidence related to the leak's impact has yet to be compiled, but trash associated with the 2011 tsunami that led to the nuclear disaster was found as far away as Alaska's Prince William Sound.[164] In addition to the very real problems associated with injuries, deaths, and poisons, companies and countries are no longer protected from repercussions related to risky decisions. International lawsuits are on the rise, and assets can be seized in other countries.[165]

Most of the world's governments have some sort of system in place to regulate workplace safety. In the United States, that system is the Occupational Safety and Health Administration (OSHA), which is run by the U.S. Department of Labor. OSHA was created by President Nixon in 1970, following the signing of the Occupational Safety and Health Act.[166] Beyond keeping track of occupational accidents, OSHA is responsible for regulating the safety of American workplaces through an array of policies and requirements, some of which are outlined in ■ **EXHIBIT 15.12**.[167] Since its formation, OSHA has had a significant impact on many businesses and industries.

Some companies are especially vigilant when it comes to protecting their workers. For example, "America's Safest Companies" is an annual award presented by the watchdog organization EHS to companies that take extra steps to ensure safety.

■ **EXHIBIT 15.12**

Example OSHA Regulations and Guidelines

- Use of guards on all moving parts of industrial machines[168]
- Permissible exposure limits for approximately 600 chemicals[169]
- Requirements regarding the use of personal protective equipment (e.g., gloves, clothing, earplugs, face shields, respirators) when handling chemicals and operating in industrial environments[170]
- Turning off energy sources when conducting repairs[171]
- Use of two-person crews and air sampling when working in confined spaces[172]
- Hazard communication policies that require developing and communicating information about dangerous workplace chemical products[173]
- Regulations to protect health care workers against bloodborne pathogens such as HIV and hepatitis B[174]
- Safeguards for workers in excavations or deep trenches to prevent collapses or cave-ins[175]
- Asbestos exposure safety regulations[176]

Organizations that receive this award excel at matters such as innovative solutions to workplace safety challenges, injury and illness rates below national averages, and strong safety training programs, among other criteria.[177]

Discussion Questions

1. Take two hours and walk around your school's campus. What evidence do you see that suggests the school is proactive about employee and student safety?

2. Research slavery in the world today. Who tends to be enslaved? Why do you think this is the case? How do you feel about this issue, and what can you and others do to combat it?

Objective 15.6
Define economic sustainability.

6. What Is Economic Sustainability?

Economic sustainability refers to an economy's ability to create and maintain economic conditions that foster current economic health and long-term economic development. Also referred to as sustainable development, this activity is recognized by the United Nations as a shared responsibility of both world governments and private institutions, such as businesses. Contained within the UN definition of economic sustainability are two key concepts: a focus on the needs of the world's poor, "to which overriding priority should be given"; and responsible use of natural resources in a manner that benefits present and future generations and has a positive impact on worldwide economic health and growth.[178]

The concept of sustainable development has drawn criticism from environmentalists, who dislike the way it assigns value to resources based on their usefulness to mankind, as well as from more traditional economists, who dislike the emphasis it places on efficacy and equity in the long term rather than profit now.[179] Nevertheless, economic sustainability and the notion of sustainable development are gaining popularity as concerns related to the environment, the exploitation of resources in underdeveloped nations, and the ability of future generations to enjoy a high standard of living create uncertainty and apprehension about the future.

How does a focus on sustainability impact our capitalist economic system? Are the two at odds? Not according to Al Gore and David Blood of Generation Investment Management, who are the subject of the following *Business Case* feature.

Al Gore and David Blood manage Generation Investment Management in ways that allow them to support businesses in making decisions with the long term in mind while simultaneously maintaining short-term viability. This is not easy, because for many years, short-term profitability (especially in publicly traded companies) has been the sole measure of business success. The move from a short-term orientation to a long-term orientation takes time and collaboration from virtually all stakeholders—and some companies are making this commitment.

For example, Sonoco, a South Carolina–based supplier of industrial and consumer packaging, states that "we believe that sustainability and business success are not only compatible but are inextricably linked and that by embracing both, we will benefit our shareholders for the long term."[180] Similarly, WholeSoy, a California-based maker of soybean-based products, incorporates sustainability into many of its processes and practices. For example, the company pays a living wage to all of its employees, offers company-funded health benefits, and has located its facilities near public transportation. In fact, the company proudly notes that none of its employees actually drive to work.[181]

Al Gore and David Blood

Few people would argue against environmental or social sustainability from an ethical point of view. However, can sustainability be the right ethical choice *and* the right way for firms to invest and manage their money? Al Gore and David Blood think so. Together, they run Generation Investment Management, an asset management firm that promotes sustainable capitalism.

Gore and Blood believe that the only way human civilization can continue is by taking a long-term view of how businesses impact both people and the environment. They see a combination of sustainability and commercial acumen as the key to long-term value and business success.[182] The philosophy behind Generation Investment Management's simple but transformational solution is that rather than looking at a long checklist of sustainability criteria, a business should develop a strategy that incorporates both a focus on business initiatives that meet market needs and a focus on sustainability—thereby positively impacting profitability in the long term as well as the short term.[183] When asked for examples of successful companies that have implemented this approach, Blood states the following:

> A company like Johnson Controls, for example . . . [has] a focus on the demand side [of] energy efficiency. About 50 percent of its business is batteries for hybrid cars and products to run buildings efficiently, the other 50 percent is automotive interiors and controls. We think it's the former that's going to be growing and driving that company. They understand that their products will help reduce their clients' environmental footprint. This strategy is completely revenue driven.[184]

Another example of a project that reflects Gore and Blood's philosophy is in Mexico, where homebuilders are linking demographic trends, environmentally sustainable construction practices, and the demand for affordable housing.[185] Yet another example is Unilever's Project Shakti, a rural entrepreneurship program.[186] This program involves the creation of self-help groups in Indian villages, where Unilever recruits people to become salespersons called *shakti amma*. These individuals go to surrounding villages to sell products and distribute health information. This is helpful because it provides the people (largely women) with an income, and it also gives Unilever access to rural areas—markets that are traditionally very difficult for outsiders to reach.[187]

Despite these good examples, investing in long-term sustainability is still far from mainstream.[188] This is partly because it requires a mind-set change from corporations as vehicles for short-term profit gain to corporations as important drivers of long-term sustainability within and beyond their boundaries. Another mind-set change is to shift from a focus on *stockholders* to a focus on *stakeholders*.[189] In addition, Gore and Blood believe that we need to shift our collective mind-set toward acknowledging that every organization's successes and challenges have numerous immediate and long-term effects on world economic, social, and political systems.[190]

Gore and Blood also state that we need to bridge the disconnect between sustainability indicators and financial indicators. Actions and investments that support long-term sustainability cost money, and they can negatively impact profitability in the short term—something many companies avoid at all costs. However, Gore and Blood's position is that unless companies take these actions, the long-term sustainability of not only the business but also the environment and the communities it serves is at risk.[191]

Gore and Blood see a powerful link between focusing on sustainability, long-term financial success, and a company's reputation and attractiveness to customers and employees.[192] Their question is not whether businesses can learn to successfully put sustainability at the forefront of their strategy, but rather how fast and how effectively they can do it.

Ashoka is another company dedicated to promoting economic sustainability. Founded in Washington, DC, in 1980 by Bill Drayton, Ashoka began with the premise that "the most effective way to promote positive social change is to invest in social entrepreneurs who have innovative solutions to society's problems that are sustainable and replicable, both nationally and globally."[193] A social entrepreneur is a person who identifies social issues and organizes people, resources, and networks to address these problems. Once Ashoka locates such individuals, it chooses some of them to be "fellows." The company then supports each fellow with guidance, expertise, and funding as he or she launches and grows a business.

One Ashoka fellow, chosen in 2008, is Molly Barker. With Ashoka's help, Barker founded Girls on the Run, an organization that helps girls and women eliminate the social barriers they face and helps them make positive choices while reducing risky behavior. Today, the venture has many sponsors, including Kellogg, New Balance, Goody, and Horizon Fitness, which together fund Girls on the Run's $1.5 million annual budget.

All of these examples show that more and more sectors of society are becoming concerned with the long-term economic viability of communities, organizations, and industries.

As we become more interconnected globally in our businesses and organizations, governments will play a significant role in encouraging sustainability at every level. Meanwhile, the scientific and not-for-profit communities provide research, innovation, and watchdog functions, and many businesses and organizations are increasingly facing the issues proactively rather than simply complying with rules and regulations. Perhaps most importantly, individuals—such as you, your friends, and your colleagues—are working to ensure that environmental, social, and economic sustainability become lasting ways of life.

Discussion Questions

1. What is your definition of a successful organization? When formulating your answer, consider economic sustainability and the organization's impact on all of its stakeholders.

2. Research the largest city near your home. What programs exist in the city to support economic development? What programs or policies get in the way of economic development?

Objective 15.7
Define corporate social responsibility.

7. What Is Corporate Social Responsibility?

In this section, we will consider the historical roots of corporate social responsibility and how it is defined today. **Corporate social responsibility (CSR)** is a form of corporate self-regulation that builds sustainability and public interest into business decision making and activities. CSR is the term used to describe how businesses and institutions address environmental, social, and economic sustainability.

Corporate social responsibility (CSR)
A form of corporate self-regulation that builds sustainability and public interest into business decision making and activities.

Corporate social responsibility has its roots in corporate philanthropy. The word *philanthropy* is derived from the Greek words *phil*, which means "love," and *anthropos*, which means "mankind." So, philanthropy is a word that means "to love mankind."[194] In a practical sense, **philanthropy** means giving money, time, services, or products in the service of supporting people's well-being. Philanthropy is not a new idea and it continues today, as you can see in ■ **EXHIBIT 15.13**.

Philanthropy
Giving money, time, services, or products in the service of supporting people's well-being.

■ **EXHIBIT 15.13**

Famous Philanthropists Past and Present	
Name	**Philanthropic Efforts**
Benjamin Franklin	Franklin is credited with being the father of American philanthropy. In 1727, he founded a 12-person club called Junto, which evolved into a think tank for philanthropic ideas. His newspaper, the *Philadelphia Gazette*, was routinely used for mobilization of the public, recruitment of volunteers, and fund-raising. Among his many public service works, Franklin founded the University of Pennsylvania, the country's first public library, the country's first volunteer fire department, and a hospital.[195]
Andrew Carnegie	The Scottish-American magnate was known as a ruthless baron of the steel industry and a devout Christian. After selling out his share of U.S. Steel in 1901, he became heavily involved in activism for world peace, giving away most of his vast fortune. He created the Carnegie Endowment for International Peace in 1910 with a gift of $10 million. The following year, he created the Carnegie Corporation of New York "to promote the advancement and diffusion of knowledge and understanding." Another foundation, the Carnegie Institute, operates four museums in Pittsburgh, including the Andy Warhol Museum. He also founded what is now known as Carnegie Mellon University.[196]

(continued)

■ **EXHIBIT 15.13** *(continued)*

Famous Philanthropists Past and Present

Name	Philanthropic Efforts
Bill and Melinda Gates	The cofounder of Microsoft has given more money to charity than anyone in history. Bill Gates set up the Bill and Melinda Gates Foundation in 2000, and in 2008, it had a $34 billion endowment to improve global health and learning. Warren Buffet donated an additional $31 billion to the foundation in 2008—at the time, half of his fortune. The foundation has paid out more than $20 billion since its inception.[197]
Bono	The lead singer of the immensely popular rock band U2 has been internationally recognized for his ongoing philanthropic efforts. He was involved in Band Aid and Live Aid in 1984 and 1985 to raise money for famine relief in Ethiopia. In 2002, he cofounded DATA (Debt, AIDS, Trade in Africa) to work for equality and justice in Africa through debt relief, improving trade, and fighting the AIDS epidemic.[198]
Jet Li	Li Lianjie is better known as Jet Li, the famous Chinese director and actor of martial arts films. Li founded the Jet Li One Foundation shortly after he became ambassador for the Red Cross Society of China. His interest in philanthropy was greatly influenced by a near-death experience when he and his four-year-old daughter were caught in a tsunami in 2004. The foundation's four principles are education, health, care for the environment, and relief of poverty. It works closely with the Red Cross to meet these goals.[199]
Marcos de Moraes	De Moraes, a dynamic Brazilian businessman, has focused on education with his foundations Zip Educação and Instituto Rukha. Through his institutions, he has worked to take children off the streets and enroll them in school. He has also provided free Web services to 6 million students. De Moraes works with a global circle of philanthropists called the Synergos organization.[200]
Rohini Nilekani	Nilekani, social activist and journalist wife of Infosys CEO Nandan Nilekani, began to look for ways of productively giving away money as soon as it started rolling in. She built two foundations: the Akshara Foundation, which is dedicated to education, and the Arghyam Trust, which focuses on clean water.[201]
Warren Buffett	The self-made billionaire believes "there are an unlimited number of good things to be done in the world" and seeks out organizations that are in synch with his goals when considering where to invest his philanthropic dollars. To that end, Buffet has given more than $30 billion to the Bill and Melinda gates foundation. He has also donated undisclosed amounts to San Francisco's antipoverty Glide Foundation, to efforts to revitalize impoverished neighborhoods in New Orleans and around the country, and to the philanthropic work of his three children.[202]

Owners of companies and other wealthy individuals often donate money to philanthropic organizations, partly out of a sense of civic duty, a commitment to sustainability, or to create goodwill throughout the community. Is philanthropy, however, the only measure of CSR? Giving money isn't enough to brand a leader or a an organization as socially responsible, and in fact there are other important ways companies engage in CSR. For example, in one notable study, five common dimensions emerged: environmental, social, economic, stakeholder, and voluntariness (willingness). As you can see in ■ **EXHIBIT 15.14**, these dimensions cover a broad set of definitions and ways of expressing commitment to CSR.

■ **EXHIBIT 15.14**

Dimensions of Corporate Social Responsibility

Dimension	Context	How Companies Talk about the Dimension
Environmental	The natural environment	"A cleaner environment" "Environmental stewardship"
Social	The relationship between corporations and society	"Contribute to a better society" "Consider the full scope of impact on communities" "Integrate social concerns in business operations"

(continued)

■ **EXHIBIT 15.14** *(continued)*

Dimensions of Corporate Social Responsibility

Dimension	Context	How Companies Talk about the Dimension
Economic	Socioeconomic or financial elements of operation	"Contribute to economic development" "Preserving profitability while also thinking about the future"
Stakeholder	All stakeholders or stakeholder groups	"There are many stakeholders we need to consider" "How we interact with our employees, suppliers, customers, and communities matters a lot"
Voluntariness (willingness)	Whether or not actions are prescribed by law	"We engage in CSR because it's the right thing to do" "We are acting on our values and ethics, beyond legal obligations"

Source: Based on a report from the United Nations World Summit on Sustainable Development, August 26–September 4, 2002. Retrieved May 27, 2010, from http://www.un.org/events/wssdsummaries/envdevj8.htm.

Leadership Perspective

● **Mary McNevin**
President of McCain
Learning Center
"It's all about caring for
our key stakeholders. . ."

CSR is a pillar within McCain Foods' strategic business model, guiding business decisions and how the company relates to its employees, customers, consumers, suppliers, and communities in which it operates. Mary McNevin, Vice-President of Talent and Organization Development has a keen sense of what it means to incorporate social responsibility into everything everyone does at the company. They describe the company's approach this way:

We build our pillars of Corporate Social Responsibility— Respecting the Environment, Inspiring Wellness, and Positively Impacting Our People—into everything we do. It's all about caring for our key stakeholders and focusing our efforts on ensuring that we do the right things in the right way to benefit both these stakeholders and our shareholders. For example, we have a global energy reduction program—the Search for Joules—which reduced our energy consumption by 5 percent between 2005 and 2009, as well as a similar water reduction program called the Search for Pools.

We also focus on the communities where we work and do business. For example, vegetable agronomy and the transfer of knowledge to contract growers have played key roles in McCain Foods' worldwide success. Our role is to share our

research, knowledge, and expertise with our grower partners to ensure their operations have the least impact on the environment and deliver quality product and a profitable return. In India, for example, farming is traditionally done manually, but after McCain's arrival just 10 years ago, partner growers have learned the technology of sowing and reaping with machines and the value of applying fertilizers. The result has been record breaking, with yields from one acre of land once averaging 1 to 10 tons of potatoes increasing to 15 tons today. Further, McCain has helped reduce farmers' expenditures by 35 percent and increase income by 104 percent. In China, where similar initiatives were implemented when we entered this market in 1998, our supply of raw product, which was 100 percent grown by McCain corporate farms just three years ago, is 95 percent supplied by the local growing community today.

Mary McNevin adds: *We focus on developing our people into leaders at all levels of the organization. We target traditional leadership development, and we also help people to see how their actions are tied to a higher purpose. For example, if someone has a passion for clean water, then we support them in discovering how they can lead an initiative at their manufacturing plant. Or, maybe their passion is the alleviation of hunger—they can then apply their leadership skills in one of our programs, like the St. Joseph's Food Bank. If people can tap into their spirit and what they are passionate about, work becomes so much more than "just a job."*

Source: Personal interviews with Mary McNevin conducted by Annie McKee, 2009 and 2012.

One outstanding example of a company that is building CSR into everything it does is McCain Foods Limited, a Canadian-based company that manufactures and distributes frozen foods around the world.

Mary McNevin explains what corporate social responsibility really means. She shows us that, in fact, this approach is not an add-on, or a nice-to-have, or something to do so you look good. It's essential to good business.

Discussion Questions

1. Consider this quote: "If you think you are too small to make an impact, try going to bed with a mosquito in the room" (attributed to various authors). In light of the quote, do you think all companies should be involved in CSR, regardless of their size? Why or why not?

2. Do you donate time or money to causes in which you believe?

8. How Can Companies Approach Corporate Social Responsibility?

Objective 15.8
List steps companies can take to be socially responsible.

Many people want to do business with companies that make social responsibility part of their core values. And, they can readily find out if a company acts in a socially responsible way or not.[203] By the same token, many investors and employees also prefer to interact with a company that has a firm foothold in socially responsible approaches.[204] After all, would you want to work for a firm that you knew was not socially responsible? How would you feel if your employer was constantly in the news for ethical violations, unfair labor practices, or environmental contamination? Of course, leaders do not want to be in the headlines for engaging in socially irresponsible practices. The high costs of bad publicity are immeasurable for individuals and companies alike.

CSR Is a Choice

It would seem that CSR makes sense, but there are many competing priorities in organizations, and CSR can easily slip to last place. This is especially true when a company is experiencing financial strain due to economic conditions, competition, or the need to invest in innovations or new technology. When it comes down to it, CSR is a choice—a choice in which all stakeholders have a say. Scholars note that the justification for CSR should not lie in its relation to the bottom line but rather to principles of social justice.[205]

Many companies have discovered that engaging in CSR is most powerful when it is at the heart of strategy.[206] Take global pharmaceutical company Johnson & Johnson (J&J), which focused on corporate social responsibility long before it was popular. Known simply as "the Credo," J&J's mission statement was created by Robert Wood Johnson in 1943. As you can see in ■ **EXHIBIT 15.15**, the Credo spells out how the company should operate in light of its obligations to individuals who use or administer its products, its stakeholders, and society. The Credo begins with a focus on doctors, nurses, patients, mothers and fathers, and anyone who uses the company's products, then moves to employees, communities, and the environment. It *ends* with stockholders and business management—where many companies both start and end.[207]

As the J&J Web site states, "Our Credo is more than just a moral compass. We believe it's a recipe for business success. The fact that Johnson & Johnson is one of only a handful of companies that have flourished through more than a century of change is proof of that."[208]

■ **EXHIBIT 15.15**

The Johnson & Johnson Credo

We believe our first responsibility is to the doctors, nurses and patients,
to mothers and fathers and all others who use our products and services.
In meeting their needs everything we do must be of high quality.
We must constantly strive to reduce our costs
in order to maintain reasonable prices.
Customers' orders must be serviced promptly and accurately.
Our suppliers and distributors must have an opportunity
to make a fair profit.
We are responsible to our employees,
the men and women who work with us throughout the world.

Everyone must be considered as an individual.
We must respect their dignity and recognize their merit.
They must have a sense of security in their jobs.
Compensation must be fair and adequate,
and working conditions clean, orderly and safe.
We must be mindful of ways to help our employees fulfill
their family responsibilities.
Employees must feel free to make suggestions and complaints.
There must be equal opportunity for employment, development
and advancement for those qualified.
We must provide competent management,
and their actions must be just and ethical.
We are responsible to the communities in which we live
and work and to the world community as well.

We must be good citizens — support good works
and charities and bear our fair share of taxes.
We must encourage civic improvements and better health and education.
We must maintain in good order
the property we are privileged to use,
protecting the environment and natural resources.
Our final responsibility is to our stockholders.

Business must make a sound profit.
We must experiment with new ideas.
Research must be carried on, innovative programs developed
and mistakes paid for.
New equipment must be purchased, new facilities provided
and new products launched.
Reserves must be created to provide for adverse times.
When we operate according to these principles,
the stockholders should realize a fair return.

Source: Johnson & Johnson. Our Credo. Retrieved April 10, 2010, from http://www.jnj.com/wps/wcm/connect/
c7933f004f5563df9e22be1bb31559c7/our-credo.pdf?MOD=AJPERES.

Countless companies have discovered that it actually makes economic sense to engage in socially responsible activities. From the board of directors to the senior executive team, from managers to each and every employee, CSR is enacted—or not—every day. Many companies take CSR very seriously. In fact, one recent study showed that about half of the people holding jobs that ensure that a company is socially responsible reported directly to the CEO or to a board member.[209] This is an indication that companies take CSR seriously.

Many people, managers, and leaders look at CSR from the perspective that it is the right thing to do—and also the smart thing to do. But how does a firm determine if it is successful in its CSR efforts? This is not an easy question to address, because CSR is both a stance and the sum of all actions every manager, employee, and leader takes on a day-to-day basis. Let's look at how approaches to CSR can be evaluated.

Common Approaches to CSR

How can we really know whether a company is engaged in CSR in a meaningful way? Let's look at how scholars have categorized various approaches to CSR. The visible behaviors associated with these approaches enable us to evaluate how a company is dealing with CSR. ■ **EXHIBIT 15.16** illustrates a continuum of these four approaches.

■ **EXHIBIT 15.16**
Organizations can approach corporate social responsibility in at least four different ways.

Obstructionist	Defensive	Accommodative	Proactive

THE OBSTRUCTIONIST APPROACH

With the obstructionist approach, a firm gives little or no attention to social responsibility. For managers in these companies, social responsibility takes a distant backseat to profits and operations. Obstructionists engage in unethical and sometimes illegal actions in order to hide their socially irresponsible behavior.

One early example of the obstructionist approach occurred in 1892 at Andrew Carnegie's Homestead Steel Mill, when 3,000 workers went on strike in pursuit of higher wages and safer working conditions. Instead of talking to the workers and trying to come to an agreement, the company hired a private army to stop the strikers. The confrontation between the workers and the strikers led to the deaths of 12 people. Even in the late 1800s, such an extreme approach was uncommon.[210] It is interesting to note that later in life, Carnegie was a champion of some aspects of social responsibility.

THE DEFENSIVE APPROACH

If a company takes a defensive approach to CSR, then it is only engaging in those activities that it is legally required to do. It won't necessarily try to hide anything or go to extremes, but it will comply only with the minimum legal requirements. Food companies and restaurants that failed to provide caloric content, ingredients, or percent daily values until legal requirements dictated their compliance are examples of firms that used the defensive approach.

THE ACCOMMODATIVE APPROACH

In an accommodative approach, the organization is more positive in its view of social responsibility. In this case, it does everything that it is legally required to do, but it also goes beyond this by addressing those areas that leaders feel are important and ethical. For example, the standard for a particular industry may be that only 1 out of 20 executive positions are held by women. Using an accommodative approach, a firm may make an effort to have 25 percent of its executive positions filled by women.

THE PROACTIVE APPROACH

As the name suggests, a proactive approach means that a company is actively engaging in socially responsible activities and attempting to set the highest industry standard possible. The goal is for the company to be the leader in the industry and the epitome of social responsibility.

Interface Global, a manufacturer of carpet and floor tiles, uses a proactive approach to CSR. In 1994, Interface CEO Ray Anderson read Paul Hawken's book *The Ecology of Commerce* and had an epiphany about how he could, and must, make his company sustainable. He immediately set out to achieve "Mission Zero." Mission Zero is Interface's promise to "eliminate any impact Interface has on the environment by 2020." Of his efforts, Anderson says:

> *Costs are down, not up, dispelling a myth and exposing the false choice between the economy and the environment, products are the best they have ever been, because sustainable design has provided an unexpected wellspring of innovation, people are galvanized around a shared higher purpose, better people are applying, the best people are staying and working with a purpose, the goodwill in the marketplace generated by our focus on sustainability far exceeds that which any amount of advertising or marketing expenditure could have generated.*[211]

The debate about CSR and its relationship to business strategy has been going on for decades. Some people believe business is for business and that any focus on environmental, social, or economic sustainability actually *harms* a company's ability to provide goods and services—thereby harming people. However, growing intolerance for compromised business ethics, and the meltdown of the economy that began in 2007—people are far less tolerant of businesses that are simply out for themselves. Taking a more positive viewpoint, there is increasing evidence that far from being bad for business, CSR is good for business. It's a double win: good for business *and* the right thing to do.

Discussion Questions

1. Does your school have an articulated stance on its approach to CSR? What is it? Do you believe that it is an appropriate stance? Why or why not?

2. Consider Johnson & Johnson's Credo: Stockholders and business practices are listed last, after individuals who use the product, employees, communities, and the environment. Argue for and against this order of priorities (e.g., Why might this be good for business? How might it inhibit business?)

Objective 15.9
Define HR's role in sustainability and corporate social responsibility.

HR Leadership Roles

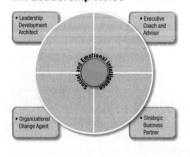

9. What Is HR's Role in Sustainability and Corporate Social Responsibility?

HR leaders have the opportunity to contribute to building sustainable organizations through fostering responsible practices that improve the bottom line for the organization while motivating employees. One way in which they can do this is to be aware of, and willing to use, technology in ways that minimize travel and commuting. HR can also help organize programs that foster a culture that supports social sustainability by supporting employees in providing service to their local communities or through activities that support global citizenship.

Telecommuting

One way to reduce our dependency on oil and decrease emissions is to provide employees with the opportunity and freedom to telecommute. In December 2010, President Obama signed the Telework Enhancement Act, a bipartisan law that requires each government agency to establish telework policies authorizing employees to telework under specific guidelines, which include training to prepare workers for telework.[212] The law is having an effect on the number of employees in government who telework. However, by far, the largest percentage of teleworkers can be found in private, for-profit business.[213]

In 2011, nearly half of U.S. workers held jobs that were compatible with at least part-time telework.[214] According to Forrester Research, "Fueled by broadband adoption, better collaboration tools, and growing management experience, the U.S. telecommuting ranks will swell to 63 million by 2016. Those 29 million new telecommuters lined up five abreast would stretch from New York to LA! . . . The impact of this expanding remote workforce is far-reaching: It will force firms to expand their digital footprints, harness new social software, crisply define their culture, and examine their real estate and energy policies."[215]

Considering the monetary advantages telecommuting offers employers and the personal advantages it offers employees, it is easy to understand why this practice has become so popular.[216] Telecommuting also offers environmental advantages. In fact, some states offer incentives to companies that allow employees to telecommute as a way of making this environmentally friendly work phenomenon more attractive to employers.[217]

One obvious benefit of telecommuting is the fact that it decreases the number of cars on the road, thus decreasing fuel consumption and automobile emissions. Some estimates even suggest that as many as 1.35 billion gallons of gas and 26 billion pounds of carbon dioxide emissions could be saved if every employee who was able telecommuted approximately two days per week.[218]

The energy savings, however, are not strictly limited to automotive gas consumption. Fewer cars, trains, and buses need to be produced when more people telecommute, meaning less energy is expended in their production, and fewer office buildings require heat, air conditioning, and light. Beyond energy consumption, telecommuting also means less consumption of land surface area for buildings, parking lots, and roadways, which could equate to more green space and parks in communities nationwide.[219]

One might argue, of course, that construction of fewer cars, buildings, and offices will negatively impact the economy, because it means fewer jobs. This is probably true. However, as manufacturing jobs decline, we will concurrently see a rise in jobs related to technology and the green economy. Think about it: People who are working from home will require better information and telecommunications technology, as well as other products and services that allow them to work effectively far from the organization.

One potential downside to the increase in telecommuting is that it opens the door to more outsourcing. The "permanent temporary workforce" is becoming a reality, and increasing numbers of people are now working as individual contractors instead of as long-term employees.[220] In fact, approximately 26 percent of the U.S. workforce fit this category as of 2010.[221]

What's the problem with this? Contract workers often do not have typical employee benefits, such as sick days, paid vacation, or employer-supported health insurance. They don't get severance when they are laid off, and they are easier to lay off because neither the company nor the employee has built the kind of bond that is typical in an employee–employer relationship. In essence, economic sustainability (in the short term, at least) wins out in this model. The employees—and ultimately, social sustainability—may be the big losers.

HR has a tremendous challenge as this and similar trends emerge. The challenge is to find new and innovative ways to support all three pillars of sustainability—to foster economic viability for the organization, while also attending to the environment and treating employees in ways that are fair, just, and equitable.

Supporting CSR through Employee Service Programs

HR can also look for ways in which the company can support the larger community by providing needed services. In its broadest sense, service is giving of oneself without any expectation of a return. Many companies sponsor programs that allow employees to serve their local communities, stakeholders, or even the global community. For

Service
Giving of oneself without any expectation of a return.

Global citizenship
Involves understanding one's place in and one's impact on the world community and engaging in activities that support global environmental, social, and economic sustainability.

example, companies may organize to serve their local communities by sponsoring service days when employees can volunteer at an event that helps the community instead of going to work. Some firms provide the expertise of their employees to community groups. For instance, an accountant may assist a community theater with its financial records, a human resources manager may help recruit volunteers at a thrift shop, or employees might use their business expertise to help local not-for-profit boards of directors.

Service can be organized to support people and groups far from home as well, enabling employees to act as global citizens. Global citizenship involves understanding one's place in and one's impact on the world community and engaging in activities that support global environmental, social, and economic sustainability. One company that is making strides in global citizenship is eBay, the online auction firm. eBay has launched three different programs that help people around the world. First, Micro-Place is a service that connects the working poor with investors through micro-loans. Investors need only put up a minimum of $20 to invest in a start-up small business. Second, WorldofGood.com, owned by eBay, is a Web site where customers can purchase from fair trade manufacturers and other socially responsible organizations. Buyers know that purchases made through this site support fair labor practices. Third, eBay allows sellers to donate part or all of the proceeds from sales to any of 18,000 certified nonprofit organizations around the world.[222]

To see some different ways in which companies can give back to the community and the world, let's look at pharmaceutical company Eli Lilly. Eli Lilly, headquartered in Indianapolis, won the U.S. Spirit Award from the United Way in 2009. Lilly's contributions included the following:

- Lilly employees volunteered more than 160,000 hours in 2008 during their Global Day of Service. Volunteers in more than 55 countries made it one of the largest single-day initiatives undertaken by any U.S.-based company.
- More than 600 Lilly employees were recruited as tutors to fourth- and fifth-grade students.
- Lilly donated approximately 5,000 volunteer hours of skills-based Six Sigma training to nonprofits.[223]

Some companies make it easy for employees to serve. A small business and accounting consulting firm in the Cleveland area, Skoda Minotti, even pays employees for the time they spend volunteering with local organizations. In one recent year, employees of the company logged more than 1,700 hours volunteering.[224] Or another example: Employees of Allied Bank, a financial institution located in Pakistan, contributed portions of their salaries and provided food, clothing, and medicine to victims of the earthquake that struck the region in October 2005.[225]

The benefits to communities that receive such services are clear. What's less obvious, but also very important, is that people who engage in service activities reap tremendous benefits as well. From learning new skills, to learning how to work cross culturally with people whose backgrounds are very different from your own, to the sheer satisfaction you can derive from giving of yourself—service is worth it.

Discussion Questions

1. Have you ever provided service to your community through volunteer work sponsored by your school or workplace? What did you do? What did your community get from this experience? What did you get?

2. What is your role as a global citizen? How does service work help you as a future employee?

10. What Can We All Do to Support Sustainability and Corporate Social Responsibility?

The massive social and technological changes currently under way have resulted in the need for us to recognize that we are fundamentally interconnected, and that our individual and organizational activities have impact far beyond ourselves or the walls of our offices. What that means for all of us is that we have to become conscious of how important sustainability and social responsibility really are. From global warming to business ethics to economic woes around the world, we are facing serious problems that will take all of our efforts to address. We all need to understand how our organizations affect our communities and the world, and we must be ready to do something if, in fact, we—or our organizations—are causing damage to the environment, society, or the long-term economic viability of our communities.

We can all be part of the solution to the challenges we face in our world today. One thing you can do right now is to begin to see yourself as a steward of the environment, a servant to the people you lead, and a member of the communities you touch. In other words, you can begin to see yourself as a servant leader.

First coined by Robert Greenleaf in 1970, the term **servant leadership** describes a leadership style in which the leader seeks to serve followers and stakeholders, as opposed to dominating them.[226] Greenleaf's concept of servant leadership grew out of a Herman Hesse novel (*Siddhartha*) that inspired him to consider servitude and leadership not as opposites but as two roles that operate dynamically.[227] According to Greenleaf, a servant leader is a servant first—a person who has the desire to serve as his or her first priority. A servant leader makes sure that the most pressing needs of others are taken care of. Servant leadership is an approach that starts with concern for the welfare of others and sincere and selfless motivation behind our actions—which almost always brings tremendous loyalty, commitment, and outstanding contributions from the people we serve.[228]

Servant leadership
A leadership style in which the leader seeks to serve followers and stakeholders, as opposed to dominating them.

Many times, we think of leaders who get other people to do things for them. In this model, however, doing for others comes first. This is empowering for followers: As their needs are addressed, people begin to grow and become more mature and self-reliant.

The Greenleaf Center has identified 10 ways in which you can enact servant leadership:[229]

- Listening
- Empathy
- Healing
- Awareness
- Persuasion
- Conceptualization
- Foresight
- Stewardship
- Commitment to the growth of people
- Building community.

As you can see, many of the qualities of a servant leader are related to emotional intelligence. Are you a servant leader? How do you demonstrate your servant leadership? How do you find out what others on the team need, and what do you do about this? Why do you think people follow you? These questions are important for every leader, no matter what position you hold. Learning to lead means learning to serve—at home, in our communities, and in our businesses.

Discussion Questions

1. In your own words, take time to define each of the 10 ways in which a team leader can enact servant leadership.

2. Think about an opportunity you have to lead (formally or informally) at work or in school. If you decided to truly enact servant leadership, what three things might you do differently in this situation?

11. A Final Word on Sustainability and Corporate Social Responsibility

Environmental, social, and economic sustainability are very complex topics that generate passion and commitment all over the world in families, communities, nations, and businesses. These topics generate controversy as well. In this chapter, you have learned how our world is coming together in dialogue and debates about how we can cooperate to ensure that our actions support healthy communities and businesses. This dialogue will no doubt continue throughout your lifetime. This means that you have a wonderful opportunity to shape how today's businesses and organizations will contribute to future generations.

EXPERIENCING Leadership

LEADING IN A GLOBAL WORLD
Kyoto and Climate Change

Since the Kyoto Protocol took effect, the UN has held regular meetings to chart progress and set new objectives and goals as economic and environmental variables change. The conference is always hosted by a different country. In 2009, it was held in Copenhagen, Denmark; 2010 in Cancun, Mexico; 2011, in Durban, South Africa; and 2012 in Doha, Qatar. Some conferences have ended in hope (Durban), while others have ended in frustration (Copenhagen).

1. Review the objectives and goals of the last three UN Climate Change Conferences. What did the participating countries agree to at the most recent conferences? What did they disagree about? What are the impacts of these agreements and disagreements?

2. Choose three key indicators of progress by the participating countries and three key indicators that much work still needs to be done. Be sure to consider which nations are key to driving climate change progress and which nations are hindering progress. In addition, pay attention to alterations and adjustments to the conference's objectives and goals from one conference to the next.

LEADING WITH EMOTIONAL INTELLIGENCE
Commitment to Compassion

Companies can approach social responsibility in a variety of ways. Your text offers four common approaches: obstructionist, defensive, accommodative, and proactive. In most instances, companies have a choice—not a mandate—to give back to the community or address social injustices, and many companies choose to do so because they feel it is the right thing to do.

Because the number of people who insist that the companies they do business with are socially responsible is growing rapidly, CSR can actually be very profitable. However, a company should not just get on the CSR bandwagon to increase market share or improve its public image. How can you determine if a company is proactively making an effort to make the world a better place or just going along for the ride?

1. In a group or on your own, research the CSR policies of two of your favorite companies. Most company Web sites now have a separate tab for social responsibility/philanthropy. Dig into their efforts and try to determine whether they are serious about CSR or perhaps just riding along on the PR bandwagon.

2. While researching the validity of their CSR/philanthropic claims, be sure to ask yourself whether the companies are genuinely proactive or perhaps merely accommodative in their approaches? Is CSR a part of the companies' mission and vision statements? Do their claims to CSR/philanthropy hold up under your research scrutiny?

3. When your research is complete, rate your companies from 1 to 10 on a "commitment to compassion" scale, with 1 being "Scrooge, Inc." and 10 being "Mother Teresa, Inc."

LEADING WITH CRITICAL THINKING SKILLS
Is It Just Me, or Is It Getting Warmer?

The topics of global warming and climate change have been hot news items for the last decade. Proponents of global warming observe that the rise in Earth's temperature is primarily the result of human activity. Opponents to the global warming theory say that it is a natural cycle and humans have had very little if any impact on the rise of temperatures. So who's right?

Pretend that you have been selected to be an adviser to the President's Commission on Environmental Sustainability. Your task will be to advise the commission on your findings concerning global warming—that is, whether it is being caused by human activity or is just a natural cycle independent of human activity.

1. In a group or on your own, research both sides of the global warming issue. Identify five to seven strong talking points around global warming as a human-caused phenomenon and five to seven points that argue for global warming as a natural phenomenon.

2. Decide what advice you will give to the commission. Use your critical thinking skills to determine where the evidence is the most clear and objective. Remember to ask yourself the following questions: How reliable are my sources? Is there a hidden agenda to either argument? What has been overlooked or omitted by both sides? What has been perhaps overemphasized by both sides and why?

ETHICAL LEADERSHIP
Suffer the Little Children

There are countries around the world that engage in slavery and child labor to produce the goods they ship to U.S. companies for distribution. The U.S. Department of Labor's Bureau of International Labor Affairs publishes reports identifying offending countries and the industries in which they engage child labor. As a result, companies and consumers can make informed buying decisions. Unfortunately, more and more U.S. companies are using overseas suppliers, like garment factories in Malaysia, Central America, and India, that employ children in sweatshops to make clothing for U.S. retail sales outlets.[230]

In a group or on your own, discuss the ethics of employing children in factories. Consider the following questions, as well as those that are important to you: What are the arguments against and the arguments in favor of child labor? Is child labor simply an economic reality for many developing countries? Are there any circumstances that might make child labor acceptable?

KEY TERMS

Sustainability, *p. 561*
Global warming, *p. 562*
Greenhouse effect, *p. 562*
Environmental sustainability, *p. 568*
Social sustainability, *p. 568*
Economic sustainability, *p. 568*

Kyoto Protocol, *p. 575*
Green economy, *p. 578*
Green-collar jobs, *p. 578*
Corporate social responsibility (CSR), *p. 592*
Philanthropy, *p. 592*

Service, *p. 599*
Global citizenship, *p. 600*
Servant leadership, *p. 601*

MyManagementLab

Go to **mymanagementlab.com** for Auto-graded writing questions as well as the following Assisted-graded writing questions:

15-1. What are some likely environmental implications of the rapid industrialization currently under way in large, powerful countries like China and India? What are some environmental consequences in these countries that you already know about? In your own country?

15-2. Search the Internet for information about businesses that foster or support economic sustainability. Is there a common thread with respect to these organizations' philosophies or work? If so, what is it? If not, why do you think differences exist?

15-3. Mymanagementlab Only — comprehensive writing assignment for this chapter.

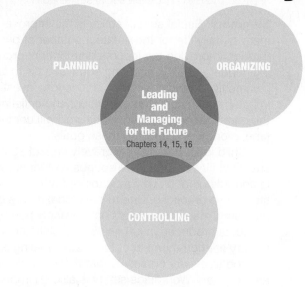

1. Why Are Sustainability and Corporate Social Responsibility Important in Today's World? (p. 560)

Objective: Explain why sustainability and corporate social responsibility are important in today's world.

Summary: The increasing interconnectedness of the world has brought sustainability and corporate social responsibility to the forefront of the business agenda. This interconnectedness is the result of advances in technology, economic interdependence, and continued industrialization. The changes we are experiencing in much of the world are positive; unfortunately, they can also have negative consequences for the environment, our society, and the economy. As a result, it is crucial that leaders understand the ways in which their organizations impact the planet and its people.

2. What Is Sustainability? (pp. 561–568)

Objective: Define sustainability.

Summary: Sustainability is the ability of current generations to meet their needs without compromising the ability of future generations to do the same. This is not a new concept; in fact, many tribal peoples practiced sustainability for thousands of years. The stakes are higher today, however, as climate change, shifts in economic power due to industrialization, lapses in business ethics, and global economic crises put people all over the planet at risk. Therefore, curbing trends related to things like global warming and questionable business practices is no longer just the responsibility of corporations and governments, but of each and every responsible citizen.

3. What Are the Three Pillars of Sustainability? (pp. 568–571)

Objective: List and describe the three pillars of sustainability.

Summary: According to the United Nations, the three pillars of sustainability are environmental sustainability, social sustainability, and economic sustainability. Each of these pillars has a major impact on organizations, communities, and the people of the world. More and more companies are attending to issues of sustainability in order to protect their stakeholders, environment, and communities, as well as to avoid disasters. Some companies are even being recognized for their efforts through tracking projects like the Global 100 Most Sustainable Corporations.

4. What Is Environmental Sustainability? (pp. 572–583)

Objective: Define environmental sustainability.

Summary: Environmental sustainability is the preservation of environmental resources and biodiversity, creation of sustainable access to safe air and drinking water, and the like. The conservation and ecology movements in the United States were early attempts at environmental sustainability, and they resulted in the creation of government agencies like the National Park Service and the Environmental Protection Agency. As nations seek to find ways to collaborate around environmental issues, other problems, such as dwindling fossil fuels, add even more complexity. There are many positive outcomes of the world's leaders attending to environmental sustainability, including the promotion of green energy technologies.

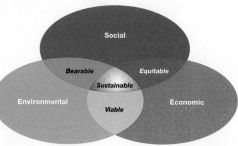

5. What Is Social Sustainability?
(pp. 583–590)

Objective: Define social sustainability.

Summary: Social sustainability is the improvement of daily life for the greatest number of people through improving fair income distribution; promoting gender equality; ensuring equal access to land ownership, employment, and education; investing in basic health care and education; and enlisting the participation of beneficiaries who will contribute time, money, and effort to these goals.

Child labor and slavery gravely impact social sustainability, and they are serious problems even in countries that closely monitor and attempt to stop these practices. Due to the global nature of our economy, many consumers unknowingly purchase products produced in nations where child labor and slavery are commonplace. Fair trade labeling is one method to assure ourselves that these practices are not used. Workplace safety is also an important aspect of social sustainability today; far too many accidents and deaths at work means that safety should be a priority for every company.

6. What Is Economic Sustainability?
(pp. 590–592)

Objective: Define economic sustainability.

Summary: Economic sustainability is an economy's capacity to regularly produce outcomes consistent with long-term economic development. Such long-term development can be difficult to achieve in the modern business world, where short-term profit has traditionally been the measure of success. However, more and more large and small companies recognize that profitability and sustainability are inextricably linked. These companies, in turn, are positively impacting the environment, health, and well-being of both local and global communities.

8. How Can Companies Approach Corporate Social Responsibility? (pp. 595–598)

Objective: List steps companies can take to be socially responsible.

Summary: In today's world where there is ready public access to information, companies have a strong motive for choosing to be socially responsible. CSR builds goodwill with customers, employees, governments, and communities. Four approaches to CSR have been identified: the obstructionist approach, which ignores CSR; the defensive approach, which does the bare minimum in terms of CSR; the accommodative approach, in which CSR activities are above average; and the proactive approach, where a company attempts to set the industry standard for CSR.

Obstructionist **Defensive** **Accommodative** **Proactive**

7. What Is Corporate Social Responsibility? (pp. 592–595)

Objective: Define corporate social responsibility.

Summary: Corporate social responsibility (CSR) is a form of corporate self-regulation that builds sustainability and public interest into business decision-making activities. Corporate social responsibility has a long history, with its roots in philanthropy. At its best, CSR is the smart thing to do in terms of the bottom line and the right thing to do in terms of serving stakeholders. This is why corporations have found that it makes financial sense to embrace CSR.

9. What Is HR's Role in Sustainability and Corporate Social Responsibility? (pp. 598–600)

Objective: Define HR's role in sustainability and corporate social responsibility.

Summary: HR can have a powerful effect on an organization's CSR efforts. For example, work design can include telecommuting, which provides clear environmental and economic benefits but potential social downfalls as more and more people work as contractors without traditional employee benefits. In addition, HR professionals can look for ways to incorporate service into organizational CSR activities. Creating programs that allow employees to serve local and global communities is beneficial for everyone involved.

10. What Can We All Do to Support Sustainability and Corporate Social Responsibility? (pp. 601–602)

Objective: Describe steps you can take to support sustainability and corporate social responsibility.

Summary: The first step in supporting sustainability, corporate social responsibility, and service is understanding how your company's actions affect current and future generations. To be part of the solution now, you can begin to see yourself as a servant leader. This approach to leadership requires you to serve followers and stakeholders and be sincerely concerned about their welfare. Servant leadership revolves around selfless motivation, generates loyalty among followers, and can be incredibly fulfilling.

11. A Final Word on Sustainability and Corporate Social Responsibility (p. 602)

Summary: We are in the midst of a massive global transformation that is improving on a daily basis our ability to communicate, live, and work. Our global population is also expanding, and it is important that we use our knowledge and skills to support ourselves and our planet in the midst of this boom. Many old ways of doing things have become inadequate, wasteful, and even harmful, and we must challenge ourselves to change. By working together as a single global community and utilizing our collective knowledge, resources, and abilities in responsible ways, we can learn how to manage these challenges.

CHAPTER 16

Managing and Leading for Tomorrow:

A Focus on Your Future

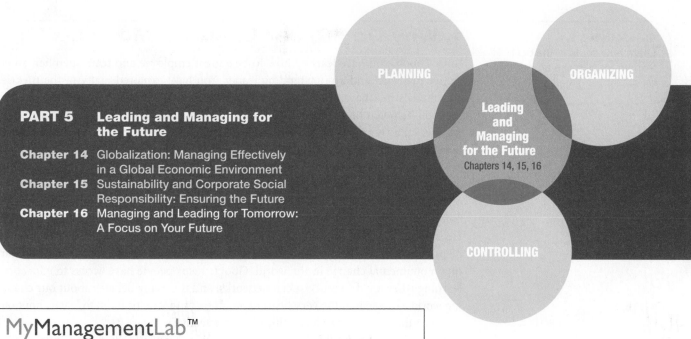

PLANNING

ORGANIZING

Leading and Managing for the Future
Chapters 14, 15, 16

CONTROLLING

MyManagementLab™

⭐ **Improve Your Grade!**

Over 10 million students improved their results using the Pearson MyLabs. Visit **mymanagementlab.com** for simulations, tutorials, and end-of-chapter problems.

Chapter Outline

Chapter Objectives

16.1 Learn how some of the best leaders today make an impact on others.

16.2 Understand ways in which management must change.

16.3 Take actions toward becoming a resonant leader.

16.4 Develop your leadership skills.

1. Why Do "Great Leaders Move Us"?[1]

In this book, you have learned how to be a great employee and team member, an effective manager, and an outstanding leader. You have explored many of the theories and models that have guided us for decades as well as new ideas and new research that will help you be successful in our changing world. In this chapter, you will have another opportunity to learn about your leadership strengths, things you would like to develop, and contributions you can make at school, in your community, at work, and in the world. Before we turn to a model and some exercises that will help you learn more about yourself, consider the Leadership Perspective feature, where you will hear from one of the most brilliant, insightful, and funny leaders we have ever met: Chade-Meng Tan—better known as "Meng"—of Google. Meng has been with Google from the start. He is one of the great minds that came together with a dream of something that would help the world. We are so used to Google now that it is easy to forget that it is part of a monumental change in the world. Google helps people have access to education, learning (they are different), social networks, and the many debates about our changing world. Google is at the very heart of an industry that helps us all to learn about our world so that we can then lead ethically and effectively.

Meng's book, *Search Inside Yourself,*[4] helps us understand that change, even change in the world, comes from within. Let's hear his wisdom in the *Leadership Perspective* feature.

Meng is a *real* leader, and he has powerful advice for the rest of us. Part of the reason his advice is so good is that he points us toward very new ways of thinking about work, management, and leadership. Like Meng, it's time for all of us to start thinking differently

Leadership Perspective

● **Chade-Meng Tan**
Google's 'Jolly Good Fellow'
"There are a lot of leaders who are just good enough to get things done. But they can't create break-throughs."

Meng grew up in Singapore. He was a brilliant student and then a much-sought after engineer. After attending graduate school at the University of California at Santa Barbara, Meng became one of the early engineers at Google. He focused his keen mind and bound-less energy on building teams that helped to build Google's first mobile search service, ensure quality in Google's search systems, and several other notable contributions. One of these contributions was as Google's official greeter. In this role he became known to many as Meng, the "Jolly Good Fellow (Which Nobody Can Deny)." In this role, he's hosted many of the world's celebrities and dignitaries.[2]

After several years leading engineering teams, Meng moved to Google University and is now part of the Talent Group. One of his favorite programs is called Search Inside Yourself—"a mind-fulness-based emotional intelligence program" which he hopes will contribute to world peace in a meaningful way.[3] He and a number of colleagues developed this program to help Googlers to become better leaders, better people and ultimately to "help bring about world peace." Meng's humor is legend, but about

some things, including contributing to world peace, he's not kid-ding. He believes that each of us can contribute to the world in many ways, and if we start with learning about ourselves, we will indeed help to bring peace and justice to the world in our own ways. Meng doesn't see any contradiction at all in being a leader in business and helping to solve the world's big social problems.

What Meng has to say about leadership is not only smart and funny, it's wise:

Being a leader humbles you, in a way that motivates you to help people. Leadership is essentially about character and compassion.

It's hard to measure character. What would you say—"In order to be a good leader you need 10 percent more char-acter?" It's not that easy to quantify. You have to do the right thing. That's character. You have to realize that you can't do anything alone. You have to be big enough and have a strong enough ego to know you can do something, and that you are small enough—egoless enough—to know you need other people. You need to let go of total control, while still making things happen, and let go of your ego while still holding onto your belief in yourself.

There are a lot of leaders who are just good enough to get things done. But they can't create breakthroughs. To cre-ate breakthroughs you need to be able to create a sense of exhilarating discomfort, and to operate with egoless-ego and selfless glory. This is the exact opposite of becoming

Continued on next page >>

Perspectives Continued

obsessed with yourself (what those just-get-things-done leaders often do).

And compassion is the antidote to excessive self obsession. Compassion has three parts:

- Cognitive: "I understand you,"
- Emotion: "I feel for you," and
- Motivation: "I want to help you."

When you are engaged in compassionate endeavors, people are inspired by you. They want to be near you, and they want to help you. If you are a leader who people like

and respect, and your "heart is in the right place," you can do a lot.

Meng's final words were perhaps the most inspiring—he talked about fun and happiness, and how all of us should be able to experience fun and happiness at work.

Happiness is a state of mind that frees you to do a lot. Good leaders need to be happy. Good leaders need to be fun. I want to see every workplace in the world to be a fountain of happiness and enlightenment.

Source: Personal interviews with Chade-Meng Tan conducted by Annie McKee, 2009 and 2012.

about what it means to be successful at work. We live in a world that is very different from that in which many management theories and practices were developed. Today, the opportunities and challenges presented by changes in information and telecommunications technology, global warming, and the call for ethical and responsible business require us to find new ways of working, managing, and leading. Let's take one last look at what leading scholars call for when it comes to management in the twenty-first century.

Discussion Questions

1. When you wake up for the day are you generally excited about the work you have to do, or are you resentful of work's challenges? How can you create a positive perception of your work?

2. Look back through all the leaders featured in the Leadership Perspective sections of this book. Who can you relate to the best? Who inspires you the most? What life lessons did you gain from these leaders?

2. What Are "Moon Shots for Management"?[5]

Objective 16.2
Understand ways in which management must change.

In 2008, the *Harvard Business Review* published a report of an ambitious project undertaken by scholars, business leaders, and consultants to compile a list of the top priority challenges for twenty-first century management research and practice. The report, called "Moon Shots for Management," identified 25 changes and challenges we need to address if we are to learn how to manage and lead our organizations more responsibly.[6]

As you can see in ■ **EXHIBIT 16.1**, the report calls for some very bold changes in how we understand management. Several of the "moon shots" are related to overcoming the limitations of the twentieth-century focus on scientific management, while others are directed toward furthering the agenda of business ethics, organizational culture, organizational learning, and strategy. Let's consider some of the main points of this report.

Perhaps because the brainstorming session that spawned this report came on the heels of the worst global economic disaster since the Great Depression of the 1930s, the number one challenge in the report is to ensure that management's activities serve a purpose higher than mere accumulation of wealth. The group stated that business goals *must* be socially significant. In fact, the top three moon shots are focused on management ethics, such as finding ways of embedding the ideas of community and citizenship into management processes and reconstructing the philosophical foundations of management to take greater advantage of knowledge from other disciplines, including biology, theology, and political science.

■ **EXHIBIT 16.1**

Moon Shots for Management: Important Challenges for Twenty-First Century Management, as Identified by Top Scholars, Business Leaders, and Consultants

1. *Ensure that the work of management serves a higher purpose.* Management, both in theory and practice, must orient itself to the achievement of noble, socially significant goals.

2. *Fully embed the ideas of community and citizenship in management systems.* There is a need for processes and practices that reflect the interdependence of all stakeholder groups.

3. *Reconstruct management's philosophical foundations.* To build organizations that are more than merely efficient, we need to draw lessons from such fields as biology, political science, and theology.

4. *Eliminate the pathologies of formal hierarchy.* There are advantages to natural hierarchies, where power flows up from the bottom and leaders emerge instead of being appointed.

5. *Reduce fear and increase trust.* Mistrust and fear are toxic to innovation and engagement and must be wrung out of management systems.

6. *Reinvent the means of control.* To transcend the discipline-versus-freedom trade-off, control systems have to encourage control from within rather than constraints from without.

7. *Redefine the work of leadership.* The notion of the leader as a heroic decision maker is untenable. Leaders must be recast as social-systems architects who enable innovation and collaboration.

8. *Expand and exploit diversity.* We must create a management system that values diversity, disagreement, and divergences as much as conformance, consensus, and cohesion.

9. *Reinvent strategy making as an emergent process.* In a turbulent world, strategy making must reflect the biological principles of variety, selection, and retention.

10. *De-structure and disaggregate the organization.* To become more adaptable and innovative, large entities must be disaggregated into smaller, more malleable units.

11. *Dramatically reduce the pull of the past.* Existing management systems often mindlessly reinforce the status quo. In the future, they must facilitate innovation and change.

12. *Share the work of setting direction.* To engender commitment, the responsibility for setting goals must be distributed through a process in which share of voice is a function of insight, not power.

13. *Develop holistic performance measures.* Existing performance metrics must be recast because they give inadequate attention to the capabilities that drive success in the creative economy.

14. *Stretch executive time frames and perspectives.* We need to discover alternatives to compensation and reward systems that encourage managers to sacrifice long-term goals for short-term gains.

15. *Create a democracy of information.* Companies need information systems that equip every employee to act in the interests of the entire enterprise.

16. *Empower the renegades and disarm the reactionaries.* Management systems must give more power to employees whose emotional equity is invested in the future rather than the past.

17. *Expand the scope of employee autonomy.* Management systems must be redesigned to facilitate grassroots initiatives and local experimentation.

18. *Create internal markets for ideas, talent, and resources.* Markets are better than hierarchies at allocating resources, and companies' resource allocation processes need to reflect this fact.

19. *Depoliticize decision making.* Decision processes must be free of positional biases and should exploit the collective wisdom of the entire organization and beyond.

20. *Better optimize trade-offs.* Management systems tend to force either-or choices. Hybrid systems that subtly optimize key trade-offs are needed.

21. *Further unleash human imagination.* Much is known about what engenders human creativity. This knowledge must be better applied in the design of management systems.

22. *Enable communities of passion.* To maximize employee engagement, management systems must facilitate the formation of self-defining communities of passion.

23. *Retool management for an open world.* Value-creating networks often transcend the firm's boundaries and can render traditional power-based management tools ineffective. New management tools are needed for building and shaping complex ecosystems.

24. *Humanize the language and practice of business.* Management systems must give as much credence to such timeless human ideals as beauty, justice, and community as they do to the traditional goals of efficiency, advantage, and profit.

25. *Retrain managerial minds.* Managers' deductive and analytical skills must be complemented by conceptual and systems-thinking skills.

Source: Hamel, Gary. 2009. Moon shots for management. *Harvard Business Review* 87(2): 91–98.

Two other moon shots are interesting in that they challenge some of the more dysfunctional behaviors that have been rampant in our organizations for decades. These moon shots call for eliminating the pathologies related to hierarchical power so that leaders and leadership practices emerge in a more organic manner. They also call for the elimination of fear and mistrust, which are toxic to innovation.

Some of the moon shots for management listed in Exhibit 16.1 are familiar, and the best leaders and organizations have been seeking to implement them for some time now. Others are new, and it's up to all of us to define exactly what they mean in practice.

Discussion Questions

1. Given all that you have learned in this course about changes in societies, technologies, and the world's economies, what bold, new approaches to managing and leading can you imagine? Create three recommendations that are specific, actionable and different from those discussed in this section.

2. Choose one of the moon shots, or one that you believe should be added to the list, and identify five actions *you* can take now to address the issue/challenge/change.

---

3. How Can You Continue Your Journey to Becoming a Resonant Leader?

Objective 16.3
Take actions toward becoming a resonant leader.

Our vision for this book is to truly help you be a powerful and positive leader. You don't need to wait to do this. It is our profound hope that you will see yourself as a leader *now*, rather than thinking you have to wait until later in your career. To conclude, we'd like to share a few final ideas, and then suggest some ways to continue your journey to becoming a resonant leader.

First, as we have emphasized throughout this book, everyone needs to be a leader today. As our organizations and management systems foster greater autonomy, empowerment, and input into decision-making processes at all levels, you will need to be a leader each and every day—often without the benefit of a formal title. This means you need to explore the secrets of great leadership: social and emotional intelligence, ethics, and responsible use of power. You need to make these your very own.

Second, you can embrace change and be part of the solution, as opposed to being part of the problems we face in our organizations and in the world today. Change is constant in life and work—fighting it does no good and is destructive. You have the opportunity to develop your capacity for adaptability, flexibility, and optimism; these qualities will help your organization and your local and global communities face today's challenges with courage, as well as maximize the opportunities available to all of us.

Third, you must focus on how you can strive to help the groups, organizations, and communities to which you belong. For too long, too many people have used their leadership and influence to further their own agendas or to benefit *their* group, *their* organization, *their* community or nation. Internal competition, self-serving agendas, fear, and mistrust have been prevalent for too long. It takes courage to refuse to play the game this way—you'll have to stand up for what's right, even when it's inconvenient or risky. Each of us has the responsibility to use our leadership for good and for others.

Fourth, you can and you must demand that the organizations with which you do business and where you work support your values and ethics. In this day and age, employees and consumers can easily find out what companies are doing vis-à-vis the environment, society, and the broader economy. Learning to do the right thing with the right people in the right way takes initiative, self-management, and the ability to inspire others to join you. You can and must make your voice heard.

Fifth, you need to become a lifelong learner. Social, economic, political, and technological changes will not slow down, nor will globalization. You have the opportunity to learn every single day from people who are very different from yourself. Don't miss the opportunity. It is up to you, and you alone, to tap into your natural curiosity, imagination, and passion, and to make learning a part of life and work every day.

You can prepare yourself for these challenges in a number of ways. In the next section we share how you can tap into your dreams and your passion, learn a bit more about your leadership strengths and challenges, and chart a course for the future.

Discussion Questions

1. Where in your life can you start to take up leadership roles and responsibilities? How will you demonstrate leadership—and to whom? How will this behavior help others?

2. Consider the organizations where you go to school, do business, or work. Do they support *your* values and ethics? How so? If they do not, what can or should you do about it? How can you stand up for your values and ethics in organizational life?

Objective 16.4
Develop your leadership skills.

4. What Can You Do to Develop Your Leadership?

By taking this course and reading this textbook, you have taken a huge step toward becoming a more effective leader. You are now equipped with the knowledge of what makes a great leader as well as the challenges we face in our world today. You have the information you need to be successful at work and as a global citizen.

If you are like most people, however, it is sometimes hard to translate knowledge into actions. For example, just reading about emotional intelligence, ethics, how to be more inclusive of others' perspectives, or how to use power doesn't mean that you will simply improve overnight. The same thing is true for skills related to communication, planning, decision making, organizing, controlling resources, and working in a virtual world or a diverse, global organization. Learning the skills that go along with this knowledge takes deliberate and focused action.

Most of the time when people attempt to learn something new (especially something related to work, like leadership skills), they start with a focus on what's not working: "I'm not a good team leader." "My communication skills are terrible." "I lose my temper all the time and get in trouble at work." We all have these kinds of thoughts sometimes, and often we try to act on them to improve. But have you ever noticed how hard it is to stay focused on a goal when we are trying to overcome a deficiency? Let's use examples from life to illustrate this point. Pick one of the following—something you have faced:

- "I need to lose weight."
- "I need to quit smoking."
- "I need to study more and party less."

If you are like most people, some of the feelings that go along with goals like this are "I'm too fat," "I'll die if I don't quit smoking," or "I'm going to fail this semester unless I stop going out with my friends so much." However compelling these feelings might be, new research tells us that thoughts and feelings like these make it very hard to stay focused on a goal.[7] This is because of the emotions that accompany these thoughts: They tend to be negative, self-critical, and pessimistic. These kinds of feelings cause us to want to get away from whatever is making us feel that way. It's the fight-or-flight response—in the face of a threat, even a psychological one, most people shut down and focus only on what will allow them to escape the threat or the source of pain. This means that when it comes to goals, negative thoughts and feelings are usually not helpful and, in fact, can interfere with achieving our goals, especially if the goals are challenging.

Making Leadership Development Fun—and Effective

So what can you do? Our research indicates that if you want to make meaningful and lasting changes in the skills and competencies related to leadership, you need to first focus on why these changes are important to you. You need to develop a powerful and positive view of the future—one where the changes you envision will help you live the life you want and become your "ideal self." This is the beginning of a process that noted scholar Richard Boyatzis has been studying for several decades, called "intentional change"—which you read about in Chapter 7.[8]

Now it's time to apply intentional change to your own life. As you can see in ■ **EXHIBIT 16.2**, intentional change begins with identifying your life vision and your ideal self. The hope, excitement, and other positive emotions this vision sparks actually provide you with energy and resilience—enough so that you can do the hard (and sometimes emotional) work of looking at both your strengths and your weaknesses. Looking at your real self—where you are today in your life, what's working and what's not—takes resilience and courage. Once you have a balanced and clear view of your real self, it is easy to see where some of the gaps are, and you can create a learning plan that is truly meaningful to you.

■ EXHIBIT 16.2
The intentional change model charts a path to your future.

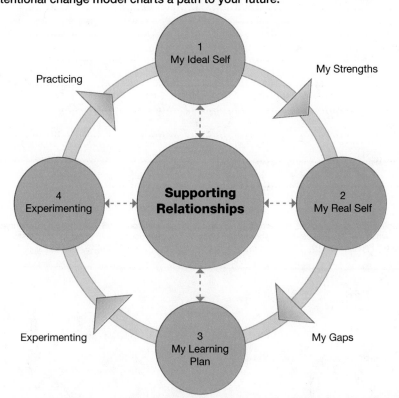

Source: Goleman, Daniel, Richard Boyatzis, and Annie McKee. 2002. *Primal Leadership.* Boston: Harvard Business School Press, p. 110. © 2002 Daniel Goleman. For more information on Intentional Change Theory see Boyatzis, Richard E. 2006. Intentional change theory from a complexity perspective. *Journal of Management Development* 25(7): 607–623.

To give you a head start on this process, the next section includes several exercises that will help deepen your self-awareness by exploring your ideal self and where you are now. They'll also help you practice writing a learning goal.

Exploring Your Vision and What You Want to Change

Here are seven exercises that will help you begin the process of becoming a better leader (■ **EXHIBITS 16.3** through **16.9**). The first few exercises will help you identify what is most important to you—your values and beliefs. Once you complete these exercises, you can review the various exercises throughout this book that have enabled you to envision your future. Next, you will explore who you are today. Finally, you will take stock of your strengths and weaknesses. You will probably see a pattern in what you have written. You'll see some themes in what you say you want to be and do in life and how your strengths can help you get there. Maybe you will even see some gaps that you would like to close or some things you would like to learn.

■ **EXHIBIT 16.3**

The Lottery: If I Could, I Would . . .

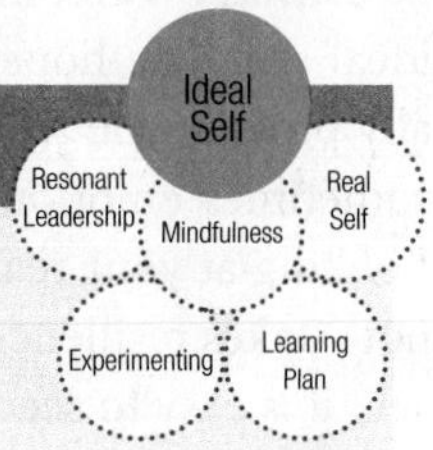

You just won the super lottery and received 50 million dollars or the equivalent in your currency after tax. How would your life and work change?

....

....

....

....

....

....

....

....

....

....

Source: Adapted from Annie McKee, Richard Boyatzis, and Frances Johnston. 2008. *Becoming a resonant leader: Develop your emotional intelligence, renew your relationships, and sustain your effectiveness* (p. 79). Boston: Harvard Business School Press.

■ **EXHIBIT 16.4**

My Life in the Year 20___

Project yourself into the future. It is 10 years from today. Picture what you most hope your life and work will be on that day.

In 20___, I am ___ years old.

If I am working, my work is best described as ....

....

....

My major work responsibilities are ....

....

....

The people I will see or talk to today include ....

....

....

The people with whom I live and socialize are ....

....

....

My most important possessions are ....

....

....

If someone were describing me to a friend today, they would say that I am .....

....

....

When I have some free time, I spend it ....

....

....

My leisure or fun activities in a typical week include ....

....

....

At least once a year, I try to ....

....

....

Source: Adapted from Annie McKee, Richard Boyatzis, and Frances Johnston. 2008. *Becoming a resonant leader: Develop your emotional intelligence, renew your relationships, and sustain your effectiveness* (p. 81). Boston: Harvard Business School Press.

◼ **EXHIBIT 16.5**

My Fantasy Job

This is an opportunity to imagine yourself doing the kind of work that you sometimes wonder about: "What would it be like if I were doing X?"

Make believe that:

1. You enter a new machine called a Neurophysiological Remaker. Using genetic reengineering and non-invasive neural implants, a few minutes inside the machine gives you the body, knowledge, and capability to do any job—and do it well.

2. You have been given the financial resources to do any job you want, and you are free of all personal, social, and financial responsibilities.

List several jobs that you would love to do or try. Consider a wide variety of jobs like those in other countries and jobs in sports, music, medicine, politics, agriculture, and religion. Consider jobs you have heard about or seen in the movies or on television.

....
....
....
....
....
....

Choose the three jobs in your list that most interest you or seem the most exciting or rewarding. Describe each of them below, including what you would enjoy or look forward to the most about each job.

1. _____
   _____

2. _____
   _____

3. _____
   _____

(continued)

■ **EXHIBIT 16.5 *(Continued)***

My Fantasy Job

Sometimes a person describes a fantasy job as one he or she really wants to do. Other times, the job represents some interesting or exciting activities or conditions. In other words, sometimes it is not the job that is the fantasy, but some aspect of it or conditions under which the job is done.

As you read your descriptions of the jobs you would most like to do or try, do you notice themes or patterns? How are these different jobs similar? Are there activities (such as being outdoors) that are part of each? Are there conditions of the work (such as working with a team) that are part of each? Are there outcomes (such as being famous) that are a part of each? List those themes or patterns below.

....

....

....

....

....

....

....

....

....

....

....

....

....

....

....

....

....

....

Source: Adapted from Annie McKee, Richard Boyatzis, and Frances Johnston. 2008. *Becoming a resonant leader: Develop your emotional intelligence, renew your relationships, and sustain your effectiveness* (pp. 82–83). Boston: Harvard Business School Press.

■ **EXHIBIT 16.6**

My Values

Beliefs, Principles, and Personal Characteristics That Guide My Life

Below is a list of values, beliefs, or personal characteristics for your consideration. Each of the steps in this process will help you identify which are most important to you and which are guiding principles in your life. It is difficult to choose, of course, because many of these values and characteristics will be at least somewhat important to you. It is also hard to choose because you might find yourself thinking, "I should value X and put it first on my list," even though it really isn't. So, force yourself to choose, and choose based on your true feelings, not the "shoulds" in life.

You might find it useful to determine degrees of importance by imagining how you would feel if you were forced to give up believing in or acting on a particular value, belief, or personal characteristic. Or, think about how you would feel if your life really revolved around certain values, beliefs, or characteristics. How would this make you feel? Sometimes, you might find it helpful to consider two values at a time, asking yourself about the relative importance of one over the other.

1. Start by circling the fifteen or so values that are most important to you.
2. Then, from this list of fifteen or so, identify the ten that are the most important to you and write them in a list.
3. From this list of ten, circle the five that are the most important to you.

List of Values, Beliefs, or Desirable Personal Characteristics

Accomplishment	Control	Independence	Reliable
Achievement	Cooperation	Improving society	Religion
Adventure	Courageous	Innovative	Respectful
Affection	Courteous	Integrity	Responsible
Affectionate	Creativity	Intellectual	Restrained
Affiliation	Dependable	Involvement	Salvation
Ambitious	Disciplined	Imagination	Self-controlled
Assisting others	Economic security	Joy	Self-reliance
Authority	Effective	Leisurely	Self-respect
Autonomy	Equality	Logical	Sincerity
Beauty	Excitement	Love	Spirituality
Belonging	Fame	Loving	Stability
Broad minded	Family happiness	Mature love	Status
Caring	Family security	National security	Success
Challenge	Forgiving	Nature	Symbolic
Cheerful	Free choice	Obedient	Taking risks
Clean	Freedom	Order	Teamwork
Comfortable life	Friendship	Peace	Tidy
Companionship	Fun	Personal development	Tender
Compassion	Genuineness	Pleasure	Tranquility
Competent	Happiness	Polite	Wealth
Competitiveness	Health	Power	Winning
Contribution to others	Helpfulness	Pride	Wisdom
Conformity	Honesty	Rational	Other:
Contentedness	Hope	Recognition	_____

(continued)

■ **EXHIBIT 16.6 (Continued)**

My Values

My Ten Most Important Values

1. _____
2. _____
3. _____
4. _____
5. _____

6. _____
7. _____
8. _____
9. _____
10. _____

Finally, rank each of your five most important values, beliefs, or characteristics with "1" being the most important value to you and "5" being the least important of these five important values.

1. _____
2. _____
3. _____

4. _____
5. _____

Source: Adapted from Annie McKee, Richard Boyatzis, and Frances Johnston. 2008. *Becoming a resonant leader: Develop your emotional intelligence, renew your relationships, and sustain your effectiveness* (pp. 90–91). Boston: Harvard Business School Press.

■ **EXHIBIT 16.7**

Strengths I See in Myself

Strengths can be elements that you were born with or things you have learned. They are extremely valuable or useful abilities, assets, or qualities. What are your strengths? What do you consider your character assets?

Complete this sentence: I am a person who...

....

....

List ten things that have served you well and of which you are most proud. For each strength, notice the sensations or feelings that come up for you as you write it down and reflect on your successes.

My Strengths	Sensations/Feelings
1. _____	_____
2. _____	_____
3. _____	_____
4. _____	_____
5. _____	_____

(continued)

■ **EXHIBIT 16.7** *(Continued)*

Strengths I See in Myself

My Strengths   Sensations/Feelings

6. _____   _____

7. _____   _____

8. _____   _____

9. _____   _____

10. _____   _____

Do any of these sensations or feelings surprise you? Why do these things stand out to you?

....

....

....

....

....

Summarize what you consider to be personal and leadership strengths. These elements are likely to be things you enjoy about yourself, and which others like about you. They are energizers for you.

....

....

....

....

....

....

....

....

Source: Adapted from Annie McKee, Richard Boyatzis, and Frances Johnston. 2008. *Becoming a resonant leader: Develop your emotional intelligence, renew your relationships, and sustain your effectiveness* (pp. 132–134). Boston: Harvard Business School Press.

■ **EXHIBIT 16.8**

Personal Balance Sheet

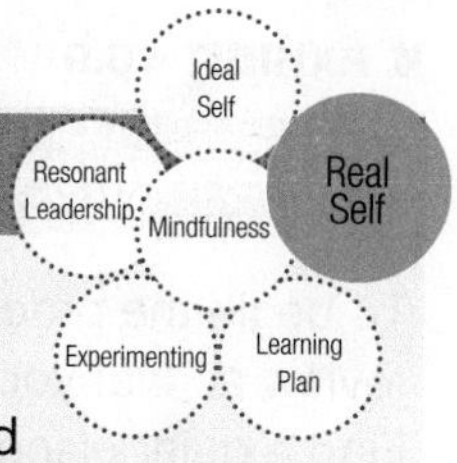

Like assessing the value of a business, a balance sheet is a way to summarize our personal assets and liabilities. Using all of the assessments and reflection you have done so far and the form that follows, we invite you to create your Personal Balance Sheet.

My Assets	My Liabilities
My Distinctive Strengths—things I know I do well and strengths that **others see in me**	**My Current Limitations**—things I know that I don't do well and **I want to do better**
My Potential Strengths—things I could do better or more often if I focused, or things I do well in some situations and could begin to apply more broadly	**My Weaknesses**—things that I know I don't do well and **want to change**
My Enduring Dispositions That Support Me—this includes traits, habits, behaviors that I do not want to change and that help me to be successful	**My Enduring Dispositions That Sometimes Get in My Way**—this includes traits, habits, behaviors that I do not want to change and that sometimes cause me to be less effective

Source: Adapted from Annie McKee, Richard Boyatzis, and Frances Johnston. 2008. *Becoming a resonant leader: Develop your emotional intelligence, renew your relationships, and sustain your effectiveness* (p. 150). Boston: Harvard Business School Press.

■ **EXHIBIT 16.9**

My Learning Edge

To begin the process of articulating learning goals, it helps to review all that you have learned and done so far in this book. Find a quiet place to sit, and go back through the exercises. Think about your Personal Vision, which you have worked on in this chapter and throughout this book, and then look at your Personal Balance Sheet. Read some of your notes about your past, your present, and your future.

What stands out to you about how your current strengths will help you move toward your Personal Vision for life and work?

....
....
....
....

Are there gaps between who you are now and who you want to be in the future or how you want to live your life?

....
....
....
....

What major changes might you need to make if you are to achieve your vision?

....
....
....
....

Identify two to five themes of what you would like to do, be, or achieve.

....
....
....
....
....
....
....

Source: Adapted from Annie McKee, Richard Boyatzis, and Frances Johnston. 2008. *Becoming a resonant leader: Develop your emotional intelligence, renew your relationships, and sustain your effectiveness* (pp. 163–164). Boston: Harvard Business School Press.

As a result of these exercises (and this course!) you probably have a lot of ideas about how you can be effective in the many roles you will play at work. As you think about this, it helps to remember *why* you want to be effective: your purpose in life, the special talents and gifts that you bring, and the contributions you can make.

Discussion Questions

1. Which exercises did you find the most revealing? Why do you think the exercises were capable of doing that? In working through the exercises, what were you surprised to learn about yourself?
2. What does lifelong learning mean to you? How will you evoke curiosity, avoid complacency, and engage others with the intention of learning from them?

5. A Final Word on Managing Yourself

Our world needs all that you can give: your brilliance and creativity, values and ethics, enthusiasm, hope, and inspiration. We are facing some very big challenges today—as a leader, you can help your organization and your community rectify the mistakes of the past and step into a new and exciting era.

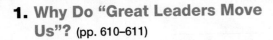

1. Why Do "Great Leaders Move Us"? (pp. 610–611)

Objective: Learn how some of the best leaders today make an impact on others.

Summary: Being a great leader is about more than knowing leadership theories. Chade-Meng Tan of Google exemplifies this and points out that egoless-ego, compassion, and fun are essential for truly inspiring followers. This type of inspiration is especially important in light of the challenges facing the world today.

2. What Are "Moon Shots for Management"? (pp. 611–613)

Objective: Understand ways in which management must change.

Summary: Moon shots for management are guidelines that encourage us to lead responsibly and shift away from antiquated forms of management toward ethical and community-oriented behavior. The moon shots seek to eliminate many of the dysfunctions seen in today's organizations—such as stifling hierarchies—so power can be used for good. Moon shots are not designed to be a specific set of instructions; rather, they are guiding principles that must be interpreted meaningfully by individual organizations and their leaders.

3. How Can You Continue Your Journey to Becoming a Resonant Leader? (pp. 613–614)

Objective: Take actions toward becoming a resonant leader.

Summary: Leadership is not a distant career goal; it is a journey that you can begin now. As autonomy and empowerment become the norm in organizations, you need to lead, embrace change, and become a lifelong learner in order to solve organizational and community problems. It is also essential that you use your power as a leader to benefit those around you and ensure that your organization lives up to your personal values and ethics.

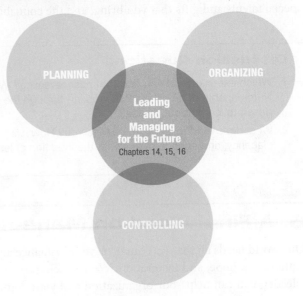

5. A Final Word on Managing Yourself (p. 625)

Summary: You are in a position to help your organizations and community today. The world needs all your talents, competencies, and creativity as we face tremendous challenges and opportunities.

4. What Can You Do to Develop Your Leadership? (pp. 614–625)

Objective: Develop your leadership skills.

Summary: Translating leadership theory into action can be tough, particularly if you set goals that focus solely on personal deficiencies. In order for you to achieve meaningful change, you need to think positively about your ideal self and engage in the process of intentional change. This process involves identifying your personal vision, exploring who you are, and planning to develop strengths that are meaningful to you.

MyManagementLab

Go to **mymanagementlab.com** for Auto-graded writing questions as well as the following Assisted-graded writing questions:

16-1. Do you find any of the moon shots for managers particularly important? Why?

16-2. What aspects of your life or work are currently in transition or changing? What can you do to embrace these changes positively—to become part of the future rather than hold onto the past?

16-3. Mymanagementlab Only — comprehensive writing assignment for this chapter.

Endnotes

Chapter 1

1. McKee, Annie, Richard Boyatzis, and Frances Johnston. 2008. *Becoming a resonant leader*. Boston: Harvard Business School Press.
2. Barton, Dominic. 2011. Capitalism for the long term. *Harvard Business Review* 89(3): 84–91.
3. Creative Commons. "Creative Commons and Open Educational Resources." Retrieved May 8, 2012, from http://wiki.creativecommons .org/Creative_Commons_and_Open_Educational_Resources; Friesen, Norm. *Open Educational Resources: New Possibilities for Change and Sustainability*. 2009. Vol. 10, 2009.
4. Barton, Dominic. 2011. Capitalism for the long term.
5. Goleman, Daniel, Richard Boyatzis, and Annie McKee. 2002. *Primal leadership*. Boston: Harvard Business School Press; McKee, Annie, and Richard Boyatzis. 2005. *Resonant leadership*. Boston: Harvard Business School Press.
6. McKee, Annie, et al. 2008. *Becoming a resonant leader*.
7. Mintzberg, Henry. 1975. *The nature of managerial work*. New York: Harper and Row.
8. Ibid.
9. Hollander, Edwin P. 1992. Leadership, followership, self, and others. *Leadership Quarterly* 3(1): 43–54; Van Vugt, Mark, Robert Hogan, and Robert B. Kaiser. 2008. Leadership, followership, and evolution: Some lessons from the past. *American Psychologist* 63(3): 182–96.
10. Kellerman, Barbara. 2008. *Followership: How followers are creating change and changing leaders*. Boston: Harvard Business School Press.
11. Kellerman, Barbara. 2007. What every leader needs to know about followers. *Harvard Business Review* 85(12): 84–91.
12. Ibid.
13. Kellerman, Barbara. 2012. *The end of leadership*. New York: HarperCollins.
14. Useem, Michael. 2003. *Leading up: How to lead your boss so you both win*. New York: Three Rivers Press; Hooley, Tristram. 2009. Followership. *Adventures in Career Development* (July 19). Retrieved March 10, 2010, from http://adventuresincareerdevelopment.posterous.com/followership.
15. Bennis, Warren. 2001. The challenges of leadership in the modern world: Introduction to the Special Issue. *American Psychologist* 62(1): 2–5.
16. Littrell, Romie F. 2007. Influences on employee preferences for empowerment practices by the "ideal manager" in China. *International Journal of Intercultural Relations* 31(1): 87–110.
17. Pina e Cunha, Miguel, and Arménio Rego. 2010. Complexity, simplicity, simplexity. *European Management Journal* 28(2): 85–94.
18. Fombrun, Charles J., Noel M. Tichy, and Mary Anne Devanna. 1984. *Strategic human resource management*. New York: Wiley.
19. Hendry, Chris, and Andrew Pettigrew. 1990. Human resource management: An agenda for the 1990s. *International Journal of Human Resource Management* 1(1): 17–43; Huselid, Mark A., Susan E. Jackson, and Randall S. Schuler. 1997. Technical and strategic human resource management effectiveness as determinants of firm performance. *The Academy of Management Journal* 40(1): 171–88; Schuler, Randall S., and Susan E. Jackson. 2007. *Strategic human resource management*. 2nd ed. Malden, MA: Blackwell.
20. Boyatzis, Richard E. 2008. Leadership development from a complexity perspective. *Consulting Psychology Journal: Practice and Research* 60(4): 298–313.
21. McKee, Annie, et al. 2008. *Becoming a resonant leader*.
22. Rage against the machine. (Cover Story). 2011. *The Economist* 400(8756): 13-13.
23. Barton, Dominic. 2011. Capitalism for the long term. *Harvard Business Review* 89(3): 84-91.
24. FitzGerald, Niall. April 27, 2012. Acceptance Speech for Business Alumnus of the Year Award. University College, Dublin.
25. Paraphrased from Rage against the machine. (Cover Story). 2011. *The Economist* 400(8756): 13-13.
26. Ibid.

Chapter 2

1. Boyatzis, Richard E. 2008. Competencies in the 21st century (Guest Editorial). *Journal of Management Development* 27(1): 5–12; Spencer, Lyle M., and Signe M. Spencer. 1993. *Competence at work: Models for superior performance*. New York: John Wiley and Sons; Boyatzis, Richard E. 1982. *The competent manager: A model for effective performance*. Hoboken, NJ: Wiley-Interscience.
2. Goleman, Daniel, Richard Boyatzis, and Annie McKee. 2004. *Primal Leadership: Realizing the Power of Emotional Intelligence*. Boston: Harvard Business School Press.
3. McClelland, David C. 1973. Testing for competence rather than for "intelligence." *American Psychologist* 28: 1–14.
4. Thorndike, R. L., and E. Hagen. 1959. *10,000 careers*. New York: Wiley.
5. Boyatzis, R. 2008. Competencies in the 21st century.
6. Ibid.
7. Ibid.
8. Ibid.
9. Boyatzis, R.. 2008. Competencies in the 21st century; Spencer, L., and S. Spencer. *Competence at work: Models for superior performance*. Boyatzis, R. *The competent manager*.
10. Ibid.
11. Goleman, D. 1995. *Emotional intelligence*. New York: Bantam Books; Goleman, D. 2006. *Social intelligence*. New York: Bantam Books.
12. McKee, Annie, Richard Boyatzis, and Frances Johnston. 2008. *Becoming a resonant leader: Develop your emotional intelligence, renew your relationships, sustain your effectiveness*: Harvard Business School Press.
13. Boyatzis, R., and A. McKee. 2005. *Resonant leadership: Sustaining yourself and connecting with others through mindfulness, hope, and compassion*. Boston: Harvard Business School Press.
14. Gardner, H. 1983. *Frames of mind: The theory of multiple intelligences*. New York: Basic Books; Bar-On, R. 1997. *Bar-On Emotional Quotient Inventory: Technical manual*. Toronto: Multi-Health Systems; Goleman, *Emotional intelligence*; Bar-On, Reuven. 1988. "The Development of a Concept of Psychological Well-Being." Rhodes University.
15. Goleman, D., R. Boyatzis, and A. McKee. 2002. *Primal leadership*. Boston: Harvard Business School Press; McKee, A. et al. 2008. *Becoming a resonant leader*. Boston: Harvard Business School Press; Goleman, D. 1998. *Working with emotional intelligence*. New York: Bantam Books.
16. Goleman et al., *Primal leadership*; Boyatzis and McKee, *Resonant leadership*.
17. Goleman, *Social intelligence*.
18. Goleman et al., *Primal leadership*; Boyatzis and McKee, *Resonant leadership*; McKee et al., *Becoming a resonant leader*; Lewis, Thomas, Fari Amini, and Richard Lannon. 2000. *A general theory of love*. New York: Random House.
19. McKee et al., *Becoming a resonant leader* p. 31.
20. Nummenmaa, L., J. Hirvonen, et al. 2008. Is emotional contagion special? An fMRI study on neural systems for affective and cognitive empathy. *NeuroImage* 43(3): 571–580; Iacoboni, M. The mirror neuron revolution: Explaining what makes humans social. *Scientific American* July 1, 2008. Retrieved February 28, 2012, from http://www.scientificamerican.com/ article.cfm?id=the-mirror-neuron-revolut.
21. Butcher, David, and Martin Clarke. 2008. *Smart management: Using politics in organisations*. Basingstoke, UK: Palgrave.
22. Runde, Craig E., and Tim A. Flanagan. 2007. *Becoming a competent leader: How you and your organization can manage conflict effectively*. San Francisco, CA: John Wiley & Sons.
23. French and Raven: French, J. R. P., and B. Raven. 1959. "The Bases of Social Power." *In Studies of Social Power*, edited by D. Cartwright. 150–67. Ann Arbor, MI: University of Michigan, Institute for Social Research.
24. Goleman et al., *Primal leadership*.
25. Source: interview with Annie McKee, 2012.

26. Bowne, D. E., and E. E. Lawler. 1992. Empowerment of service workers: What, why, how and when. *Sloan Management Review* 33(3): 31–39; Pastor, J. 1996. Empowerment: What it is and what it is not. *Empowerment in Organizations* 4(2): 5–7.

27. Spreitzer, G. M. 2007. Giving peace a chance: Organizational leadership, empowerment, and peace. *Journal of Organizational Behavior* 28: 1077–95.

28. Bakker, A. B. 2005. Flow among music teachers and their students: The crossover of peak experiences. *Journal of Vocational Behavior* 66: 26–44; Reeve, J., H. Jang, D. Carrell, S. Jeon, and J. Barch. 2004. Enhancing students' engagement by increasing teachers' autonomy support. *Motivation and Emotion* 28: 147–69; Ouchi, W. G. 1981. *Theory Z: How American business can meet the Japanese challenge.* Reading, MA: Addison-Wesley.

29. Spreitzer, G. M. 1995. Psychological empowerment in the workplace: dimensions, measurement, and validation. *Academy of Management Journal* 38: 1442–65.

30. Lucas, Victoria, Heather K. Spence Laschinger, and Carol Wong. 2008. The impact of emotional intelligent leadership on staff nurse empowerment: The moderating effect of span of control. *Journal of Nursing Management* 16: 964–73; Erstad, M. 1997. Empowerment and organizational change. *International Journal of Contemporary Hospitality* 9(7): 325–33.

31. Ouchi, William. G. 1981. *Theory Z: How American business can meet the Japanese challenge.* Reading, MA: Addison-Wesley.

32. Ibid.

33. Pellegrini, E. K., and T. A. Scandura. 2008. Paternalistic leadership: A review and agenda for future research. *Journal of Management* 34(3) 566–93.

34. Forrester, R. 1993. Empowerment, *Academy of Management Executive* 14: 67–90.

35. Manning, George, and Kent Curtis. 2003. The Art of Leadership, p. 133. Boston, Mass.: McGraw-Hill/Irwin.

36. Beck, Sanderson. 2004. Greece & Rome to 30 BC. *Iscrates, Aristotle, and Diogenes.* Retrieved August 7, 2009, from http://www.san.beck.org/EC22-Aristotle.html.

37. Wills, Garry. 2001. *Saint Augustine's childhood.* New York: Penguin Putnam.

38. Ferguson, W. C. 1997. Ethical foundations. *Executive Excellence* 14(6): 16.

39. Rokeach, Milton. 1973. *The nature of human values.* New York: Free Press.

40. Epstein, Edwin M. 1989. Business ethics, corporate good citizenship and the corporate social policy process: A view from the United States. *Journal of Business Ethics* 8(8): 583–95.

41. AICPA code of professional conduct: Preamble. Retrieved February 26, 2010, from http://www.aicpa.org/About/code/et_50.html.

42. Bauman, Zygmunt. 1998. *Globalization: The human consequences.* NewYork: Columbia University Press.

43. Ess, Charles. 2006. Ethical pluralism and global information ethics. *Ethics and Information Technology* 8(4): 215–26.

44. Bauman, Zygmunt. 1993. *Postmodern ethics.* Blackwell, Oxford.

45. Sarbanes-Oxley Act. Retrieved July 9, 2009, from http://en.wikipedia.org/wiki/Sarbanes-Oxley_Act.

46. U.S. Department of State. International Anticorruption and Good Governance Act. Retrieved February 26, 2010, from http://www.state.gov/j/inl/rls/rpt/c6696.htm.

47. "AT&T to Pay $756,000 for Religious Bias against Jehovah's Witnesses." U.S. Equal Employment Opportunity Commission. Retrieved November 19, 2012, from http://www.eeoc.gov/eeoc/newsroom/release/10-23-07.cfm.

48. Clegg, Stewart, Martin Kornberger, and Carl Rhodes. 2007. Business ethics as practice. *British Journal of Management* 18(2): 107–22.

49. Brin, S., and L. Page. Google code of conduct. Retrieved July 5, 2009, from http://investor.google.com/conduct.html.

50. Madoff investment scandal. Retrieved March 4, 2012, from http://www.wikipedia.com; Appelbaum, Binyamin, David S. Hilzenrath, and Amit R. Paley. 2008, December 13. All just one big lie. *Washington Post.* Retrieved September 10, 2009, from http://www.washingtonpost.com/wp-dyn/content/article/2008/12/12/AR2008121203970.html?hpid=topnews.

51. Biggs, Barton. 2009, January 13. The Affinity Ponzi scheme. *Newsweek.* Retrieved August 13, 2009, from http://www.newsweek.com/id/177679.

52. Madoff trading statement. November 2008. Retrieved February 26, 2010, from http://www.scribd.com/doc/8976754/Madoff-Trading-Statement-November-2008.

53. Arvedlund, Erin E. 2001, May 7. Don't ask, don't tell. *Barron's.* Retrieved February 26, 2010, from http://online.barrons.com/article/SB989019667829349012.html.

54. Appelbaum, et al. All just one big lie; Sherwell, Philip. 2010, December 11. "Son of Disgraced Financier Bernard Madoff Found Dead on Anniversary." *The Telegraph,* http://www.telegraph.co.uk/finance/financetopics/bernard-madoff/8196243/Bernard-Madoffs-son-Mark-found-dead.html.

55. Henriques, Diana B. 2009. Madoff Is Sentenced to 150 Years for Ponzi Scheme (September 29). New York Times. Retrieved November 7, 2012, from http://www.nytimes.com/2009/06/30/business/30madoff.html?pagewanted=all accessed February 24, 2012.

56. McClean, Elkind, and Alex Gibney. 2005. *Enron: The smartest guys in the room.* Directed by Alex Gibney. Distributed by Columbia Pictures.

57. Halbesleben, Jonathon R. B., Anthony R. Wheeler, and M. Ronald Buckley. 2005. Everybody else is doing it, so why can't we? Pluralistic ignorance and business ethics education. *Journal of Business Ethics* 56(4): 385–98.

58. Hardin, Garrett. 1968. The tragedy of the commons. *Science* 162(3859): 1243–48.

59. Kohs, S. C., and K. W. Irle. 1920. Prophesying army promotion. *Journal of Applied Psychology* 4(1): 73–87; Tead, Ordway. 1929. *Human nature and management.* New York: McGraw-Hill; Page, David P. 1935. Measurement and prediction of leadership. *American Journal of Sociology* 41(1): 31–43; Bellingrath, George C. 1930. *Qualities associated with leadership in the extra-curricular activities of the high school.* New York: Teacher's College Contributions to Education; Gowin, E. B. 1927. *The executive and his control of men.* New York: Macmillan Company.

60. Jenkins, W. O. 1947. A review of leadership studies with particular reference to military problems. *Psychological Bulletin* 44: 54–79.

61. Contributors to Exhibit 2.10, (individual contributions undifferentiated): Bass, Bernard M. 1990. *Bass & Stogdill's handbook of leadership: Theory, research and managerial applications.* New York: The Free Press; Kirkpatrick, Shelley A., and Edwin A. Locke. 1991. Leadership: Do traits matter? *Academy of Management Executive* 5(2): 48–60; Mishra, Aneil K. 1996. Organizational responses to crises: The centrality of trust. In *Trust in organizations,* ed. Roderick M. Kramer and Thomas Tyler, 261–87. Newbury Park, CA: Sage; Bryman, A. 1993. *Charisma and leadership in organizations.* London: Sage; George, Jennifer M. 2000. Emotions and leadership: The role of emotional intelligence. *Human Relations* 53(8): 1027–55; Judge, Timothy A., and Joyce E. Bono. 2000. Five-factor model of personality and transformational leadership. *Journal of Applied Psychology* 85(5): 751–65; Mumford, Michael D., Stephen J. Zaccaro, Francis D. Harding, T. Owen Jacobs, and Edwin A. Fleishman. 2000. Leadership skills for a changing world: Solving complex social problems. *Leadership Quarterly* 11(1): 11–35; Conger, Jay A., and Rabindra N. Kanungo. 1987. Towards a behavioral theory of charismatic leadership in an organizational setting. *Academy of Management Review* 12: 637–47; Conger, Jay A., and Rabindra N. Kanungo. 1994. Charismatic leadership in organizations: Perceived behavioral attributes and their measurement. *Journal of Organizational Behavior* 15(5): 439–52; Hartog, Deanne N., Robert J. House, Paul J. Hanges, and S. Antonio Ruiz-Quintanilla. 1999. Culture specific and cross-culturally generalizable implicit leadership theories: Are attributes of charismatic/transformational leadership universally endorsed? *Leadership Quarterly* 10(2): 219–56; Covey, S. R. 1996. Three roles of the leader in the new paradigm, in *The leader of the future: New visions, strategies, and practices for the next era,* ed. F. Hesselbein, M. Goldsmith, and R. Beckhard, 149–59. New York: Jossey Bass; Covey, S. R. 1990. *Principle-centered leadership.* New York: Simon and Schuster; Russell, Robert F., and A. Gregory Stone. 2002. A review of servant leadership attributes: Developing a practical model. *Leadership & Organization Development Journal* 23(3/4): 145–57; Zaccaro, S. J., C. Kemp, and P. Bader. 2004. Leader traits and attributes. In *The nature of leadership,* ed. J. Antonakis, A. T. Cianciolo, and R. J. Sternberg, 101–24. Thousand Oaks, CA: Sage; Zaleznik, Abraham. 1992. Managers and leaders: Are they different? *Harvard Business Review* (March–April): 126–35; Goleman et al. *Primal leadership.*

62. Ibid.

63. Fleishman, E. A. 1957. A leader behavior description for industry, in *Leader behavior: Its description and measurement,* ed. R. M. Stogdill and A. E. Coons. Columbus, OH: Bureau of Business Research; Fleishman, E. A., E. F. Harris, and H. E. Burtt. 1955. *Leadership and supervision in*

industry. Columbus, OH: Bureau of Educational Research, Ohio State University; Fleishman, E. A., and D. A. Peters. 1962. Interpersonal values, leadership attitudes, and managerial success. *Personnel Psychology* 15: 127–43. See also Fiedler, F. E. 1958. *Leader attitudes and group effectiveness*. Urbana, IL: University of Illinois Press.

64. Fleishman, E. 1973. Twenty years of consideration and structure, in *Current developments in the study of leadership: A centennial event*, ed. E. A. Fleishman and J. Hunt, 1–40. Carbondale, IL: Southern Illinois University Press.

65. Likert, R. 1979. From production- and employee-centeredness to systems 1–4. *Journal of Management* 5: 628–41.

66. Blake and Mouton, *The managerial grid*; Blake, R., and J. Mouton. 1978. *The new managerial grid*. Houston, TX: Gulf Publishing Co; Blake, R. R., and J. S. McCanse. 1991. *The managerial grid illuminated: Leadership dilemmas grid solutions*. Houston, TX: Gulf Publishing Co.; Blake, R., and J. Mouton. 1994. *The managerial grid*. Houston, TX: Gulf Publishing Co; McKee, R. K., and B. Carlson. 1999. *The power to change*. Austin, TX: Grid International, Inc.

67. Fiedler, F. E. 1967. *A theory of leadership effectiveness*. New York: McGraw-Hill.

68. Fiedler, F. 1965. Engineer the job to fit the manager. *Harvard Business Review* 43(5): 115–22; Fiedler, F., and M. M. Chemers. 1984. *Improving leadership effectiveness: The leader match concept* (rev. ed.). New York: Wiley.

69. Hersey, P., and K. Blanchard. 1982. *Management of organizational behavior*. Englewood Cliffs, NJ: Prentice Hall.

70. House, R. J. 1971. A path-goal theory of leader effectiveness. *Administrative Science Quarterly* 16: 321–38; Wofford, J. C., and L. Z. Liska. 1993. Path-goal theories of leadership: A meta-analysis. *Journal of Management* 19: 857–76.

71. Keller, R. 1989. Test of path-goal theory of leadership with need for clarity as moderator in research and development organizations. *Journal of Applied Psychology* 74: 208–12.

72. Kerr, S., and J. M. Jermier. 1978. Substitutes for leadership: Their meaning and measurement. *Organizational Behavior and Human Performance* 22: 375–403.

73. Burns, James M. 1978. *Leadership*. New York: HarperCollins.

74. Milz, Mary. 2011, March 31. Brad Stevens: From Lilly PR man to Butler hoops. *WTHR.com*. Retrieved March 8, 2012, from http://www.wthr.com/story/14360449/brad-stevens-from-lilly-pr-man-to-butler-hoops.

75. Butlersports.com. Men's Basketball: Brad Stevens. Retrieved on March 8, 2012, from http://www.butlersports.com/sports/m-baskbl/mtt/stevens_brad00.html.

76. Butlersports.com. Brad Stevens Profile. Retrieved on March 8, 2012, from http://butlersports.cstv.com/sports/m-baskbl/mtt/stevens_brad00.html.

77. Butlersports.com. Men's Basketball: Brad Stevens. Retrieved on March 8, 2012, from http://www.butlersports.com/sports/m-baskbl/mtt/stevens_brad00.html.

78. Schultz, Jordan. 2011, April 5. Can Brad Stevens Turn Butler Into A True National Power? *The Huffington Post*. Retrieved March 8, 2012, from http://www.huffingtonpost.com/2011/04/05/can-brad-stevens-turn-butler_n_845166.html.

79. Ibid.

80. Winn, Luke. 2012, January 12. Butler enduring difficult season as poor shooting derails high hopes. *SI.com*. Retrieved March 8, 2012, from http://sportsillustrated.cnn.com/2012/writers/luke_winn/01/27/butler.crossroads/index.html.

81. Bloomgarden, Kathy. 2007. *Trust: The secret weapon of effective business leaders*. New York: St. Martin's Press; Useem, Michael. 2006. How well-run boards make decisions. *Harvard Business Review* 84(6): 130–38.

82. Conger, J. A., and R. N. Kanungo, eds. 2008. *Charismatic leadership in organizations*. Thousand Oaks, CA: Sage Publications.

83. Lever, W. H. Prosperity-sharing versus profit sharing in relation to workshop management. *The Economic Review (Christian Social Union)* 11(1901): 17; FitzGerald, Niall. 2011. Perlmutter Award Acceptance Speech. Delivered on October 31, 2011, at Brandeis University.

84. http://www.unilever.com/brands/

85. McKee, Annie, and Frances Johnston. *The four HR leadership roles* (Elkins Park, PA: Teleos Leadership Institute, 2010) slides.

86. Green, Michael, and Erin McGill. State of the Industry, 2011. In ASTD's *Annual review of workplace learning and development data*, edited by Laurie Miller, 70 pp. Alexandria, VA: American Society for Training & Development, 2011.

87. Carrick, Laurie A. 2010. Demystifying the EI Quick Fix. *T+D* 64(11): 60–63.

88. George, B., P. Sims, A. N. McLean, and D. Mayer. 2007. Discovering your authentic leadership. *Harvard Business Review* 85(2): 129–38.

89. Avolio, Bruce J., and William L. Gardner. 2005. Authentic leadership development: Getting to the root of positive forms of leadership. *Leadership Quarterly* 16(3): 315–38.

90. Kernis, Michael H. 2003. Toward a conceptualization of optimal self-esteem. *Psychological Inquiry* 14(1): 1–26.

91. Gillespie, Nicole A., and Leon Mann. 2004. Transformational leadership and shared values: The building blocks of trust. *Journal of Managerial Psychology* 19(6): 588–607; Hosmer, Larue Tone. 1995. The connecting link between organizational theory and philosophical ethics. *Academy of Management Review* 20(2): 379–403.

92. Gillespie and Mann, Transformational leadership and shared values.

93. Brown, Michael E., and Linda K. Treviño. 2005. Ethical leadership: A social learning perspective for construct development and testing. *Organizational Behavior and Human Decision Processes* 97: 117–34.

94. Waddock, Sandra. 2007. Leadership integrity in a fractured knowledge world. *Academy of Management Learning & Education* 6(4): 543–57.

95. Palanski, Michael E., and Francis J. Yammarino. 2009. Integrity and leadership: A multi-level conceptual framework. *Leadership Quarterly* 20(3): 405–20.

96. Redmoon, Ambrose H. 1991. No peaceful warriors! *Gnosis: A Journal of the Western Inner Traditions* 21(Fall): 40–45.

97. Hightower, Jim, and Susan DeMarco. 2008. *Swim against the current: Even a dead fish can go with the flow*. Hoboken, NJ: John Wiley & Sons.

98. Kouzes, J., and B. Posner. 2003. *The leadership challenge*. New York: Jossey-Bass.

99. Ibid.

Chapter 3

1. Latham, Gary P., and Craig C. Pinder. 2005. Work motivation theory and research at the dawn of the twenty-first century. *Annual Review of Psychology* 56: 485–516.

2. Frankl, Victor. 1963. *Man's search for meaning*. New York: Pocket Books.

3. Csikszentmihalyi, Mihaly. 1975. *Beyond boredom and anxiety: Experiencing flow in work and play*. San Francisco: Jossey-Bass; Csikszentmihalyi, Mihaly. 1990. *Flow: The psychology of optimal experience*. New York: HarperCollins; Keller, J., and H. Bless. 2008. Flow and regulatory compatibility: An experimental approach to the flow model of intrinsic motivation. *Personality and Social Psychology Bulletin* 34: 196–209.

4. Adapted from Nakamura, Jeanne, and Mihaly Csikszentmihalyi. 2002. The concept of flow. In *Handbook of positive psychology*, ed. R. Snyder and Shane Lopez. Oxford: Oxford University Press.

5. Boyatzis, Richard, and Annie McKee. 2005. *Resonant leadership: Renewing yourself and connecting with others through mindfulness, hope and compassion*. Boston: Harvard Business School Press; Snyder, C. R., K. L. Rand, and D. R. Signon. 2002. Hope theory: A member of the positive psychology family. In *Handbook of positive psychology*, ed. C. R. Snyder and S. J. Lopez, 257–76. New York: Oxford University Press.

6. Boyatzis and McKee, *Resonant leadership*; Snyder, C. R., C. Harris, J. R. Anderson, S. A. Holleran, L. M. Irving, S. T. Sigmon, L. Yoshinobu, J. Gibb, C. Langelle, and P. Harney. 1991. The will and the ways. *Journal of Personality and Social Psychology* 60: 570–85.

7. Boyatzis and McKee, *Resonant leadership*.

8. Goleman, Daniel, Richard Boyatzis, and Annie McKee. 2002. *Primal leadership: Realizing the power of emotional intelligence*. Boston: Harvard Business School Press.

9. Csikszentmihalyi. *Beyond boredom and anxiety*.

10. Ryan, Richard M., and Edward L. Deci. 2000. Self-determination theory and the facilitation of intrinsic motivation, social development, and well-being. *American Psychologist* (January): 68–78; Deci, E., and R. Ryan. 2008. Facilitating optimal motivation and psychological well-being across life's domains. *Canadian Psychology* 49: 14–23; Deci, Edward L., and Richard M. Ryan, eds. 2002. *Handbook of self-determination research*. Rochester, NY: University of Rochester Press; Deci, Edward L., and Richard M. Ryan. 1985. *Intrinsic motivation and self-determination in human behavior*. New York: Plenum Press; Mruk, Christopher J. 2006.

Self-esteem research, theory, and practice. New York: Springer Publishing Company.

11. Deci, Edward L., and Richard M. Ryan. 2008. Self-determination theory: A macrotheory of human motivation, development, and health. *Canadian Psychology* 49(3): 183; Guay, Frédéric, Catherine F. Ratelle, and Julien Chanal. 2008. Optimal learning in optimal contexts: The role of self-determination in education. *Canadian Psychology* 49(3): 233–40; Joussemet, Mireille, Renée Landry, and Richad Koestner. 2008. A self-determination theory perspective on parenting. *Canadian Psychology* 49(3): 194–200; Baard, Paul P., Edward L. Deci, and Richard M. Ryan. 2004. Intrinsic need satisfaction: A motivational basis of performance and well-being in two work settings. *Journal of Applied Social Psychology* 34(10): 2045–68.

12. Deci and Ryan, *Intrinsic motivation*.

13. Gagné, Marylène, and Edward L. Deci. 2005. Self-determination theory and work motivation. *Journal of Organizational Behavior* 26: 331–62.

14. Deci, Edward L. 1972. Intrinsic motivation, extrinsic reinforcement, and inequity. *Journal of Personality and Social Psychology* 22(1): 113–20.

15. Rotter, J. B. 1954. *Social learning and clinical psychology*. New York: Prentice Hall; Rotter, Julian B. 1966. Generalized expectancies for internal versus external control reinforcement. *Psychological Monographs: General and Applied* 80(1): 1–28.

16. Thurstone, L. L. 1934. The vectors of the mind. *Psychological Review* 41: 1–32; Goldberg, L. R. 1981. Language and individual differences: The search for universals in personality lexicons, *Review of personality and social psychology, Vol. 2*, ed. L. Wheeler, 141–165. Beverly Hills, CA: Sage; Allport, G. W., and H. S. Odbert. 1936. Trait names: A psycholexical study. *Psychological Monographs* 47: 211; Cattell, R. B. 1946. *The description and measurement of personality*. New York: World Book; Norman, W. T. 1963. Toward an adequate taxonomy of personality attributes: Replicated factor structure in peer nomination personality ratings. *Journal of Abnormal and Social Psychology* 66: 574–83; McCrae, R. R., and P. T. Costa. 1987. Validation of the five-factor model of personality across instruments and observers. *Journal of Personality and Social Psychology* 52(1): 81–90.

17. Bono, J. E., and T. A. Judge. 2004. Personality and transformational and transactional leadership: A meta-analysis. *Journal of Applied Psychology* 89(5): 901–10; Barrick, M. R., G. L. Stewart, and M. Piotrowski. 2002. Personality and job performance: Test of the mediating effects of motivation among sales representatives. *Journal of Applied Psychology* 87(1): 43–51.

18. Maslow, Abraham. 1968. *Toward a psychology of being*. New York: D. Van Nostrand Co.

19. Wahba, Mahmoud A., and Lawrence G. Bridwell. "Maslow Reconsidered: A Review of Research on the Need Hierarchy Theory." *Organizational Behavior and Human Performance* 15, no. 2 (1976): 212–40.

20. Alderfer, Clayton P. 1972. *Existence, relatedness, and growth: Human needs in organizational settings*. New York: Free Press.

21. Herzberg, Frederick. 1959. *The motivation to work*. New York: Wiley.

22. Wall, Toby D., and Geoffrey M. Stephenson. 1970. Herzberg's two-factor theory of job attitudes: A critical evaluation and some fresh evidence. *Industrial Relations Journal* 1(3): 41–65.

23. Herzberg, F., B. Mausner, and B. B. Snyderman. 1959. *The motivation to work*. New York: Wiley; Parker, Sharon K., and Toby D. Wall. 1998. Work design: Learning from the past and mapping a new terrain. In *Handbook of industrial, work, and organizational psychology, Vol. 1*, ed. Neil Anderson, Deniz S. Ones, Handan K. Sinangil, and Chockalingam Viswesvaran, 90–109. Thousand Oaks, CA: Sage Publications.

24. McClelland, David C. 1985. *Human motivation*. Glenview, IL: Scott Foresman and Company; Wheatley, Margaret. 1999. *Leadership and the new science: Discovering order in a chaotic world*. San Francisco: Berrett-Koehler; Wheatley, Margaret. 2005. *Finding our way: Leadership for uncertain times*. San Francisco: Berrett-Koehler; Boyatzis, Richard. 2006. An overview of intentional change from a complexity perspective. *Journal of Management Development,* 25(7): 607–623; Goleman, Daniel, ed. 2003. *Destructive emotions: How can we overcome them? A scientific dialogue with the Dalai Lama*. New York: Bantam Books.

25. Hofer, Jan, Athanasios Chasiotis, Wolfgang Friedlmeier, Holger Busch, and Domingo Campos. 2005. The measurement of implicit motives in three cultures: Power and affiliation in Cameroon, Costa Rica, and Germany. *Journal of Cross-Cultural Psychology* 36: 689–716; Sokolowski, Kurt, Heinz-Dieter Schmalt, Thomas A. Langens, and Rosa M. Puca. 2000. Assessing achievement, affiliation, and power motives all at once:

The multi-motive grid (MMG). *Journal of Personality Assessment* 74(1): 126–45; Yamaguchi, Ikushi. 2003. The relationships among individual differences, needs and equity sensitivity. *Journal of Managerial Psychology* 18(4): 324–44.

26. McClelland, David C. 1982. The need for power, sympathetic activation, and illness. *Motivation and Emotion,* 6(1): 31–41; McKee, Annie, Richard Boyatzis, and Frances Johnston. 2008. *Becoming a Resonant Leader: Develop your emotional intelligence, renew your relationships and sustain your effectiveness*. Boston: Harvard Business Press.

27. Blount, Rachel. "U.S. Olympic Swimming Trials; Bold Choices; U.S. Swimmer Michael Phelps, Only 19, Has Won 20 National Titles and Holds Three World Records. No Wonder He Has Grand Plans for the Summer Games.(Sports)." *Star Tribune*, 2004.

28. McClelland, D. C. 1961. *The achieving society*. New York: Van Nostrand-Rheinhold.

29. Boyatzis and McKee, *Resonant leadership*; McClelland, *Human motivation*, 1982, p. 71.

30. McClelland, D. C., W. N. Davis, R. Kalin, and H. E. Wanner. 1972. *The drinking man*. New York: Free Press; Schultheiss, O. C., K. L. Campbell, and D. C. McClelland. 1999. Implicit power motivation moderates men's testosterone response to imagined and real dominance success. *Hormones and Behavior* 36: 234–41.

31. Ibid.

32. Schultheiss, Campbell, and McClelland. Implicit poor motivation moderates men's testosterone reponse to imagined and real dominance success.

33. Brown, Michael E., and Linda K. Treviño. 2006. Socialized charismatic leadership, values congruence, and deviance in work groups. *Journal of Applied Psychology* 91(4): 954–62; Kanungo, Rabindra N., and Manuel Mendonca. 1996. *Ethical dimensions in leadership*. Beverly Hills, CA: Sage Publications.

34. Mandela, Nelson, interviewed and presented on video http://www .youtube.com/watch?v=ODQ4WiDsEBQ.

35. Nussbaum, Barbara. 2003. African culture and Ubuntu: Reflections of a South African in America. *World Business Academy* 17: 1; Nussbaum, Barbara. 2003. Ubuntu: Reflections of a South African in our common humanity. *Reflections* 4: 4; Nussbaum, Barbara. 2003. Ubuntu and business…reflections and questions. *World Business Academy* 17: 3.

36. Newenham-Kahindi, Aloysius. "The Transfer of Ubuntu and Indaba Business Models Abroad." *International Journal of Cross Cultural Management* 9, no. 1 (2009): 87–108.

37. McKee, Annie, Frances Johnston, Eddy Mwelwa, and Suzanne Rotondo. 2009. Resonant leadership for results: An emotional and social intelligence program for change in South Africa and Cambodia. In *Handbook for developing emotional and social intelligence*, ed. Marcia Hughes, Henry L. Thompson, and James Bradford Terrel, 49–71. San Francisco: Pfeiffer.

38. McClelland, *The achieving society*; McClelland, D. C. 1975. *Power: The inner experience*. New York: Irvington; Murray, Henry A. 1938. *Explorations in personality*. New York: Oxford University Press.

39. Aronow, Edward, Kim Weiss, and Marvin Reznikoss. 2001. *A practical guide to the Thematic Apperception Test: The TAT in clinical practice*. Philadelphia: Taylor and Francis.

40. McClelland, David C. 1958. Methods of measuring human motivation. In *Motives in fantasy, action and society*, ed. John W. Akinson, 12–13. Princeton, NJ: D. Van Nostrand Co..

41. Polk, Denise M. "Evaluating Fairness: Critical Assessment of Equity Theory." In *Theories in social psychology*, edited by Derek Chadee, 163–91. Malden, MA: Blackwell Publishing, 2011; Adams, J. Stacey. 1965. Inequity in social exchange. In *Advances in experimental social psychology, Vol. 2*, ed. Leonard Berkowitz, 267–99. New York: Academic Press.

42. Festinger, Leon. 1957. *A theory of cognitive dissonance*. Stanford, CA: Stanford University Press; Brehm, Jack, and Arthur Cohen. 1962. *Explorations in cognitive dissonance*. New York: Wiley.

43. Brown, Michael E., and Linda K. Treviño. 2006. Ethical leadership: A review and future directions. *Leadership Quarterly* 17: 595–616.

44. Schor, Juliet. 1991. *The overworked American*. New York: Basic Books.

45. Schoen, John W. 2009, August 11. Americans working much harder—for less pay. *MSNBC*. Retrieved December 11, 2009, from http://www .msnbc.msn.com/id/32374533/ns/business-eye_on_the_economy.

46. Goleman et al., *Primal leadership*; Lewis, Thomas, Fari Amini, and Richard Lannon. 2000. *A general theory of love*. New York: Random House.

47. Vroom, Victor H. 1964. *Work and motivation.* New York: Wiley; Atkinson, J. W. 1958. Towards experimental analysis of human motivation in terms of motives, expectancies, and incentives. In *Motives in fantasy, action and society,* ed. J. W. Atkinson, 288–305. New York: D. Van Nostrand Co.

48. Galbraith, Jay, and Larry L. Cummings. 1967. An empirical investigation of the motivational determinants of past performance: Interactive effects between instrumentality, valence, motivation and ability. *Organizational Behavior and Human Performance* 2: 237–57.

49. Altvater, Elmar. 2003. The growth obsession. In *2002: A world of contradiction, socialist register 2002,* ed. Leo Panitch and Colin Leys, 73–92. London: Merlin Press.

50. Barton, Dominic. 2011. "Capitalism for the Long Term." *Harvard Business Review* 89(3): 84–91.

51. Latham, Gary, and Edwin Locke. 1990. *A theory of goal setting and task performance.* Englewood Cliffs, NJ: Prentice Hall; Latham, G., and Edwin Locke. 2002. Building a practically useful theory of goal setting and task motivation. *American Psychologist* 57(9): 705–17; Locke, Edwin A., and Gary P. Latham. 2006. "New Directions in Goal-Setting Theory." *Current Directions in Psychological Science* 15(5): 265–68.

52. Locke, Edwin. 1968. Toward a theory of task motivation and incentives. *Organizational Behavior and Human Performance* 3(2): 157–89.

53. Doran, George T. 1981. There's a S.M.A.R.T. way to write management's goals and objectives. *Management Review* 70(11): 35–36.

54. Vermeeren, Douglas. 2005, July 3. Want to be a top achiever? Stop setting goals! *My Article Archive.* Retrieved July 9, 2009, from http://www.myarticlearchive.com/articles/7/305.htm.

55. Siegert, Richard J., and William J. Taylor. 2004. Theoretical aspects of goal-setting and motivation in rehabilitation. *Disability and Rehabilitation* 26(1): 1–8.

56. Skinner, B. F. 1971. *Beyond freedom and dignity.* New York: Alfred A. Knopf; Thorndike, E. L. 1911. *Animal intelligence: Experimental studies.* New York: Macmillan.

57. Braithwaite, John. 2000. Shame and criminal justice. *Canadian Journal of Criminology* 42(3): 281–98; Tangney, June P. 1990. Assessing individual differences in proneness to shame and guilt: Development of the self-conscious affect and attribution inventory. *Journal of Personality and Social Psychology* 59(1): 102–11.

58. Kohn, Alfie. 1994. The risks of rewards. *ERIC Digests,* ED376990, 1–6.

59. Bandura, Albert. 1969. Social-learning theory of identificatory processes. In *Handbook of socialization theory and research,* ed. David A. Goslin, 213–62. Chicago: Rand McNally & Co.; Bandura, Albert. 1977. *Social learning theory.* Englewood Cliffs, NJ: Prentice Hall; Bandura, Albert. 1977. Self-efficacy: Toward a universal theory of behavioral change. *Psychological Review* 84(2): 191–215.

60. Tarde, G. 1903. *The laws of imitation.* New York: Henry Holt and Co.; Vygotsky, Lev S. 1962. *Thought and language.* Cambridge, MA: MIT Press; Vygotsky, L. S. 1978. *Mind in society.* Cambridge, MA: Harvard University Press; Bandura, A. 1965. Vicarious processes: A case of no-trial learning. In *Advances in experimental social psychology, Vol. 2,* ed. L. Berkowitz, 1–57. New York: Academic Press.

61. Rotter, J. B. 1954. *Social learning and clinical psychology.* Englewood Cliffs, NJ: Prentice Hall.

62. Bandura, Albert, Dorothea Ross, and Sheila A. Ross. 1961. Transmission of aggression through imitation of aggressive models. *Journal of Abnormal and Social Psychology* 63: 575–82.

63. Bandura, Albert. 1986. *Social foundations of thought and action: A social cognitive theory.* Englewood Cliffs, NJ: Prentice Hall.

64. Bandura Albert. 1997. *Self-efficacy: The exercise of control.* New York: H. Freeman.

65. Bandura, Albert. 1997. Self-efficacy: Toward a unifying theory of behavioral change. *Psychological Review* 84(2): 191–215.

66. Pajares, Frank. 2004. Albert Bandura: Biographical sketch. Retrieved August 5, 2009, from http://www.uky.edu/~eushe2/Bandura/bandurabio.html.

67. Bandura, Albert. 1994. Self-efficacy, in *Encyclopedia of human behavior.,* Vol. 4, ed. V.S. Ramachaudran, 71–81. New York: Academic Press.

68. Bandura, Albert. 1973. Social learning theory of aggression, in *The control of aggression,* ed. John F. Knutson, 201–52. Piscataway, NJ: Transaction Publishers.

69. "100 Best Companies to Work For." *CNN Money* (2012). Retrieved May 25, 2012, from http://money.cnn.com/magazines/fortune/best-companies/.

70. Google Inc. 2009. The Google culture. Retrieved September 12, 2009, from http://www.google.com/corporate/culture.html.

71. Ibid; Kumar, Reshma. 2008, August 24. Google's free food being cut. *Silicon Valley WebGuild.* Retrieved September 23, 2009, from http://www.webguild.org/2008/08/googles-free-food-being-cut.php.

72. The most desirable employers. 2009. *BusinessWeek.* Retrieved September 12, 2009, from http://bwnt.businessweek.com/interactive_reports/most_desirable_employers/index.asp.

73. Battelle, John. 2005, December 1. The 70 percent solution. *CNNMoney.com.* Retrieved September 12, 2009, from http://money.cnn.com/magazines/business2/business2_archive/2005/12/01/8364616/index.htm; Princeton University. 2008, December 22. Princeton University learning process. *Learning & Development.* Retrieved September 12, 2009, from http://www.princeton.edu/hr/l&d/l&d_learning_process.htm; Casnocha, B. 2009, April 24. Success on the side. *The American.* Retrieved September 12, 2009, from http://www.american.com/archive/2009/april-2009/Success-on-the-Side.

74. Help wanted: Google. 2008, January 22. *CNNMoney.com.* Retrieved March 16, 2010, from http://money.cnn.com/galleries/2008/fortune/0801/gallery.BestCo_Google_help.fortune/7.html.

75. Battelle, John. The 70 percent solution.

76. Google Inc. 2011, March 17. "Google '20-Percent Time' Going to Help Japan," Retrieved May 31, 2012, http://www.google.com/hostednews/afp/article/ALeqM5hoT9bl2rJLD_GQe8oRBz51xvxrwA?docId=CNG.ec8adac15de3a8c766bb1f548b5c44b7.bd1.

77. Manyika, James. "Google's View on the Future of Business: An Interview with Ceo Eric Schmidt" *McKinsey Quarterly* (2008). Retrieved July 23, 2012, from http://www.mckinseyquarterly.com/Googles_view_on_the_future_of_business_An_interview_with_CEO_Eric_Schmidt_2229.

78. Kirkman, Bradley L., and Debra L. Shapiro. 1997. The impact of cultural values on employee resistance to teams: Toward a model of globalized self-managing work team effectiveness. *Academy of Management Review* 22(3): 730–57.

79. Hackman, J. R., and G. R. Oldham. 1976. Motivation through the design of work: Test of a theory. *Organizational Behavior and Human Performance* 16: 250–79.

80. Heathfield, Susan M. 2008. Five factors every employee wants from work. *Human_Resources_About.com.* Retrieved July 16, 2009, from http://humanresources.about.com/od/managementtips.

81. Goleman et al. *Primal leadership;* Boyatzis and McKee, *Resonant leadership.*

82. Preston, Stephanie D., and Frans B. M. de Waal. 2002. Empathy: Its ultimate and proximate bases. *Behavioral Brain Science* 25: 1–72; de Vignemont, Frederique, and Tania Singer. 2006. The empathic brain: How, when and why? *Trends in Cognitive Sciences* 10(10): 435–41; Hoffman, M. L. 2000. *Empathy and moral development: Implications for caring and justice.* New York: Cambridge University Press.

83. Goleman, Daniel. 2006. *Social intelligence: The new science of human intelligence.* New York: Bantam Dell; Boyatzis and McKee, *Resonant leadership;* Goleman et al., *Primal leadership.*

84. Kao, H. S. R., and N. Sek-Hong. 1997. Work motivation and culture. In *Motivation and culture,* ed. D. Munro, J. F. Schumaker, and S. C. Carr, 119–32. New York: Routledge.

85. Thinkexist.com Sigmund Freud Quotes. Retrieved 2009, November 14, from http://thinkexist.com/quotation/love_and_work_are_the_cornerstones_of_our/166402.html.

Chapter 4

1. Pearce, Terry. 2003. *Leading out loud: Inspiring change through authentic communication.* San Francisco, CA: Jossey-Bass; Boyatzis, Richard, and Annie McKee. 2005. Primal and *Resonant leadership: Renewing yourself and connecting with others through mindfulness, hope and compassion.* Boston: Harvard Business School Press.

2. Yu, Eileen 2007, August 29. A blog into Schwartz's mind. Accessed March 21, 2012, from ZDNet, http://www.zdnetasia.com/a-blog-into-schwartzs-mind-62031604.htm.

3. McKee, Annie, Richard Boyatzis, and Frances Johnston. 2008. *Becoming a resonant leader: Develop your emotional intelligence, renew your relationships, sustain your effectiveness.* Harvard Business School Press Books.

4. Klein, E. 1969. *Klein's comprehensive etymological dictionary of the English language.* Stockholm: Elsevier.

5. Chomsky, Noam. 1988. *Language and problems of knowledge: The Managua lectures,* p. 183. Cambridge, MA: MIT Press; Chomsky, Noam. 2005. Three factors in language design. *Linguistic Inquiry* 36(1): 1–22; Chomsky, Noam. 2006. *Language and mind.* Cambridge: Cambridge University Press.

6. Corballis, Michael C. 2002. *From hand to mouth: The origins of language,* p. 3. Princeton, NJ: Princeton University Press.

7. Deacon, Terrence W. 1997. *The symbolic species: The co-evolution of language and the brain.* New York: W. W. Norton & Company; Merlin, Donald. 1991. *Origins of the modern mind: Three stages in the evolution of culture and cognition.* Boston: Harvard University Press; Lieberman, Paul. 1991. *Uniquely human: Speech, thought, and selfless behavior.* Boston: Harvard University Press.

8. World Federation of the Deaf Homepage. Retrieved April 2, 2010, from http://www.wfdeaf.org.

9. Gallaudet University FAQ Page. Retrieved April 2, 2010, from http://library.gallaudet.edu/Library/Deaf_Research_Help/Frequently_Asked_Questions_(FAQs)/Sign_Language/ASL_Ranking_and_Number_of_Speakers.html.

10. Ibid.

11. Ibid.

12. Sutton-Spence, Rachel, and Bencie Woll. 1999. *The linguistics of British Sign Language: An introduction.* Cambridge: Cambridge University Press.

13. British Deaf Association. 1975. *Gestuno: International sign language of the deaf.* Carlisle, England: BDA.

14. Birdwhistell, Ray L. 1970. *Kinesics and context: Essays on body motion communication.* Philadelphia: University of Pennsylvania Press.

15. Mehrabian, Albert, and Susan R. Ferris. 1967. Inference of attitudes from nonverbal communication in two channels. *Journal of Consulting Psychology* 3(3): 248–52.

16. McKee, Annie, Richard Boyatzis, and Frances Johnston. 2008. *Becoming a resonant leader: Develop your emotional intelligence, renew your relationships, and sustain your effectiveness.* Boston: Harvard Business School Press; Boyatzis, Richard, and Annie McKee. 2005. *Resonant leadership: Renewing yourself and connecting with others through mindfulness, hope and compassion.* Boston: Harvard Business School Press; Goleman, Daniel, Richard Boyatzis, and Annie McKee. 2002. *Primal leadership: Realizing the power of emotional intelligence.* Boston: Harvard Business School Press; Pearce, *Leading out loud*; Lewis, Thomas, Fari Amini, and Richard Lannon. 2000. *A general theory of love.* New York: Random House.

17. Ekman, Paul. 1975. *Unmasking the face: A guide to recognizing emotions from facial clues.* Upper Saddle River, NJ: Prentice Hall; Ekman, Paul. 2005. *Emotions in the human face.* Oxford: Oxford University Press.

18. Ibid.

19. King, L. A., and R. A. Emmons. 1990. Conflict over emotional expression: Psychological and physical correlates. *Journal of Personality and Social Psychology* 58: 864–77.

20. Ekman, Paul. 1985. *Telling lies: Clues to deceit in the marketplace, politics, and marriage.* London: W. W. Norton & Company.

21. Emmons, R. A., and P. M. Colby. 1995. Emotional conflict and well-being: Relation to perceived availability, daily utilization, and observer reports of social support. *Journal of Personality and Social Psychology* 68: 947–59.

22. Katz, I. M., and J. D. Campbell. 1994. Ambivalence over emotional expression and well-being: Nomothetic and idiographic tests of the stress-buffering hypothesis. *Journal of Personality and Social Psychology* 67: 513–24; King, L. A., and R. A. Emmons. 1990. Conflict over emotional expression: Psychological and physical correlates. *Journal of Personality and Social Psychology* 58: 864–77; Emmons and Colby, Emotional conflict and well-being.

23. George, Jennifer. 2000. Emotions and leadership: The role of emotional intelligence. *Human Relations* 53(8): 1027–55.

24. Goffman, Erving. 1959. *The presentation of self in everyday life.* New York: Doubleday.

25. Goffman, Erving. 1955. On face-work: An analysis of ritual elements in social interaction. *Journal for the Study of Interpersonal Processes* 18: 213–31.

26. Brown, Penelope, and Stephen C. Levinson. 1987. *Politeness: Some universals in language usage.* New York: Cambridge University Press.

27. Ibid.

28. Ibid.

29. Wilbur, Ken. 1996. *A brief history of everything.* Boston: Shambhala Publications, Inc.

30. Cross, Rob, Andrew Parker, and Stephen P. Borgatti. 2002. *A bird's-eye view: Using social network analysis to improve knowledge creation and sharing.* Somers, NY: IBM Institute for Business Value.

31. Shannon, Claude, and Warren Weaver. 1949. *The mathematical theory of communication.* Urbana, IL: University of Illinois Press.

32. Schramm, Wilbur. 1954. How communication works. In *The process and effects of communication,* ed. Wilbur Schramm, 3–26. Urbana, IL: University of Illinois Press.

33. Berlo, David K. 1960. *Process of communication: An introduction to theory and practice.* New York: Holt, Rinehart and Winston.

34. Shannon and Weaver, *The mathematical theory of communication.*

35. Mortensen, C. David. 1972. *Communication: The study of human communication.* New York: McGraw-Hill.

36. Roszak, Theodore. 1986. *The cult of information.* Berkeley, CA: University of California Press.

37. Schramm, How communication works.

38. Berlo, David K. 1960. *Process of communication: An introduction to theory and practice.* New York: Holt, Rinehart and Winston.

39. The Associated Press. 2012, March 4. Conflicting accounts over Afghan Quran burnings. Retrieved April 19, 2012, from http://www.usatoday.com/news/world/story/2012-03-03/official-quran-burnings/53340562/1.

40. Daft, R., R. Lengel, and L. Trevino. 1987. Message equivocality, media selection, and manager performance: Implications for information systems. *MIS Quarterly* 17: 355–66; Rice, R. 1992. Task analyzability, use of new media, and effectiveness: A multi-site exploration of media richness. *Organization Science* 3: 475–500.

41. Carlson, John R., and Robert W. Zmud. 1999. Channel expansion theory and the experiential nature of media richness perceptions. *Academy of Management Review* 42(2): 153–70.

42. Reinfeld, Fred. 1966. *Pony express.* New York: Macmillan.

43. Carter, Kimberly A. 2003. Type me how you feel: Quasi-nonverbal cues in computer-mediated communication. *ETC: A Review of General Semantics* 60(1): 29–40.

44. Richards, Howard, and Harris Makatsoris. 2002. The metamorphosis to dynamic trading networks and virtual corporations. In *Managing virtual web organizations in the 21st century: Issues and challenges,* ed. Ulrich Franke, 65. Hershey, PA: Idea Publishing Group.

45. Gibson, Cristina B., and Susan G. Cohen. 2003. *Virtual teams that work,* p. 220. San Francisco, CA: John Wiley and Sons.

46. Friedman, Barry A., and Lisa J. Reed. 2007. Workplace privacy: Employee relations and legal implications of monitoring employee e-mail use. *Employee Responsibilities and Rights Journal* 19(2): 75–83; Allen, Myria W., Stephanie J. Coopman, Joy L. Hart, and Kasey L. Walker. 2007. Workplace surveillance and managing privacy boundaries. *Management Communication Quarterly* 21(2): 172–200; Halpern, David, Patrick J. Reveille, and Donald Grunewald. 2008. Management and legal issues regarding electronic surveillance of employees in the workplace. *Journal of Business Ethics,* 80(2): 175–80.

47. Linden Research, Inc. 2009. How meeting in Second Life transformed IBM's technology elite into virtual world believers. Retrieved September 12, 2009, from http://secondlifegrid.net/casestudies/IBM.

48. IT News Online. 2008. IBM opens IBM virtual healthcare island on Second Life. *IT News Online* (February 25).

49. Linden Research, How meeting in Second Life transformed IBM's technology elite.

50. Ibid.

51. Marche, Stephen. May 2012. Is Facebook making us lonely? *The Atlantic Monthly*: 67–69.

52. Ibid.

53. Ibid.

54. Beechler, Schon L., and Allan Bird. 1998. *Japanese multinationals abroad: Individual and organizational learning,* p. 118. New York: Oxford University Press.

55. Adler, Carlye. 2003. Colonel Sanders' march on China. *Time Magazine.* Retrieved March 31, 2010, from http://www.time.com/time/magazine/article/0,9171,543845,00.html.

56. Agha, Asif. 2007. *Language and social relations.* Cambridge: Cambridge University Press.

57. Labov, William. 1966. *The social stratification of English in New York City.* Washington, DC: Center for Applied Linguistics.

58. Agha, *Language and social relations.*

59. Trompenaars, Fons, and Charles Hampden-Turner. 1998. *Riding the waves of culture: Understanding diversity in global business.* New York: McGraw-Hill.

60. Hymes, Dell. 2001. On communicative competence. In *Linguistic anthropology: A reader,* ed. Allesandro Duranti. Malden, MA: Blackwell Publishers.

61. Hargie, Owen, and David Dickson. 2004. *Skilled interpersonal communication: Research, theory and practice.* New York: Routledge.

62. Ting-Toomey, Stella, and Atsuko Kurogi. 1998. Facework competence in intercultural conflict: An updated face-negotiation theory. *International Journal of Intercultural Relations* 22(2): 187–225.

63. Ibid.

64. Kouzmin, Alexander, and Nada Korac-Kakabadse. 1997. From phobias and ideological prescription: Towards multiple models in transformation management for socialist economies in transition. *Administration and Society* 29(2): 139–88.

65. Ibid.

66. Kouzmin, Alexander, R. Leivesley, and A. Carr. 1996. From managerial dysfunction, towards communicative competence: Re-discovering dramaturgy and voice in communicating risk. In *Handbook of administrative communication,* ed. J. L. Garnett and A. Kouzmin, 661–79. New York: Marcel Dekker; Kouzmin, Alexander, and Nada Korac-Kakabadse. 2000. Mapping institutional impacts of lean communication in lean agencies: Information technology, illiteracy, and leadership failure. *Administration and Society* 32(1): 29–69.

67. Catalyst. 2003. *Women in U.S. corporate leadership: 2003.* New York.

68. Matsa, David A., and Amalia R. Miller. 2011. Chipping away at the glass ceiling: Gender spillovers in corporate leadership. *American Economic Review* 101(3): 635–39.

69. Trompenaars and Hampden-Turner, *Riding the waves of culture.*

70. Hall, Edward Twitchell. 1966. *The Hidden Dimension.* Garden City, NY: Doubleday.

71. Landis, Dan. 2008. Globalization, migration into urban centers, and cross-cultural training. *International Journal of Intercultural Relations* 32(4): 337–48.

72. Hall, Edward T. 1976. *Beyond culture.* Oxford: Anchor Books.

73. Thomas, David A. 2004. Diversity as strategy. *Harvard Business Review* 82(9): 98–108.

74. Gray, John. 1999. *Men are from Mars, women are from Venus.* New York: HarperCollins; Tannen, Deborah. 1990. *You just don't understand: Women and men in conversation.* New York: William Morrow.

75. Gilligan, Carol. 1984. New maps of development: New visions of maturity, in *Annual progress in child psychiatry and child development, 1983,* ed. Stella Chess and Alexander Thomas, 98–116. New York: Brunner/Mazel.

76. Tannen, Deborah. 1986. *That's not what I meant: How conversational style makes or breaks relationships.* New York: Random House.

77. Brody, Leslie R. 2000. The socialization of gender differences in emotional expression: Display rules, infant temperament, and differentiation. In *Gender and emotion: Social psychological perspectives,* ed. Agneta H. Fischer, 24–47. New York: Cambridge University Press; Hall, Judith A., Jason D. Carter, and Terrence G. Horgan. 2000. Gender differences in nonverbal communication of emotion. In *Gender and emotion: Social psychological perspectives,* ed. Agneta H. Fischer, 97–117. New York: Cambridge University Press.

78. Lakoff, Robin. 1973. Language and woman's place. *Language in Society* 2(1): 45–80.

79. Ibid.

80. Tannen, D. 1994. *Talking from 9 to 5: How women's and men's conversational styles affect who gets heard, who gets credit, and what gets done.* New York: William Morrow & Co.

81. Oakley, Judith G. 2000. Gender-based barriers to senior management positions: Understanding the scarcity of female CEOs. *Journal of Business Ethics* 27: 321–34.

82. Claes, Marie-Thérèse. 1999. Women, men, and management styles. *International Labour Review* 138(4): 431–46; Boyatzis and McKee, *Resonant leadership.*

83. Ridgeway, Cecelia L., and Lynn Smith-Lovin. 1999. The gender system and interaction. *Annual Review of Sociology* 25: 191–216.

84. Keeter, Scott, and Paul Taylor. 2009. The Millenials. *Pew Research Center Publications* (December 11). Retrieved May 23, 2012, from http://pewresearch.org/pubs/1437/millennials-profile.

85. Meister, Jeanne C., and Karie Willyerd. 2010. Mentoring Millennials. (Cover Story). *Harvard Business Review* 88(5): 68–72; Johnson, Bonnie. Generation Y's guide to working with older generations. *Agri Marketing* (2011): 22–23; Gavatorta, Steve. 2012. It's a Millennial thing. *T+D* 66(3): 58–65.

86. Randstad USA. 2008. *Limited interaction among generations in the workplace identified as key indicator of coming skilled worker crisis.* Atlanta, GA: Randstad, U.S.A.

87. De Mare, G. 1989. Communicating: The key to establishing good working relationships. *Waterhouse Review* 33: 30–37.

88. Crampton, Suzanne M., John W. Hodge, and Jitendra M. Mishra. 1998. The informal communication network: Factors influencing grapevine activity. *Public Personnel Management* 27(4): 569–83.

89. Keyes, Ralph. 2006. *The quote verifier: Who said what, where, and when.* New York: St. Martin's Press.

90. Byrne, Dennis. 2010. When all else fails, blame the system. *Chicago Tribune* (January 4). Retrieved January 11, 2010, from http://www.chicagotribune.com/news/opinion/chi-oped0105byrnejan05,0,6556064.column.

91. Milbank, Dana. 2010. Obama administration says there was no smoking gun before attempted airline bombing. *Washington Post* (January 8). Retrieved January 11, 2010, from http://www.washingtonpost.com/wp-dyn/content/article/2010/01/07/AR2010010704069.html?hpid=topnews.

92. Weick, Karl E. 2004. A bias for conversation: Acting discursively in organizations, in *The Sage handbook of organizational discourse,* ed. David Grant, Cynthia Hardy, Cliff Oswick, and Linda Putnam, 405. Thousand Oaks, CA: Sage Publications.

93. Davenport, Thomas H., and Laurence Prusak. 1998. *Working knowledge: How organizations manage what they know,* p. 5. Boston: Harvard Business School Press.

94. Gabriel, Yiannis. 2000. *Storytelling in organizations: Facts, fictions, and fantasies.* New York: Oxford University Press.

95. Forster, Nick, Martin Cebis, Sol Majteles, Anurag Mathur, Roy Morgan, Janet Preuss, Vinod Tiwari, and Des Wilkinson. 1999. The role of storytelling in organizational leadership. *Leadership and Organizational Development Journal* 20(1): 11–17.

96. Kouzes, J., and B. Posner. 2005. *The leadership challenge.* New York: Jossey-Bass.

97. Grice, H. P. 1975. Logic and conversation. In *Syntax and semantics. Vol. 1: Speech acts,* ed. P. Cole and J. L. Morgan, 41–58. New York: Academic Press.

98. Brown and Levinson, Politeness: Some universals in language usage; Grice, Logic and conversation.

99. Weick, A bias for conversation.

100. Cross, Rob, Andrew Parker, and Stephen P. Borgatti. 2002. *A bird's-eye view: Using social network analysis to improve knowledge creation and sharing.* Somers, NY: IBM Institute for Business Value.

Chapter 5

1. McCaskey, Michael B. 1974. A contingency approach to planning: Planning with goals and planning without goals. *Academy of Management Journal* 17(2): 281–91; McCaskey, Michael B. 1977. Goals and direction in personal planning. *Academy of Management Review* 2(3): 454–62; McKee, Annie. 1991. *Individual differences in planning for the future.* Dissertation. Cleveland, OH: Case Western Reserve University.

2. Online Etymology Dictionary. Teleos. Retrieved April 2, 2010, from http://www.etymonline.com/index.php?search=teleos&searchmode=none.

3. Mintzberg, Henry. 1994. *The rise and fall of strategic planning: Reconceiving roles for planning, plans, planners,* p. 12. New York: The Free Press.

4. Ibid.

5. Wang, Xuemei. 1994. Learning planning operators by observation and practice, in *Proceedings of the Second International Conference on AI Planning Systems, AIPS-94,* pp. 335–340. Chicago, IL.

6. McCaskey, A contingency approach to planning; McCaskey, Goals and direction in personal planning.

7. Online Etymology Dictionary. Plan. Retrieved October 2, 2009, from http://www.etymonline.com/index.php?term=plan.

8. Lane, Terry, and Leslie P. Kaelbling. 2001, August 4–10. Toward hierarchical decomposition for planning in uncertain environments. Workshop on planning under uncertainty and incomplete information, International Joint Conferences on Artificial Intelligence, Seattle, WA.

9. Lakoff, George, and Mark Johnson. 1980. *Metaphors we live by*. Chicago: University of Chicago Press.

10. *The American Heritage Dictionary of the English Language*, 4th ed. 2006. Boston: Houghton Mifflin Company.

11. Online Etymology Dictionary. "Goal." Retrieved December 1, 2009, from http://www.etymonline.com/index.php?search=goal&search mode=none.

12. Doran, George T. 1981. There's a S.M.A.R.T. way to write management's goals and objectives. *Management Review* 70(11): 35–36.

13. Sarasvathy, S. D., and S. Kotha. 2001. Effectuation in the management of Knightian uncertainty: Evidence from the Realnetworks case, in *Research on Management and Entrepreneurship, Vol. 1*, ed. J. Butler, 31-62. Greenwich, CT: IAP Inc.

14. Helmert, M., P. Haslum, and J. Hoffmann. 2007. Flexible abstraction heuristics for optimal sequential planning, in *Proceedings of ICAPS 2007*, pp. 176-183. Menlo Park, CA: AAAI Press.

15. Markov, A. A. 1913/2006. Classical text in translation: An example of statistical investigation of the text "Eugene Onegin" concerning the connection of samples in chains. *Science in Context* 19(4): 591–600; Markov, A. A. 1971. Extension of the limit theorems of probability theory to a sum of variables connected in a chain. Reprinted in Appendix B of *Dynamic probabilistic systems, Vol. 1: Markov chains*, ed. R. Howard. New York: John Wiley and Sons.

16. Watkin, Michael, and Christopher Rozell. 2004. *A Markov chain analysis of black jack*. Course material for Math 502 at Rice University (26 pp.). Retrieved September 29, 2009, from http://www-ece.rice.edu/~crozell/courseproj/MCBJ.pdf.

17. Wack, Pierre. 1985. Scenarios: Uncharted waters ahead. *Harvard Business Review* 63(5): 74.

18. Centers for Disease Control. 2012. Seasonal Flu Vaccine. Retrieved April 5, 2012, from http://www.cdc.gov/flu/about/qa/fluvaccine.htm#flu-vaccines; World Health Organization. 2012. Global Action Plan for Influenza Vaccines: GAP Objectives. Retrieved April 5, 2012, from http://www.who.int/influenza_vaccines_plan/objectives/en/.

19. Abrahams, Jeffrey. 1999. *The mission statement book: 301 corporate mission statements from America's top companies*, 2d ed., p. 14. Berkeley, CA: Ten Speed Press.

20. Big Brothers Big Sisters. About us. Retrieved October 21, 2009, from http://www.bbbs.org/site/c.diJKKYPLJvH/b.1539781/k.4319/Mentors__The_Largest_Youth_Mentoring_Programs_from_Big_Brothers_Big_Sisters.htm.

21. Toyota Website FAQ. Retrieved October 21, 2009, from http://www.toyota.com/help/faqs/company-what_are_toyotas_mission_and_vision_statements.html.

22. Stovall, Steven Austin. 2009. Is your vision a hallucination? *Podiatry Management* 28(1): 142.

23. Personal Interview with Annie McKee, May 31, 2012.

24. Manasse, A. Lorri. 1985. Vision and leadership: Paying attention to intention. *Peabody Journal of Education* 63(1): 150–73.

25. Personal Interview with Annie McKee, May 31, 2012.

26. Stovall, Steven Austin. 2009. Change your culture, change YOUR future. *Bed Times* 134(12): 10.

27. Malnight, Tom. 2008. *Strategically engaging your organization: Assessing your current reality*. Lausanne, Switzerland: IMD International, 5 pp.

28. Ibid.

29. Honan, Mathew. 2008, March 24. Photo Essay: Unlikely Places Where Wired Pioneers Had Their Eureka! Moments. *Wired*, 8 pp. Retrieved August 6, 2012, from http://www.wired.com/culture/lifestyle/multimedia/2008/03/ff_eureka?slide=4&slideView=7.

30. Ibid.

31. Von Hippel, Eric, Stefan Thomke, and Mary Sonnack. 1999. Creating breakthroughs at 3M. *Harvard Business Review* (September). Retrieved September 12, 2009, from http://hbr.harvardbusiness.org/1999/09/creating-breakthroughs-at-3m/ar/1.

32. Ibid.

33. Beinhocker, Eric D. 2006. The adaptable corporation. *McKinsey Quarterly Review* (May). Retrieved September 12, 2009, from http://www.mckinseyquarterly.com/The_adaptable_corporation_1757.

34. Expert Choice Inc. 2009. 3M case study. Retrieved September 12, 2009, from http://www.expertchoice.com/xres/uploads/resource-center-documents/3M_casestudy.pdf.

35. Donlon, J. 2009. Best companies for leaders. *ChiefExecutive.net*. (January 31.) Retrieved September 12, 2009, from http://chiefexecutive.net/best-companies-for-leaders.

36. Ibid.

37. Von Hippel et al., Creating breakthroughs at 3M.

38. Shor, Rita. 2009. Managed innovation: 3M's latest model for new products—Guest editorials. *Manufacturing and Technology News*. Retrieved March 20, 2010, from http://www.manufacturingnews.com/news/editorials/shor.html.

39. Ibid.

40. Courtney, Hugh, John T. Horn, and Jayarta Kar. 2009. Getting into your competitor's head. *McKinsey Quarterly Review* (February). Retrieved September 12, 2009, from http://www.mckinseyquarterly.com/Getting_into_your_competitors_head_2281.

41. Aufreiter, Nora A., Teri L. Lawver, and Candace D. Lun. 2000. A new way to market. *McKinsey Quarterly Review* (May). Retrieved September 12, 2009, from http://www.mckinseyquarterly.com/A_new_way_to_market_801.

42. Casnocha, Ben. 2009. Success on the side. *The American* (April 24). Retrieved September 12, 2009, from http://www.american.com/archive/2009/april-2009/Success-on-the-Side.

43. Costello, Brid, and Jennifer Weil. 2008. Annick Goutal outlines global growth strategy. *Women's Wear Daily* 196(128): 21; Annick Goutal Paris. About Annick Goutal. Retrieved May 25, 2012, from http://www.annickgoutal.com/en/infos/pos.aspx

44. Laube, James, and Daniel Sogg. 2004. Wine giant to acquire Mondavi for $1 billion. *Wine Spectator* 29(15): 14.

45. Landi, Heather. 2007. 'Tis the season...for mergers and acquisitions. *Beverage World* 126(12): 10.

46. Yanow, Dvora. 2000. Seeing organizational learning: A cultural view. *Organization Articles* 7(2): 24–268.

47. "2011 Annual Report." 276 pp: Bank of America Corporation, 2011. Retrieved May 25, 2012, from http://media.corporate-ir.net/Media_Files/IROL/71/71595/AR2011.pdf.

48. Daimler. 2007, May 14. Cerberus Takes Over Majority Interest in Chrysler Group and Related Financial Services Business for EUR 5.5 Billion (7.4 billion) from DaimlerChrysler. Retrieved May 22, 2010, from http://www.daimler.com/dccom/0-5-7145-1-858191-1-0-0-0-0-0-11979-0-0-0-0-0-0-0.html.

49. Puranam, Phanish, Harbir Singh, and Maurizio Zollo. 2006. Organizing for innovation: Managing the coordination-autonomy dilemma in technology acquisitions. *Academy of Management Journal* 49(2): 263–80.

50. Piekkari, R., E. Vaara, J. Tienari, and R. Säntti. 2005. Integration or disintegration? Human resource implications of the common corporate language decision in a crossborder merger. *International Journal of Human Resource Management* 16(3): 333–47; Vaara, E., J. Tienari, R. Piekkari, and R. Santti. 2005. Language and the circuits of power in a merging multinational corporation. *Journal of Management Studies* 42(3): 595–623.

51. Thomas, Chris A. 2008. Bridging the gap between theory and practice: Language policy in multilingual organizations. *Language Awareness* 17(4): 307–25.

52. San Francisco Bay Joint Venture. Retrieved October 19, 2009, from http://www.sfbayjv.org.

53. Walmart Stores.com: India. Retrieved March 30, 2010, from http://walmartstores.com/aboutus/276.aspx?p=251.

54. Walmart Stores.com: India Fact Sheet. Retrieved May 24, 2012, from http://walmartstores.com/download/1996.pdf.

55. PTI. 2011, November 25. FDI in retail: I will set Walmart stores on fire, threatens Uma Bharati. *The Times of India*. Retrieved March 26, 2012, from http://articles.timesofindia.indiatimes.com/2011-11-25/india/30440799_1_retail-sector-uma-bharati-fdi.

56. Gulati, Ranjay, and Harbir Singh. 1998. The architecture of cooperation: Managing coordination costs and appropriation concerns in strategic alliances. *Administrative Science Quarterly* 43(4): 781–814.

57. Grossman, Lev. 2007. Invention of the year: The iPhone. *Time South Pacific (Australia/New Zealand edition)*: 44.

58. Boguslauskas, Vytautas, and Goda Kvedaraviciene. 2009. Difficulties in identifying company's core competencies and core processes. *Inzinerine Ekonomika-Engineering Economics* 62(2): 75–81.

59. Porter, Michael E. 1979. How competitive forces shape strategy. *Harvard Business Review* 57(2): 137–45; Porter, Michael E. 2008.

The five competitive forces that shape strategy. *Harvard Business Review* 86(1): 79–93.

60. Green Car Congress. 2011, April 6. Toyota sells one-millionth Prius in the US. Retrieved April 19, 2012, from http://www.greencarcongress .com/2011/04/prii-20110406.html#more.

61. State of the Union: Can the Euro Zone Survive Its Debt Crisis? In *Economist Intelligence Unit Special Report*, 46 pp. London, March 2011. Retrieved March 26, 2012, from http://www.eiu.com/public/topical_ report.aspx?activity=reg&campaignid=eurodebt.

62. CBS News. 2012, July 31. Gluten-Free Diet Fad: Are Celiac Disease Rates Actually Rising? Retrieved August 6, 2012, from http://www.cbsnews .com/8301-504763_162-57483789-10391704/gluten-free-diet-fad-are-celiac-disease-rates-actually-rising/.

63. Gillin, Paul. 2007. Twitter strikes community chord. *B to B* 92(15): 11.

64. The United States Environmental Protection Agency. 2011, December 16. Texas Oil Company Sentenced to Pay $12 Million for Clean Air Act Violations and Obstruction Crimes in Louisiana/Sentence Is the Largest Eve Criminal Fine in Louisiana for Air Pollution. Retrieved March 26, 2012, from http://yosemite.epa.gov/opa/admpress.nsf/ 6427a6b7538955c585257359003f0230/224a2af1ec8927c7852579670063 837a!OpenDocument.

65. Farouk, Dalia. 2011, December 31. Egypt Tourism's Revenues Dropped 30 Per Cent in 2011. Retrieved March 27, 2012, from ahramonline, http://english.ahram.org.eg/NewsContent/3/12/30574/ Business/Economy/Egypt-tourisms-revenues-dropped--per-cent-in-.aspx.

66. UPS My Choice^SM. Retrieved April 6, 2012, from http://www.ups.com/ mychoice/index.html.

67. IBM Tops Green Company List. 2011, October 18. *Newsweek*, Retrieved April 6, 2012, from http://www.globe-net.com/articles/2011/october/19/ ibm-tops-us-green-company-list/; United States Environmental Protection Agency. Summary of 2011 Award Winners' Programs. U.S. Environmental Protection Agency, Retrieved April 6, 2012, from http://www .epa.gov/osw/partnerships/wastewise/events/2011awards.htm#toyota.

68. Porter, How competitive forces shape strategy.

69. Ibid.

70. Nalebuff, B. J., and A. M. Brandenburger. 1996. *Co-opetition*. London: HarperCollins.

71. ALC. 2009. A website's work is *never* done. *The Rest of the Story* 4(1): 6–7. Retrieved May 25, 2012, from http://www.alc.com/newsletters/ ALC_Spring09.pdf.

72. Braddock, Rick. 2009. Lessons of Internet marketing from FreshDirect. *Wall Street Journal* (May 11). Retrieved May 25, 2012, from http:// online.wsj.com/article/SB124205175154206817.html.

73. Mitchell, Ronald K., Bradley R. Agle, and Donna J. Wood. 1997. Toward a theory of stakeholder identification and salience: Defining the principle of who and what really counts. *Academy of Management Review* 22(4): 853–86.

74. Freeman, R. E. 1984. *Strategic management: A stakeholder approach*. Boston: Pitman.

75. UNESCO-IHE–UNEP/GPA. 1970. Stakeholder analysis I. Retrieved October 5, 2009, from http://www.training.gpa.unep.org/content .html?id=109.

76. *The ripple effect: Why failure of the Big 3 is not an option*. 2008. Report published by the Office of the House Majority Leader, compiled by House Representative Carolyn B. Maloney. Retrieved October 19, 2009, from http://majorityleader.house.gov/docUploads/TheRippleEffect121008.pdf.

77. Durbin, Dee-Ann. 2011. Chrysler to pay back all but $1.3B of bailout. *The Associated Press* (June 3). Retrieved May 23, 2012, from http:// www.usatoday.com/money/autos/2011-06-03-chrysler-bailout-government_n.htm.

78. Stetler, Brian. 2011. Netflix, in Reversal, Will Keep Its Services Together. *The New York Times* (October 10). Retrieved May 25, 2012, from http:// mediadecoder.blogs.nytimes.com/2011/10/10/netflix-abandons-plan-to-rent-dvds-on-qwikster/.

79. How a new strategic plan saved a century-old nonprofit. 2005. *Nonprofit World* 23(4): 1.

80. Ginter, Peter M., Andrew C. Ruck, and W. Jack Duncan. 1985. Planners' perceptions of the strategic management process. *Journal of Management Studies* 22(6): 582.

81. National Association of Home Builders. 2012. New and Existing Home Sales, U.S. Retrieved April 11, 2012, from http://www.nahb.org/ fileUpload_details.aspx?contentID=55761&fromGSA=1

82. Ireland, Duane R., Michael A. Hitt, Richard A. Bettis, and Deborah A. De Porras. 1987. Strategy formulation processes: Differences in perceptions of strength and weaknesses indicators and environmental uncertainty by managerial level. *Strategic Management Journal* 8: 469–85.

83. Barney, Jay B. 1995. Looking inside for competitive advantage. *Academy of Management Executives* 9(4): 49–61.

84. Earls, Alan. 2009. BASF procurement gets deep into R&D. *Purchasing* 138(6): 31–33.

85. Hill, Terry, and Roy Westbrook. 1997. SWOT analysis: It's time for a product recall. *Long Range Planning* 30(1): 46–52.

86. Houben, G., K. Lenie, and K. Vanhoof. 1999. A knowledge-based SWOT-analysis system as an instrument for strategic planning in small and medium sized enterprises. *Decision Support Systems* 26: 125–35.

87. Hill and Westbrook, SWOT analysis.

88. Hambrick, Donald C., Ian C. MacMillan, and Diana L. Day. 1982. Strategic attributes and performance in the BCG matrix—A PIMS-based analysis of industrial product businesses. *Academy of Management Journal* 25(3): 511.

89. MarketResearch.com. 2012. Market Research Projects Smartphone Market Growth at 19% CAGR Through 2016. *Yahoo! Finance* (April 11). Retrieved May 25, 2012, from http://finance.yahoo.com/news/market-research-projects-smartphone-market-080800406.html; Wilcox, Joe. 2012. iPhone saves smartphone market. *Betanews* (February). Retrieved on May 25, 2012, from http://betanews.com/2012/02/15/iphone-saves-smartphone-market/.

90. Calandro, Joseph, and Scott Lane. 2007. A new competitive analysis tool: The relative profitability and growth matrix. *Strategy and Leadership* 35(2): 30–38.

91. Bruner, Jerome S. 1956/2005. On perceptual readiness, in *Social cognition: Key readings*, ed. D. L. Hamilton, 108–14. New York: Psychology Press.

92. Bossidy, Larry, and Ram Charan. 2002. *Execution: The discipline of getting things done*. New York: Crown Publishing Group.

93. Charan, Ram, and Geoffrey Colvin. 1999, June 21. Why CEOs fail. *Fortune* 139(12): 68–80.

94. Mankins, Michael C., and Richard Steele. 2005. Turning great strategy into great performance. *Harvard Business Review* 83(7/8): 1–11.

95. Killing, Peter, Tom Malnight, and Tracy Keys. 2005. *Must-win battles: Creating the focus you need to achieve your key business goals*. Upper Saddle River, NJ: Wharton School Publishing.

96. Stovall, Steven Austin. 2006. *Cases in human resources management*. Cincinnati, OH: Atomic Dog Publishing.

97. Dwyer, Jim, and Kevin Flynn. 2005. *102 minutes: The untold story of the fight to survive inside the twin towers*. New York: Times Books.

98. Marquez, Jessica. 2006. Learning from 9/11 recovery. *Workforce Management* 85(17): 1–36.

99. Stovall, Steven Austin. 2006.

100. Needleman, Sarah. 2009. A new job just a tweet away. *Wall Street Journal Online*. Retrieved March 30, 2010, from http://tweetmyjobs .com/docs/wsj.pdf.

101. Margolis, Howard. 1987. *Patterns, thinking and cognition: A theory of judgment*. London: University of Chicago Press.

102. Kass, Steven J., Daniel A. Herschler, and Michael A. Companion. 1991. Training situational awareness through pattern recognition in a battlefield environment. *Military Psychology* 3(2): 105–12.

103. Wiig, Karl M. 2003. *A knowledge model for situation-handling*. Arlington, TX: Knowledge Research Institute.

104. Langer, Ellen J. 1989. *Mindfulness*, p. xiv. Reading, MA: Addison-Wesley/Addison Wesley Longman. Quote from abstract retrieved October 9, 2009, from http://psycnet.apa.org/psycinfo/1989-97542-000.

Chapter 6

1. Drake, R. A. 1987. Effects of gaze manipulation on aesthetic judgments: Hemisphere priming of affect. *Acta Psychologica* 65: 91–99; Merckelbach, Harald, and Patricia Van Oppen. 1989. Effects of gaze manipulation on subjective evaluation of neutral and phobia-relevant stimuli. *Acta Psychologica* 70: 147–51; Schiff, Bernard B., and Sandra A. Rump. 1995. Asymmetrical hemispheric activation and emotion: The effects of unilateral forced nostril breathing. *Brain and Cognition* 29: 217–31.

2. Boyatzis, Richard, and Annie McKee. 2005 *Resonant leadership: Renewing yourself and connecting with others through mindfulness, hope and compassion*. Boston: Harvard Business School Press; Goleman, Daniel, Richard Boyatzis, and Annie McKee. 2002. *Primal leadership*. Boston: Harvard Business School Press.

3. Soelberg, Peer. 1966. Unprogrammed decision making. *Academy of Management Proceedings*, pp. 3–16.

4. March, James G., and Chip Heath. 1994. *A primer on decision making: How decisions happen.* New York: The Free Press.

5. Bornat, Richard. 2005. *Proof and disproof in formal logic: An introduction for programmers.* New York: Oxford University Press.

6. Ibid.

7. Abelson, Robert P., Roger C. Schank, and Ellen J. Langer, eds. 1994. *Beliefs, reasoning, and decision making: Psycho-logic in honor of Bob Abelson.* Hillsdale, NJ: Lawrence Erlbaum Associates.

8. Fiske, S. T., and P. W. Linville. 1980. What does the schema concept buy us? *Personality and Social Psychology Bulletin* 6: 543–57.

9. Piaget, Jean. 1970. Piaget's theory. In *Carmichael's manual of child psychology, Vol. 1,* 3d ed., ed. P. H. Mussen. New York: Wiley.

10. Ibid.

11. Greenwald, Anthony G., and Mahzarin R. Banaji. 1995. Implicit social cognition: Attitudes, self-esteem, and stereotypes. *Psychological Review* 102(1): 4–27.

12. Thorndike, Edward L. 1920. A constant error on psychological rating. *Journal of Applied Psychology* 4: 25–29; Rozenzweig, Phil. 2007. *The halo effect… and the eight other business delusions that deceive managers.* New York: The Free Press.

13. Asch, Solomon. 1946/2005. Forming impressions of personality, in *Social cognition: Key readings in social psychology,* ed. David L. Hamilton, 362–71. New York: Psychology Press.

14. Nisbett, R. E., and T. D. Wilson. 1977. Telling more than we can know: Verbal reports on mental processes. *Psychological Review* 84(3): 231–59.

15. Bechara, Antoine. 2004. The role of emotion in decision making: Evidence from neurological patients with orbitofrontal damage. *Brain and Cognition* 55(1): 30–40.

16. Porges, Stephen W. 1998. Love: An emergent property of the mammalian autonomic nervous system. *Psychoneuroendocrinology* 23(8): 837–61.

17. Critchley, Hugo D., Rebecca Elliott, Christopher J. Mathias, and Raymond J. Dolan. 2000. Neural activity relating to generation and representation of galvanic skin conductance responses: A functional magnetic resonance imaging study. *Journal of Neuroscience* 20(8): 3033–40.

18. Read, Stephen J., and Carol L. Miller. 1994. Dissonance and balance in belief systems: The promise of parallel constraint satisfaction processes and connectionist modeling approaches. In *Beliefs, reasoning, and decision making: Psycho-logic in honor of Bob Abelson,* ed. Robert P. Abelson, Roger C. Schank, and Ellen J. Langer. New York: Lawrence Erlbaum Associates.

19. Tversky, Amos, and Daniel Kahneman. 1981. The framing of decisions and the psychology of choice. *Science* 211(4481): 453–58.

20. Time for Change. 2010. Definition of intuition—What is intuitive decision making? Retrieved March 23, 2010, from http://timeforchange.org/definition-of-intuition-intuitive.

21. Ibid.

22. Burke, L. A., and M. K. Miller. 1999. Taking the mystery out of intuitive decision making. *Academy of Management Executive* 13(4): 91–99; Dane, Erik, and Michael G. Pratt. Exploring intuition and its role in managerial decision making. *Academy of Management Review* 32(1): 33–54; Epstein, Seymour. 1990. Cognitive-experiential self-theory, in *Handbook of personality: Theory and research,* ed. L. Pervin, 165–92. New York: Guilford Press.

23. Dane and Pratt, Exploring intuition.

24. Simon, Herbert A. 1987. Making management decisions: The role of intuition and emotion. *Academy of Management Executive* 1(1): 57–64.

25. Ibid.

26. Epstein, Seymour. 1994. Integration of the cognitive and the psycho-dynamic unconscious. *American Psychologist* 49: 709–24. Hogarth, Robin M. 2005. Deciding analytically or trusting your intuition? The advantages and disadvantages of analytic and intuitive thought, in *The routines of decision-making,* ed. T. Betsch and S. Haberstroh, 67–82. Mahwah, NJ: Lawrence Erlbaum Associates.

27. Hammond, Kenneth R., Robert M. Hamm, Janet Grassia, and Tamra Pearson. 1987. Direct comparison of the efficacy of intuitive and analytical cognition in expert judgment. *IEEE Transactions on Systems, Man, and Cybernetics* 17: 753–70.

28. Goleman, Daniel, and Richard Boyatzis. 2008. Social intelligence and the biology of leadership. *Harvard Business Review* 86(9): 74–81.

29. Sadler-Smith, Eugene. 2008. The role of intuition in collective learning and the development of shared meaning. *Advances in Developing Human Resources* 10(4): 494–508.

30. Nicosia, F. 1966. *Consumer decision processes.* Englewood Cliffs, NJ: Prentice Hall.

31. Lacey, Hoda. 2006. Don't let your bosses make wrong decisions. *Travel Trade Gazette UK and Ireland* (2701): 45.

32. Simon, Herbert. 1957. *Models of man: Social and rational—Mathematical essays on rational human behavior in a social setting.* New York: Wiley; Roach, John M. 1979. Decision making is a "satisficing" experience. *Management Review* 68(1): 8.

33. Retrieved April 5, 2012, from http://www.google.com/#hl=en&safe=off&sclient=psy-ab&q=%22decision+making%22&oq=%22decision+making%22&aq=f&aqi=g4&aql=&gs_l=hp.3.0l4.1718l16430l0l16733l2 00l52l1l0l0l3l3l378l5221l34j15j1j1l53l0.frgbld.&pbx=1&bav=on.2,or.r_gc.r_pw.r_qf.,cf.osb&fp=d1cb6253d6261c3c&biw=1600&bih=728.

34. Kant, Immanuel. 1785/1993. *Grounding for the metaphysics of morals,* 3d ed. Trans. James W. Ellington. Indianapolis, IN: Hackett.

35. Simon, *Models of man.*

36. Ibid; March, James G. 1978. Bounded rationality, ambiguity, and the engineering of choice. *Bell Journal of Economics* 9(2): 587–608.

37. Simon, *Models of man;* March, Bounded rationality, ambiguity, and the engineering of choice; Kahneman, Daniel, and Amos Tversky. 2004. Prospect theory: An analysis of decision under risk, in *Preference, belief, and similarity,* ed. Amos Tversky, 549–82. Cambridge: Massachusetts Institute of Technology.

38. Kahneman, Daniel and Amos Tyersky. 2004. Prospect theory: an analysis of decision under risk, in *Preface, belief, and similarity,* ed. A. Tversky, pp. 549–589. Cambridge, MA. MIT Press; Weary, Gifford, Stephanie J. Tobin, and John A. Edwards. 2010. *The Causal Uncertainty Model Revisited; Handbook of the Uncertain Self,* ed. Robert M. Arkin, Kathryn C. Oleson, and Patrick J. Carroll. New York: Psychology Press.

39. Kahneman, Daniel. 2003. Maps of bounded rationality: Psychology for behavioral economics. *American Economic Review* 93(5): 1449–75.

40. Kahneman, Maps of bounded rationality.

41. Simon, *Models of man;* Roach, Decision making is a "satisficing" experience.

42. Juran, Joseph M. 1975. The non-Pareto principle—Mea culpa. *Quality Progress* 8: 8–9; Bunkley, Nick. 2008. Joseph Juran, 103, pioneer in quality control, dies. *New York Times* (March 3): 23.

43. Emiliani, M. L. 2000. Cracking the code of business. *Management Decision* 38(2): 60–79.

44. Watson, G. B., and E. M. Glaser. 1994. *Watson-Glaser Critical Thinking Appraisal Form S manual.* San Antonio, TX: Harcourt Brace.

45. Taylor, Chris. 2005. It's a wiki, wiki world. *Time Magazine* (May 29). Retrieved September 12, 2009, from http://www.time.com/time/magazine/article/0,9171,1066904-1,00.html.

46. Miller, Robin ("Roblimo"). 2004, July 24. Wikipedia founder Jimmy Wales responds. *Slashdot.org.* Retrieved September 12, 2009, from http://interviews.slashdot.org/article.pl?sid=04/07/28/1351230.

47. McCarthy, Tom. 2012. Encyclopedia Britannica halts print publication after 244 years. *The Guardian* (March 13). Retrieved April 23, 2012, from http://www.guardian.co.uk/books/2012/mar/13/encyclopedia-britannica-halts-print-publication.

48. Cunningham, Ward. 2003. Correspondence on the etymology of Wiki (November). Retrieved September 12, 2009, from http://c2.com/doc/etymology.html.

49. Taylor, It's a wiki, wiki world.

50. Solar Navigator. 2006. Wikipedias or wiki world. Retrieved September 12, 2009, from http://www.solarnavigator.net/wikipedias.htm.

51. Taylor, It's a wiki, wiki world.

52. Tapscott, D., and A. D. Williams. 2006. *Wikonomics: How mass collaboration changes everything.* New York: Portfolio.

53. Sigenthaler, John. 2005, December 4. Truth can be at risk in the world of the web. *The Tennessean.*

54. Hammond, John S., Ralph L. Keeney, and Howard Raiffa. 1998. The hidden traps in decision making. *Harvard Business Review* 76(5): 47–58.

55. Edwards, M. O. 1966. Tips on solving problems creatively. *Management Review* 55(3): 28.

56. Rowe, Gene, and George Wright. 1999. The Delphi technique as a forecasting tool: Issues and analysis. *International Journal of Forecasting* 15(4): 353–75.

57. Ibid.
58. Langer, Ellen J. 1997. *The power of mindful learning.* Reading, MA: Perseus Books; Kabat-Zinn, Jon. 1990. *Full catastrophe living: Using the wisdom of your body and mind to face stress, pain and illness.* Cambridge, MA: Perseus Publishing.
59. McKee, Annie, Richard, Boyatzis, and Frances Johnston. 2008. *Becoming a resonant leader: Develop your emotional intelligence, renew your relationships and sustain your effectiveness.* Boston: Harvard Business School Press.
60. Boyatzis, Richard, and Annie McKee. 2005. *Resonant leadership: Renewing yourself and connecting with others through mindfulness, hope and compassion.* Boston: Harvard Business School Press; Goleman, Daniel, Richard Boyatzis, and Annie McKee. 2002. *Primal leadership.* Boston: Harvard Business School Press.
61. Ruggiero, V. R. 1996. *Becoming a critical thinker.* Boston, MA: Houghton Mifflin.
62. Argyris, C., and D. Schön. 1978. *Organizational learning: A theory of action perspective.* Reading, MA: Addison Wesley; Argyris, C., and D. Schön. 1974. *Theory in practice: Increasing professional effectiveness.* San Francisco, CA: Jossey-Bass; Forrester, J. W. 1971. *World dynamics.* Cambridge, MA: MIT Press.
63. Argyris, Chris. 1976. *Increasing leadership effectiveness.* New York: Wiley.
64. Andrews, Robert. 1989. *The Concise Columbia Dictionary of Quotations.* New York: Columbia University Press.

Chapter 7

1. Whorf, Benjamin. 1940. Science and linguistics. *Technology Review (MIT)* 42(6): 229–31, 247–48.
2. Goodwin, Charles. 1996. Practices of color classification. *Ninchi Kagaku* (Cognitive Studies: Bulletin of the Japanese Cognitive Science Society) 3(2): 62–82.
3. Wallechinsky, David, and Irving Wallace. 1978. *The people's almanac #2, issue 2.* New York: William Morrow and Company.
4. Ramachandran, Vilayanur S. The Neurons That Shaped Civilization, TED: Ideas Worth Spreading. TEDIndia, 2009.
5. James, Jesse. 2009. Career transitioning not just a symptom of the economy (November 1). *AC Associated Content.* Retrieved January 31, 2010, from http://www.associatedcontent.com/article/2346770/career_transitioning_not_just_a_symptom.html?cat=3.
6. Bureau of Labor Statistics. 2008. Employee Tenure Summary (September 26). Retrieved May 10, 2010, from http://www.bls.gov/news.release/tenure.nr0.htm.
7. Ibid.
8. Waring, Paul. 2008. Coaching the brain. *The Coaching Psychologist* 4(2): 10–16.
9. Goleman, Daniel, Richard E. Boyatzis, and Annie McKee. 2002. *Primal leadership: Learning to lead with emotional intelligence.* Boston: Harvard Business School Press.
10. Ibid.
11. Boyatzis, Richard E. 2006. An overview of intentional change from a complexity perspective. *Journal of Management Development* 25(7): 607–23; Howard, Anita. 2006. Positive and negative emotional attractors and intentional change. *Journal of Management Development* 25(7): 657–70; Boyatzis, Richard, and Annie McKee. 2005. *Resonant leadership: Renewing yourself and connecting with others through mindfulness, hope and compassion.* Boston: Harvard Business School Press.
12. Dolan, S. L., S. Garcia, and A. Auerbach. 2003. Understanding and managing chaos in organizations. *International Journal of Management* 20(1): 23–35; Van der Ven, Andrew H., and Marshall S. Poole. 1995. Explaining development and change in organizations. *Academy of Management Review* 20(3): 510–40.
13. McKee, Annie, Richard Boyatzis, and Frances Johnston. 2008. *Becoming a resonant leader.* Cambridge: Harvard University Press.
14. Ibid.
15. Seligman, Martin. 1998. *Learned optimism: How to change your mind and your life.* New York: Pocket Books.
16. Ibid.
17. Boyatzis and McKee. 2005. *Resonant leadership;* Seligman, Martin. *Learned optimism.*
18. Boyatzis, Richard, and Annie McKee. 2005. *Resonant leadership.* Boston, MA: Harvard University Press. Boyatzis, An overview of intentional change theory from a complexity perspective; Boyatzis, Richard E. 2001. Developing emotional intelligence, in *The emotionally intelligent workplace,* eds. C. Cherniss, R. E. Boyatzis, and D. Goleman, 234–53. San Francisco, Jossey-Bass.
19. Boyatzis, An overview of intentional change theory from a complexity perspective; Boyatzis, Developing emotional intelligence. Kolb, David A., and Richard E. Boyatzis. 1970. Goal setting and self-directed behavior change. *Human Relations* 23(5): 439–57; Boyatzis, Richard E. 2008. Leadership development from a complexity perspective. *Consulting Psychology Journal* 60(4): 298–313.
20. Goleman et al., *Primal leadership;* Boyatzis, Richard E., and Kleio Akrivou. 2006. The ideal self as the driver of intentional change. *Journal of Management Development* 25(7): 139.
21. Goleman et al., *Primal leadership;* Boyatzis and Akrivou, The ideal self as the driver of intentional change.
22. Goleman, Daniel, Richard Boyatzis, and Annie McKee. 2002. *Reawakening your passion for work.* Boston: Harvard Business School Press.
23. New York Institute for Gestalt Therapy. Home page. Retrieved May 10, 2010, from http://www.newyorkgestalt.org/index/html.
24. Critchley, B., and D. Casey. 1989. Organizations get stuck too. *Leadership and Organization Development Journal* 10(4): 3–12.
25. Kepner, Elaine. 1980. Gestalt group process. In *Beyond the hot seat: Gestalt approaches to group,* ed. Bud Feder and Ruth Ronall, 5–25. Highland, NY: Gestalt Journal Press; Kolb, David. 1984. *Experiential learning: Experience as the source of learning and development.* Upper Saddle River, NJ: Prentice Hall.
26. Interview with Frances Johnston, January 2010.
27. Johnston, Frances, and Eddy Mwelwa. 2009. Making the HIV/AIDS problem visible in Cambodia. In *Mending the world,* ed. Joseph Melnick and Edwin C. Nevis, 287–309. Bloomington, IN: Xlibris Publishing.
28. United States Agency for International Development. USAID/Cambodia. Retrieved May 10, 2010, from http://www.usaid.gov/our_work/global_health/aids/Countries/asia/cambodia_profile.pdf.
29. Ibid.
30. *CIA World Factbook,* Cambodia. Retrieved May 10, 2010, from https://www.cia.gov/library/publications/the-world-factbook/geos/countrytemplate_cb.html.
31. Bauman, Zygmunt. *Liquid times: Living in an age of uncertainty.* Cambridge: Polity Press, 2007.
32. Friedman, Thomas L. 2011. A Theory of Everything (Sort of). *The New York Times* (August 13). Retrieved May 18, 2012, from http://www.nytimes.com/2011/08/14/opinion/sunday/Friedman-a-theory-of-everyting-sort-of.html.
33. Whiteman, Hilary. "Asia Facing 'Epidemic' of Worker Deaths, Report Warns." *cnn.com.* Retrieved April 28, 2012. http://www.cnn.com/2012/04/28/world/asia/asia-workers-occupational-disease/index.html?eref=rss_latest&utm_source=feedburner&utm_medium=feed&utm_campaign=Feed%3A+rss%2Fcnn_latest+%28RSS%3A+Most+Recent%29.
34. Friedman, Thomas L. 2008. *Hot, flat and crowded: Why we need a green revolution and how it can renew America.* New York: Farrar, Straus and Giroux.
35. Rifkin, Jeremy. 2010. *The empathic civilization: The race to global consciousness in a world in crisis.* New York: Tarcher-Penguin.
36. Chouinard, Yvon. 1993. Patagonia: The next hundred years. In *Sacred trusts: Essays on stewardship and responsibility,* ed. M. Katkis, 112–121. San Francisco: Mercury House.
37. Sustainable Energy Solutions. 2011. Patagonia goes greener at CA campus with solar array (October 12). Retrieved May 4, 2012, from http://www.sccleanenergy.com/tag/patagonia-solar-array/; Stevenson, Seth. 2012. Patagonia's Founder Is America's Most Unlikely Business Guru. *The Wall Street Journal* (April 26). Retrieved May 4, 2012, from http://online.wsj.com/article/SB100014240527023035134045773522214 65986612.html.
38. Trading Economics. United States. GDP. Retrieved August 6, 2012, from http://www.tradingeconomics.com/united-states/gdp-growth.
39. News India. 2012. India growth drops to slowest in nearly three years. *BBC* (February 29). Retrieved June 5, 2012, from http://www.bbc.co.uk/news/world-asia-india-17201132; Perkowski, Jack. 2012. China's Economy Is Slowing, But.... *Forbes* (June 5). Retrieved June 5, 2012, from http://www.forbes.com/sites/jackperkowski/2012/06/05/chinas-economy-is-slowing-but/.
40. Friedman, Thomas. 2005. *The world is flat.* New York: Farrar, Straus and Giroux.

41. Anderson, Chris. 2008. *The long tail: Why the future of business is selling less of more.* New York: Hyperion Books; Bauman, Zygmunt. 2007. *Consuming life.* Cambridge: Polity Press; Watson, Joe. 2006. *Without excuses: Unleash the power of diversity to build your business.* New York: St. Martin's Press.

42. Norton, Seth W. 2004. Towards a more general theory of franchise governance, in *Economics and management of franchising networks,* ed. J. Windsperger adn G. Hendrikse, pp. 17–37. New York: Physica-Verlag Heidelberg.

43. Disney. Walt Disney Imagineering. Retrieved May 15, 2012, from http://wdi.disneycareers.com/en/career-areas/overview/.

44. Thomas, David A. 2004. "Diversity as Strategy." Harvard Business Review 82(9): 98–108.

45. Avery, Derek R., Patrick F. McKay, David C. Wilson, and Scott Tonidandel. 2007. Unequal attendance: The relationships between race, organizational diversity cues, and absenteeism. *Personnel Psychology* 60(4): 875–902.

46. Charney, Richard J., Madeleine L.S. Loewenberg, Karen Ainslie, Claire Darbourne, Paul Griffin, Katrin Scheicht, and Leanne Nickels. 2011. Diversity Laws: A Global Overview. *Norton Rose.* Retrieved July 30, 2012, from http://www.nortonrose.com/knowledge/publications/51599/diversity-laws-a-global-overview.

47. Anderson, *The long tail.*

48. Google Finance. Amazon.com. Retrieved July 30, 2012, from http://www.google.com/finance?client=ob&q=NASDAQ:AMZN.

49. Thomas, David A., and Robin J. Ely. 2007. Making differences matter, in *The Jossey-Bass reader on educational leadership,* ed. Michael Fullan, p. 270. San Francisco: Jossey-Bass.

50. Sylvia Ann Hewlett Associates LLC. 2009. Creating a Sustainable Inclusion & Diversity Strategy: Build on Your Company's Goals and Strengths. Retrieved May 15, 2012, from http://www.cisco.com/web/about/ac49/ac55/white_paper_Diversity_102709.pdf.

51. Great Places to Work. 2011. World's Best Multinational Workplaces. Retrieved May 15, 2012, from http://www.greatplacetowork.com/best-companies/worlds-best-multinationals/list-of-the-25-best-from-2011.

52. Beattie, Geoffrey. 2012. *Our racist heart? An exploration of unconscious prejudice in everyday life.* New York: Routledge.

53. Data are from the US Current Population Survey 2010. Accessed May 6, 2012, from http://www.census.gov/.

54. Bureau of Labor Statistics. Retrieved February 1, 2010, from http://www.bls.gov/cps/cpsaat39.pdf.

55. Fortune. 2009. Women CEOs. (May 4). Retrieved February 11, 2010, from http://money.cnn.com/magazines/fortune/fortune500/2009/womenceos.

56. Ibid.

57. Bureau of Labor Statistics. Retrieved August 6, 2012, from http://www.bls.gov/cps/cpsaat39.pdf.

58. Catalyst. 2012. Statistical Overview of Women in the Workplace. Retrieved May 18, 2010, http://www.catalyst.org/publication/219/statistical-overview-of-women-in-the-workplace.

59. Data collected from the United States Census Bureau. Retrieved May 15, 2012, from http://www.census.gov/population/international/data/idb/informationGateway.php.

60. Ibid.

61. Ibid.

62. Ibid.

63. Ibid.

64. Chakravarthy, B., and P. Lorange. 2008. Driving renewal: The entrepreneur manager. *Journal of Business Strategy* 29: 14–21.

65. Nadler, David A., and Michael L. Tushman. 1989. Organizational frame bending: Principles for managing reorientation. *The Academy of Management Executive* 3(3): 194–204.

66. General Electric. Our history. Retrieved January 26, 2010, from http://www.ge.com/company/history/index.html; General Electric Company. Retrieved January 26, 2010, from http://www.fundinguniverse.com/company-histories/General-Electric-Company-Company-History.html.

67. General Electric. Ecomagination. Retrieved May 10, 2010, from http://ge.ecomagination.com/index.html.

68. Cassano, Erik. 2011. How Bill Ford Jr. led Ford Motor Co. through the recession. *SmartBusiness* (March 1). Retrieved May 18, 2011, from http://www.sbnonline.com/2011/03/bill-ford-jr-on-the-future-of-his-brand-the-business/?paging=1.

69. Blow-Ups Happen. 2012. *The Economist* 402(8775): 10–14.

70. Frogland-The boiled frog. Retrieved May 10, 2010, from http://allaboutfrogs.org/stories/boiled.html.

71. Krugman, Paul. 2009. Reagan did it. *New York Times* (May 31). Retrieved January 28, 2010, from http://www.nytimes.com/2009/06/01/opinion/01krugman.html?_r=1.

72. Stiglitz, Joseph E. 2009. Capitalist fools. *Vanity Fair* (January). Retrieved January 28, 2010, from http://www.vanityfair.com/magazine/2009/01/stiglitz200901.

73. Labaton, Stephen. 2008. Agency's '04 rule let banks pile up new debt. *New York Times* (October 2). Retrieved January 28, 2010, from http://www.nytimes.com/2008/10/03/business/03sec.html?em.

74. Holmes, Steven A. 1999. Fannie Mae eases credit to aid mortgage lending. *New York Times* (September 30). Retrieved January 28, 2010, from http://www.nytimes.com/1999/09/30/business/fannie-mae-eases-credit-to-aid-mortgage-lending.html; Board of Governors of the Federal Reserve System. Open Market Operations. Retrieved May 10, 2010, from http://www.federalreserve.gov/fomc/fundsrate.htm. Federal Deposit Insurance Corporation. 2006. Challenges and FDIC efforts related to predatory lending. Report No. 06-011. Arlington, VA: FDIC. Retrieved January 28, 2010, from http://www.fdicoig.gov/reports06/06-011.pdf.

75. Andrews, Edmund L. 2008. Greenspan concedes error on regulation. *New York Times* (October 23). Retrieved February 1, 2010, from http://www.nytimes.com/2008/10/24/business/economy/24panel.html.

76. Ip, Greg. 2008. His legacy tarnished, Greenspan goes on defensive. *Wall Street Journal* (April 8). Retrieved March 11, 2010, from http://online.wsj.com/article/SB120760341392296107.html.

77. Bartlett, Bruce. 2009. Who saw the housing bubble coming? *Forbes.com* (January 2). Retrieved February 1, 2010, from http://www.anderson.ucla.edu/faculty/edward.leamer/documents/01-02-2009%20Forbes%20-%20Who%20saw%20bubble%20coming.pdf.

78. CSI: Credit crunch. 2007, October 20. *The Economist* 385(8551): 4–8.

79. Joint Center for Housing Studies of Harvard University. 2008. The state of the nation's housing 2008. President and fellows of Harvard College. Retrieved January 28, 2010, from http://www.jchs.harvard.edu/publications/markets/son2008/son2008.pdf; Labaton, Agency's '04 rule let banks pile up new debt.

80. Engdahl, F. William. 2004. Is a USA economic collapse due in 2005? *Centre for Research on Globalisation.* Retrieved February 1, 2010, from http://www.globalresearch.ca/articles/ENG407A.html.

81. Glass, Ira. 2009, April 5. This American life: Giant pool of money wins Peabody. *Public Radio International.* Retrieved February 1, 2010, from http://www.pri.org/business/giant-pool-of-money.html.

82. Volcker, Paul A. 2005. An economy on thin ice. *Washington Post* (April 10). Retrieved March 11, 2010, from http://www.washingtonpost.com/wp-dyn/articles/A38725-2005Apr8.html.

83. BBC News. 2003. Buffett warns of investment "time bomb." Retrieved January 28, 2010, from http://news.bbc.co.uk/2/hi/business/2817995.stm.

84. Salmon, Felix. 2009. Recipe for disaster: The formula that killed Wall Street. *Wired Magazine* 17 (February 23). Retrieved January 28, 2010, from http://www.wired.com/techbiz/it/magazine/17-03/wp_quant.

85. Associated Press. 2012, April 23. Half of new graduates are jobless or underemployed. Retrieved on May 25, 2012, from http://www.usatoday.com/news/nation/story/2012-04-22/college-grads-jobless/54473426/1.

86. "The Employment Situation —April 2012." edited by Bureau of Labor Statistics: U.S. Department of Labor, 2012.

87. "The State of Small Businesses Post Great Recession: An Analysis of Small Businesses between 2007 and 2011." Dun & Bradstreet, 2011.

88. Google Public Data. 1996–2012. GDP Growth Rate. Retrieved August 6, 2012, from http://www.google.com/publicdata/explore?ds=d5bncppjof8f9_&met_y=ny_gdp_mktp_kd_zg&idim=country:GRC&dl=en&hl=en&q=greece+gdp+growth+rate#!ctype=l&strail=false&bcs=d&nselm=h&met_y=ny_gdp_mktp_kd_zg&scale_y=lin&ind_y=false&rdim=region&idim=country:GRC&ifdim=region&tstart=832219200000&tend=1273982400000&hl=en_US&dl=en&ind=false

89. *CIA world factbook,* Germany. Retrieved May 18, 2012, from https://www.cia.gov/library/publications/the-world-factbook/geos/gm.html.

90. Orol, Ronald D. 2012. FDIC: Bank profits at highest levels since 2007. *The Wall Street Journal MarketWatch* (May 24). Retrieved June 5, 2012, from http://articles.marketwatch.com/2012-05-24/

economy/31832758_1_bank-profits-problem-list-bank-net-income; MSNBC. 2012. JP Morgan's Dimon: 'I understand the frustration' (May 11). Retrieved June 5, 2012, from http://marketday.msnbc.msn .com/_news/2012/05/11/11659940-jp-morgans-dimon-i-understand-the-frustration?lite.

91. Lewin, Kurt. 1951/1964. *Field theory in social science: Selected theoretical papers.* New York: Harper Torchbooks.

92. Ibid., 229.

93. Burnes, Bernard. 2004. Kurt Lewin and complexity theories: Back to the future? *Journal of Change Management* 4(4): 309–25.

94. Lewin, Kurt. 1943. Psychological ecology. In *Field theory in social science,* 1952, ed. D. Cartwright. London: Social Science Paperbacks; Lewin, Kurt. 1947. Frontiers in group dynamics. In *Field theory in social science,* 1952, ed. D. Cartwright. London: Social Science Paperbacks; Burnes, Kurt Lewin and complexity theories.

95. Levy, Steven. 2005. Honey, I shrunk the iPod. A lot. *Newsweek* 146(12): 58.

96. Ibid; Sutton, R. L. 2001. The weird rules of creativity. *Harvard Business Review* 79(8): 94–103.

97. Ibid. Schein, Edgar H. 2002. Models and tools for stability and change in human systems. *Reflections* 4(2): 13.

98. Lewin, Kurt. 1952. Group decision and social change. In *Readings in social psychology,* ed. G. E. Swanson, T. N. Newcomb, and E. L. Hartley. New York: Holt; Schein, E. H. 1987. *Organizational culture and leadership.* San Francisco: Jossey-Bass.

99. Vaill, Peter. 1989. *Managing as a performing art: New ideas for a world of chaotic change.* San Francisco: Jossey-Bass.

100. Shea, Gregory, and Robert Gunther. 2009. *Your job survival guide: A manual for thriving in change.* Upper Saddle River, NJ: Pearson Education.

101. Vaill, Peter. 1996. *Learning as a way of being: Strategies for survival in a world of permanent white water.* San Francisco: Jossey-Bass.

102. Kotter, John P. 2012. *Leading Change, 2nd ed.* Boston, Mass.: Harvard Business Review Press.

103. Herper, Matthew, and Peter Kang. 2006. The world's ten best-selling drugs. *Forbes* (March 22). Retrieved January 29, 2010, from http://www .forbes.com/2006/03/21/pfizer-merck-amgen-cx_mh_pk_0321topdrugs .html.

104. Pfizer. Appendix A: 2011 Financial Report. Retrieved August 9, 2012 from http://www.pfizer.com/files/annualreport/2011/financial/ financial2011.pdf.

105. Bristol-Myers Squibb. Growth through Innovation: 2011 Annual Report. Retrieved August 9, 2012 from http://www.bmsfrance.fr/IMG/ pdf/bristolmyerssquibb_2011_annualreport_web.pdf.

106. AstraZeneca. Annual Report and Form 20-F Information 2011: Therapy Area Review: Gastrointestinal. Retrieved August 9, 2012 from http:// www.astrazeneca-annualreports.com/2011/documents/pdfs/gastroin- testinal.pdf; AstraZeneca. Annual Report and Form 20-F Information 2010: Therapy Area Review: Gastrointestinal. Retrieved August 9, 2012 from http://www.astrazeneca-annualreports.com/documents/2010/ therapy_review_area_factsheets/gastrointestinal.pdf; AstraZeneca. Condensed Consolidated Statement of Comprehensive Income (2011). Retrieved August 9, 2012 from http://www.astrazeneca.com/cs/ Satellite?blobcol=urldata&blobheader=application%2Fpdf&blobheader name1=Content-Disposition&blobheadername2=MDT-Type&blobhea dervalue1=inline%3B+filename%3DFigures.pdf&blobheadervalue2=abi nary%3B+charset%3DUTF-8&blobkey=id&blobtable=MungoBlobs&bl obwhere=1285632537830&ssbinary=true.

107. Shea, Gregory P. 2001. Leading change. In *Medicine and business: Bridging the gap,* ed. S. Rovin, p. 47. Gaithersburg, MD: Aspen Publishers.

108. Personal correspondence with Gregory Shea, January 30, 2010.

109. Thomas, Chris A., and Brett Lee. 2010. Language liaisons: Language planning leadership in health care. *Language Problems and Language Planning,* 34. In press.

110. Wharton ebuzz. Innovation requires change. Retrieved January 28, 2010, from http://executiveeducation.wharton.upenn.edu/ebuzz/0611/ classroom.html.

111. Livingston, Jessica. 2008. Riding the waves during the recession: An interview with authors Gregory Shea and Robert Gunther. *Human Resource iQ* (September 29). Retrieved November 26, 2012, from http:// www.humanresourcesiq.com/business-strategies/articles/riding-the- waves-during-the-recession-an-interview/.

112. Green, Peter S. 2009. Merrill's Thain said to pay $1.2 million to decora- tor. (January 23). *Bloomberg.com.* Retrieved March 11, 2010, from http://

www.bloomberg.com/apps/news?pid=20601087&sid=aFcrG8er4FRw& refer=home.

113. Touryalai, Halah. 2011. Bank of America's Latest Peril: Losing Merrill Lynch. *Forbes* (September 2). Retrieved June 5, 2012, from http://www .forbes.com/sites/halahtouryalai/2011/09/02/bank-of-americas-latest- peril-losing-merrill-lynch/.

114. Burke, W. Warner. 1987. *Organization development: A normative view.* Reading, MA: Addison-Wesley.

115. French, Wendell. 1969. Organization development: Objectives, assump- tions, and strategies. *California Management Review* 12: 23–34.

116. Hinkley, Stanley R. 2006. A history of organization development. In *NTL handbook of organization development and change: Principles, practices, and perspectives,* ed. Brenda B. Jones and Michael Brazzel, 28–45. San Francisco: Pfeiffer; Weisbord, M. R. 2004. *Productive workplaces revisited: Dignity, meaning and community in the 21st century.* San Francisco: Pfeiffer.

117. Cummings, T. G., and C. G. Worley. 2009. *Organization development and change.* Mason, OH: South-Western Cengage Learning.

118. Ibid.

119. McGregor, Douglas, and Joel Cutcher-Gershenfield. 2006. *The human side of enterprise.* New York: McGraw-Hill.

120. Leskiw, Sheri-Lynne, and Parbudyal Singh. 2007. Leadership devel- opment: Learning from best practices. *Leadership and Organization Development Journal* 28(5): 444–64.

121. Lewin, Kurt. 1946. Action research and minority problems. *Journal of Social Issues* 2(4): 34–46.

122. Raelin, Joseph A. 1997. Action Learning and Action Science: Are they different? *Organizational Dynamics* 26(1): 21–34.

123. Reason, P., and H. Bradbury, eds. 2008. *Sage handbook of action research: Participative inquiry and practice,* 2d ed. London: Sage Publications; Reason, Peter, Gill Coleman, David Ballard, Michelle Williams, Margaret Gearty, Carole Bond, Chris Seeley, and Esther Maughan McLachlan. 2009. Insider Voices: Human Dimensions of Low Carbon Technology. *Lowcarbonworks Centre for Action Research in Professional Practice* 132. Retrieved November 26, 2010, from http://www.bath.ac.uk/ management/news_events/pdf/lowcarbon_insider_voices.pdf.

124. Freire, P. 1970. *Pedagogy of the oppressed.* New York: Herder & Herder.

125. Lewin, Action research and minority problems; Burnes, Kurt Lewin and complexity theories.

126. Reason, Peter, and Hilary Bradbury. 2001. Inquiry and participation in search of a world worth of human aspiration, in *Handbook of action research: Participative inquiry and practice,* eds. P. Reason and H. Bradbury, 1–14. Thousand Oaks, CA: Sage Publications; McKee, Annie, and Frances Johnston. 2006. The impact and opportunity of emotion in organizations, in *The NTL Handbook of Organizational Development and Change,* eds. B. B. Jones and M. Brazzel, 407–423. San Francisco: Pffeifer; London, Anne (Annie McKee), and McMillan, Cecilia. 1992. Discovering social issues: Organizational development in a multicultural community. *Journal of Applied Behavioral Sciences* 28: 445–460.

127. Kemmis, Stephen, and Robin McTaggart. 2005. Participatory action research: Communicative action and the public sphere, in *SAGE handbook of qualitative research,* ed. Norman K. Denzin and Yvonna S. Lincoln, 559–604. Thousand Oaks, CA: Sage Publications.

128. Schwaninger M. 2000. Managing complexity: The path toward intelli- gent organizations. *Systemic Practice and Action Research* 13(2): 207–41; Schwaninger, Markus. 2004. Methodologies in conflict: Achieving synergies between system dynamics and organizational cybernetics. A cyberkinetic model to enhance organizational intelligence. *Systems Research and Behavioral Science* 21: 411; Schwaninger, Markus. 2003. A cybernetic model to enhance organizational intelligence. *Systems Analysis Modelling Simulations* 43(1): 53–65.

129. Boyatzis and McKee. *Resonant leadership*; Boyatzis, Richard E., A. Baker, D. Leonard, K. Rhee, and L. Thompson. 1995. Will it make a difference? Assessing a value-based, outcome oriented, competency- based professional program, in *Innovation in professional education: Steps on a journey from teaching to learning,* ed. Richard E. Boyatzis, S. S. Cowen, and D. A. Kolb, 167–202. San Francisco: Jossey-Bass; Boyatzis, Richard E., and Argun Saatcioglu. 2008. A 20-year view of trying to develop emotional, social and cognitive intelligence compe- tencies in graduate management education. *Journal of Management Development* 27(1): 92–108.

130. McKee, Annie, Richard Boyatzis, and Frances Johnston. 2008. *Becoming a resonant leader: Develop your emotional intelligence, renew your relationships, and sustain your effectiveness.* Boston: Harvard Business School Press.

131. Bunch, Kay J. 2007. Training failure as a consequence of organizational culture. *Human Resource Development Review* 6(1): 142–63.

132. Buchanan, D., and D. Boddy. 1992. *The expertise of the change agent.* New York: Prentice Hall.

133. Dawson, P. 1994. *Organizational change: A processual approach.* London: Paul Chapman; Hardy, C. 1994. *Managing strategic action: Mobilizing change—concepts, readings and cases.* London: Sage; Hardy, S. 1996. Understanding power: Bringing about strategic change. *British Journal of Management* 7 (Special Issue): S3–S16; Kanter, R. M. 1983. *The change masters: Corporate entrepreneurs at work.* London: Allen & Unwin; Pettigrew, A. M. 1985. *The awakening giant: Continuity and change in Imperial Chemical Industries.* Oxford: Blackwell.

134. Balogun, Julia, Pauline Gleadle, Veronica H. Hailey, and Hugh Willmott. 2005. Managing change across boundaries: Boundary-shaking practices. *British Journal of Management* 16(4): 261–78.

135. Ibid., 263.

136. Goleman, Daniel. 1995. *Emotional intelligence.* New York: Bantam Books; Goleman, Daniel. 1998. *Working with emotional intelligence.* New York: Bantam Books.

137. Cangemi, Joseph P., Bill Burga, Harold Lazarus, Richard L. Miller, and Jaime Fitzgerald. The real work of the leader: A focus on the human side of the equation. *Journal of Management Development* 27(10): 1026–36; Vakola, M., I. Tsaousis, and I. Nikolaou. 2004. The role of emotional intelligence and personality variables on attitudes toward organizational change. *Journal of Managerial Psychology* 19(2): 88–110.

138. Boyatzis and McKee, *Resonant leadership.*

139. Ibid.

Chapter 8

1. D'Aveni, Richard A. 1994. *Hypercompetition: Managing the dynamics of strategic maneuvering.* New York: The Free Press.

2. Wiggins, Robert R., and Timothy W. Ruefli. 2005. Schumpeter's Ghost: Is Hypercompetition Making the Best of Times Shorter? *Strategic Management Journal* 26(10): 887-911.

3. Ibid.

4. Bogner, William C., and Pamela S. Barr. 2000. Making sense in hypercompetitive environments: A cognitive explanation for persistence of high velocity competition. *Organization Science* 11(2): 212–26.

5. Amar, A. D., Carsten Hentrich, and Vlatka Hlupic. 2009. To be a better leader, give up authority. *Harvard Business Review* 87(12): 22–24, 126.

6. Silverthorne, Sean. 2012. The High Risks of Short-Term Management. *Harvard Business School Working Knowledge* (2012): 2 pp., Retrieved May 17, 2012, from http://hbswk.hbs.edu/pdf/item/6965.pdf.

7. Dietrich, Arne. 2004. The cognitive neuroscience of creativity. *Psychonomic Bulletin and Review* 11(6): 1011–26.

8. Ibid.

9. Ibid.

10. Krashen, Stephen. 1985. *The input hypothesis: Issues and implications.* White Plains, NY: Longman; Carson, Shelley H., and Ellen J. Langer. 2006. Mindfulness and self-acceptance. *Journal of Rational-Emotive and Cognitive Behavior Therapy* 24(1): 29–43.

11. Dietrich, The cognitive neuroscience of creativity.

12. Langer, E. J., and M. Moldoveanu. 2000. The construct of mindfulness. *Journal of Social Issues* 56(1): 1–9.

13. Carson and Langer, Mindfulness and self-acceptance; Csikszentmihalyi, Mihaly. *Finding flow: The psychology of engagement with everyday life.* New York: Basic Books. 1997.

14. Dietrich, The cognitive neuroscience of creativity.

15. Sutton, Robert I. 2001. The weird rules of creativity. *Harvard Business Review* 79(8): 94–103.

16. Deci, E. L., and R. M. Ryan. 1995. Human autonomy: The basis for true self-esteem. In *Efficacy, agency, and self-esteem,* ed. M. Kemis, 31–49. New York: Plenum; Carson and Langer, Mindfulness and self-acceptance.

17. Sutton, The weird rules of creativity.

18. McKee, Annie, Richard Boyatzis, and Frances Johnston. 2008. *Becoming a resonant leader: Develop you emotional intelligence, renew your relationships and sustain your effectiveness.* Boston: Harvard Business School Press.

19. Mölle, Mattias, Lisa Marshall, Werner Lutzenberger, Reinhard Pietrowsky, Horst L. Fehm, and Jan Born. 1996. Enhanced dynamic complexity in the human EEG during creative thinking. *Neuroscience Letters* 208: 61–64.

20. Indefrey, P., and W. J. Levelt. 2004. The spatial and temporal signatures of word production components. *Cognition* 92(1–2): 101–44.

21. Cattell, R. 1971. *Abilities: Their structure, growth, and action.* New York: Houghton-Mifflin; Guilford, J. P. 1975. Creativity: A quarter century of progress, in *Perspectives in creativity,* ed. I. A. Taylor and J. W. Getzels, 37–59. Chicago: Aldine.

22. Dietrich, Arne. 2007. Who's afraid of a neuroscience of creativity? *Methods* 42(1): 22–27.

23. Ibid.

24. Ibid.

25. Dietrich, The cognitive neuroscience of creativity.

26. Corballis, Michael C. 1980. Laterality and myth. *American Psychologist* 35(3): 288.

27. Weaver, Catherine. 2009. IPE's split brain. *New Political Economy* 14(3): 337–46.

28. Fink, Andreas, Mathias Benedek, Roland H. Grabner, Beate Staudt, and Aljoscha C. Neubauer. 2007. Creativity meets neuroscience: Experimental tasks for the neuroscientific study of creative thinking. *Methods* 42(1): 68–76.

29. Dietrich, The cognitive neuroscience of creativity.

30. Fink et al., Creativity meets neuroscience.

31. Ibid.

32. Dietrich, The cognitive neuroscience of creativity.

33. Damasio, A. R. 1994. *Descartes' error: Emotion, reason, and the human brain.* New York: Putnam.

34. Scase, Richard. 2009. "Herding cats": Managing creativity. *Market Leader* 44: 58–61.

35. Nussbaum, Bruce, Robert Berner, and Diane Brady. 2005. Get creative! *BusinessWeek* 3945: 60–68.

36. Lehrer, Jonah. 2012. Groupthink. *New Yorker* 87(46): 22–27.

37. Nemeth, Charlan J., Bernard Personnaz, Marie Personnaz, and Jack A. Goncalo. 2004. The liberating role of conflict in group creativity: A study in two countries. *European Journal of Social Psychology* 34(4): 365–74.

38. Goldenberg, Olga, and Jennifer Wiley. 2011. Quality, conformity, and conflict: Questioning the assumptions of Osborn's Brainstorming Technique. *Journal of Problem Solving* 3(2): 96–118; Kohn, Nicholas W., and Steven M. Smith. 2011. Collaborative fixation: Effects of others' ideas on brainstorming. *Applied Cognitive Psychology* 25(3): 359–71.

39. Nemeth, Charlan J., et al. The Liberating Role of Conflict in Group Creativity.

40. Mostert, Nel M. 2007. Diversity of the mind as the key to successful creativity at Unilever. *Creativity and Innovation Management* 16(1): 93–100.

41. ASAE & the Center for Association Leadership. Idea bank: A room of their own. 2006. *Associations Now* 2(2): 13.

42. Leichtman Research Group, Inc. 2012. Actionable Research on the Broadband, Media & Entertainment Industries. Retrieved July 31, 2012, from http://www.leichtmanresearch.com/research/notes04_2012.pdf.

43. Stelter, Brian. 2011. Comcast-NBC Deal Wins Federal Approval. *The New York Times* (January 18). Retrieved July 31, 2012, from http://mediadecoder.blogs.nytimes.com/2011/01/18/f-c-c-approves-comcast-nbc-deal/.

44. Comcast. Internet Essentials FAQs. Retrieved May 17, 2012, from http://www.internetessentials.com/faq/default.aspx

45. Drucker, Peter. 1993. *Post-capitalist society,* p. 38. New York: HarperCollins.

46. Yahoo! Finance. Netflix, Inc. (NFLX). Retrieved May 11, 2010, from http://finance.yahoo.com/q?s=NFLX.

47. Netflix. About Netflix. Retrieved May 11, 2010, from http://cdn-0.nflximg.com/us/pdf/Consumer_Press_Kit.pdf.

48. Ibid.

49. Netflix. Netflix Prize. Retrieved May 11, 2010, from http://www.netflixprize.com.

50. Liedtke, Michael. 2012. "Price Hike Still Haunts Netflix One Year Later." *CIO Today* (July 16). Retrieved July 31, 2012, from http://www.cio-today.com/news/Price-Hike-Still-Haunts-Netflix-Stock/story.xhtml?story_id=1000098K0ZRG&full_skip=1.

51. Hulu. More About Hulu. Retrieved May 17, 2012, from http://www.hulu.com/about.

52. Salzman, Alex. 2008. *What gets Seventh Generation's "director of corporate consciousness" out of bed in the morning?* (May 19). Retrieved September 12, 2009, from http://www.alternativechannel.tv/blog/en/comments/what_gets_seventh_generations_director_of_corporate_consciousness_out_of_bed.

53. Heimert, Chrystie. 2009. Seventh Generation names PepsiCo/Quaker Oats veteran as CEO (June 1). Retrieved September 12, 2009, from http://www.csrwire.com/press/press_release/27044-Seventh-Generation-Names-PepsiCo-Quaker-Oats-Veteran-as-CEO.

54. Seventh Generation, Inc. Company profile. Retrieved March 14, 2010, from LexisNexis Corporate Affiliations Database.

55. Heimert, Seventh Generation Names PepsiCo/Quaker Oats Veteran as CEO.

56. Seventh Generation, Inc. About Seventh Generation. Retrieved September 12, 2009, from http://www.seventhgeneration.com/about.

57. Ibid.

58. Werbach, Adam. 2009. When sustainability means more than "green." *McKinsey Quarterly* (July). Retrieved September 12, 2009, from http://www.mckinseyquarterly.com/When_sustainabillity_means_more_than_green_2404.

59. Rushe, Dominic. 2009. Eco firm Seventh Generation is riding high in Obama revolution. *Sunday Times* (February 15). http://business.timesonline.co.uk/tol/business/entrepreneur/article5733543.ece.

60. Ibid.

61. Werbach, When sustainability means more than "green."

62. Hollender, Jeffrey. 2008. Corporate consciousness report 2008. Retrieved September 7, 2009, from http://www.seventhgeneration.com.

63. Fast Company. 2012. The world's most innovative companies. Retrieved July 31, 2012, from http://www.fastcompany.com/most-innovative-companies/2012/full-list.

64. Volberda, Henk W. 1996. Toward the flexible form: How to remain vital in hypercompetitive environments. *Organization Science* 7(4): 359–74.

65. Swisher, Kara. 1998. *AOL.Com: How Steve Case beat Bill Gates, nailed the Netheads, and made millions in the war for the Web*, 1st ed. New York: Times Books. Snow, Nancy. 2012. Citizen Arianna: The Huffington Post / Aol Merger: Triumph or Tragedy?. Nimble Books, 2012.

66. AOL. 2012. Retrieved May 30, 2012, from http://corp.aol.com/.

67. Rich, Ben, and Leo Janos. 1996. *Skunk Works: A personal memoir of my years at Lockheed*. Boston: Little, Brown and Company.

68. Ibid.

69. Kiley, David. 2009. Putting Ford on fast-forward. *BusinessWeek* (October 26). Retrieved February 24, 2010, from http://www.thefreelibrary.com/PUTTING+FORD+ON+FAST+FORWARD-a01612033904.

70. Kowal, Eric. 2008. Army suggestion program can thicken your wallet. *U.S. Army Military News* (November 21). Retrieved February 28, 2010, from http://www.army.mil/article/14451/. Army Suggestion Program. 2008. Leading Change. Retrieved July 31, 2012, from http://www.hqda.army.mil/leadingchange/AIEP/ASP.htm.

71. Disney. Walt Disney Imagineering. Retrieved May 11, 2010, from http://corporate.disney.go.com/careers/who_imagineering.html.

72. Ibid.

73. Marling, Karal. 1997. *Designing Disney's theme parks*. New York: Flammarion.

74. Disney. ImagiNations. Retrieved May 11, 2010, from http://disney.go.com/disneycareers/imaginations.

75. Online Etymology Dictionary. Entrepreneur. Retrieved May 11, 2010, from http://www.etymonline.com/index.php?search=entrepreneur&searchmode=none.

76. McClelland, D. C. 1961. *The achieving society*. Princeton, NJ: D. Van Nostrand Company.

77. Lemke, C., and B. Lesley. 2009. *Advance 21st century innovation in schools through smart, informed state policy*. Los Angeles: The Metiri Group; Soriano, D. R., and J. M. C. Martínez. 2007. Transmitting the entrepreneurial spirit to the work team in SMEs: The importance of leadership. *Management Decision* 45(7): 1102–22; Blair, Tony, and Gerhard Schröder. 2003. Europe: The third way/Die neue mitte, in *The new Labour reader*, ed. A. Chadwick and R. Heffernan. Malden, MA: Blackwell Publishing.

78. World Economic Forum. 2012. Forum Blog: Social Entrepreneurs en route to Davos (January 28). Retrieved August 10, 2012 from http://forumblog.org/2012/01/social-entrepreneurs-en-route-to-davos/.

79. SBA Office of the Advocacy. Frequently Asked Questions. SBA Office of the Advocacy. Retrieved May 17, 2012, from http://www.sba.gov/sites/default/files/sbfaq.pdf.

80. ABC News/Money. Photos: Celebrity entrepreneurs. Retrieved May 11, 2010, from http://abcnews.go.com/Business/popup?id=4941699.

81. Mattern, Joanne. Kim Kardashian: Reality Tv Star. *Contemporary Lives*. Minneapolis, Minn.: ABDO Pub. Co., 2012.

82. ROCNATION 2012. The Official Website of Roc Nation—J-Z. Retrieved May 22, 2012, from http://rocnation.com/jayz/; Harry Bradford. 2012. JAY-Z: We Don't Want to Knock Anyone in America for Being Successful. *The Huffington Post* (May 15). Retrieved May 22, 2012, from http://www.huffingtonpost.com/2012/05/15/jay-z-dont-knock-successful_n_1518320.html.

83. Tyra. Tyra Mail Blog. Retrieved May 22, 2012, from http://www.typef.com/tyra/blog/; Guzman, Mark. 2011. Tyra Banks Enrolls at Harvard Business School. *The Harvard Crimson* (February 16). Retrieved July 31, 2012, from http://www.thecrimson.com/article/2011/2/16/program-banks-baugher-opm/.

84. BusinessInsider. 2011, June 9. 10 Incredibly Successful Celebrity Entrepreneurs. Retrieved May 22, 2012, from http://www.businessinsider.com/10-celebrity-entrepreneurs-and-their-businesses-2011-6#robert-de-niro-6.

85. The Oprah Winfrey Leadership Academy Foundation. Building a dream. Retrieved May 11, 2010, from http://oprahwinfreyleadershipacademy.o-philanthropy.org/site/PageServer?pagename=owla_about.

86. NBC Chicago. Sean Penn to Receive Peace Summit Award in Chicago. Retrieved May 22, 2012, from http://www.nbcchicago.com/news/local/Sean-Penn-to-Receive-Peace-Summit-Award-in-Chicago-143308516.html.

87. Make It Right Foundation. Our Work and Progress. Retrieved May 22, 2012, from http://www.makeitrightnola.org/.

88. Resnick, Rosalind. 2009. Can you handle the risk? Make sure your risk tolerance and investment strategy align. *Entrepreneur Magazine* (January). Retrieved February 28, 2010, from http://www.entrepreneur.com/magazine/entrepreneur/2009/january/199022.html.

89. Hornaday, John A., and John Aboud. 1971. Characteristics of successful entrepreneurs. *Personnel Psychology* 24(2): 141–53.

90. Hines, John L. 2004. Characteristics of an entrepreneur. *Surgical Neurology* 61(4): 407–08.

91. Lans, Thomas, Harm Biemans, Jos Verstegen, and Martin Mulder. 2008. The influence of the work environment on entrepreneurial learning of small-business owners. *Management Learning* 39(5): 597–613.

92. Robison, Jennifer. 2008. Will social entrepreneurship save the world? *Gallup Management Journal Online*. Retrieved February 24, 2010, from http://gmj.gallup.com/content/112915/will-social-entrepreneurship-save-world.aspx#1.

93. Mobiles in Malawi. "Going global" and www.jobsa.org. Retrieved May 11, 2010, from http://mobilesinmalawi.blogspot.com.

94. Ibid.

95. Banks, Ken, and Josh Nesbit. 2008. Witnessing the human face of mobile in Malawi. *PC World Business Center* (June 27). Retrieved February 28, 2010, from http://www.pcworld.com/businesscenter/article/147679/witnessing_the_human_face_of_mobile_in_malawi.html; http://www.frontlinesms.com/what; http://www.kiwanja.net.

96. Medic Mobile. 2012. Our Team. Retrieved May 25, 2012, from http://medicmobile.org/team/.

97. Forum for the Future. FT Climate Change Challenge. Retrieved May 11, 2010, from http://www.forumforthefuture.org/FT-climate-challenge.

98. KYOTO: Free is the sun. KYOTO Retrospective. Retrieved May 11, 2010, from http://www.kyoto-energy.com/history.html.

99. Ibid; Forum for the Future. FT Climate Change Challenge. Retrieved May 11, 2010, from http://www.forumforthefuture.org/FT-climate-challenge.

100. Ibid.

101. Kyoto Energy. 2012. Kyoto Products. Retrieved May 25, 2012, from http://kyoto-energy.com/products.html.

102. Ibid.

103. Ashoka.org. Ashoka facts. Retrieved April 26, 2010, from http://www.ashoka.org/facts.

104. Ashoka. 2012. Fellows. Retrieved May 31, 2012, from https://www.ashoka.org/fellow/james-nguo.

105. Oloo, Mark. 2012. UNESCO Fetes Kenyan for Linking Villages with Ict. *Standard Digital* (March 25). Retrieved May 31, 2012, from http://www.standardmedia.co.ke/?id=2000054853&articleID=2000054853.

106. Parker, S. C. 2009. Intrepreneurship or entrepreneurship? *Journal of Business Venturing* 24(5): 519–32.

107. McCrae, N. 1982. Intrapreneurial now. *The Economist* (April 17): 67–72.

108. Pinchot, Gifford. 1999. *Intrapreneuring in action*, p. 1. San Francisco: Berrett-Koehler Publishers.

109. Entrepreneurs in the U.S. economy. 2007. *Monthly Labor Review* 130, (12): 38.

110. Help wanted: A mix of skills. 2006. *eWeek* 23(28): 46.

111. Nelson, S. J., Birchard, B. Raffone, I., and Schrange, M. Starting new businesses–Inside the organization. 1999. *Harvard Management Update* 4(12): 1.

112. SBA Office of Advocacy. Frequently asked questions. Retrieved August 6, 2012, from http://www.sba.gov/sites/default/files/sbfaq.pdf.

113. Small Business Administration. How to write a business plan. Retrieved February 24, 2010, from http://www.sba.gov/smallbusinessplanner/plan/writeabusinessplan/SERV_WRRITINGBUSPLAN.html.

114. Kahn, Sharon. 2009. The venture game. *Fortune Small Business* 19(4): 60.

115. National Venture Capital Association. 2009. Frequently asked questions about venture capital. Retrieved February 24, 2010, from http://www.nvca.org/index.php?option=com_content&view=article&id=119&Itemid=147.

116. Ibid.

117. Zoltners, Andris A., Prabhakant Sinha, and Sally E. Lorimer. 2006. Match your sales force structure to your business life cycle. *Harvard Business Review* 84(7/8): 83.

118. Lippitt, Gordon L., and Warren H. Schmidt. 1967. Crises in a developing organization. *Harvard Business Review* 45: 102–12.

119. Zoltners et al., Match your sales force structure to your business life cycle.

120. Quinn, Robert E., and Kim Cameron. 1983. Organization life cycles and shifting criteria of effectiveness: Some preliminary evidence. *Management Science* 29(1): 33–51; Teeter, Ryan A., and Karen S. Whelan-Berry. 2008. My firm versus our firm: The challenge of change in growing the small professional service firm. *Journal of Business Inquiry* 7(1): 43–52.

121. Teeter and Whelan-Berry. My firm versus our firm; Churchill, N. C., and V. L. Lewis. 1983. The five stages of business growth. *Harvard Business Review* 61(3): 30–50.

122. Dodge, H. Robert, Sam Fullerton, and John E. Robbins. 1994. Stage of the organizational life cycle and competition as mediators of problem perception for small businesses. *Strategic Management Journal* 15(2): 121–34.

123. Azides, I. 1979. Organizational passages: Diagnosing and treating life cycle problems in organizations. *Organizational Dynamics* 9: 3–24.

124. Quinn and Cameron, Organization life cycles and shifting criteria of effectiveness.

125. How to pay the piper. 2003. *Economist* 367(8322): 62.

126. Ambrosek, Renee. 2007. *Shawn Fanning: The founder of Napster*. New York: Rosen Publishing Group; Weiss, Joseph W. 2009. *Business ethics: A stakeholder and issues management approach*. Mason, OH: South-Western Cengage Learning; Napster profile. Retrieved March 14, 2009, from Lexis-Nexis Corporate Affiliations Database.

127. Pepitone, Julianne. 2011. Today Is Napster's Last Day of Existence. *CNN Money* (November 30.). Retrieved May 17, 2012, from http://money.cnn.com/2011/11/30/technology/napster_rhapsody/?source=cnn_bin.

128. Knaup, Amy E. 2005. Survival and longevity in the business employment dynamics data. *Monthly Labor Review* 128(5): 51.

129. Clifford, Catherine. 2011. States with Worst Business Failure Rates *CNN Money* (May 20 Retrieved May 17, 2012, from http://money.cnn.com/2011/05/19/smallbusiness/small_business_state_failure_rates/index.htm.

130. Williams, Geoff. 2007. Dead zone. *Entrepreneur* 35(3): 76.

131. Henricks, Mark. 2008. Do you really need a business plan? *Entrepreneur* 36(12): 92.

132. Diamond, Mike. 2006. Why companies fail. *Reeves Journal: Plumbing, Heating, Cooling* 86 (10): 103.

133. Levinson, Jay Conrad, and Al Lautenslager. 2005. Mind over market. *Entrepreneur* 33(3): 66.

134. Colombo, George. 2004. Are you really listening to your customers? *Business Credit* 106(6): 66.

135. U.S. Patent and Trademark Office. Patent applications filed. Retrieved August 2, 2009, from http://www.uspto.gov/web/offices/com/annual/2008/oai_05_wlt_02.html.

136. U.S. Copyright Office. Frequently asked questions. Retrieved April 7, 2010, from http://www.copyright.gov/help/faq/faq-duration.html#duration.

137. Charan, Ram. 2008. Stop whining, start thinking. *BusinessWeek* 4097: 58.

138. Buzan, Tony, and Berry Buzan. 1996. *The mind map book*. New York: Penguin.

139. Cross, Jay. 2005. Useful things. *Chief Learning Officer* 4(6): 14.

140. Ibid.; Buzan, Tony, and Raymond Keene. 1994. *Buzan's book of genius: And how to unleash your own*. London: Random House.

141. Global Human Capital Journal. 17 enterprise visionaries release 2010 predictions for social networks, web 2.0. Retrieved May 11, 2010, from http://globalhumancapital.org/?p=1103.

Chapter 9

1. Department of Treasury. Publication 557: Tax exempt status for your organization. Retrieved May 14, 2010, from http://www.irs.gov/pub/irs-pdf/p557.pdf.

2. Useem, Jerry. 2005. 1914: Ford offers $5 a day. *Fortune* 151(13): 65.

3. Plato. 1946. *The republic*, trans. Benjamin Jowett. Cleveland: World Publishing Company.

4. Smith, Adam. 1776. *The wealth of nations*. Lawrence, KS: Digireads.

5. Taylor, Frederick W. 1911. *The principles of scientific management*. Ithaca: Cornell University Library.

6. Burgess, Thomas F. 1994. Making the leap to agility. *International Journal of Operations and Production Management* 14(11): 23–34.

7. Readman, Jeff, Brian Squire, John Bessant, and Steve Brown. 2006. The application of agile manufacturing for customer value. *Journal of Financial Transformation* 18 (2006): 133–41.

8. Siegel-Jacobs, Karen, and J. Frank Yates. 1996. Effects of procedural and outcome accountability on judgment quality. *Organizational Behavior and Human Decision Making* 65(1): 1–17.

9. 8 USC § 1103: Powers and duties of the secretary, undersecretary, and the attorney general. Cornell Law School Legal Information Institute. Retrieved May 18, 2012, from http://www.law.cornell.edu/uscode/text/8/1103.

10. Brafman, Ori, and Rod A. Beckstrom. 2006. *The starfish and the spider: The unstoppable power of leaderless organizations*. New York: The Penguin Group.

11. Emery, Merrelyn. 2000. The current version of Emery's open systems theory. *Systemic Practice and Action Research* 13(5): 623–43.

12. Starnes, Becky J. 2000. Achieving competitive advantage through the application of open systems theory and the development of strategic alliances: A guide for managers of not-for-profit organizations. *Journal of Not-for-Profit and Public Sector Marketing* 8(2): 15.

13. Katz, D., and R. L. Kahn. 1978. *The social psychology of organizations*. New York: John Wiley & Sons.

14. Long, Mark, and Angel Gonzalez. 2010. Transocean seeks limit on liability. *Wall Street Journal* (May 13). Retrieved May 17, 2010, from http://online.wsj.com/article/SB10001424052748704635204575241852606380696.html; Efstathiou, Jim. 2010. BP, Halliburton, Transocean blame each other in Gulf oil spill. *Bloomberg Businessweek* (May 10). Retrieved May 17, 2010, from http://www.businessweek.com/news/2010-05-10/bp-halliburton-transocean-blame-each-other-in-gulf-oil-spill.html.

15. King, Leo. 2011. Bp £24bn Lawsuits Claim Contractors Failed to Use Modelling Software Properly. *ComputerWorld UK* (April 21). Retrieved (insert date of retrieval) http://www.computerworlduk.com/news/it-business/3275978/bp-24bn-lawsuits-claim-contractors-failed-to-use-modelling-software-properly/.

16. Fahey, Jonathan, and Chris Kahn. 2012. BP Begins to Put Spill Behind It with Settlement. *Boston Globe* (March 3). Retrieved May 18, 2012, from http://articles.boston.com/2012-03-03/news/31119946_1_deepwater-horizon-oil-spill-gulf-oil.

17. Morand, David A. 1995. The role of behavioral formality and informality in the enactment of bureaucratic versus organic organizations. *Academy of Management Review* 20(4): 831–72; Harvey, Edward. 1968. Technology and the structure of organization. *American Sociological Review* 33(2): 247–59; McCaskey, Michael B. 1974. A contingency approach to planning: Planning with goals and planning without goals. *Academy of Management Journal* 17(2): 281–91; Burns, T., and G. M. Stalker. 1961. *The management of innovation*. Tavistock: London.

18. Covin, Jeffrey G., Dennis P. Slevin, and Randall L. Schultz. 1994. Implementing strategic missions: Effective strategic, structural and tactical

choices. *Journal of Management Studies* 31(4): 481–505; Morand, The role of behavioral formality and informality; McCaskey, A contingency approach to planning; Burns and Stalker, *The management of innovation*.

19. Morgan, Gareth. 1998. *Images of organization*, p. 40. Thousand Oaks, CA: Sage.

20. Ibid.

21. Dooley, Kevin J. 1997. A complex adaptive systems model of organization change. *Nonlinear Dynamics, Psychology, and Life Sciences* 1(1): 69–97.

22. Weick, Karl E. 2002. The aesthetic of imperfection in orchestras and organizations, in *Organizational improvisation*, ed. Ken N. Kamoche, Miguel Pina e Cunha, and Joao Vieira da Cunha, 163-180. London: Routledge.

23. Van Baalen, Peter J., and Paul C. van Fenema. 2009. Instantiating global crisis networks: The case of SARS. *Decision Support Systems* 47: 277–86.

24. World Health Organization. Summary of probable SARS cases with onset of illness from 1 November 2002 to 31 July 2003. Retrieved April 27, 2010, from http://www.who.int/csr/sars/country/ table2004_04_21/en/index.html.

25. Van Baalen and van Fenema. 2009. Instantiating global crisis networks.

26. Wouter, Dessein, and Tano Santos. 2006. Adaptive organizations. *Journal of Political Economy* 114(5): 956–95.

27. Ibid., 956.

28. Adams, Guy. 2012. Nutrition: America Awakens to the Sour Taste of 'Pink Slime'. *The Independent* (March 18). Retrieved May 18, 2012, http:// www.independent.co.uk/life-style/food-and-drink/news/nutrition- america-awakens-to-the-sour-taste-of-pink-slime-7593484.html.

29. Morgan, *Images of organization*.

30. Brafman and Beckstrom, *The starfish and the spider*.

31. Ibid.

32. Realuyo, Celina B. 2011. Assessing Our Counterterrorism Investment. *The Journal of International Security Affairs* 21. Retrieved May 18, 2012, from http://www.securityaffairs.org/issues/2011/21/realuyo.php.

33. Brafman and Beckstrom, The starfish and the spider.

34. Ibid.

35. *CIA World Factbook*. Zambia. Retrieved August 7, 2012, from https:// www.cia.gov/library/publications/the-world-factbook/geos/za.html; Google Public Data. Retrieved August 7, 2012, from http://www.google .com/publicdata/explore?ds=d5bncppjof8f9_&met_y=sp_pop_gr ow&idim=coutry:ZMB&dl=en&hl=en&q=zambia+population+g rowth#!ctype=l&strail=false&bcs=d&nselm=h&met_y=sp_pop_ totl&scale_y=lin&ind_y=false&rdim=region&idim=country:ZMB &ifdim=region&tstart=1028692800000&tend=1312689600000&hl= en_US&dl=en&ind=false.

36. Hitt, Michael A., R. Duane Ireland, and Robert E. Hoskisson. 2009. *Strategic management: Competitiveness and globalization: Concepts and cases*. St. Paul, MN: South-Western Cengage Learning; Stalk, George, and Jill E. Black. 1994. The myth of the horizontal organization. *Canadian Business Review* 21(4): 26–29.

37. Tiernan, Siobhan D., Patrick C. Flood, Eamonn P. Murphy, and Stephen J. Carroll. 2002. Employee reactions to flattening organizational structures. *European Journal of Work and Organizational Psychology* 11(1): 47–67.

38. Ibid.

39. Stalk and Black, The myth of the horizontal organization; Cornelissen, Joep, Tibor van Bekkum, and Betteke van Ruler. 2006. Corporate com- munications: A practice-based theoretical conceptualization. *Corporate Reputation Review* 9(2): 114–33.

40. Virtual Advisor. Designed chaos: An interview with David Kelley, founder and CEO of IDEO. Retrieved May 20, 2010, from http:// www.va-interactive.com/inbusiness/editorial/bizdev/articles/ideo .html.

41. IDEO. IDEO fact sheet. Retrieved May 20, 2010, from http://www.ideo .com/to-go/fact-sheet/.

42. Designed chaos: An interview with David Kelley, founder and CEO of IDEO.

43. Tiernan et al., Employee reactions to flattening organizational structures.

44. Hitt et al., *Strategic management*.

45. Cornelissen et al., Corporate communications.

46. Hitt et al., *Strategic management*; Stalk and Black, The myth of the hori- zontal organization.

47. Tiernan et al., Employee reactions to flattening organizational structures.

48. Fortune Brands. Homepage. Retrieved June 6, 2012, from http://www .fortunebrands.com/.

49. Malone, Thomas W. 1987. Modeling coordination in organizations and markets. *Management Science* 33(10): 1317–32.

50. Cross, R., A. Parker, and S. P. Borgatti. 2002. A bird's-eye view—Using social network analysis to improve knowledge creation and sharing. *IBM Institute for Knowledge-Based Organizations*. Retrieved from http:// www-304.ibm.com/jct03001c/services/learning/solutions/pdfs/.

51. Carpenter, Mason. 2009. *An executive's primer on the strategy of social networks*. New York: Business Expert Press; Cross et al., A bird's-eye view.

52. Chandler, Alfred D. 1990. *Strategy and structure: Chapters in the history of the industrial en-terprise*. Cambridge, MA: MIT Press; Hall, David J., and Maurice A. Saias. 1980. Strategy fol-lows structure! *Strategic Management Journal* 1(2): 149–63.

53. Hall and Saias. Strategy follows structure! 155.

54. Hall and Saias, Strategy follows structure!; Miller, Danny. 1986. Configurations of strategy and structure: Towards a synthesis. *Strategic Management Journal* 7(3): 233–49; Pacheco, Jorge M., Arne Traulsen, and Martin A. Nowak. 2006. Coevolution of strategy and structure in complex networks with dynamical linking. *Physical Review Letters* 97: 25.

55. Creative Commons. About. Retrieved May 27, 2012, from http:// creativecommons.org/about.

56. Fiat. Fiat Completes Acquisition of Chrysler Equity from Canada and the U.S. Department of the Treasury. Retrieved June 4, 2012, from http://www.fiatspa.com/en-US/media_center/FiatDocuments/2011/ July/Fiat_acquista_partecipazioni_in_Chrysler_del_Canada_e_del_ Tesoro_Usa_ing.pdf; Higgins, Tim, and David Welch. 2012. Fiat Buys Rest of U.S.'s Chrysler Stake, Right to UAW Shares. *Bloomberg Business- week* (June 3). Retrieved June 4, 2012, from http://www.businessweek .com/news/2011-06-03/fiat-buys-rest-of-u-s-s-chrysler-stake-right-to- uaw-shares.html.

57. Chrysler Press Release. 2011. Chrysler Brand Launches New Marketing and Advertising Campaign. Retrieved June 4, 2012, from http://www .media.chrysler.com/newsrelease.do;jsessionid=B9AB8DB3A96CA13E8 5C8AB35BD25ECB8?&id=10512&mid=23.

58. Healey, James R. 2010. 7 New Fiat Models Bound for U.S.; 9 Chryslers to Go Abroad. *USA Today* (April 21). Retrieved June 4, 2012, from http:// www.usatoday.com/money/advertising/2010-04-21-fiat-splits_N.htm.

59. Marcum, Ed. 2012. Knox Businesses Find Ways of Dealing with Fuel Price Hike. *KnoxNews.com* (March 6). Retrieved June 4, 2012, from http://www.knoxnews.com/news/2012/mar/06/knoxvillians-coping- with-high-prices-at-the-pump/?print=1.

60. Sherefkin, Robert. 2007. Dauch to U.S. industry: Don't fear trouble. *Automotive News* 81(6239): 30.

61. Woodward, Joan. 1966. *Management and technology*. London: HM Stationary Office.

62. FindLaw. Local start-up requirements for small businesses. Retrieved May 14, 2010, from http://smallbusiness.findlaw.com/starting-business/ starting-business-licenses-permits/starting-business-licenses-permits- local.html.

63. Crain, Nicole V., and W. Mark Crain. 2010. The Impact of Regulatory Costs on Small Firms. *Small Business Administration*. Retrieved June 4, 2012, from http://archive.sba.gov/advo/research/rs371tot.pdf.

64. Internal Revenue Service. Limited liability company (LLC). Retrieved April 27, 2010, from http://www.irs.gov/businesses/small/ article/0,,id=98277,00.html.

65. Ibid.

66. *Trustees of Dartmouth College v. Woodward*, 17 U.S. (4 Wheaton) 518 (1819); Menez, Joseph Francis, John R. Vile, and Paul Charles Bartholemew. 2004. *Summaries of leading cases on the Constitution*. Lanham, ME: Rowman & Littlefield.

67. Internal Revenue Service. Definition of corporation—Section 527 political organizations. Retrieved April 27, 2010, from http://www.irs .gov/charities/political/article/0,,id=204994,00.html.

68. Internal Revenue Service. S corporations. Retrieved April 27, 2010, from http://www.irs.gov/businesses/small/article/0,,id=98263,00.html.

69. Ibid.

70. Standard Legal Law Library. S-corporations: Eliminating "double taxation." Retrieved May 17, 2010, from http://www.standardlegal.com/ law-library/S-Corporation.html.

71. S-Corp.org. About. Retrieved May 18, 2012, from http://www.s-corp .org/about/.

72. Internal Revenue Service. Limited liability company (LLC).

73. Ibid.

74. Folta, Paul H. 2005. Cooperative joint ventures: Savvy foreign investors may wish to consider the benefits of this flexible investment structure. *China Business Review* (January–February): 18–23; The Business Reading Room. Glossary and acronyms. Retrieved June 6, 2012, from http://www.rmauduit.com/glossary-con.html.

75. Pekar, Peter, and Marc S. Margulis. 2003. Equity alliances take center stage: The emergence of a new corporate growth model. *Ivey Business Journal Online* (May/June). Retrieved November 28, 2012, from http://wwwold.iveybusinessjournal.com/view_article.asp?intArticle_ID=418

76. Ibid.

77. Beshel, Barbara. An introduction to franchising. *International Franchise Association Educational Foundation*. Retrieved December 15, 2009, from http://franchise.org/uploadedFiles/Franchise_Industry/Resources/Education_Foundation/Intro%20to%20Franchising%20Student%20Guide.pdf.

78. International Licensing Industry Merchandisers' Association. Introduction to licensing. Retrieved December 15, 2009, from http://www.licensing.org/education/licensing-introduction.php.

79. International Licensing Industry Merchandisers' Association. Why license? Retrieved December 15, 2009, from http://www.licensing.org/education/why-license.php.

80. International Licensing Industry Merchandisers' Association. Types of licensing. Retrieved December 15, 2009, from http://www.licensing.org/education/licensing-types.php.

81. Ibid.

82. Beshel, An introduction to franchising.

83. CBSNews.com. 2009. Food fight: Burger King franchisees sue (November 12). Retrieved December 15, 2009, from http://www.cbsnews.com/stories/2009/11/12/business/main5631870.shtml; Chun, Janean. 2011. Burger King Franchisees Dismiss Lawsuit Over $1 Cheeseburger (April 18). *AOL Small Business*. Retrieved May 22, 2012, from http://smallbusiness.aol.com/2011/04/18/burger-king-franchisees-dismiss-lawsuit-over-1-cheeseburger/.

84. Investor Glossary. Wholly owned subsidiary. Retrieved December 16, 2009, from http://www.investorglossary.com/wholly-owned-subsidiary.htm.

85. The Free Dictionary. Subsidiary, in *Legal dictionary*. Retrieved December 16, 2009, from http://legal-dictionary.thefreedictionary.com/Wholly+owned+subsidiary.

86. West Virginia University College of Business and Economics. International strategy: Entry modes. Retrieved December 16, 2009, from http://www.be.wvu.edu/divmim/mgmt/insch/International%20Strategy-1.ppt.

87. The Free Dictionary, Subsidiary.

88. Ibid.

89. Chang, Peng S. 1995. International joint ventures vs. wholly owned subsidiaries. *Multinational Business Review* (Spring). Retrieved December 16, 2009, from http://findarticles.com/p/articles/mi_qa3674/is_199504/ai_n8729617/.

90. Aveda Customer Service. Frequently asked questions. Retrieved January 6, 2010, from http://www.aveda.com/customerservice/faq.tmpl; Canedy, Dana. 1997. Estée Lauder is acquiring maker of natural cosmetics. *New York Times* (November 20). Retrieved January 6, 2010, from http://www.nytimes.com/1997/11/20/business/Estée-lauder-is-acquiring-maker-of-natural-cosmetics.html?pagewanted=1.

91. Company profile: Aveda. 2009/2010. *GreenMoney Journal* 18:2. Retrieved January 6, 2010, from http://www.greenmoneyjournal.com/article.mpl?newsletterid=11&articleid=86; Sacks, Danielle. 2007. It's easy being green. *Fast Company* (December 19). Retrieved January 6, 2010, from http://www.fastcompany.com/magazine/85/aveda.html.

92. West Virginia University College of Business and Economics, International strategy: Entry modes.

93. The Free Dictionary, Subsidiary.

94. Chang, International joint ventures vs. wholly owned subsidiaries.

95. Reuer, Jeffrey J., Africa Ariño, and Antoni Valverde. The perfect "pre-nup" to strategic alliances: A guide to contracts. *Association of Strategic Alliance Professionals Best Practice Bulletins*. Retrieved December 16, 2009, from http://www.strategic-alliances.org/membership/memberresources/bestpracticebulletin.

96. Small Business Notes. Strategic alliances. Retrieved December 16, 2009, from http://www.smallbusinessnotes.com/operating/leadership/strategicalliances.html.

97. Small Business Notes. Strategic alliances.

98. Reuer et al., The perfect "pre-nup" to strategic alliances.

99. Wharton Executive Education. Strategic alliances: Creating growth opportunities. Wharton School at the University of Pennsylvania. Retrieved December 16, 2009, from http://executiveeducation.wharton.upenn.edu/open-enrollment/strategy-management-programs/strategic-alliances-growth-opportuities.cfm.

100. Caltech Industrial Relations Center. Strategic alliances. California Institute of Technology. Retrieved December 16, 2009, from http://www.irc.caltech.edu/p-105-strategic-alliances.aspx.

101. Small Business Notes, Strategic alliances.

102. PepsiCo. Our history: 1991 milestones. Retrieved January 6, 2010, from http://www.pepsico.com/Company/Our-History.html#block_1991.

103. Reference for Business. Strategic alliances, in *Encyclopedia of business*, 2d ed. Retrieved January 6, 2010, from http://www.referenceforbusiness.com/encyclopedia/Sel-Str/Strategic-Alliances.html.

104. Food and Drink Europe. 2003. Unilever, PepsiCo join forces to meet ice tea challenge (October 15). Retrieved January 6, 2010, from http://www.foodanddrinkeurope.com/Products-Marketing/Unilever-PepsiCo-join-forces-to-meet-ice-tea-challenge.

105. Starbucks, Pepsi, and Unilever partner to grow the Tazo® tea ready to drink business. 2008. *Starbucks Newsroom*. Retrieved May 18, 2012, from http://news.starbucks.com/article_display.cfm?article_id=30.

106. PepsiCo. Our history: 2009 milestones. Retrieved May 20, 2010, from http://www.pepsico.com/Company/Our-History.html#block_2009.

107. Lipton Joins Grammy Award-Winning Trio Lady Antebellum To Support The Rebuilding Of Henryville, Ind. 2012. *PR Newswire*. Retrieved May 18, 2012, from http://www.marketwatch.com/story/lipton-joins-grammy-award-winning-trio-lady-antebellum-to-support-the-rebuilding-of-henryville-ind-2012-05-02.

108. Gompers, Samuel, and Florence Calvert Thorne. *Seventy years of life and labor; an autobiography*, 2 volumes. New York: E.P. Dutton & company, 1925.

109. AFL-CIO. About the AFL-CIO. Retrieved May 21, 2012, from http://www.aflcio.org/About.

110. AFL-CIO. Global Unions. Retrieved May 21, 2012, from http://www.aflcio.org/About/Global-Unions.

111. Union Member Summary. 2012. Bureau of Labor Statistics Economics News Release USDL-12-0094 (January 27). Retrieved May 21, 2012, from http://www.bls.gov/news.release/union2.nr0.htm.

112. Trade Unions. 2012. *European Trade Union Institute* Retrieved May 21, 2012, from http://www.worker-participation.eu/National-Industrial-Relations/Across-Europe/Trade-Unions2.

113. Pretoria, South Africa. 2012. Quarterly Labour Force Survey: Quarter 1, 2012. Retrieved May 21, 2012, from http://www.datafirst.uct.ac.za/catalogue3/index.php/catalog/219.

114. Stovall, Steven Austin. 2006. *Cases in human resources management*. Cincinnati, OH: Atomic Dog.

115. Gabarro, John J., and John P. Kotter. 1993. Managing your boss. *Harvard Business Review* 71(3): 150–7; Useem, Michael. 2001. *Leading up: How to lead your boss so you both win*. New York: Crown.

116. Bickel, Janet. 2007. Managing "up": Achieving an effective partnership with your boss. *Academic Physician and Scientist* (February): 4–5.

117. Ibid.

118. Ibid.

Chapter 10

1. Katzenbach, Jon R., and Douglas K. Smith. 1993. The discipline of teams. *Harvard Business Review* 71(2): 111–20; Katzenbach, J. R., and D. K. Smith. 2003. *The wisdom of teams: Creating the high-performance organization*. New York: HarperCollins Publishers; Wheelan, Susan A. 2010. *Creating effective teams: A guide for members and leaders*. Thousand Oaks, CA: Sage.

2. Philadelphia Police Department. Charles H. Ramsey. Retrieved May 15, 2010, from http://www.phillypolice.com/about/leadership/charles-h-ramsey/.

3. Information in this case derived from a personal interview with Annie McKee, 2010.

4. Lewin, Kurt. 1951. *Field theory in social science*. New York: Harper.

5. Lewin, Kurt, Ronald Lippitt, and Ralph White. 1939. Patterns of aggressive behavior in experimentally created "social climates." *Journal of Social Psychology* 10: 271–99; White, Ronald K., and Ralph Lippitt. 1968. Leader behavior and member reaction in three "social climates,"

in *Group dynamics: Research and theory*, 3d ed., ed. D. Cartwright and A. Zander, 318–35. New York: Harper & Row.

6. Ibid.

7. Van Vugt, Mark, Sarah F. Jepson, Claire M. Hart, and David De Cremer. 2004. Autocratic leadership in social dilemmas: A threat to group stability. *Journal of Experimental Social Psychology* 40(1): 1–13.

8. De Cremer, David. 2006. Affective and motivational consequences of leader self-sacrifice: The moderating effect of autocratic leadership. *Leadership Quarterly* 17(1): 79–93.

9. Gastil, John, Stephanie Burkhalter, and Laura W. Black. 2007. Do juries deliberate? A study of deliberation, individual difference, and group member satisfaction at a municipal courthouse. *Small Group Research* 38(3): 337–59.

10. Fricher, Josef. 2006. *Laissez-faire leadership versus empowering leadership in new product development*, p. 1. Aalborg, Denmark: Danish Centre for Philosophy and Science Studies.

11. Ibid.

12. Bennis, W., and H. Shepard, 1956. A theory of group development. *Human Relations* 9: 415–37; Tuckman, B. W., 1965. Developmental sequence in small groups. *Psychological Bulletin* 63: 384–99.

13. Tuckman, Developmental sequence in small groups. *Psychological Bulletin* 63: 384–99.

14. Tuckman, Bruce W., and Mary Ann C. Jensen. 1977. Stages of small group development revisited. *Group and Organizational Studies* 2: 419–27.

15. Wheelan, Susan A. 1994. *Group processes: A developmental perspective.* Boston: Allyn and Bacon; Wheelan, Susan A., Barbara Davidson, and Felice Tilin. 2003. Group development across time: Reality or illusion? *Small Group Research* 34: 223–45; Tuckman, Developmental sequence in small groups, 384–99; Cissna, Kenneth N. 1984. Phases in Group Development. *Small Group Research* 15(1): 3-32.

16. Wheelan, Susan A. 2010. *Creating effective teams: A guide for members and leaders.* Thousand Oaks, CA: Sage; Bion, W. R. 1952. Group dynamics: A review. *International Journal of Psychoanalysis* 33(2): 235–47; Bion, W. R. 1961. *Experience in groups.* New York: Basic Books; Cholden, L. 1953. Group therapy with the blind. *Group Psychotherapy* 6: 21–29.

17. Bennis and Shepard, A theory of group development.

18. Dias de Figueiredo, António, and Afonso Ana Paula. 2006. Context and learning: A philosophical framework, in *Managing learning in virtual settings: The role of context,* ed. António Dias de Figueiredo and Afonso Ana Paula. Hershey, PA: IGI Global.

19. Benne, Kenneth D., and Paul Sheats. 1948. Functional roles of group members. *Journal of Social Issues* 4(2): 41–49.

20. Johnson, D. W., and F. P. Johnson. 1975. *Joining together: Group theory and group skills.* Upper Saddle River, NJ: Prentice-Hall.

21. Adapted from Johnson, D. W., and F. P. Johnson, 1975. *Joining together: Group theory and Group skills.* Upper Saddle River, NJ: Prentice-Hall.

22. Ibid.

23. Zimbardo, Philip G. 2009. Stanford prison experiment: A simulation study of the psychology of imprisonment conducted at Stanford University. Retrieved April 30, 2010, from http://www.prisonexp.org/.

24. Zimbardo, Stanford prison experiment; Haney, Craig, Curtis Banks, and Philip Zimbardo. 1973. Interpersonal dynamics in a simulated prison. *International Journal of Criminology and Penology* 1: 69–97.

25. Zimbardo, Philip. 2007. *The Lucifer effect: Understanding how good people turn evil.* New York: Random House; Zimbardo, Stanford prison experiment; Haney et al., Interpersonal dynamics in a simulated prison.

26. Zimbardo, *The Lucifer effect.*

27. Personal interview with Annie McKee, 2010.

28. Druskat, Vanessa U., and Steven B. Wolff. 2001. Building the emotional intelligence of groups. *Harvard Business Review* 79(3): 80–91

29. Merriam-Webster Dictionary Online. Status. Retrieved April 2, 2010, from http://www.merriam-webster.com/dictionary/status.

30. Lin, Nan. 2001. *Social capital: A theory of social structure and action.* New York: Cambridge University Press.

31. Boyd, Danah. 2008. Why youth (heart) social network sites: The role of networked publics in teenage social life, in *Youth, identity, and digital media,* ed. David Buckingham, 119–42. Cambridge, MA: The MIT Press.

32. Agha, Asif. 2007. *Language and social relations.* Cambridge: Cambridge University Press.

33. Bourdieu, Pierre. 1983. The forms of capital, in *Handbook of theory and research for the sociology of education,* ed. John G. Richardson, 241–58. New York: Greenwood Press; Asante, Molefi, and Alice Davis. 1985. Black and white communication: Analyzing work place encounters. *Journal of Black Studies* 16: 77–93; Kirchmeyer, Catherine, and Aaron Cohen. 1992. *Group and Organization Management* 17(2): 153–170.

34. French, John R. P., and Bertram Raven. The bases of social power, in *The international library of leadership,* vol. 2, ed. J. Thomas Wren, Douglas A Hicks, and Terry L Price, 150–67. Northampton, MA: Edward Elgar Publishing, Inc.

35. Tolbert, Mary Ann Rainey, and Jonno Hanafin. 2006. Use of Self in OD Consulting: What Matters Is Presence., in *The NTL handbook of organization development and change: Principles, practices, and perspectives,* ed. Brenda B. Jones and Michael Brazzel, 69–82. San Francisco: Pfeiffer.

36. Mead, Margaret. 1977. *Sex and temperament in three primitive societies,* p. 322. London: Routledge.

37. Progoff, Ira. 1999. *Jung's psychology and its social meaning.* London: Routledge.

38. Myers-Briggs Foundation. Sensing or intuition. Retrieved April 5, 2010, from http://www.myersbriggs.org/my-mbti-personality-type/mbti-basics/sensing-or-intuition.asp; Golden LLC. Golden Personality Type Profiler frequently asked questions. Retrieved April 5, 2010, from http://www.goldenllc.com/about_GPTP_FAQ.htm.

39. Progoff, Jung's psychology and its social meaning; Myers-Briggs Foundation. Thinking or feeling. Retrieved April 5, 2010, from http://www.myersbriggs.org/my-mbti-personality-type/mbti-basics/thinking-or-feeling.asp; Golden LLC, Golden Personality Type Profiler frequently asked questions.

40. Myers-Briggs Foundation. Extraversion or introversion. Retrieved April 5, 2010, from http://www.myersbriggs.org/my-mbti-personality-type/mbti-basics/extraversion-or-introversion.asp; Golden LLC, Golden Personality Type Profiler frequently asked questions.

41. Myers-Briggs Foundation. Judging or perceiving. Retrieved April 5, 2010, from http://www.myersbriggs.org/my-mbti-personality-type/mbti-basics/judging-or-perceiving.asp; Golden LLC, Golden Personality Type Profiler frequently asked questions.

42. Golden LLC. About Golden LLC Products. Retrieved April 29, 2010, from http://www.goldenllc.com/About_GPTP.htm; Golden Personality Type Profiler frequently asked questions.

43. Kolb, David. 1984. *Experiential learning: Experience as the source of learning and development.* Englewood Cliffs, NJ: Prentice-Hall.

44. Kolb, David A. 1999. *Learning style inventory: Technical manual.* Boston: Hay/McBer.

45. Kolb, *Experiential learning.*

46. Greiner, Walter. 2001. *Quantum mechanics: An introduction.* New York: Springer.

47. Smith, Kenwyn K., and David N. Berg. 1987. *Paradoxes of group life: Understanding conflict, paralysis, and movement in group dynamics.* San Francisco: Jossey-Bass.

48. Ibid.

49. Ibid.

50. Ibid, 135.

51. Ibid.

52. Ibid.

53. Katzenbach and Smith. *The wisdom of teams,* xiii.

54. Katzenbach and Smith. The discipline of teams.

55. Ibid; Katzenbach, Jon R., and Douglas K. Smith. 1994. Teams at the top. *McKinsey Quarterly* 1: 71–79.

56. Katzenbach and Smith. *The wisdom of teams.*

57. Ibid.

58. Ibid.

59. Ibid.

60. Hackman, Richard. 1987. The design of work teams, in *Handbook of organizational behavior,* ed. J. Lorsch. Englewood Cliffs, NJ: Prentice Hall; Hackman, J. R., and C. G. Morris. 1978. Group Tasks, Group Interaction Process, and Group Performance Effectiveness: A Review and Proposed Integration, in *Group Processes,* ed. L. Berkowitz, 1–55. New York: Academic Press.

61. Karau, S. J., and K. D. Williams. 1993. Social loafing: A meta-analytic review and theoretical integration. *Journal of Personality and Social Psychology* 65: 681–706.

62. Asch, Solomon E. 1951. Effects of group pressure upon the modification and distortion of judgments, in *Groups, leadership and men,* ed.

H. Guetzkow, 177–90. Pittsburgh, PA: Carnegie Press; Asch, Solomon E. 1955. Opinions and social pressure. *Scientific American* 193(5): 31–35; Asch, S. E. 1956. Studies of independence and conformity: A minority of one against a unanimous majority. *Psychological Monographs* 70(9): (Whole No. 416).

63. Ibid.

64. Hodges, Bert H., and Anne L. Geyer 2006. A nonconformist account of the Asch experiments: Values, pragmatics, and moral dilemmas. *Personality and Social Psychology Review* 10(1): 2–19.

65. Janis, I. L., and L. Mann. 1977. *Decision making: A psychological analysis of conflict, choice, and commitment*, p. 129. New York: The Free Press.

66. Sims, Ronald R. 1992. Linking groupthink to unethical behavior in organizations. *Journal of Business Ethics* 11: 651–62; Adler, Stephen J. 2009. Beware groupthink on the economy. *Business Week* (February 16) 00077135, Issue 4119.

67. Argyris, Chris. 1977. Double-loop learning in organizations. *Harvard Business Review* 55(5): 115–25.

68. Asch, Solomon E. 1951. Effects of group pressure upon the modification and distortion of judgments; Asch, Solomon E. 1955. Opinions and social pressure; Asch, Solomon E. 1956. Studies of independence and conformity: A minority of one against a unanimous majority.

69. Napier, Matti K., and Rodney W. Gershenfield. 2007. *Groups: Theory and experience*, 7th ed, p. 133. Hillside, NJ: Lawrence Erlbaum Associates.

70. Jassawalla, Avan R., and Hemant C. Sashittal. 1993. Building collaborative cross-functional new product teams. *Academy of Management Executive* 13(3): 50–63.

71. Blanchard, Kendall. *The Ritual of sport: An introduction*. Westport, CT: Greenwood Publishing Group, 1995.

72. Aquino, Karl, and Stefan Thau. 2009. Workplace victimization: Aggression from the target's perspective. *Annual Review of Psychology* 60(1): 717–41.

73. Jehn, Karen A. 1997. A qualitative analysis of conflict types and dimensions in organizational groups. *Administrative Science Quarterly* 42(3): 530–57.

74. Jehn, Karen A., and Elizabeth A. Mannix. 2001. The dynamic nature of conflict: A longitudinal study of intergroup conflict and group performance. *Academy of Management* 44(2): 238–51.

75. Paulas, P. B., and B. A. Nijistad. 2003. *Group creativity: Innovation thought collaboration*. Oxford, UK: Oxford University Press; Laughlin, P. R., M. L. Zanderr, E. M. Knievel, and T. K. Tan. 2003. Groups perform better than the best individuals on letter-to-numbers problems: Informative equations and effective strategies. *Journal of Personality and Social Psychology* 85: 684–94.

76. Hardin, Russell. 1995. *One for all: The logic of group conflict*. Princeton, NJ: Princeton University Press.

77. Ansari, Shahzad, Frank Wijen, and Barbara Gray. 2009. Averting the 'tragedy of the commons': An institutional perspective on the construction and governance of transnational commons. *Academy of Management Proceedings* 2009: 1–6; Hardin, Garrett. 1968. The tragedy of the commons. *Science* 162(3859): 1243–1248.

78. Brehmer, B. 1976. Social judgment theory and the analysis of interpersonal conflict. *Psychological Bulletin* 83: 985–1003.

79. De Drue, C. K. W., and L. R. Weingart. 2003. Task versus relationship conflict, team performance, and team member satisfaction: A meta-analysis. *Journal of Applied Psychology* 86: 1191–201.

80. Jehn, Karen A., and Elizabeth A. Mannix. 2001. The dynamic nature of conflict: A longitudinal study of intragroup conflict and group performance. *Academy of Management*, 44(2): 238–251.

81. Ibid.

82. Roughan, Nicole. "Relative Authority." SSRN eLibrary (2011).

83. Wei, Yinghong, Gary L. Frankwick, and Binh H. Nguyen. 2012. Should firms consider employee input in reward system design? The effect of participation on market orientation and new product performance. *Journal of Product Innovation Management*.

84. Smith and Berg, *Paradoxes of group life*. 29, no. 4 (2012): 546–58.

85. Greenhaus, Jeffrey H., and Nicholas J. Beutell. 1985. Sources of conflict between work and family roles. *Academy of Management Review* 10(1): 76–88.

86. Smith and Berg, *Paradoxes of group life*.

87. Ibid.

88. FAMU band's suspension extended a year after hazing death. May 14, 2012. *USA Today*. Retrieved May 22, 2012, from http://www.usatoday.com/news/education/story/2012-05-14/famu-florida-band-hazing/54954384/1.

89. Tindale, R. S., A. Dykema-Engblade, and E. Wittkowski. 2005. Conflict within and between groups, in *Handbook of group research and practice*, ed. S. Wheelan. Thousand Oaks, CA: Sage.

90. Deutsch, M. 1973. *The resolution of conflict*. New Haven, CT: Yale University Press.

91. Harvard Business Essentials. 2003. *Negotiation*. Boston: Harvard Business School Publishing.

92. Ibid.

93. McKee, Annie, Richard Boyatzis, and Frances Johnston. 2008. *Becoming a resonant leader: Develop your emotional intelligence, renew your relationships and sustain your effectiveness*. Boston: Harvard Business School Press.

94. Hargie, Owen, and David Dickson. 2004. *Skilled interpersonal communication: Research, theory and practice*. New York: Routledge; Barbara, Dominick A. 1959. The art of listening. *Communication Quarterly* 7(1): 5–7; West, Richard, and Lynn H. Turner. 2006. *Understanding interpersonal communication: Making choices in changing times*. Boston: Wadsworth Cengage Learning.

95. Rogers, Carl R., and Richard E. Farson. 1987. Active listening, in *Communication in business today*, ed. R.G. Newman, M.A. Danziger, and M. Cohen. Washington, DC: Heath and Company.

96. Hoppe, Michael H. 2006. *Active listening: Improve your ability to listen and lead*. Greensboro, NC: Center for Creative Leadership.

97. Goodwin, Charles. 2007. Participation, stance and affect in the organization of activities. *Discourse & Society* 18(1): 53–73.

98. Rogers and Farson, Active listening.

99. Hill, Gayle W. 1982. Group versus individual performance: Are $N + 1$ heads better than one? *Psychological Bulletin* 91(3): 517–39.

100. Ibid.

101. Janus, Irving L. 1982. *Groupthink: Psychological studies of policy decisions and fiascoes*. Boston: Houghton Mifflin. Cox, Taylor H., and Stacey Blake. 1991. Managing cultural diversity: Implications for organizational competitiveness. *Academy of Management Executive* 5(3): 45–56.

Chapter 11

1. Kumar, Krishnan. 1995. *From post-industrial to post-modern society: New theories of the contemporary world*, 62. Malden, MA: Blackwell Publishing.

2. Ramachandran, Vilayanur S.V. "The Neurons That Shaped Civilization." In TEDIndia: TED Talks, 2009. Retrieved May 23, 2012, from http://www.ted.com/talks/vs_ramachandran_the_neurons_that_shaped_civilization.html.

3. Rifkin, Jeremy. 2010. *The empathic civilization: The race to global consciousness in a world in crisis*. New York: Jeremy P. Tarcher/Penguin.

4. Ramachandran, Vilayanur S.V. "The Neurons That Shaped Civilization." In TEDIndia: TED Talks, 2009. Retrieved May 23, 2012, from http://www.ted.com/talks/vs_ramachandran_the_neurons_that_shaped_civilization.html.

5. Rifkin, *The empathic civilization*.

6. Thomas, Chris Allen. 2009. Using technology to reintegrate learning and doing: IBM's approach and its implications for education, in *Handbook of research on e-learning applications for career and technical education: Technologies for vocational training, 2009*, ed. Victor Wang, 59–70. Hershey, PA: IGI Global; Liu, Jianxun, Shensheng Zhang, and Jinming Hu. 2005. A case study of an inter-enterprise workflow-supported supply chain management system. *Information and Management* 42(3): 441–54.

7. Thomas, Using technology to reintegrate learning and doing.

8. Lustig, Myron W., and Jolene Koestner. 1996. *Intercultural competence: Interpersonal communication across cultures*. New York: HarperCollins College Publishers.

9. McKee, Annie, Richard Boyatzis, and Frances Johnston. 2008. *Becoming a resonant leader: Develop your emotional intelligence, renew your relationships and sustain your effectiveness*. Boston: Harvard Business School Press.

10. Reich, Robert. 2008. *The work of nations: Preparing ourselves for 21st century capitalism*. New York: Simon and Schuster.

11. Emery, F. 1959. *Characteristics of sociotechnical systems*. London: Tavistock Institute for Human Relations; Herbst, P. G. 1974. *Sociotechnical design*. London: Tavistock Institute for Human Relations.

12. Trist, Eric L., and K. W. Bamforth. 1951. Some social and psychological consequences of the long wall method of coal-getting. *Human Relations* 4(1): 3–38.

13. Emery, F. L., and E. L. Trist. 1969. Socio-technical systems, in *Systems thinking,* ed. F. E. Emery, 281–96. London: Penguin; Pasmore, William, Carole Francis, Jeffrey Haldeman, and Abraham Shani. 1982. Sociotechnical systems: A North American reflection on empirical studies of the seventies. *Human Relations* 35(12): 1179–1204; Damanpour, Fariborz, and William M. Evan. 1984. Organizational innovation and performance: The problem of "organizational lag." *Administrative Science Quarterly* 29(3): 392–409.

14. Damanpour, Fariborz, and William M. Evan. 1984. Organizational Innovation and Performance: The Problem of "Organizational Lag". *Administrative Science Quarterly* 29, no. 3 (1984): 392–409.

15. Mokyr, Joel. 1999. Editor's introduction: The new economic history and the Industrial Revolution, in *The British Industrial Revolution: An economic perspective,* ed. Joel Mokyr, 1–31. Boulder, CO: Westview Press.

16. Landes, David. 1999. The fable of the dead horse; or, the Industrial Revolution revisited, in *The British Industrial Revolution: An economic perspective,* ed. Joel Mokyr, 128–59. Boulder, CO: Westview Press.

17. Gay, Peter. 1977. *The Enlightenment: An interpretation,* Vol. 2. New York: Norton.

18. Smith, Adam. 2000. *The wealth of nations,* p. 15. New York: Modern Library.

19. Smith, *The wealth of nations.*

20. Marx, Karl. 1988. *The Communist manifesto,* ed. Frederic L. Bender. New York: W. W. Norton.

21. Landes, David. 1969. *The unbound Prometheus: Technological change and industrial development in Western Europe from 1750 to the present.* New York: Cambridge University Press.

22. Drucker, Peter F. 1942. *The future of industrial man.* Omaha, NE: John Day Company.

23. Adams, Brooks. 1901. The new Industrial Revolution. *Atlantic Monthly* (February): 165; Lauck, W. Jett. 1929. *The new Industrial Revolution and wages.* New York: Funk and Wagnalls.

24. Eltis, David, and Stanley L. Engerman. 2000. The Importance of Slavery and the Slave Trade to Industrializing Britain. *The Journal of Economic History* 60(1): 123–44.

25. Braudel, Fernand. 1979. *Civilization and capitalism: 15th–18th century.* Berkeley: University of California Press.

26. Lovejoy, Paul E. 1983. *Transformations in slavery: A history of slavery in Africa.* New York: Cambridge University Press; Encyclopædia Britannica Guide to Black History. 2009. Slavery. Retrieved December 30, 2009, from http://www.britannica.com/blackhistory/article-24156.

27. Rothenberg, Paula S. 2006. *Beyond borders: Thinking critically about global issues.* New York: Worth Publishers.

28. Know India. 2008. Indian freedom struggle (1857–1947). Retrieved December 31, 2009, from http://india.gov.in/knowindia/history_freedom_struggle.php; Rothenberg, *Beyond borders.*

29. Amin, Samir. 1976. *Unequal development.* New York: Monthly Review Press.

30. Know India, Indian freedom struggle.

31. Amin, *Unequal development.*

32. Wood, Michael. 2000. *Conquistadors.* Los Angeles: University of California Press.

33. Rieger, Joerg. 2007. *Christ and empire: From Paul to post-colonial times.* Minneapolis, MN: Fortress Press.

34. O'Brien, Patrick Karl. 1997. Intercontinental trade and the development of the Third World since the Industrial Revolution. *Journal of World History* 8(1): 75–133.

35. Ibid.

36. Maddison, Angus. Explaining the economic performance of nations, 1820–1989, in *Convergence of productivity: Cross-national studies and historical evidence,* ed. William J. Baumol, Richard R. Nelson, and Edward N. Wolff, 20–61. New York: Oxford University Press.

37. Hirschman, Albert O. 1968. The political economy of import-substituting industrialization in Latin America. *Quarterly Journal of Economics* 82(1): 1–32; Naim, Moises. 1993. Latin America: Post-adjustment blues. *Foreign Policy* 92: 133–150.

38. Teng, Ssu-yü, and John King Fairbank. 1954. *China's response to the West: A documentary survey, 1839–1923.* Boston: President and Fellows of Harvard College.

39. Wong, Kam C. 2000. Black's theory on the behavior of law revisited IV: The behavior of Qing law. *International Journal of the Sociology of Law* 28: 327–374.

40. Goldstone, Jack A. 1996. Gender, work, and culture: Why the Industrial Revolution came early to England but late to China. *Sociological Perspectives* 39(1): 1–21.

41. Ibid.

42. Lavely, W., and R. Bin Wong. 1990. *Population and resources in modern China: Institutions in the balance.* Unpublished manuscript; Lavely, W., and R. Bin Wong. 1992. Family division and mobility in North China. *Comparative Studies in Society and History* 3(4): 439–463.

43. Machlup, Fritz. 1962. *The production and distribution of knowledge in the United States.* Princeton, NJ: Princeton University Press.

44. Bell, D. 1973. *The coming of post-industrial society,* 127. New York: Basic Books.

45. Foundation on Economic Trends. The hydrogen economy. Retrieved January 19, 2010, from http://www.foet.org/lectures/lecture-hydrogen-economy.html.

46. Anderson, Kurt. 2009. *Reset: How this crisis can restore our values and renew America.* New York: Random House.

47. Corporate Affiliations. Intel hierarchy. Retrieved May 11, 2010, from http://corporateaffiliations.ecnext.com.

48. Liu et al., A case study of an inter-enterprise workflow-supported supply chain management system.

49. Bureau of Labor Statistics. 2012. *Manufacturing: NAICS 31-33.* Washington, DC: United States Department of Labor. Retrieved May 23, 2012, from http://data.bls.gov/timeseries/CES3000000001?data_tool=XGtable.

50. Bell, *The coming of post-industrial society*; Friedman, Thomas. 2006. *The world is flat.* New York: Farrar, Straus, and Giroux.

51. Quinn, James B. 1999. Strategic outsourcing: Leveraging knowledge capabilities. *Sloan Management Review* 40(4): 9–21.

52. Ackman, Dan. 2002. Dock deal historic in more ways than one. *Forbes* (November 25). Retrieved January 4, 2010, from http://www.forbes.com/2002/11/25/cx_da_1125topnews.html.

53. Sridhar, V. 2002. Locked out of the docks. *Frontline* 19: 23. Retrieved January 4, 2010, from http://www.thehindu.com/fline/fl1923/stories/20021122001408800.htm.

54. Arabe, Katrina C. 2002. The aftermath of the West Coast port shutdown. *Industry Market Trends* (December 12). Retrieved January 4, 2010, from http://news.thomasnet.com/IMT/archives/2002/12/the_aftermath_o.html.

55. Kelleher, James R. March 12, 2011. Up to 100,000 protest Wisconsin law curbing unions. *Reuters.* Retrieved July 22, 2012, from http://www.reuters.com/article/2011/03/13/usa-wisconsin-idUSN1227540420110313

56. Maley, Mark. June 14, 2011. UPDATE: Unions Sue to Block Supreme Court's Reinstatement of Controversial Budget Repair Bill. *Shorewood Patch.* Retrieved July 22, 2012, from http://shorewood.patch.com/articles/high-court-reinstates-controversial-budget-repair-bill.

57. Hafner, Katie, and Matthew Lyon. 1996. *Where wizards stay up late: The origins of the Internet.* New York: Touchstone.

58. Tomlinson, Ray. The first network email. Retrieved January 5, 2010, from http://openmap.bbn.com/~tomlinso/ray/firstmailframe.html.

59. Leiner, Barry M., et al. 2009. A brief history of the Internet. *ACM SIGCOMM Computer Communication Review* 39(5): 22–31.

60. Berners-Lee, Tim, Robert Cailliau, A. Lontonen, H. F. Nielsen, and A. Secret. 1994. The world-wide web. *Communications of the ACM* 37: 76–82.

61. Ibid.

62. Google. Corporate history. Retrieved December 22, 2009, from http://www.google.com/corporate/history.html; Google. The official Google blog. Retrieved April 10, 2010, from http://googleblog.blogspot.com/2008/07/we-knew-web-was-big.html.

63. O'Reilly, Tim. 2005. *What is Web 2.0: Design patterns and business models for the next generation of software.* Sebastopol, CA: O'Reilly Media. Retrieved April 10, 2010, from http://www.oreillynet.com/pub/a/oreilly/tim/news/2005/09/30/what-is-web-20.html?page=1.

64. Shuen, Amy. 2008. *Web 2.0: A strategy guide.* Sebastopol, CA: O'Reilly Media.

65. Ibid.

66. LaRosa, Paul and Maria Cramer. 2009. *Seven Days of Rage: The Deadly Crime Spree of the Craigslist Killer.* Pocket Books: New York; Craigslist. About: Factsheet. Retrieved August 15, 2012 from http://www.craigslist.org/about/factsheet.

67. Angie's List. *Wikipedia*. Retrieved on July 22, 2012, from http://en .wikipedia.org/wiki/Angie%27s_List#cite_note-Amateur-4.

68. Hayes, Brian. 2009. Cloud computing: As software migrates from local PCs to distant Internet servers, users and developers alike go along for the ride. *Communications of the ACM* 51(7): 9–11.

69. TechTarget.com. Cloud computing. Retrieved December 31, 2009, from http://searchcloudcomputing.techtarget.com/sDefinition/0,,sid201_ gci1287881,00.html.

70. Google. GoogleApps. Retrieved April 10, 2010, from http://www.google .com/apps/intl/en/business/index.html#utm_campaign=en&utm_ source=en-ha-na-us-bk&utm_medium=ha&utm_term=google%20apps.

71. Amazon Web Services. Amazon Elastic Compute Cloud. Retrieved April 10, 2010, from http://aws.amazon.com/ec2.

72. Apple. Mobileme. Retrieved April 10, 2010, from http://www.apple .com/mobileme.

73. Gruber, Harold. 2005. *The economics of mobile telecommunications*. New York: Cambridge University Press.

74. CTIA. 2009. Background on CTIA's semi-annual wireless industry survey. Retrieved January 19, 2009, from http://files.ctia.org/pdf/CTIA_ Survey_Midyear_2009_Graphics.pdf; People's Daily Online. 2009. Over 700 million mobile phone users in China (September 3). Retrieved January 19, 2009, from http://english.people.com.cn/90001/ 90778/90857/90860/6747627.html; Telecom Regulatory Authority of India. 2009. Telecom subscription data as on 30th November 2009. Retrieved January 19, 2009, from http://www.trai.gov.in/WriteReadData/ trai/upload/PressReleases/712/pr23dec09no79.pdf.

75. CAPITALFM NEWS. May 23, 2012. China's mobile phone users hit 1.03b. Retrieved May 23, 2012, from http://www.capitalfm.co.ke/news/ 2012/05/chinas-mobile-phone-users-hit-1-03b/.

76. McKee, Annie, and Richard Boyatzis. 2005. *Resonant leadership: Renewing yourself and connecting with others through mindfulness, hope and compassion*, 24. Boston: Harvard Business School Press.

77. Vartiainen, Matti. 2006. Mobile virtual work—Concepts, outcomes, and challenges, in *Mobile virtual work: A new paradigm?*, ed. J. H. Erik Andriessen and Matti Vartiainen. New York: Springer.

78. Lucas, Henry C. 1994. The role of information technology in organization design. *Journal of Management Information Systems*, 10 (4): 7.

79. PUBLIC LAW 111–292. Retrieved May 24, 2012, from http://www.gpo .gov/fdsys/pkg/PLAW-111publ292/pdf/PLAW-111publ292.pdf.

80. Jones, Jeffrey M. 2006. One in three U.S. workers have "telecommuted" to work. *Gallup* (August 16). Retrieved December 28, 2009, from http:// www.gallup.com/poll/24181/One-Three-US-Workers-Telecommuted-Work.aspx.

81. Ibid.

82. BusinessDictionary.com. Hoteling. Retrieved April 10, 2010, from http://www.businessdictionary.com/definition/hoteling.html.

83. Rees, Paul. 2008. Shifting sands. *Communications Review* 13: 2.

84. Richards, Howard, and Harris Makatsoris. 2002. The metamorphosis to dynamic trading networks and virtual corporations, in *Managing virtual web organizations in the 21st century: Issues and challenges*, ed. Ulrich Franke, 75. Hershey, PA: Idea Publishing Group.

85. McDaniel, Christie L. 2008. Removing space and time: Tips for managing the virtual workplace, in *Handbook of research on virtual workplaces and the new nature of business practices*, ed. Pavel Zemliansky. Hershey, PA: IGI Global.

86. Nemiro, Jill, Lori Bradley, Michael M. Beyerlein, and Susan Beyerlein, eds. 2008. *The handbook of high-performance virtual teams*. San Francisco: Jossey-Bass.

87. Burn, Janice, Peter Marshall, and Martin Barnett. 2002. *E-business strategies for virtual organizations*. Woodburn, MA: Butterworth-Heinemann.

88. Fiol, C. Marlene, and Edward J. O'Conner. 2005. Identification in face-to-face, hybrid, and pure virtual teams: Untangling the contradictions. *Organization Science* 16(1): 19–32.

89. Nemiro, Jill. 2000. The glue that binds creative virtual teams, in *Knowledge management and new organization forms: A framework for business model innovation*, 102. Hershey, PA: Idea Group Publishing.

90. Malhotra, Arvind, Ann Majchrzak, Robert Carman, and Vern Lott. 2001. Radical innovation without collocation: A case study at Boeing-Rocketdyne. *MIS Quarterly* 25(2): 229–49.

91. Braga, David, Steve Jones, and Dennis Bowyer. 2008. Problem solving in virtual teams, in *The handbook of high-performance virtual teams: A toolkit for collaborating across boundaries*, ed. Jill Nemiro, Michael M. Beyerlein, Lori Bradley, and Susan Beyerlein, 391–404. San Francisco: Jossey-Bass.

92. Lucas, The role of information technology in organization design.

93. Wilson, Jeanne M., Susan G. Straus, and Bill McEvily. 2005. All in due time: The development of trust in computer-mediated and face-to-face teams. *Organizational Behavior and Human Decision Processes* 99(1): 16–33.

94. Bergiel, Blaise J., Erich B. Bergiel, and Phillip W. Balsmeir. 2008. Nature of Virtual Teams: A Summary of Their Advantages and Disadvantages. *Management Research News* 31(2): 99-110.

95. Ibid; Hertel, Guido, Susanne Geister, and Udo Konradt. 2005. Managing Virtual Teams: A Review of Current Empirical Research. *Human Resource Management Review* 15(1): 69-95.

96. Thomas, Dominic, and Robert Bostrom. 2010. Building Trust and Co-operation through Technology Adaptation in Virtual Teams: Empirical Field Evidence. *EDPACS* 42(5): 1-20.

97. Ibid.

98. Hinrichs, Gina, Jane Seiling, and Jackie Stavros. 2008. Sensemaking to create high-performing virtual teams, in *The handbook of high-performance virtual teams: A toolkit for collaborating across boundaries*, ed. Jill Nemiro, Michael M. Beyerlein, Lori Bradley, and Susan Beyerlein, 131–52. San Francisco: Jossey-Bass.

99. Ronfeldt, David. 1996. *Tribes, institutions, markets, networks: A framework about societal evolution*. Santa Monica, CA: RAND; Arquilla, John, and David Ronfeldt. 1996. *The advent of netwar*, 30. Santa Monica, CA: RAND National Defense Research Institute.

100. Sculley, John. 1992. Quoted in Forbes ASAP. *Forbes* 150(13): 26.

101. DeSanctis, Geraldine, and Peter Monge. 1998. Communication process for virtual organizations. *Journal of Computer-Mediated Communication*: 3(4): 2.

102. Burn et al., *E-business strategies for virtual organizations*.

103. Katzy, Bernhard, Chungyan Zhang, and Hermann Löh. 2005. Reference models for virtual organizations, in *Virtual organizations: Systems and practices*, ed. Luis M. Camarinha-Matos, Hamideh Afsarmanesh, and Martin Ollus, 45–58. New York: Springer Science+Business Media.

104. Netflix. Finish Netflix free trial sign up. Retrieved April 10, 2010, from http://www.netflix.com/NRD/Xbox?mqso=80025846.

105. Burn et al., *E-business strategies for virtual organizations*, 46.

106. Katzy et al., Reference models for virtual organizations.

107. Burn et al., *E-business strategies for virtual organizations*, 46.

108. Katzy et al., Reference models for virtual organizations.

109. Bitcoin P2P Digital Currency. Retrieved June 12, 2012, from http:// bitcoin.org/; Lyons, Daniel. 2011. The Web's Secret Cash. *The Daily Beast* (June 19). Retrieved June 12, 2012, from http://www .thedailybeast.com/newsweek/2011/06/19/the-web-s-secret-cash .html; Bitcoin Exchange Rates. *Bitcoin Prices*. Retrieved June 12, 2012, from http://bitcoinprices.com/.

110. Sienkiewicz, Stan. 2001. *Credit cards and payment efficiency*. Philadelphia: Federal Reserve Bank of Philadelphia.

111. Moore, David W. 2002. Only one in six Americans is without a credit card. *Gallup* (May 22). Retrieved January 20, 2010, from http://www.gallup.com/ poll/6067/Only-One-Six-Americans-Without-Credit-Card.aspx.

112. Ibid.

113. Merzer, Martin. 2010. 1 in 10 Has Given up—or Lost—Credit Cards in Past 8 Months. CreditCards.com. Retrieved May 24, 2012, from http:// www.creditcards.com/credit-card-news/poll-1-in-10-americans-gives-up-loses-credit-cards-1276.php.

114. Woolsey, Ben, and Matt Schulz. 2012. Credit Card Statistics, Industry Facts, Debt Statistics. *CreditCards.com*. Retrieved May 24, 2012, from http://www.creditcards.com/credit-card-news/credit-card-industry-facts-personal-debt-statistics-1276.php.

115. Hayashi, Fumiko, Richard Sullivan, and Stuart E. Weiner. 2003. *A guide to the ATM and debit card industry*. Kansas City, MO: Federal Reserve Bank of Kansas City.

116. Ibid.

117. Robat, Cornelis, ed. 2006. ATM automatic teller machines. *The history of computing project*. Retrieved January 20, 2010, from http://www .thocp.net/hardware/atm.htm.

118. Furst, Karen, William W. Lang, and Daniel E. Nolle. 2002. Internet banking. *Journal of Financial Services Research* 22(1): 95–117.

119. ING Bank of Canada. ING Direct. Retrieved April 10, 2010, from http:// www.ingdirect.ca/en/; Wikipedia. ING Group. Retrieved April 10, 2010, from http://en.wikipedia.org/wiki/ING_Direct.

120. ING Direct. About us. Retrieved June 12, 2012, from http://home.ingdirect.com/about/about.asp.

121. Online Banking: Full Report—Best Internet-Only Banks. *Consumersearch*. Retrieved June 12, 2012, from http://www.consumersearch.com/online-banking/best-internet-only-banks; Ally. Banking with Ally. Retrieved June 12, 2012, from http://www.ally.com/bank/online-banking/; FNBO Direct. Online Savings. Retrieved June 12, 2012, from https://www.fnbodirect.com/01d/html/en/personal/faqs/online_savings.html.

122. PayPal. About us. Retrieved April 10, 2010, from https://www.paypal-media.com/aboutus.cfm.

123. Kiva.org. About us. Retrieved April 10, 2010, from http://www.kiva.org/about.

124. Kiva.org. Loans that change lives. Retrieved April 10, 2010, from http://media.kiva.org/KIVA_brochure_6.1.07.pdf.

125. Kiva.org. 2012. Statistics Retrieved June 1, 2012, http://www.kiva.org/about/stats.

126. Ibid.

127. Central Intelligence Agency. World Factbook: United States. Retrieved May 31, 2012, from https://www.cia.gov/library/publications/the-world-factbook/geos/us.html; Central Intelligence Agency. World Factbook: Uganda. Retrieved May 31, 2012, from https://www.cia.gov/library/publications/the-world-factbook/geos/ug.html; Central Intelligence Agency. World Factbook: Democratic Republic of the Congo. Retrieved May 31, 2012, from https://www.cia.gov/library/publications/the-world-factbook/geos/cg.html.

128. Fusich, Monica. 2005. In Style: Fashion Plates from 1792 to World War I: Selections from the Little Bower Collection. *Special Collections, Henry Madden Library, California State University* (December). Retrieved June 12, 2012, from http://zimmer.csufresno.edu/~monicaf/index.htm.

129. Coopey, R., Sean O'Connell, and Dilwyn Porter. *Mail Order Retailing in Britain: A Business and Social History*. Oxford; New York: Oxford University Press, 2005.

130. Spector, Robert. *Amazon.com: Get big fast: Inside the revolutionary business model that changed the world*. New York: Random House.

131. Amazon.com. Sell on Amazon. Retrieved April 10, 2010, from http://www.amazonservices.com/content/sell-on-amazon.htm?ld=AZFSSOA.

132. Collier, Marsha. 2009. *eBay for dummies*. Indianapolis, IN: Wiley Publishing.

133. Bates, T. 2001. National strategies for e-learning in post-secondary education and training, in *Fundamentals for educational planning*, no. 70, 1–135. Paris: United Nations Educational, Scientific and Cultural Organization (UNESCO).

134. Zemsky, R., and W. Massey. 2004. *Thwarted innovation: A Learning Alliance report*, 11. West Chester, PA: Learning Alliance. Retrieved January 6, 2010, from http://www.immagic.com/eLibrary/ARCHIVES/GENERAL/UPENN_US/P040600Z.pdf.

135. Riswadkar, Amit, and A. V. Riswadkar. 2009. Balancing the risks of remote working: Walking the telecommuting line. *John Liner Review* 23(2): 89–94.

136. Ibid.

137. Bernthal, Paul R., Karen Colteryahn, Patty Davis, Jennifer Naughton, William J. Rothwell, and Rich Wellins. 2004. *Mapping the future: New workplace learning and performance competencies*. Alexandria, VA: ASTD Press.

138. Offstein, Evan H., and Jason M. Morwick. 2009. *Making telework work: Leading people and leveraging technology for high-impact results*. Boston, MA: Nicholas Breatley Publishing.

139. Ibid.

140. United Sample. 2011. I Can't Get My Work Done! How Collaboration & Social Tools Drain Productivity. Retrieved August 9, 2012, from http://cdn.mainsoft.com/21/24/Distraction_Survey_Results_US.pdf

141. Information Overload Research Group. Homepage. Retrieved May 12, 2010, from http://iorgforum.org.

142. Information Overload Research Group. February 3, 2011. Information Overload Research Group Takes Aim at Data Deluge in 2011. Retrieved May 24, 2012, from http://iorgforum.org/about-iorg/media-releases/.

143. Richtel, Lost in e-mail, tech firms face self-made beast.

144. Eggen, Dan, Karen DeYoung, and Spencer S. Hsu. 2009. Plane suspect was listed in terror database after father alerted U.S. officials. *Washington Post* (December 27). Accessed April 10, 2010, from http://www.washingtonpost.com/wp-dyn/content/article/2009/12/25/AR2009122501355_2.html?sid=ST2009122601151.

145. Malhotra, Yogesh. 2000. *Knowledge management and new organization forms: A framework for business model innovation*, 11. Hershey, PA: Idea Group Publishing.

146. Bradley, Tony. December 21, 2011. Pros and Cons of Bringing Your Own Device to Work. *PC World* (2011). Retrieved May 29, 2012, from http://www.pcworld.com/businesscenter/article/246760/pros_and_cons_of_bringing_your_own_device_to_work.html.

147. Bernabei, Lynne, and Alan R. Kabat. July 23, 2012. Invasions of Privacy. *The National Law Journal* (2012). Retrieved July 24, 2012, from http://www.law.com/jsp/nlj/PubArticleNLJ.jsp?id=1202563811801&Invasions_of__privacy&slreturn=20120624172037.

148. Boyatzis et al., *Resonant leadership*.

149. Duarte, Deborah L., and Nancy Tennant Snyder. 2006. *Mastering virtual teams: Strategies, tools, and techniques that succeed*. San Francisco: Jossey-Bass.

150. Hinrichs et al., Sensemaking to create high-performing virtual teams.

151. Hertel, G., U. Konradt, and B. Orlikowski. 2004. Managing distance by interdependence: Goal setting, task interdependence and team-based rewards in virtual teams. *European Journal of Work and Organizational Psychology* 13: 1–28.

152. Duarte and Snyder, *Mastering virtual teams*.

153. Kayworth, T. R., and D. E. Leidner. 2001. Leadership effectiveness in global virtual teams. *Journal of Management Information Systems* 18: 7–40.

154. Kirkman, B. L., B. Rosen, P. E. Tesluk, and C. B. Gibson. 2004. The impact of team empowerment on virtual team performance: The moderating role of face-to-face interaction. *Academy of Management Journal* 47: 175–92.

155. Cascio, Wayne. 2000. Managing a virtual workplace. *Academy of Management Executive*, 14 (3): 84.

156. Friedman, *The world is flat*.

157. International Telecommunication Union. Cambodia. Retrieved April 10, 2010, from http://www.itu.int/ITU-D/icteye/Reporting/ShowReportFrame.aspx?ReportName=/WTI/InformationTechnologyPublic&RP_intYear=2008&RP_intLanguageID=1; ITU Telecom World. 2011. ICT Facts and Figures. Retrieved August 9, 2012, from http://www.itu.int/ITU-D/ict/facts/2011/material/ICTFactsFigures2011.pdf.

158. World Summit on the Information Society. 2006. Report of the Tunis phase of the World Summit on the Information Society: Tunis, Kram Palexpo, November 16–18, 2005. Retrieved December 22, 2009, from http://www.itu.int/wsis/index-p2.html.

159. Symantec press release. September 7, 2011. Norton Study Calculates Cost of Global Cybercrime: $114 Billion Annually. http://www.symantec.com/about/news/release/article.jsp?prid=20110907_02.

Chapter 12

1. Bruce, J. C. *The 'Rogue' Myth: Demon Traders or Convenient Scapegoats?* South Carolina: CreateSpace, 2010.

2. Seligson, Susan. 2012. How Does a Bank Lose $5.8 Billion? *BU Today* (July 24). Retrieved July 26, 2012, from http://www.bu.edu/today/2012/how-does-a-bank-lose-billions/.

3. Moore, Michael J., and Dawn Kopecki. 2012. Dimon Saw $1 Billion Potential Loss When He Made 'Teapot' Remark. *Bloomberg* (July 13). Retrieved August 10, 2012, from http://www.bloomberg.com/news/2012-07-13/dimon-saw-1-billion-potential-loss-when-he-made-teapot-remark.html.

4. Marx, Karl. 1959. *The economic and philosophic manuscripts of 1844*. Trans. Martin Milligan. Moscow: Progress Publishers.

5. Taylor, Frederick Winslow. 1911. *Principles of scientific management*. New York: Harper and Brothers.

6. Stewart, Matthew. 2009. *The management myth: Why the experts keep getting it wrong*. New York: Norton.

7. Ibid.

8. Follett Foundation. 2010. Mary Parker Follett. Retrieved April 5, 2010, from http://www.follettfoundation.org/mpf.htm.

9. Mockler, Robert J. 1970. *Readings in management control*. New York: Appleton-Century-Crofts; Graham, Pauline, ed. 2003. *Mary Parker Follett: Prophet of management*. Frederick, MD: Beard Books.

10. Goleman, Daniel, Richard E. Boyatzis, and Annie McKee. 2002. *Primal leadership: Learning to lead with emotional intelligence*. Boston: Harvard Business School Press; Boyatzis, Richard, and Annie McKee. 2005. *Resonant leadership; Renewing yourself and connecting with others through*

mindfulness, hope and compassion. Boston: Harvard Business School Press; Bowen, Benjamin, and David Bowen. 1995. *Winning the service game.* Boston: Harvard Business School Press.

11. Mayo, Elton. 1977. *The Human Problems of an Industrial Civilization. Work, Its Rewards and Discontents.* New York: Arno Press; Follett, Mary Parker. 1924. *Creative Experience.* New York: Longmans, Green and co.; Follett, Mary Parker. 1918. *The New State, Group Organization the Solution of Popular Government.* New York: Longmans, Green and co.; Drucker, Peter F. 1995. *The Future of Industrial Man.* New Brunswick, N.J., U.S.A.: Transaction Publishers; Morgan, Gareth. 2006. *Images of Organization.* Updated ed. Thousand Oaks: Sage Publications.

12. Spreitzer, Gretchen M. 1995. Psychological, Empowerment in the Workplace: Dimensions, Measurement and Validation. *Academy of Management Journal* 38(5): 1442-65; Cameron, Kim S., and Gretchen M. Spreitzer. *The Oxford Handbook of Positive Organizational Scholarship.* Oxford Library of Psychology. New York: Oxford University Press, 2012.

13. Boyatzis and McKee, *Resonant leadership.*

14. Smith, Vernon. 2003. Constructivist and ecological rationality. *American Economic Review* 93(111): 485–508.

15. Coffey, Laura T. 2008. Chocoholics sour on new Hershey's formula. *MSNBC* (September 19). Retrieved April 16, 2010, from http://www.msnbc.msn.com/id/26788143.

16. Greenberg, Paul. 2010, The Impact of CRM 2.0 on Customer Insight. *The Journal of Business & Industrial Marketing* 25(6): 410-19.

17. Otley, David. 1999. Performance management: A framework for management control systems research. *Management Accounting Research* 10: 363–82.

18. Ibid.

19. Hope, Jeremy, and Robin Fraser. 2003. *Beyond Budgeting: How managers can break free from the annual performance trap.* Boston: Harvard Business School Press.

20. Peelen, Ed. 2005. *Customer relationship management.* Upper Saddle River, NJ: Financial Times/Prentice Hall; Heskett, James, W. Earl Sasser, and Leonard Schlesinger. 1997. *The service profit chain.* New York: Free Press.

21. Jayachandran, Satish, Subhash Sharma, Peter Kaufman, and Pushkala Raman. 2005. The role of relational information processes and technology use in customer relationship management. *Journal of Marketing* 69 (October): 177–92.

22. Davenport, Thomas H., and James E. Short. 1990. The new industrial engineering: Information technology and business process redesign. *Sloan Management Review* (Summer): 11–26.

23. Davenport, *Process innovation,* 1.

24. Hammer, Michael, and James Champy. 2001. *Reengineering the corporation: A manifesto for business revolution,* 35. New York: HarperCollins.

25. Hammer, Michael. 1990. Reengineering work: Don't automate, obliterate. *Harvard Business Review* 68(4): 104–12.

26. Hammer and Champy, *Reengineering the corporation,* 21.

27. Davenport and Short, The new industrial engineering; Davenport, Thomas. 1993. *Process innovation: Reengineering work through information technology.* Boston: Harvard Business School Press.

28. Raymond, Louis, Francios Bergeron, and Suzanne Rivard. 1998. Determinants of business process reengineering success in small and large enterprises. *Journal of Small Business Management* 36(1): 72–85.

29. Goel, Sanjay, and Chen, Vicki. 2008. Integrating the global enterprise using Six Sigma: Business process reengineering at General Electric Wind Energy. *International Journal of Production Economics* 113: 914–27.

30. Wikipedia. Total quality management. Retrieved August 14, 2009, from http://en.wikipedia.org/wiki/TQM.

31. Antony, Jiju. Pros and cons of Six Sigma: An academic perspective. Retrieved October 28, 2009, from http://www.onesixsigma.com/node/7630.

32. Acuity Institute. Lean Six Sigma Black Belt certification. Retrieved April 16, 2010, from http://www.acuityinstitute.com/six-sigma-blackbelt.html.

33. Imai, Masaaki. 1986. *Kaizen: The key to Japan's competitive success.* New York: McGraw Hill.

34. Acuity Institute. Lean Six Sigma Black Belt certification.

35. Henderson, K.M. and Evans, J.R. 2000. Successful implementation of Six Sigma: benchmarking, General Electric Company. *Benchmarking: An International Journal* 7 (4): 260-81.

36. Choi, Bong, Jongweon Kim, Byung-hak Leem, Chang-Yeol Lee, and Han-kuk Hong. 2012. Empirical Analysis of the Relationship between Six Sigma Management Activities and Corporate Competitiveness. *International Journal of Operations & Production Management* 32(5): 528-50.

37. Hindo, Brian. 2007. At 3M, a struggle between efficiency and creativity. *Business Week* (June 6). Retrieved October 28, 2009, from http://www.businessweek.com/magazine/content/07_24/b4038406.htm?chan=top+news_top+news+index_best+of+bw.

38. Ruffa, Stephen A. 2008. *Going lean: How the best companies apply lean manufacturing principles to shatter uncertainty, drive innovation, and maximize profits.* New York: AMACOM.

39. Brady, J. E., and T. T. Allen. 2006. Six Sigma literature: A review and agenda for future research. *Quality and Reliability Engineering International* 22: 335–67.

40. Womac, James P., Daniel T. Jones, and Daniel Roos. 1990. *The machine that changed the world: The story of lean production.* New York: Rawson Associates.

41. Ohno, Taiichi. 1995. *Toyota Production System: Beyond large-scale production.* New York: Productivity Press.

42. Trent, Robert J. *End-to-end lean management: A guide to complete supply chain improvement.* Fort Lauderdale, FL: J. Ross Publishing.

43. Ibid.; Brun, Yuriy, and Nenad Medvidovic. 2007. Fault and adversary tolerance as an emergent property of distributed systems' software architectures. Paper presented at 2007 Workshop on Engineering Fault Tolerant Systems, Dubrovnik, Croatia, September 4. Retrieved March 20, 2010, from http://portal.acm.org/citation.cfm?id=1316550.1316557.

44. International Organization for Standardization. ISO 9000 and ISO 14000. Retrieved December 2, 2009, from http://www.iso.org/iso/iso_catalogue/management_standards/iso_9000_iso_14000.htm.

45. American Society for Quality. Organization-wide approaches: ISO 9000 and other standards. Retrieved December 2, 2009, from http://www.asq.org/learn-about-quality/iso-9000/overview/overview.html.

46. International Organization for Standardization. ISO 14000:2004 and SMEs. Retrieved December 2, 2009, from http://www.iso.org/iso/iso_catalogue/management_standards/iso_9000_iso_14000/iso_14001_2000_and_smes.htm.

47. American Society for Quality, Organization-wide approaches: ISO 9000 and other standards.

48. ISO9000Council.org. Welcome to ISO9000Council.org. Retrieved April 5, 2010, from http://www.iso9000council.org.

49. International Organization for Standardization. Quality management principles. Retrieved December 2, 2009, from http://www.iso.org/iso/iso_catalogue/management_standards/iso_9000_iso_14000/qmp.htm.

50. ISO9000Council.org, Welcome to ISO9000Council.org.

51. Ibid.

52. The International Organization for Standardization (ISO). ISO 9001-Quality management systems-Requirements. Retrieved July 26, 2012, from http://www.iso.org/iso/iso-survey2010.pdf

53. Ibid.

54. Minority Business Development Agency. ISO 14000 Standards. U.S. Department of Commerce. Retrieved December 2, 2009, from http://www.mbda.gov/?id=5&bucket_id=163&content_id=2478&well=entire_page.

55. Hanson, Arthur J. Global green standards. International Institute for Sustainable Development. Retrieved December 2, 2009, from http://www.iisd.org/greenstand/default.htm.

56. International Organization for Standardization. ISO 14000 essentials. Retrieved December 2, 2009, from http://www.iso.org/iso/iso_catalogue/management_standards/iso_9000_iso_14000/iso_14000_essentials.htm.

57. Hanson, Global green standards.

58. International Organization for Standardization. Certification. Retrieved December 2, 2009, from http://www.iso.org/iso/iso_catalogue/management_standards/certification.htm; Minority Business Development Agency, ISO 14000 Standards.

59. Zorpas, Antonis. 2010. Environmental Management Systems as Sustainable Tools in the Way of Life for the Smes and Vsmes. *Bioresource Technology* 101(6): 1544-57.

60. International Organization for Standardization. ISO 9000 essentials. Retrieved December 2, 2009, from http://www.iso.org/iso/iso_catalogue/management_standards/iso_9000_iso_14000/iso_9000_essentials.htm.

61. ISO9000Council.org, Welcome to ISO9000Council.org.

62. Baldrige National Quality Program. The Malcolm Baldrige National Quality Improvement Act of 1987—Public Law 100-107. National Institute of Standards and Technology. Retrieved December 2, 2009, from http://www.baldrige.nist.gov/Improvement_Act.htm.

63. Baldrige National Quality Program. Biography of Malcolm Baldrige. National Institute of Standards and Technology. Retrieved December 2, 2009, from http://www.baldrige.nist.gov/Biography.htm.

64. National Institute of Standards and Technology. Frequently asked questions about the Malcolm Baldrige National Quality Award. Retrieved December 2, 2009, from http://www.nist.gov/public_affairs/factsheet/baldfaqs.htm.

65. Turner, Sam. 2009. Baldrige criteria can help utility industry: How the Baldrige Criteria for Performance Excellence can help today's utility industry meet tomorrow's challenges. *Quality Digest* (November 12). Retrieved December 2, 2009, from http://www.qualitydigest.com/inside/quality-insider-article/baldrige-criteria-can-help-utility-industry.html.

66. National Institute of Standards and Technology, Frequently asked questions.

67. Nguyen, Vu, Ronald Lee, and Kaushik Dutta. 2006. An aspect architecture for modeling organizational controls in workflow systems. Paper presented at DESRIST conference, February 24–25, Claremont, CA, 172–191.

68. Ferner, Anthony. 2007. The underpinnings of "bureaucratic" control systems: HRM in European multinationals. *Journal of Management Studies* 37(4): 521–40.

69. Frost, Peter. 2003. *Toxic emotions at work.* Boston: Harvard Business School Press.

70. Ouchi, William G. 1979. A conceptual framework for the design of organizational control mechanisms. *Management Science* 25(9): 833–48.

71. Eisenhardt, Kathleen M. 1985. Control: Organizational and economic approaches. *Management Science* 31(2): 134–49.

72. Leifer, Richard, and Peter K. Mills. 1996. An information processing approach for deciding upon control strategies and reducing control loss in emerging organizations. *Journal of Management* 22(1): 113–37.

73. Snell, Scott A. 1992. Control theory in strategic human resource management: The mediating effect of administrative information. *Academy of Management Journal* 35(2): 292–327.

74. Ouchi, William G. 1977. The relationship between organizational structure and organizational control. *Administrative Science Quarterly* 20: 95–113.

75. Horngren, Charles T. 2006. *Cost accounting: A managerial emphasis,* 12th ed. Upper Saddle River, NJ: Prentice-Hall.

76. Simons, Robert. 1994. *Levers of control: How managers use innovative control systems to drive strategic renewal.* Boston: Harvard Business School Press.

77. Ferreira, Aldónio, and David Otley. 2009. The Design and Use of Performance Management Systems: An Extended Framework for Analysis. *Management Accounting Research* 20(4): 263–82.

78. Simons, Robert. 1994. Levers of control: How managers use innovative control systems to drive strategic renewal. Boston: Harvard Business School Press.

79. Widener, S.K. 2007. An Empirical Analysis of the Levers of Control Framework. *Accounting, Organizations and Society* 32: 757–88.

80. McCaig, Linda F., and Eric W. Nawar. 2006. National Hospital Ambulatory Medical Care Survey: 2004 Emergency Department Summary. *Advance Data from Vital and Health Statistics* 372. Retrieved November 29, 2012, from http://www.cdc.gov/NCHS/data/ad/ad372.pdf

81. Niska, Richard, Farida Bhuiya, and Jianmin Xu. 2010. National Hospital Ambulatory Medical Care Survey: 2007 Emergency Department Summary. 32 pages: National Health Statistics Reports.

82. Emergency Department: Patient Perspectives on American Health Care, in Pulse Report, 28 pages. South Bend, IN, 2010. Retrieved July 26, 2012, from http://www.pressganey.com/Documents_secure/Pulse%20Reports/2010_ED_Pulse_Report.pdf?viewFile.

83. Berglöf, Erik, and Ernst-Ludwig von Thadden. 1999. The changing corporate governance paradigm: Implications for transition and developing countries, in *Corporate governance and globalization: Long range planning issues,* ed. Stephen S. Cohen and Gavin Boyd, 275–306. Northampton, MA: Edward Elgar Publishing.

84. Schleifer, Andrei, and Robert W. Vishny. 1997. A survey of corporate governance. *Journal of Finance* 52(2): 737–83.

85. Jensen, Michael. 1998. *Foundations of organisational strategy.* Boston: Harvard Business School Press.

86. Civil Rights Act of 1964. Title VII: Equal employment opportunities. 42 USC Chapter 21.

87. U.S. House of Representatives. USC Chapter 98. Retrieved May 12, 2010, from http://uscode.house.gov/download/pls/15C98.txt.

88. Senator Charles E. Schumer. January 22, 2007. Schumer, Bloomberg Report: NY in danger of losing status as world financial center within 10 years without major shift in regulation and policy. Retrieved November 28, 2012, from http://schumer.senate.gov/new_website/record.cfm?id=267787&.

89. Malone, Michael S. 2008. Washington Is Killing Silicon Valley. *Wall Street Journal* (December 22). Retrieved May 29, 2012, from http://online.wsj.com/article/SB122990472028925207.html; America as Number Two. 2012. *Wall Street Journal* (January 4). Retrieved May 29, 2012, from http://online.wsj.com/article/SB100014240529702047202045 7712905231747614.html.

90. Taylor, William C. 2006. To charge up customers, put customers in charge. *New York Times* (June 18). Retrieved November 11, 2009, from http://www.nytimes.com/2006/06/18/business/yourmoney/18mgmt.html.

91. Ibid.

92. Lindberg, Oliver. 2009. The secrets behind Threadless "success." *techradar.com* (May 28). Retrieved September 12, 2009, from http://www.techradar.com/news/internet/the-secrets-behind-Threadless-success-602617.

93. Ibid.

94. Chafkin, Max. 2008. The customer is the company. *Inc.* (July 1). Retrieved September 12, 2009, from http://www.inc.com/magazine/20080601/the-customer-is-the-company.html.

95. Ibid.

96. Ibid.

97. Otley, David. 1999. Performance Management: A Framework for Management Control Systems Research. *Management Accounting Research* 10(4): 363-82.

98. Ibid.

99. Kaplan, Robert S., and David P. Norton. 1996. *The Balanced Scorecard: Translating strategy into action.* Boston: Harvard Business School Press.

100. Goleman et al. *Primal leadership;* Frost, P., J. Dutton, M. Worline, and A. Wilson. 2000. Narratives of compassion in organizations, in *Emotion in organizations,* ed. S. Fineman. Thousand Oaks, CA: Sage Publications; Graen, G., and M. Uhl-Bien. 1995. Relationship-based approach to leadership development of leader-member exchange (LMX) theory of leadership over 25 years: Applying a multi-level, multi-domain perspective. *Leadership Quarterly* 6: 219–47; Higgins, M. C., and K. E. Kram. 2001. Reconceptualizing mentoring at work: A developmental network perspective. *Academy of Management Review* 26(2): 264–88; Kanov, J. M., S. Maitlis, M. C. Worline, J. E. Dutton, P. J. Frost, and J. M. Lilius. 2004. Compassion in organizational life. *American Behavioral Scientist* 47(6): 808–27.

101. Drucker, Peter F. 1954. *The practice of management.* New York: Harper & Brothers.

102. Romani, Paul N. 1997. MBO by any other name is still MBO. *Supervision* 58(12): 6–8.

103. Thomas, Gail Fann, Roxanne Zolin, and Jackie L. Hartman. 2009. The central role of communication in developing trust and its effect on employee involvement. *Journal of Business Communication* 46(3): 291.

104. Kram, Kathy E. 1996. A relationship approach to career development, in *The career is dead—Long live the career.* San Francisco: Jossey-Bass.

105. McKee, A., and R. E. Boyatzis. 2008. *Becoming a resonant leader: Develop your emotional intelligence, renew your relationships, and sustain your effectiveness.* Boston: Harvard Business School Press.

106. Lewis, Kristi M. 2000. When leaders display emotion: How followers respond to negative emotional expression of male and female leaders. *Journal of Organizational Behavior* 21(special issue): 221–34.

107. Ibid.

108. Langer, Ellen. 1989. *Mindfulness.* Reading, MA: Addison-Wesley.

Chapter 13

1. Mead, Margaret. 1953. *Cultural patterns and technical change,* 9–10. Deventer, Holland: UNESCO.

2. Hofstede, Geert. 1980/1984. *Culture's consequences: International differences in work-related values,* 14. Newbury Park, CA: Sage Publications.

3. Mead, R. 1994. *International management: Cross-cultural dimensions.* Oxford: Blackwell Business.

4. Hofstede, Geert. 1998. Attitudes, values, and organizational culture: Disentangling the concepts. *Organization Studies* 19(3): 477–92; Rokeach, Milton. 1972. *Beliefs, attitudes, and values.* San Francisco: Jossey-Bass.

5. Lagarde, Emmanuel, Catherine Enel, Karim Seck, Aïssatou, Gueye-Ndiaye, Jean-Pierre Piau, Gilles Pison, Valerie Delaunay, Ibrahima Ndoye, and Souleymane Mboup. 2000. Religion and protective behaviors towards AIDS in rural Senegal. *AIDS* 14: 2027–33.

6. Finkelstein, S. 2002. The DaimlerChrysler merger. Business case no. 1-0071. Retrieved April 17, 2010, from http://mba.tuck.dartmouth.edu/pdf/2002-1-0071.pdf.

7. CSL Behring. About CSL Behring. Retrieved April 17, 2010, from http://www.cslbehring.com/about.

8. Unilever. Powered by people. Retrieved April 17, 2010, from http://www.unilever.com/careers; ExxonMobil. Country, regional business and brand sites. Retrieved April 17, 2010, from http://www.exxonmobil.com/corporate/about_where_countries.aspx; Nike. Careers. Retrieved November 18, 2009, from http://www.nikebiz.com/careers.

9. Teleos Leadership Institute. Who we are. Retrieved November 18, 2009, from http://www.teleosleaders.com/teleos_who_we_are.html.

10. Schein, E. H. 1985. *Organizational culture and leadership.* San Francisco: Jossey-Bass.

11. Schein, *Organizational culture and leadership;* Likert, R. 1961. *New patterns of management.* New York: McGraw-Hill; Gregory, B. T., S. G. Stanley, A. A. Armenakis, and C. L. Shook. 2009. Organizational culture and effectiveness: A study of values, attitudes, and organizational outcomes. *Journal of Business Research* 62: 673–79.

12. Pfeffer, J. 1981. Management as symbolic action: The creation and maintenance of organizational paradigms, in *Research in organizational behavior,* vol. 3, ed. L. L. Cummings and B. M. Staw, 1–52. Greenwich, CT: JAI Press.

13. Hofstede, *Culture's consequences;* Hofstede, Geert. 1994. The business of international business is culture. *International Business Review* 3(1): 1–14.

14. Hofstede, Geert, and Michael H. Bond. 1988. The Confucius connection: From cultural roots to economic growth. *Organizational Dynamics* 16: 5–21; Franke, Richard H., Geert Hofstede, and Michael H. Bond. 2002. National culture and economic growth. In *Handbook of cross-cultural management,* ed. Martin J. Gannon and Karen L. Newman, 5–15. Malden, MA: Blackwell Publishers.

15. Hofstede, *Culture's consequences.*

16. Hofstede, Geert, Bram Neuijen, Denise D. Ohayv, and Saunders Geert. 1990. Measuring organizational cultures: A qualitative and quantitative study across twenty cases. *Administrative Science Quarterly* 35(2): 286–317; Chinese Culture Connection. 1987.

17. Ibid; Yeh, Ryh-Song, and John J. Lawrence. 1995. Individualism and Confucian dynamism: A note on Hofstede's cultural root to economic growth. *Journal of International Business Studies* 26(3): 655–69; Hofstede and Bond, The Confucius connection; Chinese values and the search for culture-free dimensions of culture. *Journal of Cross-Cultural Psychology* 18: 143–64.

18. House, Robert, Paul J. Hanges, Mansour Javidan, and Peter W. Dorfman, eds. 2004. *Culture, leadership, and organizations: The GLOBE study of 62 societies.* Thousand Oaks, CA: Sage Publications.

19. Ibid.

20. Javidan, M., and R. J. House. 2001. Cultural acumen for the global manager: Lessons from Project GLOBE. *Organizational Dynamics* (Spring): 289–305.

21. *Baker v. Nelson,* 291 Minn. 310 (1971).

22. Freedom to Marry.org. States. Retrieved August 11, 2009, from http://www.freedomtomarry.org/states.php.

23. National Conference of State Legislatures. Defining Marriage: Defense of Marriage Acts and Same-Sex Marriage Laws. Retrieved August 16, 2012, from http://www.ncsl.org/issues-research/human-services/same-sex-marriage-overview.aspx.

24. Lee, Carol E. 2012. Obama Backs Gay Marriage. *Wall Street Journal* (May 10). Retrieved May 29, 2012, from http://online.wsj.com/article/SB10001424052702304070304577394332545729926.html.

25. Lewis, Gregory B. 2005. Same-sex marriage and the 2004 presidential election. *PS: Political Science and Politics* 38: 195–99.

26. Yanow, Dvora. 2000. Seeing organizational learning: A cultural view. *Organization Articles* 7(2): 247–68.

27. Quinn, R. E., and J. A. Rohrbaugh. 1983. A spatial model of effectiveness criteria: Towards a competing values approach to organizational analysis. *Management Science* 29: 363–77; Quinn, R. E., and G. M. Spreitzer. 1991. The psychometrics of the competing values culture instrument and an analysis of the impact of organizational culture on quality of life, in *Research in organizational change and development,* vol. 5, ed. R. W. Woodman and W. A. Pasmore, 115–42. Greenwich, CT: JAI Press; Cameron, K. S., and S. J. Freeman. 1991. Cultural congruence, strength, and type: Relationships to effectiveness, in *Research in organizational change and development,* vol. 5, ed. R. W. Woodman and W. A. Pasmore, 23–58. Greenwich, CT: JAI Press.

28. Cameron, Kim S., and Robert E. Quinn. 2006. *Diagnosing and changing organizational culture: Based on the competing values framework.* San Francisco: Jossey-Bass.

29. Gregory et al., Organizational culture and effectiveness; Quinn, R. E. 1988. *Beyond rational management.* San Francisco: Jossey-Bass; Cameron, Kim S. 1984. Cultural congruence, strength, and type: Relationships to effectiveness. Working Paper No. 401b, Graduate School of Business Administration, University of Michigan; Denison, D. R., and G. M. Spreitzer. Organizational culture and organizational development: A competing values approach, in *Research in organizational change and development,* vol. 5, ed. R. W. Woodman and W. A. Pasmore, 1–21. Greenwich, CT: JAI Press; Cameron, K. S., R. E. Quinn, J. Degraff, and A. V. Thakor. 2006. *Creating values in leadership.* Northampton, MA: Edward Elgar; Cameron, K. S., and R. E. Quinn. 1999. *Diagnosing and changing organizational cultures.* New York: Addison-Wesley.

30. Gregory et al., Organizational culture and effectiveness.

31. Ibid.; Quinn, R. E., *Beyond rational management.*

32. Kotter, J., and J. Heskett. 1992. *Corporate culture and performance.* New York: Free Press; O'Reilly, C. A., and J. A. Chatman. 1996. Culture as social control: Corporations, culture and commitment, in *Research in organizational behavior,* vol. 18, ed. B. M. Staw and L. L. Cummings, 157–200. Greenwich, CT: JAI Press.

33. Pascale, R. 1985. The paradox of "corporate culture": Reconciling ourselves to socialization. *California Management Review* 27: 26–41; Posner, B.,J. Kouzes, and W. Schmidt. 1985. Shared values make a difference: An empirical test of corporate culture. *Human Resource Management* 24: 293–309.

34. Sorenson, J. B. 2002. The strength of corporate culture and the reliability of firm performance. *Administrative Science Quarterly* 47: 70–91. Denison, Daniel R. 1984. Bringing corporate culture to the bottom line. *Organizational Dynamics* 13(2): 4–22; Denison, Daniel R. 1990. *Corporate culture and organizational effectiveness.* New York: Wiley; Gordon, G., and N. DiTomaso. 1992. Predicting corporate performance from organizational culture. *Journal of Management Studies* 29: 783–98.

35. Collins, C., and J. Porras. 2002. *Built to last: Successful habits of visionary companies.* New York: HarperCollins; Schrodt, Paul. 2002. The relationship between organizational identification and organizational culture: Employee perceptions of culture and identification in a retail sales organization. *Communication Studies* 53: 189–202.

36. Martin, Joanne, Peter J. Frost, and Olivia A. O'Neill. 2006. Organizational culture: Beyond struggles for intellectual dominance, in *The handbook of organisation studies,* 2d ed., ed. S. R. Clegg, C. Hardy, T. B. Lawrence, and W. R. Nord, 725–53. Newbury Park, CA: Sage Publications.

37. Shrivastava, P. 1985. Integrating strategy formulation with organizational culture. *Journal of Business Strategy* 5: 103–11.

38. Sørensen, Jesper B. 2002. The strength of corporate culture and the reliability of firm performance. *Administrative Science Quarterly* 47(1): 70–91.

39. Gordon, George G. 1991. Industry determinants of organizational culture. *Academy of Management Review* 16(2): 396–415.

40. Michel, Alexandra, and Stanton Wortham. 2008. *Bullish on uncertainty: How organizational cultures transform participants.* New York: Cambridge University Press.

41. Dakan, Myles. 2007. What is uchi, what is soto: The cultural implications of Japanese grammar. *Daily Gazette* (February 12). Retrieved September 12, 2009, from http://daily.swarthmore.edu/2007/2/12/what-is-uchi-what-is-soto-the-cultural-implications-of-japanese-grammar.

42. Jones, Dell. 2008. Some firms' fertile soil grows crop of future CEOs. *USA Today* (January 1).

43. Byrne, John A., and Gary McWilliams. 1993. The alumni club to end all alumni clubs. *Businessweek* (September 20). Retrieved September 12, 2009, from http://www.businessweek.com/archives/1993/b333748.arc.htm.

44. Ibid.

45. Ibid.

46. Hirst, Clayton. 2002. The might of the McKinsey mob. *The Independent* (January 20). Retrieved April 23, 2010, from http://www.independent.co.uk/news/business/analysis-and-features/the-might-of-the-mckinsey-mob-664081.html.

47. Byrne, John A. 2002. Inside McKinsey. *BusinessWeek* (July 8). Retrieved September 12, 2009, from http://www.businessweek.com/magazine/content/02_27/b3790001.htm.

48. Schein, *Organizational culture and leadership.*

49. Ibid., 3–27.

50. Highlights of Women's Earnings in 2010. Washington, DC: Bureau of Labor Statistics, 2011. Retrieved May 16, 2012, from http://www.bls.gov/cps/cpswom2010.pdf.

51. Yanow, Dvora. 2000. Seeing organizational learning: A cultural view. *Organization Science* 7(2): 247–68; Lytle, James H. 1996. The inquiring manager. *Phi Delta Kappan* 77(10): 664–66.

52. Pettigrew, A. M. 1979. On studying organizational cultures. *Administrative Science Quarterly* 24: 570–81.

53. Bowles, M. L. 1989. Myth, meaning, and work organization. *Organization Studies* 10(3): 405–21.

54. Schein, E. H. 1983. The role of the founder in creating organizational culture. *Organization Dynamics* (Summer): 13–28.

55. Rogers, William. 1969. *Think: A biography of the Watsons and IBM.* New York: Stein & Day.

56. Martin, Joanne, Martha S. Feldman, and Mary Jo Hatch. 1983. The uniqueness paradox in organizational stories. *Administrative Science Quarterly* 28(3): 438–53.

57. Durkheim, E. 1965. *The elementary forms of religious life.* New York: Free Press.

58. Martin, Joanne. 1990. Deconstructing organizational taboos: The suppression of gender conflict in organizations. *Organization Science* 1(4): 339–59.

59. Kallio, Tomy J. 2007. Taboos in corporate social responsibility discourse. *Journal of Business Ethics* 74: 165–75.

60. Ibid.

61. Kontakt: The Arts and Civil Society Program of Erste Group. Cold War and Coca-Cola. Retrieved April 23, 2010, from http://www.kontakt.erstegroup.net/report/stories/Issue20_07_Kalter+Krieg+und+Coca+Cola/en.

62. LaTour, Kathryn, Michael S. LaTour, and George M. Zinkhand. 2009. Coke is it: How stories in childhood memories illuminate an icon. *Journal of Business Research* 63(3): 328–36.

63. Barley, Stephen R. 1983. Semiotics and the study of occupational and organizational cultures. *Organizational Culture* 28(3): 393–413; Eco, Umberto. 1986. *Semiotics and the philosophy of language.* Bloomington, IN: Indiana University Press.

64. Wiktionary.com. Glossary of military slang. Retrieved November 29, 2012, from http://en.wiktionary.org/wiki/Appendix:Glossary_of_military_slang.

65. Thomas, Chris Allen. 2008. Bridging the gap between theory and practice: Language policy in multilingual organizations. *Language Awareness* 17(4): 307–25.

66. Kallio, Taboos in corporate social responsibility discourse.

67. Yanow, Seeing organizational learning; Reason, Peter. *Human inquiry in action: Developments in new paradigm research.* Thousand Oaks, CA: Sage; Schein, Edgar H. 2001. Clinical inquiry/research, in *Handbook of action research,* ed. Peter Reason and Hilary Bradbury, 228–237. Thousand Oaks, CA: Sage; Lytle, The inquiring manager.

68. Plato, and Benjamin Jowett. 1901. *The Republic of Plato : An Ideal Commonwealth.* The World's Great Classics. Rev. ed. New York: The Colonial Press.

69. London, Anne (Annie McKee) and M. C. McMillen. 1993. Discovering social issues: Organization development in a multicultural community. *Journal of Applied Behavioral Sciences* 28(3): 445–60.

70. Goleman, Daniel, Richard E. Boyatzis, and Annie McKee. 2002. *Primal leadership: Realizing the power of emotional intelligence,* 198–200. Boston: Harvard Business School Press.

71. Cooperrider, David L. 2004. Appreciative inquiry: New horizons in strength-based organization development, in *Sixth annual best of organizational development summit,* 79–107. Burlington, MA: Linkage Inc.; Cooperrider, D. L., and S. Srivasta. 1987. Appreciative inquiry in

72. organizational life, in *Research in organizational change and development,* Vol. 1, ed. R. W. Woodman and W. A. Pasmore, 129–69. Greenwich, CT: JAI Press.

72. Gustavson, Bjørn. 2001. Theory and practice: The mediating discourse, in *Handbook of action research,* ed. Peter Reason and Hilary Bradbury, 17–26. Thousand Oaks, CA: Sage Publications; Hult, M., and S. Lennung. 1980. Towards a definition of action research: A note and bibliography. *Journal of Management Studies* 17(2): 242–50.

73. Weick, Karl E., and Robert E. Quinn. 1999. Organizational change and development. *Annual Review of Psychology* 50: 361–86.

74. Kent, William E. 1990. Putting up the Ritz: Using culture to open a hotel. *Cornell Hotel and Restaurant Administration Quarterly* 31(3): 16–24.

75. Enz, C. A., and J. A. Signaw. 2000. Best practices in service quality. *Cornell Hotel and Restaurant Administration Quarterly* 41: 20–29.

76. Locander, W. B., F. Hamilton, D. Ladik, and J. Stewart. 2002. Developing a leadership-rich culture: The missing link to creating a market-focused organization. *Journal of Market-Focused Management* 5: 149–63.

77. Catalyst. 2008. 2008 census of women corporate officers and top earners of the Fortune 500. *Catalyst Research Report.* Retrieved August 20, 2009, from http://www.catalyst.org/file/266/cote_ca_09.pdf.

78. Catalyst. 2001. *2001 Catalyst census of women board directors.* Retrieved August 20, 2009, from http://www.catalyst.org/file/77/2001%20catalyst%20wbd.pdf; Catalyst. 2012. 2011 Catalyst census: Fortune 500 women board directors. Retrieved August 16, 2012, from http://www.catalyst.org/file/533/2011_fortune_500_census_wbd.pdf.

79. Toossi, Mitra. 2007. Employment outlook: 2006–2016. Labor force projections to 2016: More workers in their golden years. *Monthly Labor Review* (November). Washington, DC: Bureau of Labor Statistics. Retrieved August 20, 2009, from http://www.bls.gov/opub/mlr/2007/11/art3full.pdf.

80. Judy, Richard W., and Carol D'Amico. 1997. *Workforce 2020: Work and workers in the twenty-first century.* Indianapolis, IN: Hudson Institute.

81. Ibid.

82. Ely, R. J., and D. A. Thomas. 2001. Cultural diversity at work: The effects of diversity perspectives on work group processes and outcomes. *Administrative Science Quarterly* 46: 229–73.

83. Diversity Inc. Why is Johnson & Johnson number one? Retrieved July 29, 2009, from http://www.diversityinc.com/public/5449.cfm; Diversity Inc. Announcing the ninth annual Diversity Inc. Top 50 companies for diversity. Retrieved July 29, 2009, from http://www.diversityinc.com/public/5530.cfm.

84. The DiversityInc Top 50 Companies for Diversity 2012. No. 11: Johnson & Johnson. Retrieved May 29, 2012, from http://diversityinc.com/2012-diversityinc-top-50/johnson-johnson/.

85. Diversity Inc., Announcing the ninth annual Diversity Inc. Top 50 companies for diversity.

86. Posner, B., J. Kouzes, and W. Schmidt. 1985. Shared values make a difference: An empirical test of corporate culture. *Human Resource Management* 24: 527–38.

87. Singhapakdi, Anusorn, and Scott J. Vitell. 2007. Institutionalization of ethics and its consequences: A survey of marketing professionals. *Journal of the Academy of Marketing Science* 35(2): 284–94.

88. Vitell, S. J., and A. Singhapakdi. 2008. The role of ethics institutionalization in influencing organizational commitment, job satisfaction, and esprit de corps. *Journal of Business Ethics* 81: 343–53.

89. Ramos, Luis. 2009. Outside-the-box ethics. *Leadership Excellence* 26: 19.

90. Ibid.

91. Tse, Tomoeh M. 2009. Judge surprises Madoff deputy by denying bail. *Washington Post* (August 13). Retrieved August 13, 2009, from http://www.washingtonpost.com/wp-dyn/content/article/2009/08/12/AR2009081202970.html?hpid=sec-business.

92. Brown, S. L., and K. M. Eisenhardt. 1998. *Competing on the edge: Strategy as structured chaos.* Boston: Harvard Business School Press; O'Reilly, C. A., J. Chatman, and D. F. Caldwell. 1991. People and organizational culture: A profile comparison approach to assessing person-organization fit. *Academy of Management Journal* 14: 487–516; Scott, S. G., and R. A. Bruce. 1994. Determinants of innovative behavior: A path model of individual innovation in the workplace. *Academy of Management Journal* 37: 580–607; Van de Ven, A., E. D. Polley, R. Garud, and S. Venkataraman. 1999. *The innovation journey.* New York: Oxford University Press.

93. Woodman, R. W., J. E. Sawyer, and R. W. Griffin. 1993. Toward a theory of organizational creativity. *Academy of Management Review* 18: 293–321.

94. Chandler, G. N., C. Keller, and D. W. Lyon. 2000. Unraveling the determinants and consequences of an innovative-supportive organizational culture. *Entrepreneurship Theory and Practice* (Fall): 59–76.

95. Sevier, Laura. 2009. Cleaner Planet Plan: A green wash or greenwash? *The Ecologist* (August 18). Retrieved August 20, 2009, from http://www .theecologist.org/blogs_and_comments/commentators/other_comments/ 305015/cleaner_planet_plan_a_green_wash_or_greenwash.html.

96. Global 100. 2009. The Global 100 most sustainable corporations in the world. Retrieved August 20, 2009, from http://www.global100.org.

97. Campaign for Real Beauty. 2006. *Evolution: A Dove film*. Retrieved August 20, 2009, from http://www.dove.us/#/features/videos/default .aspx[cp-documentid=7049579].

98. Boyatzis, Richard, and Annie McKee. 2005 *Resonant leadership: Sustaining yourself and connecting with others through mindfulness, hope, and compassion.* Boston: Harvard Business School Press.

99. Pawar, B. S. 2008. Two approaches to workplace spirituality facilitation: A comparison and implications. *Leadership and Organization Development Journal* 29: 544–67; Giacalone, R. A., and C. L. Jurkiewicz, eds. 2003. *Handbook of workplace spirituality and organizational performance.* New York: M. E. Sharpe.

100. Google search results for "workplace spirituality," August 13, 2009.

101. Pawar, Two approaches to workplace spirituality facilitation; Corner, P. D. 2009. Workplace spirituality and business ethics. *Journal of Business Ethics* 85: 377–89.

102. Duchon, Dennis, and Donde A. Plowman. 2005. Nurturing spirit at work: Impact on work unit performance. *Leadership Quarterly* 16: 807–33.

103. Driscoll, Cathy, and Margaret McKee. 2007. Restoring a culture of ethical and spiritual values: A role for leader storytelling. *Journal of Business Ethics* 73: 205–17; Corner, Workplace spirituality and business ethics.

104. Konz, Gregory N. P., and Francis X. Ryan. 1999. Maintaining an organizational spirituality: No easy task. *Journal of Organizational Change Management* 12(3): 200–10.

105. Fry, Louis W. 2003. Toward a theory of spiritual leadership. *Leadership Quarterly* 14: 693–727.

106. U.S. Equal Employment Opportunity Commission. 2002. Facts about sexual harassment (June 27). Retrieved April 6, 2010, from http://www .eeoc.gov/facts/fs-sex.html.

107. Ibid.

108. Ibid.

109. Dobbin, Frank, and Erin L. Kelly. 2007. How to stop harassment: Professional construction of legal compliance in organizations. *American Journal of Sociology* 112(4): 1203–1243.

110. National Women's Law Center. Sexual harassment in the workplace. Retrieved April 17, 2010, from http://www.nwlc.org/details .cfm?id=459&section=employment; U.S. Equal Employment Opportunity Commission. 2009. Sexual harassment charges: EEOC and FEPAs combined: FY 1997–FY 2008. Retrieved April 17, 2010, from http:// www.eeoc.gov/eeoc/statistics/enforcement/sexual_harassment.cfm; Texas Association Against Sexual Assault. 2008. Confronting sexual harassment brochure (October 1). Retrieved April 6, 2010, from http:// www.taasa.org/member/pdfs/csh-eng.pdf.

111. U.S. Equal Employment Opportunity Commission. Sexual Harassment Charges.

112. U.S. Metric Systems Correction Board. 1994. Sexual harassment in the federal workplace: Trends, progress, continuing challenges. Retrieved April 6, 2010, from http://www.mspb.gov/netsearch/viewdocs.aspx?doc number=253661&version=253948&application=ACROBAT.

113. Faley, Robert H., Deborah E. Knapp, Gary A. Kustis, Cathy L. Z. Dubois, Jill Young, and Brian Polin. 2006. Estimating the organizational costs of same-sex sexual harassment: The case of the U.S. Army. *International Journal of Intercultural Relations* 30(5): 557–77.

114. MSNBC. 2008. Pentagon releases sexual harassment data (March 14). Retrieved May 30, 2012, from http://www.msnbc.msn.com/id/23636487/ ns/us_news-military/t/pentagon-releases-sexual-harassment-data/.

115. Goleman et al., *Primal leadership*.

116. Boyatzis, Richard E. 1998. *Thematic analysis: Transforming qualitative information*. Thousand Oaks, CA: Sage.

117. Keyton, Joann. 2005. *Communication and organizational culture*. Thousand Oaks, CA: Sage.

118. Goleman, Daniel. 2006. *Social intelligence: The new science of human relationships*. New York: Bantam Books.

119. Earley, P. Christopher, and Elaine Masakowski. 2004. Cultural intelligence. *Harvard Business Review* (October): 139.

120. Earley, P. Christopher, and Ang Soon. 2003. *Cultural intelligence: Individual interactions across cultures*. Palo Alto, CA: Stanford University Press.

121. Brislin, Richard, Reginald Worthley, and Brent Macnab. 2006. Cultural intelligence: Understanding behaviors that serve people's goals. *Group and Organization Management* 31(1): 40–55.

122. Goleman et al., *Primal leadership*.

123. Ibid., 218–19.

124. Ibid., 219.

125. Ibid., 219–20.

126. Kolodinsky, Robert, Robert Giacalone, and Carole Jurkiewicz. 2008. Workplace Values and Outcomes: Exploring Personal, Organizational, and Interactive Workplace Spirituality. Journal of Business Ethics 81(2): 465-80.

127. Schein, Edgar H. 2009. *The Corporate Culture Survival Guide*. New and rev. ed. San Francisco, CA: Jossey-Bass.

128. Hsieh, Tony. 2010. *Delivering Happiness: A Path to Profits, Passion, and Purpose*, 1st ed. New York: Business Plus.

129. Smith, G. 2012. Why I Am Leaving Goldman Sachs. *New York Times* (March 14). Retrieved November 29, 2012, from http://www.nytimes .com/2012/03/14/opinion/why-i-am-leaving-goldman-sachs.html? pagewanted=all.

130. Smith, Greg. 2012. Why I Am Leaving Goldman Sachs. *The New York Times* (March 14). Retrieved electronically August 16, 2012, from http:// www.nytimes.com/2012/03/14/opinion/why-i-am-leaving- goldman-sachs.html?_r=2&pagewanted=all.

131. Martin, Courtney E., and John Cary. 2012. Greg Smith to Goldman Sachs: A New Era in Wall Street Ethics. *Christian Science Monitor*, (March 20). Retrieved August 16, 2012, from http://www.csmonitor .com/Commentary/Opinion/2012/0320/Greg-Smith-to-Goldman- Sachs-A-new-era-in-Wall-Street-ethics.

Chapter 14

1. Srinivasan, T. N. *Globalization: Is It Good or Bad?* Palo Alto, CA: Stanford Institute for Economic Policy Research, 2002.

2. Samuelson, Robert. 2008. A baffling global economy. *Washington Post* (July 16). Retrieved April 13, 2010, from http://www.washingtonpost .com/wp-dyn/content/article/2008/07/15/AR2008071502428.html; Parker, J. 2009. Burgeoning Bourgeoisie. *The Economist* (February 12), Retrieved May 1, 2012, from http://www.economist.com/node/ 13063298; Dobbs, Richard, Jeremy Oppenheim, and Fraser Thompson. 2012. Mobilizing for a Resource Revolution. (Cover Story). *McKinsey Quarterly*, no. 1 (2012): 28–42.

3. BBC News. 2001. Globalisation: Good or bad? *Talking Point* (July 25). Retrieved February 8, 2010, from http://news.bbc.co.uk/2/hi/ talking_point/1444930.stm.

4. Friedman, Thomas L. 2000. *The Lexus and the olive tree*. New York: Farrar, Straus and Giroux.

5. Della Porta, Donatella. 2006. *The global justice movement: Cross-national and transnational perspectives*. New York: Paradigm; Juris, Jeffrey S. 2008. *Networking futures: The movements against corporate globalization*. Durham, NC: Duke University Press.

6. Stiglitz, Joseph. 2004. Economic, social, and cultural rights: The right to food. Report prepared for the United Nations Commission on Human Rights. Retrieved February 8, 2010, from http://www.unhchr.ch/Huridocda/ Huridoca.nsf/0/34441bf9efe3a9e3c1256e6300510e24/$FILE/G0410777.pdf.

7. Stiglitz, Joseph, and Andrew Charlton. 2005. *Fair trade for all: How trade can promote development*. New York: Oxford University Press.

8. Zeleny, Milan. 2012. High Technology and Barriers to Innovation: From Globalization to Relocalization. *International Journal of Information Technology & Decision Making* 11(2): 441-56.

9. Retrieved August 21, 2012, from http://smallbusinesssaturday.com/.

10. Friedman, Thomas L. 2006. *The world is flat*, 422. New York: Farrar, Straus, and Giroux.

11. Reich, Robert. 2007. *Supercapitalism*, 7. Knopf: New York.

12. Hoovers. McDonald's Corporation. Retrieved April 19, 2012, from http://proxy.library.upenn.edu:2825/H/company360/overview.html? companyId=10974000000000.

13. Nathan, Andrew J., and Robert S. Ross. 1997. *The Great Wall and the empty fortress: China's search for security*, 13. New York: W. W. Norton.

14. U.S. Department of Defense. Military casualty information. Retrieved April 27, 2010, from http://siadapp.dmdc.osd.mil/personnel/CASUALTY/ vietnam.pdf.

15. Friedman, *The world is flat*, 53.

16. ActionForex.com. 2012. 1973 Oil Crisis. Retrieved April 25, 2012, from http://www.actionforex.com/articles-library/financial-glossary/1973-oil-crisis-20041204320/.

17. U.S. Department of State Office of the Historian. Milestones: 1969–1976: OPEC Oil Embargo, 1973–1974. Retrieved April 25, 2012, from http://history.state.gov/milestones/1969-1976/OPEC.

18. CIA World Factbook. 2012. Brunei. Retrieved June 4, 2012, from https://www.cia.gov/library/publications/the-world-factbook/geos/bx.html; U.S. Department of State. 2012. Brunei. Retrieved June 4, 2012, from http://www.state.gov/r/pa/ei/bgn/2700.htm.

19. Khouri, Rami G. 2006. In Khartoum, the Refrain of Arab Failure. *The Daily Star* (March 31). Retrieved April 25, 2012, from http://yaleglobal.yale.edu/content/khartoum-refrain-arab-failure

20. Ibid.

21. Nazir, Sameena, and Leigh Tomppert. 2004. *Women's Rights in the Middle East and North Africa: Citizenship and Justice*. Lanham, MD: Rowman & Littlefield; Kelly, Sanja, and Julia Breslin. 2010. *Women's Rights in the Middle East and North Africa: Progress Amid Resistance*, 2010 ed. New York: Publisher.

22. Gardner, Robert, Peter Ferdinand, and Stephanie Lawson. 2009. Box 17.4: The rise of Al Qaeda and Islamic militancy, in *Introduction to politics*. New York: Oxford University Press. Retrieved April 25, 2012, from http://www.oup.com/uk/orc/bin/9780199231331/01student/case1/174alqaeda/.

23. Abbas, M. 2011. Times names Bouazizi person of 2011. Reuters (it.) (December 28). Retrieved from http://uk.reuters.com/article/2011/12/28/uk-times-bouazizi-idUKTRE7BR0CE20111228.

24. Blight, G., S. Pulham, et al. 2012. Arab Spring: An interactive time-line of Middle East protests. *The Guardian* US (January 5). Retrieved February 21, 2012, from http://www.guardian.co.uk/world/interactive/2011/mar/22/middle-east-protest-interactive-timeline.

25. Syrian revolution comes to Damascus as rebels openly patrol the streets. February 13, 2012. *The Telegraph*. Retrieved February 21, 2012, from http://www.telegraph.co.uk/news/worldnews/middleeast/syria/9080666/Syrian-revolution-comes-to-Damascus-as-rebels-openly-patrol-the-streets.html.

26. Syrian regime in demolition mode. November 6, 2012. *The Nation*. Retrieved November 6, 2012, from http://www.nation.com.pk/pakistan-news-newspaper-daily-english-online/international/06-Nov-2012/syrian-regime-in-demolition-mode

27. Weisert, Drake. 2001. Coca-Cola in China: Quenching the thirst of a billion. *The China Business Review*, July–August. Retrieved June 4, 2012, from https://www.chinabusinessreview.com/public/0107/weisert.html.

28. "The World Trade Organization...". edited by The World Trade Organization, 8. Geneva, Switzerland. Retrieved November 9, 2008, from http://www.wto.org/english/res_e/doload_e/inbr_e.pdf

29. World Trade Organization. World trade report 2008. Retrieved December 29, 2009, from http://www.wto.org/english/res_e/booksp_e/anpre_e/wtr08-2b_e.pdr.

30. Cass, Deborah Z. 2005. *The constitutionalization of the World Trade Organization: legitimacy, democracy, and community in the international trading system*, p. 266. International economic law series. Oxford University Press: New York.

31. BBC News. 2012. Profile: G8. Retrieved June 14, 2012, from http://news.bbc.co.uk/2/hi/americas/country_profiles/3777557.stm.

32. Giles, Chris. 2009. G20 yet to deliver on early promise. *Financial Times* (November 8). Retrieved April 13, 2010, from http://www.ft.com/cms/s/8e834f02-cc63-11de-8e30-00144feabdc0,Authorised=false.html?_i_location=http%3A%2F%2Fwww.ft.com%2Fcms%2Fs%2F0%2F8e834f02-cc63-11de-8e30-00144feabdc0.html&_i_referer=http%3A%2F%2Fsearch.ft.com%2Fsearch%3FqueryText%3DG20%2BYet%2Bto%2BDeliver%2Bon%2BEarly%2BPromise%26aje%3Dtrue%26dse%3D%26dsz%3D%26x%3D9%26y%3D7.

33. World Economic Forum, Frequently asked questions; World Economic Forum. What is the role of business in advancing economic development and social progress? Retrieved December 18, 2009, from weforum.org/en/initiatives/index.htm.

34. About ECOSOC. Retrieved November 6, 2012, from http://www.un.org/en/ecosoc/about/index.shtml

35. Ruggerio, Renato. October 16, 1995. Growing complexity in international economic relations demands broadening and deepening of multilateral trading system. Paul-Henri Spaack Lecture, Harvard University. Retrieved December 29, 2009, from http://www.wto.org/english/news_e/pres95_e/pr025_e.htm.

36. Gale, Colin, and Jasbir Kaur. 2002. *The textile book*. New York: Berg.

37. Business.gov. Trade agreements. Retrieved December 10, 2009, from http://www.business.gov/expand/import-export/trade-agreements.

38. Business.gov. Import/export. Retrieved December 10, 2009, from http://www.business.gov/expand/import-export; Business.gov, Trade agreements.

39. Retrieved from CIA World Factbook https://www.cia.gov/library/publications/the-world-factbook/rankorder/2089rank.html?countryName=UnitedStates&countryCode=us&regionCode=noa&rank=118#us.

40. Europe without Frontiers. Retrieved November 6, 2012, from http://europa.eu/about-eu/eu-history/1990-1999/index_en.htm.

41. Clark, Cynthia, and Elaine Turney. 2003. *Encyclopedia of tariffs and trade in U.S. history*, 280. Westport, CT: Greenwood Press; Teslick, Lee Hudson. 2009. NAFTA's economic impact. *Council on Foreign Relations* (July 7). Retrieved April 13, 2010, from http://www.cfr.org/publication/15790/#p4.

42. CAFTA Intelligence Center. Home page. Retrieved May 27, 2010, from http://www.caftaintelligencecenter.com/; World Trade Organization. DOHA development agenda. Retrieved April 13, 2010, from http://tcbdb.wto.org/trta_project.aspx?prjCode=113-0439-03-B&benHostId=116.

43. Goodman, Joshua. 2007. South American presidents agree to form UNASUR bloc. *Bloomberg.com* (May 23). Retrieved April 13, 2010, from http://www.bloomberg.com/apps/news?pid=20601087&sid=abWOMOeJUK7Y&refer=home.

44. Association of Southeast Asian Nations. Overview. Retrieved April 13, 2010, from http://www.aseansec.org/about_ASEAN.html; Association of Southeast Asian Nations. 2007. 13th ASEAN summit press statement (November 20). Retrieved April 13, 2010, from http://app.mti.gov.sg/data/article/11702/doc/AEC%20BLUEPRINTPressRelease%28final%29%28formatted%29.pdf.

45. Asia-Pacific Economic Cooperation. Achievements and benefits. Retrieved April 13, 2010, from http://www.apec.org/apec/about_apec/achievements_and_benefits.html.

46. European Union. Countries. Retrieved November 6, 2012, from http://europa.eu/about-eu/countries/index_en.htm.

47. Decision-Making in the European Union. Retrieved November 6, 2012, from http://europa.eu/about-eu/basic-information/decision-making/index_en.htm.

48. CIA World Factbook: World. Retrieved. November 6, 2012, from https://www.cia.gov/library/publications/the-world-factbook/geos/ee.html

49. Samuelson, A baffling global economy.

50. Major foreign holders of treasury securities. Retrieved May 2, 2012, from http://www.treasury.gov/resource-center/data-chart-center/tic/Documents/mfh.txt.

51. China Says Ready to Help Solve EU Debt Crisis. February 14, 2012. *EUBusiness* Retrieved May 2, 2012, from http://www.eubusiness.com/news-eu/china-finance-debt.f6g.

52. The History of the European Union. Retrieved (date retrieved), from http://europa.eu/about-eu/eu-history/index_en.htm.

53. CIA World Factbook: The European Union. Retrieved (date retrieved), from https://www.cia.gov/library/publications/the-world-factbook/geos/ee.html.

54. Data gathered from Europa: Gateway to the European Union, accessed at http://europa.eu/index_en.htm

55. Riot rage: Athens protesters throw firebombs, police shoot tear gas. September 26, 2012. *RT*. Retrieved November 6, 2012, from http://rt.com/news/greece-strike-demonstration-athens-011/.

56. Paris, Costas. 2012. Greece Seen Facing ?30 Billion Shortfall. *Wall Street Journal* (July 27). Retrieved July 27, 2012, from http://online.wsj.com/article/SB10000872396390443931404577552971586204232.html?mod=googlenews_wsj.

57. Global Financial Stability Report: The Quest for Lasting Stability. Washington, DC, 2012. Retrieved July 27, 2012, from http://www.imf.org/External/Pubs/FT/GFSR/2012/01/pdf/text.pdf.

58. Ibid.

59. New Setbacks, Further Policy Action Needed. *World Economic Outlook Update: International Monetary Fund, 2012*. Retrieved July 27, 2012, from http://www.imf.org/external/pubs/ft/weo/2012/update/02/pdf/0712.pdf.

60. Panckhurst, Paul. 2012. China Pledges Sustained Euro Holdings with Plan to Invest in Bailout Funds. *Bloomberg News* (February 15), Retrieved

May 2, 2012, from http://www.bloomberg.com/news/2012-02-14/eu-s-van-rompuy-welcomes-china-s-interest-in-aiding-europe.html.

61. Hazlitt, Henry, and Steve Forbes. *Economics in One Lesson*, 50th anniversary ed. Benicia: Laissez Faire Books, 1996; Trahan, Francois, and Katherine Krantz. *The Era of Uncertainty: Global Investment Strategies for Inflation, Deflation, and the Middle Ground.* Hoboken, N.J.: J. Wiley, 2011.

62. Reuer, Jeffrey J., Africa Ariño, and Antoni Valverde. The perfect "pre-nup" to strategic alliances: A guide to contracts. *Association of Strategic Alliance Professionals best practice bulletins.* Retrieved December 16, 2009, from http://www.strategic-alliances.org/membership/memberresources/bestpracticebulletin.

63. Beshel, Barbara. An introduction to franchising. *International Franchise Association Educational Foundation.* Retrieved December 15, 2009, from http://franchise.org/uploadedFiles/Franchise_Industry/Resources/Education_Foundation/Intro%20to%20Franchising%20Student%20Guide.pdf.

64. Investor Glossary. Wholly-owned subsidiary. Retrieved December 16, 2009, from http://www.investorglossary.com/wholly-owned-subsidiary.htm.

65. Brown, Erika. 2004. The global startup. *Forbes.com* (November). Retrieved December 16, 2009, from http://www.forbes.com/forbes/2004/1129/150.html; Presutti, Manuela, Alberto Onetti, and Vincenza Odorici. Serial entrepreneurship and born-global new ventures: A case study. *Biblioteca.net.* Retrieved December 16, 2009, from http://amsacta.cib.unibo.it/2477/1/Serialentrepreneurshipbornglobal.pdf.

66. Huntington, S. P. 1993. The clash of civilizations? *Foreign Affairs* 72(3): 22–49.

67. Pieterse, J. N. 2009. *Globalization and culture: Global mélange.* Lanham, MD: Rowman and Littlefield Publishers.

68. Ritzer, G. 1993. *The McDonaldization of society: An investigation into the changing character of contemporary social life.* Thousand Oaks, CA: Pine Forest Press.

69. Karp, Jonathan. 1996. Food for Politics. *Far Eastern Economic Review* 159(43): 72.

70. Pieterse, *Globalization and culture.*

71. Export.gov. FAQ: Export basics. Retrieved December 10, 2009, from http://www.export.gov/faq/eg_main_017487.asp.

72. Spencer, Earl P. 1995. EuroDisney: What happened? What's next? *Journal of International Marketing* 3(3). Retrieved January 7, 2010, from http://www.jstor.org/pss/25048611.

73. Blalock, Marty. 2005. Listen up: Why good communication is good business. *Wisconsin Business Alumni Update* (December). Retrieved January 7, 2010, from http://www.bus.wisc.edu/update/winter05/business_communication.asp; Recklies, Dagmar. EuroDisney—Case study I. *Themanager.org.* Retrieved January 7, 2010, from http://themanager.org/ME/Disney_1.htm.

74. Liddle, Alan. 1992. Guests walk a not-so-fine line at EuroDisney's attractions. *Nation's Restaurant News* (November 23). Retrieved January 7, 2010, from http://findarticles.com/p/articles/mi_m3190/is_n47_v26/ai_12941855/?tag=content;col1.

75. Less a Sleeping Beauty, more a rude awakening at EuroDisney. 2004 *The Independent* (August 8). Retrieved January 7, 2010, from http://www.independent.co.uk/news/business/analysis-and-feature/less-a-sleeping-beauty-more-a-rude-awakening-at-euro-disney-555756.html; Blalock, Listen up.

76. *The Independent,* Less a Sleeping Beauty, more a rude awakening at EuroDisney.

77. Euro Disney S.C.A. Reports 2011 Results. *PR Newswire.* In *BC-Euro-Disney-SCA:* Y, 2011.

78. Neate, Rupert, Christian Sylt, and Caroline Reid. 2012. Disneyland Paris Celebrates 20th Birthday ?1.9bn in Debt. *The Guardian* (April 11). Retrieved June 4, 2012, from http://www.guardian.co.uk/world/2012/apr/11/disneyland-paris-20th-birthday-debt.

79. Adamson, Thomas. Disneyland Paris Fetes 20th after Rocky Childhood. April 01. Retrieved June 4, 2012, from http://abclocal.go.com/wpvi/story?section=news/national_world&id=8603519.

80. Vodafone Group Plc Annual Report for the Year Ended 31 March 2011. 156: Vodafone, 2012; Interim Management Statement for the Quarter Ended 31 December 2011. 10: Vodafone, 2012.

81. Vodafone. About Vodafone. Retrieved April 13, 2010, from http://www.vodafone.com/start/about_vodafone.html.

82. Sourcingmag.com. Outsourcing—What is outsourcing? Retrieved December 17, 2009, from http://www.sourcingmag.com/content/what_is_outsourcing.asp.

83. Morgan, Robert. 2011. Trends in Outsourcing Deals for 2012. *Computer Weekly* 8; Infosys Dives on Soft Outlook. Date. *Investors Business Daily.* volume and issue: A01.

84. Stanley, David. Tuna Canneries. *Publication Date.* Retrieved January 31, 2010, from http://www.americansamoa.southpacific.org/americansamoa/canneries.html.

85. Furchtgott-Roth, Diana. 2009. Thousands lost jobs due to higher federal minimum wage. *Reuters.* (May 14). Retrieved January 31, 2010, from http://blogs.reuters.com/great-debate/2009/05/14/thousands-lose-jobs-due-to-higher-federal-minimum-wage/.

86. American Samoa grateful for minimum wage increase delaying bill. October 3, 2010. *Radio New Zealand International.* Retrieved May 2, 2012, from http://www.rnzi.com/pages/news.php?op=read&id=56208.

87. American Samoa and Commonwealth of the Northern Marianas Islands: Employment, Earnings, and Status of Key Industries since Minimum Wage Increases Began, in *Report to Congressional Committees,* 142. Washington, DC: United States Government Accountability Office, 2011.

88. Gurufocus.com. January 13, 2013. Seven Companies with Unrivaled Economies of Scale. Retrieved July 30, 2012, from http://www.gurufocus.com/news/158280/7-companies-with-unrivaled-economies-of-scale.

89. The NIST Definition of Cloud Computing. *National Institute of Science and Technology.* Retrieved 24 July 2012, from http://csrc.nist.gov/publications/nistpubs/800-145/SP800-145.pdf; UPS Fact Sheet. Publishing Organization. Retrieved November 12, 2012, from http://pressroom.ups.com/Fact+Sheets/UPS+Fact+Sheet.

90. Knorr, Eric, and Galen Gruman. What Cloud Computing Really Means. *InfoWorld.* Retrieved July 24, 2012, from http://www.infoworld.com/d/cloud-computing/what-cloud-computing-really-means-031; Mell, Peter, and Timothy Grance. The Nist Definition of Cloud Computing. 7 pages. Gaithersburg, MD: National Institute of Standards and Technology, 2011.

91. Freedman, Jennifer M. 2012. Arab Spring Unrest Sent 2011 Tourism Down 30% in Egypt, Tunisia. *Bloomberg* (March 6). Retrieved November 6, 2012, from http://www.bloomberg.com/news/2012-03-06/arab-spring-unrest-sent-2011-tourism-down-30-in-egypt-tunisia.html; Direct Investment in Egypt Slumps in First Quarter 2011. Date. *AhramOnline*: Al-Ahram Establishment. Retrieved, from URL. Retrieved May 20, 2012, from http://english.ahram.org.eg/NewsContent/3/12/17525/Business/Economy/Direct-investment-in-Egypt-slumps-in-first-quarter.aspx

92. de Soto, Hernando. 2011. Egypt's Economic Apartheid. *Wall Street Journal* - Eastern Edition 257(27): A15.

93. de Soto, Hernando. *The mystery of capital: Why capitalism triumphs in the West and fails everywhere else.* New York: Basic Books, 2000.

94. Chubb, Daniel. 2010. Honda recall joined by Peugeot: Cars made with Toyota. *Product Reviews News.* (January 10). Retrieved February 1, 2010, from http://www.product-reviews.net/2010/01/31/honda-recall-joined-by-peugeot-cars-made-with-toyota/.

95. Woodyard, C. 2010. Pontiac Vibe: Overlooked step-sister in Toyota recall? *USA Today* (February 1). Retrieved February 1, 2010, from http://content.usatoday.com/communities/driveon/post/2010/02/pontiac-vibe-overlooked-step-sister-intoyota-recall/1?loc=interstitialskip.

96. U.S. Congressional Budget Office. 2004. What accounts for the decline in manufacturing employment? Retrieved February 7, 2010, from http://www.cbo.gov/ftpdocs/50xx/doc5078/02-18-ManufacturingEmployment.pdf.

97. Manufacturing: NAICS 31–33. *Bureau of Labor Statistics,* Retrieved May 3, 2012, from http://www.bls.gov/iag/tgs/iag31-33.htm.

98. Aspray, W., F. Mayadas, and M. Y. Vardi. 2006. *Globalization and offshoring of software: A report of the ACM Job Migration Task Force.* New York: Association for Computing Machinery.

99. Istrate, Emilia, Jonathan Rothwell, and Bruce Katz. *Export Nation: How U.S. Metros Lead U.S. Growth and Boost Competitiveness.* Washington, DC: Brookings Institution, 2010.

100. http://www.eaton.com/Eaton/index.htm accessed May 29, 2012.

101. Top 100 Global Innovators. 20 pp: ThomsonReuters, 2011. Retrieved June 5, 2012, from http://top100innovators.com/; Baldinger, Michael, and Markus Nöthiger. 2011. The Sustainability Yearbook 2011. 118 pp: Sustainable Asset Management/PriceWaterhouseCoopers. Retrieved June 5, 2012, from http://www.sam-group.com/images/SAM_Yearbook_2011_tcm794-290391.pdf.

102. Elliott, Dominic. 2009. Fundamentals drive the "BRIC" rebound. *Wall Street Journal* (July 27). Retrieved April 13, 2010, from http://online.wsj.com/article/SB124864236547882043.html.

103. Gross Domestic Product 2010. *World Bank Data*. Retrieved May 3, 2012, from http://siteresources.worldbank.org/DATASTATISTICS/Resources/GDP.pdf.

104. Retrieved May 3, 2012, from https://www.cia.gov/library/publications/the-world-factbook/rankorder/rawdata_2119.txt.

105. Retrieved May 3, 2012, from http://siteresources.worldbank.org/DATASTATISTICS/Resources/GDP.pdf.

106. Retrieved May 3, 2012, from https://www.cia.gov/library/publications/the-world-factbook/rankorder/rawdata_2001.txt.

107. Retrieved May 3, 2012, from https://www.cia.gov/library/publications/the-world-factbook/rankorder/rawdata_2004.txt.

108. Retrieved May 3, 2012, from https://www.cia.gov/library/publications/the-world-factbook/rankorder/rawdata_2054.txt.

109. Retrieved May 3, 2012, from https://www.cia.gov/library/publications/the-world-factbook/rankorder/rawdata_2066.txt.

110. Retrieved May 3, 2012, from https://www.cia.gov/library/publications/the-world-factbook/rankorder/rawdata_2102.txt.

111. Dataset retrieved May 3, 2012, from International Telecommunications Union: www.itu.int/ITU-D/ict/statistics/material/.../EstimatedInternetUsers00-09.xls.

112. Retrieved May 3, 2012, from http://data.un.org/Data.aspx?d=SOWC&f=inID%3A74.

113. https://www.cia.gov/library/publications/the-world-factbook/rankorder/rawdata_2087.txt.

114. Retrieved May 3, 2012, from https://www.cia.gov/library/publications/the-world-factbook/rankorder/rawdata_2078.txt.

115. Retrieved May 3, 2012, from https://www.cia.gov/library/publications/the-world-factbook/rankorder/rawdata_2186.txt.

116. Retrieved May 3, 2012, from https://www.cia.gov/library/publications/the-world-factbook/rankorder/rawdata_2079.txt.

117. Watkins, Thayer. The economic history of Brazil: Booms and busts of Brazilian history. *San Jose State University Department of Economics*. Retrieved January 27, 2010, from http://www.sjsu.edu/faculty/watkins/brazil1.htm.

118. Fausto, Boris. 1999. *A Concise History of Brazil*. New York: Cambridge University Press.

119. History World. The history of Brazil. Retrieved January 27, 2010, from http://www.historyworld.net/wrldhis/PlainTextHistories.asp?groupid=891&HistoryID=aa88.

120. Ibid. April 4, 2000. Brazilian economic performance since 1500: A comparative view. Paper presented at XIII Forum de Liberdade. Retrieved January 27, 2010, from http://www.ggdc.net/maddison/ARTICLES/Brazil_500.pdf.

121. Ibid; Watkins, Thayer. The economic system of corporatism. *San Jose State University Department of Economics*. Retrieved January 28, 2010, from http://www.sjsu.edu/faculty/watkins/corporatism.htm.

122. Fausto, Boris. *A Concise History of Brazil*.

123. Vignogna, Mary E. 2000. The Brazilian economic crisis. *Augusta State University*. Retrieved January 27, 2010, from http://www.aug.edu/pkp/2000/conf-2000-vignogna.PDF; History World, The history of Brazil.

124. Brazilian economic performance since 1500.

125. U.S. Department of State. 2009. Background note: Brazil. Retrieved January 29, 2010, from http://www.state.gov/r/pa/ei/bgn/35640.htm.

126. Federal Research Division, U.S. Library of Congress. 1997. *A country study: Brazil*. Retrieved January 29, 2010, from http://lcweb2.loc.gov/frd/cs/brtoc.html.

127. U.S. Department of State, Background note: Brazil.

128. Schemo, Diana Jean. 1999. Tense times on front line of Brazil's battle on hyperinflation. *New York Times* (January 20). Retrieved January 29, 2010, from http://www.nytimes.com/1999/01/20/world/tense-times-on-front-line-of-brazil-s-battle-on-hyperinflation-empty-shops.html?pagewanted=1; Hornbeck, J. F., 2006. Brazilian trade policy and the United States. *CRS report for Congress* (February 3). Retrieved January 29, 2010, from http://www.nationallawcenter.org/assets/crs/RL33258.pdf; Joffe-Walt, Chana. 2010. How Fake Money Saved Brazil. *Planet Money*: National Public Radio.

129. Schemo, Tense times on front line.

130. Roett, Riordan. 2011. *The New Brazil*. Washington, D.C.: The Brookings Institution Press.

131. Columbia Electronic Encyclopedia. 2007. Brazil: History. Retrieved January 29, 2010, from http://www.infoplease.com/ce6/world/A0857011.html.

132. U.S. Department of State, Background note: Brazil.

133. Ibid.

134. Welch, John H. 2012. Brazil under Dilma: Forward, backward, or status quo? *Brazil Under Rousseff Task Force* (January 13). University of Miami Center for Hemispheric Policy. Retrieved April 3, 2012, from https://www6.miami.edu/hemispheric-policy/Task_Force_Papers/Welch-BrazilUnderDilma-FINAL.pdf.

135. Ibid; U.S. Department of State, Background note: Brazil; Trading Economics: Brazil Inflation Rate. Retrieved November 12, 2012, from http://www.tradingeconomics.com/brazil/inflation-cpi.

136. Welch, John H. Brazil under Dilma; U.S. Department of State, Background note: Brazil.

137. Douradina. January 19, 2012. Mário Gazin ensina a criar valores. Retrieved May 4, 2012, from http://www.douradina.pr.gov.br/noticias/ler/6/mario-gazin-ensina-a-criar-valores.html.

138. Roett, Riordan. *The New Brazil*.

139. Downie, Andrew. 2008. Brazil's counterattack on biofuels. *Time* (April 28). Retrieved February 1, 2010, from http://www.time.com/time/world/article/0,8599,1735644,00.html.

140. Clive Cookson. 2012. A Tank of Sugar: How Brazil Runs on Biofuel. *FT Magazine* (April 28). Retrieved May 4, 2012, from http://www.ft.com/intl/cms/s/2/6d4ea098-8e67-11e1-b9ae-00144feab49a.html#axzz1tuPMFNfS.

141. Execbrazil.com Mining Sector Overview: Brazil. Retrieved November 12, 2012, from http://execbrazil.com/miningsectoroverview.

142. Clendenning, Alan. 2007. Offshore discovery could make Brazil major oil exporter. *USA Today* via Associated Press (November 9). Retrieved February 1, 2010, from http://www.usatoday.com/money/industries/energy/2007-11-09-brazil-oil_N.htm.

143. U.S. Department of State, Background note: Brazil.

144. 2010 Minerals Yearbook: NIOBIUM (COLUMBIUM) AND TANTALUM. USGS. Retrieved November 12, 2012, from http://minerals.usgs.gov/minerals/pubs/commodity/niobium/myb1-2010-niobi.pdf; Tantalum - Raw Materials and Processing. TIC. Accessed November 12, 2012, from http://tanb.org/tantalum.

145. U.S. Department of State, Background note: Brazil.

146. Brookings Institution. July 13, 2009. Brazil in the global crisis: Still a rising economic superpower? Washington, DC. Retrieved April 13, 2010, from http://www.brookings.edu/~/media/Files/events/2009/0713_brazil/20090713_brazil.pdf; U.S. Department of State, Background note: Brazil.

147. Hornbeck, *Brazilian trade policy and the United States*.

148. U.S. Department of State, Background note: Brazil.

149. Brazil Institute. 2009. The evolving configuration of the October 2010 elections. *Woodrow Wilson International Center for Scholars*, 2011. Retrieved February 1, 2010, from http://brazilportal.wordpress.com/2009/09/11/paulo-sotero-on-election-possibilities-in-brazil/.

150. Ibid.

151. Ibid.; Valdes, Constanza. 2006. Brazil emerges as major force in global meat markets. *U.S. Department of Agriculture Amber Waves Magazine* (April). Retrieved February 1, 2010, from http://www.ers.usda.gov/AmberWaves/April06/Findings/Brazil.htm; U.S. Department of Agriculture. December 11, 2009. Countries/products eligible for export to the United States. Retrieved February 1, 2010, from http://www.fsis.usda.gov/pdf/Countries_Products_Eligible_for_Export.pdf.

152. Federal Research Division, U.S. Library of Congress. 1996. *A country study: Russia*. Retrieved May 28, 2010, from http://memory.loc.gov/frd/cs/rutoc.html.

153. Ibid.

154. Ibid.

155. Ibid.

156. Ibid.

157. BBC News. December 31, 1999. Yeltsin's resignation speech. Retrieved April 13, 2010, from http://news.bbc.co.uk/2/hi/world/monitoring/584845.stm.

158. Rutland, Peter. 2005. Putin's economic record. In *Developments in Russian politics*, vol. 6, ed. S. White, Z. Y. Gitelman, and R. Sakwa. Durham, NC: Duke University Press.

159. Gee, Alastair. 2008. Rising anti-Americanism in Russia. *U.S. News and World Report* (January 18). Retrieved January 30, 2010, from http://www.usnews.com/articles/news/world/2008/01/18/rising-anti-americanism-in-russia.html.

160. Knight, Amy. 2008. The truth about Putin and Medvedev. *New York Review of Books* (May 15). Retrieved January 26, 2010, from http://www.nybooks.com/articles/21353.

161. Fishman, Mikhail. 2009. Who's the boss now? *Newsweek* (May 15). Retrieved January 26, 2010, from http://www.newsweek.com/id/197789.

162. Russia: After the Protests. *Business Eastern Europe* 41(10): 1.

163. Economists Doubt Russia's Right to Be in the BRIC Club. *Russia Briefing* (September 13). Retrieved May 4, 2012, from http://russia-briefing.com/news/economists-to-doubt-russias-right-to-be-in-the-bric-club.html/.

164. Meyer, Henry, and Ilya Arkhipov. 2011. Russian 'Petro-Economy' Doesn't Belong among BRICs, Krugman Says. *Bloomberg* (September 9). Retrieved May 4, 2011, from http://www.bloomberg.com/news/2011-09-09/russian-petro-economy-doesn-t-belong-among-brics-krugman-says.html.

165. Beyrle, John. 2009. Russia and America's shared economic future. *Embassy of the United States to Russia.* Retrieved January 30, 2010, from http://moscow.usembassy.gov/beyrlerem042909.html.

166. *CIA World Factbook.* Russia. Retrieved January 28, 2010, from https://www.cia.gov/library/publications/the-world-factbook/geos/rs.html.

167. Ibid; Rapoza, Kenneth. 2011. Russian Law Seeks to Lower Abortion Numbers. *Forbes,* (May 30). Retrieved June 5, 2012, from http://www.forbes.com/sites/kenrapoza/2011/05/30/russian-law-seeks-to-lower-abortionnumbers/; Russia Must Tackle 'Critical' Suicide Rate: Experts. *The Raw Story* (October 20). Retrieved June 5, 2012, from http://www.rawstory.com/rs/2011/10/20/russia-must-tackle-critical-suicide-rate-experts/.

168. Friedman, *The world is flat.*

169. Stelzer, Irwin. 2010. Investments will remain a gamble until rule of law comes to Russia. *Wall Street Journal* (January 4). Retrieved April 13, 2010, from http://online.wsj.com/article/SB10001424052748704152804574627841894245048.html; Pan, Philip. 2008. Financial crisis in Russia raises stakes for Putin. *Washington Post* (September 21). Retrieved January 27, 2010, from http://www.washingtonpost.com/wp-dyn/content/article/2008/09/20/AR2008092001858.html.

170. SandHill.com. February 20, 2006. Best practices: Offshoring and outsourcing. Retrieved April 13, 2010, from http://www.sandhill.com/opinion/daily_blog.php?id=27&post=125.

171. Moser, Evelyn, and Nestmann, Thorsten. August 20, 2007. Russia's Financial Sector: Financial Deepening Will Support Long-Term Growth. *Deutsche Banks Research Report.* Retrieved January 27, 2010, from "http://www.dbresearch.com/PROD/DBR_INTERNET_EN-PROD/PROD0000000000214153.pdf" http://www.dbreasearch.com/PROD/DBR_INTERNET)EN-PROD/PROD0000000000214153.pdf.

172. Mozarjaplata.ru. 2012. 2011. Retrieved June 5, 2012, from http://translate.google.com/translate?hl=en&sl=ru&u=http://www.mojazarplata.ru/main/srednemesjachnaja-nominalnaja-nachislennaja-zarabotnaja-plata/&prev=/search%3Fq%3D.mojazarplata.ru/main/srednemesjachnaja-nominalnaja-nachislennaja%26hl%3Den%26safe%3Doff%26tbo%3Dd%26biw%3D1600%26bih%3D728&sa=X&ei=zD6dUM3-N5DU0gGNjoCgDQ&ved=0CDQQ7gEwAA; Friedman. The World is Flat.

173. Aron, Leon. 2002. Russia reinvents the rule of law. *AEI Russian Outlook* (Spring). Retrieved January 27, 2010, from http://siteresources.worldbank.org/INTLAWJUSTINST/Resources/aronRussiaJudicial-Reform.pdf; Collins, James, and Anton Ivanov. April 3, 2009. Rule of law in Russia. Public dialogue sponsored by the Carnegie Endowment for International Peace. Retrieved January 27, 2010, from http://www.carnegieendowment.org/events/?fa=eventDetail&id=1314; Edwards, Lynda. 2009. Russia claws at the rule of law. *ABA Journal* (July 1). Retrieved January 27, 2010, from http://www.abajournal.com/magazine/article/russia_claws_at_the_rule_of_law/.

174. Cappelli, Peter, Harbir Singh, Jitendra Singh, and Michael Useem. 2010. *The India way: How India's top business leaders are revolutionizing management.* Boston: HBP; Spencer, Signe M., Tharuma Rajah, S.A. Naryayan, Seetharaman Lmohan, and Gaurav Lahiri. 2010. *The Indian CEO: A portrait of excellence.* Los Angeles: Response Business Books from Sage; Thatchenkery, Tojo Joseph, and Keimei Sugiyama. *Making the invisible visible: Understanding leadership contributions of Asian minorities in the workplace.* New York: Palgrave Macmillan, 2011.

175. Columbia Electronic Encyclopedia, 6th ed. Year. India: History. Retrieved (November 30), from http://www.infoplease.com/encyclopedia/world/india-history.html.

176. U.S. Department of State, Background note: India. Accessed November 28, 2012, from http://www.state.gov/r/pa/ei/bgn/3454.htm.

177. *Columbia Electronic Encyclopedia,* India: History.

178. Ibid.

179. United Nations Population Division. 1999. The twenty most populous countries in 1950, 1999, and 2050. Retrieved February 2, 2010, from http://www.un.org/esa/population/pubsarchive/india/20most.htm; *Columbia Electronic Encyclopedia,* India: History; Singh, Manmohan. 2005. Of Oxford, economics, empire, and freedom. *The Hindu* (July 10). Retrieved February 2, 2010, from http://www.hindu.com/2005/07/10/stories/2005071002301000.htm.

180. British Broadcasting Corporation. December 3, 1998. India: The economy. Retrieved February 3, 2010, from http://news.bbc.co.uk/2/hi/south_asia/55427.stm.

181. Ibid.

182. *Columbia Electronic Encyclopedia.* 2007. India: History. Retrieved February 2, 2010, from http://www.infoplease.com/ce6/world/A0858782.html.

183. U.S. Department of State, Background note: India.

184. *Columbia Electronic Encyclopedia,* India: History.

185. British Broadcasting Corporation, India: The economy.

186. Organization for Economic Cooperation and Development (OECD). 2007. *Policy brief: Economic survey of India* (October). Retrieved February 3, 2010, from http://www.oecd.org/dataoecd/17/52/39452196.pdf.

187. OECD, *Policy brief*; Singh, Kulwindar. 2005. Foreign direct investment in India: A critical analysis of FDI from 1991–2005. *Center for Civil Society*, New Delhi. Retrieved February 3, 2010, from http://unpan1.un.org/intradoc/groups/public/documents/APCITY/UNPAN024036.pdf; CIA World Factbook. Retrieved May 4, 2012, from https://www.cia.gov/library/publications/the-world-factbook/rankorder/2198rank.html.

188. Gross Domestic Product 2010. World Bank Data. Retrieved May 3, 2012, from http://siteresources.worldbank.org/DATASTATISTICS/Resources/GDP.pdf; CIA World Factbook, Retrieved May 4, 2012, from https://www.cia.gov/library/publications/the-world-factbook/rankorder/2001rank.html?countryName=India&countryCode=in&regionCode=sas&rank=4#in.

189. *CIA world factbook,* India.

190. U.S. Department of State, Background note: India.

191. Crisil Cuts India's GDP Growth Forecast to 6.5%. *Business Standard*, June 4, 2012. Retrieved June 5, 2012, from http://business-standard.com/india/news/crisil-cuts-indias-gdp-growth-forecast-to-65/166709/on.

192. "Potential for Investment in India." Accessed November 28, 2012, from http://www.indembassy.be/potential_investment.html.

193. Indian Biotechnology Sector – Overview. 5 pages. New Delhi: European Business and Technology Centre, 2011.

194. "Potential for Investment in India." Accessed November 28, 2012, from http://www.indembassy.be/potential_investment.html.

195. *CIA world factbook,* India.

196. Bhargava, Rajat, Rajat Gupta, and Babar Khan. 2005. Unearthing India's mineral wealth. *McKinsey Quarterly* (September). Retrieved February 3, 2010, from http://www.mckinseyquarterly.com/Energy_Resources_Materials/Strategy_Analysis/Unearthing_Indias_mineral_wealth_1657?gp=1.

197. OECD, *Policy brief.*

198. "India's Role in World Agriculture." 11: European Commission, 2007.

199. Joshi, Harsh. 2010. India's taste for inflation fight. *Wall Street Journal* (January 30). Retrieved February 2, 2010, from http://online.wsj.com/article/SB100014240527487033890004575032663512689570.html.

200. Data gathered from International Monetary Fund country database. Retrieved. May 7, 2012, from http://www.imf.org/external/pubs/ft/weo/2012/01/weodata/weoselgr.aspx.

201. Joshi, India's taste for inflation fight.

202. United Nations, Department of Economic and Social Affairs: Population Division, Population Estimates and Projections Section. Retrieved May 7, 2012, from http://esa.un.org/unpd/wpp/population-pyramids/population-pyramids.htm.

203. Friedman, *The world is flat.*

204. Cappelli, Singh, Singh, and Useem. The India way: How India's top business leaders are revolutionizing management.

205. "International Student Enrollment Increased by 5 Percent in 2010/11, Led by Strong Increase in Students from China." Institute of International Education, http://www.iie.org/Who-We-Are/News-and-Events/Press-Center/Press-Releases/2011/2011-11-14-Open-Doors-International-Students.

206. *CIA world factbook, India; British Broadcasting Corporation, India: The economy.*

207. Singh, Avantika. 2009. Growth of the middle class in India: Implications for domestic tourism. HVS (January 13). Retrieved February 3, 2010, from http://www.4hoteliers.com/4hots_fshw.php?mwi=3690.

208. Nath, Kamal. 2010. India's road to progress. *Wall Street Journal* (January 26). Retrieved February 2, 2010, from http://online.wsj.com/article/SB10001424052748703808904575026043518922322.html.

209. Wikipedia.org. List of countries by English-speaking population. Retrieved February 3, 2010, from http://en.wikipedia.org/wiki/List_of_countries_by_English-speaking_population.

210. U.S. Department of State, Background note: India; Majumder, Sanjoy. 2006. Furor reflects India's caste complexities. *BBC News* (May 20). Retrieved February 3, 2010, from http://news.bbc.co.uk/2/hi/south_asia/4998274.stm.

211. Republican China. Retrieved February 1, 2010, from http://www-chaos.umd.edu/history/republican.html#nationalism.

212. Hsü, Immanuel C. Y. 2000. *The Rise of Modern China*, 6th ed. New York: Oxford University Press.

213. Ibid; Mayhew, B. 2004. *Shanghai*. United Kingdom: Lonely Planet.

214. 2000. Fairbank and Twitchett, *The Cambridge history of China*.

215. Ibid.

216. Ibid.

217. MacFarquhar, R., J. K. Fairbank, and D. Twitchett. 1991. *Cambridge history of China: The People's Republic, part 2: Revolutions within the Chinese Revolution, 1966–1982*. Cambridge: Cambridge University Press.

218. Ibid.

219. Ibid.

220. Beam, Christopher. 2009. Tussle in Tiananmen Square. *Slate* (June 3). Retrieved February 1, 2010, from http://www.slate.com/id/2219697/.

221. Ibid.

222. Ibid. Friedman, *The world is flat*.

223. Organization for Economic Cooperation and Development (OECD). 2006. *OECD investment policy reviews China: Open policies towards mergers and acquisitions*. Paris: OECD Publications.

224. CIA World Factbook. Foreign Direct Investment. Retrieved May 7, 2012, from https://www.cia.gov/library/publications/the-world-factbook/rankorder/rawdata_2198.txt.

225. Zakaria, Fareed. 2005. Does the future belong to China? *Newsweek* (May 9). Retrieved February 3, 2010, from http://www.newsweek.com/id/51964.

226. British Petroleum. 2011. BP Statistical Review of World Energy. Retrieved May 7, 2012, from http://www.bp.com/assets/bp_internet/globalbp/globalbp_uk_english/reports_and_publications/statistical_energy_review_2011/STAGING/local_assets/pdf/statistical_review_of_world_energy_full_report_2011.pdf; World Steel Association Crude Steel Production 2000–2009. Retrieved May 7, 2012, from http://www.worldsteel.org/dms/internetDocumentList/statistics-archive/production-archive/steel-archive/steel-annually/Annual-steel-2000-2009/document/Annual%20steel%202000-2009.pdf.

227. US State Department Human Rights Report 2010: China. Retrieved May 7, 2012, from http://www.state.gov/j/drl/rls/hrrpt/2010/index.htm.

228. *CIA world factbook*. 2011. China. Retrieved November 9, 2012, from https://www.cia.gov/library/publications/the-world-factbook/geos/ch.html.

229. Human Rights Watch. 2009. *World report*. New York: Seven Stories Press.

230. Hodgson, Ann. 2007. China's middle class reaches 80 million. *Euromonitor International* (July 25). Retrieved February 3, 2010, from http://www.euromonitor.com/Chinas_middle_class_reaches_80_million.

231. Reynolds, James. 2007. Wifeless future for China's men. *BBC News*. (February 12). Retrieved February 3, 2010, from http://news.bbc.co.uk/2/hi/6346931.stm.

232. Friedman, *The world is flat*.

233. Malone, Robert. 2006. America's most polluted cities. *Forbes.com* (March 22). Retrieved February 3, 2010, from http://www.forbes.com/2006/03/21/americas-most-polluted-cities-cx_rm_0321pollute.html.

234. Friedman, *The world is flat*.

235. China Gateway. Protecting your intellectual property rights (IPR) in China. Retrieved February 3, 2010, from http://www.mac.doc.gov/China/Docs/businessguides/IntellectualPropertyRights.htm.

236. Wikipedia.org. Pet food recalls. Retrieved February 3, 2010, from http://en.wikipedia.org/wiki/2007_pet_food_recalls#Affected_brands; Wikipedia.org. Chinese export recalls. Retrieved February 3, 2010, from http://en.wikipedia.org/wiki/2007_Chinese_export_recalls#Mattel; Bogdanich, Walt. 2007. Chinese chemicals flow unchecked onto world drug market. *New York Times* (October 31).

Retrieved January 11, 2010, from http://www.nytimes.com/2007/10/31/world/asia/31chemical.html.

237. Personal interview with Mwitwa Muyembe conducted by Annie McKee, 2012.

238. Teleos Leadership Institute. Executive coach development program: Core competencies. Retrieved April 7, 2010, from http://www.coachfederation.org/research-education/icf-credentials/core-competencies.

239. Zander, L. 2005. Communication and country clusters: A study of language and leadership preferences. *International Studies of Management and Organization* 35(1): 83–103; Kogut, B., and U. Zander. 1992. Knowledge of the firm, combinative capabilities, and the replication of technology. *Organization Science* 3(3): 383–97.

240. Harzing, A.-W., and A. J. Feely. 2008. The language barrier and its implications for HQ-subsidiary relationships. *Cross-Cultural Management* 15(1): 49–61; Zander, Communication and country clusters.

241. FedEx Corporation. June 19, 2012. About FedEx. Retrieved August 23, 2012 from http://about.van.fedex.com/fedex_corporation.

242. Leahey, Colleen. 2011. 25 Best Global Companies to Work For. *Fortune*, (October 28). Retrieved May 8, 2012, from http://money.cnn.com/galleries/2011/fortune/1110/gallery.best_companies_global.fortune/index.html

243. Gallagher, Paul. 2009. Beyond the Borders. *Human Resource Executive Online, 2009*. Retrieved May 8, 2012, from http://www.hreonline.com/HRE/story.jsp?storyId=298518365

244. Smith, Tess. 2011. Brazil Volunteer Experience Sparks Fedex Global Leadership Corps. *Center for Corporate Citizenship, 2011*. Retrieved May 8, 2012, from http://blogs.bcccc.net/2011/10/brazil-volunteer-experience-sparks-fedex-global-leadership-corps/

245. Retrieved May 8, 2012, from http://cdcdevelopmentsolutions.org/newsletter/april-2012/fedex-global-leadership-corps-in-bangalore-india.

246. Sims, Ronald R. 2003. *Ethics and corporate social responsibility: Why giants fall*. Westport, CT: Greenwood Publishing.

247. Chippendale, Paul. 2001. *On values, ethics, morals, and principles*. Retrieved February 8, 2010, from http://www.minessence.net/AVI_Accred/pdfs/ValuesEthicsPrinciples.PDF.

248. Franke, J., and N. Nicholson. 2002. Who shall we send? Cultural and other influences on the rating of selection criteria for expatriate assignments. *International Journal of Cross Cultural Management* 2(1): 21–36.

249. Zander, Communication and country clusters.

250. Wyatt, Edward. 2011. Former Siemens executives are charged with bribery. *The New York Times* (December 13). Retrieved August 23, 2012 from http://www.nytimes.com/2011/12/14/business/global/former-siemens-executives-charged-with-bribery.html; Matthews, C.M. 2012. A Former Siemens Exec Settles with SEC, Another Fights. *The Wall Street Journal* (October 19). Retrieved November 9, 2012, from http://blogs.wsj.com/corruption-currents/2012/10/19/a-former-siemens-settles-with-sec-another-fights/.

Chapter 15

1. United Nations General Assembly. September 15, 2005. 2005 World Summit Outcome, Resolution A/60/1. Retrieved May 29, 2012, from http://data.unaids.org/Topics/UniversalAccess/worldsummitoutcome_resolution_24oct2005_en.pdf.

2. Interface. What is sustainability? Retrieved April 26, 2010, from http://www.interfaceglobal.com/Sustainability/What-is-Sustainability-.aspx.

3. United Nations. *Our common future, chapter 2: Towards sustainable development*. Retrieved April 26, 2010, from http://www.un-documents.net/ocf-02.htm.

4. Vasey, Daniel E. 1992. *An ecological history of agriculture, 10,000 B.C.–A.D. 10,000*. Ames: Iowa State University Press.

5. Kradin, Nikolay N. 2002. Nomadism, evolution, and world-systems: Pastoral societies in theories of historical development. *Journal of World-Systems Research* 8(3): 368–88.

6. Dawkins, Richard. 2004. *The ancestor's tale: A pilgrimage to the dawn of evolution*. New York: Houghton-Mifflin Company.

7. Saitoti, Tepilit Ole, and Carol Beckwith. 1949. *Maasai*. New York: Abradale Press.

8. Maasai Association. Maasai ceremonies and rituals. Retrieved November 3, 2009, from http://www.maasai-association.org/ceremonies.html.

9. Berntsen, John L. 1976. The Maasai and their neighbors: Variables of interaction. *African Economic History* 2: 1–11.

10. Anderson, David M. 1993. Cow power: Livestock and the pastoralist in Africa. *African Affairs* 92(366): 121–33.

11. Maasai Association, Maasai ceremonies and rituals.

12. Fagan, Brian. 2000. *The little ice age: How climate made history, 1300–1850*. New York: Basic Books.

13. Revkin, Andrew. 2009. Skeptics dispute climate worries and each other. *New York Times* (March 8). Retrieved April 26, 2010, from http://www.nytimes.com/2009/03/09/science/earth/09climate.html.

14. Kaufman, Darrell S., David P. Schneider, Nicholas P. McKay, Caspar M. Ammann, Raymond S. Bradley, Keith R. Briffa, Gifford H. Miller, et al. 2009. Recent Warming Reverses Long-Term Arctic Cooling. *Science* 325 (5945): 1236–39.

15. United Nations Intergovernmental Panel on Climate Change (IPCC). 2007. Summary for policymakers, in *Climate change 2007: The physical science basis. Contribution of Working Group I to the Fourth Assessment Report of the Intergovernmental Panel on Climate Change*, ed. S. Solomon, D. Qin, M. Manning, Z. Chen, M. Marquis, K. B. Averyt, M. Tignor, and H. L. Miller. Cambridge, UK: Cambridge University Press.

16. Pittock, I. B. 2007. The enhanced greenhouse effect: Threats to Australia's water resources. *Journal of the Australian Water Association* (August): 36–38; Morales, Pablo, Thomas Hickler, David P. Rowell, Benjamin Smith, and Martin T. Sykes. 2007. Changes in European ecosystem productivity and carbon balance driven by regional climate model output. *Global Change Biology* 13: 108–22; Seidel, Dian J., Qiang Fu, William J. Randel, and Thomas J. Reichler. 2008. Widening of the tropical belt in a changing climate. *Nature Geoscience* 1: 21–24. Retrieved January 23, 2010, from http://www.arl.noaa.gov/documents/JournalPDFs/SeidelEtAl.ngeo.2007.38.pdf; The National Aeronautics and Space Administration Goddard Institute for Space Studies. 2012. Earth's Energy Budget Remained Out of Balance Despite Unusually Low Solar Activity (January 30). Retrieved May 29, 2012, from http://www.giss.nasa.gov/research/news/20120130b/.

17. Twicken, Joe. 1999. Greenhouse effect. Retrieved April 29, 2010, from http://nova.stanford.edu/projects/mod-x/id-green.html.

18. National Aeronautics and Space Administration. 2012. GISS surface temperature analysis. Retrieved June 1, 2012, from http://data.giss.nasa.gov/gistemp/graphs_v3/.

19. Table adapted from United Nations Intergovernmental Panel on Climate Change (IPCC). 2007. Synthesis report, in *Climate change 2007: Contribution of Working Groups I, II, and III to the Fourth Assessment Report of the Intergovernmental Panel on Climate Change*, ed. R. K. Pachauri and A. Reisinger. Geneva: IPCC.

20. Sierra, Katherine, and Nathan Hultman. 2012. Green Growth Innovation: Toward a New Architecture for Developing Countries. *The Brookings Institution* (May 2012). Retrieved May 29, 2012, from http://www.brookings.edu/research/papers/2012/05/green-growth-innovation-sierra-hultman.

21. Harvey, Fiona. 2012. Bonn Climate Talks End in Discord and Disappointment. *The Guardian* (May 25).

22. UN News Centre. 2012. Development cooperation will play key role in gaining sustainable development. UN (May 12). Retrieved May 29, 2012, from http://www.un.org/apps/news/story.asp?NewsID=41989&Cr=sustainable+development&Cr1=.

23. Sierra, Katherine, and Nathan Hultman. 2012. Green Growth Innovation: Toward a New Architecture for Developing Countries. *The Brookings Institution* (May 2012). Retrieved May 29, 2012, from http://www.brookings.edu/research/papers/2012/05/green-growth-innovation-sierra-hultman.

24. Leber, Jessica. 2010. Indonesia Walks a 'Tricky' Path Toward Growth and Sustainability. *The New York Times* (March 22). Retrieved May 30, 2012, from http://www.nytimes.com/cwire/2010/03/22/22climatewire-indonesia-walks-a-tricky-path-toward-growth-22444.html?pagewanted=all.

25. Ibid.

26. Robertson, Delia. 2012. *African Leaders Discuss Roadmap for Sustainable Development* (May 24). Retrieved May 30, 2012, from http://www.voanews.com/content/african-leaders-discuss-roadmap-to-sustainable-development/940457.html.

27. Woods, Penny. 2012. Rio+20 should prioritise sustainable agriculture, says Caroline Spelman. *The Guardian* (May 24). Retrieved May 30, 2012, from http://www.guardian.co.uk/global-development/2012/may/24/rio-20-sustainable-agriculture-caroline-spelman?newsfeed=true.

28. Ibid.

29. Moore, Malcolm. 2011. Apple's child labour issues worsen. *The Telegraph* (February 15). Retrieved May 30, 2012, from http://www.telegraph.co.uk/technology/apple/8324867/Apples-child-labour-issues-worsen.html.

30. Miller, George. 2004. Everyday low wages: The hidden price we all pay for Wal-mart. *A report by the Democratic staff of the Committee on Education and the Workforce* (February 16). Retrieved January 23, 2010, from http://www.wakeupwalmart.com/facts/miller-report.pdf.

31. Asian American Press. March 10, 2012. Walmart employees speak out about poverty wages at LA welfare office. Retrieved May 30, 2012, from http://aapress.com/editorial/walmart-employees-speak-out-about-poverty-wages-at-la-welfare-office/.

32. Mills, Elinor. 2008. Jerry Yang lobbies for release of Chinese dissidents. *BusinessWeek* (February 25). Retrieved January 23, 2010, from http://www.businessweek.com/globalbiz/content/feb2008/gb20080225_248127.htm?campaign_id=rss_daily.

33. Anderson, Jenny and Heather Timmons. 2007. Why a U.S. Subprime Mortgage Crisis Is Felt Around the World. *The New York Times* (August 31). Retrieved May 30, 2012, from http://www.nytimes.com/2007/08/31/business/worldbusiness/31derivatives.html?pagewanted=all.

34. FitzGerald, Niall. 2006. Why the investment climate for Africa deserves U.S. support: A response to the "CGD Note: The Investment Climate Facility for Africa: Does it deserve U.S. support?" Retrieved January 23, 2010, from http://www.cgdev.org/doc/commentary/ICFResponseC-GDNote.pdf.

35. FitzGerald, Niall. 2009. Corporate responsibility in the twenty-first century. Tyburn Lecture, May 20, Tyburn Convent, London.

36. Eichler, Alexander. 2012. Warren Buffett On the Environment, Businesses Can't Take 'Shortcuts'. *The Huffington Post* (April 3), Retrieved June 8, 2012, from http://www.huffingtonpost.com/2012/04/03/warren-buffett-environmental-regulations_n_1399846.html.

37. United Nations General Assembly. 2005. 2005 world summit outcome (Resolution A/60/1) (September 15). Retrieved November 2, 2009, from http://daccess-dds-ny.un.org/doc/UNDOC/GEN/N05/487/60/PDF/N0548760.pdf?OpenElement.

38. United Nations Millennium Development Goals. Goal 7: Ensure environmental sustainability. Retrieved April 26, 2010, from http://www.un.org/millenniumgoals/environ.shtml.

39. United Nations. Information management for social aspects of sustainable development training module. Retrieved April 26, 2010, from www.un.org/esa/sustdev/natlinfo/indicators/idsd/workshops/workshop10-27-31/02_TRAINING%20MODULE.doc.

40. United Nations Economic Commission for Africa. Transforming Africa's economies, 18. Retrieved April 26, 2010, from www.uneca.org/eca_resources/Publications/books/transforming_africas_economies/ECA_Overview_03.pdf.

41. United Nations Educational, Scientific, and Cultural Organization. 2007. The UN decade of education for sustainable development (DESD 2005–2014): The first two years. Paris: UNESCO. Retrieved April 26, 2010, from http://unesdoc.unesco.org/images/0015/001540/154093e.pdf.

42. United Nations. 2002. World Summit on Sustainable Development (August 26–September 4). Retrieved May 27, 2010, from http://www.un.org/events/wssd/summaries/envdevj8.htm.

43. Basham, Brian. 2012. The Loons Are Ok — So Far, but DNR Is Looking at Long-Range Impact of Gulf Oil Spill. *Detroit Lakes Online*, (May 23). Retrieved June 1, 2012, from http://www.dl-online.com/event/article/id/67723/.

44. Center for Catastrophic Risk Management, U.C. Berkeley. 2011. Final Report on the Investigation of the Macondo Well Blowout, 124. Retrieved June 1, 2012, from http://ccrm.berkeley.edu/pdfs_papers/bea_pdfs/DHSGFinalReport-March2011-tag.pdf.

45. Muyembe, Chikasha. 2012. Cooperatives in Zambia, in McKee, Annie. *Management: A Focus on Leaders, first edition*. Upper Saddle River: Prentice Hall, 2012.

46. Lanhelle, Oluf. October 29, 2010. Economic Sustainability: The Norwegian Experience, in *CELM Breakfast*. West Perth, Australia: Centre for Engineering Leadership and Management.

47. Broughton, Edward. 2005. The Bhopal disaster and its aftermath. *Environmental Health* 4(6).

48. Ibid.

49. Author. 2010. The Slow Pursuit of Justice. *The Economist* 395 (8688): 43–43.

50. Broughton, The Bhopal disaster and its aftermath.

51. Ibid.

52. Stott, Matthew. 2011. London 2012: British nurse challenges Coe to see victims of Bhopal for himself. *Sports Beat* (December 5). Retrieved June 5, 2012, from http://www.morethanthegames.co.uk/london-2012/0515945-london-2012-british-nurse-challenges-coe-see-victims-bhopal-himself.

53. Kumar, S. 2004. Victims of gas leak in Bhopal seek redress on compensation. *British Medical Journal* 329(7462): 366; Lahri, Tripti. 2010. Three things for the Bhopal Panel to consider. *The Wall Street Journal* (June 16). Retrieved June 16, 2010, from http://blogs.wsj.com/indiarealtime/2010/06/16/three-things-for-the-bhopal-panel-to-consider/.

54. Bhopal Medical Appeal. Poisoned water: Corporate, municipal, and medical neglect condemn many to death. Retrieved January 19, 2010, from http://www.bhopal.org/index.php?id=111.

55. Power, M. 2004. The poison stream: Letter from Kerala. *Harper's* (August): 51–61.

56. Carbide waste to go: HC. 2008. *Times of India* (December 16). Retrieved January 19, 2010, from http://timesofindia.indiatimes.com/India/Carbide_waste_to_go_HC/articleshow/3847412.cms.

57. Japan. 2012. *The New York Times* (April 27). Retrieved June 1, 2012, from http://topics.nytimes.com/top/news/international/countriesandterritories/japan/index.html.

58. Global 100. Why We Do It. Retrieved June 8, 2012, from http://www.global100.org/about-us/why-we-do-it.html.

59. Mills, Enos A. 1917. *Your national parks.* Cambridge, MA: Houghton-Mifflin Company.

60. National Park Service. Frequently asked questions. Retrieved November 5, 2009, from http://www.nps.gov/faqs.htm.

61. Crandall, Robert W. 2008. Pollution controls, in *Concise encyclopedia of economics.* Library of Economics and Liberty. Retrieved August 31, 2009, from http://www.econlib.org/library/Enc/PollutionControls.html.

62. United States Environmental Protection Agency. 2009. Environmental progress. Retrieved January 24, 2010, from http://www.epa.gov/earthday/history.htm#1.

63. United States Environmental Protection Agency. Timeline. Retrieved April 26, 2010, from http://www.epa.gov/history/timeline/index.htm.

64. Barr, Christopher D. and Francesca Dominici. 2010. Cap and trade legislation for greenhouse gas emissions. *JAMA* (January 6). 303(1): 69–70. Retrieved June 1, 2012, from http://www.ncbi.nlm.nih.gov/pmc/articles/PMC2913286/.

65. United States Environmental Protection Agency. Laws that we administer. Retrieved May 22, 2010, from http://www.epa.gov/lawsregs/laws/index.html.

66. United Nations Framework Convention on Climate Change. Kyoto Protocol. Retrieved November 7, 2009, from http://unfccc.int/kyoto_protocol/items/2830.php.

67. Carey, John. 2009. Obama's cap and trade plan. *Bloomberg Businessweek* (March 5). Retrieved April 26, 2010, from http://www.businessweek.com/magazine/content/09_11/b4123022554346.htm.

68. The White House. Energy and environment. Retrieved June 11, 2012, from http://www.whitehouse.gov/issues/energy-and-environment.

69. United Nations Framework Convention on Climate Change. Clean development mechanism. Retrieved November 7, 2009, from http://unfccc.int/kyoto_protocol/mechanisms/clean_development_mechanism/items/2718.php.

70. United Nations Framework Convention on Climate Change. Joint implementation. Retrieved November 7, 2009, from http://unfccc.int/kyoto_protocol/mechanisms/joint_implementation/items/1674.php.

71. United Nations Framework Convention on Climate Change, Kyoto Protocol.

72. CO_2 Emissions from Fuel Combustion Highlights. Paris: International Energy Agency (IEA), 2011, 134 pages.

73. The world's top 25 greenhouse gas emitters. 2008. *Reuters* (November 25).Retrieved April 11, 2010, from http://www.alertnet.org/thenews/newsdesk/LP343601.htm.

74. Global Carbon Project. 2008. Carbon budget and trends 2007. Retrieved September 26, 2008, from http://www.globalcarbonproject.org.

75. Lomborg, Bjørn. 2007. *Cool it: The skeptical environmentalist's guide to global warming.* New York: Alfred A. Knopf.

76. 105th Congress 1st Session. S. Res. 98. Retrieved April 26, 2010, from http://frwebgate.access.gpo.gov/cgi-bin/getdoc.cgi?dbname=105_cong_bills&docid=f:sr98ats.txt.pdf.

77. Northrop, Michael, and David Sassoon. 2009. Ambitious actions by the states push U.S. toward climate goals. *Environment 360* (December 8). Retrieved December 8, 2009, from http://www.e360.yale.edu/content/feature.msp?id=2219.

78. Xinhua News. 2009. Global efforts to fight climate change—from Rio de Janeiro to Copenhagen. *China.org.cn* (December 7). Retrieved January 19, 2010, from http://www.china.org.cn/environment/Copenhagen/2009-12/07/content_19019633.htm.

79. Friedman, Lisa. 2009. The major players in the Copenhagen talks and their positions. *New York Times* (December 8). Retrieved December 8, 2009, from http://www.nytimes.com/cwire/2009/12/08/08climatewire-the-major-players-in-the-copenhagen-talks-an-45792.html.

80. Aljazeera. China attacks rich states at summit. 2009. *Aljazeera.net* (December 9). Retrieved December 9, 2009, from http://english.aljazeera.net/news/europe/2009/12/2009128234918828775.html.

81. Talley, Ian. 2009. EPA declares greenhouse gases a danger. *Wall Street Journal* (December 8). Retrieved December 8, 2009, from http://online.wsj.com/article/SB20001424052748703558004574582190625776518.html; Dlouhy, Jennifer A., and Matthew Tresaugue. 2009. EPA declares greenhouse gases pose health risk. *San Francisco Chronicle* (December 8). Retrieved December 8, 2009, from http://www.sfgate.com/cgi-bin/article.cgi?f=/c/a/2009/12/08/MNDA1B0I89.DTL&type=health.

82. National Public Radio. 2009. UN climate chief urges avoiding blame over summit. (December 23). Retrieved January 19, 2010, from http://www.npr.org/templates/story/story.php?storyId=120160589; Memmott, Mark. 2009. Obama in Copenhagen; climate talks in disarray; urges "action over inaction." National Public Radio (December 18). Retrieved January 19, 2010, from http://www.npr.org/blogs/thetwo-way/2009/12/obama_in_copenhagen_climate_ch.html; Indo-Asian News Service. 2009. Last day of Copenhagen summit, hope fizzling out. *IBN Live* (December 18). Retrieved January 19, 2010, from http://ibnlive.in.com/news/last-day-of-copenhagen-summit-hope-fizzling-out/107355-11.html.

83. Aljazeera. China attacks rich states at summit; Vidal, John. 2009. Copenhagen: Leaked draft deal widens rift between rich and poor nations. *The Guardian* (December 9). Retrieved December 9, 2009, from http://www.guardian.co.uk/environment/2009/dec/09/copenhagen-summit-danish-text-leak.

84. United Nations Framework Convention on Climate Change. 2009. Draft decision -/CP.15: Copenhagen Accord (December 18). Retrieved January 19, 2010, from http://unfccc.int/resource/docs/2009/cop15/eng/l07.pdf.

85. Schneider, Keith. 2009. Climate agreement not accepted, but Copenhagen conference makes it "operational." *Copenhagen Insider* (December 19). Retrieved January 19, 2010, from http://copenhagen.nationaljournal.com/2009/12/climate-agreement-not-accepted.php; Taylor, Paul. 2010. E.U. seeks to regain influence on response to climate change. *New York Times* (January 15). Retrieved January 19, 2009, from http://www.nytimes.com/2010/01/16/business/global/16iht-inside16.html.

86. Canada Pulls out of Kyoto Protocol. December 12, 2011. *The Guardian.* Retrieved June 1, 2012, from http://www.guardian.co.uk/environment/2011/dec/13/canada-pulls-out-kyoto-protocol.

87. Harvey, Fiona. 2012. Bonn Climate Talks End in Discord and Disappointment. *The Guardian* (May 25). Retrieved June 1, 2012, from http://www.guardian.co.uk/environment/2012/may/25/bonn-climate-talks-end-disappointment?newsfeed=true.

88. *CIA world factbook 2012.* Country comparison: Oil consumption. Retrieved June 1, 2012, from https://www.cia.gov/library/publications/the-world-factbook/rankorder/2174rank.html.

89. Mouawad, Jad. 2008. Oil prices pass record set in '80s, but then recede. *New York Times* (March 3). Retrieved January 22, 2010, from http://www.nytimes.com/2008/03/03/business/worldbusiness/03cnd-oil.html?_r=1&hp.

90. Ibid.

91. "Monthly Oil Market Report: May 2012." 76 pp.: Organization of the Petroleum Exporting Countries, 2012. Retrieved June 1, 2012, from http://www.opec.org/opec_web/static_files_project/media/downloads/publications/MOMR_May_2012.pdf.

92. Hubbert, M. K. 1956. *Nuclear energy and the fossil fuels.* Presented at the Spring Meeting of the Southern District, American Petroleum Institute, Plaza Hotel, San Antonio, Texas, March 7–9. Retrieved January 22, 2010, from http://www.hubbertpeak.com/hubbert/1956/1956.pdf; Brandt, Adam R. 2007. Testing Hubbert. *Energy Policy* 35: 3074–88.

93. Salazar, Ken. 2009. Statement before the U.S. Senate Energy and Natural Resources Committee regarding energy development on the public lands and outer continental shelf (March 17). Retrieved October 15, 2009, from http://www.doi.gov/news/speeches/2009_03_17_speech.cfm.

94. Wilber, Tom. *Under the Surface: Fracking, Fortunes and the Fate of the Marcellus Shale*. Ithaca: Cornell University Press, 2012; Miller, Debra A. Pollution. *Current Controversies*. Detroit: Greenhaven Press, 2012.

95. Whitesides, John. 2012. Insight: In Ohio, "fracking" boom a delicate issue for Obama. *Reuters* (May 16). Retrieved June 1, 2012, from http://www.reuters.com/article/2012/05/16/us-usa-campaign-ohio-fracking-idUSBRE84F17520120516.

96. Obama Administration Announces Green Button Program: Makes Energy Use Transparent, Forges Cleantech Business Innovation. 2012. *Sustainable Business.com News* (March 22). Retrieved on June 1, 2012, from http://www.sustainablebusiness.com/index.cfm/go/news.display/id/23534.

97. Geman, Ben. 2012. Senate Republicans take aim at Obama gas 'fracking' regulations. *The Hill* (March 29). Retrieved on June 11, 2012, from http://thehill.com/blogs/e2-wire/e2-wire/218969-senate-republicans-take-aim-at-federal-gas-fracking-rules; Farnham, Alan. 2012. So, Drill Already: Obama to Oil Industry. *ABC News* (May 17). Retrieved June 11, 2012, from http://abcnews.go.com/Business/obama-tells-oil-industry-drill-idle-leased-land/story?id=16363021.

98. McLean-Conner, Penni. 2009. Green-collar jobs. *Electric Light and Power* 87(3): 10.

99. Giller, Chip. 2008. The future of green jobs. *NOW on PBS* (November 14). Retrieved April 26, 2010, from http://www.pbs.org/now/shows/445/green-jobs.html.

100. Bureau of Labor Statistics. March 22, 2012. Green Goods and Services News Release. Retrieved June 4, 2012, from http://www.bls.gov/news.release/ggqcew.htm.

101. Hethcock, Bill. 2012. UNT's Apogee Stadium wins Green Project Deal of the Year. *Dallas Business Journal* (April 27). Retrieved June 4, 2012, from http://www.bizjournals.com/dallas/print-edition/2012/04/27/unts-apogee-stadium-wins-green.html.

102. United States Environmental Protection Agency. Cleaning up the nation's hazardous waste sites. Retrieved June 4, 2012, from http://www.epa.gov/superfund/.

103. United States Environmental Protection Agency. National Priorities List (NPL). Retrieved June 4, 2012, from http://www.epa.gov/superfund/sites/npl/index.htm.

104. Fairley, Peter. 2007. Nuclear wasteland. *IEEE Spectrum* (February). Retrieved January 24, 2010, from http://spectrum.ieee.org/energy/nuclear/nuclear-wasteland.

105. World Nuclear Association. Nuclear power in France. Retrieved June 4, 2012, from http://www.world-nuclear.org/info/inf40.html.

106. Ibid.

107. Ibid.

108. Ibid.

109. United States Senate Committee on Energy and Natural Resources. 1988. *Nuclear Waste Policy Amendments of 1987*. Washington, DC.

110. *Washington Post*. 2009. Editorial: Mountain of trouble: Mr. Obama defunds the nuclear repository at Yucca Mountain. Now what? (March 8). Retrieved January 24, 2010, from http://www.washingtonpost.com/wp-dyn/content/article/2009/03/07/AR2009030701666.html; Hargreaves, Steve. 2011. Nuclear waste: Back to Yucca Mountain? *CNNMoney* (July 11). Retrieved June 4, 2012, from http://money.cnn.com/2011/07/06/news/economy/nuclear_waste/index.htm.

111. United States Fish and Wildlife Service. 2008. A history of the Endangered Species Act of 1973. Retrieved April 11, 2010, from http://www.fws.gov/Endangered/factsheets/history_ESA.pdf.

112. United States Fish and Wildlife Service. Species reports. Retrieved June 4, 2012, from http://ecos.fws.gov/tess_public/pub/boxScore.jsp.

113. United States Fish and Wildlife Service. 2009. ESA basics. Retrieved November 9, 2009, from http://www.fws.gov/Endangered/factsheets/ESA_basics.pdf.

114. Pimm, Stuart L., and Peter Raven. 2000. Biodiversity: Extinction by numbers. *Nature* 403 (February 24): 843–45.

115. Ibid.

116. Ibid.; Walter, K. S., and H. J. Gillett. 1998. IUCN red list of threatened plants. Gland, Switzerland: International Union for Conservation of Nature; Collar, N. J., M. J. Crosby, and A. J. Stattersfield. 1994. *Birds to watch 2*. Washington, DC: Smithsonian Institution Press.

117. Sax, Dov F., and Steven D. Gaines. 2008. Species invasions and extinction: The future of native biodiversity on islands. *Proceedings of the National Academy of Sciences* 105(1): 11490–97.

118. Ibid.

119. Baldwin, Paul H., Charles W. Schwartz, and Elizabeth R. Schwartz. 1952. Life history and economic status of the mongoose in Hawai'i. *Journal of Mammalogy* 33(3): 335–56.

120. Englund, R. A., D. J. Preston, A. E. Vorsino, S. Myers, and L. L. Englund. 2009. Results of the 2007–2008 alien species and wekiu bug (*Nysius wekiuicola*) surveys on the summit of Mauna Kea, Hawai'i Island. Final report prepared for Office of Mauna Kea Management, University of Hawaii at Hilo.

121. Johnson, Jim. 2009. Ford holds the line on enviro initiatives. *Waste and Recycling News* 15(8): 15.

122. Toyota. Prius 10. Retrieved April 26, 2010, from http://www.toyota.com/prius-hybrid/.

123. MacDonald, Jay. 2005. Hummer tax break gets hammered. *Bankrate.com* (January 20). Retrieved April 26, 2010, from http://www.bankrate.com/brm/itax/biz_tips/20030403a1.asp.

124. United States Department of Transportation. August 26, 2009. DOT 133-09: Cash for Clunkers wraps up with nearly 700,000 car sales and increased fuel efficiency. Retrieved April 26, 2010, from http://www.cars.gov/files/official-information/August26PR.pdf.

125. Healey, James R. 2009. Q&A: How the "cash-for-clunker" plan would work." *USA Today* (June 10). Retrieved April 26, 2010, from http://www.usatoday.com/money/autos/2009-05-11-chrysler-gm-cash-clunkers_N.htm.

126. United States Department of Transportation, DOT 133-09.

127. McKenzie, Stephen. 2004. Social sustainability: Towards some definitions. *Hawke Research Institute Working Paper Series* 27: 1–25. Retrieved September 11, 2009, from http://www.unisa.edu.au/hawkeinstitute/publications/downloads/wp27.pdf.

128. Our Mission. Novica. Retrieved June 11, 2012, from http://www.novica.com/info/index.cfm?action=ourmission.

129. Hindman, Hugh D. 2002. *Child labor: An American history*. New York: M. E. Sharpe.

130. List of Goods Produced by Child Labor or Forced Labor. 56 pages. Washington, D.C.: U.S. Department of Labor, 2011.

131. Bureau of International Labor Affairs. 2010. List of Goods Produced by Child Labor or Forced Labor. U.S. Department of Labor. Retrieved June 4, 2012, from http://www.dol.gov/ilab/programs/ocft/pdf/2010TVPRA.pdf.

132. Montero, David. 2006. Nike's dilemma: Is doing the right thing wrong? A child labor dispute could eliminate 4,000 Pakistani jobs. *Christian Science Monitor* (December 22). Retrieved January 22, 2010, from http://www.csmonitor.com/2006/1222/p01s03-wosc.html?s=u.

133. Ibid.

134. Fair Trade Organization. 2009. Principles of the fair trade federation members. Retrieved January 22, 2010, from http://www.fairtradefederation.org/ht/d/sp/i/8447/pid/8447.

135. Knox, Robert. 2010. Fair trade importer says it's ripe for success. *Boston Globe* (January 4). Retrieved January 22, 2010, from http://www.boston.com/business/articles/2010/01/04/fair_trade_importer_says_its_ripe_for_success/; Huybrechts, Benjamin. 2012. *Fair Trade Organizations and Social Enterprise: Social Innovation through Hybrid Organization Models*. Routledge Studies in Management, Organizations and Society. New York: Routledge; Linton, April. 2012. *Fair Trade from the Ground Up: New Markets for Social Justice*. Seattle: University of Washington Press. DeCarlo, Jacqueline. 2011. *Fair Trade and How It Works. Contemporary Issues*. New York: Rosen Pub.

136. Quirk, Joel. 2008. *Unfinished business: A comparative survey of historical and contemporary slavery*. Paris: UNESCO. Retrieved January 18, 2009, from http://www.unesco.org/culture/pdf/UnfinishedBusinessReport2008.pdf.

137. H.R. 2478 (111th): Lord's Resistance Army Disarmament and Northern Uganda Recovery Act of 2009. Retrieved June 1, 2012, from http://www.govtrack.us/congress/bills/111/hr2478/text.

138. Retrieved June 1, 2012, from http://www.kony2012.com/.

139. Garlan, Yvon. 1988. *Slavery in ancient Greece*. Ithaca, NY: Cornell University Press.

140. Patterson, Orlando. 1982. *Slavery and social death: A comparative study*. Boston: Harvard University Press.

141. Ibid.

142. Archer, Leonie. 1988. *Slavery and other forms of unfree labor*. London: Routledge.

143. Jones, Pete. 2012. Kony 2012: Invisible Children prepares Cover the Night stunt amid criticism. *The Guardian* (April 20). Retrieved June 1, 2012, from http://www.guardian.co.uk/world/2012/apr/20/kony-2012-cover-night-campaign; http://invisiblechildren.com/movedc/accessed 11 3 12.

144. Miller, Max. 2010. Transcript: Interview with Kevin Bales (September 24). Retrieved June 4, 2012, from http://bigthink.com/ideas/24523.

145. Klein, Herbert S. 2010. *The Atlantic slave trade*. New York: Cambridge University Press.

146. *Every child counts: New global estimates on child labour*. 2002. Geneva: International Labour Office.

147. Belser, P. 2005. *Forced labour and human trafficking: Estimating the profits*. Geneva: International Labour Office.

148. Bhatnagar, Rakesh. 2010. Stop sex tourism, Supreme Court tells govt. *DNA* (January 15). Retrieved January 22, 2010, from http://www.dnaindia.com/india/report_stop-sex-tourism-supreme-court-tells-govt_1335320.

149. Kahng, Grace. 2011. Sex slavery in America: One girl's nightmare. *Today News* (February 3). Retrieved June 4, 2012, from http://today.msnbc.msn.com/id/41409991/ns/today-today_news/t/sex-slavery-america-one-girls-nightmare/.

150. European Commission. 2001. Research based on case studies of victims of trafficking in human beings in three EU member states, i.e., Belgium, Italy, and the Netherlands. Commission on the European Communities, DG Justice and Home Affairs, Hippocrates JA/2001/HIP/023.

151. U.S. Department of State. 2011. Trafficking in Persons Report 2011: Country Narratives: Countries N Through Z (June 28). Retrieved June 8, 2012, from http://www.state.gov/j/tip/rls/tiprpt/2011/164233.htm.

152. Larsen, Rozanne. 2011. U.S. Human Trafficking Incidents, 2008–2010. *Journalist's Resource* (May 20). Retrieved June 8, 2012, from http://journalistsresource.org/studies/government/criminal-justice/human-trafficking/.

153. U.S. Department of State. 2011. Trafficking in Persons Report 2011: Country Narratives: Countries N Through Z (June 27). Retrieved August 20, 2012 from http://www.state.gov/j/tip/rls/tiprpt/2011/164233.htm.

154. U.S. Department of State. 2012. Trafficking in Persons Report 2012: Country Narratives: T-Z and Special Case (June 19). Retrieved July 31, 2012 from http://www.state.gov/documents/organization/192598.pdf.

155. United States Department of Labor. 2009. The Department of Labor's list of goods produced by child labor or forced labor. Washington, DC. Retrieved January 22, 2010, from http://www.dol.gov/ilab/programs/ocft/pdf/2009TVPRA.pdf.

156. List of Goods Produced by Child Labor or Forced Labor. 56 pages. Washington, D.C.: U.S. Department of Labor, 2011. Retrieved July 30, 2012, from http://www.dol.gov/ilab/programs/ocft/PDF/2011TVPRA.pdf.

157. Ibid; United States Department of Labor. 2009. The Department of Labor's list of goods produced by child labor or forced labor. Washington, DC. Retrieved January 22, 2010, from http://www.dol.gov/ilab/programs/ocft/pdf/2009TVPRA.pdf..

158. Stephens, Hugh W. 1997. *The Texas City disaster, 1947*. Austin: University of Texas Press.

159. The American Experience. Timeline: Deadliest Workplace Accidents. *PBS.org*. Retrieved June 4, 2012, from http://www.pbs.org/wgbh/americanexperience/features/timeline/triangle/.

160. Plant shut amid lead poisoning fear. December 29, 2009. *Press Association*. Retrieved January 22, 2010, from http://www.google.com/hostednews/ukpress/article/ALeqM5jND__CRpbPhlUdAP6KKN6VYywLww.

161. Symonds, Peter. 1997. *Industrial inferno: The story of the Thai toy factory fire*. Sydney: Labour Press Books.

162. The American Experience. Timeline: Deadliest Workplace Accidents. *PBS.org*. Retrieved June 4, 2012, from http://www.pbs.org/wgbh/americanexperience/features/timeline/triangle/.

163. Medvedev, Zhores. 1990. *The legacy of Chernobyl*. New York: W. W. Norton & Company.

164. Safina, Carl. 2011. In Japan, will sea dilute radiation pollution? *CNN* (April 7). Retrieved June 11, 2012, from http://articles.cnn.com/2011-04-07/opinion/safina.radiation.water.leak.japan_1_cesium-water-leak-radiation?_s=PM:OPINION; Rosen, Yereth. 2012. Alaskan crews gear up to tackle Japan tsunami debris. *Reuters* (May 24). Retrieved June 11, 2012, from http://articles.chicagotribune.com/2012-05-24/news/sns-rt-us-tsunami-trash-alaskabre84o01j-20120524_1_japan-tsunami-debris-alaska-coast-fukushima-daiichi.

165. Thousands protest reopening of Indorayon pulp plant. 2003. *Down to Earth* 56 (February). Retrieved January 22, 2010, from http://dte.gn.apc.org/56tpl.htm.

166. Occupational Safety and Health Administration. OSHA mission. Retrieved January 22, 2010, from http://www.osha.gov/oshinfo/mission.html.

167. Occupational Safety and Health Administration. OSHA regulations. Retrieved November 7, 2009, from http://www.osha.gov/pls/oshaweb/owasrch.search_form?p_doc_type=STANDARDS&p_toc_level=0&p_keyvalue=.

168. Occupational Safety and Health Administration. Machine guarding. Retrieved April 26, 2010, from http://www.osha.gov/SLTC/machine-guarding/index.html.

169. Occupational Safety and Health Administration. Permissible exposure limits. Retrieved April 26, 2010, from http://www.osha.gov/SLTC/pel/index.html.

170. Occupational Safety and Health Administration. Brownfields safety standards. Retrieved April 26, 2010, from http://www.osha.gov/SLTC/brownfields/standards.html.

171. Occupational Safety and Health Administration. Control of hazardous energy. Retrieved April 26, 2010, from http://www.osha.gov/SLTC/controlhazardousenergy/index.html.

172. Occupational Safety and Health Administration. Confined spaces. Retrieved April 26, 2010, from http://www.osha.gov/SLTC/confinedspaces/.

173. Occupational Safety and Health Administration. 1910.1200(a). Retrieved April 26, 2010, from http://www.osha.gov/pls/oshaweb/owadisp.show_document?p_table=STANDARDS&p_id=10099.

174. Occupational Safety and Health Administration. Blood borne pathogens. Retrieved April 26, 2010, from http://www.osha.gov/SLTC/bloodbornepathogens/index.html.

175. Occupational Safety and Health Administration. Confined spaces. Retrieved April 26, 2010, from http://www.osha.gov/pls/oshaweb/owadisp.show_document?p_table=DIRECTIVES&p_id=1659.

176. Occupational Safety and Health Administration. OSHA Instruction CPL 2.87. Retrieved April 26, 2010, from http://www.osha.gov/pls/oshaweb/owadisp.show_document?p_table=STANDARDS&p_id=9995.

177. America's safest companies. 2009. *EHS Today*. Retrieved January 22, 2010, from http://ehstoday.com/safety/asc/.

178. United Nations General Assembly. 1987. Report of the World Commission on Environment and Development. Annex to document A/42/427—Development and International Co-operation: Environment (December 11). Geneva: United Nations Department of Economic and Social Affairs. Retrieved September 10, 2009, from http://www.un-documents.net/wced-ocf.htm.

179. Foy, George. 1990. Economic sustainability and the preservation of environmental assets. *Environmental Management* 12(6): 771–78.

180. Sonoco. Sustainability statement. Retrieved April 26, 2010, from http://www.sonoco.com/sonoco/Home/Sustainability/sus_sustainability_statement.htm.

181. Whole Soy Company. Sustainability statement. Retrieved June 4, 2012, from http://www.wholesoyco.com/about-us/sustainability-statement.

182. Does it add value? 2004. *The Economist* (November 13). Retrieved September 13, 2009, from http://www.highbeam.com/doc/1G1-124864188.html.

183. Oppenheim, Jeremy, and Lenny T. Mendoca. 2007. Investing in sustainability: An interview with Al Gore and David Blood. *McKinsey Quarterly* (May). Retrieved September 13, 2009, from http://www.mckinseyquarterly.com/Investing_in_sustainability_An_interview_with_Al_Gore_and_David_Blood_2005.

184. Ibid.

185. Ibid.

186. Unilever. 2009. India: Creating rural entrepreneurs. Retrieved September 12, 2009, from http://www.unilever.com/sustainability/casestudies/economic—development/creating-rural-entrepreneurs.aspx.

187. Aithal, Rajesh. 2009. Project Shakti going global. Marketing in India Blog (January 9). Retrieved January 24, 2010, from http://rajeshaithal.blogspot.com/2009/01/project-shakti-going-global.html.

188. Lydenberg, Steve, and Graham Sinclair. 2009. Mainstream or daydream? The future for responsible investing. *Journal of Corporate Citizenship* 33: 47–67.

189. Ibid.

190. Oppenheim and Mendoca, Investing in sustainability.

191. Ibid.

192. Ibid.

193. Ashoka.org. Ashoka facts. Retrieved April 26, 2010, from http://www.ashoka.org/facts.

194. Etymology Online. Philanthropy. Retrieved June 1, 2010, from http://www.etymonline.com/index.php?search=philanthropy&searchmodenone.

195. Grimm, Robert T. 2002. *Notable American philanthropists: Biographies of giving and volunteering.* Westport, CT: Greenwood Publishing Group.

196. Ibid.

197. Bill and Melinda Gates Foundation. 2009. Foundation fact sheet. Retrieved January 22, 2010, from http://www.gatesfoundation.org/about/Pages/foundation-fact-sheet.aspx.

198. National Constitution Center. 2007. 2007 Liberty Medal recipients. Retrieved January 24, 2010, from http://constitutioncenter.org/libertymedal/recipient_2007.html; Tyrangiel, Josh. 2002. Can Bono save the world? *Time.* Retrieved January 24, 2010, from http://www.time.com/time/covers/1101020304/story.html.

199. One Foundation. Retrieved January 24, 2010, from http://www.onefoundation.cn/html/en/beneficence_01.htm; Interview: Jet Li. 2009. *Alliance Magazine* (December 1). Retrieved January 24, 2010, from http://www.alliancemagazine.org/en/content/interview-jet-li.

200. McGee, Suzanne. 2009. The 25 best givers. *Barron's* (November 30). Retrieved January 24, 2010, from http://online.barrons.com/article/SB125935466529866955.html#articleTabs_panel_article%3D1.

201. Nilekani, Nandan. 2009. *Imagining India: The idea of a renewed nation.* London: Penguin.

202. Wilhelm, Ian. 2010. Warren Buffet Shares his Philanthropic Philosophy. The *Chronicle of Philanthropy* (March 8). Retrieved June 5, 2012 from http://philanthropy.com/blogs/prospecting/warren-buffett-shares-his-philanthropic-philosophy/21672

203. Weeks, Edward. 2006. Why firms should embrace CSR. *Lawyer* (December 4): 33.

204. Luo, Xueming, and C. B. Bhattacharya. 2006. Corporate social responsibility, customer satisfaction, and market value. *Journal of Marketing* 70(1): 1–18.

205. Margolis, Joshua D., Hillary A. Elfenbein, and James P. Walsh. 2007. Does it pay to be good? A meta-analysis and redirection of research on the relationship between corporate social and financial performance. Working paper. Boston: Harvard Business School.

206. Garrett, Paul. 2003. Why it pays to be good. *Utility Week* 19(17): 16.

207. McClenahen, John S. 2005. Defining social responsibility. *Industry Week* 254(3): 64–65.

208. Johnson & Johnson. Our Credo. Retrieved April 11, 2010, from http://www.jnj.com/connect/about-jnj/jnj-credo/.

209. Williams, Nadia. 2008. CSR profession no longer the poor relation. *Personnel Today*, 47.

210. Barney, William L. 2006. *A companion to 19th century America.* Malden, MA: Blackwell Publishing, Ltd.

211. Interface. Toward a more sustainable way of business. Retrieved October 15, 2009, from http://www.mondaneum.org/pt/node/393.

212. BarackObama.com. Investing in America's future: Barack Obama and Joe Biden's plan for science and innovation. Retrieved October 15, 2009, from http://www.barackobama.com/pdf/issues/FactSheet Science.pdf; PUBLIC LAW 111–292. Retrieved May 24, 2012, from http://www.gpo.gov/fdsys/pkg/PLAW-111publ292/pdf/PLAW-111publ292.pdf.

213. Lister, Kate, and Tom Harnish. 2011. The State of Telework in th U.S.: How Individuals, Business, and Government Benefit. *Telework Research Network.*

214. Ibid.

215. Schadler, Ted, Matthew Brown, and Sara Burnes. 2011. "US Telecommuting Forecast, 2009 to 2016." *Forrester Research, Inc.*

216. Abate, Tom. 2008. Group touts telecommuting's green benefits. *San Francisco Chronicle* (April 22). Retrieved September 24, 2009, from http://www.sfgate.com/cgi-bin/article.cgi?f/c/a/2008/04/22/BUEC1087U5.DTL.

217. Telework. 2000. Telework (telecommuting): The benefits—and some issues! *European Telework Online* (January 25). Retrieved September 14, 2009. http://www.eto.org.uk/faq/faq03.htm.

218. Abate, Group touts telecommuting's green benefits.

219. Telecommuting Safety and Health Benefits Institute. 1994. Ten advantages to telecommuting: In the areas of conserving energy, protecting the environment, promoting family values, and enhancing worker safety. Retrieved September 14, 2009, from http://www.gilgordon.com/telecommutesafe/telebenefits.html.

220. Coy, Peter, Michele Conlin, and Moira Herbst. 2010. The permanent temporary workforce. *Business Week* (January 18). Retrieved April 26, 2010, from http://www.businessweek.com/magazine/content/10_03/b4163032935448_page_4.htm.

221. Ibid.

222. eBay. Sustainability. Retrieved April 26, 2010, from http://pages.ebay.com/aboutebay/socialventures.html.

223. United Way of America. Eli Lily and Company responds to U.S. economic challenges, donating millions of dollars, volunteer hours, and life-saving medicines. Retrieved October 15, 2009, from http://www.liveunited.org/NCL/upload/Master_Release_FINAL.PDF.

224. Delivering on the promise. 2008. *Smart Business Cleveland* 20(5): 48.

225. Allied Bank. Corporate and social responsibility statement. Retrieved June 1, 2010, from http://www.abl.com/thebank/pdf/annual_report2005/corporate_social_responsibity_statement.pdf.

226. Greenleaf, Robert. 2002. *Servant leadership.* New York: Paulist Press.

227. Greenleaf, Robert K. 1977. *Servant leadership: A journey into the nature of legitimate power and greatness.* Mahwah, NJ: Paulist Press; Hesse, Herman. 1922/2002. *Siddhartha,* trans. Joachim Neugroschel and Ralph Freedman. New York: Penguin.

228. Jaramillo, Fernando, Douglas B. Grisaffe, Lawrence B. Chonko, and James A. Roberts. 2009. Examining the impact of servant leadership on sales force performance. *Journal of Personal Selling and Sales Management* 29(3): 257–75.

229. Greenleaf Center. 1999. *Servant-leadership.* Advanced American Communications, Inc. Retrieved August 21, 2009, from http://www.trainingabc.com/xcart/product_files/P/ServantLeadershipLG.pdf.

230. United States Department of Labor. Year of pub. Child Labor in the Apparel Sector. Retrieved August 8, 2012, from URL. http://www.dol.gov/ilab/media/reports/iclp/apparel/1c.htm.

Chapter 16

1. Goleman, Daniel, Richard E. Boyatzis, and Annie McKee. 2002. *Primal leadership: Learning to lead with emotional intelligence.* Boston: Harvard Business School Press.

2. Tan, Chade-Meng. *Search inside yourself: Google's guide to enhancing productivity, creativity, and happiness.* New York: HarperOne, 2012.

3. Lohr, Steve. 2007. Hey, who's he? With Gwyneth? The Google guy. *New York Times* (September 1). Retrieved May 27, 2010, from http://www.nytimes.com/2007/09/01/technology/01google.html.

4. Tan, Chade-Meng. Search inside yourself: Google's guide to enhancing productivity, creativity, and happiness.

5. Hamel, Gary. 2009. Moon shots for management. *Harvard Business Review* 87(2): 91–98.

6. Ibid.

7. McKee, Annie, Richard Boyatzis, and Frances Johnston. 2008. *Becoming a resonant leader: Develop your emotional intelligence, renew your relationships, and sustain your effectiveness.* Boston: Harvard Business School Press.

8. Boyatzis, Richard E. 2006. An overview of intentional change from a complexity perspective. Journal of Management Development 25(7): 607–23; Howard, Anita. 2006. Positive and negative emotional attractors and intentional change. Journal of Management Development 25(7): 657–70; Boyatzis, Richard, and Annie McKee. 2005. Resonant leadership: Renewing yourself and connecting with others through mindfulness, hope and compassion. Boston: Harvard Business School Press.

Name Index

Page numbers in *italic* indicate exhibits or special features (Business Cases or Leadership Perspectives)

A

Abate, Tom, 666n216, 666n218
Abbas, M., 657n23
Abelson, Robert P., 638n7, 638n18
Aboud, John, 643n89
Abrahams, Jeffrey, 636n19
Ackman, Dan, 649n52
Adams, Brooks, 649n23
Adams, Guy, 645n28
Adams, John Stacey, *71*, 77
Adamson, Thomas, 658n79
Adler, Carlye, 634n55
Aeschylus, 131
Afsarmanesh, Hamideh, 650n103
Agata, Bonaventure, *66*
Agha, Asif, 634n56, 635n58, 647n32
Agle, Bradley R., 637n73
Ainslie, Karen, 640n46
Aïssatou, Gueye-Ndiaye, 654n5
Aithal, Rajesh, 665n187
Akrivou, Kleio, 639nn20–21
Alderfer, Clayton, *71*, 73, 632n20
Alexandra, Michel, 654n40
Allen, Myria W., 634n46
Allen, T.T., 652n39
Allport, G.W., 632n16
Altvater, Elmar, 633n49
Amar, A.D., 645n5
Ambrosek, Renee, 644n126
Amin, Samir, 649n29, 649n31
Amini, Fari, 632n46
Ammon, Hans-Christoph, 569
Ana Paula, Afonso, 647n18
Anderson, Chris, 640n41, 640n47
Anderson, David M., 661n10
Anderson, Jenny, 662n33
Anderson, Kurt, 649n46
Anderson, Neil, 632n23
Anderson, Ray, 597–598
Andrews, Edmund L., 640n75
Andrews, Robert, 639n64
Andriessen, J.H. Erik, 650n77
Ang Soon, 656n120
Anmmann, Caspar M., 662n14
Ansari, Shahzad, 648n77
Antonakis, J., 630nn61–62
Antony, Jiju, 652n31
Aquino, Karl, 648n72
Arabe, Katrina C., 649n54
Archer, Leonie, 665n142
Argyris, C., 639nn62–63, 648n67
Ariño, Africa, 646n95, 658n62
Arkhipov, Ilya, 660n164
Arkin, Robert M., 638n38
Arne Traulsen, 645n54
Aron, Leon, 660n173

Aronow, Edward, 632n39
Arquilla, John, 650n99
Arthur Andersen, 43
Arvedlund, Erin E., 630n53
Asante, Molefi, 647n33
Asch, Solomon E., 365, 638n13, 647nn62–63, 648n68
Aspray, W., 658n98
Atkinson, J.W., 633n47
Auerbach, A., 639n12
Aufreiter, Nora A., 636n41
Avery, Derek R., 640n45
Averyt, K.B., 662n15
Avolio, Bruce J., 631n89
Azides, I., 644n123

B

Baard, Paul P., 632n11
Bader, P., 630nn61–62
Baker, A., 641n129
Baker, Jack, 479
Bakker, A.B., 630n28
Baldwin, Paul H., 664n119
Bales, Kevin, 586
Ballard, David, 641n123
Balogun, Julia, 642nn134–135
Balsmeir, Philip W., 650n94
Bamforth, Ken W., 386, 649n12
Banaji, Mahzarin R., 638n11
Bandura, Albert, 86–87, 633n59, 633nn62–65, 633nn67–68
Banks, Ken, 274, 643n95
Banks, Tyra, 273
Barch, J., 630n28
Barker, Molly, 591
Barley, Stephen R., 655n63
Barnett, Martin, 409, 650n87
Barney, Jay B., 637n83
Barney, William L., 666n210
Barr, Christopher D., 666n64
Barr, Pamela S., 642n4
Barrick, M.R., 632n17
Bartlett, Bruce, 640n77
Barton, Dominic, 629n2, 629n4, 629n23, 630n50
Basham, Brian, 662n43
Bass, Bernard M., 630nn61–62
Bates, T., 651n133
Battelle, John, 633n73, 633n75
Bauman, Zygmunt, 630n42, 630n44, 639n31, 640n41
Baumol, William J., 649n36
Beam, Christopher, 661n220
Beattie, Geoffrey, 640n52
Bechara, Antoine, 638n15
Beck, Sanderson, 630n36
Beckwith, Carol, 661n7
Beckhard, R., 630nn61–62
Beckstrom, Rod A., 307, 644n10, 645nn30–31, 645nn33–34
Beckwith, Carol, 661n7
Beechler, Schon L., 634n54
Beinhocker, Eric D., 636n33

Bell, Daniel, 392, 649n44, 649n50
Bellingrath, George C., 630n59
Belser, P., 665n147
Benedek, Mathias, 642n28
Benne, Kenneth D., 647n19
Bennis, W., 647n12
Bennis, Warren, 12, 629n15, 647n17
Berg, David N., 359–360, 647nn47–52, 648n84, 648nn86–87
Bergeron, Francois, 652n28
Bergiel, Blaise J., 650n94
Bergiel, Erich B., 650n94
Berglof, Erik, 653n83
Berlo, David K., 634n33, 634n38
Bernabei, Lynne, 651n147
Bernardo, Dolores, 5–6
Berner, Robert, 642n35
Berners-Lee, Tim, 394, 649nn60–61
Bernthal, Paul R., 651n137
Berntsen, John L., 661n9
Bertuzzi, Stefano, *69–70*
Beshel, Barbara, 646n77, 646n82, 658n63
Bessant, John, 644n7
Betsch, T., 638n26
Bettis, Richard A., 637n82
Beutell, Nicholas J., 648n85
Beyerlein, Michael M., 650n86, 650n91, 650n98
Beyerlein, Susan, 650n86, 650n91, 650n98
Beyrle, John, 660n165
Bhargava, Rajat, 660n196
Bhatnagar, Rakesh, 665n148
Bhattacharya, C.B., 666n204
Bhuiya, Farida, 653n81
Biemans, Harm, 643n91
Biggs, Barton, 630n51
bin Laden, Osama, 308
Bion, W.R., 647n15
Birchard, B., 644n111
Bird, Allan, 634n54
Birdwhistell, Ray L., 106, 634n14
Black, Jill E., 645n36, 645n39
Black, Laura W., 647n9
Blair, Tony, 643n77
Blake, Robert, 47, 631n66
Blake, Stacey, 648n101
Blalock, Marty, 658n73
Blanchard, Ken, 47, 631n69
Blanchard, Kendall, 648n71
Bless, H., 631n3
Blight, G., 657n24
Blood, David, *591–592*
Bloomgarden, Kathy, 631n81
Blount, Rachel, 632n27
Boddy, D., 643n132
Bogner, William C., 642n4
Boguslauskas, Vytautas, 636n58
Bohmerin, Jon, 274
Bond, Carole, 641n123
Bond, Michael, H., 654n14, 654n17
Bono, *593*
Bono, J.E., 632n17

Company/Organization

Glossary/Index